The Growing Child

the Growing Child

Denise Boyd
Houston Community College

Helen Bee

Allyn & Bacon

Boston New York San Francisco
Mexico City Montreal Toronto London Madrid Munich Paris
Hong Kong Singapore Tokyo Cape Town Sydney

This book is dedicated to my two favorite growing children,
Mackenzie and Madeleine.
—D.B.

Senior Acquisitions Editor:	Stephen Frail
Series Editorial Assistant:	Kerri Hart-Morris
Senior Development Editor:	Christina Lembo
Marketing Manager:	Nicole Kunzmann
Production Editor:	Claudine Bellanton
Editorial Production Service:	Lifland et al., Bookmakers
Manufacturing Buyer:	JoAnne Sweeney
Electronic Composition:	Modern Graphics, Inc.
Interior Design:	Glenna Collett, Jean Hammond, and Joyce Weston
Photo Researcher:	Rachel Lucas
Cover Administrator/Designer:	Kristina Mose-Libon

Library of Congress Cataloging-in-Publication Data

Boyd, Denise Roberts.
The growing child / Denise Boyd, Helen Bee.
p. cm.
ISBN 978-0-205-54596-4
1. Child development. I. Bee, Helen L., 1939– II. Title.
RJ131.B68 2010
618.92—dc22

2008052511

10 9 8 7 6 5 4 3 2 1 WEB 13 12 11 10 09

Allyn & Bacon is an imprint of

www.pearsonhighered.com

ISBN-10: 0-205-54596-3
ISBN-13: 978-0-205-54596-4

Brief Contents

Contents

THE WHOLE CHILD IN FOCUS

At the end of Unit One, we visit the Changs again, this time in the delivery room.

Unit Two Infancy and Toddlerhood 96

THE WHOLE CHILD IN FOCUS
In Unit Two, we meet 6-month-old Federico and Hector, his stay-at-home father.

THE WHOLE CHILD IN FOCUS
We look back at Federico's development over the past 2 years.

Unit Three Early Childhood 182

THE WHOLE CHILD IN FOCUS
We meet 2-year-old Madeleine, who loves to dance.

THE WHOLE CHILD IN FOCUS
We look back at how Madeleine, now 6 years old, has changed and grown.

Unit Four Middle Childhood 286

THE WHOLE CHILD IN FOCUS

We meet Jamal, a 6-year-old boy just learning how to ride his bicycle.

THE WHOLE CHILD IN FOCUS

We trace Jamal's development as he grows into a confident 12-year-old.

Unit Five Adolescence 382

THE WHOLE CHILD IN FOCUS

We meet eighth-grade best friends Cho and Michelle, two girls trying to establish their independence.

13

14

THE WHOLE CHILD IN FOCUS

We rejoin Cho and Michelle as they begin planning for college and life after high school.

Features

DEVELOPMENTAL SCIENCE IN THE CLINIC

DEVELOPMENTAL SCIENCE IN THE CLASSROOM

DEVELOPMENTAL SCIENCE AT HOME

Preface

A great textbook informs students, helps them retain what they have read, and helps them apply the principles the book teaches in the real world. Fortunately for most instructors who teach child development, students approach the task of learning about childhood and adolescence with a natural desire to find explanations for their own and others' behavior. As I have learned over the course of my 20 years of teaching developmental psychology, successful teaching strategies build on that natural desire, but they also encourage students to think more deeply about development. My goal is to incorporate this approach to teaching into the textbooks that I co-author.

Although students' natural interest in development helps them learn some of the content of a child development course, most are not motivated by intellectual curiosity when they enroll in the class. In my child development classes, students come from a variety of backgrounds, including education, human services, health careers, and criminal justice majors, and most take the course because it fulfills a degree requirement. Consequently, one of the significant challenges that I and others who teach such students face is to find a textbook that successfully integrates the practical concerns of readers whose primary goal is to learn how to work effectively with children and adolescents with the kind of comprehensive treatment of theories and research that most instructors believe should be included in a child development course.

Another challenge facing instructors is getting students to keep in mind the *whole child* in a course whose syllabus is segmented by both domain (cognitive, physical, and socioemotional) and age (infancy and toddlerhood, early childhood, middle childhood, and adolescence). Students tend to forget that development does not happen in a vacuum.

Finally, in an era in which educators are increasingly called upon to document what their students are learning and how well they are learning it, a text that supports instructors' assessment needs is vital. Students also have self-assessment needs; they often have limited time to study and want a text and ancillary program that teaches them strong study skills and helps them perform well in the course.

Features of the Textbook

The Growing Child will address three key needs of instructors in ways that will also facilitate students' learning of course content.

Need #1: Support Instructors' Assessment and Students' Self-Assessment Needs. The textbook's pedagogical system is adapted from the SQ3R study method (survey, question, read, review, rehearse) to support student learning. Several textbook features make up the SQ3R system:

A learning system organized around numbered **learning objective** questions ensures that both students and instructors know exactly which skills are covered in each section. It also helps students organize and retain the material as they read the textbook.

Chapter 4

Physical Development and Health in Infancy

Perceptual Skills

Studying Perceptual Development

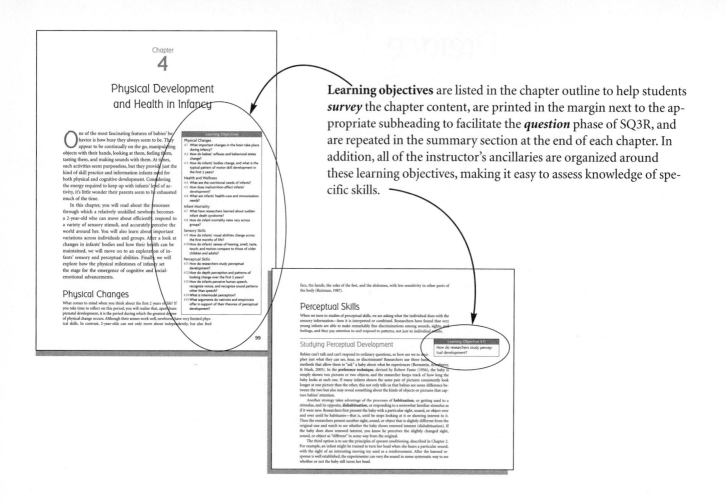

Learning objectives are listed in the chapter outline to help students ***survey*** the chapter content, are printed in the margin next to the appropriate subheading to facilitate the ***question*** phase of SQ3R, and are repeated in the summary section at the end of each chapter. In addition, all of the instructor's ancillaries are organized around these learning objectives, making it easy to assess knowledge of specific skills.

The end-of-chapter **Test Prep Center**, which integrates a summary organized around the learning objectives with a built-in study guide, facilitates the ***review*** and ***rehearse*** phases of SQ3R and supports active learning of text content.

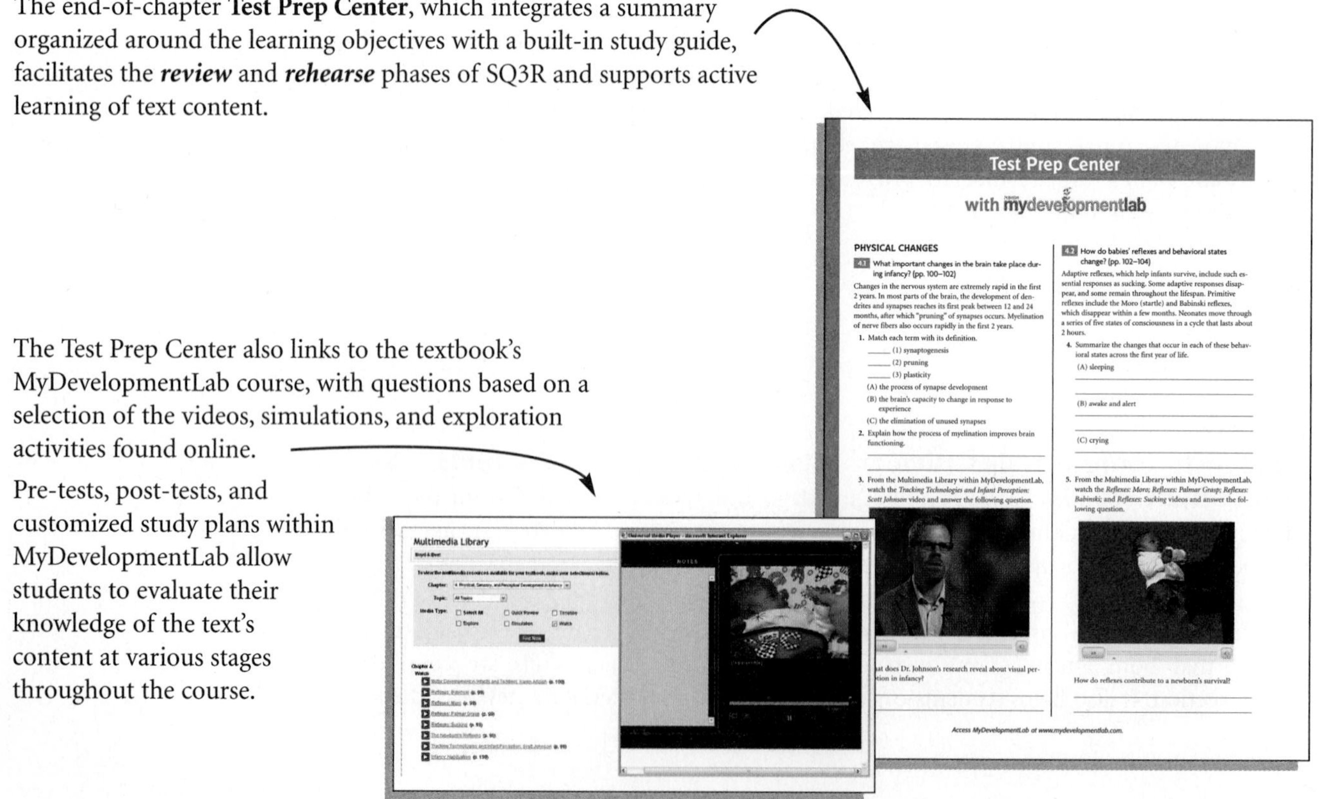

The Test Prep Center also links to the textbook's MyDevelopmentLab course, with questions based on a selection of the videos, simulations, and exploration activities found online.

Pre-tests, post-tests, and customized study plans within MyDevelopmentLab allow students to evaluate their knowledge of the text's content at various stages throughout the course.

The **Comprehensive Practice Test**, a complete test of content from all 15 chapters found at the back of the book, allows students to practice for midterm and/or final exams.

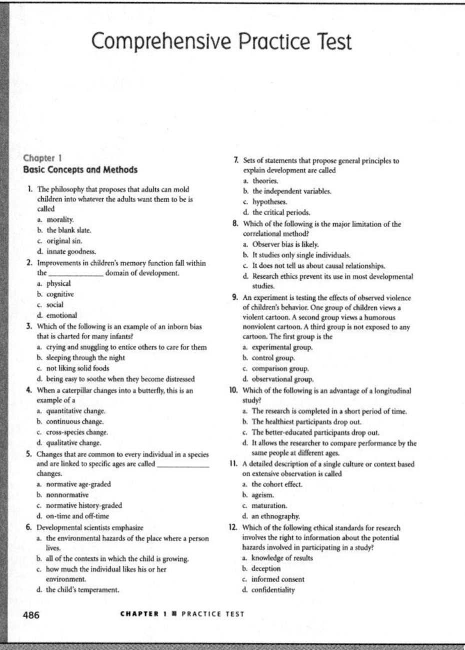

Comprehensive Practice Test

Chapter 1
Basic Concepts and Methods

1. The philosophy that proposes that adults can mold children into whatever the adults want them to be is called
   a. morality.
   b. the blank slate.
   c. original sin.
   d. innate goodness.
2. Improvements in children's memory function fall within the ______________ domain of development.
   a. physical
   b. cognitive
   c. social
   d. emotional
3. Which of the following is an example of an inborn bias that is charted for many infants?
   a. crying and snuggling to entice others to care for them
   b. sleeping through the night
   c. not liking solid foods
   d. being easy to soothe when they become distressed
4. When a caterpillar changes into a butterfly, this is an example of a
   a. quantitative change.
   b. continuous change.
   c. cross-species change.
   d. qualitative change.
5. Changes that are common to every individual in a species and are linked to specific ages are called ______________ changes.
   a. normative age-graded
   b. nonnormative
   c. normative history-graded
   d. on-time and off-time
6. Developmental scientists emphasize
   a. the environmental hazards of the place where a person lives.
   b. all of the contexts in which the child is growing.
   c. how much the individual likes his or her environment.
   d. the child's temperament.
7. Sets of statements that propose general principles to explain development are called
   a. theories.
   b. the independent variables.
   c. hypotheses.
   d. the critical periods.
8. Which of the following is the major limitation of the correlational method?
   a. Observer bias is likely.
   b. It studies only single individuals.
   c. It does not tell us about causal relationships.
   d. Research ethics prevent its use in most developmental studies.
9. An experiment is testing the effects of observed violence of children's behavior. One group of children views a violent cartoon. A second group views a humorous nonviolent cartoon. A third group is not exposed to any cartoon. The first group is the
   a. experimental group.
   b. control group.
   c. comparison group.
   d. observational group.
10. Which of the following is an advantage of a longitudinal study?
    a. The research is completed in a short period of time.
    b. The healthiest participants drop out.
    c. The better-educated participants drop out.
    d. It allows the researcher to compare performance by the same people at different ages.
11. A detailed description of a single culture or context based on extensive observation is called
    a. the cohort effect.
    b. ageism.
    c. maturation.
    d. an ethnography.
12. Which of the following ethical standards for research involves the right to information about the potential hazards involved in participating in a study?
    a. knowledge of results
    b. deception
    c. informed consent
    d. confidentiality

486 CHAPTER 1 ■ PRACTICE TEST

A **marginal glossary** of bold-faced key terms provides additional support for student learning.

Infant Mortality

Researchers formally define **infant mortality** as death within the first year after birth. In the United States, about 7 babies out of every 1,000 die before age 1 (Kochanek & Martin, 2004). The rate has been declining steadily for the past several decades (down from 30 per 1,000 in 1950), but the United States continues to have a higher infant mortality rate than other industrialized nations. Almost two-thirds of these infant deaths occur in the first month of life and are directly linked to either congenital anomalies or low birth weight (Kochanek & Martin, 2004).

Sudden Infant Death Syndrome

Learning Objective 4.7
What have researchers learned about sudden infant death syndrome?

After the death of a spouse, the death of a child, especially when the death is unexpected, is the most distressing source of bereavement there is for most adults (see *Developmental Science in the Clinic* on page 110). Parents' questions about the cause of their child's death are a natural part of the grief process. In the case of the loss of an infant, few parents find the answers they are looking for, because most deaths after the first month of life are the result of SIDS. **Sudden infant death syndrome (SIDS)**, in which an apparently healthy infant dies suddenly and unexpectedly, is the leading cause of death in the United States among infants between 1 month and 1 year of age (Task Force on Sudden Infant Death Syndrome, 2005). Physicians have not yet uncovered the basic cause of SIDS, but there are a few clues. For one thing, it is more common in the winter when babies may be suffering from viral infections that cause breathing difficulties. In addition, babies with a history of *sleep apnea*—brief periods when their breathing suddenly stops—are more likely to die from SIDS (Kercsmar, 1998). Episodes of apnea may be noticed by medical personnel in the newborn nursery, or a nonbreathing baby may be discovered by her parents in time to be resuscitated. In such cases, physicians usually recommend using electronic breathing monitors that will sound an alarm if the baby stops breathing again while asleep.

infant mortality death within the first year of life

sudden infant death syndrome (SIDS) a phenomenon in which an apparently healthy infant dies suddenly and unexpectedly

CHAPTER 4 ■ PHYSICAL DEVELOPMENT AND HEALTH IN INFANCY 109

Electronic flashcards on MyDevelopmentLab (an online study and homework system) allow students to test their knowledge of these terms.

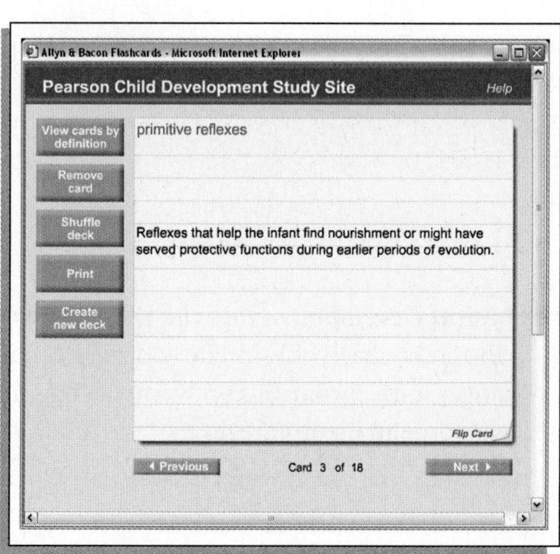

Need #2: Focus the Reader on the Development of the Whole Child. A unique ***Whole Child in Focus* theme** emphasizes that the different domains of development (physical, cognitive, and socioemotional) interact with one another and the child's environment to produce different developmental pathways. Several unit and chapter features together implement the *Whole Child* theme:

Each of the five **unit openers** relates the story of a family, child, or pair of friends that will serve as a *Whole Child* context for thinking about the research presented within the subsequent three chapters.

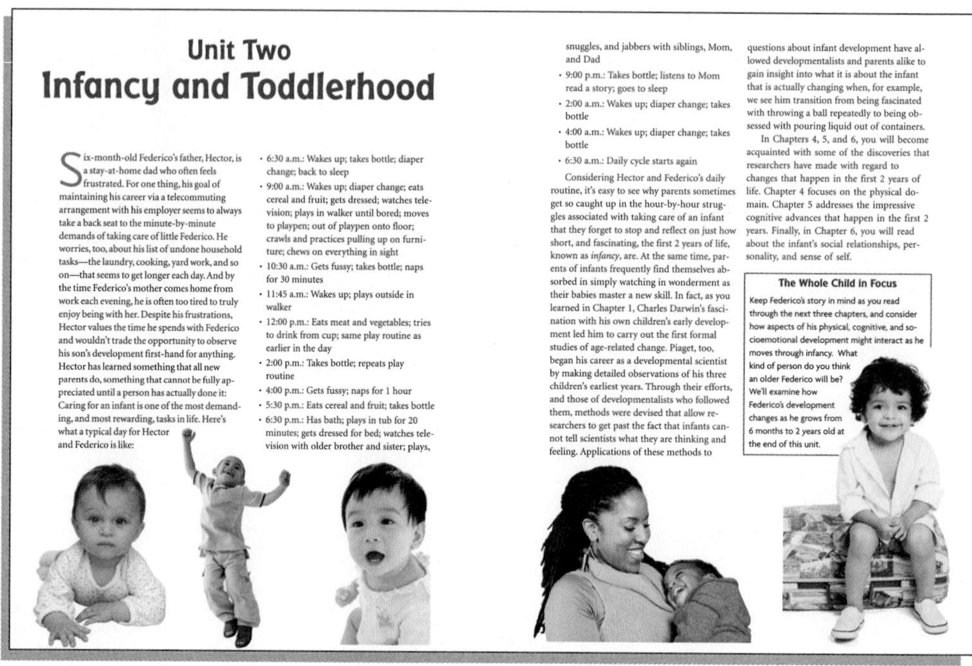

Unit Two

Infancy and Toddlerhood

Six-month-old Federico's father, Hector, is a stay-at-home dad who often feels frustrated. For one thing, his goal of maintaining his career via a telecommuting arrangement with his employer seems to always take a back seat to the minute-by-minute demands of taking care of little Federico. He worries, too, about his list of undone household tasks—the laundry, cooking, yard work, and so on—that seems to get longer each day. And by the time Federico's mother comes home from work each evening, he is often too tired to truly enjoy being with her. Despite his frustrations, Hector values the time he spends with Federico and wouldn't trade the opportunity to observe his son's development first-hand for anything. Hector has learned something that all new parents do, something that cannot be fully appreciated until a person has actually done it: Caring for an infant is one of the most demanding, and most rewarding, tasks in life. Here's what a typical day for Hector and Federico is like:

- 6:30 a.m.: Wakes up; takes bottle; diaper change; back to sleep
- 9:00 a.m.: Wakes up; diaper change; eats cereal and fruit; gets dressed; watches television; plays in walker until bored; moves to playpen; out of playpen onto floor; crawls and practices pulling up on furniture; chews on everything in sight
- 10:30 a.m.: Gets fussy; takes bottle; naps for 30 minutes
- 11:45 a.m.: Wakes up; plays outside in walker
- 12:00 p.m.: Eats meat and vegetables; tries to drink from cup; same play routine as earlier in the day
- 2:00 p.m.: Takes bottle; repeats play routine
- 4:00 p.m.: Gets fussy; naps for 1 hour
- 5:30 p.m.: Eats cereal and fruit; takes bottle
- 6:30 p.m.: Has bath; plays in tub for 20 minutes; gets dressed for bed; watches television with older brother and sister; plays, snuggles, and jabbers with siblings, Mom, and Dad
- 9:00 p.m.: Takes bottle; listens to Mom read a story; goes to sleep
- 2:00 a.m.: Wakes up; diaper change; takes bottle
- 4:00 a.m.: Wakes up; diaper change; takes bottle
- 6:30 a.m.: Daily cycle starts again

Considering Hector and Federico's daily routine, it's easy to see why parents sometimes get so caught up in the hour-by-hour struggles associated with taking care of an infant that they forget to stop and reflect on just how short, and fascinating, the first 2 years of life, known as *infancy*, are. At the same time, parents of infants frequently find themselves absorbed in simply watching in wonderment as their babies master a new skill. In fact, as you learned in Chapter 1, Charles Darwin's fascination with his own children's early development led him to carry out the first formal studies of age-related change. Piaget, too, began his career as a developmental scientist by making detailed observations of his three children's earliest years. Through their efforts, and those of developmentalists who followed them, methods were devised that allow researchers to get past the fact that infants cannot tell scientists what they are thinking and feeling. Applications of these methods to questions about infant development have allowed developmentalists and parents alike to gain insight into what it is about the infant that is actually changing when, for example, we see him transition from being fascinated with throwing a ball repeatedly to being obsessed with pouring liquid out of containers.

In Chapters 4, 5, and 6, you will become acquainted with some of the discoveries that researchers have made with regard to changes that happen in the first 2 years of life. Chapter 4 focuses on the physical domain. Chapter 5 addresses the impressive cognitive advances that happen in the first 2 years. Finally, in Chapter 6, you will read about the infant's social relationships, personality, and sense of self.

The Whole Child in Focus

Keep Federico's story in mind as you read through the next three chapters, and consider how aspects of his physical, cognitive, and socioemotional development might interact as he moves through infancy. What kind of person do you think an older Federico will be? We'll examine how Federico's development changes as he grows from 6 months to 2 years old at the end of this unit.

THE WHOLE CHILD IN FOCUS

How did the combination of Federico's maturing brain and developing fine motor skills almost result in an accident? Find out on page 179.

***Whole Child in Focus* callouts** appear in the margins of each of the chapters, along with questions to remind students to think about the whole child/children introduced at the beginning of the unit.

Physical Development and the Whole Child

Your study of the infancy period so far has focused on the physical domain. In addition to learning about the changes in infants' bodies and motor skills that take place during this period, you have read about some of the important issues in infant health and have learned a bit about the development of sensory and perceptual skills. Now it is time to consider how some of the milestones of the physical domain set the stage for the emergence of a few of the most important cognitive and socioemotional advances across the first 2 years of life.

Cognitive Functioning

In Chapter 5, you will read about one of the most important milestones of infant cognitive development: *object permanence*, or the understanding that objects continue to exist when they cannot be directly observed. An infant with object permanence knows that his favorite toy exists and can think about it even when he cannot see it. Object permanence is thought to enable infants to separate their own mental world from the physical

Physical Development and the Whole Child is a section that appears at the end of each physical development chapter. By discussing how changes in the brain and body impact cognitive and socioemotional development, it emphasizes that the three strands of development are interactive rather than independent of one another.

The *Whole Child* theme is capped off in two two-page spreads at the end of each unit.

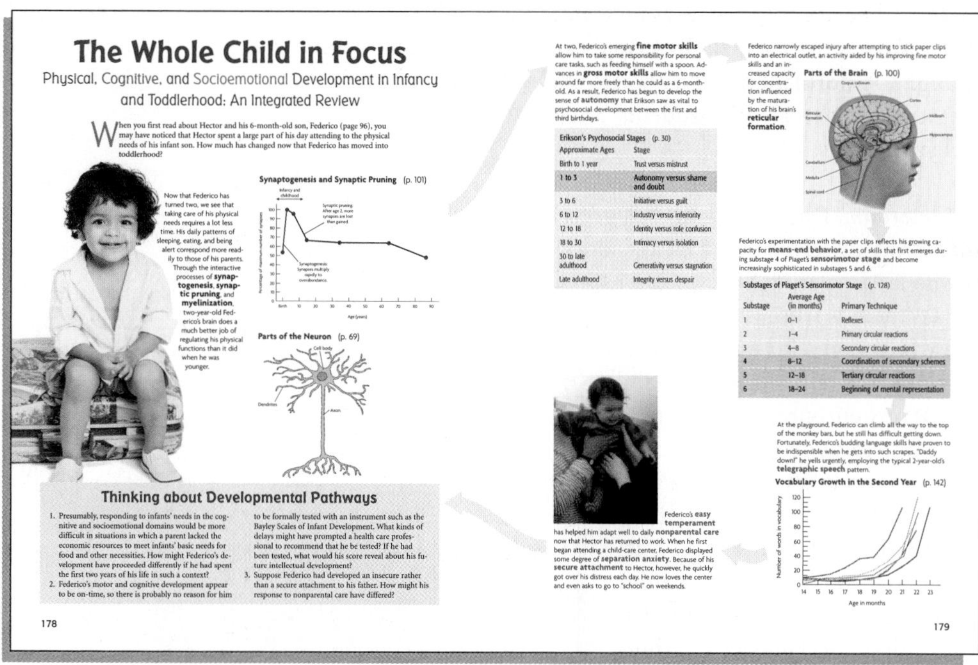

The Whole Child in Focus

Physical, Cognitive, and Socioemotional Development in Infancy and Toddlerhood: An Integrated Review

When you first read about Hector and his 6-month-old son, Federico (page 96), you may have noticed that Hector spent a large part of his day attending to the physical needs of his infant son. How much has changed now that Federico has moved into toddlerhood?

Now that Federico has turned two, we see that taking care of his physical needs requires a lot less time. His daily patterns of sleeping, eating, and being alert correspond more readily to those of his parents. Through the interactive processes of **synaptogenesis**, **synaptic pruning**, and **myelinization**, two-year-old Federico's brain does a much better job of regulating his physical functions than it did when he was younger.

Synaptogenesis and Synaptic Pruning (p. 101)

Parts of the Neuron (p. 69)

Thinking about Developmental Pathways

1. Presumably, responding to infants' needs in the cognitive and socioemotional domains would be more difficult in situations in which a parent lacked the economic resources to meet infants' basic needs for food and other necessities. How might Federico's development have proceeded differently if he had spent the first two years of his life in such a context?
2. Federico's motor and cognitive development appear to be on-time, so there is probably no reason for him to be formally tested with an instrument such as the Bayley Scales of Infant Development. What kinds of delays might have prompted a health care professional to recommend that he be tested? If he had been tested, what would his score reveal about his future intellectual development?
3. Suppose Federico had developed an insecure rather than a secure attachment to his father. How might his response to nonparental care have differed?

178

At two, Federico's emerging **fine motor skills** allow him to take some responsibility for personal care tasks, such as feeding himself with a spoon. Advances in **gross motor skills** allow him to move around far more freely than he could as a 6-month-old. As a result, Federico has begun to develop the sense of **autonomy** that Erikson saw as vital to psychosocial development between the first and third birthdays.

Erikson's Psychosocial Stages (p. 30)

Approximate Ages	Stage
Birth to 1 year	Trust versus mistrust
1 to 3	**Autonomy versus shame and doubt**
3 to 6	Initiative versus guilt
6 to 12	Industry versus inferiority
12 to 18	Identity versus role confusion
18 to 30	Intimacy versus isolation
30 to late adulthood	Generativity versus stagnation
Late adulthood	Integrity versus despair

Federico narrowly escaped injury after attempting to stick paper clips into an electrical outlet, an activity aided by his improving fine motor skills and an increased capacity for concentration influenced by the maturation of his brain's **reticular formation**.

Parts of the Brain (p. 100)

Federico's experimentation with the paper clips reflects his growing capacity for **means-end behavior**, a set of skills that first emerges during substage 4 of Piaget's **sensorimotor stage** and become increasingly sophisticated in substages 5 and 6.

Substages of Piaget's Sensorimotor Stage (p. 128)

Substage	Average Age (in months)	Primary Technique
1	0–1	Reflexes
2	1–4	Primary circular reactions
3	4–8	Secondary circular reactions
4	**8–12**	**Coordination of secondary schemes**
5	**12–18**	**Tertiary circular reactions**
6	**18–24**	**Beginning of mental representation**

At the playground, Federico can climb all the way to the top of the monkey bars, but he still has difficult getting down. Fortunately, Federico's budding language skills have proven to be indispensible when he gets into such scrapes. "Daddy down!" he yells urgently, employing the typical 2-year-old's **telegraphic speech** pattern.

Vocabulary Growth in the Second Year (p. 142)

Federico's **easy temperament** has helped him adapt well to daily **nonparental care** now that Hector has returned to work. When he first began attending a child-care center, Federico displayed some degree of **separation anxiety**. Because of his **secure attachment** to Hector, however, he quickly got over his distress each day. He now loves the center and even asks to go to "school" on weekends.

179

The Whole Child in Focus uses narrative storytelling and a targeted review of chapter visuals to examine how the interaction of the physical, cognitive, and socioemotional domains has influenced the development of the child introduced in the unit opener.

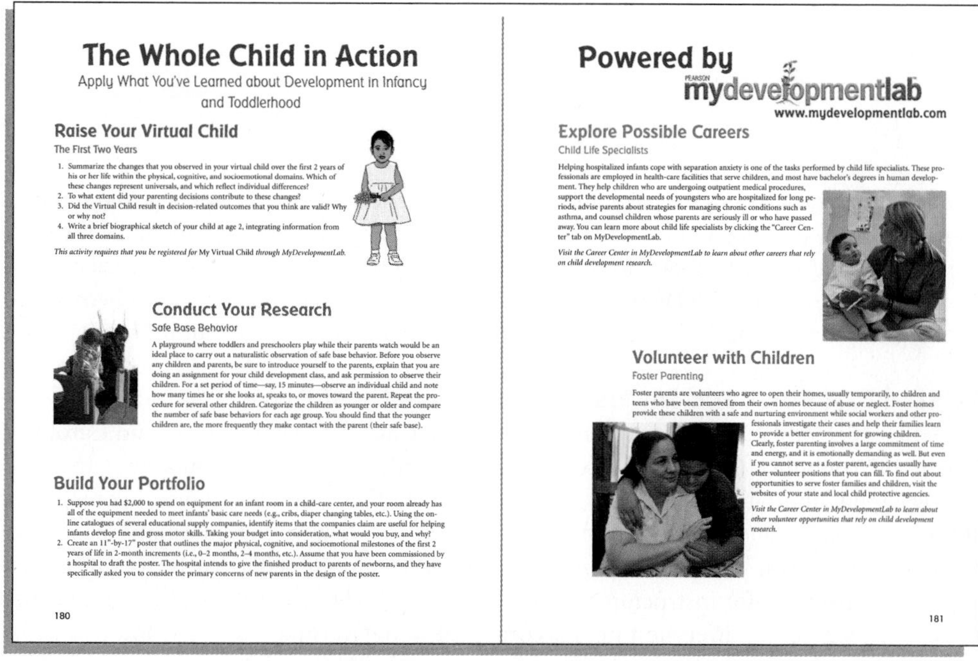

The Whole Child in Action

Apply What You've Learned about Development in Infancy and Toddlerhood

Raise Your Virtual Child

The First Two Years

1. Summarize the changes that you observed in your virtual child over the first 2 years of his or her life within the physical, cognitive, and socioemotional domains. Which of these changes represent universals, and which reflect individual differences?
2. To what extent did your parenting decisions contribute to these changes?
3. Did the Virtual Child result in decision-related outcomes that you think are valid? Why or why not?
4. Write a brief biographical sketch of your child at age 2, integrating information from all three domains.

This activity requires that you be registered for My Virtual Child *through MyDevelopmentLab.*

Conduct Your Research

Safe Base Behavior

A playground where toddlers and preschoolers play while their parents watch would be an ideal place to carry out a naturalistic observation of safe base behavior. Before you observe any children and parents, be sure to introduce yourself to the parents, explain that you are doing an assignment for your child development class, and ask permission to observe their children. For a set period of time—say, 15 minutes—observe an individual child and note how many times he or she looks at, speaks to, or moves toward the parent. Repeat the procedure for several other children. Categorize the children as younger or older and compare the number of safe base behaviors for each age group. You should find that the younger children are, the more frequently they make contact with the parent (their safe base).

Build Your Portfolio

1. Suppose you had $2,000 to spend on equipment for an infant room in a child-care center, and your room already has all of the equipment needed to meet infants' basic care needs (e.g., cribs, diaper changing tables, etc.). Using the online catalogues of several educational supply companies, identify items that the companies claim are useful for helping infants develop fine and gross motor skills. Taking your budget into consideration, what would you buy, and why?
2. Create an 11"-by-17" poster that outlines the major physical, cognitive, and socioemotional milestones of the first 2 years of life in 2-month increments (i.e., 0–2 months, 2–4 months, etc.). Assume that you have been commissioned by a hospital to draft the poster. The hospital intends to give the finished product to parents of newborns, and they have specifically asked you to consider the primary concerns of new parents in the design of the poster.

180

Powered by

PEARSON mydevelopmentlab

www.mydevelopmentlab.com

Explore Possible Careers

Child Life Specialists

Helping hospitalized infants cope with separation anxiety is one of the tasks performed by child life specialists. These professionals are employed in health-care facilities that serve children, and most have bachelor's degrees in human development. They help children who are undergoing outpatient medical procedures, support the developmental needs of youngsters who are hospitalized for long periods, advise parents about strategies for managing chronic conditions such as asthma, and counsel children whose parents are seriously ill or who have passed away. You can learn more about child life specialists by clicking the "Career Center" tab on MyDevelopmentLab.

Visit the Career Center in MyDevelopmentLab to learn about other careers that rely on child development research.

Volunteer with Children

Foster Parenting

Foster parents are volunteers who agree to open their homes, usually temporarily, to children and teens who have been removed from their own homes because of abuse or neglect. Foster homes provide these children with a safe and nurturing environment while social workers and other professionals investigate their cases and help their families learn to provide a better environment for growing children. Clearly, foster parenting involves a large commitment of time and energy, and it is emotionally demanding as well. But even if you cannot serve as a foster parent, agencies usually have other volunteer positions that you can fill. To find out about opportunities to serve foster families and children, visit the websites of your state and local child protective agencies.

Visit the Career Center in MyDevelopmentLab to learn about other volunteer opportunities that rely on child development research.

181

The Whole Child in Action encourages students to interact with children, both virtually and face to face. Students are given guidance on raising a *Virtual Child* within MyDevelopmentLab, conducting research in a child-care center or classroom, building a professional portfolio, and working or volunteering with kids.

Need #3: Balance Research, Theory, and Application, and Address Needs of Different Students. A series of boxed essays integrate theory and research into solutions to real-world problems that arise in three applied contexts: classrooms, health-care settings, and families. Information about careers in developmental science both in the text and in MyDevelopmentLab calls students' attention to the professionals who implement these solutions.

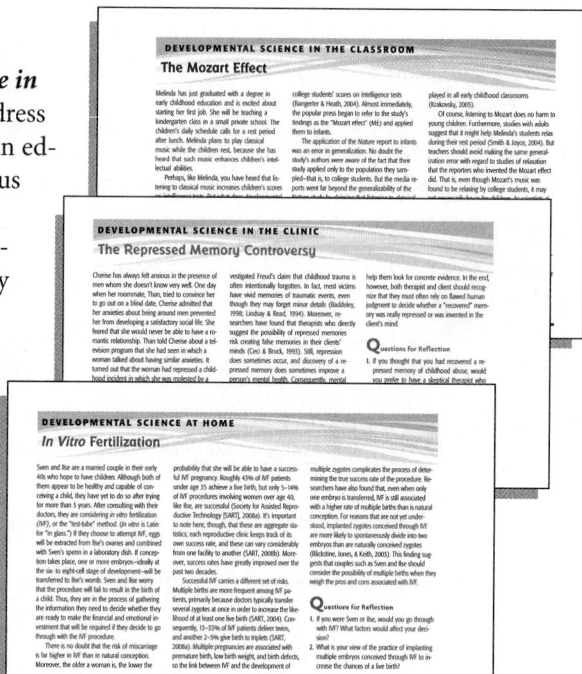

- ***Developmental Science in the Classroom, Developmental Science in the Clinic***, and ***Developmental Science at Home*** boxed essays address practical concerns of students who are preparing for professions in education and health care, as well as students who would like to focus on parenting issues. Each of these boxes presents a problem in a real-world context and then discusses the relevant theories and research. Questions at the end of the box encourage readers to apply the theories and research to the problem presented in the mini-vignette. In one of these boxes, for example, students read about a first-year teacher who is alarmed by the degree of prejudice that is demonstrated by the 6-year-olds in her class. The box then moves to a discussion of how young children acquire such attitudes and what parents and teachers can do to moderate them. At the end of the box, readers are challenged to think of ways the teacher can apply these ideas to the problems she sees in her classroom.
- An online **Career Center** on MyDevelopmentLab works together with the end-of-unit *Whole Child in Action* applications to provide information on potential career options and Web links to job sites in these fields.

Teaching and Learning Package

The teaching and learning package has been designed to support the text's goals outlined above. All of the instructor and student supplements are organized around the same learning objectives found in the textbook to provide a cohesive teaching and learning experience. All assessments (Test Bank, MyDevelopmentLab, textbook Test Prep Center) have been thoroughly and carefully checked for accuracy and consistency with the content in the textbook.

Printed Test Bank and MyTest Computerized Test Bank (Printed Test Bank ISBN: 0-205-72405-1) Mary Kay Reed of York College of Pennsylvania and Carol LaLiberte of Asnuntuck Community College have provided a *Test Bank* containing approximately 1500 thoroughly checked questions, including multiple-choice, completion (fill-in-the-blank), and Whole Child integrative critical essays. Test questions have also been written to test student comprehension of select multimedia assets found within MyDevelopmentLab, for instructors who wish to make MyDevelopmentLab a central component of their course. Every test item is correlated to the learning objectives introduced in the textbook. All questions are accompanied by the correct answer, a page reference, a difficulty ranking, and a question-type designation.

The *Test Bank* is also available in Pearson MyTest, www.pearsonmytest.com (access code required), a powerful assessment generation program that helps instructors easily create and print quizzes and exams. Questions and tests can be authored online, allowing instructors ultimate flexibility and the ability to efficiently manage assessments anytime, anywhere.

Instructor's Manual with CD-ROM (ISBN: 0-205-72406-X) Prepared by Kathleen Bey of Palm Beach Community College, the *Instructor's Manual* is a wonderful tool for classroom preparation and management. The "easy-to-find" format includes detailed cross-references to features in the *Instructor's Manual* as well as to other print and media supplements and outside teaching resources. Each chapter includes the following resources:

- An Integrated Teaching Outline, with summaries of key concepts
- Teaching objectives
- List of key terms
- Lecture material, including outlines and suggested discussion topics, with references to pertinent activities in the *Instructor's Manual* and videos from the Allyn & Bacon video library
- Classroom activities and demonstrations
- A list of video, media, print, and Web resources

The appendix includes a compilation of handouts and video offerings.

PowerPoint™ Presentation (ISBN: 0-205-72407-8) Eileen Roth of Glendale College has prepared a PowerPoint presentation that is an exciting interactive tool for use in the classroom. Each chapter includes the following:

- Key points covered in the textbook
- Images from the textbook, with demonstrations

The PowerPoint files are available on the Instructor's Resource Center (www.pearsonhighered.com/IRC) for your convenience. Please contact your Pearson representative if you do not have access to the Instructor's Resource Center.

Transparencies for Human Development (ISBN: 0-205-40747-1) Approximately 125 full-color acetates allow instructors to enhance classroom lecture and discussion.

MyDevelopmentLab (www.mydevelopmentlab.com) The APA strongly recommends student self-assessment tools and the use of embedded questions and assignments (see http://www.apa.org/ed/eval_strategies.html for more information). In keeping with these recommendations, Pearson's MyDevelopmentLab offers students useful and engaging self-assessment tools and offers instructors flexibility in assessing and tracking student progress. For instructors, MyDevelopmentLab is a powerful tool for assessing student performance and adapting course content to students' changing needs—without investing additional time or resources. Students benefit from an easy-to-use site on which they can test themselves on key content, track their progress, and utilize an individually tailored study plan. MyDevelopmentLab includes an eBook plus multimedia tutorials, audio, video, simulations, animations, and controlled assessments to completely engage students and reinforce learning.

MyDevelopmentLab is designed with instructor flexibility in mind; you decide the extent of integration into your course—from independent self-assessment for students to total course management. By transferring faculty members' most time-consuming tasks—content delivery, student assessment, and grading—to automated tools, MyDevelopmentLab enables faculty to spend more quality time with students. Instructors are provided with the results of student diagnostic tests in a gradebook and can view performance of individual students or an aggregate report on their class. Instructors can access the remediation activities students receive within their customized study plans and can also link to extra lecture notes, video clips, and activities that reflect the content areas their class is struggling with. Instructors can bring these resources to class or easily post them online for students to access.

With the publication of *The Growing Child* comes a new generation of MyDevelopmentLab, with dozens of improvements and new features that make MyDevelopmentLab both more powerful and easier to use. Some highlights of the new MyDevelopmentLab course include the following:

- MyVirtualChild, an interactive simulation that allows students to raise a virtual child from birth to age 17 and monitor the effects of their parenting decisions over time. *The Whole Child in Action* sections of this textbook include questions that prompt students to reflect on the decisions they made within the simulation.
- GradeTracker for the website version of MyDevelopmentLab, to track students' performance on quizzes
- A new, more flexible, powerful, and intuitive platform for the course management version of MyDevelopmentLab
- A redesigned eBook that gives students the option to highlight passages and access media content directly from the eBook page
- A new interactive Timeline tool that vividly illustrates key dates in the history of psychology through text, audio, and video
- Redesigned Flash Cards for reviewing key terms, with audio to help students with pronunciation of difficult terminology
- Continued improvements to the design, course content, and grading system based on direct customer feedback

For technical support for any of your Pearson products, you and your students can contact http://247.pearsoned.com.

Course Management Use these preloaded, customizable content and assessment items—available in Blackboard, WebCT, and other formats—to teach your online courses. Contact your Pearson representative for additional details.

Development: Journey through Childhood and Adolescence CD-ROM (ISBN: 0-205-39568-6) This multimedia learning tool is available to be packaged with the text or sold separately. It includes eight units that cover development from the prenatal period through adolescence and introduce all of the biological, cognitive, and psychosocial changes that occur along the way. Clips include footage of live births, interviews with adolescents and the elderly, and toddlers learning to walk. In addition, audio clips, flash animations, and 3-D video animations accompany the footage. Written by Dr. Kelly Welch of Kansas State University, the CD-ROM includes several exercises for students, such as "drag-and-drop" activities, multiple-choice quizzes, flash cards of glossary terms, journal writing, and instant feedback exercises called "Mad Minutes."

Insights into Human Development Video (ISBN 0-205-46624-9) This video is available to accompany *The Growing Child*. The video highlights important high-interest topics in human development, including imagination in early childhood, motivation and school success, and aggression in adolescent romantic relationships. A video user's guide, with critical thinking questions and Web resources, is available to support the use of the video in the classroom.

Study Card for Child Development (Chronological) (ISBN: 0-205-43508-4) Colorful, affordable, and packed with useful information, the Study Card makes studying easier, more efficient, and more enjoyable. Course information is distilled down to the basics, helping students quickly master the fundamentals, review a subject for understanding, or prepare for an exam. The Study Card is laminated for durability.

Acknowledgments

Creating a textbook that informs and challenges students is a daunting task, one that could not be accomplished without the help of a dedicated team of professionals. Senior Acquisitions Editor Stephen Frail was responsible for the vision that guided the development of *The Growing Child* from beginning to end, under the direction of Editor-in-Chief Susan Hartman. Developmental Editors Sharon Geary, Julie Swasey, and Christina Lembo played indispensible roles in bringing our goals for the text to fruition. The production staff for Allyn & Bacon, especially Production Editor Claudine Bellanton, shepherded the manuscript through the long process through which a manuscript becomes a book. Copyeditor Sally Lifland added polish and precision to the manuscript and page proofs. Finally, if instructors are unaware of our book and its unique features, the book will be unable to fulfill its mission of helping students understand child and adolescent development. Thus, we are grateful to our marketing team at Allyn & Bacon, Nicole Kunzmann, Jeanette Koskinas, and Brandy Dawson, for introducing our text to the people for whom we wrote it.

Thanks also to the following reviewers, who provided invaluable feedback:

Carolyn Adams-Price, Mississippi State University
Michelle D. Bannoura, Hudson Valley Community College
Michelle Beasley, Southwest Tennessee Community College
Kathleen Bey, Palm Beach Community College
Catherine Caldwell-Harris, Boston University
Cathy Cody, Asheville-Buncombe Technical Community College
Timothy Croy, Eastern Illinois University
Sharon DeLeon, Fullerton College
Carol Michler Detmer, Middle Tennessee State University
Eugene Geist, Ohio University
Christine Grela, McHenry County College
Sandra Hellyer, Ball State University
Carol LaLiberte, Westfield State College
Dawn S. Munson, Elgin Community College
Mary Kay Reed, York College of Pennsylvania
Kathleen A. Reid, California State University, Fresno
Eileen Roth, Glendale College
Patricia J. Sawyer, Middlesex Community College
Kristen K. Williams, Ball State University

Denise Boyd

The Growing Child

Unit One
Foundations

Like most couples who are expecting their first child, Todd and Lisa Chang are both excited and daunted by the prospect of bringing into the world a tiny human being who will be totally dependent on them for some time to come. Their transition to parenthood is made all the more momentous by the position they occupy at the intersection of two very different cultures. Both were born in the United States to parents who emigrated from China. In everyday terms, Todd and Lisa vary little from parents-to-be in other American ethnic groups. Yet, the prospect of becoming parents has awakened in them a desire to rediscover their cultural roots so that they can pass them on to their child.

Whenever the issue of culture is raised, most of us think in terms of differences. Cultural differences are important, of course, and you will learn about many such variations in the chapters to come. However, developmental science has also shed a great deal of light on the aspects of human development that are similar across cultures.

For example, you might be surprised to learn that there is general agreement across cultures with respect to two broad classes of developmental goals (LeVine, 1974). First,

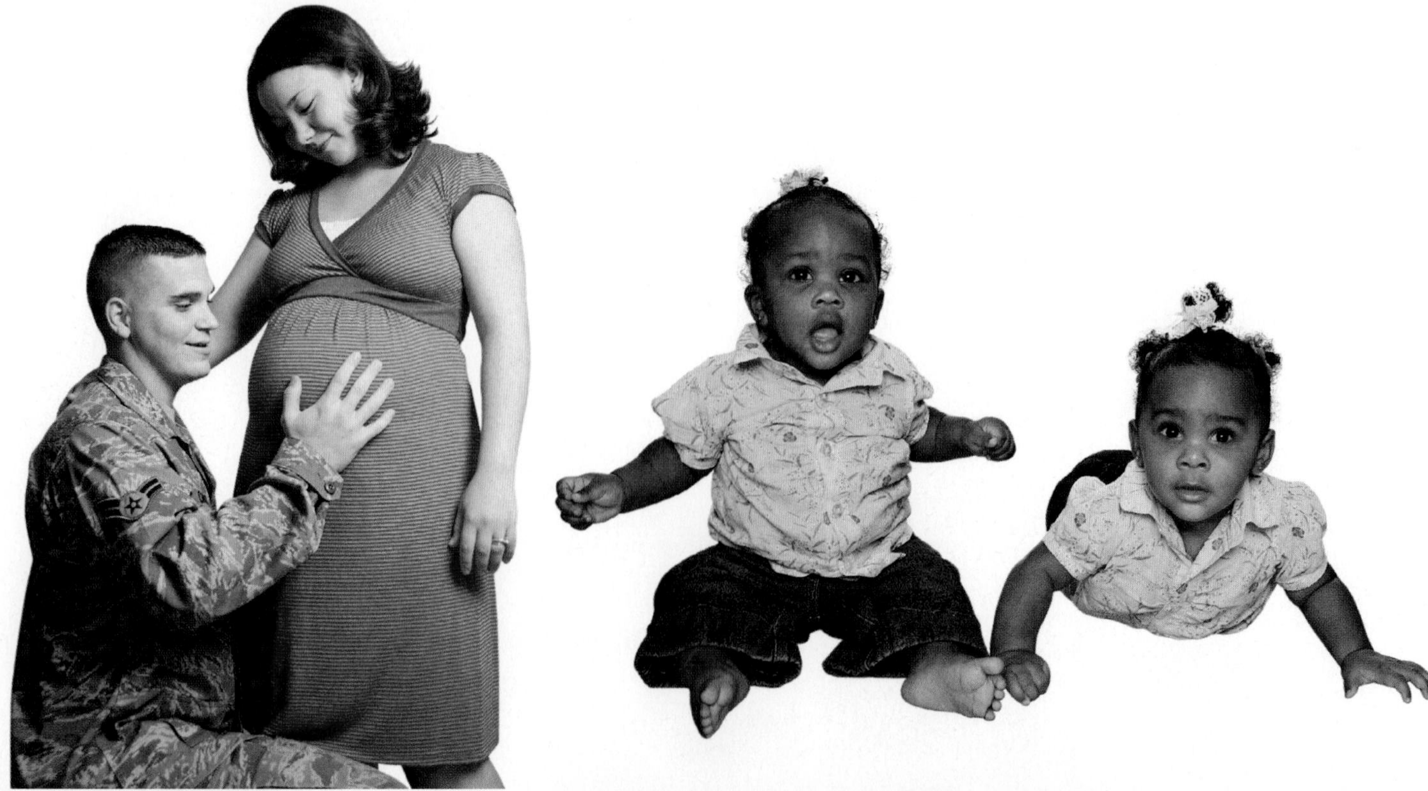

parents place a high priority on the physical survival of their young. That's why parents the world over make enormous sacrifices, often endangering themselves, to keep their children physically safe and healthy. Second, parents and the larger societies in which families are embedded devote considerable resources to teaching children the skills that they need to survive in adulthood. Nowadays, these skills include literacy, numeracy, and other academic skills that are needed for economic independence. But adults also help children learn how to do domestic chores, when to recognize that an apology is in order, and how to cope when a teacher or peer doesn't seem to like them.

When we move into another broad class of child-rearing goals, those that address the connection between the individual and the society in which she lives, ideas begin to diverge. Some groups focus on teaching children that the highest goal in life is to contribute to the good of the group as a whole, whereas others place a higher priority on independence, self-sufficiency, and individual achievement. Such differences have led to varying views of the role and importance of childhood and adolescence to the whole of the human lifespan: Is childhood a period of innocence during which protection from corruption can ensure that each child will grow up to be a productive member of society? Is it a time when parents must teach children to curb inborn impulses so that they will be unlikely to harm others or themselves when they attain the freedom that comes with adulthood? Or is it a period during which society can shape its young members to fill the adult roles that are vital to the society's survival?

Philosophers' attempts to answer such questions gave birth to developmental science. In the first chapter in this unit, you will read about their ideas and how the union of philosophy and the scientific method gave rise to the field of developmental psychology. You will also learn about the methods that developmental scientists use to study age-related change. In Chapter 2, we will turn our attention to long-standing and contemporary theories that guide the study of child development. Finally, the fascinating process through which a single fertilized egg develops into a newborn infant is the topic of Chapter 3.

The Whole Child In Focus

Keep the Changs' story in mind as you read through the next three chapters, and consider how their lives will change as they prepare for and then welcome their new baby into the world. Does everything turn out the way they expected? We'll learn more about Lisa's pregnancy and the new addition to the Chang family at the end of this unit.

LIMON

Chapter

1

Basic Concepts and Methods

The last time you saw a child or teenager whom you hadn't seen for a while, the chances are good that you made an observation like "He's grown so much since the last time I saw him" or "She's turned into a beautiful young lady." Such comments suggest that we humans are natural observers of the ways in which we change with age. But we also notice characteristics that seem to stay the same over time. We might say, "He's always had a mean streak" or "She's always been such a sweet child." And our powers of observation don't stop with simple descriptions. We also come up with theories to explain our observations. Have you ever said something like "They don't discipline that child; no wonder she's such a brat" or "He's really smart, just like his father; I guess it runs in the family"?

Scientists who study human development do precisely the same things. Their goal is to produce observations and explanations that can be applied to as wide a range of human beings and as many contexts as possible. To accomplish this goal, they study both change and stability. In addition, they make predictions about development and use scientific methods to test them. Finally, most hope that their findings can be used to positively influence the development of individual human beings.

In this chapter, you will learn how the science of human development came into being. You will also learn about the key issues in the scientific study of development. In addition, when you finish reading the chapter, you will be acquainted with the research designs and methods used by developmentalists.

Learning Objectives

An Introduction to Human Development

- 1.1 What ideas about development were proposed by early philosophers and scientists?
- 1.2 What major domains and periods do developmental scientists use to organize their discussions of child and adolescent development?

Key Issues in the Study of Human Development

- 1.3 How do developmentalists view the two sides of the nature-nurture debate?
- 1.4 What is the continuity-discontinuity debate?
- 1.5 How do the three kinds of age-related change differ?
- 1.6 How does consideration of the contexts in which change occurs improve scientists' understanding of child and adolescent development?

Research Methods and Designs

- 1.7 What are the goals of scientists who study child and adolescent development?
- 1.8 What descriptive methods are used by developmental scientists?
- 1.9 What is the primary advantage of the experimental method?
- 1.10 How do cross-sectional, longitudinal, and sequential research designs differ?
- 1.11 Why is cross-cultural research important to the study of human development?
- 1.12 What are the ethical standards that developmental researchers must follow?

An Introduction to Human Development

The field of **developmental science** is the application of scientific methods to the study of age-related changes in behavior, thinking, emotion, and personality. As such, developmental science draws upon theories and research from several different disciplinary perspectives. These include psychology, sociology, anthropology, and economics, as well as biology and medicine.

Long before scientific methods were used to study development, though, philosophers offered a variety of explanations for the differences they observed in individuals of different ages. In the 19th century, early pioneers in the study of human behavior applied scientific methods to questions about age-related change. Their efforts led to useful ways of categorizing important issues in the study of development and revealed a wealth of data suggesting that child development is a highly complex process.

Learning Objective 1.1

What ideas about development were proposed by early philosophers and scientists?

Philosophical and Scientific Roots

Early philosophers' ideas about development were derived from spiritual authorities, general philosophical orientations, and deductive logic. Typically the philosophers focused on why babies, who appear quite similar, grow up to vary widely, and they were primarily concerned with the moral dimensions of development. In the 19th century, though, people who wanted to better understand human development turned to science.

LESSON XXXII.

VERBS.—REVIEW.

1. Name the mode of each verb in these sentences:
   1. Bring me some flowers.
   2. I must not be careless.
   3. Who is the King of Glory?
   4. Can that be the man?
   5. The pupils have recited well.
   6. Passionate men are easily irritated.
   7. Do not walk so fast.
   8. The prize cannot be obtained without labor.
   9. Idleness often leads to vice.
   10. Live for something.
   11. In all climates, spring is beautiful.
   12. I would have gone if I had known that I was needed.
   13. If we would seem true, we must be true.

This page from the *Hoenshel's Complete Grammar*, published in 1895, illustrates the influence of the doctrine of original sin on education and child-rearing. Statements that promote religious and moral principles are embedded in this exercise on verbs. The idea was that the goals of teaching grammar to children and shaping their spiritual development could be, and should be, accomplished simultaneously.

Original Sin, the Blank Slate, and Innate Goodness The Christian doctrine of *original sin*, often attributed to 4th-century philosopher Augustine of Hippo, taught that all humans are born with a selfish nature. Advocates of the original sin view argued that, to reduce the influence of this inborn tendency toward selfishness, parents and teachers must help children realize their need for spiritual rebirth and provide them with religious training. Thus, from this perspective, developmental outcomes, both good and bad, are the result of each individual's struggle to overcome an inborn tendency to act immorally when doing so somehow benefits the self.

By contrast, 17th-century English philosopher John Locke drew upon a broad philosophical approach known as *empiricism* when he claimed that the mind of a child is a *blank slate*. Empiricism is the view that humans possess no innate tendencies and that all differences among humans are attributable to experience. As such, the blank slate view suggests that adults can mold children into whatever they want them to be. Therefore, differences among adults can be explained in terms of differences in their childhood environments rather than as a result of a struggle to overcome any kind of inborn tendencies, as the original sin view proposed.

Different still was the *innate goodness* view proposed by 18th-century Swiss philosopher Jean-Jacques Rousseau. He claimed that all human beings are naturally good and seek out experiences that help them grow (Ozmon & Craver, 1986). Rousseau believed that children need only nurturing and protection to reach their full potential. Good developmental outcomes happen when a child's environment doesn't interfere with her attempts to nurture her own development. In contrast, poor outcomes occur when a child is frustrated in her efforts to express the innate goodness with which she was born. Thus, the innate goodness and original sin approaches share the view that development involves a struggle between internal and

developmental science the application of scientific methods to the study of age-related changes in behavior, thinking, emotion, and personality

external forces. In contrast to both, the blank slate view sees the child as a passive recipient of environmental influences.

Early Scientific Theories The 19th century brought an explosion of interest in how scientific methods might be applied to questions that previously had been thought to be in the domain of philosophy. Charles Darwin, for example, became well known for proposing the idea that the wide variety of life forms that exist on Earth evolved gradually as a result of the interplay between environmental factors and genetic processes. Moreover, Darwin proposed that studying children's development might help scientists better understand the evolution of the human species. To that end, Darwin and other like-minded scientists kept detailed records of their own children's early development (called *baby biographies*), in the hope of finding evidence to support the theory of evolution (Lamb, Bornstein, & Teti, 2002). These were the first organized studies of human development, but critics claimed that studying children for the purpose of proving a theory might cause observers to misinterpret or ignore important information.

Charles Darwin, who fathered 10 children, initiated the scientific study of childhood. He used the same scientific methods that led to the discoveries on which he based his theory of evolution to make and record daily observations of his children's development.

G. Stanley Hall of Clark University wanted to find more objective ways to study development. He used questionnaires and interviews to study large numbers of children. His 1891 article entitled "The Contents of Children's Minds on Entering School" represented the first scientific study of child development (White, 1992).

Hall agreed with Darwin that the milestones of childhood were similar to those that had taken place in the development of the human species. He thought that developmentalists should identify **norms**, or average ages at which developmental milestones are reached. Norms, Hall said, could be used to learn about the evolution of the species as well as to track the development of individual children. In 1904, Hall published *Adolescence: Its Psychology and Its Relations to Physiology, Anthropology, Sociology, Sex, Crime, Religion and Education.* This book introduced the idea that adolescence is a unique developmental period.

Arnold Gesell's research suggested the existence of a genetically programmed sequential pattern of change (Gesell, 1925; Thelen & Adolph, 1992). Gesell used the term **maturation** to describe such a pattern of change. He thought that maturationally determined development occurred regardless of practice, training, or effort. For example, infants don't have to be taught how to walk—they begin to do so on their own once they reach a certain age. Because of his strong belief that many important developmental changes are determined by maturation, Gesell spent decades studying children and developing norms. He pioneered the use of movie cameras and one-way observation devices to study children's behavior. Gesell's findings became the basis for many tests that are used today to determine whether individual children are developing normally (see *Developmental Science in the Clinic* on page 8).

THE WHOLE CHILD IN FOCUS

What milestone, or *norm*, did the Changs' baby have to reach before being discharged from the hospital? Find out on page 93.

norms average ages at which developmental milestones are reached

maturation the gradual unfolding of a genetically programmed sequential pattern of change

The Domains and Periods of Development

Learning Objective 1.2

What major domains and periods do developmental scientists use to organize their discussions of child and adolescent development?

Scientists who study age-related changes often use three broad categories, called *domains of development*, to classify those changes. The **physical domain** includes changes in the size, shape, and characteristics of the body. For example, developmentalists study the physiological processes associated with puberty. Also included in this domain are changes in how individuals sense and perceive the physical world, such as the gradual development of depth perception over the first year of life.

Changes in thinking, memory, problem-solving, and other intellectual skills are included in the **cognitive domain**. Researchers working in the cognitive domain study topics as diverse as how children learn to read and why memory functions improve so

physical domain changes in the size, shape, and characteristics of the body

cognitive domain changes in thinking, memory, problem-solving, and other intellectual skills

DEVELOPMENTAL SCIENCE IN THE CLINIC

The Importance of Norms

Like many new parents, Derrick and Tracy purchased an infant care book that included information about the normal sequence of infant development. They delighted in noting that their newborn son, Blake, seemed to be capable of doing everything that a newborn should be able to do. The book said that he should begin to try to roll over between 1 and 2 months of age, so, as the weeks passed, they eagerly looked for signs that the little boy was trying to roll over. When no such signs had appeared by the time the baby reached the 2-month mark, Derrick and Tracy were comforted by the book's emphasis on individual differences. By 3 months, though, they were beginning to worry.

Derrick and Tracy shared their concerns with the nurse practitioner to whom they usually went for Blake's well-baby check-ups. Like that of most health-care professionals who work with infants and children, the nurse practitioner's policy with regard to parental concerns of this kind was to carry out a formal assessment of the infant's development (Overby, 2002). As a result, she decided to administer the *Denver Developmental Screening II (Denver II)* to Blake.

The Denver II is a *norm-referenced* test of infant and early childhood development (Frankenburg & Dodds, 1990). Norm-referenced tests compare an individual child's performance to that of others of the same age. The norms themselves are based on data that the tests' authors collect on hundreds or even thousands of healthy children. Each test provides health-care professionals with a standard for determining whether further evaluation is needed. For example, the Denver II manual recommends that a child be referred for more thorough testing if he fails to exhibit skills that are typical for 90% of children of his age (Kauffman, 2005).

The establishment of developmental norms did not prove to be as valuable to the study of human evolution as G. Stanley Hall and others had hoped. Nevertheless, the concept of norms turned out to be one of the most useful ideas in the history of developmental science. Norms that are determined through careful and thorough empirical studies help professionals such as Blake's nurse practitioner identify potential problems earlier than they might otherwise. Early identification is of vital importance in cases in which a child's developmental delays are caused by some kind of curable disease process. Even for children whose delays are the result of conditions that cannot be treated, early identification helps families identify the strategies and resources that they will need to ensure that a child with a disability will reach his full developmental potential.

Questions for Reflection

1. If you were the parent of an infant who appeared to have a developmental delay, what kind of "self-talk" do you think you would engage in before speaking to a health-care professional about the problem?
2. Why do the norms for tests such as the Denver II need to be based on studies of large numbers of children?

---

dramatically in adolescence. They also examine the ways in which individual differences among children and adults, such as differences in intelligence test scores, are related to other variables within this domain. By contrast, the **socioemotional domain** includes changes in variables that are associated with the relationship of an individual to the self and to others. For instance, studies of children's social skills fall into the socioemotional domain, as does research on individual differences in personality and individuals' beliefs about themselves.

Using domain classifications helps to organize discussions of human development. However, it is always important to remember that the three domains do not function independently. For instance, when a boy goes through puberty, which is a change in the physical domain, his ability to think abstractly (cognitive domain) and his feelings about potential romantic partners (socioemotional domain) change as well.

In addition to classifying developmental events according to domains, developmental scientists also use a system of age-related categories known as *periods of development*. The first of these periods, the *prenatal period*, is the only one that has clearly defined biological boundaries at its beginning and end; it begins at conception and ends at birth. The next period, *infancy*, begins at birth and ends when children begin to use language to communicate, a milestone that marks the start of *early childhood*. Thus, while infancy begins at birth for all children, its end point can vary from one child to another. A social event, the child's entrance into school or some other kind of formal training, marks the transition from early to *middle childhood*. Consequently, cultures vary to some degree with regard to when early childhood ends and middle childhood begins.

socioemotional domain change in variables that are associated with the relationship of an individual to the self and others

By contrast, a biological milestone, puberty, signals the end of middle childhood and the beginning of *adolescence*. Still, the timing of this transition varies across individuals. And when does adolescence end? One way of answering this question is by noting that different cultures set different legal boundaries for the end of adolescence and the beginning of adulthood. For instance, a person must be 18 years of age to join the military without parental permission in the United States, but 16 is the age of majority for military service in the United Kingdom. Even within one culture, such as the United States, legal adulthood is defined differently for different activities: 16 for driving, 17 or 18 for criminal accountability, 18 for signing contracts, 21 for buying alcohol, and 24 for economic independence with regard to college financial aid.

Despite the difficulties involved in defining the various periods of development, they can still serve as a useful system for organizing the study of development. As a result, this textbook is organized around them. For our purposes, the first 2 years after birth constitute infancy. Early childhood is defined as the years between 2 and 6. Our chapters on middle childhood discuss development between the ages of 6 and 12. Adolescence is defined as the years from 12 to 18.

Key Issues in the Study of Human Development

There are several key issues that cut across all of the domains and periods of development. These include the relative contributions of biological and environmental factors to development and the presence or absence of stages. In addition, one researcher might propose that a specific change is common to all human beings, while another might propose that the change in question occurs under some conditions but not others. Researchers debate, too, the degree to which the settings in which development occurs contribute to developmental outcomes.

Nature versus Nurture

Learning Objective 1.3

How do developmentalists view the two sides of the nature-nurture debate?

Some early developmentalists thought of change as resulting from *either* forces outside the person *or* forces inside the person. The debate about the relative contributions of biological processes and experiential factors to development is known as the **nature-nurture debate**. In struggling with this important issue, psychologists have moved away from either/or approaches toward more subtle ways of looking at both types of influences. For example, the concept of **inborn biases** is based on the notion that children are born with tendencies to respond in certain ways. Some of these inborn biases are shared by virtually all children, such as the sequence in which children acquire spoken language—single words precede two-word sentences, and so on (Pinker, 2002).

Other inborn biases may vary from one individual to another. Even in the early days of life, for example, some infants are relatively easy to soothe when they become distressed, while others are more difficult to console. Whether these inborn patterns are coded in the genes, are created by variations in the prenatal environment, or arise through some combination of the two, the basic point is that a baby is not a blank slate at birth. Babies seem to start life prepared to seek out and react to particular kinds of experiences (Thompson & Goodvin, 2005).

Thinking on the nurture side of the issue has also become more complex. For example, modern developmentalists have accepted the concept of *internal models of experience.* The key element in this concept is the idea that the effect of a particular experience depends not on any objective properties of the experience but rather on the individual's *interpretation* of it, the meaning the individual attaches to that experience. For instance, suppose a friend says to you, "Your new haircut looks great; it's a lot nicer when it's short like that." Your friend intends to pay you a compliment, but you also hear an implied criticism ("Your hair used to look awful"), so your reactions, your feelings, and even your relationship with your friend are affected by how you interpret the comment—not by what your friend meant or by the objective qualities of the remark.

nature-nurture debate the debate about the relative contributions of biological processes and experiential factors to development

inborn biases the notion that children are born with tendencies to respond in certain ways

Learning Objective 1.4

What is the continuity-discontinuity debate?

Continuity versus Discontinuity

Another key issue in the study of human development is the *continuity-discontinuity* issue. The question is whether age-related change is primarily a matter of amount or degree (the *continuity* side of the debate) or more commonly involves changes in type or kind (the *discontinuity* side). For example, a 2-year-old is likely to have no individual friends among her playmates, while an 8-year-old is likely to have several. We could think of this as a **quantitative change** (a change in amount) from zero friends to some friends. This view implies that the qualitative aspects of friendship are the same at every age—or, as developmentalists would express it, changes in friendship are *continuous* in nature. Alternatively, we could think of the difference in friendships from one age to another as a **qualitative change** (a change in kind or type)—from disinterest in peers to interest or from one sort of peer relationship to another. In other words, from this perspective, changes in friendships are *discontinuous* in that each change represents a change in the quality of a child's relationships with peers. Thus, friendships at age 2 are quite different from friendships at age 8 in ways that cannot be captured by describing them solely in terms of the number of friends a child has.

Of particular significance is the idea that, if development consists only of additions (quantitative change), then the concept of **stages**, qualitatively distinct periods of development, is not needed to explain it. However, if development involves reorganization or the emergence of wholly new strategies, qualities, or skills (qualitative change), then the concept of stages may be useful. As you'll learn in Chapter 2, one of the important differences among theories of development is whether they assume development occurs in stages or is primarily continuous in nature.

Learning Objective 1.5

How do the three kinds of age-related change differ?

Three Kinds of Change

Age-related changes are a part of our everyday lives, so much so that we often give them little thought. Yet, have you ever thought about the difference between a human being's first step and his or her first date? Clearly, both are related to age, but they represent fundamentally different kinds of change. Generally, developmental scientists think of each age-related change as falling into one of three categories.

Normative age-graded changes are universal; that is, they are common to every individual in a species and are linked to specific ages. Some universal changes, like a baby's first steps, happen because we are all biological organisms subject to a genetically programmed maturing process. The infant who shifts from crawling to walking and the adolescent who goes through puberty are following a plan that is an intrinsic part of the physical body, most likely something in the genetic code itself.

However, some changes are universal because of shared experiences. A social clock also shapes all (or most) lives into shared patterns of change (Helson, Mitchell, & Moane, 1984). In each culture, the **social clock**, or a set of age norms, defines a sequence of normal life experiences, such as the right time to begin toilet-training, the age at which children are expected to dress themselves, and expectations regarding school-aged children's capacity for doing homework without adult supervision.

Equally important as a source of variation in life experience are historical forces, which affect each generation somewhat differently. Such changes are called **normative history-graded changes**. Social scientists use the word **cohort** to describe a group of individuals who are born within some fairly narrow span of years and thus share the same historical experiences at the same times in their lives. For instance, during the 1980s, a type of instruction called *whole language* was the dominant method of teaching reading in the United States, whereas *phonics* became the predominant teaching strategy during the 1990s. As a result, the literacy skills of adults who attended elementary school in the 1980s are different from those of adults who received their early education in the 1990s. The differences stem from method-of-instruction-based variations in the normative history-graded changes that both cohorts went through when they were in elementary school.

quantitative change a change in amount

qualitative change a change in kind or type

stages qualitatively distinct periods of development

normative age-graded changes changes that are common to every member of a species

social clock a set of age norms that defines a sequence of normal life experiences

normative history-graded changes changes that occur in most members of a cohort as a result of factors at work during a specific, well-defined historical period

cohort a group of individuals who share the same historical experiences at the same times in their lives

nonnormative changes changes that result from unique, unshared events

Finally, **nonnormative changes** result from unique, unshared events. One clearly unshared event in each person's life is conception; the combination of genes each individual receives at conception is unique. Thus, genetic differences—including physical characteristics such as body type and hair color as well as genetic disorders—represent one category of individual differences. Characteristics influenced by both heredity and environment, such as intelligence and personality, constitute another class of individual differences.

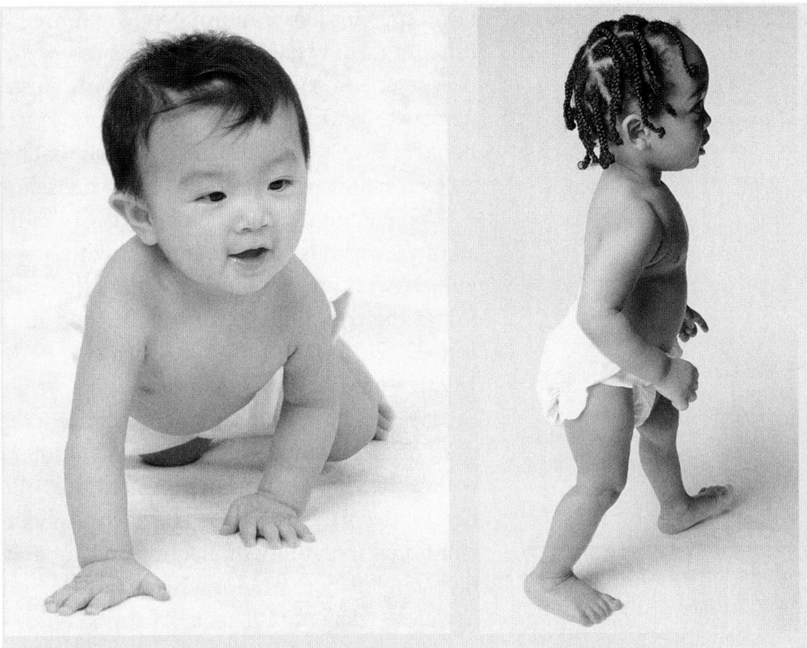

The shift from crawling to walking is an example of a normative age-graded change.

Other individual differences are the result of the timing of a developmental event. Child development theorists have adopted the concept of a **critical period**. The idea is that there may be specific periods in development when an organism is especially sensitive to the presence (or absence) of some particular kind of experience.

Most knowledge about critical periods comes from animal research. For baby ducks, for instance, the first 24–48 hours or so after hatching is a critical period for the development of a following response. Newly hatched ducklings will follow any duck or any other moving object that happens to be around them at that critical time. If nothing is moving at that critical point, they don't develop any following response at all (Hess, 1972).

critical period a specific period in development when an organism is especially sensitive to the presence (or absence) of some particular kind of experience

The broader concept of a **sensitive period** is more common in the study of human development. A sensitive period is a span of months or years during which a child may be particularly responsive to specific forms of experience or particularly influenced by their absence. For example, the period from 6 to 12 months of age may be a sensitive period for the formation of parent-infant attachment.

sensitive period a span of months or years during which a child may be particularly responsive to specific forms of experience or particularly influenced by their absence

Atypical development is another kind of individual change. Atypical development (also known as *abnormal behavior*, *developmental psychopathology*, or *maladaptive development*) refers to deviation from a typical, or "normal," developmental pathway in a direction that is harmful to an individual. One type of atypical development in the cognitive domain is *mental retardation*, a condition in which a child displays intellectual capabilities that are far below those of other children of the same age. In the socioemotional domain, some children have *autism spectrum disorders* that interfere with the development of social relationships.

atypical development development that deviates from the typical developmental pathway in a direction that is harmful to the individual

Contexts of Development

Learning Objective 1.6

How does consideration of the contexts in which change occurs improve scientists' understanding of child and adolescent development?

In recent decades, developmental scientists have become increasingly aware of the importance of looking beyond a child's immediate family for explanations of development. According to this view, often called the **ecological approach**, we must understand the context in which the child is growing: the neighborhood and school, the occupations of the parents and their level of satisfaction in these occupations, the parents' relationships with each other and their own families, and so on. For example, a child growing up in a neighborhood where drugs and violence are a part of everyday life is coping with a set of problems radically different from those of a child in a relatively safe neighborhood.

ecological approach the view that children's development must be studied and understood within the contexts in which it occurs

A good example of research that examines a larger system of influences is Gerald Patterson's work on the origins of delinquency (Patterson, Capaldi, & Bank, 1991; Patterson, DeBaryshe, & Ramsey, 1989). His studies show that parents who use poor discipline techniques and poor monitoring are more likely to have noncompliant children. Once established, such a behavior pattern has repercussions in other areas of the child's life, leading to peer rejection and difficulty in school. These problems, in turn, are likely to push the young person toward delinquency (Dishion, Patterson, Stoolmiller, & Skinner, 1991; Vuchinich, Bank, & Patterson, 1992). So a pattern that began in the family is maintained and exacerbated by interactions with peers and with the school system, as suggested in Figure 1.1.

When considering the contexts of development, however, we have to keep in mind that all of the various contexts interact with one another and with the characteristics of the individuals who are developing within them. Along these lines, some developmentalists have found the concepts of *vulnerability* and *resilience* to be useful (Garmezy, 1993; Garmezy & Rutter, 1983; Masten, Best, & Garmezy, 1990; Moen & Erickson, 1995; Rutter, 1987; Werner, 1995). **Vulnerability** encompasses factors within a child herself or in her environment that cause her to have a higher risk of experiencing poor developmental outcomes than other children do. **Resilience**, the opposite of vulnerability, refers to the collective effects of factors within the child or her environment that offer some protection from the effects of such vulnerabilities. For instance, a child who is born with vulnerabilities such as a tendency toward emotional irritability or alcoholism probably also possesses some protective factors, such as high intelligence, good physical coordination, or physical attractiveness, that tend to make her more resilient in the face of stress. These vulnerabilities and protective factors then interact with the child's environment, so the same environment can have quite different effects, depending on the qualities the child brings to the interaction.

vulnerability factors within the individual or the environment that increase the risk of poor developmental outcomes

resilience factors within the individual or the environment that moderate or prevent the negative effects of vulnerabilities

The combination of a highly vulnerable child and a poor or unsupportive environment produces by far the most negative outcomes (Horowitz, 1990). Either of these two negative conditions alone—a vulnerable child or a poor environment—can be overcome. A resilient child in a poor environment may do quite well, since he can find and take advantage of all the stimulation and opportunities available; similarly, a vulnerable child may do quite well in a

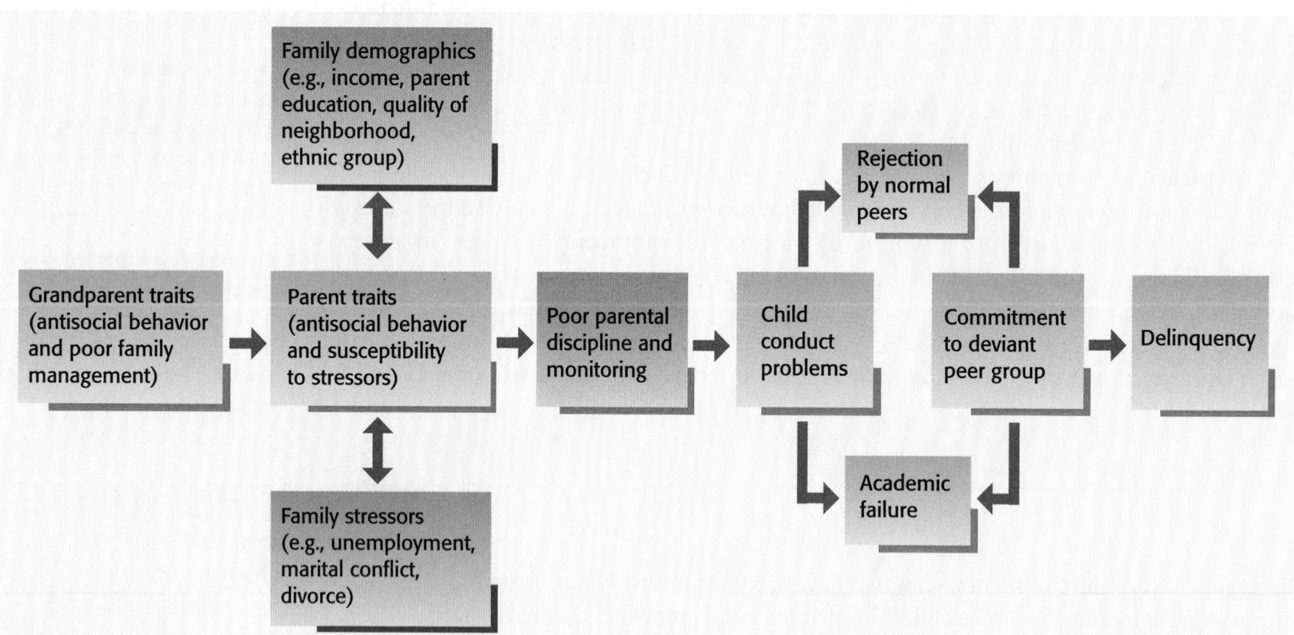

Figure 1.1 Patterson's Model of Antisocial Development

Patterson's model describes the many factors that influence the development of antisocial behavior. The core of the process, in this model, is the interaction between the child and the parent (the red box). One might argue that the origin of antisocial behavior lies in that relationship. But Patterson argues that there are larger ecological, or contextual, forces that are also "causes" of the child's delinquency, some of which are listed in the two blue boxes on the left.

(*Source*: Patterson, G. R., DeBaryshe, B. D., and Ramsey, E., 1989. "A Developmental Perspective on Antisocial Behavior," *American Psychologist, 44*, pp. 331 and 332. Copyright © 1989 by the American Psychological Association. Adapted by permission of the American Psychological Association and B. D. DeBaryshe.)

highly supportive environment in which parents help him overcome or cope with his vulnerabilities. The "double whammy"—being a vulnerable child in a poor environment—leads to very poor outcomes for the child.

Many children who grow up in poverty-stricken neighborhoods are high achievers who are well adjusted. Developmentalists use the term *resilient* to refer to children who demonstrate positive developmental outcomes despite being raised in high-risk environments.

The characteristics of the larger society in which a child's family and neighborhood are embedded matter as well. The term *culture* has no commonly agreed-on definition, but in essence it describes some system of meanings and customs, including values, attitudes, goals, laws, beliefs, moral guidelines, and physical artifacts of various kinds, such as tools, forms of dwellings, and the like. Furthermore, to be called a culture, a system of meanings and customs must be shared by some identifiable group, whether that group is a subsection of some population or a larger unit, and must be transmitted from one generation of that group to the next (Betancourt & Lopez, 1993; Cole, 1992). Culture shapes not only the development of individuals, but also the ideas about what normal development is.

For example, researchers interested in adolescence often study dating behavior. But their findings do not apply to teens in cultures in which dating does not occur, such as those in which parents choose whom adolescents will marry when they reach adulthood. Consequently, developmentalists must be aware that research findings regarding links among dating behavior, sexual activity, and the development of romantic relationships do not constitute universal changes. Instead, they represent developmental experiences that are culturally specific.

One final aspect of the context within which an individual's development occurs involves gender. Two individuals can be quite similar with regard to their individual characteristics and the environment within which they grow up. However, if one is female and the other male, they will experience the interaction between their characteristics and their environment differently. As you will learn in a later chapter, for example, the effects of the earliness or lateness with which a child goes through puberty depend on gender. Thus, early and late puberty have different meanings for boys and girls.

Research Methods and Designs

The easiest way to understand research methods is to look at a specific question and consider the alternative ways it could be answered. Suppose we wanted to answer the following question: "What causes children's attention spans to increase as they get older?" How might we go about it?

The Goals of Developmental Science

Learning Objective 1.7
What are the goals of scientists who study child and adolescent development?

Researchers who study child and adolescent development use the scientific method to achieve four goals: to describe, to explain, to predict, and to influence human development from conception to adolescence. To *describe* development is simply to state what happens. For example, we might measure how long children of different ages pay attention to something and come up with a descriptive statement such as "Children's attention spans get longer as they get older."

Explaining development involves telling why a particular event occurs. To generate explanations, developmentalists rely on **theories**—sets of statements that propose general principles of development. Students often say that they dislike reading about theories; what they want are the facts. However, theories are important because they help us look at facts from different perspectives. For example, "Older children have longer attention spans than younger children do because of changes in the brain that happen as children get older" is a statement

theories sets of statements that propose general principles of development

that attempts to explain the fact of age-related gains in attention span from a biological perspective. Alternatively, we could explain older children's superior attention spans from an experiential perspective, hypothesizing that attention span improves with age because older children have had more time to practice paying attention than younger children have.

Useful theories produce *predictions* researchers can test, or **hypotheses**, such as "If changes in the brain cause children's attention spans to increase, then children whose brain development is ahead of that of their peers should also have longer attention spans." To test the biological hypothesis, we would have to measure some aspect of brain structure or function as well as attention span. Then we would have to find a way to relate one to the other.

We could test the experiential explanation of attention-span improvement by comparing children of the same age who differ in the amount of practice they get in paying attention. For example, we might hypothesize that the experience of learning to play a musical instrument enhances children's ability to attend. If we compare instrument-playing and non–instrument-playing children of the same age and find that those who have musical training do better on tests of attention than their agemates who have not had musical training, the experiential perspective gains support.

If both the biological and the experiential hypotheses are supported by research, they provide far more insight into age-related attention-span change than would either hypothesis alone. In this way, theories add tremendous depth to psychologists' understanding of the facts of human development and provide information that can be used to influence development. As a result, theories make an important contribution to the final goal of developmental science, that of *influencing* children's development.

Let's say, for example, that a child is diagnosed with a condition that can affect the brain, such as epilepsy. If research has shown that brain development and attention span are related, we can use tests of attention span to make judgments about how much her medical condition may have already influenced her brain. If developmental scientists have found that experience affects attention span as well, we may be able to provide her with training that will help her overcome attention-span problems that are likely to arise in the future.

No matter which of these goals underlies the purpose of a particular study, to be most useful, a study must be *generalizable*. That is, its results must apply to individuals other than those who participated in the investigation. As a rule, the findings of any particular study can be generalized only to the *population* represented by the *sample* of individuals who participated in it (see *Developmental Science in the Classroom*). For instance, the results of a study of attention span in 6-year-olds conducted in an affluent private school cannot be generalized to 6-year-olds who live in low-income neighborhoods and attend public schools.

Researchers approach the generalizability issue in three ways. First, when possible, they do everything within their power to recruit participants who represent the population to which they hope to apply their findings. Second, when developmental scientists publish the results of their studies, they provide information about the characteristics of their samples and the populations they represent, noting any limitations on the generalizability of their results. Third, as is true in all sciences, *replication* is required before developmental scientists accept any finding and regard it as generalizable. For instance, to address the limitations of the attention-span study involving 6-year-olds enrolled in an affluent private school, a researcher could repeat the study in low- and middle-income schools. If the findings hold up across schools, regardless of participants' incomes, then the study will be deemed generalizable.

Learning Objective 1.8
What descriptive methods are used by developmental scientists?

Descriptive Methods

A researcher interested in studying the relationship between age and attention span must decide how to go about finding relationships between *variables*. Variables are characteristics that vary from person to person, such as height, intelligence, and personality. When two or more variables vary together, there is some kind of relationship between them. The hypothesis that attention span increases with age involves two variables, attention span and age, and suggests a relationship between them. There are several ways of identifying such relationships.

hypothesis a testable prediction based on a theory

DEVELOPMENTAL SCIENCE IN THE CLASSROOM

The Mozart Effect

Melinda has just graduated with a degree in early childhood education and is excited about starting her first job. She will be teaching a kindergarten class in a small private school. The children's daily schedule calls for a rest period after lunch. Melinda plans to play classical music while the children rest, because she has heard that such music enhances children's intellectual abilities.

Perhaps, like Melinda, you have heard that listening to classical music increases children's scores on intelligence tests. But what does developmental science say? You may be surprised to learn that there is no scientific support whatsoever for this notion (Krakovsky, 2005). So, why do so many people believe it?

Stanford University researchers Adrian Bangerter and Chip Heath have found that the widespread belief that classical music raises children's IQ scores originated with a 1993 report of a study that was published in the prestigious scientific journal *Nature* (Rauscher, Shaw, & Ky, 1993) in which researchers reported that listening to a Mozart sonata appeared to temporarily raise college students' scores on intelligence tests (Bangerter & Heath, 2004). Almost immediately, the popular press began to refer to the study's findings as the "Mozart effect" (ME) and applied them to infants.

The application of the *Nature* report to infants was an error in generalization. No doubt the study's authors were aware of the fact that their study applied only to the population they sampled—that is, to college students. But the media reports went far beyond the generalizability of the *Nature* study by claiming that listening to classical music increased infants' scores on intelligence tests. Ironically, too, for more than a decade, reporters have ignored numerous carefully designed research studies clearly showing that there is no such thing as the ME (Chabris, 1999; Crncec, Wilson, & Prior, 2006; Jones & Zigler, 2002; Krakovsky, 2005; McKelvie & Low, 2002; Steele, Bass, & Crook, 1999). As a result, many popular books and Internet sites devoted to child development continue to promote the idea that listening to music by Mozart raises infants' intelligence test scores and recommend that his music be routinely played in all early childhood classrooms (Krakovsky, 2005).

Of course, listening to Mozart does no harm to young children. Furthermore, studies with adults suggest that it might help Melinda's students relax during their rest period (Smith & Joyce, 2004). But teachers should avoid making the same generalization error with regard to studies of relaxation that the reporters who invented the Mozart effect did. That is, even though Mozart's music was found to be relaxing by college students, it may not necessarily be so for children. As scientists always say, "More research is needed."

Questions for Reflection

1. In your opinion, why are people willing to accept reports such as those about the Mozart effect uncritically?
2. How would you explain the generalization error that was made in the case of the ME to a kindergarten teacher who believed that she should play music by Mozart in her classroom in order to raise her students' IQs?

Case Studies **Case studies** are in-depth examinations of single individuals. To test the hypothesis about attention span and age, we could use a case study comparing one individual's scores on tests of attention span in early and middle childhood. Such a study might tell us a lot about the development of attention span in the individual studied, but we wouldn't know if our findings applied to others.

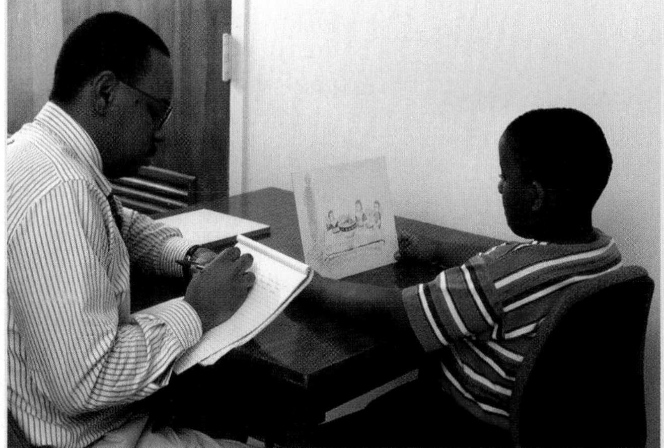

Psychologists who conduct case studies gather detailed information about a single child. Their data often include the results of psychological tests.

Still, case studies are extremely useful in making decisions about individuals. For example, to find out whether a child has mental retardation, a psychologist would conduct an extensive case study involving tests, interviews of the child's parents, behavioral observations, and so on. Case studies are also frequently the basis of important hypotheses about the effects of unusual developmental events, such as head injuries and strokes.

Naturalistic Observation When psychologists use **naturalistic observation** as a research method, they observe people in their normal environments. For instance, to find out more about attention span in children of different ages, a researcher could observe them in their homes or schools. Such studies provide developmentalists with information about psychological processes in everyday contexts.

The weakness of naturalistic observation, however, is observer bias. For example, if the researcher who is observing preschoolers is convinced that most of them have short attention spans, she is likely to ignore any behavior that goes against this view. Because of observer bias, naturalistic observation studies often use "blind" observers, who don't know what the

case study an in-depth examination of a single individual

naturalistic observation the process of studying people in their normal environments

research is about. In most cases, for the sake of accuracy, researchers use two or more observers so that the observations of each observer can be checked against those of the other(s).

Like case studies, naturalistic observation studies are limited in the extent to which the results can be generalized. In addition, naturalistic observation studies are very time-consuming. They must be repeated in a variety of settings so that researchers can be sure people's behavior reflects development and not the influences of a specific environment.

Laboratory Observation **Laboratory observation** differs from naturalistic observation in that the researcher exerts some degree of control over the environment. In a laboratory observation study of attention span, a researcher might observe how long children of different ages pay attention to different kinds of stimuli in the absence of the kinds of distractions that are present in natural settings, such as playgrounds and classrooms. To this end, the researcher could limit the number of children who are in the laboratory at the same time or choose to observe each child alone. Such a study would help the researcher determine whether it is actually the length of their attention spans that distinguishes younger from older children or age-related variations in the capacity for screening out distractions.

Correlations A **correlation** is a relationship between two variables that can be expressed as a number ranging from −1.00 to +1.00. A zero correlation indicates that there is no relationship between the two variables. A positive correlation means that high scores on one variable are usually accompanied by high scores on the other. The closer a positive correlation is to +1.00, the stronger the relationship between the variables. Two variables that change in opposite directions have a negative correlation, and the nearer the correlation is to −1.00, the more strongly the two are connected.

To understand positive and negative correlations, think about the relationship between temperature and the use of air conditioners and heaters. Temperature and air conditioner use are positively correlated. As the temperature climbs, the number of air conditioners in use goes up. Conversely, temperature and heater use are negatively correlated. As the temperature decreases, the number of heaters in use goes up.

If we wanted to test the hypothesis that age is related to attention span, we could use a correlation. All that would be necessary would be to administer tests of attention span to children of varying ages and calculate the correlation between test scores and ages. If there was a positive correlation between age and the number of minutes that children paid attention to a particular stimulus, then we could say that our hypothesis had been supported. Conversely, if there was a negative correlation—if older children paid attention to the stimulus, on average, for a shorter period of time than younger children did—then we would have to conclude that our hypothesis had not been supported.

Useful as they are, though, correlations have a major limitation: They do not indicate causal relationships. For example, even a high positive correlation between attention span and age would tell us only that performance on attention tests and age were connected in some way. It wouldn't tell us what caused the connection. It might be that older children understand the task instructions better than their younger counterparts. In order to identify a cause, we have to carry out experiments. Armed with this knowledge, you can become a critical consumer of news reports that make causal claims on the basis of correlational studies (see *Developmental Science at Home*).

laboratory observation observation of behavior under controlled conditions

correlation a relationship between two variables that can be expressed as a number ranging from −1.00 to +1.00

Learning Objective 1.9

What is the primary advantage of the experimental method?

The Experimental Method

An **experiment** is a study that tests a causal hypothesis. Suppose that we think age differences in attention span are caused by younger children's failure to use attention-maintaining strategies, such as ignoring distractions. We could test this hypothesis by providing attention training to one group of children and no training to another group. If the trained children got higher scores on attention tests than they did before training and the no-training group showed no change, we could claim that our hypothesis had been supported.

experiment a study that tests a causal hypothesis

DEVELOPMENTAL SCIENCE AT HOME

Correlation versus Causation

Three-year-old Mina loves to play with the other children at her child-care center and can't wait to get to "school" each morning. But her mother, Christina, is worried about reports she has heard on the news about the possible harmful effects of child care on children's development. Like most parents, Christina wants what is best for her child, but she also needs to work. She wonders how to find a balance between Mina's need for quality time with Mom and her family's economic needs.

When research results are at variance with our personal values or with the decisions we have made about our lives, many of us respond by saying either "I agree with that study" or "I don't agree with that study." A better approach is to learn to use knowledge of research methods to become a "critical consumer" of research. For example, suppose Christina is a friend of yours and, knowing that you are taking a course in child development, she asks you for advice regarding the news report about which she is concerned. After reading this chapter, you should know that only an experiment can produce the kind of proof that Christina needs. To demonstrate that child care causes behavior problems, researchers would have to randomly assign infants to child-care and home-care groups. You should be aware that such a study would be unethical and, therefore, impossible. Thus, a news report may claim that a study showing a correlation between child care and behavior problems demonstrates that one causes the other, but you, the critical consumer, should know better. Once you make Christina aware of the scientific merits of the study, she can move forward with balancing such findings with her own values and priorities to make decisions about how she wants to raise her child.

Questions for Reflection

1. How would you apply the ideas in this discussion to interpreting a news report about a study "proving" that being raised by a single parent is harmful to young children?
2. If such a study were reported, what variables other than single parenthood itself might explain the results?

A key feature of an experiment is that participants are assigned randomly to one of two or more groups. In other words, chance determines which group each participant is placed in. When participants are randomly assigned to groups, the groups have equal amounts of variation with respect to characteristics such as intelligence, personality traits, height, weight, and health status. Consequently, none of these variables can affect the outcome of the experiment.

Participants in the **experimental group** receive the treatment the experimenter thinks will produce a particular effect, while those in the **control group** receive either no special treatment or a neutral treatment. The presumed causal element in the experiment is called the **independent variable**, and the characteristic or behavior that the independent variable is expected to affect is called the **dependent variable**.

Applying these terms to the attention-training experiment may help you better understand them. The group that receives the attention training is the experimental group, while those who receive no instruction form the control group. Attention training is the variable that we, the experimenters, think will cause differences in attention span, so it is the independent variable. Performance on attention tests is the variable we are using to measure the effect of the attention training. Therefore, performance on attention tests is the dependent variable.

Experiments are essential for understanding many aspects of development. But two special problems in studying child development limit the use of experiments. First, many of the questions developmentalists want to answer have to do with the effects of unpleasant or stressful experiences—for example, abuse or prenatal exposure to alcohol or tobacco. For obvious ethical reasons, researchers cannot manipulate these variables. For example, they cannot ask one set of pregnant women to have two alcoholic drinks a day and others to have none. To study the effects of such experiences, developmentalists must rely on nonexperimental methods, like correlation.

Second, the independent variable developmentalists are often most interested in is age itself, and they cannot assign participants randomly to age groups. Researchers can compare the attention spans of 4-year-olds and 6-year-olds, but the children differ in a host of ways other than their ages. Older children have had more and different experiences. Thus, unlike psychologists studying other aspects of behavior, developmental psychologists cannot systematically manipulate many of the variables they are most interested in.

To get around this problem, developmentalists can use any of a number of strategies, sometimes called *quasi-experiments*, in which they compare groups without assigning the

experimental group the group in an experiment that receives the treatment the experimenter thinks will produce a particular effect

control group the group in an experiment that receives either no special treatment or a neutral treatment

independent variable the presumed causal element in an experiment

dependent variable the characteristic or behavior that is expected to be affected by the independent variable

participants randomly. Cross-sectional comparisons (which you will read about in the next section) are a form of quasi-experiment. So are studies in which researchers select naturally occurring groups that differ in some dimension of interest, such as children whose parents choose to place them in child-care programs and children whose parents keep them at home. Such comparisons have built-in problems, because groups that differ in one way are likely to be different in other ways as well. Families who place their children in child care are likely to be poorer, are more likely to have only a single parent, and may have different values or religious backgrounds than those who rear their children at home. If researchers find that the two groups of children differ in some fashion, is it because they have spent their daytime hours in different places or because of these other differences in their families? Such comparisons can be made a bit cleaner if the comparison groups are initially selected so that they are matched on those variables that researchers think might matter, such as income, marital status, or religion. But a quasi-experiment, by its very nature, will always yield more ambiguous results than will a fully controlled experiment.

Learning Objective 1.10

How do cross-sectional, longitudinal, and sequential research designs differ?

Designs for Studying Age-Related Changes

In addition to deciding which method to use, developmental scientists must also determine how to incorporate age into their research design. There are three general strategies: (1) Study different groups of people of different ages, using what is called a **cross-sectional design**; (2) study the same people over a period of time, using a **longitudinal design**; (3) combine cross-sectional and longitudinal designs in some fashion in a **sequential design**.

Cross-Sectional Designs To study attention span with a cross-sectional design, we might select groups of participants at each of several ages, such as groups of 2-, 5-, 8-, and 11-year-olds. If we find that each group demonstrates a longer average attention span than all the groups that are younger, we may be tempted to conclude that attention span does increase with age, but we cannot say this conclusively on the basis of cross-sectional data, because these children differ not only in age but also in cohort. The differences in attention span might reflect educational differences and not actually be linked to age or development. Furthermore, cross-sectional studies cannot tell us anything about sequences of change over age or about the consistency of individual behavior over time, because each child is tested only once. Still, cross-sectional research is very useful because it can be done relatively quickly and can give indications of possible age differences or age changes.

Longitudinal Designs Longitudinal designs seem to solve the problems that arise with cross-sectional designs, because they follow the same individuals over a period of time. For example, to examine our attention-span hypothesis, we could test a particular group of children first at age 2, then at age 5, next at age 8, and finally at age 11. Such studies look at sequences of change and at individual consistency or inconsistency over time. And because these studies compare the same people at different ages, they get around some obvious aspects of the cohort problem.

However, longitudinal designs have several major difficulties. One problem is that longitudinal designs typically involve giving each participant the same tests over and over again. Over time, people learn how to take the tests. Such practice effects may distort the measurement of any underlying developmental changes.

Another significant problem with longitudinal studies is that not everyone sticks with the program. Some participants drop out; others die or move away. As a general rule, the healthiest and best-educated participants are most likely to stay, and that fact biases the results, particularly if the study continues into adulthood.

Longitudinal studies don't totally solve the cohort problem either. For example, one famous study, the Oakland Growth Study, followed individuals born between 1918 and 1928 into old age. Consequently, the study's participants experienced certain major historical

cross-sectional design a research design in which groups of people of different ages are compared

longitudinal design a research design in which people in a single group are studied at different times in their lives

sequential design a research design that combines cross-sectional and longitudinal comparisons of development

events, such as the Great Depression and World War II, which probably influenced their development. So, we don't know whether the ways in which they changed across these years, when they were children and teenagers, were caused by developmental processes or by the unique historical period in which they were growing up.

Sequential Designs One way to avoid the shortcomings of both cross-sectional and longitudinal designs is to use a sequential design. To study our attention-span question using a sequential design, we would begin with at least two age groups. One group might include 2- to 4-year-olds, and the other might have 5- to 7-year-olds. We would then test each group over a number of years, as illustrated in Figure 1.2. Each testing point beyond the initial one provides two types of comparisons. Age-group comparisons yield the same kind of information as a cross-sectional study would. Comparisons of the scores or behaviors of participants in each group to their own scores or behaviors at an earlier testing point produce longitudinal evidence at the same time.

Group	Age at testing point 1	Age at testing point 2	Age at testing point 3
A	5 to 7	8 to 10	11 to 13
B	2 to 4	5 to 7	8 to 10

Figure 1.2
A Hypothetical Sequential Study

A hypothetical sequential study of attention span across ages 2 to 13.

Sequential designs also allow for comparisons of cohorts. Notice in Figure 1.2, for example, that those in Group A are 5 to 7 years old at testing point 1, and those in Group B are 5 to 7 years old at testing point 2. Likewise, Group A members are 8 to 10 at point 2, and their counterparts in Group B are this age at point 3. If same-age comparisons of the two groups reveal that their average attention spans are different, the researchers have evidence that, for some reason, the two cohorts differ. Conversely, if the groups perform similarly, the investigators can conclude that their respective performances represent developmental characteristics rather than *cohort effects*, results that reflect the historical forces to which a particular sample is exposed. Moreover, if both groups demonstrate similar age-related patterns of change over time, the researchers can conclude that the developmental pattern is not specific to any particular cohort. Finding the same developmental pattern in two cohorts provides psychologists with stronger evidence than either cross-sectional or longitudinal data alone.

Cross-Cultural Research

Learning Objective 1.11
Why is cross-cultural research important to the study of human development?

Increasingly common in human development research are studies comparing cultures or contexts, a task that researchers approach in several ways. One method of study, borrowed from the field of anthropology, is the ethnographic method. An **ethnography** is a detailed description of a single culture or context based on extensive observation. Often the observer lives in the culture or context for a period of time, perhaps as long as several years. Each ethnographic study is intended to stand alone, although it is sometimes possible to combine information from several different studies to see whether similar developmental patterns exist in the various cultures or contexts.

ethnography a detailed description of a single culture or context

Alternatively, investigators may attempt to compare two or more cultures directly, by testing children or adults in each of the cultures with the same or comparable measures. Sometimes this involves comparing groups from different countries. Sometimes the comparisons are between subcultures within the same country; for example, increasingly common in the United States is research involving comparisons of children or adults living in different ethnic groups or communities, such as African Americans, Hispanic Americans, Asian Americans, and European Americans.

Ethnographers often interact in everyday settings with members of the cultures they study.

Cross-cultural research is important to the study of child and adolescent development for two reasons. First, developmentalists want to identify universal changes—that is, predictable events or processes experienced by individuals in all cultures. Developmentalists don't want to make a general statement about development—such as "attention span increases with age"—if the phenomenon in question happens only in certain cultures. Without cross-cultural research, it is impossible to know whether studies involving North Americans and Europeans apply to people in other parts of the world.

Second, one of the goals of developmentalists is to produce findings that can be used to improve people's lives. Cross-cultural research is critical to this goal as well. For example, developmentalists know that children in cultures that emphasize the community more than the individual are more cooperative than children in more individualistic cultures. However, to use this information to help all children learn to cooperate, they need to know exactly how adults in such cultures teach their children to be cooperative. Cross-cultural research helps developmentalists identify specific variables that explain cultural differences.

research ethics guidelines researchers follow to protect the rights of animals used in research and humans who participate in studies

Learning Objective 1.12

What are the ethical standards that developmental researchers must follow?

Research Ethics

No matter which of the research strategies summarized in Table 1.1 a researcher chooses to use, he is ethically bound to conduct his research according to a well-established set of rules. **Research ethics** are the guidelines researchers fol-

Table 1.1 Research Methods and Designs

Method	Description	Advantages	Limitations
Case Study	In-depth study of one or a few individuals using observation, interviews, or psychological testing	Provides in-depth information; important in the study of unusual events	Results may not generalize beyond the case that is studied; time-consuming; subject to misinterpretation
Naturalistic Observation	Observation of behavior in natural settings	Participants behave naturally	Researchers' expectations can influence results; little control over conditions
Laboratory Observation	Observation of behavior in controlled settings	Enables precise measurement of variables under controlled conditions	Observer bias may influence results
Correlational Study	Determination of a mathematical relationship between two variables	Assesses strength and direction of relationships	Cause and effect cannot be demonstrated
Experiment	Random assignment of participants to control and experimental groups; manipulation of independent (causal) variable	Identifies cause-effect relationships	Results may not generalize to nonresearch settings; many variables cannot be studied
Cross-Sectional Design	Studying participants of different ages at one time	Allows quick access to data about age differences	Individual differences and cohort effects are ignored
Longitudinal Design	Studying participants in one group several times	Tracks developmental changes in individuals and groups	Time-consuming; findings may apply only to the group studied
Sequential Design	Study that combines both longitudinal and cross-sectional components	Collects cross-sectional and longitudinal data relevant to the same hypothesis	Time-consuming; attrition rates across groups differ
Cross-Cultural Research	Research that either describes culture or includes culture as a variable	Generates information about universality and culture-specificity of age-related changes	Time-consuming; constructing tests and methods that are equally valid in different cultures is difficult

low to protect the rights of animals used in research and humans who participate in studies. Ethical guidelines are published by professional organizations such as the American Psychological Association, the American Educational Research Association, and the Society for Research in Child Development. Universities, private foundations, and government agencies have review committees that make sure all research sponsored by the institution is ethical. Guidelines for animal research include the requirement that animals be protected from unnecessary pain and suffering. Further, researchers must demonstrate that the potential benefits of their studies to either human or animal populations will be greater than any potential harm to animal subjects.

Ethical standards for research involving human participants address the following major concerns:

Protection from Harm. It is unethical to do research that may cause participants permanent physical or psychological harm. Moreover, if the possibility of temporary harm exists, researchers must provide participants with some way of repairing the damage. For example, if the study will remind subjects of unpleasant experiences, like rape, researchers must provide them with counseling.

Informed Consent. Researchers must inform participants of any possible harm and have them sign a consent form stating that they are aware of the risks of participating. In order for children to participate in studies, their parents must give permission after the researcher has informed them of possible risks. Children older than 7 must also give their own consent. If the research takes place in a school or child-care center, an administrator representing the institution must consent. In addition, both children and adults have the right to discontinue participation in a study at any time. Researchers are obligated to explain this right to children in language they can understand.

Confidentiality. Participants have the right to confidentiality. Researchers must keep the identities of participants confidential and must report their data in such a way that no particular piece of information can be associated with any specific participant. The exception to confidentiality is when children reveal to researchers that they have been abused in any way by an adult. In most states, all citizens are required to report suspected cases of child abuse.

Knowledge of Results. Participants, their parents, and the administrators of institutions in which research takes place have a right to a written summary of a study's results.

Deception. If deception has been a necessary part of a study, participants have the right to be informed about the deception as soon as the study is over.

Test Prep Center

with mydevelopmentlab

AN INTRODUCTION TO HUMAN DEVELOPMENT

1.1 What ideas about development were proposed by early philosophers and scientists? (pp. 6–7)

The philosophical concepts of original sin, the blank slate, and innate goodness have influenced Western ideas about human development. Darwin studied child development to gain insight into evolution. G. Stanley Hall published the first scientific study of child development and introduced the concepts of norms and adolescence.

1. Classify each of the following statements as consistent with (A) the original sin view, (B) the blank slate view, or (C) the innate goodness view.

    ______ (1) Children are born morally neutral, with no inclination toward either good or evil.

    ______ (2) Children are born with an inclination toward evil.

    ______ (3) Children are born with an inclination toward good.

2. What methods did each of these theorists use to study development?

Theorist	Methods of Studying Development
Charles Darwin	
G. Stanley Hall	
Arnold Gesell	

3. Explain what is meant by this statement: Developmental science is an interdisciplinary field.

____

____

4. From the Multimedia Library within MyDevelopmentLab, read the *Charles Darwin* biography and answer the following question.

In Darwin's view, how do organisms acquire adaptive characteristics, and what are the advantages of acquiring these characteristics?

____

____

1.2 What major domains and periods do developmental scientists use to organize their discussions of child and adolescent development? (pp. 7–9)

Theorists and researchers classify age-related change according to three broad categories: the physical, cognitive, and socioemotional domains. The major periods are prenatal, infancy, early childhood, middle childhood, and adolescence.

5. Based on your own experiences with children and adolescents, give an example of a developmental event in each of the three domains of development for each of the four major developmental periods.

Period	Developmental Event		
	Physical	Cognitive	Socioemotional
Infancy (Birth to 2)			
Early childhood (2 to 6)			
Middle childhood (6 to 12)			
Adolescence (12 to 18)			

KEY ISSUES IN THE STUDY OF HUMAN DEVELOPMENT

1.3 How do developmentalists view the two sides of the nature-nurture debate? (p. 9)

Historically, developmentalists argued that development was affected by either nature or nurture, but now they believe that every developmental change is a product of both.

6. What is the difference between an inborn bias and an internal model of experience?

____

____

7. From the Multimedia Library within MyDevelopmentLab, watch the *Genetic Time Clock* video and answer the following question.

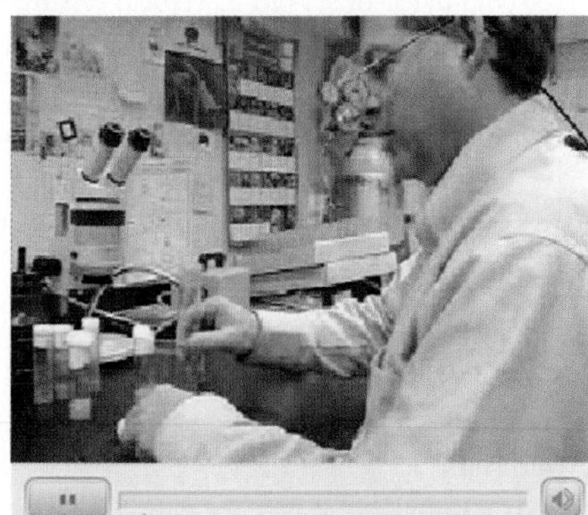

How does the experiment described in the video exemplify the current view of developmentalists regarding the nature-nurture debate?

____

____

1.4 What is the continuity-discontinuity debate? (p. 10)

This debate centers on the question of whether change is a matter of amount or degree or a matter of type or kind. Some developmentalists emphasize qualitative, or discontinuous, changes, whereas others focus on quantitative, or continuous, changes. Theorists who focus on qualitative changes usually propose explanations of development that include stages.

8. Classify each of the following statements as consistent with (A) continuity (quantitative change) or (B) discontinuity (qualitative change) in development.

______(1) The average 6-year-old is taller than the average 5-year-old.
______(2) Four-year-olds use language to communicate, but 4-month-olds do not.
______(3) Twelve-year-olds think more logically than 4-year-olds do.
______(4) The average 7-year-old has a larger vocabulary than the average 5-year-old does.
______(5) At some point during puberty, an adolescent becomes capable of conceiving a child.

1.5 How do the three kinds of age-related change differ? (pp. 10–11)

Normative age-graded changes are those that are experienced by all human beings. Normative history-graded changes are common to individuals who have similar cultural and historical experiences. Nonnormative changes, such as the timing of experiences, can lead to individual differences in development.

9. Give an example of each kind of change.

Type of Change	Example
Normative age-graded	
Normative history-graded	
Nonnormative	

1.6 How does consideration of the contexts in which change occurs improve scientists' understanding of child and adolescent development? (pp. 11–13)

The contexts of development include both individual variables and the settings within which development occurs (e.g., family, neighborhood, culture). Individual traits and contexts interact in complex ways to influence development.

10. List five examples of contexts that should be taken into account when trying to understand an individual child's development.

(1) _______________
(2) _______________
(3) _______________
(4) _______________
(5) _______________

RESEARCH METHODS AND DESIGNS

1.7 What are the goals of scientists who study child and adolescent development? (pp. 13–14)

Developmental psychologists use scientific methods to describe, explain, and predict age-related changes and individual differences. Most also want to use research results to positively influence people's lives.

11. Write Y in the blank if this is a goal of scientists who study human development. Write N if it is not.

______(1) To develop practical strategies that can be used to positively influence development
______(2) To determine which theory of development is true
______(3) To explain the basic facts of development
______(4) To accurately describe the process of development
______(5) To develop theories and test hypotheses
______(6) To predict developmental outcomes

1.8 What descriptive methods are used by developmental scientists? (pp. 14–16)

Case studies and naturalistic observation provide a lot of important information, but it usually isn't generalizable to other individuals or groups. Laboratory observations provide researchers with more control over the settings in which behavior occurs than naturalistic observation does. Correlational studies measure relationships between variables. They can be done quickly, and the information they yield is more generalizable than that from case studies or naturalistic observation.

12. From the Multimedia Library within MyDevelopmentLab, explore *Correlations Do Not Show Causation* and answer the following question.

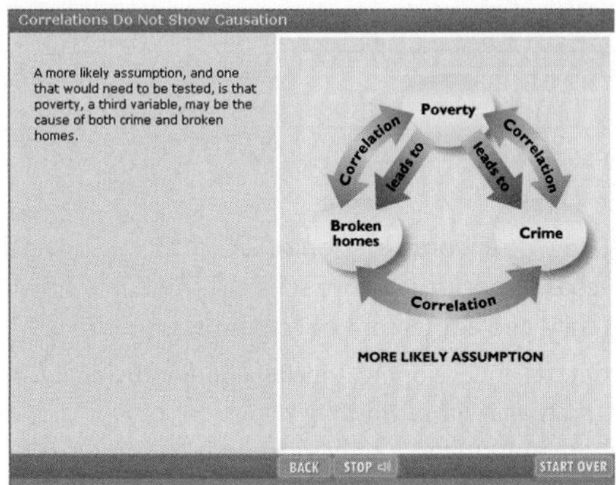

What factors might account for the correlation between family structure and crime? (Hint: One such factor might be that children in single-parent homes receive less supervision than those in two-parent homes.)

____

____

1.9 What is the primary advantage of the experimental method? (pp. 16–18)

To test causal hypotheses, it is necessary to use experimental designs in which participants are assigned randomly to experimental or control groups.

13. From the Multimedia Library within MyDevelopmentLab, run through the *Distinguishing Independent and Dependent Variables* simulation and answer the following question.

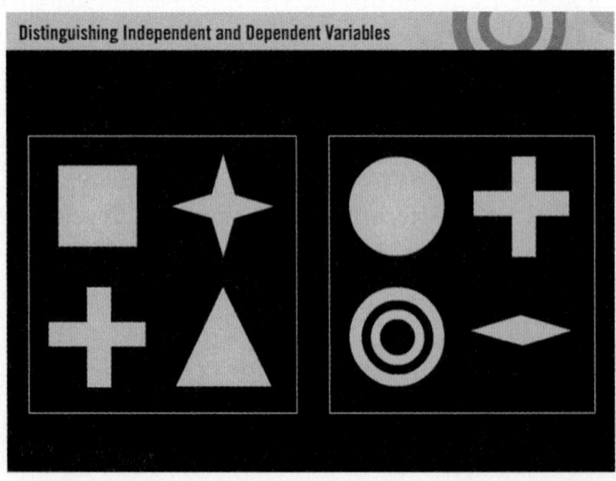

In an experiment, a researcher manipulates the (independent/dependent) variable and measures its effects on the (independent/dependent) variable.

1.10 How do cross-sectional, longitudinal, and sequential research designs differ? (pp. 18–19)

In cross-sectional studies, separate age groups are each tested once. In longitudinal designs, the same individuals are tested repeatedly over time. Sequential designs combine cross-sectional and longitudinal comparisons.

14. Match each research method to its definition.

_______(1) One group studied over time
_______(2) Manipulated independent variable
_______(3) Behavior observed in controlled settings
_______(4) In-depth study of single individual
_______(5) Behavior observed in typical settings
_______(6) Two or more age groups studied at the same time
_______(7) Mathematical relationship between two variables
_______(8) Two or more age groups studied over time

(A) naturalistic observation
(B) case study
(C) laboratory observation
(D) correlation
(E) experiment
(F) cross-sectional
(G) longitudinal
(H) sequential

15. List the advantages and disadvantages of each method of studying age-related change.

Method	Advantages	Disadvantages
Cross-sectional		
Longitudinal		
Sequential		

1.11 Why is cross-cultural research important to the study of human development? (pp. 19–20)

Cross-cultural research helps developmentalists identify universal factors and cultural variables that affect development.

16. From the Multimedia Library within MyDevelopmentLab, watch the *Grandparents and Culture* video and answer the following question.

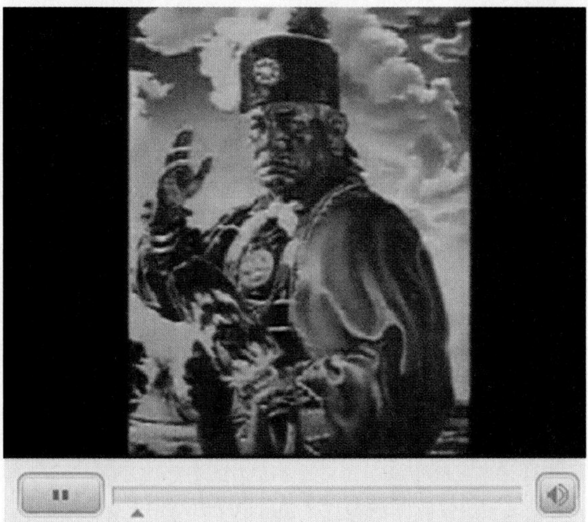

Suppose a group of researchers conducted a study of the influence of grandparents on children's development that included only European American families, and they concluded that grandparents are of little importance. Would their results apply to all cultures? Why or why not?

____

____

1.12 What are the ethical standards that developmental researchers must follow? (pp. 20–21)

Ethical principles governing psychological research include protection from harm, informed consent, confidentiality, knowledge of results, and protection from deception.

17. Explain what researchers must do to meet ethical standards in each area listed in the table.

Issue	What Researchers Must Do
Protection from Harm	
Informed Consent	
Confidentiality	
Knowledge of Results	
Deception	

18. From the Multimedia Library within MyDevelopmentLab, run through the *Ethics in Psychological Research* simulation and answer the following question.

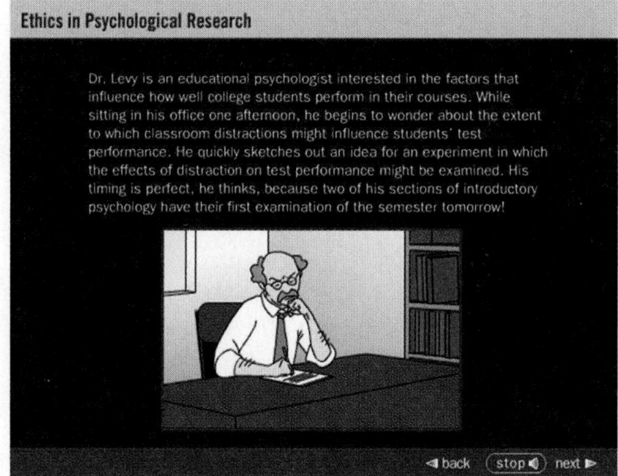

Is deception in research always unethical? Why or why not?

____

____

For answers to the questions in this chapter, turn to page 503. For a list of key terms, turn to page 530.

Succeed with PEARSON mydevelopmentlab

Do You Know All of the Terms in This Chapter?
Find out by using the Flashcards. Want more practice? Take additional quizzes, try simulations, and watch video to be sure you are prepared for the test!

Chapter

2

Theories of Development

As you learned in Chapter 1, developmental psychologists use theories to formulate hypotheses, or testable answers, to "why" questions about behavior. It is helpful to categorize these theories by type. At the broadest level are three families of theories—psychoanalytic theories, learning theories, and cognitive theories. Theories within each of these families attempt to provide developmentalists with comprehensive explanations of just about every facet of human development. Additionally, theories that deal with the biological foundations of development and interactions between these factors and the environment extend developmentalists' understanding of age-related changes beyond that provided by the three major families of theories. Thus, the most comprehensive explanations of developmental phenomena often include ideas from the psychoanalytic, learning, and cognitive approaches as well as from biological and contextual theories.

This chapter will introduce you to the three major families of theories. These theories will come up again and again as you make your way through this book. This chapter will also acquaint you with other theoretical trends in the field of human development, and you will learn how developmental psychologists compare theories.

Learning Objectives

Psychoanalytic Theories

2.1 What are the main ideas of Freud's theory?
2.2 What is the conflict associated with each of Erikson's psychosocial stages?
2.3 What are the strengths and weaknesses of psychoanalytic theories?

Learning Theories

2.4 How did Watson condition Little Albert to fear white, furry objects?
2.5 How does operant conditioning occur?
2.6 In what ways does social-cognitive theory differ from other learning theories?
2.7 How well do the learning theories explain development?

Cognitive Theories

2.8 How does cognitive development progress, according to Piaget?
2.9 How did Vygotsky use the concepts of scaffolding and the zone of proximal development to explain cognitive development?
2.10 How does information-processing theory explain the findings of developmental psychologists such as Piaget?
2.11 What are some of the important contributions and criticisms of cognitive theories?

Biological and Ecological Theories

2.12 How do behavior geneticists explain individual differences?
2.13 What kinds of behaviors are of interest to ethologists and sociobiologists?
2.14 What is the main idea of Bronfenbrenner's bioecological theory?

Comparing Theories

2.15 What assumptions do the three families of theories make about development?
2.16 On what criteria do developmentalists compare the usefulness of theories?
2.17 What is eclecticism?

Psychoanalytic Theories

Every parent knows it's a constant struggle to keep babies from putting everything in their mouths. Why do babies exhibit this behavior? One way of explaining this seemingly odd phenomenon would

psychoanalytic theories theories proposing that developmental change happens because of the influence of internal drives and emotions on behavior

be to suggest that infants derive more physical pleasure from mouthing objects than from manipulating them with other parts of their bodies. Such an approach would most likely belong to the family of **psychoanalytic theories**, a school of thought that originated with Viennese physician Sigmund Freud (1856–1939). Psychoanalytic theorists believe that developmental change happens because internal drives and emotions influence behavior.

Learning Objective 2.1
What are the main ideas of Freud's theory?

Freud's Psychosexual Theory

Most of Freud's ideas about development were derived from his work with adults who were suffering from serious mental disorders. These patients' memories of their early experiences constituted the primary source of data upon which Freud based his theory. One of his most important conclusions about his patients' memories was that behavior is governed by both conscious and unconscious processes. The most basic of these unconscious processes is an internal drive for physical pleasure that Freud called the libido. He believed the libido to be the motivating force behind most behavior.

id in Freud's theory, the part of the personality that comprises a person's basic sexual and aggressive impulses; it contains the libido and motivates a person to seek pleasure and avoid pain

ego according to Freud, the thinking element of personality

superego Freud's term for the part of personality that is the moral judge

Freud also argued that personality has three parts. The **id** contains the libido and operates at an unconscious level; the id is a person's basic sexual and aggressive impulses, which are present at birth. The **ego**, the conscious, thinking part of personality, develops in the first 2 to 3 years of life. One of the ego's jobs is to keep the needs of the id satisfied. For instance, when a person is hungry, it is the id that demands food immediately, and the ego is supposed to find a way to obtain it. The **superego**, the portion of the personality that acts as a moral judge, contains the rules of society and develops near the end of early childhood, at about age 6. Once the superego develops, the ego's task becomes more complex. It must satisfy the id without violating the superego's rules.

The ego is responsible for keeping the three components of personality in balance. According to Freud, a person experiences tension when any of the three components is in con-

DEVELOPMENTAL SCIENCE IN THE CLINIC

The Repressed Memory Controversy

Cherise has always felt anxious in the presence of men whom she doesn't know very well. One day when her roommate, Than, tried to convince her to go out on a blind date, Cherise admitted that her anxieties about being around men prevented her from developing a satisfactory social life. She feared that she would never be able to have a romantic relationship. Than told Cherise about a television program that she had seen in which a woman talked about having similar anxieties. It turned out that the woman had repressed a childhood incident in which she was molested by a neighbor. Once a therapist helped her recall the incident, she was able to overcome her anxieties and was now happily married. Cherise began to wonder whether she might have repressed such a memory, and she made an appointment to talk to a therapist at the university counseling center.

When Cherise meets with the therapist, she will likely learn that memory researchers have investigated Freud's claim that childhood trauma is often intentionally forgotten. In fact, most victims have vivid memories of traumatic events, even though they may forget minor details (Baddeley, 1998; Lindsay & Read, 1994). Moreover, researchers have found that therapists who directly suggest the possibility of repressed memories risk creating false memories in their clients' minds (Ceci & Bruck, 1993). Still, repression does sometimes occur, and discovery of a repressed memory does sometimes improve a person's mental health. Consequently, mental health professionals face a dilemma. Should they ignore the possibility of a repressed memory or risk creating a false one?

Therapists address the dilemma by obtaining training in techniques that can bring out repressed memories without directly suggesting that such memories exist. For example, when clients believe they have recalled a repressed event, therapists help them look for concrete evidence. In the end, however, both therapist and client should recognize that they must often rely on flawed human judgment to decide whether a "recovered" memory was really repressed or was invented in the client's mind.

Questions for Reflection

1. If you thought that you had recovered a repressed memory of childhood abuse, would you prefer to have a skeptical therapist who educated you about research findings showing that such memories are rarely forgotten or one who was supportive and helped you search for evidence of the abuse? Explain your preference.
2. How could Freud's concepts of the id, ego, and superego be used to explain Cherise's anxiety about being with men?

flict with another. For example, if a person is hungry, the id may motivate her to do anything to find food, but the ego—her conscious self—may be unable to find any. Alternatively, food may be available, but the ego may have to violate one of the superego's moral rules to get it. In such cases, the ego may generate *defense mechanisms*, or ways of thinking about a situation that reduce anxiety. For instance, the ego, according to Freud, can cause memories of traumatic events to be repressed, or pushed down into the unconscious component of personality (see *Developmental Science in the Clinic*).

Many of Freud's patients had memories of sexual feelings and behavior in childhood. This led Freud to believe that sexual feelings are important to personality development. Based on his patients' childhood memories, Freud proposed a series of **psychosexual stages** through which a child moves in a fixed sequence determined by maturation (see Table 2.1). In each stage, the libido is centered on a different part of the body. In the infant, the mouth is the focus of the drive for physical pleasure; the stage is therefore called the *oral stage*. As maturation progresses, the libido becomes focused on the anus (hence, the *anal stage*) and later the genitals (the *phallic stage* and eventually the *genital stage*).

Optimal development, according to Freud, requires an environment that will satisfy the unique needs of each period. For example, the infant needs sufficient opportunity for oral stimulation. An inadequate early environment will result in *fixation*, characterized by behaviors that reflect unresolved problems and unmet needs. Thus, as you might guess from looking at the list of stages in Table 2.1, emphasis on the formative role of early experiences is a hallmark of psychoanalytic theories.

Freud's most controversial idea about early childhood is his assertion that children experience sexual attraction to the opposite-sex parent during the phallic stage (ages 3 to 6). Freud borrowed names for this conflict from Greek literature. Oedipus was a male character who was involved in a romantic relationship with his mother. Electra was a female character who had a similar relationship with her father. Thus, for a boy, the Oedipus complex involves a conflict between his affection for his mother and his fear of his father; for a girl, the Electra complex pits her bond with her father against her anxiety over the potential loss of her mother's love. In both genders, the conflict is resolved by abandoning the quest to possess the opposite-sex parent in favor of identification with the same-sex parent. In other words, the phallic stage reaches a successful conclusion when boys develop a desire to be like their fathers and girls begin to view their mothers as role models.

psychosexual stages Freud's five stages of personality development through which children move in a fixed sequence determined by maturation; the libido is centered on a different body part in each stage

Table 2.1 Freud's Psychosexual Stages

Stage	Approximate Ages	Focus of Libido	Major Developmental Task	Some Characteristics of Adults Fixated at This Stage
Oral	Birth to 1 year	Mouth, lips, tongue	Weaning	Oral behavior, such as smoking and overeating; passivity and gullibility
Anal	1 to 3 years	Anus	Toilet training	Orderliness, obstinacy or messiness, disorganization
Phallic	3 to 6 years	Genitals	Resolving Oedipus/Electra complex; identifying with same-sex parent	Vanity, recklessness, sexual dysfunction or deviancy
Latency*	6 to 12 years	None	Developing defense mechanisms; identifying with same-sex peers	None
Genital	12+	Genitals	Achieving mature sexual intimacy	Adults who have successfully integrated earlier stages should emerge with sincere interest in others and mature sexuality.

*Freud thought that the latency period was not really a psychosexual stage, because libido is not focused on the body during this period; therefore, fixation is impossible.

Learning Objective 2.2

What is the conflict associated with each of Erikson's psychosocial stages?

Erikson's Psychosocial Theory

Many of Freud's critics accepted his assertion that unconscious forces influence development, but they questioned his rather gloomy view that childhood trauma nearly always leads to emotional instability in adulthood. Later theorists, known as neo-Freudians, proposed ideas that built on the strengths of Freud's theory but tried to avoid its weaknesses. Erik Erikson (1902–1994) is the neo-Freudian theorist who has had the greatest influence on the study of development (Erikson, 1950, 1959, 1980b, 1982; Erikson, Erikson, & Kivnick, 1986; Evans, 1969). Erikson shared most of Freud's basic assumptions, but he placed more emphasis on the cultural demands associated with children's ages, such as the demand that the child become toilet trained at about age 2 or that the child learn school skills at age 6 or 7. Each stage, then, centers on a particular crisis, or social task. Thus, Erikson called his stages **psychosocial stages** rather than psycho*sexual* stages (see Table 2.2).

THE WHOLE CHILD IN FOCUS

What did the Changs do to help their baby develop a sense of trust very early in life? Find out on page 93.

psychosocial stages Erikson's eight stages, or crises, of personality development in which inner instincts interact with outer cultural and social demands to shape personality

The first crisis, *trust versus mistrust*, occurs during the first year of life, when the child must develop a sense of basic trust in the predictability of the world and in his ability to affect the events around him. Erikson believed that the behavior of the major caregiver (usually the mother) is critical to the child's successful or unsuccessful resolution of this task. Children who reach the end of the first year with a firm sense of trust are those whose parents are loving and respond predictably and reliably to the child.

Erikson saw the child's greater mobility during the toddler years as forming the basis for the next crisis, *autonomy versus shame and doubt*, during which she develops a sense of independence. But if the child's efforts at independence are not carefully guided by the parents and she experiences repeated failure or ridicule, then the results of all the new opportunities for exploration may be shame and doubt instead of a basic sense of self-control and self-worth.

Next, during the *initiative versus guilt* crisis, the child tries out his new cognitive skills and attempts to conquer the world around him. He may try to go out into the street on his

Table 2.2 Erikson's Psychosocial Stages

Approximate Ages	Stage	Positive Characteristics Gained and Typical Activities
Birth to 1 year	Trust versus mistrust	Hope; trust in primary caregiver and in one's own ability to make things happen (secure attachment to caregiver is key)
1 to 3	Autonomy versus shame and doubt	Independence; new physical skills lead to demand for more choices, most often seen as saying "no" to caregivers; child learns self-care skills such as toileting
3 to 6	Initiative versus guilt	Purpose; ability to organize activities around some goal; more assertiveness and aggressiveness (Oedipus/Electra conflict with parent of same sex may lead to guilt)
6 to 12	Industry versus inferiority	Competence; cultural skills and norms, including school skills and tool use (failure to master these leads to sense of inferiority)
12 to 18	Identity versus role confusion	Fidelity; adaptation of sense of self to pubertal changes, consideration of future choices, achievement of a more mature sexual identity, and search for new values
18 to 30	Intimacy versus isolation	Love; person develops intimate relationships beyond adolescent love; many become parents
30 to late adulthood	Generativity versus stagnation	Care; people rear children, focus on occupational achievement or creativity, and train the next generation; turning outward from the self toward others
Late adulthood	Ego integrity versus despair	Wisdom; person conducts a life review, integrates earlier stages, and comes to terms with basic identity; self-acceptance

own; he may take a toy apart and then find he can't put it back together and throw the parts at his mother. The risk is that the child may go too far in his forcefulness or that the parents may restrict and punish too much—either of which can produce guilt. The ideal interaction between parent and child is certainly not total indulgence, but too much guilt can inhibit the child's creativity and interactions with others.

The beginning of schooling is the major force ushering in the *industry versus inferiority* stage. The child is now faced with the need to win approval by developing specific competences—learning to read, to do math, and to succeed at other school skills. Ideally, the child should have sufficient success to encourage a sense of competence but should not place so much emphasis on competence that failure is unacceptable or that she becomes a "workaholic."

The task during puberty is a major one in which the adolescent reexamines his identity and the roles he must occupy, a crisis that Erikson called *identity versus role confusion*. Erikson suggested that two "identities" are involved—a sexual identity and an occupational identity. Peers are helpful to an adolescent's attempts to establish both. What should emerge for the adolescent from this period is an integrated sense of self, of what one wants to do and be, and of one's appropriate sexual role.

Adhering to group norms regarding which clothes are "in" and "out" is one of the ways in which Erikson says teenagers begin to construct a sense of identity that distinguishes them from their parents.

In contrast to Freud's, Erikson's stages extend beyond the childhood and adolescent years. In the first of the three adult stages, the young adult confronts the crisis of *intimacy versus isolation*. Erikson defined intimacy as "the ability to fuse your identity with someone else's without fear that you're going to lose something yourself" (Erikson, in Evans, 1969). In the second adult stage, middle-aged men and women face the crisis of *generativity versus stagnation*, which is "primarily the concern in establishing and guiding the next generation" (Erikson, 1963, p. 267). Finally, elderly adults or those who are younger but who are faced with a terminal illness must resolve the crisis of *ego integrity versus despair*. In this stage, the individual reviews her life and, if satisfied with the results, achieves ego integrity. If not, the person experiences despair.

Evaluation of Psychoanalytic Theories

Learning Objective 2.3

What are the strengths and weaknesses of psychoanalytic theories?

Psychoanalytic theories such as Freud's and Erikson's, summarized in Table 2.3 on page 32, have several attractive aspects. Most centrally, they highlight the importance of the child's earliest relationships with caregivers. Furthermore, they suggest that the child's needs change with age, so parents and other caregivers must continually adapt to the changing child. One of the implications of this is that we should not think of "good parenting" as an unchanging quality. Some people may be very good at meeting the needs of an infant but less capable of dealing with teenagers' identity struggles. The child's eventual personality and her overall mental health thus depend on the interaction pattern that develops in a particular family. The idea of changing needs is an extremely attractive element of these theories, because more and more of the research in developmental psychology is moving developmentalists toward just such a conception of the process.

Psychoanalytic theories have also given psychologists a number of helpful concepts, such as the unconscious, the ego, and identity, which have become a part of everyday language as well as theory. Moreover, psychologists are taking a fresh look at Freud's ideas about the importance of defense mechanisms in coping with anxiety (Cramer, 2000). Freud is also usually credited with the invention of psychotherapy, which is still practiced today. An additional strength of the psychoanalytic perspective is the emphasis on continued development during adulthood found in Erikson's theory. His ideas have provided a framework for a great deal of new research and theorizing about adult development.

Table 2.3 Psychoanalytic Theories

Theory	Main Idea	Evaluation: Strengths	Evaluation: Weaknesses
Freud's Psychosexual Theory	Personality develops in five stages from birth to adolescence; in each stage, the need for physical pleasure is focused on a different part of the body.	Emphasizes importance of experiences in infancy and early childhood; provides psychological explanations for mental illness	Sexual feelings are not as important in personality development as Freud claimed.
Erikson's Psychosocial Theory	Personality develops through eight life crises across the entire lifespan; a person finishes each crisis with either a good or a poor resolution.	Helps explain the role of culture in personality development; is important in lifespan psychology; provides useful description of major themes of personality development at different ages	Describing each period in terms of a single crisis is probably an oversimplification.

The major weakness of psychoanalytic theories is the fuzziness of many of their concepts. For example, how could researchers detect the presence of the id, ego, superego, and so on? Without more precise definitions, it is extremely difficult to test these theories, despite their provocative explanations of development.

Learning Theories

Psychologist John Watson (1878–1958) offered ideas about human development that were very different from those of Freud and other psychoanalysts. Watson believed that, through manipulation of the environment, children could be trained to be or do anything (Jones, 1924; Watson, 1930). To refer to this point of view, Watson coined the term **behaviorism**, which defines development in terms of behavior changes caused by environmental influences. As Watson put it,

> Give me a dozen healthy infants, well-formed, and my own specified world to bring them up in and I'll guarantee to take any one at random and train him to become any type of specialist I might select—doctor, lawyer, merchant, chief, and yes, even beggerman and thief, regardless of his talents, penchants, abilities, vocations, and race of his ancestors. (1930, p. 104)

behaviorism the view that defines development in terms of behavior changes caused by environmental influences

Watson's views represent a way of thinking about development that is common to the family of **learning theories**. These theories assert that development results from an accumulation of experiences. As you will see, however, each of the learning theories has a distinctive way of explaining how experience shapes development.

Learning Objective 2.4

How did Watson condition Little Albert to fear white, furry objects?

Classical Conditioning

Watson based many of his ideas about the relationship between learning and development on the work of Russian physiologist and Nobel prize winner Ivan Pavlov (1849–1936). Pavlov discovered that organisms can acquire new signals for existing responses (behaviors). The term **classical conditioning** refers to this principle. Each incidence of learning begins with a biologically programmed stimulus-response connection, or *reflex*. For example, salivation happens naturally when you put food in your mouth. In classical conditioning terms, the food is the *unconditioned (unlearned, natural) stimulus*; salivating is an *unconditioned (unlearned, natural) response.*

learning theories theories that assert that development results from an accumulation of experiences

classical conditioning learning that results from the association of stimuli

Stimuli presented just before or at the same time as the unconditioned stimulus are those which are likely to be associated with it. For example, most foods have odors, and to get to your mouth, food has to pass near your nose. Thus, you usually smell food before you taste it. Food odors eventually become *conditioned (learned) stimuli* that elicit salivation. In effect, they act as a signal to your salivary glands that food is coming. Once the connection between food odors and salivation has been established, smelling food triggers the salivation response even when you do not actually eat the food. When a response occurs reliably in connection with a conditioned stimulus in this way, it is known as a *conditioned (learned) response.*

For Watson, Pavlov's principles of classical conditioning held the key to understanding human development. He viewed developmental change as nothing more than the acquisition of connections between stimuli and responses. To prove his point, Watson set out to show that he could use the principles of classical conditioning to cause an infant to develop a new emotional response to a stimulus. Watson's hapless subject, 11-month-old "Little Albert," was exposed to sudden loud noises while he played with a white rat, a stimulus that had fascinated him when it was first introduced. As a result of the pairing of the rat with the noises, however, Albert learned to fear the rat so thoroughly that he cried hysterically at the mere sight of the rodent. Moreover, he generalized his fear of the rat to other white, fuzzy objects such as a rabbit, a fur coat, and a Santa Claus mask.

As you might guess, Watson's experiment would be regarded as unethical by today's standards. Moreover, few developmentalists would agree with Watson's assertion that classical conditioning explains all of human development. Yet the Little Albert experiment demonstrated that classical conditioning may indeed be the source of developmental changes that involve emotional responses. For this reason, classical conditioning continues to have a place in the study of human development. It is especially important in infancy. Because a child's mother or father is present so often when nice things happen, such as when the child feels warm, comfortable, and cuddled, the mother and father usually serve as conditioned stimuli for pleasant feelings, a fact that makes it possible for the parents' presence to comfort a child. Moreover, classical conditioning is the basis of several useful therapies for anxiety problems (see *Developmental Science in the Classroom* below).

DEVELOPMENTAL SCIENCE IN THE CLASSROOM

Systematic Desensitization

Dr. Rawlins is a psychologist who works in a large urban school district. The children she works with suffer from a wide range of emotional problems, but one of the most common is *school refusal*, a condition in which a child refuses to go to school. When confronted with a case of school refusal, Dr. Rawlins begins by determining whether there is a concrete reason for the child to refuse, such as a fear of being bullied. If such a reason is found, she works with the child's teachers and school administrators to address the problem. In most cases of school refusal, however, children do not want to go to school because they feel anxious in the school setting, just as some adults refuse to fly because they feel anxious on board an airplane (Kauffman, 2005). You might be surprised to learn that the mechanisms at work in John Watson's experiment with Little Albert hold the key to one way of helping children overcome school refusal.

Recall that Little Albert learned to associate a neutral stimulus, a rat, with a stimulus to which his inborn reflexes predisposed him to respond fearfully, a loud noise. Psychologists speculate that children who refuse to go to school because of anxiety are exhibiting a similar pattern. For some reason, the neutral stimulus of school has become associated with stimuli that naturally provoke anxious responses in children. Thus, psychologists reason that children's fear of school can be unlearned through the same stimulus-response mechanism that produced it.

Like many psychologists, Dr. Rawlins uses a technique called *systematic desensitization* to help children with school refusal learn to respond to the school setting differently (Kauffman, 2005; Wolpe, 1958). She begins by teaching the child how to control his respiration rate and muscular contractions in order to achieve a state of physical relaxation. Afterward, Dr. Rawlins helps him learn to "switch on" his relaxation response in connection with each step in the sequence of events that are involved in getting to and staying in school. For example, he will first learn to intentionally relax while getting ready for school. Next, he will practice intentionally relaxing while waiting for the bus, and then while he is on the bus. Once at school, the therapist will encourage him to initiate his relaxation response in front of the school entrance. The final step will be to learn to intentionally relax in the classroom and to initiate the relaxation response whenever he experiences feelings of anxiety during the school day. As a result, the child will learn to associate going to school with the relaxation responses rather than with anxiety.

Questions for Reflection

1. How could systematic desensitization be used to help a child who was bitten by a dog overcome her subsequent fear of all dogs?
2. What actions on the part of parents, teachers, or peers might prevent a child with school refusal from benefiting from systematic desensitization?

Learning Objective 2.5

How does operant conditioning occur?

Skinner's Operant Conditioning

Another behavioral approach to development may be found in a set of learning principles known collectively as **operant conditioning**, a term coined by B. F. Skinner (1904–1990), the most famous proponent of this theory (Skinner, 1953, 1980). Operant conditioning involves learning to repeat or stop behaviors because of the consequences they bring about. **Reinforcement** is anything that follows a behavior and causes it to be repeated. **Punishment** is anything that follows a behavior and causes it to stop.

A *positive reinforcement* is a consequence (usually involving something pleasant) that follows a behavior and increases the chances that the behavior will occur again. For example, if you buy a scratch-off lottery ticket and win $100, you will probably be more willing to buy another ticket in the future than you would if you hadn't won the money.

Negative reinforcement occurs when an individual learns to perform a specific behavior in order to cause something unpleasant to stop. For example, coughing is an unpleasant experience for most of us, and taking a dose of cough medicine usually stops it. As a result, when we begin coughing, we reach for the cough syrup. The behavior of swallowing a spoonful of cough syrup is reinforced by the cessation of coughing.

operant conditioning learning to repeat or stop behaviors because of their consequences

reinforcement anything that follows a behavior and causes it to be repeated

punishment anything that follows a behavior and causes it to stop

Positive and negative reinforcement often interact in complex ways in real-life contexts. For example, most people understand that paying attention to a preschooler's whining is likely to increase it, an example of positive reinforcement. However, parents learn to attend to whining preschoolers because whining is irritating, and responding to it usually makes it stop. In other words, like taking cough syrup for an annoying cough, the parents' behavior of responding to whining is negatively reinforced by its consequence—namely, that the child *stops* whining.

In contrast to both kinds of reinforcement, punishment stops a behavior. Sometimes punishments involve eliminating nice things—taking away TV privileges, for example. However, punishment may also involve unpleasant things such as scolding. Like reinforcement,

DEVELOPMENTAL SCIENCE AT HOME

Unintended Consequences

Every night at bedtime, 5-year-old Keira uses every ploy she can think of to avoid going to sleep. Numerous trips to the bathroom, heart-rending pleas for just one more story, and seemingly endless requests for hugs and kisses have become a part of Keira's nightly routine. The final act of this drama, which gets slightly longer each evening, is repeated every night. Keira's parents reach their breaking point and say "no more" to all of the girl's requests, whereupon Keira initiates a frenzy of kicking, screaming, and crying until exhaustion finally puts her to sleep. Her parents have tried everything they can think of to shorten the process of putting Keira to bed, all to no avail. But they hope that a new approach in which Keira earns stickers for going to bed without protesting will do the trick.

Most parents use consequences to try to change their children's behavior. But most don't realize how easy it is to create unintended consequences if they don't understand all of the mechanisms that are involved in learning from consequences. For example, consider the case of a mother whose 3-year-old son repeatedly demands her attention while she is fixing dinner. The mother doesn't want to reinforce this behavior, so she tries to ignore the boy the first six or eight times he calls to her or tugs at her clothes. But after the ninth or tenth repetition, with his voice getting whinier each time, she can't stand it any longer and finally says something like "All right! What do you want?" Since the mother has ignored most of her son's demands, you might think she has not been reinforcing them. But what the mother has created is a *partial reinforcement schedule,* the same kind of schedule that motivates a gambler to keep on plugging coins into a slot machine in the hope that the big pay-off is coming with the next pull of the lever.

So, what's happening in Keira's case? Notice that the bedtime drama gets longer each night, which means it's being reinforced in some way. Without intending to, Keira's parents are reinforcing her antics by gradually lengthening the amount of time that they are willing to allow her to manipulate them. Consequently, their sticker strategy is unlikely to change Keira's behavior unless they also change the way they respond to the behaviors that she exhibits which allow her to avoid going to bed.

Questions for Reflection

1. If Keira's parents asked for your advice, how would you advise them to modify their plan for using stickers to change their daughter's nightly routine?
2. To what degree is negative reinforcement responsible for Keira's parents' responses to her bed-avoidance behaviors?

punishment is defined by its effect; consequences that do not stop behavior can't be properly called punishments.

An alternative way to stop an unwanted behavior is **extinction**, which is the gradual elimination of a behavior through repeated nonreinforcement. If a teacher succeeds in eliminating a student's undesirable behavior by ignoring it, the behavior is said to have been extinguished.

Laboratory research involving animals was important in the development of Skinner's operant-conditioning theory.

Such examples illustrate the complex manner in which reinforcements and punishments operate in the real world. In laboratory settings, operant conditioning researchers usually work with only one participant or animal subject at a time; they needn't worry about the social implications of behaviors or consequences. They can also control the situation so that a particular behavior is reinforced every time it occurs. In the real world, *partial reinforcement*—reinforcement of a behavior on some occasions but not others—is more common. Studies of partial reinforcement show that people take longer to learn a new behavior under partial reinforcement conditions; once established, however, such behaviors are very resistant to extinction (see *Developmental Science at Home*).

extinction the gradual elimination of a behavior through repeated nonreinforcement

Bandura's Social-Cognitive Theory

Learning Objective 2.6

In what ways does social-cognitive theory differ from other learning theories?

Learning theorist Albert Bandura (b. 1925), whose ideas are more influential among developmental psychologists than those of the conditioning theorists, argues that learning does not always require reinforcement (1977a, 1982, 1989). Learning may also occur as a result of watching someone else perform some action and receiving reinforcement or punishment for that action. Learning of this type, called **social learning** or **modeling**, is involved in a wide range of behaviors. For example, observant school children learn to distinguish between strict and lenient teachers by observing teachers' reactions to the misbehavior of children who are risk-takers—that is, those who act out

social learning (modeling) learning that results from seeing a model reinforced or punished for a behavior

Modeling is an important source of learning for both children and adults. What behaviors have you learned by watching and copying others?

without having determined how teachers might react. As a result, when in the presence of strict teachers, observant children suppress forbidden behaviors such as talking out of turn and leaving their seats without permission. By contrast, when they are under the authority of lenient teachers, these children may display just as much misbehavior as their risk-taking peers.

However, learning from modeling is not an entirely automatic process. Bandura points out that what an observer learns from watching someone else will depend on two cognitive elements: what she pays attention to and what she is able to remember. Moreover, to learn from a model, an observer must be physically able to imitate the behavior and motivated to perform it on her own. Because attentional abilities, memory, and physical capabilities change with age, what a child learns from any given modeled event may be quite different from what an adult learns from an identical event (Grusec, 1992).

According to Bandura, a child learns not only overt behavior, but also ideas, expectations, internal standards, and self-concepts, from models. At the same time, he acquires expectancies about what he can and cannot do—which Bandura (1997) calls *self-efficacy*. Once those standards and those expectancies or beliefs have been established, they affect his behavior in consistent and enduring ways. For example, self-efficacy beliefs influence our overall sense of well-being and even our physical health.

Learning Objective 2.7

How well do the learning theories explain development?

Evaluation of Learning Theories

Several implications of learning theories, summarized in Table 2.4, are worth emphasizing. First, learning theories can explain both consistency and change in behavior. If a child is friendly and smiling both at home and at school, learning theorists would explain the child's behavior by saying that the child is being reinforced for that behavior in both settings. It is equally possible to explain why a child is happy at home but miserable at school. We need only hypothesize that the home environment reinforces cheerful behavior but the school setting does not.

Learning theorists also tend to be optimistic about the possibility of change. Children's behavior can change if either the reinforcement system or their beliefs about themselves change. So, problem behavior can be modified.

Table 2.4 Learning Theories

		Evaluation	
Theory	**Main Idea**	**Strengths**	**Weaknesses**
Pavlov's Classical Conditioning	Learning happens when neutral stimuli become so strongly associated with natural stimuli that they elicit the same response.	Is useful in explaining how emotional responses such as phobias are learned	Explanation of behavior change is too limited to serve as comprehensive theory of human development.
Skinner's Operant Conditioning	Development involves behavior changes that are shaped by reinforcement and punishment.	Provides the basis for many useful strategies for managing and changing human behavior	Humans are not as passive as Skinner claimed; the theory ignores hereditary and cognitive, emotional, and social factors in development.
Bandura's Social-Cognitive Theory	People learn from models; what they learn from a model depends on how they interpret the situation cognitively and emotionally.	Helps explain how models influence behavior; explains more about development than other learning theories do because of addition of cognitive and emotional factors	The theory does not provide an overall picture of development.

The great strength of learning theories is that they seem to give an accurate picture of the way in which many behaviors are learned. It is clear that both children and adults learn through conditioning and modeling. Bandura's addition of mental elements to learning theory adds further strength, since it allows an integration of learning models and other approaches.

However, the learning theorists' approach is not really developmental; it doesn't tell us much about change with age, either in childhood or in adulthood. Even Bandura's variation on learning theory does not tell us whether there are any changes with age in what a child can learn from modeling. Thus, learning theories help developmentalists understand how specific behaviors are acquired but do not contribute to an understanding of age-related change.

Cognitive Theories

The family of theories known as **cognitive theories** emphasizes mental aspects of development, such as logic and memory. Have you ever watched a baby throw things out of her mother's shopping cart? No matter how many objects she drops, she watches each one intently as if she has no idea where it's going to land. Why do babies engage in repetitive actions of this kind? One reason might be that they use their motor skills (throwing things) and senses (watching them) to build mental pictures of the world around them. Thus, infants drop objects and watch them fall until they have learned all they can from this behavior; then they move on to a more mature way of interacting with the world.

cognitive theories theories that emphasize mental processes in development, such as logic and memory

Piaget's Cognitive-Developmental Theory

Learning Objective 2.8

How does cognitive development progress, according to Piaget?

One of the most influential theories in the history of developmental psychology is that of Swiss developmentalist Jean Piaget (1896–1980). Originally educated as a natural scientist, Piaget spent six decades studying the development of logical thinking in children. Because of the popularity of Watson's views, psychologists in the United States paid little attention to Piaget's work. During the late 1950s, however, American developmentalists "discovered" Piaget. From then on, developmental psychologists in the United States began to focus on children's thinking more than on how environmental stimuli influence their behavior.

Piaget based many of his ideas on naturalistic observations of children of different ages on playgrounds and in schools.

Piaget was struck by the fact that all children seem to go through the same sequence of discoveries about their world, making the same mistakes and arriving at the same solutions (Piaget, 1952, 1970, 1977; Piaget & Inhelder, 1969). For example, all 3- and 4-year-olds seem to think that if water is poured from a short, wide glass into a taller, narrower one, there is then more water, because the water level is higher in the narrow glass than it was in the wide glass. In contrast, most 7-year-olds realize that the amount of water has not changed. To explain such age differences in reasoning, Piaget proposed several concepts that continue to guide developmental research.

A pivotal idea in Piaget's model is that of a **scheme**, an internal cognitive structure that provides an individual with a procedure to follow in a specific circumstance. For example, when you pick up a ball, you use your picking-up scheme. Piaget proposed that each of us begins life with a small repertoire of sensory and motor schemes, such as looking, tasting, touching, hearing, and reaching. As we use each scheme, it becomes better adapted to the world; in

scheme in Piaget's theory, an internal cognitive structure that provides an individual with a procedure to use in a specific circumstance

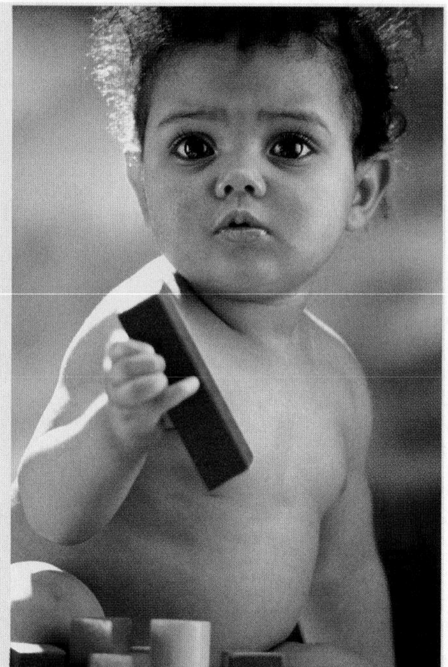
Using Piaget's terminology, we would say that this infant is assimilating the object to her grasping scheme.

other words, it works better. During childhood and adolescence, mental schemes allow us to use symbols and think logically. Piaget proposed three processes to explain how children get from built-in schemes such as looking and touching to the complex mental schemes used in childhood, adolescence, and adulthood.

Assimilation is the process of using schemes to make sense of experiences. Piaget would say that a baby who grasps a toy is assimilating it to his grasping scheme. The complementary process is **accommodation**, which involves changing the scheme as a result of some new information acquired through assimilation. When the baby grasps a square object for the first time, he will accommodate his grasping scheme so that the next time he reaches for a square object, his hand will be more appropriately bent to grasp it. Thus, the process of accommodation is the key to developmental change. Through accommodation, we improve our skills and reorganize our ways of thinking.

Equilibration is the process of balancing assimilation and accommodation to create schemes that fit the environment. To illustrate, think about infants' tendency to put things in their mouth. In Piaget's terms, they assimilate objects to their mouthing scheme. As they mouth each one, their mouthing scheme changes to include the instructions "*Do* mouth this" or "*Don't* mouth this." The accommodation is based on mouthing experiences. A pacifier feels good in the mouth, but a dead insect has an unpleasant texture. So eventually, the mouthing scheme says it's okay to mouth a pacifier, but it's not okay to mouth a dead insect. In this way, an infant's mouthing scheme attains a better fit with the real world.

Piaget's research suggested to him that logical thinking evolves in four stages. During the *sensorimotor stage*, from birth to 24 months, infants use their sensory and motor schemes to act on the world around them. In the *preoperational stage*, from 24 months to about age 6, youngsters acquire symbolic schemes, such as language and fantasy, that they use in thinking and communicating. Next comes the *concrete operational stage*, during which 6- to 12-year-olds begin to think logically and become capable of solving problems, such as the one illustrated in Figure 2.1. The last phase is the *formal operational stage*, in which adolescents learn to think logically about abstract ideas and hypothetical situations.

Table 2.5 describes these stages more fully; you will read about each of them in detail later in the book. For now, it is important to understand that in Piaget's view, each stage grows out of the one that precedes it, and each involves a major restructuring of the child's way of thinking. It's also important to know that research has confirmed Piaget's belief that the sequence of the stages is fixed. However, children progress through them at different rates. In addition, some individuals do not attain the formal operational stage in adolescence or even in adulthood. Consequently, the ages associated with the stages are approximations.

assimilation the process of using a scheme to make sense of an event or experience

accommodation changing a scheme as a result of some new information

equilibration the process of balancing assimilation and accommodation to create schemes that fit the environment

Table 2.5 Piaget's Cognitive-Developmental Stages

Approximate Ages	Stage	Description
Birth to 24 months	Sensorimotor	The baby understands the world through her senses and her motor actions; she begins to use simple symbols, such as single words and pretend play, near the end of this period.
24 months to 6 years	Preoperational	By age 2, the child can use symbols both to think and to communicate; he develops the abilities to take others' points of view, classify objects, and use simple logic by the end of this stage.
6 to 12	Concrete operational	The child's logic takes a great leap forward with the development of new internal operations, such as conservation and class inclusion, but is still tied to the known world; by the end of the period, she can reason about simple "what if" questions.
12+	Formal operational	The child begins to manipulate ideas as well as objects; he thinks hypothetically and, by adulthood, can easily manage a variety of "what if" questions; he greatly improves his ability to organize ideas and objects mentally.

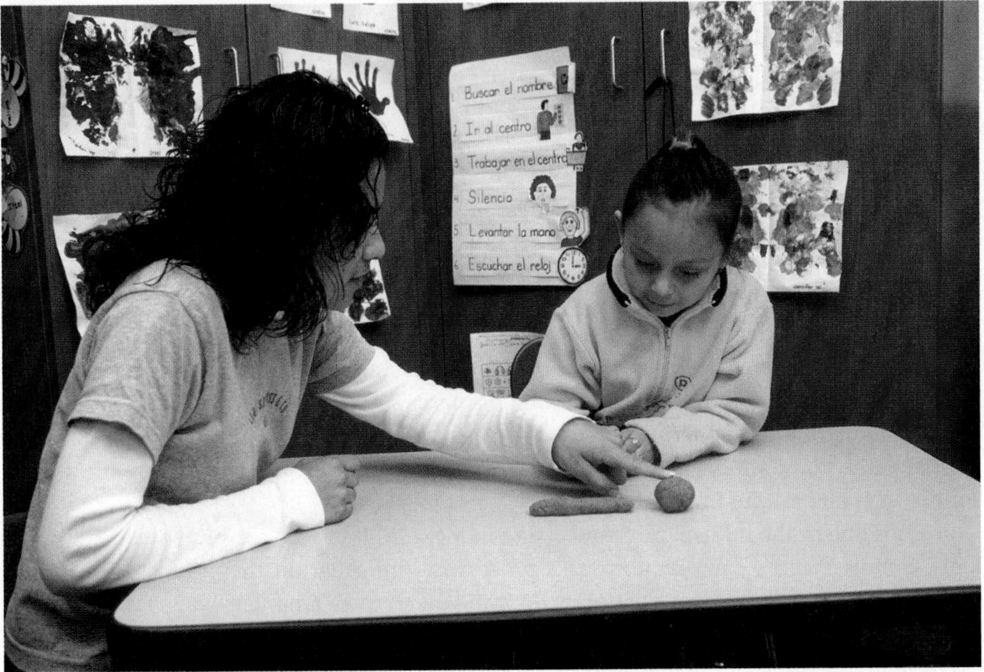

Figure 2.1 A Conservation Task

In one of the problems Piaget devised, a child is shown two clay balls of equal size and asked if they both contain the same amount of clay. Next, the researcher rolls one ball into a sausage shape and asks the child if the two shapes still contain the same amount of clay. A preoperational child will say that one now contains more clay than the other and will base her answer on their appearance: "The sausage has more because it's longer now." A concrete operational thinker will say that the two still contain the same amount of material because no clay was added or taken away from either.

(Photo: Will Hart)

sociocultural theory Vygotsky's view that complex forms of thinking have their origins in social interactions rather than in an individual's private explorations

Vygotsky's Sociocultural Theory

Learning Objective 2.9

How did Vygotsky use the concepts of scaffolding and the zone of proximal development to explain cognitive development?

Lev Vygotsky's **sociocultural theory** asserts that complex forms of thinking have their origins in social interactions rather than in the child's private explorations, as Piaget thought. According to Vygotsky (1886–1934), children's learning of new cognitive skills is guided by an adult (or a more skilled child, such as an older sibling) who structures the child's learning experience, a process Vygotsky called *scaffolding*. For example, parents of a beginning reader provide a scaffold when they help him sound out new words. To create an appropriate scaffold, the adult must gain and keep the child's attention, model the best strategy, and adapt the whole process to the child's *zone of proximal development* (Landry, Garner, Swank, & Baldwin, 1996; Rogoff, 1990). Vygotsky used this term to signify the set of tasks that are too hard for the child to do alone but that can be managed with guidance.

Vygotsky's ideas have important educational applications. Like Piaget's, Vygotsky's theory suggests the importance of opportunities for active exploration. But assisted discovery would play a greater role in a Vygotskian than in a Piagetian classroom; the teacher would provide the scaffolding for children's discovery through questions, demonstrations, and explanations (Tharp & Gallimore, 1988). To be effective, the assisted discovery processes would have to be within the zone of proximal development of each child.

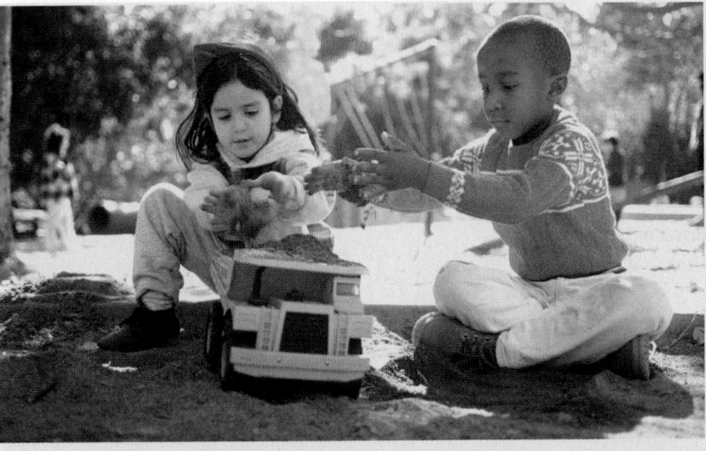

Developmental psychologist Lev Vygotsky hypothesized that social interactions among children are critical to both cognitive and social development.

Learning Objective 2.10

How does information-processing theory explain the findings of developmental psychologists such as Piaget?

Information-Processing Theory

The goal of **information-processing theory** is to explain how the mind manages information (Klahr, 1992). Theorizing about and studying memory processes are central to information-processing theory. Most memory research assumes that the human memory is made up of multiple components. The idea is that information moves through these components in an organized way (see Figure 2.2). The process of understanding a spoken word serves as a good example. First, you hear the word when the sounds enter your *sensory memory*. Your experiences with language allow you to recognize the pattern of sounds as a word. Next, the word moves into your *short-term memory*, the component of the memory system where all information is processed. Thus, short-term memory is often called *working memory*. Knowledge of the word's meaning is then called up out of *long-term memory*, the component of the system where information is permanently stored, and placed in short-term memory, where it is linked to the word's sounds to enable you to understand it.

According to the information-processing model, children who are presented with problems such as Piaget's conservation tasks process the information they need to solve such problems in their short-term memories. As you will learn in Chapter 8, a great deal of research has shown that younger children's short-term memories are both more limited in capacity and less efficient than those of older children (Kail, 1990). Consequently, some developmentalists have used information-processing theory to explain Piaget's stages. Their theories are called **neo-Piagetian theories** because they expand on Piaget's theory rather than contradict it (Case, 1985, 1997). According to neo-Piagetians, older children and adults can solve complex problems like those in Piaget's research because they can hold more pieces of information in their short-term memories at the same time than younger children can.

Learning Objective 2.11

What are some of the important contributions and criticisms of cognitive theories?

Evaluation of Cognitive Theories

Research based on cognitive theories, especially the work of Piaget, has demonstrated that simplistic views, such as those of the conditioning theorists, cannot explain the development of the complex phenomenon that is logical thinking. Moreover, Piaget's research findings have been replicated in virtually every culture and in every cohort of children since his work was first published in the 1920s. Thus, not only did he formulate a theory that forced psychologists to think about child development in a new

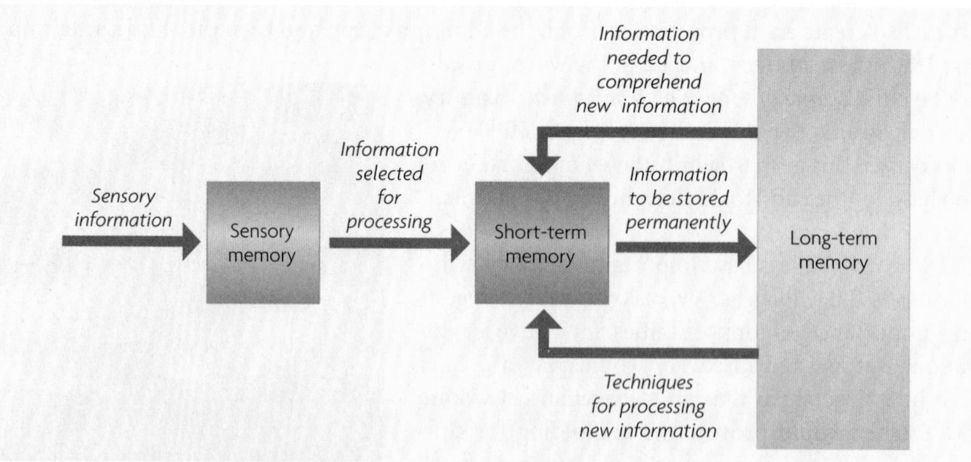

Figure 2.2 The Information-Processing System

Information-processing research on memory is based on the assumption that information moves into, out of, and through the sensory, short-term, and long-term memories in an organized way.

information-processing theory a theoretical perspective that explains how the mind manages information

neo-Piagetian theory an approach that uses information-processing principles to explain the developmental stages identified by Piaget

way; he also provided a set of findings that were impossible to ignore and difficult to explain. In addition, he developed innovative methods of studying children's thinking that continue to be important today (Kuhn, 2008).

Nevertheless, Piaget turned out to be wrong about some of the ages at which children develop particular skills. As you will see in later chapters, researchers have found that children develop some intellectual skills at earlier ages than Piaget's findings suggested. Furthermore, Piaget was probably wrong about the generality of the stages themselves. Most 8-year-olds, for example, show concrete operational thinking on some tasks but not on others, and they are more likely to show complex thinking on familiar than on unfamiliar tasks. Thus, the whole process seems to be a great deal less stage-like than Piaget proposed.

At present, there is insufficient evidence to either support or contradict most of Vygotsky's ideas (Thomas, 2000). However, studies have shown that children in pairs and groups do produce more sophisticated ideas than individual children who work on problems alone (Tan-Niam, Wood, & O'Malley, 1998). Moreover, researchers have found that young children whose parents provide them with more scaffolding during the preschool years exhibit higher levels of achievement in elementary school than peers whose parents provide less support of this kind (Neitzel & Stright, 2003). Thus, future research may support the conclusion that Vygotsky's theory constitutes an important contribution to a full understanding of human development.

In contrast to Vygotsky's theory, the information-processing approach to cognitive development has received a great deal of empirical support (Lamb & Lewis, 2005). These findings have helped to clarify some of the cognitive processes underlying Piaget's findings. Furthermore, they have greatly enhanced developmentalists' understanding of human memory. However, critics of information-processing theory point out that much information-processing research involves artificial memory tasks such as learning lists of words. Therefore, say critics, research based on the information-processing approach doesn't always accurately describe how memory works in the real world. Consequently, just as Piaget did, information-processing theorists may underestimate children's capabilities with regard to real-world tasks.

Piagetians claim that information-processing theory emphasizes explanations of single cognitive tasks at the expense of a comprehensive picture of development. Finally, critics of both cognitive theories say that they ignore the role of emotions in development. The cognitive theories are summarized in Table 2.6.

Table 2.6 Cognitive Theories

		Evaluation	
Theory	Main Idea	Strengths	Weaknesses
Piaget's Cognitive-Developmental Theory	Reasoning develops in four universal stages from birth through adolescence; in each stage, the child builds a different kind of scheme.	Helps explain how children of different ages think about and act on the world	The stage concept may cause adults to underestimate children's reasoning abilities; there may be additional stages in adulthood.
Vygotsky's Sociocultural Theory	Linguistic and social factors in cognitive development are emphasized.	Incorporates group learning processes into explanations of individual cognitive development	There is insufficient evidence to support most ideas.
Information-Processing Theory	The mind manages information using memory processes; information flows through sensory, short-term and long-term memory; memory processes change with age, causing changes in memory function; these changes happen because of both brain maturation and practice.	Helps explain how much information people of different ages can manage at one time and how they process it; provides a useful framework for studying individual differences in people of the same age	Much research involves artificial memory tasks; the theory doesn't always accurately describe how memory works in the real world.

Biological and Ecological Theories

Theories that propose links between physiological processes and development represent one of the most important current trends in developmental psychology (Parke, 2004). Some of these theories focus on individual differences, whereas others deal with universal aspects of development. All of them, to varying degrees, address the manner in which environmental factors interact with physiological processes.

Learning Objective 2.12

How do behavior geneticists explain individual differences?

Behavior Genetics

Behavior genetics focuses on the effect of heredity on individual differences. Traits or behaviors are believed to be influenced by genes when those of related people, such as children and their parents, are more similar than those of unrelated people. Behavior geneticists have shown that heredity affects a broad range of traits and behaviors, including intelligence, shyness, and aggressiveness.

Furthermore, the contributions of heredity to individual differences are evident throughout the lifespan. For example, researchers in the Netherlands have been studying a number of variables in identical and fraternal twins for several decades. You'll learn in Chapter 3 that identical twins are particularly important in genetic research because they have exactly the same genes. Moreover, it's useful to compare them to twins who are nonidentical because these individuals share the same environment but do not have the same genes. As you can see in Figure 2.3, the Dutch researchers have found that IQ scores of identical twins are more strongly correlated than those of fraternal (nonidentical) twins from early childhood until middle age. Interestingly, such findings show that the environment affects IQ scores as well, but that its effects may be transient. This conclusion is suggested by the fact that the IQ scores of fraternal twins are more strongly correlated in childhood, when they are living together, than in adulthood, when they do not share the same environment.

behavior genetics the study of the role of heredity in individual differences

Behavior geneticists also study how individuals' genetic makeup influences the environments in which they are developing, a phenomenon that occurs via one or both of two routes (Caspi & Moffitt, 2006). First, the child inherits his genes from his parents, who also create the environment in which he is growing up. So a child's genetic heritage may predict something about his environment. For example, parents who themselves have high IQ scores are not only likely to pass their "good IQ" genes on to their children; they are also likely to create a richer, more stimulating environment for those children. Similarly, children who inherit a tendency toward aggression or hostility from their parents are likely to live in a family environment that is high in criticism and negativity—because those are expressions of the parents' own genetic tendencies toward aggressiveness or hostility (Reiss, 1998).

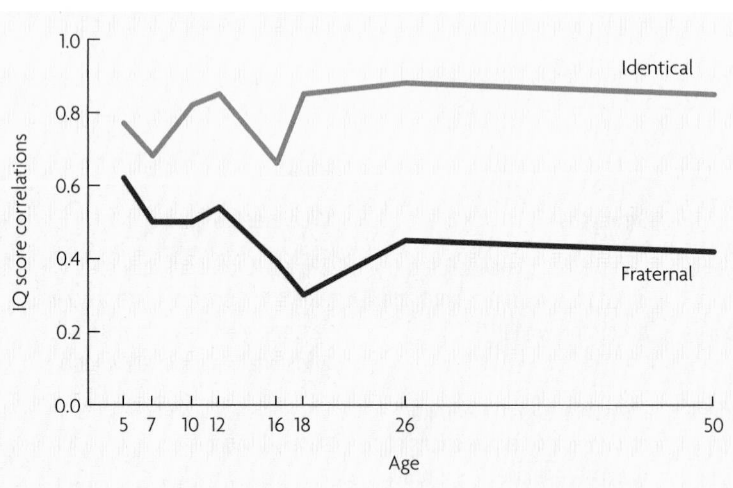

Figure 2.3 IQs of Fraternal and Identical Twins

This figure illustrates the combined findings of several longitudinal and cross-sectional studies of Dutch twins (Posthuma, de Geus, & Boomsma, 2003). You will notice that in childhood, when fraternal twins share the same environment, their IQ scores are more strongly correlated than in adulthood, when they presumably no longer live together. By contrast, the IQ scores of identical twins are even more strongly correlated in adulthood than during the childhood years. This pattern suggests conclusions about both heredity and environment. Specifically, at least with regard to IQ scores, the influence of heredity appears to increase with age, while that of the environment declines.

Second, each child's unique pattern of inherited qualities affects the way she behaves with other people, which in turn affects the way adults and other children respond to her. A cranky or temperamentally difficult baby may receive fewer smiles and more scolding than a placid, even-tempered one; a genetically brighter child may demand more personal attention, ask more questions, or seek out more complex toys than a less bright child (Saudino & Plomin, 1997). Furthermore, children's interpretations of their experiences are affected by all their inherited tendencies, including not only intelligence but also temperament or pathology (Plomin, Reiss, Hetherington, & Howe, 1994).

Ethology and Sociobiology

Learning Objective 2.13

What kinds of behaviors are of interest to ethologists and sociobiologists?

The relationship between individuals and the settings in which they develop is the emphasis of *ecological theories*, perspectives that view development as resulting from the degree to which genes help or hinder individuals' efforts to adapt to their environments. One such theory, known as **ethology**, focuses on the study of animals in their natural environments. Ethologists emphasize genetically determined survival behaviors that are assumed to have evolved through natural selection. For example, nests are necessary for the survival of young birds. Therefore, ethologists say, evolution has equipped birds with nest-building genes.

Likewise, the young of many species are vulnerable to predators, so their genes direct them to form a relationship with a more mature member of the species very early in life. One such relationship results from a process called *imprinting*, in which newborns of some species learn to recognize the characteristics of a protective organism within the first hours of life. Ethologist Konrad Lorenz (1903–1989) studied imprinting among animals extensively (Lorenz, 1935). He learned that young ducklings and geese, for example, imprint on any moving object to which they are exposed during the critical period for imprinting (24 to 48 hours after hatching). In fact, one of the best-known images in the field of ethology is that of Lorenz himself being followed by several goslings who had imprinted on him.

Similarly, ethologists believe that emotional relationships are necessary to the survival of human infants (Bowlby, 1969, 1980). They claim that evolution has produced genes that cause humans to form these relationships. For example, most people feel irritated when they hear a newborn crying. Ethologists say the baby is genetically programmed to cry in a certain way, and adults are genetically programmed to get irritated when they hear it. The caretaker responds to a crying baby's needs in order to remove the irritating stimulus of the noise. As the caretaker and infant interact, an emotional bond is created between them. Thus, genes for crying in an irritating manner increase infants' chances of survival.

ethology a perspective on development that emphasizes genetically determined survival behaviors presumed to have evolved through natural selection

sociobiology the study of society using the methods and concepts of biology; when used by developmentalists, an approach that emphasizes genes that aid group survival

Sociobiology is the study of society using the methods and concepts of biological science. When applied to human development, sociobiology emphasizes genes that aid group survival. Sociobiologists claim individual humans have the best chance for survival when they live in groups. Therefore, they claim, evolution has provided humans with genetic programming that helps us cooperate.

To support their views, sociobiologists look for social rules and behaviors that exist in all cultures. For example, every society has laws against murder. Sociobiologists believe that humans are genetically programmed to create rules based on respect for other people's lives. Evolution has selected these genes, they claim, because people need to respect each other's lives and be able to cooperate.

Critics of ethology and sociobiology claim that these theories underestimate the impact of the environment. Moreover, these theories are difficult to test. How can researchers test ethological theorists' claim that infant-caregiver attachment is universal because it has survival value, for example? Finally,

Lorenz found that once a gaggle of newly hatched geese had imprinted on him, they followed him wherever he went.

critics say that these theories ignore the fact that societies invent ways of enhancing whatever behaviors might be influenced by universal genetic programming. For instance, as sociobiologists hypothesize, genes may be involved in the universal prohibition of murder, but societies invent strategies for preventing it. Moreover, these strategies differ across societies and in their effectiveness.

Learning Objective 2.14

What is the main idea of Bronfenbrenner's bioecological theory?

Bronfenbrenner's Bioecological Theory

Another approach gaining interest in developmental science is Urie Bronfenbrenner's **bioecological theory**, which explains development in terms of relationships between people and their environments, or contexts, as Bronfenbrenner calls them (Bronfenbrenner, 1979, 1993). Bronfenbrenner (1917–2005) attempts to classify all the individual and contextual variables that affect development and to specify how they interact.

According to Bronfenbrenner, the contexts of development are like circles within circles (see Figure 2.4). The outermost circle, the *macrosystem* (the cultural context), contains the values and beliefs of the culture in which a child is growing up. For example, a society's beliefs about the importance of education exist in the cultural context.

The next level, the *exosystem* (the socioeconomic context), includes the institutions of the culture that affect children's development indirectly. For example, funding for education exists in the socioeconomic context. The citizens of a specific nation may strongly believe that all children should be educated (cultural context), but their ability to provide universal education may be limited by the country's wealth (socioeconomic context).

bioecological theory Bronfenbrenner's theory that explains development in terms of relationships between individuals and their environments, or interconnected contexts

The *microsystem* (the immediate context) includes those variables to which people are exposed directly, such as their families, schools, religious institutions, and neighborhoods. The *mesosystem* is made up of the interconnections between these components. For example, the specific school a child attends and her own family are part of the microsystem. Her parents' involvement in her school and the response of the school to their involvement are part of the mesosystem. Thus, the culture a child is born into may strongly value quality education. Moreover, her nation's economy may provide ample funds for schooling. However, her own education will be more strongly affected by the particular school she attends and the connections—or lack thereof—between her school and her family. Thus, the child's immediate context may be either consistent with the cultural and socioeconomic contexts or at odds with them.

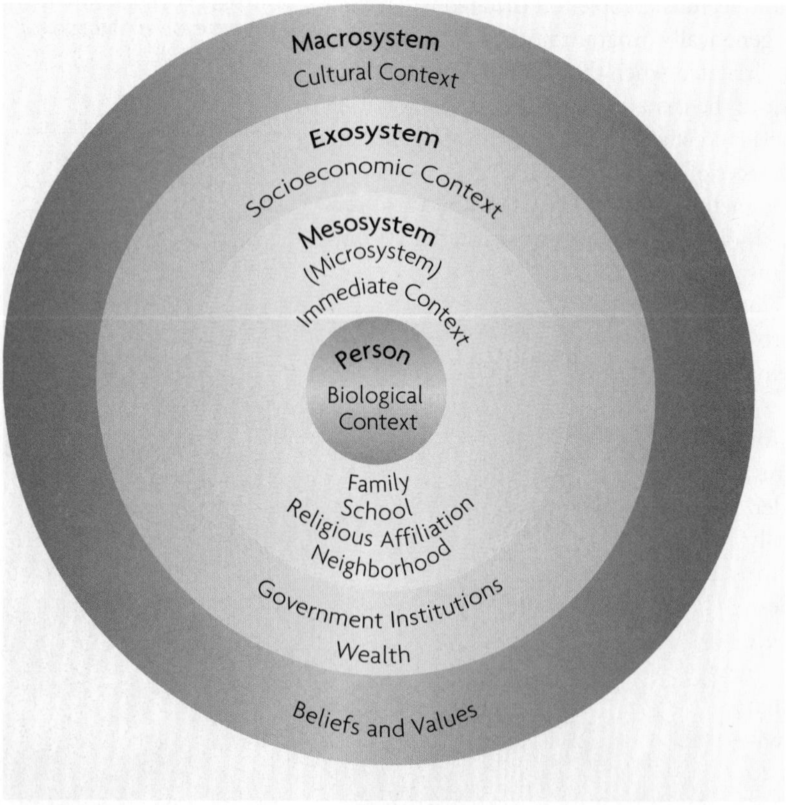

Finally, the child's genetic makeup and developmental stage—her *biological context*—also influence her development. For example, a student who hasn't mastered the skill of reading isn't likely to benefit from an enriched literature program. Thus, her culture, the socioeconomic situation, the school she attends, and her own family may all be geared toward providing a quality education. However, her ability to benefit from it will be determined by the degree to which her education fits her individual needs.

Figure 2.4 Bronfenbrenner's Contexts of Development

Bronfenbrenner's bioecological theory proposes that people are exposed to interconnected contexts that interact in complex ways to influence development.

Bronfenbrenner's bioecological theory provides a way of thinking about development that captures the complexity of individual and contextual variables. To date, its greatest contribution to developmental science has been its emphasis on the need for research examining interactions among these variables (Thomas, 2000). For example, bioecological theory has helped developmentalists understand that studies of infant child care can't just compare infants in child care to infants in home care. Such studies must also consider family variables, such as parents' educational level, and child-care variables, such as the ratio of caretakers to infants. Since the 1980s, an increasing number of such studies have appeared.

Comparing Theories

After learning about theories, students usually want to know which one is right. However, developmentalists don't think of theories in terms of right or wrong; instead, they compare theories on the basis of their assumptions and how useful they are in promoting understanding of development. Today's developmentalists often don't adhere to a single theory but take an approach that taps the strengths of each of the major theoretical perspectives.

Assumptions About Development

Learning Objective 2.15
What assumptions do the three families of theories make about development?

When we say that a theory assumes something about development, we mean that it holds some general perspective to be true. We can think of a theory's assumptions in terms of its answers to three questions about development.

One question addresses the *active or passive* issue: Is a person active in shaping his own development, or is he a passive recipient of environmental influences? Theories that claim a person's actions on the environment are the most important determinants of development are on the active side. Cognitive theories, for example, typically view development this way. In contrast, theories on the passive side, such as those of Pavlov and Skinner, maintain that development results from the environment acting on the individual.

As you learned in Chapter 1, the *nature versus nurture* question—How do nature and nurture interact to produce development?—is one of the most important in developmental science. All developmental theories, while admitting that both nature and nurture are involved in development, make assumptions about their relative importance. Theories claiming that biology contributes more to development than does environment are on the nature side of the question. Those that view environmental influences as most important are on the nurture side. Other theories assume that nature and nurture are equally important, and that it is impossible to say which contributes more to development.

You may also recall from Chapter 1 that the *continuity versus discontinuity* issue—Does development happen continuously or in stages?—is a source of debate among developmentalists. Theories that do not refer to stages assert that development is a stable, continuous process. Stage theories, on the other hand, emphasize change more than stability. They claim that development happens in leaps from lower to higher steps.

Ethologists assert that the first 2 years of life are a critical period for the establishment of relationships between infants and caregivers.

Table 2.7 on page 46 lists the assumptions made by each of the three major families of theories regarding these issues. Because each theory is based on different assumptions, each implies a different approach to studying development. Consequently, research derived from each theory tells us something different about development. Moreover, a theory's assumptions shape the way it is applied in the real world. For example, a teacher who approached instruction from the

Table 2.7 How Theories Answer Three Questions About Development

Theories	Active or Passive?	Nature or Nurture?	Stability or Change?
Psychoanalytic Theories			
Psychosexual Theory	Passive	Nature	Change (stages)
Psychosocial Theory	Passive	Both	Change
Learning Theories			
Classical Conditioning	Passive	Nurture	Stability (no stages)
Operant Conditioning	Passive	Nurture	Stability
Social-Cognitive Theory	Active	Nurture	Stability
Cognitive Theories			
Cognitive-Developmental Theory	Active	Both	Change
Sociocultural Theory	Active	Both	Change
Information-Processing Theory	Active	Both	Both

cognitive perspective would create a classroom in which children could experiment to some degree on their own. He would also recognize that children differ in ability, interests, developmental level, and other internal characteristics. He would believe that structuring the educational environment is important, but would assume that what each student ultimately learns will be determined by her own actions on the environment.

Alternatively, a teacher who adopted the learning perspective would guide and reinforce children's learning very carefully. Such a teacher would place little importance on ability differences among children. Instead, she would try to accomplish the same instructional goals for all children through proper manipulation of the environment.

Learning Objective 2.16

On what criteria do developmentalists compare the usefulness of theories?

Usefulness

Developmentalists also compare theories with respect to their usefulness. You should be aware that there is a fair amount of disagreement among developmentalists on exactly how useful each theory is. Nevertheless, there are a few general criteria most psychologists use to evaluate the usefulness of a theory.

One way to evaluate usefulness is to assess a theory's ability to generate predictions that can be tested using scientific methods. For example, as you have learned, one criticism of Freud's theory is that of his claims are difficult to test. In contrast, when Piaget claimed that most children can solve concrete operational problems by age 7, he made an assertion that is easily tested. Thus, Piaget's theory is viewed by many developmentalists as more useful in this sense than Freud's. Vygotsky, learning theorists, and information-processing theorists also proposed testable ideas. By contrast, according to some developmental psychologists, current biological and ecological theories are weak because they are difficult to test (Thomas, 2000).

Another criterion by which to judge the usefulness of a theory is its *heuristic* value, the degree to which it stimulates thinking and research. In terms of heuristic value, Freud's and Piaget's theories earn equally high marks. Both are responsible for an enormous amount of theorizing and research on human development, often by psychologists who strongly disagree with them. In fact, all of the theories in this chapter are important heuristically.

Yet another way of evaluating a theory's usefulness, though, is in terms of its practical value. In other words, a theory may be deemed useful if it provides solutions to problems. Based on this criterion, the learning and information-processing theories seem to stand out because they provide tools that can be used to influence behavior. A person who suffers from anxiety attacks, for example, can learn to use biofeedback, a technique derived from conditioning theories, to manage anxiety. Similarly, a student who needs to learn to study more effectively can get help from study-skills courses based on information-processing research.

Ultimately, of course, no matter how many testable hypotheses or practical techniques a theory produces, it has little or no usefulness to developmentalists if it doesn't explain the basic facts of development. Based on this criterion, learning theories, especially classical and operant conditioning, are regarded by many developmentalists as somewhat less useful than other perspectives (Thomas, 2000). Although they explain how specific behaviors may be learned, they cannot account for the complexity of human development, which can't be reduced to connections between stimuli and responses or between behaviors and reinforcers.

As you can see, the point of comparing theories is not to conclude which one is true. Instead, such comparisons help to reveal the unique contribution each can make to a comprehensive understanding of human development.

Eclecticism

Learning Objective 2.17
What is eclecticism?

Today's developmental scientists try to avoid the kind of rigid adherence to a single theoretical perspective that was characteristic of theorists such as Freud, Piaget, and Skinner. Instead, they emphasize **eclecticism**, the use of multiple theoretical perspectives to explain and study human development (Parke, 2004).

To better understand the eclectic approach, think about how ideas drawn from several sources might help us better understand a child's disruptive behavior in school. Observations of the child's behavior and her classmates' reactions may suggest that her behavior is being rewarded by the other children's responses (a behavioral explanation). Deeper probing of the child's family situation may indicate that her acting-out behavior is an emotional reaction to a family event such as divorce (a psychoanalytic explanation).

The interdisciplinary nature of today's developmental science also contributes to eclecticism. For instance, an anthropologist might suggest that the rapid-fire communication media found in almost every home nowadays (e.g., televisions, computers) require children to develop attention strategies that differ from those that are appropriate for classroom environments. As a result, children today exhibit more disruptive behavior in school than children in past generations because of the mismatch between the kinds of information delivery to which they are accustomed at home and those which are found in school.

By adopting an eclectic approach, developmentalists can devise more comprehensive theories from which to derive questions and hypotheses for further research. In other words, their theories and studies may more closely match the behavior of real people in real situations.

eclecticism the use of multiple theoretical perspectives to explain and study human development

Test Prep Center

with mydevelopmentlab

PSYCHOANALYTIC THEORIES

2.1 What are the main ideas of Freud's theory? (pp. 28–29)

Freud emphasized that behavior is governed by both conscious and unconscious motives and that the personality develops in steps: The id is present at birth, whereas the ego and the superego develop in childhood. Freud proposed psychosexual stages, which highlight the formative role of early experiences.

1. Suppose that you are thinking about putting a scoop of ice cream on top of the piece of apple pie you are about to eat. Which of the statements below would be made by your id? by your ego? by your superego?

   ______ (1) "Ice cream? Are you kidding me? It's bad enough that you're eating pie. If the fat, sugar and cholesterol in that dessert don't kill you, they'll definitely make you sick. Maybe you should have another helping of salad instead."

   ______ (2) "Wow! Will one piece of pie be enough? Make sure there's enough for seconds before you start eating. If not, make a run to the store first so you can really enjoy yourself."

   ______ (3) "Here's an idea. Just eat half a piece of pie. That will help to make up for the extra calories in the ice cream. You can skip dessert tomorrow night and work out for an extra half-hour."

2. Summarize each of Freud's five psychosexual stages by completing the following table.

Name of Stage	Age	Focus of Libido	Developmental Task	Characteristics of Fixation in Adulthood
Oral				
Anal				
Phallic				
Latency				
Genital				

2.2 What is the conflict associated with each of Erikson's psychosocial stages? (pp. 30–31)

Erikson proposed that personality develops in eight psychosocial stages over the course of the lifespan: trust versus mistrust, autonomy versus shame and doubt, initiative versus guilt, industry versus inferiority, identity versus role confusion, intimacy versus isolation, generativity versus stagnation, and ego integrity versus despair.

3. Summarize each of Erikson's eight psychosocial stages by completing the following table.

Name of Stage	Age	Positive Characteristics Gained and Typical Activities	Conflict Associated with Stage
Trust versus mistrust			
Autonomy versus shame and doubt			
Initiative versus guilt			
Industry versus inferiority			
Identity versus role confusion			
Intimacy versus isolation			
Generativity versus stagnation			
Ego integrity versus despair			

2.3 What are the strengths and weaknesses of psychoanalytic theories? (pp. 31–32)

Psychoanalytic theories emphasize the importance of children's early relationships and the ever-changing nature of their needs. Psychoanalytic concepts, such as the unconscious and identity, have contributed to psychologists' understanding of development. However, these theories propose many ideas that are difficult to test.

4. Why are the major concepts of psychoanalytic theory difficult to test?

   ____

   ____

LEARNING THEORIES

2.4 How did Watson condition Little Albert to fear white, furry objects? (pp. 32–33)

Classical conditioning—learning through association of stimuli—helps explain the acquisition of emotional responses. Using these principles, Watson paired a white rat with sudden loud noises to condition a fear of white rats in Little Albert, who generalized his fear to other white, furry objects.

5. Through what process do food odors become conditioned stimuli that cause the body to respond, in the same way that it does to the foods with which they are associated?

____

____

6. From the Multimedia Library within MyDevelopmentLab, explore *Classical Conditioning of Little Albert* and answer the following question.

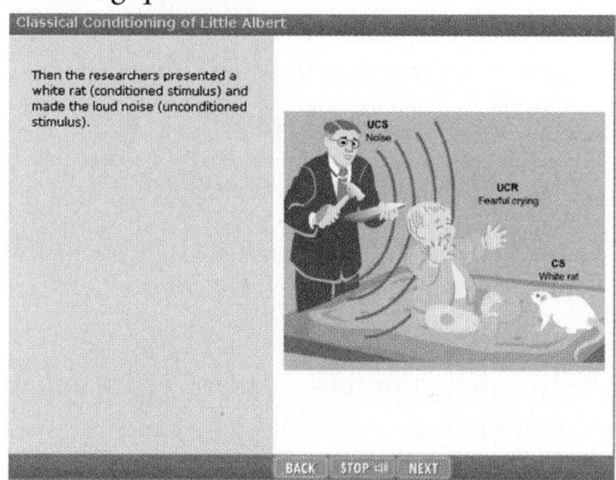

What were the unconditioned stimulus, unconditioned response, conditioned stimulus, and conditioned response in Watson's Little Albert experiment?

____

____

2.5 How does operant conditioning occur? (pp. 34–35)

Operant conditioning involves learning to repeat or stop behaviors because of their consequences. However, consequences often affect behavior in complex ways in the real world.

7. A mother wants her daughter to clean her room. Write the operant conditioning term that matches the action: positive reinforcement, negative reinforcement, or punishment.

   ______ (1) If she cleans her room, she doesn't have to do the dishes.

   ______ (2) If she cleans her room, she can go to the movies.

   ______ (3) If she does not clean her room, she cannot watch TV.

8. How might a father use extinction to stop his son's whining?

____

____

2.6 In what ways does social-cognitive theory differ from other learning theories? (pp. 35–36)

Bandura's social-cognitive theory places more emphasis on mental elements than other learning theories do and assumes a more active role for the individual.

9. What factors influence the degree to which a child learns a behavior from watching a model?

____

____

10. From the Multimedia Library within MyDevelopmentLab, watch the *Bandura's Bobo Doll Experiment* video and answer the following question.

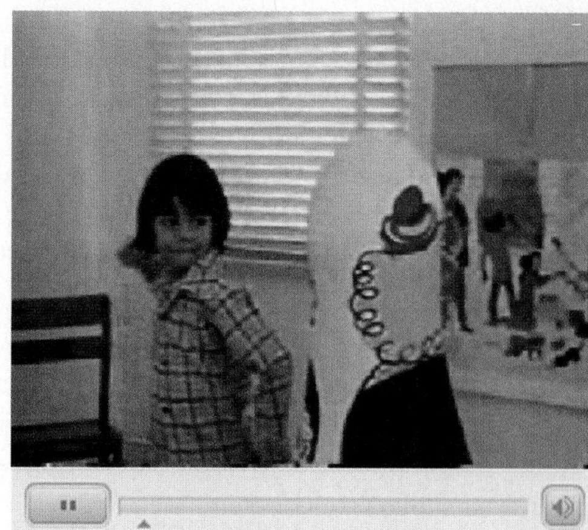

Do you think Bandura's studies would have had the same outcome if he had recruited children who had been habitually exposed to aggressive behavior? Why or why not?

____

____

2.7 How well do the learning theories explain development? (pp. 36–37)

Learning theories provide useful explanations of how behaviors are acquired but fall short of a truly comprehensive picture of age-related change in human development.

11. Why do many developmentalists argue that learning theories don't explain development very well?

____

____

COGNITIVE THEORIES

2.8 How does cognitive development progress, according to Piaget? (pp. 37–39)

Piaget focused on the development of logical thinking. He discovered that such thinking develops across four stages: the sensorimotor, preoperational, concrete operational, and formal operational stages. He proposed that movement from one stage to another is the result of changes in mental frameworks called schemes.

12. Describe Piaget's cognitive-developmental stages listed in the following table.

Stage	Average Ages	Description
Sensorimotor		
Preoperational		
Concrete operational		
Formal operational		

2.9 How did Vygotsky use the concepts of scaffolding and the zone of proximal development to explain cognitive development? (p. 39)

Vygotsky claimed that cognitive development arises from social interactions. Of particular value are interactions between children and older individuals in which the older individuals provide children with scaffolding, or structured learning experiences that helps them achieve cognitive goals. An appropriate scaffold is adapted to the child's zone of proximal development. Through this process, children advance to higher levels of cognitive development.

13. Vygotsky proposed that complex forms of thinking develop as a result of the child's ________________.

14. From the Multimedia Library within MyDevelopmentLab, watch the *Zone of Proximal Development: Cognitive* video and answer the following question.

How would the behavior of the children in the video fit Vygotsky's description of the zone of proximal development?

____

____

2.10 How does information-processing theory explain the findings of developmental psychologists such as Piaget? (p. 40)

Information-processing theory attempts to explain how the mind manages information using intellectual processes such as memory and problem-solving. The theory suggests that there are both age and individual differences in the efficiency with which humans use their information-processing systems.

15. Match each component of the information-processing system to its description.

______ (1) sensory memory

______ (2) short-term memory

______ (3) long-term memory

(A) all information is processed here

(B) information is permanently stored here

(C) the senses recognize information here

2.11 What are some of the important contributions and criticisms of cognitive theories? (pp. 40–41)

Cognitive theories highlight the complexity of logical thinking. Research has confirmed the sequence of skill development outlined in Piaget's cognitive-developmental theory but suggests that the timing and generality of Piaget's stages are questionable; young children are more capable of logical thinking than Piaget believed. Ideas based on sociocultural theory have been embraced by many educators. Information-processing theory has been important in explaining how the mind manages information but has been criticized for the narrowness of its scope. In general, cognitive theories ignore the role of emotion in development.

16. Match each cognitive theory with its definition.

______ (1) cognitive-developmental theory

______ (2) sociocultural theory

______ (3) information-processing theory

(A) Vygotsky's view that complex forms of thinking have their origins in social interactions rather than in an individual's private explorations

(B) the theory that proposes four stages of cognitive development

(C) a theoretical perspective that explains how the mind manages information

BIOLOGICAL AND ECOLOGICAL THEORIES

2.12 How do behavior geneticists explain individual differences? (pp. 42–43)

Behavior geneticists study the influence of heredity on individual differences and the ways in which individuals' genes influence their environments.

17. From the Multimedia Library within MyDevelopmentLab, watch the *Twin Studies* video and answer the following question.

What have researchers learned from twin studies about the role of heredity in intelligence and achievement?

____

____

2.13 What kinds of behaviors are of interest to ethologists and sociobiologists? (pp. 43–44)

Ethologists study genetically determined traits and behaviors that help animals adapt to their environments. Sociobiologists emphasize the genetic basis of behaviors that promote the development and maintenance of social organizations in both animals and humans.

18. How do ethologists explain the function of a newborn's crying?

____

____

19. How do sociobiologists explain the finding that all societies prohibit murder?

____

____

2.14 What is the main idea of Bronfenbrenner's bioecological theory? (pp. 44–45)

Bronfenbrenner's bioecological theory categorizes environmental factors into contexts and then explores the interactions between those contexts and the individual.

20. Match each of Bronfenbrenner's contexts with its definition.

______ (1) macrosystem ______ (3) microsystem

______ (2) exosystem ______ (4) mesosystem

(A) interconnections between microsystem and exosystem

(B) values and beliefs of the culture

(C) institutions that affect development indirectly

(D) variables and institutions that affect development directly

COMPARING THEORIES

2.15 What assumptions do the three families of theories make about development? (pp. 45–46)

Theories vary in how they answer three basic questions: Are individuals active or passive in their own development? How do nature and nurture interact to produce development? Does development happen continuously or in stages?

21. Categorize each theory below according to its assumptions on the three basic questions about human development.

Theories	Active/ Passive	Nature/ Nurture	Continuity/ Discontinuity
Psychosexual			
Psychosocial			
Classical Conditioning			
Operant Conditioning			
Social-Cognitive			
Cognitive-Developmental			
Sociocultural			
Information-Processing			

2.16 On what criteria do developmentalists compare the usefulness of theories? (pp. 46–47)

Useful theories allow psychologists to devise hypotheses to test their validity, are heuristically valuable, provide practical solutions to problems, and explain the facts of development.

22. Explain how each of the following criteria influences the usefulness of a theory.

(A) Testability

____

____

(B) Heuristic value

____

____

(C) Solutions for real-world problems

____

____

(D) Explanation of the basic facts of development

____

____

2.17 What is eclecticism? (p. 47)

Developmentalists who take an eclectic approach use theories derived from all the major families, as well as those of many disciplines, to explain and study human development.

23. Mark each statement as True or False with regard to eclecticism.

______ (1) A method for determining which theory is true

______ (2) Influenced by the interdisciplinary nature of contemporary developmental science

______ (3) Contributes to comprehensive explanations of development

______ (4) A strategy for eliminating theories that are false

______ (5) The use of multiple theoretical perspectives to explain development

For answers to the questions in this chapter, turn to page 505. For a list of key terms, turn to page 530.

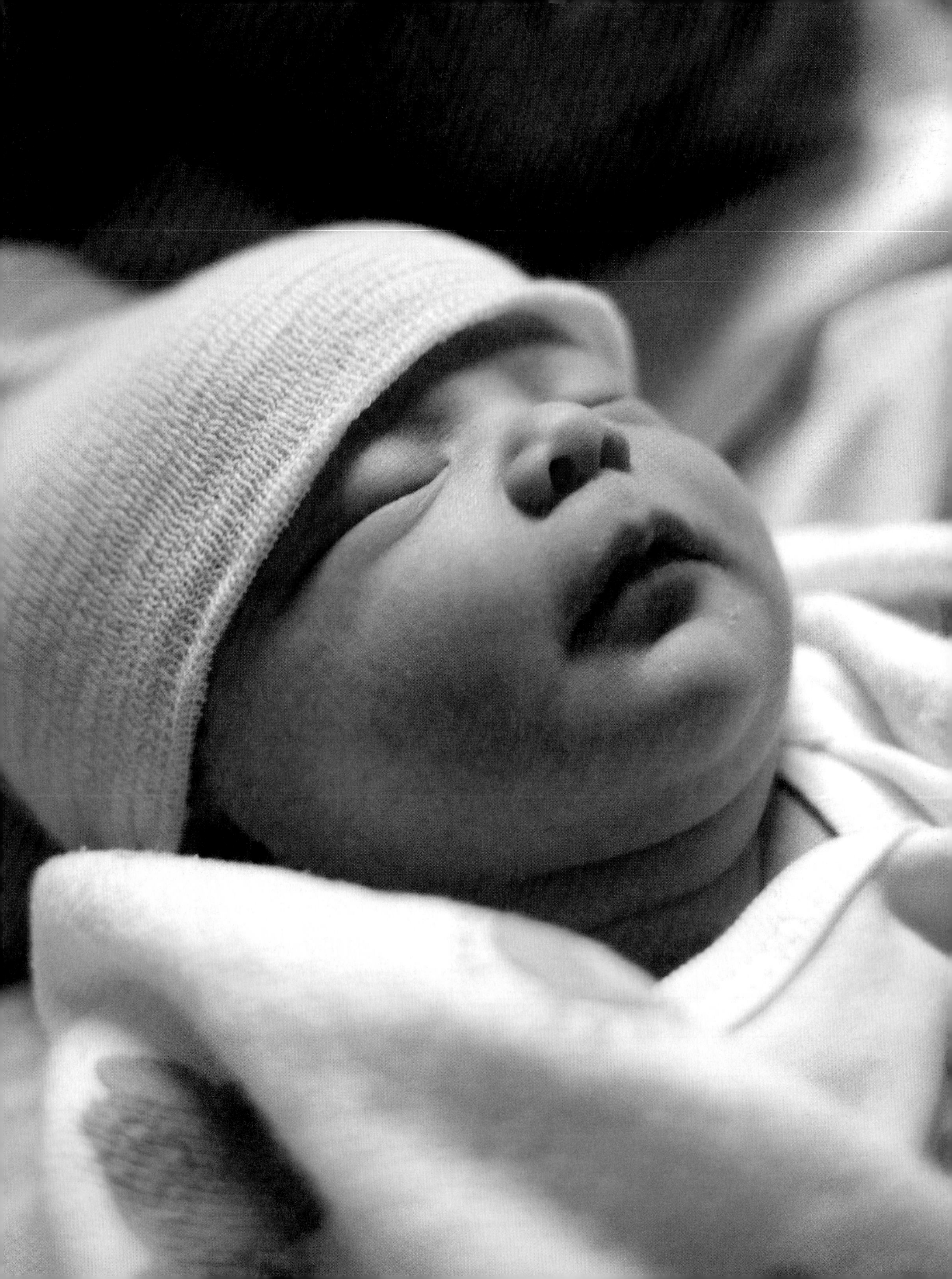

Chapter 3

Prenatal Development and Birth

The story of human development begins with the union of two sets of genes. Soon afterward, a dance in which nature and nurture are partners begins, one that shapes the first 40 weeks of human development. In the context of this dance, a single cell is transformed into a crying, but curious, newborn making his or her debut in the outside world.

Until recently, much of the dance was hidden from view. Thanks to rapidly evolving techniques that allow scientists to observe the earliest moments of development both in the laboratory and inside a mother's body, researchers are gaining insight into prenatal developmental processes that were shrouded in mystery just a few decades ago. As you explore this chapter, you will become acquainted with some of these insights and, we hope, gain a greater appreciation for the amazing process of prenatal development.

In this chapter, you will learn about conception, prenatal development, and birth. First, you will read about the process of conception and the rules governing the transmission of genetic traits from parent to child. Then comes a discussion of genetic and chromosomal disorders, followed by a discussion of the milestones of pregnancy and prenatal development. Next is an overview of the negative effects of drugs, diseases, and other such factors on prenatal development. Finally, you will learn about the process of birth itself.

Learning Objectives

Conception and Genetics
- 3.1 What are the characteristics of the zygote?
- 3.2 In what ways do genes influence development?

Genetic and Chromosomal Disorders
- 3.3 What are the effects of the major recessive, dominant, and sex-linked diseases?
- 3.4 How do trisomies and other disorders of the autosomes and sex chromosomes affect development?

Pregnancy and Prenatal Development
- 3.5 What are the characteristics of each trimester of pregnancy?
- 3.6 What happens in each stage of prenatal development?
- 3.7 How do male and female fetuses differ?
- 3.8 What behaviors have scientists observed in fetuses?

Problems in Prenatal Development
- 3.9 How do teratogens affect prenatal development?
- 3.10 What are the potential adverse effects of tobacco, alcohol, and other drugs on prenatal development?
- 3.11 What are the risks associated with teratogenic maternal diseases?
- 3.12 What other maternal factors influence prenatal development?
- 3.13 How do physicians assess and manage fetal health?

Birth and the Neonate
- 3.14 What kinds of birth choices are available to expectant parents?
- 3.15 What happens in each of the three stages of labor?
- 3.16 What do physicians learn about a newborn from the Apgar and Brazelton scales?
- 3.17 Which infants are categorized as low birth weight and what risks are associated with this classification?

Conception and Genetics

The first step in the development of an individual human being happens at conception, when each of us receives a combination of genes that will shape our experiences throughout the rest of our lives.

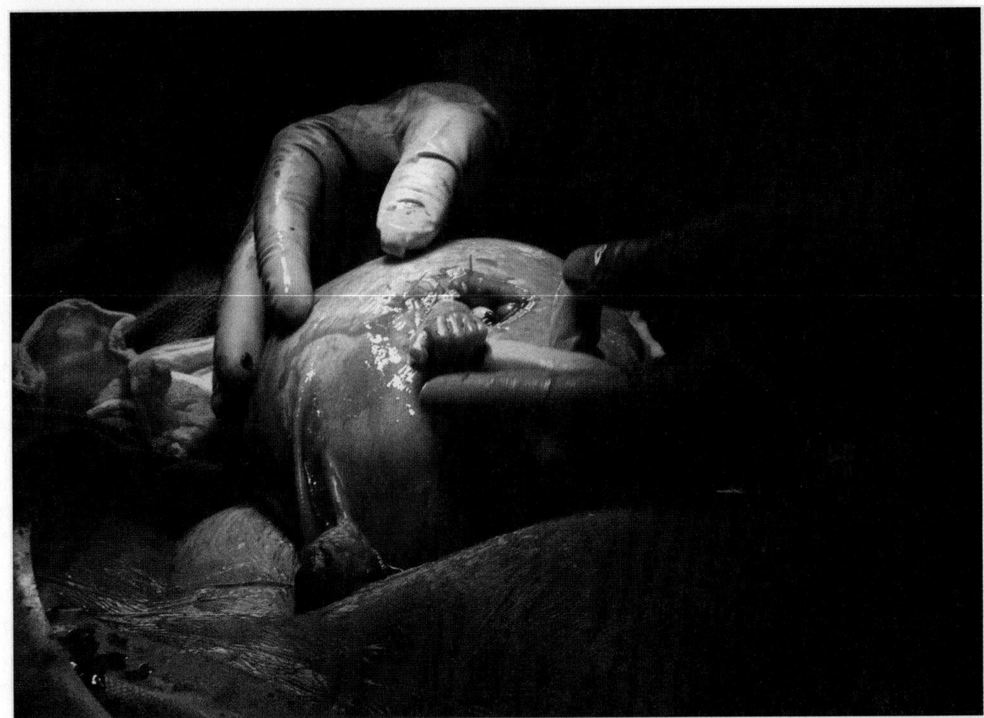

A photographer snapped this amazing photo showing the tiny hand of a 21-week-old fetus grasping the finger of the surgeon who had just completed an operation to correct a serious malformation of the fetus's spine. New technologies have not only allowed for the development of prenatal treatment strategies for correcting birth defects, but also revealed many features of prenatal development that were unimaginable just a few decades ago.

Learning Objective 3.1

What are the characteristics of the zygote?

The Process of Conception

Ordinarily, a woman produces one *ovum* (egg cell) per month from one of her two ovaries, roughly midway between menstrual periods. If the ovum is not fertilized, it travels from the ovary down the *fallopian tube* toward the *uterus*, where it gradually disintegrates and is expelled as part of the menstrual fluid. However, if a couple has intercourse during the crucial few days when the ovum is in the fallopian tube, one of the millions of sperm ejaculated as part of each male orgasm may travel the full distance through the woman's vagina, cervix, uterus, and fallopian tube and penetrate the wall of the ovum.

chromosomes strings of genetic material in the nuclei of cells

gametes cells that unite at conception (ova in females; sperm in males)

zygote single cell created when sperm and ovum unite

deoxyribonucleic acid (DNA) chemical material that makes up chromosomes and genes

genes pieces of genetic material that control or influence traits

Chromosomes, DNA, and Genes As you probably know, every cell in the human body contains 23 pairs of **chromosomes**, or strings of genetic material. However, sperm and ova, collectively called **gametes**, contain 23 single (unpaired) chromosomes. At conception, chromosomes in the ovum and the sperm combine to form 23 pairs in an entirely new cell called a **zygote**.

Chromosomes are composed of molecules of **deoxyribonucleic acid (DNA)**. Each chromosome can be further subdivided into segments called **genes**, each of which influences a particular feature or developmental pattern. A gene controlling some specific characteristic always appears in the same place (the *locus*) on the same chromosome in every individual of the same species. For example, the locus of the genes that determine whether a person's blood is type A, B, AB, or O is on chromosome 9.

Determination of Sex Twenty-two pairs of chromosomes, called *autosomes*, contain most of the genetic information for the new individual. The 23rd pair, the *sex chromosomes*, determine the sex. One of the two sex chromosomes, the *X chromosome*, is one of the largest chromosomes in the body and carries a large number of genes. The other, the *Y chromosome*, is quite small and contains only a few genes. Zygotes containing two X chromosomes develop into females, and those containing one X and one Y chromosome develop into males. Since the cells in a woman's body contain only X chromosomes, all her ova carry X chromosomes. Half of a man's sperm contain X chromosomes; the other half contain Y chromosomes. Consequently, the sex of the new individual is determined by the sex chromosome in the sperm.

How do chromosomal differences become physical differences between males and females? Sometime during the 4 to 8 weeks following conception, the *SRY gene* on the Y chromosome signals the male embryo's body to begin secreting hormones called *androgens.* These hormones cause male genitals to develop. If androgens are not present, female genitals develop no matter what the embryo's chromosomal status is. Likewise, female embryos that are exposed to androgens, via either medications that the mother is taking or a genetic disorder called *congenital adrenal hyperplasia,* can develop male-appearing external genitalia. Development of the **gonads**, testes in males and ovaries in females, also depends upon the presence or absence of androgens. Prenatal androgens also influence the developing brain and may play a role in the development of sex differences in cognitive functioning and in the development of sexual orientation (Lippa, 2005). We will explore these topics in greater detail in later chapters.

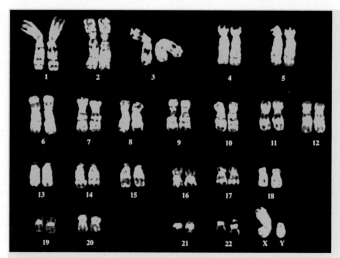

Each cell in the human body has 23 pairs of chromosomes in its nucleus. The 23 single chromosomes in a female gamete, or egg, combine with the 23 single chromosomes in a male gamete, or sperm, to create a new, genetically unique array of 23 pairs of chromosomes that contain all of the instructions needed to guide the development of a human being from conception forward and that will influence him or her throughout life.

Multiple Births In most cases, human infants are conceived and born one at a time. However, in about 4 out of every 100 births, more than one baby is born, usually twins. Two-thirds of twins are *fraternal twins,* or twins that come from two sets of ova and sperm. Such twins, also called *dizygotic twins* (meaning that they originate from two zygotes), are no more alike genetically than any other pair of siblings and need not even be of the same sex.

The remaining one-third of twins are *identical twins* (*monozygotic,* or arising from one zygote). Identical twins result when a single zygote, for unknown reasons, separates into two parts, each of which develops into a separate individual. Because identical twins develop from the same zygote, they have identical genes. Research involving identical twins is one of the major investigative strategies in the field of behavior genetics.

gonads sex glands (ovaries in females; testes in males)

Over the past 30 years, the annual number of multiple births has increased about 66% in the United States (National Center for Health Statistics [NCHS], 2005; Martin et al., 2005). One reason for the increase is that the number of women over 35 giving birth for the first time has grown. There are two factors that underlie the association between multiple births and maternal age (Reynolds, Schieve, Martin, Jeng, & Macaluso, 2003). First, for reasons that researchers don't yet understand, women are far more likely to naturally conceive twins and other multiples after age 35. Second, women over 35 are more likely than younger women to experience difficulty becoming pregnant and, thus, are more likely to be treated with fertility-enhancing drugs and to use other assisted reproductive techniques (see *Developmental Science at Home* on page 56). Women of all ages who use fertility drugs and/or employ

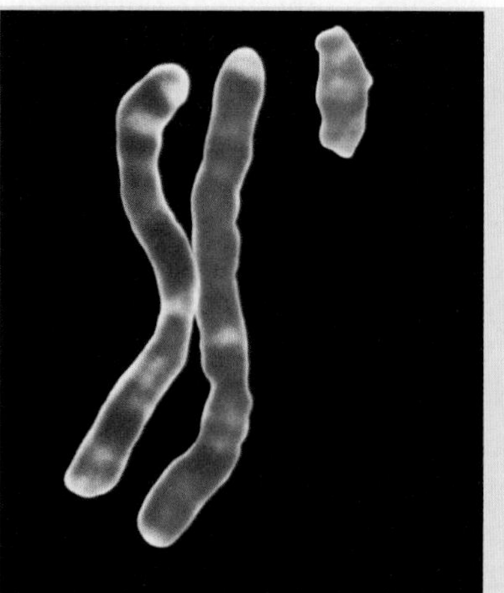

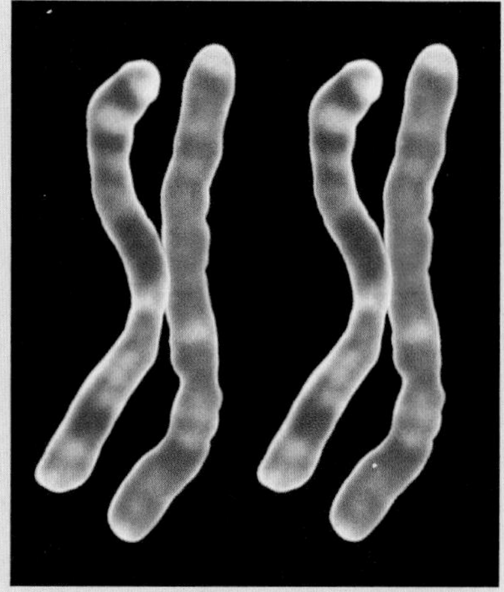

The X chromosome is quite large and carries thousands of genes. By contrast, the Y chromosome is very small and carries little genetic information. The mismatch between the genetic material on the X and Y chromosomes leaves males more vulnerable to some genetic disorders than females are. That's because if a female has a harmful gene on one of her X chromosomes, it is likely to be balanced by a corresponding gene on her other X chromosome that either blocks or minimizes the effects of the harmful gene. (Left: male; right: female.)

DEVELOPMENTAL SCIENCE AT HOME

In Vitro Fertilization

Sven and Ilse are a married couple in their early 40s who hope to have children. Although both of them appear to be healthy and capable of conceiving a child, they have yet to do so after trying for more than 3 years. After consulting with their doctors, they are considering *in vitro* fertilization *(IVF)*, or the "test-tube" method. (*In vitro* is Latin for "in glass.") If they choose to attempt IVF, eggs will be extracted from Ilse's ovaries and combined with Sven's sperm in a laboratory dish. If conception takes place, one or more embryos—ideally at the six- to eight-cell stage of development—will be transferred to Ilse's womb. Sven and Ilse worry that the procedure will fail to result in the birth of a child. Thus, they are in the process of gathering the information they need to decide whether they are ready to make the financial and emotional investment that will be required if they decide to go through with the IVF procedure.

There is no doubt that the risk of miscarriage is far higher in IVF than in natural conception. Moreover, the older a woman is, the lower the probability that she will be able to have a successful IVF pregnancy. Roughly 43% of IVF patients under age 35 achieve a live birth, but only 5–14% of IVF procedures involving women over age 40, like Ilse, are successful (Society for Assisted Reproductive Technology [SART], 2008a). It's important to note here, though, that these are aggregate statistics; each reproductive clinic keeps track of its own success rate, and these can vary considerably from one facility to another (SART, 2008b). Moreover, success rates have greatly improved over the past two decades.

Successful IVF carries a different set of risks. Multiple births are more frequent among IVF patients, primarily because doctors typically transfer several zygotes at once in order to increase the likelihood of at least one live birth (SART, 2004). Consequently, 13–33% of IVF patients deliver twins, and another 2–5% give birth to triplets (SART, 2008a). Multiple pregnancies are associated with premature birth, low birth weight, and birth defects, so the link between IVF and the development of multiple zygotes complicates the process of determining the true success rate of the procedure. Researchers have also found that, even when only one embryo is transferred, IVF is still associated with a higher rate of multiple births than is natural conception. For reasons that are not yet understood, implanted zygotes conceived through IVF are more likely to spontaneously divide into two embryos than are naturally conceived zygotes (Blickstine, Jones, & Keith, 2003). This finding suggests that couples such as Sven and Ilse should consider the possibility of multiple births when they weigh the pros and cons associated with IVF.

Questions for Reflection

1. If you were Sven or Ilse, would you go through with IVF? What factors would affect your decision?
2. What is your view of the practice of implanting multiple embryos conceived through IVF to increase the chances of a live birth?

assisted reproductive techniques to become pregnant are more likely to deliver multiples than women who conceive naturally.

Learning Objective 3.2
In what ways do genes influence development?

How Genes Influence Development

At conception, the genes from the father contained in the sperm and those from the mother in the ovum combine to create a unique genetic blueprint—the **genotype**—that characterizes the new individual. The **phenotype** is the individual's whole set of actual characteristics. One way to remember the distinction is that the phenotype can be identified by directly observing the individual. For example, you can easily see that a woman has brown eyes, which are part of her phenotype. Her genotype, though, can't be so easily determined. In many cases, you have to know her parents' and offsprings' eye color to find out whether she carries genes for another eye color, because complex rules govern the way genotypes influence phenotypes.

genotype the unique genetic blueprint of each individual

phenotype an individual's particular set of observable characteristics

dominant-recessive pattern pattern of inheritance in which a single dominant gene influences a person's phenotype but two recessive genes are necessary to produce an associated trait

Dominant and Recessive Genes The simplest genetic rule is the **dominant-recessive pattern**, in which a single dominant gene strongly influences phenotype. Table 3.1 lists several normal phenotypical traits and indicates whether they arise from dominant, recessive, or many genes. People whose chromosomes carry either two dominant or two recessive genes are referred to as *homozygous*. Those with one dominant and one recessive gene are said to be *heterozygous*.

If a child receives a single dominant gene for a trait from one parent, the child's phenotype will include the trait determined by that gene. In contrast, a child's phenotype will include a recessive trait only if she inherits a recessive gene from both parents. For example, geneticists have found that the curliness of hair is controlled by a single pair of genes (see

Figure 3.1). The gene for curly hair is dominant; therefore, if a man has curly hair, his genotype includes at least one gene for curly hair and half of his sperm carry this gene. Conversely, straight hair is recessive, so a straight-haired man's genotype must include two straight-hair genes for his phenotype to include straight hair. Geneticists also know that the only kind of hair type a straight-haired father can pass on to his children is straight hair, because all his sperm carry recessive, straight-hair genes.

In addition, human geneticists have learned that both dominant and recessive genes differ in expressivity, meaning that the degree to which any gene influences phenotypes varies from person to person. For example, all individuals who have the gene for curly hair don't have equally curly hair. So, even when a child receives a dominant gene for curly hair from her father, the amount and type of curl in her hair probably won't be exactly the same as his.

Table 3.1 Genetic Sources of Normal Traits

Dominant Genes	Recessive Genes	Polygenic (many genes)
Freckles	Flat feet	Height
Coarse hair	Thin lips	Body type
Dimples	Rh-negative blood	Eye color
Curly hair	Fine hair	Skin color
Nearsightedness	Red hair	Personality
Broad lips	Blond hair	
Rh-positive blood	Type O blood	
Types A and B blood		
Dark hair		

Source: Tortora & Grabowski, 1993.

Blood type is also determined by a dominant-recessive pattern of inheritance. Because a person must have two recessive genes to have type O blood, the genotype of every person who has this blood type is clear. Likewise, the only way a person can have type AB blood is if her genotype includes one gene for type A and one for type B. However, the genotype of people with type A or B blood is not obvious because types A and B are dominant. Thus, when a person's phenotype includes either type A or type B blood, one of the person's blood-type genes must be for that type, but the other could be for some other type. However, if a type A father and a type B mother produce a child with type O, each

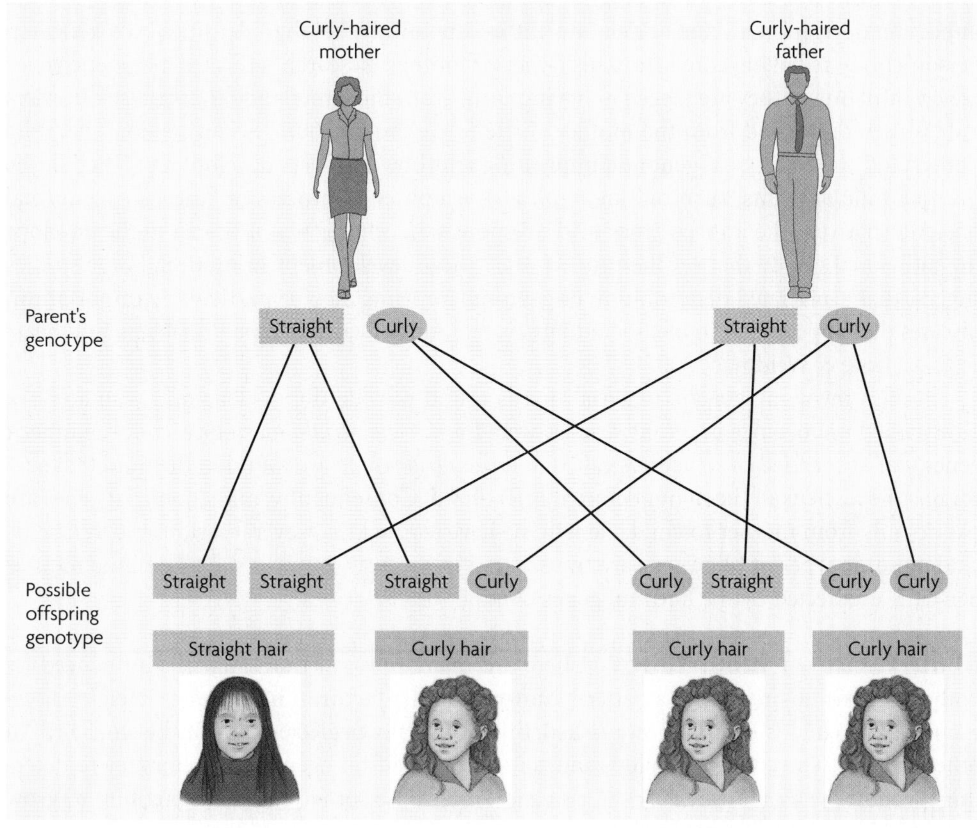

Figure 3.1
The Genetics of Hair Type

Examples of how the genes for curly and straight hair pass from parents to children.

of them carries a gene for type O, because the child must receive one such recessive gene from each parent to have the type O phenotype.

Polygenic Inheritance With **polygenic inheritance**, many genes influence the phenotype. There are many polygenic traits in which the dominant-recessive pattern is also at work. For example, geneticists believe that children get three genes for skin color from each parent (Tortora & Grabowski, 1993). Dark skin is dominant over light skin, but the skin colors also blend together. Thus, when one parent is dark-skinned and the other is fair-skinned, the child will have skin that is somewhere between the two. The dark-skinned parent's dominant genes will ensure that the child will be darker than the fair parent, but the fair-skinned parent's genes will prevent the child from having skin as dark as that of the dark-skinned parent.

Eye color is another polygenic trait with a dominant-recessive pattern (Tortora & Grabowski, 1993). Scientists don't know for sure how many genes influence eye color. They do know, however, that these genes don't cause specific colors. Instead, they cause the colored part of the eye to be dark or light. Dark colors (black, brown, hazel, and green) are dominant over light colors (blue and gray). However, blended colors are also possible. People whose chromosomes carry a combination of genes for green, blue, and gray eyes have eye colors that are blends of these colors. Likewise, genes that cause different shades of brown can combine their effects to make children's eye-color phenotypes different from those of their brown-eyed parents.

Many genes influence height, and they are not subject to a dominant-recessive pattern of inheritance. Most geneticists believe that each height gene has a small influence over a child's size (Tanner, 1990).

Other Types of Inheritance You probably learned about dominant and recessive traits in high school biology and came away with the impression that they represented the only rules governing how genotypes are expressed as phenotypes. But there are several other modes of genetic transmission; two of them have gained an increasing amount of attention in recent years. For instance, geneticists have been aware of the process of *genomic imprinting* for some time, but recent technological advances have enabled them to more fully study its impact on development. A genomic imprint is a chemical label that identifies each gene in a person's body as having come from his father or mother. Research indicates that some genes are harmful only if they are tagged as having come from the father and others cause disorders only if they originated from the mother (Jirtle & Weidman, 2007). Scientists don't yet fully understand the process of genomic imprinting and how it affects development. It could be that genomic imprints "turn on" an atypical developmental process or "turn off" a normal one. Alternatively, the imprints may evoke responses in other genes or tissues in the developing individual's body that set the process of atypical development in motion. Some studies suggest that age-related deterioration of genomic imprints may be particularly important in diseases that appear later in life, including several kinds of cancer, Type II diabetes, and heart disease (Jirtle & Weidman, 2007).

Studies involving genetic material that is found outside the nucleus of a woman's ova have gained importance in recent years as well. In *mitochondrial inheritance*, children inherit genes that are carried in structures called *mitochondria* which are found in the fluid that surrounds the nucleus of the ovum before it is fertilized. Consequently, mitochondrial genes are passed only from mother to child. Geneticists have learned that several serious disorders, including some types of blindness, are transmitted in this way. In most such cases, the mother herself is unaffected by the harmful genes (Amato, 1998).

Multi-Factorial Inheritance There are many physical traits that are influenced by both genes and environment, a pattern known as **multi-factorial inheritance**. Height is one example. If a child is ill, poorly nourished, or emotionally neglected, he may be smaller than others his age. Thus, when a child is shorter than 97% of his agemates, doctors try to determine whether he is short because of his genes or because something is causing him to grow poorly (Sulkes, 1998; Tanner, 1990).

polygenic inheritance
pattern of inheritance in which many genes influence a trait

multi-factorial inheritance
inheritance affected by both genes and the environment

As discussed in Chapter 1, psychological traits such as intelligence and personality are influenced by both heredity and environment. Thus, they result from multi-factorial inheritance. But just how do genes and environment work together to produce variations in such traits? A set of five general principles proposed by Michael Rutter and his colleagues (1997) can help organize our thinking about this question:

- "*Individuals differ in their reactivity to the environment*" (p. 338). Some individuals are highly reactive, highly sensitive to stress or strangeness; others react with much less volatility.
- "*There is a two-way interplay between individuals and their environments*" (p. 338). It is important not to think of this process as a one-way street. Influences go back and forth.
- "*The interplay between persons and their environments needs to be considered within an ecological framework*" (p. 339). Although our research nearly always treats environmental events—such as divorce—as if they were constant, they are not. Such events vary as a function of culture, poverty, family structure, and a whole host of other variables.
- "*People process their experiences rather than just serve as passive recipients of environmental forces*" (p. 339). It is the meaning each person attaches to an experience that governs the effect, not the experience itself. Thus, the "same" experience can have widely differing effects, depending on how the individual interprets it.
- "*People act on their environment so as to shape and select their experiences*" (p. 339). For instance, a child with a genetic predisposition toward shyness may choose not to play organized sports. As a result, he will not have the same opportunity to gain information about his athletic (and presumably genetic) talents as a more outgoing child who enjoys being in groups. Because of his choice, the shy child will have fewer opportunities than the outgoing child to learn and practice athletic skills.

Genetic and Chromosomal Disorders

Did you know that when a pregnant woman goes into labor, there is about a 97% chance that she will deliver a healthy baby? Of the 3% of births in which the health of a newborn is impaired or seriously threatened, about 30% are the result of harmful genes or errors in the process of early development that have altered a child's chromosomal makeup (CDC, 2005).

Genetic Disorders

Learning Objective 3.3
What are the effects of the major recessive, dominant, and sex-linked diseases?

Many disorders appear to be transmitted through the operation of dominant and recessive genes (see Table 3.2). *Autosomal disorders* are caused by genes located on the autosomes (chromosomes other than sex chromosomes). The genes that cause *sex-linked disorders* are found on the X chromosome.

Table 3.2 Some Genetic Disorders

Autosomal Dominant Disorders	Autosomal Recessive Disorders	Sex-Linked Recessive Disorders
Huntington's disease	Phenylketonuria	Hemophilia
High blood pressure	Sickle-cell disease	Fragile-X syndrome
Extra fingers	Cystic fibrosis	Red-green color blindness
Migraine headaches	Tay-Sachs disease	Missing front teeth
Schizophrenia	Kidney cysts in infants	Night blindness
	Albinism	Some types of muscular dystrophy
		Some types of diabetes

Sources: Amato, 1998; Tortora & Grabowski, 1993.

Autosomal Disorders Most disorders caused by recessive genes are diagnosed in infancy or early childhood. For example, a recessive gene causes a baby to have problems digesting the amino acid phenylalanine. Toxins build up in the baby's brain and cause mental retardation. This condition, called *phenylketonuria (PKU)*, is found in about 1 in every 10,000 babies (Nicholson, 1998). If a baby consumes no foods containing phenylalanine, however, she will not develop mental retardation. Milk is one of the foods PKU babies can't have, so early diagnosis is critical. For this reason, most states require all babies to be tested for PKU soon after birth.

Like many recessive disorders, PKU is associated with ethnicity. White babies are more likely to have the disorder than infants in other groups. Similarly, West African and African American infants are more likely to have *sickle-cell disease*, a recessive disorder that causes red blood cell deformities (Scott, 1998). In sickle-cell disease, the blood can't carry enough oxygen to keep the body's tissues healthy. Few children with sickle-cell disease live past the age of 20, and most who survive to adulthood die before they are 40 (Scott, 1998).

Almost one-half of West Africans have either sickle-cell disease or *sickle-cell trait* (Amato, 1998). Persons with sickle-cell trait carry a single recessive gene for sickle-cell disease, which causes a few of their red blood cells to be abnormal. Thus, doctors can identify carriers of the sickle-cell gene by testing their blood for sickle-cell trait. Once potential parents know they carry the gene, they can make informed decisions about future childbearing. In the United States, about 1 in 650 African Americans has sickle-cell disease, and 1 in 8 has sickle-cell trait. The disease and trait also occur more frequently in Americans of Mediterranean, Caribbean, Indian, Arab, and Latin American ancestry than in those of European ancestry (Wong, 1993).

About 1 in every 3,000 babies born to Jewish couples of Eastern European ancestry has another recessive disorder, *Tay-Sachs disease*. By the time he is 1 to 2 years old, a baby with Tay-Sachs is likely to have severe mental retardation and be blind. Very few survive past the age of 3 (Painter & Bergman, 1998).

Disorders caused by dominant genes, such as *Huntington's disease*, are usually not diagnosed until adulthood (Amato, 1998). This disorder causes the brain to deteriorate and affects both psychological and motor functions. Until recently, children of people with Huntington's disease had to wait until they became ill themselves to know for sure that they carried the gene. There is now a blood test to identify the Huntington's gene. Thus, people who have a parent with this disease can now make better decisions about their own childbearing, as well as prepare themselves to live with a serious disorder when they get older.

Sex-Linked Disorders Most sex-linked disorders are caused by recessive genes (see Figure 3.2). One fairly common sex-linked recessive disorder is *red-green color blindness*. People with this disorder have difficulty distinguishing between the colors red and green when these colors are adjacent. The prevalence of red-green color blindness is 8% in men and .5% (½ percent) in women (National Library of Medicine, 2008). Most people learn ways of compensating for the disorder and thus live perfectly normal lives.

A more serious sex-linked recessive disorder is *hemophilia*. The blood of people with hemophilia lacks the chemical components that cause blood to clot. Thus, when a person with hemophilia bleeds, the bleeding doesn't stop naturally. Approximately 1 in 5,000 baby boys is born with this disorder, which is almost unknown in girls (Scott, 1998).

About 1 in every 1,500 males and 1 in every 2,500 females have a sex-linked disorder called *fragile-X syndrome* (Amato, 1998). A person with this disorder has an X chromosome with a "fragile," or damaged, spot. Fragile-X syndrome can cause mental retardation that becomes progressively worse as a child gets older (Adesman, 1996). In fact, experts estimate that 5–7% of all males with mental retardation have fragile-X syndrome (Zigler & Hodapp, 1991).

Figure 3.2
Sex-Linked Inheritance

Compare this pattern of sex-linked transmission of a recessive disease (hemophilia) with the pattern shown in Figure 3.1.

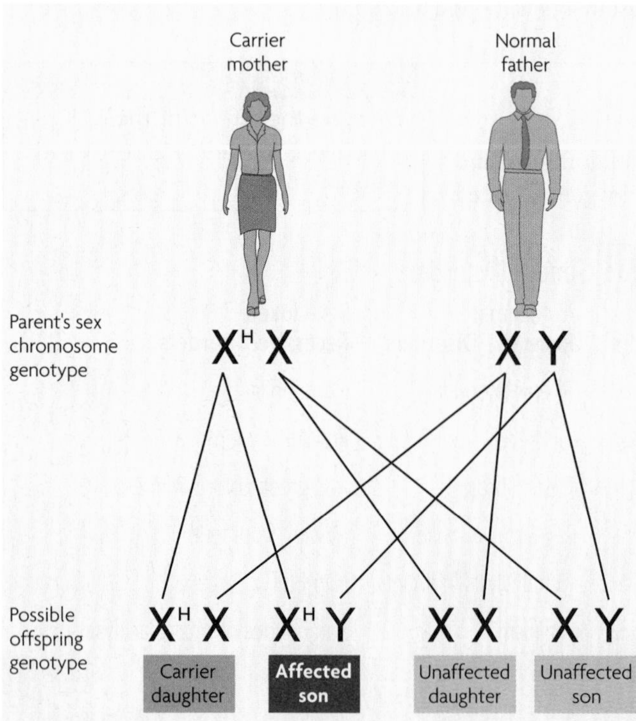

Chromosomal Errors

Learning Objective 3.4

How do trisomies and other disorders of the autosomes and sex chromosomes affect development?

A variety of problems can be caused when a child has too many or too few chromosomes, a condition referred to as a *chromosomal error* or *chromosomal anomaly*. Like genetic disorders, these are distinguished by whether they involve autosomes or sex chromosomes.

Trisomies A *trisomy* is a condition in which a child has three copies of a specific autosome. The most common is *trisomy 21*, or *Down syndrome*, in which the child has three copies of chromosome 21. Roughly 1 in every 800–1,000 infants is born with this abnormality (Nightingale & Goodman, 1990). These children have mental retardation and have distinctive facial features, smaller brains, and often other physical abnormalities such as heart defects (Haier et al., 1995).

The risk of bearing a child with trisomy 21 is greatest for mothers over 35. Among women aged 35–39, the incidence of Down syndrome is about 1 in 280 births. Among those over 45, it is as high as 1 in 50 births (D'Alton & DeCherney, 1993).

Scientists have identified children with trisomies in the 13th and 18th pairs of chromosomes as well (Amato, 1998). These disorders have more severe effects than trisomy 21. Few children with trisomy 13 or trisomy 18 live past the age of 1 year. As with trisomy 21, the chances of having a child with one of these disorders increase with a woman's age.

Sex-Chromosome Anomalies A second class of anomalies is associated with the sex chromosomes. The most common is an XXY pattern, called *Klinefelter's syndrome*, that occurs in 1 or 2 out of every 1,000 males (Amato, 1998). Affected boys don't look different from unaffected boys, but they have underdeveloped testes and, as adults, very low sperm production. Many have language and learning disabilities. At puberty, these boys experience both male and female changes. For example, their penises enlarge and their breasts develop.

A single-X pattern (X0), called *Turner syndrome*, may also occur. Individuals with Turner syndrome are anatomically female but show stunted growth and are usually sterile. Without hormone therapy, they do not menstruate or develop breasts at puberty. About one-fourth have serious heart defects (Amato, 1998). These girls also show an imbalance in their cognitive skills: They often perform particularly poorly on tests that measure spatial ability but usually perform at or above normal levels on tests of verbal skill (Golombok & Fivush, 1994).

Neither Klinefelter's nor Turner syndrome is associated with the mother's age. However, older mothers are more likely to produce normal-appearing girls with an extra X chromosome and boys with an extra Y chromosome (Amato, 1998). Females with an XXX pattern, about 1 in every 1,000 female births, are usually of normal size but develop more slowly than their peers (Amato, 1998). Many, though not all, have poor verbal abilities, score low on intelligence tests, and do more poorly in school than other groups with sex-chromosome anomalies (Bender, Harmon, Linden, & Robinson, 1995).

Approximately 1 in 1,000 boys has an extra Y chromosome. Most are taller than average and have large teeth. They usually experience normal puberty, and they have no difficulty fathering children (Amato, 1998). Developmentalists now know that it is only a myth that an extra Y chromosome causes below-average intelligence and high aggression (Tortora & Grabowski, 1993).

This child shows the distinctive facial features of a child with Down syndrome.

Pregnancy and Prenatal Development

The process that ends with the birth of a baby involves two sets of experiences: those of the pregnant woman and those of the developing zygote, embryo, and fetus. *Pregnancy* is the physical condition in which a woman's body is nurturing a developing embryo or fetus. *Prenatal development*, or *gestation*, is the process that transforms a zygote into a newborn.

Learning Objective 3.5

What are the characteristics of each trimester of pregnancy?

The Mother's Experience

Pregnancy is customarily divided into trimesters, three periods of 3 months each (see Table 3.3).

First Trimester Pregnancy begins when the zygote implants itself in the lining of the woman's uterus (also called the *womb*). The zygote then sends out chemical messages that cause the woman's menstrual periods to stop. Some of these chemicals are excreted in her urine, making it possible to diagnose pregnancy within a few days after conception. Other chemicals cause physical changes, such as breast enlargement.

The *cervix* (the narrow, lower portion of the uterus, which extends into the vagina) thickens and secretes mucus that serves as a barrier to protect the developing embryo from harmful organisms that might enter the womb through the vagina. The uterus begins to shift position and put pressure on the woman's bladder, causing her to urinate more often. This and other symptoms, like fatigue and breast tenderness, may interfere with sleep. Another common early symptom of pregnancy is *morning sickness*—feelings of nausea, often accompanied by vomiting, that usually occur in the morning.

Table 3.3 Milestones of Pregnancy

Trimester	Events	Prenatal Care	Serious Problems
First trimester: From first day of last menstrual period (LMP) to 12 weeks	Missed period Breast enlargement Abdominal thickening	Confirmation of pregnancy Calculation of due date Blood and urine tests (and other tests if needed) Monthly doctor visits to monitor vital functions, uterine growth, weight gain, sugar and protein in urine	Ectopic pregnancy Abnormal urine or blood tests Increased blood pressure Malnutrition Bleeding Miscarriage
Second trimester: From 13 weeks after LMP to 24 weeks after LMP	Weight gain "Showing" Fetal movements felt Increased appetite	Monthly doctor visits continue Ultrasound to measure fetal growth and locate placenta	Gestational diabetes Excessive weight gain Increased blood pressure Miscarriage 13 to 20 weeks Premature labor 21 weeks
Third trimester: From 25 weeks after LMP to beginning of labor	Weight gain Abdominal enlargement Breast discharge	Weekly visits beginning at 32nd week Ultrasound to assess position of fetus Pelvic exams to check for cervical dilation	Increased blood pressure Bleeding Premature labor Bladder infection

Sources: Hobbs & Ferth, 1993; Kliegman, 1998; Tortora & Grabowski, 1993.

Prenatal care during the first trimester is critical to prevent birth defects, because all of the baby's organs form during the first 8 weeks. Early prenatal care can identify maternal conditions, such as sexually transmitted diseases, that may threaten prenatal development. Doctors and nurses can also urge women to abstain from drugs and alcohol early in prenatal development, when such behavior changes may prevent birth defects.

Early prenatal care can also be important to the pregnant woman's health. For example, a small number of zygotes implant in one of the fallopian tubes instead of in the uterus, a condition called *ectopic pregnancy*. Early surgical removal of the zygote is critical to the woman's future ability to have children.

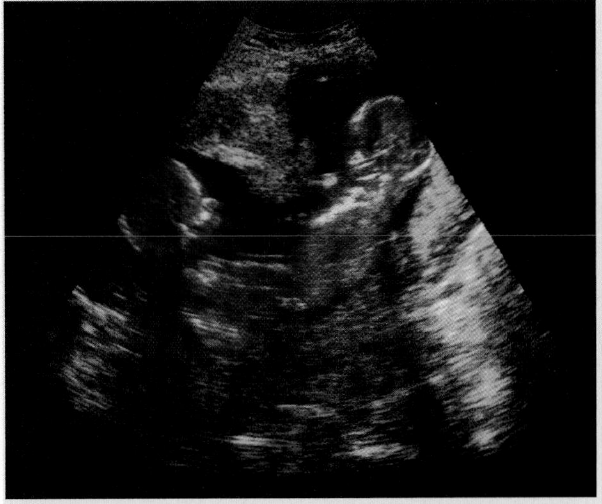
Ultrasound examinations are especially helpful in tracking the progress of multiple pregnancies.

About 15% of pregnancies end in *miscarriage*, or *spontaneous abortion*. From the woman's point of view, an early miscarriage is similar to a menstrual period, although feelings of discomfort and blood loss are usually greater. Medical care is always necessary after a miscarriage because the woman's body may fail to completely expel the embryo.

Second Trimester During the second trimester of pregnancy, from week 13 through week 24, morning sickness usually disappears, resulting in increases in appetite. The pregnant woman gains weight, and the uterus expands to accommodate the fetus, which is growing rapidly. Consequently, the woman begins to "show" sometime during the second trimester. She also begins to feel the fetus's movements, usually at some point between the 16th and 18th weeks.

At monthly clinic visits, doctors monitor both the mother's and the baby's vital functions and keep track of the growth of the baby in the womb. Ultrasound tests are usually performed, and the sex of the baby can be determined after about the 13th week. Monthly urine tests check for *gestational diabetes*, a kind of diabetes that happens only during pregnancy. Women who have any kind of diabetes, including gestational diabetes, have to be carefully monitored during the second trimester because their babies may grow too rapidly, leading to premature labor or a baby that is too large for vaginal delivery. The risk of miscarriage drops in the second trimester. However, a few fetuses die between the 13th and 20th weeks of pregnancy.

THE WHOLE CHILD IN FOCUS

What were the results of Lisa Chang's ultrasound examination? Find out on page 92.

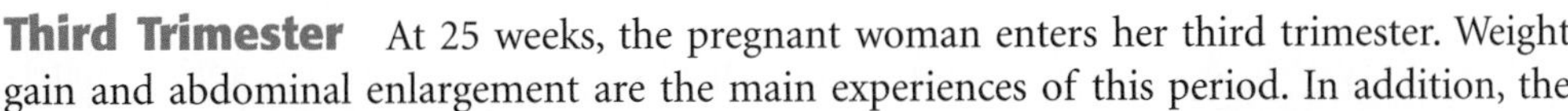

Third Trimester At 25 weeks, the pregnant woman enters her third trimester. Weight gain and abdominal enlargement are the main experiences of this period. In addition, the woman's breasts may begin to secrete a substance called *colostrum* in preparation for nursing.

Most women begin to feel more emotionally connected to the fetus during the third trimester. Individual differences in fetal behavior, such as hiccupping or thumb-sucking, sometimes become obvious during the last weeks of pregnancy. These behaviors may be observed during ultrasound tests, which produce increasingly clear images of the fetus. In addition, most women notice that the fetus has regular periods of activity and rest.

Supportive partners, friends, and relatives can help third-trimester mothers-to-be maintain positive attitudes and balance negative emotions, which often accompany their feelings of physical awkwardness, against the anticipated joy of birth.

Monthly prenatal doctor visits continue in the third trimester until week 32, when most women begin visiting the doctor's office or clinic once a week. Monitoring of blood pressure is especially important, as some women develop a life-threatening condition called *toxemia of pregnancy* during the third trimester. This condition is signaled by a sudden increase in blood pressure and can cause a pregnant woman to have a stroke.

Learning Objective 3.6

What happens in each stage of prenatal development?

Prenatal Development

In contrast to the trimesters of pregnancy, the three stages of prenatal development are defined by specific developmental milestones and are not of equal length. Moreover, the entire process follows two developmental patterns, which you can see at work in the photographs in Table 3.4. With the **cephalocaudal pattern**, development proceeds from the head down. For example, the brain is formed before the reproductive organs. With the **proximodistal pattern**, development happens in an orderly way from the center of the body outward to the extremities. In other words, structures closer to the center of the body, such as the rib cage, develop before the fingers and toes.

The Germinal Stage The first 2 weeks of gestation, from conception to *implantation*, constitute the **germinal stage**. During this stage, cells specialize into those that will become the fetus's body and those that will become the structures needed to support its development. Cell division happens rapidly, and by the 4th day, the zygote contains dozens of cells.

On day 5, the cells become a hollow, fluid-filled ball called a *blastocyst*. Inside the blastocyst, cells that will eventually become the embryo begin to clump together. On day 6 or 7, the blastocyst comes into contact with the uterine wall, and by the 12th day, it is completely buried in the uterine tissue, a process called **implantation**. Some of the cells of the blastocyst's outer wall combine with cells of the uterine lining to begin creating the **placenta**, an organ that allows oxygen, nutrients, and other substances to be transferred between the mother's and baby's blood. The placenta's specialized structures bring the mother's and baby's blood close to each other without allowing them to mix.

Like the zygote, the placenta secretes chemical messages (hormones) that stop the mother's menstrual periods and keep the placenta connected to the uterus. Other placental hormones allow the bones of the woman's pelvis to become more flexible, induce breast changes, and increase the mother's metabolism rate. At the same time, the blastocyst's inner cells begin to specialize. One group of cells will become the **umbilical cord**, the organ that connects the embryo to the placenta. Vessels in the umbilical cord carry blood from the baby to the mother and back again. Other cells will form the yolk sac, a structure that produces blood cells until the embryo's blood-cell-producing organs are formed. Still others will become the **amnion**, a fluid-filled sac in which the baby floats until just before it is born. By the 12th day, the cells that will become the embryo's body are also formed.

The Embryonic Stage The **embryonic stage** begins at implantation, approximately the 3rd week after conception, and continues until the end of week 8. By the time many women first suspect a pregnancy, usually 3 weeks after conception, the embryo's cells are starting to specialize and come together to form the foundations of all the body's organs. For example, the cells of the nervous system, the **neurons**, form a structure called the *neural tube*, from which the brain and spinal cord will develop. A primitive heart and the forerunners of the kidneys also develop during week 3, along with three sacs that will become the digestive system.

In week 4, the end of the embryo's neural tube swells to form the brain. Spots that will become the eyes appear on the embryo's head, and its heart begins to beat. The backbone and ribs become visible as bone and muscle cells move into place. The face starts to take shape, and the endocrine system begins to develop.

By week 5, the embryo is about ¼ inch long, 10,000 times larger than the zygote. Its arms and legs are developing rapidly. Five fingers are visible on its hands. Its eyes have corneas and lenses, and its lungs are beginning to develop.

In week 6, the embryo's brain begins to produce patterns of electrical activity, and the embryo moves in response to stimuli. During week 7, the embryo begins to move spontaneously (Joseph, 2000). It has a visible skeleton and fully developed limbs. The bones are beginning to harden and the muscles are maturing; by this point, the embryo can maintain a semi-upright

cephalocaudal pattern growth that proceeds from the head downward

proximodistal pattern growth that proceeds from the middle of the body outward

germinal stage the first stage of prenatal development, beginning at conception and ending at implantation (approximately 2 weeks)

implantation attachment of the blastocyst to the uterine wall

placenta specialized organ that allows substances to be transferred from mother to embryo and from embryo to mother, without their blood mixing

umbilical cord organ that connects the embryo to the placenta

amnion fluid-filled sac in which the fetus floats until just before it is born

embryonic stage the second stage of prenatal development, from week 3 through week 8, during which the embryo's organ systems form

neurons specialized cells of the nervous system

Table 3.4 Milestones in Prenatal Development

Stage/Time Frame	Milestones	
Day 1: Conception	Sperm and ovum unite, forming a zygote containing genetic instructions for the development of a new and unique human being.	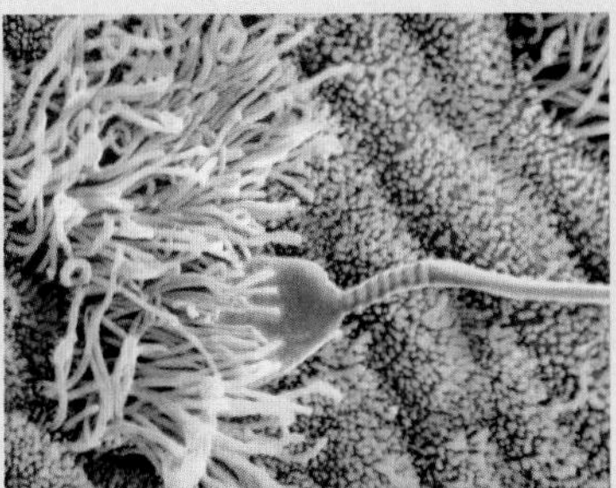 Sperm and egg
Days 6 to 12: Implantation	The zygote burrows into the lining of the uterus. Specialized cells that will become the placenta, umbilical cord, and embryo are already formed.	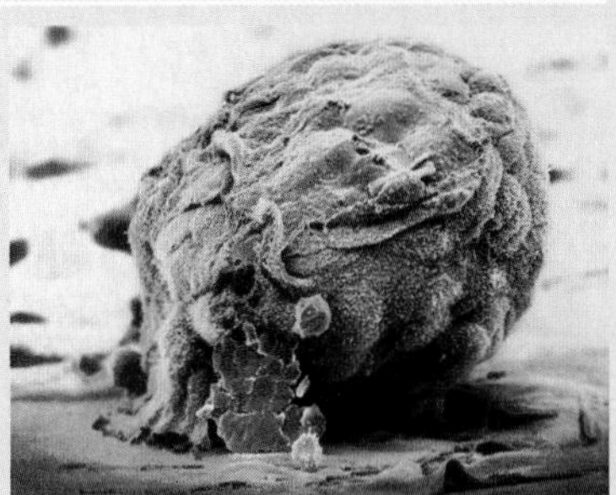 Zygote
Weeks 3 to 8: Organogenesis	All of the embryo's organ systems form during the 6-week period following implantation.	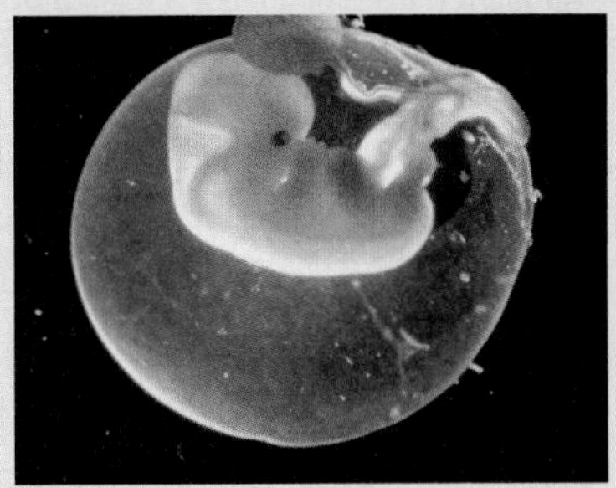 6-week embryo
Weeks 9 to 37: Growth and Organ Refinement	By week 12 or 13, most fetuses can be identified as male or female. Changes in the brain and lungs make viability possible by week 24; optimal development requires an additional 14 to 16 weeks in the womb. Most neurons form by week 28, and connections among them begin to develop shortly thereafter. In the last 8 weeks, the fetus can hear and smell, is sensitive to touch, and responds to light. Learning is also possible.	

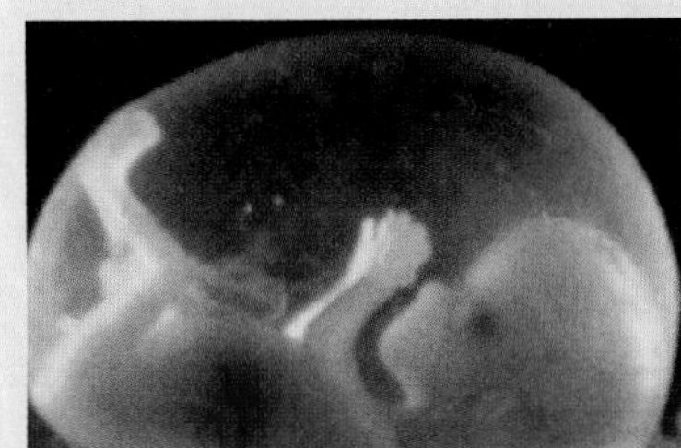
12-week fetus

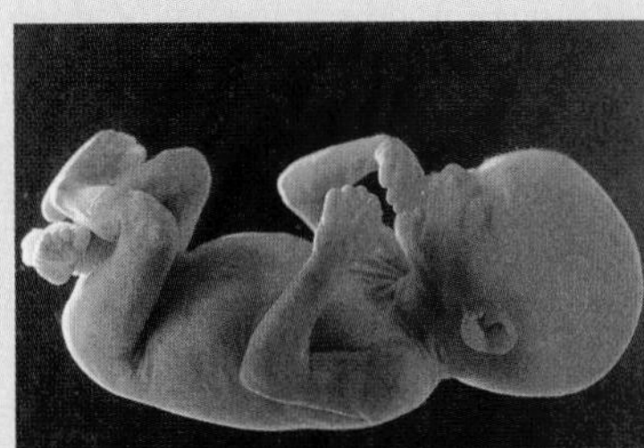
14-week fetus

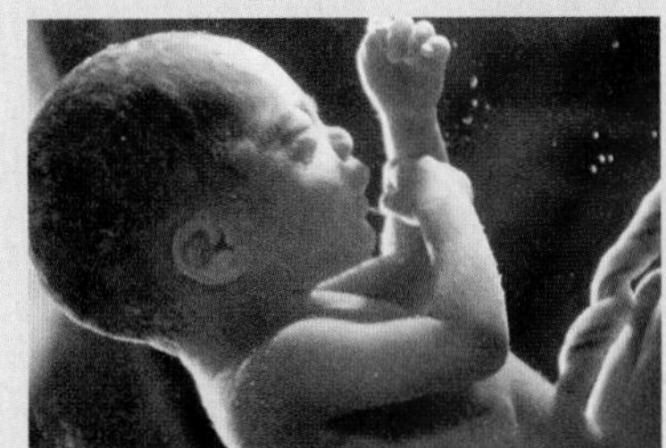
Well-developed fetus (age not given)

Sources: Kliegman, 1998; Tortora & Grabowski, 1993.

posture. The eyelids seal shut to protect the developing eyes. The ears are completely formed, and x-rays can detect tooth buds in the jawbones.

During the last week of the embryonic stage, week 8, the liver and spleen begin to function. These organs allow the embryo to make and filter its own blood cells. Its heart is well developed and efficiently pumps blood to every part of the body. The embryo's movements increase as the electrical activity in its brain becomes more organized. Connections between the brain and the rest of the body are also well established. The embryo's digestive and urinary systems are functioning. By the end of week 8, **organogenesis**, the technical term for organ development, is complete.

The Fetal Stage The final phase is the **fetal stage**, beginning at the start of week 9 and continuing until birth. The fetus grows from a weight of about 1/4 ounce and a length of 1 inch to a baby weighing about 7 pounds and having a length of about 20 inches, who is ready to be born. In addition, this stage involves refinements of the organ systems that are essential to life outside the womb (see Table 3.5).

By the end of week 23, a small number of babies have attained **viability**, the ability to live outside the womb (Moore & Persaud, 1993). However, most babies born this early die, and those who do survive struggle for many months. Remaining in the womb just 1 week longer, until the end of week 24, greatly increases a baby's chances of survival. The extra week probably allows time for lung function to become more efficient. In addition, most brain structures are completely developed by the end of the 24th week. For these reasons, most experts accept 24 weeks as the average age of viability.

organogenesis process of organ development

fetal stage the third stage of prenatal development, from week 9 to birth, during which growth and organ refinement take place

viability ability of the fetus to survive outside the womb

The Fetal Brain As you learned earlier, the foundational structures of all of the body's organ systems are formed during the embryonic stage. Yet most of the formation and finetuning of the brain take place during the fetal stage. Recall that neurons, the specialized cells of the nervous system, begin developing during the embryonic stage in week 3. But the pace of neural formation picks up dramatically between the 10th and 18th weeks, in a process known as *neuronal proliferation.*

Table 3.5 Milestones of the Fetal Stage

Period	What Develops
Weeks 9–12	Fingerprints; grasping reflex; facial expressions; swallowing and rhythmic "breathing" of amniotic fluid; urination; genitalia
Weeks 13–16	Hair follicles; responses to mother's voice and loud noises; 8–10 inches long; weighs 6 ounces
Weeks 17–20	Fetal movements felt by mother; heartbeat detectable with stethoscope; lanugo (hair) covers body; eyes respond to light introduced into the womb; eyebrows; fingernails; 12 inches long
Weeks 21–24	Vernix (oily substance) protects skin; lungs produce surfactant (vital to respiratory function); most fetuses attain viability at some point during this period, although most born before week 24 don't survive
Weeks 25–28	Recognition of mother's voice; regular periods of rest and activity; 14–15 inches long; weighs 2 pounds; good chance of survival if born now
Weeks 29–32	Very rapid growth; antibodies acquired from mother; fat deposited under skin; 16–17 inches long; weighs 4 pounds; excellent chance of survival if delivered now
Weeks 33–36	Movement to head-down position for birth; lungs mature; 18 inches long; weighs 4–5 pounds; virtually 100% chance of survival if delivered
Week 37	Full-term status; 19–21 inches long; weighs 5-6 pounds

Between the 13th and 21st weeks, the newly formed neurons migrate to the parts of the brain where they will reside for the rest of the individual's life (Chong et al., 1996). While migrating, neurons consist only of **cell bodies**, the part of the cell that contains the nucleus and in which all the cell's vital functions are carried out (see Figure 3.3). Once they have reached their final destinations in the fetal brain, the neurons begin to develop connections. These connections, called **synapses**, are tiny spaces between neurons across which neural impulses travel from one neuron to the next. Several changes in fetal behavior signal that the process of synapse formation is underway. For instance, the fetus exhibits alternating periods of activity and rest and begins to yawn (Walusinski, Kurjak, Andonotopo, & Azumendi, 2005; see Figure 3.4). When observed, these changes tell physicians that fetal brain development is proceeding normally.

Synapse formation requires the growth of two neuronal structures. **Axons** are tail-like extensions that can grow to be several feet in length. **Dendrites** are tentacle-like branches that extend out from the cell body (see Figure 3.3). Dendrite development is thought to be highly sensitive to adverse environmental influences such as maternal malnutrition and defects in placental functioning (Dieni & Rees, 2003).

Simultaneously with neuronal migration, **glial cells** begin to develop. These cells are the "glue" that hold the neurons together to give shape to the brain's major structures. As glial cells develop, the brain begins to assume a more mature appearance, one that can be observed using *magnetic resonance imaging (MRI)* and other modern technologies that you will read more about later in the chapter (see Figure 3.5 on page 68).

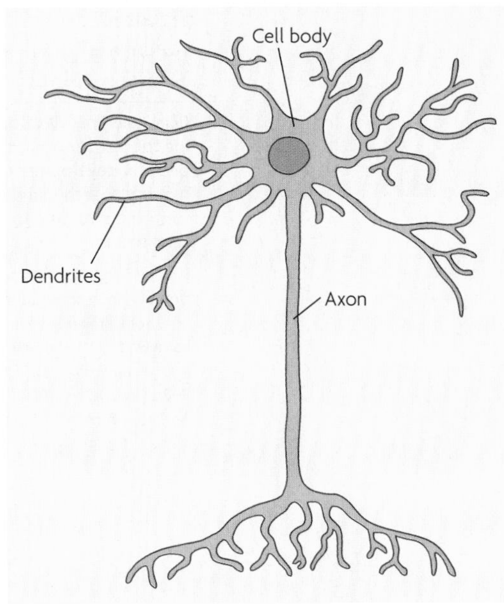

Figure 3.3 **Parts of the Neuron**

The structure of a single developed neuron. The cell bodies are the first to be developed. Axons and dendrites develop later and continue to increase in size and complexity for several years after birth.

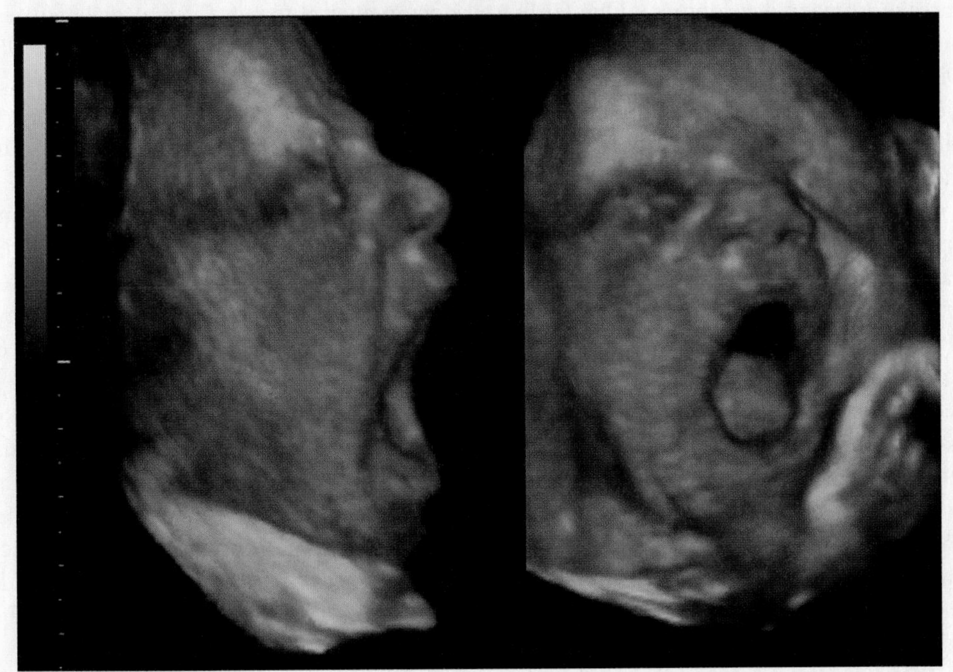

Figure 3.4 **Fetal Yawning**

Fetal yawning appears between the 10th and 15th week. Its presence signals the beginning of sleep stages in the fetal brain.

(*Source*: From O. Walusinski et al., "Fetal yawning: A behavior's birth with 4D US revealed," *The Ultrasound Review of Obstetrics and Gynecology*, 5 (2005): 210–217. Reprinted with permission.)

cell body the part of a neuron that contains the nucleus and is the site of vital cell functions

synapses tiny spaces across which neural impulses flow from one neuron to the next

axons tail-like extensions of neurons

dendrites branch-like protrusions from the cell bodies of neurons

glial cells the "glue" that holds neurons together to give form to the structures of the nervous system

Figure 3.5
A Normal Third-Trimester Fetal Brain

Glial cells that develop during the last few months of prenatal development hold neurons together and give form and structure to the fetal brain.

(*Source*: Reprinted with permission of Anderson Publishing, Ltd., from: Brown SD, Estroff JA, Barnewolf CE. "Fetal MRI." *Applied Radiology*, 33:2 (2004): 9–25. Copyright © 2004, Anderson Publishing, Ltd.)

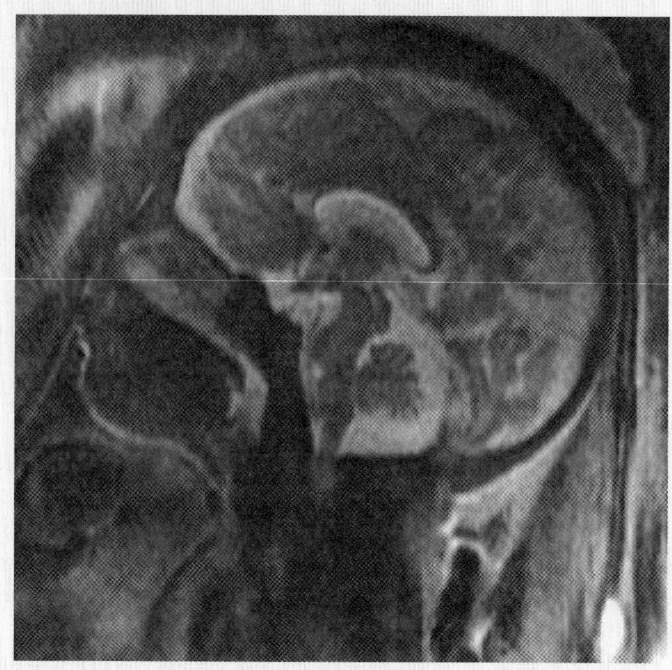

Learning Objective 3.7

How do male and female fetuses differ?

Sex Differences

Because prenatal development is strongly influenced by maturational codes that are the same for both males and females, there are only a few sex differences in prenatal development. One fairly well-documented difference is that male fetuses, on average, are more physically active (DiPietro, Hodgson, Costigan, & Johnson, 1996; DiPietro, Hodgson, Costigan, Hilton, & Johnson, 1996). Further, activity level is fairly stable from the fetal stage through childhood (Accardo et al., 1997). This means that the sex differences in children's activity level you'll read about in later chapters probably begin in the womb.

Subtle sex differences in prenatal brain development probably contribute to different patterns of growth hormone secretions in adolescence as well. Researchers have linked prenatal hormones to sex differences in the dominance of the right and left hemispheres of the brain, physical aggression, and connections between brain and motor patterns (Pressman, DiPietro, Costigan, Shupe, & Johnson, 1998; Todd, Swarzenski, Rossi, & Visconti, 1995).

Developmentalists aren't sure why, but female fetuses appear to be more sensitive to external stimulation and to advance more rapidly in skeletal development (Groome et al., 1999; Tanner, 1990). Female infants are about 1–2 weeks ahead in bone development at birth, even though newborn boys are typically longer and heavier. Female superiority in skeletal development persists through childhood and early adolescence, causing girls to acquire many coordinated movements and motor skills, especially those involving the hands and wrists, earlier than boys. The gap between the sexes gets wider every year until the mid-teens, when boys catch up and surpass girls in general physical coordination.

Boys are more vulnerable to all kinds of prenatal problems. Many more boys than girls are conceived—from 120 to 150 male embryos to every 100 female ones—but more of the males are spontaneously aborted. At birth, there are about 105 boys for every 100 girls. Male fetuses also appear to be more sensitive to variables such as marijuana and maternal stress, which may negatively affect prenatal development (Bethus, Lemaire, Lhomme, & Goodall, 2005; Wang, Dow-Edwards, Anderson, Minkoff, & Hurd, 2004).

Prenatal Behavior

Learning Objective 3.8

What behaviors have scientists observed in fetuses?

In recent years, techniques such as ultrasound imaging have provided researchers with a great deal of information about fetal behavior. Some researchers suggest that establishing norms for fetal behavior would help health-care providers better assess fetal health (Nijhuis, 2003). Thus, in recent years, the number of research studies examining fetal behavior has increased significantly. These studies have revealed some rather remarkable findings, some of which are shown in Figure 3.6.

For one thing, researchers have discovered that the fetus can distinguish between familiar and novel stimuli by the 32nd or 33rd week (Sandman, Wadhwa, Hetrick, Porto, & Peeke, 1997). In one study, pregnant women recited a short children's rhyme out loud each day from week 33 through week 37. In week 38, researchers played a recording of either the rhyme the mother had been reciting or a different rhyme and measured the fetal heart rate. Fetal heart rates dropped during the familiar rhyme, but not during the unfamiliar rhyme, suggesting that the fetuses had learned the sound patterns of the rhyme recited by their mothers (DeCasper, Lecaneut, Busnel, Granier-DeFerre, & Maugeais, 1994).

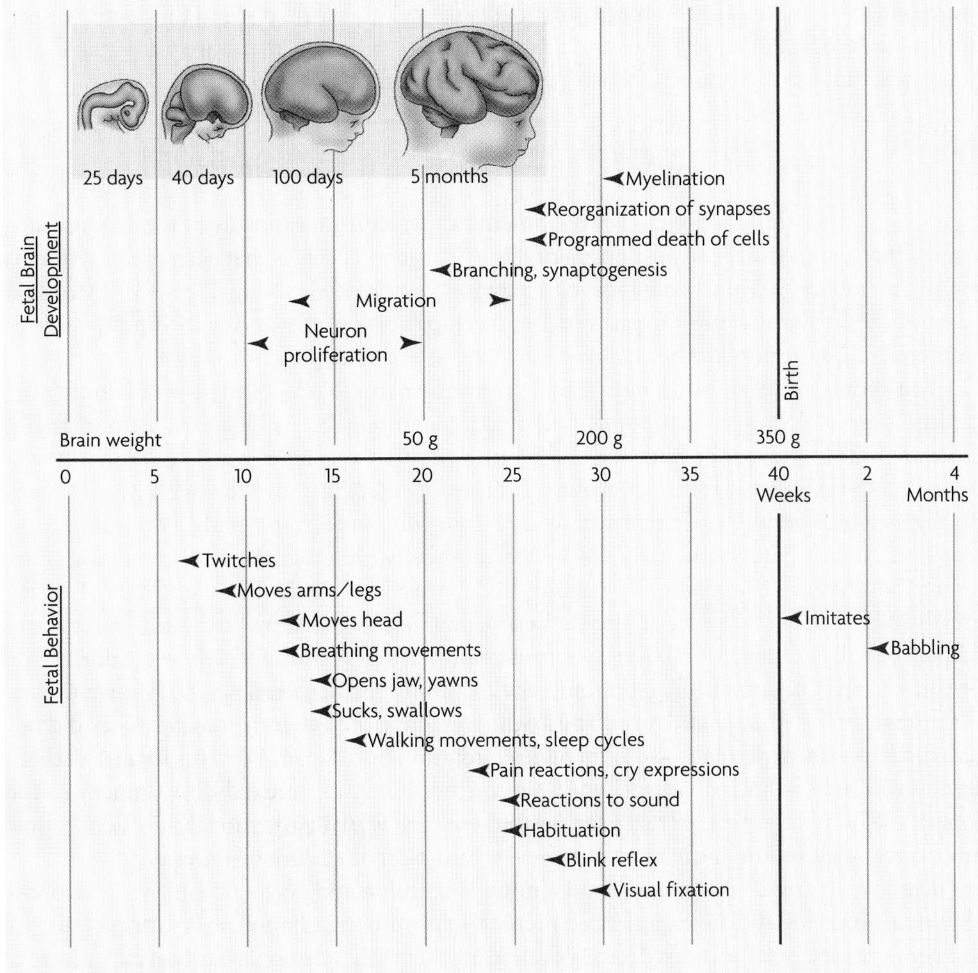

Figure 3.6 Correlations Between Fetal Behavior and Brain Development

Researchers have discovered numerous correlations between fetal brain development and behavior.

(*Source*: From O. Walusinski et al., "Fetal yawning: A behavior's birth with 4D US revealed," *The Ultrasound Review of Obstetrics and Gynecology*, 5, (2005): 210–217. Reprinted with permission.)

Evidence for fetal learning also comes from studies in which newborns appear to remember stimuli to which they were exposed prenatally. In a classic study of prenatal learning, pregnant women read Dr. Seuss's classic children's story *The Cat in the Hat* out loud each day for the final 6 weeks of their pregnancies. After the infants were born, they were allowed to suck on special pacifiers that turned a variety of sounds off and on. Each kind of sound required a special type of sucking. Researchers found that the babies quickly adapted their sucking patterns in order to listen to the familiar story, but did not increase their sucking in order to listen to an unfamiliar story (DeCasper & Spence, 1986). In other words, babies preferred the sound of the story they had heard *in utero* (in the womb).

Stable individual differences in behavior are also identifiable in fetuses. Longitudinal studies have shown that very active fetuses tend to become children who are very active. Moreover, these children are more likely to be labeled "hyperactive" by parents and teachers. In contrast, fetuses that are less active than average are more likely to become children who have mental retardation (Accardo et al., 1997).

Problems in Prenatal Development

Prenatal development is not immune to outside influences, as you'll see in this section. Keep in mind that most of the problems you'll read about are very rare, many are preventable, and many need not have permanent consequences for the child.

Learning Objective 3.9
How do teratogens affect prenatal development?

How Teratogens Influence Development

Deviations in prenatal development can result from exposure to **teratogens**, substances that cause damage to an embryo or fetus. The general rule is that each organ system is most vulnerable to harm when it is developing most rapidly, as shown in Figure 3.7 (Moore & Persaud, 1993). Because most organ systems develop most rapidly during the first 8 weeks of gestation, this is the period when exposure to teratogens carries the greatest risk.

You should recall from Chapter 1 that *critical periods* are phases when a developing organism is especially sensitive to some kind of external influence. As Figure 3.7 demonstrates, there are critical periods in both the embryonic and the fetal stages when certain body systems are especially sensitive to teratogens. If drugs or infections interfere with development during a critical period, a particular body structure will not form properly. For example, researchers found that Japanese people whose mothers were pregnant with them when the atomic bombs were dropped on Hiroshima and Nagasaki at the end of World War II varied greatly in how they responded to the environmental hazard posed by the bombs' radioactive fallout (Schull & Otake, 1997). Many of those who were in the 8th to 15th week, during the period of rapid neuronal formation and the beginning of neuronal migration, were born with irreversible mental retardation. Those who were between the 16th and 25th week did not have higher-than-expected rates of mental retardation, but they did exhibit higher levels of seizure disorders than individuals who were further along in prenatal development at the time of the bombings. Fetuses that were beyond the 25th week in gestational age did not show any degree of elevation in the rates of mental retardation or seizure disorders.

Despite the trends that were found among Hiroshima and Nagasaki survivors, remarkably, many individuals who experienced prenatal exposure to radiation, even during the critical periods, were born without defects of any kind. Such cases demonstrate that many factors contribute to the effects that a particular teratogen has on prenatal development. Two such factors are the duration and intensity of teratogen exposure. A single, brief exposure to even the most powerful teratogen may have little or no impact on development. However, if a single exposure is particularly intense—that is, if the "dose" of the teratogen is high—then it may be sufficient to cause damage. Among the Japanese atomic bomb survivors, the farther the person's mother was from the actual impact sites of the two bombs, the less likely the person was to develop mental retardation or a seizure disorder. However, exposures of low intensity may be harmful if they occur over an extended period of time. For this reason, special precautions must be taken by pregnant women who are likely to be exposed to even minimal

teratogens substances, such as viruses and drugs, that can cause birth defects

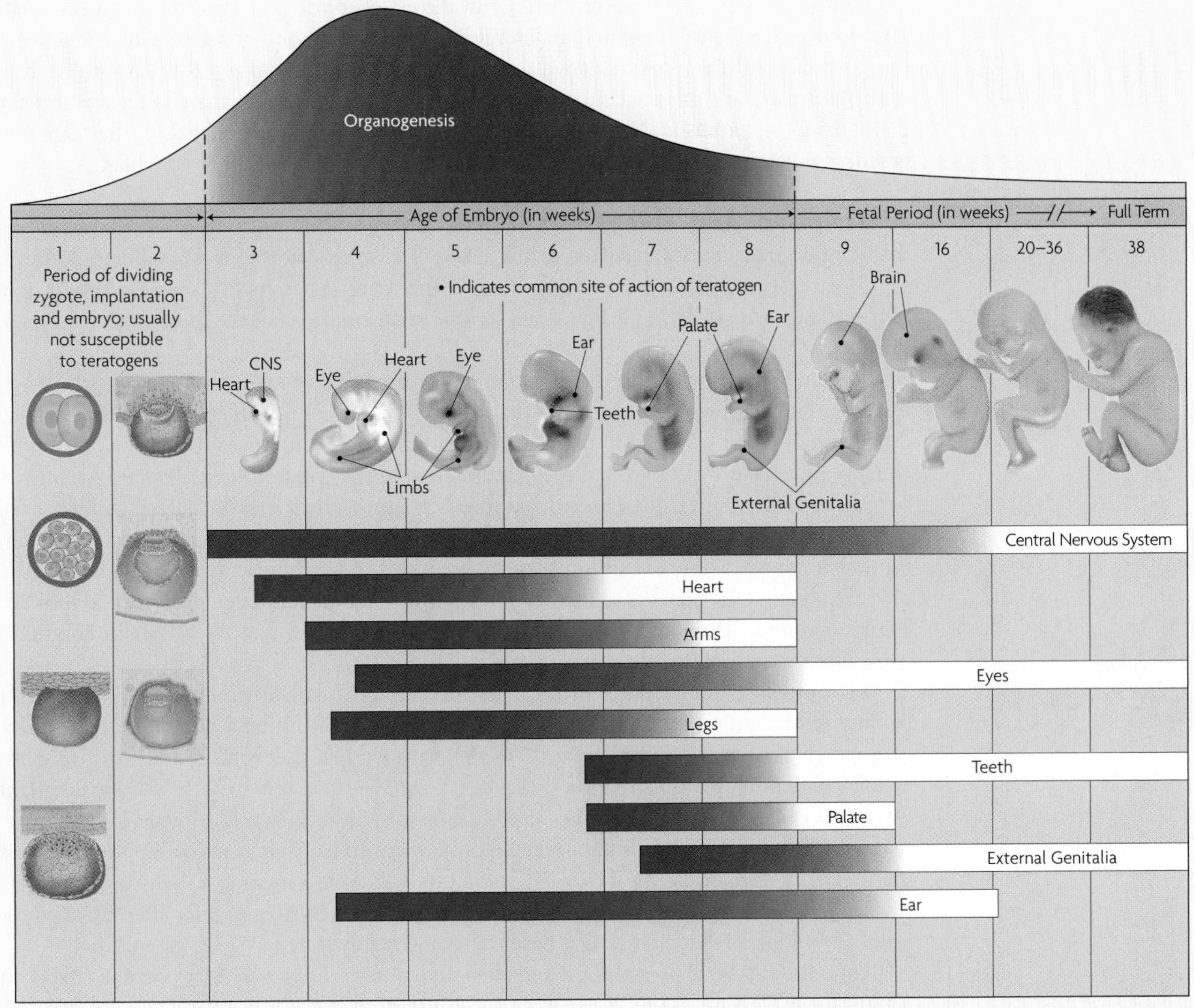

Figure 3.7 The Timing of Teratogen Exposure

The timing of teratogen exposure is crucial. Notice that teratogens have the most impact during the embryonic stage, except on certain body parts such as the brain and ears, which continue to be at risk for teratogenic effects because they continue to grow and develop during the fetal period.

(*Source*: C. Moore, J. Barresi, and C. Thompson, "The cognitive basis of future-oriented prosocial behavior," *Social Development*, 7 (1998): 198–218. Reprinted with permission.)

doses of radiation or other potentially harmful substances that are a part of their everyday working environments.

Finally, researchers have hypothesized that fetuses vary widely in their susceptibility to teratogens. These differences are thought to arise from genes that moderate or block the effects of some kinds of harmful substances. For instance, studies involving various strains of laboratory mice have shown that some strains are completely immune to teratogens that cause serious facial deformities in others (Syska, Schmidt, & Schubert, 2004).

Drugs

Learning Objective 3.10

What are the potential adverse effects of tobacco, alcohol, and other drugs on prenatal development?

Any drug, including many whose safety we take for granted (e.g., antibiotics), can be teratogenic. That is why doctors always ask women of childbearing age whether they might be pregnant before prescribing medication for them. Unless a drug is absolutely necessary to a woman's health, doctors recommend avoiding drugs of any kind during pregnancy. However, sorting out the effects of drugs (prescription and nonprescription, legal and illegal) on prenatal development has proven to be an immensely challenging task because many pregnant women take multiple drugs. Also, other factors, such as maternal stress, lack of social support, or poverty and poor prenatal care, often accompany illegal drug use (Johnson, Nusbaum, Bejarano, & Rosen, 1999). Nevertheless, there are several drugs that seem to affect infant development, independent of other variables.

Prescription and Over-the-Counter Drugs You may have heard about the thalidomide tragedy that occurred in the 1960s. The drug involved was a mild tranquilizer that doctors prescribed to pregnant women who were experiencing severe symptoms of morning sickness. Sadly, the drug caused serious malformations of the limbs in thousands of fetuses that were exposed to it (Vogin, 2005).

In general, doctors advise against taking any unnecessary medicines during pregnancy. But some pregnant women must take drugs in order to treat health conditions that may be threatening to their own and to their unborn child's life. For instance, pregnant women with epilepsy must take anticonvulsant medication because the seizures themselves are potentially harmful to the unborn child. Other drugs that pregnant women may have to risk taking, even though they can be harmful, include medications that treat heart conditions and diabetes, those that control asthma symptoms, and some kinds of psychiatric drugs. In all such cases, physicians weigh the benefits of medication against potential teratogenic effects and look for a combination of drug and dosage that will effectively treat the mother's health condition while placing her unborn child at minimal risk.

In contrast to prescription drugs, most people, pregnant or otherwise, take over-the-counter medicines on a casual, as-needed basis without consulting a doctor. Many of these drugs, such as acetaminophen, are safe for pregnant women unless taken to excess (Organization of Teratology Information Specialists, 2005). However, experts advise pregnant women to discuss the medicines they usually take with physicians at the outset of their pregnancies. These discussions should deal with both drugs and any vitamins or supplements that the pregnant woman usually takes. Their doctors will advise them as to which of the substances are safe and which are risky. Often, too, physicians can suggest safer alternatives. Typically, most look to older drugs that have been thoroughly tested (Vogin, 2005).

For a list of several prescription and over-the-counter drugs and their possible effects on a fetus, see Table 3.6.

Illegal Drugs Significant numbers of pregnant women the world over take various illegal drugs. The drug most frequently used is marijuana. The infants of twice-weekly marijuana smokers suffer from tremors and sleep problems. They seem to have little interest in their surroundings for up to 2 weeks after birth (Brockington, 1996). Moreover, at age 6, children who had experienced prenatal exposure to marijuana are shorter on average than 6-year-olds whose mothers did not use marijuana during pregnancy (Cornelius, Goldschmidt, Day, & Larkby, 2002).

Both heroin and methadone, a drug often used in treating heroin addiction, can cause miscarriage, premature labor, and early death (Brockington, 1996). Further, 60–80% of babies born to heroin- or methadone-addicted women are addicted to these drugs as well. Addicted babies have high-pitched cries and suffer from withdrawal symptoms, such as irritability, uncontrollable tremors, vomiting, convulsions, and sleep problems. These symptoms may last as long as 4 months.

The degree to which heroin and methadone affect development depends on the quality of the environment in which babies are raised. Babies who are cared for by mothers who continue to be addicted themselves usually don't do as well as those whose mothers stop using drugs or who are raised by relatives or foster families (Schuler, Nair, & Black, 2002). By age 2, most heroin- or methadone-addicted babies in good homes are developing normally.

Use of cocaine, in either powder or "crack" form, by pregnant women is linked to many kinds of developmental problems in their children (Chatlos, 1997; Ornoy, 2002). However,

Table 3.6 Additional Prescription and Over-the-Counter Drugs and Their Effects

Teratogens	Possible Effects on Fetus
Accutane/Vitamin A	Facial, ear, heart deformities
Streptomycin	Deafness
Penicillin	Skin disorders
Tetracycline	Tooth deformities
Diet pills	Low birth weight

Sources: Amato, 1998; Kliegman, 1998.

most cocaine-using pregnant women are poor and abuse multiple substances, making it difficult to separate the effects of cocaine from those of poverty and other drugs. Some studies suggest that cocaine alone has no long-term effects on cognitive or social development (Kilbride, Castor, Hoffman, & Fuger, 2000; Phelps, Wallace, & Bontrager, 1997; Richardson, Conroy, & Day, 1996). However, other research has demonstrated that prenatal exposure to cocaine, especially when women use it several times a week, leads to a variety of developmental problems in infants (Brown, Bakeman, Coles, Sexson, & Demi, 1998; Madison, Johnson, Seikel, Arnold, & Schultheis, 1998; Mayes, Cicchetti, Acharyya, & Zhang, 2003; Schuler & Nair, 1999). Still other studies indicate that cocaine-exposed infants' problems may seem to be minimal when the children are assessed individually in researchers' laboratories. However, in complex environments such as school classrooms, their difficulties become more apparent (Betancourt et al., 1999).

The mixed findings on prenatal exposure to cocaine probably mean that this drug interacts with other environmental factors to produce a complex set of effects. For example, a cocaine-exposed infant who receives good follow-up care and whose mother discontinues her drug use may be less likely to suffer than another who receives little or no such care and is raised by a drug-using mother. Consequently, health professionals suggest that the development of cocaine-exposed babies should be closely monitored and that interventions should be tailored to fit the individual circumstances and characteristics of each infant (Kilbride et al., 2000).

Tobacco The correlation between smoking during pregnancy and an infant's birth weight has been well documented by researchers. Infants of mothers who smoke are on average about half a pound lighter at birth than infants of nonsmoking mothers (Fourn, Ducic, & Seguin, 1999; Mohsin, Wong, Bauman, & Bai, 2003). Prenatal exposure to tobacco may also have long-term effects on children's development. Some studies suggest that there are higher rates of learning problems and antisocial behavior among children whose mothers smoked during pregnancy (Fergusson, Horwood, & Lynskey, 1993; Tomblin, Smith, & Zhang, 1997; Visscher, Feder, Burns, Brady, & Bray, 2003). Moreover, children of women who smoked during pregnancy are more likely than their schoolmates to be diagnosed with attention-deficit hyperactivity disorder (Linnet et al., 2003; Thapar et al., 2003).

Alcohol In the face of mounting evidence documenting the detrimental effects of alcohol on prenatal development, the safest course for pregnant women is to drink no alcohol at all. For example, researchers have found that 6-year-olds who were prenatally exposed to alcohol are smaller than their non-alcohol-exposed peers (Cornelius, Goldschmidt, Day, & Larkby, 2002). In fact, studies show that alcohol can even adversely affect an ovum prior to ovulation or during its journey down the fallopian tube to the uterus. Likewise, a zygote can be affected by alcohol even before it has been implanted in the uterine lining (Kaufman, 1997).

Children with fetal alcohol syndrome have distinctive features.

Mothers who are heavy drinkers or alcoholics are at significant risk of delivering infants with *fetal alcohol syndrome (FAS)*. These children are generally smaller than normal, with smaller brains. They frequently have heart defects and hearing losses, and their faces are distinctive, with a somewhat flattened nose and often an unusually long space between nose and mouth (Church, Eldis, Blakley, & Bawle, 1997; Ornoy, 2002). As children, adolescents, and adults, they are shorter than normal and have smaller heads, and their intelligence test scores indicate mild mental retardation. Indeed, FAS is one of the most frequent causes of retardation in the United States, exceeding even trisomy 21 according to some studies (Streissguth et al., 1991). FAS children who do not have mental retardation often have learning and behavior difficulties (Mattson & Riley, 1999; Mattson, Riley, Gramling, Delis, & Jones, 1998; Meyer, 1998; Uecker & Nadel, 1996). Moreover, these problems can persist into adolescence and adulthood (Kerns, Don, Mateer, & Streissguth, 1997; Olson, Feldman, Streissguth, Sampson, & Bookstein, 1998; Ornoy, 2002).

Learning Objective 3.11

What are the risks associated with teratogenic maternal diseases?

Maternal Diseases

Several viruses pass through the placental filters and attack the embryo or fetus directly. For example, *rubella*, or *German measles*, causes a short-lived mild reaction in adults but may be deadly to a fetus. Most infants exposed to rubella in the first 4–5 weeks show some abnormality, compared with only about 10% of those exposed in the final 6 months of pregnancy (Moore & Persaud, 1993). Deafness, cataracts, and heart defects are the most common abnormalities. Because the possible effects of rubella are so severe, doctors now recommend that all women of childbearing age be vaccinated against the disease (American College of Obstetrics and Gynecology [ACOG], 2002). However, the vaccine may also be teratogenic. For this reason, the American College of Obstetrics and Gynecology suggests that women wait at least one month after receiving the vaccine before they begin trying to conceive.

HIV, the virus that causes AIDS, is one of many sexually transmitted organisms that can be passed directly from mother to fetus. The virus may cross the placenta and enter the fetus's bloodstream, or the infant may contract the virus in the birth canal during delivery. Only about a quarter of infants born to HIV-infected mothers become infected, although scientists don't yet know how to predict which infants will contract the virus (Abrams et al., 1995; Annunziato & Frenkel, 1993). Transmission appears to be more likely when the mother has AIDS than when she is HIV-positive but not yet ill (Abrams et al., 1995). In addition, HIV-positive pregnant women who take the drug AZT have a markedly lower risk of transmitting the disease to their children—as low as 8% (Prince, 1998).

Infants who acquire HIV from their mothers typically become ill within the first 2 years of life (Prince, 1998). The virus weakens children's immune systems, allowing a host of other infectious agents, such as the bacteria that cause pneumonia and meningitis, to attack their bodies. Even children who remain symptom-free must restrict their exposure to viruses and bacteria. For example, HIV-positive children cannot be immunized with vaccines that utilize live viruses, such as the polio vaccine (Prince, 1998).

Other sexually transmitted diseases (STDs), including *syphilis, genital herpes, gonorrhea*, and *cytomegalovirus*, cause a variety of birth defects. Unlike most teratogens, the bacterium that causes syphilis is most harmful during the last 26 weeks of prenatal development and causes eye, ear, and brain defects. Genital herpes is usually passed from mother to infant during birth. One-third of infected babies die, and another 25–30% suffer blindness or brain damage. Thus, doctors usually deliver the babies of women who have herpes surgically. Gonorrhea, which can cause the infant to be blind, is also usually transmitted during birth. For this reason, doctors usually treat the eyes of newborns with a special ointment that prevents damage from gonorrhea.

Table 3.7 Additional Maternal Diseases and Their Effects

Teratogens	Possible Effects on Fetus
Cancer	Fetal or placental tumor
Toxoplasmosis	Brain swelling, spinal abnormalities
Chicken pox	Scars, eye damage
Parvovirus	Anemia
Hepatitis B	Hepatitis
Chlamydia	Conjunctivitis, pneumonia
Tuberculosis	Pneumonia or tuberculosis

Sources: Amato, 1998; Kliegman, 1998.

THE WHOLE CHILD IN FOCUS

Why did Lisa Chang avoid contact with one of her nephews during her pregnancy? Find out on page 92.

A much less well-known sexually transmitted virus is *cytomegalovirus (CMV)*, which is in the herpes group. As many as 60% of all women carry CMV, but most have no recognizable symptoms. Of babies whose mothers are infected with CMV, 1–2% become infected prenatally. When the mother's disease is in an active phase, the transmission rate is more like 40–50% (Blackman, 1990). About 2,500 babies born each year in the United States display symptoms of CMV and have a variety of serious problems, including deafness, central nervous system damage, and mental retardation (Blackman, 1990).

For a list of other maternal diseases and their possible effects on a fetus, see Table 3.7.

Other Maternal Influences on Prenatal Development

Learning Objective 3.12

What other maternal factors influence prenatal development?

Other maternal characteristics that can adversely affect prenatal development include the mother's diet, her age, and her mental and physical health.

Diet Some specific nutrients are vital to prenatal development. One is folic acid, a B vitamin found in beans, spinach, and other foods. Inadequate amounts of this nutrient are linked to neural tube defects, such as *spina bifida* (Daly, Kirke, Molloy, Weir, & Scott, 1995). The potential negative effects of insufficient folic acid occur in the very earliest weeks of pregnancy, before a woman may know she is pregnant. So it is important for women who plan to become pregnant to obtain at least 400 micrograms of this vitamin daily, the minimum required level.

It is also important for a pregnant woman to take in sufficient overall calories and protein to prevent malnutrition. A woman who experiences malnutrition during pregnancy, particularly during the final 3 months, has an increased risk of delivering a low-birth-weight infant who will have intellectual difficulties in childhood (Mutch, Leyland, & McGee, 1993). In addition, researchers have identified prenatal malnutrition, along with a variety of obstetrical complications, as an important risk factor in the development of mental illnesses in adulthood (Neugebauer, Hoek, & Susser, 1999; Susser & Lin, 1992).

The impact of maternal malnutrition appears to be greatest on the developing nervous system—a pattern found in studies of both humans and other mammals. For example, rats whose caloric intake has been substantially restricted during the fetal and early postnatal periods show a pattern described as *brain stunting*, in which both the weight and the volume of the brain are reduced. They also develop fewer dendrites and show less rich synaptic formation (Pollitt & Gorman, 1994). In human studies of cases in which prenatal malnutrition has been severe enough to cause the death of the fetus or newborn, effects very similar to those seen in the rat studies have been observed. That is, these infants had smaller brains and fewer and smaller brain cells (Georgieff, 1994).

Reproductive technology has enabled women who are well past their child-bearing years to give birth. After 10 years of fertility treatments, this 67-year-old Romanian woman delivered twin girls and became the world's oldest first-time mother.

Age Have you heard sensationalized media reports about women giving birth in their 50s and even into their 60s? Such late-in-life births are very rare, but it is nonetheless the case that the average age at which women give birth for the first time has increased over the past few decades. In 1970, the average age at which a woman delivered her first child was 21.4 years in the United States. By contrast, in 2003, the average was 25.1 years (Martin et al., 2005). One effect of this trend, as you have already learned, is that the number of multiple births each year has increased dramatically.

In most cases, older mothers have uncomplicated pregnancies and deliver healthy babies, but the risks associated with pregnancy do increase somewhat as women get older (Martin et al., 2005). Their babies are also at greater risk of weighing less than 5.5 pounds at birth, a finding that is partly explained by the greater incidence of multiple births among older mothers. Still, infants born to women over the age of 35, whether single or multiple birth, are at higher risk of having problems such as heart malformations and chromosomal disorders.

At the other end of the age continuum, when comparing the rates of problems seen in teenage mothers with those among mothers in their 20s, almost all researchers find higher rates among the teens. However, teenage mothers are also more likely to be poor and less likely to receive adequate prenatal care, so it is very hard to sort out the causal factors (Martin et al., 2005). Nevertheless, researchers have found higher rates of adverse pregnancy outcomes even among middle-class teenage mothers who received good prenatal care (Fraser, Brockert, & Ward, 1995). Moreover, the children of teenage mothers are more likely than children of women who are older to exhibit learning and behavior problems in school (Levine, Pollack, & Comfort, 2001).

Chronic Illnesses Chronic illnesses, whether emotional or physical, can also affect prenatal development. For example, long-term severe depression and other mood disorders can lead to slow fetal growth and premature labor (Weinstock, 1999). Moreover, developmentalists have learned that depressed mothers are less likely to feel attached to their fetuses. At least one study suggested that infants whose mothers do not develop a prenatal attachment to them are less socially responsive than other infants of the same age (Oates, 1998).

Conditions such as heart disease, diabetes, lupus, hormone imbalances, and epilepsy can also affect prenatal development negatively (Kliegman, 1998; McAllister et al., 1997; Sandman, Wadhwa, Chicz-DeMet, Porto, & Garite, 1999). In fact, one of the most important goals of the new specialty of *fetal-maternal medicine* is to manage the pregnancies of women who have such conditions in ways that will support the health of both mother and fetus. For example, pregnancy often makes it impossible for a diabetic woman to keep her blood sugar levels under control. In turn, erratic blood sugar levels may damage the fetus's nervous system or cause it to grow too rapidly (Allen & Kisilevsky, 1999; Kliegman, 1998). To prevent such complications, a fetal-maternal specialist must find a diet, a medication, or a combination of the two that will stabilize the mother's blood sugar but will not harm the fetus. Similarly, fetal-maternal specialists help women who have epilepsy balance their own need for anticonvulsant medication against possible harm to the fetus.

Environmental Hazards There are a number of substances found in the environment that may have detrimental effects on prenatal development. For example, women who work with mercury (e.g., dentists, dental technicians, semiconductor manufacturing workers) are advised to limit their exposure to this potentially teratogenic substance (March of Dimes, 2004). Consuming large amounts of fish may also expose pregnant women to high levels of mercury (because of industrial pollution of the oceans and waterways). Fish may also contain elevated levels of another problematic industrial pollutant known as polychlorinated biphenyls, or PCBs. For these reasons, researchers recommend that pregnant women limit their consumption of fish, especially fresh tuna, shark, swordfish, and mackerel (March of Dimes, 2004).

There are several other environmental hazards that pregnant women are advised to avoid (March of Dimes, 2004):

- *Lead*, found in painted surfaces in older homes, pipes carrying drinking water, lead crystal glassware, and some ceramic dishes
- *Arsenic*, found in dust from pressure-treated lumber
- *Cadmium*, found in semiconductor manufacturing facilities
- *Anesthetic gases*, found in dental offices, outpatient surgical facilities, and hospital operating rooms
- *Solvents*, such as alcohol and paint thinners
- *Parasite-bearing substances*, such as animal feces and undercooked meat, poultry, or eggs

Maternal Emotions Some psychologists have suggested that maternal emotions can affect prenatal development. Their rationale is that stressful psychological states such as anxiety and depression lead to changes in body chemistry. In a pregnant woman, these changes result in both qualitative and quantitative differences in the hormones and other chemicals to which the fetus is exposed.

As persuasive as this idea may be, the question of whether maternal emotional states such as anxiety and depression affect prenatal development remains open. For example, one study found children of mothers who reported high levels of psychological distress during pregnancy to be more emotionally negative at both 6 months and 5 years of age than children of nondistressed mothers (Martin, Noyes, Wisenbaker, & Huttunen, 1999). But critics claim that the real connection is a matter of maternal genes and/or parenting style: Emotionally negative mothers may simply be more likely to have children who are less emotionally positive than their peers.

One fairly consistent finding, however, is that the fetuses of severely distressed mothers tend to grow more slowly than others (Linnet et al., 2003; Paarlberg, Vingerhoets, Passchier, Dekker, & van Geign, 1995). Developmentalists do not really know whether this effect results directly from emotion-related hormones or is an indirect effect of the mother's emotional state. A stressed or depressed mother may eat less, or her weakened immune system may limit her ability to fight off viruses and bacteria—either of these situations may retard fetal growth. Consequently, many psychologists suggest that providing stressed and/or depressed pregnant women with social support and counseling may lead to improvements in both maternal and fetal health (Brockington, 1996).

Fetal Assessment and Treatment

Learning Objective 3.13

How do physicians assess and manage fetal health?

Ultrasonography has become a routine part of prenatal care in the United States because of its usefulness in monitoring fetal growth. (Ultrasound images are produced by the echoes that result from bouncing sound waves off of internal tissues.) Other tests, including *chorionic villus sampling (CVS)* and *amniocentesis*, can be used to identify chromosomal errors and many genetic disorders prior to birth (see Figure 3.8 on page 78). With CVS, cells are extracted from the placenta and used in a variety of laboratory tests during the early weeks of prenatal development. With amniocentesis, which is done between weeks 14 and 16 of a woman's pregnancy, a needle is used to extract amniotic fluid containing fetal cells. Fetal cells filtered out of the fluid are then tested in a variety of ways to diagnose chromosomal and genetic disorders.

THE WHOLE CHILD IN FOCUS

What did Lisa Chang discover after undergoing amniocentesis during her pregnancy? Find out on page 92.

Both tests are associated with an increased risk of miscarriage. CVS is used most often when a medical condition in the mother necessitates early diagnosis of fetal abnormalities

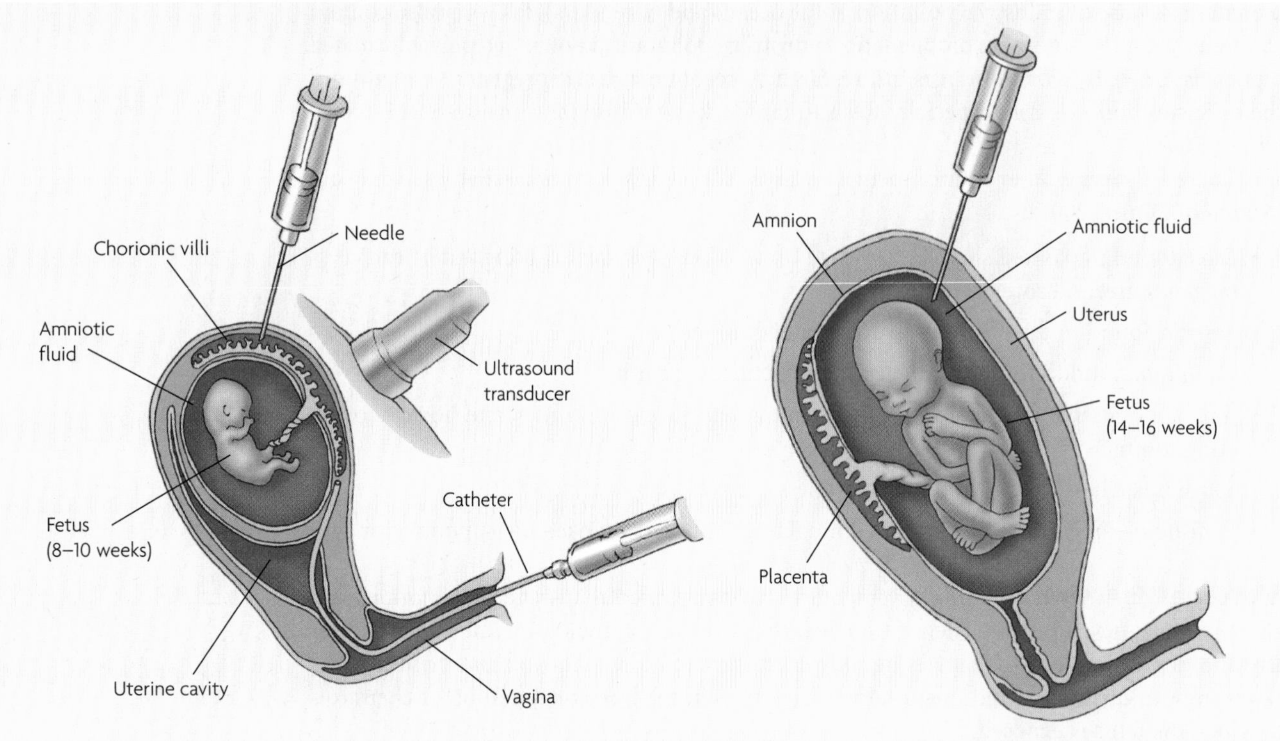

Figure 3.8 **Two Methods of Prenatal Diagnosis**

In chorionic villus sampling (left), placental cells are extracted through a hollow needle inserted in the mother's abdomen. These cells can then be used in a variety of laboratory analyses to determine whether the fetus is healthy. In amniocentesis, a similar technique is used to extract cells from the fluid that surrounds the fetus. These cells are used to create a chromosomal map that can help physicians identify several different kinds of birth defects.

(Curry, 2002). In general, amniocentesis carries a lower risk of miscarriage and fetal injury than CVS does. Thus, it is usually the preferred prenatal diagnostic technique and is routinely recommended as a screening tool for Down syndrome and other chromosomal abnormalities in pregnant women over age 35.

There are also many laboratory tests that use maternal blood, urine, and/or samples of amniotic fluid to help health-care providers monitor fetal development. For example, the presence of a substance called *alpha-fetoprotein* in a pregnant woman's blood is associated with a number of prenatal defects, including abnormalities in the brain and spinal cord. Doctors can also use a laboratory test to assess the maturity of fetal lungs (Kliegman, 1998). This test is critical when doctors have to deliver a baby early because of the mother's health.

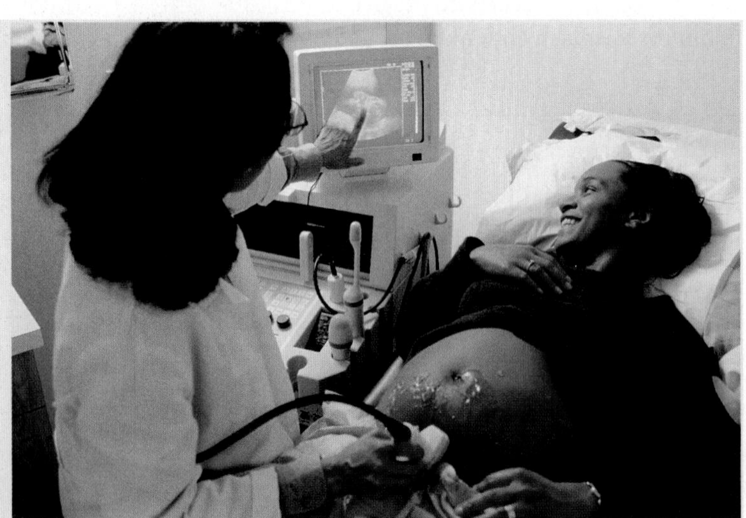

Ultrasound tests allow doctors to identify the fetus's sex, diagnose fetal deformities and growth problems, and determine the fetus's position in the uterus.

Fetoscopy involves insertion of a tiny camera into the womb to directly observe fetal development. Fetoscopy makes it possible for doctors to correct some kinds of defects surgically (Kliegman, 1998). Likewise, fetoscopy has made such techniques as fetal blood transfusions and bone marrow transplants possible. Specialists also use fetoscopy to take samples of blood from the umbilical cord. Laboratory tests performed on fetal blood samples can assess fetal organ function, diagnose genetic and chromosomal disorders, and detect fetal infections (Curry, 2002). For example, fetal blood tests can help doctors identify a bacterial infection that is causing a fetus to grow too slowly. Once diagnosed, the infection can be treated by injecting antibiotics into the amniotic fluid (so that they will be swallowed by the fetus) or into the umbilical cord (Kliegman, 1998).

Researchers have examined how prenatal diagnosis affects parents-to-be. Compared to parents who did not know prior to birth about the disabilities their 1-year-olds would have, parents whose infants' difficulties were diagnosed prenatally report greater feelings of stress and depression (Hunfeld et al., 1999). However, specialists in fetal medicine suggest that the negative emotional effects of prenatal diagnosis can be moderated by providing parents-to-be with counseling and specific information about treatment at the time the diagnosis is made, rather than waiting until after the birth.

Birth and the Neonate

Once gestation is complete, the fetus must be born—an event that holds some pain as well as a good deal of joy for most parents.

Birth Choices

Learning Objective 3.14
What kinds of birth choices are available to expectant parents?

In most places around the world, tradition dictates how babies are delivered. However, in industrialized countries, especially the United States, hospital deliveries became routine in the second half of the 20th century. Today, however, parents in such societies have several choices as to where the birth will take place, who will attend their baby's birth, and whether medication will be used to manage the physical discomforts of labor and delivery.

The Location of Birth and Birth Attendants One choice parents must make is where the baby is to be born. In most of the industrialized world, women deliver their babies in specialized maternity clinics. However, in the United States, there are four alternatives in most communities:

- A traditional hospital maternity unit
- A birth center or birthing room located within a hospital, which provides a more homelike setting for labor and delivery and often allows family members to be present throughout
- A free-standing birth center, like a hospital birth center except that it is located apart from the hospital, with delivery typically attended by a midwife rather than (or in addition to) a physician
- The mother's home

More than 99% of babies in the United States are born in hospitals (Martin et al., 2005). Thus, much of what researchers know about out-of-hospital births comes from studies in Europe. For example, in the Netherlands, a third of all deliveries occur at home (Eskes, 1992). Home deliveries are

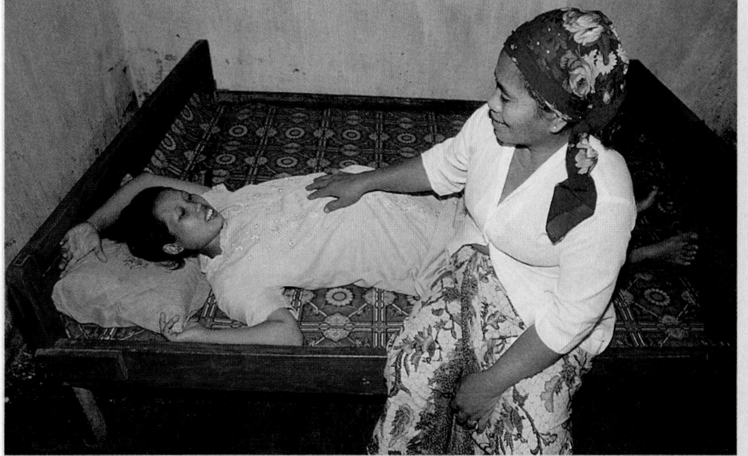

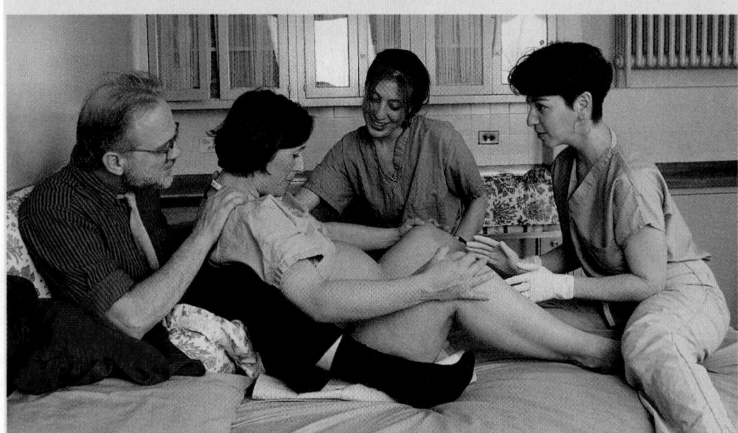

In the developing world, tradition determines where a baby is born and who attends the birth. Hospital deliveries are common in the United States, but many hospitals offer parents the option of delivering their babies in nonsurgical settings such as the birthing room pictured above.

encouraged for uncomplicated pregnancies during which the woman has received good prenatal care. When these conditions are met, with a trained birth attendant present at delivery, the rate of delivery complications or infant problems is no higher than for hospital deliveries.

Certified nurse-midwives are registered nurses who have specialized training that allows them to care for pregnant women and deliver babies. *Certified midwives* have training in midwifery but are not nurses. Instead, most received training in other health-care professions, such as physical therapy, before becoming certified midwives. In Europe and Asia, nurse-midwives and certified midwives have been the primary caretakers of pregnant women and newborns for many years. By contrast, in the United States, physicians provide prenatal care and deliver babies for 91% of women (Martin et al., 2005).

Drugs During Labor and Delivery One key decision for expectant mothers concerns whether to use drugs during labor and delivery. *Analgesics* may be given during labor to reduce pain. *Sedatives* or *tranquilizers* can be administered to reduce anxiety. *Anesthesia*, when used, is usually given later in labor to block pain, either totally (general anesthesia) or in certain portions of the body (local anesthesia such as an epidural).

Studying the causal links between drug use during labor and delivery and the baby's later behavior or development has proven to be difficult. First, it's clear that nearly all drugs given during labor pass through the placenta, enter the fetal bloodstream, and may remain there for several days. Not surprisingly, then, infants whose mothers have received any type of drug are typically slightly more sluggish, gain a little less weight, and spend more time sleeping in the first few weeks than do infants of nondrugged mothers (Maurer & Maurer, 1988).

Second, there are no consistently observed effects from analgesics and tranquilizers beyond the first few days, and only hints from a few studies of long-term effects of anesthesia (Rosenblith, 1992). Given such contradictory findings, only one specific piece of advice seems warranted: If you are a new mother who received medication during childbirth, bear in mind that your baby was also drugged and that this will affect her behavior in the first few days. If you allow for this effect and realize that it will wear off, your long-term relationship with your child is likely to be unaffected.

Many fathers take prenatal classes like the one pictured so that they can provide support to their partners during labor.

Nevertheless, many women choose to avoid drugs altogether. The general term *natural childbirth* is commonly used to refer to this particular choice. This approach is also often called the *Lamaze method*, after the physician who popularized the notion of natural childbirth and devised a variety of pain management techniques. In natural childbirth, women rely on psychological and behavioral methods of pain management rather than on pain-relieving drugs.

Natural childbirth involves several components. First, a woman selects someone, usually the baby's father, to serve as a labor coach. *Prepared childbirth classes* psychologically prepare the woman and her labor coach for the experience of labor and delivery. For example, they learn to use the term *contraction* instead of *pain*. Further, believing that her baby will benefit from natural childbirth provides the woman with the motivation she needs to endure labor without the aid of pain-relieving medication. Finally, relaxation and breathing techniques provide her with behavioral responses that serve to replace the negative emotions that typically result from the physical discomfort of contractions. Aided by her coach, the woman focuses attention on her breathing rather than on the pain.

The Physical Process of Birth

Learning Objective 3.15
What happens in each of the three stages of labor?

Labor is typically divided into three stages (see Figure 3.9 on page 82). Stage 1 covers the period during which two important processes occur: dilation and effacement. The cervix (the opening at the bottom of the uterus) must open up like the lens of a camera (*dilation*) and also flatten out (*effacement*). At the time of actual delivery, the cervix must normally be dilated to about 10 centimeters (about 4 inches).

Customarily, stage 1 is itself divided into phases. In the *early* (or *latent*) phase, contractions are relatively far apart and typically are not too uncomfortable. In the *active* phase, which begins when the cervix is 3 to 4 centimeters dilated and continues until dilation has reached 8 centimeters, contractions are closer together and more intense. The last 2 centimeters of dilation are achieved during a phase usually called *transition*. It is this phase, when contractions are closely spaced and strong, that women typically find the most painful. Fortunately, transition is also ordinarily the shortest phase.

Figure 3.10 on page 83 shows the typical length of these various phases of labor for first births and later births. What the figure does not convey is the wide individual variability that exists. Among women delivering a first child, stage 1 may last as few as 3 hours or as many as 20 (Biswas & Craigo, 1994; Kilpatrick & Laros, 1989).

At the end of the transition phase, the mother will normally have the urge to help the infant emerge by "pushing." When the birth attendant (physician or midwife) is sure the cervix is fully dilated, she or he will encourage this pushing, and stage 2 of labor, the actual delivery, begins. The baby's head moves past the stretched cervix, into the birth canal, and finally out of the mother's body. Most women find this part of labor markedly less distressing than the transition phase because at this point they can assist the delivery process by pushing. Stage 2 typically lasts less than an hour and rarely takes longer than 2 hours. Stage 3, also typically quite brief, is the delivery of the placenta (also called the *afterbirth*) and other material from the uterus.

Cesarean Deliveries Sometimes it is necessary to deliver a baby surgically through incisions made in the abdominal and uterine walls. There are several situations that justify the use of this operation, called a **cesarean section** (or **c-section**). A *breech presentation*, in which an infant's feet or bottom is delivered first, represents one of the most compelling reasons for a c-section because it is associated with collapse of the umbilical cord (ACOG, 2001). Other factors that call for the procedure include fetal distress during labor, labor that fails to progress in a reasonable amount of time, a fetus that is too large to be delivered vaginally, and maternal health conditions that may be aggravated by vaginal delivery (e.g., cardiovascular disease, spinal injury) or may be dangerous to a vaginally delivered fetus (e.g., herpes).

cesarean section (c-section) delivery of an infant through incisions in the abdominal and uterine walls

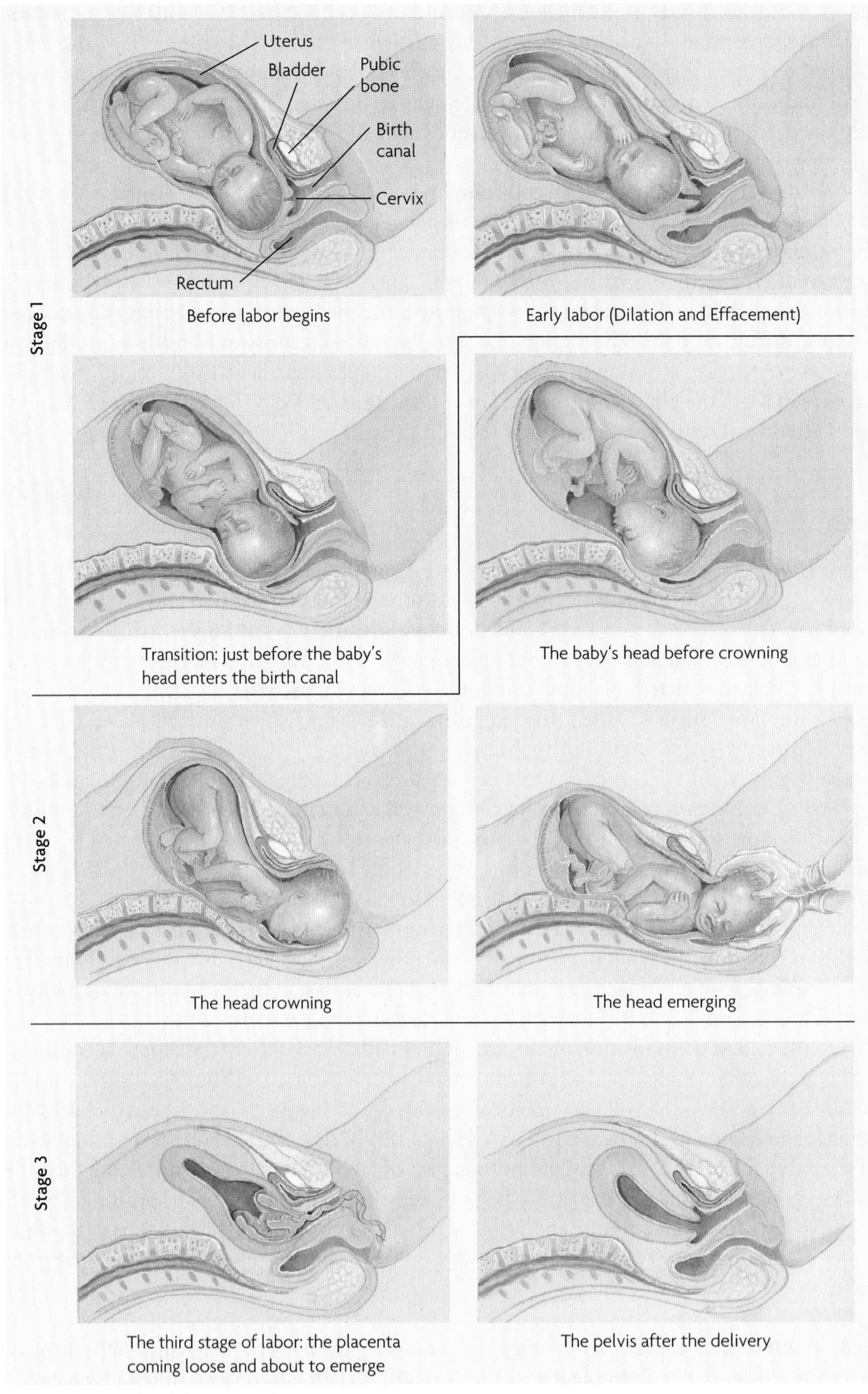

Figure 3.9 **The Three Stages of Labor**

The sequence of steps during delivery is shown clearly in these drawings.

Many observers claim that the current rate of cesarean deliveries in the United States is too high. The National Center for Health Statistics (Martin et al., 2005) reports that just over 27% of all deliveries in 2003 in the United States involved a cesarean section. Critics of the frequency with which c-sections occur say that many of these operations are unnecessary. Are their claims justified?

One factor behind current c-section statistics is that, as you learned earlier, more older women are having babies (Joseph et al., 2003). These women are more likely to conceive twins and other multiples. In such cases, surgical delivery almost always increases the odds in favor of the babies' postnatal health. Thus, the benefits of cesarean delivery outweigh its risks.

By contrast, a recent survey of hospital records found that nearly one-fourth of c-sections performed in 2002 in the United States were entirely elective (Hall, 2003). In these cases, women who had no medical problems and who were carrying healthy fetuses requested a surgical delivery, and their physicians complied. The ethics committee of the American College of Obstetrics and Gynecology (2004a) has ruled that elective surgical deliveries are ethical as long as the practitioner is certain that, for the patients who request them, vaginal deliveries carry equal risk. Advocates of elective cesareans say that the surgery spares women from future problems associated with vaginal delivery, such as urinary incontinence.

But should cesarean delivery be thought of as just another birth option? Critics say that the possible benefits of elective cesareans do not justify exposing women to their risks (Hall, 2003). They claim that many obstetric patients do not realize that a c-section is major surgery and carries the same risks as other abdominal operations. These risks include allergic reactions to anesthetic, infection, accidental injuries to other organs (as well as to the fetus), and excessive blood loss. Consequently, these critics believe that elective cesarean delivery represents a poorly informed choice on the part of the patient and an irresponsible practice on the part of the physician.

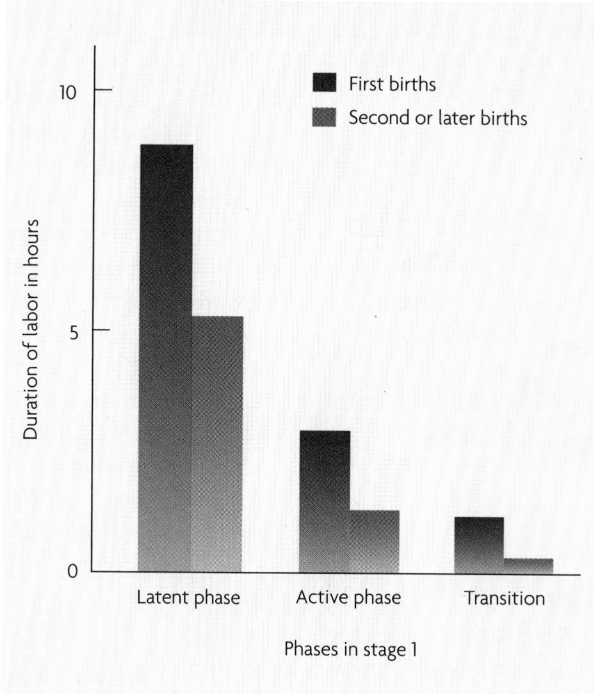

Figure 3.10 Duration of Labor in First and Second Births

Typical pattern of the duration of the phases of stage 1 labor for first births and subsequent births.

(*Source*: Based on Biswas & Craigo, "The course and conduct of normal labor and delivery." In A. H. DeCherney & M. L. Pernoll (Eds.), *Current Obstetric and Gynecologic Treatment*, 1994, from Figures 10-16, p. 216, and 10-17, p. 217. Reprinted by permission of The McGraw-Hill Companies.)

Birth Complications During the process of birth, some babies go into *fetal distress*, signaled by a sudden change in heart rate. In most cases, doctors don't know why a baby experiences fetal distress. However, one cause of distress is pressure on the umbilical cord. For example, if the cord becomes lodged between the baby's head and the cervix, each contraction will push the baby's head against the cord. The collapsed blood vessels can no longer carry blood to and from the baby. When this happens, the baby experiences **anoxia**, or oxygen deprivation. Anoxia can result in death or brain damage, but doctors can prevent long-term effects by acting quickly to surgically deliver infants who experience distress (Handley-Derry et al., 1997).

Infants may also dislocate their shoulders or hips during birth. Some experience fractures, and in others, nerves that control facial muscles are compressed, causing temporary paralysis on one side of the face. Such complications are usually not serious and resolve themselves with little or no treatment.

If a laboring woman's blood pressure suddenly increases or decreases, a cesarean delivery may be indicated. In addition, sometimes labor progresses so slowly that women remain in stage 1 for more than 24 hours. This can happen if the infant's head is in a position that prevents the infant from exerting enough pressure on the cervix to force it open. In such cases, surgery is indicated, because continuing labor can cause permanent damage to the mother's body.

After birth, most women require a period of a month or so to recover. During this time, the mother's body experiences a variety of hormonal changes including those required for nursing and for returning to the normal menstrual cycle. A few women experience a period of depression after giving birth. However, most recover quickly, both physically and emotionally, from the ordeal of pregnancy and birth.

anoxia oxygen deprivation experienced by a fetus during labor and/or delivery

Learning Objective 3.16

What do physicians learn about a newborn from the Apgar and Brazelton scales?

Assessing the Neonate

A baby is referred to as a **neonate** for the first month of life. The health of babies born in hospitals and birth centers, as well as most who are delivered at home by professional midwives, is usually assessed with the *Apgar scale* (Apgar, 1953). The baby receives a score of 0, 1, or 2 on each of five criteria, listed in Table 3.8. A maximum score of 10 is fairly unusual immediately after birth, because most infants are still somewhat blue in the fingers and toes at that stage. At a second assessment, usually 5 minutes after birth, however, 85–90% of infants score 9 or 10. A score of 7 or better indicates that the baby is in no danger. A score of 4, 5, or 6 usually means that the baby needs help establishing normal breathing patterns; a score of 3 or below indicates a baby in critical condition.

THE WHOLE CHILD IN FOCUS

How did the Changs' new baby score on the Apgar scale? Find out on page 93.

Health professionals often use the *Brazelton Neonatal Behavioral Assessment Scale* to track a neonate's development over about the first 2 weeks following birth (Brazelton, 1984). A health professional examines the neonate's responses to stimuli, reflexes, muscle tone, alertness, cuddliness, and ability to quiet or soothe herself after being upset. Scores on this test can be helpful in identifying children who may have significant neurological problems.

Learning Objective 3.17

Which infants are categorized as low birth weight and what risks are associated with this classification?

Low Birth Weight and Preterm Birth

Classification of a neonate's weight is another important factor in assessment. All neonates below 2,500 grams (about 5.5 pounds) are classified as having **low birth weight (LBW)**. Most LBW infants are *preterm*, or born before the 38th week of gestation. The proportion of LBW infants is particularly high in the United States, where about 12% of newborns are preterm and 8% of newborns weigh less than 2,500 grams (Martin et al., 2005). Multiple fetuses—which, as you learned earlier in the chapter, are increasing in frequency in the industrialized world—are especially likely to result in preterm birth.

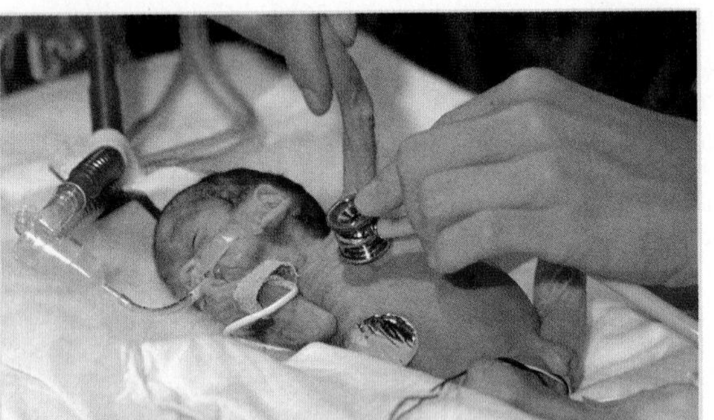

LBW infants' chances of survival are better when they receive care in a neonatal intensive care unit.

However, it is possible for an infant to have completed 37 weeks or more of gestation and still be an LBW baby. In addition, some preterm babies weigh the right amount for their gestational age, while others are smaller than expected. These *small-for-date neonates* appear to have suffered from retarded fetal growth and, as a group, have poorer prognoses than do infants who weigh an appropriate amount for their gestational age.

Table 3.8 The Apgar Scale

	Score Assigned		
Aspect Observed	0	1	2
Heart rate	Absent	< 100 beats per minute	> 100 beats per minute
Respiratory rate	No breathing	Weak cry and shallow breathing	Good cry and regular breathing
Muscle tone	Flaccid	Some flexion of extremities	Well-flexed extremities
Response to stimulation of feet	None	Some motion	Crying
Color	Blue; pale	Body pink, extremities blue	Completely pink

Source: Handbook of Infant Development, Joy D. Osofsky (Ed.). Copyright © 1987 John Wiley & Sons Ltd. Reproduced with permission.

neonate term for babies between birth and 1 month of age

low birth weight (LBW) newborn weight below 5.5 pounds

DEVELOPMENTAL SCIENCE IN THE CLINIC

Singing to the LBW Newborn

Dana works as a nurses' aide in the neonatal intensive care unit (NICU) of a large hospital. All of the infants in Dana's unit were born prematurely and have serious medical conditions. She has noticed that many parents sing to these newborn babies. In her training program, Dana learned that premature infants are more sensitive to stimulation than full-term infants are. As a result, she wonders whether the NICU staff should discourage parents from singing.

Singing to newborns is a behavior that has been found everywhere in the world (Rock, Trainor, & Addison, 1999). Moreover, being sung to appears to make important contributions to low birth weight babies' development (Standley, 2002). One study found that preterm newborns in a neonatal intensive care nursery who were sung to three times a day for 20 minutes over a 4-day period ate more, gained weight faster, and were discharged from the hospital earlier than infants who were not sung to (Coleman, Pratt, Stoddard, Gerstmann, & Abel, 1997). Remarkably, too, the physiological functioning of babies who were sung to (as measured by variables such as oxygen saturation levels in their bloodstreams) was superior. However, the greatest effect of parents' singing and babies' reactions to it may be communication of a mutual "I love you" message that helps to establish a lasting emotional bond between parent and child, a bond that is equally important for preterm and full-term infants (Bergeson & Trehub, 1999). Thus, Dana should encourage parents who are so inclined to sing to the fragile babies in her NICU.

Questions for Reflection

1. How could the research on singing to premature infants be put into practice in neonatal intensive care units in nondisruptive ways?
2. If you were responsible for helping parents of newborns understand the value of singing to their babies, how would you explain the relevant research to them?

LBW infants display markedly lower levels of responsiveness at birth and in the early months of life. Those born more than 6 weeks early also often suffer from *respiratory distress syndrome* (also referred to as *hyaline membrane disease*). Their poorly developed lungs cause serious breathing difficulties. In 1990, physicians began treating this problem by administering *surfactant*, the chemical that makes it possible for the lungs to exchange oxygen and carbon dioxide in the blood, to preterm neonates who are found to be deficient in the substance. As a result, the rate of death among very-low-birth-weight infants has been reduced by about 30%, and respiratory distress syndrome is no longer the leading cause of neonatal death among premature infants (Corbet, Long, Schumacher, Gerdes, & Cotton, 1995; Lynch, 2004; Schwartz, Anastasia, Scanlon, & Kellogg, 1994). Furthermore, support for newborn LBW babies' socioemotional needs improves their chances for survival (see *Developmental Science in the Clinic*).

With adequate parental and educational support, the majority of LBW babies who weigh more than 1,500 grams (about 3 pounds) and who are not small-for-date catch up to their normal peers within the first few years of life, although they do so at widely varying rates (Hill, Brooks-Gunn, & Waldfogel, 2003). But those below 1,500 grams remain smaller than normal and have significantly higher rates of long-term problems (Weindrích, Jennen-Steínmetz, Laucht, & Schmidt, 2003). Still, the degree to which the environment supports the physical, cognitive, and socioemotional needs of LBW infants contributes to their chances of survival and to their status later in childhood.

An LBW neonate's general health also makes a difference. For example, LBW babies who experience bleeding in the brain immediately after birth are more likely to have later problems (Bendersky & Lewis, 1994). The economic circumstances of an LBW infant's family matter as well. Children in low-income families are more likely to suffer from long-term effects of low birth weight, such as attention problems, than are those who grow up in more affluent homes (Breslau & Chilcoat, 2000).

THE WHOLE CHILD IN FOCUS

Why did the Changs choose to deliver at a hospital with a neonatal intensive care unit? Find out on page 93.

Boys are more likely than girls to show long-term effects of low birth weight. In fact, one recent study involving more than 700 6-year-olds found a higher rate of learning disabilities and other problems in LBW boys than among their normal-birth-weight (NBW) peers (Johnson & Breslau, 2000). By contrast, LBW girls did not differ at all from their NBW counterparts. The difference between LBW and NBW boys persisted when they were examined again at age 11 (see *Developmental Science in the Classroom* on page 86).

DEVELOPMENTAL SCIENCE IN THE CLASSROOM

Premature Birth and School Problems

Monique's 6-year-old son, Ramon, is a first-grader who seems to love school. However, almost every day, Monique receives a note from the boy's teacher regarding his classroom behavior and academic performance. It seems that Ramon has been having temper tantrums which suggest that he has little tolerance for frustration, and he is far behind his peers in reading and math skills. Recently, Monique met with the school psychologist and revealed that Ramon was born 12 weeks prematurely. The psychologist suggested that Ramon's birth status might be linked to his problems in the classroom.

Thankfully, two-thirds to three-fourths of premature infants are indistinguishable from peers by the time they reach school age (Bowen, Gibson, & Hand, 2002; Foulder-Hughes & Cooke, 2003a). But the remainder experience difficulties in school like Ramon's. The two critical predictive factors for such children seem to be birth weight and gestational age (Foulder-Hughes & Cooke, 2003b; McGrath & Sullivan, 2002). The lower a child's birth weight and the earlier the gestational age at which he was born, the greater the risk that he will exhibit school problems. Researchers have found that children who were born prior to the 27th week and who weighed less than 2.2 pounds are far more likely to suffer from problems in elementary school than LBW children who were born later and/or weighed more than 2.2 pounds (Shum, Neulinger, O'Callaghan, & Mohay, 2008). Moreover, this difference persists through fourth grade in many cases. However, research also shows that these children do show progress over time, suggesting that their difficulties do not necessarily indicate the presence of a permanent disability (Fussell & Burns, 2007).

For these reasons, once the school psychologist learned that Ramon was born very prematurely, she probably began to think of his problems as developmental in nature rather than as evidence of a lifelong disorder. This conclusion will shape the interventions that she recommends. Monique is likely to be advised that her son is moving through the same milestones that other children do, albeit at a slower rate and via a pathway that isn't quite as straight as that of children who are born at full term. Thus, he is likely to respond to the same kinds of parenting strategies and school interventions that more typically developing children do; it just may take longer for him to show the effects.

Questions for Reflection

1. In your opinion, given Ramon's birth status, should Monique adopt a "he'll-grow-out-of-it" attitude toward his school problems? Why or why not?
2. Should the school adjust its academic and behavioral expectations for Ramon? If so, what kinds of adjustments do you think are appropriate, and at what age do you think he should be expected to perform at the same level as his peers?

Test Prep Center

with mydevelopmentlab

CONCEPTION AND GENETICS

3.1 What are the characteristics of the zygote? (pp. 54–56)

At conception, the 23 chromosomes from the sperm join with the 23 chromosomes from the ovum to form a new cell that contains the set of 46 chromosomes that will then be reproduced in each cell of the new individual.

1. Match each term with its definition.

_______(1) chromosomes

_______(2) zygote

_______(3) gonads

_______(4) gametes

_______(5) genes

_______(6) dizygotic

(A) cells that unite at conception

(B) strings of genetic material

(C) pieces of genetic material that control or influence traits

(D) describes twins that develop from two fertilized ova

(E) sex glands

(F) sperm and ovum unite to form 23 pairs of chromosomes in this entirely new cell

3.2 In what ways do genes influence development? (pp. 56–59)

Geneticists distinguish between the genotype (the pattern of inherited genes) and the phenotype (the individual's observable characteristics). Genes are transmitted from parents to children according to complex rules that include the dominant-recessive pattern, polygenic inheritance, genomic imprinting, mitochondrial inheritance, and multi-factorial inheritance.

2. Describe each type of inheritance.

Inheritance	Description
Polygenic	
Genomic imprinting	
Mitochondrial	
Multi-factorial	

GENETIC AND CHROMOSOMAL DISORDERS

3.3 What are the effects of the major recessive, dominant, and sex-linked diseases? (pp. 59–60)

Recessive disorders affect individuals early in life, often leading to mental retardation and/or early death. These disorders include phenylketonuria, Tay-Sachs disease, cystic fibrosis, and sickle-cell disease. Dominant disorders are not usually manifested until adulthood. Huntington's disease, a fatal affliction of the nervous system, is one such disorder. Hemophilia and fragile-X syndrome are serious sex-linked disorders that affect males far more often than females; fragile-X syndrome can cause progressive mental retardation.

3. Albinism is more likely to develop (early in life/in adulthood) because it is a (recessive/dominant) disorder, while schizophrenia is more likely to develop (early in life/in adulthood) because it is a (recessive/dominant) disorder.

3.4 How do trisomies and other disorders of the autosomes and sex chromosomes affect development? (p. 61)

Abnormal numbers of chromosomes and damage to chromosomes cause a number of serious disorders, including Down syndrome. Sex-chromosome anomalies may affect sexual development and certain aspects of intellectual functioning.

4. From the Multimedia Library within MyDevelopmentLab, watch the *Down Syndrome: Enhancing Development* video and answer the following question.

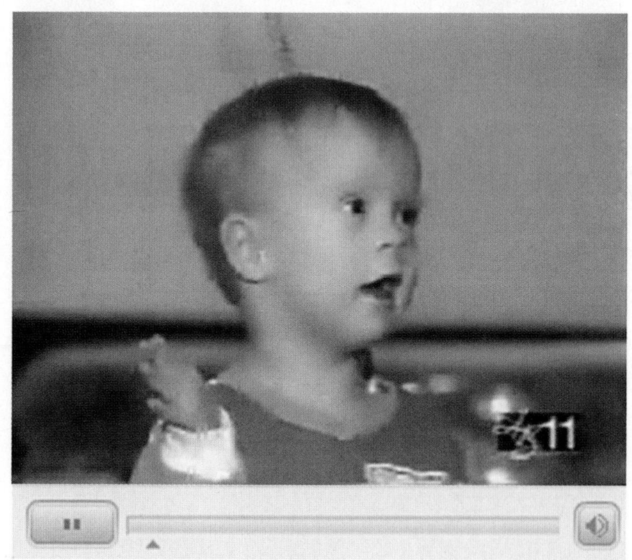

What techniques do teachers and therapists use to help children with Down syndrome achieve their full developmental potential?

____

____

PREGNANCY AND PRENATAL DEVELOPMENT

3.5 What are the characteristics of each trimester of pregnancy? (pp. 62–63)

During the first trimester, a woman experiences morning sickness, breast enlargement, and fatigue. As the woman's abdomen enlarges during the second trimester, her pregnancy becomes noticeable. She feels fetal movements for the first time and experiences an increase in her appetite. During the third trimester, the woman gains weight and may experience breast discharge in preparation for nursing.

5. Label each item on the list as characteristic of the (A) first, (B) second, or (C) third trimester of pregnancy.

_______(1) ectopic pregnancy

_______(2) weekly doctor visits

_______(3) gestational diabetes

_______(4) ultrasound to assess position of fetus

_______(5) premature labor

_______(6) ultrasound to locate placenta

6. From the Multimedia Library within MyDevelopmentLab, watch the *Second Trimester* video and answer the following question.

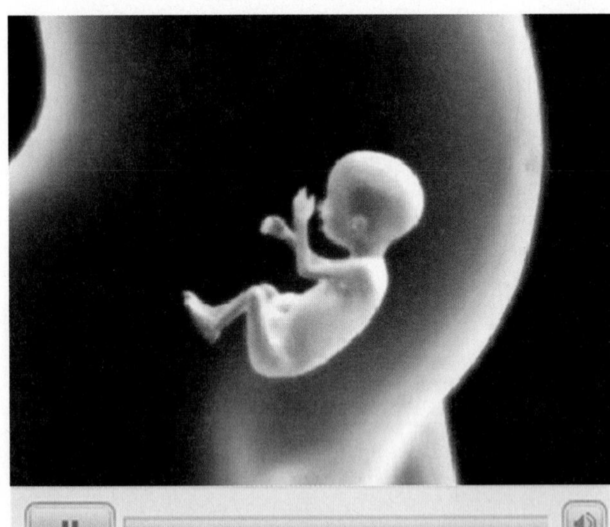

Why doesn't the pregnant woman feel fetal movements in the first trimester?

____

____

3.6 What happens in each stage of prenatal development? (pp. 64–68)

During the germinal phase, from conception to the end of week 2, the zygote travels down the fallopian tube to the uterus and implants itself in the uterine wall. During the embryonic phase, from week 3 through week 8, organogenesis occurs. From week 9 through the end of pregnancy, the fetal stage, the fetus grows larger, and the structure and functioning of the various organs is refined.

7. From the Multimedia Library within MyDevelopmentLab, watch the *Period of the Zygote* video and answer the following question.

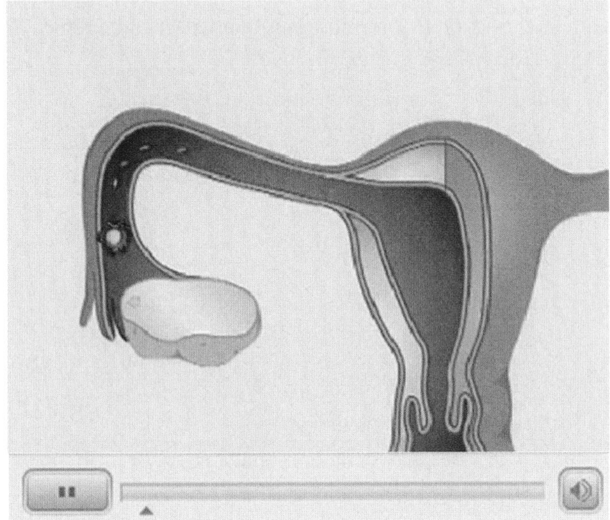

Where does conception usually occur?

____

____

3.7 How do male and female fetuses differ? (p. 68)

Male fetuses are more active than their female counterparts. They also develop more slowly and are more vulnerable to most of the potentially negative influences on prenatal development.

8. Describe some of the differences between male and female skeletal development?

____

____

3.8 What behaviors have scientists observed in fetuses? (pp. 69–70)

The fetus is responsive to stimuli and appears to learn in the womb. Prenatal temperamental differences (for example, activity level) persist into infancy and childhood, and some aspects of the prenatal sensory environment may be important to future development.

9. Write a Y in the blank next to behaviors and sensory abilities that are typical in fetuses. Write an N by those that are not seen in fetuses.

_______(1) imitation

_______(2) hearing

_______(3) blinking

_______(4) sucking

_______(5) babbling

_______(6) breathing

_______(7) movement

PROBLEMS IN PRENATAL DEVELOPMENT

3.9 How do teratogens affect prenatal development? (pp. 70–71)

Teratogens exert greater effects on development during critical periods when specific organ systems are developing. The duration and intensity of exposure to a teratogen, as well as variations in genetic vulnerability, contribute to teratogenic effects.

10. In most cases, teratogens are most harmful during the ________ period of prenatal development.

3.10 What are the potential adverse effects of tobacco, alcohol, and other drugs on prenatal development? (pp. 71–74)

Drugs such as alcohol and nicotine appear to have harmful effects on the developing fetus, often resulting in lower birth weights and learning and behavior difficulties. The effects of drugs depend on the timing of exposure, the dosage, and the quality of the postnatal environment.

11. "Under no circumstance should pregnant women take prescription or over-the-counter drugs." Agree or disagree with this statement, and explain the reasons for your opinion.

____

____

12. Describe the potentially harmful effects of each substance in the table.

Drug	Effect
Heroin	
Cocaine	
Marijuana	
Tobacco	
Alcohol	

13. From the Multimedia Library within MyDevelopmentLab, watch the *Fetal Alcohol Damage* video and answer the following question.

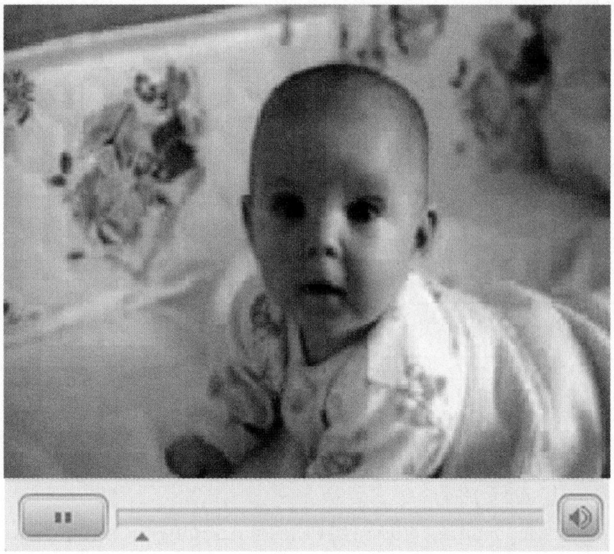

Why is alcohol harmful in the later weeks of prenatal development?

____

____

3.11 What are the risks associated with teratogenic maternal diseases? (pp. 74–75)

Some diseases contracted by the mother may cause abnormalities or disease in the child. These include rubella, AIDS, syphilis, gonorrhea, genital herpes, and CMV.

14. Match each disease with its potentially harmful effect(s) on prenatal development. (Diseases can have more than one harmful effect.)

_______(1) rubella

_______(2) HIV

_______(3) syphilis

_______(4) genital herpes

_______(5) cytomegalovirus

(A) blindness

(B) AIDS

(C) death

(D) heart defects

(E) brain damage

(F) deafness

(G) mental retardation

3.12 What other maternal factors influence prenatal development? (pp. 75–77)

If the mother suffers from poor nutrition, her fetus faces increased risk of low birth weight in infancy and intellectual difficulties in childhood. Older mothers and very young mothers run increased risks, as do their infants. Long-term, severe depression or chronic physical illnesses in the mother may also increase the risk of complications of pregnancy or difficulties in the infant.

15. Briefly explain the association between each variable in the table below and prenatal development.

Variable	Association with Prenatal Development
Diet	
Age	
Chronic illnesses	
Environmental hazards	
Maternal emotions	

3.13 How do physicians assess and manage fetal health? (pp. 77–79)

Techniques such as fetoscopy, ultrasonography, chorionic villus sampling, and amniocentesis are used to diagnose chromosomal and genetic disorders and, along with laboratory tests, identify problems in fetal development. A few such problems can be treated prior to birth with surgery and/or medication.

16. Explain how each prenatal assessment works.

Test	How It Works
Ultrasonography	
Alpha-fetoprotein	
Chorionic villus sampling	
Fetoscopy	
Fetal blood tests	
Amniocentesis	

BIRTH AND THE NEONATE

3.14 What kinds of birth choices are available to expectant parents? (pp. 79–81)

Parents can now decide where the birth will take place, who will be present, and if pain medication will be used. In the United States, most babies are delivered in hospitals by physicians. For uncomplicated, low-risk pregnancies, delivery at home or in a birthing center is as safe as hospital delivery.

17. Fill in the table with the choices available in each category to a woman giving birth.

Category	Choices Available
Location	
Pain relief	
Birth attendants	

3.15 What happens in each of the three stages of labor? (pp. 81–83)

The normal birth process has three stages: dilation and effacement of the cervix, delivery, and placental delivery.

18. From the Multimedia Library within MyDevelopmentLab, watch the *Labor and Birth* video and answer the following question.

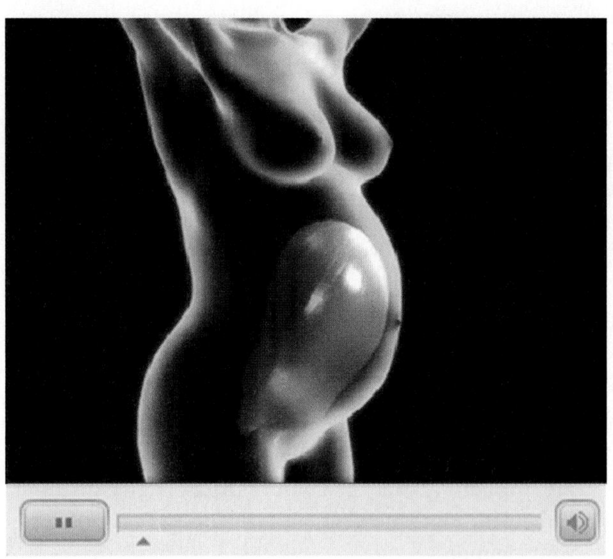

What triggers the start of labor?

____

____

3.16 What do physicians learn about a newborn from the Apgar and Brazelton scales? (p. 84)

Doctors, nurses, and midwives use the Apgar scale to assess a neonate's health immediately after birth and the Brazelton

Neonatal Behavioral Assessment Scale to track a newborn's development over the first 2 weeks of life. The Brazelton Scale is helpful in identifying significant neurological problems.

19. What Apgar score would be assigned to a newborn for each of the following characteristics, and what would be his total score?

_______(1) heart rate less than 100 beats per minute
_______(2) weak cry, shallow breathing
_______(3) some flexion of extremities
_______(4) responds to stimulation of feet with crying
_______(5) pale color
_______(6) total Apgar score

3.17 Which infants are categorized as low birth weight and what risks are associated with this classification? (pp. 84–86)

Neonates weighing less than 2,500 grams are designated as having low birth weight. The lower the weight, the greater the risk of significant lasting problems, such as low intelligence test scores or learning disabilities.

20. Which of these newborns has the best chance of survival? Which has the poorest chance of survival?

(A) girl born at 32 weeks weighing 4.5 pounds
(B) boy born at 38 weeks weighing 4.5 pounds
(C) boy born at 28 weeks weighing 2 pounds

21. From the Multimedia Library within MyDevelopmentLab, watch the *Technological Miracles* video and answer the following question.

In what ways do the lungs of premature infants function differently from those of full-term infants, and how does the treatment shown in the video help?

____

____

For answers to the questions in this chapter, turn to page 507. For a list of key terms, turn to page 530.

Succeed with PEARSON **mydevelopmentlab**

Do You Know All of the Terms in This Chapter?
Find out by using the Flashcards. Want more practice? Take additional quizzes, try simulations, and watch video to be sure you are prepared for the test!

The Whole Child in Focus

The Foundations of Physical, Cognitive, and Socioemotional Development: An Integrated Review

At the beginning of Unit One, we introduced you to Todd and Lisa Chang, an Asian American couple expecting their first child (page 2). Not wanting to leave anything to chance, the Changs researched how they might increase the odds of a healthy pregnancy and birth. Let's see how things turned out.

Lisa altered her diet to be certain that the baby's nutritional needs were met during the **prenatal period**. Lisa and Todd also made a conscious effort to limit their exposure to **teratogens**. When one of her nephews came down with chicken pox, Lisa avoided contact with him until she was sure he had fully recovered.

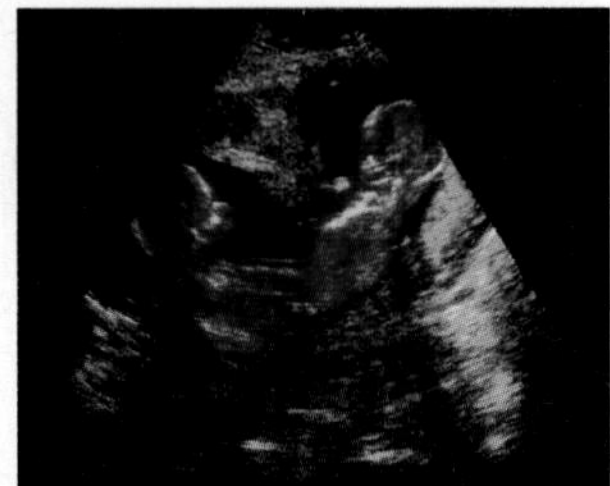

Lisa's 16-week **ultrasound** examination revealed a surprise: Lisa was carrying twins! The babies shared a single **placenta**, suggesting that they were **identical twins**. However, because of their position during the test, the ultrasound technician was unable to determine their gender.

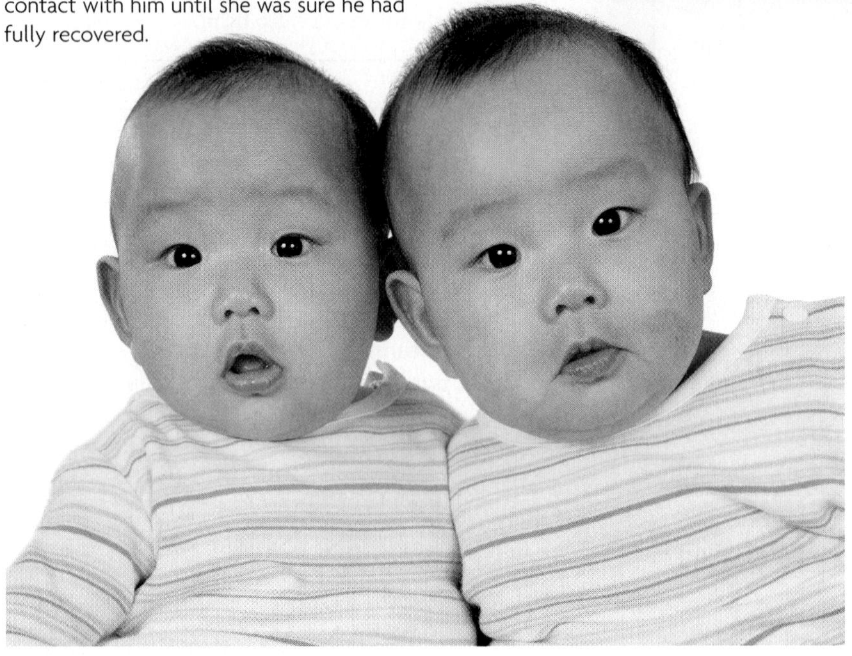

Thinking about Developmental Pathways

1. In what ways might the Chang twins' arrival in the world have been different if they had been born as singleton siblings rather than as twins? What if the amniocentesis had revealed the presence of a chromosomal disorder?
2. Before the twins were born, Todd and Lisa decided that it was important to pass on their cultural heritage to them. How do you think the girls' future development will be affected by the Changs' decision, and how would their development be affected if the Changs had decided to ignore their cultural heritage in their children's upbringing?
3. The Changs recognize that some of the decisions they have made about parenting may have to be changed in the future, depending on their daughters' characteristics. How would their children's development be affected if they had agreed on an approach that was more similar to the blank slate view of development that you learned about in Chapter 1?

Because Lisa was in her mid-thirties, her doctor recommended that she undergo **amniocentesis** to be certain that neither of the twins had a chromosomal disorder such as **Down syndrome**. Thankfully, the test indicated that the twins' chromosomes were entirely normal. It also revealed that both were girls, and **DNA** tests showed that they had indeed developed from a single **zygote**.

Amniocentesis (p. 78)

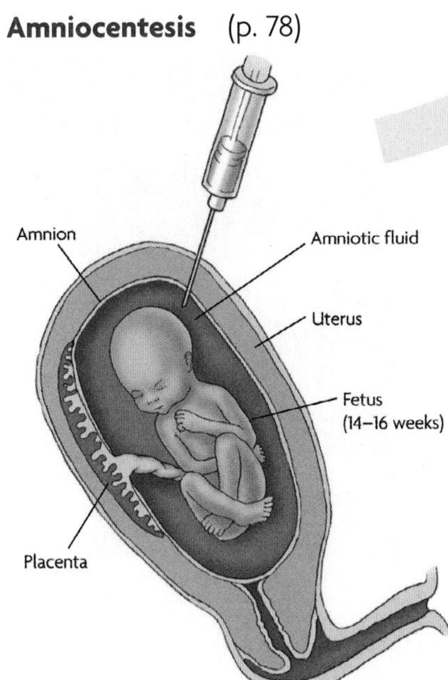

The doctor advised the couple that a **cesarean section** would likely be required to deliver the twins. Because the risk of **premature labor** is higher for twins than for single pregnancies, the doctor recommended that the delivery take place at a hospital with state-of-the-art surgical facilities and a **neonatal intensive care unit**.

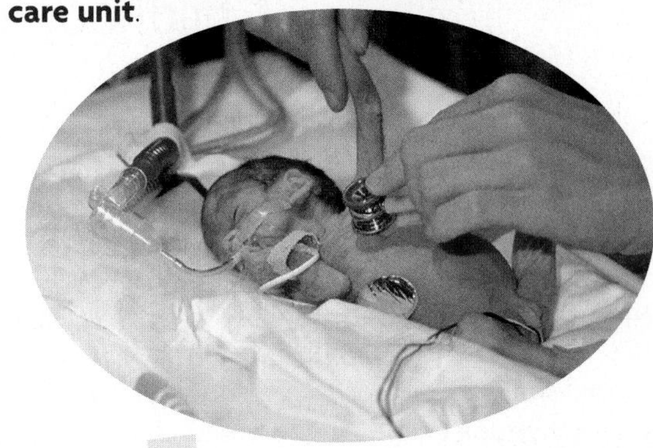

The Apgar Scale (p. 84)
Aspect Observed
Heart rate
Respiratory rate
Muscle tone
Response to stimulation of feet
Color

(*Source:* Francis, Self, & Horowitz, 1987, pp. 731–732)

The twins were born four weeks early and weighed just under four pounds each, which, while appropriate for their gestational age, met the criteria for **low birth weight**. Both girls obtained good scores on the **Apgar scale**, so the prognosis for their future development was good. Even so they were kept in the hospital when Lisa was discharged a week later.

Todd and Lisa visited the girls every day, feeding them, talking and singing to them, and holding them and stroking their backs, thereby creating a pattern of parental responsiveness that would facilitate the twins' resolution of Erikson's **trust versus mistrust** crisis.

Erikson's Psychosocial Stages (p. 30)

Approximate Ages	Stage
Birth to 1 year	**Trust versus mistrust**
1 to 3	Autonomy versus shame and doubt
3 to 6	Initiative versus guilt
6 to 12	Industry versus inferiority
12 to 18	Identity versus role confusion
18 to 30	Intimacy versus isolation
30 to late adulthood	Generativity versus stagnation
Late adulthood	Integrity versus despair

The doctor explained to the Changs that healthy preterm babies are released from the hospital once they reach 5.5 pounds because the average fetus weighs between 5 and 6 pounds when it reaches 37 weeks—the age **norm** at which fetuses are considered "full-term." At 3 weeks the twins reached this critical milestone and were discharged from the hospital.

The Whole Child in Action

Apply What You've Learned about the Foundations of Childhood Development

Raise Your Virtual Child

Become a Virtual Parent

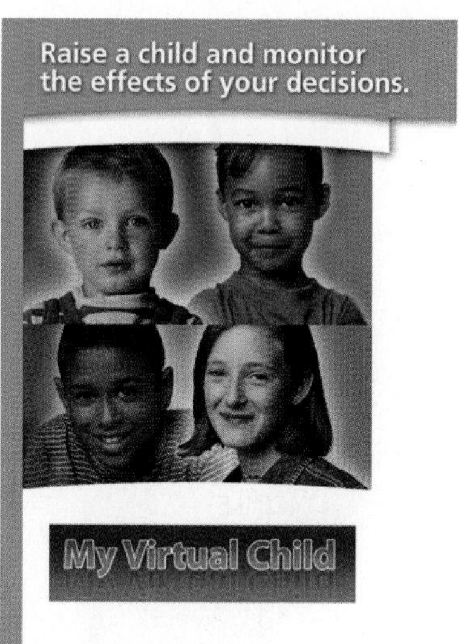

Raise a child and monitor the effects of your decisions.
My Virtual Child

"My Virtual Child" is an online learning tool that is included in MyDevelopmentLab. It allows you to raise a child from birth to 18 years of age. At the outset, the program gives your child some characteristics. As your child grows, the program prompts you to make some parenting decisions. Your child's inborn characteristics and your parenting decisions—and the interactions between these two sets of factors—show themselves over time, sometimes subtly and sometimes rather dramatically. The child will also display universal milestones within the physical, cognitive, and socioemotional domains. The program includes a variety of questions and writing assignments that prompt you to appreciate and think about the "whole child" at various ages. To get started, access My Virtual Child in MyDevelopmentLab and take the first steps toward becoming a cyber-parent. But keep in mind that the virtual child tends to simplify development to achieve its instructional goals. Thus, as you are getting acquainted with the program, give some thought to the differences between cyber-parenting and actual parenting, and consider how you might change the virtual child to make it more like the real thing.

This activity requires that you be registered for My Virtual Child *through MyDevelopmentLab.*

Conduct Your Research

Culture and Informal Theories of Development

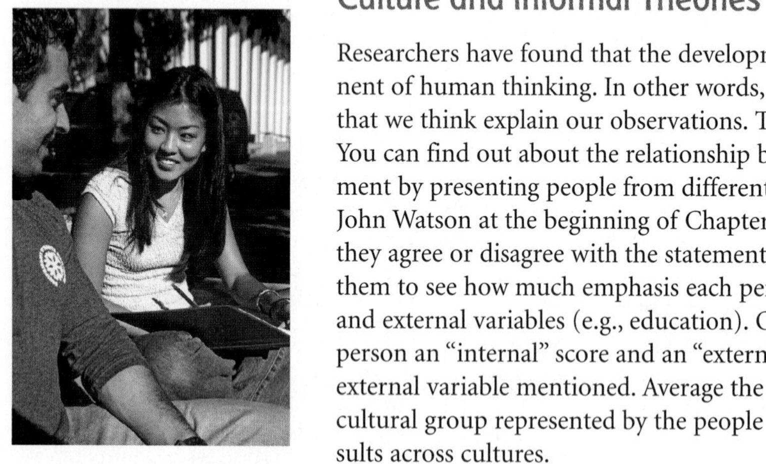

Researchers have found that the development of psychological theories is a basic component of human thinking. In other words, we observe human behavior and develop ideas that we think explain our observations. These ideas are often strongly influenced by culture. You can find out about the relationship between culture and informal theories of development by presenting people from different backgrounds with the statement attributed to John Watson at the beginning of Chapter 2 (see page 32) and asking them to explain why they agree or disagree with the statement. Write down or record their responses and analyze them to see how much emphasis each person places on internal variables (e.g., intelligence) and external variables (e.g., education). One way of analyzing them would be to give each person an "internal" score and an "external" score by assigning 1 point for each internal and external variable mentioned. Average the internal scores and the external scores within each cultural group represented by the people included in your study, and then compare the results across cultures.

Build Your Portfolio

1. Design a presentation on the original sin, blank slate, and innate goodness approaches to child development. In your presentation, explain how these three philosophies might be manifested in the practices of teachers and/or parents.
2. Use the information on theories of development in Chapters 1 and 2 as the basis of an essay that outlines your personal view of child development.

Powered by

PEARSON
mydevelopmentlab™

www.mydevelopmentlab.com

Explore Possible Careers

Certified Nurse Midwives

As discussed in Chapter 3, many women these days choose to deliver their babies at home. Most home deliveries are supervised by professional midwives. There are several credentials for midwives. One such credential, the certificate in nurse midwifery, is awarded to registered nurses who complete postgraduate training in midwifery and who pass a national certification exam. According to the American College of Nurse Midwives (ACNM), registered nurses must have a 4-year degree in nursing (BSN) to be admitted to a midwifery program. Consequently, nursing students who are interested in midwifery should enroll in a 4-year rather than a 2-year degree program. In addition, some midwifery programs admit only students who have had experience working in a hospital labor and delivery unit. Once certified, nurse midwives can practice independently, work in a hospital, or be employed in a physician's private practice. For more information on nurse midwifery, click on the "Career Center" tab in MyDevelopmentLab.

Visit the Career Center in MyDevelopmentLab to learn about other careers that rely on child development research.

Volunteer with Children

Adult Literacy Volunteer

Helping an illiterate adult learn to read can be fulfilling, but it can also have far-reaching, multigenerational effects. Why? Because many illiterate adults are parents, and improvements in their academic skills change the microsystem in which their children are growing up. Not only are literate parents more knowledgeable, but acquiring the ability to read enables them to improve the family's standard of living by providing them with access to new employment opportunities. As a result, the new reader's children may develop higher aspirations for themselves and, ultimately, their own children. In most communities, libraries, religious institutions, community centers, and other organizations offer free literacy classes in which the teachers are volunteers. These programs provide training for volunteers, so all that you need to get started is a desire to help others and the knowledge that helping just one adult learn to read has the potential to change many children's lives.

Visit the Career Center in MyDevelopmentLab to learn about other volunteer opportunities that rely on child development research.

Unit Two
Infancy and Toddlerhood

Six-month-old Federico's father, Hector, is a stay-at-home dad who often feels frustrated. For one thing, his goal of maintaining his career via a telecommuting arrangement with his employer seems to always take a back seat to the minute-by-minute demands of taking care of little Federico. He worries, too, about his list of undone household tasks—the laundry, cooking, yard work, and so on—that seems to get longer each day. And by the time Federico's mother comes home from work each evening, he is often too tired to truly enjoy being with her. Despite his frustrations, Hector values the time he spends with Federico and wouldn't trade the opportunity to observe his son's development first-hand for anything. Hector has learned something that all new parents do, something that cannot be fully appreciated until a person has actually done it: Caring for an infant is one of the most demanding, and most rewarding, tasks in life. Here's what a typical day for Hector and Federico is like:

- 6:30 a.m.: Wakes up; takes bottle; diaper change; back to sleep
- 9:00 a.m.: Wakes up; diaper change; eats cereal and fruit; gets dressed; watches television; plays in walker until bored; moves to playpen; out of playpen onto floor; crawls and practices pulling up on furniture; chews on everything in sight
- 10:30 a.m.: Gets fussy; takes bottle; naps for 30 minutes
- 11:45 a.m.: Wakes up; plays outside in walker
- 12:00 p.m.: Eats meat and vegetables; tries to drink from cup; same play routine as earlier in the day
- 2:00 p.m.: Takes bottle; repeats play routine
- 4:00 p.m.: Gets fussy; naps for 1 hour
- 5:30 p.m.: Eats cereal and fruit; takes bottle
- 6:30 p.m.: Has bath; plays in tub for 20 minutes; gets dressed for bed; watches television with older brother and sister; plays,

snuggles, and jabbers with siblings, Mom, and Dad

- 9:00 p.m.: Takes bottle; listens to Mom read a story; goes to sleep
- 2:00 a.m.: Wakes up; diaper change; takes bottle
- 4:00 a.m.: Wakes up; diaper change; takes bottle
- 6:30 a.m.: Daily cycle starts again

Considering Hector and Federico's daily routine, it's easy to see why parents sometimes get so caught up in the hour-by-hour struggles associated with taking care of an infant that they forget to stop and reflect on just how short, and fascinating, the first 2 years of life, known as *infancy*, are. At the same time, parents of infants frequently find themselves absorbed in simply watching in wonderment as their babies master a new skill. In fact, as you learned in Chapter 1, Charles Darwin's fascination with his own children's early development led him to carry out the first formal studies of age-related change. Piaget, too, began his career as a developmental scientist by making detailed observations of his three children's earliest years. Through their efforts, and those of developmentalists who followed them, methods were devised that allow researchers to get past the fact that infants cannot tell scientists what they are thinking and feeling. Applications of these methods to questions about infant development have allowed developmentalists and parents alike to gain insight into what it is about the infant that is actually changing when, for example, we see him transition from being fascinated with throwing a ball repeatedly to being obsessed with pouring liquid out of containers.

In Chapters 4, 5, and 6, you will become acquainted with some of the discoveries that researchers have made with regard to changes that happen in the first 2 years of life. Chapter 4 focuses on the physical domain. Chapter 5 addresses the impressive cognitive advances that happen in the first 2 years. Finally, in Chapter 6, you will read about the infant's social relationships, personality, and sense of self.

The Whole Child in Focus

Keep Federico's story in mind as you read through the next three chapters, and consider how aspects of his physical, cognitive, and socioemotional development might interact as he moves through infancy. What kind of person do you think an older Federico will be? We'll examine how Federico's development changes as he grows from 6 months to 2 years old at the end of this unit.

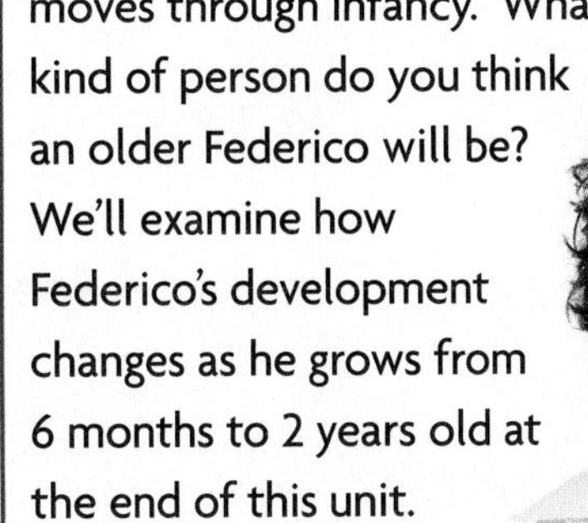

Chapter

4

Physical Development and Health in Infancy and Toddlerhood

Learning Objectives

Physical Changes
- 4.1 What important changes in the brain take place during infancy?
- 4.2 How do babies' reflexes and behavioral states change?
- 4.3 How do infants' bodies change, and what is the typical pattern of motor skill development in the first 2 years?

Health and Wellness
- 4.4 What are the nutritional needs of infants?
- 4.5 How does malnutrition affect infants' development?
- 4.6 What are infants' health-care and immunization needs?

Infant Mortality
- 4.7 What have researchers learned about sudden infant death syndrome?
- 4.8 How do infant mortality rates vary across groups?

Sensory Skills
- 4.9 How do infants' visual abilities change across the first months of life?
- 4.10 How do infants' senses of hearing, smell, taste, touch, and motion compare to those of older children and adults?

Perceptual Skills
- 4.11 How do researchers study perceptual development?
- 4.12 How do depth perception and patterns of looking change over the first 2 years?
- 4.13 How do infants perceive human speech, recognize voices, and recognize sound patterns other than speech?
- 4.14 What is intermodal perception?
- 4.15 What arguments do nativists and empiricists offer in support of their theories of perceptual development?

One of the most fascinating features of babies' behavior is how busy they always seem to be. They appear to be continually on the go, manipulating objects with their hands, looking at them, feeling them, tasting them, and making sounds with them. At times, such activities seem purposeless, but they provide just the kind of skill practice and information infants need for both physical and cognitive development. Considering the energy required to keep up with infants' level of activity, it's little wonder their parents seem to be exhausted much of the time.

In this chapter, you will read about the processes through which a relatively unskilled newborn becomes a 2-year-old who can move about efficiently, respond to a variety of sensory stimuli, and accurately perceive the world around her. You will also learn about important variations across individuals and groups. After a look at changes in infants' bodies and how their health can be maintained, we will move on to an exploration of infants' sensory and perceptual abilities. Finally, we will explore how the physical milestones of infancy set the stage for the emergence of cognitive and social-emotional advancements.

Physical Changes

What comes to mind when you think about the first 2 years of life? If you take time to reflect on this period, you will realize that, apart from prenatal development, it is the period during which the greatest degree of physical change occurs. Although their senses work well, newborns have very limited physical skills. In contrast, 2-year-olds can not only move about independently, but also feed themselves and, to the dismay of many parents, get themselves into all kinds of precarious situations. A 2-year-old still has a long way to go before he reaches physical maturity. But his brain is racing ahead of the rest of his body, a developmental pattern that accounts for the typical "top-heavy" appearance of toddlers.

Learning Objective 4.1

What important changes in the brain take place during infancy?

The Brain and Nervous System

The brain and the nervous system develop rapidly during the first 2 years. Figure 4.1 shows the main structures of the brain. At birth, the midbrain and the medulla are the most fully developed. These two parts, both in the lower part of the skull and connected to the spinal cord, regulate vital functions such as heartbeat and respiration, as well as attention, sleeping, waking, elimination, and movement of the head and neck—all actions a newborn can perform at least moderately well. The least-developed part of the brain at birth is the **cortex**, the convoluted gray matter that wraps around the midbrain and is involved in perception, body movement, thinking, and language.

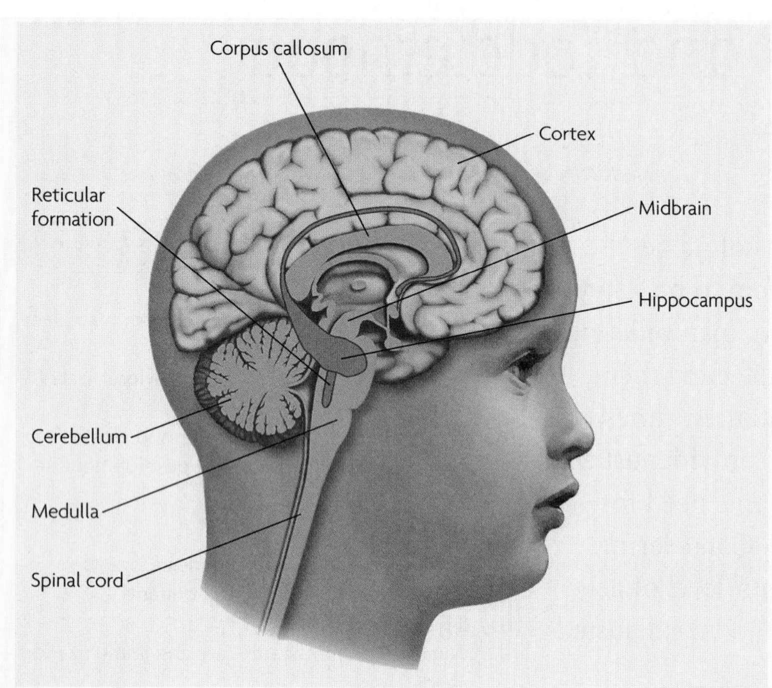

Figure 4.1
Parts of the Brain

The medulla and the midbrain are largely developed at birth. In the first 2 years after birth, it is primarily the cortex that develops, with each neuron going through an enormous growth of dendrites and a vast increase in synapses.

cortex the convoluted gray matter that wraps around the midbrain and is involved in perception, body movement, thinking, and language

synapses connections between neurons

synaptogenesis the process of synapse development

pruning the process of eliminating unused synapses

plasticity the ability of the brain to change in response to experience

Synaptic Development You'll recall from Chapter 3 that all brain structures are composed of two basic types of cells: neurons and glial cells. Millions of these cells are present at birth, and **synapses**, or connections between neurons, have already begun to form (Monk, Webb, & Nelson, 2001). Synapse development results from growth of both dendrites and axons (look back at Figure 3.3 on page 69). **Synaptogenesis**, the creation of synapses, occurs rapidly in the cortex during the first few years after birth, resulting in a quadrupling of the overall weight of the brain by age 4 (Spreen, Risser, & Edgell, 1995). However, synaptogenesis is not smooth and continuous. Instead, it happens in spurts.

Typically, each synaptic growth spurt generates many more connections between neurons than the individual actually needs. Thus, each burst of synaptogenesis is followed by a period of **pruning** in which unnecessary pathways and connections are eliminated (Huttenlocher, 1994). For example, each muscle cell seems to develop synaptic connections with several motor neurons (nerve cells that carry impulses to muscles) in the spinal cord. As the infant works to gain control over his movements, some of these connections are used repeatedly while others are ignored. Soon, the unused connections die off, or get "pruned" by the system. Once the pruning process is completed, each muscle fiber is connected to only one motor neuron.

This cycle of synaptogenesis followed by pruning continues through the lifespan (see Figure 4.2). With each cycle, the brain becomes more efficient. Consequently, a 1-year-old actually has denser dendrites and synapses than an adult does, but the 1-year-old's network operates far less efficiently than that of the adult. However, efficiency comes at a price. Because infants have more unused synapses than adults, they can bounce back from a host of insults to the brain (e.g., malnutrition, head injury) much more easily than an adult. Neuroscientists use the term **plasticity** to refer to the brain's ability to change in response to experience.

Developmentalists draw several important implications from the cyclical synaptogenesis–pruning feature of neurological development. First, it seems clear that brain development follows the old dictum "Use it or lose it." A child growing up in a rich or intellectually challeng-

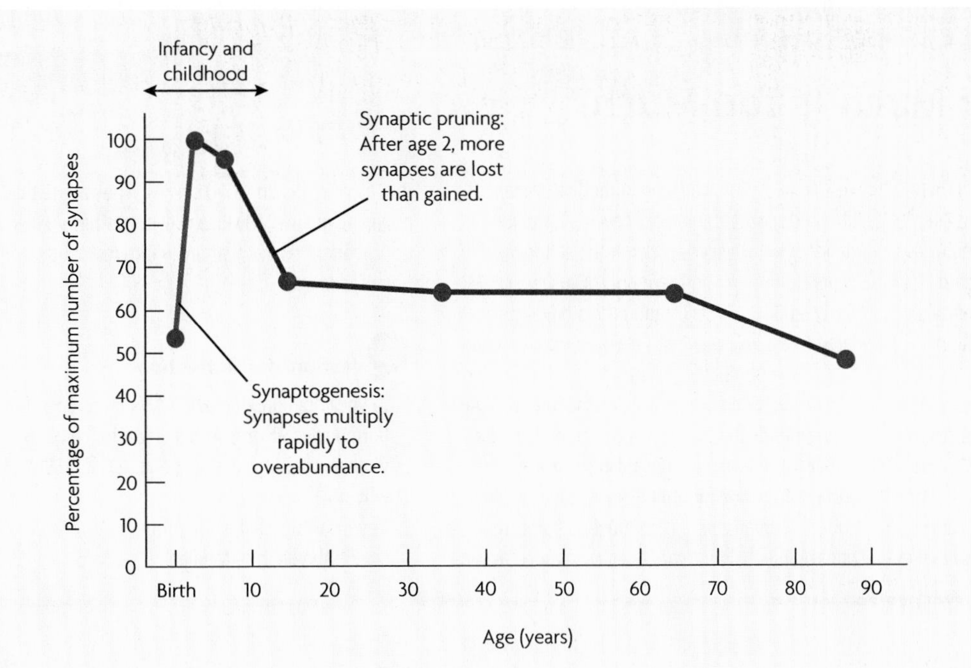

Figure 4.2
Synaptogenesis and Synaptic Pruning

Synaptogenesis occurs at a rapid rate for the first 2 years of life and is followed by a period of pruning that decreases synaptic density in the child's brain. Synaptic density remains fairly stable across the lifespan until the later adulthood years.

(*Source*: Cook, CHILD DEVELOPMENT: PRINCIPLES & PERSPECTIVES, Figure 4.9, © 2009. Reproduced by permission of Pearson Education, Inc.)

ing environment will retain a more complex network of synapses than one growing up with fewer forms of stimulation. The evidence to support this proposal comes from several kinds of research, including work with animals. For example, rats that were in highly stimulating environments as infants have a denser network of neurons, dendrites, and synaptic connections in adulthood than rats not raised in such settings (e.g., Escorihuela, Tobena, & Fernández-Teruel, 1994). Animal studies also show that enriched environments help the young brain overcome damage caused by teratogens such as alcohol (Hannigan, O'Leary-Moore, & Berman, 2007).

In addition, as mentioned earlier, the brains of infants possess greater plasticity than those of older children and adults. Paradoxically, though, the period of greatest plasticity is also the period in which the child may be most vulnerable to major deficits—just as a fetus is most vulnerable to teratogens during the time of most rapid growth of any body system (Uylings, 2006). Thus, a young infant needs sufficient stimulation and order in his environment to maximize the early period of rapid growth and plasticity (de Haan, Luciana, Maslone, Matheny, & Richards, 1994). A really inadequate diet or a serious lack of stimulation in the early months may thus have subtle but long-range effects on the child's later cognitive progress. Some have even argued that watching too much television in the early months may impede brain development (see *Developmental Science in the Classroom* on page 102).

Finally, new information about the continuation of synaptogenesis and pruning throughout the lifespan has forced developmental psychologists to change their ideas about the links between brain development and behavior. If the brain were almost completely organized by age 2, as most developmentalists believed until recently, it would seem logical to assume that whatever developments occurred after that age were largely the product of experience. But researchers now know that changes in psychological functioning are linked to changes in the brain throughout the entire human lifespan (Huttenlocher & Dabholkar, 1997).

THE WHOLE CHILD IN FOCUS

How did the development of Federico's brain over the first 2 years of his life affect his father? Find out on page 178.

Myelination Another crucial process in the development of neurons is the creation of sheaths, or coverings, around individual axons, which insulate them from one another electrically and improve their conductivity. These sheaths are made of a substance called myelin; the process of developing the sheath is called **myelination**.

The sequence of myelination follows both *cephalocaudal* (head-to-tail) and *proximodistal* (torso-to-limbs) patterns. For example, nerves serving muscle cells in the neck and shoul-

myelination a process in neuronal development in which sheaths made of a substance called myelin gradually cover individual axons and electrically insulate them from one another to improve the conductivity of the nerve

DEVELOPMENTAL SCIENCE IN THE CLASSROOM

TV for Tots: How Much Is Too Much?

During a recent visit with his pediatrician, Lorne, a single father who is raising a 1-year-old daughter, expressed concern about the amount of time the infants in his daughter's child-care center spend watching television. He said that the workers at the center explained that they play only educational videos. However, Lorne told the doctor that he became alarmed when he heard that the American Academy of Pediatrics (AAP) recommends that children under age 2 watch no television at all, because television interferes with normal brain development.

The doctor explained that researcher Dimitri Christakis and his colleagues' studies show that excessive television watching in the first 3 years of life predisposes children to develop attention-deficit hyperactivity disorder in the school-age years (Christakis, Zimmerman, DiGiuseppe, & McCarty, 2004). Christakis and others have speculated that a link between television watching and brain development is responsible for this finding. As a result, to err on the side of caution, the AAP recommends that caregivers discourage children under the age of 2 from watching television (American Academy of Pediatrics, 2001). Moreover, the organization recommends that caregivers engage infants in interactive activities such as talking, playing, reading, and singing. They argue that engaging in such activities with adults has greater educational benefits than even the best "educational" videos.

Questions for Reflection

1. In your opinion, does the AAP's recommendation to severely restrict television for children younger than 2 years of age go too far? Why or why not?
2. In your view, what is the proper role of television in the life of a toddler?

---

ders are myelinated earlier than those serving the abdomen. As a result, babies can control their head movements before they can roll over. Myelination is most rapid during the first 2 years after birth, but it continues at a slower pace throughout childhood and adolescence. For example, the parts of the brain that are involved in vision reach maturity by the second birthday (Lippé, Perchet, & Lassonde, 2007), whereas those that govern motor movements are not fully myelinated until a child is about 6 years old (Todd, Swarzenski, Rossi, & Visconti, 1995).

Other structures take even longer to become myelinated. For example, the **reticular formation** is the part of the brain responsible for keeping your attention on what you're doing and for helping you sort out important and unimportant information. Myelination of the reticular formation begins in infancy but continues in spurts across childhood and adolescence. In fact, the process isn't complete until a person is in her mid-20s (Spreen, Risser, & Edgell, 1995). Consequently, during the first 2 years, infants improve their ability to focus on a task. Likewise, a 12-year-old is much better at concentrating than an infant but is still fairly inefficient when compared to an adult.

reticular formation the part of the brain that regulates attention

adaptive reflexes reflexes, such as sucking, that help newborns survive

Learning Objective 4.2

How do babies' reflexes and behavioral states change?

Reflexes and Behavioral States

Changes in the brain result in predictable changes in babies' reflexes, sensory capacities, and patterns of waking and sleeping. In fact, such changes—or their lack—can be important indicators of nervous system health.

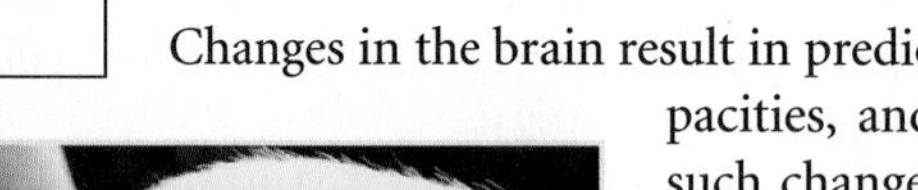

This 4-week-old baby is using the inborn adaptive reflex of sucking.

Reflexes Humans are born with several reflexes, as shown in Table 4.1. **Adaptive reflexes** help infants survive. Some, such as automatically sucking any object that enters the mouth, disappear in infancy or childhood. Others protect us against harmful stimuli over the whole lifespan. These include withdrawal from a painful stimulus and the opening and closing of the pupil of the eye in response to variations in brightness. Weak or absent adaptive reflexes in neonates suggest that the brain is not functioning properly and that the baby requires additional assessment.

Table 4.1 Examples of Primitive and Adaptive Reflexes

Reflex	Stimulation	Response	Developmental Pattern
Tonic neck	While baby is on his back and awake, turn his head to one side.	Baby assumes a "fencing" posture, with arm extended on the side toward which the head is turned.	Primitive; fades by 4 months
Grasping	Stroke baby's palm with your finger.	Baby makes a strong fist around your finger.	Primitive; fades by 3 to 4 months
Moro	Make a loud sound near baby, or let baby "drop" slightly and suddenly.	Baby extends legs, arms, and fingers; arches back; and draws back head.	Primitive; fades by about 6 months
Stepping	Hold baby under her arms with her feet just touching a floor or other flat surface.	Baby makes step-like motions, alternating feet as in walking.	Primitive; fades by about 8 weeks in most infants
Babinski	Stroke sole of baby's foot from toes toward heel.	Baby fans out toes.	Primitive; fades between 8 and 12 months
Rooting	Stroke baby's cheek with your finger or nipple.	Baby turns head toward the touch, opens mouth, and makes sucking movements.	Adaptive; after 3 weeks, transforms into a voluntary head-turning response

The purposes of **primitive reflexes**, so called because they are controlled by the less sophisticated parts of the brain (the medulla and the midbrain), are less clear. For example, if you make a loud noise or startle a baby in some other way, you'll see her throw her arms outward and arch her back, a pattern that is part of the Moro, or startle, reflex. Stroke the bottom of her foot and she will splay out her toes and then curl them in, a reaction called the Babinski reflex (see Table 4.1). By 6 to 8 months of age, primitive reflexes begin to disappear. If such reflexes persist past this age, the baby may have some kind of neurological problem (DiMario, 2002).

Behavioral States Researchers have described five different states of sleep and wakefulness in neonates. Most infants move through these states in the same sequence: from deep sleep to lighter sleep and then to alert wakefulness and fussing. After they are fed, they become drowsy and drop back into deep sleep. The cycle repeats itself about every 2 hours.

Neonates sleep as much as 80% of the time, as much in the daytime as at night (Sola, Rogido, & Partridge, 2002). By 8 weeks of age, the total amount of sleep per day has dropped somewhat and signs of day/night sleep rhythms (called circadian rhythms) become evident. Babies of this age begin to sleep through two or three 2-hour cycles in sequence without coming to full wakefulness, and thus are often said to have started to "sleep through the night." By 6 months, babies are still sleeping a bit over 14 hours per day, but sleep is more regular and predictable. Most have clear nighttime sleep patterns and nap during the day at more predictable times.

Of course, babies vary a lot around these averages. Of the 6-week-old babies in one study, there was one who slept 22 hours per day and another who slept only 8.8 hours per day (Bamford et al., 1990). (Now, that must have been one tired set of parents!) And some babies do not develop a long nighttime sleep period until late in the first year of life. Moreover, cultural beliefs play an important role in parents' responses to infants' sleep patterns. For example, parents in the United States typically see a newborn's erratic sleep cycle as a behavior problem that requires "fixing" through parental intervention (Harkness, 1998). As a result, they focus a great deal of attention on trying to force babies to sleep through the night. In

primitive reflexes reflexes, controlled by "primitive" parts of the brain, that disappear during the first year of life

contrast, European parents are more likely to regard newborns' patterns of sleeping as manifestations of normal development and expect babies to acquire stable sleep patterns naturally, without parental intervention, during the first 2 years.

Infants have different cries for pain, anger, and hunger. The basic cry, which often signals hunger, usually has a rhythmical pattern: cry, silence, breath, cry, silence, breath, with a kind of whistling sound often accompanying the in-breath. An anger cry is typically louder and more intense, and the pain cry normally has a very abrupt onset—unlike the other two kinds of cries, which usually begin with whimpering or moaning.

Cross-cultural studies suggest that crying increases in frequency over the first 6 weeks and then tapers off (St. James-Roberts, Bowyer, Varghese, & Sawdon, 1994). Moreover, parents across a variety of cultures use very similar techniques to soothe crying infants. Most babies stop crying when they are picked up, held, and talked or sung to. Getting a baby to suck on a pacifier also usually helps. Some parents worry that picking up a crying baby will lead to even more crying. But research suggests that prompt attention to a crying baby during the first 3 months actually leads to less crying later in infancy (Sulkes, 1998).

For the 15–20% of infants who develop **colic**, a pattern involving intense bouts of crying totaling 3 or more hours a day, for no immediately apparent reason such as hunger or a wet diaper, nothing seems to help. Typically, colic appears at about 2 weeks of age and then disappears spontaneously at 3 to 4 months (Coury, 2002). The crying is generally worst in late afternoon or early evening. Neither psychologists nor physicians know why colic begins or why it stops without any intervention. It is a difficult pattern to live with, but the good news is that it does go away.

On average, neonates are awake and alert for a total of only 2 to 3 hours each day, and this time is unevenly distributed over a 24-hour period. In other words, the baby may be awake for 15 minutes at 6:00 a.m., another 30 minutes at 1:00 p.m., another 20 minutes at 4:00 p.m., and so on. Over the first 6 months, advances in neurological development enable infants to remain awake and alert for longer periods of time as their patterns of sleeping, crying, and eating become more regular.

Learning Objective 4.3
How do infants' bodies change, and what is the typical pattern of motor skill development in the first 2 years?

Growth, Motor Skills, and Developing Body Systems

Did you know that half of all the growing you do in your life happens before you are 2 years old? In other words, a 2-year-old's height is approximately half of what her height will be when she reaches physical maturity, a remarkable rate of growth considering that attainment of the second half of her adult height will be spread over a period of 10 to 12 years. But infants' bodies don't just change in size. There are many qualitative changes, such as those involving motor skills, that happen during this period as well. As you read about them, recall from Chapter 3 and earlier in this chapter that physical development proceeds from the head downward (*cephalocaudal* pattern) and from the center of the body outward (*proximodistal* pattern).

Growth and Motor Skills Babies grow 10–12 inches and triple their body weight in the first year of life. By age 2 for girls and about 2½ for boys, toddlers are half as tall as they will be as adults. This means that a 2- to 2½-year-old's adult height can be reliably predicted by doubling his or her current height. But 2-year-olds have proportionately much larger heads than do adults—which they need to hold their nearly full-sized brains.

Children acquire an impressive array of motor skills in the first 2 years. *Gross motor skills* include abilities, such as crawling, that enable the infant to get around in the environment. *Fine motor skills* involve use of the hands, as when a 1-year-old stacks one block on top of another. Table 4.2 summarizes developments in each of these areas over the first 24 months.

colic an infant behavior pattern involving intense daily bouts of crying totaling 3 or more hours a day

Table 4.2 Milestones of Motor Development in the First 2 Years

Age (in months)	Gross Motor Skills	Fine Motor Skills
1	Stepping reflex; lifts head slightly	Holds object placed in hand
2–3	Lifts head up to 90-degree angle when lying on stomach	Begins to swipe at objects in sight
4–6	Rolls over; sits with support; moves on hands and knees ("creeps"); holds head erect while in sitting position	Reaches for and grasps objects
7–9	Sits without support; crawls	Transfers objects from one hand to the other
10–12	Pulls self up and walks grasping furniture, then walks alone; squats and stoops; plays pat-a-cake	Shows some signs of hand preference; grasps a spoon across palm but has poor aim when moving food to mouth
13–18	Walks backward, sideways; runs (14–20 months); rolls ball to adult; claps	Stacks two blocks; puts objects into small container and dumps them out
19–24	Walks up and down stairs, two feet per step; jumps with both feet off ground	Uses spoon to feed self; stacks 4 to 10 blocks

Sources: Capute et al., 1984; Den Ouden et al., 1991; Overby, 2002.

Throughout infancy, girls are ahead of boys in some aspects of physical maturity. For example, the separate bones of the wrist appear earlier in girls than in boys (Tanner, 1990). This means that female infants may have a slight advantage in the development of fine motor skills such as self-feeding. Typically, boys are found to be more physically active and acquire gross motor skills faster than girls do.

THE WHOLE CHILD IN FOCUS

How did the combination of Federico's maturing brain and developing fine motor skills almost result in an accident? Find out on page 179.

Explaining Motor Skill Development Despite gender differences in the rate of physical development, the sequence of motor skill development is virtually the same for all children, even those with serious physical or mental handicaps. Children with mental retardation, for example, move through the various motor milestones more slowly than typically developing children do, but they do so in the same sequence. Such consistencies support the view that motor development is controlled by an inborn biological timetable (Thelen, 1995).

The late Esther Thelen (1941–2004) suggested that the inborn timetable for motor skill development interacts with other aspects of physical development (Thelen, 1996). As an example of her **dynamic systems theory**, the notion that several factors interact to influence development, she often cited the disappearance, at 4 months of age, of the *stepping reflex*—the tendency among very young infants to attempt to take steps when they are placed in an upright position with their feet touching a flat surface. Thelen noted that infants gain a proportionately substantial amount of weight at about the same time that they no longer show the stepping reflex. She hypothesized that infants no longer exhibit the stepping reflex because their muscles are not yet strong enough to handle the increased weight of their legs. True walking, according to Thelen, emerges both as a result of a genetic plan for motor skill development and because of a change in the ratio of muscle strength to weight in infants' bodies. The latter change is strongly influenced by environmental variables, especially nutrition. Thus, the streams of influence that are incorporated into dynamic systems theory include inborn genetic factors and environmental variables, such as the availability of adequate nutrition.

Wayne Dennis's (1960) classic early study of children raised in Iranian orphanages presaged Thelen's theory. His work demonstrated that babies who were routinely placed on their backs in cribs learned to walk eventually, but they did so about a year later than babies in less restrictive settings. Research involving infants living in normal environments supports the notion that experience influences motor development. In one such study, very young babies

dynamic systems theory the view that several factors interact to influence development

The striking improvements in motor development in the early months are easy to illustrate. Between 6 and 12 months of age, babies progress from sitting alone to crawling to walking.

who were given more practice sitting were able to sit upright longer than those without such practice (Zelazo, Zelazo, Cohen, & Zelazo, 1993). Opportunities to practice motor skills seem to be particularly important for young children who have disorders, such as cerebral palsy, that impair motor functioning (Kerr, McDowell, & McDonough, 2007). Consequently, developmentalists are fairly certain that severely restricting a baby's movement slows down acquisition of motor skills, and many are beginning to accept the idea that a baby's movement experiences in normal environments may also influence motor skill development.

Developing Body Systems During infancy, bones change in size, number, and composition. Changes in the number and density of bones in particular parts of the body are responsible for improvements in coordinated movement. For example, at birth, the wrist contains a single mass of cartilage; by 1 year of age, the cartilage has developed into three separate bones. The progressive separation of the wrist bones is one of the factors behind gains in fine motor skills over the first 2 years. Wrist bones continue to differentiate over the next several years until eventually, in adolescence, the wrist has nine separate bones (Tanner, 1990).

The process of bone hardening, called *ossification*, occurs steadily, beginning in the last weeks of prenatal development and continuing through puberty. Bones in different parts of the body harden in a sequence that follows the typical proximodistal and cephalocaudal patterns. Motor development depends to a large extent on ossification. Standing, for example, is impossible if an infant's leg bones are too soft, no matter how well developed the muscles and nervous system are.

The body's full complement of muscle fibers is present at birth, although the fibers initially are small and have a high ratio of water to muscle (Tanner, 1990). In addition, a newborn's muscles contain a fairly high proportion of fat. By 1 year of age, the water content of an infant's muscles is equal to that of an adult's, and the ratio of fat to muscle tissue has begun to decline (Tershakovec & Stallings, 1998). Changes in muscle composition lead to increases in strength that enable 1-year-olds to walk, run, jump, climb, and so on.

The lungs also grow rapidly and become more efficient during the first 2 years (Kercsmar, 1998). Improvements in lung efficiency, together with the increasing strength of heart muscles, give a 2-year-old greater *stamina*, or ability to maintain activity, than a newborn. Consequently, by the end of infancy, children are capable of engaging in fairly long periods of sustained motor activity without rest (often exhausting their parents in the process!).

Health and Wellness

Babies depend on the adults in their environments to help them stay healthy. Specifically, they need the right foods in the right amounts, and they need regular medical care.

Nutrition

Learning Objective 4.4

What are the nutritional needs of infants?

As discussed in *Developmental Science at Home* below, most experts agree that breast-feeding is superior to formula-feeding for most infants. Yet infants who cannot be nursed for one reason or another typically thrive on high-quality infant formulas that are properly sterilized (Furman et al., 2004; Tershakovec & Stallings, 1998). Moreover, there are a wide variety of formulas available today to fulfill the requirements of infants who have special needs, such as those who are lactose-intolerant.

Up until 4 to 6 months, babies need only breast milk or formula accompanied by appropriate supplements (Taveras et al., 2004). For example, pediatricians usually recommend iron supplements for most babies over 4 months of age and vitamin B12 supplements for infants whose nursing mothers are vegetarians (Tershakovec & Stallings, 1998). Doctors may recommend supplemental formula-feeding for infants who are growing poorly.

There is no evidence to support the belief that solid foods encourage babies to sleep through the night. In fact, early introduction of solid food can interfere with nutrition. Pediatricians usually recommend withholding solid foods until a baby is 4 to 6 months old. The first solids should be single-grain cereals, such as rice cereal, with added iron. Parents should introduce a baby to no more than one new food each week. By following a systematic plan, parents can easily identify food allergies (Tershakovec & Stallings, 1998).

Malnutrition

Learning Objective 4.5

How does malnutrition affect infants' development?

Malnutrition in infancy can seriously impair a baby's brain because the nervous system is the most rapidly developing body system during the first 2 years of life. *Macronutrient* malnutrition results from a diet that contains too few calories. Macronutrient malnutrition is the world's leading cause of death among children under the age of 5 (Tershakovec & Stallings, 1998).

DEVELOPMENTAL SCIENCE AT HOME

Breast or Bottle?

Expectant mother Suzanne found it easy to decide where she wanted to give birth and whom she wanted to serve as her labor coach. Now, her greatest worries center around how she will feed her baby. She has heard that breast-feeding is best, but she expects to return to work within a few weeks after the birth. Consequently, she is leaning toward bottle-feeding but is seeking information that will reassure her that her baby will develop properly on formula.

All parents, like Suzanne, want to do what's best for their babies, and developmentalists today generally agree that breast-feeding is superior to bottle-feeding for meeting infants' nutritional needs (Overby, 2002). However, not all mothers *can* breast-feed. Some have an insufficient milk supply; others suffer from medical conditions that require them to take drugs that may filter into breast milk and harm the baby. Furthermore, viruses, including HIV, can be transmitted from mother to child through breast milk. And what about adoptive mothers?

Developmentalists are quick to reassure mothers who can't nurse that their babies will most likely develop as well as breast-fed infants. However, it is important to understand that, after several decades of extensive research in many countries, experts agree that, for most infants, breast-feeding is substantially superior nutritionally to bottle-feeding (Taveras et al., 2004). Breast-feeding is associated with a number of benefits. For one, breast milk contributes to more rapid weight and size gain (Prentice, 1994). On average, breast-fed infants are less likely to suffer from such problems as diarrhea, gastroenteritis, bronchitis, ear infections, and colic, and they are less likely to die in infancy (Barness & Curran, 1996; Beaudry, Dufour, & Marcoux, 1995; Golding, Emmett, & Rogers, 1997a, 1997b; López-Alarcón, Villapando, & Fajardo, 1997). Breast milk also appears to stimulate better immune system function, and it may protect infants from becoming overweight in later years (Dietz, 2001; Pickering et al., 1998). For these reasons, physicians strongly recommend breast-feeding if it is at all possible, even if the mother can nurse for only a few weeks after birth or if her breast milk must be supplemented with formula feedings (Tershakovec & Stallings, 1998).

Questions for Reflection

1. If Suzanne were your friend and asked you for advice regarding this important decision, what would you tell her?
2. The research linking breast-feeding to obesity prevention was correlational. What other variables might explain this relationship?

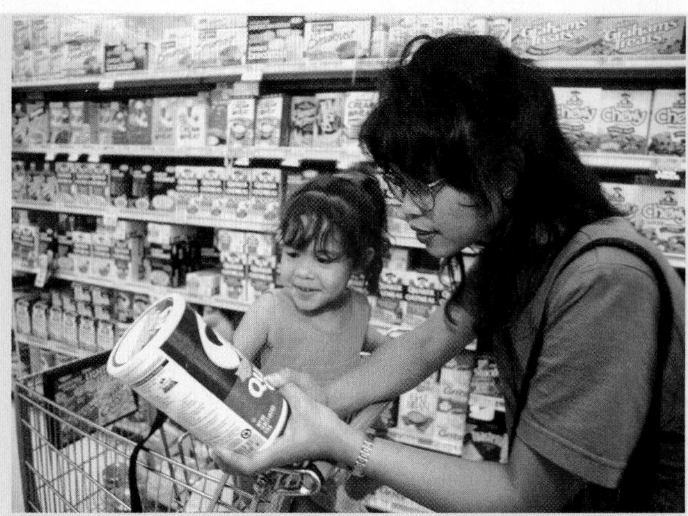

The goal of nutritional support programs for low-income mothers and children, such as the WIC program in the United States, is to prevent infant malnutrition. These programs may save taxpayers money in the long run, because malnutrition interferes with early brain development, thereby increasing the likelihood of learning problems and the need for special education services later in childhood.

When the calorie deficit is severe, a disease called *marasmus* results. Infants with marasmus weigh less than 60% of what they should at their age, and many suffer permanent neurological damage from the disease. Most also suffer from parasitic infections that lead to chronic diarrhea. This condition makes it very difficult to treat marasmus by simply increasing an infant's intake of calories. However, a program of dietary supplementation with formula, combined with intravenous feedings and treatment for parasites, can reverse marasmus (Tershakovec & Stallings, 1998).

Some infants' diets contain almost enough calories, but not enough protein. Diets of this type lead to a disease called *kwashiorkor*, which is common in countries where infants are weaned too early to low-protein foods. Kwashiorkor-like symptoms are also seen in children who are chronically ill because of their bodies' inability to use the protein from the foods they eat. Like marasmus, kwashiorkor can lead to a variety of health problems as well as permanent brain damage (Tershakovec & Stallings, 1998).

Growth rate studies of poor children in the United States suggest that a small number of them suffer from macronutrient malnutrition (Tanner, 1990). In addition, a small proportion of infants have feeding problems, such as a poorly developed sucking reflex, that place them at risk for macronutrient malnutrition (Wright & Birks, 2000). However, most nutritional problems in industrialized societies involve *micronutrient malnutrition*, a deficiency of certain vitamins and/or minerals. For example, about 65% of infants and children in the United States have diets that are low enough in iron to cause anemia (Tershakovec & Stallings, 1998). Calcium deficiency, which results in poor bone health, is also becoming more common in the United States (Tershakovec & Stallings, 1998). Such deficiencies, although more common among the poor, are found in children of all economic levels.

Micronutrient malnutrition in infancy, especially when it leads to iron-deficiency anemia, may impede both social and language development (Guesry, 1998; Josse et al., 1999). Interestingly, researchers found that supplementing anemic infants' diets with iron led to improved scores on measures of social development but not language development, suggesting that the cognitive effects of anemia may be irreversible. Consequently, most public health officials support efforts to educate parents about the micronutritional needs of infants and children.

Learning Objective 4.6

What are infants' health-care and immunization needs?

Health Care and Immunizations

Infants need frequent medical check-ups. Much of well-baby care may seem routine, but it is extremely important to development. For example, during routine visits to the doctor's office or health clinic, babies' motor skills are usually assessed. An infant whose motor development is less advanced than expected for his age may require additional screening for developmental problems such as mental retardation (Sulkes, 1998).

One of the most important elements of well-baby care is vaccination of the infant against a variety of diseases. Although immunizations later in childhood provide good protection, the evidence suggests that immunization is most effective when it begins in the first month of life and continues through childhood and adolescence (Umetsu, 1998). Even adults need occasional "booster" shots to maintain immunity.

In the United States, the average baby has seven respiratory illnesses in the first year of life. Interestingly, research in a number of countries shows that babies in child-care centers have about twice as many infections as those reared entirely at home, with those in small-group child care falling somewhere in between, presumably because babies cared for in group settings are exposed to a wider range of germs and viruses (Collet et al., 1994; Hurwitz, Gunn, Pinsky, & Schonberger, 1991; Lau, Uba, & Lehman, 2002). In general, the more people a baby is exposed to, the more often he is likely to be sick.

Neuropsychologists have suggested that the timing of respiratory illnesses that can lead to ear infections is important. Many note that infants who have chronic ear infections are more likely than their peers to have learning disabilities, attention disorders, and language deficits during the school years (Asbjornsen et al., 2005). These psychologists hypothesize that, because ear infections temporarily impair hearing, they may compromise the development of brain areas that are essential for language learning during the first 2 years of life (Spreen, Risser, & Edgell, 1995). Thus, most pediatricians emphasize the need for effective hygiene practices in child-care centers, such as periodic disinfection of all toys, as well as prompt treatment of infants' respiratory infections.

As recently as 1992, only 55% of children in the United States had received the full set of immunizations—a schedule that includes three separate injections of hepatitis vaccine, four of diphtheria/tetanus/pertussis, three of influenza, three of polio, and one each of measles/rubella and varicella zoster virus vaccines (Committee on Infectious Diseases, 1996). Vaccination against hepatitis A is also recommended in some cities (Centers for Disease Control [CDC] National Immunization Program, 2000). In 1995, an intensive media campaign sponsored by the federal government and the American Academy of Pediatrics (AAP) was put into place. As a result, the U.S. vaccination rate had risen to more than 90% by 1999 and continued to rise in the early years of the 21st century (CDC National Immunization Program, 2000; Rosenthal et al., 2004). Public health officials believe that continued educational efforts, both in the media and by health-care professionals who work directly with infants and their families, are necessary to prevent the immunization rate from returning to pre-campaign levels.

Infant Mortality

Researchers formally define **infant mortality** as death within the first year after birth. In the United States, about 7 babies out of every 1,000 die before age 1 (Kochanek & Martin, 2004). The rate has been declining steadily for the past several decades (down from 30 per 1,000 in 1950), but the United States continues to have a higher infant mortality rate than other industrialized nations. Almost two-thirds of these infant deaths occur in the first month of life and are directly linked to either congenital anomalies or low birth weight (Kochanek & Martin, 2004).

Sudden Infant Death Syndrome

Learning Objective 4.7
What have researchers learned about sudden infant death syndrome?

After the death of a spouse, the death of a child, especially when the death is unexpected, is the most distressing source of bereavement there is for most adults (see *Developmental Science in the Clinic* on page 110). Parents' questions about the cause of their child's death are a natural part of the grief process. In the case of the loss of an infant, few parents find the answers they are looking for, because most deaths after the first month of life are the result of SIDS. **Sudden infant death syndrome (SIDS)**, in which an apparently healthy infant dies suddenly and unexpectedly, is the leading cause of death in the United States among infants between 1 month and 1 year of age (Task Force on Sudden Infant Death Syndrome, 2005). Physicians have not yet uncovered the basic cause of SIDS, but there are a few clues. For one thing, it is more common in the winter when babies may be suffering from viral infections that cause breathing difficulties. In addition, babies with a history of *sleep apnea*—brief periods when their breathing suddenly stops—are more likely to die from SIDS (Kercsmar, 1998). Episodes of apnea may be noticed by medical personnel in the newborn nursery, or a nonbreathing baby may be discovered by her parents in time to be resuscitated. In such cases, physicians usually recommend using electronic breathing monitors that will sound an alarm if the baby stops breathing again while asleep.

infant mortality death within the first year of life

sudden infant death syndrome (SIDS) a phenomenon in which an apparently healthy infant dies suddenly and unexpectedly

DEVELOPMENTAL SCIENCE IN THE CLINIC

When an Infant Dies

Morgan recently lost her 2-month-old son to sudden infant death syndrome (SIDS). After the baby's death, she was determined to continue living as normal a life as possible, despite the overwhelming grief she felt. To that end, she went back to work immediately after the funeral and kept up all of her social activities. She also forced herself to attend family gatherings, even though she feared having to talk about the experience. To her dismay, her co-workers and relatives kept their distance from her, as if they didn't know what to say to her about her child's death. Morgan was torn between the relief she felt over not having to talk too much about what had happened and a desperate need for others to somehow acknowledge her loss.

When she discussed her concerns with a professional counselor, Morgan learned that her experiences are typical of those of parents who have lost an infant. The counselor explained that when an older child dies, parents, family members, and the child's friends build reminiscences on their overlapping relationship histories with the child. They share anecdotes about the child's personality, favorite activities, and so on. Such devices help everyone in the child's relationship network release the child psychologically, a process that helps the child's parents deal with their own profound grief. But with an infant, there is little or no relationship history to draw on. The parents, of course, feel deep emotions of attachment, but the cognitive elements that help parents cope with the loss of a child are absent.

Because friends and relatives are usually less knowledgeable about the deceased infant than the parents are, they often simply avoid talking about the child altogether. As a result, bereaved parents of a dead infant often have a greater need for support from family, friends, and health professionals than even they themselves realize (Vaeisaenen, 1998). Thus, health professionals have compiled a few guidelines that can be useful to family members or friends in supporting parents who have lost an infant (Wong, 1993):

- Don't try to force bereaved parents to talk about their grief or the infant if they don't want to.
- Always refer to the deceased infant by name.
- Express your own feelings of loss for the infant, if they are sincere.
- Follow the parents' lead in engaging in reminiscences about the baby.
- Discourage the parents from resorting to drugs or alcohol to manage grief.
- Assure grieving parents that their responses are normal and that it will take time to resolve the emotions associated with losing an infant.
- Don't pressure the parents to "replace" the baby with another one.
- Don't offer rationalizations (e.g., "Your baby's an angel now") that may offend the parents.
- Do offer support for the parents' own rationalizations.
- Be aware that the infant's siblings, even those who are very young, are likely to experience some degree of grief.

Questions for Reflection

1. If you were one of Morgan's co-workers or relatives, how do you think you would behave toward her in everyday situations?
2. What sort of "mental script" could you develop from the recommendations above that would be helpful to friends and relatives of a person who has lost a child?

SIDS is also more frequent among babies who sleep on their stomachs or sides, especially on a soft or fluffy mattress, pillow, or comforter (Task Force on Sudden Infant Death Syndrome, 2005). The American Academy of Pediatrics, along with physicians' organizations in many other countries, recommends that healthy infants be positioned on their backs to sleep. During the first 2 years after this recommendation was introduced, there was a 12% overall drop in SIDS cases in the United States, with even more dramatic declines of as much as 50% in areas where the recommendation was widely publicized (Spiers & Guntheroth, 1994). In England, Wales, New Zealand, and Sweden, major campaigns to discourage parents from placing their babies in the prone position (on their stomachs) were also followed by sharp drops in SIDS rates (Gilman, Cheng, Winter, & Scragg, 1995). Another important contributor is smoking by the mother during pregnancy or by anyone in the home after the child's birth. Babies exposed to such smoke are about four times as likely to die of SIDS as are babies with no smoking exposure (CDC, 2006c).

Imaging studies of the brains of infants at high risk for SIDS, such as those who display sleep apnea in the early days of life, suggest that myelination progresses at a slower rate in these children than in others who do not exhibit such risk factors (Morgan et al., 2002). Babies' patterns of sleep reflect these neurological differences and also predict SIDS risk. Infants who show increasingly lengthy sleep periods during the early months are at lower risk of dying from SIDS than babies whose sleep periods do not get much longer as they get older (Cornwell & Feigenbaum, 2006). Likewise, autopsies of SIDS babies have revealed that their brains often show signs of delayed myelination.

Group Differences in Infant Mortality

Learning Objective 4.8

How do infant mortality rates vary across groups?

Infant mortality rates, including deaths attributable both to congenital abnormalities and to SIDS, vary widely across racial groups in the United States, as shown in Figure 4.3 (Heron et al., 2008; Matthews, 2005). Rates are lowest among Asian American infants; about 5 of every 1,000 such infants die each year. Among White babies, the rate is 5.5 per 1,000. The groups with the highest rates of infant death are Native Hawaiian Americans (9 per 1,000), Native Americans (9.1 per 1,000), and African Americans (13.3 per 1,000). One reason for these differences is that infants in these groups are two to three times more likely to suffer from congenital abnormalities and low birth weight—the two leading causes of infant death in the first month of life—than babies in other groups. Furthermore, SIDS is also two to three times as common in these groups.

Because babies born into poor families are more likely to die than those born into families that are better off economically, some observers have suggested that poverty explains the higher rates of infant death among Native Americans (including Native Hawaiian Americans) and African Americans, the groups with the highest rates of poverty. However, infant mortality rates among Hispanic groups suggest that the link between poverty and infant mortality is complex. The average infant mortality rate among Mexican American, Cuban American, and South and Central American populations is only about 5.6 per 1,000 (MacDorman & Atkinson, 1999). These groups are almost as likely to be poor as African Americans and Native Americans. By contrast, Americans of Puerto Rican ancestry are no more likely to be poor than other Hispanic American groups, but the infant mortality rate in this group is 7.9 per 1,000.

Interestingly, mortality rates among the babies of immigrants of all groups are lower than those of U.S.-born infants. This finding also challenges the poverty explanation for group differences in infant mortality, because immigrant women are more likely to be poor and less likely to receive prenatal care than are women born in the United States (MacDorman & Atkinson, 1999; NCHS, 2006). Many researchers suggest that lower rates of tobacco and alcohol use among women born outside the United States may be an important factor.

Access to prenatal care is another factor that distinguishes ethnic groups in the United States (NCHS, 2006). As you can see in Figure 4.4 on page 112, the two groups with the highest

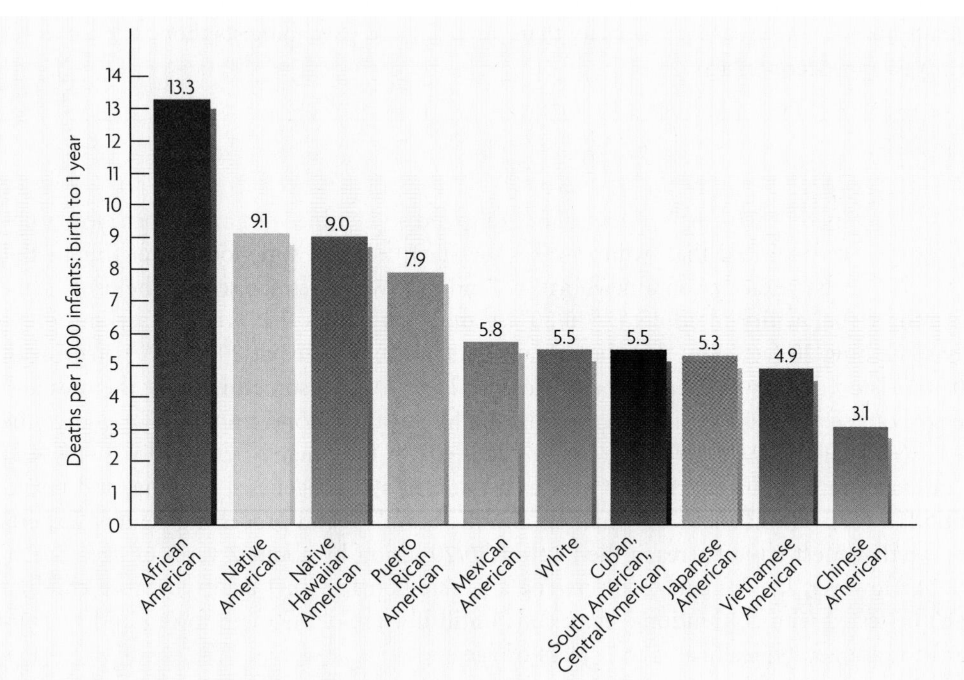

Figure 4.3
Group Differences in Infant Mortality

As you can see, infant mortality rates vary widely across U.S. ethnic groups.

(*Sources*: Heron et al., 2008; Kochanek & Smith, 2004; MacDorman & Atkinson, 1999; Matthews, 2005.)

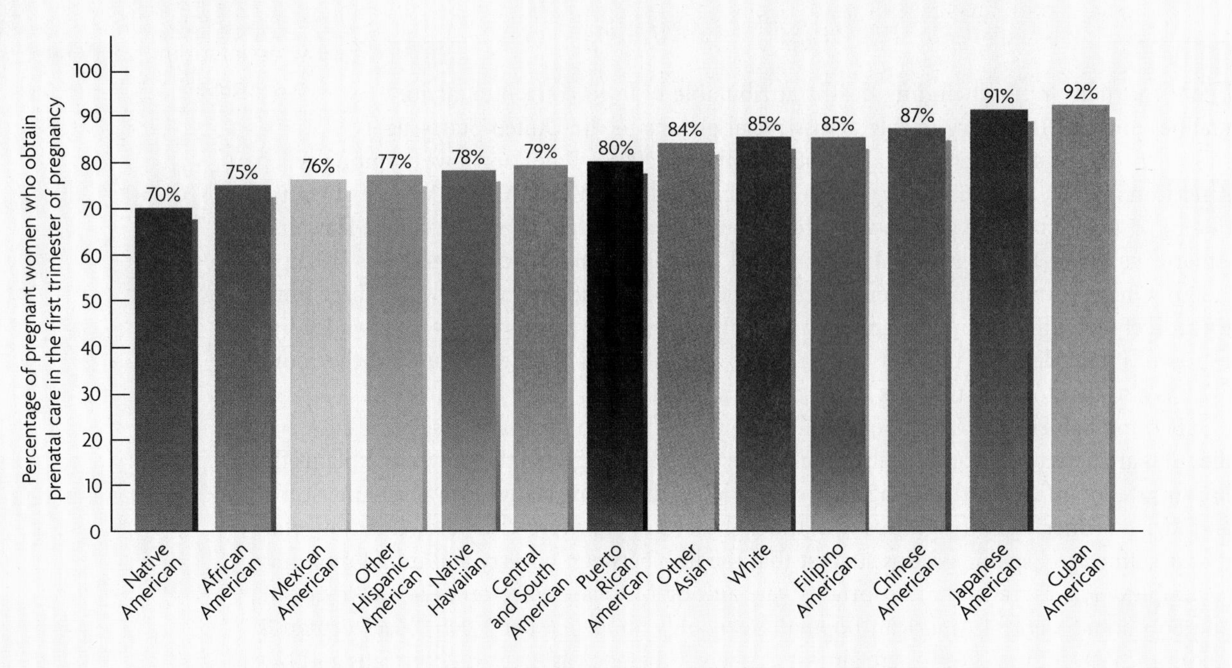

Figure 4.4
Early Prenatal Care and Ethnicity

Wide disparities exist across ethnic groups with regard to access to prenatal care. Note that Native Americans and African Americans, the two groups with the highest rates of infant mortality, are the least likely of all ethnic groups in the United States to obtain prenatal care in the first trimester.

(*Source*: National Center for Health Statistics, 2007b.)

infant mortality rates, African Americans and Native Americans, are also those who are least likely to obtain prenatal care in the first trimester of pregnancy. Thus, the links among poverty, ethnicity, and infant mortality may be partly explained by access to prenatal care.

Sensory Skills

When we study sensory skills, we are asking just what information the sensory organs receive. Does the structure of the eye permit infants to see color? Are the structures of the ear and the cortex such that a very young infant can discriminate among different pitches? The common theme running through all of what you will read in this section is that newborns and young infants have far more sensory capacity than physicians or psychologists thought even as recently as a few decades ago.

Learning Objective 4.9
How do infants' visual abilities change across the first months of life?

Vision

If you have ever had the chance to spend some time with a newborn, you probably noticed that, while awake, she spent a lot of time looking at things. But what, exactly, can a newborn see, and how well does she see it? The usual standard for **visual acuity** in adults is "20/20" vision. This means that you can see and identify something 20 feet away that the average person can also see at 20 feet. A person with 20/100 vision, in contrast, has to be as close as 20 feet to see something that the ordinary person can see at 100 feet. In other words, the higher the second number, the poorer the person's visual acuity. At birth, the infant's acuity is in the range of 20/200 to 20/400, but it improves rapidly during the first year as a result of synaptogenesis, pruning, and myelination in the neurons that serve the eyes and the brain's vision processing centers. Experts believe that most children reach the level of 20/20 vision by about 2 years of age (Keech, 2002). However, it's difficult to determine an infant's true visual acuity because children can't be tested with conventional eye exams until they are old enough to respond verbally to the examiner, typically at 4 to 5 years of age.

visual acuity how well one can see details at a distance

Researchers have established that the types of cells in the eye (cones) necessary for perceiving red and green are clearly present by 1 month (and perhaps present at birth); those required for perceiving blue are probably present by then as well (Bornstein et al., 1992). Thus, infants can and do see and discriminate among various colors. Indeed, researchers have determined that infants' ability to sense color, even in the earliest weeks of life, is almost identical to that of adults (Pereverzeva, Hui-Lin Chien, Palmer, & Teller, 2002).

Newborns are pretty nearsighted, so they can focus very well at about 8 to 10 inches—just the distance between a parent's face and the baby's eyes when the baby is held for feeding.

The process of following a moving object with your eyes is called **tracking**, and you do it every day in a variety of situations. You track the movement of other cars when you are driving; you track as you watch a friend walk toward you across the room; a baseball outfielder tracks the flight of the ball so that he can catch it. Because a newborn infant can't yet move independently, a lot of her experiences with objects are with things that move toward her or away from her. If she is to have any success in recognizing objects, she has to be able to keep her eyes on them as they move; she must be able to track. Classic research by Richard Aslin (1987) and others shows that tracking is initially fairly inefficient but improves quite rapidly. Infants younger than 2 months show some tracking for brief periods if the target is moving very slowly, but somewhere around 6 to 10 weeks a shift occurs, and babies' tracking becomes skillful rather quickly.

Hearing and Other Senses

Learning Objective 4.10

How do infants' senses of hearing, smell, taste, touch, and motion compare to those of older children and adults?

As you learned in Chapter 3, babies can hear long before they are born. However, like vision, hearing improves considerably in the early months of life. The other senses follow a similar course.

Hearing Although children's hearing improves up to adolescence, newborns' **auditory acuity** is actually better than their visual acuity. Research evidence suggests that, within the general range of pitch and loudness of the human voice, newborns hear nearly as well as adults do (Ceponiene et al., 2002). Only with high-pitched sounds is their auditory skill less than that of an adult; such a sound needs to be louder to be heard by a newborn than to be heard by older children or adults (Werner & Gillenwater, 1990).

Another basic auditory skill that exists at birth but improves with age is the ability to determine the location of a sound. Because your two ears are separated from each other, sounds arrive at one ear slightly before the other, which allows you to judge location. Only if a sound comes from a source equidistant from the two ears (the "midline") does this system fail. In this case, the sound arrives at the same time to the two ears and you know only that the sound is somewhere on your midline. We know that newborns can judge at least the general direction from which a sound has come because they will turn their heads in roughly the right direction toward the sound. Finer grained location of sounds, however, is not well developed at birth. For example, Barbara Morrongiello has observed babies' reactions to sounds played at the midline and then sounds coming from varying degrees away from the midline. Among infants 2 months old, it takes a shift of about 27 degrees off of midline before the baby shows a changed response; among 6-month-olds, only a 12-degree shift is needed; by 18 months, discrimination of a 4-degree shift is possible—nearly the skill level seen in adults (Morrongiello, 1988; Morrongiello, Fenwick, & Chance, 1990).

tracking the smooth movements of the eye used to follow the track of a moving object

auditory acuity how well one can hear

Smelling and Tasting The senses of smell and taste have been studied much less than vision and hearing, but we do have some basic knowledge. The two senses are intricately related in infants, just as they are in adults—that is, if you cannot smell for some reason (for example, because you have a cold), your taste sensitivity is also significantly reduced. Taste is detected by the taste buds on the tongue, which register four basic flavors: sweet, sour, bitter, and salty. Smell is registered in the mucous membranes of the nose and has nearly unlimited variations.

Newborns appear to respond differentially to all four of the basic flavors (Crook, 1987). Some of the clearest demonstrations of this come from an elegantly simple set of early studies by Jacob Steiner (Ganchrow, Steiner, & Daher, 1983; Steiner, 1979). Newborn infants who had never been fed were photographed before and after flavored water was put into their mouths. By varying the flavor, Steiner could determine whether the babies reacted differently to different tastes. As you can see in Figure 4.5, babies responded quite differently to sweet, sour, and bitter flavors. Newborns can also taste *umami*, the characteristic flavor that comes from adding monosodium glutamate (MSG) to food and is typical of high-protein foods that are high in glutamates (e.g., meat, cheese). Generally, newborns express pleasure when researchers test them for umami sensitivity (Nicklaus, Boggio, & Issanchou, 2005). Some researchers speculate that newborns' preferences for umami-flavored and sweet foods explain their attraction to breast milk, a substance that is naturally rich in sugars and glutamates.

Senses of Touch and Motion The infant's senses of touch and motion may well be the best developed of all. Certainly these senses are sufficiently well developed to get the baby fed. If you look back at the list of reflexes in Table 4.1 (page 103), you'll realize that the rooting reflex relies on a touch stimulus to the cheek while the grasping reflex relies on a touch to the palm of the hand. Babies appear to be especially sensitive to touches on the mouth, the

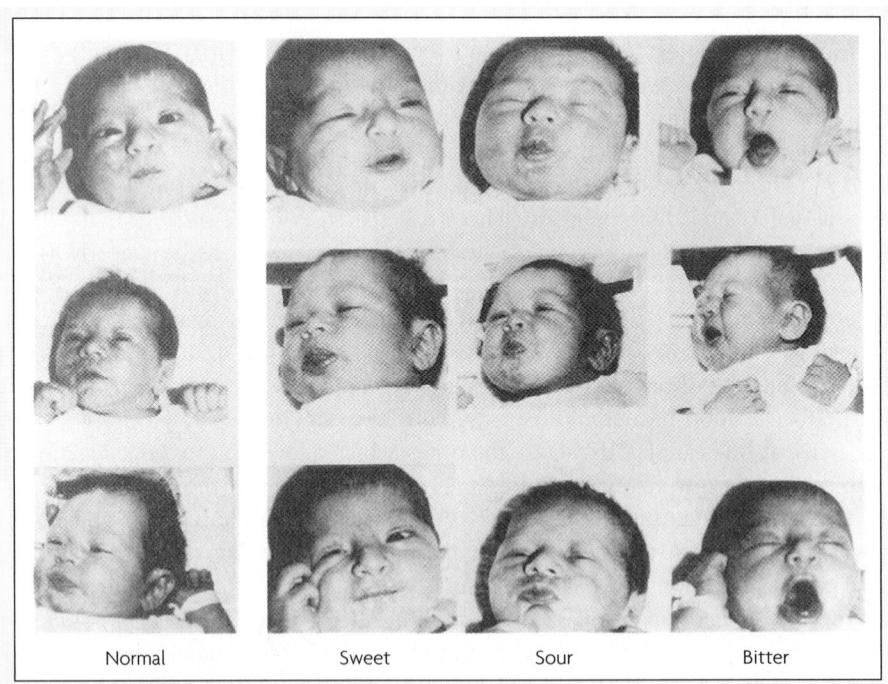

Figure 4.5 **Taste Responses in Newborns**

These are three of the newborns Steiner observed in his experiments on taste response. The left-hand column shows the babies' normal expressions; the remaining columns show the change in expression when they were given sweet, sour, and bitter tastes. What is striking is how similar the expressions are for each taste.

(*Source*: This figure was first published in *Advances in Child Development and Behavior*, Vol. 13, H. W. Reese and L. P. Lipsitt, "Human Facial Expressions in Response to Taste and Smell Stimulation", Copyright Academic Press, 1979. Reprinted by permission.)

face, the hands, the soles of the feet, and the abdomen, with less sensitivity in other parts of the body (Reisman, 1987).

Perceptual Skills

When we turn to studies of perceptual skills, we are asking what the individual does with the sensory information—how it is interpreted or combined. Researchers have found that very young infants are able to make remarkably fine discriminations among sounds, sights, and feelings, and they pay attention to and respond to patterns, not just to individual events.

Studying Perceptual Development

Learning Objective 4.11
How do researchers study perceptual development?

Babies can't talk and can't respond to ordinary questions, so how are we to decipher just what they can see, hear, or discriminate? Researchers use three basic methods that allow them to "ask" a baby about what he experiences (Bornstein, Arterberry, & Mash, 2005). In the **preference technique**, devised by Robert Fantz (1956), the baby is simply shown two pictures or two objects, and the researcher keeps track of how long the baby looks at each one. If many infants shown the same pair of pictures consistently look longer at one picture than the other, this not only tells us that babies see some difference between the two but also may reveal something about the kinds of objects or pictures that capture babies' attention.

Another strategy takes advantage of the processes of **habituation**, or getting used to a stimulus, and its opposite, **dishabituation**, or responding to a somewhat familiar stimulus as if it were new. Researchers first present the baby with a particular sight, sound, or object over and over until he habituates—that is, until he stops looking at it or showing interest in it. Then the researchers present another sight, sound, or object that is slightly different from the original one and watch to see whether the baby shows renewed interest (dishabituation). If the baby does show renewed interest, you know he perceives the slightly changed sight, sound, or object as "different" in some way from the original.

The third option is to use the principles of *operant conditioning*, described in Chapter 2. For example, an infant might be trained to turn her head when she hears a particular sound, with the sight of an interesting moving toy used as a reinforcement. After the learned response is well established, the experimenter can vary the sound in some systematic way to see whether or not the baby still turns her head.

Looking

Learning Objective 4.12
How do depth perception and patterns of looking change over the first 2 years?

One important question to ask about visual perception is whether the infant perceives his environment in the same way as older children and adults do. Can he judge how far away an object is by looking at it? Does he visually scan an object in an orderly way? Developmentalists believe that infants' patterns of looking at objects tell us a great deal about what they are trying to gain from visual information.

Depth Perception One of the perceptual skills that has been most studied is depth perception. An infant needs to be able to judge depth in order to perform all kinds of simple tasks, including judging how far away an object is so that he can reach for it, how far it is to the floor if he has ideas about crawling off the edge of the couch, or how to aim a spoon toward a bowl of chocolate pudding.

It is possible to judge depth using any (or all) of three rather different kinds of information: First, *binocular cues* involve both eyes, each of which receives a slightly different visual image of an object; the closer the object is, the more different these two views are. In addition, of course, information from the muscles of the eyes tells you something about how far

preference technique a research method in which a researcher keeps track of how long a baby looks at each of two objects shown

habituation a decline in attention that occurs because a stimulus has become familiar

dishabituation responding to a somewhat familiar stimulus as if it were new

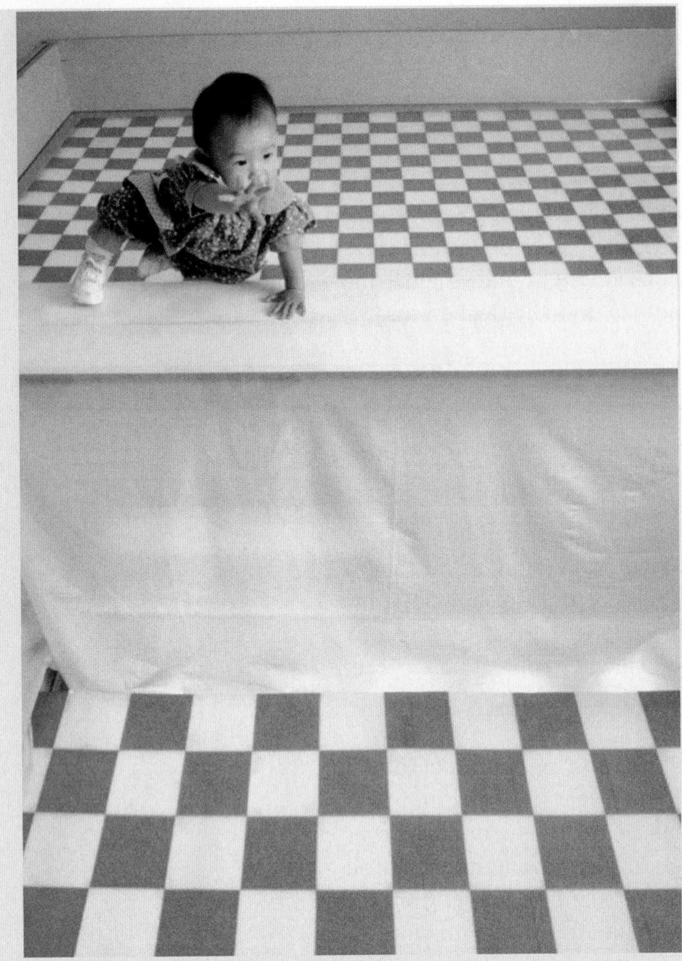

In an experiment using a visual cliff apparatus like the one used by Gibson and Walk, Mom tries to entice her baby out onto the "cliff" side. But because the infant can perceive depth, she fears that she will fall if she comes toward her, so she stays put, looking concerned.

away an object may be. Second, pictorial information, sometimes called *monocular cues*, requires input from only one eye. For example, when one object is partially in front of another one, you know that the partially hidden object is farther away—a cue called *interposition*. The relative sizes of two similar objects, such as two telephone poles or two people you see in the distance, may also indicate that the smaller-appearing one is farther away. *Linear perspective* (like the impression that railroad lines are getting closer together as they get farther away) is another monocular cue. Third, *kinetic cues* come from either your own motion or the motion of some object: If you move your head, objects near you seem to move more than objects farther away (a phenomenon called *motion parallax*). Similarly, if you see objects moving, such as a person walking across a street or a train moving along a track, closer objects appear to move over larger distances in a given period of time.

How early can an infant judge depth, and which of these cues does he use? This is still an active area of research, so the answer is not final. The best conclusion at the moment seems to be that kinetic information is used first, perhaps by about 3 months of age; binocular cues are used beginning at about 4 months; and linear perspective and other pictorial (monocular) cues are used last, perhaps at 5 to 7 months (Bornstein, 1992; Yonas, Elieff, & Arterberry, 2002).

In a remarkably clever early study, Eleanor Gibson and Richard Walk (1960) devised an apparatus called a *visual cliff*. You can see from the photograph that it consists of a large glass table with a white runway in the middle. On one side of the runway is a checkerboard pattern immediately below the glass; on the other side—the "cliff" side—the checkerboard is several feet below the glass. The baby could judge depth here by several means, but it is primarily kinetic information that is useful, since the baby in motion would see the nearer surface move more than the farther surface. If a baby has no depth perception, she should be equally willing to crawl on either side of the runway, but if she can judge depth, she should be reluctant to crawl out on the cliff side.

Since an infant had to be able to crawl in order to be tested in the Gibson and Walk procedure, the original subjects were all 6 months old or older. Most of these infants did not crawl out on the cliff side but were quite willing to crawl out on the shallow side. In other words, 6-month-old babies have depth perception.

What about younger infants? The traditional visual cliff procedure can't give us the answer, since the baby must be able to crawl in order to "tell" us whether he can judge depth. With younger babies, researchers have studied kinetic cues by watching the babies react to apparently looming objects. Most often, the baby observes a film of an object moving toward him, apparently on a collision course. If the infant has some depth perception, he should flinch, move to one side, or blink as the object appears to come very close. Such flinching has been observed in 3-month-olds (Yonas & Owsley, 1987). Most experts now agree that this is about the lower age limit of depth perception.

What Babies Look at In the first 2 months, a baby's visual attention is guided by a search for meaningful patterns (Bornstein, Arterberry, & Mash, 2005). A baby scans the world around her until she comes to a sharp light-dark contrast, which typically signals the edge of some object. Once she finds such an edge, the baby stops searching and moves her eyes back and forth across and around the edge. Motion also captures a baby's attention at this age, so she will look at things that move as well as things with large light-dark contrast. Between 2 and 3 months, when the cortex has developed more fully, the baby's attention seems to shift from where an object is to what an object is. Babies this age begin to scan rapidly across an entire figure rather than getting stuck on edges. As a result, they spend more time looking for patterns.

One early study that illustrates this point particularly well comes from the work of Albert Caron and Rose Caron (1981), who used stimuli like those in Figure 4.6 in a habituation procedure. Each baby was first shown a series of pictures that shared some particular relationship—for example, a small figure positioned above a larger version of the same figure (small over big). After the baby stopped being interested in these training pictures (that is, after he habituated), the Carons showed him another figure (the test stimulus) that either followed the same pattern or followed some other pattern. If the baby had really habituated to the pattern of the original pictures (small over big), he should show little interest in stimuli like test stimulus A in Figure 4.6 ("Ho hum, same old boring small over big thing"), but he should show renewed interest in test stimulus B ("Hey, here's something new!"). Caron and Caron found that 3- and 4-month-old children did precisely that. So even at this early age, babies find and pay attention to patterns, not just specific stimuli.

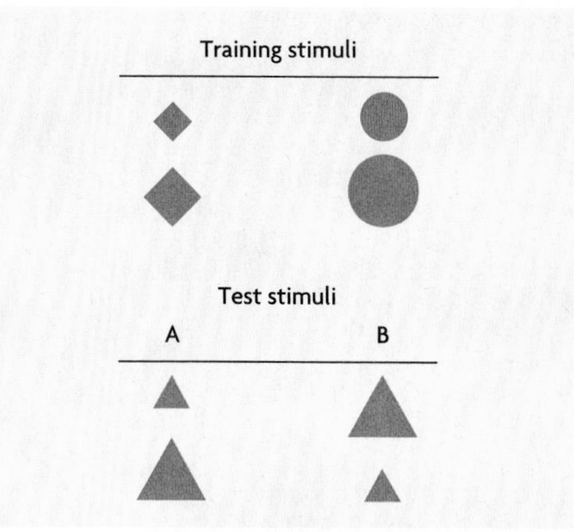

Figure 4.6 **Pattern Recognition in Infants**

In the Carons' study, the researchers first habituated each baby to a set of training stimuli (all "small over large" in this case). Then they showed each baby two test stimuli: one that had the same pattern as the training stimuli (A) and one that had a different pattern (B). Babies aged 3 and 4 months showed renewed interest in stimulus B but not stimulus A, indicating that they were paying attention to the pattern and not just specific stimuli.

(*Source*: This figure was published in *Pre-Term Birth and Psychological Development*, by S. Friedman and M. Sigman, "Processing of Relational Information as an Index of Infant Risk," by A. J. Caron and R. F. Caron, pp. 227–228, Copyright Academic Press, 1981. Reprinted by permission.)

Although there is little indication that faces are uniquely interesting patterns to infants—that is, babies do not systematically choose to look at faces rather than at other complex patterns—babies clearly prefer some faces to others. They prefer attractive faces, and they also prefer their mother's face from the earliest hours of life, a finding that has greatly surprised psychologists, although it may not surprise you (Langlois, Roggman, & Reiser-Danner, 1990).

Beyond the issue of preference, we also have the question of just what it is that babies are looking at when they scan a face. Before about 2 months of age, babies seem to look mostly at the edges of faces (the hairline and the chin), a conclusion buttressed by the finding by Pascalis and his colleagues (1995) that newborns could not discriminate Mom's face from a stranger's if the hairline was covered. After 4 months, however, covering the hairline did not affect the baby's ability to recognize Mom. In general, babies appear to begin to focus on the internal features of a face, particularly the eyes, at about 2 to 3 months.

Listening

Learning Objective 4.13

How do infants perceive human speech, recognize voices, and recognize sound patterns other than speech?

When we turn from looking to listening, we find similarly intriguing indications that very young infants not only make remarkably fine discriminations among individual sounds but also pay attention to patterns. Early studies established that as early as 1 month, babies can discriminate between speech sounds like *pa* and *ba* (Trehub & Rabinovitch, 1972). Studies using conditioned head-turning responses have shown that by perhaps 6 months of age, babies can discriminate between two-syllable "words," like *bada* and *baga*, and can even respond to a syllable that is hidden inside a string of other syllables, like *tibati* or *kobako* (Fernald & Kuhl, 1987; Goodsitt, Morse, Ver Hoeve, & Cowan, 1984; Morse & Cowan, 1982). Even more remarkable, the quality of the voice making the sound doesn't seem to matter. By 2 or 3 months of age, babies respond to individual sounds as the same, whether they are spoken by a male or a female or by an adult or a child (Marean, Werner, & Kuhl, 1992). Research also indicates that infants can rapidly learn to discriminate between words and nonwords in

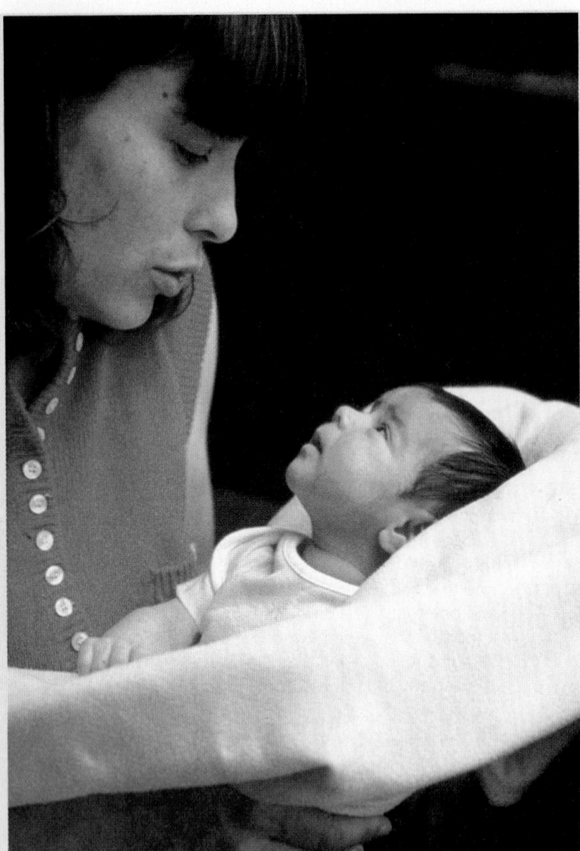

Newborns recognize their mother's voice and by 1 month of age can discriminate between syllables such as *ba* and *pa*.

artificial languages researchers invent strictly for the purpose of such experiments (Aslin, Saffran, & Newport, 1998).

Even more striking is the finding that babies are actually better at discriminating some kinds of speech sounds than adults are. Each language uses only a subset of all possible speech sounds. Japanese, for example, does not use the *l* sound that appears in English; Spanish makes a different distinction between *d* and *t* than occurs in English. It turns out that up to about 6 months of age, babies can accurately discriminate all sound contrasts that appear in any language, including sounds they do not hear in the language spoken to them. At about 6 months of age, they begin to lose the ability to distinguish pairs of vowels that do not occur in the language they are hearing; by age 1, the ability to discriminate nonheard consonant contrasts begins to fade (Polka & Werker, 1994). Interestingly, however, neuroimaging studies show that the neural networks that underlie this acquired restriction on speech perception become more flexible, or plastic, in elementary school children who receive instruction in a new language (Nelson, Haan, & Thomas, 2006). So, the narrowing of speech perception that has been found at the end of the first year may not necessarily be permanent. Clearly, too, it is dependent on experience.

Newborns also seem to be able to discriminate between individual voices. DeCasper and Fifer (1980) found that the newborn can tell the mother's voice from another female voice (but not the father's voice from another male voice) and prefers the mother's voice. Moreover, there is a correlation between gestational age and maternal voice recognition: Premature infants are less likely to recognize their mother's voice than are babies born at term (DeRegnier, Wewerka, Georgieff, Mattia, & Nelson, 2002). Thus, *in utero* learning appears to be responsible for newborns' preference for the maternal voice.

Learning Objective 4.14

What is intermodal perception?

Combining Information from Several Senses

If you think about the way you receive and use perceptual information, you'll realize that you rarely have information from only one sense at a time. Psychologists have been interested in knowing how early an infant can combine such information. An even more complex issue is determining how early a baby can learn something via one sense and transfer that information to another sense (for example, recognize solely by feel a toy he has seen but never before felt). This skill is usually called **intermodal perception**.

Research findings show that intermodal perception is possible as early as 1 month and becomes common by 6 months (Rose & Ruff, 1987). Moreover, research comparing these skills in children born prematurely and those born at term suggests that basic maturational processes play an important role in their development (Espy et al., 2002). Research also suggests that intermodal perception is important in infant learning. One group of researchers found that babies who habituated to a combined auditory-visual stimulus were better able to recognize a new stimulus than infants who habituated to either the auditory or the visual stimulus alone (Bahrick & Lickliter, 2000). For example, suppose you played a videotape of someone singing for one baby, played the videotape without the sound for another, and played an audio recording of the song for a third. Research suggests that the first baby would recognize a change in either the singer (visual stimulus) or the song (auditory stimulus) more quickly than would either of the other two infants.

intermodal perception formation of a single perception of a stimulus based on information from two or more senses

In older infants, intermodal perception can be readily demonstrated, not only between touch and sight but also between other modalities such as sound and sight. For instance, in several delightfully clever early experiments, Elizabeth Spelke (1979) showed that 4-month-old infants can connect sound rhythms with movement. She showed babies two films simultaneously, one depicting a toy kangaroo bouncing up and down and the other showing a donkey bouncing up and down, with one of the animals bouncing at a faster rate. Out of a loudspeaker located between the two films she played a tape recording of a rhythmic bouncing sound that matched the bounce pattern of one of the two animals. In this situation, babies showed a preference for looking at the film showing the bounce rate that matched the sound.

An even more striking illustration of the same basic process comes from the work of Jeffery Pickens (1994). He showed 5-month-old babies two films side by side, each displaying a train moving along a track. Then out of a loudspeaker he played engine sounds of various types, such as that of an engine getting gradually louder (thus appearing to come closer) or gradually fainter (thus appearing to be moving away). The babies in this experiment looked longer at a picture of a train whose movement matched the pattern of engine sounds. That is, they appeared to have some understanding of the link between the pattern of sound and the pattern of movement—knowledge that demonstrates not only intersensory integration but also a surprisingly sophisticated understanding of the accompaniments of motion.

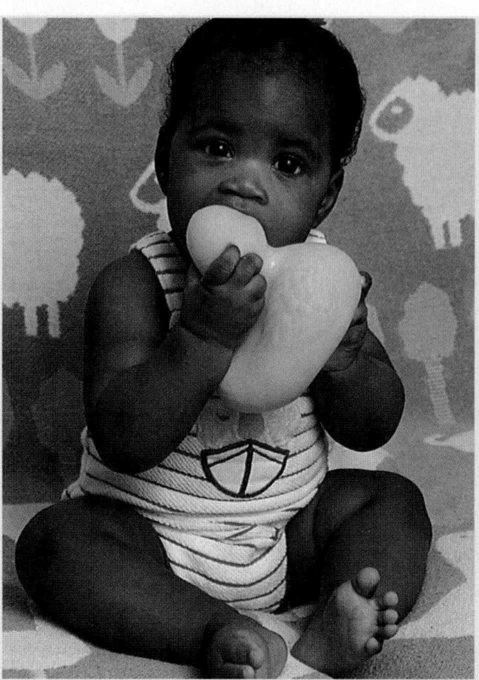
Even though 7-month-old Leslie is not looking at this toy while she chews on it, she is nonetheless learning something about how it ought to look based on how it feels in her mouth and in her hands—an example of intermodal perception.

Explaining Perceptual Development

Learning Objective 4.15

What arguments do nativists and empiricists offer in support of their theories of perceptual development?

The study of perceptual development has been significant because it has been a key battleground for the dispute about nature versus nurture. **Nativists** claim that most perceptual abilities are inborn, while **empiricists** argue that these skills are learned. There are strong arguments for both positions.

In support of the nativists' argument, researchers have found more and more skills that are present from the earliest days of life outside the womb: Newborns have good auditory acuity, poor but adequate visual acuity, excellent tactual and taste perception. They have at least some color vision and at least rudimentary ability to locate the source of sounds around them. More impressive still, they are capable of making quite sophisticated discriminations from the earliest days of life, including identifying their mother by sight, smell, or sound.

On the other side of the ledger, however, we find evidence from research with other species that some minimal level of experience is necessary to support the development of the perceptual systems. For example, animals deprived of light show deterioration of the whole visual system and a consequent decrease in perceptual abilities (Hubel & Weisel, 1963). Likewise, animals deprived of auditory stimuli display delayed or no development of auditory perceptual skills (Dammeijer, Schlundt, Chenault, Manni, & Anteunis, 2002).

We can best understand the development of perceptual skills by thinking of it as the result of an interaction between inborn and experiential factors. A child is able to make visual discriminations between people or among objects within the first few days or weeks of life. The specific discriminations she learns and the number of separate objects she learns to recognize, however, will depend on her experiences. A perfect example of this is the newborn's ability to discriminate her mother's face from a very similar woman's face. Such a discrimination must be the result of experience, yet the capacity to make the distinction must be built in. Thus, as is true of virtually all dichotomous theoretical disputes, both sides are correct. Both nature and nurture are involved.

nativists theorists who claim that perceptual abilities are inborn

empiricists theorists who argue that perceptual abilities are learned

Physical Development and the Whole Child

Your study of the infancy period so far has focused on the physical domain. In addition to learning about the changes in infants' bodies and motor skills that take place during this period, you have read about some of the important issues in infant health and have learned a bit about the development of sensory and perceptual skills. Now it is time to consider how some of the milestones of the physical domain set the stage for the emergence of a few of the most important cognitive and socioemotional advances across the first 2 years of life.

Cognitive Functioning

In Chapter 5, you will read about one of the most important milestones of infant cognitive development: *object permanence*, or the understanding that objects continue to exist when they cannot be directly observed. An infant with object permanence knows that his favorite toy exists and can think about it even when he cannot see it. Object permanence is thought to enable infants to separate their own mental world from the physical world. Its emergence is strongly associated with synaptogenesis and increased oxygenation of the blood in the frontal lobes of the brain (Baird et al., 2002; Kagan & Herschkowitz, 2005).

Moreover, classic studies showing that infants with motor disabilities develop object permanence more slowly than babies without disabilities suggest that the motor skills that infants acquire in the first year allow them to manipulate objects in ways that contribute to the development of object permanence (Eagle, 1975). Similarly, studies of children who have visual impairments indicate that "on-time" acquisition of object permanence depends on a healthy visual system (Lewis, 2002). In addition, the emergence of intermodal perception in the middle of the first year, regardless of an infant's status with regard to disabilities, is foundational to the development of object permanence (Schweinle & Wilcox, 2003).

The advances in speech perception that you read about in this chapter are, of course, vital to the milestones of early language development that are outlined in Chapter 5, but so are other aspects of physical development. Recall that the development of the infant's perceptual system is driven by a search for meaningful patterns. Each language has a consistent way of associating gestures and other elements of nonverbal communication with verbal expressions. The infant's advancing motor skills allow him to produce and reproduce the gestures that he observes, and his growing perceptual system enables him to create appropriate patterns of combined verbal and nonverbal expressions in order to make himself understood (Blake, Osborne, Cabral, & Gluck, 2003).

Socioemotional Functioning

As you will learn in Chapter 6, *attachment* is the emotional bond that develops between an infant and her primary caregivers. One of the infant's primary tools in the creation of this bond is her tendency to cry when she needs care—one of the behavioral states you learned about in this chapter. When she cries, the caregiver usually responds, resulting in the creation of an opportunity for social interaction, the cornerstone of the development of attachment. Likewise, as the infant becomes more capable of moving around, she can seek out such opportunities by doing things such as following a sibling from one room to another.

Looking Ahead

In the remaining chapters devoted to infancy, you will learn about the impressive advances in cognitive and socioemotional skills that occur during the first 2 years. Remember, though, that dividing development up in this way makes it seem as if age-related changes take place on separate, parallel tracks; but, while each track is distinctive from the others in important ways, the tracks also interact with one another. Therefore, as you read about the cognitive and socioemotional milestones of infancy, remember that they are facilitated by advances in the physical domain and, in turn, contribute to changes in the physical domain.

THE WHOLE CHILD IN FOCUS

To trace how the physical, cognitive, and socioemotional domains work together to influence Federico's development, see *The Whole Child in Focus* on page 178.

Test Prep Center

with PEARSON mydevelopmentlab

PHYSICAL CHANGES

4.1 What important changes in the brain take place during infancy? (pp. 100–102)

Changes in the nervous system are extremely rapid in the first 2 years. In most parts of the brain, the development of dendrites and synapses reaches its first peak between 12 and 24 months, after which "pruning" of synapses occurs. Myelination of nerve fibers also occurs rapidly in the first 2 years.

1. Match each term with its definition.

______ (1) synaptogenesis

______ (2) pruning

______ (3) plasticity

(A) the process of synapse development

(B) the brain's capacity to change in response to experience

(C) the elimination of unused synapses

2. Explain how the process of myelination improves brain functioning.

____

____

3. From the Multimedia Library within MyDevelopmentLab, watch the *Tracking Technologies and Infant Perception: Scott Johnson* video and answer the following question.

What does Dr. Johnson's research reveal about visual perception in infancy?

____

____

4.2 How do babies' reflexes and behavioral states change? (pp. 102–104)

Adaptive reflexes, which help infants survive, include such essential responses as sucking. Some adaptive responses disappear, and some remain throughout the lifespan. Primitive reflexes include the Moro (startle) and Babinski reflexes, which disappear within a few months. Neonates move through a series of five states of consciousness in a cycle that lasts about 2 hours.

4. Summarize the changes that occur in each of these behavioral states across the first year of life.

(A) sleeping

____

____

(B) awake and alert

____

____

(C) crying

____

____

5. From the Multimedia Library within MyDevelopmentLab, watch the *Reflexes: Moro; Reflexes: Palmar Grasp; Reflexes: Babinski;* and *Reflexes: Sucking* videos and answer the following question.

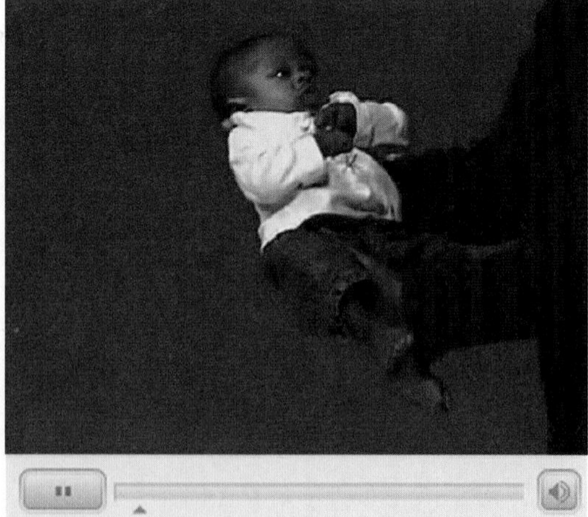

How do reflexes contribute to a newborn's survival?

____

____

4.3 How do infants' bodies change, and what is the typical pattern of motor skill development in the first 2 years? (pp. 104–106)

During infancy, bones increase in size, number, and density; muscle fibers become larger and contain less water. Stamina improves as the lungs grow and the heart gets stronger. Motor skills improve rapidly in the first 2 years, as the baby moves from creeping to crawling to walking to running and becomes able to grasp objects.

6. List the gross and fine motor skills associated with each age range in the table below.

Age	Gross Motor Skills	Fine Motor Skills
1 month		
2–3 months		
4–6 months		
7–9 months		
10–12 months		
13–18 months		
19–24 months		

7. From the Multimedia Library within MyDevelopmentLab, watch the *Motor Development in Infants and Toddlers: Karen Adolph* video and answer the following question.

What does cross-cultural research suggest about the order in which infants acquire motor skills?

____

____

HEALTH AND WELLNESS

4.4 What are the nutritional needs of infants? (p. 107)

Breast-feeding has been shown to be better for a baby nutritionally than bottle-feeding. For the first 4 to 6 months, breast milk or formula accompanied by appropriate supplements is sufficient to meet all of an infant's nutritional needs. Solid foods should be introduced gradually, one at a time, so that the cause of any allergic reaction can be easily identified.

8. From the Multimedia Library within MyDevelopmentLab, watch the *Infant Perception* video and answer the following question.

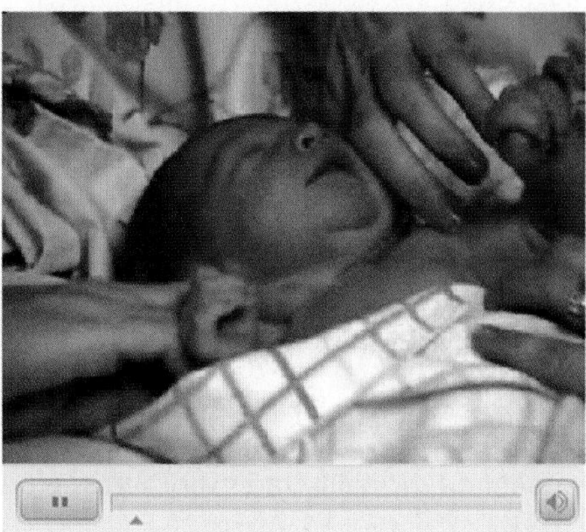

In what way is breast-feeding associated with the development of taste?

____

____

4.5 How does malnutrition affect infants' development? (pp. 107–108)

Macronutrient malnutrition results from a diet that contains too few calories, whereas micronutrient malnutrition is caused by a diet that has sufficient calories but lacks specific nutrients, vitamins, or minerals. Infants whose daily caloric intake is severely restricted develop marasmus; those who do not get enough protein suffer from kwashiorkor. Both types of malnutrition can result in neurological damage.

9. Label each case of malnutrition as (A) macronutrient malnutrition, (B) micronutrient malnutrition, (C) kwashikor, or (D) marasmus.

______ (1) Jerome's diet is deficient in calcium and vitamin C.

______ (2) Because she doesn't get enough to eat, 8-year-old Nala's weight is equivalent to that of an average 4-year-old.

______ (3) George's diet is so low in protein that he is at risk of permanent brain damage.

______ (4) This type of malnutrition is the world's leading cause of death among children under age 5.

4.6 What are infants' health-care and immunization needs? (pp. 108–109)

Babies need regular check-ups and a variety of immunizations. Prompt treatment of respiratory infections is crucial.

10. Explain why the following statement is false: Healthy infants don't need to go to the doctor.

____

____

INFANT MORTALITY

4.7 What have researchers learned about sudden infant death syndrome? (pp. 109–110)

Sudden infant death syndrome is the most common cause of death between 1 month and 1 year of age in the United States. Risk factors for SIDS include sleeping on the stomach, sleep apnea, and exposure to tobacco smoke before and after birth.

11. Write Y next to risk factors for SIDS, and write N next to characteristics that are not risk factors for SIDS.

_____ (1) infants' showing increasingly lengthy sleep periods as they get older

_____ (2) winter birth

_____ (3) family history of lung cancer

_____ (4) sleeping on a firm mattress with no pillow

4.8 How do infant mortality rates vary across groups? (pp. 111–112)

African American, Native Hawaiian American, and Native American children are more likely to die in the first year of life than children in other U.S. racial groups; they are also more likely to have congenital anomalies and low birth weight. Poverty seems a likely explanation, but the relationship between low income and infant mortality is complex.

12. Number these groups in accordance with their rates of early prenatal care, with 1 indicating the highest percentage receiving care.

_____ (1) Japanese Americans

_____ (2) White Americans

_____ (3) Native Americans

_____ (4) Chinese Americans

_____ (5) African Americans

_____ (6) Mexican Americans

13. What role does sudden infant death syndrome (SIDS) play in group differences in infant mortality?

____

____

SENSORY SKILLS

4.9 How do infants' visual abilities change across the first months of life? (pp. 112–113)

Color vision is present by 1 month and perhaps at birth. Visual acuity and visual tracking skills are relatively poor at birth and then develop rapidly during the first few months.

14. From the Multimedia Library within MyDevelopmentLab, watch the *Infant Perception* video and answer the following question.

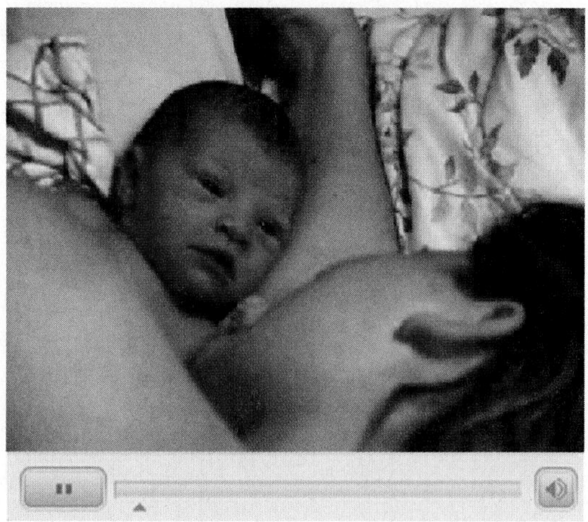

How do the newborn's visual abilities compare to his other sensory skills, and how does vision change over the first year of life?

____

____

4.10 How do infants' senses of hearing, smell, taste, touch, and motion compare to those of older children and adults? (pp. 113–115)

Basic auditory skills are fully developed at birth; acuity is good for the range of the human voice, and the newborn can locate at least the approximate direction of sounds. The sensory capacities for smelling, tasting, and the senses of touch and motion are also well developed at birth.

15. How do the newborn's auditory abilities compare to his other sensory skills?

____

____

PERCEPTUAL SKILLS

4.11 How do researchers study perceptual development? (p. 115)

In the preference technique, researchers track how long babies look at each of a pair of stimuli. Habituation involves exposing babies to a stimulus until they are no longer interested in it. The purpose is to see whether the babies will then respond to a new stimulus that is only slightly different from the original one (dishabituation). By using operant conditioning, researchers train babies to perform behaviors such as turning their heads in response to a specific stimulus. Then the researchers vary the stimulus slightly; if babies do not respond as they have been trained to do, then the researchers know that they can tell the difference between the original and the new stimulus.

16. From the Multimedia Library within MyDevelopmentLab, watch the *Infancy: Habituation* video and answer the following question.

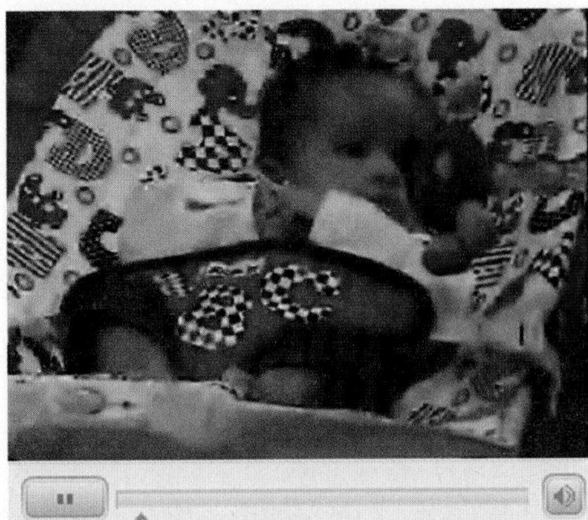

How does the infant in the video demonstrate habituation and dishabituation?

____

____

4.12 How do depth perception and patterns of looking change over the first 2 years? (pp. 115–117)

Depth perception is present in at least rudimentary form by 3 months. Babies use kinetic cues initially, then binocular cues, and finally pictorial (monocular) cues by about 5 to 7 months. Visual attention appears to follow definite rules, even in the first hours of life. Babies can discriminate the mother's face from other faces, and the mother's voice from other voices, almost immediately after birth.

17. From the Multimedia Library within MyDevelopmentLab, explore *The Visual Cliff* and answer the following question.

Why does a baby with depth perception stop crawling when she gets to the visual cliff?

____

____

4.13 How do infants perceive human speech, recognize voices, and recognize sound patterns other than speech? (pp. 117–118)

From the beginning, babies appear to attend to and discriminate among speech contrasts present in all possible languages. By the age of 1 year, the infant makes fine discriminations only among speech sounds salient in the language he is actually hearing. By 6 months, babies also attend to and discriminate among different patterns of sounds, such as melodies or speech inflections.

18. From the Multimedia Library within MyDevelopmentLab, explore *Infants' Perceptual and Cognitive Milestones* and answer the following question.

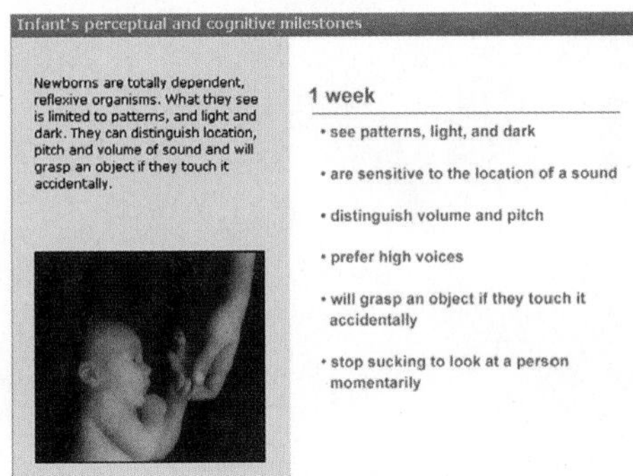

What are the milestones of auditory perceptual development across the first 12 months of life?

____

____

4.14 What is intermodal perception? (pp. 118–119)

Studies show that infants can learn something via one sense and transfer it to another sense, a skill known as intermodal perception.

19. What role does intermodal perception play in infant learning?

____

____

4.15 What arguments do nativists and empiricists offer in support of their theories of perceptual development? (p. 119)

A central issue in the study of perceptual development continues to be the nature-nurture controversy. Many basic perceptual abilities, including strategies for examining objects, appear to be built into the system at birth or to develop as the brain develops over the early years. But specific experiences are required both to maintain the underlying system and to learn fundamental discriminations and patterns.

20. Label these statements as consistent with the (A) nativist or (B) empiricist view of perceptual development.

______ (1) Perceptual skills are inborn.

______ (2) Perceptual skills are learned.

______ (3) The development of perceptual skills depends on experience.

______ (4) Newborns can make perceptual discriminations.

For answers to the questions in this chapter, turn to page 509.
For a list of key terms, turn to page 530.

Succeed with

Do You Know All of the Terms in This Chapter?
Find out by using the Flashcards. Want more practice? Take additional quizzes, try simulations, and watch video to be sure you are prepared for the test!

Chapter 5

Cognitive Development in Infancy and Toddlerhood

Advertisements for books, videos, and expensive toys often make parents wonder whether they're providing their infant with the stimulation needed for optimal intellectual development. But the influence of experience on cognitive development is most evident in cases in which a dramatic disruption in environmental support—malnourishment, child abuse, lead poisoning, or the like—impedes intellectual development. Researchers have known for some time that extraordinary amounts of intellectual stimulation do little, if anything, to enhance cognitive development in healthy infants (Bruer, 1999). Thus, anxious parents can rest easy knowing that research shows that what babies need to fulfill their intellectual potential are caretakers who respond to all of their needs and who avoid narrowly focusing on a specific developmental outcome, such as maximizing their scores on the intelligence tests they will take when they start school.

In this chapter, you will learn about Piaget's explanation of the universal changes in thinking that happen in the first 2 years of life, as well as how other theorists explain his research findings. You will also read about learning and memory during these years and about the beginnings of language. Individual differences in intelligence among infants will be discussed as well.

Learning Objectives

Cognitive Changes

5.1 What are the important milestones of Piaget's sensorimotor stage?

5.2 What are some of the challenges offered to Piaget's explanation of infant cognitive development?

5.3 What does research tell us about infants' understanding of objects?

Learning, Categorizing, and Remembering

5.4 When are babies able to learn through classical conditioning, operant conditioning, and observing models?

5.5 How does categorical understanding change over the first 2 years?

5.6 How does memory function in the first 2 years?

The Beginnings of Language

5.7 What are the behaviorist, nativist, and interactionist explanations of language development?

5.8 What are some of the environmental influences on language development?

5.9 How do infants' sounds, gestures, and understanding of words change in the early months of life?

5.10 What are the characteristics of toddlers' first words?

5.11 What kinds of sentences do children produce between 18 and 24 months of age?

5.12 What kinds of individual differences are evident in language development?

5.13 How does language development vary across cultures?

Measuring Intelligence in Infancy

5.14 How is intelligence measured in infancy?

Cognitive Changes

The remarkable cognitive advances that happen in infancy are highly consistent across environments. Of course, 2-year-olds are still a long way from cognitive maturity, but some of the most important steps toward that goal are taken in the first 2 years of life.

Learning Objective 5.1

What are the important milestones of Piaget's sensorimotor stage?

Piaget's View of the First 2 Years

Recall from Chapter 2 that Piaget assumed that a baby *assimilates* incoming information into the limited array of *schemes* she is born with—looking, listening, sucking, grasping—and *accommodates* those schemes based on her experiences. He called this form of thinking *sensorimotor intelligence*. The **sensorimotor stage** is the period during which infants develop and refine sensorimotor intelligence. (See Table 5.1.)

sensorimotor stage Piaget's first stage of development, in which infants use information from their senses and motor actions to learn about the world

primary circular reactions Piaget's phrase to describe a baby's simple repetitive actions in substage 2 of the sensorimotor stage, organized around the baby's own body

Sensorimotor Stage In Piaget's view, the newborn who is in substage 1 of the sensorimotor stage is entirely tied to the immediate present, responding to whatever stimuli are available. She forgets events from one encounter to the next and does not appear to plan. Substage 2 (from roughly 1 to 4 months) is marked by the beginning of the coordinations between looking and listening, between reaching and looking, and between reaching and sucking that are central features of the 2-month-old's means of exploring the world. The technique that distinguishes substage 2 is **primary circular reactions**, the many simple repetitive actions seen at this time, each organized around the infant's own body. For example, the baby may accidentally suck his thumb one day, find it pleasurable, and repeat the action.

Table 5.1 Substages of Piaget's Sensorimotor Stage

Substage	Average Age (in months)	Primary Technique	Characteristics
1	0–1	Reflexes	Use of built-in schemes or reflexes such as sucking or looking. Primitive schemes begin to change through very small steps of accommodation. Limited imitation, no ability to integrate information from several senses.
2	1–4	Primary circular reactions	Further accommodation of basic schemes, as the baby practices them endlessly–grasping, listening, looking, sucking. Beginning coordination of schemes from different senses, so the baby now looks toward a sound and sucks on anything he can reach and bring to his mouth. But the baby does not yet link his body actions to results outside his body.
3	4–8	Secondary circular reactions	The baby becomes much more aware of events outside her body and makes them happen again in a kind of trial-and-error learning. Scientists are unsure whether babies this young understand the causal links yet, however. Imitation may occur, but only of schemes already in the baby's repertoire. The baby will look for a partially hidden toy but lacks true object permanence.
4	8–12	Coordination of secondary schemes	Clear intentional means-end behavior. The baby not only goes after what he wants but may combine two schemes to do so, such as moving a pillow aside to reach a toy (object permanence). Imitation of novel behavior occurs.
5	12–18	Tertiary circular reactions	"Experimentation" begins, in which the infant tries out new ways of playing with or manipulating objects. Very active, very purposeful trial-and-error exploration.
6	18–24	Beginning of mental representation	Development of use of symbols to represent objects or events. The child understands that the symbol is separate from the object. As a result, infants in this stage are able to solve problems by thinking about them. Moreover, deferred imitation becomes possible because it requires the ability to represent internally the event to be imitated.

In substage 3 (from about 4 to 8 months), the baby engages in **secondary circular reactions**, repeating some action in order to trigger a reaction outside her own body. The baby coos and Mom smiles, so the baby coos again to get Mom to smile again. These initial connections between body actions and external consequences seem to be simple, almost mechanical links between stimuli and responses. However, in substage 4, the 8- to 12-month-old baby shows the beginnings of understanding causal connections, at which point she moves into exploratory high gear. One consequence of this new drive to explore is **means-end behavior**, or the ability to keep a goal in mind and devise a plan to achieve it. Babies show this kind of behavior when they move one toy out of the way to gain access to another. The end is the toy they want; the means to the end is moving the other toy.

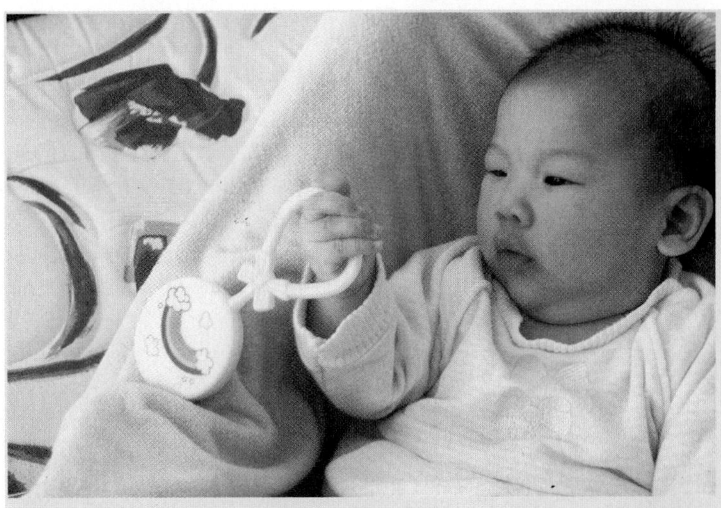
Four-month-old Andrea may be showing a secondary circular reaction here, shaking her hand repeatedly to hear the sound of the rattle. A learning theorist would say that the pleasure she experiences from hearing the sound is reinforcing her hand-shaking behavior.

In substage 5, from about 12 to 18 months, exploration of the environment becomes more focused with the emergence of **tertiary circular reactions**. In this pattern, the baby doesn't merely repeat the original behavior but tries out variations of it. He may try out many sounds or facial expressions to see if they will trigger Mom's smile, or he may try dropping a toy from several heights to see if it makes different sounds or lands in different places. At this stage, the baby's behavior has a purposeful, experimental quality. Nonetheless, Piaget thought that the baby still did not have mental symbols to stand for objects in this substage.

The ability to manipulate mental symbols, such as words or images, marks substage 6, which lasts from roughly 18 months to 24 months of age. This new capacity allows the infant to generate solutions to problems simply by thinking about them, without the trial-and-error behavior typical of substage 5. As a result, means-end behavior becomes far more sophisticated than in earlier stages. For example, a 24-month-old who knows there are cookies in the cookie jar can figure out how to get one. Furthermore, she can find a way to overcome just about any obstacle placed in her path (Bauer, Schwade, Wewerka, & Delaney, 1999). If her parents respond to her climbing on the kitchen counter in pursuit of a cookie by moving the cookie jar to the top of the refrigerator, the substage 6 toddler's response will likely be to find a way to climb to the top of the refrigerator. Thus, changes in cognition are behind the common impression of parents and other caregivers that 18- to 24-month-olds cannot be left unsupervised, even for very short periods of time.

THE WHOLE CHILD IN FOCUS

What skills did Federico display that are characteristic of Piaget's sensorimotor substages? Find out on page 179.

Object Permanence

You know that this book continues to exist even when you are unable to see it—an understanding that Piaget called **object permanence**. In a series of studies, many of which involved his own children, Piaget discovered that babies acquire this understanding gradually during the sensorimotor period. According to his observations, replicated frequently by later researchers, the first hint of object permanence is evident at about 2 months of age (in substage 2). Suppose you show a toy to a child of this age and then put a screen in front of the toy and remove the toy. When you then remove the screen, the baby will show some indication of surprise, as if he knows that something should still be there. The child thus seems to have a rudimentary expectation about the permanence of an object. But infants of this age show no signs of searching for a toy that has fallen over the side of the crib or that has disappeared beneath a blanket or behind a screen.

In substage 3 (at about 6–8 months), however, babies will look over the edge of the crib for dropped toys or on the floor for spilled food. (In fact, babies of this age may drive their parents nuts playing "dropsy" from the high chair.) Infants of this age will also search for

secondary circular reactions repetitive actions in substage 3 of the sensorimotor period, oriented around external objects

means-end behavior purposeful behavior carried out in pursuit of a specific goal

tertiary circular reactions the deliberate experimentation with variations of previous actions that occurs in substage 5 of the sensorimotor period

object permanence the understanding that objects continue to exist when they can't be seen

After babies acquire object permanence, they become fascinated with activities that involve putting objects into containers that partially or fully obscure the objects from view.

partially hidden objects. If you put a baby's favorite toy under a cloth but leave part of it sticking out, the infant will reach for the toy, which indicates that in some sense he "recognizes" that the whole object is there even though he can see only part of it. But if you cover the toy completely with the cloth or put it behind a screen, the infant will stop looking for it and will not reach for it, even if he has seen you put the cloth over it.

This behavior changes again between 8 and 12 months, in substage 4. Infants of this age will reach for or search for a toy that has been covered completely by a cloth or hidden by a screen. Thus, by 12 months, most infants appear to grasp the basic fact that objects continue to exist even when they are no longer visible (see *Developmental Science in the Clinic*).

However, substage 4 infants' understanding of where a hidden object might be found is limited by the **A-not-B error**. This flaw in logic leads infants to look for an object in the place where it was last seen (position A) rather than in the place to which they have seen a researcher move it (position B) (Flavell, 1963). In substage 5, infants' searching strategies are somewhat more logical. For instance, if they see a researcher move a hidden object from behind screen A to behind screen B, they will immediately look for it behind screen B. However, if they see a researcher hide an object in her hand and immediately move the hand behind screen A, dropping the object out of view, they will persist in searching for the object in the researcher's hand just as substage 4 infants do. This error is not resolved until substage 6. Thus, infants' full understanding of the behavior of objects and their connections to the spaces in which they appear and can possibly appear does not emerge until near the end of the second year of life.

Imitation Piaget also studied infants' ability to imitate the actions of others. He observed that as early as the first few months of life, infants could imitate actions they could see them-

DEVELOPMENTAL SCIENCE IN THE CLINIC

Object Permanence and Developmental Surveillance

A simple test of object permanence is a part of the routine well-baby exam that Dr. Poneru does with 12-month-old infants. He allows the baby to play with a small stuffed bear that he keeps in the pocket of his lab coat. When he puts the bear back into his pocket, he says, "Where's the bear?" If the infant looks for the bear in his pocket, then Dr. Poneru is fairly confident that her development in the cognitive domain is on track. If the infant does not look for the bear, then Dr. Poneru is likely to carefully track the child's intellectual progress over the next several months and recommend her for further testing if she continues to lag behind her peers.

Developmental scientists have known for some time that a delay in acquiring object permanence is strongly associated with a later diagnosis of mental retardation (e.g., Wachs, 1975). Consequently, many pediatricians, like Dr. Poneru, assess an infant's understanding of object permanence, along with other cognitive and language skills, during well-baby exams (Overby, 2002). Informal procedures of this kind are called *developmental surveillance*, and they represent a critical step toward identifying children who are at risk of mental retardation and other developmental disabilities earlier than they might be otherwise (American Academy of Pediatrics [AAP], 2006).

At present, more than 80% of cases of mental retardation are not diagnosed until after children enter school (DSM-IV TR, 2000). Health-care professionals are committed to changing that statistic through the implementation of effective developmental surveillance procedures. The American Academy of Pediatrics suggests that doctors track changes in infants' cognitive and language skills across the first 2½ years (AAP, 2006). They recommend that infants who show signs of lagging behind their peers in these domains be given standardized screening tests during the 30-month-old well-child exam. Those who perform more poorly on these tests than do their agemates should be referred for further evaluation. The AAP hopes that widespread implementation of these procedures will increase the numbers of at-risk infants who are referred to school-based early intervention programs.

Questions for Reflection

1. How might physicians incorporate parents' observations into the developmental surveillance process?
2. How would you explain Dr. Poneru's hidden-bear task to a parent who didn't understand the reason for the doctor's use of it?

selves make, such as hand gestures. But he found that they could not imitate other people's facial gestures until substage 4 (8–12 months). This second form of imitation seems to require some kind of intermodal perception, combining the visual cues of seeing the other's face with the kinesthetic cues (perceptions of muscle motion) from one's own facial movements. Piaget argued that imitation of any action that wasn't already in the child's repertoire did not occur until about 1 year, and that **deferred imitation**—a child's imitation of some action at a later time—was possible only in substage 6, since deferred imitation requires some kind of internal representation.

Challenges to Piaget's View

Learning Objective 5.2
What are some of the challenges offered to Piaget's explanation of infant cognitive development?

Many studies since Piaget's time have suggested that he underestimated the cognitive capacity of infants. By changing the methods used to measure object permanence, for instance, researchers have found that younger infants understand object movements better than Piaget suggested. Moreover, studies have shown that imitation appears at younger ages than Piaget's research implied.

Object Permanence In Piaget's studies of object permanence, infants were judged as having object permanence if they moved a blanket in order to retrieve a hidden object. You may recall from Chapter 4 that infants are unable to grasp and move objects in this way until they are 7 to 9 months old. Thus, Piaget's methods made it impossible to tell whether younger infants failed to exhibit object permanence because they were physically unable to perform the task of moving the blanket.

Thanks to the advent of computers, researchers have been able to measure infants' understanding of objects in ways that do not depend on motor skill development. In many post-Piagetian studies of object permanence, researchers have used computer technology to keep track of how infants' eyes respond when researchers move objects from one place to another. These "looking" studies have demonstrated that babies as young as 4 months show clear signs of object permanence if a visual response rather than a reaching response is used in the test (Baillargeon, 1987, 1994; Baillargeon & DeVos, 1991; Baillargeon, Spelke, & Wasserman, 1985). Moreover, many studies have examined how infants respond to a moving object that temporarily disappears behind a screen (e.g., Rosander & von Hofsten, 2004). In these studies, most 5-month-olds immediately looked to the other side of the screen when the moving object disappeared behind it and were delighted when it reappeared. These findings indicate that infants are holding some kind of representation of the hidden object in mind when it is behind the screen, the essence of object permanence. Nevertheless, such studies typically show that younger infants' understanding of object permanence is tied to the specific experimental situation. By contrast, babies who are nearing or past their first birthday understand object permanence sufficiently to use it across all kinds of situations, such as when they playfully hide objects from themselves and delight in "finding" them.

Findings like these have sparked renewed discussion of the nature-versus-nurture issue (e.g., Diamond, 1991; Fischer & Bidell, 1991; Karmiloff-Smith, 1991). Piaget assumed that a baby came equipped with a repertoire of sensorimotor schemes, but his most fundamental theoretical proposal was that the child constructed an understanding of the world based on experience. In contrast, recent theorizing suggests that the development of object permanence is more a process of elaboration than one of discovery. Newborns may have considerable awareness of objects as separate entities that follow certain rules (Valenza, Leo, Gava, & Simion, 2006). Certainly, all the research on the perception of patterns suggests that babies pay far more attention to relationships between events than Piaget's model supposed. Still, no one would argue that a baby came equipped with a full-fledged knowledge of objects or a well-developed ability to experiment with the world.

A-not-B error substage 4 infants' tendency to look for an object in the place where it was last seen (position A) rather than in the place to which they have seen a researcher move it (position B)

deferred imitation imitation that occurs in the absence of the model who first demonstrated it

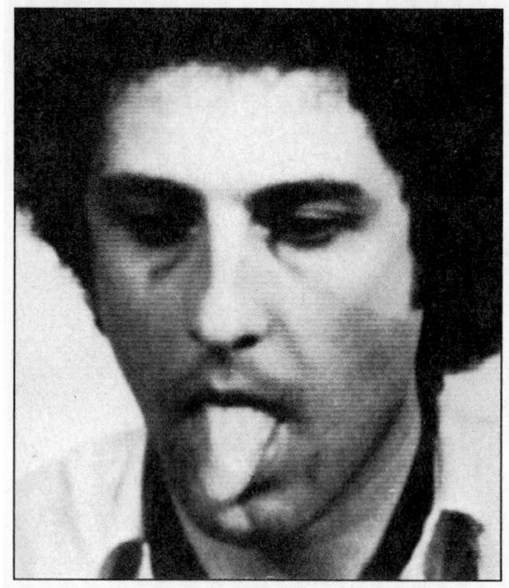

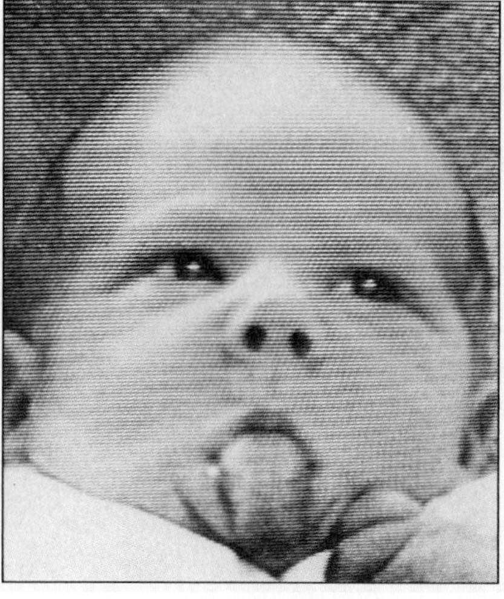

Figure 5.1 Imitation in Newborns

Although researchers still disagree on just how much newborns will imitate, everyone agrees that they will imitate the gesture of tongue protrusion, demonstrated here by Andrew Meltzoff from the earliest study of this kind.

(*Source*: From A. N. Meltzoff and M. K. Moore, "Imitation of facial and manual gestures by human neonates," *Science*, 198 (1977): 838–850. Reprinted by permission.)

Imitation With respect to imitation, Piaget's proposed sequence has been supported. Imitation of someone else's hand movement or an action with an object seems to improve steadily, starting at 1 or 2 months of age; imitation of two-part actions develops much later, perhaps around 15–18 months (Poulson, Nunes, & Warren, 1989). Yet there are two important exceptions to this general confirmation of Piaget's theory: Infants imitate some facial gestures in the first weeks of life, and deferred imitation seems to occur earlier than Piaget proposed.

Several researchers have found that newborn babies will imitate certain facial gestures—particularly tongue protrusion, as shown in Figure 5.1 (Anisfeld, 1991). This seems to happen only if the model sits with his tongue out, looking at the baby, for a fairly long period of time, perhaps as long as a minute. But the fact that newborns imitate at all is striking—although it is entirely consistent with the observation that quite young babies are capable of tactile-visual intermodal transfer, or perception.

Most studies of deferred imitation also support Piaget's model. However, some research indicates that infants as young as 6 weeks of age can defer imitation for at least a few minutes (Bremner, 2002). Moreover, studies show that babies as young as 9 months can defer their imitation for as long as 24 hours (Herbert, Gross, & Hayne, 2006; Meltzoff, 1988). By 14 months, toddlers can recall and imitate someone's actions as much as 2 days later (Hanna & Meltzoff, 1993).

These findings are significant for several reasons. First, they make it clear that infants can and do learn specific behaviors through modeling, even when they have no chance to imitate the behavior immediately. In addition, these results suggest that babies may be more skillful than Piaget thought. Clearly, too, more abilities than he suggested may be built in from the beginning and develop continuously, rather than in stages, throughout infancy (Courage & Howe, 2002).

Learning Objective 5.3

What does research tell us about infants' understanding of objects?

Alternative Approaches

The many challenges to Piaget's characterization of infant thinking have led some developmental researchers to investigate object permanence within the more general context of infants' understanding of what objects are and how they behave. Researchers use the term **object concept** to refer to this understanding. The most thorough and clever work on the development of the object concept has been done by Elizabeth Spelke and her colleagues (Spelke, 1982, 1985; Spelke, von Hofsten, & Kestenbaum, 1989). Spelke believes that babies are born with certain built-in assumptions that guide their interactions with objects. One of these is the assumption that when two surfaces are connected to each other, they belong to the same object; Spelke calls this the *connected surface principle*. For instance, you know that all sides of your textbook are connected together in a single, solid object.

object concept an infant's understanding of the nature of objects and how they behave

In Spelke's early studies of this phenomenon (e.g., Spelke, 1982), she first habituated some 3-month-old babies to a series of displays of two objects; other babies were habituated to the sight of one-object displays. Then the babies were shown two objects touching each other, such as two square blocks placed next to each other so that they created a rectangle. Under these conditions, the babies who had been habituated to two-object displays showed renewed interest, clearly indicating that they "saw" this display as different, presumably as a single object. Babies who had seen the one-object displays during habituation showed no renewed interest.

In later experiments, Spelke (1991) used the **violation of expectations method**, a research strategy in which an infant is habituated to a display that depicts the movement of an object and then is shown another display in which the object moves in a way that goes against what the infant expects to happen. She demonstrated that babies as young as 2 and 3 months old are remarkably aware of what kinds of movements objects are capable of. Two-month-old babies were repeatedly shown a series of events like the one shown schematically in the "familiarization" section in the upper part of Figure 5.2: A ball was rolled from the left-hand side to the right and disappeared behind a screen. The screen was then taken away, and the baby could see that the ball was stopped against the wall on the right. After the baby got bored looking at this sequence (habituated), he or she was tested with two variations, one "consistent" and one "inconsistent." In the consistent variation, a second wall was placed behind the screen and the sequence run as before, except that now when the screen was removed, the ball could be seen resting up against the nearer wall. In the inconsistent variation, the ball was surreptitiously placed on the far side of the new wall. When the screen was removed, the ball was visible in this presumably impossible place. Babies in this experiment were quite uninterested in the consistent condition but showed sharply renewed interest in the inconsistent condition, as you can see in the lower part of Figure 5.2, which shows the actual results of this experiment.

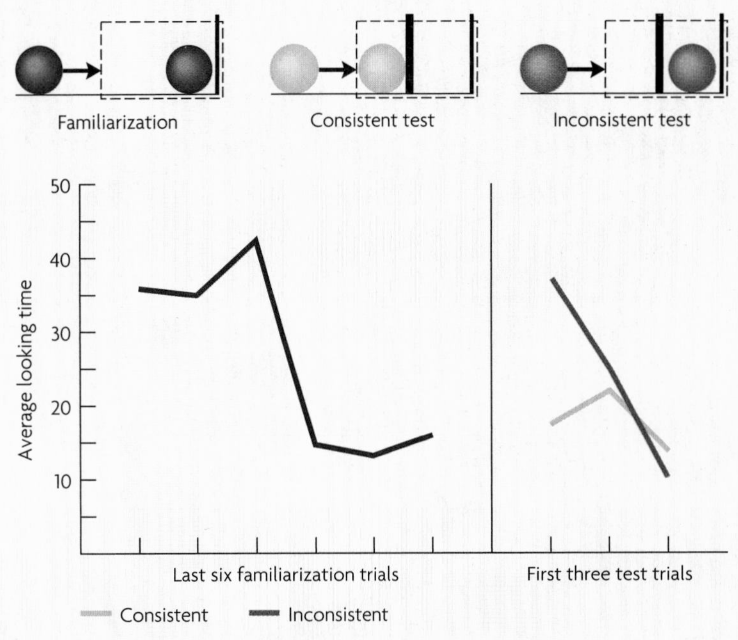

Figure 5.2 Spelke's Classic Study of Object Perception

The top part of the figure shows a schematic version of the three conditions Spelke used. The graph below shows the actual results. You can see that the babies stopped looking at the ball and screen after a number of familiarization trials, but they showed renewed interest in the inconsistent version—a sign that the babies saw it as somehow different or surprising. The very fact that the babies found the inconsistent trial surprising is evidence that infants as young as 2 months have far more knowledge about objects and their behavior than most developmentalists had thought.

(*Source*: Copyright © 1991. From "Physical Knowledge in Infancy: Reflections of Piaget's Theory," by E. S. Spelke, in S. Carey and R. Gelman (Eds.), *The Epigenesis of Mind: Essays on Biology and Cognition.* Reproduced by permission of Lawrence Erlbaum Associates Inc., a division of Taylor & Francis Group.)

violation of expectations method a research strategy in which researchers move an object in one way after having taught an infant to expect it to move in another

Other researchers, such as Renée Baillargeon (1994), argue that knowledge about objects is not built in, but that strategies for learning are innate. According to this view, infants initially develop basic hypotheses about the way objects function—how they move, how they connect to one another. Then these early basic hypotheses are quite rapidly modified based on the baby's experience with objects. For example, Baillargeon finds that 2- to 3-month-old infants are already operating with a basic hypothesis that an object will fall if it isn't supported by something, but they have no notion of how much support is required. By about 5 months of age, this basic hypothesis has been refined, so they understand that the smiling-face block in part (a) of Figure 5.3 will stay supported but the block in part (b) will not (Baillargeon, 1994).

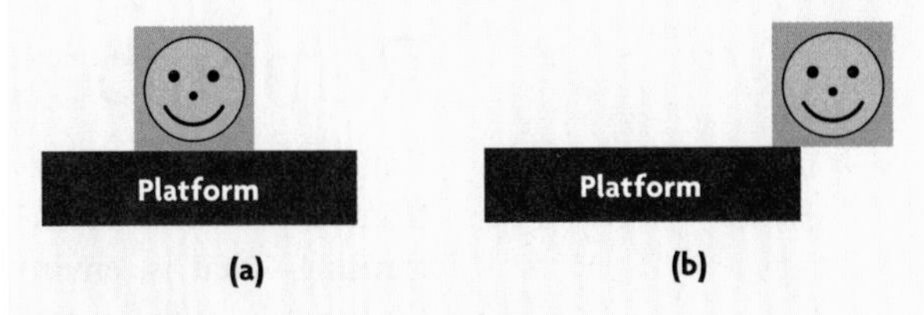

Figure 5.3 Baillargeon's Study of Object Stability Perception

Renée Baillargeon's research suggests that 2- and 3-month-old babies think that the smiling-face block will not fall under either of these conditions, but by 5 months, they realize that only the condition shown in (a) is stable. In condition (b), the block will fall.

(*Source*: From "How Do Infants Learn About the Physical World?" by Renée Baillargeon, *Current Directions in Psychological Science*, Vol. 3, No. 5 (October 1994), p. 134, Fig. 1. Reprinted by permission.)

Figure 5.4 **Toddler's Understanding of Object Movement**

Researchers use devices such as this one to find out whether toddlers can predict that a moving object will be stopped by the barrier that protrudes above the wall of doors. Children younger than 3 typically fail to identify the door behind which the object will be found.

However, other psychologists question Baillargeon's conclusions. For example, developmental psychologist Leslie Cohen and his associates have conducted similar experiments with 8-month-olds and argue that infants respond to the stimuli used in such studies on the basis of novelty, rather than because of an understanding of stable and unstable block arrangements (Cashon & Cohen, 2000). Such varying interpretations demonstrate just how difficult it is to make inferences about infants' thinking from their interactions with physical objects.

Recent research has also examined the degree to which infants can make practical use of their understanding of objects and object movement. For example, several studies have shown that 2-year-olds experience difficulty when they are required to use this understanding to search for a hidden object (Keen, 2003). In one study, 2-, 2.5-, and 3-year-olds were shown displays similar to those in the top portion of Figure 5.2 and responded in exactly the same way as younger infants to the consistent and inconsistent displays (Berthier, DeBlois, Poirier, Novak, & Clifton, 2000). Next, a board in which there were several doors took the place of the screen; however, the barrier protruded several inches above this board (see Figure 5.4). Across several trials, children were shown the ball rolling behind the board and were asked to open the door behind which they thought the ball would be found. Even though the children could clearly see behind which door the barrier was placed in every trial, none of the 2-year-olds and only a few of the 2.5-year-olds were able to succeed at this task, in contrast to the large majority of 3-year-olds. Developmentalists interpret such results to mean that young infants' understanding of objects is the foundation upon which the object concept is gradually constructed and applied to real-world interaction with objects over the first 3 years of life (Keen, 2003).

Learning, Categorizing, and Remembering

Generally, the term *learning* is used to denote permanent changes in behavior that result from experience. From the first moments following birth, babies exhibit evidence of learning—that is, environmental forces change their behaviors. However, babies also actively organize their interactions with these forces, as research examining categorization and memory clearly shows.

Learning Objective 5.4

When are babies able to learn through classical conditioning, operant conditioning, and observing models?

Conditioning and Modeling

Learning of emotional responses through classical conditioning processes may begin as early as the first week of life. For example, in classic research, pediatrician Mavis Gunther (1955, 1961) found that inexperienced mothers often held nursing newborns in ways that caused the babies' nostrils to be blocked by the breast. Predictably, the babies reflexively turned away from the breast in response to the sensation of smothering. During future nursing sessions, babies who had experienced the smothering sensation while nursing at their mother's right breast refused to nurse on the right side; babies who had associated the smothering sensation with the left breast displayed the opposite pattern of refusal. Gunther hypothesized that classical conditioning was at work in such cases. She developed an intervention based on principles of stimulus-response learning to help babies "unlearn" the response of turning away from the breast they had learned to associate with the sensation of smothering.

Newborns also clearly learn by operant conditioning. Both the sucking and the head-turning response have been increased by the use of reinforcements such as sweet liquids or the sound of the mother's voice or heartbeat (Moon & Fifer, 1990). At the least, the fact that conditioning of this kind can take place means that the neurological wiring needed for operant learning is present at birth. Results like these also tell developmentalists something about which reinforcements are effective with very young children; it is surely highly significant for the mother-infant interaction that the mother's voice is an effective reinforcer for virtually all babies.

Infants can also learn by watching models, especially in their second year. In one study, 10- and 12-month-olds were randomly assigned to two learning groups (Provasi, Dubon, & Bloch, 2001). "Observers" first watched an adult demonstrate how to find a toy by lifting the lids of various containers and then were allowed to play with the containers. "Actors" played with the containers on their own. Researchers found that in both age groups observers were more proficient than actors at finding the toy. However, the effect was much more pronounced among the older infants.

Schematic Learning

Learning Objective 5.5

How does categorical understanding change over the first 2 years?

Schematic learning is the organizing of experiences into expectancies, or "known" combinations. These expectancies, often called *schemas*, are built up over many exposures to particular experiences. Once formed, they help the baby to distinguish between the familiar and the unfamiliar.

One kind of schematic learning involves categories. Research suggests that by 7 months of age, and perhaps even earlier, infants actively use categories to process information (Pauen, 2000). For example, a 7-month-old is likely to habituate to a sequence of 10 animal pictures and, if the next picture is of another animal, will not show surprise or look at it any longer than the first 10. If, however, researchers show the baby a picture of a human after 10 animal pictures, the baby will look surprised and gaze at the picture longer. The same thing is likely to happen if researchers show an infant several pictures of humans and then switch to an animal picture.

Such findings suggest that infants build and use categories as they take in information. However, categorical organization as a cognitive tool is not well developed in 7-month-olds. For one thing, infants of this age clearly do not understand the difference between lower-level and higher-level categories. "Dogs" and "animals," for example, can both be thought of as categories, but the higher-level one ("animals") includes the lower-level one. Thus, categories such as "animals" are referred to as *superordinates*. Researchers have found that infants respond to superordinate categories before they display reactions to basic-level categories (Pauen, 2002). In other words, 7- or 8-month-olds view "animals" and "furniture" as different categories, but not "dogs" and "birds." By contrast, 12-month-olds appear to understand both types of categories.

Still, 12-month-olds don't yet know that basic-level categories such as "dogs" and "birds" are nested within the superordinate category "animals." The concept that smaller categories are nested within larger ones, or *hierarchical categorization*, is demonstrated to some degree by 2-year-olds (Diesendruck & Shatz, 2001). However, full understanding of this kind of categorization is not typical until age 5 or so and is linked to language development and experiences with using words as category labels (Malabonga & Pasnak, 2002; Omiya & Uchida, 2002).

schematic learning organization of experiences into expectancies, called schemas, which enable infants to distinguish between familiar and unfamiliar stimuli

Learning Objective 5.6

How does memory function in the first 2 years?

Memory

You have probably heard that it is impossible to form memories while you are sleeping, so playing tapes of your textbook while you sleep is not likely to help you perform well on your next exam. However, newborns do appear to be able to remember auditory stimuli to which they are exposed while sleeping (Cheour et al., 2002). This is just one of several interesting characteristics of infant memory.

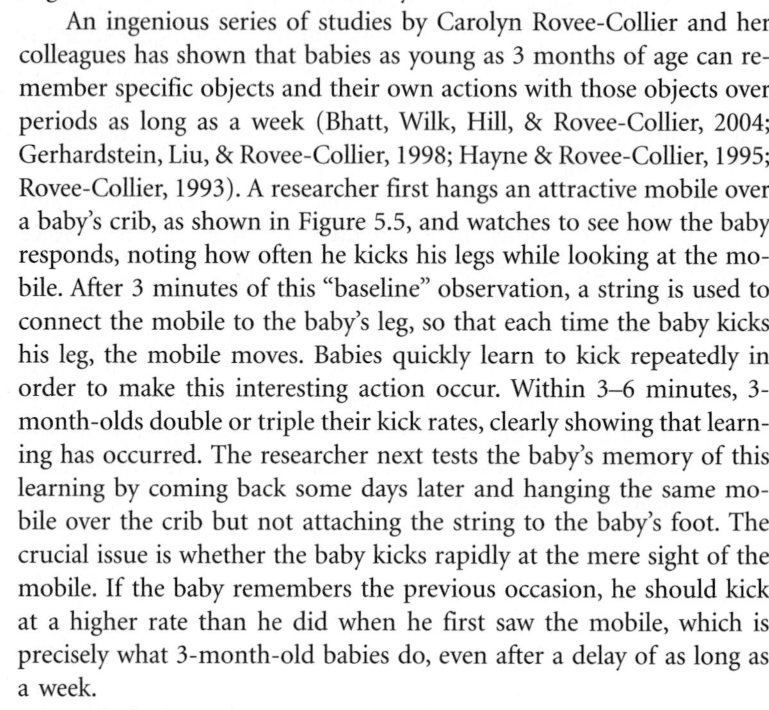

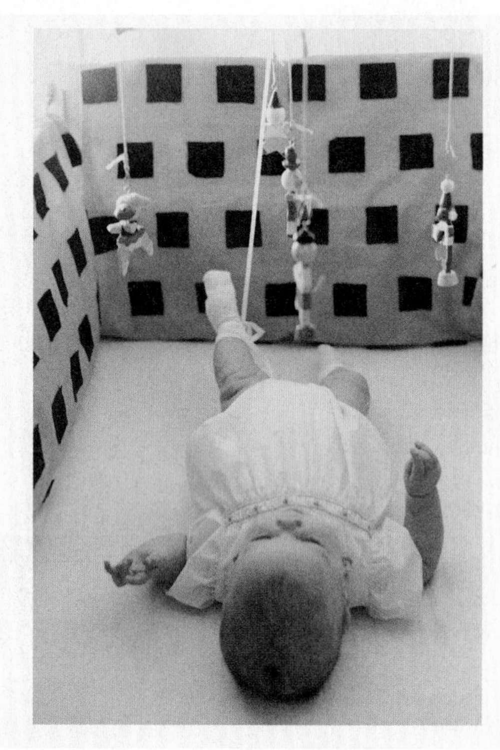

Figure 5.5 Rovee-Collier's Study of Infant Memory

This 3-month-old baby in one of Rovee-Collier's memory experiments will quickly learn to kick her foot in order to make the mobile move. And several days later, she will remember this connection between kicking and the mobile.

(*Source*: Rovee-Collier, "The capacity for long-term memory in infancy," *Current Directions in Psychological Science*, 2, 1993, p. 131. Reprinted by permission.)

An ingenious series of studies by Carolyn Rovee-Collier and her colleagues has shown that babies as young as 3 months of age can remember specific objects and their own actions with those objects over periods as long as a week (Bhatt, Wilk, Hill, & Rovee-Collier, 2004; Gerhardstein, Liu, & Rovee-Collier, 1998; Hayne & Rovee-Collier, 1995; Rovee-Collier, 1993). A researcher first hangs an attractive mobile over a baby's crib, as shown in Figure 5.5, and watches to see how the baby responds, noting how often he kicks his legs while looking at the mobile. After 3 minutes of this "baseline" observation, a string is used to connect the mobile to the baby's leg, so that each time the baby kicks his leg, the mobile moves. Babies quickly learn to kick repeatedly in order to make this interesting action occur. Within 3–6 minutes, 3-month-olds double or triple their kick rates, clearly showing that learning has occurred. The researcher next tests the baby's memory of this learning by coming back some days later and hanging the same mobile over the crib but not attaching the string to the baby's foot. The crucial issue is whether the baby kicks rapidly at the mere sight of the mobile. If the baby remembers the previous occasion, he should kick at a higher rate than he did when he first saw the mobile, which is precisely what 3-month-old babies do, even after a delay of as long as a week.

Such findings demonstrate that the young infant is more cognitively sophisticated than developmentalists (and Piaget) had supposed. At the same time, these studies support Piaget's view that infants show systematic gains in the ability to remember over the months of infancy. Two-month-olds can remember their kicking action for only 1 day, 3-month-olds can remember it for over a week, and 6-month-olds can remember it longer than 2 weeks.

However, early infant memories are strongly tied to the specific context in which the original experience occurred (Barr, Marrott, & Rovee-Collier, 2003; Bhatt et al., 2004; Houston & Jusczyk, 2003). Even 6-month-olds do not recognize or remember the mobile if the context is changed even slightly—for example, by hanging a different cloth around the crib in which the infant is tested. However, Rovee-Collier and her colleagues have also learned that lost infant memories can be "reactivated" with the use of cues that remind the baby of the association between a behavior, such as kicking, and a stimulus, such as a mobile (Bearce & Rovee-Collier, 2006). Thus, babies do remember more than Piaget believed, but their memories are highly specific. With age, their memories become less and less tied to specific cues or contexts.

The Beginnings of Language

Most of us think of "language" as beginning when the baby uses her first words, at about 12 months of age. But all sorts of important developments precede the first words. Before we look at these developments, though, we'll look at the various theoretical perspectives that try to explain them.

Theoretical Perspectives

> **Learning Objective 5.7**
> What are the behaviorist, nativist, and interactionist explanations of language development?

The nature-nurture debate is alive and well in discussions of language development. The child's amazing progress in this domain in the early years of life has been explained from both behaviorist and nativist points of view and as part of the larger process of cognitive development.

The Behaviorist View In the late 1950s, B. F. Skinner, the scientist who formulated operant conditioning theory, suggested a behaviorist explanation of language development (Skinner, 1957). He claimed that language development begins with babbling. While babbling, babies accidentally make sounds that somewhat resemble real words as spoken by their parents. Parents hear the word-like sounds and respond to them with praise and encouragement, which serve as reinforcers. Thus, word-like babbling becomes more frequent, while utterances that do not resemble words gradually disappear from babies' vocalizations. Skinner further hypothesized that parents and others respond to grammatical uses of words and do not respond to nongrammatical ones. As a result, correct grammar is reinforced and becomes more frequent, but incorrect grammar is extinguished through nonreinforcement.

At first glance, Skinner's theory might appear to make sense. However, systematic examination of the interactions between infants and parents reveals that adults do not reinforce babies' vocalizations in this manner. Instead, parents and others respond to all of a baby's vocalizations and even sometimes imitate them—a consequence that, according to operant conditioning theory, should prolong babbling rather than lead to the development of grammatical language. Skinner's mistake was that his theory was not based on observations of language development but rather on his assumption that the principles of operant conditioning underlie all human learning and development. Of course, findings that challenge Skinner's extreme views do not mean that the environment has no effect on language development. Language activities such as reading aloud contribute to children's linguistic proficiency (see *Developmental Science in the Classroom*).

DEVELOPMENTAL SCIENCE IN THE CLASSROOM

The Importance of Reading to Toddlers

Greg is a certified early childhood educator. When he was pursuing his degree, he assumed that he would be teaching kindergartners, so he developed an impressive repertoire of strategies for teaching pre-literacy skills to 4- and 5-year-olds. However, the only job that he was offered after graduation was one that required him to spend half of each day teaching a group of 2-year-olds from low-income homes. Now he is wondering how he can utilize his pre-literacy training with such young children.

Greg might be surprised to learn that 2-year-olds enjoy and benefit from many of the same pre-literacy activities as older preschoolers. For instance, a classic series of studies by G. J. Whitehurst and his colleagues suggests that interactive reading can have powerful effects on a toddler's language development. In their first study, Whitehurst's team of researchers trained some parents to read picture books to their toddlers and to interact with them using a strategy Whitehurst calls *dialogic reading*, which involves the use of questions that can't be answered by pointing (Whitehurst et al., 1988). For example, a parent reading a story about Winnie the Pooh might say, "There's Eeyore. What's happening to him?" Other parents were encouraged to read to their children, but were given no special instructions about how to read. After a month, the children who had experienced dialogic reading showed a larger gain in vocabulary than did the children in the comparison group.

Whitehurst later replicated this study in day-care centers for poor children in both Mexico and New York City and in a large number of Head Start classrooms (Valdez-Menchaca & Whitehurst, 1992; Whitehurst et al., 1994; Whitehurst, Fischel, Crone, & Nania, 1995). Greg can put Whitehurst's findings to work in his classroom by engaging in dialogic reading with his young pupils. In the process, he will provide an important bridge between spoken and written language for children who will face the developmental task of acquiring literacy in just a few short years.

Questions for Reflection

1. What would you say to a person who claimed that reading to infants or toddlers was a waste of time because of their limited language skills?
2. If a toddler doesn't want to be read to, do you think his parents or teachers should try to get him interested in books? If so, how do you think they should go about it?

The Nativist View Have you ever heard a child say "I breaked it" instead of "I broke it" or "foots" instead of "feet"? Such utterances constitute the biggest challenge to behaviorists' explanations of language development, because there is no way that they could be acquired through imitation. Moreover, when parents correct these errors, children often persist in using them or further overregularize them (e.g., "I broked it" or "feets"). Linguist Noam Chomsky used examples such as these to refute Skinner's theory (Chomsky, 1959). Chomsky argued that the only possible explanation for such errors was that children acquire grammar rules before they master the exceptions to them. Further, Chomsky proposed a nativist explanation for language development: Children's comprehension and production of language are guided by an innate language processor that he called the **language acquisition device (LAD)**, which contains the basic grammatical structure of all human language. In effect, the LAD tells infants what characteristics of language to look for in the stream of speech to which they are exposed. Simply put, the LAD tells babies that there are two basic types of sounds—consonants and vowels—and enables them to properly divide the speech they hear into the two categories so that they can analyze and learn the sounds that are specific to the language they are hearing. Chomsky supported the existence of the LAD with evidence compiled over hundreds of years by field linguists, which demonstrated that all human languages have the same grammatical forms. He also argued that the LAD is species-specific—that is, nonhuman species do not have one and, therefore, cannot learn grammatical language.

Another influential nativist, Dan Slobin (1985a, 1985b), proposed that babies are preprogrammed to pay attention to the beginnings and endings of strings of sounds and to stressed sounds—a hypothesis supported by research (e.g., Morgan, 1994). Together, these operating principles would help to explain some of the features of children's early grammar. In English, for example, the stressed words in a sentence are normally the verb and the noun—precisely the words that English-speaking children use in their earliest sentences. In Turkish, on the other hand, prefixes and suffixes are stressed, and Turkish-speaking children learn both very early. Both of these patterns make sense if we assume that the preprogrammed rule is not "verbness" or "nounness" or "prefixness" but "pay attention to stressed sounds."

The Interactionist View Clearly, nativist explanations like those of Chomsky and Slobin are more consistent than Skinner's view with both research findings and our everyday communication experiences with young children. Even so, some theorists argue that language development is part of the broader process of cognitive development and is influenced by both internal and external factors. These theorists are known as **interactionists**. There are two common threads that run through the interactionists' theories. First, interactionists believe that infants are born with some kind of biological preparedness to pay more attention to language than to other kinds of information. Second, interactionists argue that, rather than having a neurological module that is specific to language (i.e., an LAD), the infant's brain has a generalized set of tools that it employs across all of the subdomains of cognitive development. These tools allow infants to extract general principles from all kinds of specific experiences, including those that they have with language. Consequently, some interactionists argue that the nativists have paid too little attention to the role that the social context plays in language development (Tomasello, 1999), while others point out that nativist theories fail to capture the degree to which language and cognition develop interdependently (Bowerman, 1985).

One prominent proponent of this interdependent view, Melissa Bowerman, puts the proposition this way: "When language starts to come in, it does not introduce new meanings to the child. Rather, it is used to express only those meanings the child has already formulated independently of language" (1985, p. 372). Even more broadly, Lois Bloom argues that from the beginning of language, the child's intent is to communicate, to share the ideas and concepts in his head. He does this as best he can with the gestures or words he knows, and he learns new words when they help him communicate his thoughts and feelings (1993, 1997; Bloom & Tinker, 2001).

One type of evidence in support of this argument comes from the observation that it is children, not mothers, who initiate the majority of verbal exchanges (Bloom, 1997). Further evidence comes from studies showing links between achievements in language development

language acquisition device (LAD) an innate language processor, theorized by Chomsky, that contains the basic grammatical structure of all human language

interactionists theorists who argue that language development is a subprocess of general cognitive development and is influenced by both internal and external factors and the child's broader cognitive development. For example, symbolic play, such as drinking from an empty cup, and imitation of sounds and gestures both appear at about the same time as the child's first words, suggesting some broad "symbolic" understanding that is reflected in a number of behaviors. In children whose language is significantly delayed, both symbolic play and imitation are usually delayed as well (Bates, O'Connell, & Shore, 1987; Ungerer & Sigman, 1984).

A second example occurs later: At about the point at which two-word sentences appear, we also see children begin to combine several gestures into a sequence in their pretend play, such as pouring imaginary liquid, drinking, and then wiping the mouth. Those children who are the first to show this sequencing in their play are also the first to show two- or three-word sentences in their speech (e.g., McCune, 1995; Shore, 1986).

Influences on Language Development

Learning Objective 5.8

What are some of the environmental influences on language development?

Developmentalists now understand how the environment influences language development better than they did when Skinner and Chomsky began their historic debate in the 1950s. Moreover, the increasing emphasis on the interactionist approach has led researchers to examine the kinds of environmental influences to which children are exposed during different phases of language development. For example, adults and older children speak differently to infants than they do to preschoolers, a way of speaking that researchers call **infant-directed speech (IDS)**. This pattern of speech is characterized by a higher pitch than that which is exhibited by adults and children when they are not speaking to an infant. Moreover, adults speaking to infants and young children repeat a lot, introducing minor variations ("Where is the ball? Can you see the ball? Where is the ball? There is the ball!"). They may also repeat the child's own sentences but in slightly longer, more grammatically correct forms—a pattern referred to as an *expansion* or a *recasting*. For example, if a child said "Mommy sock," the mother might recast it as "Yes, this is Mommy's sock," or if a child said "Doggie not eating," the parent might say "The doggie is not eating."

We also know that babies as young as a few days old can discriminate between IDS and adult-directed speech and that they prefer IDS, whether it is spoken by a female or a male voice (Cooper & Aslin, 1994; Pegg, Werker, & McLeod, 1992). This preference exists even when IDS is being spoken in a language other than the one normally spoken to the child. Janet Werker and her colleagues (1994), for example, have found that both English and Chinese infants prefer to listen to infant-directed speech, whether it is spoken in English or in Cantonese (one of the major languages of China). Other studies by Werker indicate that IDS helps infants identify the sounds in their mothers' speech that are specific to the language they are learning (e.g., the English schwa, the Spanish rolled *r*) by emphasizing those sounds more than others (Werker et al., 2007).

Infant-directed speech may also be important to grammar development. The quality of IDS that seems to be particularly attractive to babies is its high pitch. Once the child's attention is drawn by this special tone, the very simplicity and repetitiveness of the adult's speech may help the child to pick out repeating grammatical forms. Children's attention also seems to be drawn to recast sentences. For example, Farrar (1992) found that a 2-year-old was two or three times more likely to imitate a correct grammatical form when he heard his mother recast his own sentences than when the mother used that same correct grammatical form in her normal conversation. Experimental studies confirm this effect of recastings. Children who are deliberately exposed to higher rates of specific types of recast sentences seem to learn the modeled grammatical forms more quickly than those who hear no recastings (Nelson, 1977).

Developmentalists also know that children whose parents talk to them often, read to them regularly, and use a wide range of words in their speech differ from children whose parents do not. These children begin to talk sooner, develop larger vocabularies, use more complex sentences, and learn to read more readily when they reach school age (Hart & Risley, 1995; Huttenlocher, 1995; Snow, 1997). Thus, the sheer quantity of language a child hears is a significant factor.

infant-directed speech (IDS) the simplified, high-pitched speech used by adults with infants and young children

Finally, poverty is related to language development. By age 4, the difference in vocabulary between poor and better-off children is already substantial, and the gap only widens over the school years. Catherine Snow (1997) found that 4-year-old children reared in poverty use shorter and less complex sentences than do their better-off peers. Many factors no doubt contribute to these differences, but the richness and variety of the language a child hears are obviously highly significant. Of all these factors, how often a child is read to may be one of the most critical.

Learning Objective 5.9

How do infants' sounds, gestures, and understanding of words change in the early months of life?

Early Milestones of Language Development

From birth to about 1 month of age, the sound an infant makes most commonly is a cry, although she also produces other fussing, gurgling, and satisfied sounds. Over the next few months, the number of ways in which a baby can express herself expands tremendously. Although some of these may seem to be of little consequence, each of the early milestones of language development makes a unique contribution to the language skills that all healthy children achieve in the first few years of life.

First Sounds and Gestures At about 1 or 2 months, the baby begins to make some laughing and **cooing** vowel sounds. Sounds like this are usually signals of pleasure and may exhibit a lot of variation in tone, running up and down in volume or pitch. Consonant sounds appear at about 6 or 7 months, frequently combined with vowel sounds to make a kind of syllable. Babies of this age seem to play with these sounds, often repeating the same sound over and over (such as *babababababa* or *dahdahdah*). This sound pattern is called **babbling**, and it makes up about half of babies' noncrying sounds from about 6 to 12 months of age (Mitchell & Kent, 1990).

Any parent can tell you that babbling is a delight to listen to. It also seems to be an important part of the preparation for spoken language. For one thing, infants' babbling gradually acquires some of what linguists call the intonational pattern of the language they are hearing—a process one developmental psychologist refers to as "learning the tune before the words" (Bates et al., 1987). Infants do seem to develop at least two such "tunes" in their babbling: babbling with a rising intonation at the end of a string of sounds seems to signal a desire for a response, while a falling intonation requires no response.

Gestures are just one of several skills in infants' repertoire of communicative skills.

A second important thing about babbling is that when babies first start babbling, they typically babble all kinds of sounds, including some that are not part of the language they are hearing. But at about 9 or 10 months, their sound repertoire gradually begins to narrow down to the set of sounds they are listening to, with the nonheard sounds dropping out (Oller, 1981). Findings like these do not prove that babbling is necessary for language development, but they certainly make it look as if babbling is part of a connected developmental process that begins at birth.

Another part of that process appears to be a kind of gestural language that develops at around 9 or 10 months. At this age, babies begin "demanding" or "asking" for things using gestures or combinations of gestures and sound. A 10-month-old baby who apparently wants you to hand her a favorite toy may stretch and reach for it, opening and closing her hand while making whining or whimpering sounds. Interestingly, infants of this age use gestures in this way whether they are exposed to spoken language or sign language. At about the same age, babies enter into those gestural games much loved by parents: "pat-a-cake," "soooo big," and "wave bye-bye" (Bates, O'Connell, & Shore, 1987).

cooing repetitive vocalizing of vowel sounds, particularly the *uuu* sound

babbling repetitive vocalizing of consonant-vowel combinations by an infant

Word Recognition Recent research has shown that babies begin to store individual words in their memories at around 8 months of age (Jusczyk & Hohne, 1997). By 9 or 10 months, most can understand the meanings of 20–30 words; this ability to understand words is known as **receptive language.** In the next few months, the number of words understood increases dramatically. In one investigation, researchers asked hundreds of mothers about their babies' understanding of various words. Reportedly, 10-month-olds understood an average of about 30 words; for 13-month-olds, the number was nearly 100 words (Fenson et al., 1994).

These babies probably haven't yet spoken their first words, but chances are they already understand quite a few. Receptive language usually develops before expressive language.

But how do babies separate a single word from the constant flow of speech to which they are exposed? Many linguists have proposed that a child can cope with the monumentally complex task of word learning only because he applies some built-in biases or *constraints* (Baldwin, 1995; Golinkoff, Mervis, & Hirsh-Pasek, 1994; Jusczyk & Hohne 1997; Markman, 1992; Waxman & Kosowski, 1990). For example, the child may have a built-in assumption that words refer to objects or actions but not both.

Learning a language's patterns of word stress may also help babies identify words. Recent research suggests that infants discriminate between stressed and unstressed syllables fairly early—around 7 months of age—and use syllable stress as a cue to identify single words (Jusczyk, Houston, & Newsome, 1999). For example, first-syllable stress, such as in the word *market*, is far more common in English than second-syllable stress, such as in the word *garage*. Thus, when English-learning infants hear a stressed syllable, they may assume that a new word is beginning. This strategy would help them single out a very large number of individual English words.

All of this information reveals a series of changes that seem to converge by 9 or 10 months: the beginning of meaningful gestures, the drift of babbling toward the heard language sounds, imitative gestural games, and the first comprehension of individual words. It is as if the child now understands something about the process of communication and is intending to communicate to adults.

The First Words

Learning Objective 5.10

What are the characteristics of toddlers' first words?

If you have ever studied another language, you probably understood the language before you could produce it yourself. Likewise, the 9- to 10-month-old infant understands far more words than she can say. **Expressive language**—the ability to produce, as well as understand and respond to, meaningful words—typically appears at about 12 or 13 months (Fenson et al., 1994). The baby's first word is an event that parents eagerly await, but it's fairly easy to miss. A word, as linguists usually define it, is any sound or set of sounds that is used consistently to refer to some thing, action, or quality. This means that a child who uses *ba* consistently to refer to her bottle is using a word, even though it isn't considered a word in English.

Often, a child's earliest words are used in specific situations and in the presence of many cues. The child may say "bow-wow" or "doggie" only in response to such promptings as "How does the doggie go?" or "What's that?" Typically, this early word learning is very slow, requiring many repetitions for each word. In the first 6 months of word usage, children may learn as few as 30 words. Most linguists have concluded that this earliest word-use phase involves learning each word as something connected to a set of specific contexts. What the child has apparently not yet grasped is that words are symbolic—they refer to objects or events.

Very young children often combine a single word with a gesture to create a "two-word meaning" before they use two words together in their speech. For example, a child may point to his father's shoe and say "Daddy," as if to convey "Daddy's shoe" (Bates et al., 1987). In such cases, meaning is conveyed by the use of gesture and body language combined with a word.

receptive language comprehension of spoken language

expressive language the ability to use sounds, signs, or symbols to communicate meaning

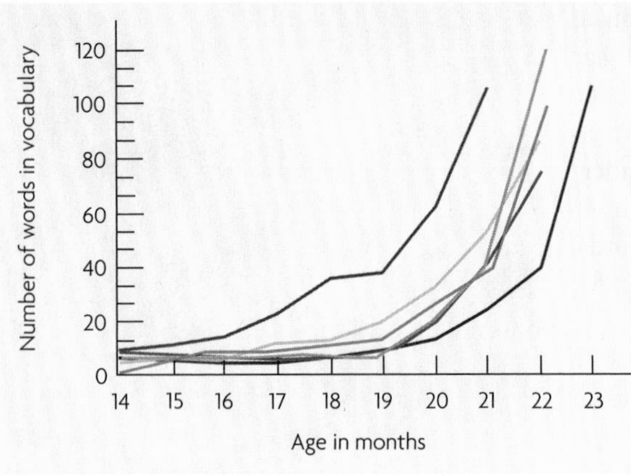

Figure 5.6 Vocabulary Growth in the Second Year

Each of the lines in this figure represents the vocabulary growth of one of the children studied longitudinally by Goldfield and Reznick. The six children shown here each acquired new words in the most common pattern: slow initial growth followed by a fairly rapid spurt.

(*Source*: Adaptation of Table 3, "Early Lexical Acquisition: Rate, Content, and the Vocabulary Spurt," by B. Goldfield and J. Reznick, in *Journal of Child Language, 17*, pp. 171–183. Reprinted with permission of Cambridge University Press.)

Linguists call these word-and-gesture combinations **holophrases**, and children use them frequently between 12 and 18 months of age.

Between 16 and 24 months, after the early period of very slow word learning, most children begin to add new words rapidly, as if they have figured out that things have names. Developmentalists refer to this period as the **naming explosion**. In this period, children seem to learn new words with very few repetitions, and they generalize these words to many more situations. According to one large cross-sectional study based on mothers' reports, the average 16-month-old has a speaking vocabulary of about 50 words; for a 24-month-old, the total has grown to about 320 words (Fenson et al., 1994).

For most children, the naming explosion is not a steady, gradual process; instead, vocabulary "spurts" begin at about the time the child has acquired 50 words. This pattern, observed by several researchers, is illustrated in Figure 5.6, which shows the vocabulary growth curves of six children studied longitudinally (Bloom, 1993; Goldfield & Reznick, 1990). Not all children show precisely this pattern, but a rapid increase over a period of a few months is typical.

THE WHOLE CHILD IN FOCUS

How did Federico use his budding language skills at the playground? Find out on page 179.

Most observers agree that the bulk of new words learned during this early period of rapid vocabulary growth are names for things or people: *ball, car, milk, doggie, he.* Action words tend to appear later (Gleitman & Gleitman, 1992). One study involving a large group of children suggested that as many as two-thirds of the words children knew by age 2 were nouns, and only 8.5% were verbs (Fenson et al., 1994). It appears that infants lack the ability to consistently associate words with actions until about 18 months of age (Casasola & Cohen, 2000). Recent cross-linguistic research also suggests that, compared to Korean-speaking parents, English-speaking parents emphasize nouns more than verbs in speaking and reading to infants (Choi, 2000). Thus, the pattern of learning nouns before verbs may be influenced by the characteristics of the language being learned, as well as by the behavior of mature speakers as they speak to infants.

Learning Objective 5.11

What kinds of sentences do children produce between 18 and 24 months of age?

The First Sentences

Research suggests that sentences appear when a child has reached a threshold vocabulary of around 100 to 200 words (Fenson et al., 1994). For most children, this threshold is crossed at between 18 and 24 months of age. Their first sentences have several distinguishing features: They are short, generally two or three words, and they are simple. Language development researcher Roger Brown coined the term **telegraphic speech** to refer to this pattern (Brown & Bellugi, 1964). Nouns, verbs, and adjectives are usually included, but virtually all grammatical markers (which linguists call **inflections**) are missing. At the beginning, for example, children learning English do not normally use the *-s* ending for plurals or put the *-ed* ending on verbs to make the past tense.

It is also clear that even at this earliest stage children create sentences following rules—not adult rules, to be sure, but rules nonetheless. They focus on certain types of words and put them together in particular orders. They also manage to convey a variety of different meanings with their simple sentences. For example, young children frequently use a sentence made up of two nouns, such as *Mommy sock* or *sweater chair* (Bloom, 1973). The child who says "Mommy sock" may mean either *This is Mommy's sock* or *Mommy is putting a sock on my foot* (Bloom, 1973). Thus, to understand what a child means by a two-word sentence, it is necessary to know the context in which it occurred.

holophrases combinations of gestures and single words used to convey more meaning than can be conveyed by just the word alone

naming explosion the period when toddlers experience rapid vocabulary growth, typically beginning between 16 and 24 months

telegraphic speech simple two-word sentences that usually include a noun and a verb

inflections additions to words that change their meaning (e.g., the *s* in toys, the *ed* in waited)

Table 5.2 Language Development in the First Two Years

Age	Milestone
2–3 months	Makes cooing sounds when alone; responds with smiles and cooing when talked to
6 months	Babbles; utters phonemes of all languages
9–10 months	Focuses on the phonemes, rhythm, and intonation of the language spoken in the home; has a receptive vocabulary of 20 to 30 words
12 months	Expressive language emerges; says single words
12–18 months	Uses word-gesture combinations and variations in intonation (holophrases)
18–24 months	Uses two-word sentences (telegraphic speech); expressive vocabulary grows from 100 to 300+ words

Individual Differences in Language Development

Learning Objective 5.12

What kinds of individual differences are evident in language development?

The sequences of development of language you've read about (shown in Table 5.2) are accurate on the average, but the speed with which children acquire language skills varies widely. One factor influencing this rate is the number of languages to which a child has daily exposure (see *Developmental Science at Home*). There also seem to be important style differences.

DEVELOPMENTAL SCIENCE AT HOME

One Language or Two?

Juan and Luisa, a Mexican American couple, are the proud parents of a 3-month-old girl. Both are fluent in Spanish and English, and they want to use both languages in their home so that their daughter will be bilingual as well. Juan and Luisa know that being bilingual is of enormous value to adults, but, knowing that language and cognitive development are interrelated, they wonder whether bilingualism will hamper their daughter's intellectual development in any way.

Research suggests that there are cognitive advantages and disadvantages to growing up bilingual. On the positive side, being bilingual seems to have no impact on early language milestones such as babbling (Oller, Eilers, Urbano, & Cobo-Lewis, 1997). Also, infants in bilingual homes readily discriminate between the two languages both phonologically and grammatically from the earliest days of life (Bosch & Sebastian-Galles, 1997; Holowka, Brosseau-Lapré, & Petitto, 2002; Koeppe, 1996). In preschool and elementary school children, being bilingual is associated with a clear advantage in metalinguistic ability, the capacity to think about language (Bialystok, Shenfield, & Codd, 2000; Mohanty & Perregaux, 1997).

On the negative side, infants in bilingual homes reach some milestones later than those learning a single language. For example, bilingual infants' receptive and expressive vocabularies are as large as those of monolingual infants, but the words they know are divided between two languages (Patterson, 1998). Consequently, they are behind monolingual infants in word knowledge no matter which language is considered, a difference that persists into the school years. In addition, most children do not attain equal fluency in both languages (Hakansson, Salameh, & Nettelbladt, 2003). As a result, they tend to think more slowly in the language in which they are less fluent (Bernardo & Calleja, 2005; Chincotta & Underwood, 1997). When the language in which they are less fluent is the language in which their schooling is conducted, they are at risk for learning problems (Anderson, 1998; Thorn & Gathercole, 1999). Therefore, parents who choose to speak two languages with their infants should probably take into account their ability to fully support the children's acquisition of fluency in both languages.

Clearly, the advantages in adulthood of being bilingual are substantial, and these advantages may outweigh any disadvantages experienced in childhood. Bilingual parents need to balance the various advantages and disadvantages, as well as their long-term parenting goals, to reach an informed decision about the kind of linguistic environment to provide for their infants and children.

Questions for Reflection

1. What kind of linguistic environment would you provide for your child if you were in the same position as Juan and Luisa?
2. In your opinion, how likely is it that the little girl will achieve her parents' goal of fluency in two languages? What factors will influence her eventual level of fluency in each language?

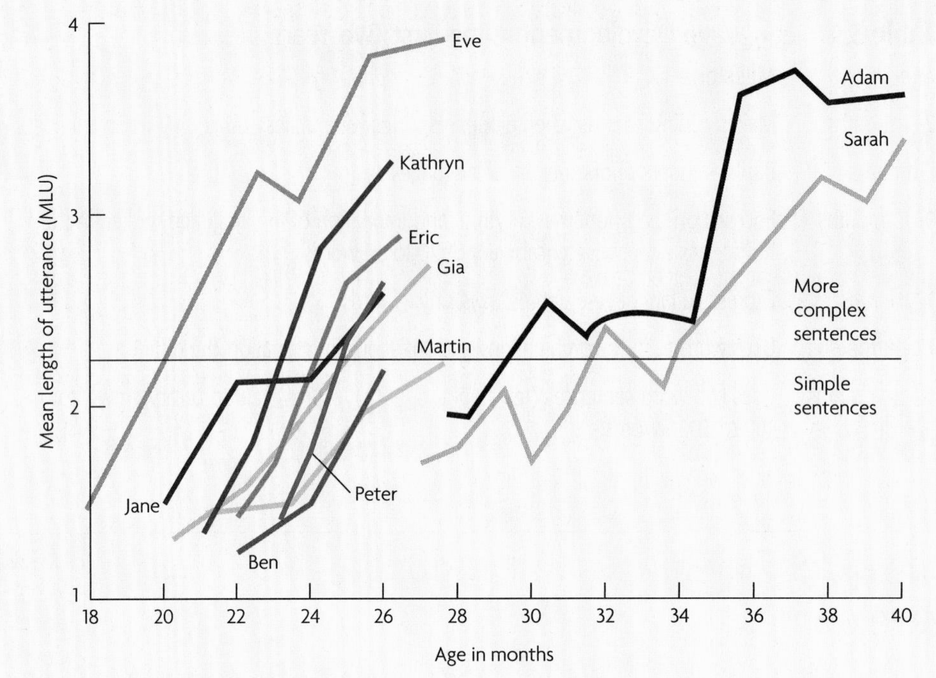

Figure 5.7 Variations in the Rate of Language Acquisition

The 10 children whose language is charted here, studied by three different linguists, moved at markedly different times from simple one- and two-word sentences to more complex sentences.

(*Sources*: Adapted from *A First Language: The Early Stages*, p. 55, Fig. 1, by Roger Brown; copyright © 1973 by the President and Fellows of Harvard College, reprinted by permission of Harvard University Press. Lois Bloom, *Language Development from Two to Three*, p. 92, Table 3.1; copyright © 1991; reprinted by permission of Cambridge University Press. I. K. Blake, "Language Development and Socialization in Young African-American Children," *Cross-Cultural Roots of Minority Children*, Greenfield and Cocking, Eds., p. 169, Table 9.1 and p. 171, Fig. 9.1; copyright © 1994; reprinted by permission of Lawrence Erlbaum Associates, Inc., a division of Taylor and Francis Group.)

Differences in Rate Some children begin using individual words at 8 months, others not until 18 months; some do not use two-word sentences until 3 years or even later. You can see the range of normal variation in sentence construction very clearly in Figure 5.7, which shows the average sentence length (referred to by linguists as the **mean length of utterance** or **MLU**) of 10 children, each studied longitudinally. Eve, Adam, and Sarah were studied by Roger Brown (1973); Jane, Martin, and Ben (all African American children) by Ira Blake (1994); and Eric, Gia, Kathryn, and Peter by Lois Bloom (1991). The figure includes a line at the MLU level that normally accompanies a switch from simple, uninflected two-word sentences to more complex forms. You can see that Eve made this transition earliest, at about 21 months; Adam and Sarah passed over this point about a year later.

More than half of children who talk late eventually catch up. The subset of those who do not catch up is made up primarily of children who also have poor receptive language (Bates, 1993; Thal, Tobias, & Morrison, 1991). This group appears to remain behind in language development and perhaps in cognitive development more generally. In practical terms, this means that if your child—or a child you care for—is significantly delayed in understanding as well as speaking language, you should seek professional help to try to diagnose the problem and begin appropriate intervention.

mean length of utterance (MLU) the average number of meaningful units in a sentence

expressive style a style of word learning characterized by low rates of noun-like terms and high use of personal-social words and phrases

Differences in Style Katherine Nelson (1973) was the first developmentalist to point out that some toddlers use an **expressive style** when learning language. Such children's early vocabulary is not made up predominantly of noun-like words. Instead, most of their early words are linked to social relationships rather than objects. They often learn pronouns (*you, me*) early and use many more of what Nelson calls "personal-social" words, such as *no, yes, want,* or *please.* Their early vocabulary may also include some multiword strings, like *love you* or *do it* or *go away.* In contrast, among children who use what Nelson calls a **referential style**, early vocabulary is made up predominantly of names for things or people.

Elizabeth Bates and her colleagues (1988; Thal & Bates, 1990) argue that referential-style children are, in some sense, more cognitively oriented. They are drawn to objects, spend more of their time in solitary play with objects, and interact with other people more often around objects. They are much more likely to show a clear spurt in vocabulary development in the early stages, adding many object names in a very short space of time, as if they—more than expressive children—have understood the basic principle that things have names. Such children are also advanced in their ability to understand complex adult language.

Expressive-style toddlers, on the other hand, are oriented more toward people and toward social interactions. Their early words and sentences include a lot of strings of words that are involved in common interactions with adults. Since many such strings include grammatical inflections, expressive children's early language often sounds more advanced than that of referential children, but their vocabularies are typically smaller, with no obvious growth spurt.

Just how these differences come about is still not clear. The most obvious possibility is that a child's early language is a reflection of the type of language she is hearing. There is some evidence, for example, that referential-style children, more than expressive-style children, have mothers who spend time naming objects and describing the environment (e.g., Furrow & Nelson, 1984; Goldfield, 1993). Yet it is also likely that the quality of the mother's speech is at least partially a response to the child's own language quality or style rather than—or in addition to—being a cause of it. Thus, referential children appear to elicit much more noun naming and equivalent referential speech from the mother than do expressive-style children (Pine, Lieven, & Rowland, 1997).

Language Development Across Cultures

Learning Objective 5.13

How does language development vary across cultures?

Studies in a wide variety of language communities, including Turkish, Serbo-Croatian, Hungarian, Hebrew, Japanese, a New Guinean language called Kaluli, German, and Italian, have revealed important similarities in language development (Maitel, Dromi, Sagi, & Bornstein, 2000). Babies the world over coo before they babble; all babies understand language before they can speak it; babies in all cultures begin to use their first words at about 12 months.

Moreover, holophrases appear to precede telegraphic speech in every language, with the latter beginning at about 18 months. However, the specific word order that a child uses in early sentences is not the same for all children in all languages. In some languages, a noun/verb sequence is fairly common; in others, a verb/noun sequence may be heard. In addition, particular inflections are learned in highly varying orders from one language to another. Japanese children, for example, begin very early to use a special kind of marker, called a pragmatic marker, that tells something about the feeling or the context. In Japanese, the word *yo* is used at the end of a sentence when the speaker is experiencing some resistance from the listener; the word *ne* is used when the speaker expects approval or agreement. Japanese children begin to use these markers very early, much earlier than children whose languages contain other types of inflections.

Most strikingly, there are languages in which there seems to be no simple two-word-sentence stage in which the children use no inflections. Children learning Turkish, for example, use essentially the full set of noun and verb inflections by age 2 and never go through a stage of using uninflected words. Their language is simple, but it is rarely ungrammatical from the adult's point of view (Aksu-Koc & Slobin, 1985; Maratsos, 1998).

referential style a style of word learning characterized by emphasis on things and people and their naming and description

Measuring Intelligence in Infancy

Learning Objective 5.14

How is intelligence measured in infancy?

As you will learn in Chapter 8, psychologists have designed many instruments that measure **intelligence** in children and adults, which is an individual's ability to take in information and use it to adapt to the environment. However, it is quite difficult to create a test that can effectively measure intelligence in infants. Tests that measure intelligence in infancy, including the widely used **Bayley Scales of Infant Development**, assess primarily sensory and motor skills (Bayley, 1969, revised 1993). For example, 3-month-old infants are challenged to reach for a dangling ring; older babies are observed as they attempt to put cubes in a cup (9 months) or build a tower of three cubes (17 months). Some more clearly cognitive items are also included; for example, uncovering a toy hidden by a cloth is a test item used with 8-month-old infants to measure an aspect of object permanence.

Bayley's test and others like it have proven to be helpful in identifying infants and toddlers with serious developmental delays (Dezoete, MacArthur, & Tuck, 2003; Gardner et al., 2006). But as more general predictive tools for forecasting later IQ or school performance, such tests have not been nearly as useful as many had hoped. For example, the typical correlation between a Bayley test score at 12 months old and an intelligence test score at 4 years old is only about .20 to .30 (e.g., Bee et al., 1982)—hardly substantial enough to be used for predicting intellectual performance at later ages. On the whole, it appears that what is measured on typical infant intelligence tests is not the same as what is tapped by commonly used childhood or adult intelligence tests (Colombo, 1993). The most recent version of the test, the Bayley-III (Bayley, 2006), includes items that address cognitive and language development in addition to those that assess sensory and motor skills. Future research will determine whether it better predicts future intellectual performance than previous versions of the test have been found to.

intelligence the ability to take in information and use it to adapt to the environment

Bayley Scales of Infant Development the best-known and most widely used test of infant "intelligence"

Recent research has indicated that habituation tasks have potential as measures of infant intelligence. For example, if a baby is shown an object or a picture over and over, how many exposures does it take before the infant stops showing interest? The speed with which such habituation/recognition takes place may reveal something about the efficiency of the baby's perceptual/cognitive system and its neurological underpinnings. And if such efficiency lies behind some of the characteristics that psychologists call intelligence, then individual differences in rate of habituation in the early months of life may predict later intelligence test scores. That is exactly what some of the research examining links between measures of habituation in infants has found (Rose & Feldman, 1995; Rose, Feldman, & Jankowski, 2004; Slater, 1995).

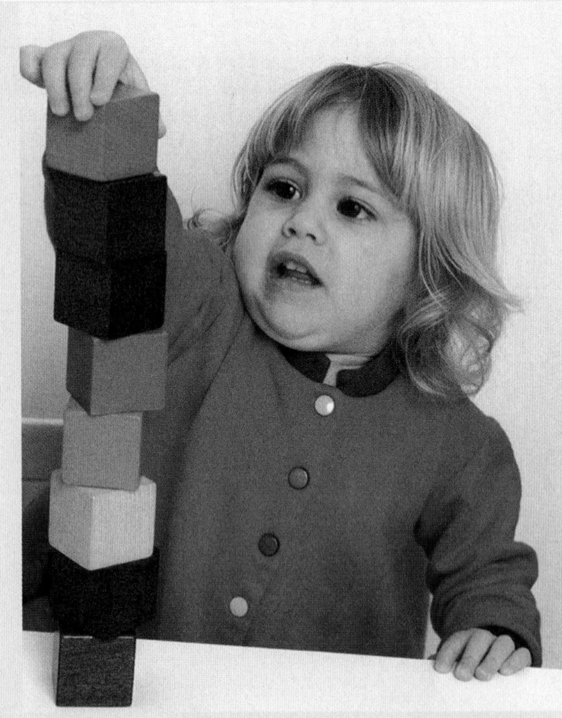

At 22 months, Katherine would clearly pass the 17-month item on the Bayley Scales of Infant Development that calls for the child to build a tower of three blocks.

Might such findings provide developmentalists with a useful test of infant intelligence? Some developmentalists believe that they will. For example, psychologist Joseph Fagan has developed a standardized test of habituation rate known as the Fagan Test of Infant Intelligence (Fagan & Detterman, 1992). Fagan argues that tests of habituation rate—also known as novelty preference and visual recognition—are particularly appropriate for individuals who are incapable of responding to conventional tests such as the Bayley scales (Fagan, 2000). For example, infants who have cerebral palsy can't perform many of the tasks required by the Bayley scales. However, they are fully capable of viewing visual stimuli and exhibiting habituation to them. Fagan's research and that of others has shown that the Fagan test is a useful measure of cognitive function among such special populations (Fagan & Detterman, 1992; Gaultney & Gingras, 2005; Smith, Fagan, & Ulvund, 2002).

However, research examining the usefulness of the Fagan test with typically developing infants has produced mixed results. Some studies have shown that infants' scores on the test are correlated with later measures of intelligence and specific cognitive skills such as language comprehension (Andersson, 1996; Thompson, Fagan, & Fulker, 1991). Others have found that the Fagan test is poorly correlated with later measures of such variables (Cardon & Fulker, 1991; Tasbihsazan, Nettelbeck, & Kirby, 2003). Thus, the final determination as to the usefulness of habituation rate as a standardized measure of intelligence in infancy has yet to be made.

Test Prep Center

with mydevelopmentlab

COGNITIVE CHANGES

5.1 What are the important milestones of Piaget's sensorimotor stage? (pp. 128–131)

Piaget described the sensorimotor infant as beginning with a small repertoire of basic schemes, from which she moves toward symbolic representation in a series of six substages. The most important cognitive milestone of this stage is object permanence.

1. Label each of the following as a (A) primary circular reaction, (B) secondary circular reaction, or (C) tertiary circular reaction.

   ______ (1) Reina has discovered that sucking her thumb makes her feel good.

   ______ (2) Keisha kicks the rails of her crib in order to make the mobile above it move and make noise.

   ______ (3) Whenever Joey's mother gives him a sippy cup filled with juice, he turns the cup upside down and watches the juice slowly trickle out through the spout.

   ______ (4) When Michael's hand touches an object, he tries to grasp it.

   ______ (5) Lucy likes to play with tennis balls and delights in throwing round fruits such as tangerines and plums on the floor in what appears to be an effort to determine whether they will bounce.

   ______ (6) Ten-month-old Lauren laughs when she sees her 3-year-old brother cover his ears in response to her intentional screams.

2. How would Piaget explain the fact that 12-month-old Jarrett always looks for his ball in his toy box after he watches it roll under the sofa?

   ____

   ____

3. From the Multimedia Library within MyDevelopmentLab, watch the *Sensorimotor Stage* video and answer the following question.

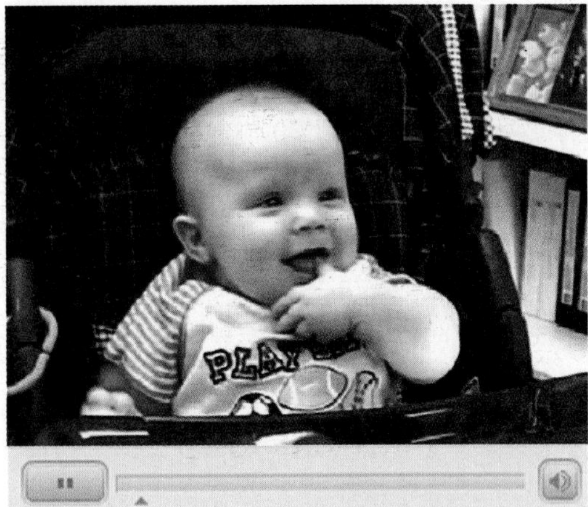

   What kinds of cognitive skills do children acquire in the first two years of life?

   ____

   ____

4. From the Multimedia Library within MyDevelopmentLab, watch the *Object Permanence* video and answer the following question.

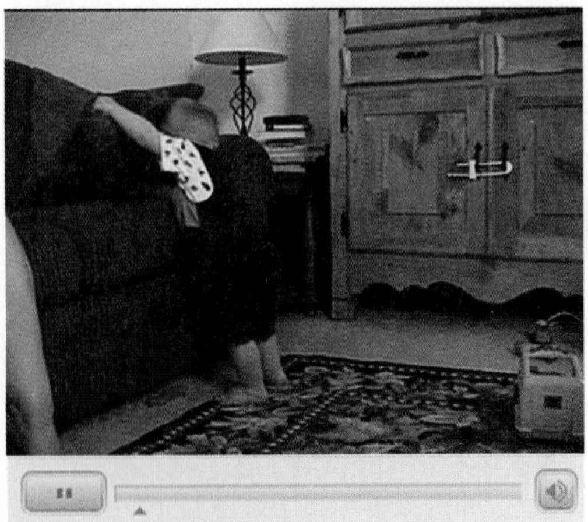

The infant's motor skills suggest that he is about a year old. How would his response to the hidden toys be different if he were only 8 months old?

____

____

5.2 What are some of the challenges offered to Piaget's explanation of infant cognitive development? (pp. 131–132)

More recent research suggests that Piaget underestimated infants' capabilities, as well as the degree to which some concepts may be inborn.

5. Briefly summarize the research findings that have challenged Piaget's views on the developmental milestones listed in the table.

Milestone	Findings
Object permanence	
Imitation	

5.3 What does research tell us about infants' understanding of objects? (pp. 132–134)

Developmentalists such as Spelke and Baillargeon have studied object permanence within the context of infants' global understanding of objects. Their research shows that Piaget underestimated how much younger infants know about objects and their movements.

6. How have the studies of Elizabeth Spelke and Renée Baillargeon contributed to developmentalists' understanding of how the object concept develops in infancy?

____

____

LEARNING, CATEGORIZING, AND REMEMBERING

5.4 When are babies able to learn through classical conditioning, operant conditioning, and observing models? (pp. 134–135)

Within the first few weeks of life, babies are able to learn through classical conditioning and operant conditioning. Infants also learn by observing models, especially in their second year of life.

7. Match each type of learning with its definition

_______ (1) classical conditioning

_______ (2) operant conditioning

_______ (3) modeling

(A) learning through reinforcement

(B) stimulus-response learning

(C) learning by observing others

5.5 How does categorical understanding change over the first 2 years? (p. 135)

From an early age, infants use categories to organize information. The sophistication of these categories, as well as an understanding of how they relate to each other, increases over the first 2 years of life.

8. Schematic learning is defined as ____________________.

5.6 How does memory function in the first 2 years? (p. 136)

Three- and 4-month-old infants show signs of remembering specific experiences over periods of as long as a few days or a week, indicating that they have developed some form of internal representation well before Piaget supposed. Early memories appear to be linked to the specific context in which they were formed, a limitation that diminishes as infants get older.

9. Mark each statement as True or False with regard to memory functioning in the first 2 years.

_______ (1) Infants can remember stimuli to which they are exposed while they are sleeping.

_______ (2) Three-month-olds' memories for objects and actions last for about 24 hours.

_______ (3) Infants' memories of events are linked to the contexts in which the events occur.

THE BEGINNINGS OF LANGUAGE

5.7 What are the behaviorist, nativist, and interactionist explanations of language development? (pp. 137–139)

Behaviorist theories of language development claim that infants learn language through parental reinforcement of wordlike sounds and correct grammar. Nativists say that an innate language processor helps infants learn language rules. Interactionists say that language development is a subprocess of cognitive development.

10. From the Multimedia Library within MyDevelopmentLab, watch the *Language Learning* video and answer the following question.

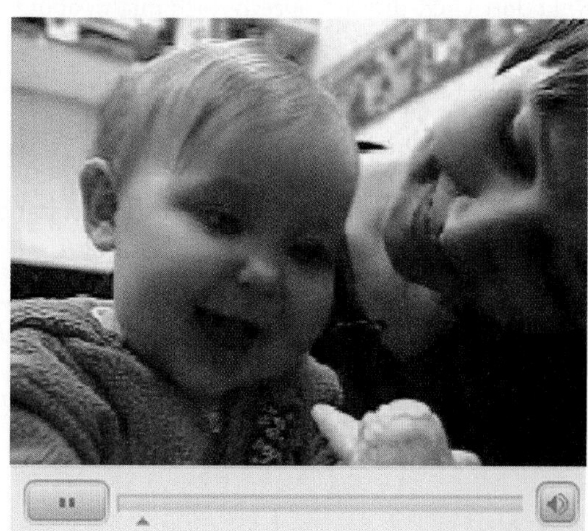

In what ways do the research findings shown in the video support the interactionist approach to language development?

____

____

5.8 What are some of the environmental influences on language development? (pp. 139–140)

High-pitched infant-directed speech (IDS) attracts infants' attention to the simple, repetitive, and expanded expressions that adults use to help them learn language and grammar. The amount of verbal interaction that takes place between infants and mature speakers through talking and reading is another influence. Poverty is associated with delays in language development.

11. List three ways in which parents can influence language development.

(A) ____

(B) ____

(C) ____

12. From the Multimedia Library within MyDevelopmentLab, watch the *Child-Directed Speech* video and answer the following question.

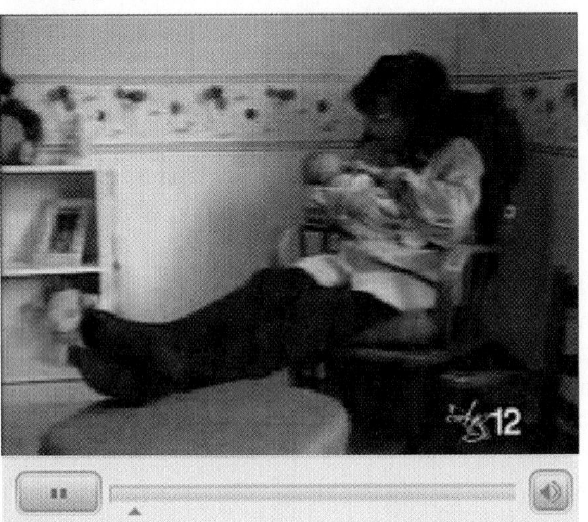

What does child-directed speech teach infants about language?

____

____

5.9 How do infants' sounds, gestures, and understanding of words change in the early months of life? (pp. 140–141)

Babies' earliest sounds are cries, followed at about 2 months by cooing, then at about 6 months by babbling. At 9 months, babies typically use meaningful gestures and can understand a small vocabulary of spoken words.

13. Explain the concept of constraints on word learning.

____

____

5.10 What are the characteristics of toddlers' first words? (pp. 141–142)

The first spoken words, usually names for objects or people, typically occur at about 1 year, after which toddlers add words slowly for a few months and then rapidly.

14. The period between 16 and 24 months is known as the ________. Explain why this term is applied to this phase of language development.

____

____

5.11 What kinds of sentences do children produce between 18 and 24 months of age? (p. 142)

Simple two-word sentences appear in children's expressive language at about 18 months; this pattern is referred to as telegraphic speech.

15. Write Y if the sentence could be a toddler's first sentence (telegraphic speech) and N if it could not be.

_______ (1) Kitty bite.

_______ (2) The balls are bouncing.

_______ (3) Daddy home.

_______ (4) Mommy leave.

_______ (5) Mommy cooked dinner.

_______ (6) The dog is under the bed.

5.12 What kinds of individual differences are evident in language development? (pp. 143–145)

The rate of language development varies from one child to another. In addition, some toddlers display an expressive style in early word learning, while others show a referential style.

16. Describe individual differences in the rate and style of language development in the table below.

Differences in...	Description
Rate	
Style	

5.13 How does language development vary across cultures? (p. 145)

Early word learning seems to follow similar patterns in all cultures. However, the word order of a child's telegraphic speech depends on which language he is learning. Language inflections are learned in highly varying orders.

17. Discuss the evidence for these two statements:

(A) Language development is highly consistent across cultures.

____

____

(B) Language development varies across cultures.

____

____

MEASURING INTELLIGENCE IN INFANCY

5.14 How is intelligence measured in infancy? (pp. 146–147)

Infant intelligence tests are not strongly related to later measures of intelligence. Measures of basic information-processing skills in infancy, such as rate of habituation, may be better correlated with later intelligence test scores.

18. Explain why each statement is false.

(A) Scores on infant intelligence tests are useful for predicting academic achievement in later childhood.

____

____

(B) Infant intelligence tests are of little use.

____

____

(C) New tests of intelligence that are based on differences in habituation rates are more useful for studying the development of intelligence in healthy infants than in infants who have disabilities.

____

____

For answers to the questions in this chapter, turn to page 511. For a list of key terms, turn to page 530.

Succeed with PEARSON **mydevelopmentlab**

Do You Know All of the Terms in This Chapter?
Find out by using the Flashcards. Want more practice? Take additional quizzes, try simulations, and watch video to be sure you are prepared for the test!

Chapter 6

Social and Personality Development in Infancy and Toddlerhood

Infancy is the period during which parents and children experience more physical closeness than at any other time in development. Proximity is pleasurable for both parents and babies, but it is also practical. For one thing, a mother or father usually has to carry out other duties while simultaneously caring for a baby. For another, keeping babies close by helps parents protect them from harm. Practical considerations aside, proximity contributes to the development of strong emotional bonds between infants and caregivers. Physical closeness provides parents with many opportunities to comfort and show affection for infants. It also allows them to interact with their infant by exchanging smiles, frowns, or silly faces.

In the context of frequent physical contact, interactions between infants and the social world around them lay the foundations for development in the social/personality domains that are the topics of this chapter. We will first review divergent ideas proposed by psychoanalytic theorists about the first 2 years; then we will consider the process of attachment. A look at the infant's emerging personality and sense of self comes next, followed by a discussion of the effects of nonparental care on infants' development.

Learning Objectives

Theories of Social and Personality Development

6.1 How do Freud's and Erikson's views of personality development in the first year of life differ?

6.2 What are the main ideas of attachment theory?

Attachment

6.3 How does synchrony affect parent-infant relations?

6.4 What are the four phases of attachment and the behaviors associated with them?

6.5 What are the variables that contribute to the development and stability of the four types of attachment?

6.6 What characteristics might affect a parent's ability to establish an attachment relationship with an infant?

6.7 What are the long-term consequences of attachment quality?

6.8 In what ways do patterns of attachment vary across cultures?

Personality, Temperament, and Self-Concept

6.9 On which dimensions of temperament do most developmentalists agree?

6.10 What are the roles of heredity, neurological processes, environment, and gender in the formation of temperament?

6.11 How do the subjective self, the objective self, and the emotional self develop during the first 2 years?

Effects of Nonparental Care

6.12 Why is it difficult to study the effects of nonparental care on development?

6.13 What might be the effects of nonparental care on cognitive development?

6.14 What does research suggest about the risks of nonparental care with respect to social development?

6.15 What variables should be taken into account in interpretations of research on nonparental care?

Theories of Social and Personality Development

Psychologists have used all of the theoretical perspectives you learned about in Chapter 2 to formulate hypotheses about infants' social and personality development. However, the two most influential perspectives on these issues are the psychoanalytic and the ethological perspectives.

Learning Objective 6.1

How do Freud's and Erikson's views of personality development in the first year of life differ?

Psychoanalytic Perspectives

You may remember from Chapter 2 that Freud proposed a series of psychosexual stages that extend from birth through adolescence, during which individuals attempt to satisfy certain basic drives in different ways. In the oral stage, from birth to age 1, infants derive satisfaction through the mouth. Freud believed that the weaning process should be managed in such a way that the infant's need to suck is neither frustrated nor overgratified. The consequences of either, Freud claimed, would be fixation at this stage of development (look back at Table 2.1 on page 29).

THE WHOLE CHILD IN FOCUS

How did Federico's father help him develop a sense of autonomy? Find out on page 179.

Freud also emphasized the symbiotic relationship between the mother and young infant, in which the two behave as if they were one. He believed that the infant did not understand herself to be separate from her mother. Thus, another result of a gratifying nursing period followed by a balanced weaning process, Freud thought, was the infant's development of a sense of both attachment to and separation from the mother.

Erikson went beyond Freud's view. Nursing and weaning are important, he conceded, but they are only one aspect of the overall social environment. Erikson claimed that responding to the infant's other needs by talking to him, comforting him, and so on was just as important. He proposed that the first year is a period during which the infant learns to trust the world around him or becomes cynical about the social environment's ability to meet his needs—the *trust versus mistrust stage.*

Harlow's ingenious research demonstrated that infant monkeys became attached to a terrycloth-covered "mother" and would cling to it rather than to a wire mother that provided them with food.

One of the best-known studies in developmental psychology demonstrated that Erikson's view of infant development was more accurate than Freud's (Harlow & Zimmerman, 1959). In this study, infant monkeys were separated from their mothers at birth. The experimenters placed two different kinds of "surrogate" mothers in their cages. The monkeys received all their feedings from a wire mother with a nursing bottle attached. The other mother was covered with soft terrycloth. The researchers found that the monkeys approached the wire mother only when hungry. Most of the time, they cuddled against the cloth mother, and they ran to it whenever they were frightened or stressed. Subsequent studies with human infants correlating maternal feeding practices with infant adjustment suggested that infants' social relationships are not based solely on either nursing or weaning practices (Schaffer & Emerson, 1964).

Learning Objective 6.2

What are the main ideas of attachment theory?

Ethological Perspectives

You may recall from Chapter 2 that the ethological perspective claims that all animals, including humans, possess innate predispositions that strongly influence their development. Thus, the ethological approach to social and personality development proposes that evolutionary forces have endowed infants with genes that predispose them to form emotional bonds with their caregivers, an approach known as **attachment theory**. Consequently, in contrast to psychoanalysts, ethologists view the infant's capacity for forming social relationships as highly resistant to environmental forces such as variations in the quality of parenting. However, ethologists do claim that the first 2 years of life constitute a sensitive period for the formation of such relationships. They say that infants who fail to form a close relationship with a caregiver before the age of 2 are at risk for future social and personality problems.

attachment theory the view that infants are biologically predisposed to form emotional bonds with caregivers and that the characteristics of those bonds shape later social and personality development

Because they hypothesize that early emotional bonds influence later social and personality development, ethological perspectives have been very influential in the study of development in this domain across the entire lifespan. In John Bowlby's terminology, infants create different *internal models* of their relationships with parents and other key adults (Bowlby, 1969). These models include such elements as the child's confidence (or lack of it) that the attachment figure will be available or reliable, the child's expectation of rebuff or affection, and the child's sense of assurance that the attachment figure is really a safe base for exploration. The internal model begins to be formed late in the child's first year of life and becomes increasingly elaborated and better established through the first 4 or 5 years. By age 5, most children have a clear internal model of the mother (or other primary caregiver), a self model, and a model of relationships. Once formed, such models shape and explain experiences and affect memory and attention. Children notice and remember experiences that fit their models and miss or forget experiences that don't match. As Piaget might say, a child more readily assimilates data that fit the model. More importantly, the model affects the child's behavior: The child tends to re-create, in each new relationship, the pattern with which he is familiar. This tendency to re-create the parent-infant relationship in each new relationship, say Bowlby and other ethologists, continues into adulthood. For this reason, ethologists believe that, for example, poor communication between adult romantic partners may result from maladaptive communication patterns that developed between one of the individuals and his or her early caregivers.

Attachment

Somehow, in the midst of endless diaper changes, food preparation, baths, and periods of exhaustion that exceed anything they have ever experienced before, the overwhelming majority of parents manage to respond to their infants in ways that foster the development of an attachment relationship. An **attachment** is an emotional bond in which a person's sense of security is bound up in the relationship. To understand the attachment between parent and infant, it is important to look at both sides of the equation—at the development of both the parents' bond to the child and the child's attachment to the parents.

attachment the emotional bond between parents and infants, from which infants derive security

synchrony a mutual, interlocking pattern of attachment behaviors shared by a parent and child

The Parents' Attachment to the Infant

Learning Objective 6.3
How does synchrony affect parent-infant relations?

Contact between mother and infant immediately after birth does not appear to be either necessary or sufficient for the formation of a stable long-term affectional bond between them (Wong, 1993). What is essential in the formation of that bond is the opportunity for mother and infant to develop a mutual, interlocking pattern of attachment behaviors called **synchrony**, a process that is somewhat like a conversation. The baby signals his needs by crying or smiling; he responds to being held by quieting or snuggling; he looks at his parents when they look at him. The mother, in turn, enters into the interaction with her own repertoire of caregiving behaviors.

The father's bond with the infant, like the mother's, seems to depend more on the development of synchrony than on contact immediately after birth. Aiding the development of such mutuality is the fact that fathers seem to have the same repertoire of attachment behaviors as do mothers. In the early weeks of the baby's life, fathers touch, talk to, and cuddle their babies in the same ways that mothers do (Parke & Tinsley, 1981). After the first weeks of the baby's life, however, signs of a kind of specialization of parental behaviors begin to emerge. Fathers spend more time playing with the baby, with more physical roughhousing; mothers spend more time in routine caregiving and also talk to and smile at the baby more (Walker, Messinger, Fogel, & Karns, 1992).

Fathers engage in physical play with infants more often than mothers do.

By 6 months, infants display distinctive patterns of responding to these mother-father differences (Feldman, 2003). Signs of positive emotional states, such as smiling, appear gradually and subtly when babies are interacting with their mothers. In contrast, babies laugh and wriggle with delight in short, intense bursts in interactions with their fathers. Again, this isn't a matter of babies' preference for one parent or the other. Instead, such results mean that infants

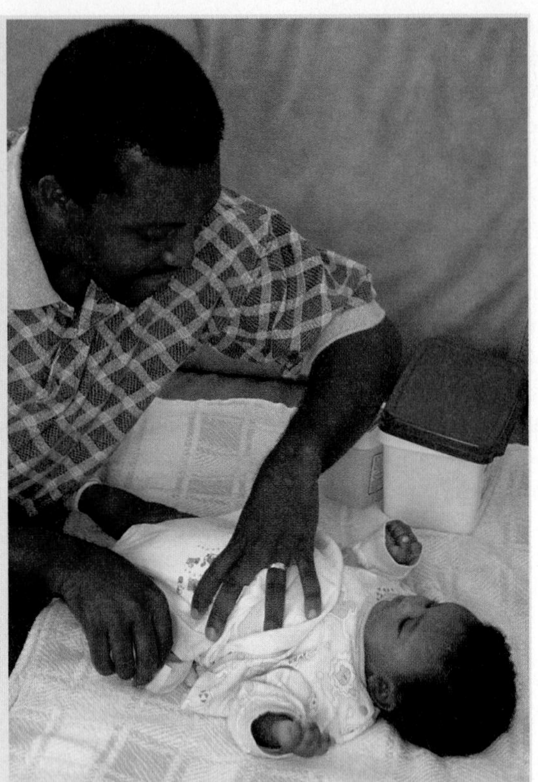

Dads like this one, who get involved with the day-to-day care of their babies, seem to develop stronger attachment relationships with their babies.

recognize the same behavioral differences in mothers and fathers that developmental scientists do when they observe parental behavior. In fact, some researchers have noted that measures of attachment behaviors based on typical mother-infant interactions may cause researchers to inappropriately conclude that fathers are less involved with babies than are mothers and, therefore, less important to infants' development (Lewis & Lamb, 2003). To the contrary, research clearly indicates that babies benefit tremendously when both kinds of interaction are available to them.

Learning Objective 6.4

What are the four phases of attachment and the behaviors associated with them?

The Infant's Attachment to the Parents

Like the parent's bond to the baby, the baby's attachment emerges gradually and is based on her ability to discriminate between her parents and other people. As you learned in Chapters 3 and 4, an infant can recognize her mother's voice prior to birth. By the time the baby is a few days old, she recognizes her mother by sight and smell as well (Cernoch & Porter, 1985; Walton, Bower, & Bower, 1992). Thus, the cognitive foundation for attachment is in place within days after birth. Advances in memory and in reasoning, particularly object permanence, provide additional cognitive support for attachment. As you'll see, attachment develops gradually as the infant moves through a series of universal stages that parallel those that emerge in the cognitive domain.

Establishing Attachment Bowlby suggested four phases in the development of the infant's attachment (Bowlby, 1969). Bowlby and other ethologists claim that these phases appear over the first 24 to 36 months of life in a fixed sequence that is strongly influenced by genes present in all healthy human infants (see Chapter 2). The infant exhibits a distinctive set of attachment-related behaviors and interaction patterns in each phase:

- *Phase 1: Nonfocused orienting and signaling (birth to 3 months).* Babies exhibit behaviors, such as crying, smiling, and making eye contact, that draw the attention of others and signal their needs. They direct these signals to everyone with whom they come into contact.
- *Phase 2: Focus on one or more figures (3 to 6 months).* Babies direct their "come here" signals to fewer people, typically those with whom they spend the most time, and are less responsive to unfamiliar people.
- *Phase 3: Secure base behavior (6 to 24 months).* True attachment emerges. Babies show "proximity-seeking" behaviors such as following and clinging to caregivers whom they regard as "safe bases," especially when they are anxious or injured or have physical needs such as hunger. Most direct these behaviors to a primary caregiver when that person is available and to others only when the primary caregiver, for some reason, cannot or will not respond to them or is absent (Lamb, 1981).
- *Phase 4: Internal model (24 months and beyond).* An internal model of the attachment relationship allows children older than 2 years to imagine how an anticipated action might affect the bonds that they share with their caregivers (van IJzendoorn, 2005). The internal model plays a role in later relationships with early caregivers (i.e., adult children and their parents) and in other significant relationships (i.e., romantic partnerships) throughout life.

Attachment Behaviors Once the child has developed a clear attachment in phase 3, several related behaviors also begin appearing. *Stranger anxiety* and *separation anxiety* rise in frequency until about 12 to 16 months and then decline. Infants express **stranger anxiety** with behaviors such as clinging to their mothers when strangers are present. **Separation anxiety** is evident when infants cry or protest on being separated from the mother. The research findings are not altogether consistent, but fear of strangers apparently emerges first. Separation anxiety starts a bit later but continues to be visible for a longer period. Such an increase in fear and anxiety has been observed in children from a number of different cultures and in both home-reared children and children in child care in the United States.

Another attachment behavior is **social referencing** (Walden, 1991). By roughly 10 months, infants use cues from the facial expressions of their attachment figures to help them figure out what to do in novel situations, such as when a stranger comes to visit (Hertenstein & Campos, 2004). Babies of this age will first look at Mom's or Dad's face to check for the adult's emotional expression. If Mom looks pleased or happy, the baby is likely to explore a new toy with more ease or to accept a stranger with less fuss. If Mom looks concerned or frightened, the baby responds to those cues and reacts to the novel situation with equivalent fear or concern (see *Developmental Science in the Clinic* on page 158).

Social referencing also helps babies learn to regulate their own emotions. For example, an infant who is angry because an enjoyable activity is no longer available may use his caregiver's pleasant, comforting emotional expressions to transition himself into a more pleasant emotional state. By contrast, a baby whose caregiver responds to his anger with more anger may experience an escalation in the level of his own angry feelings. Most developmentalists think that the quality of the emotional give-and-take in interactions between an infant and his caregivers is important to the child's ability to control emotions such as anger and frustration in later years (Cole, Martin, & Dennis, 2004).

THE WHOLE CHILD IN FOCUS

Why does 2-year-old Federico easily separate from his father Hector when he arrives at child care each day? Find out on page 179.

Separation anxiety signifies the formation of a true attachment relationship between an infant and her primary caregiver. Once the parent has actually left, this child will probably be content to play with the other children and will respond positively to her temporary caregivers.

stranger anxiety expressions of discomfort, such as clinging to the mother, in the presence of strangers

separation anxiety expressions of discomfort, such as crying, when separated from an attachment figure

social referencing an infant's use of others' facial expressions as a guide to his or her own emotions

DEVELOPMENTAL SCIENCE IN THE CLINIC

Reducing Infants' Anxiety

Hank is a registered nurse who works in a pediatrician's office. He has noticed that infants who are old enough to have formed an association between his presence and the unpleasant experience of getting a shot vary greatly in how much distress they show in the examining room. Some respond to his presence simply by moving closer to the parent, while others cry hysterically and have to be held down to be examined. He wonders if there is a way to prevent those who seem most sensitive from becoming so overwrought.

Research indicates that social referencing plays an important role in infants' distress in health-care settings. In other words, if a parent displays anxiety in Hank's presence, then an infant is likely to do so as well (Bernard & Cohen, 2006). Thus, one thing that Hank can do to reduce his young patients' distress is to explain the process of social referencing to their parents.

Of course, every infant is different, and some are likely to become upset no matter how careful their parents are about their own expressions of emotion. For these babies, researchers have found that distraction is helpful (Cramer-Berness, 2006). Hank's patients, then, might be less distressed if their parents brought along a few toys or books to divert their attention from the unpleasant events that they have learned to associate with going to the doctor. Moreover, as Harlow's research with infant monkeys suggests, infants derive great comfort from physical contact with their parents. If babies are held while they are examined or immunized, they may exhibit less distress.

Questions for Reflection

1. What do you think would be the best way for Hank to inform parents about the types of anxiety-reducing strategies they can use at the doctor's office?
2. What would you say to a parent who characterized her 15-month-old infant's emotional outbursts at the doctor's office as "misbehavior" that should be punished?

Learning Objective 6.5

What are the variables that contribute to the development and stability of the four types of attachment?

Variations in Attachment Quality

Virtually all babies seem to go through the four phases of attachment first identified by Bowlby, but the quality of the attachments they form differs from one infant to the next.

secure attachment a pattern of attachment in which an infant readily separates from the parent, seeks proximity when stressed, and uses the parent as a safe base for exploration

insecure/avoidant attachment a pattern of attachment in which an infant avoids contact with the parent and shows no preference for the parent over other people

insecure/ambivalent attachment a pattern of attachment in which the infant shows little exploratory behavior, is greatly upset when separated from the mother, and is not reassured by her return or efforts to comfort him or her

Secure and Insecure Attachments Variations in the quality of the first attachment relationship are now almost universally described using Ainsworth's category system (Ainsworth, Blehar, Waters, & Wall 1978). The Ainsworth system distinguishes between secure attachment and two types of insecure attachment, which psychologists assess using a procedure called the *Strange Situation.*

The Strange Situation consists of a series of eight episodes played out in a laboratory setting, typically with children between 12 and 18 months of age. The child is observed in each of the following situations:

- With the mother
- With the mother and a stranger
- Alone with the stranger
- Completely alone for a few minutes
- Reunited with the mother
- Alone again
- With the stranger again
- Reunited with the mother

Ainsworth suggested that children's reactions in these situations—particularly to the reunion episodes—showed attachment of one of three types: **secure attachment**, **insecure/avoidant attachment**, and **insecure/ambivalent attachment**. More recently, developmentalists have suggested a fourth type: **insecure/disorganized attachment** (Main & Solomon, 1990). The characteristics of each type are listed in Table 6.1.

Table 6.1 Categories of Secure and Insecure Attachment in Ainsworth's Strange Situation

Category	Behavior
Secure attachment	Child readily separates from mother and easily becomes absorbed in exploration; when threatened or frightened, child actively seeks contact and is readily consoled; child does not avoid or resist contact if mother initiates it. When reunited with mother after absence, child greets her positively or is easily soothed if upset. Clearly prefers mother to stranger.
Insecure/avoidant attachment	Child avoids contact with mother, especially at reunion after an absence. Child does not resist mother's efforts to make contact, but does not seek much contact. Shows no preference for mother over stranger.
Insecure/ambivalent attachment	Child shows little exploration and is wary of stranger. Child is greatly upset when separated from mother, but not reassured by mother's return or her efforts at comforting. Child both seeks and avoids contact at different times. May show anger toward mother at reunion and resists both comfort from and contact with stranger.
Insecure/disorganized attachment	Child seems confused or apprehensive. Child may show contradictory behavior patterns simultaneously, such as moving toward mother while keeping gaze averted.

Sources: Ainsworth et al., 1978; Carlson & Sroufe, 1995; Main & Solomon, 1990.

Whether a child cries when he is separated from his mother is not a helpful indicator of the security of his attachment. At the time of separation, some securely attached infants cry, whereas others do not; the same is true of insecurely attached infants. It is the entire pattern of the child's response to the Strange Situation that is critical, not any one response. These attachment types have been observed in studies in many different countries, and secure attachment is the most common pattern in every country.

Stability of Attachment Classification Researchers have found that the quality of a child's attachment can be either consistent or changeable. It seems that, when a child's family environment or life circumstances are reasonably consistent, the security or insecurity of her attachment also seems to remain consistent, even over many years (Hamilton, 1995; Wartner, Grossman, Fremmer-Bombik, & Suess, 1994; Weinfield & Egeland, 2004). However, when a child's circumstances change in some major way—such as when the parents divorce or the family moves—the security of the child's attachment may change as well, either from secure to insecure or the reverse. For example, in one important study, developmentalists followed one group of middle-class White children from age 1 to age 21 (Waters, Treboux, Crowell, Merrick, & Albersheim, 1995). Those whose attachment classification changed over this long interval had nearly all experienced some major upheaval, such as the death of a parent, physical or sexual abuse, or a serious illness.

The fact that the security of a child's attachment can change over time does not refute the notion of attachment as arising from an internal model. Bowlby suggested that for the first 2 or 3 years, the particular pattern of attachment a child shows is in some sense a property of each specific relationship. For example, studies of toddlers' attachments to mothers and fathers show that about 30% of the children are securely attached to one parent and insecurely attached to the other, with both possible combinations equally likely (Fox, Kimmerly, & Schafer, 1991). It is the quality of each relationship that determines the security of the child's attachment to a specific adult. If the relationship changes markedly, the security of attachment may change, too. But, Bowlby argued, by age 4 or 5, the internal model becomes more a property of the child, more generalized across relationships, and thus more resistant to change. At that point, the child tends to impose the model on new relationships, including relationships with teachers or peers.

insecure/disorganized attachment a pattern of attachment in which an infant seems confused or apprehensive and shows contradictory behavior, such as moving toward the mother while looking away from her

Learning Objective 6.6

What characteristics might affect a parent's ability to establish an attachment relationship with an infant?

Caregiver Characteristics and Attachment

Researchers have found that several characteristics of caregivers influence the attachment process. These characteristics include the caregivers' emotional responses to the infant, their marital and socioeconomic status, and their mental health.

Emotional Responsiveness Studies of parent-child interactions suggest that one crucial ingredient for secure attachment is *emotional availability* on the part of the primary caregiver (Biringen, 2000). An emotionally available caregiver is one who is able and willing to form an emotional attachment to the infant. *Contingent responsiveness* is another key ingredient of secure attachment (Isabella, 1995; Pederson & Moran, 1995; Pederson et al., 1990; Seifer, Schiller, Sameroff, Resnick, & Riordan, 1996). Parents who demonstrate contingent responsiveness are sensitive to the child's cues and respond appropriately. They smile when the baby smiles, talk to the baby when he vocalizes, pick him up when he cries, and so on (Ainsworth & Marvin, 1995). Infants of parents who display contingent responsiveness in the early months are more likely to be securely attached at age 12 months (Heinicke et al., 2000).

A low level of parental responsiveness thus appears to be an ingredient in any type of insecure attachment. However, each of the several subvarieties of insecure attachment is affected by additional distinct factors. For example, if the mother rejects the infant or regularly withdraws from contact with her, the baby is more likely to show an avoidant pattern of attachment, although the pattern also seems to occur when the mother is overly intrusive or overly stimulating toward the infant (Isabella, 1995). An ambivalent pattern is more common when the primary caregiver is inconsistently or unreliably available to the child. A disorganized/disoriented pattern seems especially likely when the child has been abused and in families in which either parent had some unresolved trauma in his or her own childhood, such as abuse or a parent's early death (Cassidy & Berlin, 1994; Main & Hesse, 1990).

Marital and Socioeconomic Status Researchers have found that infants whose parents are married are more likely to be securely attached than babies whose parents are either cohabiting or single (e.g., Rosenkrantz, Aronson, & Huston, 2004). However, the effects of marital status may be due to other characteristics of parents who choose to marry, cohabit, or remain single. Married parents typically have more education and are less likely to be poor than parents in the other groups.

In addition, married parents are, on average, older than parents in the other two groups (Rosenkrantz et al., 2004). Most of the information about the influence of maternal age on the attachment process comes from studies comparing adolescent to older mothers. These studies suggest that, with increasing age, mothers become less likely to describe their babies as "difficult" (Miller, Eisenberg, Fabes, & Shell, 1996). Moreover, older mothers display more sensitive caregiving behaviors than teenagers. Of course, teenaged mothers are likely to have less education and fewer economic resources than older mothers. Thus, it's hard to say whether age or maturity is responsible for the associations between maternal age and parenting characteristics.

Finally, marital conflict poses risks for the development of attachment. Researchers have found that 6-month-olds who are exposed to parental arguments, especially those in which parents are verbally aggressive toward each other, are more likely to display signs of emotional withdrawal than babies who are not so exposed (Crockenberg, Leerkes, & Lekka, 2007). Emotional withdrawal on the part of the infant interferes with synchrony, thereby lessening the chances that she will develop a secure attachment to her primary caregiver.

Mental Health Psychiatric illness is another caregiver characteristic that appears to be related to attachment quality (Murray et al., 1999; Teti, Gelfand, Messinger, & Isabella, 1995). Developmentalists have found that babies who interact regularly with a mother who is depressed express more negative and fewer positive emotions. Some even resist their mother's efforts to nurse them; others refuse to eat altogether (Coulthard & Harris, 2003). As a result, compared with infants of mothers without depression, a higher proportion of the infants of mothers with depression are undernourished (Rahman, Lovel, Bunn, Igbal, & Harrington, 2004). All of these effects interfere with synchrony and can predispose the infant of a mother who is depressed to develop an insecure attachment. As a result, infants of these mothers are at higher risk for later problems. For example, they are more likely than other children to exhibit either heightened aggression or social withdrawal in school (Cummings & Davies, 1994). They also are at higher risk of developing psychiatric illnesses themselves in adulthood (Maki et al., 2004).

It is important to note that maternal depression itself doesn't necessarily doom an infant to an insecure attachment. The critical factors appear to be how and to what extent depression affects mother-infant interactions. There seem to be three problematic behavior patterns in mothers who have depression. In one pattern, mothers are withdrawn and detached; they look at, touch, or talk to their babies less often and are less affectionate toward their infants than are mothers without depression (Field, 1995; Hart, Jones, Field, & Lundy, 1999). In the second pattern, mothers are overly involved with their infants, often interrupting and overstimulating them (Hart, Jones, Field, & Lundy, 1999). The third group of mothers with depression overreact and respond angrily to babies' undesirable behaviors (O'Leary, Smith, & Reid, 1999).

Of course, many mothers with depression are just as sensitive and responsive to their babies' needs as mothers who do not have depression. And, as you might expect, infants whose mothers with depression exhibit sensitive parenting behaviors are less likely to display long-term negative effects than babies of less sensitive mothers with depression (NICHD Early Child Care Research Network, 1999). In other words, when mothers who are depressed exhibit the same kinds of parenting behaviors as most mothers without depression, their emotional status doesn't appear to have negative effects on their babies' development.

Studies involving many mothers with panic disorder have shown that these mothers, like mothers with depression, exhibit behaviors that may interfere with synchrony (Warren et al., 2003). Because it is through behavior that maternal psychiatric illnesses affect infants, parent training may provide an avenue through which the potential negative effects of this caregiver characteristic can be moderated. Indeed, several studies have shown that training can increase the frequency of sensitive behaviors in mothers who are depressed and, as a result, lead to changes in infants' attachment status (van den Boom, 1994, 1995). Moreover, appropriate medications may positively affect many aspects of behaviors of mothers who are psychiatrically ill (e.g., Kaplan, Bachorowski, Smoski, & Zinser, 2001).

Long-Term Consequences of Attachment Quality

Learning Objective 6.7

What are the long-term consequences of attachment quality?

As we noted earlier, attachment theory proposes that early emotional relationships shape later ones. Thus, researchers have examined the links between Ainsworth's classification and a wide range of other behaviors in infants, children, adolescents, and adults. Dozens of studies show that children rated as securely attached to their mothers in infancy are later more sociable, more positive in their behavior toward friends and siblings, less clinging and dependent on teachers, less aggressive and disruptive, more empathetic, and more emotionally mature in their interactions in school and other settings outside the home (e.g., Carlson, Sampson, & Sroufe, 2003; Carlson & Sroufe, 1995; Jacobsen, Husa, Fendrich, Kruesi, & Ziegenhain, 1997; Leve & Fagot, 1995).

Adolescents who were rated as securely attached in infancy or who are classed as secure on the basis of interviews in adolescence are also more socially skilled, have more intimate friendships, are more likely to be rated as leaders, and have higher self-esteem and better grades (Black & McCartney, 1995; Jacobsen & Hofmann, 1997; Lieberman, Doyle, & Markiewicz, 1995; Ostoja, McCrone, Lehn, Reed, & Sroufe, 1995). Those with insecure attachments—particularly those with avoidant attachments—not only have less positive and supportive friendships in adolescence but also are more likely to become sexually active early and to practice riskier sex (Carlson, Sroufe, Egeland, 2004; O'Beirne & Moore, 1995; Sroufe, Carlson, & Schulman, 1993; Urban, Carlson, Egeland, & Sroufe, 1991).

Quality of attachment in infancy also predicts sociability through early, middle, and late adulthood (Van Lange, DeBruin, Otten, & Joireman, 1997). Moreover, one study found a link between attachment history and sexual dysfunction in adult males (Kinzl, Mangweth, Traweger, & Biebl, 1996). In fact, that investigation found that quality of attachment in infancy predicted sexual dysfunction in adulthood better than a history of sexual abuse did.

Developmentalists have also found that an adult's internal model of attachment affects his or her parenting behaviors (Crittenden, Partridge, & Claussen, 1991; Steele, Hodges, Kaniuk, Hillman, & Henderson, 2003). For example, mothers who are themselves securely attached are more responsive and sensitive in their behavior toward their infants or young children (Hammond, Landry, Swank, & Smith, 2000; van IJzendoorn, 1995). Attachment history affects parental attitudes as well. Some studies have shown that parents with a history of insecure attachment are more likely to view their infants negatively (Pesonen, Raikkonnen, Strandberg, Keltikangas-Järvinen, & Jarvenpaa, 2004). Such parents may also lack confidence in their ability to perform effectively in the parenting role (Huth-Bocks, Levendosky, Bogat, & von Eye, 2004).

Examinations of the long-term consequences of attachment quality suggest that both psychoanalysts and ethologists are correct in their assumption that the attachment relationship becomes the foundation for future social relationships. Certainly, it appears to be critical to the relationship most similar to it—the relationship an individual ultimately develops with her or his own child.

Learning Objective 6.8

In what ways do patterns of attachment vary across cultures?

Cross-Cultural Research on Attachment

Studies in a variety of countries (e.g., Posada et al., 1995) support Ainsworth's contention that some form of "secure base behavior" occurs in every child in every culture. But there is also some evidence suggesting that secure attachments may be more likely in certain cultures than in others. The most thorough analyses have come from some Dutch psychologists who have examined the results of 32 separate studies in eight different countries. Figure 6.1 presents the percentage of babies whose attachment is classified as secure, avoidant, and ambivalent for each country (van IJzendoorn & Kroonenberg, 1988). It is important to avoid overinterpreting the information in this table, because in most cases there are only one or two studies from a given country, normally with quite small samples. The single study from China, for example, included only 36 babies. Still, the findings are thought-provoking.

The most striking thing about these data is their consistency. In each of the eight countries, secure attachment is the most common pattern, found in more than half of all babies studied; in six of the eight countries, an avoidant pattern is the more common of the two forms of insecure attachment. Only in Israel and Japan is this pattern significantly reversed. How can developmentalists explain such differences?

One possibility is that the Strange Situation is simply not an appropriate measure of attachment security in all cultures. For example, because Japanese babies are rarely separated from their mother in the first year of life, being left totally alone in the midst of the Strange Situation may be far more stressful for them and might result in more intense, inconsolable crying and hence a classification of ambivalent attachment. Yet when researchers look directly at toddlers' actual behavior in the Strange Situation, they find few cultural differences in such things as proximity seeking or avoidance of mother—which gives researchers more confidence that the Strange Situation is tapping similar processes among children in many cultures (Sagi, van IJzendoorn, & Koren-Karie, 1991).

It is also possible that what people mean by a "secure" or an "avoidant" pattern is different in different cultures, even if the percentages for the categories are similar (Crittenden, 2000). German researchers, for example, have suggested that an insecure-avoidant classification in their culture may reflect not indifference in the mother, but rather explicit training toward

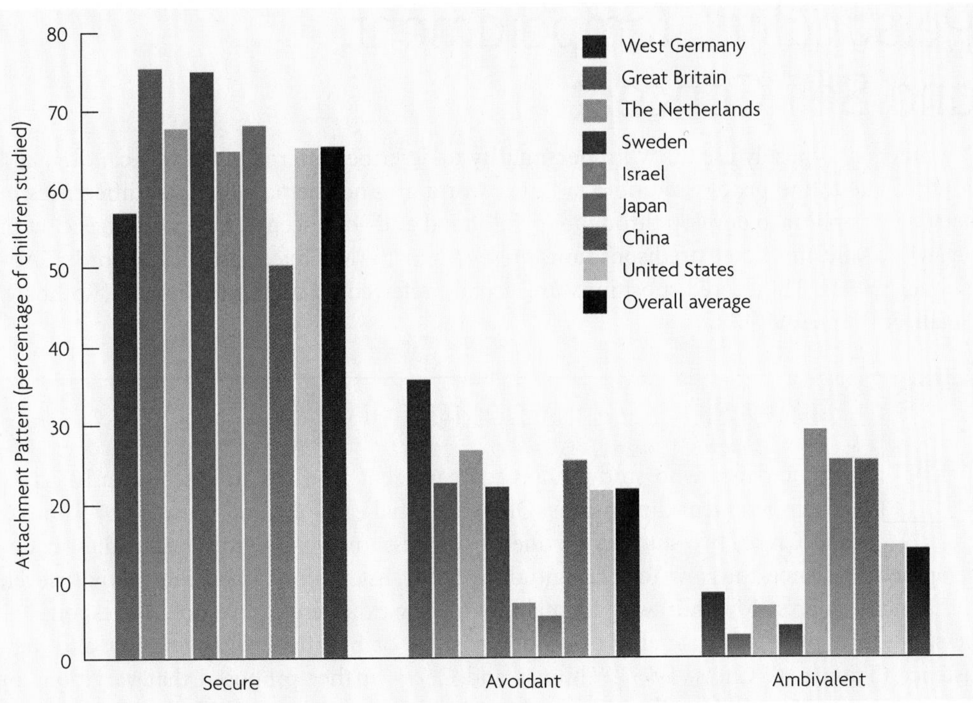

Figure 6.1 Attachment Categories Across Cultures

In a classic study, van IJzendoorn and Kroonenberg (1988) found that secure attachment was the most frequent category across several cultures.

(*Source*: Based on Table 1 of van IJzendoorn and Kroonenberg, 1998, pp. 150–151.)

greater independence for the baby (Grossmann, Grossmann, Spangler, Suess, & Unzner, 1985). Research in Israel shows that the Strange Situation attachment classification predicts a baby's later social skills in much the same way as it does for U.S. babies, which suggests that the classification system is valid in both cultures (Sagi, 1990). Physically "clingy" behavior in American preschool children is related both to a history of insecure attachment and to emotional disturbance. However, in Japanese children, it is correlated with a secure attachment history and good adjustment at preschool age (Mizuta, Zahn-Waxler, Cole, & Hiruma, 1996).

In all of the countries van IJzendoorn studied, infants typically have one caregiver, usually the mother. What would researchers find in a culture in which the child's early care was more communal? To find out, developmentalists studied a group called the Efe, who forage in the forests of Zaire (Tronick, Morelli, & Ivey, 1992). The Efe live in camps, in small groups of perhaps 20 individuals, each group consisting of several extended families, often brothers and their wives. Infants in these communities are cared for communally in the early months and years of life. They are carried and held by all the adult women and interact regularly with many different adults. If they have needs, they are tended to by whichever adult or older child is nearby; they may even be nursed by women other than the mother, although they normally sleep with the mother. The researchers reported two things of particular interest about early attachment in this group. First, Efe infants seem to use virtually any adult or older child in their group as a safe base, which suggests that they may have no single central attachment. But, beginning at about 6 months, the Efe infants nonetheless seem to insist on being with their mother more and to prefer her over other women, although other women continue to help with caregiving responsibilities. Thus, even in an extremely communal rearing arrangement, some sign of a central attachment is evident, though perhaps less dominant.

At the moment, the most plausible hypothesis is that the same factors involving mother-infant interaction contribute to secure and insecure attachments in all cultures, and that these patterns reflect similar internal models. But it will take more research in which long-term outcomes for individuals in the various categories are studied before researchers will know whether this is correct.

Personality, Temperament, and Self-Concept

Psychologists typically use the word **personality** to describe patterns in the way children and adults relate to the people and objects in the world around them. Individual differences in personality appear to develop throughout childhood and adolescence, based on a basic set of behavioral and emotional predispositions present at birth (McCrae, Costa, Ostendord, & Angleitner, 2000). These predispositions are usually referred to as **temperament** (Rothbart, Ahadi, & Evans, 2000).

Learning Objective 6.9

On which dimensions of temperament do most developmentalists agree?

Dimensions of Temperament

Psychologists who study infant temperament have yet to agree on a basic set of temperament dimensions. One influential early theory, proposed by Thomas and Chess, two authors of one of the best known longitudinal studies in developmental science, the New York Longitudinal Study, listed nine dimensions: activity level, rhythmicity, approach/withdrawal, adaptability to new experience, threshold of responsiveness, intensity of reaction, quality of mood (positive or negative), distractibility, and persistence (Thomas & Chess, 1977). Thomas and Chess further proposed that variations in these nine qualities tend to cluster into three types that can be applied to about 75% of infants. The remaining infants exhibit combinations of two or three of the main types of temperament.

- *Easy children (40% of infants).* These children approach new events positively, display predictable sleeping and eating cycles, are generally happy, and adjust easily to change.
- *Difficult children (10% of infants).* Patterns that characterize children in this category include irregular sleeping and eating cycles, emotional negativity and irritability, and resistance to change.
- *Slow-to-warm-up children (15% of infants).* Children in this group display few intense reactions, either positive or negative, and appear nonresponsive to unfamiliar people.

Other researchers have examined temperament from a trait perspective rather than a dimensional perspective. These developmentalists view an individual infant's temperament as a function of how much or how little of various characteristics she possesses. For example, an infant in whom a high level of physical activity was combined with emotional irritability would have a different temperamental profile than an infant in whom high activity was combined with a more easygoing nature.

In their classic work on the subject of temperament, researchers Arnold Buss and Robert Plomin (1984) suggested three dimensions of temperament: *activity level*, *sociability*, and *emotionality*. Since then, other researchers have proposed and investigated additional traits. While there is still some disagreement among developmentalists as to what the component characteristics of temperament are, research has revealed a few key traits (Thompson & Goodvin, 2005). *Activity level* refers to an infant's tendency to either move often and vigorously or remain passive or immobile. *Approach/positive emotionality* is a tendency to move toward rather than away from new people, things, or objects, usually accompanied by positive emotion (see *Developmental Science in the Classroom*). *Inhibition*—a tendency to respond with fear or withdrawal to new people, new situations, or new objects—is the flip side of approach. *Negative emotionality* is a tendency to respond to frustrating circumstances with anger, fussing, loudness, or irritability. Finally, *effortful control/task persistence* is an ability to stay focused, to manage attention and effort.

personality a pattern of responding to people and objects in the environment

temperament predispositions, such as activity level, that are present at birth and form the foundations of personality

DEVELOPMENTAL SCIENCE IN THE CLASSROOM

Temperamental Surgency in the Toddler Classroom

Benita works in a child-care center and is assigned to the toddler room. She has noticed that one of the tykes, an 18-month-old boy named Thomas, seems to dominate the others. The little boy is bright, cheerful, and physically active and makes friends easily. However, whenever Benita plays naming games with the toddlers, Thomas blurts out an answer whenever Benita asks "What's this?" before his peers have a chance to answer. Benita wonders whether she should make a special effort to reduce Thomas's domineering behavior.

Developmental scientists often employ Chess and Thomas's goodness-of-fit model to explain interactions between infants' temperaments and their capacity to adjust to different settings. For instance, some temperamental profiles predispose infants to adjust easily to the structure of a child-care center, whereas others increase the chances that they will develop behavior problems (De-Schipper, Tevecchio, van IJzendoorn, & Linting, 2003). In general, infants who are classified as easy according to Chess and Thomas's system more readily adjust to child-care centers than do children in the difficult category. Such research suggests that what Benita may be seeing in Thomas's behavior is a conflict between his temperament and the demands of the environment in which he is being cared for.

Research suggests that Thomas possesses an above-average level of a dimension of temperament called *surgency*, a cluster of traits that includes sociability, high activity level, generally positive emotional states, and impulsiveness (Rothbart & Putnam, 2002). Some studies suggest that surgency is observable in infants as young as 3 months of age. Moreover, surgency is a highly stable facet of temperament that persists throughout childhood and into adulthood. However, surgent children's impulsiveness predisposes them to develop behavior problems in structured settings such as child-care centers. Despite their generally positive emotional state, surgent children can become frustrated when they are prevented from behaving impulsively. In some cases, this frustration leads them to behave aggressively toward their peers. Thus, Benita's challenge is to find a way to encourage Thomas to allow the other children to respond to her questions without causing him to become so frustrated that he expresses his impulsiveness in less positive ways.

Questions for Reflection

1. How might Benita use the principles of operant conditioning that you learned about in Chapter 2 to reduce Thomas's behavior of blurting out answers?
2. If you were Thomas's parent, how would you respond if Benita expressed her concerns about his impulsive behavior to you?

Origins and Stability of Temperament

Learning Objective 6.10

What are the roles of heredity, neurological processes, environment, and gender in the formation of temperament?

Because temperamental differences appear so early in life, even during the prenatal period (see Chapter 3), it may seem that genes are entirely responsible for them. However, research suggests that both nature and nurture contribute to individual differences in temperament.

Heredity Studies of twins in many countries show that identical twins are more alike in their temperament than are fraternal twins (Rose, 1995). For example, one group of researchers studied 100 pairs of identical twins and 100 pairs of fraternal twins at both 14 and 20 months. At each age, the children's temperaments were rated by their mothers using the Buss and Plomin categories. In addition, each child's level of behavioral inhibition was measured by observing how the child reacted to strange toys and a strange adult in a special laboratory playroom. Did the child approach the novel toys quickly and eagerly or hang back or seem fearful? Did the child approach the strange adult or remain close to the mother? The correlations between temperament scores on all four of these dimensions were consistently higher for identical than for fraternal twins, indicating a strong genetic effect (Emde et al., 1992; Plomin et al., 1993).

Research showing that temperament is stable across infancy and into children's later years supports the view that temperament is strongly influenced by heredity. There is growing evidence of consistency in temperamental ratings over rather long periods of infancy and childhood. For example, Australian researchers studying a group of 450 children found that mothers' reports of children's irritability, cooperation/manageability, inflexibility, rhythmicity, persistence, and tendency to approach rather than avoid contact were all quite consistent from infancy through age 8 (Pedlow, Sanson, Prior, & Oberklaid, 1993). Similarly, in an American longitudinal study of a group of children ages 1 through 12, psychologists found strong consistency in parents' reports of their children's overall "difficultness," as well as approach versus withdrawal, positive versus negative mood, and activity level (Guerin & Gottfried, 1994a, 1994b). Other research suggests that temperamental differences are stable from the preschool years into adulthood (Caspi, 2000).

Researchers have also found considerable consistency at various ages in Jerome Kagan's measure of inhibition, which is based on direct observation of the child's behavior rather than on the mother's ratings of the child's temperament. In one study, for example, children who had been classified as inhibited at 4 months were less socially responsive to both adults and children at age 2 than were their uninhibited peers (Young, Fox & Zahn-Waxler, 1999). In Kagan's own longitudinal study, half of the children who had shown high levels of crying and motor activity in response to a novel situation when they were 4 months old were still classified as highly inhibited at age 8, and three-fourths of those rated as uninhibited at 4 months remained in that category 8 years later (Kagan, Snidman & Arcus, 1993). Subsequent studies showed that these trends continued into the children's teen and early adulthood years (Kagan & Herschkowitz, 2005).

Neurological Processes Many temperament theorists take the heredity argument a step further and trace the basic differences in behavior to variations in underlying physiological patterns (e.g., Gunnar, 1994; Rothbart, Derryberry, & Posner, 1994). For example, studies examining the genes that control the functions of two important neurotransmitters, dopamine and serotonin, support Kagan's hypothesis (Lakatos et al., 2003). These neurotransmitters regulate the brain's responses to new information and unusual situations, precisely the kinds of stimuli that appeared to overstimulate shy children in Kagan's research.

Another important neurological variable that has been found to be associated with shyness is *frontal lobe asymmetry* (Kagan & Herschkowitz, 2005). In most people, the left and right hemispheres of the frontal lobes respond similarly to new stimuli; in other words, they exhibit symmetry. In shy infants, however, the two hemispheres respond differently—that is, asymmetrically—to such stimuli. Specifically, these children exhibit higher levels of arousal in the right hemisphere than in the left (Fox, Henderson, Rubin, Calkins, & Schmidt, 2001; Henderson, Marshall, Fox, & Rubin, 2004). Such findings make it tempting to conclude that temperamental differences are based in neurological processes. Research, however, suggests that it is difficult to say whether neurological differences are a cause or an effect of temperament. Developmentalists have found that shy infants whose temperaments change over the first 4 years of life—that is, those who become more outgoing—also become less likely to exhibit the asymmetrical pattern of arousal (Fox et al., 2001).

niche-picking the process of selecting experiences on the basis of temperament

As long as securely attached infants remain physically close to their parents, they can easily manage the stresses associated with being in a large group of unfamiliar people.

Environment Critics of neurological studies point out that it is impossible to know whether such findings are causes or effects (Johnson, 2003). They argue that behavior shapes the brain. Thus, shy children may exhibit different neurological patterns than outgoing children because their exhibition of shy behavior contributes to the neural networks that developmental processes in the brain, such as pruning, allow to develop and those that are shut down due to lack of use.

Consistent with these critics' claims, researchers have found that a number of temperament-environment interactions tend to strengthen built-in qualities. For one thing, people of all ages choose their experiences, a process Sandra Scarr refers to as **niche-picking** (Scarr & McCartney, 1983). Our choices reflect our temperaments. For example, highly sociable children seek out contact with others; children low on the activity dimension are more likely to choose sedentary activities, such as putting together puzzles or playing board games, over playing baseball.

Parents may also be able to either increase or decrease the effects of an infant's inborn temperamental tendencies. In one longitudinal study, researchers videotaped play sessions in which Chinese parents interacted with their 4-year-old children (Hou, Chen, & Chen, 2005). When the children were 7 years old, the researchers found that parent behavior at age 4 predicted behavioral inhibition (shyness) at age 7. Specifically, the more controlling parents were during the play sessions, the more likely their children were to be rated as more behaviorally inhibited at age 7 than they had been at age 4. Such findings suggest that, perhaps contrary to what you might expect, parents who accept an inhibited child's temperament may contribute more to the child's ability to overcome shyness later in life than parents who try to force a child to be more outgoing. Some experts suggest that parental influences may be greatest for children who are at the extremes of a given temperamental continuum. That is, children who are extremely inhibited may be more subject to parental influence than those who are moderately so (Buss & Plomin, 1984).

Developmentalists propose that it is the **goodness-of-fit** between an infant's temperament and his environment that influences how inborn temperamental characteristics are manifested later in life (Thomas & Chess, 1977). For example, if the parents of an irritable baby boy are good at tolerating his irritability and persist in establishing a synchronous relationship with him, then his irritability doesn't lead to the development of an insecure attachment. An infant's gender may also influence how the environment responds to his temperament, as discussed in the next section.

Gender Differences In some studies, researchers have found clear gender differences in certain dimensions of temperament. You have already learned that boys and girls differ in physical activity level, and that this difference is discernible even before they are born (see Chapter 3). Researchers have also found that boys are more emotionally intense and less fearful than girls and that girls are generally more sociable (Calkins, Dedmon, Gill, Lomax, & Johnson, 2002; Gartstein & Rothbart, 2003).

Nevertheless, temperamental differences between boys and girls are much smaller than the differences perceived by parents and other adults. In one classic study, researchers found that adults viewing a videotape of an infant interpreted the baby's behavior differently depending on the gender label experimenters provided. Participants who were told the baby was a girl interpreted a particular behavior as expressing "fear." Amazingly, participants who believed the infant was a boy labeled the same behavior "anger" (Condry & Condry, 1976). More recent research employing this technique suggests that adults nowadays are somewhat less likely to stereotype infant behavior in this way, although, like their counterparts in the 1970s, they attend to and comment on motor activity more when they believe the infant under observation is a boy (Pomerleau, Malcuit, Turgeon, & Cossette, 1997).

Temperamental stereotyping may also affect the quality of the parent-infant relationship and, in turn, modify a child's inborn temperament. For example, parents of a calm, quiet girl may respond positively to her because they perceive her behavior to be consistent with their concept of "girlness." By contrast, parents of a physically active girl may develop a rejecting, disapproving attitude toward her because they view her behavior as excessively masculine. In this way, parents may unwittingly encourage girls and boys to manifest temperamental characteristics that are consistent with cultural expectations and to suppress those that are not.

goodness-of-fit the degree to which an infant's temperament is adaptable to his or her environment, and vice versa

Self-Concept

Learning Objective 6.11

How do the subjective self, the objective self, and the emotional self develop during the first 2 years?

During the same months when a baby is creating an internal model of attachment and expressing her own unique temperament, she is also developing an internal model of self. Freud suggested that the infant needs to develop a sense of separateness from her mother before she can form a sense of self. Piaget emphasized that the infant's understanding of the basic concept of object permanence is a necessary precursor for

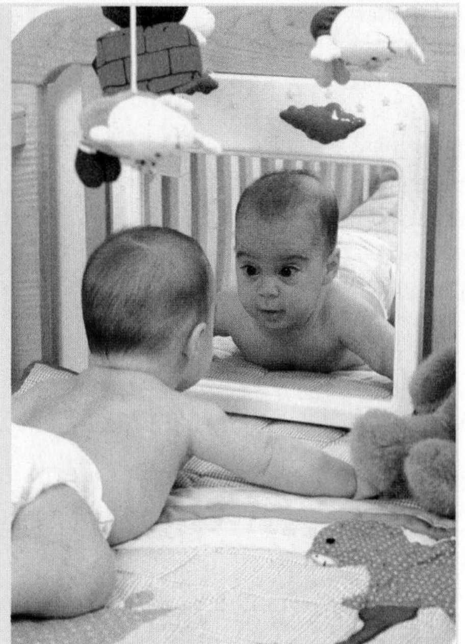

Research that has examined babies' ability to recognize themselves suggests that self-awareness develops in the middle of the second year.

the child's attaining self-permanence. Both of these aspects of early self-development reappear in more recent descriptions of the emergence of the sense of self (Lewis, 1990, 1991).

The Subjective Self The child's first task is to figure out that he is separate from others and that this separate self endures over time and space. Developmentalists call this aspect of the self-concept the **subjective self**, or sometimes the **existential self**, because the key awareness seems to be "I exist." The roots of this understanding lie in the myriad everyday interactions the baby has with the objects and people in his world that lead him to understand, during the first 2 to 3 months of life, that he can have effects on things (Lewis, 1991). For example, when the child touches a mobile, it moves; when he cries, someone responds; when he smiles, his mother smiles back. Through this process, the baby separates self from everything else and a sense of "I" begins to emerge.

By the time the infant has constructed a fairly complete understanding of object permanence, at about 8 to 12 months, the subjective self has fully emerged. Just as he is figuring out that Mom and Dad continue to exist when they are out of sight, he is figuring out—at least in some preliminary way—that he exists separately and has some permanence.

The Objective Self The second major task is for the toddler to come to understand that she is also an object in the world (Lewis, 1991). Just as a ball has properties—roundness, the ability to roll, a certain feel in the hand—so the "self" has qualities or properties, such as gender, size, a name, shyness or boldness, coordination or clumsiness. It is this self-awareness that is the hallmark of the second aspect of identity, the **objective self**, sometimes called the **categorical self** because once the child achieves self-awareness the process of defining the self involves placing oneself in a whole series of categories.

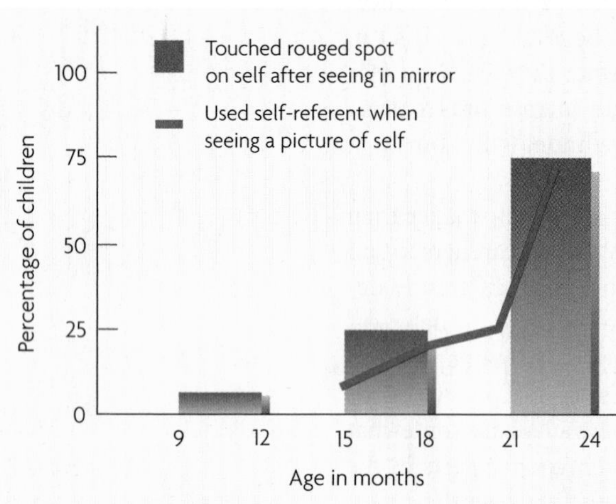

Figure 6.2 The Rouge Test

Mirror recognition and self-naming develop at almost exactly the same time.

(*Source*: From M. Lewis and J. Brooks, *The Development of Affect*, 1978, pp. 214–215. With kind permission from Springer Science and Business Media.)

It has not been easy to determine just when a child has developed the initial self-awareness that delineates the formation of the objective self. The most commonly used procedure involves a mirror. First, the baby is placed in front of a mirror, just to see how she behaves. Most infants between about 9 and 12 months old will look at their own image, make faces, or try to interact with the baby in the mirror in some way. After allowing this free exploration for a time, the experimenter, while pretending to wipe the baby's face with a cloth, puts a spot of rouge on the baby's nose and then lets the baby look in the mirror again. The crucial test of self-recognition, and thus of awareness of the self, is whether the baby reaches for the spot on her own nose, rather than the nose on the face in the mirror.

The results of a classic study using this procedure are graphed in Figure 6.2. As you can see, few of the 9- to 12-month-old children in this study touched their own nose, but three-quarters of the children aged 21 months showed that level of self-recognition, a result confirmed in a variety of other research studies, including studies in Europe (Asendorpf, Warkentin, & Baudonnière, 1996; Lewis & Brooks, 1978). Figure 6.2 also shows the rate at which children refer to themselves by name when they are shown a picture of themselves, which is another commonly used measure of self-awareness. You can see that this development occurs at almost exactly the same time as self-recognition in a mirror. Both are present by about the middle of the second year of life, a finding confirmed by other investigators (Bullock & Lütkenhaus, 1990). At this point, toddlers begin to show a newly proprietary attitude ("Mine!") toward toys or other treasured objects.

As self-awareness develops, infants begin to refer to themselves by name and, near the end of the second year, to label themselves as boys or girls. In addition, infants recognize

subjective (existential) self an infant's awareness that she or he is a separate person who endures through time and space and can act on the environment

objective (categorical) self a toddler's understanding that he or she is defined by various categories such as gender or qualities such as shyness that they belong to the "child" category. They also use categorical terms such as "good" and "big" to describe themselves. For example, a girl might say "good girl" when she obeys her parent or "big girl" when she is successful at a task like using the toilet (Stipek, Gralinski, & Kopp, 1990).

The Emotional Self Development of the **emotional self** begins when babies learn to identify changes in emotion expressed in others' faces, at 2 to 3 months of age. Initially, they discriminate emotions best when they receive information on many channels simultaneously—such as when they see a particular facial expression and hear the same emotion expressed in the adult's voice (Walker-Andrews, 1997). Moreover, in these early weeks, infants are much better at discerning the emotional expressions of a familiar face than those of an unfamiliar face (Kahana-Kalman & Walker-Andrews, 2001). By 5 to 7 months, babies begin to "read" one channel at a time, responding to facial expression alone or vocal expression alone, even when the emotions are displayed by a stranger rather than Mom or Dad (Balaban, 1995). They also respond to a much wider variety of emotions than younger infants do and can distinguish among happy, surprised, angry, fearful, interested, and sad faces (Soken & Pick, 1999; Walker-Andrews & Lennon, 1991).

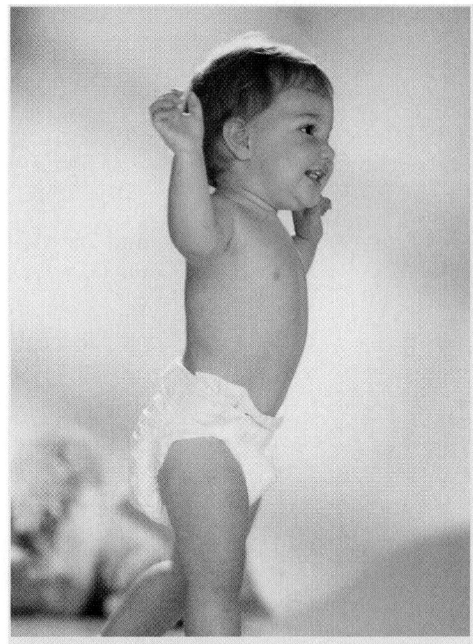

This baby's emotional reaction is best described as joy or delight rather than pride; her sense of self is not yet well enough developed that she can feel pride in learning to walk.

Near the end of the first year, infants' perceptions of others' emotions help them anticipate others' actions and guide their own behavior (Phillips, Wellman, & Spelke, 2002). For instance, they react to another infant's neutral facial expression by actively trying to elicit an emotional expression from that child (Striano & Rochat, 1999). Just as adults often work at getting a baby to smile at them, babies seem to be following the same sort of script by 8 to 10 months of age.

As the infant's understanding of others' emotions advances, it is matched by parallel progression in expression of emotions. At birth, infants have different facial expressions for interest, pain, and disgust, and an expression that conveys enjoyment develops very quickly. By the time a baby is 2 to 3 months old, adult observers can also distinguish expressions of anger and sadness, with expressions of fear appearing by 6 or 7 months (Izard et al., 1995; Izard & Harris, 1995). At about the same time, infants begin to smile more in response to human faces than to a doll's face or another inanimate object, suggesting that at this early stage the baby is already responding to the added social signals available in the human face (Ellsworth, Muir, & Hains, 1993; Legerstee, Pomerleau, Malcuit, & Feider, 1987).

Over the next several months, the infant's emotional expressions, and the behaviors that arise from them, become more sophisticated. For example, as you learned earlier in the chapter, infants who have formed an attachment to a caregiver (typically in the last few months of the first year) use the caregiver's emotions to guide their own feelings. Moreover, by this age, babies have learned to calm themselves when their caregivers behave in expected ways (Cole et al., 2004). For example, a baby who is frustrated by hunger will calm down when she sees her caregiver preparing to nurse her or to provide her with some other kind of nourishment. Finally, near the middle of the second year, at about the same time that a child shows self-recognition in the mirror, such self-conscious emotional expressions as embarrassment, pride, and shame emerge (Lewis, Allesandri, & Sullivan, 1992; Lewis, Sullivan, Stanger, & Weiss, 1989; Mascolo & Fischer, 1995).

Effects of Nonparental Care

Since the late 1970s, women in virtually every industrialized country in the world have been entering the workforce in great numbers. In the United States, the change has been particularly rapid and massive: In 1970, only 18% of U.S. married women with children under age 6 were in the labor force; at the beginning of the 21st century, 61% of such women (and more than half of women with children under age 1) were working outside the home at least part-time (NICHD

emotional self a toddler's identification of emotions expressed in others' faces and ability to regulate emotion

Early Child Care Research Network, 2003). The younger children are, the less likely they are to receive nonparental care. However, even among U.S. infants under the age of 2 years, half are cared for by someone other than a parent at least part-time (FIFCFS, 2005). Among 3- to 4-year-olds, about three-fourths receive nonparental care. The key question for psychologists is "What effect does nonparental care have on infants and young children?"

Learning Objective 6.12

Why is it difficult to study the effects of nonparental care on development?

Difficulties in Studying Nonparental Care

It might seem that the effect on infant development of this trend toward nonparental care could easily be determined by comparing babies receiving nonparental care to those cared for by their parents. However, both "nonparental care" and "parental care" are really complex interactions among numerous variables rather than single factors whose effects can be studied independently. Thus, interpretation of research on nonparental care has to take into account a variety of issues.

To begin with, in many studies an enormous range of different care arrangements are all lumped under the general title of "nonparental care" (see Figure 6.3). Infants who are cared for by grandparents in their own homes, as well as those who are enrolled in child-care centers, receive nonparental care. In addition, infants enter these care arrangements at different ages, and they remain in them for varying lengths of time. Some have the same nonparental caregiver over many years; others shift often from one care setting to another. Moreover, nonparental care varies widely in quality. Nevertheless, child-care arrangements seem to be getting somewhat more homogeneous in the United States. If this trend continues, it may become easier to study the effects of nonparental care.

According to recent surveys, the most common pattern is for a child to be cared for by a family member in the child's or family member's home (FIFCFS, 2005). Another third or so of children receiving nonparental care are cared for in *family child care.* In family child care, a person takes care of other parents' children in his or her home. Nevertheless, a majority of 3- to 6-year-olds who are cared for by relatives or in family child care are also enrolled at least part-time in some kind of child-care center or preschool. Thus, an-

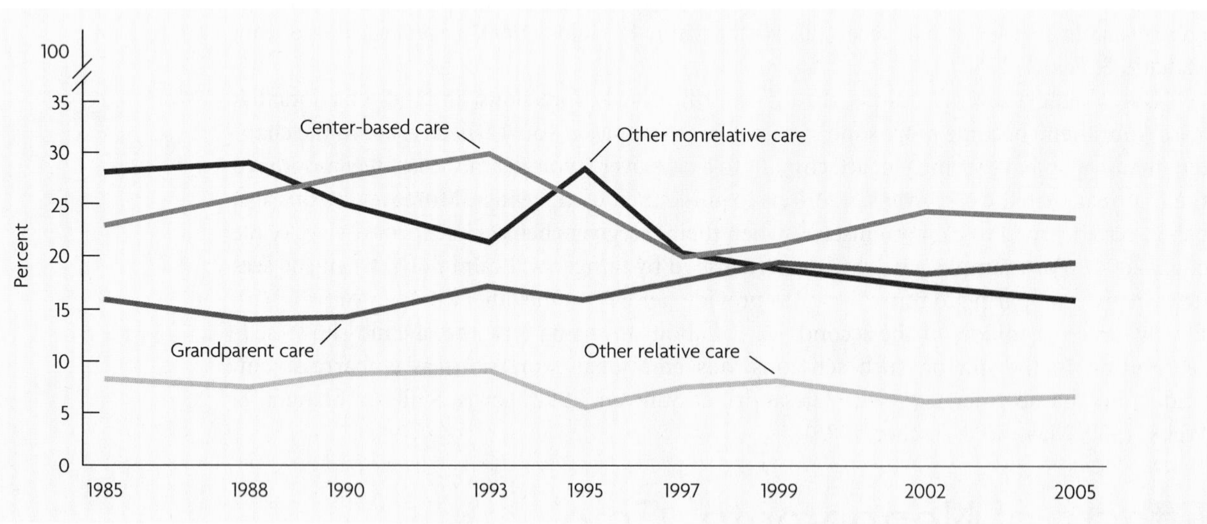

Figure 6.3 **Nonparental Care Arrangements for Children Under 4 in the United States**

Children younger than 4 years old whose mothers are employed are cared for in a variety of nonparental settings in the United States.

(*Source*: Federal Interagency Forum on Child and Family Statistics, 2007.)

other problem with studying the effects of nonparental care is that many children receive care in multiple settings.

To further complicate matters, families who place their children in nonparental care are different in a whole host of ways from those who care for their children primarily at home. How can researchers be sure that effects attributed to nonparental care are not instead the result of these other family differences? Mothers also differ in their attitudes toward the care arrangements they have made. Some mothers with children in nonparental care would rather be at home taking care of their children; others are happy to be working. Similarly, some mothers who are at home full-time would rather be working, and some are delighted to be at home. Studies of the effects of nonparental care rarely offer any information at all about the mother's level of satisfaction with her situation.

Most of the research on nonparental versus parental care has not taken these complexities into account. Researchers have frequently compared children "in child care" with those "reared at home" and assumed that any differences between the two groups were attributable to the child-care experience. Some recent studies are better, but clear answers to even the most basic questions about the impact of nonparental care on children's development are still not available. Nonetheless, because the issue is so critical, you need to be aware of what is and is not yet known.

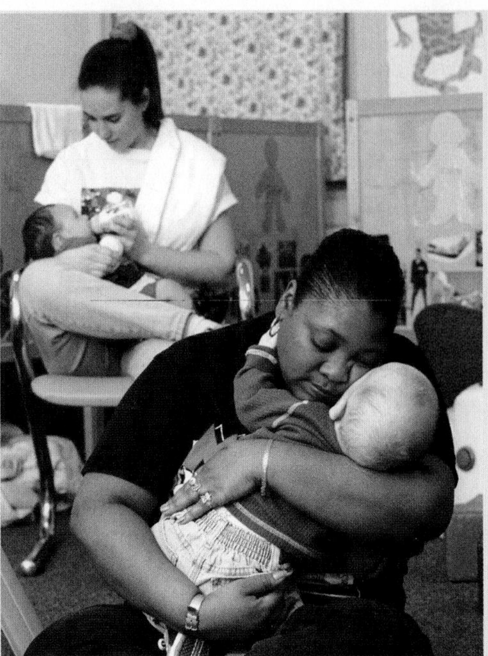

The majority of infants in the United States now experience at least some nonparental care.

Effects on Cognitive Development

Learning Objective 6.13
What might be the effects of nonparental care on cognitive development?

There is a good deal of evidence that high-quality child care has beneficial effects on many children's overall cognitive development (NICHD Early Child Care Research Network, 2006). This effect is particularly strong for children from poor families, who show significant and lasting gains in IQ and later school performance after attending highly enriched child care throughout infancy and early childhood (Campbell & Ramey, 1994; Loeb, Fuller, Kagan, & Carrol, 2003; Love et al., 2003; Ramey, 1993). Even middle-class children show some cognitive benefit when they are in high-quality child care (Peisner-Feinberg, 1995).

However, the picture is not entirely rosy. Several studies in the United States point to possible negative effects of child-care experience on cognitive development in some children, especially middle-class children. For example, in one large study of over 1,000 preschoolers, researchers found that White children—but not African American children—who had entered child care in the first year of life had lower vocabulary scores than those who had entered after age 1 (Baydar & Brooks-Gunn, 1991). Conversely, in a large study of 5- and 6-year-olds, researchers found that children from poor families who began child care before age 1 had higher reading and math scores at the start of school than did children from middle-class families who entered child care in infancy (Caughy, DiPietro, & Strobino, 1994).

How can these conflicting findings be reconciled? One fairly straightforward possibility is that the crucial issue is the discrepancy between the level of stimulation the child would receive at home and the quality of the child care. When a particular child-care setting for a given child provides more enrichment than the child would have received at home, child-care attendance has some beneficial cognitive effects; when child care is less stimulating than full-time home care would be for that child, child care has negative effects. However, there are not yet enough well-designed, large studies to make developmentalists confident that this is the right way to conceptualize the process. Consequently, the most that can be said about the effects of nonparental care on cognitive development is that it seems to be beneficial for children from impoverished environments, but research findings are mixed with respect to middle-class children.

Learning Objective 6.14

What does research suggest about the risks of nonparental care with respect to social development?

Effects on Social Development

As you have learned, the formation of an attachment relationship appears to be central to social development during infancy and in later years. Thus, one of the most important questions about nonparental care concerns its potential effects on the attachment process. Until the mid-1980s, most psychologists believed that infant child care had no negative effect on attachment. But then developmental psychologist Jay Belsky, in a series of papers and in testimony before a congressional committee, sounded an alarm (Belsky, 1985, 1992; Belsky & Rovine, 1988). Combining data from several studies, he concluded that there was a heightened risk of insecure attachment for infants who entered child care before their first birthday.

Since that time, a number of other researchers have analyzed the combined results of large numbers of studies and confirmed Belsky's original conclusion. For example, a summary of the findings of 13 different studies involving 897 infants revealed that 35% of infants who had experienced at least 5 hours per week of nonparental care were insecurely attached, compared to 29% of infants with exclusively maternal care (Lamb, Sternberg, & Prodromidis, 1992).

Another study, involving more than 1,000 infants, demonstrated that infants whose parents exhibit behaviors associated with insecure attachment, such as poor sensitivity to the child's needs, are more likely to be negatively affected by nonparental care. When all of the infants were considered together, researchers found no differences in attachment quality between those who were in nonparental care and those who were cared for at home, regardless of the age at which they entered outside care or how many hours per week they were cared for there (NICHD Early Child Care Research Network, 1998). However, when researchers looked at only those babies whose parents displayed behaviors associated with insecure attachment, such as insensitivity to the child's needs, they found that children who were home-reared were more likely to be securely attached to their caregivers than were those who were enrolled in nonparental care.

How does nonparental care affect other social relationships? Belsky argues that, when children reach school age, those who entered nonparental care during the early months of life and spent 20 or more hours per week in such care throughout early childhood are at greater risk for social problems than children who spent less time in nonparental care (Belsky, 2001, 2002). A number of studies support Belsky's view (Kim, 1997; NICHD, 2006). In fact, some research indicates that Belsky's hypothesis may have been overly optimistic with regard to the amount of nonparental care that may be harmful. One study showed that kindergartners who had spent as little as 10 hours per week in nonparental care during infancy and early childhood were more likely to display aggressiveness toward peers and disobedience toward teachers than peers who were entirely home-reared (NICHD Early Child Care Research Network, 2003). However, other studies suggest that the negative effects of nonparental care are no longer evident in children over the age of 7 (Van Beijsterveldt, Hudziak, & Boomsma, 2005).

Learning Objective 6.15

What variables should be taken into account in interpretations of research on nonparental care?

Interpreting Research on Nonparental Care

What is it about nonparental care that predisposes infants to become aggressive, disobedient kindergartners? Studies of infants' psychological responses to nonparental care may hold a clue. Researchers have found that levels of the stress hormone cortisol increase from morning to afternoon in infants who are enrolled in center-based care (Vermeer & van IJzendoorn, 2006; Watamura, Donzella, Alwin, & Gunnar, 2003). By contrast, cortisol levels decrease over the course of the day in home-reared infants. Interestingly, cortisol levels of home-reared and center-care infants are identical on weekends and holidays. Thus, some developmentalists argue that the higher levels of cortisol experienced by center-care infants affect their rapidly developing brains in ways that lead to problem behaviors. However, there is no direct evidence yet to support this hypothesis.

Some developmentalists argue that nonparental care arrangements probably vary in the degree to which they induce stress in infants and young children. In other words, they say, quality of care may be just as important as quantity of care (Maccoby & Lewis, 2003). For example, some researchers have found that, when infants are cared for in high-quality centers, the amount of time they spend in such care is unrelated to social behavior (Love et al., 2003). Thus, developmentalists urge parents, especially those who must leave their infants in center-based care for extended periods of time, to make every effort to ensure that the arrangement they choose has the characteristics discussed in the *Developmental Science at Home* feature.

Another point to keep in mind is that individual and gender differences have been found to interact with the quality and/or quantity of nonparental care. For example, infants who are behaviorally inhibited (in Jerome Kagan's terms) may be more sensitive to the stresses associated with center-based care (Watamura et al., 2003). Moreover, boys in nonparental care are more likely than girls in similar care settings to be insecurely attached to their caregivers (Crockenberg, 2003). For these reasons, more research that takes both temperament and gender into account is needed before we can say for certain that nonparental care has uniformly negative effects on children's social development (Crockenberg, 2003).

Finally, it is important to understand that, on average, the differences between children in nonparental care and their home-reared peers, both positive and negative, are very small (NICHD, 2006). Moreover, studies that have attempted to examine all of the complex variables associated with parental and nonparental care, such as parents' level of education, have shown that family variables are more important than the type of child-care arrangements a family chooses (NICHD Early Child Care Research Network, 2003).

Developmental psychologist Sandra Scarr, a leading child-care researcher, has suggested that the kind of child care parents choose is an extension of their own characteristics and parenting styles (Scarr, 1997). For example, poorly educated parents may choose child-care arrangements that do not emphasize infant learning. Similarly, parents whose focus is on intellectual development may not place a high priority on the emotional aspects of a particular child-care arrangement. Thus, Scarr claims, child-care effects are likely to be parenting effects in disguise.

DEVELOPMENTAL SCIENCE AT HOME

Choosing a Child-Care Center

Rey is a single father who needs to find someone to care for his 14-month-old son while he is at work. Up until now, Rey's mother has been caring for the boy, but she has decided to return to work herself. Rey has heard about studies showing that high-quality care can enhance children's development, but he isn't exactly sure what is meant by the term "high-quality." Here are a few pointers that Rey could use to find a high-quality child-care center (Clarke-Stewart, 1992; Howes, Phillips, & Whitebook, 1992; Scarr & Eisenberg, 1993).

- **A low teacher/child ratio.** For children younger than 2, the ratio should be no higher than 1:4; for 2- to 3-year-olds, ratios between 1:4 and 1:10 appear to be acceptable.
- **A small group size.** The smaller the number of children cared for together—whether in one room in a child-care center or in a home—the better for the child. For infants, a maximum of 6 to 8 per group appears best; for 1- to 2-year-olds, between 6 and 12 per group; for older children, groups as large as 15 or 20 appear to be acceptable.
- **A clean, colorful space, adapted to child play.** It is not essential to have lots of expensive toys, but the center must offer a variety of activities that children find engaging, organized in a way that encourages play.
- **A daily plan.** The daily curriculum should include some structure, some specific teaching, and some supervised activities. However, too much regimentation is not ideal.
- **Sensitive caregivers.** The adults in the child-care setting should be positive, involved, and responsive to the children, not merely custodial.
- **Knowledgeable caregivers.** Training in child development and infant curriculum development helps caregivers provide a child-care setting that meets criteria for good quality.

Questions for Reflection

1. What do you think Rey should do to ease his son's transition from family care to a child-care center?
2. One of the criteria is "sensitive caregivers." What kinds of caregiver behaviors might be indicative of this criterion?

Test Prep Center

with mydevelopmentlab

THEORIES OF SOCIAL AND PERSONALITY DEVELOPMENT

6.1 How do Freud's and Erikson's views of personality development in the first year of life differ? (p. 154)

Freud suggested that individual differences in personality originated in the nursing and weaning practices of infants' mothers. Erikson emphasized the roles of both mothers and fathers, as well as other adults in the infant's environment, in providing for all the infant's needs, thereby instilling a sense of trust (or cynicism) concerning the social world.

1. Classify each of the following statements as consistent with (A) Freud's or (B) Erikson's view of infant development.

   ______ (1) If the infant's needs are frustrated or overgratified, he will become fixated.

   ______ (2) Infants satisfy their desire for pleasure with their mouths.

   ______ (3) Harlow's infant monkeys preferred cloth mothers to those that had fed them.

   ______ (4) The infant and the mother have a symbiotic relationship in which the two behave as one.

6.2 What are the main ideas of attachment theory? (pp. 154–155)

Ethologists hypothesize that attachment is the foundation of later personality and social development. They further suggest that the first 2 years of life are a sensitive, or critical, period for the development of attachment.

2. Explain why each of the following statements about the ethological perspective is false.

   (A) The ethological perspective proposes that infants' desire to form emotional bonds with their caregivers is learned through modeling.

   ____

   ____

   (B) According to the ethological perspective, an infant who fails to form a close relationship with a caregiver can develop a relationship with a peer that will serve the same developmental purpose.

   ____

   ____

   (C) Ethologists believe that early relationships have little impact on relationships in adulthood.

   ____

   ____

ATTACHMENT

6.3 How does synchrony affect parent-infant relations? (pp. 155–156)

For parents to form a strong attachment relationship with an infant, what is most crucial is the development of synchrony, a set of mutually reinforcing and interlocking behaviors that characterize most interactions between parent and infant. Fathers as well as mothers form strong bonds with their infants, but fathers show more physically playful behaviors with their children than do mothers.

3. At what point in babies' development do mothers and fathers begin to behave differently toward them?

   ____

   ____

6.4 What are the four phases of attachment and the behaviors associated with them? (pp. 156–158)

Bowlby proposed that the child's attachment to a caregiver develops in four phases, beginning with rather indiscriminate aiming of attachment behaviors toward anyone within reach, through a focus on one or more figures, and then to "secure base behavior," beginning at about 6 months of age, which signals the presence of a clear attachment. In the final phase, the child develops an internal model of attachment that influences current and future close relationships.

4. Fill in the table below with information about the four phases of attachment proposed by Bowlby.

Stage	Name of Stage	Age	Attachment Behaviors
1			
2			
3			
4			

5. From the Multimedia Library within MyDevelopmentLab, watch the *Stranger Anxiety* video and answer the following question.

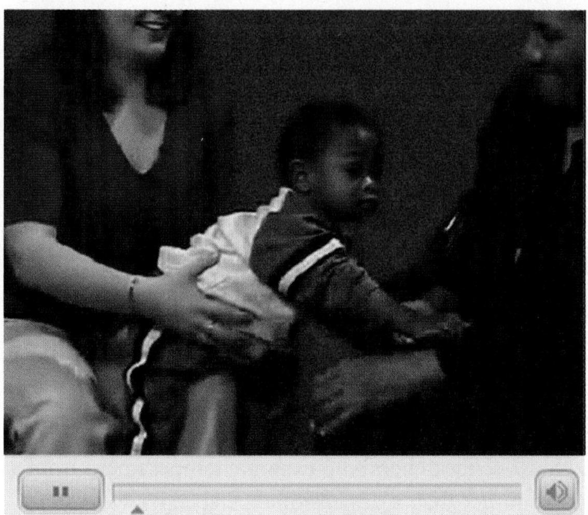

During which of Bowlby's stages would you expect to see the behaviors shown by the child in the video?

____

____

6.5 What are the variables that contribute to the development and stability of the four types of attachment? (pp. 158–159)

Children differ in the quality of their first attachments, which can be either consistent or changeable, and thus in the internal models of relationships that they develop. When a child's circumstances change in some major way, the security of the child's attachment may change as well.

6. From the Multimedia Library within MyDevelopmentLab, run through the *Attachment Classifications in the Strange Situation* simulation and classify each separation/reunion behavior pattern below according to Ainsworth's categories.

Attachment Classifications in the Strange Situation

The Strange Situation

In this task, you will classify the attachment status of children based on their behavior in the Strange Situation procedure. The strange situation is a series of separation and reunion episodes in which a child interacts with a parent and a stranger. The two reunion episodes are very important because the behaviors that occur during these episodes provide the most reliable data for classification.

stop next

______ (1) upset at separation, but not comforted by mother's return

______ (2) easily separates and greets mother positively upon return

______ (3) not upset at separation; avoids mother at reunion

______ (4) inconsistent pattern of behavior at separation and reunion

6.6 What characteristics might affect a parent's ability to establish an attachment relationship with an infant? (pp. 160–161)

Caregiver characteristics such as marital status, age, education level, and income can affect the infant's attachment quality, as can the caregiver's level of emotional responsiveness to the infant. Also, infants whose parents have psychiatric illnesses are more likely to form insecure attachments than are babies whose parents do not have these disorders.

7. Classify each statement as True or False.

______ (1) The marital status of an infant's parents is unrelated to attachment quality.

______ (2) Older mothers display more sensitive caregiving behaviors than teenaged mothers do.

______ (3) Psychiatric illness in the mother can interfere with synchrony.

______ (4) Mothers who are depressed touch their babies more often than mothers without depression do.

______ (5) Parent training can moderate the effects of maternal psychiatric illness on attachment.

6.7 What are the long-term consequences of attachment quality? (pp. 161–162)

The security of the initial attachment is reasonably stable; later in childhood, securely attached children appear to be more socially skillful and more emotionally mature. The internal model of attachment that individuals develop in infancy affects how they parent their own babies.

8. List the outcomes in each phase of development that are associated with secure attachment in infancy.

Early and Middle Childhood	Adolescence	Adulthood

6.8 In what ways do patterns of attachment vary across cultures? (pp. 162–163)

Studies in many countries suggest that secure attachment is the most common pattern everywhere, but cultures differ in the frequency of different types of insecure attachment.

9. True or False: Infants who are cared for in groups develop a preference for their own mothers. ___________

PERSONALITY, TEMPERAMENT, AND SELF-CONCEPT

6.9 On which dimensions of temperament do most developmentalists agree? (pp. 164–165)

Temperament theorists generally agree on the following basic temperament dimensions: activity level, approach/positive emotionality, inhibition, negative emotionality, and effortful control/task persistence.

10. Describe the three types of temperament proposed by Thomas and Chess.

(A) Easy

____

(B) Difficult

____

(C) Slow-to-warm-up

____

11. From the Multimedia Library within MyDevelopmentLab, watch the *Temperament: Easy* video and answer the following question.

What is it about the behavior of the child in the video that suggests that she has an easy temperament?

____

6.10 What are the roles of heredity, neurological processes, environment, and gender in the formation of temperament? (pp. 165–167)

There is strong evidence that temperamental differences have a genetic component and that they are at least somewhat stable over infancy and childhood. Gender differences in temperamental characteristics such as inhibition are also stable. However, temperament is not totally determined by heredity, neurological processes, environment, or gender. The "fit" of the parents' expectations and the child's built-in temperament shapes the child's interactions with the world and affects others' responses to the child. Temperamental characteristics that render infants difficult to manage, such as emotional negativity, may predispose them to developing insecure attachments. However, the fit between children's temperaments and their environments may be more important than temperament itself.

12. How do researchers who examine temperament from a trait rather than a dimensional perspective view an infant's temperament?

____

13. Shy infants demonstrate a pattern of brain activation known as ___________.

14. The process of choosing experiences that strengthen inborn temperamental tendencies is called ___________.

6.11 How do the subjective self, the objective self, and the emotional self develop during the first 2 years? (pp. 167–169)

The infant first begins to develop a sense of self, including the awareness of a separate self and the understanding of self-permanence (which may be collectively called the subjective self) during the first 2 to 3 months of life. Awareness of herself as an object in the world (the objective self) follows. An emotional self begins to develop at 2 to 3 months of age. The range of emotions babies experience—as well as their ability to make use of information about emotions, such as facial expressions—increases dramatically over the first year.

15. What behaviors are associated with the development of each component of the self during infancy?

Component of Self	Behaviors
Subjective/existential	
Objective/categorical	
Emotional	

EFFECTS OF NONPARENTAL CARE

6.12 Why is it difficult to study the effects of nonparental care on development? (pp. 170–171)

Comparing parental care to nonparental care is difficult because there are so many different types of nonparental care arrangements.

16. If all children who are cared for by someone other than a parent were enrolled in child-care centers, would it be easier or more difficult to study the effects of nonparental care? Why?

____

____

6.13 What might be the effects of nonparental care on cognitive development? (p. 171)

Child care often has positive effects on the cognitive development of less advantaged children, but it may have negative effects on that of more advantaged children if there is a large discrepancy between the level of stimulation in the home environment and that in the child-care center.

17. In order for a child-care setting to have a positive influence on cognitive development, it must provide children with _______________________________.

6.14 What does research suggest about the risks of nonparental care with respect to social development? (p. 172)

The impact of child care on children's social development is unclear. Some studies show a small difference in security of attachment between children in child care and those reared at home; others suggest that home-care and child-care children do not differ with respect to attachment. Some studies show children who spend more time in child care to be more aggressive. However, research indicates that family variables influence children's social development more strongly than nonparental care does.

18. True or False: Infants whose parents exhibit behaviors associated with insecure attachment, such as poor sensitivity to the child's needs, are more likely to be negatively affected by nonparental care. _______________

6.15 What variables should be taken into account in interpretations of research on nonparental care? (pp. 172–173)

Infants' physiological responses to the stresses associated with nonparental care may underlie the association of nonparental care with negative developmental outcomes. The quality of the nonparental care a child receives may be as important as the quantity. Individual and gender differences may interact with the quality of a care arrangement, the quantity of outside-the-home care a child receives, or both. Average differences between children who receive nonparental care and those who are cared for entirely in their own home are small.

19. From the Multimedia Library within MyDevelopmentLab, watch the *Day Care* video and answer the following question.

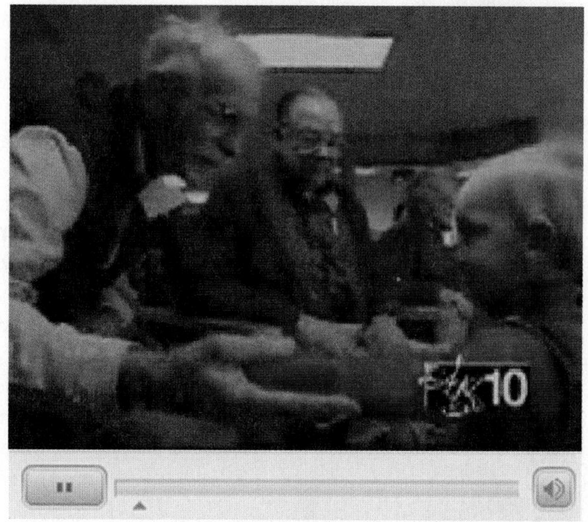

What is unique about the child-care facility in the video?

____

____

For answers to the questions in this chapter, turn to page 512. For a list of key terms, turn to page 530.

The Whole Child in Focus

Physical, Cognitive, and Socioemotional Development in Infancy and Toddlerhood: An Integrated Review

When you first read about Hector and his 6-month-old son, Federico (page 96), you may have noticed that Hector spent a large part of his day attending to the physical needs of his infant son. How much has changed now that Federico has moved into toddlerhood?

Now that Federico has turned two, we see that taking care of his physical needs requires a lot less time. His daily patterns of sleeping, eating, and being alert correspond more readily to those of his parents. Through the interactive processes of **synaptogenesis**, **synaptic pruning**, and **myelination**, two-year-old Federico's brain does a much better job of regulating his physical functions than it did when he was younger.

Synaptogenesis and Synaptic Pruning (p. 101)

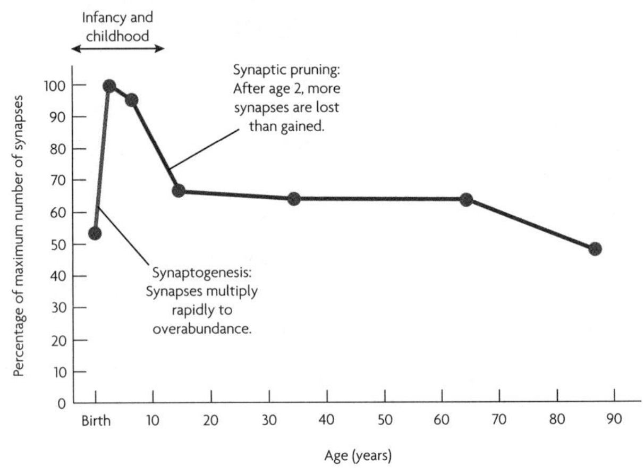

Parts of the Neuron (p. 69)

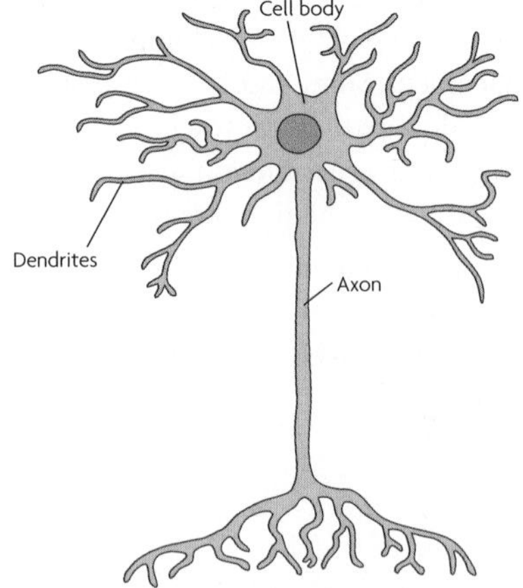

Thinking about Developmental Pathways

1. Presumably, responding to infants' needs in the cognitive and socioemotional domains would be more difficult in situations in which a parent lacked the economic resources to meet infants' basic needs for food and other necessities. How might Federico's development have proceeded differently if he had spent the first two years of his life in such a context?
2. Federico's motor and cognitive development appear to be on-time, so there is probably no reason for him to be formally tested with an instrument such as the Bayley Scales of Infant Development. What kinds of delays might have prompted a health care professional to recommend that he be tested? If he had been tested, what would his score reveal about his future intellectual development?
3. Suppose Federico had developed an insecure rather than a secure attachment to his father. How might his response to nonparental care have differed?

At two, Federico's emerging **fine motor skills** allow him to take some responsibility for personal care tasks, such as feeding himself with a spoon. Advances in **gross motor skills** allow him to move around far more freely than he could as a 6-month-old. As a result, Federico has begun to develop the sense of **autonomy** that Erikson saw as vital to psychosocial development between the first and third birthdays.

Erikson's Psychosocial Stages (p. 30)

Approximate Ages	Stage
Birth to 1 year	Trust versus mistrust
1 to 3	**Autonomy versus shame and doubt**
3 to 6	Initiative versus guilt
6 to 12	Industry versus inferiority
12 to 18	Identity versus role confusion
18 to 30	Intimacy versus isolation
30 to late adulthood	Generativity versus stagnation
Late adulthood	Integrity versus despair

Federico narrowly escaped injury after attempting to stick paper clips into an electrical outlet, an activity aided by his improving fine motor skills and an increased capacity for concentration influenced by the maturation of his brain's **reticular formation**.

Parts of the Brain (p. 100)

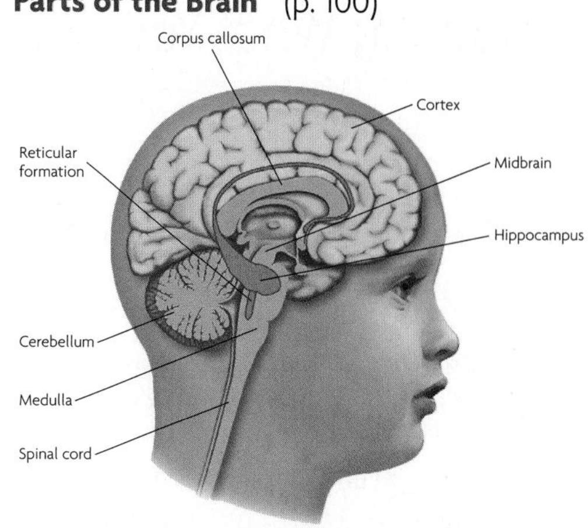

Federico's experimentation with the paper clips reflects his growing capacity for **means-end behavior**, a set of skills that first emerges during substage 4 of Piaget's **sensorimotor stage** and become increasingly sophisticated in substages 5 and 6.

Substages of Piaget's Sensorimotor Stage (p. 128)

Substage	Average Age (in months)	Primary Technique
1	0–1	Reflexes
2	1–4	Primary circular reactions
3	4–8	Secondary circular reactions
4	**8–12**	**Coordination of secondary schemes**
5	**12–18**	**Tertiary circular reactions**
6	**18–24**	**Beginning of mental representation**

Federico's **easy temperament** has helped him adapt well to daily **nonparental care** now that Hector has returned to work. When he first began attending a child-care center, Federico displayed some degree of **separation anxiety**. Because of his **secure attachment** to Hector, however, he quickly got over his distress each day. He now loves the center and even asks to go to "school" on weekends.

At the playground, Federico can climb all the way to the top of the monkey bars, but he still has difficulty getting down. Fortunately, Federico's budding language skills have proven to be indispensible when he gets into such scrapes. "Daddy down!" he yells urgently, employing the typical 2-year-old's **telegraphic speech** pattern.

Vocabulary Growth in the Second Year (p. 142)

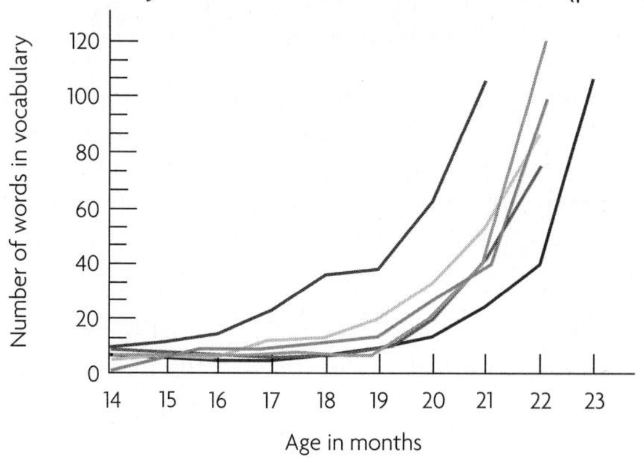

The Whole Child in Action

Apply What You've Learned about Development in Infancy and Toddlerhood

Raise Your Virtual Child

The First Two Years

1. Summarize the changes that you observed in your virtual child over the first 2 years of his or her life within the physical, cognitive, and socioemotional domains. Which of these changes represent universals, and which reflect individual differences?
2. To what extent did your parenting decisions contribute to these changes?
3. Did the Virtual Child result in decision-related outcomes that you think are valid? Why or why not?
4. Write a brief biographical sketch of your child at age 2, integrating information from all three domains.

This activity requires that you be registered for My Virtual Child *through MyDevelopmentLab.*

Conduct Your Research

Safe Base Behavior

A playground where toddlers and preschoolers play while their parents watch would be an ideal place to carry out a naturalistic observation of safe base behavior. Before you observe any children and parents, be sure to introduce yourself to the parents, explain that you are doing an assignment for your child development class, and ask permission to observe their children. For a set period of time—say, 15 minutes—observe an individual child and note how many times he or she looks at, speaks to, or moves toward the parent. Repeat the procedure for several other children. Categorize the children as younger or older and compare the number of safe base behaviors for each age group. You should find that the younger children are, the more frequently they make contact with the parent (their safe base).

Build Your Portfolio

1. Suppose you had $2,000 to spend on equipment for an infant room in a child-care center, and your room already has all of the equipment needed to meet infants' basic care needs (e.g., cribs, diaper changing tables, etc.). Using the online catalogues of several educational supply companies, identify items that the companies claim are useful for helping infants develop fine and gross motor skills. Taking your budget into consideration, what would you buy, and why?
2. Create an 11"-by-17" poster that outlines the major physical, cognitive, and socioemotional milestones of the first 2 years of life in 2-month increments (i.e., 0–2 months, 2–4 months, etc.). Assume that you have been commissioned by a hospital to draft the poster. The hospital intends to give the finished product to parents of newborns, and they have specifically asked you to consider the primary concerns of new parents in the design of the poster.

Powered by

PEARSON mydevelopmentlab™

www.mydevelopmentlab.com

Explore Possible Careers

Child Life Specialists

Helping hospitalized infants cope with separation anxiety is one of the tasks performed by child life specialists. These professionals are employed in health-care facilities that serve children, and most have bachelor's degrees in human development. They help children who are undergoing outpatient medical procedures, support the developmental needs of youngsters who are hospitalized for long periods, advise parents about strategies for managing chronic conditions such as asthma, and counsel children whose parents are seriously ill or who have passed away. You can learn more about child life specialists by clicking the "Career Center" tab on MyDevelopmentLab.

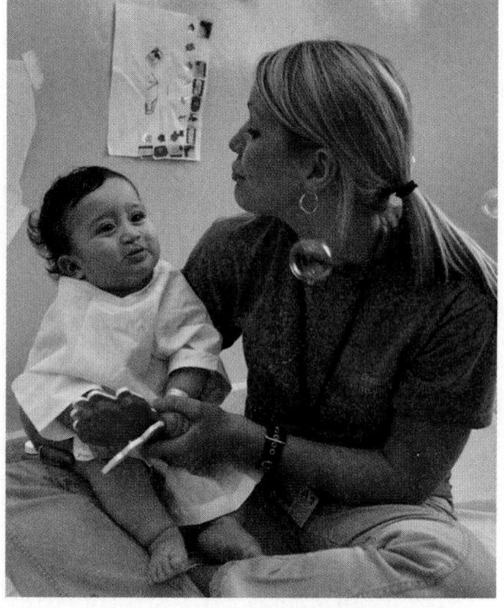

Visit the Career Center in MyDevelopmentLab to learn about other careers that rely on child development research.

Volunteer with Children

Foster Parenting

Foster parents are volunteers who agree to open their homes, usually temporarily, to children and teens who have been removed from their own homes because of abuse or neglect. Foster homes provide these children with a safe and nurturing environment while social workers and other professionals investigate their cases and help their families learn to provide a better environment for growing children. Clearly, foster parenting involves a large commitment of time and energy, and it is emotionally demanding as well. But even if you cannot serve as a foster parent, agencies usually have other volunteer positions that you can fill. To find out about opportunities to serve foster families and children, visit the websites of your state and local child protective agencies.

Visit the Career Center in MyDevelopmentLab to learn about other volunteer opportunities that rely on child development research.

Unit Three
Early Childhood

Life is never dull for Michael and Shelly, the proud parents of 2-year-old Madeleine and 6-year-old Marcy. They call themselves a "split-shift" family because Michael works during the day, and Shelly works at night. As a result, they don't have a lot of time together, but their working arrangement ensures that the two little girls are cared for by one of their parents most of the time. On weekends, the couple enjoys a "date night" while the girls' grandparents babysit, but most of their conversation revolves around the girls.

Michael and Shelly often reminisce about what an easygoing child Marcy was from the beginning. They often remark that she seems to be unusually mature for her age. For instance, when Marcy started attending a prekindergarten class, she developed a ritual that she continues to do as a first-grader. Each evening at bedtime, she chooses her clothes for school the next day and lays them out on a chair in her bedroom. Next, she places her backpack by the door so she won't forget it. Finally, she goes to the refrigerator, chooses a juice box and sets it aside from the others so that Shelly will know which kind of juice to put in her lunch box. Once the ritual is complete, Marcy heads straight to the bathroom and brushes her teeth without being told.

When discussing Madeleine, Michael and Shelly agree that she was a more challenging infant than her older sister was. They recall that she has always been moody and difficult to calm when she gets angry or upset. In fact, as her third birthday approaches, she seems to be becoming more rather than less difficult. For one thing, Madeleine hates getting up in the morning and often plops down on the floor with her arms crossed when Shelly tries to get her to eat breakfast. When she's happy, she talks nonstop, often about a group of imaginary friends that seem to accompany her everywhere and have an opinion on everything that goes on

in the family. Michael, Shelly, and Marcy enjoy Madeleine's rambling accounts of her imaginary friends, but, at times, they just wish she would be quiet. When they show that they are no longer interested in hearing about her fantasy world, Madeleine pouts, and it takes a good deal of coaxing to get her back into a positive frame of mind.

Like most parents, Michael and Shelly often ask themselves, "How can two little girls from the same family be so different?" The everyday experiences of families like this one vividly illustrate the main theme of the early childhood period: during the years between two and six, the child makes a slow but immensely important shift from dependent baby to independent child. The toddler and then the preschooler can move around easily, can communicate more and more clearly, and has a growing sense of him- or herself as a separate person with specific qualities. Thus, the temperamental characteristics that Marcy and Madeleine showed as infants are in the process of developing into full-blown personalities that differ significantly from one another.

But Marcy and Madeleine differ in more than just personality. Madeleine's imaginary friends reflect an emerging capacity for pretense that is one of the cognitive milestones of the third year of life. Marcy, by contrast, shows the school-aged child's tendency to look for and to create rules and regularity in the world around her, a developmental trend that first appears in the later years of the early childhood period and emerges as a predominant developmental theme in middle childhood. Still, their differences in personality mean that, when Madeleine reaches school age, she is likely to manifest the 6-year-old's focus on rules in ways that differ from those of her sister.

In Chapters 7, 8, and 9, you will read about some of the fascinating changes that take place between the ages of two and six. Chapter 7 deals with the physical domain. In Chapter 8, we discuss the dramatic changes in cognitive ability that take place during this period. Finally, in Chapter 9, you will read about the young child's emerging personality, sense of self, and social relationships.

The Whole Child In Focus

Keep Madeleine's story in mind as you read through the next three chapters, and consider how aspects of her physical, cognitive, and socioemotional development might interact as she moves through the early childhood period. What kind of person do you think an older Madeleine will be? We'll examine how Madeleine's development changes as she grows from 2 to 6 years old at the end of this unit.

5

Chapter

7

Physical Development and Health in Early Childhood

Watch a group of 2- to 6-year-olds on a playground and you are likely to be amazed by the pure joy they get from moving their bodies. They climb things, throw things, run, leap, and build elaborate forts out of blocks. When a child first masters any one of these skills, the utter delight and pride on the child's face is a wonder to behold. When a child is working hard on some physical skill—trying to string beads or trying to build a castle out of blocks—she is likely to have a look of intense concentration. And even when children this age are clearly exhausted, they usually refuse to stop playing.

The first topic we address in this chapter is the young child's growth and mastery of these and other physical skills. Next we turn to the health needs of young children and some of the health hazards they face during this period. Finally, we consider two atypical developmental pathways that are usually diagnosed during early childhood.

Learning Objectives

Physical Changes

7.1 How do patterns of growth change during early childhood?

7.2 What important changes happen in the brain during early childhood?

7.3 What are the arguments for the genetic and experiential explanations of handedness?

7.4 What advances in sensory and perceptual abilities occur between ages 2 and 6?

7.5 What are the major milestones of motor development between ages 2 and 6?

7.6 What kinds of sleep problems emerge during early childhood?

Health and Wellness

7.7 In what ways do eating patterns change in early childhood?

7.8 What are the health-care needs of young children?

7.9 What factors are involved in illnesses, accidents, and mortality among 2- to 6-year-olds?

7.10 What are the risk factors that are associated with abuse and neglect?

Atypical Development

7.11 What are the features and causes of mental retardation?

7.12 How do pervasive developmental disorders affect children's development?

Physical Changes

Chapter 4 chronicled the many rapid changes in the infant's body. The physical changes between ages 2 and 6 are less dramatic. Subtle though they may be, the physical changes of the early childhood period provide children with an apt foundation for the cognitive and social leaps that lie ahead of them.

Changes in Size and Shape

Learning Objective 7.1

How do patterns of growth change during early childhood?

Changes in height and weight happen far more slowly in the preschool years than in infancy. Each year, the child adds about 2 to 3 inches in height and about 6 pounds in weight. In addition, growth becomes more predictable during early childhood.

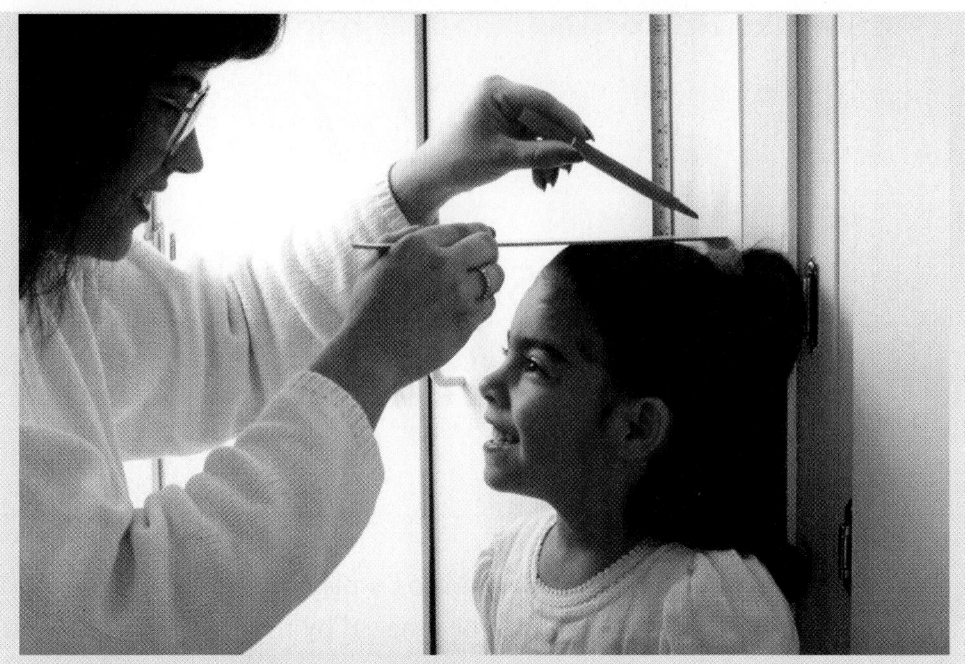
Each child establishes a stable growth curve during the early childhood years.

Growth Curves When health-care professionals measure children's height and weight, they use a statistic called a *percentile rank* to describe how the child compares to others of the same age. A **percentile rank** is the percentage of individuals whose scores on a measure are equal to or less than those of the individual child who is being described. For example, if a child's weight is at the 25th percentile, 25 percent of children of his age weigh less than he does and 75 percent weigh more. In other words, a child who is at the 25th percentile is on the small side, compared to peers. One who is at the 50th percentile is about average, and another who is at the 75th percentile is larger than most children his age.

percentile rank the percentage of individuals whose scores on a measure are equal to or less than those of the individual child who is being described

Individual children's height and weight percentile ranks can vary a great deal in the first 2 years of life. Thus, a child might accurately be described as "small for her age" at one check-up and "big for her age" at another check-up. But beginning around the age of 2 years, children's percentile ranks for height and weight begin to stabilize. Figure 7.1, which is based on longitudinal data derived from several hundred children (Mei, Grummer-Strawn, Thomp-

Figure 7.1
Growth Curve Shifts from Birth to 5 Years

This graph shows the percentage of children in each age group who show changes in the percentile ranks for their height and weight from one check-up to the next.

Source: Mei, Grummer-Strawn, Thompson, & Dietz, 2004.

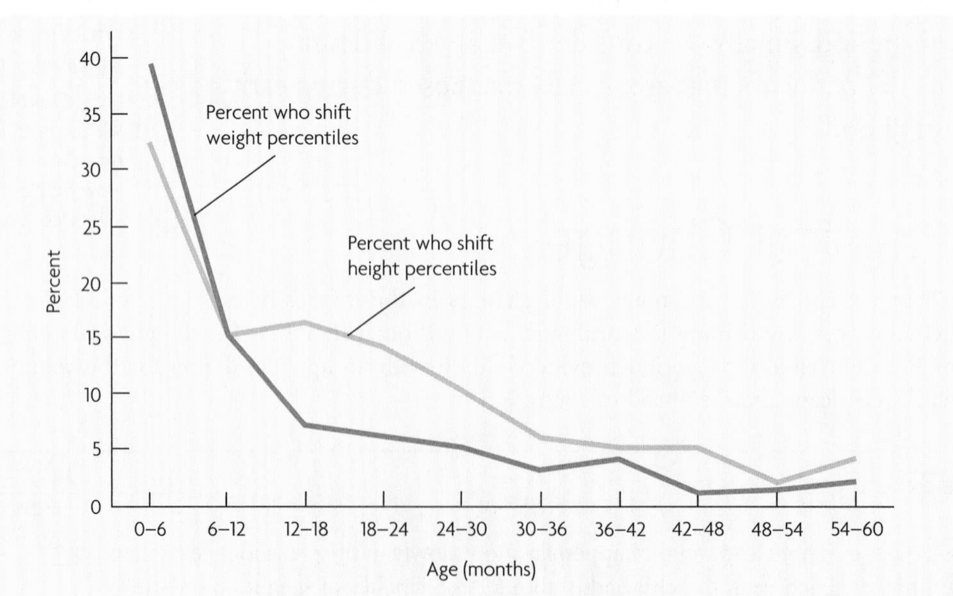

son, & Dietz, 2004), illustrates this pattern. When a child's percentile ranks for height and weight become stable, the child is said to have established his individual **growth curve**, or pattern and rate of growth.

Stable growth curves allow parents and health-care professionals to predict a child's adult height with a large degree of accuracy. If a child's growth curve is at the 25th percentile, his adult height will also be at the 25th percentile. Table 7.1 shows the predicted adult heights of 4-year-old boys and girls whose heights are at the 25th, 50th, 75th, and 95th percentile.

The growth curve is critical to assessments of children's health across the early childhood years (Overby, 2002). A downward deviation away from an established growth curve for height may be a sign that a child is suffering from an undiagnosed illness (Styne & Glaser, 2002). An upward deviation for weight may mean that the child is trending toward obesity. The importance of growth curve assessment is one reason most health-care professionals assert that it is critical to young children's health that they be examined by the same physician, or at least in the same clinic, at each check-up (Children's Hospital of Philadelphia, 2008). Clearly, without a consistent record of growth, it is impossible to make determinations about an individual child's growth curve. As a result, disorders of growth and other problems that affect growth may go undiagnosed.

Disorders of Growth When a child exhibits a stable growth curve that places her at or below the 5th percentile for both height and weight, physicians typically undertake an investigation of the child's small size (Styne & Glaser, 2002). The first step toward determining why a child is much smaller than others her age is to collect data about the child's parents. If a child's parents are of below-average height, then smallness is probably a characteristic that the child inherited from them.

Moreover, growth charts based on samples of North American or European children can be misleading when they are applied to children of Asian, Indian, or Middle Eastern ethnicity who are recent immigrants (Center for Adoption Medicine, 2008). Such children tend to be smaller, on average, than their North American and European counterparts because of the cumulative effects of generations of poor nutrition and lack of medical care. Thus, health professionals must not be too quick to jump to the conclusion that a very small child whose family recently emigrated or who was adopted into a North American or European family has a growth problem. Such children's growth should be compared to that which is typical for children in their cultures of origin (Center for Adoption Medicine, 2008).

Table 7.1 Predicting Adult Height at Age 4 Years

Percentile Rank	Height at 4 (in inches)	Height at 18 (in inches)
Boys		
25th	40	68
50th	41	70
75th	42	72
95th	43	74
Girls		
25th	38	63
50th	39	64
75th	41	66
95th	43	69

Source: CDC, 2000.

growth curve the pattern and rate of growth exhibited by a child over time

If it turns out that a small child's parents are of average or above-average size and any needed adjustments for ethnicity have been made, physicians usually monitor the child's growth carefully over several months. If the child maintains a rate of growth that is typical for children of the same age, ethnicity, and medical status, then her small size is called *idiopathic short stature*, a term that simply means that the cause of the child's small size is unknown (Rosenthal & Gitelman, 2002). As long as she continues to grow at a satisfactory rate, no treatment will be recommended.

When a child is small and grows at a much slower rate than other children his age, physicians look for some kind of abnormality or disease (Styne & Glaser, 2002). For instance, poor growth is often the first sign that a child is suffering from Turner syndrome, a chromosomal disorder in which a girl possesses only one X chromosome (see Chapter 3). Poor growth combined with rapid weight gain is also a sign of a rare genetic disorder called *Prader-Willi syndrome*, a condition that affects both physical and cognitive development.

Children who are unusually small may also be suffering from a disorder of the **endocrine system**, the body's system of glands. These glands secrete **hormones** that govern many aspects of physical growth, development, and functioning. The **pituitary gland** controls the system and is, thus, often called the *master gland*. It also secretes **growth hormone (GH)**, a hormone that controls the growth process. In some cases, children fail to grow as they should because of a GH deficiency. In such cases, children can be treated with GH injections. Growth hormone is also used to moderate the effects of Turner syndrome and Prader-Willi syndrome.

Slow growth may also be attributable to social conditions. For example, it may be an indicator of abuse or neglect, even if the abuse or neglect is not physical in nature (Black & Krishnakumar, 1999). That is, children who are verbally and/or emotionally abused or neglected may exhibit slow growth even if they are getting enough to eat. By contrast, children in low-income homes may be well supported emotionally but be receiving inadequate nutrition because of their family's lack of economic resources. In all cases in which social conditions are responsible for poor growth, interventions on the part of health professionals are critical, because most such children catch up to their peers in physical growth if the conditions in which they are developing are improved.

endocrine system glands (including the adrenals, thyroid, pituitary, testes, and ovaries) that secrete hormones governing overall physical growth and sexual maturation

hormones substances that are secreted by glands and that govern physical growth and sexual maturation

pituitary gland gland that governs the endocrine system and provides hormonal triggers for release of hormones from other glands

growth hormone (GH) the pituitary hormone that controls the growth process

corpus callosum the brain structure through which the left and right sides of the cerebral cortex communicate

lateralization the functional specialization of the left and right hemispheres of the cerebral cortex

Learning Objective 7.2

What important changes happen in the brain during early childhood?

The Brain and Nervous System

Brain growth, synapse formation, and myelination continue in early childhood, although at a slower pace than in infancy. (Recall from Chapter 4 that myelination involves the development of a fatty covering on the axons that improves the efficiency of neural impulse transmission.) However, the slower rate of growth should not be taken to mean that brain development is nearly complete. Indeed, a number of important neurological milestones are reached between the ages of 2 and 6. It is likely that these milestones represent the neurological underpinnings of the remarkable advances in thinking and language that occur during this period.

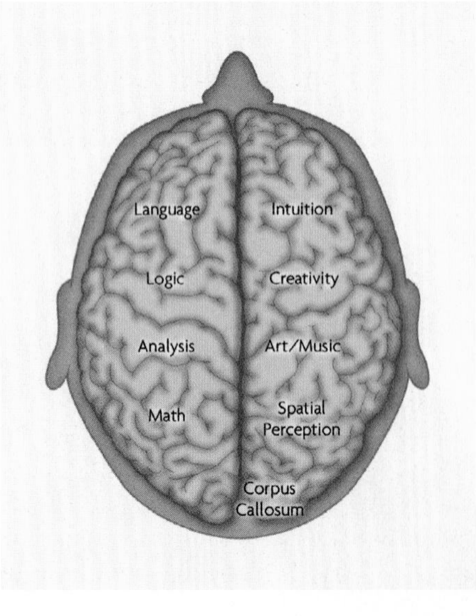

Figure 7.2
Lateralization of Brain Functions

Brain functions are lateralized as shown in the figure. Neurologists think that the basic outline of lateralization is genetically determined, whereas the specific timing of the lateralization of each function is determined by an interaction of genes and experiences.

Lateralization

The **corpus callosum**, the brain structure through which the left and right sides of the cortex communicate, grows and matures more during the early childhood years than in any other period of life (see Figure 7.2). The growth of this structure accompanies the functional specialization of the left and right hemispheres of the cortex. This process is called **lateralization**. Figure 7.2 shows how brain functions are lateralized in most people. During early childhood, advances in lateralization are linked to improvements in memory, language, and categorization skills (Kagan & Herschkowitz, 2005).

Neuroscientists suspect that the genes that all humans share dictate which functions will be lateralized and which will not. However, experience shapes the pace at which lateralization occurs. For example, in 95% of humans, language is processed in the left hemisphere. Studies of fetal responses to different kinds of sounds (i.e., language and music) show that this pattern is evident even before we are born (de Lacoste, Horvath, & Woodward, 1991). The fact that left-side processing of language appears so early in life suggests that lateralization of these functions is dictated by our genes.

Nevertheless, language functions are not as fully lateralized in fetuses as they are in children and adults. Moreover, research indicates that the degree to which these language functions are relegated to the left side of the brain is linked to language production. Preschoolers with the most advanced language skills show the highest levels of left-side lateralization of language functions (Mills, Coffey-Corina, & Neville, 1994). Of course, we don't know whether children acquire language more rapidly because their brains are lateralizing at a faster pace. It seems that the reverse is just as likely to be true—namely, that some children's brains are lateralizing language functions more rapidly because they are learning language faster. But such findings suggest that maturation and experience are both at work in the lateralization process.

The Reticular Formation and the Hippocampus Myelination of the neurons of the *reticular formation*, which you will remember from Chapter 4 as the brain structure that regulates attention and concentration, is another important milestone of early childhood brain development. It means, for example, that at age 2 children are better able to listen to a story from beginning to end than they were when they were younger. Neurons in other parts of the brain, such as the hippocampus, are also myelinated during this period (Tanner, 1990). The **hippocampus** (refer back to Figure 4.1 on page 100) is involved in the transfer of information to long-term memory. Maturation of this brain structure probably accounts for improvements in memory function across the preschool years (Rolls, 2000). For example, most preschoolers love to learn new songs, often with humorous results (e.g., "rock a pie-baby" rather than "rock-a-bye baby"). Moreover, maturation of the connections between the hippocampus and the cortex is probably responsible for the common finding that people's earliest memories involve events that happened when they were about 3 years old (Zola & Squire, 2003).

THE WHOLE CHILD IN FOCUS

What did her maturing hippocampus enable Madeleine to do by the end of the early childhood period? Find out

Handedness: Nature or Nurture?

Learning Objective 7.3

What are the arguments for the genetic and experiential explanations of handedness?

Handedness, the tendency to rely primarily on the right or left hand, is another neurological milestone of the 2- to 6-year-old period (Tanner, 1990). By examining skeletons that predate the invention of writing, archaeologists have determined that the proportions of right- and left-handers were about the same in illiterate ancient populations as among modern humans (83% right-handed, 14% left-handed, and 3% ambidextrous) (Steele & Mayes, 1995). Archaeologists made this determination by comparing the lengths of the bones in the right and left arms of ancient skeletons; the bones of the dominant arm are longer than those of the nondominant arm. Such findings suggest that the prevalence of right-handedness is likely to be the result of genetic inheritance. Moreover, geneticists at the National Cancer Institute (NCI) have identified a dominant gene for right-handedness, which they believe to be so common in the human population that most people receive a copy of it from both parents (Klar, 2003).

Further evidence for the genetic hypothesis can be found in studies demonstrating that handedness appears very early in life. In fact, some studies suggest that handedness is already well established in some fetuses, especially those who are observed sucking their thumbs during ultrasound examinations (Hepper, Wells, & Lynch, 2004). Research also indicates that clear hand preferences are evident in most children prior to their first birthday, although they don't become firmly established until the preschool years (Stroganova, Posikera, Pushina, &

hippocampus the brain structure that is involved in the transfer of information to long-term memory

handedness the tendency to rely primarily on the right or left hand

Orekhova, 2003). Research comparing children's right-hand and left-hand performance on manual tasks, such as moving pegs from one place to another on a pegboard, also supports the genetic hypothesis. Most of these studies show that older children are better at accomplishing fine motor tasks with the nondominant hand than younger children are (Dellatolas et al., 2003; Roy, Bryden, & Cavill, 2003). Findings from studies comparing nondominant hand use in children and adults follow the same pattern (Annett, 2003; Cavill & Bryden, 2003). Thus, experience in using the hands appears to moderate, rather than strengthen, the advantage of the dominant over the nondominant hand.

Clearly, heredity plays a role in handedness, but think for a moment about what happens when a person's dominant hand is damaged or lost in an accident. In most such cases, people are able to retrain the nondominant hand to become proficient at the tasks that were previously performed by the injured or missing hand, such as writing. Obviously, this means that there is some degree of neurological plasticity with regard to handedness, even if there is a strong push from nature in the direction of right-handedness in most people.

Similarly, the phenomenon of opposite-handedness in identical twins shows that heredity isn't the whole story. In 18% of identical twins, one is right-handed and the other is left-handed (Klar, 2003). If genes fully determined handedness, then identical twins would always have the same hand preference. One explanation for this finding emphasizes the crowding that occurs in a womb that is nurturing two fetuses. (Neither twin has much room to move around!) Thus, say advocates for the "crowding" hypothesis, for each twin, the arm that has the greater degree of freedom of movement during prenatal development is the one that will become dominant (Klar, 2003).

However, some genetic researchers argue that the phenomenon of opposite-handedness in identical twins fits perfectly with the findings of genetic studies (Klar, 2003). These studies suggest that 82% of humans have genes that push them in the direction of right-handedness, without regard to prenatal or postnatal experience. The remaining 18% have no genes for handedness, and, as a result, hand dominance among them is determined by experience. Hence, among the 18% of twins who lack genes for handedness, prenatal crowding may be one of many factors that influence handedness. By contrast, among those with genes for right-handedness, experiential factors are irrelevant. They are destined to be right-handed even if their positions in the womb prevent them from moving their right arms at all.

In addition, the genetic hypothesis is supported by a study that examined the link between prenatal handedness and hand preference at age 10 (Hepper, Wells, & Lynch, 2004). All of the children who exhibited right-handedness during prenatal ultrasound examinations were found to be right-handed a decade later. In contrast, only two-thirds of fetuses who seemed to be left-handed when examined in the womb were left-handed at age 10. Thus, the genetic push involved in right-handedness may be better thought of as a forceful shove, and that which is associated with left-handedness may be just a slight nudge.

Of course, what developmentalists ultimately want to know is how being left- or right-handed affects a child's development. At one time, left-handedness was regarded as a highly undesirable developmental outcome. This was due to superstitions about associations between left-handedness and the presence of evil spirits. As a result, parents and teachers encouraged left-handers to switch to right-handedness. Some children were even physically punished for failing to do so. The effects of these practices can be seen in research findings showing that the prevalence of left-handedness among elderly adults in the United States is half of what it is among those who are middle-aged and younger (Porac & Friesen, 2000). Clearly, years ago, left-handedness was a developmental risk factor. However, as evidence for the role of genetics in the development of handedness began to emerge in the middle of the 20th century, views began to change. Moreover, child-rearing authorities, such as Dr. Benjamin Spock, convinced parents and teachers that forcing a left-handed child to become right-handed was potentially damaging to the child's self-esteem. As a result of this cultural shift, most parents today don't discourage a child's tendency toward left-handedness. In fact, some may even encourage left-handedness, given the unique value of left-handedness in sports such as baseball, basketball, and football.

Allowing a child to develop handedness on the basis of his or her personal preferences is probably a good idea. Nevertheless, left-handedness is associated with poor developmental outcomes in both the cognitive domain and the socioemotional domain (Johnston, Shah, & Shields, 2007). But this association is probably the result of an underlying factor that influences both handedness and developmental outcomes. It's important to remember, too, that only a small proportion of left-handed children ever display these deficits. Consequently, parents should avoid pushing a left-handed child to be right-handed in the interest of preventing developmental problems. Even if parents succeed in switching a child's hand preference, if there is a hidden risk factor present, that factor will still be there. Thus, research aimed at finding and moderating the effects of the underlying cause of the correlation between handedness and poor developmental outcomes is needed, rather than a campaign to change children's hand preferences.

Sensory and Perceptual Abilities

Learning Objective 7.4
What advances in sensory and perceptual abilities occur between ages 2 and 6?

As you learned in Chapter 4, children's sensory and perceptual systems mature rapidly during infancy. Yet, there are still a number of important advancements that are required before the child attains adult-level skills.

Vision Children's **field of vision**, the amount of the environment that can be seen without moving the eyes, does not reach maturity until age 5 (Gabbard, 2008). Until then, children have limited *peripheral vision*, or capacity to see objects and movement outside the direct line of vision. Poor peripheral vision is probably one factor that contributes to accidents among preschoolers. Most young children are also *farsighted*; that is, they have poorer near-vision than older children and adults do. For this reason, books for young children are printed in larger type than books for older children are.

There are also a number of visual problems commonly diagnosed in early childhood that can become worse over time or interfere with the development of other skills. For this reason, most states require children who are enrolled in child-care centers or preschools to be screened for visual problems at age 4 or 5. Likewise, pediatricians include vision screening in routine well-child exams for preschoolers (Overby, 2002).

One serious condition that is found in 2 to 6% of preschoolers is **strabismus**, a misalignment of the two eyes in which one or both eyes are turned in or out (Keech, 2002). This condition interferes with the brain's ability to coordinate information from the eyes. It is also the leading cause of another serious condition, **amblyopia**, or "lazy eye," in which the brain suppresses information from one of the eyes.

In cases of *organic amblyopia*, a physical cause is present and treatment depends on the specific cause. If a damaged nerve is to blame, the condition cannot be corrected. If it is caused by a mechanical problem, such as an abnormality in the muscles that serve the lazy eye, the condition may be surgically correctable. *Functional amblyopia*, on the other hand, is acquired through experience (Yen, 2006). For instance, if a child has poorer vision in one eye than in the other, amblyopia can develop. The condition is usually corrected by patching the child's good eye, a strategy that forces his brain to rely on the lazy eye and to develop supportive neurological structures for it. When the patch is removed, the brain can then develop the structures needed to coordinate information from both eyes. About 2% of preschoolers in the United States suffer from amblyopia, either organic or functional (Yen, 2006).

Visual Perception Eye-care professionals place a high priority on diagnosing and treating strabismus and amblyopia in early childhood because both conditions interfere with the development of mature visual perception. The timing of diagnosis and treatment is vital, because **stereopsis**, the capacity to perceive depth when separate images sent to the brain by the eyes are integrated into a single image (*binocular fusion*), matures over the first 10 years of life. Tests of stereopsis are included in routine vision exams for preschoolers, as its role in

field of vision the amount of the environment that can be seen without moving the eyes

strabismus a disorder of alignment of the two eyes in which one or both eyes are turned in or out

amblyopia a disorder in which the brain suppresses information from one of the eyes ("lazy eye")

stereopsis the capacity to perceive depth by integrating separate images sent to the brain by the eyes into a single, three-dimensional image

depth perception is vital to some of the advances that occur in the gross motor domain, such as the ability to catch a ball. When young children fail to display stereopsis, health-care professionals look for undiagnosed conditions that interfere with its development. For instance, the variation in acuity between a child's eyes may be large enough to prevent the development of stereopsis without also causing amblyopia. In such cases, corrective lenses equalize the acuity of the two eyes, resulting in the development of stereopsis.

Once a child reaches age 10, stereopsis no longer can be acquired. Thus, conditions that interfere with its development must be corrected before age 10 to ensure that stereopsis will develop. Moreover, the younger a child is when these conditions are diagnosed, the more rapidly and completely she responds to treatment.

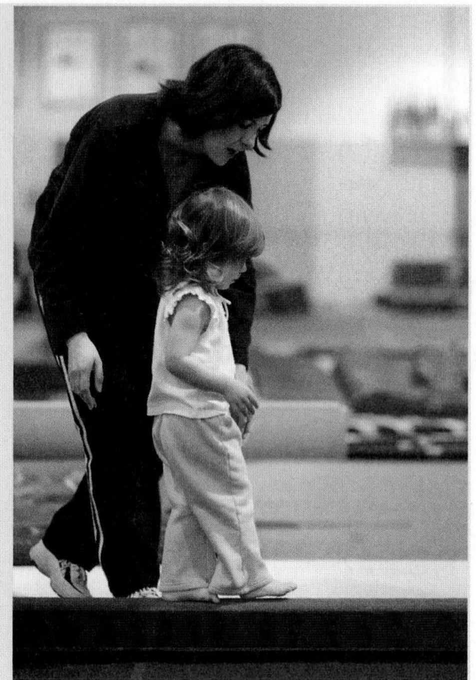

Development of the vestibular sense, along with greater motor control, allows young children to accomplish feats such as walking on a balance beam with alternating steps.

The Vestibular Sense Interactions between visual information and body sensations underlie the **vestibular sense**, the body's sense of its position in space. The vestibular sense is involved in the ability to maintain balance. The structures of the inner ear that are involved in the vestibular sense are mature before birth. However, a certain degree of maturation of the body's skeletal, muscular, and neurological systems is required before a child can achieve the milestones in Table 7.2.

Table 7.2 Balance Milestones in Early Childhood

Milestone	Age
Balances on one foot for 3 to 4 seconds	3 years
Walks on a 4-inch balance beam using alternating steps	3 years
Balances on one foot for 10 seconds	4 years
Walks on a 2-inch beam using alternating steps	4 years
Hops seven to nine times on one foot	5 years
Is proficient at two-footed, traveling hops	6 years

Sources: Dixon & Stein, 2006; Gabbard, 2008.

Hearing As you learned in Chapters 3 and 4, hearing is established prior to birth. Language development obviously depends on a child's ability to hear, so physicians use a 2-year-old's language skills as a guide to his ability to hear. If a child is not speaking at least a few words by this age, doctors typically test his hearing. However, because human speech uses a very limited range of sound levels, a child can exhibit normal language development even if he has a hearing loss. A hearing loss that involves higher-pitched sounds may not lead to impairment of a child's own speech, but it may interfere with his ability to understand others' speech, especially in a setting in which there is a great deal of background noise. Research shows that children with mild hearing losses, even if the losses involve only one ear, are more likely to fail in school than are those with normal hearing (Tharpe, 2006). Researchers are currently attempting to devise guidelines for determining whether children with mild hearing losses should be fitted with hearing aids and whether doing so will prevent them from experiencing academic difficulties (McKay, Gravel, & Tharpe, 2008). However, most experts agree that children who are diagnosed with mild hearing losses should also be assessed for cognitive and language problems so that any developmental deficits that are present as a result of the hearing loss can be remediated (Tharpe, 2007).

THE WHOLE CHILD IN FOCUS

What did Madeleine learn to do with her maturing sense of balance? Find out on page 282.

For these reasons, most physicians recommend testing a child's hearing before she starts school, and many include hearing tests in routine well-child check-ups at age 3 or 4 (Overby, 2002). Children who are enrolled in child care or preschool are also usually tested at school. Children who fail a hearing test at school or the pediatrician's office are referred to a specialist for further assessment and to determine if the hearing loss is treatable or if the child needs a hearing aid.

Hearing losses can be caused by illnesses, genetic disorders, or physical abnormalities of the inner ear. But most cases of hearing loss, regardless of the age at which they happen, result from exposure to excessive noise. Thus, the American Speech-Language-Hearing Association (ASHA) recommends that parents take steps to protect children's hearing (ASHA, 2008). The organization issues an annual report that lists toys that can damage children's

vestibular sense the body's sense of its position in space

hearing. In addition, it advises parents that children may hold noisy toys very close to their ears, thus increasing the chances of hearing loss. Headphones, too, are potentially harmful.

Motor Development

Learning Objective 7.5

What are the major milestones of motor development between ages 2 and 6?

Improvements in a child's ability to take in visual information and to maintain balance are key factors in the steady progress in gross and fine motor skills that happens during the early childhood years. These changes are listed in Table 7.3. As you can see, they are not as dramatic as those of infancy, but they enable the child to acquire skills that markedly increase his independence and exploratory ability.

Gross Motor Skills By age 5 or 6, children are running, jumping, hopping, climbing, and skipping. Most can ride a tricycle; some can ride a two-wheeled bike. The degree of confidence with which a 5-year-old uses her body for these movements is impressive, particularly in contrast to the somewhat unsteady movements of an 18-month-old.

The gross motor advances of early childhood involve not only the appearance of new skills, but also important refinements of those skills that children already possess. For example, consider how the running skills of 2-year-olds differ from those of 6-year-olds; not only do 6-year-olds run faster and stumble less than 2-year-olds, but they can turn, start, and stop more readily as well. Such improvements are the result of changes in the **fundamental movement skills** that underlie gross motor skills such as running (Gabbard, 2008). The fundamental movement skills involved in running, for example, include holding the trunk of the body at the correct angle, swinging the arms, synchronizing arm and leg movements, placing the support foot on the ground at the correct angle, bending the knee at the correct angle when the support foot contacts the ground, and so on.

You can think of a complex gross motor activity such as running as being similar to the harmonious sounds that you hear when a band plays. To produce such sounds, all of the instruments in the band have to be playing the same song in the same key and rhythmic pattern. Likewise, each of the fundamental movement skills required for running has to reach a certain threshold of development in order for a child to be capable of exhibiting a mature pattern of running. Every facet of the young child's body that contributes to physical movement—the brain's motor cortex, the spinal cord, the muscles, the joints, the bones—plays a role in the emergence of the fundamental movement skills. And each of

fundamental movement skills basic patterns of movement that underlie gross motor skills such as running

Table 7.3 Milestones of Motor Development from Age 18 Months to 6 Years

Age	Gross Motor Skills	Fine Motor Skills
18–24 months	Runs awkwardly; climbs stairs with both feet on each step; pushes and pulls boxes or wheeled toys	Shows clear hand preference; stacks four to six blocks; turns pages one at a time; picks up things without overbalancing; unscrews lid on a jar
2–3 years	Runs easily; climbs on furniture unaided; hauls and shoves big toys around obstacles	Picks up small objects; throws small ball while standing
3–4 years	Walks up stairs one foot per step; skips on two feet; walks on tiptoe; pedals and steers tricycle; walks in any direction pulling large toys	Catches large ball between outstretched arms; cuts paper with scissors; holds pencil between thumb and fingers
4–5 years	Walks up and down stairs one foot per step; stands and runs on tiptoe	Strikes ball with bat; kicks and catches ball; threads beads on a string; grasps pencil properly
5–6 years	Skips on alternate feet; walks on a line; uses slides, swings	Plays ball games well; threads needle and sews large stitches

Sources: Connolly & Dalgleish, 1989; Diagram Group, 1977; Fagard & Jacquet, 1989; Mathew & Cook, 1990; Thomas, 1990.

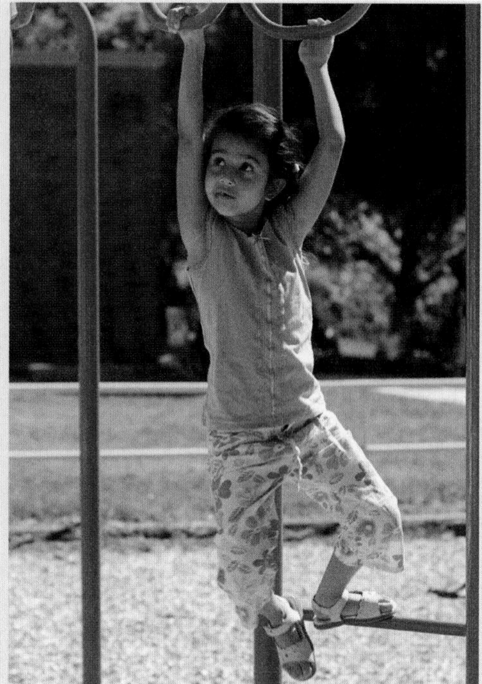

Advances in gross motor skills, such as climbing, are the products of smaller, less obvious gains in fundamental movement skills, such as the degree to which a child can flex her hips, knees, and ankles.

them is on a somewhat different maturational timetable. That's why complex skills such as running often seem to emerge overnight. One day, a child runs awkwardly, seems to trip over everything, and falls again and again. The next day, he is zipping around like a track star. In such cases, what has happened is that one of the essential fundamental movement skills has finally reached the critical threshold of readiness, correcting that one final discordant note and allowing the motor skill "band" to play a tune that observers recognize as a skilled performance ("Look at that girl go!"), with no awareness of the thousands of minute neurological, skeletal, and muscular events that contribute to it.

There is a unique set of fundamental movement patterns that underlies each of the gross motor skills that emerge during the early childhood years, and these movements serve as the foundation upon which children build sports-related skills in middle childhood. Because children acquire these movement skills through both inborn patterns of maturation and experience with different types of movement (see *Developmental Science in the Classroom*), providing young children with opportunities for gross motor development is vital to their future physical development.

Fine Motor Skills Fine motor skills also improve in these years, as shown in Table 7.3. As with skills in the gross motor domain, advances in fine motor skills represent changes in underlying movement patterns. For instance, the ability to grip a pencil effectively (see Figure 7.3) emerges after children develop the ability to touch each finger on a hand with the thumb on that hand, a movement pattern known as **finger differentiation** (Gabbard, 2008). Changes in the muscles and bones of the wrist and hand, along with maturation of the nervous system, make finger differentiation possible.

finger differentiation the ability to touch each finger on a hand with the thumb of that hand

DEVELOPMENTAL SCIENCE IN THE CLASSROOM

Movement Education

Rashad cannot remember a time in his life when he wasn't involved in organized sports in one way or another. His passion for sports led him to pursue a degree in sports management, and after graduation he landed a job as the director of a neighborhood recreation center. After organizing a team sports program for the children who attend the center's after-school program, he turned his attention to the preschoolers in the neighborhood. He wondered whether it would be better to set up a schedule of supervised free-play sessions for the children or to provide them with a more structured program that included instruction in motor skills.

When Rashad did some research to find out which approach was better, he learned that *movement education*, a formal program that teaches children fundamental movement skills, is beneficial. Experiments show that children who receive such instruction develop gross motor skills more rapidly than children who spend an equal amount of time in free play or traditional physical education programs do (Goodway & Branta, 2003). Such programs lead to improvements in gross motor skills among typically developing children and those who display delayed motor development.

To be effective, movement education must be based on a thorough understanding of early childhood motor development. In addition, teachers must take children's sensory development into account when planning activities. For example, the visual perceptual systems of young children are not yet fully mature, so they have difficulty tracking rapidly moving objects that are small and that blend in with background images (Gabbard, 2008). As a result, they are more likely to enjoy and to benefit from throwing and catching a beach ball than a tennis ball. Preschoolers' limited fine motor skills make the beach ball a better choice as well.

Because the fundamental movement skills that are acquired in early childhood are foundational to many sports and leisure activity skills that are developed in later childhood, experts on motor development argue that early motor development may be related to physical fitness later in life. They assert that children who acquire fundamental movement skills feel more confident about their ability to engage in motor activities, and, as a result, they may be more willing to participate in activities that contribute to physical fitness.

Questions for Reflection

1. Why is it necessary that a preschool movement education program be based on an understanding of early childhood motor development?
2. What role might temperament play in the finding that movement education advances children's gross motor development?

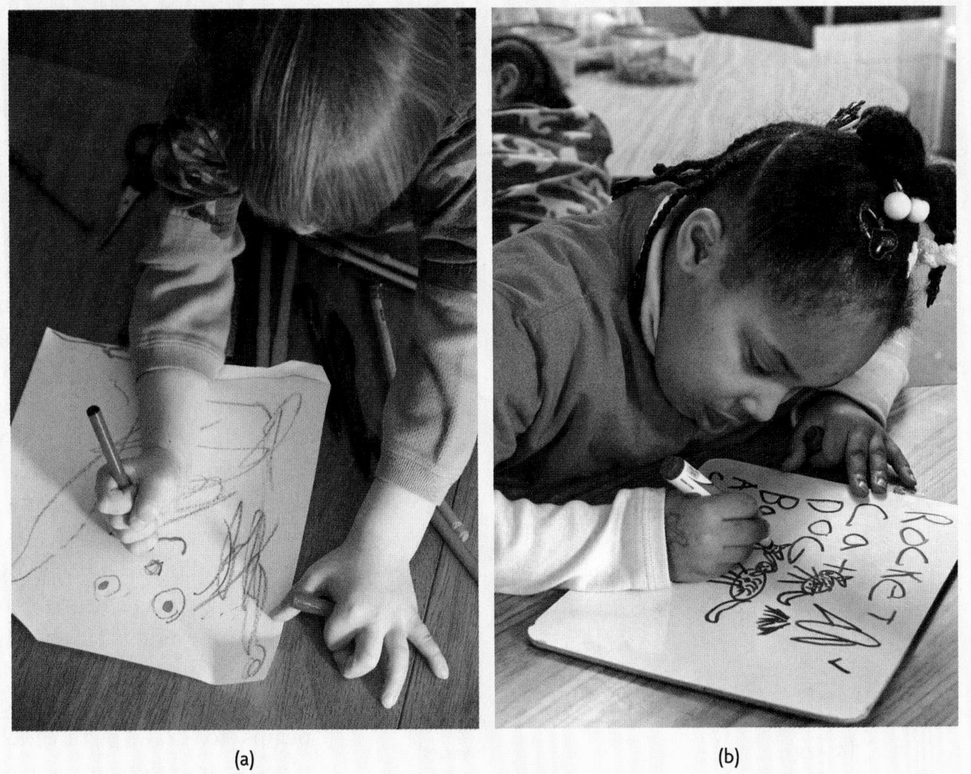

Figure 7.3 **Immature and Mature Pencil Grips**

Until age 3 or so, most children grip a pencil or crayon as shown in (a). Between 3 and 6, as finger differentiation develops, they gradually change the way they grip a writing instrument until they achieve the mature grip shown in (b).

Despite the impressive gains in fine motor skills that occur during early childhood, even the oldest preschoolers are not highly skilled at such fine motor tasks as using a pencil or crayon or cutting accurately with scissors. Research suggests that these skills do not reach mature levels until the age of 8 years or so. This is an important fact for parents and teachers of young children to understand. It is the rare kindergartner who is really skilled at such fine motor tasks as coloring within the lines in coloring books or writing letters. Younger preschoolers, of course, are even less skilled at these tasks. However, a "wait and see" strategy isn't the best approach to helping children learn to write letters and draw simple forms. Researchers have found that early training, beginning at about age 2½, can accelerate the rate at which young children acquire school-related fine motor skills such as writing letters when they go to school at age 5 or 6 (Callaghan & Rankin, 2002). A word of caution is in order, though, because the kind of early training that is most beneficial involves providing children with opportunities to use their fingers for all kinds of activities: making clay figures, stringing beads, and using appropriately sized and injury-proof tools such as tweezers and tongs. That is, if a parent wants to increase the chances that a child will easily learn to write in the early school years, she should provide the child with a wide variety of fine motor activities in early childhood (Rule & Stewart, 2002).

Experience contributes to the development of fine motor skills.

Children's drawings appear to follow the developmental sequence shown in Figure 7.4 on page 196 (Toomela, 1999). These stages were first identified in a classic study by Rhonda Kellogg (1970), who examined more than a million drawings made by children all over the world. Thus, the stages that Kellogg identified are thought to be universal.

Figure 7.4
Stages in Children's Drawing

Developmentalist Rhonda Kellogg identified four stages in young children's drawings: *scribble, shape, design,* and *pictorial.*

(*Source*: Helen Bee, *The Growing Child: An Applied Approach*, 2nd ed. Boston: Allyn & Bacon, 1999.)

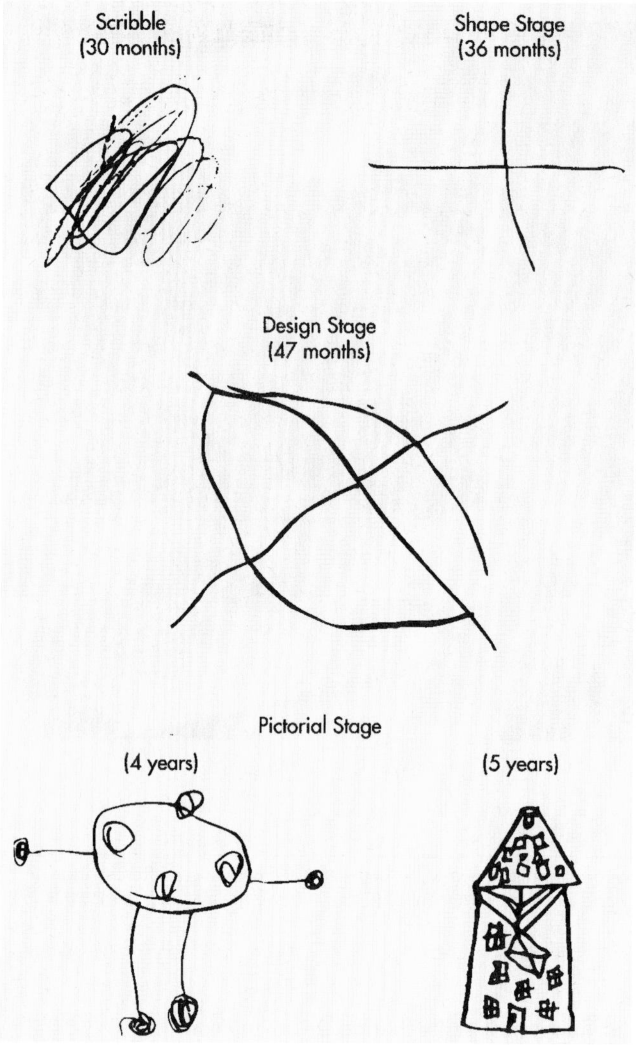

scribble stage the first of Kellogg's stages of drawing, in which children draw dots, horizontal and vertical lines, curved or circular lines, and zigzags

shape stage Kellogg's second stage, in which children intentionally draw shapes such as circles, squares, or X shapes

design stage Kellogg's third stage, in which children mix several basic shapes to create more complex designs

pictorial stage Kellogg's fourth stage, in which children begin to draw pictures of objects or events from real life

The first stage is the **scribble stage**, typically beginning between ages 18 months and 2 years. Kellogg identified 20 basic scribbles, including dots, horizontal and vertical lines, curved or circular lines, and zigzags. Collectively, these scribble patterns form the foundation of the drawings that children produce in later stages. By age 3, children enter what Kellogg called the **shape stage**, when they begin to draw particular shapes deliberately, such as circles, squares, or X shapes. This is followed quickly by the **design stage**, in which they mix several basic shapes to create more complex designs. At age 4 or 5, the child begins to draw pictures of objects or events from real life; this is the **pictorial stage**. These objects and events—humans, pets, houses, toys, birthday parties, trips to the zoo—are all made up of basic scribbles and shapes.

Changes in children's drawings seem to go hand in hand with changes in how well they understand what they're drawing (Callaghan, 1999). For example, at the scribble stage, children may create a drawing and then give it a name. In later stages, children tend to create a mental image and attempt to represent it with a drawing. Similarly, older preschoolers who understand the symbolic nature of letters—usually those beyond age 3—benefit more from instruction in letter writing than younger children do. Moreover, learning to write letters appears to help children more fully understand them (Callaghan & Rankin, 2002). Thus, research examining young children's writing demonstrates that, in some cases, physical and cognitive development are interactive processes.

Learning Objective 7.6
What kinds of sleep problems emerge during early childhood?

Sleep Patterns

Like other changes in the physical domain, changes in children's sleep patterns are less striking over the preschool years than in infancy. The typical 2-year-old sleeps 13 hours a day, including one daytime nap. By age 6, the typical child sleeps about 10 hours, with no nap (Adair & Bauchner, 1993; Needlman, 1996).

Many young children have problems with or during sleeping. These problems include bedtime struggles like the one described in the *Developmental Science at Home* discussion that follows. Problems such as nightmares, night terrors, and bed-wetting are common as well.

DEVELOPMENTAL SCIENCE AT HOME

A Good Night's Sleep for Kids (and Parents, Too!)

Every night, Luis and Ramona go through the same ordeal when they put their 3-year-old son, Manny, to bed. The boy begs to sleep with them, but they always refuse. After four or five cycles of begging and sobbing, usually spread over at least an hour, Manny finally becomes so exhausted that he can no longer stay awake. Despite his parents' consistency, Manny often gets his way. He wakes up every night around 2:00 a.m. and attempts to slip into his parents' bed without their noticing. Sometimes Luis or Ramona awakens and takes him back to bed and, in the process, initiates another round of the begging-sobbing cycle that Manny exhibits at bedtime. Other times, they both are sleeping so soundly that Manny's late-night invasion goes unnoticed, and they awaken the next morning to find him in their bed.

Manny's nighttime behavior is all too familiar to many parents of preschoolers. As explained in the *Developmental Science at Home* box in Chapter 2 (see page 34), parents sometimes unknowingly encourage such behavior. Consequently, pediatricians frequently deal with parental concerns about sleep patterns such as Manny's (Coury, 2002). Here are the bedtime strategies that most doctors recommend:

- Provide the child with a structured, predictable daytime schedule, and stick to it as closely as possible every day.
- Set a regular bedtime that is 8 to 10 hours before the desired waking time.
- Discontinue daytime naps for a child who has difficulty getting to sleep or who awakens too early in the morning.
- Establish a routine set of "settling activities" such as a bath, storybook, and goodnight kiss, and resist the child's efforts to prolong or modify the routine.
- Provide the child with a *transitional object* such as a doll or stuffed animal that is reserved especially for bedtime.

Making such adjustments can be challenging, especially when the child actively resists them. However, research confirms that these kinds of changes can significantly reduce sleep-related conflicts (Borkowski, Hunter, & Johnson, 2001). Thus, a few days or even weeks of persistence on the parents' part may pay off in years of undisturbed sleep for parents and children alike.

Questions for Reflection

1. If you were Manny's parent, what strategies would you use to try to prevent him from awakening at night and getting into your bed?
2. In your opinion, to what extent are parental concerns about where children sleep driven by cultural beliefs and standards of behavior?

Nightmares and Night Terrors **Nightmares** are most likely to occur in the second half of a child's nighttime sleep, which means they usually happen in the early morning. Although nightmares can be very distressing for the child and for the parent, they are quite normal and do not usually signify any underlying emotional or psychological problem. If they happen only occasionally, a parent should not be alarmed. However, frequent nightmares may be a response to a stressor that is present in the child's life (Dixon & Stein, 2006). Often parents know what a child is stressed about, as in the case of parents who are going through a divorce. However, if parents have no idea why a child might be experiencing frequent nightmares, they should take their concerns to a health-care professional.

Interestingly, a child's temperament and the ways in which her parents respond to it appear to contribute to nightmares. Researchers in Canada tracked the frequency of nightmares in over 900 children for 3 years (Simard, 2008). They found that only 4% of the children ever experienced nightmares. More often than not, children who had nightmares were also anxious and somewhat difficult to manage during their waking hours. These children's mothers tended to have little confidence in their ability to manage children's behavior. The researchers concluded that frequent nightmares may be a manifestation of a maladaptive pattern of interaction between young children and their caregivers. Other researchers have found that children who have frequent nightmares are more likely than their peers to have mothers who also have frequent nightmares, but there is no correlation between nightmare frequency in fathers and children (Schredl, Barthold, & Zimmer, 2006). These findings, like those of the Canadian researchers, suggest that children's nightmares are influenced in some way by the mother-child relationship or that an underlying characteristic that leads to frequent nightmares is shared by mothers and children.

nightmares frightening dreams that usually happen early in the morning and awaken the child

night terrors frightening dreams that usually happen within a couple of hours of a child's going to sleep and do not fully awaken the child

Night terrors usually occur early in the child's sleep. The child appears to awaken abruptly and may sit up in bed and scream. Despite these signs, the child whose sleep has been disturbed by a night terror does not fully awaken and is usually unable to talk sensibly about the dream. Thus, although night terrors may be frightening to parents, children typically go back to sleep almost immediately and seldom recall the incident the next morning.

Sleep researchers believe that night terrors stem from an unusually rapid transition from very deep sleep to a drowsy "twilight sleep" state (Dixon & Stein, 2006). They tend to be somewhat more likely to happen when children are physically exhausted or under unusual stress. However, night terrors are not linked to any underlying emotional problem (Kemper, 1996).

Bed-Wetting Many parents believe that once a child is out of diapers, perhaps at age 2 or 3, the child is fully "toilet trained" and should never be wet at night. In fact, children vary a lot in how long it takes them to control their bladders for as long as the 8 to 10 hours of nighttime sleep that most preschoolers need. Thus, most health-care professionals do not consider bed-wetting—or, in medical terms, *nocturnal enuresis*—to be a significant problem unless it persists past the age of 6 (Coury, 2002).

One important physical cause of enuresis is a smaller-than-normal bladder. Another is a difference in the way the child's brain signals the kidneys to make urine. A hormone called *antidiuretic hormone (ADH)* signals the kidneys to make less urine. In adults, and in children who do not suffer from enuresis, the brain makes more ADH at night, resulting in lower urine production at night. Children who wet the bed, in contrast, secrete the same amount of ADH throughout the day and night, which means they have to urinate more often in the night. These children eventually do develop the typical pattern of ADH secretion, but it is a slower developmental process for them than for the average child. In the meantime, medications and nighttime alarms that sound at the first drop of moisture on a special pad can be used to successfully manage nocturnal enuresis (Coury, 2002; Tomasi, Siracusano, Monni, Mela, & Delitala, 2001).

Health and Wellness

Early childhood is the ideal time to begin teaching children good health habits. Their rapidly advancing language skills and love of imitating others allow them to benefit from parents' verbal instructions about and demonstrations of health-related behaviors such as eating nutritious foods. Yet, early childhood is also a time when children are vulnerable to a number of problems, many of which are preventable.

Learning Objective 7.7

In what ways do eating patterns change in early childhood?

Nutrition

Because children grow more slowly during the early childhood years, they may seem to eat less than when they were babies. Moreover, food aversions often develop during the preschool years. For example, a child who loved carrots as an infant may refuse to eat them at age 2 or 3. Consequently, conflicts between young children and their parents often focus on eating behavior (Wong, 1993). Most 2- to 6-year-olds are resistant to the idea of trying new foods. Surprisingly, twin studies suggest that resistance to new foods is strongly influenced by heredity (Wardle & Cooke, 2008). These findings suggest that aversion to new foods may be a protective mechanism that helps children survive in a natural environment in which it is difficult to distinguish between safe and harmful sources of food. However, children's finicky tastes are not necessarily conducive to a healthy diet.

Nutritionists point out that it is important that parents not become so concerned about the quantity or variety of food a child consumes that they cater to his preferences for sweets and other high-calorie foods or try to force him to eat (Dixon & Stein, 2006). Many children acquire eating habits during these years that lead to later weight problems. Surveys show that 15% of children aged 2 to 5 are overweight and another 16% are at risk of becoming so by the time they reach school age (Pediatric Nutrition Surveillance, 2005). Thus, nutritionists recommend keeping a variety of nutritious foods on hand and allowing a child's appetite to be a good guide to how much food he should eat. Of course, this approach works only if young children's access to sweets and other attractive, but nonnutritious, foods is limited.

Parents should also keep in mind that young children eat only about half as much food as adults and, unlike adults, many don't consume the majority of their daily calories at regular meals (Dixon & Stein, 2006). Nutritionists suggest that concerned parents keep a daily record of what their children are actually eating for a week. In most cases, parents will find that children are consuming plenty of food.

The issue of how much fat should be included in young children's diets has been somewhat controversial in recent years (National Academies of Science Food and Nutrition Board, 2005). The controversy arises from the view that a certain amount of dietary fat is required for normal brain development. Thus, doctors in the United States are reluctant to recommend that parents restrict the fat in children's diets. However, an experiment involving several hundred Finnish children found that restricting children's daily fat intake to 30–35% of total calories beginning in infancy had no impact on brain development at age 5 (Rask-Nisillä et al., 2000). Children in the study's fat-restricted diet group displayed cognitive, motor, and sensory skills that were equivalent to those of the children whose diets were not restricted.

The quantity of fat that children in the Finnish study consumed, at 30–35% of total calories, was more than the 20–30% of total daily calories that is recommended for adults. Thus, health-conscious parents should avoid feeding children the same low-fat diet that they follow themselves. Experts agree that young children require a certain amount of dietary fat to support normal brain development (National Academies of Science Food and Nutrition Board, 2005).

Nevertheless, many dietary recommendations that are given to adults regarding fat intake are important for children as well. For example, *saturated fats*, those derived from animal sources, should be limited in the diets of both children and adults. *Trans fats* and *partially hydrogenated fats*, fats that are often found in packaged foods such as crackers and chips, should be limited as well. These three types of fats are thought to contribute to the development of heart disease later in life. By contrast, *monounsaturated fats* and *polyunsaturated fats*, such as olive and safflower oil, are believed to provide the bodies of developing children and adults alike with essential fats without increasing the risk of heart disease. In the Finnish study cited earlier, the fat in the diets of the children who consumed the fat-restricted diet consisted of about one-third saturated, one-third monounsaturated, and one-third polyunsaturated fats (Rask-Nisillä et al., 2000). At age 5, children in the fat-restricted group were found to have lower levels of *cholesterol* in their bloodstreams than children in the control group did. Cholesterol is believed to contribute to heart disease in adulthood.

Health-Care Needs

Learning Objective 7.8

What are the health-care needs of young children?

As noted earlier, keeping track of children's growth patterns helps health-care professionals determine whether children are developing normally. To get a comprehensive picture of how well a child is developing, they usually include several other types of assessments in basic well-child physical exams for preschoolers.

Well-Child Care Physicians recommend that young children be examined each year about the time of their birthdays (Overby, 2002). In addition to monitoring children's growth, physicians assess their general health and their overall developmental status.

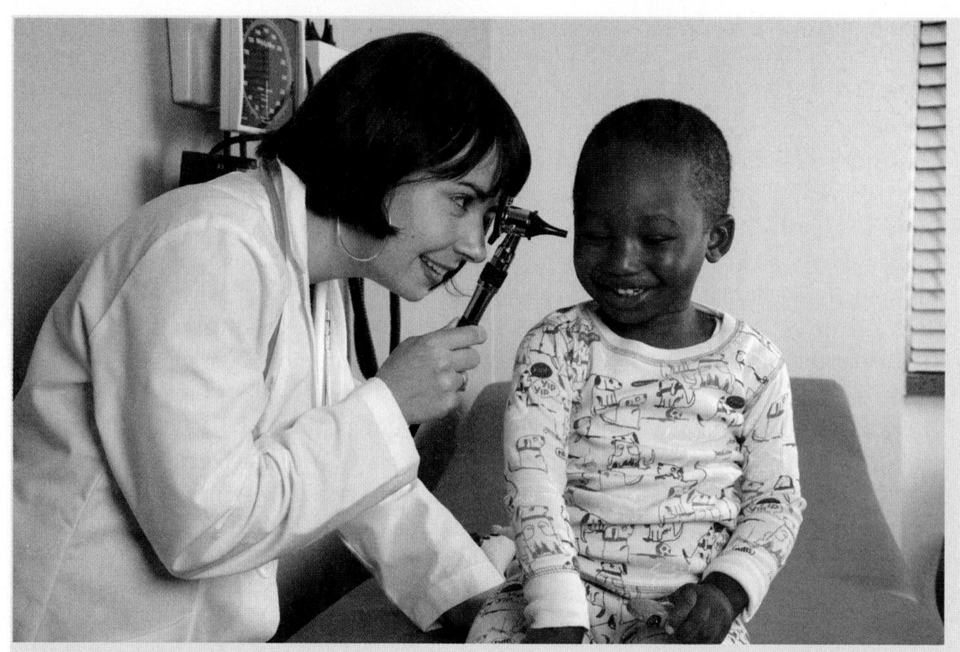

Well-child exams enable health-care professionals to monitor children's growth and administer needed immunizations.

Table 7.4 Recommended Immunization Schedule for Children from Birth to 6 Years

Vaccine	Recommended Age
Hepatitis B	Birth–18 months
Rotavirus	2–6 months
Diphtheria, Tetanus, Pertussis	Four doses: 2 months, 4 months, 6 months, 16–18 months
Haemophilus influenzae type b (Hib)	Four doses: 2 months, 4 months, 6 months, 12–15 months
Pneumococcus	Four doses: 2 months, 4 months, 6 months, 12–15 months
Polio	Three doses: 2 months, 4 months, 6–18 months
Influenza	6 months to 6 years
Measles, Mumps, Rubella	12–15 months
Varicella	12–15 months
Hepatitis A	Two doses: 12 months–2 years
Meningococcus	2–6 years

Source: AAP, 2008.

Well-child exams also provide parents with an opportunity to discuss any concerns they have about their children with their physicians.

There are a number of immunizations that must be administered during early childhood (see Table 7.4). Each state mandates a set of immunizations that children must have in order to enroll in state-licensed child-care or preschool programs. Thus, children who participate in such programs are usually up to date on all of their shots. However, children who are not enrolled in child care or preschool often fall behind in their immunizations. In addition, parents who are concerned about the possible risks associated with vaccinations are likely to delay getting their children immunized (Gust et al., 2004). Public health officials warn that delaying immunizations puts both under-immunized children and the communities in which they live at risk.

Dental Care Dentists recommend that parents begin cleaning a child's teeth as soon as they erupt in order to prevent the build-up of bacteria that cause **dental caries**, or tooth decay (cavities). At first, parents are advised to clean infants' teeth with a washcloth or infant toothbrush. Toothpaste isn't essential, but, if used, it should be a product that is specially formulated for infants and is free of fluoride. Toothpaste with fluoride should be used only after children can use toothpaste without swallowing it, a milestone that varies in age from one child to another.

dental caries tooth decay (cavities) caused by bacteria

During early childhood, dental-care responsibilities are gradually turned over to the child himself. Of course, because of the rate at which fine motor skills are acquired, toothbrushing and flossing are likely to be shared tasks for several years. For example, parents may strike a bargain with a 3-year-old in which they allow him to brush his front teeth on his own if he will agree to let them brush his back teeth. The goal is to ensure effective toothbrushing while, at the same time, helping the child develop confidence in his ability to care for his body.

Most children get their first dental check-up at around age 3 (Overby, 2002). If a child is still sucking her thumb or her fingers or a pacifier, the dentist is likely to recommend that she stop as soon as possible. Dentists are concerned about children's sucking habits because the bones around the mouth are in the process of hardening during early childhood. As a result, habitual sucking during these years leads to malformation of these bones and to misalignment of the teeth.

Strategies for stopping habitual sucking include simple measures such as having the child wear mittens or tape on the thumb. When such strategies fail, dentists sometimes install an appliance in the child's mouth that prevents sucking. Behavior modification strategies can also work, such as praising the child or giving her gold stars for increasingly longer periods without sucking. However, a parent would be wise to look at the child's stress levels before initiating any systematic attempt to eliminate her sucking habit. Eliminating or reducing some of the stresses in the child's life may make it easier for her to give up the habit.

Illnesses, Accidents, and Mortality

Learning Objective 7.9

What factors are involved in illnesses, accidents, and mortality among 2- to 6-year-olds?

Most young children visit their physician's office several times between check-ups, because of the frequency of minor illnesses during these years. Many require emergency care from time to time. Tragically, a small proportion of young children die each year, usually as the result of some kind of accident.

Illnesses In the United States, the average preschooler has four to six brief bouts of sickness each year, most often colds or the flu (Sulkes, 1998). Children who are experiencing high levels of stress or family upheaval are more likely to become ill. For example, a large nationwide study in the United States showed that children living in single-parent homes have more asthma, more headaches, and a generally higher vulnerability to illnesses of many types than do those living with both biological parents (Dawson, 1991).

In some cases, simple illnesses such as the common cold progress to more serious conditions. For instance, **otitis media (OM)**, an inflammation of the middle ear that is caused by a bacterial infection, is the leading cause of children's visits to physicians' offices in the United States (Waseem, 2007). More than 90% of children have at least one episode of OM in the first year of life, and about one-third have six or more bouts before age 7.

Thanks to antibiotic drugs, most cases of OM clear up quickly. However, physicians have become concerned in recent years about the increasing resistance to antibiotics of the bacteria that cause otitis media. As a result, many physicians now recommend a "wait-and-see" response to cases of OM (American Academy of Pediatrics [AAP], 2004). If the child develops a high fever or the infection continues for 3 to 4 days, then antibiotics are prescribed. Placebo-controlled studies suggest that 75% of cases of OM clear up on their own within 7 days of initial diagnosis (AAP, 2004).

In a few children, OM becomes chronic, defined as an episode of otitis media that remains uncured after 6 months of antibiotic treatment (Waseem, 2007). In such cases, some physicians recommend that children undergo surgery to insert tubes in the ears. The tubes allow fluid to escape from the middle ear through the ear drum.

Accidents Another danger for children is accidents. In any given year, about a quarter of all children under 5 in the United States have at least one accident that requires some kind of medical attention, and accidents are the major cause of death in preschool and school-aged

otitis media (OM) an inflammation of the middle ear that is caused by a bacterial infection

children (Heron, 2007). At every age, accidents are more common among boys than among girls, presumably because of their more active and daring styles of play. The majority of accidents among children in this age range—falls, cuts, accidental poisonings, and the like—occur at home. Automobile accidents are the second greatest source of injuries among preschoolers. Experts point out that, although parents obviously can't keep preschoolers entirely free from injuries, many are preventable. Children can wear protective gear while riding tricycles and bicycles, and in most nations parents are legally required to use car seats and restraint systems to reduce the chances that their children will be injured in an accident. Placing child-proof fencing around a swimming pool greatly reduces the chances that a child will fall into it, an accident that often results in a drowning or near-drowning when there is no adult nearby (Stevenson, Rimajova, Edgecombe, & Vickery, 2003).

Table 7.5 The Ten Substances Most Frequently Involved in Poisonings of Children Between 1 and 4 Years

Substance	Percentage of Cases
Cosmetics	13.3
Cleaning substances	9.8
Pain relievers	8.4
Foreign bodies, toys	7.4
Skin creams, lotions	7.0
Cough and cold medicines	5.7
Vitamins	3.9
Insecticides	3.7
Plants	3.7
Antacids and anti-diarrheal medicines	2.8

Source: Bronstein et al., 2007.

Poisoning When children fall or are involved in bicycle or automobile accidents, they usually receive immediate medical attention or at least first aid. By contrast, most cases of accidental poisoning are not treated until a child is quite ill (Fein, Durbin, & Selbst, 2002). In the typical case, parents bring a very sick child or one who is unconscious to a hospital emergency room and report that the child was fine just a few hours earlier. Poisoning is determined to be the cause of the child's condition by process of elimination. Cases of accidental poisoning typically follow this course because parents don't watch preschoolers as closely as they do infants and because children themselves are likely to be secretive about getting into things that they have been told to stay away from.

Half of all poisoning cases each year in the United States involve children under the age of 6 (Bronstein et al., 2007). Thankfully, only a small fraction of poisoning incidents involving young children are fatal. In 2006, for example, more than one million children were treated for accidental poisoning, and just 29 died. Nevertheless, poisoning can have long-term effects, including brain and nerve damage, so it's vital that parents and others who care for children in home settings take steps to "poison-proof" their homes. Table 7.5 lists the substances that are most often responsible for cases of accidental poisoning involving young children. The American Academy of Pediatrics (2008) recommends that caregivers take the following steps with regard to these substances in order to protect children from accidental poisoning:

- Keep poisonous substances in their original packages.
- Store all poisonous substances in locked cabinets or containers, and keep them out of the reach of children.
- Place safety latches on child-accessible cabinets that contain poisonous substances.
- Buy medicines only in child-proof containers.
- Throw away all unused and expired medications.
- Always check the label when you give a child medicine, and be sure to give the recommended dosage.

Mortality In the developing regions of the world, the most common causes of death in early childhood are infectious and parasitic diseases (World Health Organization [WHO], 2005). In Africa, for example, 18% of early childhood deaths are due to malaria and 40% are caused by diarrhea or pneumonia (UNICEF, 2008). To address this crisis, WHO is working with the governments of the world's economically advantaged countries to fund a package of humanitarian relief for Africa that aims to increase the number of health-care professionals

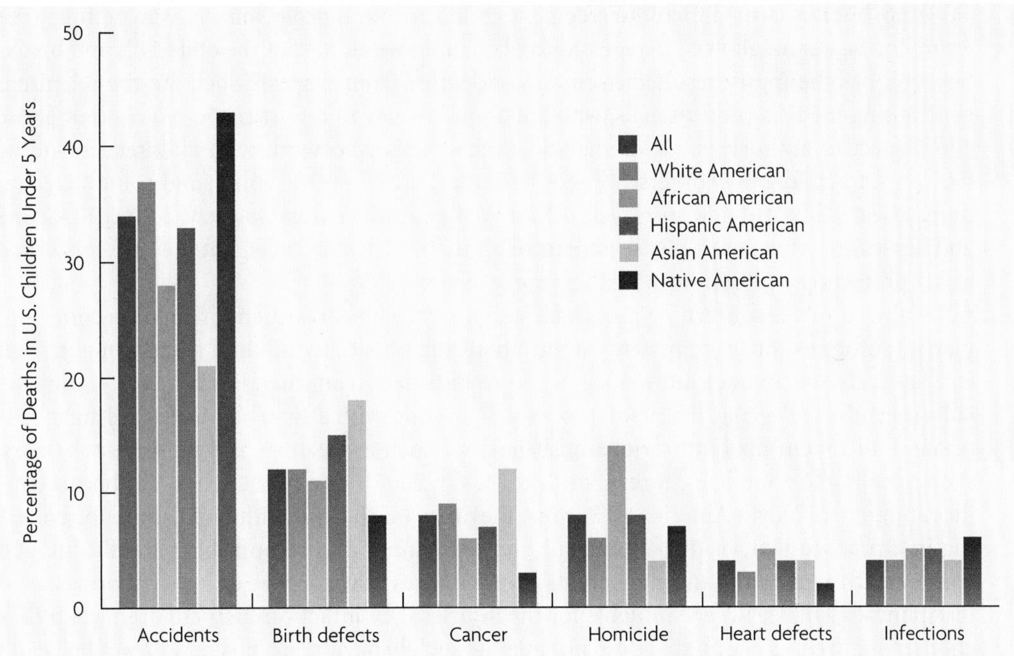

Figure 7.5
Ethnic Group Differences in Causes of Death in Children Under 5 Years

As this figure shows, accidents are the leading cause of death for young children in all ethnic groups in the United States. However, the rankings of the various causes of death vary across groups.

(*Source*: Heron, 2007.)

in the region; improve access to basic medical care, such as well-child exams and immunizations; build water treatment facilities; provide families with mosquito nets to protect them from disease-bearing insects; distribute medications that can prevent the progression of infectious diseases; supplement local food supplies with additional sources of protein, vitamins, and minerals; and educate parents about their own and their children's health-care needs. These efforts have led to dramatic declines in early childhood death among African children. Measles deaths, for example, have declined 91% since 2000, when a major immunization campaign was launched on the continent by a coalition of international organizations (Measles Initiative, 2007).

Sub-Saharan Africa is the only region in the world where early childhood mortality has increased in the last two decades (UNICEF, 2008). Under-5 mortality increased by 17% during these years. In contrast, during the same period, rates of early childhood death dropped 70% in the Americas (UNICEF, 2008). Increased mortality rates in sub-Saharan Africa are driven by the HIV/AIDS epidemic. For instance, HIV/AIDS accounted for 35% of deaths among children under 5 in South Africa in 2000, while the disease caused only 3% of under-5 deaths across the continent as a whole (Norman, Bradshaw, Schneider, Pieterse, & Groenewald, 2000; UNICEF, 2008)

In the United States, Europe, and economically advantaged Asian nations such as Japan, accidents are the leading cause of death in early childhood (Fein, Durbin, & Selbst, 2002). As Figure 7.5 shows, causes of death vary across ethnic groups in the United States. Moreover, the annual death rate among Hispanic and White preschoolers is about 2.7 per thousand; among African Americans, by contrast, the annual death rate is 4.5 per thousand. Differences across groups in children's living circumstances, such as higher poverty rates and lower rates of access to health care among African Americans, account for some of the discrepancy. However, cross-group variations in chronic diseases and homicide rates are also contributing factors.

child abuse physical or psychological injury that results from an adult's intentional exposure of a child to potentially harmful physical stimuli, sexual acts, or neglect

neglect the failure of caregivers to provide emotional and physical support for a child

Abuse and Neglect

Learning Objective 7.10
What are the risk factors that are associated with abuse and neglect?

Legally, **child abuse** is defined as physical or psychological injury that results from an adult's intentional exposure of a child to potentially harmful physical stimuli, sexual acts, or neglect (Sulkes, 1998). **Neglect** is the failure of caregivers to provide emotional and physical support for a child. Signs of abuse and neglect are listed in

Table 7.6, but it is fairly difficult to recognize child abuse and neglect in everyday settings. For example, if a parent allows a 2-year-old to play outdoors alone and the child falls and breaks her arm, has the injury resulted from an accident or from neglect? Such are the dilemmas confronting medical professionals, who are bound by law to report suspected cases of abuse and neglect to authorities. (Note that all professionals who work with children, including teachers and child-care workers, are required to report suspected abuse, and some states require private citizens to do so as well [Child Welfare Information Gateway, 2008a].) Doctors and nurses are reluctant to accuse parents of abuse in such situations, but they are concerned about protecting children from further injury (Sulkes, 1998).

Cultural values concerning acceptable and unacceptable treatment of children come into play when professionals approach parents about the possibility of child maltreatment. That is, what is abusive in one culture may not be so regarded in another. For instance, Caribbean cultures endorse *flogging*, the practice of beating a child with a switch or a stick, as an appropriate punishment for both serious misbehaviors, such as stealing, and mild misbehaviors, such as failing to complete chores (Smith & Mosby, 2003). As a result, when Caribbean families emigrate to North America or Europe, they may be charged with child abuse for engaging in a practice that, in their home culture, is regarded as a responsible parent's duty. Of course, culture notwithstanding, parents from cultures that approve of harsh approaches to discipline are still legally accountable for the injuries they inflict on their children when they choose to move to a nation that does not tolerate such behavior. For this reason, public health

Table 7.6 Signs of Child Abuse and Neglect

The Child

- Shows sudden changes in behavior or school performance
- Has not received help for physical or medical problems brought to the parents' attention
- Has learning problems (or difficulty concentrating) that cannot be attributed to specific physical or psychological causes
- Is always watchful, as though preparing for something bad to happen
- Lacks adult supervision
- Is overly compliant, passive, or withdrawn
- Comes to school or other activities early, stays late, and does not want to go home

The Parent

- Shows little concern for the child
- Denies the existence of–or blames the child for–the child's problems in school or at home
- Asks teachers or other caregivers to use harsh physical discipline if the child misbehaves
- Sees the child as entirely bad, worthless, or burdensome
- Demands a level of physical or academic performance the child cannot achieve
- Looks primarily to the child for care, attention, and satisfaction of emotional needs

The Parent and Child

- Rarely touch or look at each other
- Consider their relationship to be entirely negative
- State that they do not like each other

Source: Child Welfare Information Gateway, 2008b.

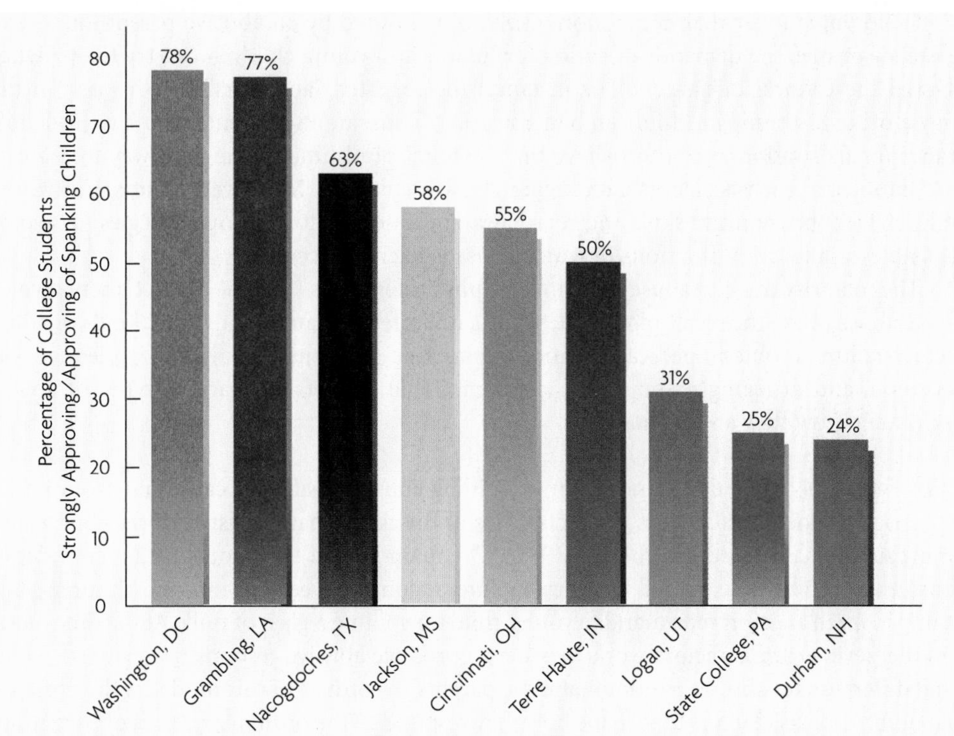

Figure 7.6
College Students' Approval of Spanking

Researchers asked college students in these locations whether they approved or disapproved of spanking. The percentages in the graph represent students who said they approved or strongly approved. As you can see, opinions about spanking vary widely from one part of the country to another.

(*Source*: Douglas, 2006.)

officials in most areas where there are large immigrant populations conduct information campaigns to educate immigrant families about acceptable forms of discipline. These campaigns are usually undertaken with the help and support of social institutions in immigrant communities, such as churches, as well as in schools and health-care facilities (New York City Children's Services, 2008).

Moreover, although it is legal throughout the United States for parents to spank their children, attitudes toward the acceptability of spanking as a routine form of punishment vary considerably from one place to another. Figure 7.6 shows the results of surveys of college students in several cities in the United States (Douglas, 2006). The researchers who carried out these surveys found a similar degree of variation among college students in Canada, where rates of approval for spanking ranged from a low of 12% in Montreal to a high of 44% in Toronto. Across Europe, rates varied from 16% in Belgium to 69% in Portugal, and in Asia, they ranged from 36% in Hong Kong to 85% in South Korea. Consequently, within cultures that we may regard as relatively homogeneous, ideas about appropriate ways of punishing children can vary quite a lot.

Looking more deeply into their findings, the researchers found two factors that predicted approval for spanking across all cultures (Douglas, 2006). The first of these factors involved students' own experiences with corporal punishment; those who had been physically punished in childhood were most likely to approve of spanking. The second factor was acceptance of spanking in the students' home cultures. That is, even among students who had not been spanked, those who came from a culture in which corporal punishment was generally regarded as acceptable were most likely to approve of spanking.

Prevalence In the United States, most cases of abuse and neglect that result in serious injury or death involve children under age 4 (CDC, 2006a). Because of the difficulties in defining abuse, it is difficult to say just how many children suffer abuse. However, research suggests that 1–5% of U.S. children are treated every year by medical professionals for injuries resulting from abuse (CDC, 2006a). Moreover, physicians estimate that abuse and/or neglect is responsible for about 10% of emergency room visits involving children under age 5 (Sulkes, 1998). Sadly, about 2,000 infants and children die as a result of abuse and/or neglect each year in the United States (CDC, 2006a).

Children younger than 5 are more likely to be injured by an abusive parent for several reasons. For one, the demands of caring for infants and young children can try the patience of even the calmest of parents. For instance, the repeated "accidents" that happen in the course of toilet-training a child can be frustrating. Thus, among parents who have little tolerance for frustration and who believe that corporal punishment is a good way to manage such problems, such accidents can trigger abusive episodes. Moreover, infants and young children lack the cognitive skills and social awareness needed to develop strategies for avoiding and escaping from situations in which abuse is likely to occur.

The majority of child abuse cases involve physical injuries (Sulkes, 1998). Others involve sexual abuse or are the result of neglect, such as underfeeding an infant. Other kinds of abuse include failure to obtain medical attention for an illness or injury, providing inadequate supervision, and drugging or poisoning children. Table 7.7 lists the various types of abuse/neglect and how they are defined.

Risk Factors One useful model for explaining abuse classifies its causes into four broad categories: sociocultural factors, characteristics of the child, characteristics of the abuser, and family stresses (Bittner & Newberger, 1981). The main idea of this model is that episodes of abuse are typically precipitated by everyday interactions between parents and children—for example, when a parent reprimands a young child for spilling a glass of milk. At the time of the episode, several causal factors work together to produce abusive responses in parents. Thus, what differentiates abusive from nonabusive parents, according to this model, is the presence of a number of risk factors that shape how they respond to the ordinary stresses of parenting.

Sociocultural factors include personal or cultural values that regard physical abuse of children as morally acceptable. Parents are more likely to be abusive if they believe that there are few, if any, moral limits on what they can do to their children physically. Sociologists suggest that such beliefs stem from cultural traditions that regard children as property rather than human beings with individual rights (Mooney, Knox, & Schacht, 2000). Moreover, parents who live in communities where others share and act on these beliefs are more likely to be abusive.

Several characteristics of children or parents may set the stage for child abuse. For example, children with physical or mental disabilities or those who have difficult tempera-

Table 7.7 Types of Child Maltreatment

Type of Abuse/Neglect	Definition
Physical abuse	Nonaccidental physical injury to the child; includes hitting, kicking, burning, biting, or any action that results in physical impairment
Neglect	Deprivation of adequate food, clothing, shelter, medical care, or supervision
Sexual abuse	Rape, molestation, or any form of sexual contact
Sexual exploitation	Employment, use, persuasion, inducement, enticement, or coercion of any child to engage in or assist another person in any sexually explicit conduct or simulation of such conduct either for the sexual gratification of an adult or for the purpose of a visual depiction of such conduct
Emotional abuse	Injury to the psychological or emotional stability of the child as expressed in depression, anxiety, withdrawal, changes in behavior, and/or school performance
Parental substance abuse	Manufacturing a controlled substance in the presence of a child; using drugs in the presence of a child; selling, distributing, or giving drugs or alcohol to a child; exhibiting impaired capacity to respond to a child's needs as a result of alcohol or drug use
Abandonment	Leaving a child in circumstances in which the child is likely to be harmed; leaving caregivers without knowledge of one's whereabouts for an extended period of time

Source: Child Welfare Information Gateway, 2007.

ments are more likely to be abused than others (Sulkes, 1998). Parents with depression, those who lack parenting skills and knowledge, those who have a history of abuse themselves, and those who are substance abusers are more likely to abuse or neglect their children (Eiden, Foote & Schuetze, 2007; Emery & Laumann-Billings, 1998). Research also shows that, compared to nonabusers, parents who are abusive are limited in their ability to empathize with others and to control their emotional reactions to others' behavior (Wiehe, 2003). In addition, mothers' live-in male partners who are not biologically related to the children in a household are more likely than biological fathers to be abusers (Daly & Wilson, 1996).

Family stressors include factors such as poverty, unemployment, and interparental conflict (CDC, 2006a; Sulkes, 1998). Keep in mind that no single factor produces abuse, but the presence of several of these variables in a particular family significantly increases the chances that the children will experience abuse.

Consequences of Abuse Some children who are frequently or severely abused develop *post-traumatic stress disorder (PTSD)* (Kendall-Tackett, Williams, & Finkelhor, 1993; Margolin & Gordis, 2000; Morrissette, 1999; Pynoos, Steinberg, & Wraith, 1995). This disorder involves extreme levels of anxiety, flashback memories of episodes of abuse, nightmares, and other sleep disturbances. For some, these symptoms persist into adulthood (Koenen, Moffitt, Poulton, Martin, & Caspi, 2007). Abused children are also more likely than nonabused peers to exhibit delays in all domains of development (Cicchetti, Rogosch, Maughan, Toth, & Bruce, 2003; Glaser, 2000; Malinosky-Rummell & Hansen, 1993; Rogosch, Cicchetti, & Aber, 1995).

On the positive side, children who are physically abused typically recover rapidly once the abuse stops. In studies involving abused and/or neglected children who were placed in foster care, developmentalists have found that differences between abused and nonabused children in physical, cognitive, and social development disappear within 1 year (Olivan, 2003). As you might suspect, though, these studies suggest that the critical factor in the catching-up process is the quality of the post-abuse environment.

Prevention Preventive strategies can be classified as primary, secondary, or tertiary. *Primary prevention* is aimed at preventing abuse from happening. For instance, educating parents about the potential consequences of some physical acts, such as the link between shaking an infant and brain damage, is primary prevention. In addition, parents need to know that injuring children is a crime, even if the intention is to discipline them. Parenting classes, perhaps as a required part of high school curricula, can help inform parents or future parents about principles of child development and appropriate methods of discipline (Mooney, Knox, & Schacht, 2000).

The goal of *secondary prevention* is to identify and intervene in situations in which abuse is likely to occur. Physicians, nurses, teachers, child-care workers, and other professionals who routinely interact with parents of infants and young children have a particularly important role to play in this kind of prevention. Parents who seem to have problems attaching to their children can sometimes be identified during medical office visits. Likewise, observers may notice inappropriate or hostile interactions between children and parents. These parents can be referred to parenting classes or to social workers for help.

Finally, the purpose of *tertiary prevention* is to protect children who are being abused from further injury. This can be accomplished through vigorous enforcement of existing child abuse laws. As noted, health-care professionals and others must report suspected abuse. And reporting is only part of the picture. Once abuse is reported, steps must be taken to protect injured children from suspected abusers. Unfortunately, in some cases, physical and legal barriers must be placed between the child and the abusive parent in order to prevent further injury. Such barriers can be implemented by removing the child from the home, incarcerating the abuser, and developing a plan for reestablishing contact between the abuser and the child if authorities deem such contact to be in the child's best interests.

Atypical Development

It's not unusual for children to exhibit problems that parents and other caregivers view as difficult. However, **atypical development** involves problems that persist for 6 months or longer and/or those that are at the extreme end of the continuum for that behavior. Two such problems that are usually diagnosed in early childhood are *mental retardation* and *pervasive developmental disorders.*

Learning Objective 7.11

What are the features and causes of mental retardation?

Mental Retardation

Mental retardation (also referred to as *developmental disability*) is diagnosed when a child's score on a standardized intelligence test falls at or below the second percentile, or in the bottom 2% of the distribution of scores. However, a low score on an intelligence test is not sufficient for a diagnosis of mental retardation. The child must also have significant problems in adaptive behavior, such as an inability to dress or feed himself or a problem getting along with others or adjusting to the demands of a regular school classroom (MacMillan & Reschly, 1997).

Cognitive Functioning of Children with Mental Retardation Some researchers interested in information processing have tried to understand normal intellectual processing by comparing the problem-solving strategies of children with mental retardation to those of children without mental retardation (Bray, Fletcher, & Turner, 1997; Calhoun & Dickerson Mayes, 2005; DeLoache & Brown, 1987). This research has led to several major conclusions about children with mental retardation:

- They process information more slowly.
- They think concretely and have difficulty with abstract reasoning.
- They require much more complete and repeated instruction in order to learn new information or a new strategy.
- They do not generalize or transfer something they have learned in one situation to a new problem or task.
- They may have difficulty with certain social skills, such as the ability to recognize and respond to facial expressions (Moore, 2001).

On simple, concrete tasks, children with mental retardation learn in ways and at rates similar to those of younger children without mental retardation. The more significant difference is in higher-order processing. Children with mental retardation can learn, but they do so more slowly and require far more task-specific instruction.

It's important to note that many of the things you have learned about child development apply to children with mental retardation. Children with intellectual disabilities go through the same Piagetian stages, although at a slower rate, and their motivational characteristics are very much like those of children without mental retardation (Blair, Greenberg, & Crnic, 2001). For example, on tasks that children without mental retardation find highly intrinsically motivating, such as learning how to play a new video game, children with mental retardation are just as likely to display high levels of intrinsic motivation. And tasks for which children without mental retardation often require extrinsic motivation, such as doing homework, children with intellectual disabilities are also likely to require parent- or teacher-provided incentives.

Causes of Retardation Children with mental retardation are often divided into two distinct subgroups, depending on the cause of the retardation. The smaller subset, making up about 15–25% of the total, is children whose retardation is caused by some evident physical damage. Included in this group are those with a genetic anomaly, such as Down syndrome, that probably causes parts of the brain associated with learning to function poorly (Penning-

atypical development developmental pathways, persisting for 6 months or longer, that are different from those of most children and/or are at the extreme end of the continuum for that behavior

mental retardation low levels of intellectual functioning (usually defined as an IQ score below 70) combined with significant problems in adaptive behavior

ton, Moon, Edgin, Stedron, & Nadel, 2003). Damage resulting in mental retardation can also be caused by a disease, a teratogen such as prenatal alcohol, or severe prenatal malnutrition; it can occur during the birth itself, from a situation such as prolonged oxygen deprivation. A small subset of children develop mental retardation as a result of an injury suffered after birth, often in an auto accident or a fall.

The majority of children with mental retardation show no obvious signs of brain damage or other physical disorder. In these cases, the cause of the retardation is some combination of genetic and environmental conditions. Typically, these children come from families in which the parents also have mental retardation and/or the home life is highly disorganized or emotionally or cognitively deprived. To be sure, in these cases, too, the child's intellectual disability may have been exacerbated by the effects of teratogens or other hazards, such as prenatal alcohol or elevated levels of prenatal or postnatal lead, but it is not thought to be attributable solely to such physical causes.

Generally speaking, the lower the intelligence test score of a child with mental retardation, the more likely it is that the cause is physical rather than environmental (Broman et al., 1987). One implication of this finding is that interventions such as enriched child-care and preschool programs are more likely to be effective in cases of milder retardation. This is not to say that educators should ignore environmental enrichment or specific early training for children whose retardation has a physical cause. Greater breadth of experience will enrich their lives and may help to bring their level of functioning closer to the top end of their full potential, allowing them to function much more independently (Spiker, 1990). But even massive early interventions are not going to bring to a typical level the cognitive functions of a child whose mental retardation is caused by a chromosomal disorder.

Pervasive Developmental Disorders

Learning Objective 7.12
How do pervasive developmental disorders affect children's development?

The defining feature of the group of disorders known as **pervasive developmental disorders (PDDs)** is the inability to form social relationships. These disorders are also known as *autism spectrum disorders*. The term "spectrum" is used because children with PDDs vary greatly in the degree to which the disorder affects their behavior. At one end of the continuum are children who lack language function, are completely incapable of forming social relationships, and have some degree of mental retardation. At the other end are children who have near-normal language and cognitive skills but whose unusual behaviors in social situations prevent them from developing the kinds of social relationships that are typical among children without PDDs.

pervasive developmental disorders (PDDs) a group of disorders that are characterized by the inability to form social relationships

One of the most important goals of educational programs for children with autism is to help them acquire communication skills. To that end, some programs teach children with autism to use sign language.

Social Functioning of Children with Pervasive Developmental Disorders

The social difficulties of individuals with PDDs usually derive from their poor communication skills and inability to understand the reciprocal, or give-and-take, aspects of social relationships. Many of these children also exhibit unusual, repetitive behaviors, such as hand-flapping. Some develop attachments to objects and become extremely anxious—or even enraged—when separated from them. Others engage in self-injurious behaviors such as head-banging. In the United States, just under 1% of all children have some kind of PDD (Kagan & Herschkowitz, 2005; NIMH, 2001). The rates are similar in European countries (Lauritsen, Pedersen, & Mortensen, 2004). The two most frequently diagnosed PDDs are *autistic disorder* and *Asperger's syndrome*.

Autistic Disorder The distinguishing symptoms that are exhibited by children with **autistic disorders** include limited or nonexistent language skills, an inability to engage in reciprocal social relationships, and a severely limited range of interests (DSM-IV TR, 2000). Most also have mental retardation, are easily distracted, are slow to respond to external stimuli, and behave impulsively (Calhoun & Dickerson Mayes, 2005). As you can see in Figure 7.7, autism rates have increased dramatically in recent years. Most experts attribute at least some of this increase to growing awareness of the disorder among teachers, health professionals, and the general public, as well as expansion of the diagnostic criteria for autism spectrum disorders (Newschaffer, Falb, & Gurney, 2005). Nevertheless, most also agree that there has been a genuine increase in the prevalence of autistic disorders, the cause of which remains unknown.

Many parents of children with autism report having noticed their children's unusual behaviors during the first few months of life. What strikes these parents is their infants' apparent lack of interest in people. However, in most cases, the disorder is not definitively diagnosed until a child's failure to develop normal language skills makes it apparent that she is on an atypical developmental path. This usually occurs between the second and third birthday.

Children with autism who are capable of some degree of normal verbal communication and whose cognitive impairments are minimal are often called high-functioning. However, these children's communicative abilities are quite poor because of their limited ability to engage in social cognition. For example, most never fully develop the ability to predict what others might be thinking (Peterson, Wellman, & Liu, 2005). Unlike most people, children with autism cannot infer that someone is angry or happy with them based on that person's facial expressions. Thus, they typically fail to understand how their statements are perceived by listeners. As a result, they are incapable of engaging in normal conversations. In addition, the pitch and intonation of their speech are often atypical. Some utter repetitive phrases, often in robot-like fashion, that are inappropriate for the situation in which they occur. Some children with autism have to be closely monitored, because they tend to engage in behaviors that can be harmful to themselves and others (see *Developmental Science in the Clinic*).

Asperger's Syndrome **Asperger's syndrome** is often thought of as a mild form of autistic disorder. The diagnostic criteria for it are highly similar to those for autistic disorder (DSM-IV TR, 2000). However, children with Asperger's syndrome have age-appropriate lan-

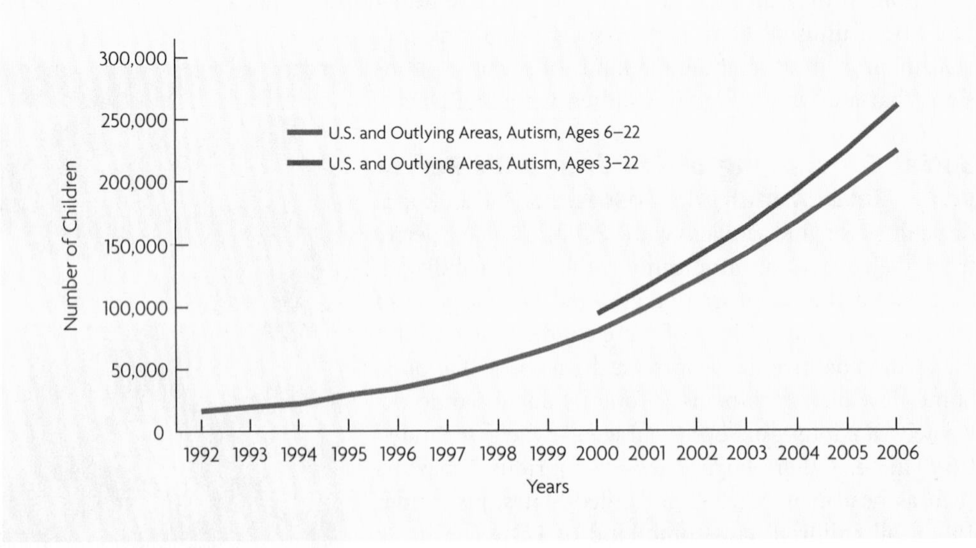

Figure 7.7 Cumulative Number of Cases of Autism in the United States from 1992 to 2006

The number of individuals under the age of 22 who are diagnosed with autism has risen dramatically over the past two decades. The cause of the increase is not known, but changes in diagnostic criteria are at least partially responsible. Individuals who would have been diagnosed with a variety of other disorders in the past are now often labeled as having autism.

(*Source*: http://www.fightingautism.org/idea/autism.php.)

autistic disorders a group of disorders that are characterized by limited or nonexistent language skills, an inability to engage in reciprocal social relationships, and a severely limited range of interests

Asperger's syndrome a disorder in which children have age-appropriate language and cognitive skills but are incapable of engaging in normal social relationships

DEVELOPMENTAL SCIENCE IN THE CLINIC

Functional Analysis of Self-Injurious Behavior

At the age of 3, Jordan was diagnosed with autistic disorder. On the advice of his neurologist, Jordan's mother enlisted the help of a behavioral consultant, a service that was available to Jordan through the local public schools. The consultant showed Jordan's mother some techniques for teaching the boy sign language. Jordan responded well to the training, and everything seemed to be going well until the day after his fourth birthday, when Jordan's mother encouraged him to put two signs together to create a sentence. He knew the signs for "car" and "go," so she demonstrated "car go" for him and attempted to get him to imitate her. To her dismay, Jordan suddenly bit his wrist so hard that it began to bleed. From that day on, whenever Jordan's mother attempted to teach him a new sign, he was cooperative, but when she tried to motivate him to combine signs, he would start biting himself. Desperate for a solution, Jordan's mother turned once again to the behavioral consultant.

The consultant assured Jordan's mother that she could devise a behavior modification plan that would eliminate, or at least reduce, Jordan's self-injurious behavior (Matson, 2008). He began by carrying out a *functional analysis* of Jordan's biting behavior. A functional analysis is accomplished by observing the problem behavior when it naturally occurs and recording the events that precede and follow it.

Once the functional analysis was complete, the consultant developed a plan for stopping Jordan's self-injurious behavior, based on his finding that the purpose of Jordan's behavior was to stop his mother from imposing new demands on him. He recommended that, whenever Jordan started biting himself, Jordan's mother stop the sign language lessons altogether instead of going back to working on individual signs. Eventually, the consultant said, Jordan would learn that, if he wanted to keep doing what he enjoyed (learning individual signs), he would have to cooperate with his mother's attempts to challenge him to combine them.

Questions for Reflection

1. In what ways are the parenting issues involved in raising a child without disabilities similar to those that were faced by Jordan's mother?
2. What kind of reinforcement is at work when Jordan's mother responds to his self-injurious behavior by abandoning her lesson in sign combinations and reverting to teaching him only individual signs? (*Hint*: Positive reinforcement is at work when an increase in behavior results from an added [usually pleasant] stimulus. Negative reinforcement is at work when an increase in behavior results from a removed [usually unpleasant] stimulus.)

guage and cognitive skills and often obtain high scores on IQ tests. Despite their normal language skills, children with Asperger's syndrome are incapable of engaging in normal social relationships because, like children with autism who are high-functioning, they usually do not develop the capacity to understand others' thoughts, feelings, and motivations.

Because of their normal language and cognitive skills, most children with Asperger's syndrome don't stand out from their peers until their second or third birthday, when other children begin to engage in cooperative play. However, since children of this age develop at different rates, children with Asperger's syndrome are often assumed to be "late bloomers" or "going through a phase." By the time they start kindergarten, though, many children with Asperger's syndrome begin to exhibit the unusual behaviors that most people associate with pervasive developmental disorders. For example, they may become intensely focused on memorizing things that have little meaning to them, such as airline flight schedules. They may also engage in obsessive behaviors, such as counting and recounting the number of squares on a checkered tablecloth. Moreover, their inability to form friendships like those of other children their age is usually quite apparent once they enter kindergarten.

Causes of Pervasive Developmental Disorders Although pervasive developmental disorders were once thought to be the result of poor parenting, it is now well established that all of these disorders are of neurological origin (Kagan & Herschkowitz, 2005). However, there is no single brain anomaly or dysfunction that is associated with PDDs. Even for the individual disorders within this category, researchers have not found a single definitive neurological marker. In a few cases, specific genetic defects are known to lead to atypical neurological development and, in turn, cause children to develop pervasive developmental disorders. For instance, fragile-X syndrome, which you may recall from Chapter 3, can cause autistic disorder. For the most part, however, the cause of PDDs remains a mystery (Kagan & Herschkowitz, 2005).

Whatever the neurological mechanisms involved in PDDs, twin studies suggest that these disorders are strongly influenced by heredity. When one identical twin is diagnosed with a PDD, there is a 70% to 90% chance that the other twin will be as well (Zoghbi, 2003). A wide variety of factors interact with genetic predispositions to trigger the appearance of these disorders (Rutter, 2005). When mothers are depressed, for example, infants have an increased risk of developing the symptoms of a PDD (Pozzi, 2003).

You may have heard that vaccines containing a form of mercury called *thimerosal* are suspected of causing autism. However, researchers generally agree that the vaccine hypothesis is unfounded (Rutter, 2005). In one important study, researchers tracked the development of more than half a million Danish children in order to compare rates of autism among those who received vaccines with thimerosal and among those who did not receive such immunizations for several years (Madsen et al., 2003). Rates of autism were found to be nearly identical in the two groups. Furthermore, these researchers found that autism rates actually increased in Denmark after thimerosal was removed from all vaccines in the late 1990s (Madsen et al., 2003). Studies in the United States and Canada show a similar pattern. Although thimerosal has been removed from the vaccines that are routinely administered to infants and children, the prevalence of autism in both countries has continued to increase (Fombonne, Zakarian, Bennett, Meng, & McLean-Heywood, 2006; Schechter & Grether, 2008). Nevertheless, sensational media reports about the hypothesized link between immunizations and autism have contributed to fears of vaccines.

Prognosis and Treatment Treatments for PDDs vary with the types and severity of the symptoms exhibited by the child (Kauffman, 2005). Most children benefit from behavior modification strategies aimed at improving their communication skills. However, in some children with PDDs, symptoms actually get worse as they get older (Sigman & McGovern, 2005). The minimal language and social skills they appear to acquire through intensive educational programs in the early years of life sometimes deteriorate markedly before they reach adulthood. Many adults with these disorders live in sheltered environments and are employed in jobs that require minimal competencies.

Some children with PDDs are taught in special education classrooms, but a growing number of them are being taught in regular classrooms along with their typically developing peers (Kauffman, 2005). However, children who display the most severe behavioral symptoms of the disorder, including self-injurious behavior, can usually spend only a limited amount of time in regular classrooms. In some cases, psychiatric medications are helpful for managing these behavior problems, but psychiatrists who specialize in treating children with PDDs recommend that behavioral approaches be tried before resorting to medication (Filipek, Steinberg-Epstein, & Book, 2006). Their reluctance to prescribe medications for children with PDDs results from the tendency of these children to respond to drugs in unpredictable ways. That is, psychiatric drugs may actually make their symptoms worse.

Like other children, youngsters with PDDs require instruction in academic skills such as reading and mathematics. The language skills of a child with a PDD are the best indicator of the degree to which he or she will benefit from academic interventions (DSM-IV TR, 2000). Consequently, children with Asperger's syndrome have the best hope of attaining independence in adulthood. Thanks to their language and cognitive skills, many are capable of high levels of academic achievement. Indeed, expert reviews of the medical records of one of the most eminent German writers of the 20th century, Robert Walser, suggest that he probably suffered from Asperger's syndrome (Fitzgerald, 2004). Despite his success, his social relationships, like those of almost all individuals with this syndrome, continued to be impaired throughout his life.

Physical Development and the Whole Child

Before moving on to the next chapter, consider what you have learned about young children up to this point. You have learned about early childhood growth patterns, advances in the motor domain and nervous system, and the factors that affect children's health. As you will see, many aspects of physical development underlie changes that occur in the cognitive and socioemotional domains during these years.

Cognitive Functioning

According to Piaget, the impressive advances in motor skills that occur during early childhood are critical to cognitive development during this period (Piaget & Inhelder, 1969). When young children build with blocks, pour sand or water from one container to another, and attempt to throw, kick, and hit different kinds of balls (e.g., a beach ball versus a tennis ball), they gain information about physical reality that enables them to better understand the relations among objects and how their actions can change those objects. Knowledge about physical reality that is acquired between ages 2 and 6 is the foundation upon which the child builds the sophisticated logical concepts that emerge at the end of the early childhood period.

Piaget also emphasized the role of brain maturation in cognitive development (Piaget & Inhelder, 1969). As you learned in this chapter, lateralization is one of the important themes of neurological development during early childhood. Lateralization is linked to advances in language development and *theory of mind*, an aspect of development that you will read about in Chapter 8 and that includes a child's understanding of other people's thoughts (Brownwell et al., 2000; Knecht, 2004). In addition, maturation of the hippocampus is related to the improvements in memory that are discussed in Chapter 8.

Socioemotional Functioning

As you learned in the chapters devoted to infancy, infants are sensitive to the emotional implications of others' facial expressions. In early childhood, children learn to categorize, label, and apply this sensitivity to social relationships. It turns out that lateralization plays a role in the development of such social perception. And, as mentioned in the discussion of changes in the brain, experience and maturation interact to produce this change. As a result of the plasticity of the brain during these early years, some kinds of experiences interfere with the development of emotional perception. Specifically, children who are abused are more sensitive to angry expressions than their nonabused peers are, and children who are institutionalized during these years are less responsive to all types of facial expressions (Nelson, Haan, & Thomas, 2006). Their differences from typically developing children come into play in the development of *empathy*, the capacity to identify with others' emotions, which you will read about in Chapter 9.

The brain's capacity for categorizing the world, another cognitive skill that is associated with lateralization, contributes to two additional sets of changes in the socioemotional domain. *Gender role development*, for example, is founded upon children's ability to categorize themselves as male or female. In addition, children's ability to categorize different kinds of rules is an important step toward the development of *moral reasoning*, the ability to make culturally based judgments about right and wrong.

THE WHOLE CHILD IN FOCUS

To trace how the physical, cognitive, and socioemotional domains work together to influence Madeleine's development, see *The Whole Child in Focus* on page 282.

Looking Ahead

In Chapters 8 and 9, you will learn about the milestones of cognitive and socioemotional functioning that happen between the ages of 2 and 6. It is worth mentioning once again that separating development into the three strands of physical, cognitive, and socioemotional functioning can distort the overall developmental process. Remember, the strands are interactive. Thus, when you are thinking about the cognitive and socioemotional advances of early childhood, keep in mind that they both depend on and contribute to the advances in physical development that you learned about in this chapter.

Test Prep Center

with PEARSON mydevelopmentlab™

PHYSICAL CHANGES

7.1 How do patterns of growth change during early childhood? (pp. 185–188)

Physical development is slower from age 2 to age 6 than it is in infancy, but it nevertheless progresses steadily. Children establish stable growth curves, which help health-care professionals identify children who may have undiagnosed diseases or growth disorders.

1. A percentile rank represents the percentage of all children whose scores on a measure are (above/below) that of an individual child.
2. It is (possible/impossible) to predict a young child's adult height.
3. A child whose height and weight fall at or below the ____ percentile may have a growth disorder.
4. Some growth disorders are caused by a deficiency of ____.

7.2 What important changes happen in the brain during early childhood? (pp. 188–189)

Significant changes in brain lateralization occur in early childhood. Myelination of the reticular formation and the hippocampus contributes to improvements in attention and memory.

5. Match each term with its definition.

    ______ (1) lateralization

    ______ (2) reticular formation

    ______ (3) hippocampus

    (A) the part of the brain involved in transferring information to long-term memory

    (B) the division of brain functions between the two hemispheres of the cortex

    (C) the part of the brain that regulates attention and concentration

6. From the Multimedia Library within MyDevelopLab, run the *Hemispheric Experiment* simulation and answer the following question.

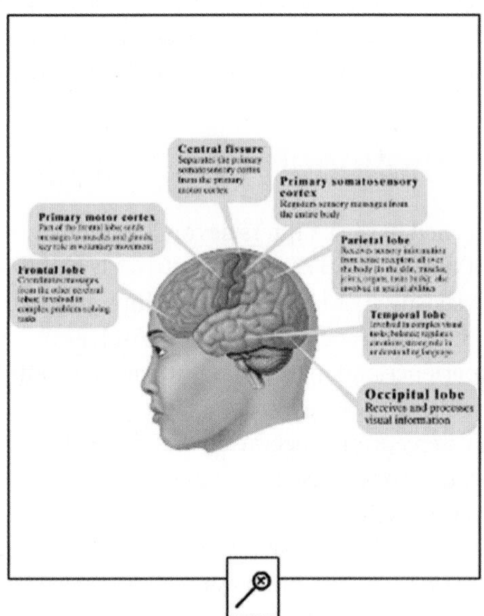

What are split-brain studies, and how do they help researchers understand the development of the brain?

____

____

7.3 What are the arguments for the genetic and experiential explanations of handedness? (pp. 189–191)

The genetic hypothesis is associated with research showing that ratios of right- and left-handers are the same in ancient and modern populations, the fact that handedness appears early in life, and genetic studies. Studies show that left-handedness is less frequent among age cohorts who were encouraged to switch hands in early childhood. Some evidence suggests that right-handedness is inherited, but left-handedness is determined by experience.

7. The finding that the proportion of right- and left-handers in the human population has been highly consistent for thousands of years supports the (nature/nurture) explanation of handedness.
8. The finding that identical twins sometimes develop different patterns of handedness supports the (nature/nurture) explanation of handedness.
9. Explain how a developmentalist might dispute the following statement: All young children should be encouraged to develop right-handedness in order to prevent them from developing problems that have been found to be correlated with left-handedness.

____

____

7.4 What advances in sensory and perceptual abilities occur between ages 2 and 6? (pp. 191–193)

Children's field of vision expands to equal that of adults, although most young children are more farsighted than older children and adults. Common vision problems include strabismus and amblyopia; diagnosis and correction of these problems helps facilitate the development of stereopsis. The vestibular sense contributes to advances in children's ability to maintain their balance under different conditions. Hearing loss in children, much of which can be attributed to noise, can lead to cognitive and language problems.

10. Match each term with its definition.

_______ (1) amblyopia

_______ (2) strabismus

_______ (3) stereopsis

_______ (4) vestibular sense

(A) a condition in which the brain suppresses the image from one eye

(B) a condition in which the eyes are misaligned

(C) the integration of images from the left and right eyes into a single, three-dimensional image

(D) the body's sense of its position in space

11. What does research suggest about the impact of mild hearing loss on academic achievement?

____

____

7.5 What are the major milestones of motor development between ages 2 and 6? (pp. 193–196)

Motor skills continue to improve gradually, with marked improvement in gross motor skills (running, jumping, climbing) and slower advances in fine motor skills.

12. List the milestones of fine and gross motor development between ages 1.5 and 6 years.

Age	Gross Motor Skills	Fine Motor Skills
18–24 months		
2–3 years		
3–4 years		
4–5 years		
5–6 years		

13. Which of Kellogg's drawing stages is each of these children likely to exhibit?

_______ (A) Dolly, who is midway between her second and third birthdays

_______ (B) Raj, who has just started kindergarten

_______ (C) Simon, who is about to turn 4

_______ (D) Shameka, who celebrated her third birthday a month ago

7.6 What kinds of sleep problems emerge during early childhood? (pp. 196–198)

Total sleep time declines from about 13 hours to 10 hours per day between the ages of 2 and 6. Common sleep problems include nightmares, night terrors, and bed-wetting.

14. Most (nightmares/night terrors) happen just before children wake up in the morning.
15. Most (nightmares/night terrors) happen shortly after children go to sleep at night.
16. In some cases, bed-wetting is caused by the secretion of (too much/too little) antidiuretic hormone (ADH) during the night.

HEALTH AND WELLNESS

7.7 In what ways do eating patterns change in early childhood? (pp. 198–199)

Slower rates of growth contribute to declines in appetite. Some children restrict their eating to one or two foods. Parents are urged not to worry about the amount of food that preschoolers eat or to try to force them to eat. They are also encouraged not to resort to feeding children unhealthy foods to increase the number of calories they consume.

17. Explain why this statement is false: In order to avoid future weight problems, young children should be fed a fat-restricted diet.

____

____

7.8 What are the health-care needs of young children? (pp. 199–201)

Children benefit from annual well-child exams. There are several immunizations that must be administered during these years.

18. Why do young children require dental care?

____

____

7.9 What factors are involved in illnesses, accidents, and mortality among 2- to 6-year-olds? (pp. 201–203)

Stress is a factor in early childhood illnesses such as colds and flu. Otitis media is a common illness among young children. Child mortality in the developing world is associated with infectious and parasitic illnesses; in industrialized nations, accidents are the most frequent cause of death.

19. Why do many physicians recommend a "wait-and-see" approach to mild, nonchronic cases of otitis media?

____

____

20. The substance most frequently involved in poisonings of 1- to 4-year-olds is ______________________.

21. The only region in the world to show an increase in child mortality in the past two decades was ______________, largely due to a(n) ______________ epidemic.

7.10 What are the risk factors that are associated with abuse and neglect? (pp. 203–207)

Children between the ages of 2 and 9 are more likely to be abused or neglected than are infants or older children. Certain characteristics of both children and parents increase the risk of abuse. Long-term consequences of abuse have been found across all domains of development.

22. Transform each of these false statements into a true statement.

(A) Most serious abuse cases involve children who are infants.

____

____

(B) Little is known about the risk factors associated with child abuse.

____

____

(C) There is no way to prevent abuse.

____

____

ATYPICAL DEVELOPMENT

7.11 What are the features and causes of mental retardation? (pp. 208–209)

Children with mental retardation show slower development and less effective information-processing strategies than peers without mental retardation. In some cases, mental retardation is the result of a physical problem or a genetic disorder. However, in most cases, the cause of a child's retardation is unknown.

23. What are the two criteria that must be met for a child to be diagnosed with mental retardation?

(A) ______________________________________

____

(B) ______________________________________

____

24. From the Multimedia Library within MyDevelopmentLab, watch the *Mental Retardation* video and answer the following question.

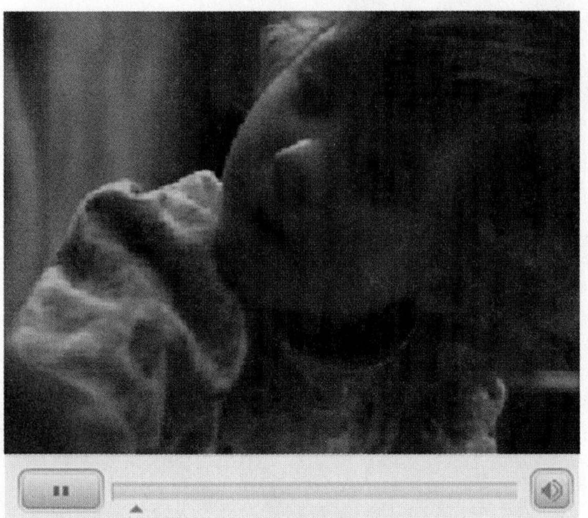

What role did the social environment play in the physical and cognitive development of the young child with mental retardation who was featured in the video?

____

____

7.12 How do pervasive developmental disorders affect children's development? (pp. 209–212)

Children with pervasive developmental disorders have impaired social relationships. Those who have autistic disorder have limited language skills and often have mental retardation. Asperger's syndrome is a milder form of autistic disorder in which children have age-appropriate language and cognitive skills.

25. List four characteristics of the behavior of children with pervasive developmental disorders.

(A) ______________________________

(B) ______________________________

(C) ______________________________

(D) ______________________________

26. Why is autism usually diagnosed earlier than Asperger's syndrome?

____

____

For answers to the questions in this chapter, turn to page 514. For a list of key terms, turn to page 531.

Chapter 8

Cognitive Development in Early Childhood

Learning Objectives

Cognitive Changes

8.1 What are the characteristics of children's thought during Piaget's preoperational stage?

8.2 How has recent research challenged Piaget's view of this period?

8.3 What is a theory of mind, and how does it develop?

8.4 How do information-processing theorists explain changes in young children's thinking?

8.5 What are the characteristics of Vygotsky's stages of early childhood cognitive development?

Changes in Language

8.6 How does fast-mapping help children learn new words?

8.7 What happens during the grammar explosion?

8.8 What is phonological awareness, and why is it important?

Differences in Intelligence

8.9 What are the strengths and weaknesses of IQ tests?

8.10 What evidence has been offered in support of the nature and nurture explanations for individual differences in IQ?

8.11 What evidence has been offered in support of the genetic and cultural explanations of group differences in IQ scores?

Early Childhood Education

8.12 How do the various approaches to early childhood education differ?

8.13 How does early childhood education influence cognitive development among economically disadvantaged children?

Watch a 1-year-old playing and you'll notice that her play is dominated by sensory explorations of objects. She seems motivated to touch and manipulate everything in her environment. If you observe a 2-year-old, you will see that a new dimension has been added to sensorimotor play—the idea that objects have names. Almost every object manipulation is accompanied by an important question for nearby adults: "Whazit?" (What is it?)

A few years later, by about age 4, sophisticated forms of pretending, such as "dress-up," become the preferred modes of play. Profound changes in the cognitive domain underlie these shifts in play behavior. In the years from 2 to 6, the period known as early childhood, the child changes from a dependent toddler, able to communicate only in very primitive ways, to a remarkably competent, communicative, social creature, ready to begin school. These changes are the subject of this chapter.

Chapter 2 acquainted you with the general principles of Piaget's theory, and in Chapter 5 you read about his view of the sensorimotor stage. In this chapter, you will learn about his discoveries of the strengths and weaknesses of children's thinking during the early childhood period, and about the efforts of other psychologists to challenge them and to find better explanations for them. But Piaget's work doesn't provide us with a full account of cognitive development in early childhood, so you will also read about momentous changes in memory functioning and language development that occur during this period. We will also look at the issues involved in the measurement of individual differences in cognitive functioning.

Cognitive Changes

If you were to visit a preschool and go from classroom to classroom observing children in free play, what kinds of activities do you think you would see? If you visited the classrooms in "chronological" order, you would see a progression of activities ranging from simple forms of constructive and pretend play among the 2-year-olds to sophisticated role-play and debates about the rules of board games among the 5- and 6-year-olds (see *Developmental Science in the Classroom*). Forms of play change over the early childhood years because children's thinking changes. At the beginning of the period, children are just beginning to learn how to accomplish goals. By the time they reach age 5 or 6, they are proficient at manipulating symbols and can make accurate judgments about others' thoughts, feelings, and behavior.

Learning Objective 8.1

What are the characteristics of children's thought during Piaget's preoperational stage?

Piaget's Preoperational Stage

According to Piaget, children acquire the **semiotic (symbolic) function** between the ages of 18 and 24 months (which, as you learned in Chapter 5, is during the final substage of the sensorimotor stage). The semiotic function is the understanding that one object or behavior can represent another—a picture of a chair represents a real chair, a child's pretending to feed a doll stands for a parent's feeding a baby, and so on. It is the cornerstone of the **preoperational stage** of cognitive development, the stage during which youngsters acquire symbolic schemes, such as language and fantasy, that they use in thinking and communicating.

DEVELOPMENTAL SCIENCE IN THE CLASSROOM

Using Children's Play to Assess Levels of Cognitive Development

The foundation that funds the child-care center for low-income families where Dona serves as director has asked her to devise a strategy for assessing the cognitive developmental status of each child who is enrolled. Their purpose is to identify children who may be suffering from some kind of developmental delay so that they can be referred to the program for at-risk preschoolers. Dona has found a reliable and valid formal test of cognitive development that she plans to give the children, but she would also like to include observational data in the assessments. She has learned that a great deal of useful information about preschoolers' cognitive development can be gleaned from observations that are geared toward a search for the following characteristics in children's play behavior (Rubin, Fein, & Vandenberg, 1983):

- **Constructive play.** By age 2 or so, children use objects to build or construct things. Piaget hypothesized that this kind of play is the foundation of a child's understanding of the rules that govern physical reality. For example, through block play, they come to understand that a tower that is broad at the top and narrow at the bottom will be unstable.
- **First pretend play.** Piaget believed that pretend play was an important indicator of a child's capacity to use symbols. The first instances of such pretending are usually simple, like pretending to drink from a toy cup. Most children exhibit some pretending at around 12 months. Between 15 and 21 months, the recipient of the pretend action becomes another person or a doll. This change signals a significant movement away from the sensorimotor stage and toward true symbolic thinking.
- **Substitute pretend play.** Between 2 and 3 years of age, children begin to use objects to stand for something altogether different. Children this age may use a broom as a horse or make "trucks" out of blocks.
- **Sociodramatic play.** Sociodramatic play, a kind of shared pretending, emerges between 3 and 4 years of age, when children are solidly in the preoperational stage. By age 4, virtually all children engage in some play of this type (Howes & Matheson, 1992).
- **Rule-governed play.** Sometime around the fifth birthday, most children begin to prefer rule-governed pretending. For example, children of this age use rules such as "Whoever is smallest has to be the baby" when playing "house." Most also enjoy simple rule-governed games such as Red Rover and Red Light, Green Light. Piaget suggested that older preschoolers' preference for rule-governed play indicates that they are about to make the transition to the next stage of cognitive development, *concrete operations*, in which they will acquire an understanding of rules (Piaget & Inhelder, 1969).

Questions for Reflection

1. Which of the research methods discussed in Chapter 1 is best suited to the study of age-related changes in children's play activities?
2. Many children have imaginary friends (a phenomenon that is considered to be entirely normal by child psychologists). In which of the stages of play would you expect to first see children inventing imaginary playmates?

You should recall from Chapter 2 that the concept of the *scheme*, an internal cognitive structure that provides an individual with a procedure to follow in a specific circumstance, is central to Piaget's explanation of cognitive development. According to Piaget, the semiotic function enables the child to acquire figurative schemes (Flavell, 1963). **Figurative schemes** are mental representations of the basic properties of objects in the world. For instance, a child is using figurative schemes when he correctly labels dogs and cats, lists their characteristics (e.g., wet noses, fur, whiskers, tails that wag), and describes their typical behaviors (e.g., barking, mewing). Knowing that dogs and cats are different kinds of animals, and that animals represent a category that is distinct from others (e.g., clothes, food, etc.), also involves figurative schemes. Such schemes enable children to understand and act on the world in more sophisticated ways than they could when they were younger and possessed only sensorimotor schemes. Nevertheless, they must also develop **operative schemes**, Piaget's term for schemes that enable children to understand the logical connections among objects in the world and to reason about the effects of transformations on them.

To better understand the impact of operative schemes on children's understanding of the world, imagine presenting a 4-year-old with a collection of toy animals in which there are seven dogs and three cats. Following the methodology that Piaget used in his classic studies of children's understanding of categories, you ask the child whether there are more dogs or more animals. Virtually all 4-year-olds will respond that there are more dogs when, of course, the correct response is that there are more animals. Children choose the larger subclass because they do not realize that, logically speaking, any combination of dogs and cats will always be more numerous than either dogs or cats alone (they lack a skill called *class inclusion*, which you will learn more about in Chapter 11). Such understandings, when they are manifested as solutions to problems, represent operative schemes that can be applied to every possible instance of a category of problems without regard to the surface characteristics of the objects involved. Thus, a child with an operative understanding of categories will answer correctly that, if there are seven daisies and three roses, there are more flowers than daisies. She will also say that, if there are twelve cars and seven trucks, there are more vehicles than cars. No matter how you change the problem, a child who has developed operative schemes for categorization will get it right, because she approaches the problem logically.

During the preoperational stage, children's figurative schemes grow by leaps and bounds. They acquire these schemes through observation and especially through the acquisition of verbal knowledge. Children as young as 2 or 3 display figurative schemes when they engage in pretend play (Walker-Andrews & Kahana-Kalman, 1999). In one kind of pretend play, children relate the characteristics of objects in the environment to figurative schemes for objects that are stored in their memories. A triangular piece of cardboard becomes an imaginary piece of pizza, and a row of blocks becomes an imaginary train. The child's actions on the objects—pretending to munch on the "pizza" or pushing the "train" along while making a noise that represents its whistle—help the child make his imaginary world more like the real one.

In sharp contrast to the rapid advances in figurative schemes that happen in early childhood, operative schemes are constructed quite slowly. Piaget claimed that the construction of operative schemes is influenced by brain maturation, experience in acting on the world, and information from others (Piaget & Inhelder, 1969). Each factor is "necessary but not sufficient" to produce operative schemes. That is, a child may have the necessary degree of brain development for a particular operative scheme, but the scheme cannot be completed until the other two factors are present. Or she may have the requisite experience and information but lack the necessary brain development. Once a scheme is in place, it has what you might think of as probationary status; the child must test it by using it to act on the world. Through practice, or *equilibration* (the process of balancing assimilation and accommodation), the scheme attains completion. Because of the complexities involved in the construction of operative schemes, young children's capacity for logic usually lags far behind their ability to use figurative schemes. Moreover, the fragmentary, or "in-progress," nature of preschoolers' operative schemes prevents them from generating valid conclusions to logical problems.

THE WHOLE CHILD IN FOCUS

Which of Madeleine's favorite activities showed that she had constructed a complex set of figurative schemes by age 6? Find out on page 283.

semiotic (symbolic) function the understanding that one object or behavior can represent another

preoperational stage Piaget's second stage of cognitive development, during which children become proficient in the use of symbols in thinking and communicating but still have difficulty thinking logically

figurative schemes mental representations of the basic properties of objects in the child's world

operative schemes mental representations that enable children to understand the logical connections among objects in their world and to reason about the effects of any changes on them

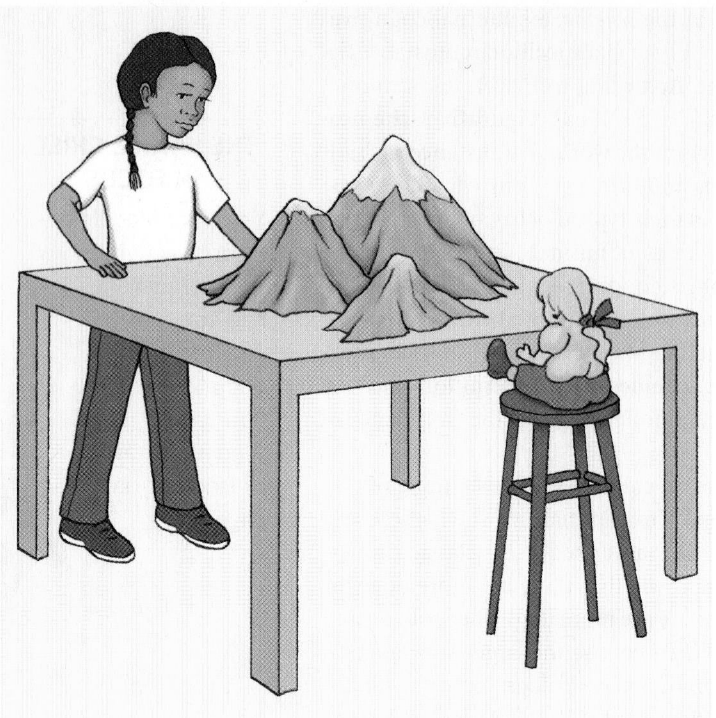

Figure 8.1
Piaget's Three Mountains Task

The experimental situation shown here is similar to one Piaget used to study egocentrism in children. The child is asked to pick out a picture that shows how the mountains look to her and then to pick out a picture that shows how the mountains look to the doll.

According to Piaget, one of several difficulties that arise from young children's lack of completed operative schemes is that they tend to look at things entirely from their own point of view, a characteristic he called **egocentrism** (Piaget, 1954). This term does not suggest that the young child is a self-centered egomaniac. It simply means that she assumes that everyone sees the world as she does. For example, while riding in the back seat of a car, a 3- or 4-year-old may suddenly call out "Look at that, Mom!"—not realizing that Mom can't see the object she's talking about. Moreover, the child doesn't realize that the car's motion prevents Mom from ever seeing the object in question. As a result, the youngster may become frustrated in her attempts to communicate with her mother about what she saw.

Figure 8.1 illustrates a classic experiment in which most young children demonstrate this kind of egocentrism. The child is shown a three-dimensional scene with mountains of different sizes and colors. From a set of drawings, she picks out the one that shows the scene the way she sees it. Most preschoolers can do this without much difficulty. Then the examiner asks the child to pick out the drawing that shows how someone else sees the scene, such as a doll or the examiner. At this point, most preschoolers choose the drawing that shows their own view of the mountains (Flavell, Everett, Croft, & Flavell, 1981; Gzesh & Surber, 1985).

Piaget also pointed out that the preschool-aged child's thinking is guided by the appearance of objects, or a reliance on figurative schemes, in forming conclusions about the world. Children may believe, for example, that any moving object is an animal of some kind. This kind of thinking reflects a child's tendency to think of the world in terms of one variable at a time, a type of thought Piaget called **centration.** Because of centration, the child reaches the conclusion that all moving objects are animals through a series of false conclusions. The premise on which these conclusions are based is the fact, evident in everyday interactions with the world, that all animals move—or, as scientists put it, have the capacity for *locomotion* (self-movement). But the preoperational thinker isn't capable of thinking of objects in terms of both their motion and their capacity for self-movement. Thus, movement, without regard to any other relevant characteristic of objects, becomes the sole criterion for distinguishing between living and nonliving objects. As a result, a child may fear a leaf that blows across the playground because he believes that the leaf is trying to follow him. Piaget used the term **animism** to refer to this particular product of preoperational logic, the attribution of the characteristics of living organisms to nonliving objects.

Some of Piaget's most famous experiments dealt with a cognitive process called **conservation**, the understanding that matter can change in appearance without changing in quantity. The ability to conserve depends on operative schemes that develop slowly across the early and middle childhood periods. Consequently, you will read about conservation in Chapter 11 as well as here. Some of the conservation tasks Piaget used, along with children's typical responses to them, are shown in Figure 8.2. As you can see, Piaget found that children rarely show any kind of conservation before age 5.

Piaget asserted that preoperational thinkers' inability to conserve is the result of their penchant for **transductive logic**, or causal inference based only on the temporal relationship between two events. Transductive logic leads children to believe that, if event A occurred shortly before event B, then event A probably caused event B. For example, if you arrange 10 pennies in a row and ask a child who knows how to count to determine how many there are, she will easily come up with the observation that there are 10 pennies. If you then stack the coins and ask her whether there are still 10 pennies, she may be perplexed. She may say that there are fewer, be-

egocentrism a young child's belief that everyone sees and experiences the world the way she or he does

centration a young child's tendency to think of the world in terms of one variable at a time

animism the attribution of the characteristics of living organisms to nonliving objects

conservation the understanding that matter can change in appearance without changing in quantity

transductive logic causal inference based only on the temporal relationship between two events (if event B happened shortly after event A, then A caused B)

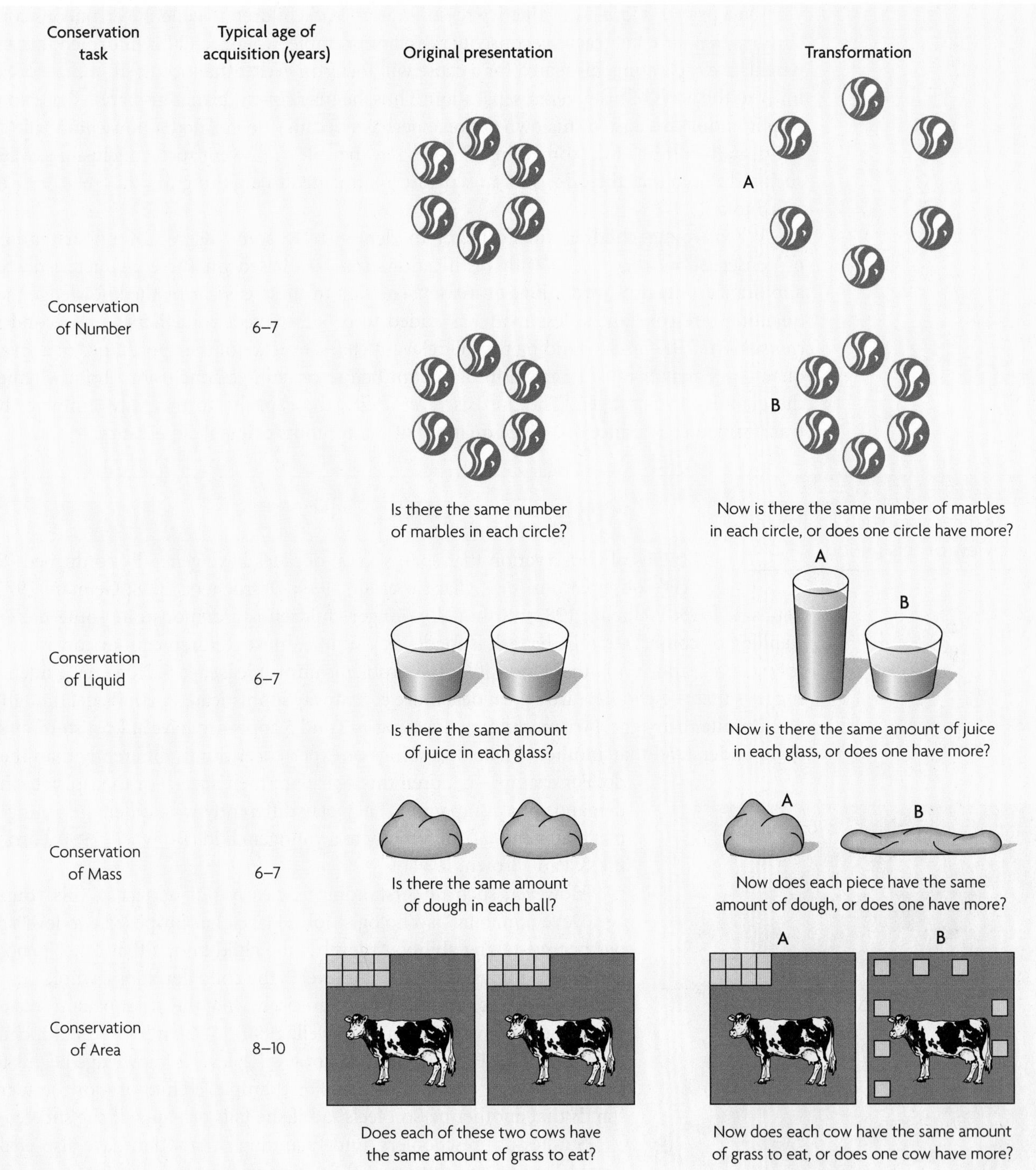

Figure 8.2 Piaget's Conservation Tasks

Piaget's research involved several kinds of conservation tasks. He classified children's responses as correct with respect to a particular task if they could correctly solve the problem and provide a logically sound reason for their answer. For example, if a child said, "The two circles of marbles are the same because you didn't add any or take any away when you moved them," the response was judged to reflect conservation. Conversely, if a child said, "The two circles are the same, but I don't know why," the response was not judged to reflect conservation.

cause of the reduction in the amount of horizontal space that is taken up by the coins (i.e., "They're not as spread out so there's less"). Or she may say that there are more, because of the increase in the amount of vertical space they occupy (i.e., "They're taller, so there's more"). In other words, transductive reasoning will lead her to hypothesize that the act of stacking the pennies caused a change in the number of pennies, and the changed appearance of the coins confirms her theory.

On a practical level, transductive reasoning can lead children to generate erroneous conclusions that have far-reaching consequences. For example, when a child is informed that his parents are separating, his search for a cause will focus on events that occurred in close proximity to the news of his parents' separation. Thus, he may conclude that his parents' relationship is ending because of his own actions, perhaps because he violated a household rule or accidentally lost or broke something. Parents may be able to prevent such conclusions by assuring children that their decision to separate is unrelated to anything the child has done or failed to do.

When young children finally begin to demonstrate some degree of understanding of conservation, they do so with justifications that are based on three characteristics of appearance-only transformations of matter. The first of these is *identity*, the knowledge that quantities are constant unless matter is added to or subtracted from them. The second is *compensation*, the understanding that all relevant characteristics of the appearance of a given quantity of matter must be taken into account before reaching a conclusion about whether the quantity has changed. The third is *reversibility*, the capacity to mentally compare the transformed appearance of a given quantity of matter to its original appearance.

Learning Objective 8.2

How has recent research challenged Piaget's view of this period?

Challenges to Piaget's View

Studies of conservation that span several decades have generally confirmed Piaget's observations (e.g., Ciancio et al., 1999; Desrochers, 2008; Gelman, 1972; Sophian, 1995; Wellman, 1982). Although younger children can demonstrate some understanding of conservation if the task is made very simple, most children cannot consistently solve conservation and other kinds of logical problems until at least age 5. However, evidence suggests that preschoolers are a great deal more cognitively sophisticated than Piaget thought.

Despite their egocentrism, children as young as 2 and 3 appear to have at least some ability to understand that another person sees things or experiences things differently than they do. For example, children this age adapt their speech or their play to the demands of a companion. They play differently with older and younger playmates and talk differently to a younger child (Brownell, 1990; Guralnik & Paul-Brown, 1984).

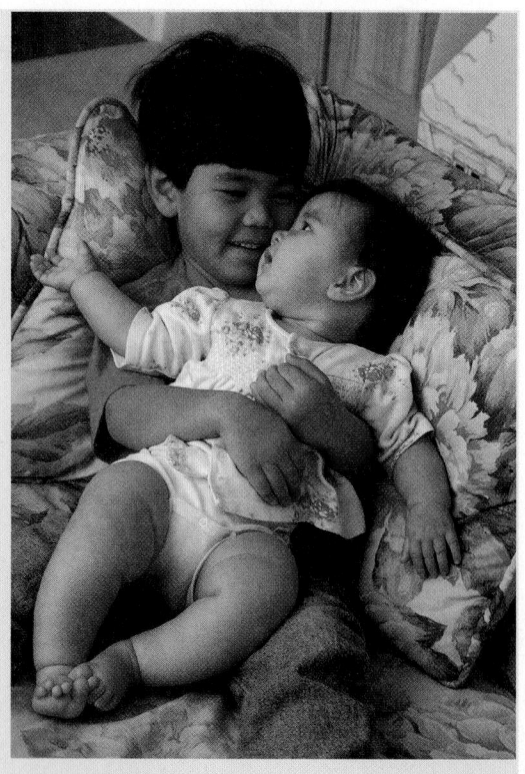

This young child is able to adapt his speech to the needs of his younger sibling, one of many indications that preschoolers are less egocentric than Piaget thought.

However, such understanding is clearly not perfect at this young age. Developmental psychologist John Flavell has proposed two levels of perspective-taking ability. At level 1, the child knows that other people experience things differently. At level 2, the child develops a whole series of complex rules for figuring out precisely what the other person sees or experiences (Flavell, Green, & Flavell, 1990). At 2 and 3 years old, children have level 1 knowledge but not level 2; level 2 knowledge begins to be evident in 4- and 5-year-olds. For example, a child of 4 or 5 understands that another person feels sad if she fails or happy if she succeeds.

Studies of preschoolers' understanding of emotion have also challenged Piaget's description of the young child's egocentrism. For example, by age 4, children learn to regulate or modulate their expressions of emotion to avoid hurting other people's feelings or causing them to get angry (Thompson & Goodvin, 2005). In addition, preschool children use emotional expressions such as crying or smiling to get things they want. These behaviors are obviously based at least in part on a growing awareness that other people judge your feelings by what they see you expressing. These behaviors wouldn't occur if children were completely incapable of looking at their own behavior from another person's perspective, as Piaget's assertions about egocentrism would suggest.

The young child's movement away from egocentrism seems to be part of a much broader change in his understanding of appearance and reality. Flavell has studied this understanding in a variety of ways

(Flavell, Green, & Flavell, 1990; Flavell, Green, Wahl, & Flavell, 1987). In the most famous Flavell procedure, the experimenter shows the child a sponge that has been painted to look like a rock. Three-year-olds will say either that the object looks like a sponge and is a sponge or that it looks like a rock and is a rock. But 4- and 5-year-olds can distinguish between appearance and reality; they realize that the item looks like a rock but is a sponge (Flavell, 1986). Thus, the older children understand that the same object can be represented differently, depending on one's point of view.

Theories of Mind

Learning Objective 8.3
What is a theory of mind, and how does it develop?

Evidence like that described in the previous section has led a number of theorists to propose that the 4- or 5-year-old has developed a new and quite sophisticated **theory of mind**, or set of ideas that describe, explain, and make predictions about others' knowledge and behavior based on inferences about their mental states.

Understanding Thoughts, Desires, and Beliefs The theory of mind does not spring forth full-blown at age 4. Toddlers as young as 18 months have some beginning understanding of the fact that people (but not inanimate objects) operate with goals and intentions (Meltzoff, 1995). By age 3, children understand some aspects of the link between people's thinking or feeling and their behavior (Higgins & Pittman, 2008). For example, they know that a person who wants something will try to get it. They also know that a person may still want something even if she can't have it (Lillard & Flavell, 1992). But they do not yet understand the basic principle that each person's actions are based on her or his own representation of reality, which may differ from what is "really" there. It is this new aspect of the theory of mind that clearly emerges between 3 and 5.

Studies that examine the **false belief principle** illustrate 3-year-olds' shortcomings in this area (Flavell, 1999). In one classic study, children were presented with a box on which there were pictures of different kinds of candy. The experimenter shook the box to demonstrate that there was something inside and then asked 3- and 4-year-olds to guess what they would find if they opened it. Regardless of age, the children guessed that the box contained candy. Upon opening the box, though, the children discovered that it actually contained crayons. The experimenter then asked the children to predict what another child who saw the closed box would believe was in it. Three-year-olds thought that the child would believe that the box contained crayons, but 4-year-olds realized that the pictures of candy on the box would lead the child to have a false belief that the box contained candy.

Similarly, 4-year-olds understand the psychological and social aspects of deception more fully than 3-year-olds do. For instance, developmentalists have known for some time that 4-year-olds are better than their 3-year-old counterparts at intentionally deceiving others (e.g., Sodian, Taylor, Harris, & Perner, 1991). Another way in which older preschoolers show that they understand deception better than younger preschoolers do is by keeping track of the reliability of others. In one of several studies comparing 3- and 4-year-olds' ability to do this, children watched videos in which, to varying degrees, adults provided inaccurate labels for objects that were familiar to the children (Pasquini, Corriveau, Koenig, & Harris, 2007). Afterward, the children were shown videos in which the same adults labeled objects with which the children were unfamiliar. Three-year-olds tended to disbelieve any adult who had made an error in labeling a familiar object; in other words, they made "all-or-none" judgments about the adults' reliability as informants. By contrast, 4-year-olds' judgments of the trustworthiness of adults in the unfamiliar-object videos were more subtle. The degree of trust that they ascribed to the adults depended on the degree of accuracy the adults had shown in the familiar-object videos. Apparently, 4-year-olds are better able to appreciate the fact that some informational errors are accidental and do not bear on the general trustworthiness of an information source. In their view, an informant's trustworthiness can be judged by his or her general tendency to give accurate information rather than a single episode in which the informant provided inaccurate information.

theory of mind a set of ideas constructed by a child or adult to describe, explain, and make predictions about other people's knowledge and behavior, based on inferences about their mental states

false belief principle an understanding that enables a child to look at a situation from another person's point of view and determine what kind of information will cause that person to have a false belief

Still, there is much that the 4-year-old doesn't yet grasp about other people's thinking. A child of this age understands that other people think, but does not yet understand that other people can think about him. The 4-year-old understands "I know that you know." But he does not yet fully understand that this process is reciprocal—namely, "You know that I know."

Understanding of the reciprocal nature of thought seems to develop between age 5 and age 7 for most children. This would seem to be a particularly important understanding, because it is probably necessary for the creation of genuinely reciprocal friendships, which begin to emerge in the elementary school years (Sullivan, Zaitchik, & Tager-Flusberg, 1994). In fact, the rate at which an individual preschooler develops a theory of mind is a good predictor of her social skills both later in early childhood and during the school years (Moore, Barresi, & Thompson, 1998; Watson, Nixon, Wilson, & Capage, 1999).

It is not until about age 6 that most children realize that knowledge can be derived through inference. For example, researchers in one study showed 4- and 6-year-olds two toys of different colors (Pillow, 1999). Next, they placed the toys in separate opaque containers. They then opened one of the containers and showed the toy to a puppet. When asked whether the puppet now knew which color toy was in each container, only the 6-year-olds said yes.

After two decades of research examining the development of theory of mind, researchers agree that there is still much to be learned. Still, a few definitive statements can be made about the sequence in which theory of mind skills emerge. First, it seems clear that children understand others' desires before they understand others' beliefs (Liu & Wellman, 2004). For instance, by the age of 3½, almost all children realize that two people can have different desires regarding the same object. They know, for instance, that one child may view an oatmeal cookie as desirable while another may not. Children's understanding of others' beliefs and how environmental cues affect their beliefs evolves gradually over the fifth and sixth year. For instance, just before their fifth birthday, but not earlier, most children come to realize that a label on a container can be misleading if a person who sees the container is unaware of another person's having replaced its contents with something other than what's on the label. The kinds of experiences that shape this sequence are the subject of much investigation.

Influences on the Development of a Theory of Mind Developmentalists have found that a child's theory of mind is correlated with his performance on Piaget's tasks, as well as on more recently developed tasks designed to assess egocentrism and appearance/reality (Melot & Houde, 1998; Yirmiya & Shulman, 1996). In addition, pretend play seems to contribute to theory of mind development. Shared pretense with other children, in particular, is strongly related to theory of mind; however, adults who engage in pretend play with children often provide them with cues and hints that provide scaffolding for theory of mind development (Dockett & Smith, 1995; Lillard, 2006a; Schwebel, Rosen, & Singer, 1999). Furthermore, children whose parents discuss emotion-provoking past events with them develop a theory of mind more rapidly than do their peers who do not have such conversations (Welch-Ross, 1997).

Language skills—such as knowledge of words like *want*, *need*, *think*, or *remember*, which express desires, feelings, and thoughts—are also related to theory of mind development (Astington & Jenkins, 1995; Green, Pring, & Swettenham, 2004; Tardif, So, & Kaciroti, 2007). Indeed, some level of language facility may be a necessary condition for the development of a theory of mind. Developmentalists have found that children in this age range simply do not succeed at false-belief tasks until they have reached a certain threshold of general language skill (Astington & Jenkins, 1999; Jenkins & Astington, 1996; Watson et al., 1999).

Moreover, research involving older children and adults with highly developed false-belief skills who are also bilingual indicates that the neural networks that support language overlap with those that support language comprehension (Kobayashi, Glover, & Temple, 2008). Studies also suggest that bilingual children have an advantage over monolingual children in performance on appearance/reality tasks (Bialystok, 2005). The mental inhibition processes that enable bilinguals to suppress their knowledge of one of the languages they speak in order to think and communicate in the other are thought to help them suppress the impulse to jump to a conclusion about an object based on its appearance. As a result, bilingual children may process the features of appearance/reality problems more thoroughly than monolingual children.

Further support for the same point comes from the finding that children with disabilities that affect language development, such as congenital deafness or autism, develop a theory of mind more slowly than others (Figueras-Costa & Harris, 2001; Harris & Leevers, 2005). Research has also demonstrated that, for children with mental disabilities, progress toward a fully developed theory of mind is better predicted by language skills than by type of disability (Bauminger & Kasari, 1999; Peterson & Siegal, 1999; Yirmiya, Eriel, Shaked, & Solomonica-Levi, 1998; Yirmiya, Solomonica-Levi, Shulman, & Pilowsky, 1996).

Theory of Mind Across Cultures Cross-cultural psychologists claim that theory of mind research in the United States and Europe may not apply to children in other cultures and have produced some preliminary evidence to support this contention (Lillard, 2006b). However, research also suggests that certain aspects of theory of mind development may be universal (Cole, 2005). For example, similar sequences of theory of mind development have been found in the United States, China, Japan, Europe, and India (Jin et al., 2002; Liu, Wellman, Tardif, & Sabbagh, 2008; Tardif & Wellman, 2000; Tardif, So, & Kaciroti, 2007; Wellman, Cross, & Watson, 2001). Critics, however, argue that most of the societies where these results have been found are industrialized and that very different findings might emerge in studies of nonindustrialized societies.

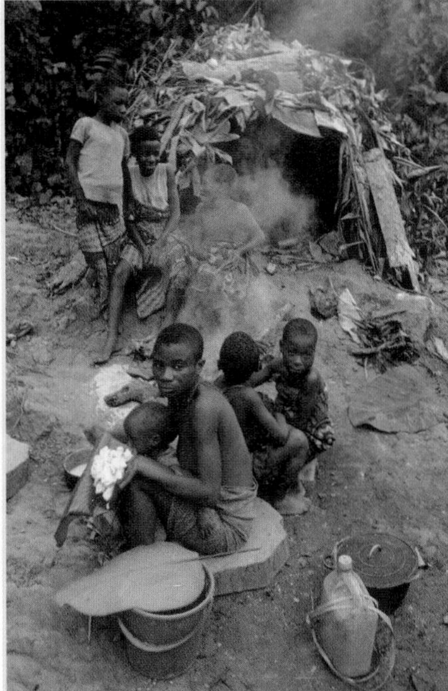

Cross-cultural research, including studies with the Cameroonian hunter-gatherer group called the Baka, suggests that all children develop a theory of mind between the ages of 3 and 5.

In response to this argument, developmentalists presented false-belief tasks to a group called the Baka, who live in the West African country of Cameroon (Avis & Harris, 1991). The Baka are hunter-gatherers who live together in camps. Each child was tested in his or her own hut, using materials with which the child was completely familiar. The child watched one adult, named Mopfana (a member of the Baka), put some mango kernels into a bowl with a lid. Mopfana then left the hut, and a second adult (also a group member) told the child they were going to play a game with Mopfana: They were going to hide the kernels in a cooking pot. Then he asked the child what Mopfana was going to do when he came back. Would he look for the kernels in the bowl or in the pot? Children between 2 and 4 years old were likely to say that Mopfana would look for the kernels in the pot, but 4- and 5-year-olds were nearly always right. Even in very different cultures, then, something similar seems to be occurring between age 3 and age 5: In these years, all children seem to develop a theory of mind.

The universal features of theory of mind have led many developmentalists to propose that a dedicated neurological structure, or *theory of mind module*, exists in the brain (Cole, 2005). This hypothesized structure generates inferences about people's behavior and the various internal and external factors that influence that behavior. The module theory explains why cross-cultural studies show a great deal of consistency in what some researchers have called the central feature of theory of mind (Cole, 2005)—that is, the ability to identify others' mental states, which universally develops across the early childhood period. However, the ways in which children's inferences are expressed and how those inferences influence children's own behavior appear to vary across cultures (Lillard, 2006b; Liu et al., 2008). Such variations result from differences in language, such as the degree to which a specific language provides words for different kinds of mental states, and variations in opportunities to discuss others' mental states.

Information Processing in Early Childhood

Learning Objective 8.4

How do information-processing theorists explain changes in young children's thinking?

During early childhood, children's cognitive advances and their capacity to use language as an aid to thinking result in rather dramatic improvements in memory function (see *Developmental Science at Home* on page 228). For instance,

DEVELOPMENTAL SCIENCE AT HOME

Leading Questions and Children's Memory

Ari was alarmed when his 4-year-old son, Micah, told him about an incident involving a neighbor that Ari believed to be a possible case of sexual molestation, so he immediately called the police. Before the police arrived, Ari received a telephone call from a social worker, who advised Ari to write down everything his son said spontaneously about the event but to avoid questioning him directly. Puzzled, Ari wondered, Who might be better than a parent to question a child about such a potentially traumatic event?

During his interview with the social worker the next day, Ari asked why she had said that he shouldn't question Micah. To begin with, the social worker explained, it's important for parents of a child who may have been abused to know that, even when they are under stress at the time of a traumatic event, young children remember it quite accurately (Peterson & Bell, 1996). Consequently, their testimony is extremely important when such cases end up in court. And in order to preserve the value of children's testimony, it's important that their memories not become distorted by leading questions.

The social worker went on to say that preschoolers' memories are more suggestible than those of older children or adults (Ceci & Bruck, 1995; Hardy & Van Leeuwen, 2004). One common way that researchers study the suggestibility factor is to show the same film to children and adults. Then, while asking questions about what the participants saw, the investigators inject a question that assumes something that didn't really happen (e.g., "He was carrying a pipe wrench when he came into the room, wasn't he?"). Young children are more affected than adults are by such misleading suggestions (Leichtman & Ceci, 1995).

The social worker also cited research showing that repeated questioning influences children's testimony (Bruck & Ceci, 1997). Even when an event did not happen, many preschoolers will say that it did after they have been asked about it many times (Ceci & Bruck, 1998; Muir-Broaddus, 1997). Thus, when an interviewer believes that some event has occurred, that belief may affect the way the interview is conducted and can influence the content of the child's recall (Ceci & Bruck, 1995).

When leading questions and misinformation come from parents, children are even more likely to incorporate the parents' version into their own free recall than they are when they are questioned by strangers (Ricci, Beal, & Dekle, 1995). For this reason, the social worker explained, professionals who work with children who have been molested tell parents to avoid directly questioning their children while at the same time encouraging them to speak spontaneously about what happened. When parents follow this advice, trained interviewers who know how to question preschoolers without unduly influencing them can have confidence in the information that they gain (Bruck, Ceci, & Hembrooke, 1998).

Questions for Reflection

1. Suppose when you pick your child up from child care, the teacher tells you that your child hit one of his classmates and asks you to talk to him about it. Based on the research regarding young children's memories, how should you proceed if you want to get the most accurate report possible about the incident from your child?
2. Think about possible conflicts between the rights of individuals who are accused of crimes and those of children who must be protected from people who would exploit them. How might research-based interviewing techniques help to protect both?

---

short-term storage space (STSS) neo-Piagetian theorist Robbie Case's term for the child's working memory

operational efficiency a neo-Piagetian term that refers to the maximum number of schemes that can be processed in working memory at one time

THE WHOLE CHILD IN FOCUS

How does Madeleine use the newfound operational efficiency that neo-Piagetian theory talks about? Find out on page 283.

most parents know that if you give a 3-year-old a list of three things to do, he is likely to forget at least one of them. By the end of the early childhood period, however, most children can remember a list of four or five items (Rosser, 1994). As a result, information-processing theorists have used memory research to support their explanations of both Piaget's original results and the more recent findings that contradict them.

Neo-Piagetian Theories One set of alternative proposals is based on the idea that children's performance on Piaget's tasks can be explained in terms of working memory limitations (Case, 1985, 1992). For example, the late Robbie Case (1944–2000), one of the best-known neo-Piagetian theorists, used the term **short-term storage space (STSS)** to refer to a child's working memory. According to Case, there is a limit on how many schemes can be attended to in STSS. He refers to the maximum number of schemes that may be put into STSS at one time as **operational efficiency**. Improvements in operational efficiency occur through both practice (doing tasks that require memory use, such as learning the alphabet) and brain maturation as the child gets older. Thus, a 7-year-old is better able to handle the processing demands of conservation tasks than is a 4-year-old because of improvements in operational efficiency of STSS.

A good example of the function of STSS may be found by examining *matrix classification*, a task Piaget often used with both young and school-aged children (see Figure 8.3). Matrix classification requires the child to place a given stimulus in two categories at the same time. Young children fail such tasks, according to neo-Piagetian theory, because they begin by processing the stimulus according to one dimension (either shape or color) and then either fail to realize that it is necessary to re-process it along the second dimension or forget to do so.

However, researchers have trained young children to perform correctly on such problems by using a two-step strategy. The children are taught to think of an orange triangle, for example, in terms of shape first and color second. Typically, instruction involves a number of training tasks in which researchers remind children repeatedly to remember to re-classify stimuli with respect to the second variable. According to Case, both children's failure prior to instruction and the type of strategy training to which they respond illustrate the constraints imposed on problem solving by the limited operational efficiency of younger children's STSS. There is room for only one scheme at a time in a young child's STSS, either shape or color. The training studies show that younger children can learn to perform correctly, but their approach is qualitatively different from that of older children. The more efficient STSS of an older child allows her to think about shape and color at the same time and, therefore, perform successfully without any training.

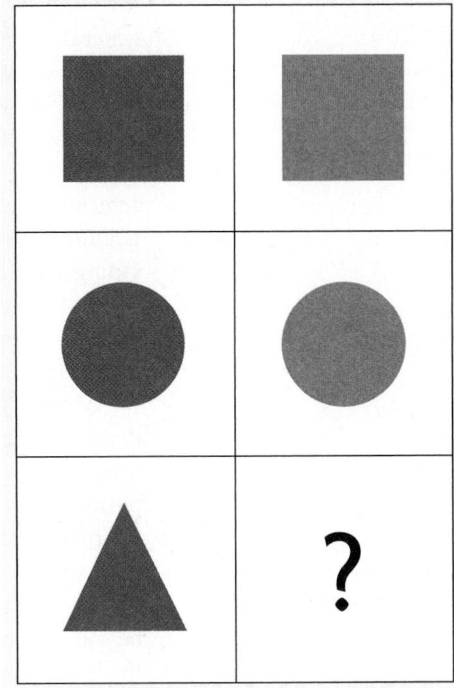

Figure 8.3 Neo-Piagetian Matrix Task

Neo-Piagetians have used Piaget's matrix classification task in strategy training studies with young children. Before training, most preschoolers say that a green triangle or an orange circle belongs in the box with the question mark. After learning a two-step strategy in which they are taught to classify each object first by shape and then by color, children understand that an orange triangle is the figure needed to complete the matrix.

Scripts, Metacognition, and Metamemory Information-processing theorists also maintain that children's ability to make efficient use of their memory system influences their performance on problem-solving tasks. For instance, **scripts**, cognitive structures underlying behaviors that are sequential in nature, emerge during early childhood. They are especially useful for managing the memory demands of tasks that involve sequential steps. For example, to brush his teeth, a preschooler must first get his toothbrush. Next, he must apply toothpaste to the brush, and so on. Establishment of a tooth-brushing script frees up the preschooler's information-processing resources so that he can focus on the quality of his brushing rather than the procedure itself.

Information-processing theorists also emphasize the importance of metamemory and metacognition. **Metamemory** is knowledge about and control of memory processes. For example, young children know that it takes longer to memorize a list of ten words than a list of five words but still aren't very good at coming up with strategies to apply to more difficult memory tasks (Kail, 1990). **Metacognition** is knowledge about and control of thought processes. For example, a child listening to a story may realize he has forgotten the main character's name and ask the reader what it is. Both knowing that the character's name has been forgotten and knowing that remembering the character's name will make the story easier to understand are forms of metacognition.

Children's use of metamemory and metacognition improves during the early childhood period. Between age 3 and age 5, for example, children figure out that in order to tell whether a sponge painted like a rock is really a sponge or a rock, a person needs to touch or hold it. Just looking at it doesn't give someone enough information (Flavell, 1993; O'Neill, Astington, & Flavell, 1992). Thus, by about age 4 or 5, children begin to grasp these processes, but they still have a long way to go. As a result, their ability to solve complex problems such as those Piaget used is limited compared to that of older children.

scripts cognitive structures that guide the performance of routine behaviors that involve a fixed sequence of events

metamemory knowledge about how memory works and the ability to control and reflect on one's own memory function

metacognition knowledge about how the mind thinks and the ability to control and reflect on one's own thought processes

Vygotsky's Sociocultural Theory

Learning Objective 8.5
What are the characteristics of Vygotsky's stages of early childhood cognitive development?

In Chapter 2, you learned about Russian psychologist Lev Vygotsky's views on development. Vygotsky's theory differs from both Piagetian and information-processing theory in its emphasis on the role of social factors in cognitive development. For example, two preschoolers working on a puzzle together discuss where the pieces belong. After a number of such dialogues, the participants internalize the discussion. It then becomes a model for an internal conversation the child uses to guide himself through the puzzle-solving process. In this way, Vygotsky suggested, solutions to problems are socially generated and learned. Vygotsky did not deny that individual learning takes place. Rather, he suggested that group learning processes are central to cognitive development. Consequently, from Vygotsky's perspective, social interaction is required for cognitive development (Thomas, 2000).

Chapter 2 described two important general principles of Vygotsky's theory. You should remember that the **zone of proximal development** includes tasks that are too difficult for the child to do alone but that she can manage with guidance. **Scaffolding** is the process of providing such guidance, much as a physical scaffold enables a painter to reach the ceiling of a room. For instance, when parents answer questions such as "Who's that?" or "What's he doing?" when they are watching a movie with a child, they help her keep track of the characters and plot to a greater degree than she would be able to manage if she were watching alone.

Vygotsky's concepts of the zone of proximal development and scaffolding have led to the development of a number of innovative practices in early childhood and elementary education. In a Vygotskian classroom, teachers use an intervention strategy called **guided participation** in which children become teachers' "apprentices" rather than passive recipients of instruction (Rogoff, 1991). For example, a teacher using a traditional approach to teaching a child to write her name might write the child's name and instruct her to copy it. In contrast, a teacher taking a sociocultural approach would share the task with the child. The task would be initiated by the child herself, and the teacher and child together would complete it, with the teacher providing whatever hints and cues the child needed to be able to form the letters and writing some of them if necessary.

Vygotsky proposed specific stages of cognitive development from birth to age 8. Each stage represents a step toward the child's internalization of the ways of thinking used by the adults around him. In the first period, between birth and age 2, called the **primitive stage**, the infant possesses mental processes similar to those of lower animals. He learns primarily through conditioning, until language begins to develop in the second year. At that point, from age 2 through age 3, he enters the **naive psychology stage**, in which he learns to use language to communicate but still does not understand its symbolic character. For example, he does not realize that any collection of sounds could stand for the object "chair" as long as everyone agreed—that is, if all English speakers agreed to substitute the word *blek* for *chair*, we could do so because we would all understand what *blek* meant.

Once the child begins to appreciate the symbolic function of language, near the end of the third year of life, he enters the **private speech stage**. In this stage, he uses language as a guide to solving problems. In effect, he tells himself how to do things. For example, a 3-year-old walking down a flight of stairs might say "Be careful" to himself. Such a statement would be the result of his internalization of statements made to him by adults and older children.

Piaget recognized the existence and importance of private speech. However, he believed that such speech disappeared as the child approached the end of the preoperational stage. In contrast, Vygotsky claimed that private speech becomes completely internalized at age 6 or 7, when children enter the final period of cognitive development, the **ingrowth stage**. Thus, he suggested that the logical thinking Piaget ascribed to older children results from their internalization of speech routines acquired from older children and adults in the social world rather than from schemes the children construct for themselves through interaction with the physical world.

Vygotsky's stages are summarized in Table 8.1. At present, there is insufficient evidence to either support or contradict most of his ideas (Thomas, 2000). However, studies have shown that young children whose parents provide them with more cognitive scaffolding during the preschool years exhibit higher levels of achievement in the early elementary grades than do peers whose parents provide less support of this kind (Neitzel & Stright, 2003). Some intriguing research on children's construction of theory of mind during social interactions lends weight to Vygotsky's major propositions. It seems that children in pairs and groups do produce more sophisticated ideas than do individual children who work on problems alone. However, the sophistication of a group's ideas appears to depend on the presence of at least

zone of proximal development the range of tasks that are too difficult for children to do alone but that they can manage with guidance

scaffolding provision, by an adult or an older child, of the guidance and assistance needed by a preschooler to accomplish tasks within the zone of proximal development

guided participation an intervention strategy in which children become teachers' apprentices rather than passive recipients of instruction

primitive stage Vygotsky's first stage, in which children between birth and age 2 think nonverbally and learn through conditioning

naive psychology stage Vygotsky's second stage, in which 2- to 3-year-olds use language but do not understand its symbolic nature

private speech stage Vygotsky's third stage, in which 3- to 6-year-olds use utterances based on internalized speech routines for self-instruction and self-monitoring

ingrowth stage Vygotsky's fourth stage, in which children 6 and older have fully internalized private speech

Table 8.1 Vygotsky's Stages of Cognitive Development

Age	Stage	Characteristics
0–2 years	Primitive	Nonverbal thought; learning through conditioning
2–3 years	Naive psychology	Language use without understanding of its symbolic nature
3–6 years	Private speech	Awareness of the symbolic nature of language; language used to communicate; utterances based on internalized language used for self-instruction and self-monitoring when solving problems
6+ years	Ingrowth	Private speech completely internalized

one fairly advanced individual child in the group (Tan-Niam, Wood, & O'Malley, 1998). Also, studies strongly support Vygotsky's hypothesis that private speech helps children solve problems (Montero & De Dios, 2006).

Changes in Language

To his credit, Piaget recognized that the overriding theme of cognitive development in the early childhood years is language acquisition. Of course, the process begins much earlier, as you learned in Chapter 5. Amazingly, though, children enter this period producing only a limited number of words and simple sentences, but leave it as accomplished, fluent speakers of at least one language.

Learning New Words

Learning Objective 8.6
How does fast-mapping help children learn new words?

The average 2½-year-old's vocabulary of about 600 words is fairly impressive when compared to the dozen or so words most 1-year-olds know (E. Bates et al., 1994). This amounts to one or two new words every day between the ages of 12 and 24 months. Impressive though this feat is, it pales in comparison to the rate of vocabulary growth among preschoolers. By the time a child goes to school at age 5 or 6, total vocabulary has risen to perhaps 15,000 words—an astonishing increase of 10 words a day (Anglin, 1995; Pinker, 1994). Moreover, word learning appears to be the engine that drives the whole process of language development. That is, the more words a child knows, the more advanced she is with regard to grammar and other aspects of language (McGregor, Sheng, & Smith, 2005). What is the impetus behind word learning?

Researchers have found that a momentous shift in the way children approach new words happens around age 3. As a result of this shift, children begin to pay attention to words in whole groups, such as words that name objects in a single class (e.g., types of dinosaurs or kinds of fruit) or words with similar meanings. In a sense, an understanding of the categorical nature of words helps children develop what we might think of as mental "slots" for new words. Once the slots are in place, children seem to automatically organize the linguistic input they receive from parents, teachers, peers, books, television programs, advertisements, and every other source of language, extracting new words with which to fill the slots as quickly as possible.

Psychologists use the term **fast-mapping** to refer to this ability to categorically link new words to real-world objects or events (Carey & Bartlett, 1978). At the core of fast-mapping, say researchers, is a rapidly formed hypothesis about a new word's meaning (Behrend, Scofield, & Kleinknecht, 2001). The hypothesis is based on information derived from children's prior knowledge of words and word categories and from the context in which the word is used. Once formed, the hypothesis is tested through use of the word in the child's own

fast-mapping the ability to categorically link new words to real-world referents

speech, often immediately after learning it. The feedback children receive in response to their use of the word helps them judge the accuracy of the hypothesis and the appropriateness of the category to which they have assumed that the word belongs. Perhaps this helps explain why preschoolers do so much talking and why they are so persistent at getting their listeners to actively respond to them.

Experimental studies have demonstrated that fast-mapping is evident as early as 18 months of age. In these studies, researchers teach toddlers new words that represent easily identifiable categories and then, after a period of time, measure their learning of related words. For example, fast-mapping should enable a child who has been taught the word *table* to acquire the word *chair* on her own more rapidly than a child who is unfamiliar with the word *table.* Such studies show that when children are tested a few weeks after receiving vocabulary instruction, they are more likely than children who were not instructed to understand and to use words that are related to, but distinct from, those they were taught (e.g., Gershkoff-Stowe & Hahn, 2007).

Learning Objective 8.7

What happens during the grammar explosion?

The Grammar Explosion

Just as the vocabulary explosion you read about in Chapter 5 begins slowly, so the **grammar explosion** of the 2- to 6-year-old period starts with several months of simple sentences such as "Mommy sock," an expression that you should recognize as *telegraphic speech* after studying Chapter 5. Telegraphic utterances lack *inflections*, additions (such as *'s*) that would tell a child's listeners that she is trying to say that the sock belongs to Mommy. Within each language community, children seem to add inflections and more complex word orders in fairly predictable sequences (Legendre, 2006). In a classic early study, Roger Brown found that the earliest inflection used by children learning English is typically *-ing* added to a verb, as in "I playing" or "Doggie running," expressions that are common in the speech of 2½- to 3-year-olds (Brown, 1973). Over the next year or so come (in order) prepositions (such as *on* and *in*), the plural *-s* on nouns, irregular past tenses (such as *broke* and *ran*), possessives, articles (*a* and *the* in English), the *-s* added to third-person verbs (such as "He wants"), regular past tenses (such as *played* and *wanted*), and various forms of auxiliary verbs (as in "I *am* going").

These 2- to 3-year-olds probably speak to each other in short sentences that include uninflected nouns and verbs.

There are also predictable sequences in the child's developing use of questions and negatives. In each case, the child seems to go through periods when he creates types of sentences that he has not heard adults use, but that are consistent with the particular set of rules he is using. For example, in the development of questions, there is a point at which the child can put a *wh-* word (*who, what, when, where, why*) at the front end of a sentence, but doesn't yet put the auxiliary verb in the right place, as in "Where you are going now?" Similarly, in the development of negatives, children go through a stage in which they add *not* or *-n't* or *no* but omit the auxiliary verb, as in "I not crying."

Another intriguing phenomenon, noted in Chapter 5, is **overregularization**, or overgeneralization. No language is perfectly regular; every language includes some irregularly conjugated verbs or unusual forms of plurals. What 3- to 4-year-olds do is apply the basic rule to all these irregular instances, thus making the language more regular than it really is (Maratsos, 2000). In English, this is especially clear in children's creation of past tenses such as *wented*, *blowed*, and *sitted* or plurals such as *teeths* and *blockses* (Fenson et al., 1994).

After children have figured out inflections and the basic sentence forms using negatives and questions, they soon begin to create remarkably complex sentences, using a conjunction

grammar explosion a period during which children rapidly acquire grammatical speech

overregularization attachment of regular inflections to irregular words, such as the substitution of *goed* for *went*

such as *and* or *but* to combine two ideas or using embedded clauses. Here are some examples from children aged 30 to 48 months (de Villiers & de Villiers, 1992, p. 379):

> I didn't catch it but Teddy did!
> I'm gonna sit on the one you're sitting on.
> Where did you say you put my doll?
> Those are punk rockers, aren't they?

When you remember that only about 18 months earlier these children were using sentences little more complex than "See doggie," you can appreciate how far they have come in a short time.

THE WHOLE CHILD IN FOCUS

How does Madeleine use invented spelling? Find out on page 283.

Phonological Awareness

Learning Objective 8.8

What is phonological awareness, and why is it important?

Certain aspects of early childhood language development, such as rate of vocabulary growth, predict how easily a child will learn to read and write when she enters school (Muter, Hulme, Snowling, & Stevenson, 2004). However, one specific component of early childhood language development, **phonological awareness**, seems to be especially important. Phonological awareness is a child's sensitivity to the sound patterns that are specific to the language being acquired. It also includes the child's knowledge of that particular language's system for representing sounds with letters. Researchers measure English-speaking children's phonological awareness with questions like these: "What would *bat* be if you took away the *b*? What would *bat* be if you took away the *b* and put *r* there instead?"

A child doesn't have to acquire phonological awareness in early childhood. It can be learned in elementary school through formal instruction (Ball, 1997; Bus & van IJzendoorn, 1999). However, numerous studies have shown that the greater a child's phonological awareness *before* he enters school, the faster he learns to read (Sodoro, Allinder, & Rankin-Erickson, 2002). In addition, phonological awareness in the early childhood years is related to rate of literacy learning in languages as varied as Korean, English, Punjabi, and Chinese (Chiappe, Glaeser, & Ferko, 2007; Chiappe & Siegel, 1999; Ho & Bryant, 1997; Huang & Hanley, 1997; McBride-Chang & Ho, 2000).

phonological awareness children's understanding of the sound patterns of the language they are acquiring and knowledge of that language's system for representing sounds with letters

invented spelling a strategy used by young children with good phonological awareness skills when they write

Phonological awareness appears to develop primarily through word play. For example, among English-speaking children, learning and reciting nursery rhymes contributes to phonological awareness (Bryant, MacLean, & Bradley, 1990; Bryant, MacLean, Bradley, & Crossland, 1990; Layton, Deeny, Tall, & Upton, 1996). For Japanese children, a game called *shiritori*, in which one person says a word and another comes up with a word that begins with its ending sound, helps children develop these skills (Kobayashi, Haynes, Macaruso, Hook, & Kato, 2005; Serpell & Hatano, 1997). Educators have found that using such games to teach phonological awareness skills to preschoolers is just as effective as more formal methods such as flash cards and worksheets (Brennan & Ireson, 1997).

Preschoolers with good phonological awareness skills—those who have learned a few basic sound-letter connections informally, from their parents or from educational TV programs or videos—often use a strategy called **invented spelling** when they attempt to write (see Figure 8.4). In spite of the many errors they make, children who use invented spelling strategies before receiving school-based instruction in reading and writing are more likely to become good spellers and readers later in childhood (Dixon & Kaminska, 2007). Thus, the evidence suggests that one of the best ways parents and preschool teachers can help young children prepare for formal instruction in reading is to engage them in activities that encourage word play and invented spelling.

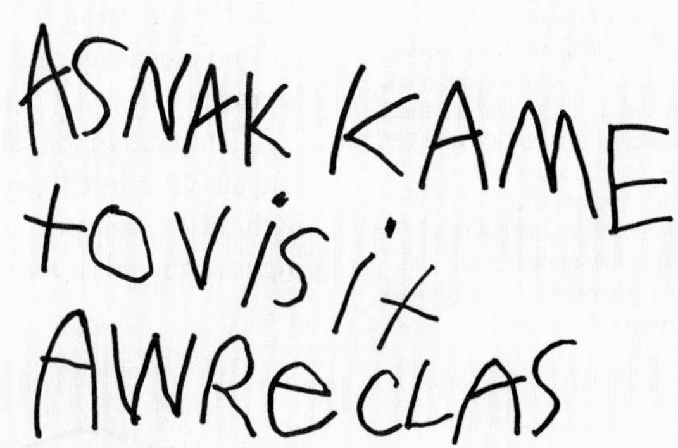

Figure 8.4 Invented Spelling

Translation: *A snake came to visit our class.* A 5-year-old used a strategy called invented spelling to write this sentence about a snake's visit (accompanied by an animal handler, we hope!) to her kindergarten class. Invented spelling requires a high level of phonological awareness. Research suggests that children who have well-developed phonological awareness skills by the time they reach kindergarten learn to read more quickly.

(Courtesy of Jerry and Denise Boyd. Used with permission.)

Differences in Intelligence

Thanks to advances in language skills, intelligence testing is far more reliable among preschoolers than among infants. Psychologists can devise tests of intelligence for preschoolers to measure their vocabulary, reasoning skills, and other cognitive processes that depend on language. Consequently, a large number of standardized tests have been developed for use with young children. However, widespread use of these tests has led to an ongoing debate about the origins of score differences and the degree to which scores can be modified.

Learning Objective 8.9

What are the strengths and weaknesses of IQ tests?

Measuring Intelligence

An important assumption in studying differences in intelligence is that these differences can be measured. Thus, it's important to understand something about the tests psychologists use to measure intelligence, as well as the meaning and stability of the scores the tests generate.

intelligence quotient (IQ) the ratio of mental age to chronological age; also, a general term for any kind of score derived from an intelligence test

The First Tests The first modern intelligence test was published in 1905 by two Frenchmen, Alfred Binet and Theodore Simon (Binet & Simon, 1905). From the beginning, the test had a practical purpose—to identify children who might have difficulty in school. For this reason, the tasks Binet and Simon devised for the test were very much like some school tasks, including measures of vocabulary, comprehension of facts and relationships, and mathematical and verbal reasoning. For example, could the child describe the difference between wood and glass? Could the young child identify his nose, his ear, his head? Could he tell which of two weights was heavier?

Lewis Terman and his associates at Stanford University modified and extended many of Binet's original tasks when they translated and revised the test for use in the United States (Terman, 1916; Terman & Merrill, 1937). The Stanford-Binet (the name by which the test is still known) initially described a child's performance in terms of a score called an **intelligence quotient**, later shortened to **IQ**. This score was computed by comparing the child's chronological age (in years and months) with his mental age, defined as the level of questions he could answer correctly. For example, a child who could solve the problems for a 6-year-old but not those for a 7-year-old would have a mental age of 6. The formula used to calculate the IQ was

Mental Age/Chronological Age × 100 = IQ

This formula results in an IQ above 100 for children whose mental age is higher than their chronological age and an IQ below 100 for children whose mental age is below their chronological age.

This system for calculating IQ is no longer used. Instead, IQ scores for the Stanford-Binet and all other intelligence tests are now based on a direct comparison of a child's performance with the average performance of a large group of other children of the same age. But the scoring is arranged so that an IQ of 100 is still average.

Figure 8.5
The Normal Curve

IQ scores form what mathematicians call a normal distribution—the famous "bell curve" you may have heard about. The two sides of a normal distribution curve are mirror images of each other. Thus, 34% of children score between 85 and 100, and another 34% score between 100 and 115. Likewise, 13% score between 70 and 85, and another 13% score between 115 and 130. A few other human characteristics, such as height, are normally distributed as well.

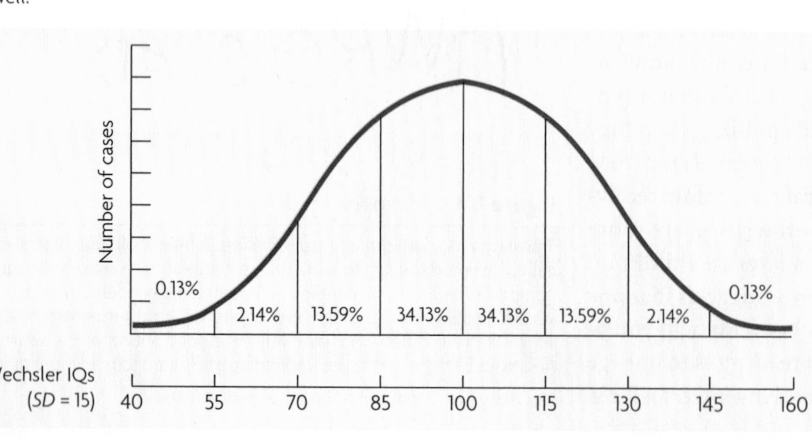

As you can see in Figure 8.5, about two-thirds of all children achieve scores between 85 and 115; roughly 96% of scores fall between 70 and 130. Children who score above 130 are often called *gifted*; those who score below 70 are normally diagnosed with *mental retardation*, although this label should not be applied unless the child also has problems with "adaptive behavior," such as an inability to dress or feed himself, a problem getting along with others, or a significant problem adapting to the demands of a regular school classroom. Some children with IQ scores in this low range are able to function in a regular schoolroom and should not be labeled as having mental retardation.

Modern Intelligence Tests The tests used most frequently by psychologists today to test children's intelligence are those developed by David Wechsler, the most recent versions of which are the *Wechsler Intelligence Scale for Children IV* (WISC-IV, for children 6 to 16) and the *Wechsler Preschool and Primary Scale of Intelligence III* (WPPSI-III, for children 2 to 7). On both of the Wechsler tests, the child is tested on several different types of problems, with each type ranging from very easy to very hard; these problems are divided into subgroups. *Verbal scales* include tasks measuring vocabulary, understanding of similarities between objects, and general knowledge about the world. *Performance scales* involve nonverbal tasks such as arranging pictures in an order that tells a story or copying a pattern using a set of colored blocks. Once children reach age 6, the Wechsler tests also include *working memory scales*, which provide psychologists with information about a child's short-term memory capacity, as well as *processing speed scales*, which provide insight into how efficiently a child processes information. Many psychologists find the Wechsler approach to be helpful, because significant differences in a child's skills across scales may indicate particular kinds of learning problems.

Stability and Predictive Value of IQ Scores The correlation between a preschooler's IQ test score and her scores on tests that measure pre-academic skills such as letter knowledge is about .70 (Wechsler, 2002). The correlation with her future grades in school is about .50 (Brody, 1992; Carver, 1990; Neisser et al., 1996). These are strong, but by no means perfect, correlations. They indicate that, on the whole, preschoolers with high IQ scores are likely to be found among the high achievers after a couple of years of schooling, and those who score low will be among the low achievers. But success in school also depends on many factors other than IQ, including motivation, interest, persistence, parental support for learning, cultural values regarding the importance of education, and a host of other variables, including the child's physical health. Because of the complex ways in which intelligence interacts with all of these variables, some children who get high scores on IQ tests in early childhood don't shine in school, whereas some children with average IQ scores do.

The relationship between school performance and IQ scores holds within each social class and racial group in the United States, as well as in other countries and cultures. Among both the poor and the middle class, and among African Americans and Hispanic Americans as well as Whites, children with higher IQs are more likely to get good grades, complete high school, and go on to college (Brody, 1992). Such findings have led a number of theorists to argue that intelligence adds to a child's resilience—a concept mentioned in Chapter 1. Numerous studies show that poor children—whether they are White, Hispanic, African American, or from another minority group—are far more likely to develop the kind of self-confidence and personal competence it takes to move out of poverty if they have higher IQs (Luthar & Zigler, 1992; Masten & Coatsworth, 1998; Werner & Smith, 1992).

At the other end of the scale, low intelligence is associated with a number of negative long-term outcomes, including delinquency in adolescence, adult illiteracy, and criminal behavior in adulthood (Baydar, Brooks-Gunn, & Furstenberg, 1993; Stattin & Klackenberg-Larsson, 1993). This is not to say that all lower-IQ individuals are illiterates or criminals—that is clearly not the case. But low IQ makes a child more vulnerable, just as a high IQ protects her against the negative influences of a variety of environmental factors (see *Developmental Science in the Clinic* on page 236).

IQ scores are also quite stable. If two tests are given a few months or a few years apart, the scores are likely to be very similar. The correlations between IQ scores from adjacent years in middle childhood, for example, are typically in the range of .80 (Wechsler, 2002). Yet this high level of predictability masks an interesting fact: Many children show quite wide fluctuations in their scores. In fact, about half of all children show noticeable changes from one testing to another and over time (McCall, 1993). Some show steadily rising scores, and some have declining ones; some show a peak in middle childhood and then a decline in adolescence. In rare cases, the shifts may cover a range as large as 40 points. When such large shifts occur after some kind of trauma, the reason for them is evident; in most cases, though, the reason is unknown.

DEVELOPMENTAL SCIENCE IN THE CLINIC

To Test or Not to Test?

Dr. Cooper is a psychologist who specializes in the assessment of children between the ages of 2 and 6 referred by pediatricians who suspect that the children may be suffering from serious cognitive developmental delays. Before signing the consent forms that Dr. Cooper requires them to sign, many parents express reservations about having their children tested at such a young age. Most of the parents tell Dr. Cooper that they have heard that IQ tests are not valid and they worry that labeling their children with an IQ score early in life will lead teachers to have low expectations for their performance.

After she explains that the results of the testing will be released only to those parties for whom parents give permission, Dr. Cooper admits that IQ tests are far from perfect. However, she also explains that, as long as the tests are used properly, intelligence tests can be very beneficial to children. Dr. Cooper points out that IQ tests are important tools for identifying children who have special educational needs, such as those who have mental retardation. There are other methods for selecting children for special programs, such as teacher recommendations, but none of the alternatives is as reliable or as valid as an IQ test for measuring that set of cognitive abilities demanded by school (Sattler, 2008). Even when a child's physical characteristics can be used to make a general diagnosis of mental retardation, as in cases of Down syndrome, an intelligence test can reveal to what degree the child is affected. This is important, Dr. Cooper explains, because effective educational interventions are based on an understanding of how an individual's disability has affected the capacity to learn. Thus, IQ tests are a critical tool in the development of individual educational plans (IEPs) for children with disabilities.

Questions for Reflection

1. In your opinion, would it be valid to base a nationwide IQ testing program for all kindergartners on research that demonstrates the usefulness of intelligence testing for children with disabilities? Why or why not?
2. If you had a child who appeared to be somewhat developmentally delayed, would you want him or her to be given an IQ test? Why or why not?

Wide swings in test scores often have more to do with children's understanding of the testing task itself than with any real change in their intellectual capabilities. For example, consider a testing situation in which a psychologist presents a 4-year-old with pictures of different types of breakfasts—perhaps a doughnut, a plate of bacon and eggs, and a bowl of granola and blueberries. Then the psychologist asks, "Which picture shows the best breakfast?" As an adult, you probably know that, in this context, *best* means "most nutritious." As a result, you would probably realize that the granola would be the appropriate choice. But a 4-year-old might interpret *best* to mean "the one you like the best." Consequently, the child would make his decision based on his own personal preferences rather than on an understanding of the academic purpose of the question. (In other words, he would choose the doughnut over either the eggs or the granola.) As children get older and have more experience with tests, they learn to interpret such questions in the manner in which they are intended by test authors. This leads to gains in test scores that are, in some cases, quite large.

Limitations of IQ Tests Before moving on to the question of the possible origins of differences in IQ, it is important to emphasize a few key limitations of IQ tests and the scores derived from them. IQ tests do not measure underlying competence. An IQ score cannot tell you (or a teacher or anyone else) that your child has some specific, fixed, underlying capacity. Traditional IQ tests also do not measure a whole host of skills that are likely to be highly significant for getting along in the world. Originally, IQ tests were designed to measure only the specific range of skills that are needed for success in school. This they do quite well. What they do not do is indicate anything about a particular person's creativity, insight, streetsmarts, ability to read social cues, or understanding of spatial relationships—or, for that matter, how well or poorly the individual's brain is functioning (Baron, 2003; Gardner, 2003).

Learning Objective 8.10

What evidence has been offered in support of the nature and nurture explanations for individual differences in IQ?

Origins of Individual Differences in Intelligence

If a couple whom you perceived to be smart conceived a child, what would you predict about their offspring's IQ scores? Most people know that differences in intelligence run in families. But why do related people seem to be alike in this regard? Is it nature or nurture that is responsible?

Evidence for Heredity Both twin studies and studies of adopted children show strong hereditary influences on IQ. Identical twins are more like each other in IQ than are fraternal twins, and the IQs of adopted children are better predicted from the IQs of their natural parents than from those of their adoptive parents (Brody, 1992; Loehlin, Horn, & Willerman, 1994; Scarr, Weinberg, & Waldman, 1993). These are precisely the findings researchers would expect if a strong genetic element were at work.

Evidence for Family Influences Adoption studies also provide some strong support for an environmental influence on IQ scores, because the IQ scores of adopted children are clearly affected by the environment in which they have grown up. The clearest evidence for this comes from a classic study of 38 French children, all adopted in infancy (Capron & Duyme, 1989). Roughly half the children had been born to better-educated parents from a higher social class, while the other half had been born to working-class or poverty-level parents. Some of the children in each group had then been adopted by parents in a higher social class, while the others grew up in poorer families. The effect of rearing conditions was evident in that the children reared in upper-class homes had IQs 15–16 points higher than those reared in lower-class families, regardless of the social-class level or education of the birth parents. A genetic effect was evident in that the children born to upper-class parents had higher IQs than those from lower-class families, no matter what kind of environment they were reared in.

When developmentalists observe how individual families interact with their infants or young children and then follow the children over time to see which ones later have high or low IQs, they begin to get some sense of the kinds of specific family interactions that foster higher scores. For one thing, parents of higher-IQ children provide them with an interesting and complex physical environment, including play materials that are appropriate for the child's age and developmental level (Bradley et al., 1989; Pianta & Egeland, 1994). They also respond warmly and appropriately to the child's behavior, smiling when the child smiles, answering the child's questions, and in myriad ways reacting to the child's cues (Barnard et al., 1989; Lewis, 1993). These kinds of parental behaviors may even help to limit the effects of poverty and other sources of family stress on children's intellectual development (Robinson, Lanzi, Weinberg, Ramey, & Ramey, 2002).

Parents of higher-IQ children also talk to them often, using language that is descriptively rich and accurate (Hart & Risley, 1995; Sigman et al., 1988). And when they play with or interact with their children, they operate in Vygotsky's zone of proximal development, aiming their conversation, their questions, and their assistance at a level just above the level the children could manage on their own, thus helping the children to master new skills (Landry, Garner, Swank, & Baldwin, 1996).

In addition, parents who appear to foster intellectual development try to avoid being excessively restrictive, punitive, or controlling, instead giving children room to explore and even opportunities to make mistakes (Bradley et al., 1989; Olson, Bates, & Kaskie, 1992). In a similar vein, these parents ask questions rather than giving commands (Hart & Risley, 1995). Most also expect their children to do well and to develop rapidly. They emphasize and press for school achievement (Entwisle & Alexander, 1990).

Nevertheless, developmentalists can't be sure that these environmental characteristics are causally important, because parents provide both the genes and the environment. Perhaps these are simply the environmental features provided by brighter parents, and it is the genes and not the environment that cause the higher IQs in their children. However, the research on adopted children's IQs cited earlier suggests that these aspects of environment have a very real impact on children's intellectual development beyond whatever hereditary influences may affect them.

Combining the Information Virtually all psychologists would agree that heredity is a highly important influence on IQ scores. Studies around the world consistently yield estimates that roughly half the variation in IQ within a given population is due to heredity

(Neisser et al., 1996; Plomin & Rende, 1991; Rogers, Rowe, & May, 1994). The remaining half is clearly due to environment or to interactions between environment and heredity.

One useful way to think about this interaction is to use the concept of **reaction range**, a range between some upper and lower boundary of functioning established by one's genetic heritage; exactly where a child will fall within those boundaries is determined by environment. Some developmental psychologists estimate that the reaction range for IQ is about 20–25 points (Weinberg, 1989). That is, given a specific genetic heritage, a child's actual IQ test performance may vary by as much as 20 or 25 points, depending on the richness or poverty of the environment in which he grows up. When the child's environment is changed for the better, the child moves closer to the upper end of his reaction range. When the environment becomes worse, the child's effective intellectual performance falls toward the lower end of his reaction range. Thus, even though intelligence as measured on an IQ test is highly heritable and falls within the reaction range, the absolute IQ score is determined by environment.

Learning Objective 8.11

What evidence has been offered in support of the genetic and cultural explanations of group differences in IQ scores?

Group Differences in Intelligence Test Scores

There appear to be a number of consistent group differences in IQ test scores and other measures of intellectual performance. For instance, Chinese and Japanese children consistently demonstrate higher performance on achievement tests—particularly math and science tests (Gonzales et al., 2004). But the finding that has been most troublesome for researchers and theorists is that in the United States, African American children consistently score lower than White children on measures of IQ. Some theorists have suggested that this difference can be traced to anatomical and physiological variations across groups (Mackintosh, 2007; Rushton & Rushton, 2003). However, this difference, which is on the order of 6 to 15 IQ points, is not found on infant tests of intelligence (which you learned about in Chapter 5) or on measures of infant habituation rate (see Chapter 4); it becomes apparent by the time children are 2 or 3 years old and persists through adolescence and adulthood (Brody, 1992; Fagan & Singer, 1983; Peoples, Fagan, & Drotar, 1995; Rowe, 2002; Rushton, Skuy, & Fridjhon, 2003). There is some indication that the size of the difference between African American and White children has been declining for several decades, but a noticeable difference persists (Neisser et al., 1996; Rushton & Jensen, 2006).

While granting that IQ is highly heritable for individuals, many developmentalists point out that the difference between average African American and White IQ scores falls well within the presumed reaction range of IQ. They emphasize that the environments in which African American and White children are typically reared differ sufficiently to account for the average difference in scores (Brody, 1992). Specifically, African American children in the United States are more likely to be born with low birth weight, to suffer from poor nutrition, and to have high blood levels of lead and are less likely to be read to or to receive a wide range of intellectual stimulation. And each of these environmental characteristics is known to be linked to lower IQ scores. Supporting this view are studies showing that African American and White adults who differ in IQ do not differ in performance on new verbal learning tasks (Fagan & Holland, 2002).

Some of the most convincing research supporting such an environmental explanation comes from mixed-race adoption studies (Scarr & Weinberg, 1983; Weinberg, Scarr, & Waldman, 1992). For example, researchers have found that African American children adopted at an early age into White middle-class families scored only slightly lower on IQ tests than did White children adopted into the same families. Similarly, regardless of race, the more education parents have, the higher their children's IQs (Sellers, Burns, & Guyrke, 2002). Thus, IQ differences in African American and White children may reflect their parents' differing amounts of experience with formal education.

reaction range a range, established by one's genes, between upper and lower boundaries for traits such as intelligence; one's environment determines where, within those limits, one will fall

Another recent entry into the debate on group differences in IQ scores is the finding that, during the 19th and 20th centuries, average IQ scores increased in every racial group throughout the industrialized world. This phenomenon is known as the **Flynn effect** because it was discovered by psychologist James Flynn (Flynn, 1999, 2003). Flynn's analyses of IQ data over several generations suggest that individuals of average IQ born in the late 19th century would have mental retardation by today's standards. If IQ is largely genetic, Flynn argues, there should be a great deal of stability in any group's average score. Because IQ scores have changed so much in a relatively short period of time, Flynn suggests that cultural changes explain the effect that bears his name. Similarly, Flynn suggests that his cross-generational studies demonstrate that cultural factors are a likely explanation for cross-group differences as well. He points out that theorists from a variety of fields—from anthropology to medicine—have posited causes for cross-generational gains in IQ such as improved nutrition, greater access to media, and universal literacy. Flynn suggests that all of these factors vary across racial as well as generational groups.

Flynn further points out that many theorists have neglected to consider cultural beliefs in their search for a hereditary basis for intelligence. For example, some psychologists have argued that the differences between Asian and American children in performance on mathematics achievement tests result not from genetic differences in capacity but from differences in cultural beliefs (Stevenson & Lee, 1990). Specifically, Asian societies place little or no value on inborn talent. Instead, they believe that hard work can modify whatever talents a person was born with. Consequently, Asian parents and teachers require students to expend a great deal of effort trying to improve themselves intellectually and do not resort to ability-based explanations of failure. This means that an individual child does not simply accept academic failure as a sign of intellectual deficit but is encouraged by adults to keep on trying. As a result, Asian children spend more time on homework and other academic activities than do children in other cultures.

In contrast, U.S. schools emphasize ability through the routine use of IQ tests to place students in high-, average-, or low-ability classes. This approach reflects American society's greater acceptance of the idea that people are limited by the amount of ability they possess and that it is unfair to ask them to do more than tests suggest they are capable of. It is likely that these complex cultural variables affect children's environments in ways that lead to differences in IQ and achievement test scores (Chang & Murray, 1995; Schneider, Hieshima, Lee, & Plank, 1994; Stevenson & Lee, 1990; Stigler, Lee, & Stevenson, 1987).

The possibility also exists that IQ test averages vary across groups because of differences in cultural experiences. Critics of IQ testing have pointed out that the tests were developed in the context of the dominant culture—namely, middle-class White culture (Guthrie, 2004). Thus, test questions emphasize skills and knowledge that are valued by middle-class Whites but that may not be valued by or relevant to other groups. Consequently, the acquisition of such skills and knowledge is not emphasized by families in nondominant groups, with the result being that their children get lower scores on intelligence tests than do children in the dominant group. The authors and publishers of contemporary IQ tests have worked diligently to ensure that the tests are as free of cultural bias as possible. The most recent editions of the Wechsler tests, for example, have been found to be less biased than the versions that were published in the early and mid-20th century (Sattler, 2001). A more recently developed test, the *Kaufman Assessment Battery for Children (KABC)*, first published in 1983 (Kaufman & Kaufman, 1983, 2004), has been praised for its lack of bias. Minority-group children tend to get higher scores on the KABC than they do on the Wechsler tests (Kaufman, Kaufman, Kaufman-Singer, & Kaufman, 2005). Thus, the KABC is used by many preschools, elementary schools, and clinicians to assess intelligence in minority-group children.

Of course, the fact that group differences in IQ or achievement test performance may be explained by appealing to the concept of reaction range, cultural beliefs, and cultural bias in the tests themselves does not make the differences disappear, nor does it make them trivial. Moreover, it's important to remember that there is the same amount of variation in IQ scores in all groups; there are many highly gifted African American children, just as there are many White children with mental retardation. Finally, the benefits of having a high IQ, as well as the risks associated with low IQ, are the same in every racial group.

Flynn effect the phenomenon of average IQ scores increasing in every racial group throughout the industrialized world during the 19th and 20th centuries

Early Childhood Education

Take a look in any preschool classroom and you're likely to see what appears to be nothing more than children being children. Preschoolers may appear to be playing, and, in their minds, that's precisely what they're doing. However, in most cases, preschool classrooms are designed in ways that enable children to accomplish important cognitive goals through engaging in activities that they are naturally interested in and enjoy.

Learning Objective 8.12

How do the various approaches to early childhood education differ?

Approaches to Early Education

The term **early childhood education** applies to programs that provide instruction to children between birth and age 8. Although there are many theoretical models in the field of early childhood education, in general they fall into two broad categories: *developmental approaches* and *academic approaches.*

Developmental Approaches The goal of **developmental approaches** is to support children through the natural course of physical, cognitive, and socioemotional development. Examples of developmental approaches with which you may be familiar are the *Waldorf* approach, the *Reggio Emilia* model, and the *Montessori* method. All of these approaches place more emphasis on the natural course of child development than they do on teaching children specific skills such as letter identification. As a result, children who attend preschools that take these approaches spend a great deal of time exploring and experimenting with educational materials.

Although there are thousands of "Montessori" schools in the United States, including some that are operated by public school systems, a true Montessori school is one that is staffed by teachers who have been specifically trained in methods and materials unique to the Montessori approach. The goal of the Montessori method, founded by Italian physician Maria Montessori in the early years of the 20th century, is to enable each child to achieve his or her full developmental potential. The main idea behind the Montessori classroom is that the child be allowed to freely choose his activities, but the range of activities available is limited to those that support the child's development. In other words, Montessori educators control the environment in ways that support the child's natural development, rather than trying to control the child himself.

To get a better understanding of how the Montessori method works, think back to what you learned in Chapter 7 about *finger differentiation*, a fundamental movement skill that children must develop before they can acquire fine motor skills such as writing. Montessori classrooms provide young children with materials that strengthen the small muscles in their hands and fingers, thereby supporting the development of finger differentiation. One activity of this type requires a few spring-type clothespins and something to clip them on, such as a piece of cardboard or a paper plate.

Because Montessori materials look like toys to children, teachers never have to say, "Susie, you need to work on your finger differentiation skills today." Instead, teachers monitor children's progress toward developmental goals and encourage children to choose activities that support the goals. In addition, Montessori teachers help children learn to cooperate and take turns using learning materials.

Academic Approaches **Academic approaches** to early childhood education focus on teaching young children the skills that they will need to succeed in elementary school. Academically oriented preschool programs employ curricula based on learning goals. Instruction tends to be teacher-directed, and the activities in which children engage are highly similar to those that are found in elementary schools.

For instance, one common goal in academic prekindergarten programs is that children learn to associate letters with the sounds they represent. Children are instructed in letter-sound relationships by teachers in a variety of ways. On one day, a teacher might conduct

early childhood education educational programs for children between birth and 8 years

developmental approach an approach to early childhood education that supports children's achievement of naturally occurring milestones

academic approach an approach to early childhood education that provides children with instruction in skills needed for success in school

whole-class sessions in which she holds up flash cards with letters and demonstrates the sounds they represent. The children imitate her a few times, and then she asks them to provide the sound for each letter as she holds up the card. On another day, a teacher might work with children in groups of three or four, asking them to look through a story book and find all the letters that represent the /m/ sound.

It is important to point out that the developmental and academic approaches are not mutually exclusive. A preschool program can include elements of both. In fact, as you might guess, it would be practically impossible to design a preschool program in which every minute of the day was taken up with academic activities, simply because of the developmental characteristics of young children. For example, recall from Chapter 7 that the reticular formation, the brain structure that controls attention, is far from mature during these years. As a result, young children simply cannot be expected to sit still, receive instruction, and complete academic tasks such as filling in blanks on worksheets for several hours each day.

Developmentally Appropriate Practices The National Association for the Education of Young Children (NAEYC) is an organization that evaluates early childhood programs and accredits those that meet its standards. The NAEYC standards do not endorse any particular approach to early childhood education. Instead, they focus on **developmentally appropriate practices**, an approach to curriculum development that takes into account the universal features of child development, individual differences across children, and the social and cultural contexts in which development occurs (NAEYC, 2006). According to these broad criteria, any kind of preschool program, regardless of its purpose or theoretical foundation, can be judged as either developmentally appropriate or inappropriate.

For example, as noted earlier, the reticular formation in the brains of young children is still immature. This is a universal that, according to the NAEYC standards, must be considered when early childhood educators design preschool programs. Thus, such programs should not depend on children's ability to pay attention to external stimuli, such as a teacher's lecture, for long periods of time. In addition, teachers should expect young children to be easily distracted and should be tolerant of their need for a great deal of repetition. Moreover, children differ in the rate at which their reticular formations mature. So, the standard of developmental appropriateness also requires that teachers be tolerant of such individual differences. Even among children of similar ages, for instance, one child may require an instruction to be repeated twice, while another may require it to be repeated seven times. The social and cultural contexts in which children are developing affect their capacity to pay attention, too, and developmentally appropriate practices require that this factor be considered in the design of the curriculum. For example, parents who are high school graduates are more likely than parents who did not complete high school to provide their children with the kinds of activities that encourage them to develop the attention skills required in preschool (Suizzo & Stapleton, 2007). Thus, when early childhood educators design programs for children whose parents are likely to be poorly educated, they should assume that such children will require a bit more time to develop needed attention skills than would be expected in a program in which most children's parents were high school graduates.

developmentally appropriate practices early childhood education practices based on an understanding of developmental universals, individual differences, and contextual variables

Early Childhood Education for Economically Disadvantaged Children

Learning Objective 8.13
How does early childhood education influence cognitive development among economically disadvantaged children?

In the United States, many government programs for economically disadvantaged children are based on the assumption that a family's economic resources can limit their ability to provide their children with preschool experiences and that such experiences are vital to supporting children's intellectual development. Public funding for such programs began in 1965 when the first version of the Elementary and Secondary Education Act (ESEA) was passed, the landmark legislation that provided

Children who attend enrichment programs like this Head Start program typically do not show lasting gains in IQ, but they are more likely to succeed in school.

federal funding to state and local education agencies. Title I of the law provided additional funding for schools that served poor families, and the law encouraged schools to use these funds for preschool programs. Thus, **Title I preschool programs** are operated by public schools. They serve economically disadvantaged children, are jointly funded by the federal government and local education agencies, and are under the supervision of the U.S. Department of Education.

Another federal preschool initiative, **Head Start**, also began in 1965. The program was based on the recommendations of a committee of child development experts that was assembled by officials in the administration of President Lyndon B. Johnson. The first actual Head Start program was a summer enrichment program for impoverished Native American children. By the end of the 1960s, the program had been expanded to include a variety of community-based preschool programs geared toward the needs of specific ethnic groups. In addition, Head Start played a critical role in the initial development of *Sesame Street.*

Like Title I programs, Head Start programs are federally funded, but they also receive funds from other sources, including state and local governments as well as private foundations. Head Start programs are governed by the U.S. Department of Health and Human Services. Most programs include health and nutritional support services to young children and their families, as well as preschool classes. The passage of Early Head Start legislation in 1995 expanded the program to include infants.

Children from economically disadvantaged families who attend Title I, Head Start, and other such preschool programs normally show gains in IQ scores while enrolled in them (Puma et al., 2005; Ludwig & Miller, 2007). However, these gains typically fade and then disappear within the first few years of school. On other kinds of measures, though, a residual effect of enriched preschool experiences can clearly be seen some years later. Children from low-income homes who attended a Head Start program or had another quality preschool experience are less likely to be placed in special education classes, less likely to repeat a grade, more likely to graduate from high school, and more likely to attend college than children from similar homes who did not attend preschool (Barnett, 1995; Darlington, 1991; Garces, Thomas, & Currie, 2002; Ludwig & Miller, 2007). One very long-term study even suggested that the impact of enriched programs may last well into adulthood. This study found that young adults who had attended a particularly good experimental preschool program, the Perry Preschool Project in Milwaukee, had higher rates of high school graduation, lower rates of criminal behavior, lower rates of unemployment, and a lower probability of being on welfare than did their peers who had not attended such a preschool (Barnett, 1993).

When the enrichment program is begun in infancy rather than at age 3 or 4, even IQ scores remain elevated into adulthood (Campbell, Ramey, Pungello, Sparling, & Miller-Johnson, 2002; Ramey & Ramey, 1998). One very well-designed and meticulously reported infancy intervention was called the Abecedarian project (Campbell & Ramey, 1994; Ramey, 1993; Ramey & Campbell, 1987). Infants from poverty-level families whose mothers had low IQs were randomly assigned either to a special child-care program or to a control group that received nutritional supplements and medical care but no special enriched child care. The special child-care program began when the infants were 6–12 weeks old and lasted until they started kindergarten. Figure 8.6 graphs the average IQ scores of the children in each of these two groups from age 2 to age 12. You can see that the IQs of the children who had been enrolled in the special program were higher at every age. Fully 44% of the control group children had IQ scores classified as borderline or retarded (scores below 85), compared with only

Title I preschool programs early childhood education programs for economically disadvantaged children that are based in public schools

Head Start community-based early childhood education programs for economically disadvantaged children that are funded by the federal government

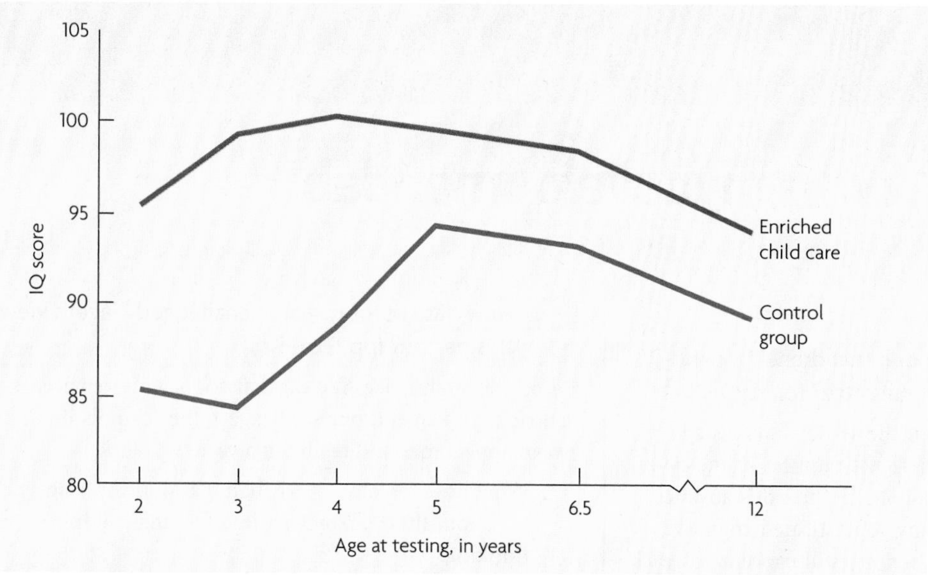

Figure 8.6 Early Education and IQ Scores

In Ramey's study, children from poverty-level families were randomly assigned in infancy to an experimental group that received special child care or to a control group, with the intervention lasting until age 5. At kindergarten, both groups entered public school. The difference in IQ between the experimental and control groups remained statistically significant even at age 12, seven years after the intervention had ended.

(*Source*: Ramey & Campbell, 1987. Figure 3, p. 135, with additional data from Ramey, 1993, Figure 2, p. 29.)

12.8% of the children who had been in the special program. In addition, children in the enriched child-care group had significantly higher scores on both reading and mathematics tests at age 12 and were only half as likely to have repeated a grade (Ramey, 1992, 1993). By age 21, participants were more likely than the control group to be enrolled in college (Campbell et al., 2002). Thus, the Abecedarian study is often cited in support of the view that public spending on preschool programs saves money in the long run.

Test Prep Center

with mydevelopmentlab

COGNITIVE CHANGES

8.1 What are the characteristics of children's thought during Piaget's preoperational stage? (pp. 220–224)

Piaget marked the transition from the sensorimotor stage to the preoperational stage at about 18–24 months, at the point when the child begins to use symbols. Despite this advance, the preschool child still lacks many sophisticated cognitive skills. In Piaget's view, such children are still egocentric, reach false conclusions because of centration, and are often fooled by appearances.

1. Match each term with its definition.

   ______ (1) semiotic function

   ______ (2) preoperational

   ______ (3) egocentrism

   ______ (4) centration

   ______ (5) conservation

   (A) thinking that focuses on one variable at a time

   (B) the belief that matter can change in appearance without changing in quantity

   (C) the kind of thinking in which children are proficient in the use of symbols but still have difficulty thinking logically

   (D) the understanding that one thing can stand for another

   (E) the belief that everyone experiences the world the same way that the self does

2. From the Multimedia Library within MyDevelopmentLab, watch the *Conservation of Liquids* video and answer the following question.

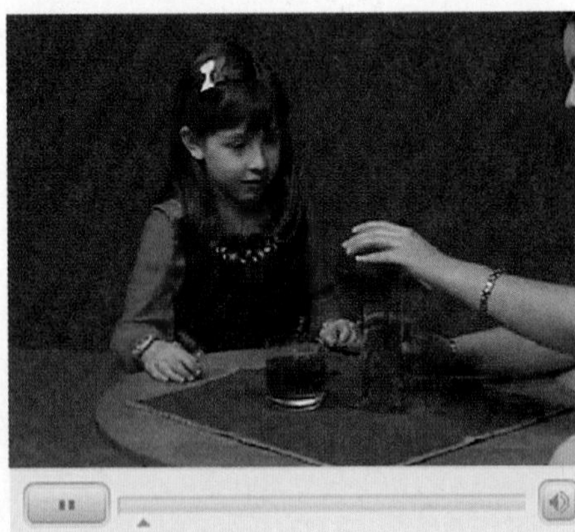

The first girl's response to the conservation problem is an example of ______________________.

8.2 How has recent research challenged Piaget's view of this period? (pp. 224–225)

Recent research makes it clear that young children are less egocentric than Piaget thought. By age 4, they can distinguish between appearance and reality in a variety of tasks.

3. What does research other than that done by Piaget say about these characteristics of young children's thinking?

Cognitive Ability	Research Findings
Conservation	
Egocentrism	
Perspective-taking	
Appearance/reality	

8.3 What is a theory of mind, and how does it develop? (pp. 225–227)

A theory of mind is a set of ideas that describe, explain, and make predictions about others' knowledge and behavior based on inferences about their mental states. By the end of early childhood, children have a well-developed theory of mind. They understand that other people's actions are based on their thoughts and beliefs. Theory of mind develops along with language skills and is associated with pretend play.

4. From the Multimedia Library within MyDevelopmentLab, watch the *Theory of Mind* video and answer the following question.

The older child in the video has mastered the __________ principle.

8.4 How do information-processing theorists explain changes in young children's thinking? (pp. 227–229)

Neo-Piagetian and information-processing theorists explain early childhood cognitive development in terms of limitations in young children's memory systems. Information-processing theorists point out that metacognition and metamemory are required for solving Piaget's conservation problems, two skill areas in which preschoolers are somewhat weak.

5. Match each term with its definition:

   ______ (1) operational efficiency

   ______ (2) metacognition

   ______ (3) metamemory

   ______ (4) scripts

   (A) knowledge about and control of thought processes

   (B) cognitive structures that underlie behaviors that are sequential in nature

   (C) knowledge about and control of memory processes

   (D) the maximum number of schemes that may be put into the child's working memory at one time

8.5 What are the characteristics of Vygotsky's stages of early childhood cognitive development? (pp. 229–231)

During the primitive stage, the infant learns primarily through conditioning. When language begins to develop, the naive psychology stage appears. Next the child enters the private speech stage, when he uses language as a guide to solving problems. In the last phase, the ingrowth stage, private speech has become completely internalized.

6. From the Multimedia Library within MyDevelopmentLab, watch the *Scaffolding* video and answer the following question.

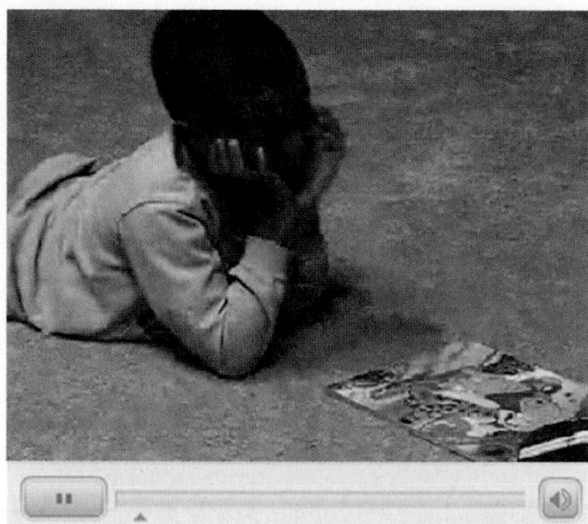

In what way does the teacher's behavior fit Vygotsky's concept of scaffolding?

____

____

CHANGES IN LANGUAGE

8.6 How does fast-mapping help children learn new words? (pp. 231–232)

Fast-mapping, the use of categories to link new words with real-world objects or events, enables young children to acquire new words rapidly.

7. How does feedback from fluent speakers help children learn new words?

____

____

8.7 What happens during the grammar explosion? (pp. 232–233)

During the grammar explosion (ages 2 to 6), children make large advances in grammatical fluency. They learn to add inflections, to form questions, to negate statements, to use conjunctions and prepositions appropriately, and to distinguish between irregular and regular verbs and plurals.

8. What is the difference between the telegraphic speech of young preschoolers and the more mature speech of older children and adults?

____

____

8.8 What is phonological awareness, and why is it important? (p. 233)

Phonological awareness is an understanding of the sound patterns of the particular language that a child acquires during early childhood. It is important in learning to read and seems to be acquired primarily through word play.

9. Mark "Y" by each example of phonological awareness and "N" by each non-example:

   ______ (1) A child recites the alphabet.

   ______ (2) A child says *cat* when asked to suggest a word that rhymes with *hat.*

   ______ (3) A child recognizes her written name.

   ______ (4) A child writes *brn* and states that she has written the word *barn.*

DIFFERENCES IN INTELLIGENCE

8.9 What are the strengths and weaknesses of IQ tests? (pp. 234–236)

Scores on early childhood intelligence tests are predictive of later school performance and are at least moderately consistent over time. The main weakness of IQ tests is that they measure only a narrow portion of intellectual ability, and interpretations of IQ scores often neglect other variables not measured by these tests that are also critical to success.

10. From the Multimedia Library within MyDevelopmentLab, watch the *Robert Guthrie: Cultural Bias* video and answer the following question.

What is Guthrie's main criticism of intelligence testing?

____

____

8.10 What evidence has been offered in support of the nature and nurture explanations for individual differences in IQ? (pp. 236–238)

Twin and adoption studies suggest that at least half the variation in IQ scores is due to genetic differences. Studies of children's home environments and studies involving children from poor families who are adopted by parents in a higher social class demonstrate that environmental variables also contribute to IQ scores.

11. What is meant by the term *reaction range*?

____

____

12. From the Multimedia Library within MyDevelopmentLab, explore *Correlations Between IQ Scores of Persons of Varying Relationships* and answer the following question.

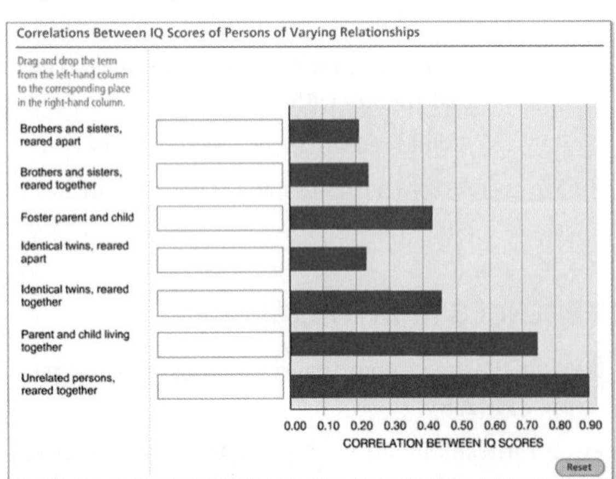

Explain why this statement is false: Twin studies prove that environment has no influence on intelligence.

____

____

8.11 What evidence has been offered in support of the genetic and cultural explanations of group differences in IQ scores? (pp. 238–239)

Theorists on the nature side of the nature-nurture debate claim that inherited physical variations across groups explain differences in IQ scores. Cultural explanations are supported by research showing that groups with lower than average IQ scores experience greater levels of exposure to risk factors such as poverty, poor nutrition, and toxic substances. The Flynn effect also demonstrates the power of cultural and historical forces in shaping IQ scores.

13. Transform each false statement into one that is true.

(A) The difference between the average intelligence test scores of White and African American children in the United States is much larger than it used to be.

____

____

(B) Most developmentalists believe that the difference between the average intelligence test scores of White and African American children in the United States is the result of genetic factors.

____

____

(C) The difference between the average intelligence test scores of White and African American children in the United States falls outside the presumed reaction range of intelligence.

____

____

14. From the Multimedia Library within MyDevelopmentLab, watch the *Cultural Influences: Robert Sternberg* video and answer the following question.

What has Sternberg found in his cross-cultural research on definitions of intelligence?

____

____

EARLY CHILDHOOD EDUCATION

8.12 How do the various approaches to early childhood education differ? (pp. 240–241)

Developmental approaches, such as the Montessori method, seek to support the attainment of naturally occurring developmental goals. Academic approaches instruct preschoolers in the skills necessary for success in elementary school. Developmentally appropriate practices are based on an understanding of developmental universals, individual differences, and the social and cultural contexts of development.

15. Classify each of these features of early childhood education programs as indicative of (A) the developmental approach or (B) the academic approach.

_______ (1) access to a climbing apparatus that encourages the development of motor skills

_______ (2) daily drilling with alphabet flash cards

_______ (3) access to adults' clothes for playing dress-up

_______ (4) daily lessons in phonological awareness

_______ (5) encouraging children to memorize addition and subtraction facts

_______ (6) access to art materials for child-directed creative projects

8.13 How does early childhood education influence cognitive development among economically disadvantaged children? (pp. 241–243)

Disadvantaged children who have been in enriched preschool programs get higher scores on IQ tests during the early childhood years, but these gains do not always persist into later childhood. However, studies show that these children are less likely to require special education services and have fewer behavior problems in elementary school than disadvantaged children who do not attend preschool. If the enrichment programs begin in infancy, IQ gains have been found to continue into the secondary school years.

16. From the Multimedia Library within MyDevelopmentLab, watch the *Windows of Opportunity for Learning* video and answer the following question.

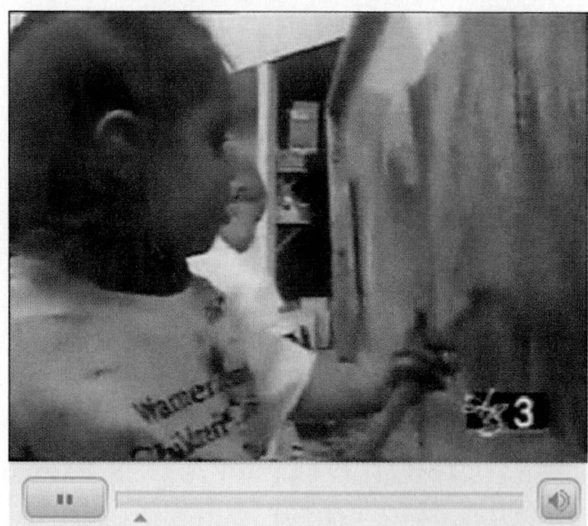

How would the researcher in the video explain the need for early childhood programs for disadvantaged children?

____

____

For answers to the questions in this chapter, turn to page 516. For a list of key terms, turn to page 531.

Chapter 9

Social and Personality Development in Early Childhood

If you asked a random sample of adults to tell you the most important characteristics of children between the ages of 2 and 6, the first thing on the list would probably be their rapidly changing social abilities during these years. Nay-saying, oppositional toddlers who spend most of their play time alone become skilled, co-operative playmates by age 5 or 6. Thus, the most obvious characteristic of 6-year-olds is how socially "grown up" they seem compared to 2-year-olds. Moreover, their blossoming physical, cognitive, and language skills have led to changes in how these children view themselves and relate to their families. Most have also broadened their social networks to include peers.

This chapter will discuss all of these changes and acquaint you with the major theoretical explanations for them. First we will review the ideas proposed by psychoanalytic theorists. Next, you will read about the very different explanations given by social-cognitive theorists. From there, we will turn to the topics of personality and gender role development. Finally, we will look at young children's relationships with others.

Learning Objectives

Theories of Social and Personality Development

9.1 What major themes of development did the psychoanalytic theorists propose for the early childhood period?

9.2 What are the findings of social-cognitive theorists with respect to young children's understanding of the social world?

Personality and Self-Concept

9.3 How does temperament change in early childhood?

9.4 What changes take place in the young child's categorical, emotional, and social selves during the preschool years?

Gender Development

9.5 How do the major theoretical orientations explain gender development?

9.6 How do children develop their concept of gender?

9.7 What are the characteristics of young children's sex-role knowledge?

9.8 How is the behavior of young children sex-typed?

Family Relationships and Structure

9.9 How does attachment change during the early childhood years?

9.10 How do parenting styles affect children's development?

9.11 How are ethnicity and socioeconomic status related to parenting style?

9.12 How is family structure related to children's development?

9.13 How does divorce affect children's behavior in early childhood and in later years?

9.14 What are some possible reasons for the relationship between family structure and development?

Peer Relationships

9.15 What are the various kinds of play exhibited by preschoolers?

9.16 What is the difference between instrumental and hostile aggression?

9.17 How do prosocial behavior and friendship patterns change during early childhood?

Theories of Social and Personality Development

What is the period of early childhood all about? One way to describe it would be to call it the "stepping out" phase, because that's precisely what 2- to 6-year-olds do. They "step out" from the safety of the strong emotional bonds that they share with their parents into the risky world of relationships with others. How do they do it? The early psychoanalysts outlined the broad themes of this foundational time of life, and the work of more recent theorists has provided us with a few details about the skills that children develop in the process of stepping out. Before we get into the details, let's look at the themes.

Learning Objective 9.1

What major themes of development did the psychoanalytic theorists propose for the early childhood period?

Psychoanalytic Perspectives

You may remember that Freud described two stages during the preschool years. The developmental task of the *anal stage* (1 to 3 years) is toilet training. That of the *phallic stage*, you may remember, is to establish a foundation for later gender and moral development by identifying with the same-sex parent. We might sum up Freud's view of the early childhood period as the time in life when young children, first, gain control of their bodily functions and, second, renegotiate their relationships with their parents to prepare for stepping out into the world of peers.

"Stepping out" is the major theme of social and personality development in early childhood. Maintaining strong bonds of affection with parents helps children feel secure enough to step out.

Erikson agreed with Freud's views on bodily control and parental relationships during the preschool years, but he placed the emphasis somewhat differently. Both of the stages Erikson identified in the preschool period (see Table 2.2, page 30) are triggered by children's growing physical, cognitive, and social skills. The stage he called *autonomy versus shame and doubt*, for example, is centered around the toddler's new mobility and the accompanying desire for autonomy. The stage of *initiative versus guilt* is ushered in by new cognitive skills, particularly the preschooler's ability to plan, which accentuates his wish to take the initiative. However, his developing conscience dictates the boundaries within which this initiative may be exercised (Evans & Erikson, 1967). For example, think about a situation in which one child wants to play with another child's toy. His sense of initiative might motivate him to simply take the toy, but his conscience will likely prompt him to find a more socially acceptable way to gain the toy. If he fails to achieve the kind of self-control that is required to maintain conformity to his conscience, the child is likely to be hampered by excessive guilt and defensiveness in future psychosocial crises.

THE WHOLE CHILD IN FOCUS

How did Madeleine develop a sense of initiative? Find out on page 283.

The key to healthy development during this period, according to Erikson, is striking a balance between the child's emerging skills and desire for autonomy and the parents' need to protect the child and control the child's behavior. Thus, the parents' task changes rather dramatically after infancy. In the early months of life, the parents' primary task is to provide enough warmth, predictability, and responsiveness to foster a secure attachment and to support basic physiological needs. But once the child becomes physically, linguistically, and cognitively more independent, the need to control becomes a central aspect of the parents' task. Too much control and the child will not have sufficient opportunity to explore; too little control and the child will become unmanageable and fail to learn the skills she will need to get along with peers as well as adults.

Learning Objective 9.2

What are the findings of social-cognitive theorists with respect to young children's understanding of the social world?

Social-Cognitive Perspectives

In contrast to the psychoanalytic tradition, **social-cognitive theory** assumes that social and emotional changes in the child are the result of—or at least are facilitated by—the enormous growth in cognitive abilities that happens during the preschool years (Macrae & Bodenhausen, 2000). Over the past three decades, psychologists have devoted a great deal of theoretical and empirical attention to determining just how the two domains are connected.

social-cognitive theory the theoretical perspective that social and emotional development in early childhood is related to improvements in the cognitive domain

Person Perception Have you ever heard a child describe a peer as "nice" or "not nice"? Preschoolers' emerging capacity for applying categories to people is called **person**

perception; basically, it is the ability to classify others. For example, by kindergarten age, children make judgments very similar to those of adults when asked to identify the most intelligent child in their class or play group (Droege & Stipek, 1993). Moreover, they describe their peers in terms of traits such as "grumpy" and "mean" (Yuill, 1997). They also make statements about other people's patterns of behavior—"Grandma always lets me pick the cereal at the grocery store." They use these observations to classify others into groups such as "people I like" and "people I don't like."

However, young children's observations and categorizations of people are far less consistent than those of older children. A playmate they judge to be "nice" one day may be referred to as "mean" the next. Developmentalists have found that young children's judgments about others are inconsistent because they tend to base them on their most recent interactions with those individuals (Ruble & Dweck, 1995). In other words, a 4-year-old girl describes one of her playmates as "nice" on Monday because she shares a cookie, but as "mean" on Tuesday because she refuses to share a candy bar. Or the child declares, "I don't like Grandma anymore because she made me go to bed early."

Preschoolers also categorize others on the basis of observable characteristics such as race, age, and gender. For example, the *cross-race effect*, a phenomenon in which individuals are more likely to remember the faces of people of their own race than those of people of a different race, is established by age 5 (Pezdek, Blandon-Gitlin, & Moore, 2003). Similarly, they talk about "big kids" (school-aged children) and "little kids" (their agemates), and they seem to know that they fit in better with the latter. Self-segregation by gender—a topic you'll read more about later in the chapter—begins as early as age 2. Likewise, young children sometimes segregate themselves according to race (see *Developmental Science in the Classroom*).

person perception the ability to classify others according to categories such as traits, age, gender, and race

DEVELOPMENTAL SCIENCE IN THE CLASSROOM

Learning and Unlearning Racial Prejudice

Mara was excited about her new job teaching prekindergarten in a school that served a multiethnic student population. She became concerned on her first day, however, when she overheard many of the 4-year-olds in her class making remarks about one another's race. Even more alarming to her was her young pupils' tendency to sort themselves according to race and to express dismay when a child of a different race sat by them or tried to join their games. Mara wanted to know how she could help her students learn to be more tolerant.

Research suggests that racial schemas are well established by age 4 to 5 (Pezdek, Blandon-Gitlin, & Moore, 2003). Once these schemas are formed, children use them to make judgments about others. These early judgments probably reflect young children's egocentric thinking. Essentially, children view those like themselves as desirable companions and those who are unlike them–in gender, race, and other categorical variables–as undesirable (Doyle & Aboud, 1995). Thus, racial prejudice may arise from the fact that children become aware of race at the same time their information-processing system begins to sort the world into "like me/not like me" categories.

Of course, cognitive development doesn't happen in a social vacuum, and by age 5 or so, most White children in English-speaking countries have acquired an understanding of their culture's racial stereotypes and prejudices (Bigler & Liben, 1993). Likewise, African American, Hispanic American, and Native American children become sensitive very early in life to the fact that people of their race are viewed negatively by many Whites. Some studies suggest that this early awareness of racial stereotypes negatively influences minority children's self-esteem (Jambunathan & Burts, 2003). It seems likely that children's observations of the race-based judgments of adults in their cultures combine with the cognitive aspects of early racial awareness to produce racial prejudice.

The key to preventing young children's racial awareness from developing into racial prejudice, psychologists say, is for preschool teachers to discuss race openly and to make conscious efforts to help children acquire nonprejudiced attitudes (Cushner, McClelland, & Safford, 1992). For example, they can make young children aware of historical realities such as slavery, race segregation, and minority groups' efforts to achieve equal rights. Teachers can also assign children of different races to do projects together. In addition, they can make children aware of each other's strengths as individuals and encourage all children to develop a positive sense of ethnic identity. In other words, even though grasping such abstract ideas may be difficult for young children, adults should model and teach that it is not necessary to devalue others in order to value oneself.

Questions for Reflection

1. How might Mara implement some of the strategies suggested here for reducing prejudice in her classroom?
2. In your view, what is the role of entertainment media in the development of racial prejudice?

Understanding Rule Categories If you attended a formal dinner at which the forks were on the right side of the plates rather than on the left, would you be upset? Probably not, because *social conventions*, such as customs that govern where to place flatware, are rules that have nothing to do with our fundamental sense of right and wrong. Consequently, most of us are not troubled when they are violated and take a dim view of people who are bothered by such trifles. By contrast, we have little tolerance for the breaking of rules that we view as having a basis in morality, such as laws that forbid stealing and unwritten rules like the one that prohibits you from flirting with your best friend's romantic partner (or with your romantic partner's best friend!). When and how did we learn to make such distinctions?

Social-cognitive theorists have found that children begin to respond differently to violations of different kinds of rules between 2 and 3 (Smetana, Schlagman, & Adams, 1993). For example, they view taking another child's toy without permission as a more serious violation of rules than forgetting to say "thank you." They also say, just as adults would in response to similar questions, that stealing and physical violence are wrong, even if their particular family or preschool has no explicit rule against them. This kind of understanding seems to develop both as a consequence of preschoolers' increasing capacity for classification and as a result of adults' tendency to emphasize transgressions that have moral overtones more than violations of customs and other arbitrary rules when punishing children (Nucci & Smetana, 1996).

Understanding Others' Intentions Would you feel differently about a person who deliberately smashed your car's windshield with a baseball bat than you would about someone else who accidentally broke it while washing your car for you? Chances are that you would be far more forgiving of the person who unintentionally broke your windshield, because we tend to base our judgments of others' behavior and our responses to it on what we perceive to be their intentions. Working from his assumptions about young children's egocentrism, Piaget suggested that young children were incapable of such discriminations.

However, more recent research has demonstrated that young children do understand intentions to some degree (Zhang & Yu, 2002). For one thing, it's quite common for preschoolers to say "It was an accident . . . I didn't mean to do it" when they are punished. Such protests suggest that children understand that intentional wrongdoing is punished more severely than unintentional transgressions of the rules.

Several studies suggest that children can make judgments about actors' intentions both when faced with abstract problems and when personally motivated by a desire to avoid punishment. For example, in a classic study, 3-year-olds listened to stories about children playing ball (Nelson, 1980), and pictures were used to convey information about intentions (see Figure 9.1). The children were more likely to label as "bad" or "naughty" the child who in-

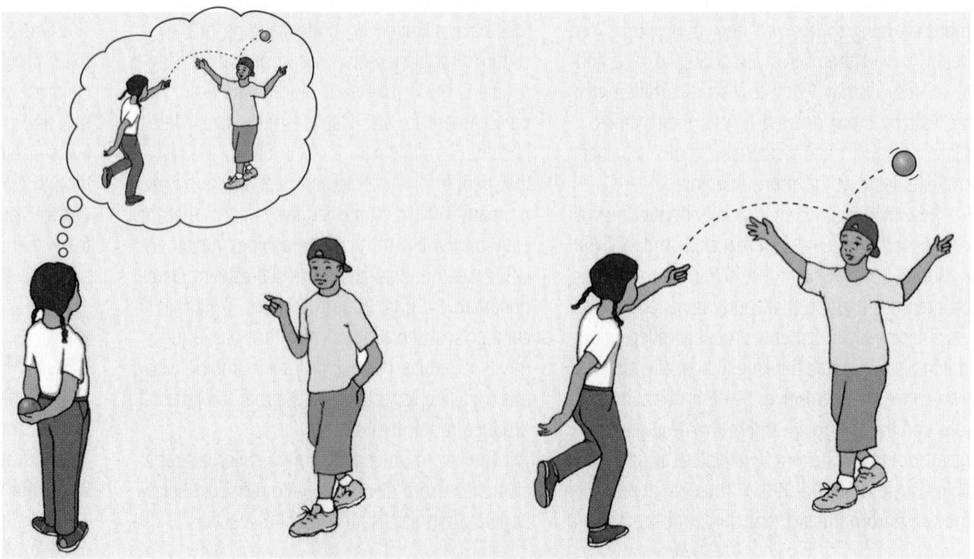

Figure 9.1
A Test of Children's Understanding of Intentionality

Pictures like these have been used to assess young children's understanding of an actor's intentions.

tended to harm a playmate than the child who accidentally hit another child in the head with the ball. However, the children's judgments were also influenced by outcomes. In other words, they were more likely to say that a child who wanted to hurt his playmate was "good" if he failed to hit the child with the ball. These results suggest that children know more about intentions than Piaget thought, but they are still limited in their ability to base judgments entirely on intentions.

Personality and Self-Concept

As young children gain more understanding of the social environment, their distinctive personalities begin to emerge. At the same time, their self-concepts become more complex, allowing them to exercise greater control over their own behavior.

From Temperament to Personality

Learning Objective 9.3
How does temperament change in early childhood?

Are you familiar with the children's game Duck, Duck, Goose? For the benefit of readers who are unfamiliar with the game, here's how it goes. A child who has been assigned the role of "it" walks around the outside of a circle of children who are seated on the floor. As "it" passes by, he touches the head of each child and calls out "duck" until he comes to the child he chooses to be the goose. The goose then has to chase "it" around the circle and try to prevent him from taking goose's seat. If the goose fails to beat "it," then she becomes "it" for the next round of the game. The difficult part of the game for many young children is waiting to be chosen to be the goose.

Activities such as Duck, Duck, Goose may seem frivolous, but they contribute to the process through which temperament becomes modified into personality during the early childhood years. A child whose temperament includes a low ranking on the dimension of effortful control (see Chapter 6), for instance, may not be able to tolerate waiting for his turn in a game of Duck, Duck, Goose (Li-Grining, 2007). If he obeys his impulse to chase "it" and jumps up from his seat before he is declared the goose, he will undoubtedly be scolded by his playmates. If his frustration leads him to withdraw from the game with the protest "I never get to be the goose!" he will miss out on the fun of participating. Either way, he will learn that controlling his impulses is more beneficial than submitting to them. A few such experiences will teach him to moderate the effects of his lack of effortful control on his social behavior. As a result, his lack of effortful control will become less prominent in the profile of characteristics that constitute his personality, and this will change how his peers respond to him. Their approval of his modified profile will encourage him to keep his impulses in check.

Similarly, children with difficult temperaments learn that the behaviors associated with difficultness, such as complaining, often result in peer rejection. As a result, many of them change their behavior to gain social acceptance. Similarly, some shy toddlers are encouraged by their parents to be more sociable (Rubin, Burgess, & Hastings, 2002). Thus, personality represents the combination of the temperament with which children are probably born and the knowledge they gain about temperament-related behavior during childhood (McCrae, Costa, Ostendord, & Angleitner, 2000; Svrakic, Svrakic, & Cloninger, 1996).

The transition from temperament to personality is also influenced by parental responses to a young child's temperament. If the parents reject a difficult child, the child is likely to emerge from the preschool years with a personality that puts him at risk for developing serious problems in social relationships, and he may suffer from cognitive deficits as well (Bates, 1989; Fish, Stifter, & Belsky, 1991). However, parents can moderate the risks associated with a difficult temperament by helping these children learn to regulate their emotions and behavior more effectively (Coplan, Bowker, & Cooper, 2003). Thus, infant temperament doesn't necessarily dictate the kind of personality a child will develop. Instead, it is one factor among many that shape an individual child's personality.

Learning Objective 9.4

What changes take place in the young child's categorical, emotional, and social selves during the preschool years?

Self-Concept

Thanks to the growing child's expanding cognitive abilities, her capacity for self-understanding improves substantially during the early childhood years. The categories to which she assigns herself become more stable and more complex at the same time. Likewise, the emotional self grows by leaps and bounds during these years, and a new component of self-concept, the social self, emerges.

The Categorical Self Ask a preschooler to describe herself, and you are likely to get an answer such as "I'm a girl." Pressed for more information, the child will add her hair color or some other physical characteristic, tell you who her friends are, or reveal who her favorite cartoon character is. These answers show that the categorical self, a concept that first emerges during infancy (see Chapter 6), is becoming more mature largely as a result of the young child's understanding of mutually exclusive categories (Kagan & Herschkowitz, 2005). For instance, it is not possible to be both a boy and a girl. Thus, a young child must settle on a categorical label for herself, one that will stay with her for the rest of her life.

Self-categorizations are a vital part of a child's sense of her own personal history as well. It is as if, once stable categorical labels are established, the child can not only project herself into a categorical future (i.e., "I am a girl; I will grow up to be a woman"), but also project self-assigned categorical labels into the past to organize a representation of her earlier life. For instance, a 5-year-old girl may not remember playing with dolls at the age of 2, but she can combine her knowledge of the world (i.e., most girls like dolls) with her self-categorization as a girl, along with her current play preferences (i.e., I like dolls), to infer that she probably enjoyed playing with dolls as a toddler. The emergence of this aspect of self-concept, an *autobiographical* sense of self, is linked to a child's theory of mind (Gergely, 2002).

emotional regulation the ability to control emotional states and emotion-related behavior

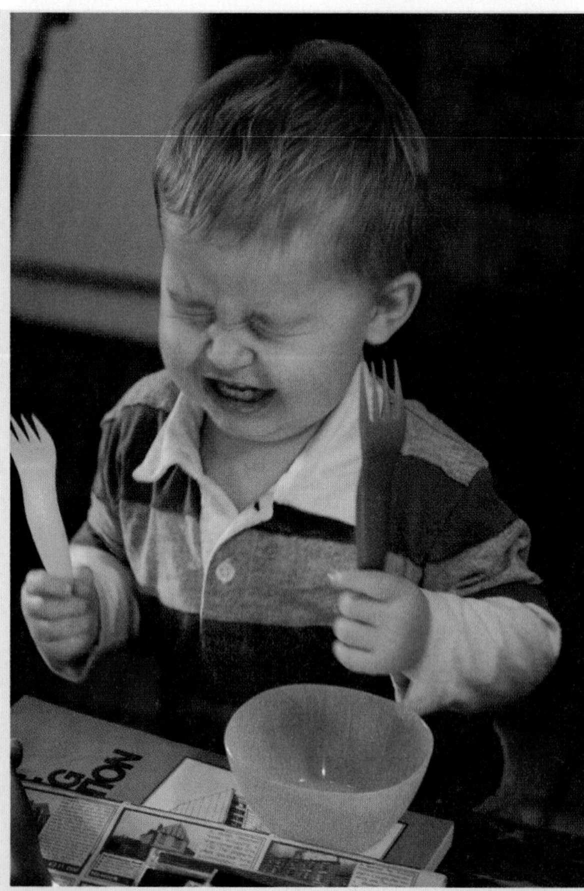
All children get upset from time to time, but they vary widely in how well they manage distressing feelings.

The Emotional Self In recent years, research examining development of the emotional self during the early childhood years has focused on the acquisition of **emotional regulation,** or the ability to control emotional states and emotion-related behavior (Hoeksma, Oosterlaan, & Schipper, 2004). For example, children exhibit emotional regulation when they find a way to cheer themselves up when they are feeling sad, or when they divert their attention to a different activity when they get frustrated with something. Recent research has shown that emotional regulation in early childhood is linked to a variety of social variables. One study showed that level of emotional regulation at age 2 predicted level of aggressive behavior at age 4 in both boys and girls (Rubin, Burgess, Dwyer, & Hastings, 2003). Predictably, preschoolers who display high levels of emotional regulation are more popular with their peers than are those who are less able to regulate their emotional behavior (Denham et al., 2003; Fantuzzo, Sekino, & Cohen, 2004). Emotional regulation skills appear to be particularly important for children whose temperaments include high levels of anger proneness (Diener & Kim, 2004). Further, longitudinal research has demonstrated that emotional regulation in early childhood is related to children's ability to obey moral rules and to think about right and wrong during the school years (Kochanska, Murray, & Coy, 1997).

The process of acquiring emotional regulation is one in which control shifts slowly from the parents to the child (Houck & Lecuyer-Maus, 2004). Here again, the child's temperament is a factor. For example, preschoolers who have consistently exhibited difficult behavior since infancy are more likely to have self-control problems in early childhood (Schmitz et al., 1999). Similarly, preschoolers who were born prematurely or who were delayed in language development in the second year of life experience more difficulties with self-control during early childhood (Carson, Klee, & Perry, 1998; Schothorst & van Engeland, 1996).

Another aspect of the emotional self involves **empathy**, the ability to identify with another person's emotional state. Empathy has two aspects: apprehending another person's emotional state or condition and then matching that emotional state oneself. An empathetic person experiences either the same feeling he imagines the other person to feel or a highly similar feeling. Empathy is negatively associated with aggression in the early childhood years; the more advanced a preschooler's capacity for empathy is, the less aggression he displays (Findlay, Girardi, & Coplan, 2006; Strayer & Roberts, 2004). Moreover, the development of empathy in early childhood appears to provide the foundation on which a more sophisticated emotion, *sympathy* (a general feeling of sorrow or concern for another person), is built in later childhood and adolescence. The most thorough analysis of the development of empathy and sympathy has been offered by Martin Hoffman (1982, 1988), who describes four broad stages, summarized in Table 9.1.

In addition to empathy, young children's emotional selves include an awareness of emotional states linked to their culture's definitions of right and wrong. These feelings, which are sometimes called the *moral emotions*, include guilt, shame, and pride (Eisenberg, 2000). Guilt is usually thought of as the emotional state that is induced when a child breaks a rule. Consequently, a child who takes a forbidden cookie will experience guilt. Feelings of shame arise when he fails to live up to expectations. For instance, most parents and teachers urge young children to share their toys. Thus, when a child behaves selfishly and is reminded about the sharing rule, he is likely to feel shame. By contrast, children feel pride when they succeed at meeting such expectations.

Research suggests that the interplay among these three emotions—and young children's awareness of them—influences the development of behavior that children's cultures regard as morally acceptable (Eisenberg, 2000). Thus, they form the foundation of later moral development. Studies suggest that these feelings evolve in the context of parent-child

empathy the ability to identify with another person's emotional state

Table 9.1 Stages in Development of Empathy Proposed by Hoffman

Stage	Description
1: Global empathy	During the first year, if the infant is around someone expressing a strong emotion, he may match that emotion–for example, by beginning to cry when he hears another infant crying.
2: Egocentric empathy	Beginning at about 12 to 18 months of age, when children have developed a fairly clear sense of their separate selves, they respond to another's distress with some distress of their own, but they may attempt to "cure" the other person's problem by offering what they themselves would find most comforting. A child may, for example, show sadness when she sees another child hurt and get her own mother to help.
3: Empathy for another's feelings	Beginning as young as age 2 or 3 and continuing through elementary school, children note others' feelings, partially match those feelings, and respond to the others' distress in nonegocentric ways. Over these years, children become able to distinguish a wider (and more subtle) range of emotions.
4: Empathy for another's life condition	In late childhood or adolescence, some children develop a more generalized notion of others' feelings and respond not just to the immediate situation but to others' general situation or plight. Thus, a young person at this level may become more distressed by another person's sadness if she knows that the sadness is chronic or that the person's general situation is particularly tragic than if she sees it as a momentary problem.

Sources: Hoffman, 1982, 1988.

relationships. Young children who do not have warm, trusting relationships with their parents are at risk of failing to develop moral emotions or of developing feelings of guilt, shame, and pride that are too weak to influence their behavior (Koenig, Cicchetti, & Rogosch, 2004).

The Social Self Another facet of a child's emerging sense of self is an increasing awareness of herself as a player in the social game. By age 2, a toddler has already learned a variety of social scripts—routines of play or interaction with others. The toddler now begins to develop some implicit understanding of her own roles in these scripts (Case, 1991). So, she may begin to think of herself as a "helper" in some situations or as "the boss" when she is telling some other child what to do.

You can see this clearly in children's sociodramatic play, as they begin to take explicit roles: "I'll be the daddy and you be the mommy," or "I'm the boss." As part of the same process, the young child also gradually comes to understand her place in the network of family roles. She has sisters, brothers, father, mother, and so forth.

Moreover, role scripts help young children become more independent. For example, assuming the "student" role provides a preschooler with a prescription for appropriate behavior in the school situation. Students listen when the teacher speaks to the class, get out and put away materials at certain times, help their classmates in various ways, and so on. Once a preschooler is familiar with and adopts the student role, he can follow the role script and is no longer dependent on the teacher to tell him what to do every minute of the day.

Gender Development

As noted earlier, preschoolers who are asked to describe themselves are likely to begin by stating whether they are boys or girls. In psychologists' terms, their tendency to do so suggests that "boy-ness" and "girl-ness" are *salient*, or important, categories for young children. Thus, one of the most fascinating developmental processes of the preschool period is the one that involves children's evolving sense of **gender**, the psychological and social associates and implications of biological sex.

Learning Objective 9.5

How do the major theoretical orientations explain gender development?

Explaining Gender Development

Developmentalists have proposed several explanations of gender development.

Psychoanalytic Explanations As you may remember from Chapter 2, Freud suggested that 3- to 6-year-olds overcome the anxiety they feel about their desires for the opposite-sex parent (the Oedipus or Electra conflict) through identification with the same-sex parent. In order to identify with the parent, the child must learn and conform to his or her sex-role concepts. Thus, according to Freud, children acquire gender through the process of identification.

The difficulty with Freud's theory is that toddlers seem to understand far more about gender than the theory would predict. For example, many 18-month-olds accurately label themselves and others as boys or girls. Likewise, clearly sex-typed behavior appears long before age 4 or 5, when psychoanalytic theories claim identification occurs.

Social-Learning Explanations Social-learning theorists have emphasized the role of parents in shaping children's gender development (Bandura, 1977a; Mischel, 1966, 1970). This notion has been far better supported by research than have Freud's ideas. Parents do seem to reinforce sex-typed activities in children as young as 18 months, not only by buying different kinds of toys for boys and girls but also by responding more positively when their sons play with blocks or trucks or when their daughters play with dolls (Fagot & Hagan, 1991; Lytton & Romney, 1991). Such differential reinforcement is particularly clear with boys, especially from fathers (Siegal, 1987).

gender the psychological and social associates and implications of biological sex

Still, helpful as it is, a social-learning explanation is probably not sufficient. In particular, parents differentially reinforce boys' and girls' behavior less than you'd expect, and probably not enough to account for the very early and robust discrimination children seem to make on the basis of gender. Even young children whose parents seem to treat their sons and daughters in highly similar ways nonetheless learn gender labels and prefer same-sex playmates.

Social-Cognitive Explanations A third alternative, social-cognitive theory, suggests that children's understanding of gender is linked to gender-related behavior. For example, one such view, based strongly on Piagetian theory, is Lawrence Kohlberg's suggestion that the crucial aspect of the process is the child's understanding of the gender concept (Kohlberg, 1966; Kohlberg & Ullian, 1974). Once the child realizes that he is a boy or she is a girl forever, he or she becomes highly motivated to learn how to behave in the way that is expected or appropriate for that gender. Specifically, Kohlberg's theory predicts that systematic same-sex imitation will become evident only after the child has shown full gender constancy. **Gender constancy** is the understanding that gender is an innate characteristic that can't be changed. Most studies designed to test this hypothesis have supported Kohlberg. Children do seem to become much more sensitive to same-sex models after they understand gender constancy (Frey & Ruble, 1992). Kohlberg's theory allows developmentalists to make highly reliable predictions about the development of children's knowledge about gender.

However, social-cognitive theory is less accurate in predicting behavior. Specifically, it can't explain the obvious fact that children show clearly different behavior, such as toy preferences, long before they have achieved full understanding of the gender concept. A newer social-cognitive theory derived from the information-processing approach is usually called *gender schema theory* (Bem, 1981; Martin, 1991; Martin & Halverson, 1981). This approach includes many of Kohlberg's ideas about how gender constancy develops, but it does a better job of predicting behavior.

Gender Schema Theory A *schema* is a mental pattern or model that is used to process information. Just as the self-concept can be thought of as a schema, so can the child's understanding of gender. According to **gender schema theory**, a gender schema begins to develop as soon as the child notices the differences between male and female, knows his own gender, and can label the two groups with some consistency—all of which happens by age 2 or 3 (Bem, 1981; Martin & Ruble, 2002). Perhaps because gender is clearly an either/or category, children seem to understand very early that this is a key distinction, so the category serves as a kind of magnet for new information. Once the child has established even a primitive gender schema, a great many experiences can be assimilated to it. Thus, as soon as this schema begins to be formed, children may begin to show preference for same-sex playmates or for gender-stereotyped activities (Martin & Little, 1990).

Preschoolers first learn some broad distinctions about what kinds of activities or behavior "go with" each gender, both by observing other children and through the reinforcements they receive from parents. They also learn a few gender scripts—whole sequences of events that are normally associated with a given gender, such as "fixing dinner" or "building with tools"—just as they learn other social scripts at about this age (Levy & Fivush, 1993). Then, between age 4 and age 6, a child learns a more subtle and complex set of associations for his own gender—what children of his own gender like and don't like, how they play, how they talk, what kinds of people they associate with. Only between the ages of 8 and 10 does the child develop an equivalently complex view of the opposite gender (Martin, Wood, & Little, 1990).

The key difference between this theory and Kohlberg's gender constancy theory is that gender schema theory asserts that children need not understand that gender is permanent to form an initial gender schema. When they do begin to understand gender constancy, at about 5 or 6, children develop a more elaborate rule, or schema, as to "what people who are like me do" and treat this rule the same way they treat other rules—as an absolute. Later, the child's application of the gender rule becomes more flexible. She knows, for example, that most boys don't play with dolls, but they can do so if they like.

gender constancy the understanding that gender is a component of the self that is not altered by external appearance

gender schema theory an information-processing approach to gender concept development that asserts that people use a schema for each gender to process information about themselves and others

Biological Approaches For a long time, developmentalists dismissed the idea that biological differences between males and females were responsible for psychological differences between them. Today, though, they are taking another look at decades-old experimental studies with animals showing that prenatal exposure to male hormones such as testosterone powerfully influences behavior after birth (Lippa, 2005). Female animals exposed to testosterone behave more like male animals; for instance, they are more aggressive than females who do not experience prenatal exposure to testosterone. Similarly, when experimenters block the release of testosterone during prenatal development of male animal embryos, the animals exhibit behavior that is more typical of the females of their species.

Hormonal influences have been proposed to explain the outcomes of cases involving boys who carry a genetic defect that causes them to develop deformed genitalia. Decades ago, a few such boys were subjected to plastic surgery to give them female-appearing genitals and were raised as girls. At that time, however, doctors did not realize that the genetic defect in question interferes only with testosterone's effects on the sex organs; the brains of these fetuses were exposed to normal amounts of testosterone throughout prenatal development (Rosenthal & Gitelman, 2002). Follow-up studies found that many of these children, when they learned of their status, sought surgery to masculinize their bodies. Moreover, even those who elected to retain the feminine identities they had been given in infancy possessed many attributes and behaviors that are more typical of males than of females (Reiner & Gearhart, 2004). Such findings support the view that hormones play some role in gender development.

gender identity the ability to correctly label oneself and others as male or female

gender stability the understanding that gender is a stable, lifelong characteristic

Learning Objective 9.6

How do children develop their concept of gender?

The Gender Concept

Children seem to develop their concept of gender in three steps. First comes **gender identity**, which is simply a child's ability to label his or her own sex correctly and to identify other people as men or women, boys or girls. By 9–12 months, babies already treat male and female faces as different categories (Fagot & Leinbach, 1993). Within the next year, they begin to learn the verbal labels that go with these categories. By age 2, most children correctly label themselves as boys or girls, and within 6–12 months, most can correctly label others as well.

Accurate labeling, though, does not signify complete understanding. The second step is **gender stability**, which is the understanding that you stay the same gender throughout life. Researchers have measured this by asking children such questions as "When you were a little baby, were you a little girl or a little boy?" or "When you grow up, will you be a mommy or a daddy?" Most children understand the stability of gender by about age 4 (Slaby & Frey, 1975) (see Figure 9.2).

Figure 9.2 Gender Stereotyping in a Child's Drawing

In describing this self-portrait, the 5-year-old artist said, "This is how I will look when I get married to a boy. I am under a rainbow, so beautiful with a bride hat, a belt, and a purse." The girl knows she will always be female and associates gender with externals such as clothing (gender stability). She is also already quite knowledgeable about gender role expectations.

(Courtesy of Jerry and Denise Boyd. Used with permission.)

The final step is the development of *true gender constancy*, the recognition that someone stays the same gender even though he may appear to change by wearing different clothes or changing his hair length. For example, boys don't change into girls by wearing dresses. It may seem odd that a child who understands that he will stay the same gender throughout life (gender stability) can nonetheless be confused about the effect of changes in dress or appearance on gender. But numerous studies, including studies of children growing up in other cultures such as Kenya, Nepal, Belize, and Samoa, show that children go through this sequence (Munroe, Shimmin, & Munroe, 1984). Moreover, it is related to general cognitive development (Trautner, Gervai, & Nemeth, 2003).

The underlying logic of this sequence may be a bit clearer if you think of a parallel between gender constancy and the concept of conservation. Conservation involves recognition that an object remains the same in some fundamental way even though it changes externally. Gender constancy is thus a kind of "conservation of gender" and is not typically understood until about 5 or 6, when children understand other conservations (Marcus & Overton, 1978).

Sex-Role Knowledge

Learning Objective 9.7
What are the characteristics of young children's sex-role knowledge?

Figuring out one's gender and understanding that it stays constant are only part of the story. Learning what goes with being a boy or a girl in a given culture is also a vital part of a child's task. Researchers have studied this in two ways—by asking children what boys and girls (or men and women) like to do and what they are like (an inquiry about gender stereotypes) and by asking children if it is okay for boys to play with dolls or girls to climb trees or do equivalent cross-sex things (an inquiry about roles).

When young children play "dress up," they reveal how much they already know about the expectations that go along with their culture's gender roles..

In every culture, adults have clear gender stereotypes. Indeed, the content of those stereotypes is remarkably similar in cultures around the world. Psychologists who have studied gender stereotypes in many different countries, including non-Western countries such as Thailand, Pakistan, and Nigeria, find that the most clearly stereotyped traits are weakness, gentleness, appreciativeness, and soft-heartedness for women and aggression, strength, cruelty, and coarseness for men (Williams & Best, 1990). In most cultures, men are also seen as competent, skillful, assertive, and able to get things done, while women are seen as warm and expressive, tactful, quiet, gentle, aware of others' feelings, and lacking in competence, independence, and logic (Williams & Best, 1990).

Studies of children show that these stereotyped ideas develop early. It would not be uncommon to hear a 3-year-old in the United States say "Mommies use the stove, and Daddies use the grill." A 4-year-old might define gender roles in terms of competencies: "Daddies are better at fixing things, but Mommies are better at tying bows and decorating." Even 2-year-olds in the United States already associate certain tasks and possessions with men and women, such as vacuum cleaners and food with women and cars and tools with men. By age 3 or 4, children can assign stereotypic occupations, toys, and activities to each gender. By age 5, children begin to associate certain personality traits, such as assertiveness and nurturance, with males or females (Martin, 1993; Serbin, Powlishta, & Gulko, 1993).

Studies of children's ideas about how men and women (or boys and girls) ought to behave add an interesting further element. For example, in an early study, a psychologist told a story to children aged 4–9 about a little boy named George who liked to play with dolls (Damon, 1977). George's parents told him that only little girls play with dolls; little boys shouldn't. The children were then asked questions about the story, such as "Why do people tell George not to play with dolls?" or "Is there a rule that boys shouldn't play with dolls?"

Four-year-olds in this study thought it was okay for George to play with dolls. There was no rule against it and he should do it if he wanted to. Six-year-olds, in contrast, thought it was wrong for George to play with dolls. By about age 9, children had differentiated between what boys and girls usually do and what is "wrong." One boy said, for example, that breaking windows was wrong and bad, but that playing with dolls was not bad in the same way: "Breaking

As gender develops, children change their views about whether it is acceptable for boys to play with dolls or for girls to play sports such as baseball.

THE WHOLE CHILD IN FOCUS

In what way is sex-role knowledge evident in Madeleine's behavior at 6 years old? Find out on page 283.

windows you're not supposed to do. And if you play with dolls, well, you can, but boys usually don't."

What this study appeared to reveal is that a 5- to 6-year-old, having figured out that gender is permanent, is searching for a rule about how boys and girls behave (Martin & Halverson, 1981). The child picks up information from watching adults, from television, from listening to the labels that are attached to different activities (e.g., "Boys don't cry"). Initially, children treat these as absolute, moral rules. Later, they understand that these are social conventions; at this point, gender concepts become more flexible and stereotyping declines somewhat (Katz & Ksansnak, 1994).

Learning Objective 9.8

How is the behavior of young children sex-typed?

Sex-Typed Behavior

The final element in the development of gender is the actual behavior children show with those of the same and the opposite sex. An unexpected finding is that **sex-typed behavior**, or different patterns of behavior among girls and boys, develops earlier than ideas about gender (Campbell, Shirley, & Candy, 2004). By 18–24 months, children begin to show some preference for sex-stereotyped toys, such as dolls for girls or trucks or building blocks for boys, which is some months before they can consistently identify their own gender (Campbell, Shirley, & Caygill, 2002; O'Brien, 1992; Serbin, Poulin-Dubois, Colbourne, Sen, & Eichstedt, 2001). By age 3, children begin to show a preference for same-sex friends and are much more sociable with playmates of the same sex—at a time when they do not yet have a concept of gender stability (Corsaro, Molinari, Hadley, & Sugioka, 2003; Maccoby, 1988, 1990; Maccoby & Jacklin, 1987) (see Figure 9.3).

sex-typed behavior different patterns of behavior exhibited by boys and girls

Not only are preschoolers' friendships and peer interactions increasingly sex-segregated; it is also clear that boy-boy interactions and girl-girl interactions differ in quality, even in these

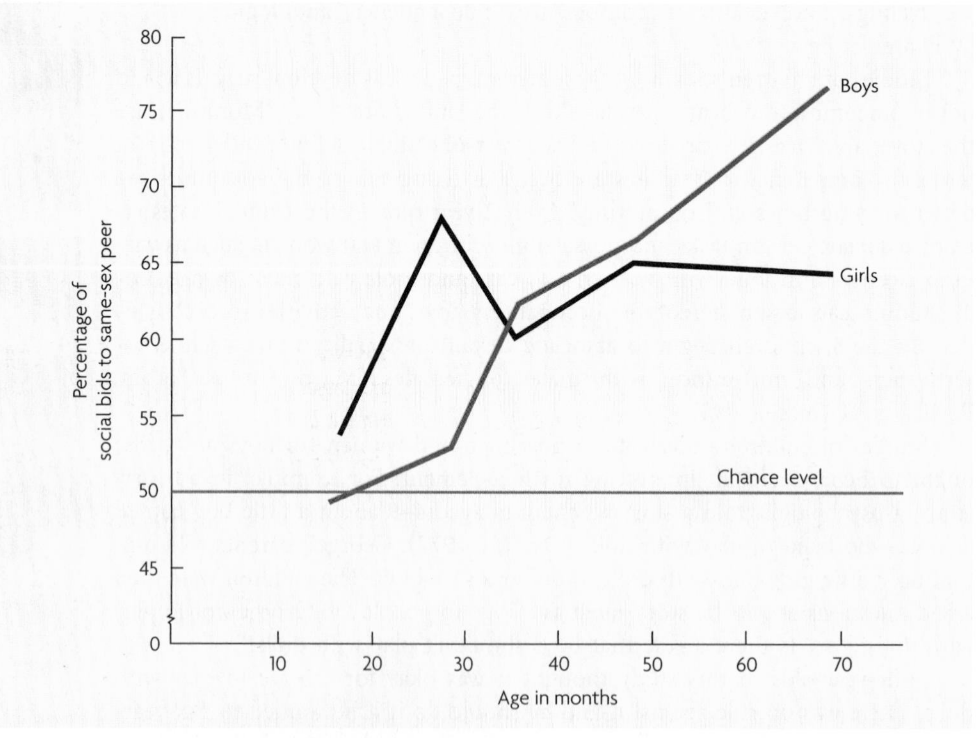

Figure 9.3 Gender and Playmate Preferences

In one classic study of playmate preferences, researchers counted how often preschool children played with same-sex and opposite-sex playmates. Children as young as 2 ½ already showed at least some preference for same-sex playmates.

(*Source*: Adaptation from *Child Development* by P. La Freniere, F. Strayer, & R. Gauthier. Figure 1, p. 1961, 1984. Reprinted by permission.)

early years. One important part of same-sex interactions seems to involve instruction in and modeling of sex-appropriate behavior. In other words, older boys teach younger boys how to be "masculine," and older girls teach younger girls how to be "feminine" (Danby & Baker, 1998).

However, these "lessons" in sex-typed behavior are fairly subtle. Eleanor Maccoby, one of the leading theorists in this area, describes the girls' pattern as an *enabling style* (Maccoby, 1990). Enabling includes such behaviors as supporting the friend, expressing agreement, and making suggestions. All these behaviors tend to foster a greater equality and intimacy in the relationship and keep the interaction going. In contrast, boys are more likely to show what Maccoby calls a *constricting*, or *restrictive*, *style*: "A restrictive style is one that tends to derail the interaction—to inhibit the partner or cause the partner to withdraw, thus shortening the interaction or bringing it to an end" (1990, p. 517). Contradicting, interrupting, boasting, and other forms of self-display are all aspects of this style. Rough-and-tumble play and play-fighting are other manifestations of boys' restrictive interaction style.

These two patterns begin to be visible in the preschool years. For example, beginning as early as age 3, boys and girls use quite different strategies in their attempts to influence each other's behavior (Maccoby, 1990). Girls generally ask questions or make requests; boys are much more likely to make demands or phrase things using imperatives ("Give me that!"). The really intriguing finding is that even at this early age, boys simply don't respond to the girls' enabling style. Thus, playing with boys yields little positive reinforcement for girls, and they begin to avoid such interactions and band together.

cross-gender behavior behavior that is atypical for one's own sex but typical for the opposite sex

Another kind of learning opportunity happens when children exhibit **cross-gender behavior**, behavior that is atypical in their culture for their gender. For example, *tomboyishness*, girls' preference for activities that are more typical for boys, is a kind of cross-gender behavior. Generally, tomboyishness is tolerated by adults and peers (Sandnabba & Ahlberg, 1999). Not surprisingly, then, cross-gender behavior is far more common among girls than boys (Etaugh & Liss, 1992). Tomboyishness does not appear to interfere with the development of a "feminine" personality in adulthood, and it may allow girls to acquire positive characteristics such as assertiveness (Burn, O'Neil, & Nederend, 1996).

In contrast, both peers and adults actively discourage boys from engaging in cross-gender behavior. Specifically, boys who play with dolls or behave in an effeminate manner are likely to elicit expressions of disapproval—or even ridicule—from children, parents, and teachers (Martin, 1991). Many adults' reactions to boys' cross-gender behavior appear to be related to the fear that it may lead to homosexuality (Sandnabba & Ahlberg, 1999).

However, it cannot be assumed that the prevalence of sex-typed play among boys is strictly the result of adult and peer influence. For one thing, sex-typed play preferences appear earlier and are more consistent in male infants, which suggests that these preferences begin to develop before environmental forces have had much chance to influence them (Blakemore, LaRue, & Olejnik, 1979). Further, by age 3, boys are likely to show an actual aversion to girls' activities—for example, by saying "yuck" when experimenters offer them toys like dolls (Bussey & Bandura, 1992). In addition, boys may prefer the

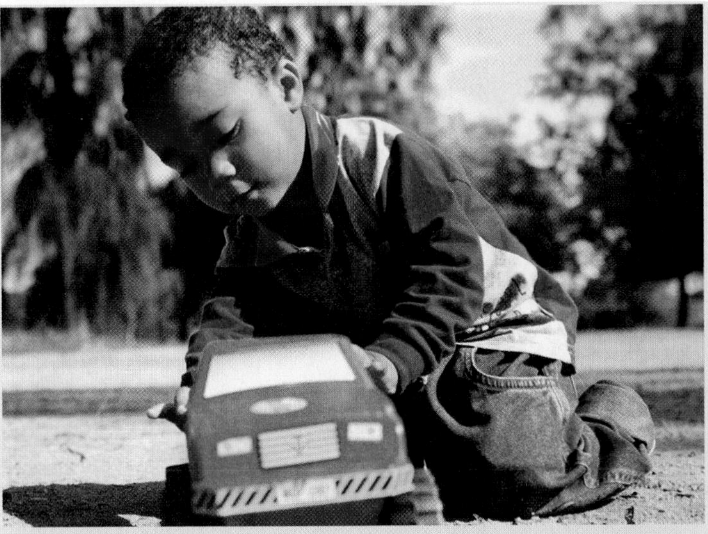

Play may provide children with opportunities to learn about gender expectations.

company of a girl who is a tomboy to that of a boy who engages in cross-gender activity (Alexander & Hines, 1994). Finally, researchers have found that it is very difficult to change boys' play preferences with modeling and reinforcement (Paley, 1986; Weisner & Wilson-Mitchell, 1990). These findings suggest that, at least for boys, sex-typed behavior is part of a complex process of identity development and not just the result of cultural modeling and reinforcement.

Family Relationships and Structure

Psychologists agree that family relationships constitute one of the most influential factors—if not the most influential factor—in early childhood development. These relationships reflect both continuity and change. The preschooler is no less attached to her family than the infant but, at the same time, is struggling to establish independence.

Learning Objective 9.9

How does attachment change during the early childhood years?

Attachment

You may remember from Chapter 6 that by 12 months of age, a baby has normally established a clear attachment to at least one caregiver. By age 2 or 3, the attachment is just as strong, but many attachment behaviors have become less visible. Three-year-olds still want to sit on Mom's or Dad's lap; they are still likely to seek some closeness when Mom returns from an absence. But when she is not afraid or under stress, a 3-year-old is able to wander farther and farther from her safe base without apparent distress. She can also deal with her potential anxiety due to separation by creating shared plans with the parents. For example, a parent might say "I'll be home after your naptime," to which the child may respond "Can we watch a movie then?" (Crittenden, 1992).

Off he goes, into greater independence. A child this age, especially one with secure attachment, is far more confident about being at a distance from his safe base.

Attachment quality also predicts behavior during the preschool years. Children who are securely attached to parents experience fewer behavior problems. Specifically, those who are insecurely attached display more anger and aggression toward both peers and adults in social settings such as child care and preschool (DeMulder, Denham, Schmidt, & Mitchell, 2000; Schmidt, DeMulder, & Denham, 2002).

For most children, the attachment relationship, whether secure or not, seems to change at about age 4. Bowlby, whose research was introduced in Chapter 6, described this new stage, or level, as a *goal-corrected partnership*. Just as the first attachment probably requires the baby to understand that his mother will continue to exist when she isn't there, so the preschooler grasps that the *relationship* continues to exist even when the partners are apart. Also at about age 4, the child's internal model of attachment appears to generalize. Bowlby argued that the child's model becomes less a specific property of an individual relationship and more a general property of all the child's social relationships. Thus, it's not surprising that 4- and 5-year-olds who are securely attached to their parents are more likely than their insecurely attached peers to have positive relationships with their preschool teachers (DeMulder et al., 2000).

At the same time, advances in the internal working model lead to new conflicts. In contrast to infants, 2-year-olds realize that they are independent contributors to the parent-child relationship. This heightened sense of autonomy brings them into more and more situations in which parents want one thing and children another. However, contrary to popular stereotypes, 2-year-olds actually comply with parents' requests more often than not. They are more likely to comply with safety requests ("Don't touch that; it's hot!") or with prohibitions about care of objects ("Don't tear up the book") than they are with requests to delay ("I can't talk to you now, I'm on the phone") or with instructions about self-care ("Please wash your hands now"). On the whole, however, children of this age comply fairly readily (Gralinski & Kopp, 1993). When they resist, it is most likely to be passive resistance—simply not doing what is asked rather than saying "no."

Parenting Styles

Learning Objective 9.10

How do parenting styles affect children's development?

Earlier we discussed the fact that temperamental differences lead children to respond differently to situations. Parents differ in temperament themselves, so, just like their children, they vary in how they respond to situations. Consider the situation in which a child resists going to bed, for example. One parent takes the nightly going-to-bed battle in stride and calmly insists that the child go to bed, even when she throws a temper tantrum. Another parent responds to the child's emotional escalation by increasing the emotional intensity of his demands, leading to all-out warfare in which the parent assures his own victory by exploiting the physical, social, and emotional control he has over the child. Yet another parent may respond permissively and allow the child to go to bed whenever she wants to. Researchers call these differences **parenting styles**—the characteristic strategies that parents use to manage children's behavior.

Of course, families vary in their responses to preschoolers' increasing demands for independence. Psychologists have struggled over the years to identify the best ways of defining parenting style. At present, the most fruitful conceptualization is one offered by developmentalist Diana Baumrind, who focuses on four aspects of family functioning: (1) warmth or nurturance, (2) clarity and consistency of rules, (3) level of expectations, which she describes in terms of "maturity demands," and (4) communication between parent and child (Baumrind, 1972). Each of these four dimensions has been independently shown to be related to various child behaviors. Children with nurturant and warm parents are more securely attached in the first 2 years of life than those with more rejecting parents; they also have higher self-esteem and are more empathetic and more responsive to others' hurts or distress; they have higher IQs, are more compliant in preschool and elementary school, do better in school, and are less likely to show delinquent behavior in adolescence or criminal behavior in adulthood (Maccoby, 1980; Maughan, Pickles, & Quinton, 1995; Simons, Robertson, & Downs, 1989; Stormshak et al., 2000).

High levels of affection can even buffer a child against the negative effects of otherwise disadvantageous environments. Several studies of children and teens growing up in poor, tough neighborhoods show that parental warmth is associated with both social and academic competence (Masten & Coatsworth, 1998). In contrast, parental hostility is linked to declining school performance and higher risk of delinquency among poor children and adolescents (Melby & Conger, 1996).

The degree and clarity of the parents' control over the child are also significant. Parents with clear rules, consistently applied, have children who are much less likely to be defiant or noncompliant. Such children are also more competent and sure of themselves and less aggressive (Kurdek & Fine, 1994; Patterson, 1980).

Equally important is the form of control the parents use. The optimal outcomes for the child occur when the parents are not overly restrictive, explain things to the child, and avoid the use of physical punishments. Children whose parents have high expectations (high "maturity demands," in Baumrind's language) also fare better. Such children have higher self-esteem and show more generosity toward others.

Finally, open and regular communication between parent and child has been linked to more positive outcomes. Listening to a child is as important as talking to him. Ideally, parents need to convey to the child that what the child has to say is worth listening to, that his ideas are important and should be considered in family decisions. Children of such parents have been found to be more emotionally and socially mature (Baumrind, 1971; Bell & Bell, 1982).

parenting styles the characteristic strategies that parents use to manage children's behavior

Although each of these characteristics of families may be significant individually, they do not occur in isolation but in combinations and patterns. In her early research, Baumrind

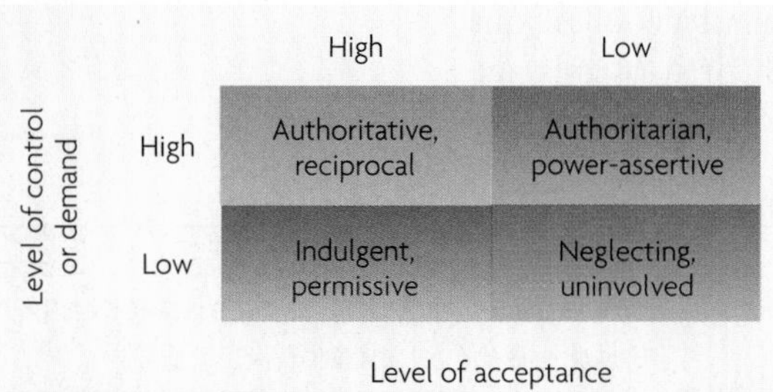

Figure 9.4
Control, Acceptance, and Parenting Style

Maccoby and Martin expanded on Baumrind's categories in this two-dimensional category system.

(*Source*: Adapted from E. E. Maccoby and J. A. Martin, 1983. "Socialization in the context of the family: Parent-child interaction." In E. M. Hetherington (Ed.), *Handbook of Child Psychology*, Fig. 2, p. 39. Reprinted by permission of John Wiley & Sons, Inc.)

identified three patterns, or styles, of parenting (Baumrind, 1967). The **permissive parenting style** is high in nurturance but low in maturity demands, control, and communication. The **authoritarian parenting style** is high in control and maturity demands but low in nurturance and communication. The **authoritative parenting style** is high in all four dimensions.

Eleanor Maccoby and John Martin have proposed a variation of Baumrind's category system, shown in Figure 9.4 (Maccoby & Martin, 1983). They categorize families on two dimensions: the degree of demand or control and the amount of acceptance versus rejection. The intersection of these two dimensions creates four types, three of which correspond quite closely to Baumrind's authoritarian, authoritative, and permissive types. Maccoby and Martin's conceptualization adds a fourth type, the **uninvolved parenting style**.

The Authoritarian Type The parent who responds to a child's refusal to go to bed by asserting physical, social, and emotional control over the child is exhibiting the authoritarian style. Children growing up in authoritarian families—with high levels of demand and control but relatively low levels of warmth and communication—do less well in school, have lower self-esteem, and are typically less skilled with peers than children from other types of families. Some of these children appear subdued; others may show high aggressiveness or other indications of being out of control. These effects are not restricted to preschool-aged children. In a series of large studies of high school students, including longitudinal studies of more than 6,000 teens, developmentalists found that teenagers from authoritarian families had poorer grades in school and more negative self-concepts than did teenagers from authoritative families, a finding that has been replicated in more recent cohorts of teens (Steinberg, Fletcher, & Darling, 1994; Steinberg, Blatt-Eisengart, & Cauffman, 2006).

The Permissive Type The permissive type of parent responds to a child's refusal to go to bed by allowing the child to go to bed whenever she wants to. Children growing up with indulgent or permissive parents also show some negative outcomes. Researchers have found that these children do slightly worse in school during adolescence and are likely to be both more aggressive (particularly if the parents are specifically permissive toward aggressiveness) and somewhat immature in their behavior with peers and in school. They are less likely to take responsibility and are less independent (Teti & Candelaria, 2002).

The Authoritative Type Authoritative parents respond to undesirable behaviors such as a child's refusal to go to bed by firmly sticking to their demands without resorting to asserting their power over the child. The most consistently positive outcomes have been associated with an authoritative pattern in which the parents are high in both control and acceptance—setting clear limits but also responding to the child's individual needs. Children reared in such families typically show higher self-esteem and are more independent, but are also more likely to comply with parental requests and may show more altruistic behavior as well. They are self-confident and achievement-oriented in school and get better grades than do children whose parents have other parenting styles (Crockenberg & Litman, 1990; Dornbusch, Ritter, Liederman, Roberts, & Fraleigh, 1987; Steinberg, Elmen, & Mounts, 1989).

The Uninvolved Type Uninvolved parents do not bother to set bedtimes for children or even to tell them to go to bed. They appear to be totally indifferent to children's behavior and to the responsibilities of parenting. The most consistently negative outcomes are associated with this fourth pattern: the uninvolved, or neglecting, parenting style. You may remember from the discussion of secure and insecure attachments in Chapter 6 that one of the family characteristics often found in infants rated as insecure/avoidant is the "emotional unavailability" of the mother. The mother may be depressed or may be overwhelmed by other problems in her life and may simply not have made any deep emotional connection with the child. Likewise, a parent may be distracted from parenting by more attractive activities. Whatever the reason, such children continue to show disturbances in their social relationships for

permissive parenting style a style of parenting that is high in nurturance but low in maturity demands, control, and communication

authoritarian parenting style a style of parenting that is high in control and maturity demands but low in nurturance and communication

authoritative parenting style a style of parenting that is high in nurturance, maturity demands, control, and communication

uninvolved parenting style a style of parenting that is low in nurturance, maturity demands, control, and communication

many years. In adolescence, for example, youngsters from neglecting families are more impulsive and antisocial, less competent with their peers, and much less achievement-oriented in school (Block, 1971; Lamborn, Mounts, Steinberg, & Dornbusch, 1991; Pulkkinen, 1982).

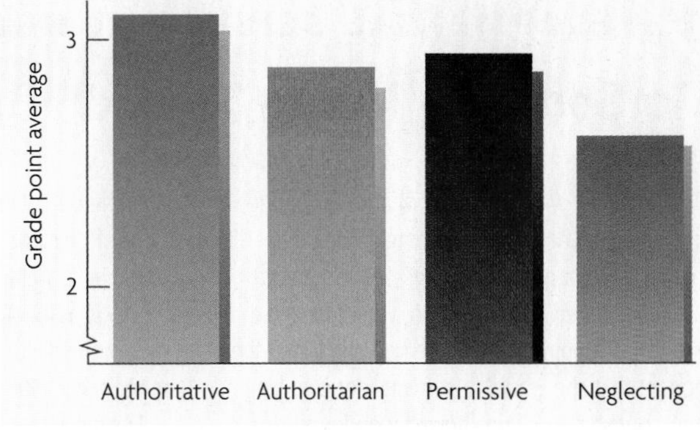

Figure 9.5 Parenting Style and Grades

Grades varied with parenting style in Steinberg and Dornbusch's study. (*Source*: Steinberg et al., 1994, from Table 5, p. 762.)

Effects of Parenting Styles Figure 9.5 illustrates the contrasting outcomes in the longitudinal study of adolescents you read about a few paragraphs back; it graphs variations in grade point average as a function of family style. In a longitudinal analysis, these same researchers found that students who described their parents as most authoritative at the beginning of the study showed more improvement in academic competence and self-reliance and the smallest increases in psychological symptoms and delinquent behavior over the succeeding 2 years. So these effects persist.

However, the effects of the family system are more complex than the figure shows. For example, authoritative parents are much more likely to be involved with their child's school, attending school functions and talking to teachers, and this involvement seems to play a crucial role in their children's better school performance. When an authoritative parent is not involved with the school, the academic outcome for the student is not so clearly positive. Similarly, the outcome for a teenager whose parent is highly involved with the school but is not authoritative is likely to be less than optimal. It is the combination of authoritativeness and school involvement that is associated with the best results (Steinberg, Lamborn, Dornbusch, & Darling, 1992).

Another set of complexities is evident in the interaction between parenting style and child temperament. For example, authoritative parents often use **inductive discipline**, a discipline strategy in which parents explain to children why a punished behavior is wrong (Hoffman, 1970). Inductive discipline helps most preschoolers gain control of their behavior and learn to look at situations from perspectives other than their own. Likewise, the majority of preschool-aged children of parents who respond to demonstrations of poor self-control, such as temper tantrums, by asserting their social and physical power—as often happens when parents physically punish children—have poorer self-control than do preschoolers whose parents use inductive discipline (Houck & Lecuyer-Maus, 2004; Kochanska, 1997b; Kochanska, Murray, Jacques, Koenig, & Vandegeest, 1996). For this and other reasons, most developmentalists are opposed to physical punishment, as discussed in the *Developmental Science at Home* feature on page 266.

However, research on inductive discipline suggests that it is not equally effective for all children. Those who have difficult temperaments or who are physically active and seem to enjoy risk taking—such as children who like to climb on top of furniture and jump off—seem to have a greater need for firm discipline and to benefit less from inductive discipline than do their peers whose temperamental make-up is different (Kochanska, 1997a). In fact, assumptions about the superiority of inductive discipline, as well as authoritative parenting in general, have been criticized by developmentalists who claim that correlations between discipline strategy and child behavior may arise simply because parents adapt their techniques to their children's behavior. Thus, parents of poorly behaved children may be more punitive or authoritarian because they have discovered that this is the kind of parenting their children need.

inductive discipline a discipline strategy in which parents explain to children why a punished behavior is wrong

Ethnicity, Socioeconomic Status, and Parenting Styles

Learning Objective 9.11

How are ethnicity and socioeconomic status related to parenting style?

Ethnicity and socioeconomic variables also interact with parenting styles. In an important, large-scale, cross-sectional study involving roughly 10,000 9th- through 12th-grade students representing four ethnic groups (White, African

DEVELOPMENTAL SCIENCE AT HOME

To Spank or Not to Spank?

Marie is at her wits' end as to what to do about her 4-year-old daughter's whining. "What that child needs is a good spanking," Marie's grandmother declared one afternoon, while the three were out shopping. Before she had children, Marie thought that she would never consider spanking them, but she now finds herself wondering whether her grandmother is right. Is Marie right to be reluctant to spank her daughter?

Surveys show that most parents believe that spanking can be an effective form of discipline if it is used sparingly and is reserved for situations in which all other disciplinary strategies have failed to achieve the desired result (Barkin, Scheindlin, Ip, Richardson, & Finch, 2007). In the short term, spanking usually does get a child to stop an undesirable behavior and temporarily reduces the likelihood that the child will repeat it (Gershoff, 2002). In the long term, however, the effects of spanking are clearly negative (American Academy of Pediatrics, 1998). Research indicates that spanking (1) models infliction of pain as a means of getting others to do what you want them to do, (2) associates the parent who spanks with the child's experience of physical pain, (3) leads to a family climate that is characterized by emotional rejection, and (4) is associated with higher levels of aggression among children who are spanked than among those who are not spanked.

For these reasons, developmentalists recommend that spanking, if it is used at all, be reserved for behaviors that are potentially harmful to the child or others (Namka, 2002). In addition, spanking, like other forms of punishment, should always be accompanied by an explanation of why the child was punished and an assurance that she is loved. Finally, experts agree that physical punishment should never under any circumstances be used to discipline children younger than 2 years of age (DYG Inc., 2004).

Thinking back to the question posed at the outset of this discussion, we must conclude that Marie's reservations about spanking her daughter are on target. Moreover, although Marie's grandmother recommended spanking, she probably told her own children, "If you don't stop whining, I won't let you watch TV" before she started searching for a paddle. Unbeknownst to Marie, her grandmother, like generations of parents before her, probably used an everyday variation of a behavior management technique that psychologists call the Premack principle after researcher David Premack, who demonstrated its effectiveness in a classic series of studies with primates and children (Premack, 1959). Thus, parents who employ the Premack principle instead of resorting to spanking can be assured of the support of grandmothers and psychologists alike.

Questions for Reflection

1. Look back at the operant conditioning principle of extinction in Chapter 2. How might it be used to diminish Marie's daughter's whining?
2. In what ways does having been spanked as a child influence an adult's views about the acceptability of spanking as a form of discipline?

American, Hispanic American, and Asian American), students answered questions about the acceptance, control, and autonomy they received from their parents (Steinberg, Mounts, Lamborn, & Dornbusch, 1991). When an adolescent described his family as above the average on all three dimensions, the family was classed as authoritative. Figure 9.6 shows the percentages of families that were classed in this way in the four ethnic groups, broken down further by the social class and intactness of the family.

You can see that the authoritative pattern was most common among White families and least common among Asian Americans, but in each ethnic group authoritative parenting was more common among the middle class and (with one exception) intact families than among single-parent or step-parent families. Furthermore, these researchers found some relationship between authoritative parenting and positive outcomes in all ethnic groups. In all four groups, for example, teenagers from authoritative families showed more self-reliance and less delinquency than did those from nonauthoritative families. However, this study, like others, found strong links between authoritative parenting style and positive outcomes only for Whites and Hispanic Americans. For Asian Americans and African Americans, the researchers found stronger connections between authoritarian style and variables such as school performance and social competence.

Studies in which children provide information about their parents' style as well as those in which researchers conduct direct observation of parents have consistently found that, in general, Asian American parents display an authoritarian style (Chao, 1994; Wang & Phinney, 1998). The finding that Asian American children score higher than their White counterparts on almost all measures of cognitive competence argues against the assumption that authoritative parenting is best. In fact, developmentalists have found a link between Asian American children's achievement and authoritarian parenting—that is, parents who have the most authoritarian parenting style have the highest-scoring children (Wang & Phinney, 1998). Similarly, authoritarian parenting has been shown to reduce the likelihood of substance abuse in both White and African American children (Broman, Reckase, & Freedman-Doan, 2006).

However, the key variable in these findings may not be ethnicity. Many studies have shown that parenting styles are grounded in parenting goals (e.g., Cheay & Rubin, 2004). Parenting goals are influenced by cultural values and by the immediate context in which parents are raising children. Consequently, it's important to know that many Asian American participants in studies comparing their parenting behaviors to those of European Americans have been recent immigrants to the United States. Thus, Asian American parents may be authoritarian in response to living in an environment that is different from the one in which they grew up, not because they are Asian. Authoritarian parenting may help them achieve two important goals: to help their children succeed economically and to enable them to maintain a sense of ethnic identity. Evidence supporting this interpretation also comes from studies of families that have emigrated to Israel, France, and Norway (Camilleri & Malewska-Peyre, 1997; Javo, Ronning, Heyerdahl, & Rudmin, 2004; Roer-Strier & Rivlis, 1998).

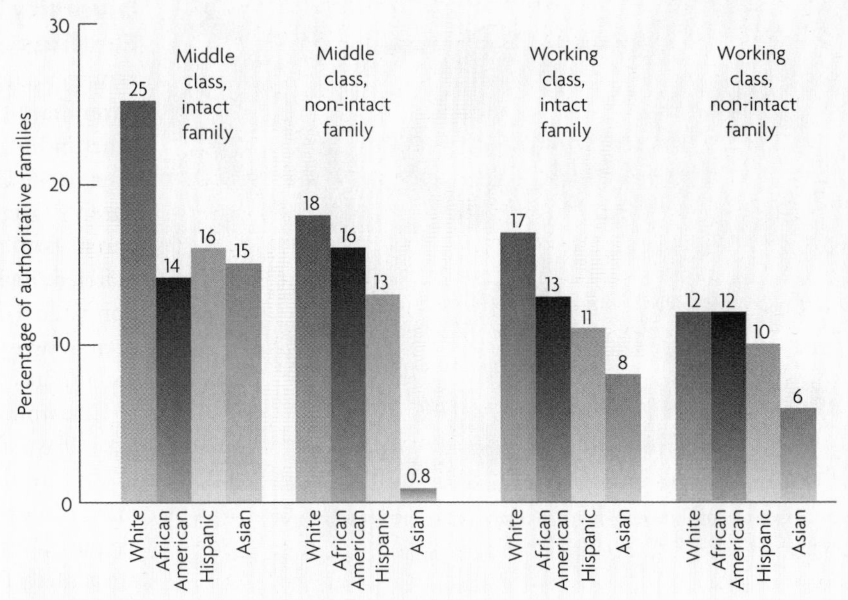

Figure 9.6 **Social Class, Ethnicity, and Parenting Style**

As this figure suggests, authoritative parenting is more common among middle-class parents as well as intact families (in which the child lives with both natural parents) of all ethnicities.

(*Source*: Steinberg et al., 1991.)

The same link between parenting goals and parenting style may help explain the greater incidence of authoritarian behavior on the part of African American parents. Specifically, African American parents are keenly aware of the degree to which social forces, such as racism, may impede their children's achievement of educational, economic, and social success. Consequently, they may adopt an authoritarian style because they believe it will enhance their children's potential for success. In fact, the correlation between authoritarian parenting and variables such as self-control among African American children suggests that they may be right (Baumrind, 1980; Broman, Reckase, & Freedman-Doan, 2006).

Another reason authoritarian parenting may be more common in African American families is that they are more likely to be poor. As Figure 9.6 shows, authoritative parenting is generally less common among working-class parents than among middle-class parents in all four major U.S. ethnic groups. It seems likely that the reason for this pattern is similar to the one mentioned above for African Americans—that is, working-class parents believe authoritarian parenting will help their children attain important goals.

Family Structure

Learning Objective 9.12

How is family structure related to children's development?

Although the two-parent family continues to be the dominant structure in the United States, the number of single-parent households has been increasing. In 1970, almost 95% of children lived in two-parent families, but by 2000, only 76% of children were living in such homes (U.S. Census Bureau, 2003a). Moreover, the proportion of single-parent families in the United States far exceeds that in other industrialized countries. For example, in Korea, Japan, and other Asian nations, only 4–8% of children live with a single parent (Martin, 1995).

Some "two-parent" households in the United States are actually those in which a child is being raised by her grandparents.

Diversity in Two-Parent and Single-Parent Families Though still the most common living arrangement for children in the United States, the two-parent family is far more diverse than in the past or in other industrialized nations. Only about half of all children in the United States live with both their biological parents (Hernandez, 1997). From 20% to 30% of two-parent families were created when a divorced or never-married single parent married another single parent or a nonparent (Ganong & Coleman, 1994). Thus, many children in two-parent households have experienced single-parenting at one time or another while growing up.

It's important to keep in mind that any set of statistics is like a snapshot of a single moment in time—it fails to capture the number of changes in family structure many children experience across their early years. For example, in some two-parent households, the "parents" are actually the child's grandparents. In most cases, custodial grandparents are caring for the children of a daughter who has some kind of significant problem, such as criminal behavior or substance abuse (Jendrek, 1993). These children are likely to have experienced a variety of living arrangements before coming to live with their grandparents. Likewise, many married parents once were single parents who had relationships with one or more live-in partners.

Single-parent households are diverse as well. In contrast to stereotypes, some single parents are very financially secure. In fact, beginning in the early 1990s, the proportion of births to single mothers increased most rapidly among middle-class professional women who actively decided to become single parents (Ingrassia, 1993). Other single parents, especially unmarried teenagers, are likely to live with their own parents (Jorgenson, 1993). Consequently, single-parent households are no more alike than are two-parent households.

Family Structure and Ethnicity Looking at family structure across ethnic groups further illustrates family diversity in the United States. You can get some feeling for the degree of variation from Figure 9.7. The figure shows estimates of the percentages of various

Figure 9.7
Ethnicity and Family Structure

Household types for U.S. children under 18 years of age.

(*Source*: U.S. Census Bureau, 2003b.)

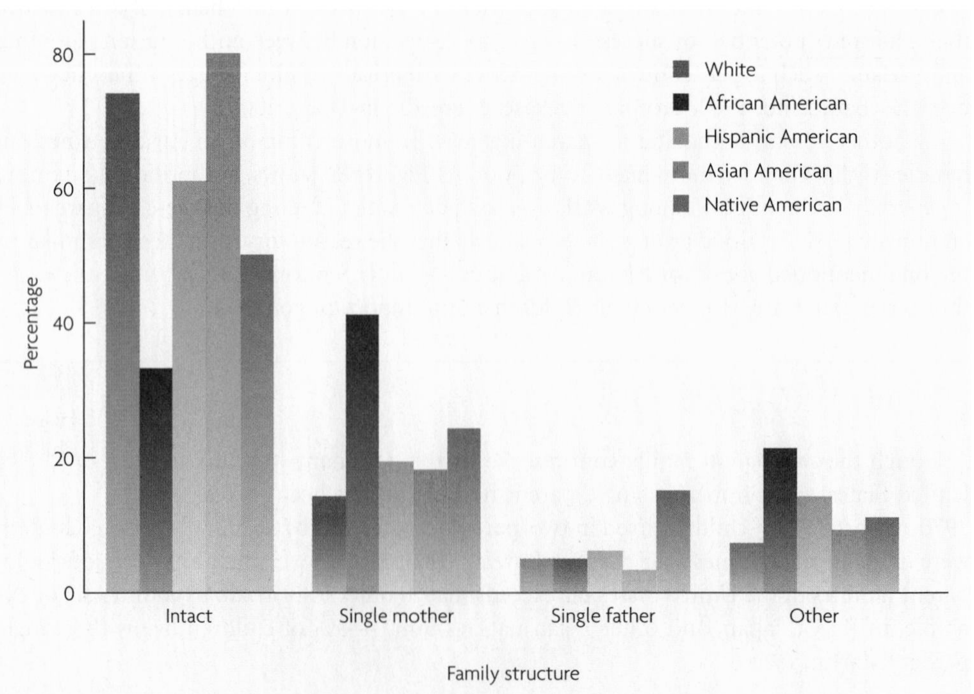

family types among White, African American, Asian American, Native American, and Hispanic American children in the United States.

You can see that single-parent families are far more common among African Americans and Native Americans than among other groups. A difference in the proportion of births to unmarried women is one contributing factor. As Figure 9.8 shows, births to single women have increased rather dramatically across all racial and ethnic groups in the United States in the past few decades. However, the rates of such births are much higher among African American and Native American women than in other groups. (By the way, in all groups, more than three-quarters of single women giving birth are over the age of 20. Thus, teenage pregnancy contributes very little to the statistics on single motherhood.)

A second factor is that, although many African American and Native American single mothers eventually marry, adults in these groups—whether parents or not—are less likely to marry. Approximately 37% of African American adults and 27% of Native American adults have never been married. Among Whites, only 18% remain single throughout their lives (U.S. Census Bureau, 1998).

Of course, statistics can't explain why African American and Native American families are more likely than those of other groups to be headed by single parents. Sociologists speculate that, in the case of African Americans, lack of economic opportunities for men renders them less able to take on family responsibilities (Cherlin, 1992). Others add that grandparents and other relatives in both groups traditionally help support single mothers. For instance, among Native Americans, a traditional cultural value sociologists call *kin orientation* views parenting as the responsibility of a child's entire family, including grandparents and aunts and uncles. As a result, Native American single parents, especially those who live in predominantly Native American communities, receive more material and emotional support than do single parents in other groups and may feel less pressure to marry (Ambert, 2001).

Other Types of Family Structures In contrast to the amount of research comparing two-parent and single-parent families, there are relatively few studies of the effects of other kinds of family structures. For example, research on custodial grandparenting tends to focus on the effects of the parenting experience on aging adults. Consequently, researchers know that grandparents' responses to children's problems are quite similar to those of

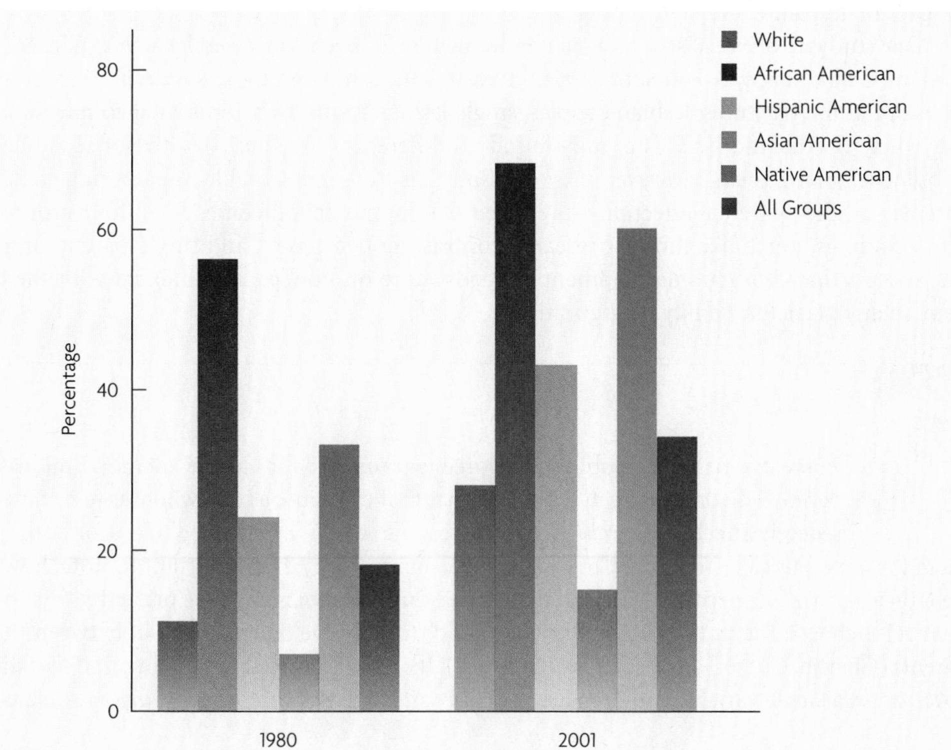

Figure 9.8
Ethnicity and Births to Unmarried Women

Percentage of births to unmarried women across racial/ethnic groups in the United States. The rate of births to unmarried women has increased across all groups in the United States over recent decades. These statistics are one reason for the growing number of school-aged and teenaged children who live in single-parent homes.

(*Source*: National Center for Health Statistics (NCHS), 2003.)

Most gay and lesbian parents are raising children who were conceived in prior heterosexual relationships. However, a growing number of couples are choosing to be parents through artificial insemination or adoption. Research suggests that the variables that contribute to effective parenting and positive developmental outcomes for children are the same regardless of the sexual orientation of a child's parents.

parents (Daly & Glenwick, 2000). However, the stresses of parenting combined with the physical effects of aging are likely to cause older adults to feel more anxious and depressed than younger adults in similar situations (Burton, 1992; Jendrek, 1993). Thus, developmentalists know something about how parenting affects older adults but very little about how children raised by grandparents fare.

Similarly, concerns about children's sex-role identity and sexual orientation have dominated research on gay and lesbian parenting (Bailey, Brobow, Wolfe, & Mikach, 1995). Studies have generally shown that children raised by gay and lesbian parents develop sex-role identities in the same way as children of heterosexual parents. They are also just as likely to be heterosexual (Golombok & Tasker, 1996).

To help answer general questions about cognitive and social development among the children of gay and lesbian parents, researchers have conducted comprehensive reviews of the small number of studies that have been done. Such reviews have examined a wide variety of studies of gay and lesbian parenting, including case studies, correlational studies, and comparisons of children in gay and lesbian families to those being raised by heterosexual parents. These reviews have typically found that the majority of studies suggest that children raised by gay and lesbian parents do not differ from those raised by heterosexuals (Fitzgerald, 1999; Patterson, 2006). However, most of the gay and lesbian participants in these studies have been raising their own biological children, who were conceived while the parents were involved in heterosexual relationships. Very few studies have involved children raised exclusively by openly gay or lesbian parents, and fewer still have compared children of gay or lesbian parents with partners to those raised by single gays or lesbians.

One study involved 80 school-aged children who had been conceived by artificial insemination (Chan, Raboy, & Patterson, 1998). Researchers compared these children across four types of family structures: lesbian couples, single lesbian mothers, heterosexual couples, and single heterosexual mothers. The study found no differences in either cognitive or social development among them. However, they did find that the same variables—parenting stress, parental conflict, parental affection—predicted developmental outcomes in all four groups. These findings, much like those of research contrasting two-parent and single-parent families, suggest that children's development depends more on how parents interact with them than on any particular family configuration.

Learning Objective 9.13

How does divorce affect children's behavior in early childhood and in later years?

Divorce

There can be little doubt that divorce is traumatic for children. Among infants, parental divorce is one of many traumas that can cause a baby who was previously securely attached to both parents to become insecurely attached to one or both of them (Waters, Merrick, Treboux, Crowell, & Albersheim, 2003). It's important to note, however, that some of the negative effects of divorce are due to factors that were present *before* the divorce, such as difficult temperament in the child or excessive marital conflict between the parents (Cherlin, Chase-Lansdale, & McRae, 1998). It's also important to keep in mind that divorce is not a single variable; children are probably affected by a multitude of divorce-related factors—parental conflict, poverty, disruptions of daily routine, involvement of the noncustodial parent, and so on (Bailey & Zvonkovic, 2003). For this reason, children whose parents separate or stay in conflict-ridden marriages may experience many of the same effects as children whose parents actually divorce (Ingoldsby, Shaw, Owens, & Winslow, 1999).

In the first few years after a divorce, children typically exhibit declines in school performance and show more aggressive, defiant, negative, or depressed behavior (Green, Anderson, Doyle, & Ridelbach, 2006). By adolescence, the children of divorced parents are more likely than their peers to engage in criminal behavior (Price & Kunz, 2003). Children living in stepparent families also have higher rates of delinquency, more behavior problems in school, and lower grades than do those in intact families (Jeynes, 2007).

The negative effects of divorce seem to persist for many years. For example, children whose parents divorce have a higher risk of mental health problems in adulthood (Chase-Lansdale, Cherlin, & Kiernan, 1995; Cherlin et al., 1998; Wallerstein & Lewis, 1998). Many young adults whose parents are divorced lack the financial resources and emotional support necessary to succeed in college, and a majority report that they struggle with fears of intimacy in relationships (Cartwright, 2006). Not surprisingly, adults whose parents divorced are themselves more likely to divorce.

As a general rule, these negative effects are more pronounced for boys than for girls. However, some researchers have found that the effects are delayed in girls, making it more difficult to associate the effects with the divorce. Consequently, longitudinal studies often find that girls show equal or even greater negative effects (Amato, 1993; Hetherington, 1991a, 1991b). Age differences in the severity of the reaction have been found in some studies but not others. For example, one longitudinal study found that the effects of divorce were most severe in a group of 12-year-olds who experienced parental divorce in early childhood rather than during their school years (Pagani, Boulerice, Tremblay, & Vitaro, 1997).

Ethnicity, incidentally, does not appear to be a causal factor here. Yes, a larger percentage of African American children grow up in single-parent families. But the same negative outcomes occur in White single-parent families, and the same positive outcomes are found in two-parent minority families. For example, the school dropout rate for White children from single-parent families is higher than the dropout rate for Hispanic American or African American children reared in two-parent families (McLanahan & Sandefur, 1994).

Many single parents manage to overcome substantial obstacles to give their children the support and supervision they need.

Learning Objective 9.14

What are some possible reasons for the relationship between family structure and development?

Understanding the Effects of Family Structure

The broadest statement psychologists can make about the effects of family structure is that, at least in the United States, research suggests that the optimal situation for children appears to be one that includes two natural parents. Never-married mothers, divorced mothers or fathers who have not remarried, and step-parents are frequently linked to less positive outcomes. Factors associated with single-parenthood, such as poverty, may help explain its negative effects on development. Still, the differences between children who never experience single-parenting and those who do are too large to be completely explained by other variables. This means that at least part of the difference is connected to the family structure itself. Thus, it's important to know just what the differences are.

Children growing up in single-parent families are about twice as likely to drop out of high school, twice as likely to have a child before age 20, and less likely to have a steady job in their late teens or early 20s (McLanahan & Sandefur, 1994). Children of adolescent mothers are particularly at risk. Differences between children of teenagers and those whose mothers are older are evident in early childhood. Preschoolers whose mothers are single teenagers display less advanced cognitive and social development than their peers (Coley & Chase-Lansdale, 1998).

How are we to understand these various findings? First, single-parenthood or divorce reduces the financial and emotional resources available to support the child. With only one parent, the household typically has only one income and only one adult to respond to the child's emotional needs. Data from the United States indicate that a woman's income drops an average of 40–50% after a divorce (Bradbury & Katz, 2002; Smock, 1993).

Second, any family transition involves upheaval. Both adults and children adapt slowly and with difficulty to subtracting adults from or adding adults to the family system (Hetherington & Stanley-Hagan, 1995). The period of maximum disruption appears to last several years, during which the parents often find it difficult to monitor their children and maintain control over them.

Perhaps most importantly, single-parenthood, divorce, and step-parenthood all increase the likelihood that the family climate or style will shift away from authoritative parenting. This shift is not uncommon in the first few years after a divorce, when the custodial parent (usually the mother) is distracted or depressed and less able to manage warm control; it occurs in stepfamilies as well, where rates of authoritative parenting are lower than in intact families.

Remember, authoritarian or neglecting parenting is linked to poor outcomes, whether it is triggered by a divorce, a stressful remarriage, the father's loss of a job, or any other stress (Goldberg, 1990). Ultimately, it is the parenting style, rather than any particular type of disruption, that is significant for the child (see *Developmental Science in the Clinic*). Many families also construct a social network called an **extended family**, a family structure that includes parents, grandparents, aunts, uncles, cousins, and so on. Extended families seem to serve a protective function for children who are growing up in single-parent homes (Wilson, 1995). Grandmothers, for example, appear to be important sources of emotional warmth for the children of teenaged mothers (Coley & Chase-Lansdale, 1998). And, as mentioned earlier, extended family members often help single and divorced mothers with financial and emotional support as well as with child care. In the United States, such networks are more common among minorities than among Whites (Harrison, Wilson, Pine, Chan, & Buriel, 1990).

Peer Relationships

What is the first thought that springs to mind when you think about 2- to 6-year-olds? Perhaps it is the phenomenon of play. Certainly, people of all ages enjoy playing, although they obviously define it differently, but it is in the early childhood period that playing is the predominant form of behavior. In the context of play, children learn the skills they need to relate to others, and they learn that relationships have both negative and positive aspects.

extended family a social network of parents, grandparents, aunts, uncles, cousins, and so on

DEVELOPMENTAL SCIENCE IN THE CLINIC

When Parents Divorce

Raj and Lena are in the process of getting divorced. They have consulted with a professional counselor, because they are concerned about how their divorce will affect their 3-year-old son. The counselor informed them about the research showing that divorce is traumatic for children and asked them if there was any hope for reconciliation. When the couple advised the counselor that they were committed to ending their marriage, she told them that, although it was impossible to eliminate all of the short-term disruptive effects of the divorce on their son, there were some specific things they could do that would soften or lessen the effects. Before going over the list of recommendations with Raj and Lena, the counselor warned them that, in the midst of the emotional upheaval that accompanies divorce, these prescriptions would not be easy to follow. However, if divorcing parents are able to do so, the counselor noted, their children are less likely to suffer long-term negative effects. Here are the counselor's recommendations:

- Try to keep the number of separate changes the child has to cope with to a minimum. If at all possible, keep the child in the same school or child-care setting and in the same house or apartment.
- The custodial parent should help the child stay in touch with the noncustodial parent. Likewise, the noncustodial parent should maintain as much contact as possible with the child, calling and seeing him regularly, attending school functions, and so on.
- Keep the open conflict to a minimum. Most of all, try not to fight in front of the child. Open conflict has negative effects on children, whether the parents are divorced or not (Boyan & Termini, 2005). Thus, divorce is not the only culprit; divorce combined with open conflict between the adults has worse effects.
- Do not use the child as a go-between or talk disparagingly about the ex-spouse to him. Children who feel caught in the middle between two parents are more likely to show various kinds of negative symptoms, such as depression or behavior problems (Buchanan, Maccoby, & Dornbusch, 1991).
- Do not expect the child to provide emotional support. Parents should maintain their own network of support and use that network liberally. They should stay in touch with friends, seek out others in the same situation, and/or join a support group.

Questions for Reflection

1. Given that divorce is traumatic for children, do you think that courts should require parents who want to divorce to go through counseling aimed at determining whether reconciliation is possible?
2. What role, if any, should a divorcing couple's extended family play in helping moderate the effects of the event on a child?

Relating to Peers Through Play

Learning Objective 9.15
What are the various kinds of play exhibited by preschoolers?

In Chapter 8, you learned about the cognitive aspects of play. But what about the social features of children's play activities?

Types of Play The social dimensions of play were outlined in a classic observational study conducted by Mildred Parten (1932). If you observe young children who are engaged in free play, you will see that Parten's stages of play continue to be useful today. At every age, children are likely to spend at least some of their time playing alone—a pattern known as **solitary play**. They may also exhibit **onlooker play**, a pattern in which they watch another child playing. However, children first begin to show some positive interest in playing with others as early as 6 months of age. If you place two babies that age on the floor facing each other, they will look at each other, touch, pull each other's hair, imitate each other's actions, and smile at each other.

By 14–18 months, two or more children play together with toys—sometimes cooperating, but more often simply playing side by side with different toys. Developmentalists refer to this as **parallel play**. Toddlers this age express interest in one another and gaze at or make noises to one another. However, it isn't until around 18 months that children engage in associative play. In **associative play**, toddlers pursue their own activities but also engage in spontaneous, though short-lived, social interactions. For example, one toddler may put down a toy to spend a few minutes chasing another, or one may imitate another's action with a toy.

By 3 or 4, children begin to engage in **cooperative play**, a pattern in which several children work together to accomplish a goal. Cooperative play can be either constructive or symbolic. A group of children may cooperate to build a city out of blocks, or they may assign roles such as "mommy," "daddy," and "baby" to one another in order to play house.

solitary play a type of play in which children play by themselves

onlooker play a type of play in which children watch another child playing

parallel play a type of play in which children play side by side but do not interact

associative play a type of play in which children both play alone and engage in brief periods of interactive play with peers

cooperative play a type of play in which several children work together to accomplish a goal

Social Skills As you learned in Chapter 8, play is related to cognitive development. Play is also related to the development of **social skills**, a set of behaviors that usually lead to being accepted as a play partner or friend by others. For example, many researchers have focused on the social skill of *group entry*. Children who are skilled in group entry spend time observing others to find out what they're doing and then try to become a part of it. Children who have poor group-entry skills try to gain acceptance through aggressive behavior or by interrupting the group. Developmentalists have found that children with poor group-entry skills are often rejected by peers (Fantuzzo, Coolahan, & Mendez, 1998). Peer rejection, in turn, is an important factor in future social development.

According to recent studies, there appear to be sex differences in the reasons for and consequences of poor group-entry skills. For example, one study found that 3-year-old girls with poorly developed group-entry skills spent more time in parallel play than in cooperative play (Sims, Hutchins, & Taylor, 1997). In contrast, girls with better group-entry skills engaged in more cooperative than parallel play. Thus, the unskilled 3-year-old girls' patterns of play placed them at risk for future developmental problems, because age-appropriate play experience in the preschool years is related to social development later in childhood (Howes & Matheson, 1992; Maguire & Dunn, 1997).

The same study found that 3-year-old boys with poor group-entry skills tended to be aggressive and were often actively rejected by peers. They typically responded to rejection by becoming even more aggressive and disruptive (Sims et al., 1997). Thus, the boys in this study seemed to be caught in a cycle: Aggressive behavior led to peer rejection, which, in turn, led to more aggression. This pattern may place boys at risk for developing an internal working model of relationships that includes aggressive behavior and, as a result, leads them to routinely respond aggressively to others in social situations.

Because of the risks associated with poor social skills, developmentalists have turned their attention to social-skills training as a preventive measure. For example, in one study, socially withdrawn 4- and 5-year-olds were taught specific verbal phrases to use when trying to gain acceptance by a group of peers (Doctoroff, 1997). In addition, their socially accepted peers were taught to remind the trained children to use their new skills. For the most part, social-skills interventions like this one lead to immediate gains in social acceptance. However, the degree to which early childhood social-skills training can prevent later social difficulties is unknown at present.

Learning Objective 9.16
What is the difference between instrumental and hostile aggression?

Aggression

Suppose you were the parent of two boys, a 4-year-old and a 6-year-old, and saw them laughing with delight while they were wrestling. What do you think might happen? You may remember a sequence of events like this one from your own childhood: First, one child "accidentally" punches the other too hard. Next, the victim's nascent sense of justice dictates that he respond in kind. Soon, what started out as fun escalates into a full-blown fight.

Interactions of this kind are common in the early childhood period and even into the early adolescent years. **Aggression** is defined as behavior that is intended to injure another person or damage an object. The emphasis on intentionality helps separate true aggression from rough-and-tumble play in which children sometimes accidentally hurt one another. Every young child shows at least some aggressive behavior, but the form and frequency of aggression change over the preschool years, as you can see in the summary in Table 9.2.

When 2- or 3-year-old children are upset or frustrated, they are most likely to throw things or hit each other. As their verbal skills improve, however, they shift away from such overt physical aggression toward greater use of verbal aggression, such as taunting or name calling, just as their defiance of their parents shifts from physical to verbal strategies.

The decline in physical aggression over these years also undoubtedly reflects the preschooler's declining egocentrism and increasing understanding of other children's thoughts and feelings. Yet another factor in the decline of physical aggression is the emergence of *dominance hierarchies*. As early as age 3 or 4, groups of children arrange themselves in well-understood *pecking orders* of leaders and followers (Strayer, 1980). They know who

social skills a set of behaviors that usually lead to being accepted as a play partner or friend by others

aggression behavior intended to harm another person or damage an object

Table 9.2 Changes in the Form and Frequency of Aggression from Age 2 to Age 8

	2- to 4-Year-Olds	4- to 8-Year-Olds
Physical aggression	At its peak	Declining
Verbal aggression	Relatively rare at 2; increases as child's verbal skills improve	Dominant form of aggression
Goal of aggression	Mostly instrumental	Mostly hostile
Occasion for aggression	Most often after conflicts with parents	Most often after conflicts with peers

Sources: Cummings, Hollenbeck, Iannotti, Radke-Yarrow, & Zahn-Waxler, 1986; Goodenough, 1931; Hartup, 1974.

will win a fight and who will lose one, which children they dare attack and which ones they must submit to—knowledge that serves to reduce the amount of actual physical aggression.

A second change in the quality of aggression during the preschool years is a shift from instrumental aggression to hostile aggression. **Instrumental aggression** is aimed at gaining some object; the purpose of **hostile aggression** is to hurt another person or gain an advantage. Thus, when 3-year-old Sarah pushes aside her playmate Lucetta in the sandbox and grabs Lucetta's bucket, she is showing instrumental aggression. When Lucetta, in turn, gets angry at Sarah and calls her a dummy, she is displaying hostile aggression.

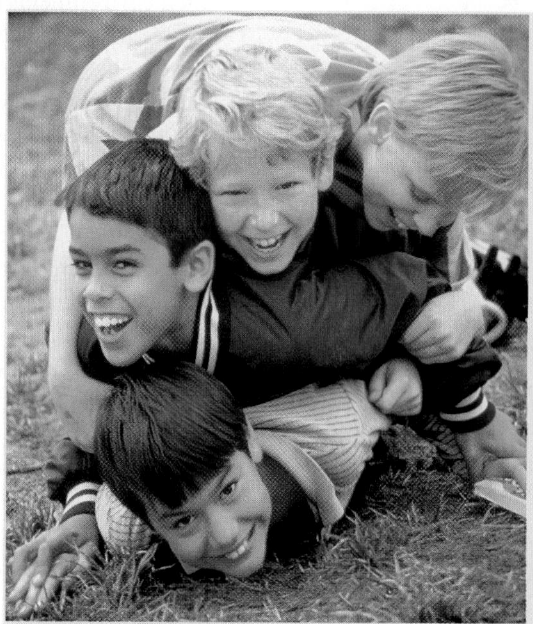

Developmentalists distinguish between true aggression (intentional harm) and the accidental injuries that often occur during normal rough-and-tumble play.

Psychologists have suggested several key factors in aggressive behavior. For example, one early group of American psychologists argued that aggression was always preceded by frustration, and that frustration was always followed by aggression (Dollard, Doob, Miller, Mowrer, & Sears, 1939). The frustration-aggression hypothesis turned out to be too broadly stated; not all frustration leads to aggression, but frustration does make aggression more likely. Toddlers and preschoolers are often frustrated—because they cannot always do what they want and because they cannot express their needs clearly—and they often express that frustration through aggression. As the child acquires greater ability to communicate, plan, and organize her activities, her frustration level declines and overt aggression drops.

Reinforcement also contributes to aggressive behavior. For instance, when Sarah pushes Lucetta away and grabs her toy, Sarah is reinforced for her aggression because she gets the toy. This straightforward effect of reinforcement clearly plays a vital role in children's development of aggressive patterns of behavior. Moreover, when parents give in to their young child's tantrums or aggression, they are reinforcing the very behavior they deplore, and they thereby help to establish a long-lasting pattern of aggression and defiance.

Modeling, too, plays a key role in children's learning of aggressive behaviors. In a classic series of studies, psychologist Albert Bandura found that children learn specific forms of aggression, such as hitting, by watching other people perform them (Bandura, Ross, & Ross, 1961, 1963). Clearly, entertainment media offer children many opportunities to observe aggressive behavior, but real-life aggressive models may be more influential. For example, children learn that aggression is an acceptable way of solving problems by watching their parents, siblings, and others behave aggressively. Indeed, parents who consistently use physical punishment have children who are more aggressive than those of parents who do not model aggression in this way (Eron, Huesmann, & Zelli, 1991). It should not be surprising that when children have many different aggressive models they learn aggressive behavior, especially if those aggressive models appear to be rewarded for their aggression.

Whatever the cause, most children become less aggressive during the preschool years. There are a few children, however, whose aggressive behavior pattern in early childhood becomes quite literally a way of life, a finding that has been supported by cross-cultural research

instrumental aggression aggression used to gain an object

hostile aggression aggression used to hurt another person or gain an advantage

(Hart, Olsen, Robinson, & Mandleco, 1997; Henry, Caspi, Moffitt, & Silva, 1996; Newman, Caspi, Moffitt, & Silva, 1997). Researchers have searched for causes of this kind of aggression, which some psychologists refer to as *trait aggression*, to distinguish it from developmentally normal forms of aggression.

Psychologists looking for a genetic basis for trait aggression have produced some supportive data (Hudziak et al., 2003; Plomin, 1990; vanBeijsterveldt, Bartels, Hudziak, & Boomsma, 2003). Others suggest that trait aggression is associated with being raised in an aggressive environment, such as an abusive family (Dodge, 1993). Family factors other than abuse, such as lack of affection and the use of coercive discipline techniques, also appear to be related to trait aggression, especially in boys (Chang, Schwartz, Dodge, & McBride-Chang, 2003; McFayden-Ketchumm, Bates, Dodge, & Pettit, 1996).

Still other developmentalists have discovered evidence that aggressive children may shape their environments in order to gain continuing reinforcement for their behavior. For example, aggressive boys as young as 4 years old tend to prefer other aggressive boys as playmates and to form stable peer groups. Boys in these groups develop their own patterns of interaction and reward each other with social approval for aggressive acts (Farver, 1996). This pattern of association among aggressive boys continues through middle childhood and adolescence.

Finally, social-cognitivists have produced a large body of research suggesting that highly aggressive children lag behind their peers in understanding others' intentions (Crick & Dodge, 1994). Research demonstrating that teaching aggressive children how to think about others' intentions reduces aggressive behavior also supports this conclusion (Crick & Dodge, 1996; Webster-Stratton & Reid, 2003). Specifically, these studies suggest that aggressive school-aged children seem to reason more like 2- to 3-year-olds about intentions. For example, they are likely to perceive a playground incident (say, one child accidentally tripping another during a soccer game) as an intentional act that requires retaliation. Training, which also includes anger management techniques, helps aggressive school-aged children acquire an understanding of others' intentions that most children learn between the ages of 3 and 5.

Similar results have been obtained in studies examining aggressive children's ability to engage in other kinds of social reasoning (Harvey, Fletcher, & French, 2001). However, developmentalists have found that, like their reasoning about intentions, aggressive children's social reasoning can be improved with training. In one study, researchers successfully used videotapes of children engaging in rough-and-tumble play to teach aggressive children how to recognize the difference between "play fighting" and aggressive acts that can cause physical pain (Smith, Smees, & Pelligrini, 2004). Thus, trait aggression may originate in some kind of deviation from the typical social-cognitive developmental path during the early childhood period, and it may be reduced with interventions aimed at returning children to that path.

Learning Objective 9.17
How do prosocial behavior and friendship patterns change during early childhood?

Prosocial Behavior and Friendships

At the other end of the spectrum of peer relationships is a set of behaviors psychologists call **prosocial behavior**. Like aggression, prosocial behavior is intentional and voluntary, but its purpose is to help another person in some way (Eisenberg, 1992). One such behavior that has been studied a great deal is **altruism**, acts motivated by the desire to help another person without expectation of reward. It changes with age, just as other aspects of peer behavior change.

Development of Prosocial Behavior Altruistic behaviors first become evident in children of about 2 or 3—at about the same time real interest in playing with other children arises. They will offer to help another child who is hurt, share a toy, or try to comfort another person (Marcus, 1986; Zahn-Waxler & Radke-Yarrow, 1982; Zahn-Waxler, Radke-Yarrow, Wagner, & Chapman, 1992). As you read in Chapter 8, children this young are only beginning to understand that others feel differently than they do—but they obviously understand enough about the emotions of others to respond in supportive and sympathetic ways when they see other children or adults hurt or sad.

prosocial behavior behavior intended to help another person

altruism acts motivated by the desire to help another person without expectation of reward

Beyond these early years, changes in prosocial behavior show a mixed pattern. Some kinds of prosocial behavior, such as taking turns, seem to increase with age. If you give children an opportunity to donate some treat to another child who is described as needy, older children donate more than younger children do. Helpfulness, too, seems to increase with age, through adolescence. But not all prosocial behaviors show this pattern. Comforting another child, for example, seems to be more common among preschoolers and children in early elementary grades than among older children (Eisenberg, 1992).

Prosocial behaviors, such as sharing, are influenced by cognitive development and by the deliberate efforts of parents and teachers to teach children to behave in such ways.

Children vary a lot in the amount of altruistic behavior they show, and young children who show relatively more empathy and altruism are also those who regulate their own emotions well. They show positive emotions readily and negative emotions less often (Eisenberg et al., 1996). They are also more popular with peers (Mayeux & Cillissen, 2003). These variations among children's levels of empathy or altruism seem to be related to specific kinds of child-rearing. In addition, longitudinal studies indicate that children who display higher levels of prosocial behavior in the preschool years continue to demonstrate higher levels of such behavior in adulthood (Eisenberg et al., 1999).

Parental Influences on Prosocial Behavior Research suggests that parental behavior contributes to the development of prosocial behavior (Eisenberg, 1992). Specifically, parents of altruistic children create a loving and warm family climate. If such warmth is combined with clear explanations and rules about what to do as well as what not to do, the children are even more likely to behave altruistically. Such parents also often explain the consequences of the child's action in terms of its effects on others—for example, "If you hit Susan, it will hurt her." Stating rules or guidelines positively rather than negatively also appears to be important; for example, "It's always good to be helpful to other people" is more effective guidance than "Don't be so selfish!"

Providing prosocial attributions—positive statements about the underlying cause for helpful behavior—helps. For example, a parent might praise a child by saying "You're such a helpful child!" or "You certainly do a lot of nice things for other people." Having heard such statements often during early childhood helps children incorporate them into their self-concepts later in childhood. In this way, parents may help create a generalized, internalized pattern of altruistic behavior in the child.

Parents of altruistic children look for opportunities for them to do helpful things. For example, they allow children to help cook, take care of pets, make toys to give away, teach younger siblings, and so forth. Finally, parental modeling of thoughtful and generous behavior—that is, parents demonstrating consistency between what they say and what they do—is another contributing factor.

Friendships Beginning at about 18 months, a few toddlers show early hints of playmate preferences or individual friendships (Howes, 1983, 1987). However, by age 3, about 20% of children have a stable playmate. By 4, more than half spend 30% or more of their time with one other child (Hinde, Titmus, Easton, & Tamplin, 1985). Thus, one important change in social behavior during early childhood is the formation of stable friendships (Hay, Payne, & Chadwick, 2004).

To be sure, these early peer interactions are still quite primitive. However, it is noteworthy that preschool friend pairs nonetheless show more mutual liking, more reciprocity, more extended interactions, more positive and less negative behavior, and more supportiveness in a novel situation than do nonfriend pairs at this same age—all signs that these relationships are more than merely passing fancies. Moreover, having had a friend in early childhood is related to social competence (Maguire & Dunn, 1997; Sebanc, 2003).

Test Prep Center

with mydevelopmentlab

THEORIES OF SOCIAL AND PERSONALITY DEVELOPMENT

9.1 What major themes of development did the psychoanalytic theorists propose for the early childhood period? (p. 250)

Freud and Erikson each described two stages of personality development during the preschool years: the anal and phallic stages in Freud's theory and the stages in which autonomy and initiative are developed in Erikson's theory. Both theories, but especially Freud's, place primary importance on the parent-child relationship.

1. How would Freud sum up the process of social and personality development in the years between 2 and 6?

____

____

2. What did Erikson believe about children's need for parental control in early childhood?

____

____

9.2 What are the findings of social-cognitive theorists with respect to young children's understanding of the social world? (pp. 250–253)

Social-cognitive theorists assert that advances in social and personality development are associated with cognitive development. Three topics of interest to such theorists are person perception, understanding of different kinds of rules, and understanding of others' intentions.

3. What does research suggest regarding Piaget's assertion that young children do not understand the difference between intentional and unintentional acts?

____

____

PERSONALITY AND SELF-CONCEPT

9.3 How does temperament change in early childhood? (p. 253)

During early childhood, children's temperaments are modified by social experiences both within and outside of the family, to form their personalities.

4. In what ways do parental responses increase or decrease the risk associated with difficult temperament?

____

____

9.4 What changes take place in the young child's categorical, emotional, and social selves during the preschool years? (pp. 254–256)

The preschooler continues to define himself along a series of objective dimensions but does not yet have a global sense of self. Children make major strides in self-control and in their understanding of their own social roles in the preschool years, as parents gradually turn over the job of control to the child.

5. Name and describe Hoffman's stages of empathy in the table below.

Stage	Description
1:	
2:	
3:	
4:	

GENDER DEVELOPMENT

9.5 How do the major theoretical orientations explain gender development? (pp. 256–258)

Psychoanalytic explanations of gender development have not received much support from researchers, as toddlers seem to understand more about gender and sex-typed behavior than Freud's theory would predict. Social-learning explanations are more persuasive but ignore the role of cognitive development. Instead, they emphasize modeling and reinforcement. Social-cognitive theories suggest that children move through gender identity, gender stability, and gender constancy stages. Gender schema theories apply information-processing principles to gender role development. Biological theories emphasize hormones and other physical factors. Social-cognitive theories explain and predict gender-related understanding and behavior better than psychoanalytic or social-learning theories.

6. From the Multimedia Library within MyDevelopmentLab, watch the *Early Gender Typing* video and answer the following question.

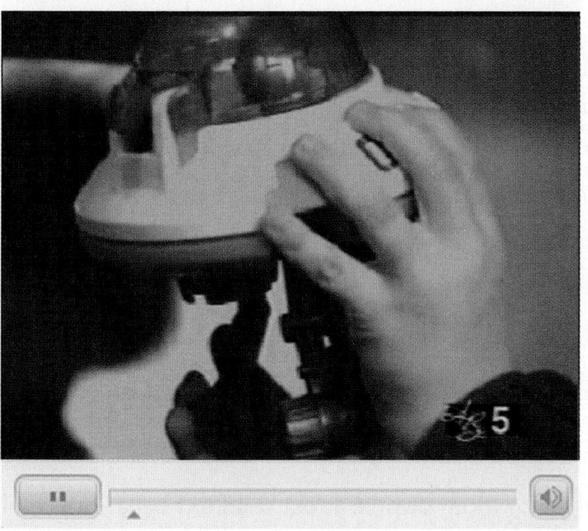

What do the research findings in the video suggest about the social learning explanation of gender development?

____

____

9.6 How do children develop their concept of gender? (pp. 258–259)

Between ages 2 and 6, most children move through a series of steps in their understanding of the concept of gender: first labeling their own and others' gender, then understanding the stability of gender, and finally comprehending the constancy of gender at about age 5 or 6.

7. At what age do children use gender to categorize others?

______

9.7 What are the characteristics of young children's sex-role knowledge? (pp. 259–260)

At about age 2, children begin to learn what is appropriate behavior for their gender. By age 5 or 6, most children have developed fairly rigid rules about what boys or girls are supposed to do and be.

8. To what extent do the rigid views of 5- and 6-year-olds influence their later views on gender-appropriate behavior?

____

____

9.8 How is the behavior of young children sex-typed? (pp. 260–262)

Children display sex-typed behavior as early as 18–24 months of age. Some theorists think children play in gender-segregated groups because same-sex peers help them learn about sex-appropriate behavior.

9. From the Multimedia Library within MyDevelopmentLab, watch the *Gender Differences: Robert Sternberg* video and answer the following question.

What has Sternberg's research shown regarding gender differences in intelligence?

____

____

FAMILY RELATIONSHIPS AND STRUCTURE

9.9 How does attachment change during the early childhood years? (pp. 262–263)

A young child has a strong attachment to the parent(s), but, except in stressful situations, attachment behaviors become less visible as the child gets older. Preschoolers refuse or defy parental influence attempts more than infants do. Outright defiance, however, declines from age 2 to age 6. Both these changes are clearly linked to the child's language and cognitive gains.

10. List the changes in attachment relationships that the text associates with each age in the table below.

Age	Change in Attachment Relationship
2–3	
4	

11. How would Bowlby explain the finding that 4- and 5-year-olds who are securely attached to their parents have generally positive relationships with their peers?

______

______

9.10 How do parenting styles affect children's development? (pp. 263–265)

Authoritative parenting, which combines warmth, clear rules, and communication with high maturity demands, is associated with the most positive outcomes for children. Authoritarian parenting has some negative effects on development. However, permissive and uninvolved parenting seem to have the least positive effects.

12. Define each parenting style, and summarize its effects on development.

Style	Definition	Effects on Development
Authoritarian		
Permissive		
Authoritative		
Uninvolved		

9.11 How are ethnicity and socioeconomic status related to parenting style? (pp. 265–267)

Asian American and African American parents are more authoritarian than those in other ethnic groups, and working-class parents in all ethnic groups tend to be authoritarian. Studies of parenting style and developmental outcomes in ethnic groups suggest that authoritative parenting may not be the best style in some situations.

13. What positive developmental outcomes are associated with authoritarian parenting among Asian Americans, African Americans, and Whites?

______

______

9.12 How is family structure related to children's development? (pp. 267–270)

Family structure affects early childhood social and personality development. Data from U.S. studies suggest that any family structure other than one that includes two biological parents is linked to more negative outcomes.

14. Transform each of these false statements into a true statement.

(A) There is a lot of evidence to suggest that children who are raised by their grandparents fare just as well as those who are raised by their parents.

______

______

(B) Children raised by gay or lesbian parents are more likely to be homosexual themselves.

______

______

15. From the Multimedia Library within MyDevelopmentLab, watch the *Co-Parenting Relationships and Socioemotional Development: Sarah Schoppe-Sullivan* video and answer the following question.

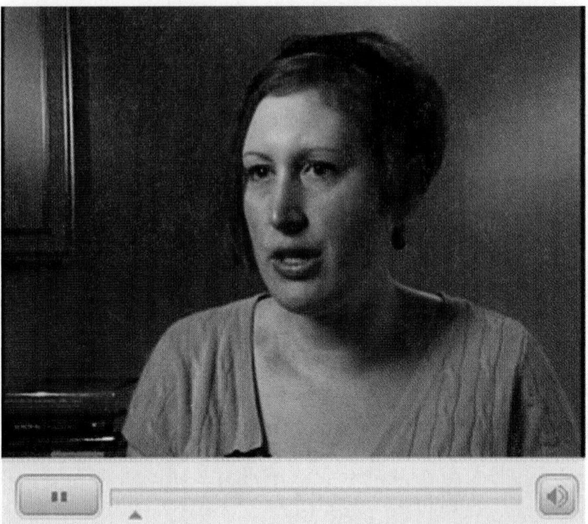

What does Schoppe-Sullivan's research suggest about the role of fathers in young children's development?

______

______

9.13 How does divorce affect children's behavior in early childhood and in later years? (pp. 270–271)

Following a divorce, children typically show disrupted behavior patterns for several years. Parenting styles also change, becoming less authoritative. However, many effects of divorce on children are associated with problems that existed before the marriage ended.

16. Briefly describe how divorce affects a young child's life in each of these areas:

(A) economic resources

______

______

(B) school performance

______

______

(C) social behavior

______

______

9.14 What are some possible reasons for the relationship between family structure and development? (pp. 272–273)

A number of variables, such as poverty, are associated with differences in family structure. However, these variables alone are insufficient to explain differences among children that are correlated with variations in family make-up.

17. How can extended families serve a protective function for children growing up in single-parent homes?

____

____

PEER RELATIONSHIPS

9.15 What are the various kinds of play that are exhibited by preschoolers? (pp. 273–274)

Play with peers is evident before age 2 and becomes increasingly important through the preschool years. At every age, children spend some time in solitary play and may exhibit onlooker play. By 14–18 months, children engage in parallel play. At 18 months, associative play is apparent. By 3 or 4, children begin to engage in cooperative play.

18. Give an example of each type of play in the table below.

Type of Play	Example
Solitary	
Onlooker	
Parallel	
Associative	
Cooperative	

19. Classify each statement as true or false.

______ (A) Children who are skilled in group entry try to become a part of what other children are doing.

______ (B) Poor social skills can lead to peer rejection.

______ (C) The consequences of poor social skills are the same for boys and girls.

______ (D) Peer rejection frequently causes aggressive children to become less so.

______ (E) Social skills are largely a product of inborn temperament, so training has little effect on them.

9.16 What is the difference between instrumental and hostile aggression? (pp. 274–276)

Instrumental aggression is aimed at gaining some object; hostile aggression is meant to hurt another person or gain an advantage.

20. Modeling plays (a key role/no role) in aggression.

21. Which type of aggression is more common between the ages of 2 and 4—instrumental or hostile—and in what ways do preschoolers display it?

____

____

9.17 How do prosocial behavior and friendship patterns change during early childhood? (pp. 276–277)

Children as young as 2 show prosocial behavior toward others, and this behavior seems to become more common as the child's ability to take another's perspective increases. Stable friendships develop between children beginning around age 3.

22. Define prosocial behavior and explain how it changes in early childhood.

____

____

23. At what age does each of these milestones in the development of friendship happen?

______ (A) More than half of children spend 30% of their time with one peer.

______ (B) Some children show hints of playmate preferences.

______ (C) About 20% of children have a stable playmate.

For answers to the questions in this chapter, turn to page 517. For a list of key terms, turn to page 531.

Succeed with PEARSON **mydevelopmentlab**

Do You Know All of the Terms in This Chapter?
Find out by using the Flashcards. Want more practice? Take additional quizzes, try simulations, and watch video to be sure you are prepared for the test!

The Whole Child in Focus

Physical, Cognitive, and Socioemotional Development in Early Childhood: An Integrated Review

Think back to the contrast between 2-year-old Madeleine and her 6-year-old sister Marcy that you read about at the beginning of this unit. Now that Madeleine has turned six, let's take a look at how her development has progressed.

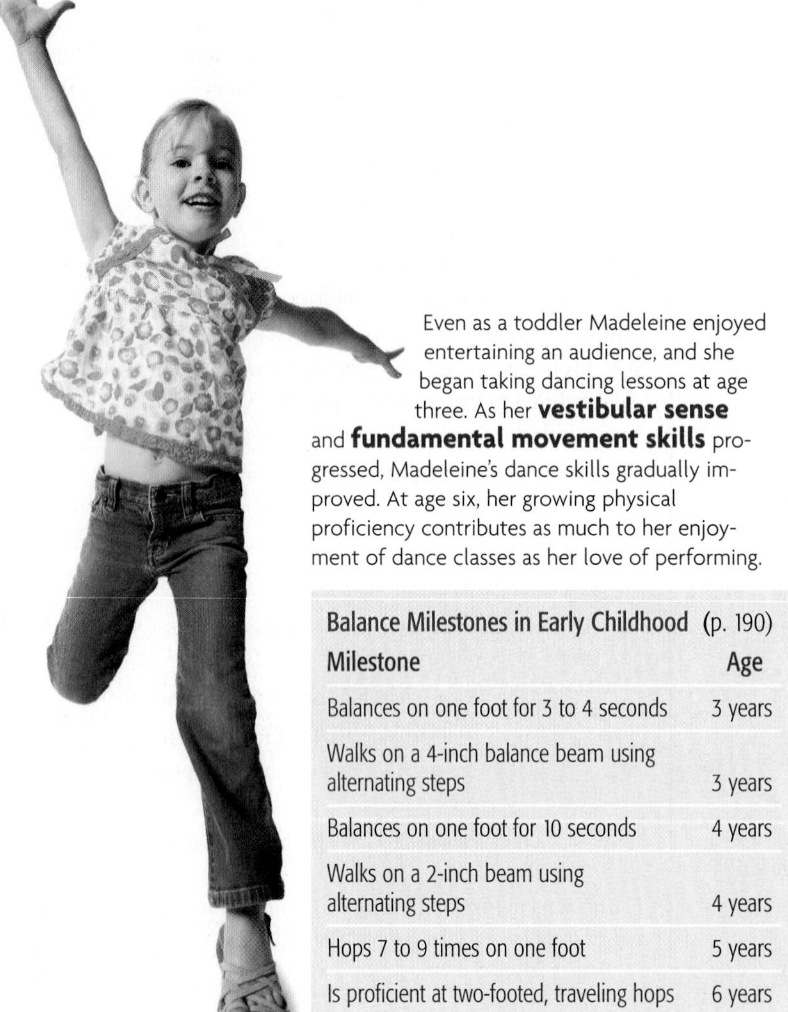

Even as a toddler Madeleine enjoyed entertaining an audience, and she began taking dancing lessons at age three. As her **vestibular sense** and **fundamental movement skills** progressed, Madeleine's dance skills gradually improved. At age six, her growing physical proficiency contributes as much to her enjoyment of dance classes as her love of performing.

Balance Milestones in Early Childhood (p. 190)

Milestone	Age
Balances on one foot for 3 to 4 seconds	3 years
Walks on a 4-inch balance beam using alternating steps	3 years
Balances on one foot for 10 seconds	4 years
Walks on a 2-inch beam using alternating steps	4 years
Hops 7 to 9 times on one foot	5 years
Is proficient at two-footed, traveling hops	6 years

Parts of the Brain (p. 100)

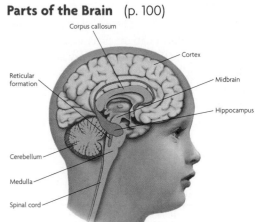

As her **hippocampus** developed, Madeleine's ability to memorize lines of text improved rapidly, which supported her growing interest in acting out stories.

Thinking about Developmental Pathways

1. As an outgoing child, Madeleine learned dance moves with her emerging motor skills. What alternative outlets for her motor abilities might she have found if she had a shy personality instead?
2. Madeleine attends a preschool employing a developmental approach. How might teachers in an academically oriented preschool respond to her desire to author stories and write them down with invented spelling? How might such responses affect her development in the socioemotional and cognitive domains?
3. Madeleine possesses good social skills, but how might her developmental outcomes in the socioemotional domain have differed if she behaved aggressively towards her peers?

Piaget's Cognitive–Developmental Stages (p. 38)	
Approximate Ages	**Stage**
Birth to 24 months	Sensorimotor
24 months to 6 years	**Preoperational**
6 to 12	Concrete operational
12+	Formal operational

At six, Madeleine often uses dolls and stuffed animals to play roles in the stories she acts out, using different voices for each character. According to Piaget, such complex forms of pretending reflect the **figurative schemes** that children develop in the **preoperational stage**.

Moreover, by age six, improvements to the **operational efficiency** of Madeleine's short-term memory allow her to keep track of the characters and plot points of stories.

The Information Processing System (p. 40)

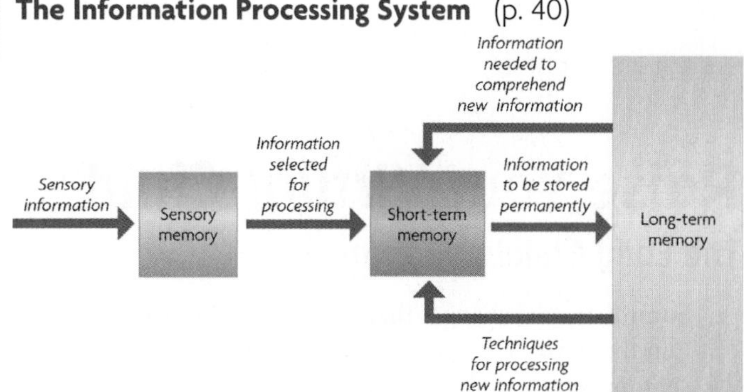

Invented Spelling (p. 231)

ASNAK KAME
tovisit
AWReCLAS

With a typical 6-year-old's understanding of others' mental states, or **theory of mind**, Madeleine has progressed from memorizing stories to creating her own. She uses her rapidly expanding vocabulary to author the stories, thanks to **fast-mapping**, and **invented spelling** skills to write them down. Madeleine attends a preschool that employs the **developmental approach** to early childhood education, and her teachers encourage her efforts.

Madeleine often takes charge of **cooperative play** activities with her peers, assigning roles to others and reminding them of how they should behave in those roles, a tendency that arises from the emerging rule-governed **operative schemes** that characterize the later years of Piaget's preoperational stage. For instance, Madeleine converts her **sex-role knowledge** into rules when she insists that children who play the "mommy" role be "nice" and those who play the "daddy" role speak with deep voices.

Erikson's Psychosocial Stages (p. 30)	
Birth to 1 year	Trust versus mistrust
1 to 3	Autonomy versus shame and doubt
3 to 6	**Initiative versus guilt**
6 to 12	Industry versus inferiority
12 to 18	Identity versus role confusion
18 to 30	Intimacy versus isolation
30 to late adulthood	Generativity versus stagnation
Late adulthood	Integrity versus despair

Other children accept Madeleine's direction because she possesses good **social skills**. Although she had a difficult temperament as a young child, with the help of the **emotional regulation** strategies she learned in preschool (e.g., use words instead of acting aggressively), she learned how to influence others without being perceived as bossy. In doing so, she achieved Erikson's early childhood psychosocial task of acquiring a sense of **initiative**.

The Whole Child in Action

Apply What You've Learned about Development in Early Childhood

Raise Your Virtual Child

The Early Childhood Years

1. Summarize the changes that you observed in your virtual child between the ages of 2 and 6 in the physical, cognitive, and socioemotional domains. Which of these changes represent universals, and which reflect individual differences?
2. To what extent did your parenting decisions contribute to these changes?
3. Did the Virtual Child result in decision-related outcomes that you think are valid? Why or why not?
4. Write a brief biographical sketch of your child at age 6, integrating information from all three domains.

This activity requires that you be registered for My Virtual Child *through MyDevelopmentLab.*

Conduct Your Research

Private Speech

As you learned in Chapter 8, Vygotsky proposed a theory of cognitive development in which private speech plays an important role. You can observe children using private speech in a preschool classroom. (Remember to get permission from school officials and from the children's parents.) Focus on one child at a time, keeping a record of the child's self-directed statements. Determine which statements appear to be for the purpose of guiding behavior, as Vygotsky suggested. An example of such a statement might be a preschooler's utterance of "this goes here" while putting a puzzle together. After you have collected data on several children, decide whether you agree with Vygotsky's emphasis on private speech.

Build Your Portfolio

1. Use the Internet to search for traditional folk tales from different cultures that involve false beliefs. For example, in the European story "The Gingerbread Man," a runaway gingerbread man is fooled by a fox and, as a result, gets eaten. In the African story "The Lion and the Hare," a rabbit's cleverness enables him to fool a lion into not eating him. Create an annotated bibliography of the tales and include information about how each could be used to facilitate theory of mind development in young children. Develop a rationale for using such stories to help children learn about cultural differences as well.
2. Develop a multimedia presentation for parents and preschool teachers that explains the development of empathy. The presentation should include a definition of empathy and an explanation of why it is important in human relationships. It should explain the factors that contribute to the development of empathy and how parents and teachers can facilitate its development. There should also be information about the risks associated with a failure to develop empathy.

Powered by

PEARSON mydevelopmentlab™

www.mydevelopmentlab.com

Explore Possible Careers

Child Development Associate

Students who are interested in a career in child care can enhance their chances for employment by obtaining a child development associate (CDA) credential. A CDA is a certified professional who works with children in child-care centers and preschools, in home child care, or as an employee of a home visitation program sponsored by an agency such as a school district. To be eligible for certification, an applicant must be at least 18 years of age, be a high school graduate, and have completed at least 120 clock hours of instruction in a formal child development educational program. Most CDAs obtain this training in a community college setting through either credit or noncredit coursework. In addition, prior to receiving the certificate, a CDA applicant must have at least 480 hours of experience working with children during the 5 years immediately prior to the date of the application. There is also an assessment process that must be completed prior to certification, which involves observations and interviews conducted by representatives of the Council for Professional Recognition. You can learn more about child development associates by clicking the "Career Center" tab in MyDevelopmentLab.

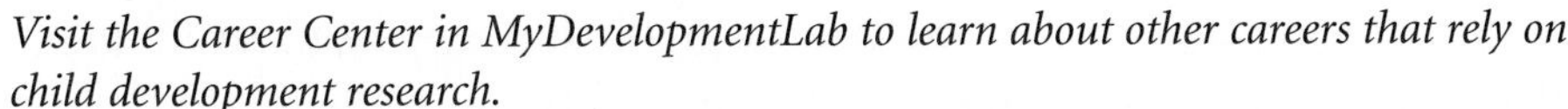

Visit the Career Center in MyDevelopmentLab to learn about other careers that rely on child development research.

Volunteer with Children

Special Olympics Coach

You have probably heard of the Special Olympics, an organization that sponsors local and national competitive sporting events for children and adults with developmental disabilities such as mental retardation and pervasive developmental disorders. Individuals over the age of 8 compete in these events, and a new program called Special Olympics Young Athletes teaches sports skills to children with disabilities between the ages of 2 and 7. All of the coaches who work with these special athletes are volunteers, so if you have a background in sports, you may be able to use your experience to help a youngster with a developmental disability experience the enjoyment and pride that go along with competing in an athletic event. Even if you don't have a background in sports, the organization needs volunteers to perform a variety of other functions.

Visit the Career Center in MyDevelopmentLab to learn about other volunteer opportunities that rely on child development research.

Unit Four
Middle Childhood

Do you remember when you learned to ride a bicycle? Perhaps your experience was similar to Jamal's. When Jamal was 6 years old, his parents bought him a small bicycle with training wheels. Jamal loved to ride up and down his street and felt incredibly grown-up when the "big kids" allowed him to ride along with them.

One day, Jamal and his new-found "bike buddies" challenged one another to ride to the top of a dirt hill at the end of their street. Their game had one simple rule: If you couldn't make it to the top, you were out. Jamal waited patiently for his turn and cheered along with the other children as each of his friends made it to the top. Finally, it was his turn. He made his way to the base of the hill and started to climb. To his dismay, though, his training wheels kept getting stuck. Each time he would jar them loose and start over, but soon the other children were yelling "You're out! Get off the hill! You have to go home now."

Feeling lower than he ever had in his life, Jamal rode home as fast as he could and begged his father to take the training wheels off his bike. Jamal's father, Raul, wasn't sure that he was ready, but, touched by the intensity of his son's plea, he reluctantly removed the training wheels. "I'll help you learn to balance," Raul said.

"No, I can do it myself," Jamal replied confidently. But on his first attempt, he tipped over sideways, and the bike landed on top of him. Humbled by his first experience, the boy agreed to accept his father's assistance.

Jamal got back on his bike and started to ride, but this time his father ran alongside and nudged him back into an upright position each time his balance started to falter. After 10 days of practicing with his father, Jamal was at last able to make it all the way to the end of the driveway without falling. At the end of his fourth trip from the garage to the end of the driveway, he cautiously ventured out into the street. To his delight, Jamal found that he was at last a true "big kid" who could ride his bicycle without

training wheels. Jamal couldn't wait to play "ride up the hill" with his friends.

At this point in your study of child development, you probably recognize that Jamal's story represents the intersection of several developmental pathways. Advances in physical development are vital to the acquisition of his bicycle-riding skills. Cognitive development is at work in his understanding of rule-based games such as the one that he and his friends had invented. But what makes Jamal's experiences unique are the emotional and behavioral responses that his personality, self-concept, and relationship history contribute to the developmental equation.

Developmental scientists haven't always appreciated the importance of the changes that occur in the socioemotional domain during middle childhood, the years between 6 and 12. The reason is that the cognitive shifts that occur during this period, especially at its beginning, are so dramatic that, for decades, research on cognitive development dominated developmental scientists' interest in this period. The essence of these shifts is movement from reliance on appearances to a search for underlying rules. The result is a powerful change in the quality of children's thinking, a change that has been noticed in every culture in the world.

In recent decades, developmental scientists have learned that the school-aged child's quest for rules extends to the social world. For instance, children's self-concepts begin to be built on systematic comparisons of their real and ideal selves. Friendship is understood as something more than just a fleeting association between playmates who happen to be near each other or to like the same toys. Gender, too, is an aspect of experience that, for the school-aged child, serves as an organizing principle around which he builds a mental representation of a rule-governed world.

In Chapters 10, 11, and 12, you will encounter these and other changes that mark the 6- to 12-year-old period as distinct from those that came before and that prepare the child for the adolescent years that lie ahead. Chapter 10 addresses the physical domain. The remarkable changes in thinking alluded to earlier are the subject of Chapter 11. And Chapter 12 delves into the socioemotional domain.

The Whole Child In Focus

Keep Jamal's story in mind as you read through the next three chapters, and consider how aspects of his physical, cognitive, and socioemotional development might interact as he moves through the middle childhood period. What kind of person do you think an older Jamal will be? We'll examine how Jamal's development changes as he grows from 6 to 12 years old at the end of this unit.

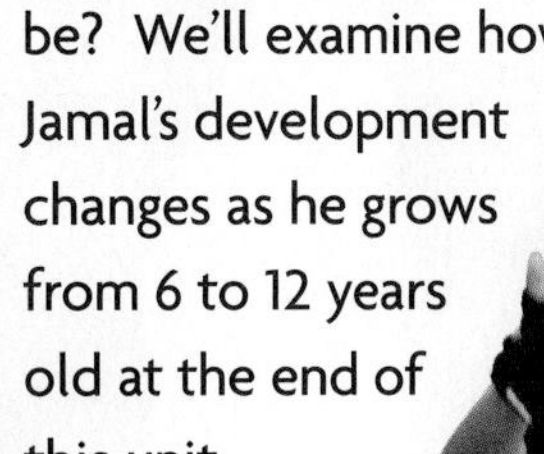

RunTex
MARATHON
Kids

Chapter 10

Physical Development and Health in Middle Childhood

School-aged children have a wonderful kind of unthinking confidence about their bodies. The wobbliness and stiffness of early childhood are gone, and the uncertainties of puberty have not yet begun. Children of this age can navigate the world with skill and begin to play sports with real enthusiasm. It is a pleasure to watch children this age on the playground or in their neighborhoods. They so often have a kind of intense joyfulness about their physical play.

The hidden changes in children's bodies that enable the movements so familiar to us—riding bikes, climbing, jumping, skipping, and so on—are the first topic taken up in this chapter. Of course, middle childhood is not without its risks and challenges, so the discussion of the physical domain in middle childhood addresses health issues next. In the final section of the chapter, you will learn about several behavioral and emotional difficulties that emerge between the ages of 6 and 12.

Learning Objectives

Physical Changes

10.1 In what ways do children's body systems change across the middle childhood period?

10.2 What changes occur in the brain during these years?

10.3 How do children's motor and perceptual skills improve between ages 6 and 12?

Health and Wellness

10.4 What are the health-care needs of school-aged children?

10.5 How do acute and chronic illnesses affect school-aged children's lives?

10.6 What trends in injuries and mortality are evident during middle childhood?

10.7 In what ways does excessive weight gain threaten the immediate and future health of school-aged children?

10.8 What are the health risks associated with type 1 and type 2 diabetes?

10.9 What is the impact of socioeconomic status on children's health?

10.10 Why is it important to encourage school-aged children to develop good health habits?

Atypical Development

10.11 What are the features of attention-deficit hyperactivity disorder, and how is it treated?

10.12 What are the characteristics of oppositional defiant disorder?

10.13 What is childhood-onset conduct disorder?

10.14 How does depression affect the lives of school-aged children?

Physical Changes

Imagine a foot race between a 6-year-old and a 12-year-old. Although there certainly could be exceptions to this generalization, the odds definitely favor the older child. In all likelihood, the 12-year-old will not only surpass the 6-year-old in speed but also display greater strength, agility, and endurance. Such differences arise from a host of hidden, qualitative changes that take place in the major systems of children's bodies between the ages of 6 and 12.

Learning Objective 10.1

In what ways do children's body systems change across the middle childhood period?

Changes in Size, Shape, and Function

Between 6 and 12, children grow 2 to 3 inches and add about 6 pounds each year. Girls in this age range are ahead of boys in their overall rate of growth. By 12, girls have attained about 94% of their adult height, while boys have reached only 84% of theirs (Tanner, 1990). Girls also have slightly more body fat and slightly less muscle tissue than boys. These are the changes that we can see, but they are driven by developmental processes that are usually hidden from view.

Bone Growth Bones mature in such a regular and predictable way that physicians use **bone age** as the best single measure of a child's physical maturation, using x-rays of the hand and wrist to judge the stage of development of wrist and finger bones. In general, bones continue to ossify, or harden, during these years, with particular activity at sites at the end of long bones (leg and arm bones as well as finger bones) called *epiphyses*. When the epiphyses have completely ossified, the bone stops growing and the child's height, arm length, and leg length are set (Tanner, 1990). These processes occur in all bones at least to some extent during the elementary school years. However, as noted in Chapter 3, girls' skeletons mature at a more rapid rate than do those of boys. By age 12, boys are, on average, about 2 years behind girls in skeletal development. That's why 12-year-old girls are closer to attaining their adult height than 12-year-old boys are.

The process of bone development gives us a powerful argument in favor of increased exercise or physical activity for children. Children who exercise more add more calcium to their bones (Greer, 2005). Calcium absorption during childhood is an important factor contributing to the level of calcium in early adults' bones. Important, too, is the fact that bone density reaches a peak in early adulthood and is stable until about age 35, when bone calcium begins to drop. This decline can be slowed down by maintaining exercise and by continuing a diet high in calcium, but the loss of calcium cannot be totally prevented. Thus, during childhood, a diet that is rich in calcium and a lifestyle that includes exercise are critical factors in adult bone health.

Hormones As you learned in Chapter 7, the endocrine system strongly influences physical growth and development. Over the middle childhood years, the glands of the endocrine system change gradually in ways that prepare the body for the momentous changes that will occur during sexual maturation, or *puberty*. For example, as Figure 10.1 shows, secretions from adrenal glands remain at very low levels until age 7 or so, when these glands begin to produce *androgens* in much greater amounts (Rosenthal & Gitelman, 2002). In Chapter 3, you learned that prenatal androgens are required for the development of male genitalia. These hormones are thought to contribute to the increase in muscle mass that children experience during middle childhood (Tanner, 1990). In addition, they play a role in bone growth and also prepare the cells of the sex glands, or *gonads*, to secrete hormones that initiate the process of puberty (more on this in Chapter 13).

Strength and Stamina As muscle mass increases in middle childhood, so does strength. Boys and girls differ in strength in two ways (Gabbard, 2008). First, boys outperform girls on measures of strength, including tasks that involve using the muscles to apply pressure to a device used to measure muscle force (such as a hand grip). Second, the ratio of strength to body size is greater among boys. Thus, boys require less effort to move their bodies through space than girls do. Both boys and girls become stronger during middle childhood, but girls do not catch up, on average. Moreover, at puberty the strength difference widens considerably in boys' favor.

Children's capacity for extended physical activity, their **stamina**, rises steeply across the middle childhood years as well (Gabbard, 2008). If you observe children on playgrounds, you will notice that preschoolers display short bursts of physical activity followed by periods of rest. School-aged children show a similar pattern, but their periods of activity are longer

bone age a measure of a child's physical maturation that is based on x-rays of the hand and wrist

stamina the capacity for extended physical activity

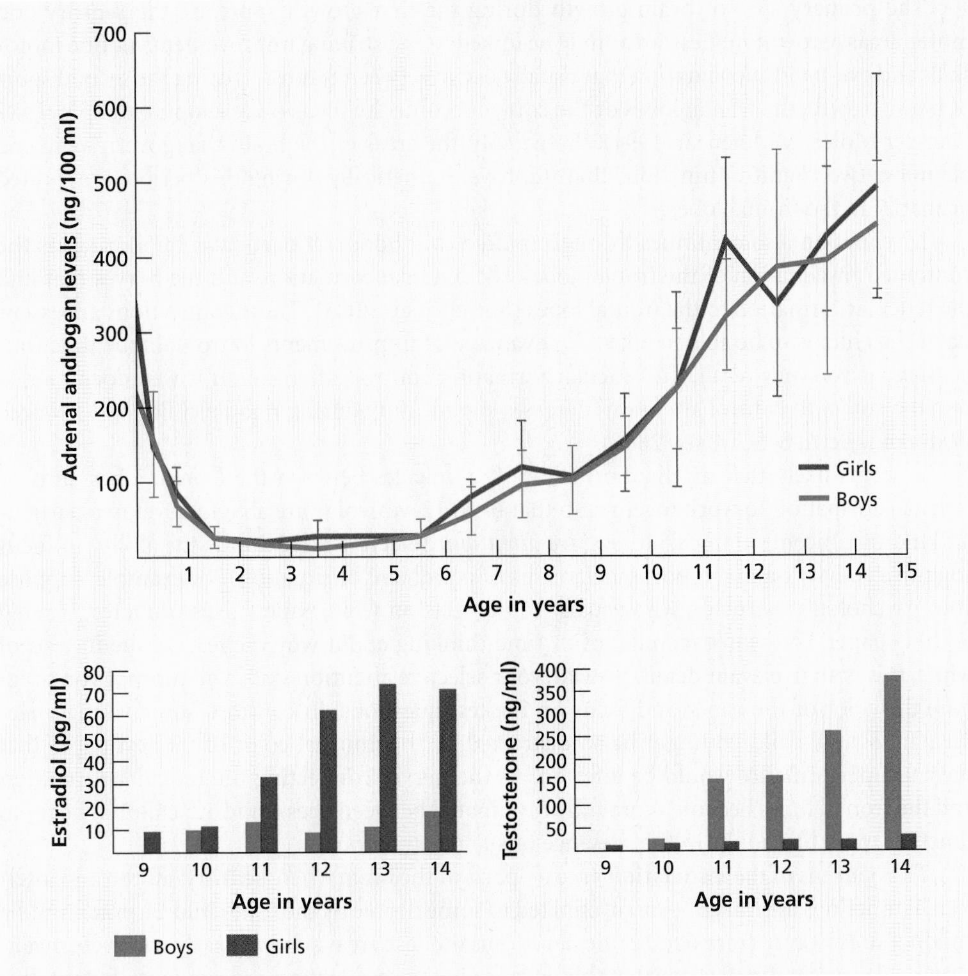

Figure 10.1 **Changes in Hormones Prior to and at Adolescence**

The top graph shows changes in adrenal androgens, which are equivalent in boys and girls; the bottom graphs show increases in estradiol for girls (in picograms per milliliter) and testosterone for boys (in nanograms per milliliter).

(*Sources*: Androgen data from M. K. McClintock and G. Herdt, from "Rethinking Puberty: The Development of Sexual Attraction," *Current Directions in Psychological Science*, Vol. 5, No. 6 (December 1996), p. 181, Fig. 2. Reprinted by permission of Blackwell Publishers. Estradiol and testosterone data from Elizabeth Susman, Fig. 2 from "Modeling Developmental Complexity in Adolescence: Hormones and Behavior in Context," *Journal of Research on Adolescence*, 7, 1997. Reprinted by permission of Blackwell Publishers.)

and their periods of rest are shorter than those of younger children because they possess more stamina.

Changes in stamina are linked to growth of the heart and lungs, which is especially evident during the later years of middle childhood. These changes enable children's bodies to take in more oxygen and to distribute it throughout the body more efficiently. During the early years of the middle childhood period, boys and girls display an equivalent degree of stamina. Both sexes show an increase in stamina around age 10, but the increase is much greater in boys than it is in girls (Gabbard, 2008). Boys retain their advantage over girls in stamina into the teen years.

The Brain and Nervous System

> **Learning Objective 10.2**
> What changes occur in the brain during these years?

Two major growth spurts happen in the brain during middle childhood (Spreen, Risser, & Edgell, 1995). In most healthy children, the first takes place between ages 6 and 8, and the second between ages 10 and 12. Both spurts involve development of new synapses as well as increases in the thickness of the cortex.

The primary sites of brain growth during the first growth spurt are the sensory and motor areas. Growth in these areas may be linked to the striking improvements in fine motor skills and eye-hand coordination that usually occur between 6 and 8. During the second spurt of brain growth, the frontal lobes of the cortex become the focus of developmental processes (van der Molen & Molenaar, 1994). Predictably, the areas of the brain that govern logic and planning, two cognitive functions that improve dramatically during this period, are located primarily in the frontal lobes.

Myelination also continues through middle childhood. Of particular importance is the continued myelination of the frontal lobes, the reticular formation, and the nerves that link the reticular formation to the frontal lobes (Sowell et al., 2003). These connections are essential if the child is to be able to take full advantage of improvements in frontal lobe functions because, as you may recall, the reticular formation controls attention. It is well documented that the ability to control attention increases significantly during middle childhood (Wetzel, Widmann, Berti, & Schröger, 2006).

It seems likely that myelination allows the linkages between the frontal lobes and the reticular formation to work together so that 6- to 12-year-olds are able to develop a particular kind of concentration called *selective attention*. **Selective attention** is the ability to focus cognitive activity on the important elements of a problem or situation. For example, suppose your psychology instructor, who usually copies tests on white paper, gives you a test printed on blue paper. You won't spend a lot of time thinking about why the test is blue instead of white; this is an irrelevant detail. Instead, your selective attention skills will prompt you to ignore the color of the paper and focus on the test questions. In contrast, some younger elementary school children might be so distracted by the unusual color of the test paper that their test performance would be affected. As the nerves connecting the reticular formation and the frontal lobes become more fully myelinated between ages 6 and 12, children begin to function more like adults in the presence of such distractions.

THE WHOLE CHILD IN FOCUS

How did Jamal use his maturing capacity for concentration? Find out on page 378.

The neurons of the **association areas**—parts of the brain where sensory, motor, and intellectual functions are linked—are myelinated to some degree by the time children enter middle childhood. However, from 6 to 12, the nerve cells in these areas achieve nearly complete myelination. Neuroscientists believe that this advance in the myelination process contributes to increases in information-processing speed. For example, suppose you were to ask a 6-year-old and a 12-year-old to identify pictures of common items—a bicycle, an apple, a desk, a dog—as rapidly as possible. Both children would know the items' names, but the 12-year-old would be able to produce the names of the items much more rapidly than the 6-year-old. Such increases in processing speed probably contribute to improvements in information-processing skills, which you'll read about in Chapter 11 (Kail, 1990; Li, Lindenberger, Aschersleben, Prinz, & Baltes, 2004). Furthermore, these improvements in memory function carry over into the socioemotional domain, because of the cognitive processes that are involved in the development of the child's self-concept and her understanding of the social world.

Studies involving children with hearing impairments suggest that the development of the association areas is strongly influenced by experience. For instance, researchers have found that the auditory association areas fail to develop in children who become deaf prior to developing spoken language (Sharma, Dorman, & Kral, 2005). In addition, development of the auditory association area is facilitated when such children's hearing is restored with *cochlear implants*. However, deaf children must receive cochlear implants prior to age 7 in order for the auditory association areas to develop sufficiently to support speech comprehension (Sharma, Dorman, & Kral, 2005; Sharma, Dorman, & Spahr, 2002).

Another important advance in middle childhood occurs in the right cerebral hemisphere, with the lateralization of **spatial perception**, the ability to identify and act on relationships between objects in space. (You should remember from Chapter 7 that *lateralization* is the process through which brain functions become assigned to one hemisphere or the other.) For example, when you imagine how a room would look with a different arrangement of furniture, you are using spatial perception. Perception of objects such as faces actually lateralizes before age 6. However, complex spatial perception, such as that needed for map reading, isn't strongly lateralized until about age 8.

selective attention the ability to focus cognitive activity on the important elements of a problem or situation

association areas parts of the brain where sensory, motor, and intellectual functions are linked

spatial perception the ability to identify and act on relationships between objects in space

A behavioral test of the lateralization of spatial perception often used by neuroscientists involves **relative right-left orientation**, the ability to identify right and left from multiple perspectives. Such tests show that most children younger than 8 know the difference between their own right and left. Typically, though, only children older than 8 understand the difference between statements like "It's on your right" and "It's on my right." Lateralization of spatial perception may be related to the increased efficiency with which older children learn math concepts and problem-solving strategies. In addition, it is correlated with performance on Piaget's conservation tasks (van der Molen & Molenaar, 1994).

Some researchers propose that differences in visual experiences explain sex differences in spatial perception and the related function of **spatial cognition**, the ability to infer rules from and make predictions about the movement of objects in space. For example, when you are driving on a two-lane road and you make a judgment about whether you have enough room to pass a car ahead of you, you are using spatial cognition. From an early age, boys score much higher than girls, on average, on such spatial tasks, perhaps because of boys' play preferences (Hyde, 2005). Some researchers argue that boys' greater interest in constructive activities such as building with blocks helps them develop more acute spatial perception. Research showing that the gender difference in spatial cognition is larger among children from middle- and high-income families than it is among low-income families seems to support this view, presumably because families with greater economic resources are better able to provide boys with the play materials that they specifically request (Bower, 2005).

relative right-left orientation the ability to identify right and left from multiple perspectives

spatial cognition the ability to infer rules from and make predictions about the movement of objects in space

Motor and Perceptual Development

Learning Objective 10.3

How do children's motor and perceptual skills improve between ages 6 and 12?

Thanks to the increasing maturity of the skeletal and muscular systems and a growing capacity for sustained activity, children become increasingly adept at skills like bike riding across the middle childhood years. The maturation of the brain that happens during these years also contributes to advances in motor skills and to the improvements in hand-eye coordination that occur in middle childhood (Thomas, Yan, & Stelmach, 2000). As a result, school-aged children perform more skillfully in activities requiring coordination of vision with body movements, such as shooting a basketball or playing a musical instrument.

THE WHOLE CHILD IN FOCUS

How has Jamal put his developing fine motor skills to good use? Find out on page 379.

Perhaps even more significant is the school-aged child's continually improving fine motor coordination. Improvements in fine motor coordination make writing possible, as well as drawing, cutting, and many other tasks and activities. Some sports skills, such as serving a tennis ball, also involve fine motor coordination. Such accomplished uses of the hands are made possible by the maturation of the wrist, which occurs more rapidly in girls than in boys (Tanner, 1990).

Advances in both gross and fine motor skills interact to allow children to develop sports skills such as hitting a baseball. Consequently, many children begin participating in organized sports around the time they enter school. However, most experts say that children should spend the early elementary school years learning and perfecting basic skills, meaning the *fundamental movement skills* discussed in Chapter 7. You may remember, for example, that the fundamental movement skills involved in running include swinging the arms, synchronizing arm and leg movements, hitting the ground with the support foot at the proper angle, and so on. Ideally, children should practice fundamental movement skills in the context of activities that are fun and that involve as much movement as possible. Among sports activities, soccer and swimming are particularly likely to meet these conditions, not only because everyone is likely to get at least some aerobic exercise but also because the basic skills are within the abilities of 6- or 7-year-olds.

School-aged children enjoy activities that allow them to practice their rapidly improving fine motor skills

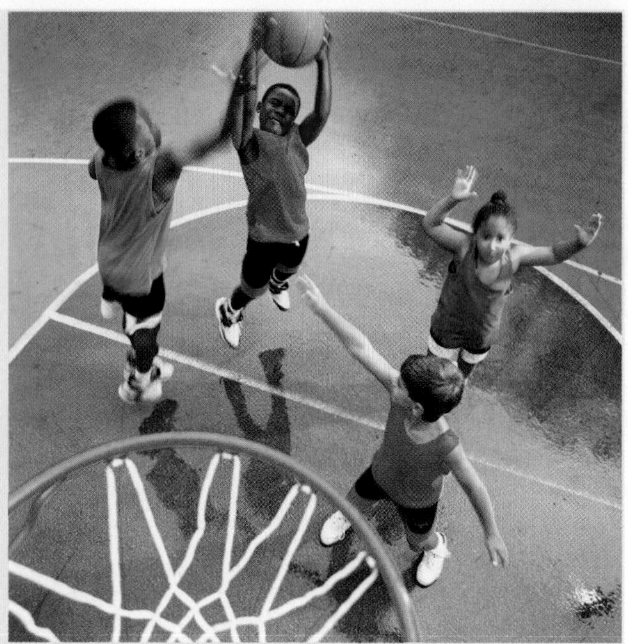

When school-aged boys and girls participate in coed sports, boys' superior strength and stamina are balanced by girls' advantage in coordination.

Baseball, in contrast, is not a good sport for most children this age because it requires well-developed eye-hand coordination to hit or catch the ball, coordination that most 7-year-olds do not yet have. By about age 10, many children are ready to play sports such as baseball and basketball, but many other sports, such as tennis, are still difficult for the average child of this age.

In addition, sports performance involves more than just motor skills. For example, children's ability to engage in any sport that involves tracking a moving object, such as a ball or a hockey puck, depends upon their ability to discriminate between the moving object and its background. This is a perceptual skill called **figure-ground perception**. It develops across the years between 4 and 13 (Gabbard, 2008). When a child has to respond to a moving object, her figure-ground perception, visual-motor coordination, and motor skills must interact effectively to allow her to intercept it. Research suggests that children's perceptual and motor abilities are sufficiently developed to perform this feat effectively at age 9 or 10 (Gabbard, 2008).

Finally, gender should also be taken into account when choosing sports for school-aged children. During middle childhood, sex differences in skeletal and muscular maturation cause girls to be better coordinated than boys are. However, as stated earlier, they have less stamina and are somewhat weaker in muscle strength than boys are. Thus, girls outperform boys in sports that require coordinated movement, such as gymnastics, and boys do better when strength and stamina are advantages, as is the case in all of the sports that involve running, jumping, kicking, and throwing (Gabbard, 2008). Further, as the *Developmental Science at Home* discussion illustrates, gender differences contribute to children's disengagement from sports at the end of the middle childhood period.

Health and Wellness

Generally speaking, most school-aged children are healthier than infants, toddlers, and young children are. They are less likely to die than at any other period of childhood, and they have fewer illnesses. However, they continue to benefit from regular medical care, and there are a few serious health concerns for this age group.

Learning Objective 10.4
What are the health-care needs of school-aged children?

Health-Care Needs of School-Aged Children

Some 80% of school-aged children in the United States visit a health-care professional's office or a clinic at least once each year (Bloom & Cohen, 2007). As you will learn later, many of these visits are the result of chronic illnesses and accidents. Yet, school-aged children continue to need annual well-child check-ups to assess their growth and to administer needed immunizations. In addition, they require regular vision and dental exams.

Vision Routine vision exams are an important part of well-child care in middle childhood. One common condition that is diagnosed as a result of these exams is **myopia**, or *nearsightedness*, a condition that results in blurred distant vision (Flynn, 1999). Corrective lenses are typically prescribed for children who are nearsighted. Myopia runs in families and is believed to be strongly influenced by heredity. Thus, if you wear glasses, your children probably will as well.

figure-ground perception the ability to discriminate between a moving object and its background

myopia a condition that results in blurred distant vision

DEVELOPMENTAL SCIENCE AT HOME

Sports for Children

At age 6, Katara could hardly wait to take part in her first soccer game. Though not the strongest player on the team, she enjoyed playing the game with friends and, until she was 11 years old, looked forward to soccer season each year. At first, 11-year-old Katara was excited about the prospect of playing soccer with her old friends. However, following the second practice session, Katara began complaining about going to practice and begged her parents to let her quit. Eventually her parents agreed, because they feared that insisting that Katara honor her commitment to the team would turn her against all forms of physical activity.

Katara's story is not unusual. Many children participate in sports for a few years and then lose interest. Why? One reason preadolescent girls like Katara stop participating in sports is that they do not want to be perceived as overly masculine. Studies have shown that athletically talented female basketball players who continue to participate in the game after puberty are those who have found a way to positively incorporate athleticism into their identities while maintaining a feminine self-perception off the court (Shakib, 2003).

A more important factor in older children's decisions to give up sports, one that applies to both boys and girls, is the strong emphasis on competition and winning in many sports programs (Anshel, 1990). Children of 6 or 7 get involved in sports more because they enjoy moving their bodies than out of any desire to defeat an opponent, but coaches in many organized sports emphasize winning rather than fun, fair play, or even basic exercise—a process sometimes called the "professionalization of play" (Hodge & Tod, 1993).

Further, amateur coaches often have a poor understanding of normal motor skills among 6- or 7-year-olds. When they see a child who does not yet throw a ball skillfully or who kicks a ball awkwardly, they label the child "clumsy" or "uncoordinated." From then on, these perfectly normal boys and girls get little playing time or encouragement. These children drop out of sports by age 10 or 11 because they have a clear impression that they are "not good enough" (Anshel, 1990).

Parents who want to encourage children to participate in organized sports should look for programs that deemphasize competition and offer skills training and encouragement to all children. They should also guard against pushing too fast or too hard to prevent children from developing the notion they can't measure up to parents' and coaches' expectations, an idea that is sure to take all the fun out of playing the game. Finally, parents should try to ensure that their daughters grow up believing that physical attractiveness isn't the most important thing in life.

Questions for Reflection

1. As the coach of a baseball team made up of 7-year-old boys and girls, how would you manage the differing ability levels and expectations of the children?
2. How might the parents of an athletically talented 11-year-old girl who wants to quit participating in sports deal with the situation?

Failing to correct myopia in school-aged children diminishes the visual information that their developing information-processing systems receive. As a result, they may miss vital learning opportunities. Moreover, myopia is progressive, so children need regular eye exams and new eyeglasses.

Some children possess excellent visual acuity but still have vision problems. *Convergence* is the movement of both eyes toward the nose in order to focus on something that is relatively close to the eyes. Because it plays an important role in reading, many eye specialists recommend that assessment of convergence be included in routine vision exams.

The 3% to 5% of school-aged children who suffer from **convergence insufficiency** are unable to move both eyes inward to the degree required to focus on near objects (Bartiss, 2007). As a result, when they try to read, they experience double vision, eye fatigue, and headaches. These symptoms cause them to avoid reading. Because children are often unable to explain what the problem is, their behavior is misinterpreted as laziness, disobedience, or evidence of an attention problem. Fortunately, when it is properly diagnosed, conversion insufficiency can be corrected with *vision therapy*, exercises that gradually alter the movement of the eyes in response to near objects (Scheiman et al., 2005).

Dental Care The loss of the primary teeth and eruption of the permanent teeth is one of the universal developmental processes that occurs during middle childhood. Children lose their first tooth around the age of 6 and the last one around 11.

Fortunately, the prevalence of dental caries (cavities) is much lower than in past cohorts of children, thanks to access to dental care and drinking water that is supplemented with *fluoride*, a mineral that prevents tooth decay. Despite declines in dental caries, children still

convergence insufficiency the inability to move both eyes inward to the degree required for focusing on near objects

need regular dental check-ups. According to the American Academy of Pediatric Dentistry (2001), regular check-ups should include assessment of the following:

- Dental-care habits
- Crowding of the permanent teeth
- Bite pattern; how the teeth come together
- Health and position of unerupted teeth (via x-rays)
- Need for orthodontic treatment
- Health and development of bones of the mouth and jaw

Learning Objective 10.5

How do acute and chronic illnesses affect school-aged children's lives?

Acute and Chronic Illnesses

About three-quarters of school children in the United States miss at least one day of school each year because of an illness or an accident (Bloom & Cohen, 2007). School-aged children suffer from essentially the same kinds of acute illnesses as preschoolers do, although ear infections become significantly less likely by school age because of the maturation of the structures of the inner ear. Chronic illnesses cause many children to miss school from time to time. Sadly, too, although overall death rates decline in this period of life, suicide appears on lists of leading causes of death in some ethnic groups.

Allergies One-quarter to one-third of children in the United States suffer from **allergies**, immune reactions to substances called *allergens* (Bloom & Cohen, 2007). Common allergens include fungal spores, pollen, animal hair, and certain foods. Some manufactured substances, including latex, can induce allergic reactions as well.

Children who have respiratory allergies experience sneezing, stuffy noses, and more frequent sinus infections than do their peers who don't have allergies (Shames, 2002). Food allergies can affect the respiratory system as well, and they may also cause troublesome rashes or gastrointestinal symptoms. Allergies are treated with environmental control—that is, by avoiding allergens. In addition, physicians prescribe *antihistamine drugs* for children who suffer from frequent allergy attacks and antibiotics for infections that follow such attacks. In severe cases, physicians prescribe *steroids* or recommend *desensitization therapy*, a procedure that involves injecting patients with small doses of allergens.

Asthma The most frequent cause of school absence for 6- to 12-year-olds is **asthma**, a chronic lung disease in which individuals experience sudden, potentially fatal attacks of breathing difficulty. According to public health officials, 14% of children in the United States have been diagnosed with asthma (Bloom & Cohen, 2007). The disease typically appears between ages 5 and 7 and is believed to be caused by hypersensitivity to allergens such as dust and animal hair (Overby, 2002).

When a child who has asthma encounters these irritants, her bronchial tube linings become inflamed. In response, large amounts of mucus are produced, the airways become blocked, and the child has to gasp for air. Researchers have recently discovered that this sequence of events is triggered when the immune systems of asthma sufferers react to environmental irritants such as dust, pet dander, pollen, and second-hand smoke as if they were bacteria or viruses that threatened to invade the cells that line the bronchial tubes and lungs (Akbari et al., 2006). This reaction results in the production of powerful "killer" cells in the bronchial tubes and lungs, causing damage to the very cells that the killer cells are supposed to protect. So far, there are no treatments available for preventing this immune response. Thus, researchers argue that the first line of defense against asthma is to help children learn to identify the irritants that trigger attacks and avoid them.

Parents, of course, play a critical role in the prevention of asthma and in the management of asthma symptoms. For instance, health-care providers typically encourage parents of children with asthma to maintain a home environment that is as free of respiratory irritants as

allergies immune reactions to substances called allergens

asthma a chronic lung disease, characterized by sudden, potentially fatal attacks of breathing difficulty

possible, especially second-hand smoke. However, a parent's level of *health literacy* can be a significant barrier to preventive efforts (Kickbusch, 2001). Health literacy is the ability to seek out, comprehend, evaluate, and communicate about health information. For example, knowing how to search the Internet for health information is a component of health literacy.

Researchers in several countries have found that variations in health literacy contribute to variations in the effectiveness of asthma treatments across socioeconomic and ethnic groups (Poureslami et al., 2007). The link between socioeonomic status and health literacy may be due to the fact that many individuals from low-SES households lack basic reading skills. As a result, one-on-one information sessions are often a more effective means of educating parents about asthma treatment than written materials are (Paasche-Orlow et al., 2005).

Ethnicity may be related to health literacy because of linguistic and cultural barriers between patients' families and caregivers. Not surprisingly, when patient education is carried out by individuals who know the language and customs of the patient's family, the health literacy barrier diminishes (Poureslami et al., 2007). However, cultural barriers to asthma prevention go beyond language and customs. For example, parents' religious beliefs influence the degree to which they adhere to children's asthma treatment regimens (Handelman, Rich, Bridgemohan, & Schneider, 2004). Such beliefs may lead them to think that their children have been miraculously cured when their asthma symptoms subside (George, 2001). As a result, they may abandon preventive measures. When physicians point out that alternating periods of wellness and sickness are typical among asthma sufferers and that preventive measures should be maintained, parents may think that these doctors are denigrating their religious beliefs. These parents may then come to distrust doctors and no longer consult with health-care professionals regarding their children's symptoms. Consequently, their children may receive care only in the midst of life-or-death crises. Sensitivity on the part of health-care professionals to patients' families' values and beliefs may help to prevent such outcomes (Poureslami et al., 2007). Moreover, when properly supported by health-care professionals, patients who have strong religious beliefs from which they draw a sense of hope about the future exhibit higher rates of adherence to medical instructions (Berg, Rapoff, Snyder, & Belmont, 2007).

Even the best, most culturally sensitive preventive measures sometimes fail to control a child's asthma symptoms. In such cases, physicians move the child to the next step, one that involves daily medication. However, the medicines used at this step can have detrimental effects on children's cognitive development (Naude & Pretorius, 2003). For this reason, most health professionals who treat asthma try to avoid using them (Overby, 2002); they want to be certain that parents and children have fully complied with lower-level treatment strategies before moving to more intense approaches. Once a child is in the midst of a full-blown asthma attack, hospitalization may be needed to prevent the attack from resulting in long-term damage to the child's lungs.

As children grow and their lung capacity increases, asthma attacks decrease in both intensity and frequency (Overby, 2002). However, about half of children with asthma continue to experience symptoms throughout their lives.

Injuries and Mortality

Learning Objective 10.6

What trends in injuries and mortality are evident during middle childhood?

You probably remember some kind of injury that occurred when you were in elementary school. Millions of such injuries occur in this age group each year. Most such injuries are minor, but some lead to lifelong impairments or death.

Accidents Falls, many of which involve wheeled sports activities such as skateboarding and biking, account for about half of injuries to school-aged children, followed by incidents in which children are accidentally hit by a ball or some other object, cuts, bicycle accidents, insect bites, dog bites, and so on (Centers for Disease Control, 2007). Many injuries occur to children who are passengers in motor vehicles as well.

Three factors seem to account for the frequency of injuries among school-aged children. First, children who are less well supervised have more accidents, whether the relative lack of supervision occurs because there is only one adult in the home, because the parents are highly stressed, or for some other reason. Second, children who are physically more active have more accidents, a group that includes boys and any child who is more physically mature than others his or her age. The sex difference is actually quite large. For instance, of the 4.5 million injuries to children aged 5 to 14 in 2001 in the United States, over 60% involved boys (Vryostek, Annest, & Ryan, 2004). Third, children whose behavior is impulsive or aggressive are more likely to have accidents (Bussing, Menvielle, & Zima, 1996).

Head injuries accompanied by some kind of change in level of consciousness (ranging from mild lethargy to a total loss of consciousness) are more common among school-aged children than any other age group (Fein, Durbin, & Selbst, 2002). In fact, about 10% of all children experience at least one such injury between the ages of 6 and 12. Motor vehicle accidents are the most common cause of head injuries in children, but bicycle accidents are another important cause. Research suggests that helmets could prevent about 85% of bicycle-related head injuries (National Center for Injury Prevention and Control, 2000).

Fortunately, the vast majority of children who experience head injuries recover fully and experience no long-term effects. However, effects can be subtle and may not be apparent immediately after the injury. Thus, physicians say that every child who experiences a trauma to the head should receive medical attention and be monitored for several days (Fein, Durbin, & Selbst, 2002).

Sports Injuries Many children in the 6- to 12-year-old age group are involved in organized sports. There is no tracking system for sports-related injuries, so estimates of the rates of such injuries depend on survey data. In one survey, parents reported the rates of injury shown in Figure 10.2. As you can see, football results in more injuries than other sports, but baseball and soccer are not far behind. Taken together, injuries that are attributable to participation in organized sports account for 9% of injury-related emergency room visits among children between the ages of 5 and 14 (United States Consumer Safety Product Commission, 2005).

Figure 10.2
Injury Rates for Different Sports

Children who play football, soccer, and baseball experience higher rates of injury than those who play softball and basketball.

(*Source*: National Safe Kids Campaign, 2000.)

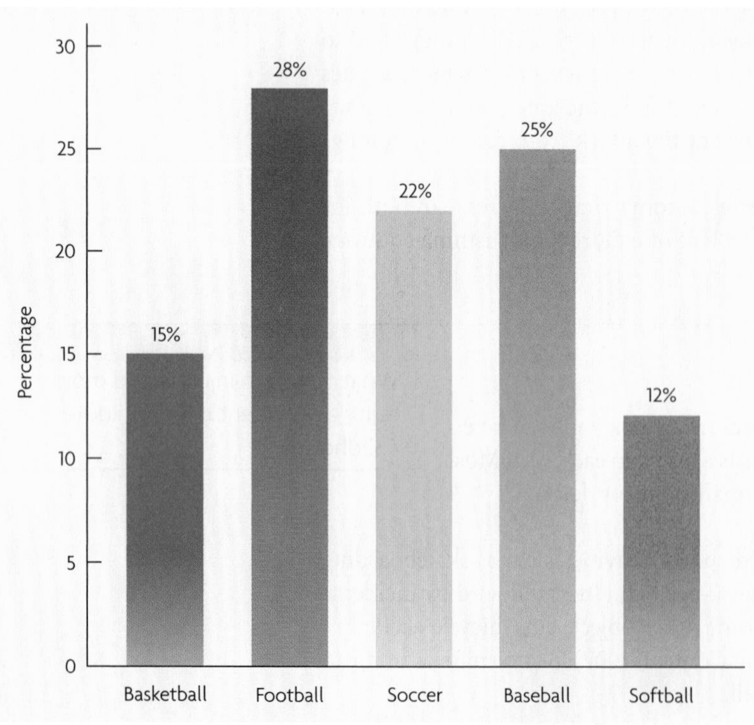

Mortality Figures 10.3 and 10.4, which parallel Figure 7.5 for the preschool period, show the leading causes of death among school-aged children in the United States. You can see in the graphs that accidents are the leading cause of death in every ethnic group, as was true among preschoolers. African American and Native American children have the highest death rates. Among African American children, 22 and 25 of every 100,000 children between 5 and 9 and 10 and 14, respectively, die each year. Among Native Americans, the mortality rates are 20 and 25 deaths per 100,000 among 5- to 9-year-olds and 10- to 14-year-olds, respectively. As you can see in Figures 10.3 and 10.4, death rates among children in these two groups are higher than those of other groups because of the comparatively high frequency of homicide among African Americans and suicides and accidents among Native Americans. As you will learn later in the chapter, correlations that link ethnicity, family economic resources, and health-related behavior contribute to these group differences.

While accidents are the number one cause of death in 5- to 14-year-olds across all ethnic groups, the second cause is *cancer*, a group of

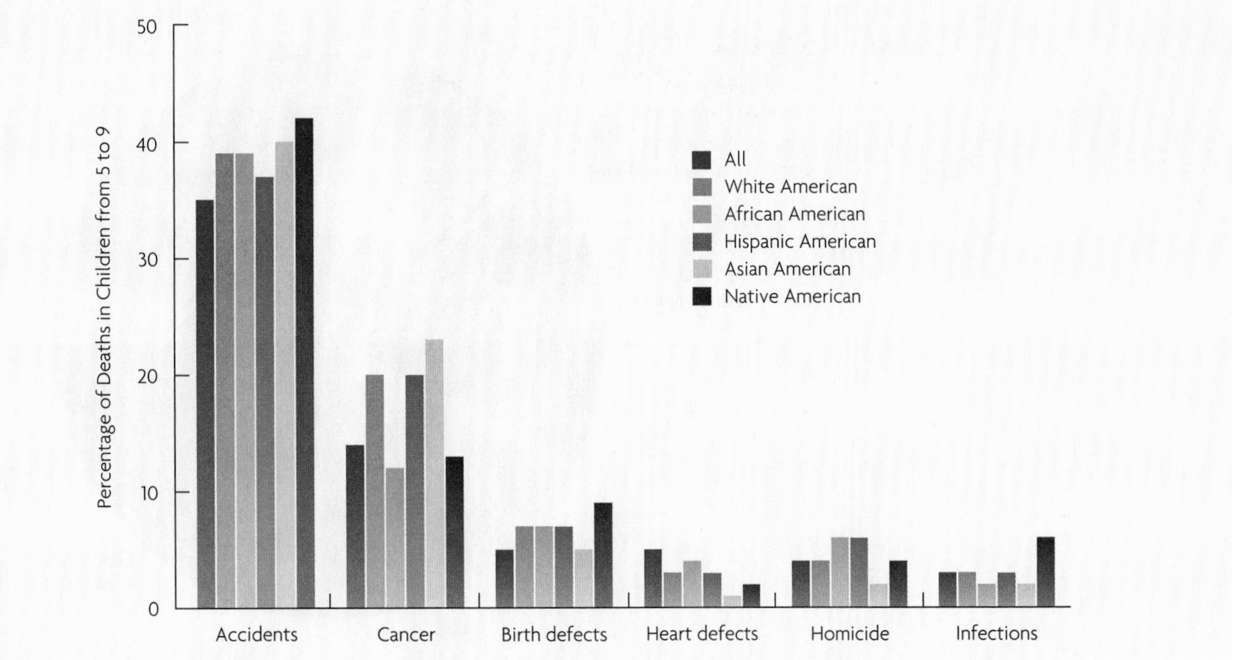

Figure 10.3 **Leading Causes of Death Among 5- to 9-Year-Olds**

As this figure shows, accidents are the leading cause of death in all ethnic groups in the United States. However, the rankings of the various causes of death vary across groups.

(*Source*: Heron, 2007.)

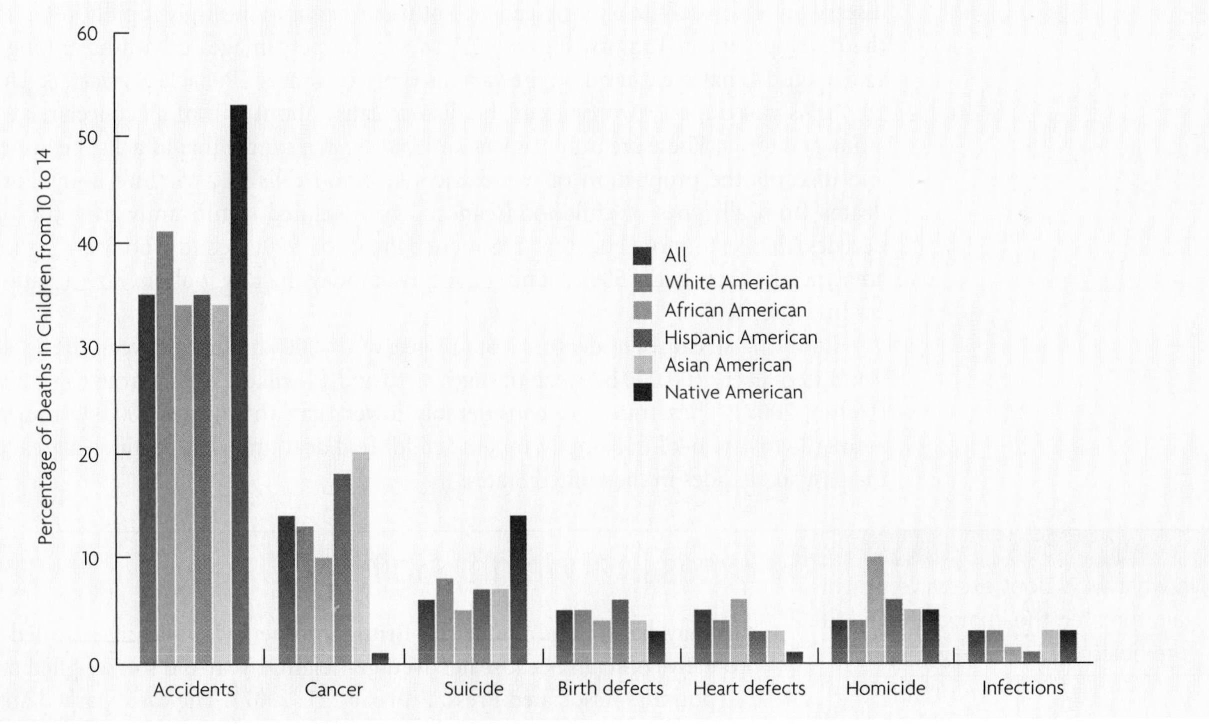

Figure 10.4 **Leading Causes of Death Among 10- to 14-Year-Olds**

Like the previous figure, this figure shows that accidents are the leading cause of death in all ethnic groups in the United States. However, as above, the rankings of the various causes of death vary across groups.

(*Source*: Heron, 2007.)

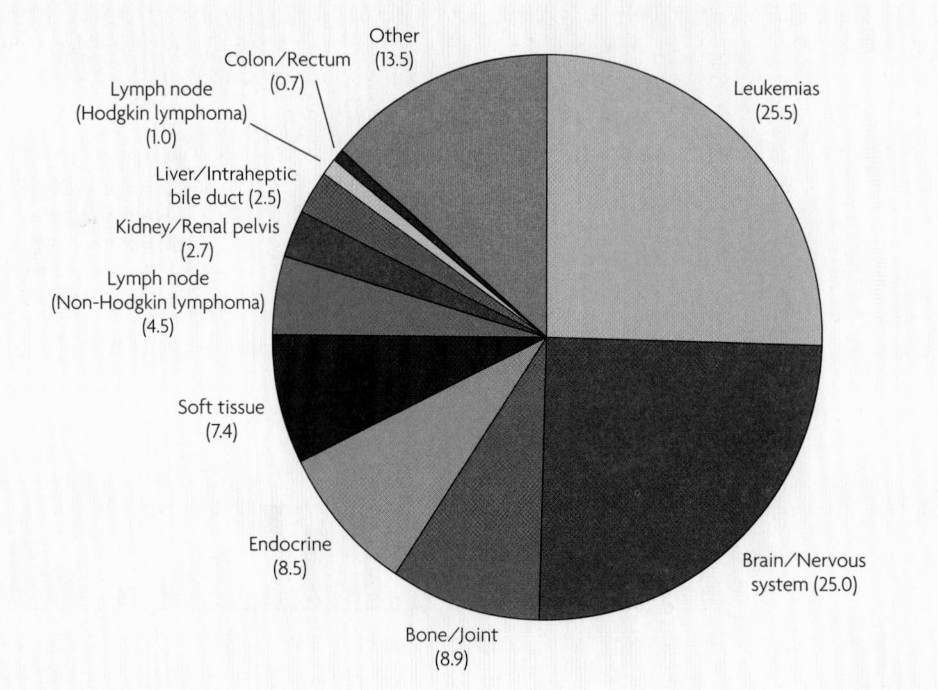

Figure 10.5 **Percentage of Childhood Cancer Deaths by Cancer Type**

Leukemia and brain cancer account for half of all childhood cancer deaths.

(*Source*: Pollack, Stewart, & Thompson, 2007.)

diseases in which cells in a particular type of tissue begin to multiply rapidly, often leading to the development of tumors. Figure 10.5 shows the percentages of deaths among children under age 14 that are caused by the various types of cancer (Pollack, Stewart, & Thompson, 2007). As you can see, two types of the disease cause about half of all cancer-related deaths among children. These are brain cancer and *leukemia*, a cancer that attacks the bone marrow and disrupts the proportion of white and red blood cells in a victim's body. Fortunately, deaths from all types of childhood cancer have declined significantly over the past three decades, thanks to more effective treatments. Prior to 1970, a child who was diagnosed with any type of cancer had a 50% chance of survival; today the rate is about 80% (National Cancer Institute, 2007).

Counting all causes of death, 15 out of every 100,000 children between the ages of 5 and 9 and 19 of every 100,000 between the ages of 10 and 14 will die each year in the United States (Heron, 2007). These rates are considerably lower than the 30 per 100,000 mortality rate among 1- to 4-year-olds. Happily, too, the childhood death rate has declined a great deal over the past six decades in the United States.

Learning Objective 10.7

In what ways does excessive weight gain threaten the immediate and future health of school-aged children?

Excessive Weight Gain

You may have heard about the British mother who was investigated by child protective officials because her average-height 8-year-old son weighed more than 200 pounds (Associated Press, February 27, 2007). The case sparked an international debate about whether a parent who allows a child to become so much heavier than he should be is guilty of child abuse. Such cases raise public awareness of the fact that **excessive weight gain** is the most serious long-term health risk of the middle childhood period. Excessive weight gain is a pattern in which children gain more weight in a year than is appropriate for their height, age, and sex. If a child gains excessive amounts of weight over a number of years, she is at risk of having weight problems and a number of serious health problems in adulthood.

excessive weight gain a pattern in which children gain more weight in a year than is appropriate for their height, age, and sex

A word about terminology is in order here, because you are probably familiar with the term *obesity* with regard to weight problems. For adults, obesity has a fixed definition that is based on the *body mass index* (*BMI*), a measure that estimates a person's proportion of body fat. Adults whose BMIs exceed 30 are classified as obese (Centers for Disease Control [CDC], 2007a). When referring to children, public health officials speak in terms of excessive weight gain, as defined above, because some degree of increase in the BMI occurs in growing children as the ratios of fat and muscle in their bodies change. Moreover, when prepubertal hormonal changes occur in the later years of middle childhood, girls' BMIs can become temporarily distorted as the accompanying accumulation of fat tissues outpaces the growth of other kinds of tissue. Thus, it would be wrong to conclude that a 10- or 11-year-old girl was obese when what was really happening was that her body was in a transitional stage. As you can see, using different terminology helps to get across the idea that the process of diagnosing weight problems is not the same in children as in adults.

To determine whether an individual child's weight gain is appropriate, health-care professionals use a measure called **BMI-for-age**, a variation on the body mass index that applies to adults (CDC, 2007a). A child's BMI-for-age is determined by calculating her BMI and comparing it to that of others her age. Different standards are used for boys and girls, because their BMIs do not increase at the same rate.

Children whose BMIs fall at the 95th percentile are considered **overweight**, and those whose BMIs fall between the 85th and 95th percentiles are classified as **at-risk-for-overweight** (CDC, 2007a). Because of growth spurts and the inherent instability of physical variables in childhood, multiple assessments are required before a child is actually classified as either overweight or at-risk-for-overweight, however. As you can see in Figure 10.6, the number of overweight children in the United States has grown at an alarming rate over the past two decades. Currently, almost one in five children between the ages of 6 and 11 is overweight (NCHS, 2007). Similar increases have been documented in every country in the world that tracks the prevalence of overweight among children (Wang & Lobstein, 2006).

Assessments of weight gain are a vitally important part of well-child care during middle childhood, because the older a child gets without stopping the pattern of excessive weight gain,

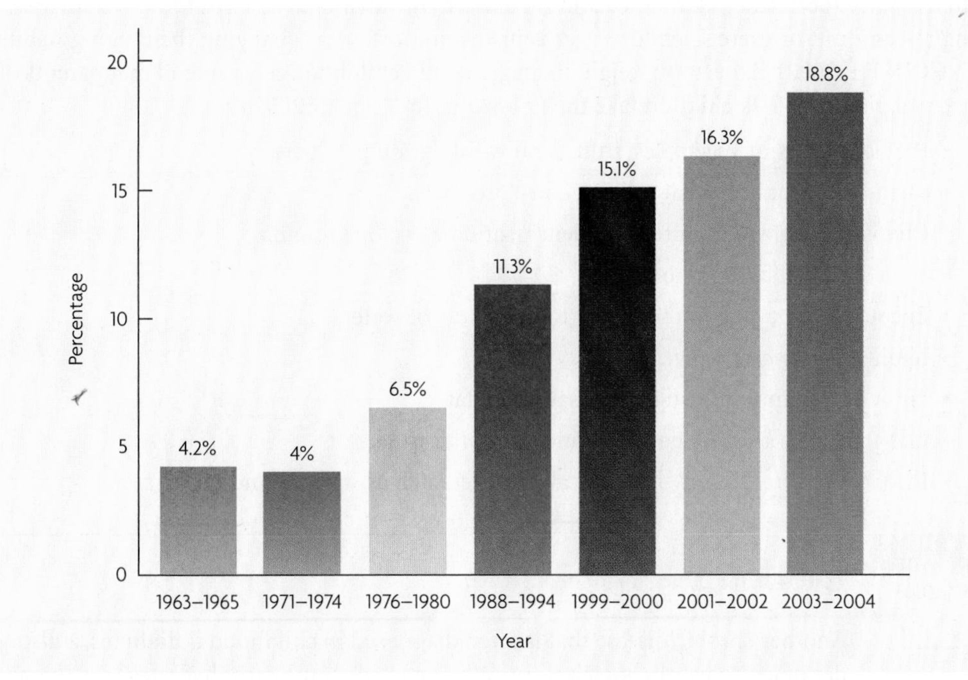

Figure 10.6 Prevalence of Overweight 6- to 11-Year-Olds in the United States

The prevalence of overweight (BMI ≥ 95th percentile) has increased dramatically in the United States over the past 40 years.

(*Source*: NCHS, 2007.)

BMI-for-age a measure that compares an individual child's BMI against established norms for his or her age group and sex

overweight a term that characterizes a child whose BMI is at the 95th percentile

at-risk-for-overweight a term that characterizes a child whose BMI is between the 85th and 95th percentiles

Many children in the industrialized world are overweight. One reason is that they consume snacks and beverages that contain a lot of sugar.

the more likely the child is to be overweight into the adult years (Magarey, Daniels, Boulton, & Cockington, 2003; Singh, Mulder, Twisk, van Mechelen, & Chinapaw, 2008). Only a fifth of overweight babies become overweight adults, but half of those who were overweight in elementary school continue to be overweight in adulthood (Serdula et al., 1993). In addition, more than half of overweight children have one or more risk factors, such as elevated levels of cholesterol or high blood pressure, that predispose them to heart disease later in life (National Center for Chronic Disease Prevention and Health Promotion [NCCDPHP], 2000). As you will learn in Chapter 13, another consequence of overweight is that it accelerates some aspects of sexual maturation in girls, such as breast development, but slows down the process in boys (Pierce & Leon, 2005; Wang, 2002).

As you might suspect, overeating or eating too much of the wrong foods causes excessive weight gain in children just as it does in adults (NCCDPHP, 2000). However, both twin and adoption studies suggest that the tendency to gain excessive amounts of weight in childhood probably results from an interaction between a genetic predisposition for obesity and environmental factors that promote overeating or low levels of activity (Stunkard, Harris, Pedersen, & McClearn, 1990; Wardle, Carnell, Haworth, & Plomin, 2008). Whatever the genetic contribution might be, research suggests that a cultural pattern of decreases in physical activity and increases in the consumption of high-calorie convenience foods has led to the current epidemic of overweight children and adults (Arluk, Swain, & Dowling, 2003; Hood & Ellison, 2003; NCCDPHP, 2000; Vandewater, Shim, & Caplovitz, 2004).

It's important to keep in mind, though, that weight-loss diets for children can be fairly risky. Because they are still growing, the nutritional needs of overweight children differ from those of overweight adults (Tershakovec & Stallings, 1998). Consequently, overweight children require special diets developed and supervised by nutritional experts. Moreover, increasing the amount of exercise children get is just as important as changing their eating habits (NCCDPHP, 2000). Experts on weight management in childhood recommend that parents of overweight and at-risk children take the following steps (CDC, 2007a):

- Provide plenty of vegetables, fruits, and whole-grain products.
- Include low-fat or nonfat milk or dairy products.
- Choose lean meats, poultry, fish, lentils, and beans for protein.
- Serve reasonably sized portions.
- Encourage everyone in the family to drink lots of water.
- Limit sugar-sweetened vegetables.
- Limit consumption of sugar and saturated fat.
- Limit children's TV, video game, and computer time.
- Involve the whole family in physical activities such as walking and bicycling.

Learning Objective 10.8

What are the health risks associated with type 1 and type 2 diabetes?

Diabetes

Another chronic disease that is often diagnosed in childhood is **diabetes**, a disorder of carbohydrate metabolism. When you consume carbohydrates (e.g., bread, candy, sugared soda), your blood sugar rises as your digestive system breaks down the constituent molecules. In response to the rise in blood sugar, your pancreas releases a hormone called *insulin* that prevents your blood sugar from rising to a level that can damage your or-

diabetes a disorder of carbohydrate metabolism

gans. In people with diabetes, this system doesn't work properly, leading to chronically high blood sugar levels, a condition that can cause extensive damage to the body's blood vessels and organs. The symptoms of diabetes include fatigue, excessive urination, and excessive thirst. Some children also have a chronic low-grade fever. Because the symptoms of diabetes are similar to those of less serious conditions, children often display symptoms for some time and undergo a variety of medical tests before the disease is diagnosed.

In **type 1 diabetes**, blood sugar rises to dangerous levels because the pancreas does not produce insulin. Moreover, the child's body is unable to use carbohydrates to produce energy. In response, muscle tissues break down, and the child loses weight. At present, researchers think that the disease process is set in motion in a genetically vulnerable child when a viral infection causes the body's immune system to produce antibodies that attack the insulin-producing cells in the pancreas (Rosenthal & Gitelman, 2002). There is no cure for type 1 diabetes, but a person with the disease can lead a normal life.

Children and teens who have type 1 diabetes must be given injections of insulin in order to prevent their blood sugar from getting too high. Their blood sugar levels must also be tested periodically so that additional insulin can be administered, if necessary. In addition, blood sugar levels sometimes fall too low after an insulin injection, and the child must eat something quickly to avoid fainting. Some children with type 1 diabetes receive insulin continuously by means of a pump that delivers the drug through a surgically implanted IV line, usually in the abdomen or hip area.

In **type 2 diabetes**, the sufferer's pancreas produces insulin, but her body does not respond to it, a condition called *insulin resistance.* The cause of type 2 diabetes hasn't been identified, but heredity does appear to play a role (Rosenthal & Gitelman, 2002). However, lifestyle factors may be equally important in the development of the disease.

At one time, type 2 diabetes was thought to exist only in adults. In recent years, however, the disease has become increasingly common among school-aged children who are just on the verge of puberty and among teenagers (Rosenthal & Gitelman, 2002). At present, one in five children with diabetes suffers from type 2 diabetes, and some studies have shown that half of all new cases of diabetes in late childhood and adolescence involve the type 2 version of the disorder. The increasing prevalence of overweight in children and teens is thought to be responsible for the rise in type 2 diabetes rates. Group differences in rates of type 2 diabetes may be explained by group differences in overweight (Mokdad et al., 2003). For instance, African American, Native American, and Hispanic American children and teens have higher rates of type 2 diabetes than do children in other groups, but they are also more likely to be overweight. Thus, the factors that contribute to excessive weight gain in these groups are also thought to contribute to diabetes rates.

In children who are overweight, the hormonal changes that precede and accompany puberty are believed to trigger some type of change in the body's fat cells that makes them resistant to the effects of insulin. Consequently, type 2 diabetes can often be successfully treated by reducing a sufferer's proportion of body fat through diet and exercise. Moreover, elimination of simple carbohydrates, such as sugar and highly refined grains, from the diet often stabilizes blood sugar levels in individuals who have the disease. If these measures fail, there are medications available that can help regulate blood sugar levels.

Controlling blood sugar levels in individuals with both types of diabetes is important because of the strong negative impact the disease often has on cardiovascular functioning. Children with diabetes are at risk of developing high blood pressure, high cholesterol, and coronary artery disease (Orchard, Costacou, Kretowski, & Nesto, 2006; Rodriguez et al., 2006). When these conditions develop in childhood, the chances of having a stroke, heart attack, or other life-threatening cardiovascular crisis in early adulthood increase dramatically. Diabetes can also cause kidney damage, a consequence that can require amputation of the lower extremities. In addition, diabetes can damage the retina, sometimes causing total blindness. The good news is that research clearly shows that early diagnosis and treatment can moderate the effects of both type 1 and type 2 diabetes (Orchard, Costacou, Kretowski, & Nesto, 2006; Rodriguez et al., 2006).

type 1 diabetes a type of diabetes in which the pancreas fails to produce insulin

type 2 diabetes a type of diabetes in which the pancreas produces insulin, but the body does not respond to it

Learning Objective 10.9

What is the impact of socioeconomic status on children's health?

Socioeconomic Status and Children's Health

In the United States, *poverty* is defined as a yearly income of less than $21,200 for a family of four (U.S. Department of Health and Human Services, 2008). As you can see in Figure 10.7, the child poverty rate in the United States declined from 22% in 1993 to 17.4% in 2006 (DeNavas-Walt, Proctor, & Smith, 2007). However, you will notice that children are more likely than those in other age groups to live in poor households. Moreover, the child poverty rate is higher in the United States than in many other industrialized countries in the world. By way of contrast, the poverty rate for children is roughly 5% in Denmark and is less than 15% in Sweden (House of Commons Work and Pensions Committee, 2006). In addition, another 39% of children in the United States live in *low-income* households, those in which the total family income is between 100% and 200% of the official federal poverty level (Douglas-Hall & Chau, 2007). Thus, more than half of all children in the United States live in families that have either insufficient funds or just enough to get by.

Characteristics of Child Poverty Child poverty rates vary across ethnic groups, as you can see in Figure 10.8. Likewise, children reared by single mothers are far more likely to be living in poverty (Evans, 2004). Research shows that children in low-income and poor households are at greater risk of a number of health problems than are their peers who are better off. This association exists in other countries as well (Currie, Shields, & Wheatley Price, 2004; Currie & Stabile, 2003).

For most children, the deleterious effects of low income on health are transient, because most families do not remain in poverty throughout their children's early years. Long-term studies suggest that about 8% of families with children in the United States experience chronic low-income status (U.S. Department of the Treasury, 2008). Similar results have been obtained in longitudinal studies in the United Kingdom (Burgess, Propper, & Rigg, 2004). Predictably, children in families that are chronically below the low-income threshold are less healthy than their peers who never experience poverty or whose families experience one or two episodes of low income (Case, Lubotsky, & Paxson, 2002; Burgess, Propper, & Rigg,

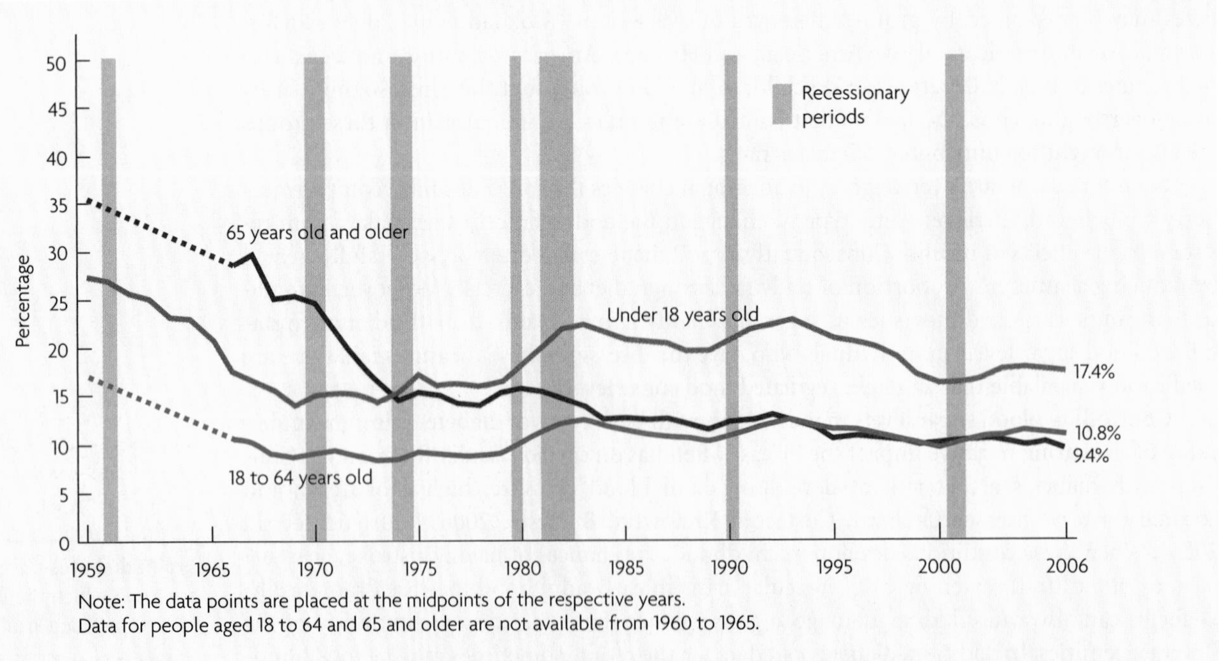

Figure 10.7 **Poverty and Age**

Children and teenagers are more likely to live in poverty than those in other age groups are.

(*Source*: DeNavas-Walt, Proctor, & Smith, 2007.)

2004). Consequently, resarchers have devoted a considerable amount of attention to finding out how a family's chronic lack of financial resources influences children's health.

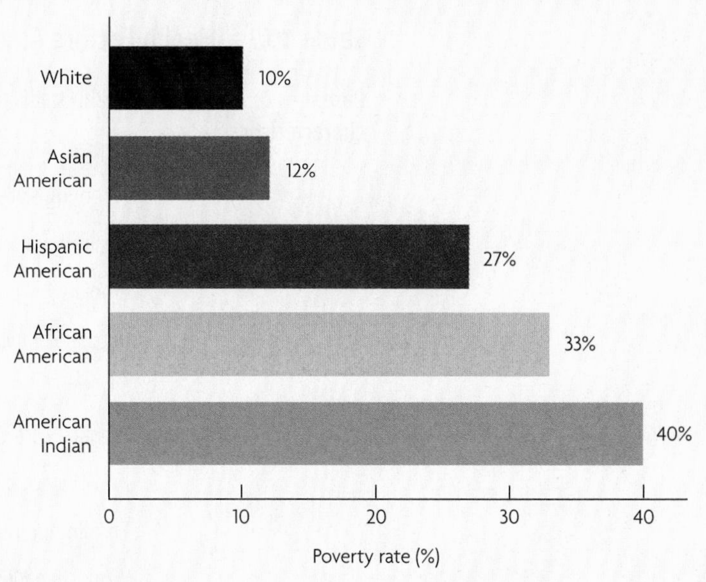

Figure 10.8
Child Poverty Rates Across Ethnic Groups in the United States, 2006

Although overall poverty rates have declined considerably in the United States over the past three decades, the rate among some ethnic groups continues to be alarmingly high.

(*Source*: From A. Douglas-Hall and M. Chau, *Basic Facts about Low-Income Children, Birth to Age 18*. Reprinted by permission of NCCP (National Center for Children in Poverty).

Risk Factors Associated with Poverty

Studies show that the link between family income and children's health is complex (Chen, 2004). As a result, researchers typically do not study income in isolation from other variables. Instead, most examine the effects of **socioeconomic status (SES)**—a collective term that includes the economic, occupational, and educational factors that influence a family's relative position in society—on children's health. Such studies show that variables such as employment status, occupation, and parental educational levels predict children's health better than income alone does. Still, identifying risk factors tells us little about why those factors are important.

One variable that has been proposed as a partial explanation of the link between SES and children's health is access to medical care. Clearly, families of lower SES, in which parents work at low-wage jobs that do not have health insurance benefits, are less able to provide their children with health care than those with better employment situations. Yet, recent studies comparing low-income and poor families in the United States to those in Canada and the United Kingdom, where all citizens have access to free health care, have failed to fully support this hypothesis (Case, Lee, & Paxson, 2007). Children in low-income and poor families across all three nations have more health problems than those in more affluent households do, although these data do show that the correlation between SES and children's health is somewhat stronger in the United States than in either Canada or the United Kingdom. Thus, access to medical care is one piece of the SES-health relationship puzzle in the United States, but it isn't the whole story.

Looking beyond access to care, researchers have identified a number of other variables that may help to explain the association between SES and children's health (Chen, 2002). For instance, tobacco use is more frequent among individuals of lower SES (Gilman, Abrams, & Buka, 2003). As a result, children in lower SES homes are more likely to be exposed to nicotine prior to birth and to second-hand smoke in the early years. Table 10.1 on page 306 lists several other such factors.

Table 10.1 includes a multitude of factors, but it's important to realize that, with few exceptions, any one of these factors alone, especially if it is experienced only temporarily, is probably insufficient to explain the relationship between SES and children's health. Imagine, though, what happens to children who are exposed to several of these factors for an extended period of time. Consider, too, that along with these SES-related health factors, children in low-income and poor households experience risk factors that children at all income levels encounter, such as whatever health-related predispositions might be in their genetic heritage (e.g., inherited diseases) and infectious agents in the environment (e.g., viruses).

Researchers use the term **cumulative risk** to describe the overall risk resulting from interactions over time among risk factors that influence children's health. To understand how cumulative risk works, consider this scenario:

> A boy is born at low birth weight because of his mother's use of tobacco during pregnancy. In the newborn nursery, he develops breathing problems. He responds well to treatment and recovers, but his early breathing difficulties have left him with a somewhat elevated risk of such problems later on. He goes home to a household in which he is exposed to second-hand smoke, a factor that elevates his risk of lung problems even more. Over the first 3 years of his life, he suffers from frequent colds, perhaps as a result of attending an overcrowded, unlicensed child-care program. His colds often progress to bronchitis. Again, he responds to treatment, but his

socioeconomic status (SES) a collective term that includes the economic, occupational, and educational factors that influence a family's relative position in society

cumulative risk the overall risk resulting from interactions over time among risk factors that influence children's health

Table 10.1 Health Factors Associated with SES

Parent characteristics	Health status and history
	Depression
	Parenting skills (e.g., consistent bedtime)
	Health habit instruction (e.g., teaching children how to brush their teeth)
	Smoking
	Substance abuse
	Obesity
	Prenatal care compliance
	Knowledge of child development
	Enrollment in available health insurance, nutritional support programs
	Work schedule
	Unemployment
	Nonparental care arrangements
	Education
Environmental characteristics	Child-proofing of environment (e.g., safety latches on cabinets)
	Cleanliness of home, neighborhood, child-care facilities
	Types of food available in the home
	Types of foods sold in neighborhood grocery stores
	Medicines available in neighborhood drug stores
	Seat belts, child safety seats in vehicles
	Mold, pollution, and other respiratory irritants
	Access to health care
	Safe, appropriate sites for motor play in neighborhood
	Safe, appropriate toys in home
	Access to high-quality child-care programs
	Level of violence in neighborhood

Source: Ashiabi & O'Neal, 2007; Burgess, Propper, & Rigg, 2004; Dowd, 2007.

> risk of breathing problems is further elevated by his medical history. In addition, he no longer responds to certain antibiotics, limiting the range of treatment options for future infections. Worrying about the child's health problems contributes to his mother's inability to quit smoking. By age 6, the boy is diagnosed with asthma and misses several days of school each month. By second grade, the boy falls behind in reading skills and is teased by his peers.

As this example shows, the accumulated, interactive influences of several risk factors can have far-reaching effects. Moreover, these effects may extend beyond the physical domain into the cognitive and socioemotional realms.

Some researchers argue that there is a cyclical component to the association between SES and children's health (Burgess, Propper, & Rigg, 2004). This cycle is perpetuated when lower-SES teens adopt behaviors such as smoking that were modeled by their parents. These behavioral decisions threaten teens' own health and that of the children they will have in the future.

Thus, many argue that, to be successful, any approach to improving the health of children who live in low-SES households must address all of the risk factors associated with SES.

Exposure to nicotine prior to birth and second-hand smoke afterward is one of the health factors associated with SES. Lower-income parents are more likely to smoke than parents of average or above-average means are.

Protective Factors Research aimed at identifying protective factors that enable some children to thrive in even the most deprived environments provides some insight into how the cycle can be broken. Studies of resilient and vulnerable children suggest that certain characteristics or circumstances may help protect some children from the detrimental effects of the cumulative stressors associated with poverty. Among the key protective factors are the following:

- High IQ of the child (Koenon, Moffitt, Poulton, Martin, & Caspi, 2007)
- Competent parenting, such as an authoritative style (good supervision or monitoring of the child seems especially important) (Eamon & Mulder, 2005)
- Parental knowledge about child development (Seo, 2006)
- An optimistic outlook (Lam, Lam, Shek, & Tang, 2004)
- Effective schools (Woolley & Grogan-Kaylor, 2006)
- A secure initial attachment of the child to the parent (Li-Grining, 2007)
- A strong community helping network, including friends, family, or neighbors (Barrow, Armstrong, Vargo, & Boothroyd, 2007)
- Stable parental employment (Terrisse, 2000)
- A strong sense of ethnic identity (Thomas, Townsend, & Belgrave, 2003)
- Participation in early childhood programs (Smokowski, Mann, Reynolds, & Fraser, 2004)

Thus, the ultimate effect that living in poverty has on the development of an individual child will depend on the combined effects of the risk and protective factors that are present in the child herself and in her environment. Poverty does not guarantee bad outcomes. But it stacks the deck against many children.

Health Habits

Learning Objective 10.10

Why is it important to encourage school-aged children to develop good health habits?

Among adults, the link between health habits and overall physical fitness is clear. Physical exercise increases fitness, and greater fitness is linked to better health. Adults who exercise even moderately live longer and are less likely to suffer from such chronic illnesses as cardiovascular disease.

Among children, the health benefits of greater fitness are less well established, although regular moderate or vigorous exercise does help to reduce or control some significant childhood medical problems. And as we noted earlier, exercise strengthens children's bones, an advantage that persists into adulthood. Nevertheless, the *habit* of exercise, established in childhood, may increase the likelihood that an individual will exercise in adulthood—a highly desirable outcome.

Physical education programs in schools have been one important mechanism for promoting fitness as well as providing training in individual sport skills. In light of the accumulating evidence on the importance of exercise in adulthood, in recent years, many physical education experts have emphasized the importance of training in **lifetime physical activities**, activities or sports that are relatively easy to pursue into adulthood because they can be done alone or with only one or two others. Such activities include swimming, walking, running, bicycling, racquet sports, aerobic dance, weight training, rowing, and skiing.

lifetime physical activities sports or activities that are relatively easy to pursue into adulthood because they can be done alone or with only one or two others

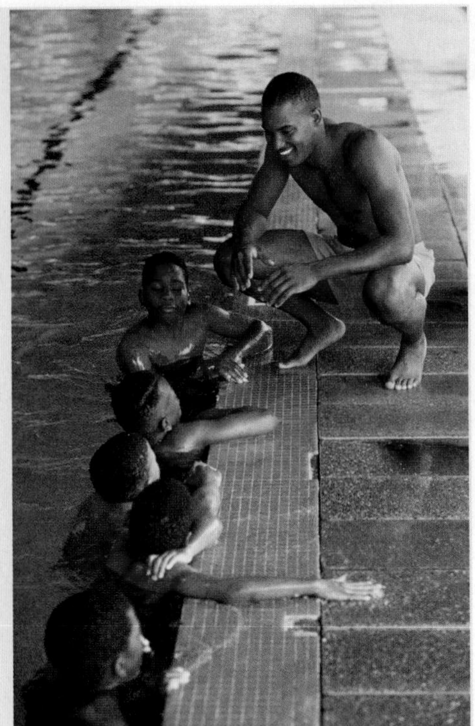

Many physical education programs emphasize health-related lifetime physical activities, such as swimming, that children can continue to enjoy and benefit from into their adult years.

Research indicates that elementary level physical education classes do tend to focus on lifetime physical activities. However, surveys show that only 12% of first-graders in the United States have daily physical education classes (National Institute for Health Care Management [NIHCM] Foundation, 2004). In addition, while physical education classes for girls at the secondary level emphasize lifetime activities, boys' classes do not (Fairclough, Stratton, & Baldwin, 2002).

Do physical education classes make a difference? It's clear that they do if we consider their immediate effects on overweight. One study found that adding just one hour of PE per week reduced the average BMI in an elementary school by 31% (NIHCM Foundation, 2004). Furthermore, medical researchers have found that cardiovascular fitness is correlated with academic performance among school-aged children (Cottrell, Northrup, & Wittburg, 2007). So, helping children improve their overall fitness levels may pay dividends in the classroom.

In order for a physical education program to have a significant impact on overall physical fitness, it has to be guided by goals based on an understanding of children's physical development. The norms included in the *FitnessGram*, a series of tests and physical fitness standards developed by the Cooper Institute in 1982, represent such goals. For instance, the FitnessGram standard for a mile run/walk is 9 to 11½ minutes for 10-year-old boys and 9½ to 12½ minutes for 10-year-old girls. Both boys and girls that age are expected to be able to do 12 curl-ups and 7 push-ups.

The FitnessGram has been updated many times since its original publication and is now accompanied by the *ActivityGram*, a system that helps teachers and parents keep track of children's physical activities and relate them to physical fitness goals. Moreover, the FitnessGram and ActivityGram have been included in the physical education curriculum standards of many states. The program has been in place in California for several years, and officials report that its implementation has led to improvements in the fitness levels of the state's public school students (California Department of Education, 2007).

Atypical Development

Most school-aged children in the United States show some kind of "problem behaviors" at one time or another (Klass & Costello, 2003). For example, parents report that 10–20% of 7-year-olds still wet their beds at least occasionally, 30% have nightmares, 20% bite their fingernails, 10% suck their thumbs, and 10% swear to such an extent that it is considered a problem. Problems like these, especially if they last only a few months, should be considered part of "normal" development (see *Developmental Science in the Clinic*). As you learned in Chapter 7, psychologists consider problem behaviors to be *atypical*, or symptomatic of a *psychological disorder*, only if they persist for 6 months or longer or if the problem is at the extreme end of the continuum for that behavior. Some disorders involve children's behavior, whereas others manifest themselves in the emotional arena.

attention-deficit hyperactivity disorder (ADHD) a behavior disorder that causes children to have difficulty attending to and completing tasks, as well as controlling impulses

Learning Objective 10.11

What are the features of attention-deficit hyperactivity disorder, and how is it treated?

Attention-Deficit Hyperactivity Disorder

The most common childhood behavioral disorder, one that afflicts as many as 18% of U.S. school children, is **attention-deficit hyperactivity disorder (ADHD)** (Visser & Lesesne, 2005). Children with ADHD are more physically active and/or less attentive than their peers. These characteristics often lead to academic and behavioral problems in school.

DEVELOPMENTAL SCIENCE IN THE CLINIC

Knowing When to Seek Professional Help

The parents of 7-year-old Lucinda sought the advice of a pediatric nurse regarding an ongoing battle they were having with their daughter. Lucinda was convinced that spaghetti and spaghetti sauce should touch each other only in a person's mouth. Consequently, she insisted on having her spaghetti served in two separate bowls, one for the pasta and another for the sauce. Furthermore, she required a spoon for the sauce and a fork for the pasta. She became hysterical at even the slightest suggestion that she try having her spaghetti in its more conventional form. Her parents had begun to worry that she might have some kind of psychological disorder and asked the nurse whether they should consult a child psychologist.

The nurse assured Lucinda's parents that her behavior was well within the bounds of normal behavior for 7-year-olds. She provided them with one of several checklists developed by experts in developmental psychopathology that help parents distinguish between behavior that is difficult to manage and behavior that may indicate a disorder for which professional care is appropriate. The checklist that the nurse gave to Lucinda's parents was published by the National Mental Health Association (available at http://www.nmha.org). Here are a few of the warning signs it includes:

- Changes in grades or behavior reports from teachers
- Changes in patterns of sleeping or eating
- Frequent stomachaches or other minor physical symptoms
- Obsessive concern with weight loss
- A sad facial expression that persists over a period of weeks
- Outbursts of rage that lead to destruction of property or aggression toward others
- Activity far in excess of that exhibited by children of the same age
- Frequent unyielding defiance of parental or teacher authority

Of course, every child who exhibits these behaviors doesn't have a serious psychological disorder. Still, when a child's pattern of difficult behavior matches one or more of these signs, parents should probably adopt the "better safe than sorry" approach and consult a mental health professional.

Questions for Reflection

1. According to the checklist, is Lucinda's spaghetti-eating behavior likely to be a sign of a psychological disorder? Why or why not?
2. What strategies might Lucinda's parents use to get her to try eating spaghetti the way most people do?

Characteristics of ADHD On many kinds of attention tasks, children with ADHD do not differ at all from normal children (Lawrence et al., 2004). They seem to vary from their normal peers in activity level, the ability to sustain attention (especially with boring and repetitive tasks), and the ability to control impulses. However, the degree of hyperactivity children with ADHD exhibit is unrelated to their performance on attention tasks. That is, a child can be very physically active and still be good at controlling his attention. Likewise, a child can be very calm yet have little ability to sustain attention. For this reason, there are now two types of ADHD: (1) the *hyperactive/impulsive type*, in which a high activity level is the main problem, and (2) the *inattentive type*, in which an inability to sustain attention is the major difficulty (DSM-IV TR, 2000). In addition, some children are diagnosed with *combined type* ADHD, signifying that they meet the criteria for both the hyperactive/impulsive and the inattentive type.

Most children with ADHD are successful in learning academic skills (Chadwick et al., 1999). However, their hyperactivity and/or inattentiveness often causes other kinds of problems. For one thing, children with both types of ADHD usually produce school work that is messy and filled with errors, causing them to get poor grades (Cahn et al., 1996). They may be disruptive in class and are often rejected by other children.

Culture, Age, Gender, and Ethnicity ADHD is diagnosed less frequently in other cultures than it is in the United States (NIMH, 2006). Critics of using medication to control ADHD symptoms suggest that this cross-national difference is the result of overuse of the diagnosis in the United States. However, some developmentalists assert that educators and mental health professionals in other nations have failed to recognize the degree to which ADHD may be prevalent in their children (Overmeyer & Taylor, 1999). Others suggest that there is a real cross-cultural difference in the incidence of ADHD. For example, a study comparing African American and South African 6-year-olds who were similar in family structure and socioeconomic status found that a larger proportion of African American children, especially boys, scored high on scales measuring hyperactivity (Barbarin, 1999).

Table 10.2 Age, Gender, Ethnicity, and ADHD

	Percentage Diagnosed with ADHD		Percentage Taking Medication for ADHD	
	Male	Female	Male	Female
Age				
4–8	6	2	4	2
9–12	14	10	9	4
13–17	14	10	7	2
Race				
White	12	5	7	3
Black	12	4	6	2
Multiracial	14	6	7	3
Other	7	2	3	1
Ethnicity				
Hispanic	5	3	2	1
Non-Hispanic	12	2	7	3
Primary Language in the Home				
English	12	5	7	3
Other	2	1	<1	<1

Source: Visser & Lesesne, 2005.

The data in Table 10.2 reveal that rates of ADHD diagnosis increase over the elementary school years. As school becomes more difficult, the characteristics of the disorder cause problems for more children. Many of those who are diagnosed in the later grades may have been able to succeed at the less challenging work in the early grades without additional help.

The table also clearly shows the striking gender difference in ADHD diagnosis and treatment. Part of this difference is due to the finding that girls are more likely to exhibit symptoms of the inattentive and combined types of ADHD than the hyperactive type (Biederman et al., 1999). Boys show the opposite pattern—that is, they are more likely to be hyperactive and disruptive. Thus, teachers and parents may be more likely to notice boys' problems and seek help for them. Girls' symptoms, in contrast, may be attributed to laziness, moodiness, or a lack of interest in school. However, the gender difference may also represent an overreaction to boys' greater general rowdiness. Thus, some speculate that gender differences in ADHD diagnosis result from the "medicalization" of typical male behavior, a view that remains controversial (Timimi & Leo, 2009).

Table 10.2 also shows that ADHD diagnosis and medication rates in the United States are consistent across White, African American, and multiracial groups. However, rates are far lower among Hispanic American children (Visser & Lesesne, 2005). This difference could be due to a real difference in children's behavior across groups, overdiagnosis in non-Hispanic groups, or underdiagnosis in Hispanic Americans. With regard to the first of these possibilities, surveys of teachers suggest that the kinds of behavior problems that lead to a diagnosis of ADHD occur just as frequently among Hispanic American children as they do in others (Ham, 2004). As for the second possible explanation, extensive surveys of parents, teachers, and health-care professionals, together with the high degree of consistency in diagnosis rates across non-Hispanic subgroups, suggest that ADHD is not overdiagnosed (Cuffe, Moore, & McKeown, 2005). The data regarding language and ADHD diagnosis shown in the table supports the third possibility: that ADHD is underdiagnosed among Hispanic American children. It is likely that language differences among parents, teachers, and health-care professionals prevent the establishment of the kind of communication among them that is needed to diagnose ADHD. In other words, Hispanic American children whose parents speak English are more likely to be diagnosed with ADHD, or, put differently, those whose families do not speak English are at increased risk of not being diagnosed and treated for this troubling condition. These findings highlight the need for multilingual professionals in schools and health-care settings.

Causes of ADHD The cause of ADHD is unknown. However, some developmentalists suggest that children with ADHD are neurologically different from their peers. Specifically, some have asserted that children with ADHD have functional deficits in the right hemisphere of the brain (Sandson, Bachna, & Morin, 2000). Others say that serotonin function is impaired in children with ADHD (Kent et al., 2002). Some type of biological factor does seem to be involved, as children who were born at 24 to 31 weeks of gestation are four to six times as likely to suffer from the symptoms of ADHD as their peers who were full-term infants (Barlow & Lewandowski, 2000). Other developmentalists hypothesize that children with ADHD require more sensory stimulation than their peers; thus, they move around more in order to get the stimulation they need (Antrop, Roeyers, Van Oost, & Buysse, 2000).

Psychologists are fairly sure that diet, environmental toxins, and brain damage are not the causes of ADHD, despite what some promoters of "cures" claim (Spreen, Risser, & Edgell, 1995). At present, most experts believe that each individual case of ADHD is caused by a complex interaction of factors unique to the specific child. These factors may include genetics, temperament, parenting styles, peer relations, the type and quality of the school a child attends, and stressors in the child's life, such as poverty, family instability, and parental mental illness.

Treating and Managing ADHD By the time their children are diagnosed with ADHD, usually upon entering school, many parents have lost confidence in their ability to control them (Barkley, 1990). Some cope with their difficult child by being extremely permissive. Others respond by becoming excessively harsh and, out of frustration, sometimes treat the child with ADHD abusively. Thus, parent training can be useful in helping parents cope with children who have ADHD.

The goal of such parenting programs is to help parents regain a sense of control (Barkley, 1990). For example, experts recommend that teachers provide parents with daily reports of their children's work in the various school subjects—language, math, social studies, and so on. Parents can then use the information to enforce a standing rule that the child must have completed all school work before watching television or doing other desired activities. Such approaches, when applied consistently, can help parents of children with ADHD manage their children's difficulties, as well as their own emotional reactions, more effectively.

As Table 10.2 shows, about half of children with ADHD take stimulant medications, such as methylphenidate (Ritalin). Medication rates are due partly to some parents' initial choices regarding treatment for the disorder. However, nonadherence to medical advice is probably a larger factor. Longitudinal studies show that one in five children who are prescribed medication for ADHD stops taking it within 4 to 6 months (Sanchez, Crismon, Barner, Bettinger, & Wilson, 2005). The primary reason for treatment termination is parents' view that their children should not be taking psychiatric medications.

Most children who do take medication for ADHD are calmer and can concentrate better (Demb & Chang, 2004; Mehta, Goodyer, & Sahakian, 2004). However, some studies show that many children's "response to the medication" may actually be due to changes in expectations on the part of their teachers and parents—a sort of self-fulfilling prophecy (Spreen et al., 1995). In addition, studies suggest that the concentration skills of children with ADHD can be improved with training. For example, one study found that, after an intensive 18-week training program, the attention skills of a group of children with ADHD were similar to those of a control group of children without attention difficulties (Semrud-Clikeman et al., 1999).

It's also important to note that medication doesn't always improve the grades of children with ADHD. For the most part, it seems that stimulant medications reduce such children's activity levels, help them control their impulses, and somewhat improve their social behavior. These effects usually result in improvements in classroom behavior and peer acceptance. Medications such as methylphenidate have the greatest effect on school grades among children whose ADHD symptoms are so severe that they interfere with actual learning (Spreen et al., 1995). For this reason, the use of stimulant medications for children who have mild or moderate ADHD symptoms is controversial. Moreover, recent studies show that many of the newer drugs that are used to treat ADHD (e.g., Adderall) are associated with changes in thinking that may increase a child's risk of developing a more serious psychological disorder (Gardner, 2007). Moreover, many of these drugs, including methylphenidate, have been found to increase the risk of cardiovascular events such as strokes and heart attacks in adults.

Learning Objective 10.12

What are the characteristics of oppositional defiant disorder?

Oppositional Defiant Disorder

Children with **oppositional defiant disorder (ODD)** display a pattern of negative, defiant, disobedient, and hostile behavior toward their parents and other authority figures that is established prior to age 8 (DSM-IV TR, 2000). Many children who suffer from ADHD are also diagnosed with ODD. Estimates of the prevalence of ODD among children with ADHD range from 21% to 60% (Austin, Reiss, & Burgdorf, 2007). Among children who are not diagnosed with ADHD, the prevalence of ODD has been estimated to fall between 2% and 16% (DSM-IV TR, 2000).

Children with ODD are difficult to manage, as you might guess. They tend to display defiant behaviors most often with the people they know best, such as their parents, siblings, teachers, and classmates. When interacting with people whom they do not know well, children with ODD often behave appropriately. For instance, many children with this disorder seem to be quite easygoing the first time they are interviewed by a psychologist or other mental health professional. Thus, diagnosing a child with ODD can be challenging. Diagnostic procedures must include assessments of the child's behavior across a variety of settings. Even so, it is not unusual for a child's parent and regular classroom teacher to report that his behavior fits the ODD profile, while others who interact less often with the child—a physical education or music teacher, for example—report having no problems with the child.

The cause of ODD is unknown, but researchers have identified several important themes in its manifestation (Tynan, 2008). As is true of ADHD, males are diagnosed with ODD more often than females are. Temperament is a factor as well; most children with ODD displayed difficult temperaments in infancy. Some studies suggest that prenatal exposure to alcohol, nicotine, and other teratogens increases a child's chances of being diagnosed with ODD. In addition, many parents of children with ODD suffer from emotional disturbances such as anxiety disorders and depression. A high degree of marital conflict is also often found among the parents of children with ODD.

If a child has both ADHD and ODD, medication may be prescribed for her ADHD symptoms, but the symptoms of ODD are treated with parent training (Tynan, 2008). Training is the treatment of choice because, by the time they consult with a mental health professional, parents of children with ODD have usually established a pattern of responding to their children's troublesome behavior that serves only to perpetuate it. Most such parents respond to their children's behavior by giving in to their demands in order to obtain brief reprieves from the children's perpetual hostility, argumentativeness, and disobedience. You should recognize this response pattern as negative reinforcement: The symptoms of ODD are an aversive stimulus that subsides temporarily when the parent gives the child whatever she wants. Thus, the behaviors of both the child and the parent are reinforced, and a maladaptive cycle is repeated each time the child misbehaves. In parent training sessions, therapists teach parents of children with ODD to break the cycle. They learn to set concrete limits for the child's behavior and to stick to promised consequences, no matter how difficult or outrageous the child's behavior becomes.

oppositional defiant disorder (ODD) a behavior disorder involving a pattern of negative, defiant, disobedient, and hostile behavior toward parents and other authority figures that is established prior to age 8

Learning Objective 10.13

What is childhood-onset conduct disorder?

Childhood-Onset Conduct Disorder

The features of oppositional defiant disorder are associated with yet another behavior disorder. **Childhood-onset conduct disorder** is a behavior disorder that includes high levels of aggression, argumentativeness, bullying, disobedience, irritability, and threatening and loud behavior that begin before a child is 10 years of age. Essentially, childhood-onset conduct disorder is diagnosed if a child has all the characteristics of ODD and also engages in threatening and/or aggressive behavior toward others and repetitively violates important social rules (e.g., stealing). Children who are diagnosed with childhood-onset conduct disorder usually exhibit problem behaviors that are more severe than those of teens who are diagnosed with *adolescent-onset conduct disorder* (discussed in Chapter 13). Moreover, the childhood-onset form of the disorder tends to persist into adolescence and adulthood, whereas the adolescent-onset form diminishes in early adulthood.

childhood-onset conduct disorder a behavior disorder involving high levels of aggression, argumentativeness, bullying, disobedience, irritability, and threatening and loud behavior that begin before age 10

Children who are diagnosed with childhood-onset conduct disorder typically begin life with a range of vulnerabilities, including difficult temperament, lower intelligence, or both (McCabe, Hough, Wood, & Yeh, 2001) In infancy, they are likely to have formed insecure/disorganized or insecure/avoidant attachments (Lyons-Ruth, 1996). In the preschool years, these children very often throw tantrums and defy parents. With peers, these children exhibit *trait aggression* (see Chapter 9)—that is, they behave aggressively toward others despite being punished by authority figures.

During the school years, these children's aggressive behavior and inability to empathize with others' feelings lead to peer rejection (Miller-Johnson, Coie, Maumary-Gremaud, & Bierman, 2002). Such peer rejection aggravates the problem, pushing the seriously aggressive child in the direction of other children with similar problems, who become the child's only supportive peer group (Shaw, Kennan, & Vondra, 1994). By adolescence, these youngsters are firmly established in delinquent or antisocial behavior, and their friends are drawn almost exclusively from among other delinquent teens (Tremblay, Masse, Vitaro, & Dobkin, 1995). They are also highly likely to display a cluster of other problem behaviors, including drug and alcohol use, truancy or dropping out of school, and early and risky sexual behavior, including having multiple sexual partners (Dishion, French, & Patterson, 1995; Wiesner, Kim, & Capaldi, 2005).

There is some indication that childhood-onset conduct disorder has a much stronger biological component than adolescent-onset conduct disorder (Oosterlaan, Geurts, Knol, & Sergeant, 2005). Thus, the preschooler who already shows defiant and oppositional behavior as well as aggressiveness may have strong inborn propensities for such behavior. Moreover, brain-imaging studies indicate that the brain structures that regulate emotion and planning in children with conduct disorder are less fully developed than those of children who do not have the disorder (Huebner et al., 2008).

Whether the child's genetic makeup and neurological deficits lead to the development of a full-fledged, persisting conduct disorder depends on the interactions between the inborn tendency and other aspects of the child's life, including the parents' ability to handle the child's early defiance as well as the general environment in which the child lives, such as inner

DEVELOPMENTAL SCIENCE IN THE CLASSROOM

Early Intervention for Childhood-Onset Conduct Disorder

Kim is a first-grade teacher who has been asked by her principal to incorporate a social/emotional education program into her classroom along with the students' daily instruction in reading, math, and other academic subjects. The principal demonstrated to Kim how the lessons in the program would help all of her students better understand, monitor, and control their emotions. However, the primary purpose of the program, the principal explained, would be to prevent first-graders who behave aggressively from developing childhood-onset conduct disorder. The new program was based on the *Fast Track Project*, a long-running research study involving hundreds of aggressive elementary school children in four different U.S. cities (Conduct Problems Research Group, 2004).

The procedures included in the Fast Track Project have proven to be useful in the prevention of childhood-onset conduct disorders (Greenberg & Kusché, 2006). In the original evaluation of the program, children were divided into experimental and control groups. In special class sessions, children in the experimental group learned how to recognize others' emotions. They also learned strategies for controlling their own feelings, managing aggressive impulses, and resolving conflicts with peers. Teachers in the program used a series of signals to help children maintain control. For example, a red card or a picture of a red traffic light indicated unacceptable behavior. A yellow card meant something like "Calm down. You're about to lose control." Parenting classes and support groups helped parents learn effective ways of teaching children acceptable behavior, rather than just punishing unacceptable behavior. In addition, parents were encouraged to maintain communication with their children's teachers. These strategies decreased the frequency of aggressive behavior among participants and enabled them to manage their emotions more effectively and to get along better with their peers (Conduct Problems Research Group, 2004).

Clearly, interventions such as the Fast Track Project require a considerable commitment of time and resources. Furthermore, they aren't effective for every child. However, they represent the best option developmentalists have to offer at this point. When balanced against the effects of conduct disorder on the lives of children who develop it and on those around them, the costs don't seem quite so extreme.

Questions for Reflection

1. What are the arguments for and against this statement: "When first-graders behave aggressively, they should be referred to programs such as the Fast Track Project rather than be punished."
2. How would you explain the benefits of the Fast Track Project to a parent who was reluctant to allow her highly aggressive first-grade child to participate in the program?

city or small town (Gottesman & Goldsmith, 1994). Parenting style matters as well; research suggests that children who develop conduct disorders have more permissive parents than do their peers (Dwairy & Menshar, 2005). Moreover, school-based programs can help prevent aggressive children from developing childhood-onset conduct disorder (see *Developmental Science in the Classroom* on page 313).

Learning Objective 10.14

How does depression affect the lives of school-aged children?

Depression

Some childhood disorders involve emotions rather than disruptive behavior. Nevertheless, in some cases, emotional disorders in children are manifested in the form of misbehavior, including many behaviors that are characteristic of attention-deficit hyperactivity disorder and oppositional-defiant disorder. Consequently, when children have behavior problems, mental health professionals often must rule out an emotional disorder as a possible cause before giving the child a diagnosis of ADHD, ODD, or childhood-onset conduct disorder. In addition, a child can be suffering from both a behavior disorder and **depression**, or feelings of sadness and despair that persist for more than 6 months.

For many years, psychiatrists took the position that children did not experience depression. This turned out to be quite wrong. Researchers have found abundant evidence that depression occurs at least occasionally among younger children. Perhaps 10% of school-aged children experience periods of deep sadness (Petersen et al., 1993). When such periods last 6 months or longer and are accompanied by other symptoms, such as disturbances of sleeping and eating and difficulty concentrating, the condition is usually referred to as **major depressive disorder (MDD)**.

When children experience feelings of deep sadness for 6 months or more, they may be diagnosed with depression.

Estimates of the frequency of major depressive disorder among children vary somewhat. The best studies suggest that, at any given time, about 1% of school-aged children have MDD (Cicchetti & Toth, 1998). During the middle childhood years, boys and girls are equally likely to be diagnosed with the disorder. Among children, bouts of MDD tend to last, on average, for 7 to 9 months, and they are highly likely to recur: As many as 90% of those who have a major depressive episode experience a recurrence within 2 years (Cicchetti & Toth, 1998). Further, depression has serious long-term consequences for children. For example, depression can interfere with learning by slowing down the speed at which the brain processes information (Calhoun & Dickerson Mayes, 2005).

The search for the developmental pathways leading to childhood depression begins with the clear finding that children growing up with parents who are depressed are much more likely than are those growing up with parents without depression to develop depression themselves (Merikangas & Angst, 1995). This finding could indicate a genetic factor, a possibility supported by at least a few studies of twins and adopted children (Petersen et al., 1993). Or, this link between parental and child depression could be explained in terms of changes in the parent-child interaction caused by the parent's depression.

Of course, not all children of parents with depression are themselves depressed. Whether a child moves along a pathway toward MDD seems to be largely a function of the number of other stresses present in the family, such as serious illness, family arguments, work stress, loss of income, job loss, or marital separation. Furthermore, the significant role of stress in the emergence of depression is clear among children whose parent or parents are not depressed. Any combination of stresses—such as the parents' divorce, the death of a parent or another loved person, a parent's loss of job, a move, and/or a change of schools—increases the likelihood of depression in the child (Chang, 2001; Compas, Ey, & Grant, 1993).

Antidepressant drugs are used to treat depression in children just as they are with adults. In most cases, these drugs are very effective. However, clinicians must closely track children's responses to them. Concerns about a link between antidepressant treatment and suicidal thinking and nonfatal suicidal behaviors in children led officials in the United States and other countries to recommend that patients younger than 18 be carefully monitored during the first few weeks of treatment (U.S. Food and Drug Administration, 2004). Thus, the use of antidepressant medications among children remains controversial.

depression feelings of sadness or despair that persist for more than 6 months

major depressive disorder (MDD) feelings of deep sadness that last 6 months or longer and are accompanied by disturbances of sleeping and eating and difficulty concentrating

Physical Development and the Whole Child

As you reflect on all you have learned about the physical changes that occur during middle childhood, you will notice that many of them are gradual. A child grows a bit taller each year, and her skills become a bit more refined with each passing birthday. Yet, when you contrast the skills of preschoolers with those of school-aged children, you get a better idea of the truly momentous nature of the leaps that distinguish middle childhood from earlier periods. These leaps in the physical domain, especially those that occur in brain development, are linked to equally dramatic advances in the cognitive and socioemotional domains. Here is a preview of what you will be reading about in Chapters 11 and 12.

Cognitive Functioning

In this chapter, you learned that the areas of the brain that are involved in planning and logic, the frontal lobes, become the focus of maturational processes during the later years of the middle childhood period. In addition, the links between the reticular formation and the frontal lobes are becoming well established, facilitating the development of selective attention. These advances enable children to reason more effectively than they could at earlier ages and to distinguish the important elements of a problem from the less important ones. Largely as a result of these changes, a powerful new form of thinking, *concrete operations*, becomes available to children.

Thanks to the maturing association areas, children can process information more rapidly. This increase in processing speed is essential to the impressive gains in memory function that occur during middle childhood. Nevertheless, if children experience a period of true depression, it is likely to interfere with these developmental processes at least temporarily.

Socioemotional Functioning

Changes in the physical and cognitive domains contribute to others in the socioemotional domain during middle childhood. For instance, selective attention plays a role in advances in *social cognition*, a child's understanding of the social world. Likewise, the school-aged child's growing ability to plan and his mastery of physical skills such as bike riding and skateboarding facilitate the development of stable peer relationships. And the penchant for rules that goes along with concrete operational thinking enables the school-aged child to engage in games and sports and motivates him to look for rules in the social world.

The search for rules influences self-concept development as well. The advances in logical thinking that occur during these years allow a child to develop an *ideal self* and compare her *actual self* to it. As you will learn in Chapter 12, such comparisons are the foundation of the child's sense of self-esteem.

A child's peer relationships and self-esteem are threatened by behavior disorders such as oppositional-defiant disorder and childhood-onset conduct disorder. Both can lead to peer rejection. In turn, peer rejection prevents children from engaging in the kinds of social interactions that are vital to the development of social cognition during middle childhood.

THE WHOLE CHILD IN FOCUS

To trace how the physical, cognitive, and socioemotional domains work together to influence Jamal's development, see *The Whole Child in Focus* on page 378.

Looking Ahead

At this point, you are probably familiar with our warnings about overemphasizing the distinctions among the physical, cognitive, and socioemotional domains. We again encourage you to keep the whole child in mind as you read about cognitive and socioemotional development in Chapters 11 and 12.

Test Prep Center

with mydevelopmentlab

PHYSICAL CHANGES

10.1 In what ways do children's body systems change across the middle childhood period? (pp. 290–291)

Physical development from age 6 to age 12 is steady and slow. Increases in height are due to growth at the ends of the body's long bones. Androgens are produced in greater quantities in preparation for puberty. Children gain in muscular strength and stamina.

1. The best measure of a child's physical maturity is ____________________.

2. Briefly describe the changes that occur during middle childhood in each of the areas listed in the table.

	Changes
Skeletal system	
Hormones	
Strength	
Stamina	

3. Mark each statement as true (T) or false (F) with regard to children's changing body systems.

    ______(A) Boys' skeletons mature at a more rapid rate than do girls' dkeletons.

    ______(B) Girls have slightly less fat and slightly more muscle tissue than boys.

    ______(C) While both boys and girls display an equal degree of stamina during the early years of middle childhood, boys show a greater increase in stamina than girls beginning at around age 10.

10.2 What changes occur in the brain during these years? (pp. 291–293)

Major brain growth spurts occur in 6- to 8-year-olds and in 10- to 12-year-olds. Neurological development leads to improvements in selective attention, information-processing speed, and spatial perception.

4. Transform these false statements into true statements.

    (A) Myelinization is complete by the time children reach middle childhood.

    ____

    ____

    (B) Lateralization is complete by the time children reach middle childhood.

    ____

    ____

5. From the Multimedia Library within MyDevelopmentLab, watch *Piano Lessons* and answer the following questions.

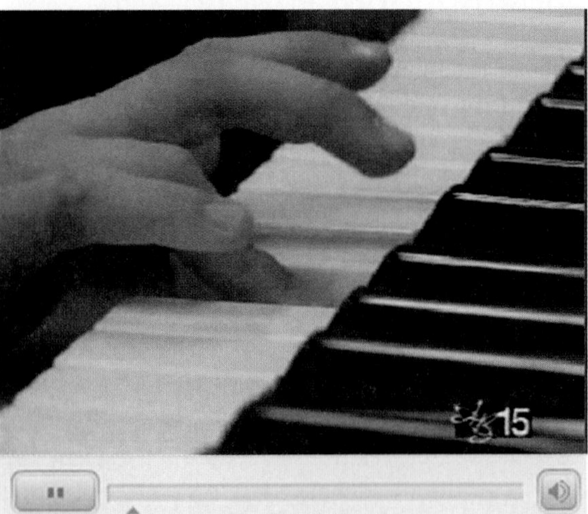

What happened to students' scores on tests of spatial perception when the school provided them with piano lessons?

____

____

What other activities might have the same effects, according to the researcher who was interviewed in the video?

____

____

10.3 How do children's motor and perceptual skills improve between ages 6 and 12? (pp. 293–294)

Maturation of children's skeletal, muscular, and neurological systems contributes to advances in both gross and fine motor skills. Children's ability to perceive figure-ground contrasts matures by the end of middle childhood. Motor and perceptual advances contribute to school-aged children's ability to acquire sports skills.

6. ______________________________ perception is the ability to distinguish between moving objects and their backgrounds.

HEALTH AND WELLNESS

10.4 What are the health-care needs of school-aged children? (pp. 294–296)

Myopia, requiring corrective lenses, is usually first diagnosed in middle childhood. Vision exams also sometimes detect convergence insufficiency, a disorder that makes it difficult for children to read and requires vision therapy. Children also need regular dental care as their primary teeth fall out and their permanent teeth erupt.

7. During middle childhood, about ________% of children in the United States visit a doctor's office or clinic at least once a year.
8. Overall, school-aged children are (healthier/less healthy) than preschool-aged children.
9. Match each of the following terms with its definition.

   ______(1) condition that causes blurry distant vision

   ______(2) condition in which the eyes cannot be turned inward to a sufficient degree to allow one to focus on near objects

   (A) myopia

   (B) convergence insufficiency

10.5 How do acute and chronic illnesses affect school-aged children's lives? (pp. 296–297)

Most school-aged children experience the same types of acute illnesses as preschoolers do, although ear infections decrease. Some develop chronic conditions such as allergies and asthma.

10. What are four different ways to treat allergies?

    (A) ______________________________

    (B) ______________________________

    (C) ______________________________

    (D) ______________________________
11. The leading health-related cause of school absences is ____________________.
12. Most health professional prefer not to prescribe daily doses of medication to children who have asthma. Why is medication usually saved for serious asthma cases only?

    ____

    ____

10.6 What trends in injuries and mortality are evident during middle childhood? (pp. 297–300)

About half of injuries to school-aged children are attributable to falls, many of which involve wheeled sports. Football is associated with higher rates of injury than other organized sports. Accidents are the leading cause of death in this age group. Correlations among ethnicity, socioeconomic status, and health-related behavior help to explain cross-group differences in deaths that are attributable to homicide, suicide, and accidents.

13. Name three factors that seem to have an effect on how often school-aged children get injured.

    (A) ______________________________

    (B) ______________________________

    (C) ______________________________
14. Transform these false statements into true statements.

    (A) African American children are less likely to die as the result of a homicide than children in other groups are.

    ____

    ____

    (B) The rate of death due to cancer is higher among Hispanic American children than any other group.

    ____

    ____

    (C) The rate of death due to accidents is lower among Native American children than any other group.

    ____

    ____

10.7 In what ways does excessive weight gain threaten the immediate and future health of school-aged children? (pp. 300–302)

Excessive weight gain is a pattern in which children gain more weight in a year than is appropriate for their height, age, and sex. A child who gains excessive amounts of weight over a number of years is at risk of having weight problems and a number of serious health problems in adulthood.

15. Match each term with its definition.

    ______(1) BMI-for-age

    ______(2) overweight

    ______(3) at-risk-for-overweight

    (A) BMI between the 85th and 95th percentiles

    (B) measure that compares a child's BMI against norms for his/her age group and sex

    (C) BMI at the 95th percentile

10.8 What are the health risks associated with type 1 and type 2 diabetes? (pp. 302–303)

In type 1 diabetes, the pancreas does not produce insulin. In type 2 diabetes, the pancreas produces insulin, but the body does not respond to it. Both types can damage the cardiovascular system and increase the chances that a child will have a serious health crisis in early adulthood. They can also seriously damage the retina and kidneys.

16. From the Multimedia Library within MyDevelopmentLab, watch *Death of the Family Dinner* and answer the following questions.

How might family eating habits increase a child's risk of developing type 2 diabetes?

____

____

How might family eating patterns make it difficult to manage the disease once a child develops it?

____

____

10.9 What is the impact of socioeconomic status on children's health? (pp. 304–307)

The combined effects of the various health-related factors associated with socioeconomic status result in the frequent finding that children in poor and low-income families are in poorer health than are their peers in average- and upper-income homes. Reasons for this include lack of health insurance and tobacco use among family members.

17. List five factors associated with both low socioeconomic status and poor health.

(A) ____

(B) ____

(C) ____

(D) ____

(E) ____

18. List five factors that may help to protect chidlren from the stressors associated with poverty.

(A) ____

(B) ____

(C) ____

(D) ____

(E) ____

10.10 Why is it important to encourage school-aged children to develop good health habits? (p. 307–308)

Health habits that are established in childhood are likely to be continued in adulthood. Good habits are known to be beneficial to adults' health, although they appear to be less important for children's health.

19. Write Y next to each activity that qualifies as a lifetime physical activity, and write N next to each that does not.

_______(1) dance

_______(2) football

_______(3) tennis

_______(4) baseball

_______(5) softball

_______(6) soccer

_______(7) swimming

ATYPICAL DEVELOPMENT

10.11 What are the features of attention-deficit hyperactivity disorder, and how is it treated? (pp. 308–311)

Children with ADHD have problems with both academic learning and social relationships. Medication, parent training, and behavior modification are useful in helping children with ADHD overcome these difficulties.

20. Psychologists consider problem behaviors to be atypical only if they persist for _______________ or longer.

21. Summarize the pros and cons of the use of stimulant drugs to treat ADHD.

Pros	Cons

22. From the Multimedia Library within MyDevelopmentLab, watch *Meet Eric: A Child with ADHD* and answer the following question.

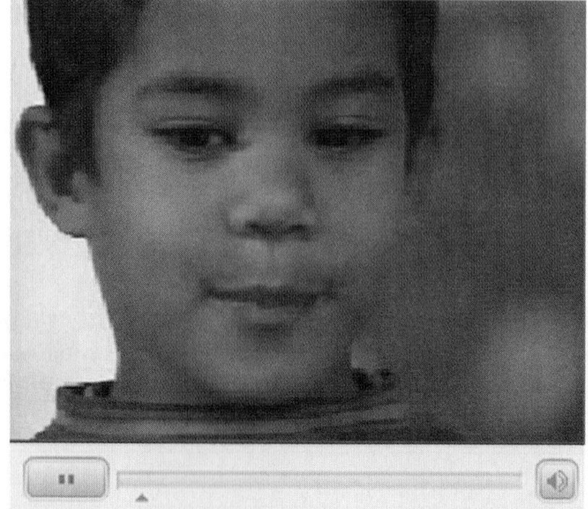

What behavioral goals did the school psychologist and teachers hope that Eric would be able to achieve?

School Psychologist: ________________________________

____

Teachers: ______________________________________

____

10.12 What are the characteristics of oppositional defiant disorder? (p. 312)

Children with oppositional defiant disorder are disobedient and hostile toward authority figures. Many children with ODD also have ADHD. Parent training is important in the treatment of ODD.

23. In order for a child to be diagnosed with oppositional defiant disorder, she must have exhibited the criteria for the disorder by age ________.

10.13 What is childhood-onset conduct disorder? (pp. 312–314)

Childhood-onset conduct disorder is a behavior disorder in which children repeatedly violate important social rules, such as prohibitions against excessive aggression and stealing. Children with this disorder often have problems that persist into adolescence and adulthood.

24. The characteristics of childhood-onset conduct disorder overlap with those of (ADHD/ODD).

10.14 How does depression affect the lives of school-aged children? (p. 314)

Children with major depressive disorder experience disturbances of sleeping and eating and have difficulty concentrating. Depression may also interfere with learning by slowing down the speed at which the brain processes information. Antidepressant medications help, but doctors must monitor children's responses to them because these drugs are sometimes associated with suicidal thinking.

25. Explain why this statement is false: Depression is easy to diagnose in children, because children who have it always appear to be sad.

____

____

For answers to the questions in this chapter, turn to page 519. For a list of key terms, turn to page 531.

Succeed with PEARSON **mydevelopmentlab**

Do You Know All of the Terms in This Chapter?
Find out by using the Flashcards. Want more practice? Take additional quizzes, try simulations, and watch video to be sure you are prepared for the test!

Chapter

11

Cognitive Development in Middle Childhood

The first day of school is viewed as one of the most important transition points in a child's life. In the United States, parents mark the occasion in a variety of ways—with new clothes, fresh school supplies, and carefully selected backpacks and lunch boxes. Some families take pictures of their children's first ride on the school bus or first classroom. All of these ways of recognizing this important milestone say to children that this day is unique, and they begin to think of themselves as "big kids" who are engaged in the serious business of going to school, rather than "little kids" who spend most of their time playing.

Throughout the industrialized world, as well as in most developing areas, the years between 6 and 12 are devoted to formal education. This universal practice is shaped by the everyday observation that the intellectual skills needed for formal learning blossom during this period. Furthermore, formal instruction, whether it involves teaching children how to care for farm animals in a traditional culture or teaching them how to read and write in an industrialized one, provides children with learning experiences that both build upon and expand their cognitive abilities.

Learning Objectives
Cognitive Changes
11.1 How do vocabulary and other aspects of language change during middle childhood?
11.2 What cognitive advantages do children gain as they move through Piaget's concrete operational stage?
11.3 What is horizontal décalage, and how does Siegler explain concrete operational thinking?
11.4 How do children's information-processing skills improve during middle childhood?
Schooling
11.5 What should be included in an effective literacy curriculum?
11.6 How do bilingual and ESL approaches to second-language instruction differ?
11.7 Why do schools administer standardized tests?
11.8 What kinds of group differences in achievement have educational researchers found?
Schooling for Children with Special Needs
11.9 Why is the term *learning disability* controversial?
11.10 How do schools meet the needs of children with developmental disabilities?
11.11 What are the educational needs of children with communication disorders?
11.12 What is inclusive education?
11.13 In what ways do the educational needs of gifted children differ from those of their peers?

Why does every society begin to formally educate children at around the age of 6? As you will learn in this chapter, children of this age are just beginning to acquire the linguistic, logical, and information-processing abilities needed for academic learning. Despite such gains, some children experience problems in school that require special education services. Others display cognitive skills that far exceed those of their peers.

Cognitive Changes

Children acquire some of the important hallmarks of mature thinking between ages 6 and 12. They learn hundreds of new words, and they learn to think logically about events in the physical and social worlds. They develop powerful memory strategies as well.

Learning Objective 11.1

How do vocabulary and other aspects of language change during middle childhood?

Language

By age 5 or 6, virtually all children have mastered the basic grammar and pronunciation of their first language, but children of this age still have a fair distance to go before reaching adult levels of fluency. During middle childhood, children become skilled at managing the finer points of grammar (Prat-Sala, Shillcock, & Sorace, 2000; Ragnarsdottir, Simonsen, & Plunkett, 1999). For example, by the end of middle childhood, most children understand various ways of saying something about the past, such as "I went," "I was going," "I have gone," "I had gone," and "I had been going." Moreover, they correctly use such tenses in their own speech.

Self-correction is largely a function of children's emerging **metalinguistic skills**, or the capacity to think and talk about language. Three-year-olds, for instance, know implicitly that, in English sentences, subjects usually precede verbs, and verbs usually precede objects. They show this knowledge when they speak in sentences that are based on the subject-verb-object pattern. But if you asked a 3-year-old to explain what's wrong with the phrase "ball boy hit," he would have difficulty, even though he could probably rearrange the words to create a grammatically correct statement. By contrast, most 8-year-olds can do both: They can reorder the phrase to turn it into a grammatical statement, and they can explain what was wrong with it. If they have studied grammar in school, they may use words such as *subject* and *verb* in these explanations. The capacity to explain grammar and the ability to attach words such as *subject* and *verb* to the grammatical elements of language are metalinguistic skills.

metalinguistic skills the capacity to think and talk about language

Across the middle childhood years, children also learn how to maintain the topic of conversation, how to create unambiguous sentences, and how to speak politely or persuasively (Anglin, 1993). All of these improvements contribute to the school-aged child's emerging mastery of conversation. By the age of 9 years, most children are fully capable of engaging in fluent conversation with speakers of any age, and their speech rates approach those of adults (Sturm & Seery, 2007).

Between 6 and 12, children also continue to add new vocabulary at the fairly astonishing rate of 5,000 to 10,000 words per year. This estimate comes from several careful studies by developmental psychologist Jeremy Anglin, who estimates children's total vocabularies by testing them on a sample of words drawn at random from a large dictionary (Anglin, 1993, 1995; Skwarchuk & Anglin, 2002). Figure 11.1 shows Anglin's estimates for first, third, and fifth grade. Anglin finds that the largest gain between third and fifth grades occurs in knowledge of the type of words he calls *derived words*—words that have a basic root to which some prefix or suffix is added, such as *happily* or *unwanted*.

Anglin argues that, at age 8 or 9, the child shifts to a new level of understanding of the structure of language, figuring out relationships between whole categories of words, such as between adjectives and adverbs (*happy* and *happily*, *sad* and *sadly*) and between adjectives and nouns (*happy* and *happiness*). Once he grasps these relationships, the child can understand and create a whole class of new words, and his vocabulary thereafter increases rapidly.

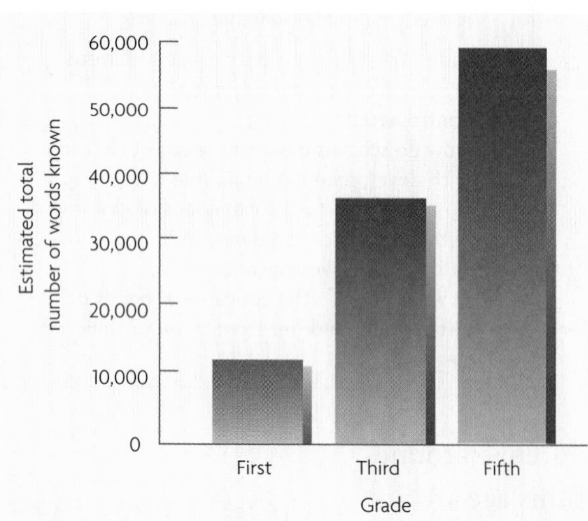

Figure 11.1 Vocabulary Growth in Middle Childhood

Anglin estimated the total vocabulary of first-, third-, and fifth-graders.

(*Source*: From J. Anglin, *Word Learning and the Growth of Potentially Knowable Vocabulary*, 1995, from Figure 6, p. 7. Reprinted with permission of the author.

Piaget's Concrete Operational Stage

Learning Objective 11.2
What cognitive advantages do children gain as they move through Piaget's concrete operational stage?

Have you ever watched a group of children being entertained by a magician? If so, you may have noticed that younger children, preoperational thinkers in Piaget's terms, don't find magic tricks to be all that interesting. As you'll recall from Chapter 8, preoperational thinkers don't really understand the rules that govern physical reality. In middle childhood, children overcome this limitation; as a result, they know that rabbits cannot be hidden in hats, and birds don't hide in the sleeves of a magician's jacket and fly out on cue. Knowing that the magician is appearing to do something that is physically impossible is what makes his performance interesting. Like adults, the school-aged child wonders, "What's the trick?"

Recall from Chapter 8 that Piaget proposed that preschool children develop *figurative*, or descriptive, schemes rapidly, as they become more proficient in the use of language. The *operative*, or logical, schemes that the young child possesses are, at worst, nonexistent or, at best, fragmentary. As a result, the 2- to 6-year-old is very good at acquiring new information but typically lacks the ability to identify the logical relationships embedded in such new information. For instance, Figure 8.2 on page 223 shows that young children perform poorly on Piaget's classic conservation tasks.

In contrast to the preschool years, the 6- to 12-year-old period has as the central theme of cognitive development the construction, application, and equilibration of the operative schemes. Thus, around the time of their 6th birthday, most children start to be capable of solving some of the simpler conservation tasks, such as conservation of number. Piaget's name for this period is the **concrete operational stage**, because the logical schemes that the child perfects during this stage involve logical relationships that can be verified in the physical, or "concrete," world. For instance, in the conservation of number task, the child can use counting to verify his logical conclusion that the number of marbles is the same whether they are arranged in a row or in a circle. Thus, this stage is devoted to the construction of schemes that enable children to think logically about objects and events in the real world.

THE WHOLE CHILD IN FOCUS

What did Jamal do to show that he was mastering the concepts associated with Piaget's concrete operational stage? Find out on page 378.

Concrete operational schemes enable a child to engage in mental processes that lead her to think about the world in an entirely different way than when she was younger. One such process is **decentration**. You learned about its opposite, *centration* (thinking in terms of single variables), in the discussion of preoperational thinking in Chapter 8. Decentration is thinking that takes multiple variables into account. As a result, the school-aged child can see that a clay ball rolled into a sausage shape is longer than it was before, but also narrower. Decentration leads her to conclude that the reduced width of the sausage shape compensates for its increased length and that it still has the same amount of clay.

Preoperational children also exhibit *irreversibility*, which is the inability to think of some transformed object as it was prior to the transformation. In contrast, concrete operational thinkers display its opposite, **reversibility**—the ability to mentally undo some kind of physical or mental transformation. Piaget thought that reversibility was the most critical of all the concrete operations. The clay sausage in a conservation experiment can be made back into a ball; water can be poured from a tall, narrow glass back into a shorter, wider glass. Understanding of the basic reversibility of actions lies behind many of the gains made during the middle childhood period. For example, if a child has mastered reversibility, then knowing that A is larger than B also tells him that B is smaller than A. The ability to understand hierarchies of classes (such as Fido, spaniel, dog, and animal) also rests on this ability to move in both directions in thinking about relationships.

Piaget also proposed that during this stage a child develops the ability to use **inductive logic**. She can go from her own experience to a general principle. For example, she can move from the observation "When a toy is added to a set of toys, it has one more than it did before" to the general principle "Adding always makes more."

Elementary school children are fairly good observational scientists, and they enjoy cataloging, counting species of trees or birds, or figuring out the nesting habits of guinea pigs. But

concrete operational stage Piaget's third stage of cognitive development, during which children construct schemes that enable them to think logically about objects and events in the real world

decentration thinking that takes multiple variables into account

reversibility the understanding that both physical actions and mental operations can be reversed

inductive logic a type of reasoning in which general principles are inferred from specific experiences

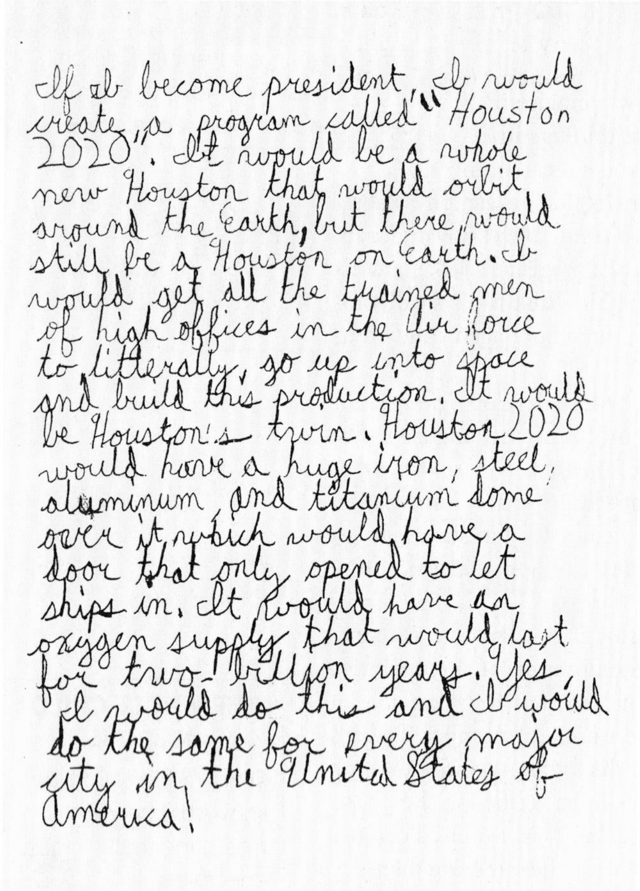

If I become president, I would create a program called "Houston 2020". It would be a whole new Houston that would orbit around the Earth, but there would still be a Houston on Earth. I would get all the trained men of high offices in the Air Force to litterally, go up into space and build this production. It would be Houston's twin. Houston 2020 would have a huge iron, steel, aluminum and titanium dome over it which would have a door that only opened to let ships in. It would have an oxygen supply that would last for two-billion years. Yes, I would do this and I would do the same for every major city in the United States of America!

Figure 11.2 **An Example of Concrete Operational Thinking**

This fifth-grader's composition illustrates the difficulty school-aged children have with deductive logic. His response to a hypothetical premise is to reinvent the world as he knows it through his own experiences or through stories about real people, places, and things. True deductive logic goes beyond what is already known.

(Courtesy of Jerry and Denise Boyd. Used with permission.)

they are not yet good at **deductive logic**, which is based on hypothetical premises and requires starting with a general principle and then predicting some outcome or observation—like going from a theory to a hypothesis. For example, in the composition in Figure 11.2, a fifth-grader responded to the question "What would you do if you were president of the United States?" Responding to such a question requires deductive, not inductive, logic; this kind of task is difficult for 6- to 12-year-olds because they must imagine things they have not experienced. The concrete operations child is good at dealing with things she can see and manipulate or can imagine seeing or manipulating—that is, she is good with concrete things; she does not do well with manipulating ideas or possibilities. Thus, as the composition illustrates, children respond to deductive problems by generating ideas that are essentially copies of the things they know about in the concrete world.

Studies all over the world have shown that children who attend school enter the concrete operational stage earlier and progress through it more rapidly than those who do not (Mishra, 2001). Schooling affects cognitive development during these years in two ways. First, it provides children with opportunities to acquire a great deal of verbal knowledge, both from the curriculum itself and from other children. Second, many academic tasks, such as learning calculation procedures, facilitate the development of logical thinking.

These studies lend weight to Piaget's claim that movement from one cognitive stage to another is not simply a matter of maturation but the result of a complex interaction between internal and environmental variables (Piaget & Inhelder, 1969). As noted in Chapter 8, a certain degree of brain maturation is required for concrete operations to emerge, but experience determines when and the degree to which a school-aged child's capacity for logical thought reaches its full potential.

Learning Objective 11.3

What is horizontal décalage, and how does Siegler explain concrete operational thinking?

Direct Tests of Piaget's View

Piaget understood that it took children some years to apply their new cognitive skills to all kinds of problems. However, other developmentalists have explained both consistencies and inconsistencies in school-aged children's reasoning as a result of their ability to use rules to solve problems.

Horizontal Décalage Researchers have generally found that Piaget was right in his assertion that concrete operational schemes are acquired gradually across the 6- to 12-year-old period, a phenomenon he called *horizontal décalage* (Feldman, 2004). (The French word *décalage* means "a shift.") Consider *conservation*, which, as you may recall from Chapter 8, is the understanding that matter can change in appearance without changing in quantity. Studies consistently show that children grasp conservation of mass or substance by about age 7. That is, they understand that the amount of clay is the same whether it is in a pancake, ball, or some other shape. They generally understand conservation of weight at about age 8, but they don't understand conservation of volume until age 11 (Tomlinson-Keasey, Eisert, Kahle, Hardy-Brown, & Keasey, 1979). (Look back at Figure 8.2 on page 223.)

Studies of classification skills show that at about age 7 or 8 the child first grasps the principle of **class inclusion**, the understanding that subordinate classes are included in larger, su-

deductive logic a type of reasoning, based on hypothetical premises, that requires predicting a specific outcome from a general principle

class inclusion the understanding that subordinate classes are included in larger, superordinate classes

perordinate classes. Bananas are included in the class of fruit, fruit is included in the class of food, and so forth. Preschool children understand that bananas are also fruit, but they do not yet fully understand the relationship between the classes.

A good illustration of all these changes comes from a classic longitudinal study of concrete operational tasks conducted by Carol Tomlinson-Keasey and her colleagues (Tomlinson-Keasey et al., 1979). They followed a group of 38 children from kindergarten through third grade, testing them with five traditional concrete operational tasks each time: conservation of mass, conservation of weight, conservation of volume, class inclusion, and hierarchical classification. You can see from Figure 11.3 that the children got better at all five tasks over the 3-year period, with a spurt between the end of kindergarten and the beginning of first grade (at about the age Piaget thought that concrete operations really arose) and another spurt during second grade.

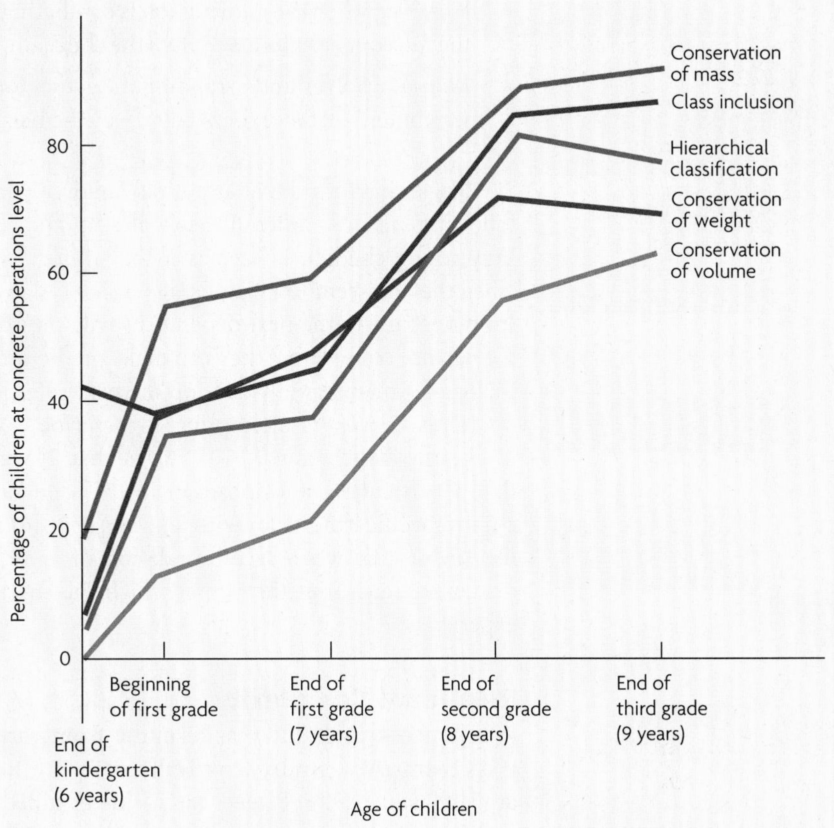

Figure 11.3 Within-Stage Development in Concrete Operations

In this classic longitudinal study, children were given the same set of concrete operational tasks five times, beginning in kindergarten and ending in third grade.

(*Source*: From C. Tomlinson-Keasey et al., "The structure of concrete operational thought," *Child Development*, 50, 1979, adapted by permission from Table 2, p. 1158.)

Concrete Operations as Rules for Problem Solving Other psychologists have conceptualized performance on concrete operational tasks in terms of rules for problem solving. For example, Robert Siegler's approach is a kind of cross between Piagetian theory and information-processing theory. He argues that cognitive development consists of acquiring a set of basic rules that are then applied to a broader and broader range of problems on the basis of experience. There are no stages, only sequences. Siegler proposes that problem-solving rules emerge from experience—from repeated trial and error and experimentation (Siegler, 1994).

Some of Siegler's own work on the development of rules illustrates how they may be acquired (Siegler & Chen, 2002). In one test, Siegler used a balance scale with a series of pegs on each side of the fulcrum at the center, like the one in Figure 11.4. The child is asked to predict which way the balance will fall, depending on the location and number of disk-shaped weights placed on the pegs. A complete solution requires the child to take into account both the number of disks on each side and the specific location of the disks.

Children do not develop such a complete solution immediately. Instead, Siegler suggests that they develop four rules, in this order:

Rule I is basically a preoperational rule, taking into account only one dimension: the number of weights. Children using this rule will predict that the side with more disks will go down, no matter which peg the disks are placed on.

Rule II is a transitional rule. The child still judges on the basis of number, except when the same number of weights appears on each side; in that case, the child takes distance from the fulcrum into account.

Rule III is basically a concrete operational rule; the child tries to take both distance and weight into account simultaneously.

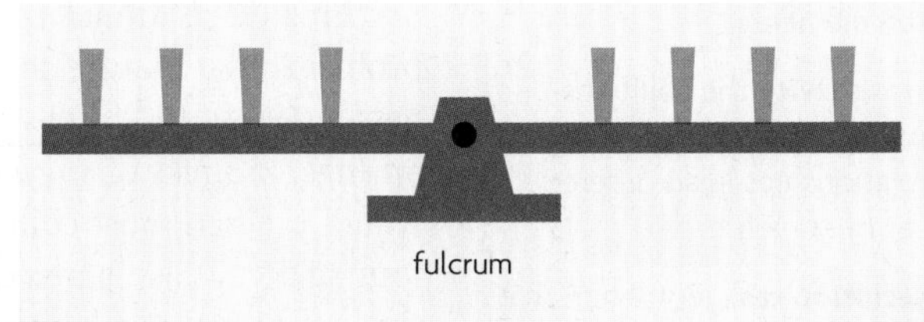

Figure 11.4 Siegler's Balance Task

This balance scale is similar to what Siegler used in his experiments.

However, when the information is conflicting (such as when the side with weights closer to the fulcrum has more weights), the child simply guesses.

Rule IV involves understanding the actual formula for calculating the combined effect of weight and distance for each side of the balance.

Siegler has found that almost all children perform on this and similar tasks as if they are following one or another of these rules, and that the rules seem to develop in the given order. Very young children behave as if they don't have a rule (they guess or behave randomly); when they do seem to begin using a rule, it is always Rule I that comes first. But progression from one rule to the next depends heavily on experience. If children are given practice with the balance scale so that they can make predictions and then check which way the balance actually falls, many rapidly develop the next rules in the sequence.

Thus, Siegler is attempting to describe a logical sequence that children follow, not unlike the basic sequence of stages that Piaget described—but Siegler's research shows that a particular child's position in the sequence depends not so much on age as on the child's specific experience with a given set of materials. In Piaget's terminology, this is rather like saying that when accommodation of some scheme occurs, it always occurs in a particular sequence, but the rate at which the child moves through that sequence depends on experience.

Relational Complexity Other studies of some of Piaget's tasks have explained children's success and failure as resulting from variations in the **relational complexity** of the tasks themselves (Andrews & Halford, 2002). Researchers who study relational complexity argue that success on Piaget's tasks is determined by both how many elements a problem has and how complicated the relationships among the elements are. Performance on Piaget's tasks improves across middle childhood, they claim, because improvements in the efficiency of the child's working memory enable him to cognitively manage more elements and more complex relationships among the elements of a problem.

One line of research on relational complexity deals with **transitivity**, the ability to make inferences about logical relationships in an ordered set of stimuli (Andrews & Halford, 1998). A simple example of a transitivity task is one in which a child is shown stick *A* and asked to compare it to a slightly shorter stick *B*. Through questioning and discussion with the experimenter, the child concludes that *A* is longer than *B*. She is then asked to compare *B* to a slightly shorter stick *C*. Once she concludes that *B* is longer than *C*, she is asked whether *A* is longer or shorter than *C*. Those children who infer that *A* must be longer than *C*, even though they did not directly compare *A* to *C*, exhibit transitivity. Researchers whose studies span three decades have found that few children younger than 6 can solve transitivity problems (Andrews & Halford, 1998; Murray & Youniss, 1968). As relational complexity theory would predict, when the complexity of transitivity problems is increased, as when sticks *B* and *C* are of equal length, even 8-year-olds have difficulty with transitivity (Andrews & Halford, 1998; Murray & Youniss, 1968). Thus, contrary to Piaget's view, there may not be a single transitivity scheme that is universally applicable to all such problems. Instead, a child's success on a transitivity problem may depend on how well the problem fits the capabilities of her information-processing system (see the next section) at a particular point in development.

Finally, relational complexity theory explains children's responses to **seriation tasks**, problems that require children to use a rule to put an array of objects in order (Piaget & Inhelder, 1969). In Piaget's classic version of the seriation task, the researcher asks the child to arrange 10 sticks of varying length from shortest to longest. As relational complexity theory would predict, most children younger than 8 create ordered sets that include only three or four sticks rather than a single ordered array that includes all of the sticks. In other words, they simplify the task by breaking it down into several less complex subtasks that they can accomplish (Halford, Bunch, & McCredden, 2007). In the process, however, they end up with an incorrect solution to the original problem.

relational complexity the number of elements in a problem and the complexity of the relationships among the elements

transitivity the ability to make inferences about logical relationships in an ordered set of stimuli

seriation task a problem that requires the ability to use a rule to put an array of objects in order

Advances in Information-Processing Skills

Learning Objective 11.4

How do children's information-processing skills improve during middle childhood?

As they progress through the middle childhood years, children are able to remember longer and longer lists of numbers, letters, or words. In fact, children's memories function so well that their testimony about events they have witnessed is usually accurate enough to be regarded as reliable in judicial proceedings. Moreover, advances in information processing are influenced by formal schooling (Cole, 2005). The memory demands of school seem to facilitate all of the improvements in information-processing skills that happen between 6 and 12.

Processing Efficiency **Processing efficiency**, the ability to make efficient use of short-term (working) memory capacity, increases steadily with age, a change that most developmentalists now see as the basis for cognitive development (Halford, Maybery, O'Hare, & Grant, 1994; Kuhn, 1992; Li et al., 2004; Swanson & Kim, 2007). The best evidence that cognitive processing becomes more efficient is that it gets steadily faster with age. Robert Kail has found virtually the same exponential increase in processing speed with age for a wide variety of tasks, including perceptual-motor tasks such as tapping in response to a stimulus (for example, pressing a button when you hear a buzzer) and cognitive tasks such as mental addition (Kail, 1991; Kail & Hall, 1994). He has found virtually identical patterns of speed increases in studies in Korea and in the United States, which adds cross-cultural validity to the argument.

Automaticity One of the most important ways in which processing efficiency grows in middle childhood is through the acquisition of **automaticity**, or the ability to recall information from long-term memory without using short-term memory capacity. For example, when children can respond "49" to the question "How much is 7 times 7?" without thinking about it, they have achieved automaticity with respect to that particular piece of information.

Automaticity is critical to efficient information processing because it frees up short-term memory space for more complex processing. Thus, the child who knows "7 times 7" automatically can use that fact in a complex multiplication or division problem without giving up any of the short-term memory space he is using to solve the problem. As a result, he is able to concentrate on the "big picture," instead of expending effort trying to recall a simple multiplication fact. Not surprisingly, researchers have found that elementary school children who have automatized basic math facts in this way learn complex computational skills more rapidly (Jensen & Whang, 1994).

Automaticity is achieved primarily through practice. For example, when babies first learn to walk, they must focus all their mental effort on the act of walking. After a few weeks of practice, walking becomes automatic, and they can think about chasing the family cat or retrieving a ball that has rolled away. Likewise, adults can think about the grocery list while driving to the supermarket, because driving skills and the routes they routinely use to get from place to place are automatized. Thus, automaticity is important to information processing throughout the lifespan. It is in middle childhood, however, that children seem to begin automatizing large quantities of information and skills at a fairly rapid rate.

Executive and Strategic Processes If you wanted to recall a list of everyday items (chair, pencil, spaghetti, tree . . .), you might consciously consider the various alternative strategies for remembering and then select the best one. You could also explain some things about how your mind works, such as which kinds of mental tasks you find most difficult. These are examples of *metacognition*—knowing about knowing or thinking about thinking—a set of skills first mentioned in Chapter 8. Metacognition is part of a large group of skills known as **executive processes**—information-processing skills that allow a person to devise and carry out alternative strategies for remembering and solving problems. Executive processes are based on a basic understanding of how the mind works. Such skills improve a great deal during middle childhood. For example, 10-year-olds are more likely than 8-year-olds to understand that attending to a story requires effort (Parault & Schwanenflugel, 2000).

THE WHOLE CHILD IN FOCUS

How do improvements in his working memory help Jamal do well in school? Find out on page 378.

processing efficiency the ability to make efficient use of short-term memory capacity

automaticity the ability to recall information from long-term memory without using short-term memory capacity

executive processes information-processing skills that involve devising and carrying out strategies for remembering and solving problems

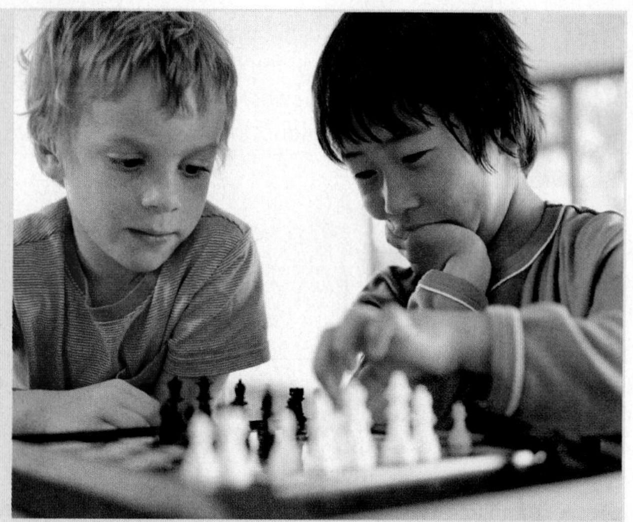

Unless they are rank novices, these school-aged chess players will remember a series of chess moves or an arrangement of chess pieces far better than adults who don't play chess.

One of the advantages of having good executive-processing skills is that they help the individual devise methods for remembering information, or **memory strategies**. Although many people possess their own unique methods for remembering, Table 11.1 lists a few common memory strategies. For the most part, these memory techniques first appear between the ages of 6 and 12.

Expertise There is a great deal of research showing that the amount of knowledge a person possesses about a particular topic—that is, one's **expertise**—makes a huge difference in how efficiently her information-processing system works. Children and adults who know a lot about a topic (dinosaurs, baseball cards, mathematics, or whatever it may be) categorize information about that topic in highly complex and hierarchical ways. They are also better at remembering and logically analyzing new information on that topic (Ni, 1998).

Even typical age differences in strategy use or memory ability disappear when the younger group has more expertise than the older group. For example, psychologist Michelene Chi, in her now-classic early study, showed that expert chess players could remember the placement of chess pieces on a board much more quickly and accurately than novice chess players, even when the expert chess players were children and the novices were adults (Chi, 1978).

However, using advanced information-processing skills in their areas of expertise doesn't seem to help children's general memory and reasoning abilities (Ericsson & Crutcher, 1990). For this reason, many information-processing psychologists now believe that an individual's information-processing skills may depend entirely on the quantity and quality of relevant information stored in long-term memory. Thus, they say, to be able to learn scientific reasoning skills, for example, children must first acquire a body of knowledge about scientific

Table 11.1 Some Common Information-Processing Strategies Used in Remembering

Strategy	Description
Rehearsal	Mental or vocal repetition; may occur in children as young as 2 years under some conditions and is common in older children and adults
Organization	Grouping ideas, objects, or words into clusters to remember them, such as "all animals," "the ingredients in the lasagna recipe," or "the chess pieces involved in the move called *castling*." This strategy is more easily applied to something a person has experience with or particular knowledge about. Two-year-olds use primitive clustering strategies.
Elaboration	Finding shared meaning or a common referent for two or more things that need to be remembered
Mnemonic	A device to assist memory; the phrase for the notes of the lines on the musical staff ("Every Good Boy Does Fine") is a mnemonic.
Systematic Searching	"Scanning" one's memory for the whole domain in which a piece of information might be found. Three- and 4-year-old children begin to do this when they search for actual objects in the real world, but they are not good at doing this in memory. So search strategies may be first learned in the external world and then applied to inner searches.

Source: Flavell, 1985.

memory strategies learned methods for remembering information

expertise the amount of knowledge one possesses about a particular topic

topics (Zimmerman, 2000). To paraphrase developmental psychologist John Flavell, expertise makes any of us, including children, look very smart; lack of expertise makes us look very dumb (Flavell, 1985).

Schooling

As noted at the outset of the chapter, formal education is under way by the time children reach the age of 6 or 7. Consequently, every society endeavors to find effective ways of teaching children the skills that they will need in adulthood. In general, studies show that teachers who display a teaching style that is similar to the approach that authoritative parents take to raising children—an approach that combines clear goals, good control, good communication, and high nurturance—are the most effective (MacIver, Reuman, & Main, 1995). In addition, at least in the United States, there is evidence that elementary schools with smaller classes, of less than 20 pupils or so, are more effective than those with larger classes (Ecalle, Magan, & Gibert, 2007). Still, quality considerations aside, because of its academic focus and the amount of time that children spend in school, formal education is one of the most important influences on the cognitive development of 6- to 12-year-olds.

Literacy

Learning Objective 11.5
What should be included in an effective literacy curriculum?

In the industrialized world, *literacy*, the ability to read and write, is the focus of education in the 6- to 12-year-old period. As you learned in Chapter 8, the skills children bring to school from their early childhood experiences may influence early reading as much as formal instruction does (Hood, Conlon, & Andrews, 2008). Especially significant among these skills is the set known as *phonological awareness* (Anthony & Lonigan, 2004; Boscardin, Muthén, Francis, & Baker, 2008; Parrila, Kirby, & McQuarrie, 2004; Schatschneider, Fletcher, Francis, Carlson, & Foorman, 2004). Across the early elementary years, phonological awareness skills continue to increase (Shu, Anderson, & Wu, 2000). Moreover, purposeful instruction in phonological awareness helps children accelerate their acquisition of phonological awareness skills (Al Otaiba et al., 2008).

All beginning readers, both those who have high levels of phonological awareness and those who know less about sounds and symbols, benefit from specific instruction in sound-letter correspondences, a type of instruction called **systematic and explicit phonics** (Armbruster, Lehr, & Osborn, 2003). *Systematic* means that instruction must follow a plan, beginning with simple, one-letter/one-sound correspondences (e.g., the letter *b* for the sound /*b*/) and moving to those that involve two or more letters. The plan must be carefully developed so that instruction corresponds in meaningful ways to the spelling system of the language that is being learned. *Explicit* means that letter-sound correspondences are taught intentionally.

systematic and explicit phonics planned, specific instruction in sound-letter correspondences

Children's experiences in school are similar the world over. The similarities help explain why cognitive-developmental research involving 6- to 12-year-olds yields pretty much the same results in all cultures where children attend school.

Effective phonics curricula also provide beginning readers with ample opportunities for daily practice in using their knowledge of sound-symbol correspondence so that they can develop automaticity. Phonics researchers argue that children cannot comprehend written language easily until they can decode it automatically and fluently (Klauda & Guthrie, 2008). Their view is based on the finding that working memory is limited in capacity. Therefore, when decoding words is automatic, working memory capacity is freed up for the task of comprehending what has been read.

Advocates for the **whole language approach**, an approach to reading instruction that places more emphasis on the meaning of written language than on its structure, say that most children are capable of inferring letter-sound correspondences on their own as long as they have enough exposure to print (Strauss & Altwerger, 2007). The key, say these educators, is to motivate children to interact with written language in meaningful and enjoyable ways. Thus, they argue that reading curricula should include high-quality children's literature, rather than phonics workbooks and "controlled vocabulary" readers featuring stories that correspond to the phonics skills that children are working on. Moreover, they recommend that teachers directly instruct children in phonics skills only when children ask questions about letters and sounds.

Research suggests that thinking that reading instruction must follow *either* the phonics *or* the whole language approach is a mistake. Thus, advocates of the **balanced approach** argue for comprehensive reading instruction that includes systematic and explicit phonics along with other instructional strategies derived from the whole language approach (Iaquinta, 2006). They argue that exposing children to good literature and helping them acquire a love of reading is an important element in any reading curriculum. And, precisely because phonics is so important, teachers have an obligation to find ways of teaching these skills in enjoyable ways. Teachers can take a cue from the whole language approach's emphasis on the personal meaningfulness of the materials that children are asked to read by writing down stories that children dictate and then helping children apply their phonics skills to reading them aloud. Likewise, some strategies for teaching phonics take advantage of children's love of games. Others use entertaining alliterative and rhyming songs to help them acquire phonics skills. In addition, children's oral language skills and vocabularies affect how rapidly and how well they learn to read. Thus, explicit instruction in both of these domains contributes to effective literacy instruction (Nation & Snowling, 2004).

Teachers who follow the balanced approach also use techniques based on Vygotsky's theory of cognitive development. For example, in *guided reading* sessions, teachers work with small groups of children on reading books that are somewhat challenging for them (recall Vygotsky's *zone of proximal development* from Chapter 2) (Iaquinta, 2006). When a child makes an error, the teacher uses the opportunity to explain a reading strategy or one of the many idiosyncrasies of written English to all of the children in the group.

As children progress through the elementary grades, several other components of reading must be addressed. Research shows that attainment of reading fluency requires that children learn about meaningful word parts, such as prefixes and suffixes (McBride-Chang, Shu, Zhou, & Wagner, 2004; Nagy, Berninger, Abbott, Vaughan, & Vermeulen, 2004). Instruction in comprehension strategies, such as identifying the main idea and purpose of a particular text, also helps (Van den Broek, Lynch, Naslund, Ievers-Landis, & Verduin, 2004). Of course, all along the way, children need to be exposed to good literature, both in their own reading and in what teachers and parents read to them.

Some of the strategies used to teach reading also help children learn writing, the other component of literacy. For example, systematic and explicit phonics instruction helps children learn to spell as well as to read (Rego, 2006). Of course, good writing involves far more than just spelling; it requires instruction and practice, just as reading does. Specifically, children need to learn about writing techniques, such as outlining and paragraph development, to become good writers. They also need to learn about language mechanics, such as grammar and appropriate uses of words, as well as how to edit their own and others' written work (Graham & Harris, 1997).

whole language approach an approach to reading instruction that places more emphasis on the meaning of written language than on its structure

balanced approach an approach to reading instruction that combines systematic and explicit phonics instruction with other strategies, derived from the whole language approach, for helping children acquire literacy

Despite educators' best efforts, some children fall behind their classmates in literacy during the early school years. In general, reading researchers have found that poor readers have problems with sound-letter combinations (Agnew, Dorn, & Eden, 2004). Thus, many children who have reading difficulties benefit from highly specific phonics approaches that provide a great deal of practice in translating letters into sounds and vice versa (Koppenhaver, Hendrix & Williams, 2007; Ryder, Tunmer, & Greaney, 2008).

However, curriculum flexibility is also important in programs for poor readers. Some do not improve when exposed to phonics approaches. In fact, programs that combine sound-letter and comprehension training, such as the Reading Recovery program, have proven to be highly successful in helping poor readers catch up, especially when the programs are implemented in the early elementary years (Hurry & Sylva, 2007). Consequently, teachers need to be able to assess the effectiveness of whatever approach they are using and change it to fit the needs of individual students.

Second-Language Learners

Learning Objective 11.6

How do bilingual and ESL approaches to second-language instruction differ?

Worldwide patterns of population growth and movement have led to tremendous increases in the number of children attending school in the United States, Canada, Great Britain, and Australia whose first language is not English. About two-thirds of these children speak English well enough to function in school, but the rest essentially do not speak English. Educators in English-speaking countries use the term **English-language learners (ELLs)** to refer to non–English-speaking children—either immigrant children or native-born children.

The number of ELLs in the United States increased from 2.5 million in 1991 to nearly 3.8 million in 2004 (National Center for Education Statistics [NCES], 2006a). As a result, at the beginning of the 21st century, 46% of all U.S. classrooms had at least one ELL, and there continues to be a shortage of qualified teachers to help these students benefit from English-only instruction (Barron & Menken, 2002). In California, Florida, Illinois, New Jersey, New York, and Texas, more than 75% of schools offer special programs for ELLs. Most such students live in large cities. For example, more than 100 languages are spoken by school children in New York City, Chicago, Los Angeles, and the suburbs of Washington, DC. Educators in these cities face a particularly difficult task in dealing not only with the large number of ELLs but also with the staggering number of languages they and their parents speak.

About 12% of ELLs, mostly those whose first language is Spanish, participate in **bilingual education**, in which instruction is given in two languages (Osorio-O'Dea, 2001). Such programs have been developed for Spanish-speaking children because they constitute nearly three-quarters of ELLs in U.S. schools (NCES, 2006a). Other English-speaking countries offer bilingual education to children from large non–English-speaking groups as well. For example, schools in Quebec, Canada, a province whose residents primarily speak French, have provided both English- and French-speaking students with bilingual education for decades.

An alternative to bilingual education is **structured immersion**, used in classrooms in which all the children speak the same non-English native language and the teacher speaks both English and the children's native language. In such classrooms, the basic instruction is in English, paced so that the children can comprehend, with the teacher translating only when absolutely necessary. French language programs of this kind for English-speaking children have been very successful in Quebec (Allen, 2004). In these programs, students are taught exclusively in French for 2 years of elementary school. During the remaining elementary years, they receive bilingual instruction. Research shows that, in the early grades, these pupils are somewhat behind monolingual English speakers in literacy skills. However, when these children reach high school age, they get higher scores on reading achievement tests than their monolingual peers.

Bilingual education and structured immersion are logistically impossible for most school districts that include ELLs. For one thing, if a school system has only a handful of students

English-language learners (ELLs) school children who do not speak English well enough to function in English-only classes

bilingual education an approach to second-language education in which children receive instruction in two different languages

structured immersion an approach to second-language instruction in which basic instruction is solely in English and a bilingual teacher translates only when absolutely necessary

who speak a particular language, it is not financially feasible to establish a separate curriculum for them. In addition, it may be impossible to find bilingual teachers for children whose language is spoken by very few people outside of their country of origin. For these reasons, about 85% of 6- to 12-year-old ELLs in the United States are enrolled in **English-as-a-second-language (ESL) programs** (Osorio-O'Dea, 2001). In ESL programs, children spend part of the day in classes to learn English and part in academic classes that are conducted entirely in English (see *Developmental Science in the Classroom*).

Research has shown that no particular approach to second-language learning is more successful than any other (Mohanty & Perregaux, 1997). There is some indication that programs that include a home-based component, such as those that encourage parents to learn the new language along with their children, may be especially effective (Koskinen et al., 2000). But it seems that any structured program, whether bilingual education or ESL, fosters higher achievement among non–English-speaking children than simply integrating them into English-only classes, an approach called **submersion**. Although most children in submersion programs eventually catch up to their English-speaking peers, many educators believe that instruction that supports children's home language and culture as well as their English-language skills enhances their overall development (Bougie, Wright, & Taylor, 2003).

English-as-a-second-language (ESL) program an approach to second-language education in which children attend classes to learn English for part of the day and then academic classes conducted entirely in English for the other part of the day

submersion the integration of non–English-speaking children into English-only classes

With respect to achievement, ELLs' performance in school is very similar to that of English-speaking children (NCES, 1997). In fact, in U.S. schools, native-born English-speaking children are more likely to fail one or more grades than are children whose home language is either Asian or European. Spanish-speaking children fail in U.S. schools at about the same rate as English speakers. Thus, there is no evidence that a child who enters school with limited English skills has any greater risk of failure than children whose first language is English.

DEVELOPMENTAL SCIENCE IN THE CLASSROOM

Age and Second-Language Learning: Is Younger Always Better?

Sheila teaches ESL to fifth-graders, most of whom have been in the United States only a few months and enter school with no knowledge of English. Other teachers in her school often comment on the daunting task that Sheila faces in teaching English to children who are already on the verge of adolescence. Most cite the widely held belief that language learning becomes more difficult with age. Yet Sheila's conversations with ESL teachers who work with younger children suggest just the opposite. Sheila's students seem to learn English more rapidly than the younger English-language learners (ELLs) in her school do. Why is that?

Researchers have found that, although it is true that those who begin learning a new language earlier in life may ultimately reach higher levels of proficiency than those who begin later do, age is not the determining factor. Kenji Hakuta and his colleagues (2003) used census data to examine relationships among English proficiency, age at entry into the United States, and educational attainment for Chinese- and Spanish-speaking immigrants. They found that immigrants' ability to learn English was better predicted by their educational backgrounds than by the age at which they entered the country. The link between education and second-language learning makes sense when considered in the light of other studies showing that the more you know about your first language—its spelling rules, grammatical structure, and vocabulary—the easier it will be for you to learn another language (Meschyan & Hernandez, 2002). You should recall from the discussion of language earlier in the chapter that these are metalinguistic abilities, a set of skills that improve significantly during middle childhood. Thus, it is likely that the superior metalinguistic skills of Sheila's fifth-graders give them an advantage over younger ESL students.

Nevertheless, there is one clear advantage to learning a new language as early in life as possible. People who are younger when they learn a new language are far more likely to be able to speak it with an appropriate accent (McDonald, 1997). One reason has to do with slight variations in neural processing in *Broca's area*, the area of the brain that controls speech production. Research by Kim and others (1997) suggested that those who learn a new language before the age of 10 or 11, or about the age of most fifth-graders, rely on the same patch of tissue in Broca's area for both of the languages they speak. In those who learn a second language at an older age, two different sections of Broca's area are active while they are performing language tasks—one section for the first language and another for the second language, a factor that is believed to account for the superior phonological performance of younger second-language learners. Consequently, although Sheila's fifth-graders' metalinguistic skills may help them learn to speak English more rapidly than younger students do, they probably will have to work harder at speaking it without an accent.

Questions for Reflection

1. What does the research cited in this discussion imply about second-language learning in adulthood?
2. How might the research on metalinguistic skills and second-language learning be used to support or to criticize bilingual education?

A cautionary note is necessary, however: An ELL does not have an increased risk of failure as long as the school provides some kind of transition to English-only instruction and school officials take care to administer all tests in the language with which the child is most familiar (Cushner et al., 1992). Providing a transition to English-only instruction is necessary to optimize the ELL's potential for achievement. Testing children in their native languages ensures that non–English-speaking children will not be misclassified as having mental retardation or learning disabilities because of their limited English skills. Beyond these requirements, ELLs represent no particular burden to U.S. schools. Moreover, it seems reasonable to conclude that their presence enriches the educational experience of children whose first language is English.

Standardized Tests

Learning Objective 11.7

Why do schools administer standardized tests?

Perhaps you remember taking standardized tests during your elementary school years. A **standardized test** is one on which each individual's performance is evaluated by comparing his or her score to the average score attained by a large sample of similar individuals. For instance, a standardized test for first-graders compares each child's score to the average achieved by a large group of first-graders who took the test prior to its publication. Most school systems in the United States administer standardized tests to students many times during their educational careers. The tests are generally of two types: achievement tests and intelligence tests.

Achievement and Intelligence Tests **Achievement tests** are designed to assess specific information learned in school, using items like those in Table 11.2. Scores are based on comparing an individual child's performance to that of other children in the same grade

Table 11.2 Sample Items from a Fourth-Grade Achievement Test

Vocabulary	Spelling
jolly old man 1. angry 2. fat 3. merry 4. sorry	Jason took the *cleanest* glass. right ______ wrong ______
Language Expression	**Mathematics Computation**
Who wants ______ books? 1. that 2. these 3. them 4. this	79 +14 149 −87 62 ×3
Reference Skills	**Mathematics**
Which of these words would be first in ABC order? 1. pair 2. point 3. paint 4. polish	What does the 3 in 13 stand for? 1. 3 ones 2. 13 ones 3. 3 tens 4. 13 tens

Source: From *Comprehensive Tests of Basic Skills*, Form S. Reprinted by permission of the publisher, CTB/McGraw-Hill, Del Monte Research Park, Monterey, CA 93940.

standardized test a test on which each individual's performance is evaluated by comparing his or her score to the average score attained by a large sample of similar individuals

achievement test a test designed to assess specific information learned in school

across the country. Critics of achievement tests point out that, although educators and parents may think of achievement tests as indicators of what children learn in school, they are actually very similar to IQ tests. For example, suppose an achievement test contains the math problem "4 × 4." A bright child who hasn't yet learned multiplication may reason his way to the correct answer of 16. Another child may give the correct answer because she has learned it in school. Still another may know the answer because he learned to multiply from his parents. Thus, critics suggest that comprehensive portfolios of children's school work may be better indicators of actual school learning than standardized achievement tests (Neill, 1998).

Most U.S. schools also require students to take intelligence tests at various points in their educational careers. These tests are usually paper-and-pencil multiple-choice tests that can be given to large numbers of children at the same time. Some critics of routine IQ testing say that such tests aren't as accurate as the individual tests you read about in Chapter 8 (Sattler, 2008). This is because many group tests require children to read, so scores reflect differences in reading ability as well as intelligence. Moreover, when children who are being tested individually become bored, psychologists can find ways of motivating them to continue. By contrast, children taking a group test may disengage from the test entirely without anyone knowing it. In such cases, children's scores are good measures of test engagement but are not good measures of their intellectual capability. Nevertheless, scores on IQ tests are often used to group children for instruction because they are strongly correlated with achievement test scores.

Two Different Views of Intelligence Some developmentalists say that the problem with relying on IQ tests to predict achievement is that they fail to provide a complete picture of mental abilities. For example, psychologist Howard Gardner proposed a **theory of multiple intelligences** (Gardner, 1983). This theory claims that there are eight types of intelligence:

- Linguistic—the ability to use language effectively
- Logical/mathematical—facility with numbers and logical problem solving
- Musical—the ability to appreciate and produce music
- Spatial—the ability to appreciate spatial relationships, such as relative distances
- Bodily kinesthetic—the ability to move in a coordinated way, combined with a sense of one's body in space
- Naturalist—the ability to make fine discriminations among the plants and animals of the natural world or the patterns and designs of human artifacts, such as tools
- Interpersonal—sensitivity to the behavior, moods, and needs of others
- Intrapersonal—the ability to understand oneself

Gardner's theory is based on observations of people with brain damage, mental retardation, and other severe mental handicaps. He points out that brain damage usually causes disruption of functioning in very specific mental abilities rather than a general decline in intelligence. He notes that many individuals with mental deficits have remarkable talents. For example, some are gifted in music, while others can perform complex mathematical computations without using a calculator or pencil and paper. Furthermore, Gardner continues to refine his model. In recent years, he has proposed that a ninth type of intelligence, one that he calls *existential* intelligence, deals with the spiritual realm and enables us to contemplate the meaning of life (Halama & Strízenec, 2004). However, critics claim that Gardner's view, although intuitively appealing, has little empirical support (Aiken, 1997).

theory of multiple intelligences Howard Gardner's theory that there are eight types of intelligence

triarchic theory of intelligence Robert Sternberg's theory that intelligence includes three components: contextual, experiential, and componential

Robert Sternberg's **triarchic theory of intelligence** proposes three components of human intelligence (Sternberg, 1988). *Contextual intelligence* has to do with knowing the right behavior for a specific situation. For example, South American street vendors, most of whom are of elementary school age but are unschooled, are good at doing practical calculations but perform poorly on more abstract, written math problems. These children are highly "intelligent" in their daily context, but in the school context they appear to lack intellectual ability.

Experiential intelligence, according to Sternberg, involves learning to give specific responses without thinking about them. For example, you can probably respond without thinking to the question "How much is 7 times 7?" Experiential intelligence enables you to come up with novel solutions to everyday problems that you haven't quite been able to solve and to recognize when a tried-and-true solution is appropriate for a new problem.

Componential intelligence is a person's ability to come up with effective strategies. To Sternberg, this is the most important component of intelligence. He claims that intelligence tests are limited in their ability to identify gifted children because they put more emphasis on "correctness" of answers than on the quality of the strategies people use to arrive at them (Sternberg, 2002).

In general, Sternberg says, IQ tests measure how familiar a child is with "school" culture. Thus, children whose cultural background does not include formal schooling perform poorly because they are unfamiliar with the context of the test. Unfortunately, their poor performance is often mistakenly interpreted as indicating that they lack intelligence (Sternberg & Grigorenko, 2006). Sternberg believes that intelligence tests should measure all three components of intelligence, and he has produced some research evidence suggesting that testing procedures based on his theory yield better performance predictions than conventional IQ tests (Sternberg, Wagner, Williams, & Horvath, 1995).

Emotional Intelligence Both Gardner's and Sternberg's theories have become important in helping educators understand the weaknesses of IQ tests. Psychologist Daniel Goleman's theory of **emotional intelligence** has also added to scientists' understanding of intelligence and achievement (Goleman, 1995). Emotional intelligence has three components: awareness of one's own emotions, the ability to express one's emotions appropriately, and the capacity to channel emotions into the pursuit of worthwhile goals. Without emotional intelligence, Goleman claims, it is impossible to achieve one's intellectual potential. Research has yet to provide support for Goleman's hypothesis (Humphrey, Curran, Morris, Farrell, & Woods, 2007). Still, research on the relationship between self-control (the third component of emotional intelligence) in early childhood and achievement in adolescence suggests that Goleman's view is correct. Children's ability to exercise control over their emotions in early childhood is strongly related to measures of academic achievement in high school (Denham, 2006).

Creativity Finally, conventional intelligence tests do not measure **creativity**, the ability to produce original, appropriate, and valuable ideas and/or solutions to problems. Although children's capacity for creativity appears to depend greatly on how much knowledge they have about a topic (Sak & Maker, 2006), researchers have found that creativity is only weakly related to IQ (Lubart, 2003).

Some developmentalists define creativity as **divergent thinking** (Guilford, 1967). A child who uses divergent thinking can provide multiple solutions to problems that have no clear answer. One creativity test, the *Alternative Uses Test* (Guilford, 1967), prompts children to think of unusual uses for everyday objects such as bricks.

However, noted creativity researcher Paul Torrance argues that such tests fail to capture all of the dimensions of creativity. To test his theory, Torrance devised the *Torrance Tests of Creative Thinking* (Torrance, 1998), in which children are presented with problems that involve interpreting pictures, interpreting verbal scenarios, and producing drawings in response to prompts. Children receive scores on four dimensions of creativity:

- Fluency—the total number of ideas generated
- Flexibility—the number of different categories represented in ideas
- Originality—the degree to which ideas are unusual, statistically speaking
- Elaboration—the amount of detail in ideas

Evidence for the validity of the Torrance Tests comes from his own longitudinal study in which children who received high scores on the test in the 1950s were found to have produced a greater number of creative accomplishments some 40 years later (Plucker, 1999). Moreover, scores on the Torrance Tests proved to be more strongly correlated with life achievements of a creative nature than were research participants' childhood IQ scores.

emotional intelligence a type of intelligence that includes awareness of one's own emotions, the ability to express emotions appropriately, and the ability to channel emotions to accomplish goals

creativity the ability to produce original, appropriate, and valuable ideas and/or solutions to problems

divergent thinking the ability to produce multiple solutions to problems that have no clear answer

Learning Objective 11.8

What kinds of group differences in achievement have educational researchers found?

Group Differences in Achievement

Although intelligence testing is a prominent feature of the educational environment, teachers and administrators are usually more concerned about what children actually learn than they are about their abilities. For this reason, a good deal of educational research focuses on finding explanations for group differences in achievement. These differences have been found across gender, ethnic groups, and cultures.

Sex Differences in Achievement Comparisons of total IQ test scores for boys and girls do not reveal consistent differences. It is only when the total scores are broken down into several separate skills that some patterns of sex differences emerge. On average, studies in the United States show that girls do slightly better on verbal tasks and at arithmetic computation and that boys do slightly better at numerical reasoning. For example, more boys than girls test as gifted in mathematics (Benbow, 1988; Lubinski & Benbow, 1992).

Encouragement from teachers and parents equal to that given to boys may help girls narrow the mathematics achievement gap.

Where might such differences come from? The explanatory options should be familiar by now. As you learned in Chapter 10, brain processes that underlie spatial perception and cognition are often argued to be the cause of sex differences in math achievement. To date, however, neurological research has failed to find sex differences in brain function large enough to explain sex differences in math achievement (Spreen et al., 1995).

So far, environmental explanations have proven to be more useful than biological theories in discussions of sex differences in mathematical or verbal reasoning. Especially in the case of mathematics, there is considerable evidence that girls' and boys' skills are systematically shaped by a series of environmental factors.

For one thing, both teachers and parents seem to believe that boys have more math ability than girls (Jussim & Eccles, 1992; Tiedemann, 2000). Thus, they are more likely to attribute a girl's success in mathematics to effort or good teaching; poor performance by a girl is attributed to lack of ability. In contrast, teachers and parents attribute a boy's success to ability and his failure to lack of application (Jussim & Eccles, 1992). Moreover, children appear to internalize these beliefs, which, in turn, influence their interest in taking math courses and their beliefs about their likelihood of achieving success in math (Eccles, Jacobs, & Harold, 1990). The cumulative effects of these differences in expectations and treatment show up in high school, when sex differences on standardized math tests usually become evident. In part, then, sex differences in math achievement test scores appear to be perpetuated by subtle family and school influences on children's attitudes.

Ethnic Differences in Achievement In the United States, differences in achievement test scores among ethnic group are similar to the differences in IQ test scores you read about in Chapter 8. Most developmentalists believe that the same factors that contribute to IQ score differences—socioeconomic status, access to prenatal care, family stability, and so on—also produce differences in measures of school performance, such as grades and achievement test scores.

In addition, group differences in learning styles may contribute to variations in achievement (Belgrave & Allison, 2005). Psychologists have learned that children who use an **analytical style** define learning goals and follow a set of orderly steps to reach them. These children are well organized, are good at learning details, and think of information in terms of "right" and "wrong." Children who use a **relational style** focus attention on "the big picture" instead of on individual bits of information.

analytical style a style of learning that involves defining learning goals and following orderly steps to reach them

relational style a style of learning that involves focusing on the "big picture" instead of on the details of a task

Consider what happens when Ayana, who has an analytical style, and Richard, who uses a relational style, both listen as their fourth-grade teacher gives instructions for a complicated project. Ayana lists every detail of the teacher's instructions and how many points each part is worth. In contrast, Richard writes down his general impression of each part of the project.

In working on the project, Ayana concentrates her effort on the parts that are worth the most points. Richard pays more attention to the aspects of the project he finds interesting. When it is finished, Ayana's project conforms more exactly to the teacher's instructions than Richard's does, and she receives a higher grade. Ayana's way of approaching school work—her analytical style—better fits school expectations, giving her an advantage over Richard. In addition, Ayana's way of learning helps her get high scores on achievement tests, which require detailed knowledge of specific information and skills.

Ethnic groups in the United States differ in the percentages of children who use each style. A higher percentage of Asian American and European American students are analytical learners. In contrast, a higher percentage of African American, Hispanic American, and Native American children are relational learners. Psychologists speculate that these learning style differences arise from historic relations among dominant and nondominant cultural groups (Hale, 2001). They argue that children in groups that have experienced oppression and discrimination develop cognitive habits that are based on the need to make rapid inferences about potentially threatening situations. As a result, they tend to favor global impressions over detailed analyses of situations and problems, a tendency that carries over into academic tasks. Thus, differences among these groups in achievement test scores and school grades may be due to the different percentages of analytical and relational learners within the groups (Serpell & Hatano, 1997).

Achievement differences may also be due to philosophical beliefs that characterize some racial and ethnic groups in the United States. For example, American culture tends to be *individualistic.* In other words, it emphasizes the achievements of individuals and encourages competition rather than cooperation. However, some U.S. subcultures place more emphasis on *interdependence*, an outlook that sociologists and anthropologists usually refer to as *collectivist* (Serpell & Hatano, 1997). In a classic study that took place in the state of Hawaii, educators tried changing their curriculum and teaching methods to better fit the collectivist emphasis of Native Hawaiian children and families. The new approach involved more group work and cooperation among students, and it apparently helped children learn more (Cushner et al., 1992). The success of such interventions suggests that educational practices in the United States may be well adapted to some groups but not others, thereby producing differences in achievement between groups for whom the educational system is a good cultural "fit" and those for whom it is not.

Feelings of hopelessness on the part of some disadvantaged students may also be a factor. For example, some African American students in the United States, discouraged by racism and lack of opportunity, believe that they won't be able to succeed economically no matter how much they learn in school (Baranchik, 2002; Ogbu, 1990). Some research suggests that these feelings influence minority children's scores on standardized tests (see *Developmental Science in the Clinic* on page 338). Educators believe schools can affect these students' beliefs by making sure textbooks and other materials accurately reflect the contributions of African Americans to American culture (Cushner et al., 1992).

Across all cultures, parental involvement is associated with high achievement.

Cross-Cultural Differences in Achievement Differences in math and science achievement between Asian children and North American children have been the focus of much study and debate. Over a 20-year period, studies have repeatedly shown that U.S. school children are significantly behind their

DEVELOPMENTAL SCIENCE IN THE CLINIC

Stereotype Threat

Dr. Jones is a clinical psychologist who works at a large children's hospital. One of her duties is to administer individual intelligence and achievement tests to children who are patients in the hospital's neurology department. When she administers a test to a child, Dr. Jones doesn't refer to it as an "intelligence" test or an "achievement" test. Instead, she tells the child what she is going to ask in concrete terms. For instance, she will say, "I'm going to ask you some questions about words" or "I'm going to ask you to solve some problems." Dr. Jones uses this approach because her goal is to get the best performance possible out of each child she tests. She believes that if children are worried about the type of test they are taking or how their performance will be judged, they aren't likely to do their best. Dr. Jones is particularly concerned about how what she says about a test might affect the performance of a child who is a member of a minority group, because she is familiar with the research on *stereotype threat*.

Psychologists Claude Steele and Joshua Aronson (Steele & Aronson, 1995) define *stereotype threat* as a subtle sense of pressure that members of a particular group feel when they are attempting to perform well in an area in which their group is characterized by a negative stereotype. According to Steele and Aronson, African American students experience stereotype threat whenever they are faced with an important cognitive test, such as a college entrance exam or an IQ test, because of the general cultural stereotype that African Americans are less intellectually able than members of other groups. In order to avoid confirming the stereotype, says the theory, African Americans avoid putting forth their best effort because to fail after having put forth one's best effort would mean that the stereotype was true.

Numerous studies have confirmed the existence of stereotype threat among both children and adults (McKown & Weinstein, 2003; Nussbaum & Steele, 2007; Steele & Aronson, 2004; Suzuki & Aronson, 2005). However, stereotype threat appears to have a smaller effect on children's test performance than it does on that of adults. Consequently, although the power of stereotype threat to influence adults' performance on cognitive tests has been well established by researchers, the jury is still out with regard to its importance in explaining group differences among children. Nevertheless, Dr. Jones believes that it is best to err on the side of caution with respect to stereotype threat. Her conclusion is that refraining from using the terms *intelligence test* and *achievement test* does not harm children or threaten their performance, whereas using those terms may cause them to be more anxious than they would be otherwise. Consequently, she intends to maintain her practice of describing the behaviors she will ask children to perform rather telling them the types of tests she is administering.

Questions for Reflection

1. Do you agree with Dr. Jones's conclusion regarding erring on the side of caution when administering tests?
2. How might parents and teachers moderate the effects of stereotype threat on children's test performance?

peers in other industrialized nations (Caslyn, Gonzales, & Frase, 1999). Yet studies also show that underlying cognitive developmental processes are very similar in Asian and North American children (Zhou & Boehm, 2004). Developmentalists speculate that the differences result from variations in both cultural beliefs and teaching methods.

With respect to cultural beliefs, developmentalists have found that North American parents and teachers emphasize innate ability, which they assume to be unchangeable, more than effort. For Asians, the emphasis is just the opposite: They believe that people can become more capable by working harder (Serpell & Hatano, 1997). Because of these differences in beliefs, this theory claims, Asian parents and teachers have higher expectations for children and are better at finding ways to motivate them to do school work. Presumably for these same reasons, Asian families spend more time teaching their children specific academic skills than North American parents do (Sijuwade, 2003).

However, teaching methods in the two cultures also vary. In one important set of studies, educational psychologists James Stigler and Harold Stevenson observed teaching strategies in 120 classrooms in Japan, Taiwan, and the United States, and they are convinced that Asian teachers have devised particularly effective modes of teaching mathematics and science (Stevenson, 1994; Stigler & Stevenson, 1991).

Japanese and Taiwanese teachers approach mathematics and science by crafting a series of "master lessons," each organized around a single theme or idea and each involving specific forms of student participation. These lessons are like good stories, with a beginning, a middle, and an end. In U.S. classrooms, by contrast, it is extremely uncommon for teachers to spend 30 or 60 minutes on a single coherent math or science lesson involving a whole class of children and a single topic. Instead, teachers shift often from one topic to another during a single math or science "lesson." They might do a brief bit on addition, then talk about measurement, then about telling time, and finally back to addition. Stigler and Stevenson also found striking differences in the amount of time teachers spend actually leading instruction for the whole class. In U.S. classrooms, teachers spent 49% of their time instructing the entire class. By contrast, group instruction occurred 74% and 90% of the time, respectively, in Japan and Taiwan.

Asian and North American math instruction also differ in their emphasis on *computational fluency*, the degree to which an individual can automatically produce solutions to simple calculation problems. A number of mathematicians and professors of mathematics claim that math instruction in the United States has been influenced more by "fads" than by a sound understanding of the role of computational fluency in mathematical problem solving (Murray, 1998). They point out that research has demonstrated that computational fluency is related both to calculation skills and to facility in solving word problems (Geary et al., 1999; Kail & Hall, 1999). Moreover, calculators are not commonly used in Asian schools. Many math educators suggest that, by the time they get to high school, U.S. students have learned to depend on calculators and, as a result, have a more difficult time learning algebra than do their Asian counterparts (Judson & Nishimori, 2005). These differences in algebra learning carry over into more advanced classes such as geometry and calculus. As a result, U.S. teens are often found to perform as well as their Asian peers with regard to mathematics concepts but fall short of them in problem solving.

The high levels of achievement attained by Asian students may be best explained by the fact that Asian teachers and parents regard instruction in computational skills as a parental responsibility and instruction in conceptual understanding as the responsibility of the school (Office of Educational Research and Improvement [OERI], 1998). Thus, by the time children enter school, they have already spent a good deal of time rehearsing basic computational facts and are ready to think more deeply about mathematical concepts. Many are taught to use an abacus, the ancient Chinese calculating device. Others begin studying mathematics in the internationally popular *Kumon* program at the age of 3 years. The Kumon program is a sequential set of timed worksheets that are designed to help children develop computational fluency through repetition. About a quarter of Japanese students continue to take Kumon classes throughout their school careers (OERI, 1998). The home-based approach to mathematics education that is common in Asian societies is effective because the amount of time needed to master computational skills varies widely from one child to another. Parents and individualized programs such as Kumon can more easily adapt their curricula to each child's unique pace of learning than schools can.

Another difference between U.S. and Asian schools, especially at the elementary level, involves the use of rewards. Because of the influence of Skinner's operant conditioning theory on education in the United States, teachers commonly use material rewards, such as stickers, to motivate children. Such rewards are effective only when they are tied to high standards, yet teachers in the United States often use them to reward students for less than optimal performance (Deci, Koestner, & Ryan, 1999; Eisenberger, Pierce, & Cameron, 1999).

In response to these criticisms, many educators say that achievement differences between North American and Asian students have been exaggerated to make U.S. schools look worse than they actually are (Berliner & Biddle, 1997). Moreover, more than 70% of American parents give grades of A or B to the nation's public schools (ABC News, 2000). Educators and parents alike often claim that Asian schools teach students to value conformity, whereas American schools place more emphasis on creativity. Indeed, some Asian educators agree that their schools have sacrificed creativity in order to attain high achievement test scores (Hatano, 1990).

Schooling for Children with Special Needs

Some children are born with or develop differences that may significantly interfere with their education unless they receive some kind of special instruction (see Table 11.3 on page 340). In the United States, 14% of all school children receive such services (NCES, 2006b). The

Table 11.3 Disabilities for Which U.S. Children Receive Special Education Services

Disability Category	Percentage of Special Education Students in the Category	Description of Disability
Learning Disability	43%	Achievement 2 or more years behind expectations, based on intelligence tests *Example*: A fourth-grader with an average IQ who is reading at a first-grade level
Communication Disorder in Speech or Language	22%	A disorder of speech or language that affects a child's education; can be a problem with speech or an impairment in the comprehension or use of any aspect of language *Example*: A first-grader who makes errors in pronunciation like those of a 4-year-old and can't connect sounds and symbols
Mental Retardation	9%	IQ significantly below average, together with impairments in adaptive functions *Example*: A school-aged child with an IQ lower than 70 who is not fully toilet-trained and who needs special instruction in both academic and self-care skills
Serious Emotional Disturbance	7%	An emotional or behavior disorder that interferes with a child's education *Example*: A child whose severe temper tantrums cause him to be removed from the classroom every day
Other Health Impairments	7%	A health problem that interferes with a child's education *Example*: A child with severe asthma who misses several weeks of school each year (Children with ADHD are included in this category.)
Autistic Disorders	3%	A group of disorders in which children's language and social skills are impaired *Example*: A child with autism who needs special training to acquire the capacity for verbal communication
Multiple Disabilities	2%	Need for special instruction and ongoing support in two or more areas to benefit from education *Example*: A child with cerebral palsy who is also deaf, thus requiring both physical and instructional adaptations
Hearing Impairment	1%	A hearing problem that interferes with a child's education *Example*: A child who needs a sign-language interpreter in the classroom
Orthopedic Impairment	1%	An orthopedic handicap that requires special adaptations *Example*: A child in a wheelchair who needs a special physical education class
Visual Impairment	0.4%	Impaired visual acuity or a limited field of vision that interferes with education *Example*: A blind child who needs training in the use of Braille to read and write

Sources: Kirk, Gallagher, & Anastasiow, 1993; NCES, 2006b.

individualized educational plan (IEP) an instructional program that has been designed to meet a child's unique needs

categories listed in Table 11.3 are defined by law, and public schools are legally obligated to provide special education services for all children who qualify. When a comprehensive assessment indicates that a child needs special education services, teachers must develop an **individualized educational plan (IEP)**, an instructional program that has been designed to meet the child's unique needs. The IEP specifies the services for which the child is eligible, the site where services will be delivered, the personnel who are responsible for delivery of services, and how progress will be measured.

Learning Disabilities

Learning Objective 11.9
Why is the term *learning disability* controversial?

The largest group of children served by U.S. special educators has some kind of **learning disability**, or difficulty in mastering a specific academic skill (most often reading), despite possessing normal intelligence and no physical or sensory handicaps. When reading is the problem skill, the term **dyslexia** is often used (even though, technically speaking, dyslexia refers to a total absence of reading). Most children with reading disabilities can read, but not as well as others their age. Moreover, it appears that their skill deficits are specific to reading—such as an inability to automatize sound-letter correspondences—rather than the result of a general cognitive dysfunction (Wimmer, Mayringer, & Landerl, 1998).

School can be a discouraging and frustrating place for a child with a learning disability.

How common such learning disabilities may be is still a matter of considerable dispute. Some experts in the field argue that up to 80% of all children classified by school systems as having learning disabilities are misclassified. They claim that only about 5 out of every 1,000 children have genuine neurologically based learning disabilities (Farnham-Diggory, 1992). The remainder who are so classified are more appropriately called slow learners or are suffering from some other problem, perhaps temporary emotional distress or poor teaching. Practically speaking, however, the term *learning disability* is used very broadly within school systems (at least within the United States) to label children who have unexpected or otherwise unexplainable difficulty with school work.

Explanations of the problem are just as subject to disagreement as its definition. One difficulty is that children labeled as having learning disabilities rarely show any signs of major brain damage on any standard neurological tests. So, if a learning disability results from a neurological problem, the neurological problem must be a subtle one. Some researchers have suggested that a large number of small abnormalities may develop in the brain during prenatal life, such as some irregularity of neuron arrangement, clumps of immature brain cells, scars, or congenital tumors. The growing brain compensates for these problems by "rewiring" around the problem areas. These rewirings, in turn, may scramble normal information-processing pathways just enough to make reading or calculation or some other specific task very difficult (Farnham-Diggory, 1992). Other experts argue that there may not be any underlying neurological problem at all. Instead, children with learning disabilities (especially reading disabilities) may simply have a more general problem with understanding the sound and structure of language (Carroll & Snowling, 2004; Share & Leiken, 2004; Torgesen et al., 1999). There is also some evidence that learning disabilities, especially dyslexia, may have a genetic basis (Gallagher, Frith, & Snowling, 2000; Turic et al., 2004).

These disagreements about both definition and explanation are (understandably) reflected in confusion at the practical level. Children are labeled as having learning disabilities and assigned to special classes, but a program that works well for one child may not work at all for another. Some parents of children with disabilities choose to homeschool (see *Developmental Science at Home* on page 342). One type of school intervention that shows promise is an approach called *reciprocal teaching*. In reciprocal teaching programs, children with learning disabilities work in pairs or groups. Each child takes a turn summarizing and explaining the material to be learned to the others in the group. A number of studies have found that, after participating in reciprocal teaching, children with learning disabilities had improved in summarization skills and memory strategies (e.g., Lederer, 2000).

A new approach to helping children who fall behind in school was included in the most recent reauthorization of special education law in 2004; experts hope it will greatly reduce the

learning disability a disorder in which a child has difficulty mastering a specific academic skill, even though she or he possesses normal intelligence and no physical or sensory handicaps

dyslexia problems in reading or the inability to read

DEVELOPMENTAL SCIENCE AT HOME

Homeschooling

The Hannigan family is concerned about their son's progress in second grade. Although Michael struggled somewhat in first grade, he was eventually able to meet the minimum requirements for promotion to second grade. Now, however, he is beginning to fall seriously behind his classmates. Michael's teachers have suggested that he might benefit from special education services, but the Hannigans are exploring the possibility of homeschooling for Michael, an option that has been enthusiastically embraced by several of their neighbors. The Hannigans' neighbors have created a variety of opportunities for their children to interact so that they do not miss out on any of the social skills that children usually learn in school. But why would a parent want to take on the daunting task of educating a child at home?

Surveys show that the most frequent reason for homeschooling is parents' belief that they can do a better job of educating their children than public or private schools can (Basham, 2001). About 8% of homeschool parents have children with disabilities and prefer teaching them at home to having them receive special education services from local schools (Basham, 2001). The one-on-one teaching these children get at home often helps them achieve more than their peers with disabilities in public schools are able to (Duvall, Delquadri, & Ward, 2004; Ensign, 1998). In addition, children with disabilities who are homeschooled don't have to deal with teasing from peers. Many homeschool parents want to be sure that their own religious and moral values are included in their children's education. Many also want to protect their children from negative peer influences or school-based crime.

Research on homeschooling is sparse. Advocates point to a small number of studies showing that homeschooled children are socially competent and emotionally well adjusted and score above average on standardized achievement tests (Ray, 1999). They further argue that homeschooled children have the opportunity to become closer to their parents than children who attend school do (Jonsson, 2003). The growing prevalence of homeschooling, which includes about 2.4% of all children in the United States, has led to the creation of a variety of extracurricular organizations, such as musical groups and athletic leagues, that serve homeschoolers exclusively. Thus, today's homeschoolers have many opportunities for interacting with peers that are highly similar to those available to children who are enrolled in school.

However, opponents of homeschooling, a group that includes most professional educators, claim that comparisons of homeschooling and public education are misleading. They point out that researchers have studied only homeschooled children whose families volunteered to participate in research studies. In contrast, most public school achievement test data are based on representative samples or on populations of entire schools.

Questions for Reflection

1. What factors would motivate you to consider homeschooling your child, and what are some reasons that you would be reluctant to do so?
2. If you were discussing homeschooling with a classmate who cited research showing that homeschoolers get higher achievement test scores than children who are enrolled in public school, how would you explain the shortcomings of such research?

---

need for special education services for children who fall behind in academic subjects (Fuchs, Fuchs, & Zumeta, 2008). This strategy, called **response to intervention (RTI)**, requires schools to implement a three-tier plan for helping such children. *Tier I* involves schoolwide efforts to prevent learning problems and to quickly intervene when problems occur. For example, testing children early in the school year to identify at-risk students and providing teachers with the materials they need to individualize instruction for them is a Tier I strategy. Tier I also includes careful monitoring of all students' progress in all subjects. *Tier II* interventions assign children to small pull-out groups in which subject-area specialists help them catch up. *Tier III* is implemented in cases in which children do not respond to Tier I and Tier II strategies. It includes the traditional services of school psychologists and special education teachers, including comprehensive assessment with psychological tests and assignment of students to special classes, if needed.

response to intervention (RTI) a three-tier plan for helping children who fall behind in school

Learning Objective 11.10
How do schools meet the needs of children with developmental disabilities?

Developmental Disabilities

Some special educators work with children who have **developmental disabilities**, conditions that impair children's functioning in school and will prevent them from living independently as adults. For instance, children with *cerebral palsy* have normal intellectual abilities but have difficulty controlling their movements. As a result, many require physical assistance with personal care functions, such as going to the restroom. Many of these children are in wheelchairs and require special equipment to write and otherwise fully participate in school.

developmental disabilities conditions that impair children's functioning in school and will prevent them from living independently as adults

Mental Retardation Children with another developmental disability, *mental retardation*, have unique educational needs. As you learned in Chapter 7, this condition is usually di-

Table 11.4 Mental Retardation as Measured on the Wechsler Scales

Classification	IQ Range	Percentage of People with Mental Retardation	Characteristics of Persons with Mental Retardation at Each Level
Mild	55–70	90%	Are able to grasp learning skills up to 6th-grade level; may become self-supporting and can be profitably employed in various vocational occupations
Moderate	40–55	6%	Probably are not able to grasp more than 2nd-grade academic skills but can learn self-help skills and some social and academic skills; may work in sheltered workshops
Severe	25–40	3%	Can be trained in basic health habits; can learn to communicate verbally; can learn through repetitive habit training
Profound	Below 25	1%	Have rudimentary motor development; may learn very limited self-help skills

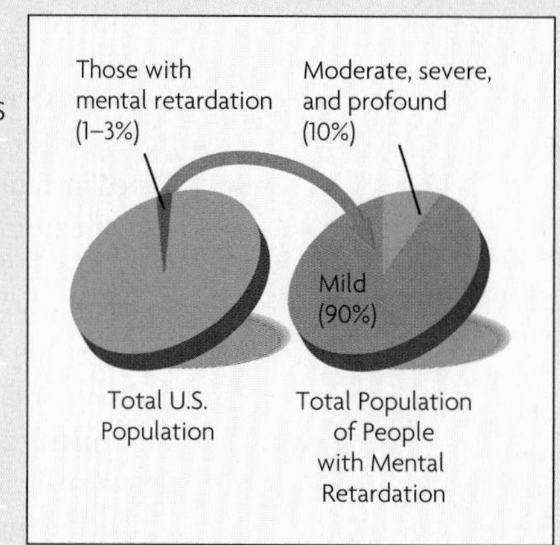

Source: Wood et al., WORLD OF PSYCHOLOGY & STUDY CARD PKG, Table 8.3 (p. 274), © 2005. Reprinted by permission of Pearson Education, Inc.

agnosed in early childhood. Because experience is so critical to the development of children with mental retardation, federal law in the United States requires that local schools provide such children with educational services beginning at birth. In infancy, these services usually take the form of home visits by child development specialists, who help parents learn how to stimulate their children's development. Beginning around age 3, most schools provide preschool programs for children with mental retardation. At age 5, children with mental retardation enter kindergarten just as other children their age do. However, the academic expectations for children with mental retardation are different from those of their agemates. Intelligence testing plays a vital role in the determination of appropriate expectations for each child with mental retardation.

For educational purposes, mental retardation is customarily divided into several IQ ranges, and different labels are attached to children in each range. As you can see in Table 11.4, the lower the IQ range, the fewer children there are. Moreover, each category is associated with different expectations with regard to school learning. However, these expectations are simply general guidelines. Special educators must work with each child individually before a valid assessment of his or her capacity for academic learning can be made.

Pervasive Developmental Disorders Special educators must also assess each child with a *pervasive developmental disorder (PDD)* individually. (You learned about this group of disorders in Chapter 7.) Like mental retardation, pervasive developmental disorders are addressed in legislation that requires schools to provide services early in life. Thus, most children with PDDs who are diagnosed in early childhood attend special education preschool programs. In these classes, special educators help children develop communication skills and appropriate social behaviors, as well as academic skills such as reading.

communication disorders problems with speech or language that interfere with a child's education

Communication Disorders

Learning Objective 11.11
What are the educational needs of children with communication disorders?

As you can see in Table 11.3, the second largest group of children served by special educators in the United States is those who have **communication disorders**, problems with speech or language that interfere with a child's education. Prior to age 8, or about third grade, the number of children diagnosed with communication disorders exceeds the number who are classified as having a learning disability. Children with these disorders are assessed and served by **speech-language pathologists (SLPs)**, professionals who are trained to diagnose communication disorders and to help children overcome them.

The category of communication disorders is a diverse one, including difficulties with speech that involve *articulation* (pronouncing sounds), *voice* (adapting the loudness of pitch of the voice to different circumstances), and *fluency* (smooth connections between speech sounds, words, and sentences). Also included are difficulties with language, such as those involving *form* (word order, word parts, parts of speech), *content* (word meanings), and *function* (or *pragmatics*). The definitions of these subgroups of communication disorders are listed in Table 11.5, along with an example of each. Notice that language disorders can involve either expressive or receptive language (look back at Chapter 5).

The first step in assessing a child who is suspected of having a communication disorder is to determine whether an underlying physical or mental condition may be causing the problem (Smith, 2007). For instance, some children who have problems with speech and/or language have an undiagnosed hearing impairment. Correcting the hearing problem to the extent possible increases the chances that intervention for the child's communication problems will be effective. Likewise, children who are born with *cleft palate*, a failure of the roof of the mouth to fully close prior to birth, have difficulty speaking until the defect is surgically corrected. And following surgery, all such children require services from SLPs to learn to speak appropriately. Many children with developmental disabilities also have communication disorders; identification of the type and severity of the developmental disability helps the SLP create an appropriate intervention plan for the particular child. There are also neurological conditions, such as brain tumors, that can interfere with the development of speech and language. Consequently, assessments of children with communication problems always require a thorough case study, which often includes both medical and psychological testing. Nevertheless, in most cases, no underlying cause for the communication disorder is found (Smith, 2007).

speech-language pathologist (SLP) professional trained to diagnose communication disorders and to help children overcome them

Table 11.5 Communication Disorders

Communication Disorder	Definition	Example
Speech Disorders		
Articulation	Abnormal production of speech sounds	Failure to pronounce */th/* correctly after age 7
Voice	Abnormal pitch, loudness, resonance, and/or duration	Excessive speech volume
Fluency	Impaired rate and/or rhythm of speech	Stuttering
Language Disorders		
Form	Abnormal word order, parts, usage	*Expressive*: Does not include past tense after age 3 *Receptive*: Does not recognize questions as distinct from statements
Content	Problems with word meaning	*Expressive*: Uses fewer words than age peers *Receptive*: Understands fewer words than age peers
Function	Problems using language in a meaningful way	*Expressive*: Does not provide enough information to listeners to be understood (compared to age peers) *Receptive*: Has poorer verbal memory than age peers

Sources: DSM-IV TR, 2000; Smith, 2007; Sanchez, 2008.

When communication disorders are diagnosed early and an appropriate intervention plan is developed, children often show dramatic improvement. This is particularly true for speech disorders. For instance, **stuttering**, a disorder of fluency in which children's speech features repeated sounds, afflicts about 1% of school-aged children and usually appears before age 5. However, until the child is in school, parents and teachers often fail to recognize it as a disorder that requires intervention. They believe that the child will "grow out of it." As a result, diagnosis and treatment of stuttering can be delayed. Such delays are unfortunate, because stuttering typically improves dramatically or disappears entirely when a child receives appropriate therapy within 3 years of the disorder's onset (Yairi & Ambrose, 2004). After 3 years, the probability that a child will recover before adolescence declines to just 15%. The consequences of failure to intervene in a timely manner go beyond the course of the disorder itself. Researchers have found that teens who stutter are more likely than their peers to be bullied (Yairi & Ambrose, 2004).

Inclusive Education

Learning Objective 11.12
What is inclusive education?

Current special education laws rest most centrally on the philosophical view that children with disabilities have a right to participate in normal school environments (e.g., Stainback & Stainback, 1985). Proponents argue that **inclusive education** aids the child with disabilities by integrating him into the nondisabled world, thus facilitating the development of important social skills as well as providing more appropriate academic challenges than are often found in separate classrooms or special programs for the disabled (Siegel, 1996). In addition, recent changes in educational law, such as the landmark 2001 *No Child Left Behind* legislation, have raised standards with regard to what all children, including those with disabilities, are expected to learn. As a result, a growing number of children with special needs are being educated in classrooms with children who do not have disabilities (Friend & Bursuck, 2006).

Schools and school districts differ widely in the specific model of inclusion they use, although virtually all models involve a team of educators, including the classroom teacher, one or more special education teachers, classroom aides, and sometimes volunteers. Some schools follow a plan called a *pull-out program*, in which the student with a disability is placed in a regular classroom only part of each day, with the remainder of the time spent working with a special education teacher in a special class or resource room. More common are *full-inclusion systems*, in which the child spends the entire school day in a regular class but receives help from volunteers, aides, or special education teachers who come to the classroom to work with the child there. In some districts, a group of children with disabilities may be assigned to a single regular classroom; in others, no more than one such child is normally assigned to any one class (Baker & Zigmond, 1995).

For teachers, the crucial question is a practical one: What works best? That is, among the many varieties of inclusion programs, can features that are consistently associated with better results or poorer results be identified? This question is extremely hard to answer. For all kinds of perfectly understandable reasons, developmentalists have little of the kind of research needed to answer it. Inclusion programs vary widely in design and serve children with diverse problems. The teachers who implement them range from highly skilled and inventive to overwhelmed and unskilled. If a particular program pattern appears to work in one school, it is often difficult to tell whether it is because of the particular teachers involved, because of the specific characteristics of the children being served, or because the program itself is especially well designed.

Given all this, it is not surprising that clear answers to many of the questions about inclusion are lacking. Still, educators and psychologists have struggled to summarize the information they do have, and most would agree with the following conclusions:

- Children with physical disabilities but no learning problem—such as children with spina bifida—make better academic gains in full-inclusion programs (Jenks, van Lieshout, & de Moor, 2008).

stuttering a disorder of fluency in which children's speech features repeated sounds

inclusive education a general term for education programs in which children with disabilities are taught in regular classrooms

- Success for children with learning disabilities in a regular classroom depends heavily on the ability of the teacher to implement an individualized program. Co-teaching arrangements appear to be particularly helpful for children with learning disabilities (Magiera & Zigmond, 2005).
- Effective inclusion programs require, at a minimum, that teachers be given extensive additional training and substantial support from specialists, aides, or volunteers (Roberts & Mather, 1995)—conditions that are very often not met because of budgetary or other reasons.

How does inclusive education affect teachers? You may be surprised by the finding that teachers who have the most positive attitudes toward inclusion also have the highest burnout rates (Talmor, Reiter, & Feigin, 2005). Researchers speculate that teachers with idealistic views of inclusion probably work very hard to help students with disabilities succeed. When their efforts meet with limited success, they may suffer from feelings of failure and incompetence and may feel emotionally drained. In some schools, teachers are provided with co-teachers who carry some of the extra burdens involved in teaching a class that includes both typically developing children and children with disabilities. This practice appears to protect some teachers against burnout (Magiera & Zigmond, 2005). Moreover, students with disabilities receive much more direct instruction when both a regular teacher and a co-teacher are available.

Finally, implementation of an inclusive education program does not relieve a school of the legal responsibility to provide a *continuum of placements* for children with special needs (Friend & Bursuck, 2006). That is, in addition to opportunities for inclusion, schools must provide these students with special, even fully individualized, classes if that is what is needed to help them achieve their full potential. For this reason, despite the undeniable trend toward greater inclusiveness, only about half of all children with special needs in the United States are placed in regular classrooms on a full-time basis (U.S. Department of Education, 2002).

Learning Objective 11.13

In what ways do the educational needs of gifted children differ from those of their peers?

Giftedness

Finally, any discussion of the schooling of children with special needs would be incomplete without consideration of those who are highly talented. Finding good programs for such children is a continuing dilemma. Consider the example of a child named Michael, described by Halbert Robinson:

> When Michael was 2 years and 3 months old, the family visited our laboratory. At that time, they described a youngster who had begun speaking at age 5 months and by 6 months had exhibited a vocabulary of more than 50 words. He started to read English when he was 13 months old. In our laboratory he spoke five languages and could read in three of them. He understood addition, subtraction, multiplication, division, and square root, and he was fascinated by a broad range of scientific constructs. He loved to make puns, frequently bilingual ones. (1981, p. 63)

Michael's IQ score on the Stanford-Binet was in excess of 180 at age 2; 2 years later, he performed as well as a 12-year-old on the test and was listed as having an IQ score beyond 220.

Definitions and Labels We can certainly all agree that Michael should be labeled as *gifted*, but defining the term precisely is difficult (Cramond, 2004). A number of authors (e.g., Gardner, 1983) have argued that people with exceptional specific talents, such as musical, artistic, mathematical, or spatial abilities, should be classed as gifted, along with those with very high IQ scores. This broadening of the definition of **giftedness** has been widely accepted among theorists, who agree that there are many kinds of exceptional ability, each of which may reflect unusual speed or efficiency with one or another type of cognitive function.

giftedness exceptional ability, such as very high intelligence and/or musical, artistic, mathematical, or spatial talents

Within school systems, however, giftedness is still typically defined entirely by IQ test scores, such as all scores above 130 or 140. Robinson suggested that it may be useful to divide the group of high-IQ children into two sets: the "garden-variety gifted," who have high IQ scores (perhaps 130 to 150) but no extraordinary ability in any one area, and the "highly gifted" (like Michael), with extremely high IQ scores and/or remarkable skill in one or more areas—a group Ellen Winner (1997) calls the *profoundly gifted*. These two groups may have quite different experiences at home and in school.

Cognitive and Social Functioning Gifted children show speedy and efficient processing on simple tasks and flexible use of strategies on more complex tasks. They learn quickly and transfer that learning broadly, and they have remarkably good problem-solving skills—they often leap directly to a solution that less gifted individuals need many intermediate steps to figure out (Sternberg & Davidson, 1985; Winner, 1997). Further, they seem to have unusually good metacognitive skills: They know what they know and what they don't know, and they spend more time than average-IQ children in planning how to go about solving problems (Dark & Benbow, 1993). Winner also notes that profoundly gifted children have a "rage to master," a powerful drive to immerse themselves in learning in some area.

Whether such advanced intellectual abilities transfer to social situations is not so well established. Many parents are concerned about placing their gifted child in a higher grade in school because of fears that the child will not be able to cope socially; others assume that rapid development in one area should be linked to rapid development in all areas.

One famous and remarkable early study of gifted children, by Lewis Terman, pointed to the latter conclusion. In the 1920s, Terman selected 1,500 children with high IQ scores from the California school system. These children—now adults in their 80s—have been followed regularly throughout their lives (e.g., Holahan, 1988; Terman, 1925; Terman & Oden, 1959). Terman found that the gifted children he studied were better off than their less gifted classmates in many ways other than school performance. They were healthier, they had wider-ranging interests, and they were more successful in later life. Both the boys and the girls in this study went on to complete many more years of education than was typical in their era, and most had successful careers as adults.

Most research suggests that gifted children have about the same risk of social or emotional problems as normal-IQ children, which means that most are well adjusted and socially adept (Vida, 2005). Optimism about the social robustness of gifted children may have to be tempered somewhat, however, in the case of the profoundly gifted subgroup. These children are often so different from their peers that they are likely to be seen as strange or disturbing. They are often socially solitary and introverted as well as fiercely independent and nonconforming; they have difficulties finding peers who can play at their level and are often quite unpopular with classmates (Kennedy, 1995). Profoundly gifted children are about twice as likely as their less gifted peers to show some kind of significant social or emotional problem (Winner, 1997). Also on the negative side of the ledger is the fact that many gifted children are so bored by school that they become disengaged and even drop out, often because their school district does not allow acceleration in grade or has no special programs for the gifted. Given the fact that skipping grades does not seem to be linked to social maladjustment (and is linked to better achievement among the gifted), it appears to make good sense to encourage accelerated schooling, if only to help ward off extreme boredom in the gifted child.

Test Prep Center

with mydevelopmentlab

COGNITIVE CHANGES

11.1 How do vocabulary and other aspects of language change during middle childhood? (p. 322)

Language development continues in middle childhood with vocabulary growth, improvements in grammar, and understanding of the social uses of language. Metalinguistic skills also improve.

1. According to Anglin, the average fifth-grader has about ______ words in his or her vocabulary.

11.2 What cognitive advantages do children gain as they move through Piaget's concrete operational stage? (pp. 323–324)

Piaget proposed that a major change in the child's thinking occurs at about age 6, when the child begins to understand powerful operations such as reversibility and decentration. The child also learns to use inductive logic, but finds using deductive logic difficult.

2. Explain how each of the following cognitive processes contributes to concrete operational thinking.

   (A) decentration

   ____

   ____

   (B) reversibility

   ____

   ____

3. From the Multimedia Library within MyDevelopmentLab, watch the *Deductive Reasoning* video and answer the following question.

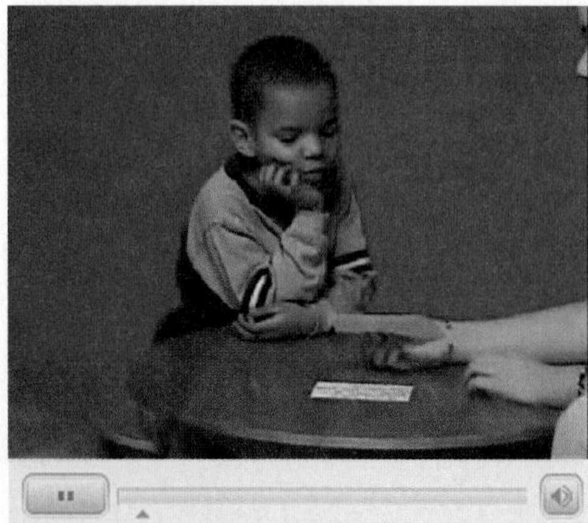

In the second reasoning problem involving a feather and a glass, why did the boy fail to follow the rule the researcher gave him?

____

____

11.3 What is horizontal décalage, and how does Siegler explain concrete operational thinking? (pp. 324–326)

Children acquire Piaget's concrete operational tasks gradually over the 6- to 12-year-old period, a pattern he called horizontal décalage. Siegler's research suggests that the "operations" Piaget observed may actually be a logical sequence of rules for solving specific types of problems. Siegler's research shows that a particular child's position in the sequence depends primarily on the child's specific experience with a given set of materials.

4. Match each of the following terms with its definition.

   ______(1) the understanding that matter can change in appearance without changing in quantity

   ______(2) the understanding that subordinate classes are included in larger, superordinate classes

   (A) class inclusion

   (B) conservation

5. Some developmentalists think that ______________ influences children's ability to solve transitivity problems.

11.4 How do children's information-processing skills improve during middle childhood? (pp. 327–329)

Most information-processing theorists conclude that there are no age-related changes in children's information-processing capacity, but there are clearly improvements in speed and efficiency. The memory demands of school seem to facilitate the improvements in information-processing skills that happen between 6 and 12.

6. In the table below, briefly summarize the information-processing benefits associated with each of the advances listed.

Advances	Benefits
Greater processing efficiency	
Automaticity	
Executive processes	
Memory strategies	
Expertise	

7. Identify each of these memory strategies.

   (A) Categorizing a grocery list by canned goods, meat, produce, etc. ______________

Access MyDevelopmentLab at www.mydevelopmentlab.com.

(B) Mentally repeating a phone number in order to remember it until you finish dialing. ______________

(C) Associating a new vocabulary word with others that have similar roots. ______________

(D) Using the first letter of each item in a list to create an acronym. ______________

SCHOOLING

11.5 What should be included in an effective literacy curriculum? (pp. 329–331)

To become literate, children need specific instruction in sound-symbol correspondences, word parts, and other aspects of written language. They also need to be exposed to literature and to have opportunities to practice their reading and writing skills.

8. What is meant by the term *balanced approach?*

____

____

9. From the Multimedia Library within MyDevelopmentLab, watch the *Early Literacy Development: Frederick Morrison* video and answer the following question.

What did Professor Morrison learn in his research on literacy that he believed should be included in elementary school teacher training?

____

____

11.6 How do bilingual and ESL approaches to second-language instruction differ? (pp. 331–333)

Children who participate in bilingual education receive academic instruction in their first language until they develop sufficient English skills to be taught in English. Those in ESL classes attend language classes in which they learn English for part of the day and then attend academic classes that are conducted entirely in English for the other part.

10. Match each English-teaching strategy with its definition.

______(1) bilingual education

______(2) English as a Second Language (ESL) program

______(3) structured immersion

______(4) submersion

(A) Children receive all instruction in English.

(B) Children receive most academic instruction in English and special instruction in English language skills.

(C) Children receive most academic instruction in English, but a teacher translates for them when necessary.

(D) Children speak two languages in class.

11. From the Multimedia Library within MyDevelopmentLab, watch the *Teaching in a Bilingual Classroom* video and answer the following question.

According to the teachers in the video, how does having cultural diversity in a classroom affect teaching?

____

____

11.7 Why do schools administer standardized tests? (pp. 333–335)

Standardized tests compare students' performance to that of a reference group. Thus, standardized achievement tests allow local school officials to compare their students' performance to that of students all over the country. Standardized tests enable administrators to track children's academic progress according to an external standard.

12. Define each type of intelligence in Gardner's theory.

Type	Definition
Linguistic	
Logical/mathematical	
Musical	
Spatial	
Bodily kinesthetic	
Naturalist	
Interpersonal	
Intrapersonal	

13. Match each type of intelligence in Sternberg's theory with its definition.

_______(1) knowing the right behavior for a particular situation

_______(2) the ability to give specific responses without thinking about them

_______(3) the ability to generate effective strategies

(A) componential

(B) contextual

(C) experiential

14. From the Multimedia Library within MyDevelopmentLab, watch the *Practical Intelligence: Robert Sternberg* video and answer the following question.

Do standardized tests measure what Sternberg called "practical" intelligence?

____

____

15. List the three components of emotional intelligence.

(A)_______________________________________

(B)_______________________________________

(C)_______________________________________

11.8 What kinds of group differences in achievement have educational researchers found? (pp. 336–339)

Boys typically do better on tests that require numerical reasoning. Girls do somewhat better on verbal tasks and at arithmetic computation. Although poverty and other social factors may play a role, ethnic differences in achievement may result from differences in learning styles, philosophical beliefs, or attitudes toward school. Differences in both cultural beliefs and teaching practices are probably responsible for cross-cultural variations in math and science achievement.

16. Classify each of the following as more typical of boys (B) or girls (G).

_______(1) scores in the gifted range on math achievement tests

_______(2) success in math attributed to effort

_______(3) success in math attributed to ability

_______(4) higher scores on tests of math computation

17. Match each of the following terms with its definition.

_______(1) a learning style associated with a tendency to focus on details

_______(2) a learning style associated with a tendency to focus on the big picture

(A) analytical style (B) relational style

18. List five factors that have been included in explanations of cross-cultural differences in academic achievement.

(A) _______________________________________

(B) _______________________________________

(C) _______________________________________

(D) _______________________________________

(E) _______________________________________

SCHOOLING FOR CHILDREN WITH SPECIAL NEEDS

11.9 Why is the term *learning disability* controversial? (pp. 341–342)

There is considerable dispute about how to identify a genuine learning disability, and some children who are labeled as learning disabled have been misclassified. Practically speaking, *learning disability* serves as a catch-all term to describe children who, for unknown reasons, do not learn as quickly as their intelligence test scores suggest they should.

19. From the Multimedia Library within MyDevelopmentLab, watch the *Dyslexia Detector* video and answer the following question.

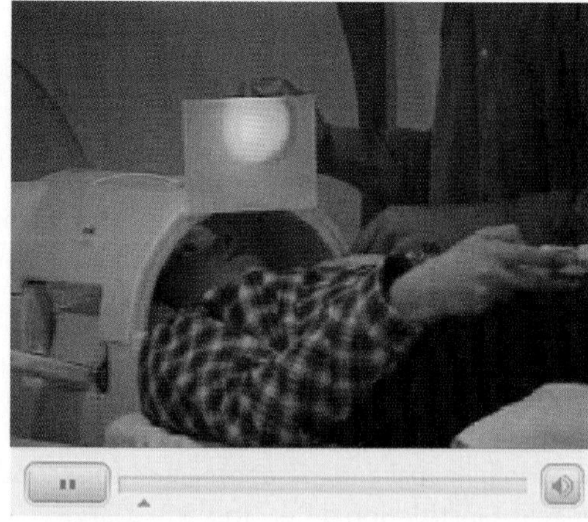

How can the test shown in the video help children at risk for learning disabilities?

____

____

11.10 How do schools meet the needs of children with developmental disabilities? (pp. 342–343)

Developmental disabilities affect children's functioning in school and prevent them from living independently as adults. Special educators must determine the unique needs of each child with a developmental disability. Intelligence testing is helpful in this regard, because it helps educators tailor academic goals to children's abilities.

20. What kinds of special services do children with cerebral palsy usually require at school?

____

____

11.11 What are the educational needs of children with communication disorders? (pp. 343–345)

Children with communication disorders have problems with speech and/or language. Some require medical intervention. Early intervention by speech-language pathologists helps children with these problems overcome them.

21. Communication disorders include difficulties with speech that involve

(A) _______________
(B) _______________
(C) _______________
(D) _______________
(E) _______________
(F) _______________

22. From the Multimedia Library within MyDevelopmentLab watch the *Special Education* video and answer the following question.

According to the teachers in the video, how did a speech language therapist support the academic development of the boy with the hearing impairment, "George"?

____

____

11.12 What is inclusive education? (pp. 345–346)

Inclusive education is a philosophy based on the belief that children with special needs are best served when they spend at least part of every school day in classrooms with children who do not have disabilities. However, inclusive education is only one component of the continuum of services that schools are legally required to offer to students with special needs.

23. What does research suggest about the type of special education services appropriate for each of these groups?

(A) Children with physical disabilities but no learning problems: _______________

____

____

(B) Children with learning disabilities: _______________

____

____

11.13 In what ways do the educational needs of gifted children differ from those of their peers? (pp. 346–347)

Gifted is a term applied to children with very high IQ scores, unusual creativity, or exceptional specific talents. Their information processing is unusually flexible and generalized. Gifted children appear to be socially well adjusted, except for a small group who are unusually gifted and have a higher risk of social and emotional problems.

24. From the Multimedia Library within MyDevelopmentLab, watch the *Giftedness: Robert Sternberg* video and answer the following question.

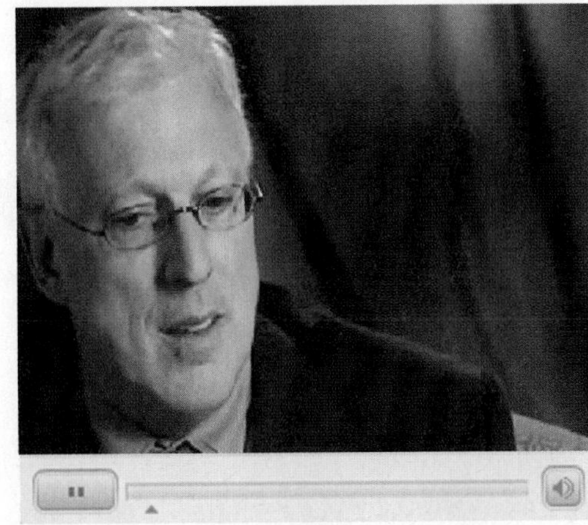

What is Professor Sternberg's primary concern about the identification of gifted children in American schools?

____

____

For answers to the questions in this chapter, turn to page 520. For a list of key terms, turn to page 531.

Succeed with PEARSON mydevelopmentlab

Do You Know All of the Terms in This Chapter?
Find out by using the Flashcards. Want more practice? Take additional quizzes, try simulations, and watch video to be sure you are prepared for the test!

Chapter 12

Social and Personality Development in Middle Childhood

Every culture in the world has a society of childhood, in which children make up their own social rules that differ from those of adult society. For example, in most U.S. school lunchrooms, food trading is common. A child who refuses to trade may be seen as "stuck up." But adults who try to talk co-workers into trading lunches are likely to be thought of as pushy or somewhat odd. Such comparisons show that children practice social competence by making up their own social rules rather than simply copying those that exist in the adult world. Creating and enforcing such rules helps children learn to look at things from other people's points of view and to cooperate.

Clearly, cognitive development provides the intellectual foundation required to engage in rule-governed activities. But what makes each child's experiences unique within the context of such universal interactions are the emotional and behavioral responses that distinctive personalities, self-concepts, and relationship histories contribute to the developmental equation. You will learn about these topics in this chapter. We will begin with a consideration of the major themes of development that uniquely mark social and personality development in the middle childhood years and the different ways in which developmentalists have explained them. Then we turn to the milestones of self-concept development and research findings in the field of social cognition. Finally, we look at social influences on the development of the school-aged child, both within and beyond the family system.

Learning Objectives

Theories of Social and Personality Development

12.1 How did the psychoanalytic theorists characterize the middle childhood years?

12.2 What are the main ideas of the trait and social-cognitive theorists?

Self-Concept

12.3 What are the features of the psychological self?

12.4 How does self-esteem develop?

Advances in Social Cognition

12.5 How does children's understanding of others change in middle childhood?

12.6 How do children in Piaget's moral realism and moral relativism stages reason about right and wrong?

The Social World of the School-Aged Child

12.7 How does self-regulation affect school-aged children's relationships with their parents?

12.8 What changes occur in children's understanding of friendships during this period?

12.9 In what ways do boys and girls interact during the middle childhood years?

12.10 What types of aggression are most common among school-aged children?

12.11 How do popular, rejected, and neglected children differ?

Influences Beyond Family and Peers

12.12 How does self-care affect girls' and boys' development?

12.13 How do television, computers, and video games affect children's development?

Theories of Social and Personality Development

Self-perceived competence is the overarching theme of social and personality development in the middle childhood years. How do children develop this critical attribute? Developmentalists representing different theoretical perspectives emphasize different sets of factors in their explanations of the development of self-perceived competence in these years.

Learning Objective 12.1

How did the psychoanalytic theorists characterize the middle childhood years?

Psychoanalytic Perspectives

When you think back to your middle childhood years, what kinds of experiences stand out? Most likely, you remember interacting with your peers and siblings. If Freud were called upon to explain how your feelings about your own competence developed, he would appeal to the emotional qualities of these interactions. Think back to the story at the beginning of this unit about a boy named Jamal who learned to ride a bicycle. When his peers taunted him after he failed to make it up the hill, Jamal was disappointed and embarrassed. However, these unpleasant emotions motivated him to learn to ride his bicycle without training wheels. According to the psychoanalytic perspective, and in line with our everyday experiences with children, children vary greatly in the ways that they respond to such situations. Some become angry and lash out at those who reject them. Others withdraw and develop a general fear of social interactions. Parents contribute to these responses. However, Freud thought that the challenge of the middle childhood years was to form emotional bonds with peers and to move beyond those that were developed with parents in earlier years. Thus, much of the modern-day research on peer rejection and other emotional features of middle childhood finds its roots in Freud's psychoanalytic approach.

THE WHOLE CHILD IN FOCUS

How have advances in the physical domain helped Jamal to resolve Erikson's crisis of industry versus inferiority? Find out on page 379.

Erik Erikson accepted Freud's view of the central role of peer relationships and the emotions that accompany them in middle childhood. He went beyond Freud's perspective, though, when he further characterized middle childhood as the period during which children experience the crisis of *industry versus inferiority*. During this stage, Erikson said, children develop a sense of their own competence through the achievement of culturally defined learning goals (see Table 2.2 on page 30). The psychosocial task of a 6- to 12-year-old is development of industry, or the willingness to work to accomplish goals. To develop industry, the child must be able to achieve the goals her culture sets for all children her age. In most countries, 6- to 12-year-olds must learn to read and write. If they fail to do so, Erikson claimed, they will enter adolescence and adulthood with feelings of inferiority. These feelings of inferiority constitute an emotional mindset that can hamper an individual's ability to achieve for the rest of her life.

Contemporary studies that stress a child's need to feel competent are in tune with Erikson's views. Many of them suggest that he was right about the link between school experiences and an emerging sense of competence. It seems that most 6- to 12-year-olds gradually develop a view of their own competence as they succeed or fail at academic tasks such as reading and arithmetic (Chapman & Tunmer, 1997; Skaalvik & Valas, 1999). Thus, their self-assessments and actual achievements are strongly correlated; that is, those who are most successful judge themselves to be competent, while those who have difficulty perceive themselves as less so. However, individual differences in children's responses to success and failure moderate the effects of the experiences themselves. Some of these differences are found in the emotional realm, as suggested earlier.

Erikson also argued that children who lack success in school can develop a sense of competence by participating in culturally valued pursuits outside of academic settings. A child who is a mediocre student, for instance, may channel his need to develop self-perceived competence into athletics. Another child who gets poor grades may do so because she spends most of her time reading books that she finds to be more interesting than her school work. Outsiders may worry about her sense of competence, but internally she has no doubts about her abilities.

The Trait and Social-Cognitive Perspectives

Learning Objective 12.2
What are the main ideas of the trait and social-cognitive theorists?

Psychoanalytic theorists have given us some compelling ideas about how individual differences in emotional responses to childhood experiences shape development and self-perceived competence. However, they tell us little about the origins of those differences. The primary goal of *trait theories*, by contrast, is to do just that. A **trait** is a stable pattern of responding to situations. This definition should remind you of our discussions of temperament in earlier chapters, because the study of infant and early childhood temperament is grounded in trait theory. By middle childhood, trait theorists argue, the various dimensions of temperament have evolved into five dimensions of personality (the so-called Big Five), which are shown in Table 12.1.

THE WHOLE CHILD IN FOCUS
Which of the Big Five traits are part of Jamal's personality? Find out on page 379.

Research suggests that trait theorists are right about the emergence of stable traits in middle childhood. Moreover, these traits are known to contribute to the development of feelings of competence. For instance, a child who is reasonably *extraverted*, or outgoing, responds to peer rejection by becoming more determined to be accepted by the group. One who is *introverted*, or shy, would likely become so emotionally distraught if taunted by her playmates that she would actively avoid social situations in the future. Still, children are not simply driven by personality-generated impulses in a mechanistic way, and trait theory leaves us wondering why extraversion doesn't always lead to social competence and why some people overcome their tendency toward introversion to become competent in the social arena.

From the social-cognitive perspective, both the psychoanalytic and the trait perspective focus on only one set of the factors that shape the development of self-perceived competence in middle childhood. Albert Bandura, for instance, proposed that the emotions described by psychoanalytic theorists and the stable patterns of responding identified by trait theorists, together with cognitive factors, constitute one of three interactive components that influence social and personality development (see Figure 12.1 on page 356) (Bandura, 1989). Bandura used the term *person component* to refer to this emotional/cognitive component. The other components of his model are the developing person's *behavior* and *environmental reinforcers*.

Bandura proposed that the personal, behavioral, and environmental components interact, in a pattern he termed **reciprocal determinism**. Each of the three components influences, and is influenced by, the other two. For example, Jamal's emotional reaction to his failure to

trait a stable pattern of responding to situations

reciprocal determinism Bandura's model in which personal, behavioral, and environmental factors interact to influence personality development

Table 12.1 The Big Five Personality Traits

Trait	Qualities of Individuals Who Show the Trait	Possible Temperament Components
Extraversion	Active, assertive, enthusiastic, outgoing	High activity level, sociability, positive emotionality, talkativeness
Agreeableness	Affectionate, forgiving, generous, kind, sympathetic, trusting	Perhaps high approach/positive emotionality, perhaps effortful control
Conscientiousness	Efficient, organized, prudent, reliable, responsible	Effortful control/task persistence
Neuroticism (Emotional Instability)	Anxious, self-pitying, tense, touchy, unstable, worrying	Negative emotionality, irritability
Openness/Intellect	Artistic, curious, imaginative, insightful, original, having wide interests	Approach, low inhibition

Sources: Ahadi & Rothbart, 1994; John, Caspi, Robins, Moffitt, & Stouthamer-Loeber, 1994, Table 1, p. 161; McCrae, Costa, Ostendorf, & Angleitner, 2000.

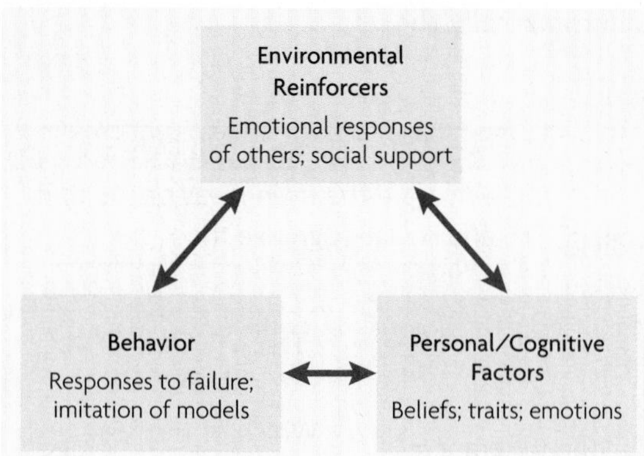

Figure 12.1 **Bandura's Reciprocal Determinism**

Bandura takes a social-cognitive view of personality. He suggests that three components—the external environment, individual behaviors, and cognitive factors, such as beliefs, expectancies, and personal dispositions—are all influenced by one another and play reciprocal roles in determining personality.

make it up the hill and his conclusion that removing the training wheels from his bike would solve his dilemma (the personal component) motivated him to head home and ask his father to remove the training wheels (the behavioral component). His father responded by removing the wheels (the environmental component). His agreeing to do so affected Jamal's emotional state (the personal component) and led him to attempt to ride the bike without his father's help (the behavioral component).

By organizing the various interactive influences the way it does, Bandura's model provides a more comprehensive explanation of how school-aged children develop ideas about the degrees of competence they possess than either the psychoanalytic or the trait theorists do. Thus, Bandura's social-cognitive approach provides us with a way of taking into account the valuable insights of the psychoanalytic theorists relative to children's emotions, as well as those of the trait theorists. And by integrating both into the three-part model that Bandura proposed, we gain a more comprehensive understanding of the mechanisms that drive the development of self-perceived competence in the middle childhood years.

Self-Concept

How much insight does a school-aged child really have into his own personality? The answer to this question depends on whether we look at the child at the beginning of the middle childhood period or near the end of it. Across the years from 6 to 12, children's understanding of themselves improves quite a bit. By the end of middle childhood, children's self-concepts include two new components: a *psychological self* and a *valued self*.

Learning Objective 12.3

What are the features of the psychological self?

The Psychological Self

The **psychological self** is a person's understanding of his or her enduring psychological characteristics. It first appears during the transition from early to middle childhood and becomes increasingly complex as the child approaches adolescence. It includes both basic information about the child's unique characteristics and self-judgments of competency.

Personality Traits Children don't use the same terminology as the trait theorists you read about earlier in the chapter, but they do describe their own personalities with increasing degrees of precision across the middle childhood years. For example a 6-year-old might use simple psychological self-descriptors such as "smart" or "dumb." By 10, a child is more likely to use comparisons in self-descriptions: "I'm smarter than most other kids" or "I'm not as talented in art as my friend" (Rosenberg, 1986; Ruble, 1987).

This developmental trend was illustrated in the results of a relatively old study of the self-concepts of 9- to 18-year-olds (Montemayor & Eisen, 1977). Children who participated were asked to give 20 answers to the question "Who am I?" The researchers found that the younger children were still using mostly surface qualities to describe themselves, as in this description by a 9-year-old:

> My name is Bruce C. I have brown eyes. I have brown hair. I have brown eyebrows. I am nine years old. I LOVE! Sports. I have seven people in my family. I have great! eye site. I have lots! of friends. I live on 1923 Pinecrest Dr. I am going on 10 in September. I'm a boy. I have a uncle that is almost 7 feet tall. My school is Pinecrest. My teacher is Mrs. V. I play Hockey! I'm almost the smartest boy in the class. I LOVE! food. I love fresh air. I LOVE school. (Montemayor & Eisen, 1977, p. 317)

psychological self an understanding of one's stable internal traits

In contrast, consider the self-description of this 11-year-old girl in the sixth grade:

> My name is A. I'm a human being. I'm a girl. I'm a truthful person. I'm not very pretty. I do so-so in my studies. I'm a very good cellist. I'm a very good pianist. I'm a little bit tall for my age. I like several boys. I like several girls. I'm old-fashioned. I play tennis. I am a very good swimmer. I try to be helpful. I'm always ready to be friends with anybody. Mostly I'm good, but I lose my temper. I'm not well-liked by some girls and boys. I don't know if I'm liked by boys or not. (Montemayor & Eisen, 1977, pp. 317–318)

This girl, like the other 11-year-olds in the study, described her external qualities, but she also emphasized psychological factors such as personality traits. Thus, as a child moves through the concrete operational period, her psychological self becomes more complex, more comparative, less tied to external features, and more centered on feelings and ideas.

Self-Efficacy As noted earlier in the chapter, middle childhood is the time when children develop perceptions of the degree to which they are competent. Albert Bandura has greatly advanced developmentalists' understanding of this crucial aspect of the psychological self. He defines **self-efficacy** as an individual's belief in her capacity to cause an intended event to occur or to perform a task (Bandura, 1997). How does self-efficacy develop?

Bandura proposed that peer models are a primary source of self-efficacy beliefs (Bandura, 1997). Bandura would say that, when Jamal observed his friends riding up the hill, he probably concluded that he could do likewise. Bandura would argue that, in order to believe that he could follow his peers' example, Jamal had to see himself as similar to them. (Recall the joy he experienced from thinking of himself as a "big kid.") Thus, *social comparisons*—the process of drawing conclusions about the self based on comparisons to others—play an integral role in the degree to which children gain insight into their own self-efficacy from observing peers. Thus, simply watching other children model success at a task is insufficient for the development of self-efficacy in a child whom outsiders see as similar to the models. The child herself must perceive that similarity in order to be influenced by the models.

Encouragement from sources of information that children value also contributes to self-efficacy. Jamal's father's willingness to let him try to ride without training wheels played a role in his feelings of self-efficacy. However, nothing influences self-efficacy more than an individual's actual experiences (Britner & Pajares, 2006). In other words, believing that you can do something is less powerful, emotionally and cognitively, than really doing it. Consequently, the final hurdle in Jamal's development of self-efficacy for bicycle riding was surmounted when he succeeded in learning to ride on his own.

The Valued Self

Learning Objective 12.4
How does self-esteem develop?

A child can have an accurate view of his personality traits, and even a solid sense of self-efficacy, but still fail to value himself as an individual. To find out why, developmentalists have studied another aspect of self-concept development in middle childhood: the emergence of the *valued self*.

The Nature of Self-Esteem A child's evaluative judgments have several interesting features. First of all, over the elementary school and high school years, children's evaluations of their own abilities become increasingly differentiated, with quite separate judgments about academic or athletic skills, physical appearance, social acceptance, friendships, romantic appeal, and relationships with parents (Harter, 1990; Marsh, Craven, & Debus, 1999). Paradoxically, however, it is when they reach school age—around age 7—that children first develop a global self-evaluation. Seven- and eight-year-olds (but not younger children) readily answer questions about how well they like themselves as people, how happy they are, or how well they like the way they are leading their lives. It is this global evaluation of one's own worth

self-efficacy the belief in one's capacity to cause an intended event to occur or to perform a task

that is usually referred to as **self-esteem**, not merely the sum of all the separate assessments a child makes about his skills in different areas.

A number of longitudinal studies of elementary school–aged children and teenagers show that self-esteem is quite stable in the short term but somewhat less so over periods of several years. The correlation between two self-esteem scores obtained a few months apart is generally about .60. Over several years, this correlation drops to about .40 (Alsaker & Olweus, 1992; Block & Robins, 1993). So, a child with high self-esteem at age 8 or 9 is likely to have high self-esteem at age 10 or 11, but self-esteem is subject to a good deal of variation. To some degree, self-esteem is more stable in girls than in boys (Heinonen, Raikkonen, & Keltikangas-Järvinen, 2003).

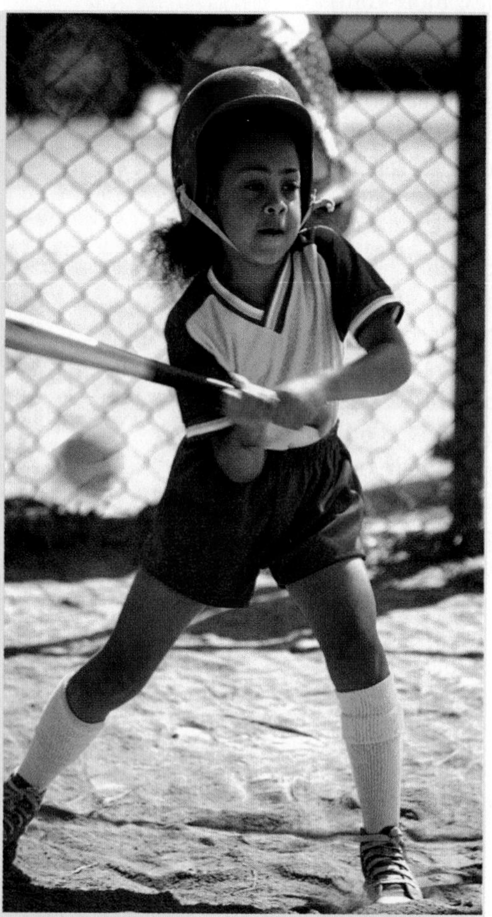
Hitting a home run will raise this girl's self-esteem only if she places a high value on being good at sports or at baseball specifically.

How Self-Esteem Develops Developmental psychologist Susan Harter (1987, 1990) has studied the development of self-esteem extensively. She has found that self-esteem is strongly influenced by mental comparisons of children's ideal selves and their actual experiences, a cognitive task that depends upon the advances in information-processing skills that you learned about in Chapter 11. However, each component of self-esteem is valued differently by different children. Thus, a child who perceives herself to have poor social skills because she is unpopular may not necessarily have low self-esteem. The degree to which her social self-assessment affects her self-esteem is influenced by how much she values social skills and popularity. In addition, she may see herself as very competent in another area—such as academic skills—which balances her lack of social skills.

The key to self-esteem, then, is the amount of discrepancy between what the child desires and what the child thinks he has achieved. Thus, a child who values sports prowess but who isn't big enough or coordinated enough to be good at sports will have lower self-esteem than will an equally small or uncoordinated child who does not value sports skill so highly. Similarly, being good at something, such as singing or playing chess, won't raise a child's self-esteem unless the child values that particular skill.

Another major influence on a child's self-esteem is the overall support the child feels she is receiving from the important people around her, particularly parents and peers (Franco & Levitt, 1998). Apparently, to develop high self-esteem, children must first acquire the sense that they are liked and accepted in their families, by both parents and siblings. Next, they need to be able to find friends with whom they can develop stable relationships. Since childhood friendships begin with shared interests and activities, children need to be in an environment in which they can find others who like the same things they do and are similarly skilled. Athletic children need other athletic children to associate with, those who are musically inclined need to meet peers who are also musical, and so on.

The separate influences of the perceived discrepancy between the ideal self and the actual self and the amount of social support are clear in the results of Harter's research on self-esteem. She asked third-, fourth-, fifth-, and sixth-graders how important it was to them to do well in each of five domains, and how well they thought they actually did in each. The total discrepancy between these sets of judgments constituted the discrepancy score. A high discrepancy score indicated that a child didn't feel he was doing well in areas that mattered to him. The social support score was based on children's replies to a set of questions about whether they thought others (parents and peers) liked them as they were, treated them as a person, and felt that they were important. Figure 12.2 shows the results for the third- and fourth-graders; the findings for the fifth- and sixth-graders are virtually identical to these results. Both sets of data support Harter's hypothesis, as does other research, including studies of African American children (Luster & McAdoo, 1995). Note that a low discrepancy score

self-esteem a global evaluation of one's own worth

alone does not protect a child completely from low self-esteem if he lacks sufficient social support. Similarly, a loving and accepting family and peer group do not guarantee high self-esteem if the youngster does not feel that he is living up to his own standards.

The criteria by which children learn to evaluate themselves vary considerably from one society to another (Miller, Wang, Sandel, & Cho, 2002; Wang & Ollendick, 2001). In individualistic cultures, like that of the United States, parents focus on helping children develop a sense of self-esteem that is based on the children's own interests and abilities. In collectivist cultures, such as China's, children are taught to value themselves based on cultural ideals about what a "good" person is.

From all of these sources, the child fashions her ideas (her internal model) about what she should be and what she is. Like the internal model of attachment, self-esteem is not fixed in stone. It is responsive to changes in others' judgments, as well as to changes in the child's own experience of success or failure. But once created, the model does tend to persist, both because the child tends to choose experiences that will confirm and support it and because the social environment—including the parents' evaluations of the child—tends to be at least moderately consistent.

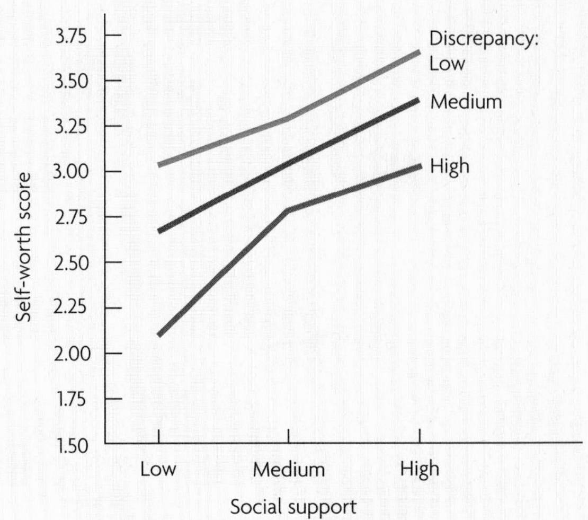

Figure 12.2
Social Support, Domain Values, and Self-Esteem

For these third- and fourth-graders in Harter's studies, self-esteem was about equally influenced by the amount of support the children saw themselves receiving from parents and peers and the degree of discrepancy between the values the children placed on various domains and the skill they thought they had in each of those domains.

(*Source*: Harter, 1987, Figure 9.2, p. 227.)

Advances in Social Cognition

To what extent did Jamal understand his peers' motivations for yelling at him when he could not make it to the top of the hill? Do you think he had any insight into why his father was reluctant to remove the training wheels from his bicycle? Children's ability to understand motivation is enhanced by the development of a theory of mind in early childhood. But by the end of the middle childhood period, children have developed a much broader understanding of others than they possessed at its beginning. Moreover, they are beginning to understand the moral aspects of social relationships.

The Child as Psychologist

Learning Objective 12.5
How does children's understanding of others change in middle childhood?

A number of early ground-breaking social-cognitive studies demonstrated that the child of this age looks beyond appearances and searches for deeper consistencies that will help him to interpret both his own and other people's behavior. Thus, like their understanding of the physical world, 6- to 12-year-olds' descriptions of other people move from the concrete to the abstract. If you ask a 6- or 7-year-old to describe others, he will focus almost exclusively on external features—what the person looks like, where he lives, what he does. This description by a 7-year-old boy, taken from a classic study of social-cognitive development, is typical:

> He is very tall. He has dark brown hair, he goes to our school. I don't think he has any brothers or sisters. He is in our class. Today he has a dark orange [sweater] and gray trousers and brown shoes. (Livesley & Bromley, 1973, p. 213)

When young children do use internal or evaluative terms to describe people, they are likely to use quite global ones, such as *nice* or *mean*, *good* or *bad*. Further, young children do not seem to see these qualities as lasting or general traits of the individual, applicable in all situations or over time (Rholes & Ruble, 1984). In other words, a 6- or 7-year-old has not yet developed a concept that might be called "conservation of personality."

Beginning at about age 7 or 8, a rather dramatic shift occurs in children's descriptions of others. The child begins to focus more on the inner traits or qualities of another person and to assume that those traits will be visible in many situations (Gnepp & Chilamkurti, 1988).

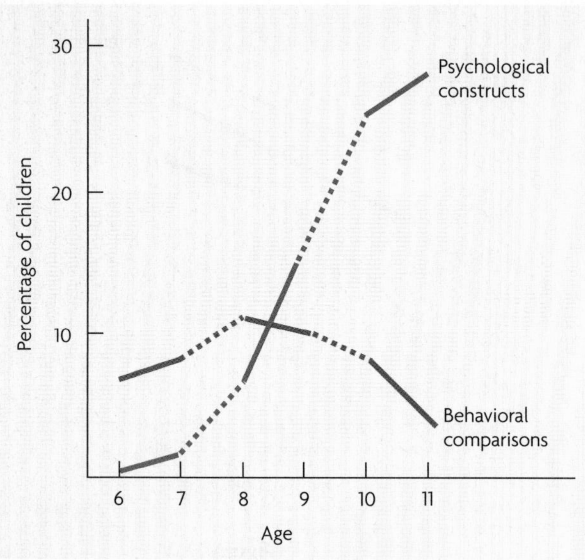

Figure 12.3
Changes in Children's Descriptions of Others

These data from Barenboim's study show the change in children's descriptions of their peers during the years of middle childhood. © The solid lines represent longitudinal data, the dashed lines cross-sectional comparisons.

(*Source*: Adapted from *Child Development* by Barenboim, Figure 1, p. 134, 1981. © The Society for Research in Child Development. Reprinted by permission of Blackwell Publishing.)

Children of this age still describe others' physical features, but their descriptions are now used as examples of more general points about internal qualities. You can see the change when you compare the 7-year-old's description given earlier with this description by a child nearly 10 years old:

> He smells very much and is very nasty. He has no sense of humour and is very dull. He is always fighting and he is cruel. He does silly things and is very stupid. He has brown hair and cruel eyes. He is sulky and 11 years old and has lots of sisters. I think he is the most horrible boy in the class. He has a croaky voice and always chews his pencil and picks his teeth and I think he is disgusting. (Livesley & Bromley, 1973, p. 217)

This description still includes many external physical features but goes beyond such concrete surface qualities to the level of personality traits, such as lack of humor and cruelty.

The movement from externals to internals in descriptions of others is well documented by research. For example, in one important early study, researchers asked 6-, 8-, and 10-year-olds to describe three other children; a year later, they asked them to do the same thing again (Barenboim, 1981). Figure 12.3 shows the results for two of the categories used in the study's data analysis. A *behavioral comparison* was any description that involved comparing a child's behaviors or physical features with those of another child or with a norm—for example, "Billy runs a lot faster than Jason" or "She draws the best in our whole class." Any statement that involved some internal personality trait—such as "Sarah is so kind" or "He's a real stubborn idiot!"—was referred to as a *psychological construct*. You can see that behavioral comparisons peaked at around age 8 but psychological constructs increased steadily throughout middle childhood.

School-aged children also understand family roles and relationships much better than younger children do. For example, by about age 9, children who live in two-parent homes understand that their parents' roles as parents are distinct from their roles as partners or spouses (Jenkins & Buccioni, 2000). Thus, a 9-year-old is better able than a 5-year-old to understand when divorcing parents say that their love for the child hasn't changed, even though their relationship with each other has ended. Emotionally, the divorce experience may be just as difficult, but school-aged children are more capable of understanding it cognitively.

Learning Objective 12.6
How do children in Piaget's moral realism and moral relativism stages reason about right and wrong?

Moral Reasoning

Children's growing understanding of the internal experiences of other people helps them develop a better understanding of how they and others think about actions that have moral implications. *Moral reasoning* is the process of making judgments about the rightness or wrongness of specific acts. As you learned in Chapter 9, children learn to discriminate between intentional and unintentional acts between age 2 and age 6. However, using this understanding to make moral judgments is another matter. Piaget claimed that the ability to use reasoning about intentions to make judgments about the moral dimensions of behavior appears to emerge along with concrete operational reasoning (Piaget, 1932).

Piaget's Moral Realism and Moral Relativism Piaget studied moral development by observing children playing games. As he watched them play, Piaget noticed that younger children seemed to have less understanding of the games' rules. Following up on these observations, Piaget questioned children of different ages about rules. Their answers led him to propose a two-stage theory of moral development (Piaget, 1932). At the beginning of the middle childhood period, children are in what Piaget termed the **moral realism stage**. They believe that the rules of games can't be changed because they come from authorities,

moral realism stage the first of Piaget's stages of moral development, in which children believe that rules are inflexible

such as parents, government officials, or religious figures. For example, one 6-year-old told Piaget that the game of marbles was invented on Noah's ark. He went on to explain that the rules can't be changed because the "big ones," meaning adults and older children, wouldn't like it (Piaget, 1965, p. 60).

Moral realists also believe that all rule violations eventually result in punishment. For example, when Piaget told children a story about a child who fell into a stream when he tried to use a rotten piece of wood as a bridge, children younger than 8 told him that the child was being punished for something "naughty" he had done in the past.

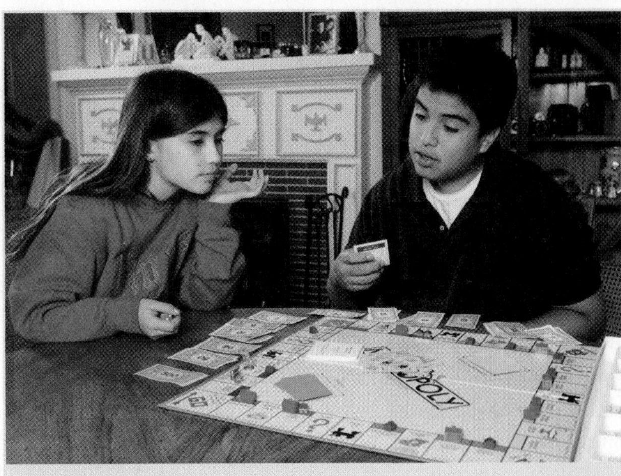

Piaget suggested that there is a connection between children's understanding of the rules by which games are played and their reasoning about moral issues.

After age 8, Piaget proposed, children move into the **moral relativism stage**, in which they learn that people can agree to change rules if they want to. They realize that the important thing about a game is that all the players follow the same rules, regardless of what those rules are. For example, 8- to 12-year-olds know that a group of children playing baseball can decide to give each batter four strikes rather than three. They understand that their agreement doesn't change the game of baseball and that it does not apply to other people who play the game. At the same time, children of this age get better at following the rules of games.

Eight- to twelve-year-olds also know that you don't get punished for rule violations unless you get caught. As a result, they view events like the one in which the child fell into the stream as accidents. They understand that accidents are not caused by "naughty" behavior. Children older than 8 also understand the relationship between punishment and intentions. For example, Piaget's research suggests that children over 8 can distinguish between a child who unintentionally left a store without paying for a candy bar and another who deliberately took one. Older children are likely to say that both children should return or pay for the candy, but only the one who intentionally stole it should be punished.

Research supports Piaget's claim that children over 8 give more weight to intentions than to consequences when making moral judgments (Zelazo, Helwig, & Lau, 1996). However, although their thinking is more mature than that of preschoolers, 6- to 12-year-olds' moral reasoning is still highly egocentric. For example, every parent has heard the exclamation "It's not fair!" when a child fails to receive the same treat or privilege as a sibling. It is rare, if not completely unknown, for a 6- to 12-year-old to protest the fairness of receiving something that a sibling didn't. Thus, school-aged children still have a long way to go with respect to mature moral reasoning (see *Developmental Science at Home* on page 362); we will return to this topic in the chapters on adolescent development.

moral relativism stage the second of Piaget's stages of moral development, in which children understand that many rules can be changed through social agreement

The Social World of the School-Aged Child

School-aged children's growing ability to understand others changes their social relationships in important ways. Children continue to be attached to parents, but they are becoming more independent. Relationships with peers become more stable, and many ripen into long-term friendships. In fact, the quality of 6- to 12-year-olds' peer relationships shapes their futures in many important ways.

Relationships with Parents

Learning Objective 12.7

How does self-regulation affect school-aged children's relationships with their parents?

Middle childhood is a period of increasing independence of child from family. Yet attachments to parents continue to be important, and relationships with

DEVELOPMENTAL SCIENCE AT HOME

Encouraging Moral Reasoning

Much to the surprise of her mother, Andrea, 8-year-old Marisol was caught stealing a package of candy from a convenience store that she passed every day when she walked home from school. The manager called Marisol's mother to report what the girl had done, and by the time Andrea arrived, the little girl was crying and pledging never to steal again. "You still have to be punished," Andrea explained and told Marisol that she was taking away all of the girl's privileges for 2 weeks. However, like most parents, Andrea wants to be sure that Marisol understands why what she did was wrong. How can parents help children learn to reason about issues of right and wrong?

In his book *Raising Good Children*, developmental psychologist Thomas Lickona reminds readers that the development of mature moral reasoning takes many years (Lickona, 1983). At the same time, he offers parents and teachers several suggestions that will help them help their 6- to 12-year-olds prepare for movement to more mature levels. Following are some of Lickona's suggestions:

- Require kids to give reasons for what they want.
- Play developmentally appropriate games with them.
- Praise them for observing social conventions such as saying "please" and "thank you."
- When punishment is necessary, provide them with an explanation, advice on how to avoid punishment in the future, and a way of repairing any damage their misbehavior has caused.
- Teach them about reciprocity: "We do nice things for you, so you should be willing to help us."
- Give them meaningful chores so that they will think of themselves as important family and community members.
- Help and encourage them to base obedience on love and respect rather than fear.
- Teach them religious and philosophical values, including the idea that some actions are right and others are wrong, regardless of circumstances.
- Challenge their egocentrism by asking questions such as "How would you feel if someone did that to you?" when they violate others' rights.
- Include them in charitable projects, such as food drives, to extend the idea of love and caring beyond their own families.

Questions for Reflection

1. Which of Lickona's suggestions are most relevant to the situation in which Marisol's mother found herself?
2. Do you agree with Andrea that it was necessary to punish the girl? If so, what additional steps do you think Andrea should take to help Marisol learn the importance of respecting others' property?

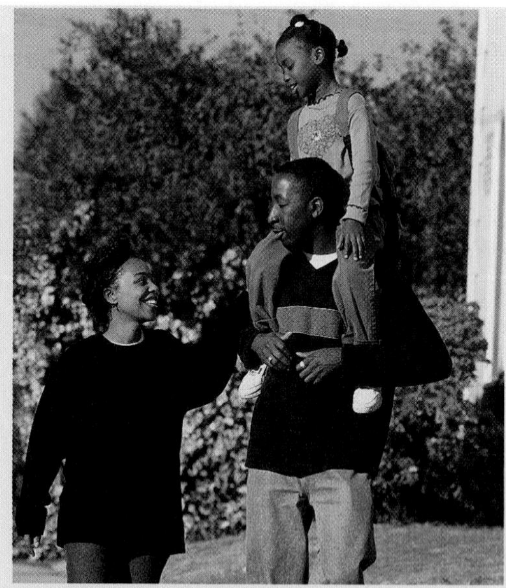

Research suggests that only children are just as well adjusted as those who have siblings.

siblings add another dimension to the social worlds of 6- to 12-year-olds who have them. (See *Developmental Science in the Clinic.*) What does change is the agenda of issues between parent and child. The parent-child agenda changes because parents of 6- to 12-year-olds recognize their children's growing capacity for **self-regulation**, the ability to conform to parental standards of behavior without direct supervision. As a result, as children get older, parents are more likely to allow them to engage in activities such as bicycle riding and skateboarding without supervision (Soori & Bhopal, 2002). However, cultures vary to some degree in the specific age at which they expect this to occur. For example, White and Hispanic parents in the United States differ in their beliefs about the average age at which school-aged children can carry out specific tasks on their own (Savage & Gauvain, 1998). It appears that Hispanic American parents have less confidence in the self-regulatory abilities of young school-aged children than White parents do. In general, though, most cultures expect 6- to 12-year-olds to be able to supervise their own behavior at least part of the time.

Some studies suggest that there are sex differences in parents' expectations with respect to self-regulatory behavior. For example, mothers make different kinds of demands on boys and girls. They appear to provide both with the same types of guidance but are likely to give boys more autonomy over their own behavior than they give girls. Nevertheless, they are likely to hold daughters to a higher standard of accountability for failure than they do sons (Pomerantz & Ruble, 1998). Developmentalists speculate that this difference may lead to stronger standards of behavior for girls in later developmental periods.

self-regulation the ability to conform to parental standards of behavior without direct supervision

Researchers have learned that there are several parenting variables that contribute to the development of self-regulation. First, parents' own ability to self-regulate is important, per-

DEVELOPMENTAL SCIENCE IN THE CLINIC

Siblings and Only Children

Guillermo and Juana are a young couple who come from a background in which large families are the rule. Guillermo's three brothers have two children each, and each of their wives is expecting another. Both of Juana's sisters have three children, and one is pregnant. Guillermo and Juana had always assumed that they would have a large family as well. However, during Juana's first pregnancy, she developed toxemia. After the birth of the couple's son, Juana's kidneys failed, and she nearly died. For these reasons, her doctor has advised her to avoid becoming pregnant again. Both Guillermo and Juana agree that they should follow the doctor's advice, but their families have told them that their son will be "spoiled" if he grows up without a brother or sister. The couple expressed their concerns about "only" children to their family pediatrician.

In response to their questions about only children, the pediatrician assured Guillermo and Juana that most studies show that only children grow up to be just as well adjusted as those who have brothers and sisters (Wang et al., 2000). Moreover, some studies have shown that only children may actually have an advantage over those who have siblings, at least with regard to cognitive development and academic achievement (Doh & Falbo, 1999; Falbo, 1992). Other studies suggest that the cognitive advantage enjoyed by only children may actually be due to birth order. First-borns (as well as the oldest surviving child in a family in which a first-born died in infancy) get higher scores, on average, on cognitive tests than later-borns do (Holmgren, Molander, & Nilsson, 2006; Kristensen & Bjerkedal, 2007). The *resource dilution hypothesis* explains these findings as the result of the progressive "watering down" of the parents' material and psychological resources with each additional birth (Downey, 2001). Thus, from this perspective, parents have the greatest influence on the oldest child, an advantage that is shared by only children and the oldest child in a multi-child family.

However, critics of the resource dilution hypothesis might advise Guillermo and Juana to consider adopting another child or making sure that their son spends plenty of time with his younger cousins, which are sure to be in plentiful supply. These critics argue that the hypothesis places too much emphasis on what later-borns take away from the family and ignores the relationship-building opportunities that these children contribute to their older siblings' development (Gillies & Lucey, 2006). For example, first-borns who have siblings outperform only children on measures of social negotiation. First-borns with younger siblings also appear to gain self-reliance skills from serving as surrogate parents for the younger siblings (Brody, Kim, Murry, & Brown, 2003). Regardless of birth order, affectionate sibling relationships moderate the effects of stressful life events such as parental divorce, and they enable children to advance more rapidly than only children do with regard to understanding others' mental states and behaviors (Gass, Jenkins, & Dunn, 2007; McAlister & Peterson, 2006). Thus, only and first-born children may get more of the kind of attention from parents that is critical to cognitive development, but having a younger sibling appears to make positive contributions to social and emotional development.

Questions for Reflection

1. What kinds of sibling relationships would harm rather than help a child's social and emotional development?
2. In what kinds of situations might you expect only children to show social skills superior to those of children who have siblings?

haps because they are providing the child with models of good or poor self-regulation (Prinstein & La Greca, 1999). Also, the degree of self-regulation expected by parents influences the child's self-regulatory behavior. Higher expectations, together with parental monitoring to make certain the expectations are met, are associated with greater self-regulatory competence (Rodrigo, Janssens, & Ceballos, 1999).

You should recall that such parental behaviors are associated with the authoritative style of parenting. Longitudinal research has demonstrated that school-aged children whose parents have been consistently authoritative since they were toddlers are the most socially competent (Baumrind, 1991). Children rated "competent" were seen as both assertive and responsible in their relationships; those rated "partially competent" typically lacked one of these skills; those rated "incompetent" showed neither. In Baumrind's (1991) study, the majority of children from authoritative families were rated as fully competent, while most of those from neglecting families were rated as incompetent.

Friendships

Learning Objective 12.8

What changes occur in children's understanding of friendships during this period?

The biggest shift in relationships during middle childhood is the increasing importance of peers. One frequent manifestation of this trend is the appearance of "best-friend" relationships. Cross-cultural studies show that best-friend relationships, and the belief that having a best friend is important, are universal features of school-aged children's social development (Schraf & Hertz-Lazarowitz, 2003). Younger children, often as early as 3 years of age, express playmate preferences (Hay, Payne, & Chadwick, 2004). Among older school-aged children, however, a best friend is much more than a playmate, reflecting these children's better understanding of the characteristics that distinguish friendships from other kinds of relationships.

THE WHOLE CHILD IN FOCUS

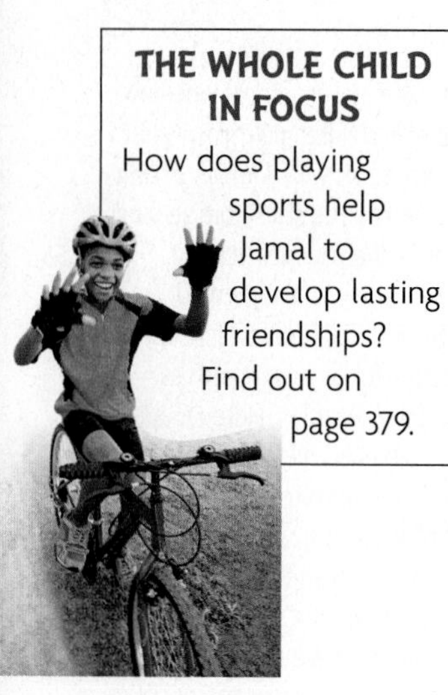

How does playing sports help Jamal to develop lasting friendships? Find out on page 379.

Social-cognitive researcher Robert Selman was one of the first to study children's understanding of friendships. He found that if you ask preschoolers and young school-aged children how people make friends, the answer is usually that they "play together" or spend time physically near each other (Damon, 1977, 1983; Selman, 1980).

In the later years of middle childhood, at around age 10, this view of friendship gives way to one in which the key concept seems to be reciprocal trust (Chen, 1997). Older children see friends as special people who possess desired qualities other than mere proximity, who are generous with each other, who help and trust each other, and so on. Figure 12.4 is a 10-year-old boy's definition of a friend. His characterization of a friend—as someone "you can trust," who will "always be there for you when you are feeling down in the dumps" and "always sit next to you at lunch"—illustrates an older child's understanding of dimensions of friendships such as trust, emotional support, and loyalty.

Researchers have examined the relationship between children's understanding of friendship and the quantity and quality of their friendships. In one such study, researchers Amanda Rose and Steven Asher (2004) presented fifth-graders with hypothetical situations in which one friend might have an opportunity to help another. In one scenario, the researchers described a child who was teased by her classmates. Rose and Asher found that children who expressed the view that children should not help others in such situations, in order to avoid putting themselves at risk of being treated similarly by peers, had fewer friends than did children who expressed the view that friends should place their relationships above concerns about how their helping behavior would affect their own social status.

Evidence of the centrality of friends to social development in middle childhood also comes from studies of children's behavior within friendships. Children are more open and more supportive when with their buddies, smiling at, looking at, laughing with, and touching one another more than they do when they are with nonfriends; they talk more with friends and cooperate and help one another more. Pairs of friends are also more successful than nonfriends in solving problems or performing some task together. Yet school-aged children are also more critical of friends and have more conflicts with them; they are more po-

My definition of a good friend
is someone who you can trust,
They will never turn their back on
you, They will always be there for
you. when you are feeling down
in the dumps, They'll try to cheer
you up, They will never forget
about you, They'll always sit
next to you at lunch,

Figure 12.4 **A 10-Year-Old's Explanation of Friendship**

This essay on friendship, written by a 10-year-old, illustrates the way older school-aged children think about friends. (Courtesy of Denise Boyd. Used with permission.)

lite with strangers (Hartup, 1996). At the same time, when conflicts with friends occur, children are more concerned about resolving them than they are about settling disagreements with nonfriends. Thus, friendship seems to represent an arena in which children can learn how to manage conflicts (Newcomb & Bagwell, 1995).

Gender Segregation

Learning Objective 12.9

In what ways do boys and girls interact during the middle childhood years?

Possibly the most striking thing about peer group interactions in the elementary school years is how gender segregated they are. This pattern seems to occur in every culture in the world and is frequently visible in children as young as 3 or 4. Boys play with boys and girls play with girls, each in their own areas and at their own kinds of games (Cairns & Cairns, 1994; Harkness & Super, 1985). In fact, gender seems to be more important than age, race, or any other categorical variable in 6- to 12-year-olds' selection of friends, and the strength of children's preference for same-sex associates increases substantially across middle childhood (Graham, Cohen, Zbikowski, & Secrist, 1998). Moreover, gender segregation is unrelated to sex differences in parenting, suggesting that it is a feature of 6- to 12-year-olds' social relationships that they construct for reasons of their own (McHale, Crouter, & Tucker, 1999).

Shared interests and activities are a critical part of friendship in the early years of middle childhood. For example, rough-and-tumble play is common in boy-boy interactions but is typically avoided by girls. Thus, based on activity preferences, boys gravitate to other boys in social situations. In so doing, they learn how to socialize with other boys but acquire few of the skills, such as self-disclosure, used by girls in their interactions (Phillipsen, 1999). Thus, boys establish stable peer groups with dominance hierarchies based on rough-and-tumble play skills (Pelligrini & Smith, 1998). A similar pattern exists for girls: Gender segregation begins with shared activity preferences but leads to the development of social skills that are more useful in interactions with other girls than in interactions with boys.

However, there are some ritualized "boundary violations" between boys' and girls' groups, such as chasing games. For example, in one universal series of interactions, a girl taunts a boy with a statement like "You can't catch me, nyah nyah." Next, the boy chases and catches her, to the delight of both of their fully supportive same-sex peer groups (Thorne, 1986). As soon as the brief cross-gender encounter ends, both girl and boy return to their respective groups. On the whole, however, girls and boys between the ages of 6 and 12 actively avoid interacting with one another and show strong favoritism toward their own gender and negative stereotyping of the opposite gender (Powlishta, 1995).

In middle childhood, boys play with boys and girls play with girls. In fact, children's play groups are more sex-segregated at this age than at any other.

Gender segregation patterns are even more pronounced in friendships during middle childhood. For example, when researchers ask children to describe the kind of playmate a fictional child would prefer, school-aged children's predictions are largely gender-based (Halle, 1999). Girls' and boys' friendships also differ in quality in intriguing ways. Boys' friendship groups are larger and more accepting of newcomers than are girls'. Boys play more outdoors and roam over a larger area in their play. Girls are more likely to play in pairs or in small, fairly exclusive groups, and they spend more playtime indoors or near home or school (Benenson, 1994; Gottman, 1986).

Sex differences also characterize the interaction between a pair of friends. Boys' friendships appear to be focused more on competition and dominance than are girls' friendships (Maccoby, 1995). In fact, among school-aged boys, researchers see higher levels of competition between pairs of friends than between strangers—the opposite of what is observed among girls.

Why do you think competition is such a strong feature of friendship interactions among boys? Do you think this is true in every culture?

Friendships between girls include more agreement, more compliance, and more self-disclosure than is true between boys. For example, "controlling" speech—a category that includes rejecting comments, ordering, manipulating, challenging, defiance, refutation, and resistance of another's attempts to control—is twice as common among pairs of 7- and 8-year-old male friends as among pairs of female friends of that age (Leaper, 1991). Among the 4- and 5-year-olds in Leaper's study, there were no sex differences in controlling speech, suggesting that these differences in interaction patterns arise during middle childhood.

None of this information should obscure the fact that the interactions of male and female friendship pairs have much in common. For example, collaborative and cooperative exchanges are the most common forms of communication in both boys' and girls' friendships in middle childhood. And it is not necessarily the case that boys' friendships are less important to them than girls' are to them. Nevertheless, it seems clear that there are gender differences in form and style that may well have enduring implications for patterns of friendship over the lifespan. Furthermore, school-aged children appear to evaluate the role of gender in peer relationships in light of other variables. For example, when asked whether a fictitious boy would prefer to play with a boy who is a stranger or with a girl who has been his friend for a while, most school-aged children say the boy would prefer to play with the friend (Halle, 1999). Such results suggest that, even though gender is clearly important in school-aged children's peer relationships, they are beginning to understand that other factors may be more important. This is yet another example of how children's growing cognitive abilities—specifically, their ability to think about more than one variable at a time—influence their ideas about the social world.

Learning Objective 12.10

What types of aggression are most common among school-aged children?

Patterns of Aggression

You may remember from Chapter 9 that physical aggression declines over the preschool years, while verbal aggression increases. In middle childhood, physical aggression becomes even less common as children learn the cultural rules about when it is acceptable to display anger or aggression and how much of a display is acceptable. In most cultures, this means that anger is increasingly disguised and aggression is increasingly controlled as children get older (Underwood, Coie, & Herbsman, 1992).

One interesting exception to this general pattern is that in all-boy pairs or groups, at least in the United States, physical aggression seems to remain both relatively high and constant over the childhood years. Indeed, at every age, boys show more physical aggression and more assertiveness than girls do, both within friendship pairs and in general (Fabes, Knight, & Higgins, 1995). Furthermore, school-aged boys often express approval for the aggressive behavior of peers (Rodkin, Farmer, Pearl, & Van Acker, 2000). Table 12.2 gives some highly representative data from a very large, carefully administered survey in Canada, in which

Table 12.2 Aggressive Behavior in Boys and Girls Ages 4 to 11

	Percentages as Rated by Teachers	
Behavior	Boys	Girls
Is mean to others	21.8	9.6
Physically attacks people	18.1	4.4
Gets in many fights	30.9	9.8
Destroys own things	10.7	2.1
Destroys others' things	10.6	4.4
Threatens to hurt people	13.1	4.0

Source: Offord, Boyle, & Racine, 1991, from Table 2.3, p. 39.

teachers completed checklists describing each child's behavior (Offord, Boyle, & Racine, 1991). It is clear that boys are described as far more aggressive on all of this study's measures of physical aggressiveness.

Results like these have been so clear and so consistent that most psychologists have concluded that boys are simply "more aggressive." But that conclusion may turn out to be wrong. Instead, girls may simply express their aggressiveness in a different way, using what has recently been labeled *relational aggression*, instead of physical aggression. Physical aggression hurts others physically or poses a threat of such damage; **relational aggression** is aimed at damaging the other person's self-esteem or peer relationships, such as by ostracism or threats of ostracism ("I won't invite you to my birthday party if you do that"), cruel gossip, or facial expressions of disdain. Children are genuinely hurt by such indirect aggression, and they are likely to express dislike for others who use this form of aggression a lot (Casas & Mosher, 1995; Cillessen & Mayeux, 2004; Cowan & Underwood, 1995; Crick & Grotpeter, 1995; Rys & Bear, 1997).

Girls are more likely than boys to use relational aggression, especially toward other girls, a difference that begins as early as the preschool years and becomes very marked by the fourth or fifth grade. For example, in one study of nearly 500 children in the third through sixth grades, researchers found that 17.4% of the girls but only 2% of the boys were rated high in relational aggression—almost precisely the reverse of what is observed for physical aggression (Crick & Grotpeter, 1995). Researchers do not yet know whether this difference in form of aggression has some hormonal/biological basis or is learned at an early age or both. They do know that higher rates of physical aggression in males have been observed in every human society and in all varieties of primates. And scientists know that some link exists between rates of physical aggression and testosterone levels (e.g., Susman et al., 1987). But the origin of girls' apparent propensity toward relational aggression is still an open question.

Retaliatory aggression—aggression to get back at someone who has hurt you—increases among both boys and girls during the 6- to 12-year-old period (Astor, 1994). Its development is related to children's growing understanding of the difference between

relational aggression aggression aimed at damaging another person's self-esteem or peer relationships

retaliatory aggression aggression to get back at someone who has hurt you

DEVELOPMENTAL SCIENCE IN THE CLASSROOM

Bullies and Victims

Mr. Najal is a principal who is determined to do something about bullying in the elementary school that he is in charge of. He is looking for an anti-bullying curriculum that can be taught by the teachers in the school as a regular part of each school day. Mr. Najal has always believed that the key to ridding a school of bullying is to find effective ways of changing the behavior of the bullies themselves. However, some of the programs that he has reviewed include a victim-education component. As a result, he is wondering whether it's a good idea to teach children how to avoid being victimized by bullies.

Research shows that, in stable peer groups, children tend to take on consistent roles—perpetrator, victim, assistant to the perpetrator, reinforcing onlooker, nonparticipant onlooker, defender of the victim, and so on (Andreou & Metallidou, 2004; Hay, Payne, & Chadwick, 2004). The occupant of each of these roles plays a part in maintaining an aggressive incident and in determining whether another aggressive interaction involving the same perpetrator and victim will occur in the future. Research also shows that victims have certain characteristics in common, including anxiety, passivity, sensitivity, low self-esteem or self-confidence, lack of humor, and comparative lack of friends (Egan & Perry, 1998; Hodges, Malone, & Perry, 1997; Olweus, 1995). Cross-cultural studies suggest that these characteristics are found among habitual victims across a wide variety of cultural settings (Eslea et al., 2004). Among boys, victims are also often physically smaller or weaker than their peers. Thus, most developmentalists would advise Mr. Najal that changing the behavior of children who are habitual victims of aggression is just as important as intervening with bullies themselves (Green, 2001).

Critics of victim-education programs argue that they send the message that the victim deserves to be bullied. Moreover, by identifying habitual victims and including them in counseling sessions and the like, the adults who are responsible for victim-training programs subject these children to further stigmatization. Thus, critics argue that programs aimed at reducing bullying should focus primarily on the bullies' behavior and should include the clear message that bullying is wrong, regardless of victims' behavior (Temko, 2005).

Questions for Reflection

1. Do you agree with the advocates or the critics of victim-education programs?
2. In your view, what role should parents play in helping victims learn to respond more effectively to bullies?

intentional and accidental actions. For example, if a child drops his pencil in the path of another child who is walking by and that child happens to kick the pencil across the floor, most 8-year-olds can identify this as an accident. Consequently, the child whose pencil was kicked feels no need to get back at the child who did the kicking. However, children over 8 view intentional harm differently. For example, let's say that one child intentionally takes another's pencil off her desk and throws it across the room. Most children over 8 will try to find a way to get back at a child who does something like this. In fact, children who don't try to retaliate in such situations are more likely to be seen as socially incompetent and to be bullied by their peers in the future (Astor, 1994) (see *Developmental Science in the Classroom* on page 367).

Peers may approve of retaliatory aggression, but most parents and teachers strive to teach children that, like other forms of intentional harm, such behavior is unacceptable. Research suggests that children can learn nonaggressive techniques for managing the kinds of situations that lead to retaliatory aggression. In one program, called PeaceBuilders, psychologists have attempted to change individual behavior by changing a school's overall emotional climate. In this approach, both children and teachers learn to use positive social strategies (Flannery et al., 2000). For example, both are urged to try to praise others more often than they criticize them. Research suggests that when such programs are integrated into students' classes every day for an entire school year or longer, aggression decreases and prosocial behavior increases. Thus, aggressive interactions between elementary school children may be common, but they do not appear to be an inevitable aspect of development.

Learning Objective 12.11

How do popular, rejected, and neglected children differ?

Social Status

Developmentalists often measure popularity and rejection by asking children to list peers they would not like to play with. They also directly observe which children are sought out or avoided on the playground. These techniques allow researchers to group children according to the degree to which they are accepted by peers—a variable often called **social status**.

Typically, researchers find three groups of children. **Popular children** are those who are named as preferred playmates by most children. Those who are named by most children as peers that they prefer to avoid are labeled **rejected children**. Children who are classified as **neglected children** do not fall into either category.

Some of the characteristics that differentiate popular children from those in the other two groups are things outside a child's control. In particular, attractive children and physically larger children are more likely to be popular (Dion & Berscheid, 1974). Conversely, being very different from her peers may cause a child to be neglected or rejected. For example, shy children usually have few friends (Fordham & Stevenson-Hinde, 1999). Similarly, highly creative children are often rejected, as are those who have difficulty controlling their emotions (Aranha, 1997; Maszk, Eisenberg, & Guthrie, 1999).

However, children's social behavior seems to be more important than looks or temperament. Most studies show that popular children behave in positive, supporting, nonpunitive, and nonaggressive ways toward most other children. They explain things, take their playmates' wishes into consideration, take turns in conversation, and are able to regulate the expression of their strong emotions. In addition, popular children are usually good at accurately assessing others' feelings (Underwood, 1997). Most are good at looking at situations from others' perspectives as well (Fitzgerald & White, 2003).

There are two types of rejected children. *Withdrawn/rejected* children realize that they are disliked by peers (Harrist, Zaia, Bates, Dodge, & Pettit, 1997). After repeated attempts to gain peer acceptance, these children eventually give up and become socially withdrawn. As a result, they often experience feelings of loneliness. *Aggressive/rejected* children are often disruptive and uncooperative and usually believe that their peers like them (Zakriski & Coie, 1996). Many appear to be unable to control the expression of strong feelings (Eisenberg et al., 1995; Pettit, Clawson, Dodge, & Bates, 1996). They interrupt their play partners more often and fail to take turns in a systematic way.

social status an individual child's classification as popular, rejected, or neglected

popular children children who are preferred as playmates by most other children in a group

rejected children children who are avoided by most other children in a group

neglected children children who are neither preferred nor avoided by most other children in a group

Aggression and disruptive behavior are often linked to rejection and unpopularity among Chinese children, just as they are among American children (Chen, Rubin, & Li, 1995; Chen, Rubin, & Sun, 1992). As you learned in Chapter 9, aggressive behavior persists into adulthood in some individuals. However, research suggests that aggression is most likely to become a stable characteristic among children who are both aggressive and rejected by peers.

Of course, not all aggressive children are rejected. Among girls, aggression, whether physical or relational, seems to lead to peer rejection consistently. Among boys, however, aggression may result in either popularity or rejection (Rodkin et al., 2000; Xie, Cairns, & Cairns, 1999). In fact, aggressiveness seems to be a fairly typical characteristic of popular African American boys.

Adults' goals for children's socialization usually include teaching them how to manage conflicts without resorting to aggression.

Interestingly, too, aggressive boys and girls, although they are typically disliked by peers, are often perceived by them as having high social status, perhaps because of their ability to manipulate others and to control social situations (Cillessen & Mayeux, 2004). This association holds for both physical and relational aggression. However, as children enter adolescence, the link between physical aggression and social status becomes weaker, while the association between relational aggression and perceived status increases in strength. This may happen because, by age 11 or 12, children regard relational aggression as a more mature form of social manipulation than physical aggression. Consequently, they may admire peers who are skilled in the use of relational aggression, even though they don't like them and prefer not to associate with them.

In addition, irrespective of aggressive boys' general popularity, their close friends tend to be aggressive as well. Furthermore, aggressiveness seems to precede these relationships. In other words, boys who are aggressive seek out boys like themselves as friends, and being friends doesn't seem to make either member of the pair more aggressive (Poulin & Boivin, 2000).

Research also suggests that children have more positive attitudes toward aggressive peers whose aggressive acts are seen as mostly retaliatory and toward those who engage in both prosocial and aggressive behavior (Coie & Cillessen, 1993; Newcomb, Bukowski, & Pattee, 1993; Poulin & Boivin, 1999). Social approval may not increase aggressiveness, but it does seem to help maintain it; interventions to reduce aggressive behavior typically have little effect on aggressive boys who are popular (Phillips, Schwean, & Saklofske, 1997).

Neglect seems to be much less stable over time than rejection; neglected children sometimes move to the popular category when they become part of a new peer group. However, children who experience prolonged neglect are more prone to depression and loneliness than are popular children (Cillessen, van IJzendoorn, van Lieshout, & Hartup, 1992; Rubin, Hymel, Mills, & Rose-Krasnor, 1991; Wentzel & Asher, 1995). The association between peer neglect and depression may be explained by recent brain-imaging studies showing that, among school-aged children, social exclusion stimulates the same area of the brain as physical pain does (Eisenberger, 2003). In addition, this tendency toward depression among neglected children may be fostered by unrealistic expectations about adults' ability to "fix" the social situation—"Why doesn't the teacher make them be my friends?" (Galanaki, 2004).

Influences Beyond Family and Peers

The daily life of the school-aged child is shaped by more than the hours he spends with his family and peers. The circumstances in which a child lives also affect him. For example, some parents are at home when children come home from school; others are still at work. A child is also affected by his family's care arrangements and by the media to which he is exposed.

Learning Objective 12.12

How does self-care affect girls' and boys' development?

After-School Care

In the United States, 7.5 million children are at home by themselves after school for an hour or more each weekday (Crockett, 2003). They are often referred to as **self-care children**. Self-care arrangements differ so much from child to child that it is impossible to say whether, as a group, self-care children differ from others. For example, some self-care children are home alone but are closely monitored by neighbors or relatives, while others are completely without supervision of any kind (Brandon, 1999). Developmentalists have learned that the effects of self-care on a child's development depend on behavioral history, age, gender, the kind of neighborhood the child lives in, and how well parents monitor the child during self-care periods (Casper & Smith, 2002; NICHD, 2004b; Posner & Vandell, 1994; Steinberg, 1986).

Research consistently demonstrates that self-care children are more poorly adjusted in terms of both peer relationships and school performance. They tend to be less socially skilled and to have a greater number of behavior problems. However, some of these differences between self-care children and others arise from the effect of self-care on children who already have social and behavioral difficulties before self-care begins. Investigators have found that children who have such problems in the preschool years, before they experience any self-care, are the most negatively affected by the self-care experience (Pettit, Laird, Bates, & Dodge, 1997).

self-care children children who are at home by themselves after school for an hour or more each day

With respect to age, most developmentalists agree that children under the age of 9 or 10 should not care for themselves. From a developmental perspective, children younger than 9 do not have the cognitive abilities necessary to evaluate risks and deal with emergencies. In fact, most cities and/or states have laws specifying the age at which a child may legally be left at home alone for long periods of time. Children who start self-care in the early elementary years are vulnerable to older self-care children in their neighborhoods who may hurt or even sexually abuse them and are more likely to have adjustment difficulties in school (Pettit et al., 1997). High-quality after-school programs can help these younger children attain a higher level of achievement (Peterson, Ewigman, & Kivlahan, 1993; Zigler & Finn-Stevenson, 1993).

The effects of after-school care depend on several factors. This child appears to be following his parents' instructions about what to do after school, a factor that helps children cope with the stress associated with caring for themselves.

Children older than 9 may be cognitively able to manage self-care, but they, too, benefit from participation in well-supervised after-school programs. Even part-time participation in supervised activities after school seems to make a difference in the adjustment of self-care children (Pettit et al., 1997). Good programs provide children with opportunities to play, do homework, and get help from adults (Posner & Vandell, 1994).

Self-care has the most negative effects for children in low-income neighborhoods with high crime rates (Marshall et al., 1997). Self-care children in such areas may use after-school time to "hang out" with socially deviant peers who are involved in criminal activity or who have negative attitudes about school. Predictably, then, the positive effects of organized after-school programs on academic achievement are greater for children in low-income neighborhoods (Mason & Chuang, 2001; Posner & Vandell, 1994).

When everything is taken into consideration, the most important factor in self-care seems to be parental monitoring. Many parents, particularly single mothers, enlist the help of neighbors and relatives to keep an eye on their self-care children (Brandon & Hofferth, 2003). Most require children to call them at work when they get home from school to talk about their school day and get instructions about homework and chores. For example, a working mother might tell a fifth-grader, "By the time I get home at 5:00, you should be finished with your math and spelling. Don't work on your history project until I get home and can help you with it. As soon as you finish your math and spelling, start the dishwasher." Research suggests that children whose periods of self-care are monitored in this way are less likely to experience the potential negative effects of self-care (Galambos & Maggs, 1991).

Media Influences

Learning Objective 12.13

How do television, computers, and video games affect children's development?

Another important feature of children's environments is the wide array of informational and entertainment media available nowadays. Televisions, computers, and video games are found in the great majority of homes in the industrialized world. How do these media affect children's development?

Television "But the kids on TV look so happy when they eat it! Don't you want me to be happy?" the 7-year-old son of one of the authors sobbed when his request for a sugary cereal was denied. The effect of advertising on children's food preferences is well documented (Chapman, Nicholas, & Supramaniam, 2006; Livingstone & Helsper, 2006). However, this is just one of several hazards associated with allowing children to watch too much TV. The association between viewing and aggressive behavior is perhaps of greatest concern.

Albert Bandura demonstrated the effects of televised violence on children's behavior in his classic Bobo doll studies (Bandura, Ross, & Ross, 1961, 1963). In these experiments, children were found to imitate adults' violent treatment of an inflatable clown that was depicted on film. Recent research suggests that such effects persist into the adult years. Psychologist L. Rowell Huesmann and his colleagues (2003) found that individuals who watched the greatest number of violent television programs in childhood were the most likely to engage in actual acts of violence as young adults. Brain-imaging studies suggest that these long-term effects may be the result of patterns of neural activation that underlie emotionally laden behavioral scripts that children learn while watching violent programming (Murray et al., 2006). These patterns of neural activation may also explain the finding that repeated viewing of TV violence leads to emotional desensitization regarding violence and to the belief that aggression is a good way to solve problems (Donnerstein, Slaby, & Eron, 1994; Funk, Baldacci, Pasold, & Baumgardner, 2004; Van Mierlo & Van den Bulck, 2004).

Of course, television isn't all bad. Researchers have found that science-oriented programs such as *Bill Nye the Science Guy* and *The Magic School Bus* are effective teaching tools (Calvert & Kotler, 2003). Likewise, programs designed to teach racial tolerance to school-aged children have consistently shown positive effects on children's attitudes and behavior (Persson & Musher-Eizenman, 2003: Shochat, 2003). However, such programs are far less popular among boys than they are among girls (Calvert & Kotler, 2003). Moreover, even among girls, their popularity declines as children progress through middle childhood years. Perhaps these findings are best summed up by adapting an old cliché: "You can lead a child to quality TV programming, but you can't make him watch it." Thus, parental regulation of television viewing is the key to ensuring that exposure to TV will have more positive than negative effects on a child's development.

In the United States, children between ages 6 and 12 spend more time watching television than they do playing.

Computers and the Internet Television is just one of several types of media to which children are exposed. Surveys show that more than 90% of school-aged children in the United States use computers on a regular basis, and about 60% regularly use the Internet (DeBell & Chapman, 2006). Computer and Internet use rates are nearly identical for boys and girls. However, a "digital divide" exists across income and ethnic groups. Among children who live in the poorest households, only 47% are regular Internet users, compared to more than 70% of children in upper-income families. Similarly, while 67% of White children and 58% of Asian American children regularly access the Internet, just under 50% of Hispanic American, African American, and Native American children do so. This divide is largely due to the fact that poor families, which are found in greater numbers among Hispanic Americans, African Americans, and Native Americans, are less likely to have a computer in their homes than are those with more economic resources. As a result, computer usage among most children in disadvantaged groups is limited to schools. Still, the proportions of children who use computers and the Internet have increased dramatically among all groups over the past decade. Most children use computers for school work, to play games, and to engage in electronic communication such as email and instant messaging (Kaiser Family Foundation, 2004).

Would you be surprised to learn that, apart from teacher-directed activities such as homework, children use computers in much the same ways as they use other environments? For the most part, children play when they are on a computer. Consequently, educators and parents need to keep an eye on children who are supposed to be doing school work on their computers and to be aware of the tendency of children to test digital boundaries—such as prohibitions against visiting chat rooms—just as they do physical boundaries.

Many developmental psychologists see children's propensity for digital play as an opportunity to learn more about the natural course of child development (Sandvig, 2006). In one study, researchers at Georgetown University provided fifth- and sixth-graders with an online, instant messaging environment in which the children created animated representations of themselves (Calvert, Mahler, Zehnder, Jenkins, & Lee, 2003). Each messaging session resembled a real-time, interactive cartoon in which the children's messages appeared in their characters' speech balloons. Some of the sessions involved children of the same gender, whereas others were mixed-gender sessions. Interestingly, the researchers found that, just as they do in face-to-face interactions, female pairs engaged in more verbal than physical interactions, and male pairs spent more time engaged in role play and physical interactions than they did in verbal interactions. However, the interactions of mixed-gender pairs resembled those of female pairs; in other words, boys tended to adopt girls' interaction styles in mixed-gender sessions. These findings invite the speculation that the anonymity offered by virtual communication frees boys from the need to behave in gender-stereotypical ways. They also show that studying children's virtual communications can help developmentalists better understand their face-to-face interactions.

Video Games Some sources claim that families spend more money on video game systems and on the games themselves than they do on any other form of entertainment ("Children spend more time . . . ," 2004). Thus, developmentalists have looked at how these games affect children's cognitive and social/emotional development. Some studies suggest that video game playing enhances children's spatial-cognitive skills and may even eliminate the well-documented gender difference in this domain (Feng, Spence, & Pratt, 2007; Greenfield, Brannon, & Lohr, 1994).

Nevertheless, research suggests even short-term exposure to violent video games in laboratory settings increases research participants' general level of emotional hostility (Anderson & Dill, 2000; Bushman & Huesmann, 2006). Apparently, increases in emotional hostility and decreases in the capacity to empathize with others, which are engendered by violent video games, are the motivating forces behind the increases in aggressive behavior that often result from playing such games for extended periods of time (Funk, Buchman, Jenks, & Bechtoldt, 2003; Gentile, Lynch, Linder, & Walsh, 2004).

Violent video games also appear to be part of an overall pattern linking preferences for violent stimuli to aggressive behavior. The more violent television programs children watch, the more violent video games they prefer—and the more aggressively they behave toward peers (Mediascope Press, 1999). This finding holds for both boys and girls; most girls aren't interested in violent games, but those who are tend to be more physically aggressive than average. Consequently, parents who notice that aggressive and violent themes characterize most of their children's leisure-time interests as well as their interactions with peers should worry about their children playing video games (Funk, Buchman, Myers, & Jenks, 2000).

Test Prep Center

with PEARSON mydevelopmentlab

THEORIES OF SOCIAL AND PERSONALITY DEVELOPMENT

12.1 How did the psychoanalytic theorists characterize the middle childhood years? (p. 354)

Freud thought that the challenge for children between ages 6 and 12 was to form emotional bonds with peers. Erikson theorized that 6- to 12-year-olds acquire a sense of industry by achieving educational goals determined by their cultures.

1. In the table below, summarize what Erikson believed to be the factors that influence the outcome of the industry versus inferiority stage and the consequences that flow from each outcome.

Industry	Inferiority

12.2 What are the main ideas of the trait and social-cognitive theorists? (pp. 355–356)

Trait theorists propose that people possess stable characteristics that emerge during middle childhood as experiences modify the dimensions of temperament. Social-cognitive theories, such as Bandura's theory of reciprocal determinism, argue that traits, and the emotional aspects of personality emphasized by psychoanalytic theories, represent one of three sets of interactive factors that shape personality: personal factors, environmental factors, and behavioral factors.

2. From the Multimedia Library within MyDevelopmentLab, explore *The Five Factor Model* and do the following matching exercise.

The Five Factor Model

Drag and drop the term from the left-hand column to the corresponding place in the right-hand column.

	______ The extent to which people are social or unsocial, talkative or quiet, affectionate or reserved
Agreeableness-antagonism	______ The extent to which people are good-natured or irritable, courteous or rude, flexible or stubborn, lenient or critical
Conscientiousness-undirectedness	______ The extent to which people are reliable or undependable, careful or careless, punctual or late, well organized or disorganized
Extraversion-introversion	______ The extent to which people are worried or calm, nervous or at ease, insecure or secure
Openness to experience	______ The extent to which people are open to experience or closed, independent or conforming, creative or uncreative, daring or timid
Neuroticism-stability	

Reset

Classify each behavior according to the Big Five personality trait that it represents.

______(1) talkativeness

______(2) kindness

______(3) worrying

______(4) curiosity

______(5) responsibility

(A) extraversion

(B) agreeableness

(C) conscientiousness

(D) neuroticism

(E) openness

3. In the following table, summarize the factors associated with each of the three components of Bandura's reciprocal determinism model of personality.

Environmental	Behavioral	Personal

SELF-CONCEPT

12.3 What are the features of the psychological self? (pp. 356–357)

Between 6 and 12, children construct a psychological self. As a result, their self-descriptions begin to include personality traits, such as intelligence and friendliness, along with physical characteristics.

4. Write "Y" by the statement that is more likely to have been made by a 6- to 12-year-old and "N" by the one that is likely to have been made by a younger child.

   ______(A) I am a boy, and I like to play with trucks.

   ______(B) I am a nice girl with brown hair, and I like school.

12.4 How does self-esteem develop? (pp. 357–359)

Self-esteem appears to be shaped by two factors: the degree of discrepancy a child experiences between goals and achievements and the degree of perceived social support from peers and parents.

5. Match each of the following terms with its definition.

   ______(1) an individual's belief in her capacity to cause an intended event to occur

   ______(2) an individual's overall sense of his value

   (A) self-efficacy

   (B) self-esteem

6. List five influences on the development of self-esteem.

   (A)____

   (B)____

   (C)____

   (D)____

   (E)____

7. Transform this false statement into one that is true: Once a child's sense of self-esteem becomes established, it is very unlikely to change in the future.

   ____

   ____

ADVANCES IN SOCIAL COGNITION

12.5 How does children's understanding of others change in middle childhood? (pp. 359–360)

Between 6 and 12, children's understanding of others' stable internal traits improves.

8. Circle each characteristic that is not likely to appear in a description of a peer given by a children who is younger than 6.

   thin brown hair smart happy mean tall

12.6 How do children in Piaget's moral realism and moral relativism stages reason about right and wrong? (pp. 360–361)

Children in the moral realism stage believe that authority figures establish rules that must be followed, under threat of punishment. Children in the moral relativism stage understand that rules can be changed through social agreement. Their moral judgment is colored more by intentions than by consequences.

9. Piaget claimed that the ability to use reasoning about intentions to make judgments about the moral dimensions of behavior appears to emerge along with ________________________.

THE SOCIAL WORLD OF THE SCHOOL-AGED CHILD

12.7 How does self-regulation affect school-aged children's relationships with their parents? (pp. 361–363)

Self-regulation is the ability to conform to parental standards of behavior without direct supervision. In middle childhood, as children become increasingly capable of self-regulation, their relationships with parents become less overtly affectionate, with fewer attachment behaviors. The strength of the attachment, however, appears to persist.

10. Briefly describe how each factor in the table contributes to self-regulation.

Factor	Contribution to Self-Regulation
Culture	
Gender	
Parenting style	

12.8 What changes occur in children's understanding of friendships during this period? (pp. 363–365)

Friendships become stable in middle childhood, with the increasing importance of peers. Children's selection of friends depends on variables such as trustworthiness as well as overt characteristics such as play preferences and gender.

11. From the Multimedia Library within MyDevelopmentLab, watch the *Child and Adolescent Friendships: Brett Laursen* video and answer the following question.

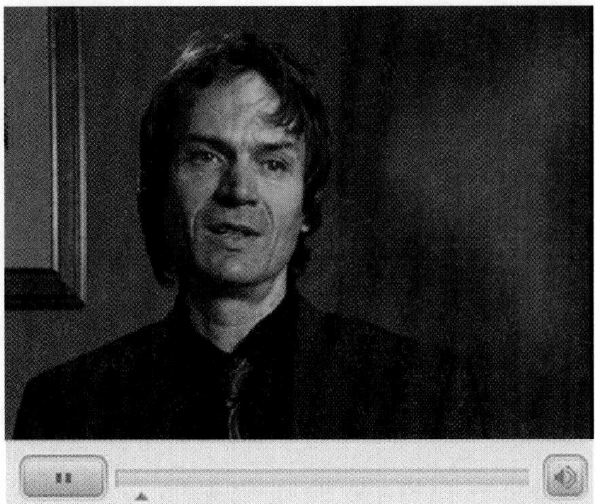

According to Professor Laursen, having friends protects children from ______________ and ______________.

12.9 In what ways do boys and girls interact during the middle childhood years? (pp. 365–366)

Gender segregation of peer groups is at its peak in middle childhood and appears in every culture. Friendships among boys and among girls appear to differ in specific ways. Boys' friendships focus on competition and dominance; girls' friendships include more agreement, compliance, and self-disclosure.

12. Classify each social behavior as more typical of (A) girls or (B) boys.

    ______(1) rough-and-tumble play

    ______(2) sharing secrets

    ______(3) interacting in groups rather than in pairs

    ______(4) welcoming newcomers into friendship groups

    ______(5) interacting in pairs or small groups more often than in large groups

13. Can any of the following examples be considered boundary violations of children's informal gender segregation rules?

    ______(A) A teacher creates mixed-gender groups for a science lesson.

    ______(B) A boy takes a girl's Barbie lunch box, runs away with it to make her chase him, and then gives it back to her.

    ______(C) Girls play together because they tend to enjoy the same activities.

12.10 What types of aggression are most common among school-aged children? (pp. 366–368)

Physical aggression declines during middle childhood, although verbal aggression increases. Boys show markedly higher levels of physical and direct verbal aggression than girls do. Girls show higher rates of relational aggression.

14. From the Multimedia Library within MyDevelopmentLab, watch the *Relational Aggression* video and answer the following question.

How does the behavior of the girls in the video fit the definition of relational aggression?

____

____

12.11 How do popular, rejected, and neglected children differ? (pp. 368–369)

Popular children are positive and supportive toward most other children, whereas rejected children are most strongly characterized by high levels of aggression or bullying. Some rejected children become socially withdrawn. Neglected children may suffer depression and loneliness.

15. From the Multimedia Library within MyDevelopmentLab, run through the *Children's Social Status* simulation and summarize the characteristics of popular, rejected, and neglected children in the table below.

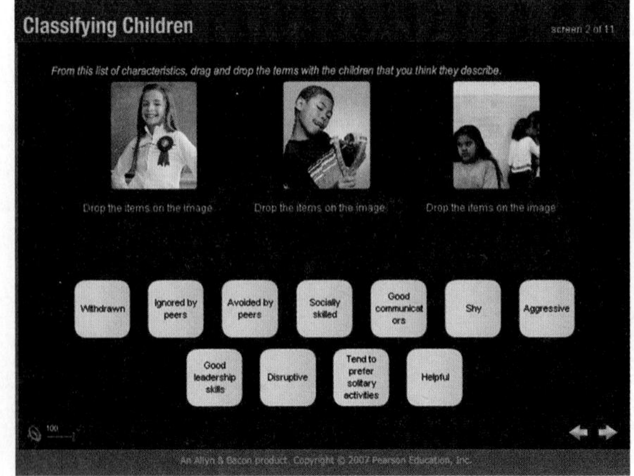

Category	Characteristics
Popular	
Rejected	
Neglected	

INFLUENCES BEYOND FAMILY AND PEERS

12.12 How does self-care affect girls' and boys' development? (pp. 370–371)

Self-care is associated with several negative effects, including problems with behavior and peer relationships. Children who live in safe neighborhoods and children whose parents closely monitor their activities after school are least likely to be negatively affected by self-care.

16. List four negative effects of self-care:

(A) ______________________________

(B) ______________________________

(C) ______________________________

(D) ______________________________

12.13 How do television, computers, and video games affect children's development? (pp. 371–373)

Experts agree that watching violence on television and playing violent video games increases the level of personal aggression or violence shown by a child. The anonymity offered by the computer may free boys from the need to behave in gender-stereotypical ways.

17. From the Multimedia Library within MyDevelopmentLab, watch the *Violence and Video Games: Douglas Gentile* video and answer the following question.

Why was Professor Gentile surprised by the results of his longitudinal study of the effects of media violence on children's aggressive behavior?

____

____

For answers to the questions in this chapter, turn to page 522. For a list of key terms, turn to page 531.

The Whole Child in Focus

Physical, Cognitive, and Socioemotional Development in Middle Childhood: An Integrated Review

When we met 6-year-old Jamal at the beginning of this unit, he was struggling to learn to ride a bicycle so that he could fit in with the school-aged children in his neighborhood. So, how has he changed now that he is 12 years old?

The "ride-up-the-hill" game that 6-year-old Jamal and his friends created reflected their emerging sense that the physical world is governed by rules, an understanding that is the core of **Piaget's concrete operational stage**. Across the middle childhood years, Jamal's concrete operational schemes have become equilibrated as a result of engaging in a variety of rule-governed activities.

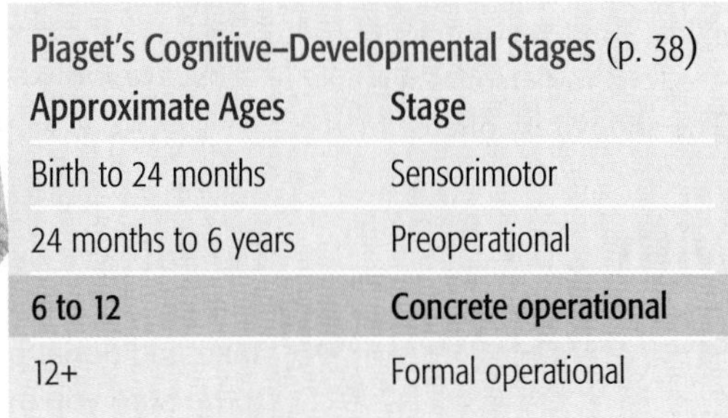

Piaget's Cognitive–Developmental Stages (p. 38)

Approximate Ages	Stage
Birth to 24 months	Sensorimotor
24 months to 6 years	Preoperational
6 to 12	**Concrete operational**
12+	Formal operational

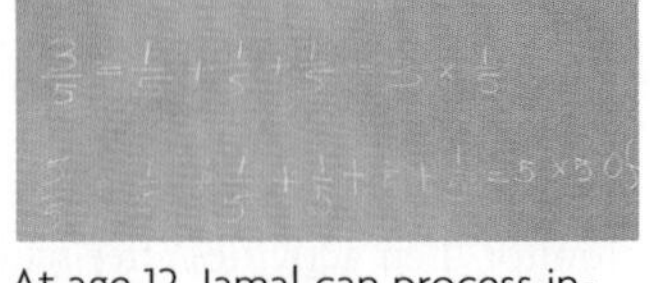

At age 12, Jamal can process information and keep track of mental tasks far better than he could at 6, thanks to his increasingly efficient **working memory**. He is also better able to learn from and enjoy rule-governed activities, such as solving math problems and playing basketball.

Thinking about Developmental Pathways

1. Our brief sketch of Jamal at age 12 suggests that he is healthy and physically fit. How might his development in all three domains have proceeded differently if he had suffered from one of the common chronic health issues of the middle childhood period, such as asthma or excessive weight gain?
2. Jamal's success in school has contributed to his development in both the cognitive and socioemotional domains. How would his development in both domains have been affected if he had displayed some kind of learning disability?
3. If Jamal tended to be extraverted rather than introverted, how might his academic interests have developed differently?

Jamal's proficiency in his favorite hobby, assembling electronic hobby kits, has advanced significantly along with his **fine motor skills**.

Jamal's **maturing brain**, especially the areas devoted to planning, enables him to complete more complex electronics projects, such as solar-powered remote control cars. **Neurological maturation** also allows him to maintain the intense levels of concentration, attention to detail, and perseverance that are required to complete his electronics projects.

Parts of the Brain (p. 100)

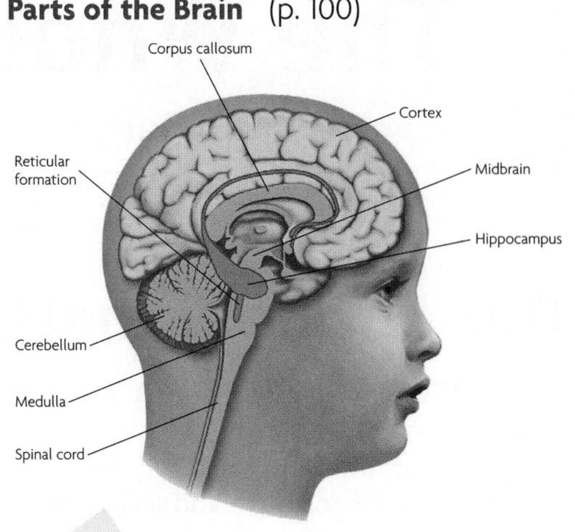

The sense of pride that Jamal feels when he finishes a kit helps him acquire the **sense of industry** that Erikson described as essential to the psychosocial development of 6- to 12-year-olds. In turn, that emerging sense of industry helps motivate him to work on the basketball skills that his **rapidly improving strength, stamina, and gross motor skills** have enabled him to acquire.

Erikson's Psychosocial Stages (p. 30)

Birth to 1 year	Trust versus mistrust
1 to 3	Autonomy versus shame and doubt
3 to 6	Initiative versus guilt
6 to 12	**Industry versus inferiority**
12 to 18	Identity versus role confusion
18 to 30	Intimacy versus isolation
30 to late adulthood	Generativity versus stagnation
Late adulthood	Integrity versus despair

The Big Five Personality Traits (p. 355)

Trait
Extraversion
Agreeableness
Conscientiousness
Neuroticism (Emotional Instability)
Openness/Intellect

Jamal puts his cognitive skills to good use in the classroom. He loves math because he prefers well defined academic tasks for which right answers can be clearly determined. His preference may stem from the **Big Five trait of conscientiousness**, a characteristic that Jamal has manifested since he was a young child. He also tends to be **introverted**, which may explain why he often enjoys spending time with a good book.

The **sense of belonging** he gains as a member of his seventh-grade basketball team has helped him develop lasting friendships. Moreover, the strong sense of **self-efficacy** for athletic activities that Jamal has gained from playing basketball has given him the confidence to try other sports, including baseball and volleyball.

The Whole Child in Action

Apply What You've Learned about Development in Middle Childhood

Raise Your Virtual Child

The Middle Childhood Years

1. Summarize the changes that you observed in your virtual child between the ages of 6 and 12 in the physical, cognitive, and socioemotional domains. Which of these changes represent universals, and which reflect individual differences?
2. To what extent did your parenting decisions contribute to these changes?
3. Did the Virtual Child result in decision-related outcomes that you think are valid? Why or why not?
4. Write a brief biographical sketch of your child at age 12, integrating information from all three domains.

This activity requires that you be registered for My Virtual Child *through MyDevelopmentLab.*

Conduct Your Research

Children's Use of Clustering Strategies

You can use a deck of playing cards to do a study of memory improvement in middle childhood. Do your research with a 7-year-old and a 10-year-old. Be sure to get the children's parents' permission before carrying out your study. Before you start, test the children to be sure that they know the names of the suits and the conventional way of referring to cards (7 of hearts, 2 of spades, etc.). For the first trial, select 12 cards, 3 from each suit, making sure that the cards all have different values. Arrange the cards in front of the child in such a way that no card is next to another of the same suit. Test each child separately, allowing 1 minute for the child to memorize the cards. When the minute has passed, take up the cards and ask each child to recall them. For the second trial, repeat the experiment with a different set of 12 cards, but tell the children that they may rearrange the cards if they think it will help their memory. The 7-year-old probably won't rearrange the cards by suit, but the 10-year-old will. This shows that the older child is attempting to use categories as a memory aid, a clustering strategy. The 10-year-old should exhibit better recall than the 7-year-old across both trials, but the difference between the two should be greater when the older child is allowed to use the clustering strategy.

Build Your Portfolio

1. Because of the popularity of inclusive education, classroom teachers must be prepared to meet the needs of children with and without disabilities. One way of doing so is to design instruction that teaches children skills and concepts through different sensory modalities. Such lessons include visual, auditory, and tactile elements. Design a lesson that teaches a skill or concept through all three modalities.
2. Most school-aged children enjoy participating in skits, and role playing can be a useful strategy for increasing children's socioemotional competence. Write three brief skits that provide children with opportunities to act out social skills such as saying "please" and "thank you," taking turns, offering assistance, and empathizing with someone who is hurt.

Powered by

PEARSON mydevelopmentlab™

www.mydevelopmentlab.com

Explore Possible Careers

Special Education Teacher

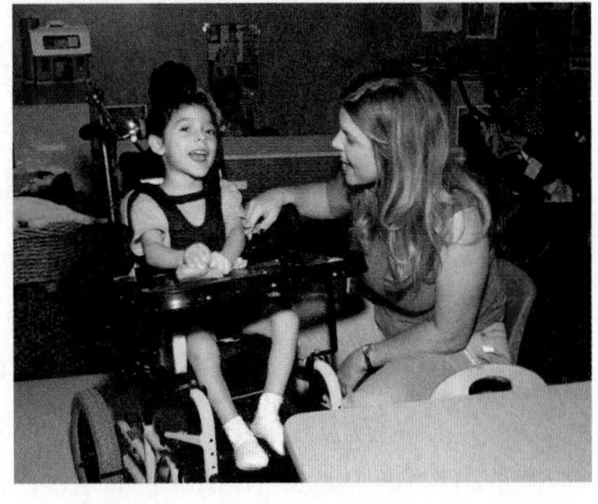

Special education teachers are trained to work with children who have disabilities. They work in a variety of settings. Most special educators are employed in public early childhood, elementary, or secondary schools. Others work in hospitals and juvenile detention facilities. Some special educators work with children with disabilities who are homebound, while others serve infants and toddlers with disabilities by helping their parents learn how to stimulate these children's development. A bachelor's degree is required, and each state has somewhat different requirements for obtaining the certification that is necessary to work in public schools. In many states, separate certificates are available for special educators who work with specific populations such as children with visual or hearing impairments. Special educators must be able to tolerate working with children who vary widely in temperament and behavior. Optimism and perseverance are helpful, along with a passion for helping others achieve. Empathy is vital for working with the parents of children with disabilities. Most special educators report that their jobs are difficult but rewarding.

Visit the Career Center in MyDevelopmentLab to learn about other careers that rely on child development research.

Volunteer with Children

Big Brothers Big Sisters

Big Brothers Big Sisters serves children over the age of 6 by pairing them with mentors, with whom they usually develop long-term relationships. Parents request Big Brothers or Big Sisters for their children for many reasons. Many parents who apply are single and are looking to broaden their children's networks of social support. Others are concerned about the peer groups with which their children have begun to associate. "Bigs and Littles," as mentor-mentee teams are called, spend a few hours together at least twice each month, engaging in casual social activities such as going to movies, playing games, or just talking. The goal of these meetings is to facilitate the development of a supportive relationship with the child. The organization hopes that Littles will view their Bigs as sources of support and as role models. Although the organization welcomes all volunteers, most local chapters have a greater need for male than for female mentors.

Visit the Career Center in MyDevelopmentLab to learn about other volunteer opportunities that rely on child development research.

Unit Five
Adolescence

Eighth-graders Cho and Michelle had been best friends since second grade. Now that they were on the verge of going to high school, the girls felt that they needed a lot more independence than their parents were willing to give them. Both had their own computers and cell phones. But when their parents denied the girls' request to attend a concert, Cho and Michelle concluded that their parents lacked respect for their emerging maturity. They made a mutual promise that each would beg, bargain, and nag until their parents finally agreed to let them go to the concert. But all their pleading was to no avail, and both concluded their failed negotiation sessions with the tragic adolescent refrain, "You never let me do anything!"

"Time for Plan B," Michelle told Cho one night as the pair lamented their severe state of deprivation. "I looked up the bus schedule online, and the 7:30 bus goes to the arena. We can sneak out and ride the bus to the concert." Cho had her doubts, though. "How can we get out early enough without anyone knowing about it?" she asked. Michelle smiled, "That's the best part of my plan. You tell your parents that you're spending the night at my house, and I'll tell mine that I'm sleeping over at your house." Cho grinned broadly, "What a great idea! But how do we get the tickets?" Michelle responded with the confidence of an accomplished petty larcenist, "I'll use my mom's credit card to buy the tickets online. I'll print out the receipt, and we can exchange it for the tickets when we get there." The girls could hardly contain their excitement as they contemplated what seemed to be a perfect plan.

On the night of the concert, Cho and Michelle executed their plan flawlessly and were riding high on an exhilarating wave of self-congratulation. As it turned out, there was just one flaw in Cho's and

Michelle's plan: The bus that they had planned to take from the arena back to their neighborhood stopped running at 10:00 p.m. As the girls stood at the bus stop in front of the arena, shivering and growing increasingly anxious, Michelle had to admit that she had forgotten to check the return route schedule. They finally reached the conclusion that they had no choice but to call their parents, who, as you might imagine, were furious. Cho's and Michelle's parents confiscated the girls' computers, cell phones, and other luxuries, and it was quite a long time before the girls were allowed to go anywhere but to school again.

Are Cho and Michelle budding criminals? Not likely, but their actions arose from a new form of thinking that is characteristic of the teen years. The powerful intellectual tools that emerge in the early teens allow adolescents to make plans and to mentally project themselves into those plans as a way of testing them. The process is similar to that of a scientist who formulates a hypothesis and devises an experiment to test it. Armed with this new way of thinking, young adolescents embark upon a period of development that is characterized by risks and opportunities. Some of their choices are good ones, but others, like those made by Cho and Michelle, reflect poor judgment. Most of teenagers' poor choices turn out to have little effect on the rest of their lives, but others can significantly alter the developmental trajectory of an adolescent's life. We look at how these risks and opportunities are manifested in the physical, cognitive, and socioemotional domains in this unit. In Chapter 13, you will learn about the maturational milestones of adolescence and how teens' decisions about a number of risky behaviors can affect their bodies for years to come. We'll also discuss physical advances that enable teens to acquire near adult level athletic skills. Cognitive gains are the subject of Chapter 14 where you learn in detail about the intellectual changes that happen during the teen years. Finally, in Chapter 15, we will turn to adolescents' changing relationships with their families and peers as well as their growing sense of personal identity.

The Whole Child In Focus

Keep Cho and Michelle's story in mind as you read through the next three chapters, and consider how aspects of each girl's physical, cognitive, and socioemotional development might interact as she moves through adolescence. What kind of person do you think an older Cho will be? What about an older Michelle? We'll examine how Cho and Michelle's development changes as they grow from 12 to 18 years old at the end of this unit.

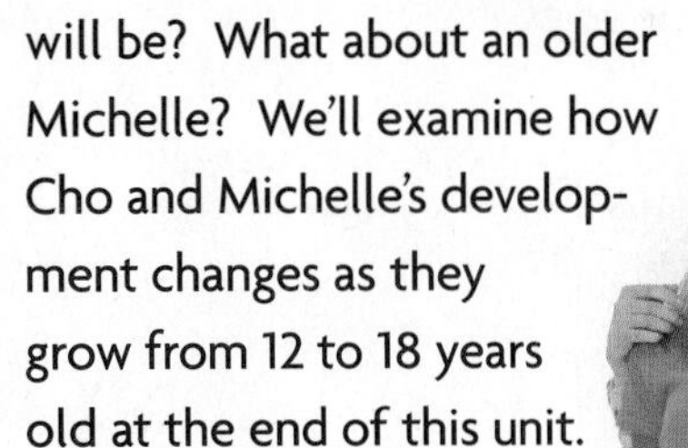

Chapter 13

Physical Development and Health in Adolescence

When you think back to your own adolescence, can you pick out a particular time, a particular age, when you began to think of yourself as an "adolescent"? Was it when you noticed the first physical changes of puberty? For many people, these changes represent the end of childhood and the beginning of a new phase of life that is clearly different from the year that came before it but, nevertheless, is considerably different from adulthood.

Adolescence is the period that lies psychologically and culturally between childhood and adulthood. As such, it is not a period that is associated with a clearly defined age range. Most cultures agree that the physical changes of puberty mark the beginning of this period. Regardless of culture, the primary task of adolescence is to prepare for participation in adult society. Thus, the end point of adolescence varies considerably across cultures and is defined by criteria from all three of the major domains of development: physical, cognitive, and socioemotional.

We will begin our study of adolescence with consideration of the momentous changes that occur in the physical domain. Understanding the changes in teenagers' bodies will enable you to better understand the emergence of sexual behavior and the many factors that influence it. From there, we will move on to the important health issues of this period of development, many of which are consequences of the choices that adolescents make about sexual behavior. Finally, we will examine a few of the mental health challenges of this period.

Learning Objectives

Physical Changes

13.1 How do the hormones, brains, and circadian rhythms of adolescents differ from those of younger children?

13.2 What changes occur in the body's size and shape during adolescence?

13.3 What are the major milestones of sexual maturity?

13.4 What are the psychological consequences of early, "on time," and late puberty for boys and girls?

Adolescent Sexuality

13.5 What are the patterns of adolescent sexual behavior in the United States?

13.6 Which teenaged girls are most likely to get pregnant?

13.7 What are some of the causes that have been proposed to explain homosexuality?

Adolescent Health

13.8 What are some of the critical nutritional issues in adolescence?

13.9 What patterns of illness exist in adolescence?

13.10 How does sensation seeking affect risky behavior in adolescents?

13.11 What patterns of drug, alcohol, and tobacco use have been found among adolescents in the United States?

13.12 What are the leading causes of death in adolescence?

Atypical Development

13.13 What are the distinguishing features of adolescent-onset conduct disorder and delinquency?

13.14 What are the characteristics and causes of eating disorders?

13.15 Which adolescents are at greatest risk of depression and suicide?

adolescence the transitional period between childhood and adulthood

Physical Changes

When we think of the physical changes of adolescence, we usually give the greatest amount of attention to the reproductive system. Reproductive changes are important, as you will see, but momentous changes occur in other systems as well.

Learning Objective 13.1

How do the hormones, brains, and circadian rhythms of adolescents differ from those of younger children?

The Endocrine and Nervous Systems

The physical change that most people associate with adolescence is the attainment of sexual maturity. Thus, it may surprise you to learn that **puberty** is a collective term that encompasses all of the changes, both seen and unseen, that are needed for reproductive maturity. These changes involve all of the body's systems, not just the reproductive organs, and the interaction between hormones and brain development that governs the entire process (Schulz & Sisk, 2006).

Hormones The process of pubertal development begins when the *pituitary gland*, the gland that controls all of the body's other glands, signals a child's adrenal gland to step up its production of androgen (see Table 13.1). This milestone, called *adrenarche*, occurs around age 7 or 8. Next, the pituitary begins secreting **gonadotrophic hormones**, hormones that stimulate the growth of ovaries in girls and testes in boys. As they grow, these glands secrete hormones that cause the sex organs to develop: *testosterone* in boys and a form of estrogen called *estradiol* in girls. Over the course of puberty, levels of testosterone increase 18-fold in boys, while levels of estradiol increase 8-fold in girls (Tanner, 1990).

The pituitary also secretes two other hormones, *thyroid stimulating hormone* and *general growth hormone*; these, along with adrenal androgen, interact with the specific sex hormones to affect growth. *Adrenal androgen*, which is chemically very similar to testosterone, plays a particularly important role for girls, triggering the growth spurt and affecting development of pubic hair. For boys, adrenal androgen is less significant, presumably because boys already have so much male hormone in the form of testosterone in their bloodstreams. Adrenal androgen is believed to play some part in the adolescent growth spurt (Tanner, 1990). Taken together, all of these hormonal changes lead to two sets of body changes: the well-known changes in the sex organs and a much broader set of changes in muscles, fat, bones, and body organs.

puberty a collective term for the physical changes that culminate in sexual maturity

gonadotrophic hormones hormones that stimulate the growth of ovaries in girls and testes in boys

The Brain By themselves, pubertal hormones are not sufficient to induce either the physical or the behavioral changes that we associate with puberty (Schulz & Sisk, 2006). Cells in the brain, the neurons, must first develop the capacity to respond to pubertal hormones before the

Table 13.1 Major Hormones That Contribute to Physical Growth and Development

Hormone(s)	Gland/Organ	Aspects of Growth Influenced
Thyroxine	Thyroid gland	Normal brain development and overall rate of growth
Adrenal androgen	Adrenal gland	Some changes at puberty, particularly the development of secondary sex characteristics in girls
Testosterone	Testes (boys)	Crucial in the formation of male genitals prenatally; also triggers the sequence of changes in primary and secondary sex characteristics at puberty in the male
Estrogen (estadiol)	Ovaries (girls)	Development of the menstrual cycle and breasts in girls; has less to do with other secondary sex characteristics than testosterone does for boys
Gonadotrophic hormones; general growth hormone; thyroid stimulating hormone	Pituitary gland	Rate of physical maturation; signals adrenal gland to secrete androgen

typical features of adolescence can appear. Furthermore, although sexual behavior may come to mind first when we think about how teens differ from younger children, the changes in cognitive behavior that are facilitated by the hormonal and neuronal changes of puberty are equally striking (Giedd, 2004). For instance, have you noticed that you are much better able to make realistic plans now than you could when you were 13 or 14? If so, then you have firsthand knowledge of the changes in the adolescent brain that facilitate planning and logic.

THE WHOLE CHILD IN FOCUS

How do advances in executive processing attributable to the prefrontal cortex help Michelle and Cho prepare for adulthood? Find out on page 474.

The first of two major adolescent growth spurts in the brain occurs between 13 and 15 (Spreen et al., 1995). During this spurt, the cerebral cortex becomes thicker, and the neuronal pathways become more efficient. In addition, more energy is produced and consumed by the brain during this spurt than in the years that precede and follow it (Fischer & Rose, 1994). For the most part, these growth and energy spurts take place in parts of the brain that control spatial perception and motor functions. Consequently, by the mid-teens, adolescents' abilities in these areas are significantly better than those of school-aged children.

Neuropsychologists Kurt Fischer and Samuel Rose believe that a qualitatively different neural network emerges during the brain growth spurt that occurs between ages 13 and 15, enabling teens to think abstractly and to reflect on their cognitive processes (Fischer & Rose, 1994). As evidence, these researchers cite numerous neurological and psychological studies revealing that major changes in brain organization show up between ages 13 and 15 and that qualitative shifts in cognitive functioning appear after age 15. They claim that the consistency of these research findings is too compelling to ignore.

The 13-to-15 spurt is also associated with profound changes in the **prefrontal cortex (PFC)** (see Figure 13.1) (Gogtay et al., 2004; Kanemura, Aihara, Aoki, Araki, & Nakazawa, 2004). The PFC is the part of the frontal lobe that is just behind the forehead. It is responsible for *executive processing*, the use of a set of information-processing skills (mentioned in Chapter 11) that enable us to consciously control and organize our thought processes. Just prior to puberty, the neurons in the PFC rapidly form new synapses with those in other parts of the brain. Over the first few years of adolescence, the brain prunes away the least efficient of these synapses (Giedd, Blumenthal, & Jeffries, 1999). As a result, by mid-adolescence, teenagers' executive-processing skills far exceed those that they exhibited during middle childhood. Moreover, studies of patients with damage to the PFC suggest that maturation of this part of the brain contributes to advances in social perception, particularly those that involve the interpretation of nonverbal information such as facial expressions (Mah, Arnold, & Grafman, 2004).

Figure 13.1
The Prefrontal Cortex

The prefrontal cortex matures rapidly during adolescence and contributes to advances in executive processing.

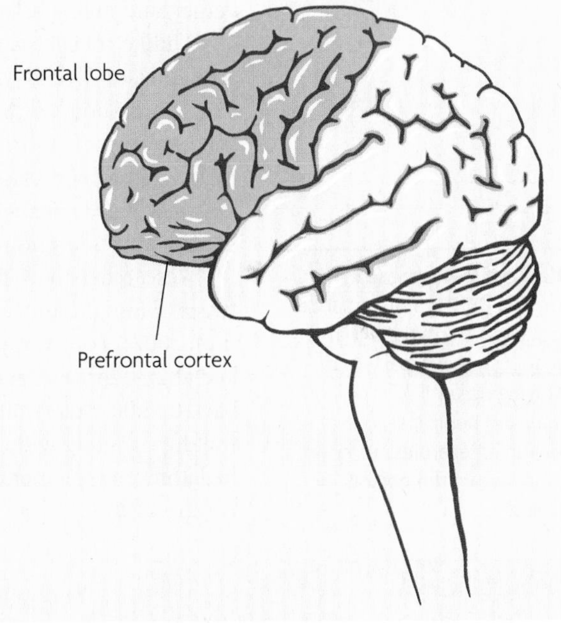

The second brain growth spurt begins around age 17 and continues into early adulthood (van der Molen & Molenaar, 1994). This time, the frontal lobes of the cortex are the focus of development (Davies & Rose, 1999). You may recall that this area of the brain controls logic and planning. Thus, it is not surprising that older teens differ from younger teens in terms of how they deal with problems and process information.

Circadian Rhythms and Sleep Changes in sleep patterns are a manifestation of the influence of the hormones of puberty on adolescents' brains. The *suprachiasmatic nucleus (SCN)* is a structure in the brain that regulates **circadian rhythms**, the regular fluctuation of bodily functions within each 24-hour period. These rhythms tie our bodily functions to the earth's light-dark cycle such that we are most alert during the daytime hours and least so when it is dark. Thus, they play a very large role in sleep patterns. Under the influence of the powerful hormones that initiate puberty, the SCN releases more *melatonin* (the substance that prompts humans to sleep) later in the day in adolescents than in either children or adults. As a result, teens tend to stay up later at night and have

prefrontal cortex (PFC) the part of the frontal lobe that is just behind the forehead and is responsible for executive processing

circadian rhythms the regular fluctuation of bodily functions within each 24-hour period

more difficulty getting up in the morning than they did earlier in their lives and will when they are adults (Crowley, Acebo, & Carskadon, 2006).

Social factors pressure teens to stay up late as well. For example, the trend toward allowing teens to have telephones, Internet connections, and entertainment media in their rooms, where they have unfettered access to them at all hours of the day and night, interacts with the rise in teens' desire to spend time with their peers and biological changes in the circadian rhythms to produce later bedtimes. Many parents think that their teens are sleeping when actually they're talking on the phone, chatting or playing games online, watching television, or listening to music. In addition, most high schools start very early in the morning in order to allow time for extracurricular activities after school. Consequently, many teens get far less than the 8 to 9 hours a night of sleep that they are thought to need (Nemours Foundation, 2007). Not surprisingly, the net effect of staying up until 3:00 a.m. and getting up for school at 6:00 a.m. is that many high school students find it quite difficult to stay awake during their classes. Moreover, lack of sleep impairs their concentration, interferes with the consolidation of new information in their memories, and disrupts girls' menstrual cycles (Sveum, 2008; Walker & Stickgold, 2006).

Many teenagers who fall into the pattern of staying up very late recognize that it is interfering with their studies. However, they often find it difficult to change their habits once **delayed sleep phase syndrome (DSPS)**, a disturbance of circadian rhythms, has set in. This happens because the SCN can reset itself to conform to habitual behaviors. Consequently, individuals with DSPS cannot fall asleep until 3:00 or 4:00 a.m., and their natural awakening time is around noon. Even when they sleep until noon, however, most individuals with DSPS become so sleepy in the afternoon that they can't stay awake. Thus, college students with DSPS find themselves sleeping through their alarms, missing their morning classes altogether, and falling asleep in their afternoon classes.

Unlike college students, most high school students are awakened by their parents. Consequently, on weekdays they can't do what their bodies want them to do—that is, they can't sleep until noon. So they drag themselves out of bed and go to school, where they struggle to keep up in their morning classes. Their feelings of sleepiness increase as the day wears on, making afternoon classes even more problematic than those that take place in the morning. On weekends, teens with DSPS stay up even later than they do on weekdays and sleep into the late afternoon hours, a practice that gives the disorder an even firmer grip on the SCN.

delayed sleep phase syndrome (DSPS) a disturbance of circadian rhythms that is manifested as a pattern of staying up until 3:00 or 4:00 a.m. and being sleepy in the daytime, regardless of how many hours the person sleeps

Researchers have found that DSPS can be reversed if teenagers avoid social activities between midnight and 3:00 a.m. and gradually move back their bedtimes (Nemours Foundation, 2007). For example, if an adolescent's usual bedtime is 3:00 a.m., she can try going to bed at 2:30 for several days. Once the 2:30 bedtime becomes habitual, she can move the time back to 2:00, then 1:30, and so on, until she achieves her desired times for falling asleep and waking up along with an acceptable degree of daytime alertness. She might also try taking a melatonin supplement an hour or so before her desired bedtime (Szeinberg, Borodkin, & Dagan, 2006).

Learning Objective 13.2

What changes occur in the body's size and shape during adolescence?

Changes in Size and Shape

You may remember from earlier chapters that babies gain in height very rapidly in infancy, adding 10 to 12 inches in length in the first year, while toddlers and school-aged children grow much more slowly. In adolescence, the body's final phase of growth occurs.

adolescent growth spurt a period during which a teenager grows rapidly to near-adult stature, usually the first observable sign of puberty

The Adolescent Growth Spurt The **adolescent growth spurt**, a period during which a teenager grows rapidly to near-adult stature, is usually the first observable sign of puberty. It is triggered by a large increase in the amount of human growth hormone released by the pituitary gland. The increase in growth hormones occurs in response to the increases in gonadotrophic hormones that you read about earlier. During the growth spurt, a teenager may grow 3 to 6 inches a year for 2 or 3 years. After the growth spurt, the adolescent again adds height and weight slowly until reaching his or her final adult size. Boys start their growth spurt later and continue longer. They catch up to the girls by age 13 or 14 and then continue growing for several more years.

The different parts of the adolescent's body do not all grow to full adult size at the same pace. This means that the shape and proportions of the adolescent's body go through a series of changes. A child's feet grow to full adult size earlier than the other parts of the body. Because of this asymmetry in the relative size of body parts, we often think of an adolescent as "awkward" or uncoordinated. However, research does not bear out this impression (Malina, 1990).

Adolescent girls reach adult height sooner than boys do because their bones grow and their joints develop more rapidly.

Skeletal Development You may remember from Chapter 10 that physical growth is linked to the process of skeletal ossification (hardening) and that most of this activity occurs at the ends of the bones, or the *epiphyses*. The adolescent growth spurt is largely the result of an acceleration of the development of the epiphyses that occurs in response to the hormonal changes of puberty (Tanner, 1990). Likewise, hormones signal the end of epiphyseal development, at which point teenagers stop growing. This happens sooner for girls than for boys. Most females reach adult height by age 16, whereas males continue growing into their late teens and early 20s (Tanner, 1990).

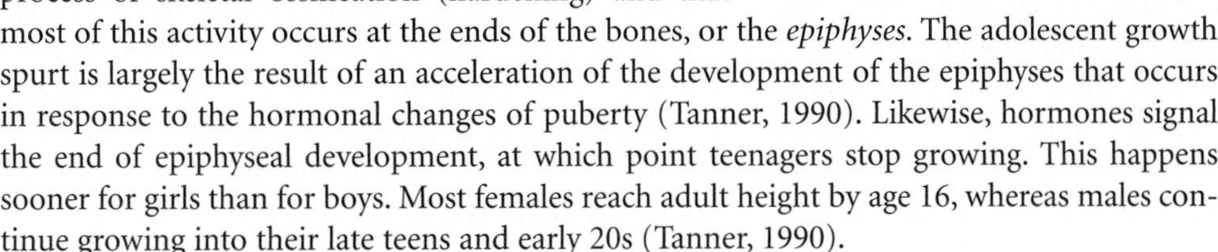

Hormonal signals are also responsible for changes in the bone structure of children's heads and faces. During the elementary school years, the size and shape of a child's jaw change when the permanent teeth come in. In adolescence, the jaw grows forward and the forehead becomes more prominent. This set of changes often gives teenagers' faces (especially boys') an angular, bony appearance, quite unlike their earlier look.

Joint development enables adolescents to achieve levels of coordination that are close to those of adults. As they did at younger ages, boys continue to lag behind girls. You may remember from earlier chapters that boys' fine motor skills are poorer than girls' because boys' wrists develop more slowly. In early adolescence, this sex difference is very large; girls achieve complete development of the wrist by their mid-teens (Tanner, 1990). A similar pattern of sex differences is evident in other joints as well, enabling early-adolescent girls to outperform boys of the same age on a variety of athletic skills that require coordination, such as pitching a softball. However, by the late teens (age 17 or 18), boys finally catch up with girls in joint development and, on average, gain superiority over them in coordinated movement.

Muscles and Fat Muscle fibers go through a growth spurt at adolescence, just as the skeleton does. The fibers become thicker and denser, so adolescents become quite a bit stronger in just a few years. Both boys and girls show this increase in strength, but the increase is much greater in boys (Buchanan & Vardaxis, 2003). This sex difference seems to be largely a result of hormone differences, although sex differences in exercise patterns or fitness may also play some role. For example, the sex difference in leg strength is much less than the difference in arm strength, a pattern that makes sense if we assume that all teenagers walk and use their legs a similar amount but that boys use their arm muscles in various sports activities more than girls do. Still, there does seem to be a basic hormonal difference as well, because we know that very fit girls and women are still not as strong as very fit boys and men.

Another major component of the body that changes during adolescence is fat, most of which is stored immediately under the skin. This *subcutaneous fat* is laid down beginning at about 34 weeks prenatally and has an early peak at about 9 months after birth. The thickness of this layer of fat then declines until about age 6 or 7, after which it rises again until adolescence.

Here, too, there is a sex difference. From birth, girls have slightly more fat tissue than boys do, and this discrepancy becomes gradually more marked during childhood and adolescence.

The size of the difference was illustrated in a classic study of Canadian youth. Between age 13 and age 17, the percentage of body weight made up of fat rose from 21.8 to 24.0% among girls but dropped from 16.1 to 14.0% among boys (Smoll & Schultz, 1990).

Other Body Systems During the teenaged years, the heart and lungs increase considerably in size, and the heart rate drops. Both of these changes are more marked in boys than in girls—additional factors making boys' capacity for sustained physical effort greater than that of girls. Before about age 12, boys and girls have similar endurance limits, although even at these earlier ages, when there is a difference it is usually boys who have greater endurance because of their lower levels of body fat. After puberty, boys have a clear advantage in endurance, as well as in size, strength, and speed (Klomsten, Skaalvik, & Espnes, 2004).

Learning Objective 13.3

What are the major milestones of sexual maturity?

Sexual Maturity

The most obvious changes of puberty are those associated with sexual maturity. Changes in **primary sex characteristics** include growth of the testes and penis in the male and of the ovaries, uterus, and vagina in the female. Such changes involve organs and functions that are required for reproduction. Changes in **secondary sex characteristics** include breast development in girls, changing voice pitch and beard growth in boys, and growth of body hair in both sexes. The appearance of both primary and secondary sex characteristics occurs in a defined sequence that is customarily divided into five stages, following a system originally suggested by J. M. Tanner (1990); examples of changes from the stages are shown in Table 13.2.

primary sex characteristics the sex organs: ovaries, uterus, and vagina in the female; testes and penis in the male

secondary sex characteristics body parts such as breasts in females and pubic hair in both sexes

menarche the beginning of the menstrual cycle

Sexual Development in Girls Studies of preteens and teens in both Europe and North America show that the various sequential changes are interlocked in a particular pattern in girls. The first steps are the early changes in breasts and pubic hair, closely followed by the peak of the growth spurt and by the development of breasts and pubic hair. First menstruation, an event called **menarche** (pronounced men-ARE-kee), typically occurs 2 years after the beginning of other visible changes and is succeeded only by the final stages of breast and pubic hair development. Among girls in industrialized countries today, menarche occurs, on average, between 12 and 13; 99% of all girls experience this event between the ages of 9 and 15 (Adelman & Ellen, 2002).

Table 13.2 Examples of Changes from Tanner's Stages of Pubertal Development

Stage	Female Breast Development	Male Genital Development
1	There is no change, except for some elevation of the nipple.	Testes, scrotum, and penis are all about the same size and shape as in early childhood.
2	Breast bud stage: breast and nipple elevate as a small mound; areolar diameter is larger than in stage 1.	Scrotum and testes are slightly enlarged; skin of the scrotum reddens and changes texture, but there is little or no enlargement of the penis.
3	Breast and areola are both enlarged and elevated more than in stage 2, but there is no separation of their contours.	Penis is slightly enlarged, at first mainly in length; testes and scrotum are further enlarged; first ejaculation occurs.
4	Areola and nipple form a secondary mound projecting above the contour of the breast.	Penis is further enlarged, with growth in breadth and development of glans; testes and scrotum are further enlarged, and scrotum skin becomes still darker.
5	Mature stage: only the nipple projects, with the areola recessed to the general contour of the breast.	Genitalia achieve adult size and shape.

Source: Petersen & Taylor, 1980, p. 127.

It is possible to become pregnant shortly after menarche, but irregular menstrual cycles are the norm for some time. In as many as three-quarters of the cycles in the first year and half of the cycles in the second and third years after menarche, a girl's body produces no ovum (Adelman & Ellen, 2002). Thus, full adult fertility develops over a period of years. Such irregularity no doubt contributes to the widespread (but false) assumption among younger teenaged girls that they cannot get pregnant.

The Secular Trend Interestingly, the timing of menarche changed rather dramatically between the mid-19th and the mid-20th century. In 1840, the average age of menarche in Western industrialized countries was roughly 17; the average dropped steadily from that time until the 1950s at a rate of about 4 months per decade among European populations, an example of what psychologists call a **secular trend** (Roche, 1979). The change was most likely caused by significant changes in lifestyle and diet, particularly increases in protein and fat intake, which resulted in an increase in the proportion of body fat in females.

Girls who are involved in activities that cause their bodies to be leaner than those of their peers experience menarche, on average, at later ages.

Data collected over much shorter periods of time in developing countries support the nutritional explanation of the secular trend. In one study, researchers found that the average age of menarche was 16 among North Korean girls who lived in squalid refugee camps (Ku et al., 2006). By contrast, studies involving impoverished groups in which food supplies suddenly increased reveal that the age of menarche can plummet from 16 to 13 within just a few years after improvements in nutrition are experienced (Khanna & Kapoor, 2004). Consequently, any change in eating patterns that affects girls' body fat, which must reach a critical value of 17% before menarche can occur, is likely to lead to a change in the age of menarche (Adelman & Ellen, 2002). But is there a lower limit on how early menarche can occur?

Exaggerated media accounts of the secular trend would have us believe that girls may someday attain sexual maturity during infancy (Viner, 2002). However, there is strong evidence for a genetic limit on the age range within which menarche may occur. Recall that, earlier in the chapter, we noted that the brain must first acquire the capacity to respond to pubertal hormones before the entire set of physical and behavioral changes we think of as typical of adolescence can emerge (Schulz & Sisk, 2006).

Studies involving thousands of girls indicate that the average age of menarche for White girls in the United States is currently about 12.8 years and that it has not changed since the mid-1940s (Kaplowitz & Oberfield, 1999; Viner, 2002). Moreover, the average age at menarche stands at 12.1 among African American girls and 12.2 among Hispanic American girls; both figures represent a drop of about 2 months since the mid-1960s (Kaplowitz & Oberfield, 1999; Wu, Mendola, & Buck, 2002). Thus, the average age at menarche for the whole population of girls in the United States was stable from 1945 to 1965 and declined about 2.5 months between 1965 and 1995 among minority girls as a result of improvements in standards of living among these generally economically disadvantaged groups (Kaplowitz & Oberfield, 1999).

Nevertheless, changes in dietary habits of children in all ethnic groups have led to some important changes in endocrine system development among school-aged and adolescent girls. That is, increased consumption of fats leads to higher proportions of body fat which, in turn, trigger hormonal changes. Because brain development prevents these hormones from stimulating full pubertal development, contemporary changes in children's diets have not significantly reduced the average age of menarche. However, these overall population trends in dietary fat consumption and increased body fat have led to declines in the average ages at which girls show secondary sex characteristics, such as the appearance of breast buds and pubic hair, in recent decades (Anderson, Dallal, & Must, 2003; Wang, 2002). On average, girls nowadays show these signs 1 to 2 years earlier than their mothers and grandmothers did,

secular trend a change, such as the decline in average age of menarche or increase in average height, that occurs in developing nations when nutrition and health improve resulting in a lengthening of the average time between the appearance of secondary sex characteristics and menarche (Parent et al., 2003).

Moreover, overweight is both a cause and a consequence of early secondary sex characteristic development, because the hormonal changes that trigger the appearance of these characteristics also signal the body's weight regulation mechanisms to increase fat stores (Pierce & Leon, 2005; Remsberg et al., 2004). Little is known about how these early hormonal shifts affect girls' later health. Several studies are under way to determine whether overweight girls who exhibit early secondary sex characteristic development are at increased risk for breast cancer, adult obesity, and heart disease (National Cancer Institute, 2006; Pierce & Leon, 2005). Interestingly, too, researchers are investigating why overweight delays pubertal development in boys and whether such delays affect boys' health later in life (Wang, 2002).

Sexual Development in Boys In boys as in girls, the peak of the growth spurt typically comes fairly late in the sequence of physical development. Studies suggest that, on average, a boy completes stages 2, 3, and 4 of genital development and stages 2 and 3 of pubic hair development before reaching the peak of the growth spurt (Adelman & Ellen, 2002). First ejaculation, or *spermarche*, occurs between 13 and 14 years of age, but the production of viable sperm does not happen until a few months after the first ejaculation. Most boys do not attain adult levels of sperm production until stage 5 of genital development. The development of a beard and the lowering of the voice occur near the end of the sequence. Precisely when in this sequence a boy begins to produce viable sperm is very difficult to determine, but it is usually just before the boy has reached the peak of the growth spurt (Adelman & Ellen, 2002).

Learning Objective 13.4

What are the psychological consequences of early, "on time," and late puberty for boys and girls?

Timing of Puberty

Although the order of physical developments in adolescence seems to be highly consistent, there is quite a lot of individual variability. In any random sample of 12- and 13-year-olds, you will find some who are already at stage 5 and others still at stage 1 in the steps of sexual maturation. We have already discussed the contributions of diet, exercise, and body fat to the timing of puberty. Researchers think that hereditary and behavioral factors also contribute to hormonal secretions in the bodies of individual teenagers, thereby influencing the timing of puberty (Dorn et al., 2003). Discrepancies between an adolescent's expectation and what actually happens determine the psychological effects of puberty. Those whose development occurs outside the desired or expected range are likely to think less well of themselves, to be less happy with their bodies and with the process of puberty. They may also display other signs of psychological distress.

Research in the United States indicates that girls who are early developers (who experience major body changes before age 10 or 11) show consistently more negative body images, such as thinking of themselves as too fat (Sweeting & West, 2002). Such girls are also more likely to get into trouble in school and at home, more likely to become sexually active, and more likely to be depressed than are girls who are average or late developers (Kaltiala-Heino, Kosunen, & Rimpela, 2003). Among boys, both very early and very late puberty are associated with depression (Kaltiala-Heino, Kosunen, & Rimpela, 2003). However, researchers have also consistently found that boys who are slightly ahead of their peers in pubertal development often occupy leadership roles and are more academically and economically successful in adulthood (Taga, Markey, & Friedman, 2006). Substance use is associated with early puberty in both girls and boys, because, based on their appearance, early maturers are often invited to join groups of older teens among whom substance use is an important social activity (Costello, Sung, Worthman, & Angold, 2007).

Research also indicates that pubertal timing interacts with a number of other variables to produce both positive and negative effects on adolescents' development. For instance, personality traits contribute to the effects of pubertal timing (Markey, Markey, & Tinsley, 2003). It appears that girls who experience early puberty and are high in the Big Five trait of openness to experience (see Chapter 12) are more likely to be sexually active at an early age than are girls who experience early puberty but do not possess this trait. Moreover, parenting moderates the effects of pubertal timing such that early-maturing boys and girls are both more likely to become involved in sexual activity and substance abuse if their parents are permissive (Costello, Sung, Worthman, & Angold, 2007).

Perhaps the most important variable moderating the effects of pubertal timing, however, is the social context in which an adolescent experiences the physical changes associated with puberty. Consider the case of girls who are involved in activities that, by their nature, inhibit development of the proportion of body fat required to initiate puberty, such as ballet and gymnastics. In these contexts, girls who are late by general cultural standards are on time for the reference group with which they spend most of their time. Thus, early puberty may cause them to believe they can no longer be successful in their chosen pursuit and may devastate their self-esteem, whereas late puberty may enhance their self-confidence and self-esteem (Brooks-Gunn, 1987; Brooks-Gunn & Warren, 1985).

Adolescent Sexuality

Puberty brings with it the hormonal changes that underlie both sexual attraction and sexual behavior. Still, these important domains of experience are not entirely controlled by hormones. Each has psychological and social components, as you will see.

Sexual Behavior

Learning Objective 13.5

What are the patterns of adolescent sexual behavior in the United States?

Most people have their first sexual encounter in the mid- to late teens (Fryar et al., 2007). However, teens vary widely in how often they have sex and in how many partners they have.

Prevalence of Sexual Behavior Figure 13.2 graphs findings from a 2005 national survey of high school students in the United States (CDC, 2006b). As you can see, boys were found to be more sexually active than girls, particularly at the younger ages. Furthermore, the proportion of sexually experienced teens increased across grades 9 to 12.

Consistent with earlier surveys, sexual experience was found to vary across racial and ethnic groups. About 67% of African American high school students reported having had sexual intercourse at least once in their lives. The rates among Hispanic American and White

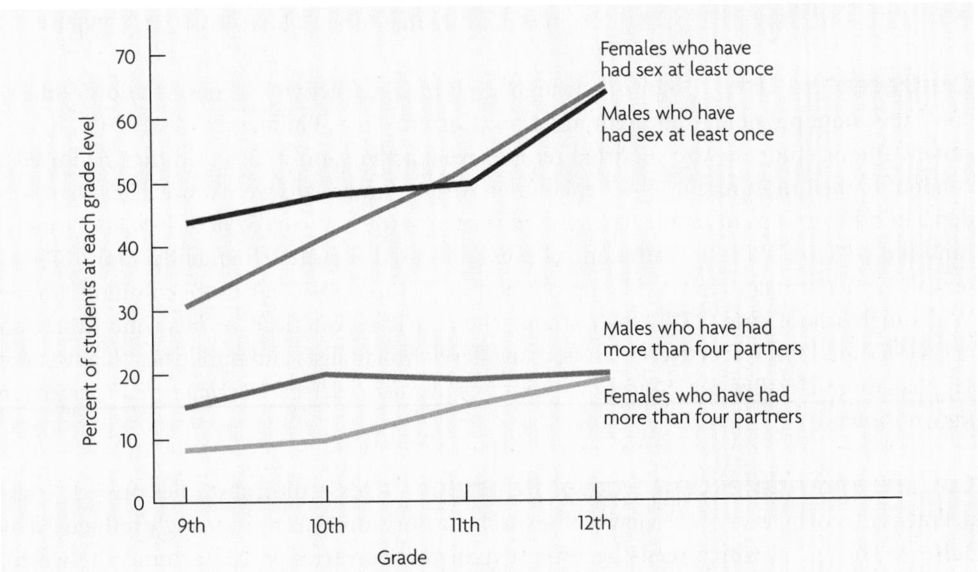

Figure 13.2
Sexual Activity Among High School Students

The graph illustrates data from a representative sample of more than 15,000 high school students interviewed in 2005.

(*Source*: CDC, 2006.)

students were 51% and 44%, respectively. African American students were more likely than Hispanic American and White teens to have had their first sexual encounter before age 13 (17% versus 7% and 4%, respectively).

There were also age and ethnic differences among students who were currently sexually active—defined as having had sex at least once within 3 months of responding to the survey. For example, roughly 41% of eleventh-grade females reported recent sexual activity, while only 20% of ninth-grade females did so. And 49% of African American students reported being sexually active currently, compared to 35% of Hispanic Americans and 32% of Whites.

Although sexual activity among boys is somewhat correlated with the amount of testosterone in the blood, social factors are much better predictors than hormones of teenagers' sexual activity (Halpern, Udry, Campbell, & Suchindran, 1993; Udry & Campbell, 1994). In fact, cross-cultural evidence suggests that the same factors are related to sexual behavior even in societies with very low rates of teenaged sexual activity, such as Taiwan (Wang & Chou, 1999). Those who begin sexual activity early are more likely to live in poor neighborhoods in which young people are not well monitored by adults. They come from poorer families or from families in which sexual activity is condoned and dating rules are lax. They are more likely to use alcohol, and many were abused and/or neglected in early childhood (Herrenkohl, Herrenkohl, Egolf, & Russo, 1998).

Among girls, those who are sexually active are also more likely to have experienced early menarche, to have problems in school, to have had their first date at a relatively early age, and to have a history of sexual abuse (Buzi, Roberts, Ross, Addy, & Markham, 2003; Ompad et al., 2006). The greater the number of risk factors present in the life of an individual teenager, the greater the likelihood that he or she will be sexually active. However, adolescents' moral beliefs and the activities in which they participate also predict their sexual activity. For example, teenagers who believe that premarital sex is morally wrong and who attend religious services frequently are less likely than their peers to become sexually active before reaching adulthood (Miller et al., 1998). Rates of sexual activity are also lower among teens who are involved in sports or other after-school pursuits than among their peers who do not participate in such activities (Savage & Holcomb, 1999). Moreover, alcohol use is associated with 25–30% of adolescent sexual encounters; thus, teens who do not use alcohol are less likely to be sexually active than are their peers who drink (CDC, 2000b).

Teens who date in early adolescence, as these middle-schoolers may be doing, are more likely to become sexually active while still in school than peers who begin dating later.

Contraceptive Use Despite their high levels of sexual activity, teenagers know remarkably little about physiology and reproduction (Carrera, Kaye, Philiber, & West, 2000). In one survey, among students who reported recent sexual activity, only 63% said they had used a condom in their most recent sexual encounter. African Americans were more likely than students in other groups to report having used condoms (69% versus 57% of Hispanic Americans and 63% of Whites). Birth control pills were used even less frequently. Only 21% of sexually active females reported being on the pill. Pill usage was far more common among White high school girls (27%) than among their African American or Hispanic American peers (9% and 11%, respectively). Thus, many developmentalists and public health advocates say that more effective sex education programs are needed (see *Developmental Science in the Classroom*).

Culture and Adolescent Sexual Behavior Cross-cultural studies provide compelling evidence in favor of the view that sexual behavior among teens is strongly influenced by culture. The age at which teens become sexually active varies widely around the world, as you can see in Figure 13.3 on page 396 (Singh, Wulf, Samara, & Cuca, 2000). The only finding

DEVELOPMENTAL SCIENCE IN THE CLASSROOM

Which Approach to Sex Education Is Most Effective?

Ms. Patel is a middle school teacher who has been asked to serve on a committee that will choose a sex education curriculum for her school district. All sixth-graders in the district will be required to participate in the program. The goal of the committee is to choose the program that is most likely to decrease students' risk of being involved in a teen pregnancy and of contracting an STD.

Ms. Patel has been reviewing the research on sex education and has learned that most developmentalists suggest programs that include training in social and decision-making skills, as well as information about sex, pregnancy, and STDs. Such programs are more likely than information-only approaches to reduce the prevalence of sexual activity and to increase the number of teens who protect themselves against disease and pregnancy when they do have sex. Programs that involve parents also appear to be more successful than those that target only teenagers (Lederman & Mian, 2003; Wilson & Donenberg, 2004). However, to Ms. Patel's dismay, she has learned that no clear consensus about the effectiveness of the various approaches to sex education has emerged, and some studies show that even carefully designed sex education programs have little or no long-term effect on adolescents' sexual behavior (Henderson et al., 2007).

The primary point of contention regarding the effectiveness of sex education programs concerns the degree to which sex education programs should emphasize abstaining from sex or using contraceptives (Santelli, Ott, Lyon, Rogers, & Summers, 2006). *Abstinence-only* programs focus on equipping teens with the social, cognitive, and communication skills they need to resist the temptation to engage in sex. *Abstinence-based* programs do so as well, but they also provide adolescents with information about reproduction, contraception, and STD prevention. *Comprehensive* programs often include sexual refusal skills as well, but their primary emphasis is on prevention of STDs and pregnancy.

Longitudinal studies suggest that abstinence-only programs are effective at delaying teens' initiation of sexual activity only under certain conditions. Such programs are effective when they are provided to younger teens who are not yet sexually active, who have already made a personal commitment to delaying sexual activity until adulthood or after marriage, whose own and whose families' religious views agree with the goals of the program, who associate with peers who are also committed to abstinence, and who are academically successful (Martino, Elliott, Collins, Kanouse, & Berry, 2008). In other words, abstinence-only programs are effective in situations in which they provide support for life goals that teens have already decided are worthwhile for reasons that have little to do with the programs themselves. Predictably, abstinence-only approaches have little effect on the behavior of teens who do not share the underlying philosophy of such programs and/or those who are older and already sexually active (Kohler, Manhart, & Lafferty, 2008). Moreover, even among teens who buy into the philosophy and goals of the abstinence-only approach, research shows a mixed pattern of results with regard to pregnancy and STD prevention. Some studies show that participants who become sexually active are no more or less likely than peers to conceive or to contract an STD (Martino et al., 2008). However, other investigations suggest that abstinence-only participants who become sexually active are at greater risk of contracting an STD or getting pregnant than their peers who participate in other types of programs, perhaps because of their lack of knowledge regarding preventive measures or because the programs cause some participants to develop unrealistic expectations about their future sexual behavior (e.g., "I'm never going to do it, so I won't plan for it") (Brückner & Bearman, 2005).

The critical factor in abstinence-based and comprehensive programs is the accuracy and breadth of the information they provide regarding the consequences of sex (Hecht & Eddington, 2003). When both types of programs provide equivalent amounts of information, research tends to show that their effects, measured in terms of outcomes such as pregnancy and STDs, do not differ. However, when abstinence-based programs focus on the benefits of abstaining from sex at the expense of information on contraception and other such topics, research tends to show that comprehensive programs are more effective (Hecht & Eddington, 2003). The age and sexual status of participants matter as well. Like abstinence-only programs, abstinence-based approaches are most likely to delay sexual activity among younger students—seventh- or eighth-graders—who are not yet sexually active (Borawski, Trapl, Lovegreen, Colabianchi, & Block, 2005). For older teens, especially those who are already sexually active, programs that provide as much information as possible about reproduction, sexuality, and methods of preventing the possible life-altering consequences of sex are most likely to influence participants' behavior, regardless of the degree to which they emphasize abstinence (Santelli et al., 2006).

Taken together, the research on sex education suggests that abstinence and contraceptive education should not be thought of in either/or terms (Borawski et al., 2005). Consequently, the American Academy of Pediatrics, the Society for Adolescent Medicine, and other such organizations, while discouraging parents and teachers from relying on abstinence-only approaches, recommend that sex education programs both encourage abstinence *and* provide information about reproduction and information about sexuality and contraception (American Academy of Pediatrics, 2001; Santelli et al., 2006). Indeed, encouraging teens to avoid becoming sexually active too early may be critical to influencing contraceptive use. The older teenagers are when they become sexually active, the more likely they are to be cognitively capable of weighing the various options and consequences associated with intercourse.

Questions for Reflection

1. What arguments could be made to parents who are reluctant to allow their children to participate in sex education classes?
2. In what way did your own experiences with sex education influence—or fail to influence—your decisions regarding sexual behavior?

that approaches universality is that boys tend to become sexually active at an earlier age than girls do, but note in the figure that there are a couple of exceptions even to this observation.

Notice, too, that first intercourse and marriage are confounded in the figure; that is, teenaged sex takes place in the context of teenaged marriage in many nations. Thus, a good argument can be made that what actually varies across cultures is not sexual behavior per se,

Figure 13.3
Percentage of 15- to 19-Year-Olds Who Have Had Sexual Intercourse Across Cultures

In some traditional cultures, teens, especially females, begin having sex at early ages because they marry sooner than is typical among their peers in industrialized countries.

(*Source*: Singh, S., et al., Gender differences in the timing of first intercourse: Data from 14 countries, *International Family Planning Perspectives*, 2000, 26(1): 21–28; 43. Figure 1.)

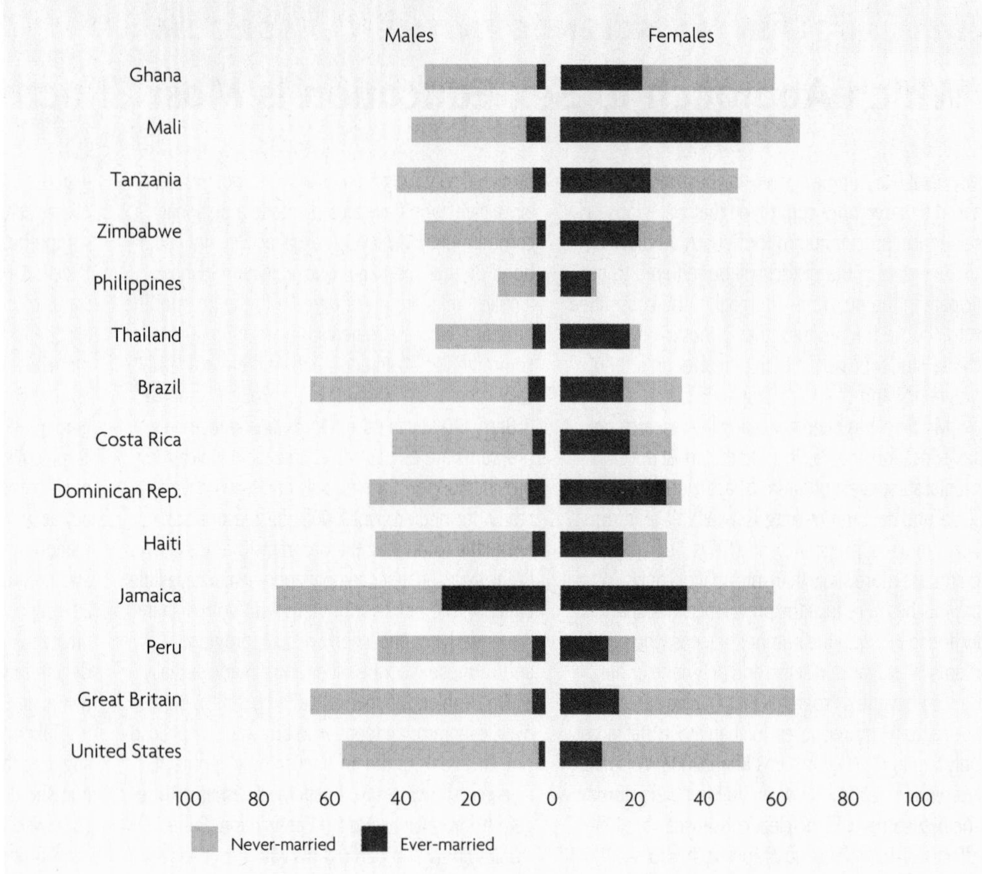

but customs regarding the appropriate age for marriage and the acceptability of premarital sex. Seen in this light, the higher rates of sexual activity among teens in Western Europe and North America could be viewed as part of a larger trend in which premarital sex has become socially acceptable (Finer, 2007).

Moreover, teenaged marriage is actively discouraged in industrialized cultures primarily for two reasons (Seiler, 2002). One reason is that teen marriages are more likely to end in divorce than are marriages that occur later in life. Longitudinal studies show that about 30% of marriages in which the bride is under the age of 18 end in divorce within the first 5 years of marriage, compared to just over 10% of those in which the woman is 25 or older (Seiler, 2002). At the 15-year mark, researchers find that nearly three-quarters of teen marriages have ended in divorce, in contrast to 40% of those involving women over age 25. The second reason is that teens who marry because of a pregnancy are far less likely to complete high school and go on to college than are those who remain single. As a result, couples who married in their teens are more likely to be living in poverty several years after the marriage than are their peers from the same ethnic and socioeconomic backgrounds who delayed marriage until they were in their 20s (Dahl, 2005). Moreover, women who married in their teens are more likely to live in poverty after the marriage dissolves than are those who married later.

Learning Objective 13.6
Which teenaged girls are most likely to get pregnant?

Adolescent Pregnancy

The rate of pregnancy among adolescents is higher in the United States than in many other industrialized countries (Ambuel, 1995; Singh & Darroch, 2000). For example, the overall annual rate is about 40 pregnancies per 1,000 teens in the United States; it is only 17 pregnancies per 1,000 in Israel and 4 per 1,000 in Japan (Martin et al., 2006; Merrick & Morad, 2002). Ethnic differences exist within the United States as well (Martin et al., 2006). Births to teenagers represent about a quarter of all births to African American women.

Among Whites, only 11% of births involve teenaged mothers; among Hispanic women, about 17% of all births are to teenagers.

However, teen pregnancy statistics can be confusing, because they usually refer to all pregnancies among women under age 20. To clarify the extent of the teen pregnancy problem, it is useful to break down the statistics by adolescent subgroups. For example, in the United States, the annual pregnancy rate is less than 1 pregnancy per 1,000 for girls younger than 15; 22 per 1,000 among girls aged 15 to 17; and 70 per 1,000 among 18- to 19-year-olds (Martin et al., 2006). Breaking down the numbers this way shows that teen pregnancy is far more frequent among older adolescents and, in fact, is most likely to happen after a girl leaves high school.

The age at which an adolescent becomes a parent is only one aspect of the teen pregnancy issue. Birth rates among teenagers have actually dropped in the entire U.S. population since the 1960s, including among 15- to 19-year-olds. What has increased is the rate of births to unmarried teens. During the 1960s, more than 80% of teens who gave birth were married. By contrast, in 2003, only 20% of teenaged mothers were married (CDC, 2004).

The proportion of teenaged mothers who eventually marry the baby's father has also declined in recent years, and again there are ethnic differences. Less than 5% of African American teen mothers marry the baby's father, compared to 26% of Hispanics and 41% of Whites (Population Resource Center, 2004). Moreover, across ethnic groups, only 17% of teen mothers maintain romantic relationships with their babies' fathers beyond the first few months after birth (Gee & Rhodes, 1999, 2003).

Whether a girl becomes pregnant during her teenaged years depends on many of the same factors that predict sexual activity in general (Miller, Benson, & Galbraith, 2001). The younger a girl is when she becomes sexually active, the more likely she is to become pregnant. Among teenaged girls from poor families, from single-parent families, and from families with relatively uneducated parents, pregnancy rates are higher (Vikat, Rimpela, Kosunen, & Rimpela, 2002). Likewise, girls whose mothers became sexually active at an early age and bore their first child early are likely to follow a similar path.

In contrast, the likelihood of pregnancy is lower among teenaged girls who do well in school and have strong educational aspirations. Such girls are both less likely to be sexually active at an early age and more likely to use contraception if they are sexually active. Girls who have good communication about sex and contraception with their mothers are also less likely to get pregnant.

When teenaged girls become pregnant, in most cases they face the most momentous set of decisions they have encountered in their young lives (see *Developmental Science in the Clinic* on page 398). About one-third of teen pregnancies across all ethnic groups end in abortion, and about 14% result in miscarriages (Alan Guttmacher Institute, 2004). Among Whites, 7% of teens carry the baby to term and place the child for adoption, but only 1% of African American teens relinquish their babies to adoptive families.

The children of teenaged mothers are more likely than children born to older mothers to grow up in poverty, with all the accompanying negative consequences for the child's optimal development (Burgess, 2005). For instance, they tend to achieve developmental milestones more slowly than infants of older mothers (Pomerleau, Scuccimarri, & Malcuit, 2003). However, the children of teenaged mothers whose own parents help with child care, finances, and parenting skills are less likely to suffer such negative effects (Birch, 1998; Uno, Florsheim, & Uchino, 1998). Moreover, social programs that provide teenaged mothers with child care and the support they need to remain in school positively affect both these mothers and their babies. Such programs also improve outcomes for teenaged fathers (Kost, 1997).

Sexual Minority Youth

Learning Objective 13.7

What are some of the causes that have been proposed to explain homosexuality?

The emergence of a physical attraction to members of the opposite sex, or *heterosexuality*, is one of the defining features of adolescence for the great majority of teenagers. For some, though, adolescence is the time when they discover—or confirm a long-standing suspicion—that they are attracted to people of the same

DEVELOPMENTAL SCIENCE IN THE CLINIC

Crisis Intervention for the Pregnant Teen

Brianna is a high school junior who recently became sexually active. She feared that she was pregnant, but she didn't know where to turn for help. Finally, after a great deal of agonizing over her situation, Brianna visited the clinic at her school, pretending to be suffering from a stomachache. In her conversation with the nurse, Brianna casually asked whether a girl who thought she was pregnant could talk to the school nurse without fearing that the nurse would tell her parents. The nurse recognized that Brianna was actually talking about herself. After some initial awkwardness, the nurse succeeded in establishing a trusting relationship with the girl, and she was able to use her crisis intervention skills to help Brianna deal with her situation.

A crisis intervention model proposed more than four decades ago continues to be helpful to health professionals in understanding and helping teens in crisis (Caplan, 1964). The first stage in a crisis, called the *initial phase*, is characterized by anxiety and confusion. Thus, the first step in crisis intervention in many teenaged pregnancies often happens when a significant adult in the teenager's life recognizes a change in behavior and questions the girl about it. Mental health professionals recommend gentle confrontation during this phase (Blau, 1996). For example, a pregnant teenager might be reminded that it isn't possible to keep a pregnancy secret for very long, but this is clearly not the time to bombard her with questions such as "How are you going to support a baby?" "What about school?," and "Aren't you going to go to college?"

The second stage of a crisis, the *escalation phase*, happens as the teenager begins to try to confront the crisis. In many cases, adolescents in this phase feel too overwhelmed to maintain daily functions such as getting to school and keeping track of homework. Teens in this phase may be responsive to helpers who simplify their decision making by directly telling them what to do. For example, a pregnant teen's mother may make a doctor's appointment for her and see that she keeps it instead of nagging her to do it herself.

The third stage of a crisis is called the *redefinition phase*. Those who are providing emotional support for the pregnant teen in this stage can help by guiding her through the process of breaking the problem down into small pieces. For the teen who wants to raise her baby, counselors or parents can divide the decisions to be made into financial and educational categories. They can help the teen identify short-term and long-term goals in each category and assist her in finding the answers to important questions. For example, in order to continue her education, she must determine the available child-care options.

Teens who leave the redefinition phase with a realistic plan of action are typically no longer in a crisis mode. However, teens who fail to redefine their problem appropriately enter the fourth crisis stage, the *dysfunctional phase*. In this stage, the pregnant adolescent either gives up hope or goes into denial. The goal of crisis intervention is to prevent either of the stage-four outcomes. The success of the entire process probably depends on whether a pregnant teen has a sensitive adult in her life who will recognize the signs of the initial phase—just one more reason why teenagers, who may seem very grown up, still need warm, authoritative parenting.

Questions for Reflection

1. In which crisis phase was Brianna when she visited the school clinic?
2. Think about how the crisis phases might be manifested in a different kind of crisis. For instance, what phase-related behaviors might be shown by a teenager who has been arrested for underage drinking?

sex (*homosexuality*) or to people of both sexes (*bisexuality*). Still others become increasingly convinced that their psychological gender is inconsistent with their biological sex (*transgenderism*).

Gay, Lesbian, and Bisexual Adolescents Surveys involving thousands of teens have found that about 92% identify themselves as exclusively heterosexual in *sexual orientation*, a person's preference for same- or opposite-sex partners (Austin et al., 2004; Remafedi, Resnick, Blum, & Harris, 1998). About 7% of teens report that they are still unsure of their sexual orientation, and 1% say that they classify themselves as exclusively gay, exclusively lesbian, or bisexual. By adulthood, 94% report being exclusively heterosexual, and just over 5% describe themselves as gay, lesbian, or bisexual, leaving only a very small proportion who are still undecided as to their sexual orientation (Langer, Arnedt, & Sussman, 2004).

Lay people and researchers alike have wondered what causes some people to develop a gay, lesbian, or bisexual orientation. Several twin studies have shown that when one identical twin is homosexual, the probability that the other twin will also be homosexual is 50–60%, whereas the concordance rate is only about 20% for fraternal twins and only about 11% for pairs of biologically unrelated boys adopted into the same family (Dawood, Pillard, Horvath, Revelle, & Bailey, 2000; Kendler, Thornton, Gilman, & Kessler, 2000). Family studies also suggest that male homosexuality runs in families—that is, the families of most gay men have a higher proportion of homosexual males than do the families of heterosexual men (Bailey et al., 1999).

Such findings strengthen the hypothesis that homosexuality has a biological basis (Dawood et al., 2000). Such evidence does not mean that environment plays no role in homosexuality. For example, when one of a pair of identical twins is homosexual, the other twin does not share that sexual orientation 40–50% of the time. Something beyond biology must be at work, although developmentalists do not yet know what environmental factors may be involved.

Prenatal hormone patterns may be one factor in homosexuality (Rahman & Wilson, 2003). For example, women whose mothers took the drug *diethylstilbestrol* (*DES*, a synthetic estrogen) during pregnancy are more likely to be homosexual as adults than are women who were not exposed to DES in the womb (Meyer-Bahlburg et al., 1995). These studies are consistent with the hypothesis that homosexuality may not be programmed in at birth or, if there is a genetic component, a hormonal trigger may be required in order for the inborn tendency to same-sex attribution to come to fruition.

Whatever the cause of variations in sexual orientation, the process through which an individual comes to realize that he or she is homosexual appears to be a gradual one. Some researchers think that the process begins in middle childhood as a feeling of doubt about one's heterosexuality (Carver, Egan, & Perry, 2004). Retrospective studies have found that many gay men and lesbians recall having had homosexual fantasies during their teen years, but few fully accepted their homosexuality while still in adolescence (Wong & Tang, 2004). Instead, the final steps toward full self-awareness and acceptance of one's homosexuality appear to take place in early adulthood.

As homosexual teens grapple with questions about their sexual orientation, many report feeling isolated from and unaccepted by their peers (Martin & D'Augelli, 2003). This may help explain why a higher proportion of homosexual than heterosexual teens suffer from depression and attempt suicide (Cato & Canetto, 2003; Savin-Williams & Ream, 2003). Many mental health professionals suggest that, to respond to these adolescents' needs, school officials provide emotional and social support for homosexual teens (Rostosky, Owens, Zimmerman, & Riggle, 2003; van Wormer & McKinney, 2003).

Social support is critical for teens who have settled on a gay, lesbian, or bisexual orientation.

Transgendered Teens **Transgendered** teens and adults are those whose psychological gender is the opposite of their biological sex. Some studies suggest that transgendered individuals may have been exposed to atypical amounts of androgens in the womb (Lippa, 2005). However, most do not have such histories, so the cause of transgenderism remains a mystery. Nevertheless, transgendered adolescents usually report that, since early childhood, they have been more interested in activities that are associated with the opposite sex than in those that are typical for their own (Lippa, 2005). However, most children who are attracted to cross-gender activities, and even those who express a desire to be of the opposite gender, do not exhibit transgenderism after puberty (Cohen-Kettenis & van Goozen, 1997). Thus, such behaviors on the part of children are not considered to be predictive of the development of transgenderism in adolescence.

Because of their fear of being stigmatized, most teens who suspect that they are transgendered keep their feelings to themselves. The denial and anger that are often expressed by family members when transgendered adolescents do venture to "come out" amplify these teens' distress (Zamboni, 2006). As a result, like gay, lesbian, and bisexual teens, transgendered teens are more likely to suffer from depression and are at higher risk of suicide than heterosexual adolescents are (Rosenberg, 2003).

Adolescent Health

For most individuals, adolescence is one of the healthiest periods of life. However, as adolescents gain independence, they encounter numerous health risks. Many of these risks flow from adolescents' behavioral choices.

Learning Objective 13.8

What are some of the critical nutritional issues in adolescence?

Nutrition

Because adolescents grow rapidly, especially in the early years of this age period, their nutritional requirements vary somewhat from those of children and adults. Calcium intake is especially critical. Some 1200 to 1500 milligrams of calcium are required each day to support skeletal development in adolescence, compared to 800 for school-aged children and 1000 to 1200 for adults (American Academy of Pediatrics, 1999). However, only 14% of adolescents consume the recommended number of servings of dairy foods (CDC, 2008). On average, adolescents in the United States take in only 700 milligrams of calcium per day.

Age-related trends in family interaction patterns help to explain this finding. Because children's beverage choices are more closely monitored than those of teens, children are more likely to drink milk than other beverages (Wang, Bleich, & Gortmaker, 2008). By contrast, teenagers consume far more sugar-sweetened beverages and fruit juices than milk because they frequent convenience stores and fast-food restaurants with their peers. Thus, teens tend to drink milk and consume other types of dairy foods only when they are at home. Calcium is found in many vegetables as well, but only 21% of teens consume the recommended number of servings of vegetables per day (CDC, 2008).

The effects of teens' consumption of sugary beverages go beyond calcium deficiencies. The rising consumption of such drinks by teens is part of a 30-year trend in which *simple carbohydrates*, the kind of carbohydrate that the body quickly converts into energy, have become the primary source of calories in adolescents' diets (Harris-Davis & Stallmann-Jorgensen, 2006). Over this same period, adolescents have become less physically active, too. When a person takes in more energy than she can expend in physical activity, the body stores the extra calories as fat. Consequently, many public health experts attribute the rising prevalence of weight problems among teenagers to the combination of increased consumption of simple carbohydrates and decreased levels of physical activity (Harris-Davis & Stallmann-Jorgensen, 2006).

Overweight is somewhat less prevalent among adolescents than it is among school-aged children (NCHS, 2007). However, the historical trend is the same one that you learned

transgendered descriptive of a person whose psychological gender is the opposite of his or her biological sex

about in Chapter 10 for school-aged children. In the early 1960s, only about 5% of teens were overweight (BMI-for-age at or above the 95th percentile) compared to about 17% today. As a result, adolescents are increasingly being diagnosed with weight-related chronic conditions such as diabetes and cardiovascular disease (Rodriguez et al., 2006; Rosenthal & Gitelman, 2002).

One factor that may explain the finding that teens are slightly less likely than school-aged children to be overweight is that many teens actively try to lose weight, including those who do not have weight problems. Dieting in adolescence represents the culmination of a trend, evident among both boys and girls as early as age 7, toward increasing awareness of the social desirability of thinness and knowledge of popular methods of weight loss (Kostanski, Fisher, & Gullone, 2004). Estimates of dieting behavior among school-aged children vary widely from one study to another, but it seems clear that many children have already attempted to lose weight before they reach adolescence. Among teenagers, surveys suggest that 40% diet regularly and 20% use extreme measures such as taking diet pills and fasting (CDC, 2006b; Neumark-Sztainer, Wall, Eisenberg, Story, & Hannan, 2006). As you will learn later in the chapter, such extreme measures can be indicative of an *eating disorder*, a serious psychological disorder that involves distortions of thinking and behavior that go far beyond habitual dieting. In most teens, however, habitual dieting is probably the result of the development, during the early teen years, of an increased capacity for self-reflection and comparisons of the self to cultural ideals (more on these trends in Chapters 14 and 15).

Illnesses

Learning Objective 13.9
What patterns of illness exist in adolescence?

The rate of acute illnesses—flu, colds, and the like—falls in the teen years. Rates of some chronic illnesses decline as well. By contrast, the incidence of asthma attacks rises in adolescence (CDC, 1996). In the process of learning to be responsible for caring for their bodies, teens with asthma sometimes forget to take prescribed medications or become convinced that they can get along without them. Consequently, the incidence of asthma attacks goes up. Most adolescents who suffer such asthma attacks learn to value compliance with medical advice more highly and change their behavior accordingly (Buston & Wood, 2000). Moreover, recent research suggests that medication reminders sent to teens as cell phone text messages are useful in helping them learn to manage their asthma-related needs (van der Meer et al., 2006).

Sexually Transmitted Diseases Predictably, as rates of sexual behavior increase among teenagers, so do the rates of **sexually transmitted diseases (STDs)**, diseases spread by sexual contact. STD rates tend to be higher among younger sexually active individuals than among those who are older. In fact, more than half of all new STD cases each year in the United States occur in 15- to 24-year-olds. The rate of one STD, *chlamydia*, is higher among teenagers than in any other age group. About 3% of sexually active 15- to 19-year-old females in the United States have chlamydia (CDC, 2007a). But chlamydia rates pale in comparison to those associated with the *human papilloma virus (HPV)*. About half of sexually active 15- to 19-year-old girls test positive for HPV, and nearly 60% of 20- to 24-year-olds are infected with the virus (Quick Stats, 2007).

By reading the entries in Table 13.3 on page 402 you can readily see that the effects of STDs can be quite severe, especially those of "silent" infections such as chlamydia and HPV, which often do not produce symptoms until they have caused a great deal of damage. Adolescents and young adults appear to be at special risk for such diseases for a variety of interacting reasons:

- The older teens get, the more likely they are to have had multiple sex partners (look back at Figure 13.2 on page 393).
- Many teens do not use condoms consistently. They may use other forms of pregnancy prevention, but only condoms protect against STDs.
- Teens, more than adults, believe that STDs are easily cured.

sexually transmitted disease (STD) a disease that is spread by sexual contact

Table 13.3 Common Sexually Transmitted Diseases

Disease	Symptoms	Treatment	Long-Term Consequences
Chlamydia	Painful urination; discharge; abdominal discomfort; one-third have no symptoms	Antibiotics	Pelvic inflammatory disease; sterility
Genital warts (HPV)	Painless growths on genitalia and/or anus	Removal of warts; no known cure	Increased risk of cervical cancer
Genital herpes	Painful blisters on genitalia	No known cure; can be controlled with various drugs	Risk of transmission to partners and to infants during birth
Gonorrhea	Discharge; painful urination	Antibiotics	Pelvic inflammatory disease
Syphilis	Sores on mouth and genitals	Antibiotics	Paralysis; brain damage; death
HIV/AIDS	Fatigue; fever; frequent infections	Antiretroviral drugs	Chronic infections; death

- Many teens who have symptoms of STDs delay treatment out of fear that their parents will find out, because of embarrassment, or because they do not know where to go for treatment.

Many teens are woefully ignorant of sexually transmitted diseases and their potential consequences, although about 90% of high school students report having learned about sexually transmitted diseases (STDs) in school (CDC, 2000; Rosenthal, Lewis, Succop, & Burklow, 1997; Sharma & Sharma, 1997). Even when they are knowledgeable about STDs, many teens lack the assertiveness necessary to resist sexual pressure from a romantic partner or to discuss condom use.

Recently, the Food and Drug Administration approved a vaccine that officials believe will protect young women against four types of HPV (CDC, 2006a). The vaccine is recommended for all females between the ages of 9 and 26. However, researchers do not yet know how long the vaccine's protective effects will last. Moreover, officials point out that there are other forms of HPV against which the vaccine offers no protection. For these reasons, public health officials state that girls and women who get the vaccine should continue to use condoms.

Efforts to develop a vaccine against the *human immune deficiency virus (HIV)*, the virus that causes *acquired immune deficiency syndrome (AIDS)*, have, so far, been unsuccessful. However, *antiretroviral drugs* interfere with HIV's ability to invade healthy cells, the process through which HIV destroys its victims' immune systems. These drugs have drastically reduced death rates associated with HIV/AIDS (Merson, 2006).

Male teens who engage in same-sex intercourse are at higher risk of contracting HIV/AIDS than other groups. Among male teens who test positive for HIV, 60% acquired the virus in this way (CDC, 2007b). Moreover, about 60% of female adolescents who test positive for HIV became infected through sexual contact with a male who had engaged in same-sex intercourse at some time in the past. Surveys showing that the disease is virtually nonexistent among homosexual male teens before age 15 but is present in about 10% of them by age 22 have prompted public health officials to heighten their efforts to educate young teens about HIV/AIDS (Valleroy et al., 2000). In addition, they have recommended universal screening for HIV for teens who engage in same-sex intercourse so that antiretroviral drugs can be prescribed as early in the course of the disease as possible. Education and screening programs are especially important among African American male teens, who account for 69% of all new cases of HIV/AIDS among 13- to 19-year-olds in the United States (CDC, 2007b).

Learning Objective 13.10

How does sensation seeking affect risky behavior in adolescents?

Sensation Seeking

Another factor that contributes to STDs and other types of health threats among teenagers is teens' beliefs about the degree to which they are vulnerable to specific risks. Teenagers appear to have what many developmentalists describe as a heightened level of **sensation seeking**, or a desire to experience increased levels of arousal such as those that accompany fast driving or the "highs" associated with drugs. Lack of maturity in the prefrontal cortex and other brain structures is viewed by some developmental scientists as the reason teens exhibit higher levels of sensation seeking than adults do (Breyer & Winters, 2005).

THE WHOLE CHILD IN FOCUS

How did Michelle channel her tendency toward sensation-seeking behavior into a positive pursuit? Find out on page 474.

Environmental factors also play a role in sensation seeking. In fact, some researchers think that risky behaviors are more common in adolescence than other periods because they help teenagers gain peer acceptance and establish autonomy with respect to parents and other authority figures (Donnenberg, Emerson, Bryant, & King, 2006). Permissive parenting contributes as well, as does alcohol use (Donnenberg et al., 2006). In addition, adolescents who are not involved in extracurricular activities at school or to whom popularity is important are more likely than their peers who value popularity less to engage in risky behavior (Carpenter, 2001; Stein, Roeser, & Markus, 1998).

The messages conveyed in the popular media about sex, violence, and drug and alcohol use may influence teens' risky behavior. In the United States, 13- to 17-year-olds spend more time watching television, listening to music, and playing video games than they do in school (Collins et al., 2004). Surprisingly, most teenagers report that their parents have few, if any, rules regarding media use (Mediascope Press, 2000). However, research indicates that media messages interact with individual differences in sensation seeking (Greene, Krcmar, Rubin, Walters, & Hale, 2002). Thus, teens who are highest in sensation seeking are those who are most strongly influenced by media portrayals of risky behavior.

The popular program *Hannah Montana* features less emphasis on sexuality than many others aimed at teens do. However, individual differences in sensation seeking influence how scenes such as this one are interpreted by viewers. Such scenes probably have little influence on most teens' behavior, but they may be interpreted by teens who are high in sensation seeking to mean that engaging in sexual behavior at a relatively early age is the key to peer acceptance and popularity.

Prime-time television programs contain about five sexual incidents per hour, and only 4% of these impart information about the potential consequences of sex (Henry J. Kaiser Family Foundation, 2005). Drugs and alcohol are even more prevalent than sex in the popular media. One survey found that of 200 movies surveyed, 98% portrayed characters using some kind of substance, and in most cases characters used more than one substance (Mediascope Press, 1999). Another group of researchers found that 51% of the films they surveyed depicted teenagers smoking (Mediascope Press, 1999). In another 46%, teenagers were shown consuming alcohol, and 3% contained images of teens using illegal drugs. Again, references to the consequences of drug or alcohol use were rare; they occurred in only 13% of the films surveyed.

Drugs, Alcohol, and Tobacco

Learning Objective 13.11

What patterns of drug, alcohol, and tobacco use have been found among adolescents in the United States?

Do you remember making some poor decisions when you were a teenager, decisions that make you wonder how you survived to adulthood? Most such decisions turn out to have little impact on teens' later lives. However, the choices that teenagers make about substance use can have life-long consequences.

As you can see in Figure 13.4 on page 404, illicit drug use is less common in recent cohorts than in past cohorts of teenagers (Johnston, O'Malley, Bachman, & Schulenberg, 2007). Researchers attribute this trend to declining approval of drug use among adolescents and to contemporary teens' better understanding of the negative consequences of taking drugs. Still, experts agree that drug use among teens continues to be a significant problem because of the risks to which teens expose themselves—such as drunk driving and the possibility of life-long addiction—when they use these substances.

Table 13.4 on page 405 lists the percentages of eighth-, tenth-, and twelfth-grade students who reported using each drug listed in the 12 months preceding the survey. Clearly, as was true in earlier cohorts, marijuana is the illicit substance that teens use most often. However, a surprising number of teenagers are using prescription drugs such as Ritalin, OxyContin, and Vicodin. Similar percentages of teens use over-the-counter drugs such as

sensation seeking a desire to experience increased levels of arousal such as those that accompany fast driving or the "highs" associated with drugs

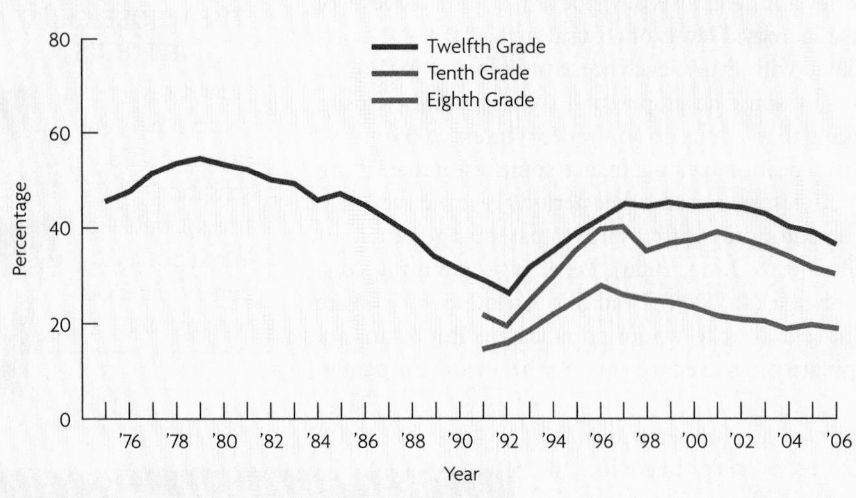

Figure 13.4
Illicit Drug Use Trends Among Teenagers

This figure shows the percentage of teens who admitted to using illicit drugs in the previous 12 months. As you can see, drug use rates have declined since the 1970s.

(*Source*: Johnston, O'Malley, Bachman, & Schulenberg, 2007.)

cough medicines. (Note that these statistics refer only to the use of these drugs for purposes other than those for which they have been medically approved.) Nevertheless, illicit drug use is far less prevalent than alcohol use among teenagers. Nearly one-third of twelfth-graders reported having been drunk in the month prior to the survey.

What makes a teenager want to use alcohol or drugs? Those who express the most interest in sensation seeking are those who are most likely to use drugs and consume alcohol (Donohew et al., 1999). Indeed, researchers have found that individual levels of sensation seeking predict peer associations—that is, teens who are high sensation seekers choose friends who are similar. Once such groups are formed, sensation seeking becomes a central feature of their activities. So, for example, if one member tries marijuana or alcohol, others do so as well. However, teens who spend a lot of time alone may also be vulnerable to substance abuse. Researchers have found that shy adolescents, particularly those who are high in neuroticism, are more likely to use alcohol and drugs than are peers who are more outgoing (Kirkcaldy, Siefen, Surall, & Bischoff, 2004).

Sensation seeking also interacts with parenting style to increase the likelihood of drug use. Authoritative parenting seems to provide sensation-seeking teenagers with protection against their reckless tendencies (Pilgrim, Luo, Urberg, & Fang, 1999). In fact, for African American adolescents, authoritative parenting may entirely negate the potential influence of drug-using peers. Moreover, parents who have realistic perceptions of the prevalence of teenaged drinking are less likely to have teenaged children who are drinkers. These parents, who are aware of the prevalence of alcohol use among adolescents, try to prevent their children from getting into situations where drinking is likely to happen, such as unsupervised social events (Bogenschneider, Wu, Raffaelli, & Tsay, 1998).

We have noted the possible role of brain maturity in sensation seeking and risky behavior, but how do alcohol and other substances affect the developing brain? One finding is that such substances lead to lowered inhibitions, just as they do in adults. However, the degree of disinhibition and the riskiness of the sensation-seeking activities that result from alcohol-induced disinhibition are greater in adolescents (Breyer & Winters, 2005). Furthermore, some studies suggest that the adolescent brain requires more alcohol, marijuana, and other drugs to experience a "high," thereby heightening the risk of immediate adverse responses and long-term dependence on these drugs. Once they become addicted to alcohol or drugs, adolescents may lose the ability to judge the value of nondrug rewards, such as grades, because of the effects of these substances on the development of the prefrontal cortex (Goldstein & Volkow, 2002). For this reason, alcohol and drugs represent enormous threats to a teenager's developmental pathway, yet another reason for parents to be vigilant in monitoring their adolescent children's activities and supporting their development in positive ways.

Sensation seeking seems to be less important in tobacco use. Surveys suggest that 12% of U.S. adolescents are regular smokers and 30% have tried smoking (Johnston et al., 2007). Smoking rates have dropped considerably since the mid-1970s, when about 30% of older teenagers were regular smokers. Researchers argue that, thanks to public education campaigns and the inclusion of antismoking information in school curricula, more teenagers are aware of the health consequences of smoking now than in earlier cohorts. Moreover, many teens report that they oppose smoking because of its potential effect on their attractiveness to potential romantic partners.

Table 13.4 Percentages of Teens Who Have Used Illicit Drugs in the Past 12 Months

Drug	Eighth-graders	Tenth-graders	Twelfth-graders
Alcohol	34	56	67
Marijuana	12	25	32
Vicodin*	3	7	10
Diet pills*	5	8	8
Tranquilizers*	3	5	7
Over-the-counter cold medicines*	4	5	7
Cocaine	2	3	5
OxyContin*	3	4	4
MDMA (Ecstasy)	1	3	4
Crack cocaine	1	1	2
Ritalin*	3	4	4
Methamphetamine	2	2	3
LSD	<1	2	2
Heroin	1	1	1

*Recreational usage outside the scope of the purpose for which the drug is medically approved.

Source: Johnston et al., 2007.

Peer influence plays an important role in teen smoking. A nonsmoking teenager is likely to take up the habit if she begins associating with a cohesive group of adolescents among whom smoking is a prominent behavior and a sign of group membership. In fact, some developmentalists advise parents that if their teenaged child's friends smoke, especially close friends with whom the child spends a lot of time, parents should probably assume that their child smokes as well (Urberg, Degirmencioglu, & Pilgrim, 1997). The period between ages 15 and 17 seems to be the time during which a teenager is most susceptible to peer influences with regard to smoking (West, Sweeting, & Ecob, 1999). Clearly, then, by monitoring the friends of their 15- to 17-year-olds and discouraging them from associating with smokers, parents may help prevent their teens from smoking (Mott, Crowe, Richardson, & Flay, 1999).

Mortality

Learning Objective 13.12
What are the leading causes of death in adolescence?

In Chapter 10, you learned that accidents are the leading cause of death among 5- to 9-year-olds and 10- to 14-year-olds. As you can see in Figure 13.5 on page 406, accidents continue to lead other causes of death among White, Hispanic American, Asian American, and Native American 15- to 19-year-olds (Heron, 2007). However, among African American teens, homicide is the leading cause of death. Notice, too, that the rate of suicide is much higher among Native American teens than it is in other groups. Moreover, the overall death rate is more than three times as high among teens than at earlier ages. About 19 of every 100,000 10- to 14-year-olds die each year, compared to 66 per 100,000 15- to 19-year-olds (Heron, 2007).

Although death rates are higher among males than females at every age, in the teen years the gender gap in mortality becomes quite large (Heron, 2007). For instance, among 10- to

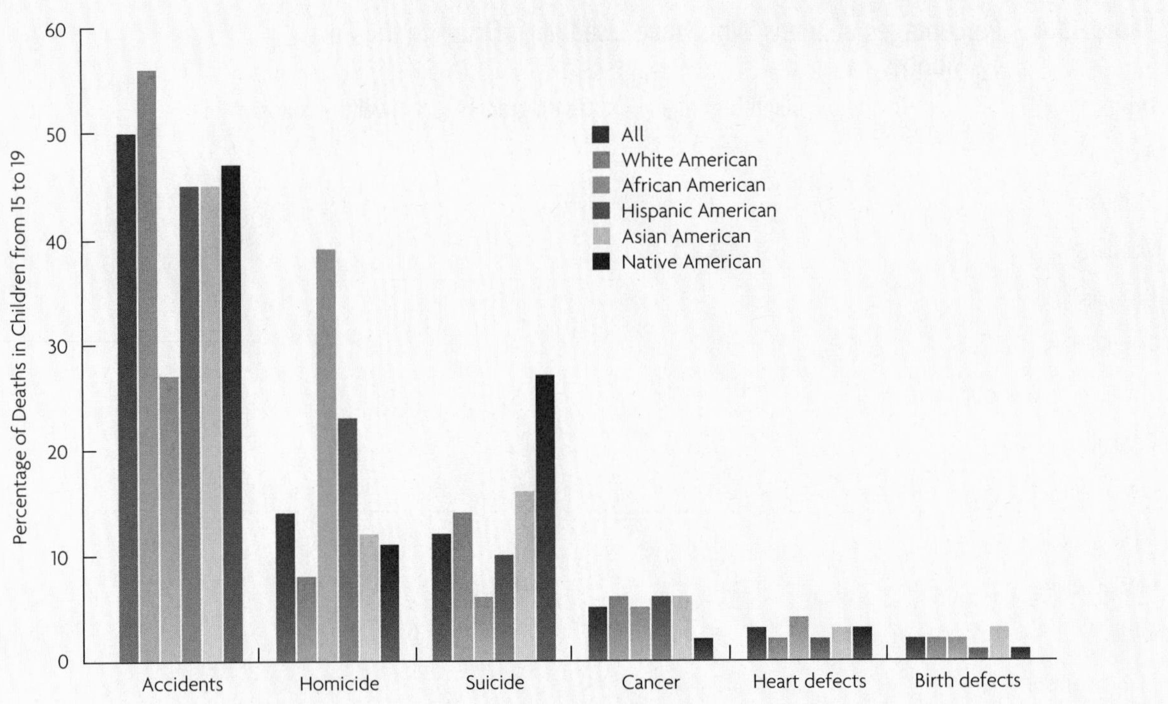

Figure 13.5
Leading Causes of Death Among 15- to 19-Year-Olds

As this figure shows, accidents are the leading cause of death among White, Hispanic American, and Asian American teens. By contrast, homicide claims the highest percentage of the lives of African American youths.

(*Source*: Heron, 2007.)

14-year-olds, the death rates for females and males are 15 and 22 per 100,000, respectively. For 15- to 19-year-olds, the respective rates are 39 and 91 per 100,000. This difference is attributable largely to the fact that homicide and suicide rates are much higher among male teens than they are among female adolescents. Just over 15 per 100,000 teenaged boys are killed in some kind of violent act each year, while only 3 per 100,000 adolescent girls die as a result of violence. The gap is almost as large for suicide, with 3 of every 100,000 teenaged girls dying as a result of suicide each year, compared to 13 of every 100,000 adolescent boys.

Gender differences aside, the overall increase in mortality in the adolescent and early adult years is due primarily to the frequency of motor vehicle accidents among young drivers. In fact, the rate of death due to motor vehicle accidents is greater among 15- to 20-year-olds than any other age group (National Highway Traffic Safety Administration [NHTSA], 2006). Male teenaged drivers are about three times as likely to die as the result of a motor vehicle accident as female adolescent drivers are.

Alcohol is a factor in 24% of fatal car crashes involving male teen drivers and 12% of fatal accidents involving female teen drivers (NHTSA, 2006). As you learned earlier in the chapter, many teens engage in risky behavior because they do not consider themselves to be vulnerable to death. Alcohol heightens these feelings of invulnerability, leading teens to be less likely to wear seat belts and more likely to speed when they drive under the influence than are adults who have been drinking. The presence of passengers in the car increases the likelihood of such high-risk behaviors, perhaps because teenaged drivers want to appear fearless to their peers.

Most states have enacted changes in driver's license laws in an effort to reduce the prevalence of fatal car crashes among teens; these changes include so-called graduated driver's licenses (Cobb, 2000). Under these laws, 16-year-olds can drive, but they must remain accident- and ticket-free for a certain period of time before they can have privileges such as driving at night. In some states, drivers under the age of 18 are not allowed to drive with a passenger under the age of 18 in the front seat.

Atypical Development

As you learned in Chapter 1, the concept of adolescence as a transitional period between childhood and adulthood was introduced into the study of human development by G. Stanley Hall. In his classic 1904 book *Adolescence: Its Psychology and Its Relations to Physiology, An-*

thropology, Sociology, Sex, Crime, Religion and Education, Hall borrowed a phrase from German literature, *sturm und drang* (storm and stress), to describe the adolescent's struggle for individuality. More than 100 years later, many people continue to think of adolescence as a period marked by instability and poor mental health. Despite this stereotype, most adolescents are mentally healthy. However, a significant minority (some 20%) of teens develop mental health problems (U.S. Department of Health and Human Services, 1999). Here we discuss three categories of disorders that appear during adolescence: conduct disorders, eating disorders, and depressive disorders.

Conduct Disorders

Learning Objective 13.13
What are the distinguishing features of adolescent-onset conduct disorder and delinquency?

As you learned in Chapter 10, *childhood-onset conduct disorder* is a pattern of behavior that begins before a child is 10 years of age and includes high levels of aggression, argumentativeness, bullying, disobedience, irritability, and threatening and loud behavior. When this pattern of behavior emerges at age 11 or later, the child is given the diagnosis of **adolescent-onset conduct disorder**. Delinquent behavior may also be apparent in teens with conduct disorder.

Adolescent-Onset Conduct Disorder In contrast to those with childhood-onset conduct disorder, teens who are diagnosed with the adolescent-onset form of the disorder tend to manifest antisocial behaviors that are milder, more transitory, and more a function of hanging out with bad companions than a deeply ingrained behavior problem. Like children with conduct disorder, teens with this pattern of problems have friends who behave similarly. However, associating with antisocial peers worsens the behavior of teens with adolescent-onset conduct disorder, whereas the behavior of younger children with this disorder remains essentially the same whether they have antisocial friends or are "loners" (Vitaro, Tremblay, Kerr, Pagani, & Bukowski, 1997). Moreover, the antisocial behavior patterns of those with adolescent-onset conduct disorder often change as their relationships change (Laird, Pettit, Dodge, & Bates, 1999). Consequently, peer influence seems to be the most important factor in the development of adolescent-onset conduct disorder.

Parenting style and other relationship variables seem to be additional factors in this type of antisocial behavior. Several studies have shown that authoritarian parenting increases the risk of adolescent-onset conduct disorder (Smith & Farrington, 2004). Thus, it may be that parents who do not balance strict supervision with recognition of teenagers' need to understand the reasons behind rules incite rebellion in some children. However, the cultural context in which parenting occurs matters as well. It seems that the combination of authoritarian parenting and a culture that endorses strict rules and strong enforcement of those rules does not increase the risk of conduct disorder in teens. For example, in most Middle Eastern societies, children whose parents display the authoritarian style are less likely to develop conduct disorder than are peers whose families' approaches to discipline do not match that of the larger culture (Dwairy, 2008).

Permissive parenting is also associated with adolescent-onset conduct disorder. Most teens who develop the disorder have parents who do not monitor them sufficiently, often because there is only one parent in the home (Office of Juvenile Justice and Delinquency Prevention [OJJDP], 2006). They are also drawn to peer groups that include teens who are experimenting with drugs or mild law breaking. After hanging out with such groups for several months, previously non-antisocial adolescents show some increase in risky behaviors, such as increased use of drugs (Berndt & Keefe, 1995; Dishion, French, & Patterson, 1995; Steinberg et al., 1994). However, when parents provide good monitoring and emotional support, their adolescent children are unlikely to exhibit antisocial behavior, even if they hang around with a tough crowd or have close friends who engage in such behavior (Brown & Huang, 1995; Mounts & Steinberg, 1995).

adolescent-onset conduct disorder a pattern of behavior that begins at age 11 or later and includes high levels of aggression, argumentativeness, bullying, disobedience, irritability, and threatening and loud behavior

delinquency a narrow category of behavior problems that includes intentional law breaking

Delinquency Unfortunately, many teens with conduct disorder, regardless of the age at which the diagnosis is made, also show **delinquency**, a narrower category of behavior problems that involves intentional law breaking. It is extremely difficult to estimate how many teenagers engage in delinquent behavior. One way to approach the problem is to look at the number of arrests—although arrest rates are arguably only the tip of the iceberg. About 6% of *juveniles*, youths between the ages of 10 and 18, were arrested in 2005 in the United States (Puzzanchera, Adams, Snyder, & Kang, 2007). From age 15 to 17, the arrest rate is closer to 10%—a higher rate than for any other age group across the entire lifespan. Many of these arrests are for relatively minor infractions, but about a third are for serious crimes, including murder, burglary, rape, and arson.

Delinquency rates are about 40% higher today than they were in the 1980s (OJJDP, 2006). Fortunately, though, the juvenile arrest rate has been on the decline in the United States since peaking in the mid-1990s. Yet the decline in overall delinquency rates over the past several years obscures a complex pattern of change. Property crimes, such as theft, have declined, while crimes against people have remained stable. Within the people crimes category, murder, aggravated assault, and offenses involving weapons have declined, but the number of arrests for simple assault (e.g., threats or other aggression that does not lead to serious bodily injury) has risen significantly. In addition, while arrests involving males have declined by 15%, arrests of females have remained stable. In fact, the overall trend among juvenile offenders, in which decreases in property crimes are accompanied by increases in people crimes, is largely attributable to a dramatic rise in arrests of female adolescents for simple assault.

Increasing rates of alcohol and drug use among girls have been blamed for the increase in people crimes perpetrated by them (Auditor General of British Columbia, 2000). However, there are many risk factors for delinquency that apply to both genders. Low IQ is one such factor (Lynam, Moffitt, & Stouthamer-Loeber, 1993). This link between IQ score and delinquency cannot be explained away by arguing that less bright delinquents are more likely to be caught. Nor is it simply an artifact of social class or ethnic differences in both delinquency and IQ, because White middle-class delinquents also have lower IQs than their nondelinquent peers. In fact, low IQ scores appear to be a genuine risk factor for delinquency, particularly for children with early-onset types of conduct disorder, for those who show more serious or violent forms of offenses, and for those who experience some school failure (Hämäläinen & Pulkkinen, 1996). The argument offered by Donald Lynam and others (1993) is that school failure reduces a young person's engagement with school and the values it represents. School failure also increases the child's or adolescent's frustration, which raises the likelihood of aggression of some kind. Thus, for many less intelligent young people, the social constraint on delinquent behavior offered by education is simply weaker.

Variations in self-esteem are also related to delinquent behavior. However, there is considerable debate as to whether low or high self-esteem predisposes an adolescent to engage in delinquent behavior. On one side, Brent Donnellan and his colleagues argue that children who develop low self-esteem in elementary school, perhaps brought on by school failure or peer rejection, are more prone to delinquency in later years (Donnellan, Trzesniewski, Robins, Moffitt, & Caspi, 2005). By contrast, Roy Baumeister and others have claimed that the development of an inappropriately high level of self-esteem during childhood, given an individual's real accomplishments, is associated with delinquency (Baumeister, Smart, & Boden, 1999). Put differently, Baumeister hypothesizes that *narcissism*, the view that one is the center of the world, is more likely to be at the center of a delinquent teen's sense of self-worth than is low self-esteem. To date, both sides have produced evidence in support of their views. As a result, Donnellan has argued that researchers should probably think of the kind of low self-esteem he measures as being qualitatively distinct from the narcissism that has been studied by Baumeister's group (Donnellan et al., 2005). He says that it is possible for a delinquent teen both to be narcissistic and to have low self-esteem when he judges himself against the criteria he knows to be part of a cultural definition of "good" people. What seems clear is that teens who display delinquent behavior have views of themselves that distinguish them from adolescents who do not engage in such behaviors.

It is important to emphasize, however, that the milder forms of delinquency do not invariably or even commonly persist into adulthood. Many teens commit only occasional delinquent acts and show no further problems in adulthood. For them, mild delinquent behavior is merely a phase. It is those who show a syndrome of delinquent acts plus high-risk behavior and come from families with low warmth and ineffective control who are quite likely to engage in criminal acts as adults.

Eating Disorders

Learning Objective 13.14

What are the characteristics and causes of eating disorders?

As we noted earlier, a sizeable proportion of adolescents in the United States diet regularly. However, dieting is quite different from an *eating disorder*, which is a category of mental disorder in which eating behaviors go far beyond most people's everyday experience with trying to lose weight (DSM-IV TR, 2000). Most importantly, individuals with eating disorders have a distorted body image that, in extreme cases, causes them to believe that they are overweight when they are actually on the verge of starvation. These disorders, which can be fatal, tend to make their first appearance in individuals' lives during the mid- to late teens. They are more common among girls than boys, but gay and lesbian youth, as well as teens who are unsure about their sexual orientation, are also at higher risk than their heterosexual peers of developing eating disorders (Austin et al., 2004).

Anorexia Nervosa Teenagers who suffer from **anorexia nervosa** engage in extreme dieting, have an intense fear of gaining weight, and are obsessed with exercising. In girls or women (who are by far the most common sufferers), the weight loss eventually produces a variety of physical symptoms associated with starvation: sleep disturbance, cessation of menstruation, insensitivity to pain, loss of hair on the head, low blood pressure, a variety of cardiovascular problems, and reduced body temperature. Between 10% and 15% of those with anorexia literally starve themselves to death; others die because of some type of cardiovascular dysfunction (Deter & Herzog, 1994).

Bulimia Nervosa **Bulimia nervosa** involves an intense concern about weight combined with twice-weekly or more frequent cycles of binge eating followed by purging, through self-induced vomiting, excessive use of laxatives, or excessive exercising (DSM-IV TR, 2000). Teens with bulimia are ordinarily not exceptionally thin, but they are obsessed with their weight, feel intense shame about their abnormal behavior, and often experience significant depression. The physical consequences of bulimia include marked tooth decay (from repeated vomiting), stomach irritation, lowered body temperature, disturbances of body chemistry, and loss of hair.

Risk Factors Some theorists have proposed biological causes for eating disorders, such as some kind of brain dysfunction. Researchers have recently identified a gene that may play a causal role in the development of anorexia nervosa (Frisch et al., 2001). Others, however, argue for a psychoanalytic explanation, such as a fear of growing up. But the most promising explanation may lie in the discrepancy between a young person's internal image of a desirable body and her or his perception of her or his own body.

Some developmentalists suggest that an emphasis on thinness as a characteristic of attractive women, which is common in Western cultures, contributes to the prevalence of eating disorders (Pelletier, Dion, & Levesque, 2004). In one approach to testing this hypothesis, 6- to 12-year-old girls' responses to images of thin, sexy women were compared to boys' reactions to images of muscular, hypermasculine men in order to find out how early children become aware of cultural stereotypes about ideal male and female body types (Murnen, Smolak, Mills, & Good, 2003). Researchers found that even the youngest children in this age group express admiration for the appearance of the models depicted in such images and that children are most interested in idealized images of adults of their own gender. However, girls are more likely than boys to compare their own appearance to that of the models. Moreover, among girls, those who are happiest with their own physical appearance are the least likely to compare their own bodies to media images of attractive women (Murnen et al., 2003; Rabasca, 1999).

These findings support the assertion of many developmentalists that girls internalize images representing what might be called the "thin ideal" during the middle childhood years and

anorexia nervosa an eating disorder characterized by self-starvation

bulimia nervosa an eating disorder characterized by binge eating and purging

use them as standards against which to compare the changes in their bodies that happen during puberty (Hermes & Keel, 2003). In fact, research shows that, by age 11, girls are significantly more dissatisfied with their bodies than boys are with theirs, and the gender gap in body satisfaction increases across the teen years (Sweeting & West, 2002). As you might expect, given these results, researchers have also found that the tendency of girls to compare themselves to the thin ideal increases as they advance through puberty (Hermes & Keel, 2003).

Cross-cultural research examining societies in which eating disorders were once unknown but have recently become major public health issues suggests that several factors interact to bring about the emergence of anorexia and bulimia (Gordon, 2001). It appears that anorexia and bulimia emerge as a society's general standard of living improves. As standards of living go up, food supplies become abundant where scarcity was once the rule. An abundance of food brings with it the emergence of overeating and overweight among some people. In response, those who have some kind of internal tendency to develop a distorted body image begin to fear that they, too, will become overweight. At the same time, access to Western media sources that promote thinness increases as a result of the culture's growing affluence. When this happens, the prevalence of both distorted body images and eating disorders increases. This pattern of eating disorder emergence has been documented in China, India, Argentina, Mexico, South Africa, South Korea, Portugal, Singapore, Turkey, and the United Arab Emirates. In all of these countries, each of which has seen a dramatic increase in standard of living and access to Western media, eating disorders were virtually unknown in 1990 but have since become a major public health problem.

Recent thinking, however, has placed more emphasis on the pre-existing psychological health of people who develop eating disorders than on cultural influences. Some researchers assert that the body images of individuals who suffer from eating disorders are the result of a general tendency toward distorted thinking (Dyl, Kittler, Phillips, & Hunt, 2006). In other words, these researchers say that people who have eating disorders tend to think in distorted ways about many things, not just their bodies. From this perspective, internalized images of the "perfect" body fuel the sales of diet products among psychologically healthy people, but they trigger a far more serious outcome, a true eating disorder, in individuals who have a tendency toward thought distortion. Thus, advertising may have a more powerful effect on an adolescent who has a general tendency toward distorted perceptions of herself and others than it does on teens who tend to view themselves and others more realistically. For instance, many young women who suffer from bulimia have also been diagnosed with *borderline personality disorder*, a psychiatric disorder in which individuals have irrational, unfounded fears that those they love will abandon them, as well as a host of other distorted perceptions (Halmi, 2003).

When this 15-year-old with anorexia looks at herself in the mirror, chances are she sees herself as "too fat," despite being obviously emaciated.

Longitudinal evidence seems to support this view. In one study, young women who had anorexia in adolescence (94% of whom had recovered from their eating disorders) were found to be far more likely than the general population to suffer from a variety of mental disorders (Nilsson, Gillberg, Gillberg, & Rastam, 1999). *Obsessive-compulsive personality disorder*, a condition characterized by an excessive need for control of the environment, seemed to be especially prevalent in this group. The study's authors stated that the young women's mental difficulties did not appear to be the result of having previously suffered from an eating disorder. Instead, both the adolescent eating disorders and the women's problems in adulthood seem to have been produced by a consistent tendency toward distorted perceptions.

Treatment Anorexia is very difficult to treat. For one thing, many teens with anorexia are good at hiding their condition (see *Developmental Science at Home*). Most are steadfast in their refusal to eat, while insisting that nothing is wrong with them. The main thrust of treatment, therefore, is to get the individual to gain weight. The patient may be admitted to a hospital, fed a controlled diet, and given rewards for small weight gains and increases in food intake. The treatment usually includes some type of psychotherapy and/or a self-help group.

Bulimia, like anorexia, is difficult to treat. Sometimes treatment is complicated by the fact that a person with an eating disorder is likely to have a personality disorder as well or be too shy to interact effectively with therapists (Goodwin & Fitzgibbon, 2002; Rosenvinge, Mat-

DEVELOPMENTAL SCIENCE AT HOME

Recognizing the Signs of an Eating Disorder

As always, Winnie was in a rush on the day she had to take her 14-year-old daughter, Lynn, to the pediatrician's office after school for a measles booster shot. Thoughts of how she could possibly get Lynn's 10-year-old brother to soccer practice on time were running through her mind as the nurse weighed and measured Lynn prior to giving her the injection. Thus, Winnie was somewhat annoyed when the nurse told her that Lynn would have to see the doctor before she could get her shot. When the pediatrician came in, he asked Winnie to leave the examining room so that he could speak to Lynn alone. A few minutes later, the doctor called her back into the room. Winnie was shocked when he asked her if she was aware that Lynn had lost 15 pounds since her last visit to the doctor's office just 6 months earlier. He pointed out that Lynn's weight, at 93 pounds, was far below that which was appropriate for her 65-inch height. Together, Lynn, Winnie, and the pediatrician discussed the possibility that Lynn might be suffering from an eating disorder.

Many parents, like Winnie, are taken aback when they learn that their child has an eating disorder, because teens with these problems are good at concealing them. Many wear baggy clothes to hide their emaciated bodies, and parents' preoccupations with their own busy lives sometimes make it easy for teens to keep such secrets. Consequently, mental health professionals suggest that all parents familiarize themselves with the warning signs associated with eating disorders. Any of the teens described below could be at risk for an eating disorder, and parents should seek professional help for a teen who exhibits several of these characteristics (helpguide.org, 2008).

- A thin teen who diets constantly
- A teen who is obsessed with calories, fat grams, weighing her food, reading nutrition labels, and so on
- A teen who pretends to eat, lies about eating, hides or throws away food, and/or makes excuses to avoid eating with others
- A teen who talks a lot about food and displays an unusual interest in food magazines and cookbooks, despite eating very little
- A teen who engages in unusual food rituals, such as cutting food into tiny pieces or insisting on eating only in certain places or at certain times
- A thin teen who complains about being "too fat" to be seen in shorts or a swimsuit
- A teen who weighs himself constantly and expresses concern about small fluctuations in weight
- A teen who is obsessed with being able to wear an extremely small clothing size when that size is clearly out of line with the teen's body type
- A teen who devotes a great deal of time to her appearance but is highly self-critical
- A teen who frequently uses laxatives or diuretics
- A teen who exercises compulsively

Questions for Reflection

1. In your opinion, what would be the best way for a parent to confront a teenager about a pattern of behavior that suggested the presence of an eating disorder?
2. How do you think that peers who do not have anorexia or bulimia unintentionally reinforce the dieting behavior of those who do have an eating disorder?

inussen, & Ostensen, 2000). Some behavior modification programs have helped extinguish bulimic behavior (Traverso, Ravera, Lagattolla, Testa, & Adami, 2000), and cognitive-behavioral therapy has been used successfully to help teens with bulimia modify their eating habits and their abnormal attitudes about body shape and weight (Wilson & Sysko, 2006).

Depression and Suicide

Learning Objective 13.15
Which adolescents are at greatest risk of depression and suicide?

As you learned in Chapter 10, *major depressive disorder (MDD)* is defined as a period of deep sadness lasting 6 months or more that affects a child's physical, cognitive, and social functioning. Epidemiological studies reveal that, at any given time, 18–30% of adolescents are in the midst of an enduring depression, with about 6% meeting the criteria for MDD (CDC, 2006b; Saluja et al., 2004; U.S. Department of Health and Human Services, 1999). Teenaged girls are twice as likely as boys to report feelings of depression, a sex difference that persists throughout adolescence and into adulthood. This sex difference has been found in a number of industrialized countries and across ethnic groups in the United States (DSM-IV TR, 2000).

Neuroimaging studies show that adolescent depression is associated with some kind of dysfunction in the pituitary gland (MacMaster & Kusumakar, 2004). But what causes the pituitary to function inappropriately in the first place? Genetic factors may be involved, as children growing up with depressed parents are much more likely to develop depression than are those growing up with nondepressed parents (Eley et al., 2004; Merikangas & Angst, 1995). The genetic hypothesis has also received support from at least a few studies of twins and adopted children (Petersen et al., 1993). However, the link between parental and child depression may also be explained in terms of the parenting behaviors of depressed parents, which you read about in earlier chapters. Furthermore, the contributions of a variety of family stressors to adolescent depression are just as clear among children whose parents are not depressed. Any combination of stresses—such as the parents' divorce, the death of a parent or another loved one, the father's loss of job, a move, a change of schools, or lack of sleep—increases the likelihood of depression or other kinds of emotional distress in the adolescent (Compas et al., 1993; D'Imperio, Dubow, & Ippolito, 2000; Fredriksen, Rhodes, Reddy, & Way, 2004).

Depression can hinder academic achievement, because it interferes with memory. For example, depressed adolescents are more likely to remember negative information than positive information (Neshat-Doost, Taghavi, Moradi, Yule, & Dalgleish, 1998). If a teacher says to a depressed adolescent, "You're going to fail algebra unless you start handing in your homework on time," the teenager is likely to remember the part about failing algebra and forget that the teacher also provided a remedy—getting homework done on time. Further, depressed adolescents seem to be less able than their nondepressed peers to store and retrieve verbal information (Horan, Pogge, Borgaro, & Stokes, 1997). Consequently, therapeutic interventions, such as antidepressant medications, may improve a depressed teenager's academic performance along with her emotional state. Most such treatments have been shown to be as effective for adolescents as they are for depressed adults (Findling, Feeny, Stansbrey, Delporto-Bedoya, & Demeter, 2004).

In some teenagers, sadly, the suicidal thoughts that often accompany depression lead to action. Surveys suggest that 17% of high school students in the United States have thought seriously about taking their own lives, and 2–8% have actually attempted suicide (CDC, 2006). A very small number of teens, about 1 in 10,000, actually succeed in killing themselves (CDC, 2007c). However, public health experts point out that many teenaged deaths, such as those that result from single-car crashes, may be counted as accidents when they are actually suicides (NCIPC, 2000).

Although depression is more common among girls, the likelihood of actually completing a suicide attempt is almost four times as high for adolescent boys as for adolescent girls. In contrast, suicide attempts are estimated to be three times more common among girls than among boys (CDC, 2007c). Girls, more often than boys, use methods that are less likely to succeed, such as self-poisoning. Factors contributing to completed suicides include the following:

- **Some triggering stressful event.** Studies of suicides suggest that this triggering event is often a disciplinary crisis with the parents or some rejection or humiliation, such as breaking up with a girlfriend or boyfriend or failing in a valued activity.
- **An altered mental state.** Such a state might be a sense of hopelessness, reduced inhibitions from alcohol consumption, or rage.
- **An opportunity.** A loaded gun in the house or a bottle of sleeping pills in the parents' medicine cabinet creates an opportunity for a teenager to carry out suicidal plans.

Physical Development and the Whole Child

The facts and figures that you have read about in this chapter illustrate the ways in which physical development is influenced by both culture and individual differences. For example, the physical changes of puberty reflect physical maturation, but they are shaped by culture and nutrition as well. Moreover, the way in which each teenager experiences puberty is influenced by cultural expectations, his peers' responses to the outward signs of puberty, and his own individual responses to the changes he observes in his body. In addition, many of the changes in the physical domain, particularly those that involve the brain, interact with cultural and individual factors to facilitate changes in the cognitive and socioemotional domains. Here is a preview of the changes in these domains that you will be reading about in Chapters 14 and 15.

Cognitive Functioning

As we noted earlier in the chapter, two major spurts occur in brain development during adolescence. These spurts involve the same kinds of neuronal branching and pruning processes that you learned about in studying infancy. They are believed to be linked to the powerful forms of thought that emerge in adolescence, particularly *hypothetico-deductive reasoning*, a kind of thinking in which a person reasons about the future consequences of a hypothetical premise. A teenager, for instance, can deduce reasonable answers to questions such as "*What if* I go to college?" and "*What if* I don't go to college?" Hypothetico-deductive thought is the cornerstone of Piaget's *formal operations* stage.

There is no doubt that the changes in the brain that occur in adolescence contribute to dramatic changes in information-processing skills as well. Recall that these changes involve the parts of the brain that we use to make plans. In the cognitive domain, the strategies that we use for managing information—for instance, outlining a textbook chapter—represent one kind of plan. As you will learn in Chapter 14, adolescents are far more proficient at such strategies than they were when they were younger.

Taken together, changes in reasoning and in information-processing skills help teens figure out how to manage their newfound capacity for sexual intimacy and reproduction. In fact, as we noted earlier, sex education programs that influence teens to delay their first sexual experience allow them the time they need to develop the cognitive skills required to make good decisions about sexual activity. Thus, influence flows in both directions between the physical and cognitive domains.

Socioemotional Functioning

Advances in the cognitive domain lead to decisive changes in adolescents' capacity for moral reasoning. Thanks to emerging cognitive skills, teens acquire the capacity to engage in *role taking*, or looking at the world from other people's perspectives, a key element in moral reasoning. In addition, formal operational thought endows teens with the capacity to think about abstractions such as justice, mercy, and other concepts that are vital to mature reasoning about moral issues.

Role taking is involved in the formation and maintenance of social relationships as well. Thus, teens establish longer lasting and more intimate friendships than younger children do. And, metaphorically speaking, walking in someone else's shoes for a bit can help teens develop their own *identity*, an understanding of what it is that distinguishes them from others. Equipped with the capacity for engaging in social relationships and a well-formed identity, teens are ready to make decisions about careers, romantic relationships, and other important aspects of their adult lives.

THE WHOLE CHILD IN FOCUS

To trace how the physical, cognitive, and socioemotional domains work together to influence Cho's and Michelle's development, see *The Whole Child in Focus* on page 474.

Looking Ahead

Again, remember that development involves interactions among the physical, cognitive, and socioemotional domains. Thus, you should read the next two chapters with all of the changes you learned about in this chapter in mind. Remember that the thinking, learning, feeling, and relating teens you will learn about in Chapters 14 and 15 are also experiencing some rather dramatic upheavals in the physical domain. Still, most emerge from adolescence with their physical and mental health intact, eager to take on the challenges of adulthood.

Test Prep Center

with mydevelopmentlab

PHYSICAL CHANGES

13.1 How do the hormones, brains, and circadian rhythms of adolescents differ from those of younger children? (pp. 386–388)

Puberty begins when the pituitary gland signals the adrenal gland to increase production of androgen. Next, the pituitary begins secreting gonadotrophic hormones. Increases in growth hormones lead to the adolescent growth spurt. The brain must develop the capacity to respond to pubertal hormones in order for them to effect these changes. There are two major brain growth spurts in adolescence: the first between ages 13 and 15 and the second between age 17 and early adulthood. Changes in hormones and in the brain lead to shifts in teens' circadian rhythms, causing them to stay up later in the evening and sleep later in the morning.

1. Complete the table.

Gland	Hormone(s)	Influence on Development
Thyroid		
Adrenal		
Testes (boys)		
Ovaries (girls)		
Pituitary		

13.2 What changes occur in the body's size and shape during adolescence? (pp. 388–390)

Puberty is accompanied by a rapid growth spurt in height and an increase in muscle mass and in fat. Boys add more muscle, and girls more fat. Growth in the heart and lungs equips teens with more stamina and endurance for physical activity than younger children have.

2. The adolescent growth spurt is the result of

____

____

13.3 What are the major milestones of sexual maturity? (pp. 390–392)

Puberty is triggered by a complex set of hormonal changes, beginning at about age 7 or 8. Very large increases in gonadotrophic hormones are central to the process. In girls, sexual maturity is achieved as early as 12 or 13. Sexual maturity is achieved later in boys, with the growth spurt occurring a year or more after the start of genital changes.

3. From the Multimedia Library within MyDevelopmentLab, watch the *Secular Trend* video and answer the following question.

Is it true that puberty is occurring at earlier ages these days? Explain your answer.

____

____

4. Classify each of the following as (A) a primary sex characteristic or (B) a secondary sex characteristic:

______(1) facial hair (boys)

______(2) maturation of the penis and scrotum

______(3) pubic hair

______(4) menarche

______(5) spermarche

______(6) breast development (girls)

13.4 What are the psychological consequences of early, "on time," and late puberty for boys and girls? (pp. 392–393)

Variations in the rate of pubertal development have some psychological effects. In general, children whose physical development occurs markedly earlier or later than they expect or desire show more negative effects than do those whose development is "on time." The former tend to think less well of themselves and to be less happy with their bodies.

5. Use the table to briefly summarize the effects of early puberty on boys and girls.

Effects on Boys	Effects on Girls

ADOLESCENT SEXUALITY

13.5 What are the patterns of adolescent sexual behavior in the United States? (pp. 393–396)

Sexual activity among teenagers has increased in recent decades in the United States. Roughly half of all U.S. teens have had sexual intercourse before they reach their last year of high school.

6. From the Multimedia Library within MyDevelopmentLab, watch the *Adolescent Sexuality: Deborah Tolman* video and answer the following question.

Why does Professor Tolman think it is important to study variables such as "sexual agency" rather than just sexual behavior itself?

____

____

13.6 Which teenaged girls are most likely to get pregnant? (pp. 396–397)

Factors that predispose girls to get pregnant include early sexual activity, being raised by a single parent, having parents with a low level of education, low socioeconomic status, and having a parent who gave birth to a child in adolescence. Factors that protect against teen pregnancy include academic achievement, high aspirations for future education and career, and good communication about sex and contraception with parents.

7. From the Multimedia Library within MyDevelopmentLab, watch the *Teen Pregnancy* video and answer the following question.

What important risk factor for pregnancy was evident in the life of the teen in the video?

____

____

13.7 What are some of the causes that have been proposed to explain homosexuality? (pp. 397–400)

Hormonal, genetic, and environmental factors have been proposed to explain homosexuality. The process of realizing one's sexual orientation is a gradual one that often isn't completed until early adulthood. Transgendered teens are those whose psychological gender differs from their biological sex. Gay, lesbian, bisexual, and transgendered adolescents must cope with peer rejection and parental anger; they have higher rates of depression and other emotional difficulties as a result.

8. From the Multimedia Library within MyDevelopmentLab, watch the *Being Gay in the U.S.* video and answer the following question.

According to the researcher, changing attitudes toward homosexuality in the United States have contributed to improvements in the ______________ of gays and lesbians.

ADOLESCENT HEALTH

13.8 What are some of the critical nutritional issues in adolescence? (pp. 400–401)

Teens need more calcium than school-aged children do, and few teens get enough. Many also consume too many simple carbohydrates and do not exercise enough to burn the added calories. The resulting increase in obesity has led to increased rates of weight-related diseases. However, many teens also diet regularly.

9. What age-related behavioral change increases the risk of calcium deficiency among teens in the United States?

____

____

13.9 What patterns of illness exist in adolescence? (pp. 401–402)

Acute illnesses decline during the teen years. Asthma attacks become more frequent as teens try to learn to manage their own medications and symptoms. Sexually active teens are vulnerable to sexually transmitted diseases.

10. The most common STD among teen girls is ______________.

13.10 How does sensation seeking affect risky behavior in adolescents? (pp. 402–403)

Adolescents have fewer acute illnesses than younger children but, because of their heightened level of sensation seeking, more injuries. In general, they show higher rates of various kinds of risky behavior, including unprotected sex, drug use, and fast driving.

11. Developmentalists hypothesize that four factors contribute to sensation seeking. These factors are

(A) ______________________________

(B) ______________________________

(C) ______________________________

(D) ______________________________

13.11 What patterns of drug, alcohol, and tobacco use have been found among adolescents in the United States? (pp. 403–405)

Illicit drug use is less common in recent cohorts of U.S. teenagers than in past cohorts; however, alcohol use is more prevalent than illicit drug use. Peer influence and shyness may contribute to drug and alcohol use; authoritative parenting can counteract negative influences. While smoking rates have dropped significantly since the mid-1990s, peers continue to play a significant role in teenage smoking.

12. Sensation seeking appears to be less important in the use of ______________ than in that of other drugs.

13. From the Multimedia Library within MyDevelopmentLab, watch the *Teen Alchoholism* video and answer the following question.

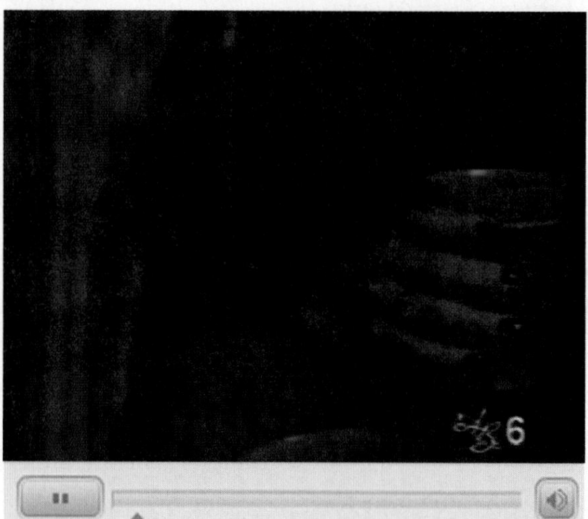

Two characteristics that are present before teens start drinking (______________ and ______________) determine whether they will develop alcoholism.

13.12 What are the leading causes of death in adolescence? (pp. 405–406)

Accidents, especially motor vehicle accidents, are the leading cause of death in adolescence among all ethnic groups other than African Americans, among whom homicide is the leading cause of death. Suicide rates are higher among Native Americans than other groups. Alcohol, speeding, and failure to use seat belts are factors in most fatal car crashes involving teen drivers.

14. What is the gender gap with regard to homicide among teens?

____

____

ATYPICAL DEVELOPMENT

13.13 What are the distinguishing features of adolescent-onset conduct disorder and delinquency? (pp. 407–409)

Adolescent-onset conduct disorder is a pattern of antisocial behaviors that is diagnosed at age 11 or later. Associated with peer influence, it often subsides by adulthood. Delinquency is a category of behavior problems that includes intentional law breaking.

15. Individuals with adolescent-onset conduct disorder are (more likely/less likely) than those with childhood-onset conduct disorder to exhibit antisocial behavior in adulthood.

16. Intentional law breaking (is/is not) an essential characteristic of adolescent-onset conduct disorder.

17. Surveys of arrest records tend to (overestimate/underestimate) adolescent delinquency rates.

13.14 What are the characteristics and causes of eating disorders? (pp. 409–411)

Eating disorders such as bulimia nervosa and anorexia nervosa are more common among teenaged girls than among teenaged boys. Some theorists hypothesize that media images of thin models and celebrities cause the body image distortions that underlie eating disorders. Others have proposed biological and socioeconomic causes. Still others emphasize the tendency of individuals with eating disorders to exhibit other kinds of distorted thoughts and comorbid psychological disorders.

18. Classify each of the following as characteristic of (A) anorexia nervosa, (B) bulimia nervosa, or (C) both.

_______(1) excessive use of laxatives

_______(2) bingeing and purging

_______(3) more common among females than males

_______(4) distorted body image

_______(5) self-starvation

_______(6) abnormally low body weight

_______(7) obsessive exercising

19. From the Multimedia Library within MyDevelopmentLab, watch the *Eating Disorders* video and answer the following question.

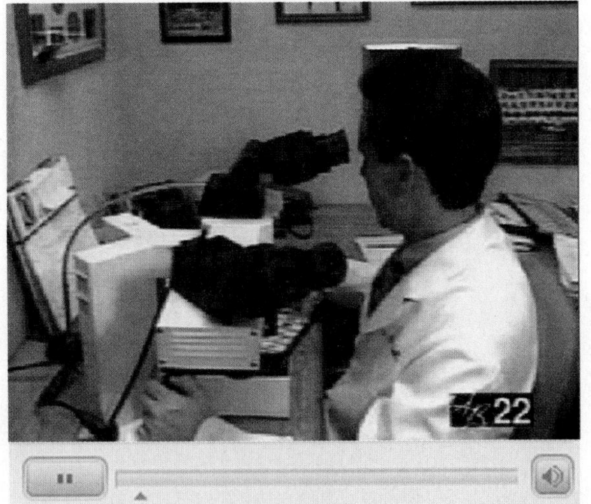

How does anorexia affect the heart?

____

____

13.15 Which adolescents are at greatest risk of depression and suicide? (pp. 411–412)

Depression and suicide are mental health problems that are common during adolescence. Both are more common among girls, although boys are more likely to succeed with a suicide attempt. Genetic factors may be involved, as children growing up with depressed parents are much more likely to develop depression than are those growing up with nondepressed parents.

20. From the Multimedia Library within MyDevelopmentLab, watch the *Depression, Reward Regions, and the Brain: Erika Forbes* video and answer the following question.

What has Professor Forbes's research revealed about teens' ability to regulate positive and negative emotions?

____

____

For answers to the questions in this chapter, turn to page 523. For a list of key terms, turn to page 532.

Succeed with PEARSON **mydevelopmentlab**

Do You Know All of the Terms in This Chapter?
Find out by using the Flashcards. Want more practice? Take additional quizzes, try simulations, and watch video to be sure you are prepared for the test!

more
to go to
DON'T LET
TEXAS GO "UP
IN SMOKE" WE WAN
TOBACCO
PREVENTION

Chapter

14

Cognitive Development in Adolescence

Learning Objectives

Piaget's Formal Operational Stage

14.1 What are the characteristics of thought in Piaget's formal operational stage?

14.2 What are some major research findings regarding Piaget's claims about the formal operational stage?

14.3 How is formal operational thinking manifested in everyday settings?

Advances in Information Processing

14.4 In what ways do executive processes improve during adolescence?

14.5 What do advances in executive processing contribute to academic learning?

Schooling

14.6 How do changes in students' goals contribute to the transition to secondary school?

14.7 What characteristics distinguish engaged students from those who are disengaged?

14.8 What variables predict the likelihood of dropping out of high school?

14.9 What are the goals of character education?

14.10 What gender and ethnic differences in science and math achievement have been found by researchers?

Entering the World of Work

14.11 What are the effects of employment on teens' lives?

14.12 What are the stages in the career decision-making process?

14.13 What factors influence adolescents' career decisions?

When people think about the teen years, the changes in the reproductive system that you learned about in Chapter 13 are probably the first developmental changes that come to mind. However, as dramatic as they are, the physical changes associated with sexual maturation are only one component of this important period. For example, if you ask an 8-year-old what she wants to be when she grows up, she is likely to say something like "a firefighter" or "a veterinarian." Ask a 15-year-old the same question, and you are likely to hear something like this: "Well, I'm thinking about several things. I know I want to go to college, but I don't know where, and I'm not sure what I want to study." Such differences reflect age-related changes in the overall quality of thought.

In this chapter, you will read about the impressive advances in thinking and memory function that happen during the teen years. You will also learn about the positive and not-so-positive aspects of the transition to secondary school. Finally, we'll look at teen employment and career development.

Piaget's Formal Operational Stage

Piaget's research led him to conclude that a new level of thinking emerges fairly rapidly in early adolescence. This new form of thought enables teens to think logically about ideas that are not tied to concrete referents in the real world. He called the stage associated with this kind of thought the **formal operational stage**. Typically, this stage is defined as the period during which adolescents develop operative schemes that enable them to reason logically

formal operational stage the fourth of Piaget's stages, during which adolescents learn to reason logically about abstract concepts

about abstract concepts. Formal operational thinking has a number of key elements and, like Piaget's earlier stages, has been both challenged and extended by later researchers.

Learning Objective 14.1

What are the characteristics of thought in Piaget's formal operational stage?

Key Elements of Formal Operational Thinking

One of the first steps in the development of formal operational thinking is for the child to extend her concrete operational reasoning abilities to objects and situations that she has not seen or experienced firsthand or that she cannot see or manipulate directly. Instead of thinking only about real things and actual occurrences, as a younger child does, a child in that formal operational stage starts to think about possible occurrences. While the preschool child plays "dress up" by putting on real clothes, the teenager thinks about options and possibilities, imagining herself in different roles—going to college or not going to college, marrying or not marrying, and so on. She can imagine future consequences of actions she might take now, so some kind of long-term planning becomes possible.

Systematic Problem Solving Another important feature of the formal operational stage is **systematic problem solving**, the ability to search methodically for an answer to a problem. To study this process, Piaget and his colleague Barbel Inhelder (Inhelder & Piaget, 1958) presented adolescents with complex tasks, mostly drawn from the physical sciences. In one of these tasks, subjects were given varying lengths of string and a set of objects of various weights that could be tied to the strings to make a swinging pendulum (see Figure 14.1). They were shown how to start the pendulum different ways—by pushing the weight with differing amounts of force and by holding the weight at different heights. The subject's task was to figure out which factor or combination of factors—length of string, weight of object, force of push, or height of push—determines the "period" of the pendulum (that is, the amount of time required for one swing). (In case you have forgotten your high school physics, the answer is that only the length of the string affects the period of the pendulum.)

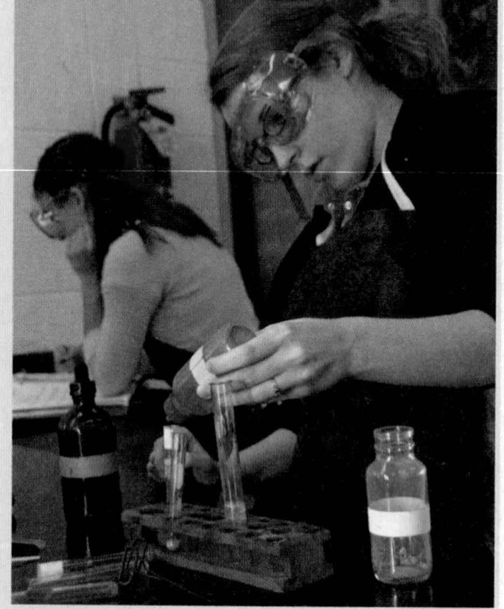

High school science classes may be one of the first places where adolescents are required to use deductive logic—a skill Piaget did not think was developed until the period of formal operations.

If you give this task to a concrete operational child, he will usually try out many different combinations of length, weight, force, and height in an inefficient way. He might try a heavy weight on a long string and then a light weight on a short string. Because he has changed both string length and weight in these two trials, there is no way he can draw a clear conclusion about either factor. In contrast, an adolescent using formal operations is likely to be more organized, attempting to vary just one of the four factors at a time. He may try a heavy object with a short string, then with a medium string, then with a long one. After that, he might try a light object with the three lengths of string. Of course, not all adolescents (or all adults, for that matter) are quite this methodical in their approach. Still, there is a very dramatic difference in the overall strategies used by 10-year-olds and 15-year-olds, and it marks the shift from concrete to formal operations.

Logic Another facet of this shift is the appearance in the adolescent's repertoire of skills in what Piaget called **hypothetico-deductive reasoning**, or the ability to derive conclusions from hypothetical premises. You may remember from Chapter 11 that Piaget suggested that a concrete operational child can use *inductive reasoning*, which involves arriving at a conclusion or a rule based on a lot of individual experiences, but performs poorly when asked to reason *deductively*. Deductive reasoning involves considering hypotheses or hypothetical premises and then deriving logical outcomes. For example, the statement "If all people are equal, then you and I must be equal" involves deductive reasoning. Although children as young as 4 or 5 can understand some deductive relationships if the premises given are factually true, both cross-sectional and longitudinal studies support Piaget's assertion that only at adolescence are young people able to understand and use basic logical relationships (Mueller, Overton, & Reene, 2001; Ward & Overton, 1990).

systematic problem solving the process of finding a solution to a problem by testing single factors

hypothetico-deductive reasoning the ability to derive conclusions from hypothetical premises

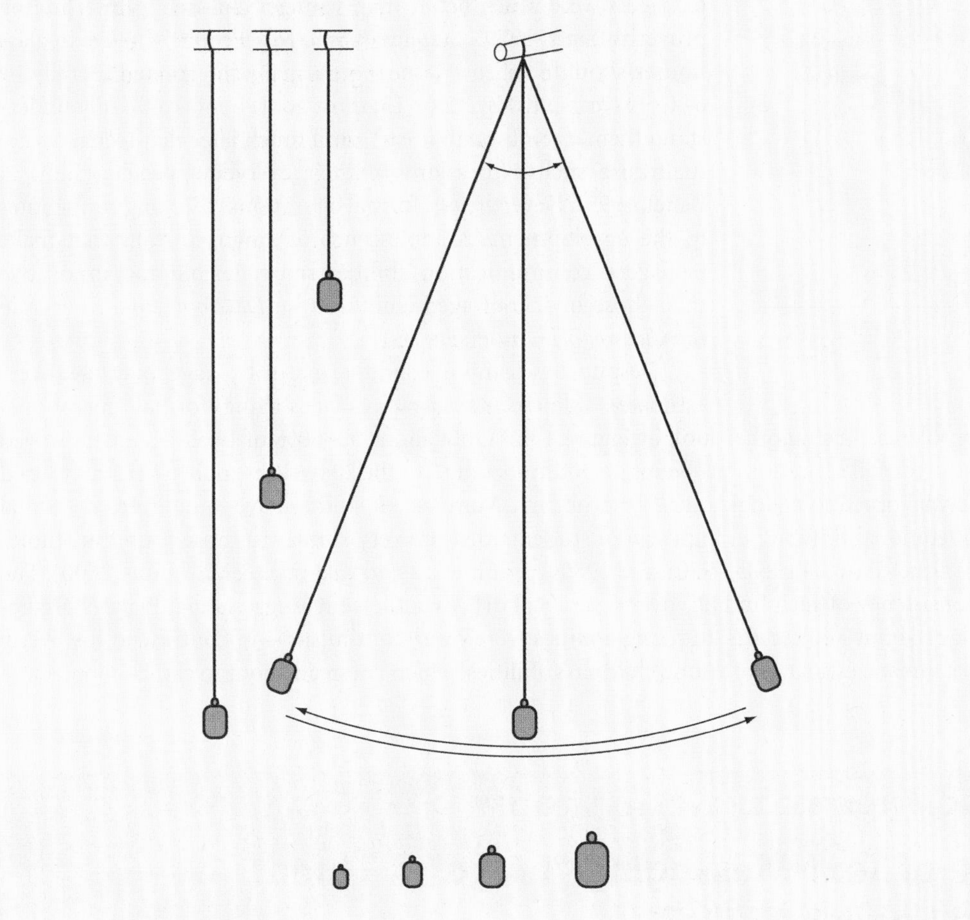

Figure 14.1 **Piaget's Pendulum Problem**

Inhelder and Piaget (1958) used these materials to study the strategies that children and teenagers used to figure out which element of a pendulum determines its period.

(*Source*: From *The Growth of Logical Thinking: From Childhood to Adolescence*, by Jean Piaget. Reprinted by permission of Basic Books, a member of Perseus Books Group.)

Direct Tests of Piaget's View

Learning Objective 14.2

What are some major research findings regarding Piaget's claims about the formal operational stage?

Developmental scientists have investigated many of Piaget's claims about formal operational reasoning. For example, in an early cross-sectional study, researchers tested 20 girls in each of four grades (sixth, eighth, tenth, and twelfth) on 10 different tasks that required one or more of what Piaget called formal operational skills (Martorano, 1977). Indeed, many of the tasks the researchers used were those Piaget himself had devised. Results on two of these tasks are graphed in Figure 14.2 on page 422. The pendulum problem is the one described earlier in this section; the balance problem requires a youngster to predict whether two different weights, hung at varying distances on each side of a scale, will balance—a task similar to the balance scale problem Siegler used (recall Figure 11.4 from page 325). To solve this problem using formal operations, the teenager must consider both weight and distance simultaneously. You can see from Figure 14.2 that older students generally did better, with the biggest improvement in scores between eighth and tenth grades (between ages 13 and 15).

Formal operational reasoning also seems to enable adolescents to understand figurative language, such as metaphors, to a greater degree. For example, one early study found that

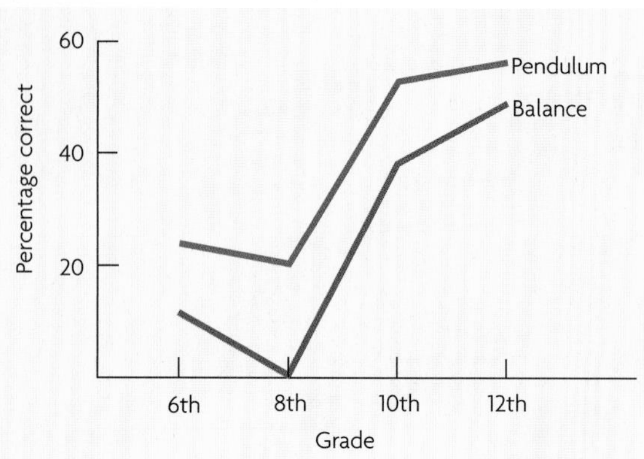

Figure 14.2
Within-Stage Development in Formal Operations

These are the results from two of the ten different formal operational tasks used in Martorano's cross-sectional study.

(*Source*: Martorano, 1977.)

teenagers were much better than younger children at interpreting proverbs (Saltz, 1979). Statements such as "People who live in glass houses shouldn't throw stones" are usually interpreted literally by 6- to 11-year-olds. By 12 or 13, most adolescents can easily understand them, even though it isn't until much later that teenagers actually use such expressions in their everyday speech (Gibbs & Beitel, 1995). Nevertheless, formal operational thinking contributes to the development in adolescence of language skills that make teenagers' communication abilities more flexible and innovative than those of school-aged children (see *Developmental Science in the Classroom*) (Andersen, 2001).

Despite these gains in cognitive maturity, Piaget may have overestimated adolescents' capacity for solving formal operational problems. Take another look at Figure 14.2: Only about 50–60% of twelfth-graders solved both formal operations problems. In addition, only 2 of the 20 twelfth-grade participants used formal operational logic on all 10 problems. More recent studies have found rates of formal operational thinking in high school students that are very similar to those found in studies conducted in the 1960s, 1970s, and 1980s (Bradmetz, 1999; Valanides & Markoulis, 2000). The consistency of such findings over several cohorts of adolescents suggests that Piaget's predictions about adolescents' thinking abilities were overly optimistic—in contrast to his overly pessimistic estimates of young children's abilities, which you read about in earlier chapters.

DEVELOPMENTAL SCIENCE IN THE CLASSROOM

Is Teenagers' Use of Text-Messaging "Lingo" a Threat to Their Standard English Skills?

Mr. Abramowitz is a ninth-grade English teacher. He has become concerned about some of the odd expressions that are showing up in his students' essays. Instead of "because," the students often write "b/c." In place of "you are," many write "u r." Although he is aware that they represent intrusions of text-messaging "lingo" into students' writing, Mr. Abramowitz always takes off points for such expressions. He worries that his students' text-messaging habits will undermine their use of standard English grammar and spelling. Are Mr. Abramowitz's concerns justified?

Psychosocial theorist Erik Erikson argued that special forms of language (*youth slang*) that are not used by older or younger individuals in the larger society help teens establish a sense of generational identity (Erikson, 1963). Generational identity, in turn, supports the development of personal identity in individual teens (more on this in Chapter 15). The current generation of youth organize their social networks around *computer-mediated communication*, which includes email, instant messaging, text messaging, and weblogs (Lenhart, Arafeh, Smith, & Macgill, 2008). Thus, the written form of contemporary youth slang reflects the conventions of computer-mediated communication (Tagliamonte & Denis, 2008).

You may be surprised to learn that the contribution of youth slang to adolescent language development may be more significant than the role it plays in identity development. *Pragmatics* is the aspect of language that includes an understanding of the influence of social context on communication. For instance, high school students do not address their teachers in the same way they do their peers. The language they use in these two situations reflects their understanding that a message must be adapted to its audience, a developmental milestone that is within the domain of pragmatics. However, research indicates that an understanding of pragmatics and applications of such understanding are clearly a "work-in-progress" during the adolescent years (Andersen, 2001). Moreover, adolescent language is more innovative than that of children or adults–that is, it includes more novel and invented expressions and words. Thus, teenagers' adoption of text lingo as a written form of youth slang involves an intersection of several developmental trends: the development of generational identity, the focus on pragmatic development that is characteristic of adolescent language development, and the tendency of teen-speak to be innovative.

It would seem that youth slang, regardless of the form it takes, should be regarded in the same way toddlers' holophrases and telegraphic speech are viewed. That is, it is an indication that the developing adolescent is engaged in a transition from a less mature to a more mature phase of language development. Youth slang is simply a tool that facilitates movement from one to the other. The good news for Mr. Abramowitz and other English teachers is that adolescents' blossoming understanding of pragmatics means that they are unlikely to forget how and when to write "because" simply because they unwittingly write "b/c" in an essay (Tagliamonte & Denis, 2008).

Questions for Reflection

1. What role did youth slang play in your own social networks in high school?
2. How would you address Mr. Abramowitz's concerns about his students' use of text-messaging lingo? What arguments might be made in favor of and against his practice of deducting points for the use of such expressions in formal essays?

In adulthood, rates of formal operational thinking increase with education. Generally, the better educated the adult participants in a study of formal operational thinking, the greater the percentage who display this kind of reasoning (Mwamwenda, 1999). Piaget's belief in the universality of formal operations may have resulted from his failure to appreciate the role of education in the development of advanced forms of thought. The current consensus among developmentalists is that all teenagers and adults without mental retardation have the capacity for formal operational thinking, but they actually acquire it in response to specific demands, such as those imposed by higher levels of education (Kuhn, 2008).

Furthermore, the fact that formal operational thinking is found more often among young people or adults in Western and other industrialized cultures can be interpreted as being due to the high levels of technology and complex lifestyles in such cultures, which demand more formal operational thought. By this argument, all neurologically healthy teenagers and adults are thought to have the capacity for formal logic, but only those whose lives demand its development will actually acquire it.

Cross-cultural research supports the assertion that most or all healthy adolescents and adults are capable of developing formal operational thinking. Several studies have shown that adolescents and adults who can solve concrete operational problems but who live in societies in which researchers have found little or no evidence of formal operations quickly grasp the logic underlying the various Piagetian tasks when experimenters explain it to them (Mishra, 1997). Following instruction, they are capable of solving a variety of such tasks.

The finding that adolescents and adults must have equilibrated concrete operational schemes before they can benefit from instruction in formal operational thinking supports Piaget's claim that the stages of cognitive development are hierarchical; that is, concrete operational schemes are the foundation upon which formal operational schemes are constructed. However, research on education, culture, and formal operational reasoning undermines the very notion of a universal "stage" of thinking in adolescence. Clearly, people whose life situations or cultures do not require formal operational thinking do not develop it. In other words, having fully developed concrete operational thinking is a *necessary but not sufficient* condition for the development of formal operational thinking. Thus, once again, we see that experience is a critical component of cognitive development. Some kind of push in the direction of formal operational thought is needed from a source outside the child himself in order for this sophisticated form of reasoning to develop, but the push will be effective only for those individuals who have equilibrated concrete operational reasoning. Thus, cross-cultural studies indicate that, in societies in which secondary schooling is universal, the appearance of formal operational thinking in adolescence is also universal (Valanides & Markoulis, 2000).

Formal Operational Thinking in Everyday Life

Learning Objective 14.3

How is formal operational thinking manifested in everyday settings?

The work of both Piaget and his critics suggests that adolescents make an impressive leap in cognitive ability when they acquire the capacity to reason deductively. Still, most teenagers require years of practice using their newfound powers of reasoning before they can apply them effectively to real-world issues.

Personal Fable Psychologist David Elkind has suggested that adolescents often deduce conclusions about themselves and others from faulty premises that are based on **adolescent egocentrism**, an adolescent's belief that her thoughts, beliefs, and feelings are unique. One component of adolescent egocentrism, Elkind said, is the **personal fable**, the belief that the events of one's life are controlled by a mentally constructed autobiography (Elkind, 1967). For example, a sexually active teenaged girl might be drawing upon such a personal fable when she says "I just don't see myself getting pregnant" in response to suggestions that she use contraception. In contrast to this inappropriately rosy view of the future, a teen who is involved in a violent street gang may say "I'll probably get shot before I make 18" when advised to leave the gang and focus on acquiring the academic skills needed to graduate from high school.

adolescent egocentrism an adolescent's belief that her or his thoughts, beliefs, and feelings are unique

personal fable the belief that the events of one's life are controlled by a mentally constructed autobiography

Research has shown that autobiographical memories, or memories of one's "life story," become more coherent and thematic during adolescence, as Elkind's theory predicts (Habermas & de Silveira, 2008). One teenager might develop her autobiography around the theme "My life was ruined when my parents divorced." For another teenager, the organizing theme might be "When I was in life science class in seventh grade, I discovered my life's calling." Such themes and the facts that teenagers focus on, and sometimes distort, to support them contribute to the development of self-concept and self-esteem during adolescence and into early adulthood.

Imaginary Audience Elkind also proposed that adolescent egocentrism drives teenagers to try out various attitudes, behaviors, and even clothing choices in front of an **imaginary audience**, an internalized set of behavioral standards usually derived from a teenager's peer group. Think about the teenaged girl who is habitually late for school because she changes clothes two or three times every day before leaving home. Each time the girl puts on a different outfit, she imagines how her peers at school will respond to it. If the imaginary audience criticizes the outfit, the girl feels she must change clothes in order to elicit a more favorable response. Similarly, a boy may spend hours in front of the mirror trimming his sideburns in an effort to achieve a look he thinks his peers will approve of.

Many developmentalists have found Elkind's imaginary audience to be helpful in explaining a variety of adolescents' everyday behaviors. However, research examining the concept has produced mixed results (Bell & Bromnick, 2003; Vartanian, 2000). Although it is true that adolescents use idealized mental models to make all kinds of decisions about their own and others' behavior, researchers have found that school-aged children sometimes exhibit similar forms of thought (Vartanian, 2001). In addition, some theorists have suggested that both the personal fable and the imaginary audience are better placed in the socioemotional domain than in the cognitive domain. Their view is based on the finding that these ways of thinking are more prominent among teens who rely on them as coping devices to deal with stressful situations such as a lack of parental support (Vartanian, 2000).

THE WHOLE CHILD IN FOCUS

What problem did Michelle and Cho solve using hypothetico-deductive reasoning? Find out on page 475.

Naïve Idealism Piaget suggested that in many adolescents, hypothetico-deductive thinking leads to an outlook he called **naïve idealism** (Piaget & Inhelder, 1969). Adolescents can use this powerful intellectual tool to think of an ideal world and to compare the real world to it. Not surprisingly, the real world often falls short of the ideal. As a result, some adolescents become so dissatisfied with the world that they resolve to change it. For many, the proposed changes are personal. For example, a teen whose parents have been divorced for years may suddenly decide she wants to live with the noncustodial parent because she expects that her life there will be better. Another may express naïve idealism by becoming involved in a political or religious organization.

Hypothetico-Deductive Thinking and Planning When adolescents first begin to use hypothetico-deductive thinking to solve problems, they often fail to consider all of the relevant variables. For instance, in one classic study, Catherine Lewis (1981) found that younger teenagers were more likely than those who were older to base solutions on incomplete formulations of problems. When Lewis asked eighth-, tenth-, and twelfth-grade students to respond to a set of dilemmas that involved a person facing a difficult decision, such as whether to have an operation to repair a facial disfigurement, 42% of the twelfth-graders, but only 11% of the eighth-graders, mentioned future possibilities in their comments. For example, in answer to the cosmetic surgery dilemma, a twelfth-grader said,

> Well, you have to look into the different things . . . that might be more important later on in your life. You should think about, will it have any effect on your future and with, maybe, the people you meet. (Lewis, 1981, p. 541)

An eighth-grader, in response to the same dilemma, said,

> The different things I would think about in getting the operation is like if the girls turn you down on a date, or the money, or the kids teasing you at school. (Lewis, 1981, p. 542)

imaginary audience an internalized set of behavioral standards usually derived from a teenager's peer group

naïve idealism the use of hypothetico-deductive thinking to conceive of an ideal world and compare the real world to it

The eighth-grader's answer focused on the here and now, on concrete things. By contrast, the twelfth-grader considered things that might happen in the future. Thus, when faced with a practical dilemma, young adolescents, most of whom can solve laboratory tasks that measure formal operational thinking, seem to use concrete rather than formal operational reasoning.

What accounts for this pattern of findings? Perhaps younger teens fail to use formal operational thinking effectively because the parts of the brain needed to connect it to everyday problems may not be sufficiently developed until the late teens. Neuroimaging studies comparing the brain activity of children, teens, and adults while they were engaged in a gambling task provide support for this hypothesis (Crone & van der Molen, 2004). However, Piaget would probably argue that young teens aren't good at applying their formal operational schemes to everyday problems because they haven't had much practice using them, a hypothesis that might also explain these neuroimaging results.

Recall that Piaget hypothesized that, when we apply a scheme to a problem, we are engaging in *assimilation*. According to his view, when teens assimilate problems to immature formal operational schemes, their failures trigger *equilibration*, the process that kicks in when schemes don't faithfully represent reality. Equilibration leads to *accommodations*, or changes in the schemes, that are put to work the next time an appropriate problem arises. Applying the accommodated scheme to a new problem initiates a new cycle of assimilation, equilibration, and accommodation. Through this back-and-forth process, teenagers' formal operational schemes become more reliable. Thus, young teens have to experiment with their formal operational schemes in the real world before they can be expected to be proficient at using them.

Advances in Information Processing

Adolescents process information faster, use processing resources more efficiently, understand their own memory processes better, and have more knowledge than do elementary school children (Kail, 1990, 1997; Kail & Ferrer, 2007). As a result, their working memories function more efficiently and they outperform school-aged children even on such simple memory tasks as recognizing faces (Gathercole, Pickering, Ambridge, & Wearing, 2004; Itier & Taylor, 2004). Moreover, they are much better at using strategies to help themselves remember things and can more easily understand and remember complex verbal information, such as that presented in a textbook.

Executive Processes

Learning Objective 14.4

In what ways do executive processes improve during adolescence?

Recall from Chapter 11 that *executive processes* are information-processing skills that allow a person to devise and carry out alternative strategies for remembering and solving problems and to maintain conscious control of her own thought processes and behavior. And you should remember from Chapter 13 that the maturation of the prefrontal cortex in early adolescence accelerates the development of these skills. As a result, teens' executive processes are far more efficient than those of younger children.

Thanks to improved executive processes, teens are better than school-aged children at attending to information that is relevant to accomplishing a goal. For example, in one classic study, 10- and 14-year-olds were instructed to do a particular activity for exactly 30 minutes (Ceci & Bronfenbrenner, 1985). Experimenters provided them with a clock and instructed them to use it to determine when they should stop. Few of the 10-year-olds periodically checked the time to see if 30 minutes had elapsed, but most of the 14-year-olds did. As a result, less than half of the younger participants succeeded in stopping on time, but more than three-quarters of the teenagers did so.

Another important skill that is facilitated by the development of executive functioning is *response inhibition*, the ability to control responses to stimuli (Luna, Garver, Urban, Lazar, & Sweeney, 2004). Response inhibition is evident in situations that call for carefully considering the impact of your answer before responding to a question, such as a job interview. Teens are less likely than school-aged children to immediately jump to a conclusion regarding the solution to a problem. Teens are likely to mentally work through the problem and be certain that they have taken into account all of the details involved in its solution before announcing that they have solved it.

As you learned in Chapter 8, metamemory skills are evident even in very young children. However, advances in metamemory are part of the overall improvement in executive processes that occurs in adolescence. In one classic study, researchers offered fifth-graders, eighth-graders, and college students the opportunity to earn money for remembering words (Cuvo, 1974). Researchers designated the words to be recalled as being worth either 1 cent or 10 cents. Fifth-graders rehearsed 1-cent and 10-cent words equally. In contrast, eighth-graders and college students put more effort into rehearsing the 10-cent words. At the end of the rehearsal period, fifth-graders recalled equal numbers of 1- and 10-cent words, while older participants remembered more 10-cent words. Further, college students outperformed eighth-graders in both rehearsal and recall. This finding suggests that the capacity to apply memory strategies selectively, based on the characteristics of a memory task, appears early in the teenaged years and continues to improve throughout adolescence.

Learning Objective 14.5

What do advances in executive processing contribute to academic learning?

Academic Learning

Adolescents' maturing executive processes enable them to approach **academic learning**, the kind of learning that is required in school, more effectively than they did in earlier years. Well-developed executive processes are critical to success in secondary school because advanced academic learning tasks often require students to process information that is removed from real-world contexts. Thus, success depends on a learner's ability to organize and mentally represent the information in a manner that will allow it to be incorporated into her existing knowledge base.

Research involving teens with attention-deficit hyperactivity disorder illustrates the key role that executive processes play in academic learning. In general, adolescents with ADHD lag behind their peers in executive process development (Biederman et al., 2008). In one study, more than one-third of teens with ADHD performed poorly on tests of such skills, compared to only 12% of teens without ADHD (Biederman et al., 2004). However, teens with ADHD whose executive-processing skills are similar to those of peers who do not have ADHD get higher scores on tests of reading and math achievement than do teens with ADHD who lack executive-processing skills.

Advances in executive processes influence academic learning in many ways, but one of the most important involves selection of appropriate strategies for learning tasks. For instance, consider the challenges associated with learning foreign language vocabulary words, a task that many high school students confront. Some students choose a simple rehearsal strategy, one that involves repeating the words and their meanings over and over. Others associate the new words with knowledge they already have stored in long-term memory, an elaborative strategy. An elaborative approach of this kind might involve associating the vocabulary words with words that students know in their own languages. Both learning strategies can be executed effectively, but the elaborative approach requires less time, is more effective, and will make the new words easier to retrieve from memory (Roediger, 2008). Thus, a student with highly developed executive-processing skills is likely to choose the elaborative strategy.

Training studies also suggest that adolescents are better able than school-aged children to recognize the value of a newly acquired learning strategy and apply it to a new learning task. In one study, researchers taught elementary school students and high school students a strategy for memorizing the manufacturing products associated with different cities (for example, Detroit/automobiles) (Pressley & Dennis-Rounds, 1980). Once participants had learned the strategy and were convinced of its effectiveness, researchers presented them with a similar task—memorizing Latin words and their English translations. Experimenters found that only the high school students made an effort to use the strategy they had just learned to ac-

academic learning the type of learning that is required in school, where information is often presented without a real-world context

complish the new memory task. The elementary school children used the new strategy only when researchers told them to and demonstrated how it could be applied to the new task. High school students' success seemed to be due to their superior ability to recognize the similarity between the two tasks—an aspect of executive functioning.

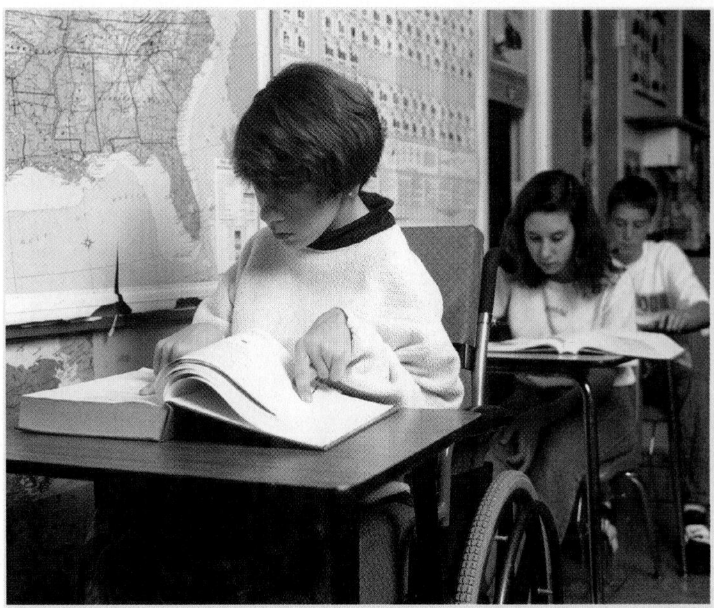
Advances in information processing lead to improvements in academic learning abilities during adolescence.

Age differences in executive processing are also evident in studies that compare school-aged children's and adolescents' processing of and memory for text. In a classic study of text processing, experimenters asked 10-, 13-, 15-, and 18-year-olds to read and summarize a 500-word passage. The researchers hypothesized that participants would use four rules in writing summaries (Brown & Day, 1983). First, they would delete trivial information. Second, their summaries would show categorical organization—that is, they would use terms such as *animals* rather than the specific names of animals mentioned in the text. Third, the summaries would use topic sentences from the text. Finally, the participants would invent topic sentences for paragraphs that didn't have them.

The results of the study suggested that participants of all ages used the first rule, because all of the summaries included more general than detailed or trivial information about the passage. However, the 10- and 13-year-olds used the other rules far less frequently than did the 15- and 18-year-olds. There were also interesting differences between the two older groups. Fifteen-year-olds used categories about as frequently as 18-year-olds did, but the oldest group used topic sentences far more effectively. This pattern of age differences suggests that the ability to summarize a text improves gradually during the second half of adolescence.

Studies of text outlining reveal a similar pattern (Drum, 1985). Both elementary and high school students know that an outline should include the main ideas of a passage along with supporting details. However, research suggests that 17-year-olds generate much more complete outlines than 14-year-olds do. Moreover, 11-year-olds' outlines usually include only a few of the main ideas of a passage and provide few or no supporting details for those main ideas.

Schooling

Do you remember your first day of secondary school? How many times did you get lost looking for a classroom? Did you carry all your books with you to avoid having to go to your locker between periods? Perhaps you forgot the combination to your locker. Such are the experiences of children who must transition from the relative simplicity of elementary school to the intimidating complexity of secondary school. Eventually, most students adjust to the new setting. Yet, as you will see, there are both benefits and costs associated with such transitions.

Transition to Secondary School

Learning Objective 14.6

How do changes in students' goals contribute to the transition to secondary school?

In many places in the world, including some in North America, children attend a lower school for 8 years before moving on to a high school for 4 years. Such an arrangement is known as an 8-4 system. Because students typically show achievement declines after entering high school, educators have developed two models that include a transitional school—a junior high school, middle school, or intermediate school—between elementary and high school. The junior high system typically includes 6 years of elementary

Some developmentalists argue that the transition to middle school or junior high school is difficult for many young adolescents because they are not developmentally ready for the secondary school model. Children who attend middle and junior high schools where close relationships between teachers and students are encouraged, as they are in elementary school, show smaller declines in achievement and self-esteem.

school followed by 3 years of junior high and 3 years of high school. The middle school model includes 5 years of elementary school, 3 years of middle school, and 4 years of high school.

Neither the junior high nor the middle school approach seems to have solved the transition problem. Students show losses in achievement and in self-esteem across both transition points in the 6-3-3 and 5-3-4 systems. Further, students in both of these systems show greater losses during the transition to high school than do those in 8-4 systems (Alspaugh, 1998; Anderman, 1998). Consequently, educators and developmentalists are currently searching for explanations and practical remedies.

Middle School One potential explanation for transition-related achievement declines associated with the transition to middle school is that students' academic goals change once they leave elementary school. Researchers classify such goals into two very broad categories: *task goals* and *ability goals*. **Task goals** are goals based on personal standards and a desire to become more competent at something. For example, a runner who wants to improve her time in the 100-meter dash has a task goal. An **ability goal** is one that defines success in competitive terms and is based on a desire to be better than another person at something. For example, a runner who wants to be the fastest person on his team has an ability goal. Longitudinal research shows that most fifth-graders have task goals, but by the time they have been in sixth grade a few months, most children have shifted to ability goals (Anderman & Anderman, 1999; Anderman & Midgley, 1997).

A student's goal influences his behavior in important ways. Task goals are associated with a greater sense of personal control and more positive attitudes about school (Anderman, 1999; Gutman, 2006). A student who takes a task-goal approach to school work tends to set increasingly higher standards for his performance and attributes success and failure to his own efforts. For example, a task goal–oriented student is likely to say he received an A in a class because he worked hard or because he wanted to improve his performance.

In contrast, students with ability goals adopt relative standards—that is, they view performance on a given academic task as good as long as it is better than someone else's. Consequently, such students are more strongly influenced by the group with which they identify than by internal standards that define good and bad academic performance. Ability goal–oriented students are also more likely than others to attribute success and failure to forces outside themselves. For example, such a student might say he got an A in a class because it was easy or because the teacher liked him. Moreover, such students are likely to have a negative view of school (Anderman, 1999).

Because middle schools emphasize ability grouping more than elementary schools do, it is likely that many middle school students change their beliefs about their own abilities during these years (Anderman, Maehr, & Midgley, 1999; Roeser & Eccles, 1998). Thus, high-achieving elementary school students who maintain their levels of achievement across the sixth-grade transition gain confidence in their abilities (Pajares & Graham, 1999). In contrast, the changes in self-concept experienced by high achievers who fail to meet expectations in middle school, as well as average and low-achieving students, do probably lead to self-esteem losses for many of them. Once an ability goal–oriented student adopts the belief that her academic ability is less than adequate, she is likely to stop putting effort into school work. In addition, such students are likely to use ineffective cognitive strategies when attempting to learn academic material (Young, 1997). Consequently, achievement suffers along with self-esteem.

Another factor that influences young adolescents' adjustment to secondary school is their perception of the school's climate. Researchers have found that many middle school stu-

task goals goals based on a desire for self-improvement

ability goals goals based on a desire to be superior to others

dents perceive their schools to be impersonal and unsupportive (Barber & Olsen, 2004). To address this perception, some schools provide students with an adult mentor, either a teacher or a volunteer from the community, to whom they are assigned for a transitional period or throughout the middle school years. In practice, the characteristics of mentoring programs vary widely (Galassi, Gulledge, & Cox, 1997). Some consist simply of giving sixth-graders the name of a teacher they can consult if they encounter any problems. At the other end of the spectrum, some mentoring programs assign each student to a teacher, who is supposed to monitor several students' daily assignment sheets, homework completion, grades, and even school supplies. The homeroom teacher also maintains communication with each child's parents regarding these issues. If a student isn't doing his math homework or doesn't have any pencils, it is the homeroom teacher's responsibility to tell his parents about the problem. The parents are then responsible for follow-up.

Research suggests that programs of this level of intensity are highly successful in improving middle school students' grades (Callahan, Rademacher, & Hildreth, 1998). Their success probably lies in the fact that the homeroom teacher functions very much like an elementary school teacher. This is significant because, despite cultural expectations to the contrary, a sixth-grader is developmentally a child, whether she is in an elementary school or a middle school. Consequently, it isn't surprising that a strategy that makes a middle school more like an elementary school—a school designed for children, not adolescents—is successful. In fact, some observers think that middle schools have failed to meet their goal of easing the transition to high school because they have simply duplicated high school organization and imposed it on students who are not developmentally ready, rather than providing them with a real transition.

One approach aimed at making middle schools truly transitional involves organizing students and teachers into teams. For example, in some schools, sixth, seventh, and eighth grades are physically separated in different wings of the school building. In such schools, each grade is a sort of school-within-a-school. Teachers in each grade-level team work together to balance the demands of different subject-area classes, assess problems of individual students, and devise parent involvement strategies. Preliminary research suggests that the team approach helps to minimize the negative effects of the middle school transition. As a result, it has become the recommended approach of the National Middle School Association in the United States (NMSA, 2004).

High School Regardless of the type of school they attended previously, the early days of high school set a general pattern of success or failure for teenagers that continues into their adult years. Numerous studies have shown that teenagers who fail one or more courses in the first year of high school are far less likely than their peers to graduate (Neild & Balfanz, 2006; Roderick & Camburn, 1999). In fact, failing ninth-grade algebra is the single most powerful predictor of dropping out of high school that researchers have identified (Balfanz & Legters, 2004). Researchers say that all too many students enter high school with weak reading skills and other deficits that make it nearly impossible for them to succeed. As a result, many fail several of their freshman classes, thereby decreasing the chances that they will graduate on time and leading them to resign themselves to leaving school as soon as their parents and/or state laws will allow them to do so.

In the United States, the pattern of ninth-grade failure coupled with abandonment of the goal of graduating from high school is especially pronounced among African American and Hispanic American students in the nation's largest cities and White students in rural areas in southern and southwestern states (Balfanz & Legters, 2004). Researchers say that the best way to reverse this pattern is to retain at-risk students in middle schools or to change the demands of the first year of high school so that at-risk students can receive the additional time and instructional support they need to develop the skills required to succeed in high school.

To address first-year high school students' need for additional academic support, some school systems have created *ninth-grade academies*, self-contained schools that are devoted entirely to ninth grade. One common feature of ninth-grade academies is a schedule that allocates extra time for reading and math classes (Morrison & Legters, 2001). By providing larger blocks of time for these courses, educators hope to increase student success rates.

Research indicates that at-risk students who attend ninth-grade academies are absent less often and require fewer disciplinary actions than do their peers at traditional schools (Philadelphia Education Fund, 2003). They also get higher scores on standardized tests and are more likely to pass freshman classes (Peasant, 2007). Moreover, longitudinal studies show that at-risk students who attend ninth-grade academies are twice as likely as peers who go to traditional schools to still be in school 2 years later (Philadelphia Education Fund, 2003).

For students who enter high school with the necessary academic skills, the transition is often a positive experience. Some psychologists point out that participation in activities usually offered only in high school allows students opportunities to develop psychological attributes that can't be acquired elsewhere. To demonstrate the point, a number of research studies had high school students use pagers to signal researchers whenever they were experiencing high levels of intrinsic motivation along with intense mental effort (Larson, 2000). The results showed that students experienced both states in elective classes and during extracurricular activities far more often than in academic classes (Larson, 2000). In other words, a student engaged in an art project or sports practice is more likely to experience this particular combination of states than is a student in a history class. Consequently, educators may be able to ease the transition to high school for many students by offering a wide variety of elective and extracurricular activities and encouraging students to participate.

Learning Objective 14.7

What characteristics distinguish engaged students from those who are disengaged?

Student Engagement in Secondary Schools

Some secondary school students benefit little from extracurricular and elective activities because they choose not to be involved in them. Research shows that secondary school students fall into two distinct groups. **Engaged students** not only enjoy school but also are involved in all aspects of it, participating in extracurricular and elective activities, doing their homework, and so on. **Disengaged students** do not enjoy school, particularly the academic part of the process, and do not participate in school activities. Steinberg (1996) argues that a child's level of engagement or disengagement is critical for the child and her future.

Family interactive style predicts academic achievement in high school. Adolescents whose parents display authoritative parenting are more likely than those with authoritarian or permissive parents to achieve academic success in high school.

Engaged Students In comparison to their disengaged peers, engaged students spend more time on homework, cut class less often, pay more attention in class, and don't cheat as often. They also tend to spend their time with other students who are engaged (or who at least do not ridicule them for making some effort in school) and they are likely to have authoritative parents who expect them to get good grades and are involved with them and with the school (Brooks-Gunn, Guo, & Furstenberg, 1993; Steinberg, 1996).

You might argue that all the relationships just described exist simply because brighter kids have an easier time with school work, and there is some truth to that. In fact, one of the best predictors of a student's academic performance in high school is his or her IQ score (Jimerson, Egeland, Sroufe, & Carlson, 2001). Bright students also have the advantage of many years of successful schooling. Such academic success fosters a greater sense of self-efficacy in these intellectually more able students, in turn increasing their sense of involvement with schooling. Yet Steinberg is also right that the sense of involvement has many other ingredients, which jointly have a strong impact on a teenager's effort and success in school.

Effort and success, in turn, predict more years of subsequent education, a link that exists among children reared in poverty as well as among the middle class (Barrett & Depinet, 1991). Those extra years of education then have a powerful effect on the career path a young person enters in early adulthood, influencing lifetime income and job success (Featherman,

engaged students secondary school students who enjoy school and are involved in all aspects of it

disengaged students secondary school students who do not enjoy school and do not participate in school activities

1980; Rosenbaum, 1984). These are not trivial effects, which is why Steinberg's conclusions about the typical level of school engagement among U.S. high school students are so disturbing.

Disengaged Students Steinberg (1996) paints quite a gloomy picture of the typical level of engagement of U.S. high school students, based on interviews with and observations of over 20,000 teenagers and their families. A high proportion don't take school or their studies seriously. Outside of class, they don't often participate in activities that reinforce what they are learning in school (such as doing their homework). The peer culture devalues academic success and scorns those students who try to do well in school. Some of the specifics that support these conclusions are summarized in Table 14.1. In some cases, disengagement has a psychological basis (see *Developmental Science in the Clinic*).

A great many parents in the United States are just as disengaged from their teenager's schooling as the children themselves are. More than half of the high school students in Steinberg's large study

Table 14.1 Steinberg's Evidence for Widespread Disengagement from Schooling Among U.S. Teenagers

- Over one-third of students said they get through the school day mostly by "goofing off with their friends."
- Two-thirds of students said they had cheated on a school test in the past year; 9 out of 10 said they had copied homework from someone else.
- The average U.S. high school student spends only about 4 hours a week on homework, whereas students in other industrialized countries spend 4 hours a *day*.
- Half the students said they did not do the homework they were assigned.
- Two-thirds of U.S. high school students hold paying jobs; half work 15 or more hours a week.
- Only about 20% of students said their friends think it is important to get good grades in school.
- Nearly 20% of students said they do not try as hard as they can in school because they are afraid of what their friends might think.

Source: Steinberg, 1996.

DEVELOPMENTAL SCIENCE IN THE CLINIC

Locus of Control

Julia's mother was at her wits' end. Her daughter, who was in the seventh grade, was failing every subject and claimed to have no idea why she was performing so poorly in school. "The teacher hates me," the girl answered when her mother asked why she was failing math.

"What about English?" her mother asked.

"English is just too hard for me. You know how I hate to read, and they expect us to read a whole book in 2 weeks in that class," Julia said. When Julia's mother suggested that she put forth more effort, the girl replied, "What good would it do? No matter how hard I try, as long as the teachers are against me and the classes are too hard, I don't have a chance."

Eager for a solution and worried about her daughter's self-esteem, Julia's mother turned to a professional counselor for help.

After interviewing Julia, the counselor concluded that the seventh-grader's self-esteem was in good shape with regard to tasks outside of school. The problem was that the theory Julia had developed to explain both her successful and her unsuccessful experiences in school was interfering with her ability to invest effort in her school work. Psychologists refer to such theories as a person's *locus of control*. A person who has an internal locus of control sees herself as capable of exerting some control over what happens to her (Rotter, 1990). As a result, such individuals study and complete most of their school work, because they recognize that their grades are the result of their own efforts. One who has an external locus of control believes that other people or uncontrollable forces such as luck determine the future. These individuals tend to believe that they have little control over outcomes, so it is useless to try to change them.

As you can probably guess, the counselor concluded that Julia had an external locus of control and developed a plan for helping her learn to make more realistic attributions, an important step toward changing her academic behavior. In discussing Julia's problems with her mother, the counselor explained that such students aren't simply being lazy or trying to avoid responsibility. Instead, their behavior is based on their beliefs about how academic achievement happens. Furthermore, they behave in ways that facilitate the confirmation of these beliefs. Thus, with every failing grade, Julia is likely to think, "I knew that teacher hated me." And with each repetition, the belief becomes a bit stronger.

The goal of counseling such students is to challenge their perceptions and to reinforce them for learning to attribute the academic outcomes they experience to their own efforts. In one study, researchers found that middle school students whose locus of control was modified through this kind of counseling maintained the effects of the counseling some 13 years later (Guangyuan, 2005). Clearly, if the attributions of students such as Julia can be changed, the counselor (or parent or teacher) who succeeds in doing so is likely to influence not only their immediate achievement but their future success as well.

Questions for Reflection

1. In your opinion, what would be a good strategy for challenging Julia's belief that she is failing math because her math teacher hates her?
2. How would you deal with Julia's belief that reading a book in 2 weeks is an unreasonable expectation?

said they could bring home grades of C or worse without their parents' getting upset; a third said their parents didn't know what they were studying at school; only about a fifth of the parents in this study consistently attended school programs. To use the terminology presented in Chapter 9, parents of disengaged students are most likely to be classed as permissive or authoritarian; parents of engaged students are most likely to be rated as authoritative (Steinberg, 1996).

Parents are not the whole story. Peer group norms and values play an equally important role. In one survey, high school students were asked why they attended school. The option "because my friends do" (68% agreeing) ran a close second to the most frequently chosen answer: "I want to graduate and go to college" (73% agreeing) (Yazzie-Mintz, 2007). Peer influences overlap with ethnicity. For instance, Steinberg found that Asian American students were more likely than African American or Hispanic American students to have friends who valued good grades and effort in school (Steinberg, 1996). African American and Hispanic American peer groups were much more likely to devalue academic effort or achievement. In these two groups, parental involvement with school or emphasis on the importance of school seemed to be undermined by peer norms. To work hard, to try to achieve, was thought of as "acting White" by many teens in these groups and was thus discouraged (Steinberg, 1996).

This problem is not unique to African American or Hispanic American students. White teens in the United States today also generally believe that high school students should not seem to be working hard—they should get by, but not show off in the process. To put it another way, the widespread peer norm or goal is the appearance of uninvolvement. Not surprisingly, many teenagers go beyond appearance and become genuinely uninvolved with their schooling, with long-term negative consequences for adult life.

School Safety Finally, the degree to which teens feel safe in secondary school strongly influences engagement. *Sexual harassment*, unwelcomed sexual advances and/or derogatory or suggestive comments of a sexual nature, is one source of anxiety for many students. In one survey, 35% of high school students reported having been sexually harassed at least once in the past 12 months (Gruber & Fineran, 2008)

Many students also worry about being victimized by aggressive peers. In the United States, surveys show that many students do not perceive their schools to be safe environments (Dinkes, Cataldi, Lin-Kelly, & Snyder, 2007). Victimization rates indicate that they have good reason to feel afraid. Respondents to one government survey involving thousands of students (Dinkes et al., 2007) reported the following occurrences over the 12 months preceding the study:

- 86% of secondary schools experienced at least one violent crime on school property during school hours.
- 43% of males and 28% of females were in at least one physical fight at or near school.
- 28% of students were bullied at least once.
- 10% of males and 3% of females brought a weapon to school at least once.
- 9% of teachers were verbally abused by a student.
- 8% of students were threatened with a weapon.
- 6% of students stayed home from school or avoided participating in a school activity because they feared being attacked.
- 3% of students reported having been the victim of a nonviolent crime (e.g., theft) in the preceding 6 months.

Experts recommend several strategies for preventing violence and other forms of victimization at school (Osher, Dwyer, & Jackson, 2004). Recall that the goal of *primary* prevention is to prevent a problem from occurring. *Secondary* prevention is designed to stop a problem before it gets out of hand, and *tertiary* prevention is implemented in situations in which some damage or harm has already occurred. With regard to violence and victimization in schools, primary prevention strategies include maintenance of high academic expectations for all students, the implementation of curricula designed to help students learn to manage conflicts with peers in socially acceptable ways, and a set of behavioral guidelines for students that make it clear that violence, bullying, and sexual harassment will not be tolerated. Secondary prevention strategies include a consistent system of discipline in which violations of school rules are dealt with in a timely and effective manner. Guidelines for removing students who repeatedly violate school rules and/or cause serious harm to others represent tertiary prevention.

Dropping Out of High School

Learning Objective 14.8

What variables predict the likelihood of dropping out of high school?

At the extreme end of the disengagement continuum are students who leave school altogether. Dropping out of high school, like academic success, results from a complex interaction of academic and social variables (Garnier, Stein, & Jacobs, 1997). Determining drop-out rates is difficult, because students are not tracked throughout their educational careers. Official estimates represent the percentage of students who are of high school age but not enrolled in school. Using that criterion, the proportion of U.S. students who drop out has declined steadily over the past few decades. About 90% of high school students in the United States receive a diploma (NCES, 2008). Hispanic Americans have the highest drop-out rate at 22%, compared with 11% for African Americans and 6% for Whites (NCES, 2008). Just under 4% of Asian Americans leave high school, and about 15% of Native American students do so (Freeman & Fox, 2005).

The manner in which drop-out estimates are calculated does not tell us how many students eventually go back to school and receive a diploma, obtain a *general educational development certificate* (GED), or complete high school in the military. Moreover, it's difficult to gauge the accuracy of the statistics. In government reports, "drop-outs" is simply a population category that includes all students of secondary school age who are not enrolled in school (Fry, 2003). Thus, it is likely that some homeschooled students and students who attend alternative programs outside the public and private school enrollment reporting systems are erroneously counted as drop-outs. Conversely, comparisons of ninth-grade public school enrollment figures for a given year to graduation rates 4 to 5 years later suggest that drop-out statistics greatly underestimate the true prevalence of leaving school prior to graduation. In some schools, such comparisons suggest that half of the students enrolled in ninth grade failed to graduate (Balfanz & Legters, 2004).

In addition, drop-out population estimates for Hispanic American adolescents include high school–aged immigrants whose purpose for coming to the United States was to find work rather than to go to school. Many of these teens have never been enrolled in U.S. schools, yet they are counted as drop-outs (Fry, 2003). When the statistics for immigrants are factored out, researchers find that only 12% of Hispanic teens who were born in the United States or who have lived in the country since they were school-aged children drop out of high school (NCES, 2008).

Ethnic differences in high school drop-out rates are associated with differences in income group. Children growing up in low-income families are considerably more likely to drop out of high school than are those from more economically advantaged families. For instance, in 2006, the drop-out rate for students whose families were in the lowest income quartile (the bottom 25%) in the United States was 11%, while that for students whose household income placed them in the top quartile was only 2% (NCES, 2008). Because Native American, Hispanic American, and African American teenagers in the United States are more likely to come from poor families, they are also more likely to drop out of school. The key factors linking income to high school completion appear to be the level of parental education, parental aspirations for children's education attainment, and children's own expectations for the future (Freeman & Fox, 2005).

Variations in teen pregnancy and parenting also help explain ethnic group differences in drop-out rates. Except in the case of Native Americans, teen birth rates across groups parallel drop-out rates. The birth rates are 8% for Hispanic Americans (meaning 8 out of every 100 Hispanic American teens give birth to a child each year), 6% for African Americans, 5% for Native Americans, 4% for Whites, and 2% for Asian Americans (Hamilton, Martin, & Ventura, 2007). Again, because school officials do not track individual students, we don't really know how many pregnant and parenting teens drop out or how many of those who drop out return to school and graduate. Moreover, it's difficult to know whether teen pregnancy is a cause or a consequence of dropping out.

Across all ethnic and income groups, young adults (16- to 25-year-olds) who dropped out of high school report that their primary reason for doing so was that their classes were uninteresting (Bridgeland, DiIulio, & Morison, 2006). Dropouts also say that the feeling that they had fallen behind and could not catch up contributed to their decision to leave school. They report that peers who were also planning to drop out influenced them, and that lack of parental monitoring played a role. Nearly three-quarters say that they regret the decision to quit school.

Peer influence is also a factor in dropping out. Teens who quit school are likely to have friends who have dropped out or who are contemplating leaving school (Staff & Kreager, 2007). Those from low-income families who associate with groups that engage in violent behavior appear to be more vulnerable to peer influence than teens in other groups. Family variables are also linked to dropping out. For example, children whose families move a lot when they are in elementary or middle school are at increased risk for dropping out of high school (Worrell, 1997).

It is important to remember, however, that the majority of students across all ethnic and income groups stay in school. Those who don't, again regardless of group, share several risk factors. Longitudinal studies show that students who have a history of academic failure, a pattern of aggressive behavior, and poor decisions about risky behavior are most likely to drop out (Cairns & Cairns, 1994; Farmer et al., 2003; Garnier et al., 1997; Jimerson, 1999). With respect to risky behavior, decisions about sexual intercourse seem to be especially critical. For girls, giving birth and getting married are strongly linked to dropping out. Another risky behavior, adolescent drug use, is also a strong predictor of dropping out (Garnier et al., 1997). In fact, alcohol and drug use better predict a high school student's grades than do the student's grades in elementary or middle school. Consequently, decisions about such risky behaviors seem to be one factor that can cause a teen to deviate from a previously positive developmental pathway.

One group of researchers has explored the possibility that, by taking into consideration several relevant factors, a general profile of high school students who are potential drop-outs can be identified. Their research has led to identification of the type of high school student who is likely to drop out: one who is quiet, disengaged, low achieving, and poorly adjusted (Janosz, Le Blanc, Boulerice, & Tremblay, 2000). Many such students display a pattern of chronic class cutting prior to dropping out (Fallis & Opotow, 2003). Thus, students who exhibit this pattern may be targeted for drop-out prevention programs.

Whatever its cause, dropping out of high school is associated with a number of long-term consequences. For instance, unemployment is higher among adults who dropped out of high school than among those who graduated, and drop-outs who do manage to find jobs earn lower wages than peers who graduate. For example, in 2006, the unemployment rate for adults who dropped out of high school was 7.1%, but the rate was just 4.4% for those with a high school diploma (U.S. Bureau of Labor Statistics, 2007). In addition, male high school drop-outs' median income was $22,151, while the median income for male high school graduates was $31,715 (Webster & Bishaw, 2007). For females, the gap was similar: $13,255 versus $20,650.

Adults who dropped out of high school are also more likely to experience depression (Hagan, 1997). Furthermore, research suggests that staying in school may be an important protective factor for boys who have poor self-regulation skills. When these poor self-regulators stay in school, they appear to be less likely than poor self-regulators who drop out to become involved in criminal activity in early adulthood (Henry et al., 1999).

Character Education

Learning Objective 14.9

What are the goals of character education?

In response to increases in the frequency of heinous crimes, bullying in schools, and generally rude behavior in everyday life, some educators argue that schools should include a **character education** curriculum, a series of lessons designed to teach students culturally acceptable ways of behaving. Critics, however, argue that emphasizing one group's notion of good character over another's might be offensive to some. Advocates of character education counter that there is a common set of values to which all human beings subscribe and that these values should form the core of a formal character education curriculum.

There is some evidence to support the position taken by those who advocate universal character education. Consider, for example, the case of the Kew Primary School in Invercargill, New Zealand (Heenan, 2005). Administrators and teachers at the school were frustrated by their limited success in using behavioral methods such as reinforcement and punishment to control troublesome student behaviors such as bullying. They sought an alternative that would help each student construct an internal sense of right and wrong, in the hope that this sense, which they called character, would lessen the need for behavioral control measures. A parent survey was one part of the process they used to develop a character education curriculum, because they wanted to be sure that the program included standards and values to which all of their students' families subscribed.

The results of the survey were astonishing, especially given the diverse nature of the school's population. Officials found that 95% of parents approved of their efforts to incorporate character education into the school's academic curriculum. Moreover, values such as truthfulness, honesty, and willingness to accept responsibility for one's actions were endorsed by 100% of parents. Endorsement of values such as respect for others' rights and property, politeness, courtesy, and kindness approached unanimity as well.

Such findings have led a number of educators to develop character education curricula that can be used by any school, regardless of the cultural make-up of its student body. One curriculum has been authored by developmental psychologist Thomas Lickona of the State University of New York at Cortland. Lickona's approach to character education is based on the assumption that 10 essential virtues comprise character (Lickona, 2004). The 10 virtues are wisdom, justice, fortitude, self-control, love, a positive attitude, hard work, integrity, gratitude, and humility. Lickona claims that, although maturational and developmental processes play important roles in the development of character, for the most part it must be deliberately and systematically transmitted to children by caring adults. His research has shown that when character education is implemented in a school, the frequency of undesirable behaviors declines. And, as an added bonus, academic achievement tends to go up.

Gender, Ethnicity, and Achievement in Science and Math

Learning Objective 14.10

What gender and ethnic differences in science and math achievement have been found by researchers?

Before leaving the topic of schooling in adolescence, we must consider differences between males and females in science and math achievement as well as differences found across ethnic groups.

Gender Differences Girls seem to be at particular risk for achievement losses after the transition to high school. For example, eighth-grade boys outscore girls in science achievement, and the gap widens substantially by the time adolescents reach tenth grade (Burkham, Lee, & Smerdon, 1997). Moreover, research suggests that the gender gap is widest among the most intellectually talented students. Nevertheless, girls possess characteristics that educators can build upon to improve their achievement in science classes. For one thing, associating with same-sex peers who are interested in and perform well in science classes influences girls' achievement in this domain (Riegle-Crumb, Farkas, & Muller, 2006). Thus, offering girls the

character education a curriculum that teaches students culturally acceptable ways of behaving

opportunity to participate in science clubs and learning communities (small groups of students who take courses together) may be an effective means of increasing their science achievement (Reid & Roberts, 2006). Furthermore, girls' choices of courses during middle school are more influenced by parental encouragement than are those of boys (Simpkins, Davis-Kean, & Eccles, 2006). Thus, parental involvement may be the key to enhancing middle school girls' interest in science and motivating them to take more advanced science courses in high school.

Clearly, cultural attitudes also influence girls' science achievement. For example, girls' and their parents' perceptions of science as a suitable career for females strongly predict girls' success in science courses (Jacobs, Finken, Griffin, & Wright, 1998). Even girls who are very high achievers in high school science have less confidence in their ability to succeed in college science courses and are, thus, less likely to pursue science majors in college (Catsambis, 1995; Guzzetti & Williams, 1996).

The gender gap in mathematics achievement widens in high school as well, although sex differences are smaller today than they were in the 1960s (Hyde, Fennema, & Lamon, 1990). Research suggests that variations in boys' and girls' approaches to problem solving may be responsible for sex differences in high school. Boys seem to be better at identifying effective strategies for solving the types of problems found on standardized math tests (Gallagher et al., 2000). Developmentalists still don't know how boys acquire this advantage, but research suggesting that important sex differences in the brain emerge in early adolescence indicates that the advantage may have a neurological basis. In addition, the fact that boys spend more time playing video games than girls do may explain some of this difference. This hypothesis is supported by research showing that playing such games improves females' scores on tests of spatial perception, an important factor in mathematics achievement (Terlecki & Newcombe, 2005) (see *Developmental Science at Home*).

DEVELOPMENTAL SCIENCE AT HOME

Girls and Video Games

Lexi and Alicia's parents are proud of their twin daughters' high scores on math achievement tests. However, they have read that girls' math scores often go down in adolescence. In an effort to support the continued development of the girls' math skills, their parents have done some research on math achievement and have learned that playing video games can help girls develop spatial cognitive skills. Consequently, they took the girls to an electronics store and offered to buy them whichever game system they preferred. But Lexi's and Alicia's responses to the offer were disappointing from their parents' perspective. When it was clear that the girls had no interest in playing video games, their parents left the store and embarked upon a search for another way to encourage the development of their daughters' math abilities.

Responses like those of Lexi and Alicia to their parents' offer to purchase video games for them are not uncommon among adolescent girls. Research from the newly emerging field of media psychology provides some possible clues as to why. Studies suggest that girls have little interest in video games because of the ways in which the games are advertised and designed.

The nonverbal cues that appear in advertisements for video games, like those for other products, are designed to foster rapid for-me/not-for-me decisions by consumers with regard to the products being advertised (Chandler, 2002). Thus, advertisements take advantage of obvious categories such as gender, race, and age. Dark or primary colors, odd camera angles, hard-driving electric guitars, deep voices, and rapidly moving, sharply focused images signal viewers that a product is intended for males (Griffiths & Chandler, 1998). By contrast, pastel colors, conventional angles, catchy jingles, high voices, and slowly moving, slightly blurry images are used to capture females' attention.

By the time children reach the age of 6 or 7, most are quite skilled at classifying advertisements by gender on the basis of these cues (Pike & Jennings, 2005). Moreover, they express more interest in products that they perceive to be gender-congruent than in those they believe to be intended for the opposite gender. These nonverbal cues are so powerful that children will say that a toy advertised with "male" nonverbal cues is for boys even if a girl is shown playing with it in a commercial.

Consequently, the ways in which video game systems and the games themselves are advertised send girls a nonverbal "this-is-not-for-you" message. And some studies show that girls, on average, are more responsive to subtle gender messages than boys are (Usher & Pajares, 2006). Girls who conform to the gender-based expectations implied by these nonverbal messages may be missing out on opportunities to develop their spatial abilities. The good news is, though, that girls also appear to be more responsive than boys to persuasive messages that tell them "you can do it." Such research suggests that the best way for Lexi and Alicia's parents to ensure that their daughters continue to score well on tests of math achievement is to provide them with plenty of verbal encouragement.

Questions for Reflection

1. In your opinion, what kinds of games and game systems would be more appealing to girls than to boys?
2. To what extent, if any, do you think the imaginary audience contributes to teenaged girls' lack of interest in video games?

Like their scientifically talented peers, mathematically gifted high school girls have considerably less confidence in their abilities than their male counterparts do, even though the girls typically get better grades (Guzzetti & Williams, 1996; Marsh & Yeung, 1998). Research demonstrates that it is girls' beliefs about their abilities that shape their interest in taking higher-level high school and college math courses (Simpkins et al., 2006). Consequently, even though girls get better grades in math than boys do, they are still less likely to take advanced courses such as calculus or to choose careers in math (Davenport et al., 1998). However, as we noted with regard to science, girls whose same-sex friends are interested in math have more confidence in their math ability and are more open to taking advanced coursework in mathematics. Studies have shown that enrolling mathematically talented middle school girls in single-sex, math-focused extracurricular activities increases their interest in the subject and their math-related confidence (Reid & Roberts, 2006).

Ethnic Group Differences As striking as the gender differences in math are, they pale in comparison to ethnic variations. For example, by the last year of high school, only a third of African American and Hispanic American students have completed 2 years of algebra. In contrast, slightly more than half of White students and two-thirds of Asian American students have taken 2 years of algebra. Further, Asian American high school students earn twice as many credits in advanced courses as White students, and three to four times as many as African American and Hispanic American students (Davenport et al., 1998).

One reason for the ethnic differences is that Asian American and White students are more likely to enter ninth grade with the skills they need to take their first algebra class. More than half of African American and Hispanic American teens are required to take remedial courses before beginning algebra, compared to about one-third of Asian American and White students (Davenport et al., 1998). Observers point out that about the same proportion of high school students across all ethnicities expect to go to college. However, it appears that Asian American and White students are much more likely to enter high school prepared to pursue college-preparatory courses (Thompson & Joshua-Shearer, 2002). Many researchers conclude that rigorous transitional classes in eighth and ninth grade might enable greater numbers of African American and Hispanic American students to complete college-preparatory math classes in high school (Gamoran, Porter, Smithson, & White, 1997).

Evidence for this position is drawn from studies involving mathematically talented students. There are large ethnic differences in high school course choices among highly able students—those who score in the top 25% of standardized math achievement tests. One study found that 100% of Asian American and 88% of White high school students scoring at this level were enrolled in advanced mathematics courses. In contrast, only 40% of mathematically talented African American and Hispanic American students were enrolled in such classes (Education Trust, 1996). It may be that high school counselors more often encourage Asian American and White students to take advanced math classes (Davenport, 1992).

Entering the World of Work

In the United States, surveys of teenagers suggest that deciding on a career is one of the central themes of adolescent development (Mortimer, Zimmer-Gembeck, Holmes, & Shanahan, 2002). And many teens believe that engaging in part-time work during high school will help them make a career decision. Yet there are many other factors that contribute to teens' decisions about their future careers.

The Effects of Teenaged Employment

Learning Objective 14.11

What are the effects of employment on teens' lives?

Parents often encourage teenagers to obtain part-time employment on the grounds that it "builds character" and teaches young people about "real life." Are they right? Research that includes several cohorts of teenagers suggests that the more hours high school students work, the more likely they are to use drugs (alcohol, cigarettes,

Many part-time jobs fail to provide teens with meaningful work experiences.

marijuana, cocaine), to display aggression toward peers, to argue with parents, to get inadequate sleep, and to be dissatisfied with life (Bachman & Schulenberg, 1993; Bachman, Safron, Sy, & Schulenberg, 2003). Moreover, as adults, individuals who worked while in high school were less likely than peers who did not work to go to college. Thus, working may actually decrease teens' chances for successful careers during adulthood, precisely the opposite of what many parents believe.

However, it is possible that teens who are inclined toward drug use, aggression, and the other negative associates of teen employment choose to work more often than their peers who are not so inclined. As a result, correlational research may overstate the negative effects of teen employment. That is, research results may represent differences between students who choose to work and those who do not rather than the effects of employment per se.

A far more positive view of the impact of teenaged employment comes from studies that take into consideration the kind of work teenagers do, as well as how many hours they spend on the job (Mortimer & Finch, 1996; Mortimer, Finch, Dennehy, Lee, & Beebe, 1995; Mortimer & Harley, 2002). These findings indicate that adolescents who have skill-based work experiences develop increased feelings of competence. In addition, those students who see themselves as gaining useful skills through their work seem to develop confidence in their ability to achieve economic success in adulthood (Grabowski, Call, & Mortimer, 2001). Only 2% of students report that having a part-time job while in high school helped them choose a career (Hurley & Thorp, 2002). Still, having a job can help teens learn responsibility, punctuality, respect for the different roles that supervisors and supervisees play in the workplace, and money management.

Learning Objective 14.12

What are the stages in the career decision-making process?

Choosing a Career

To a great extent, teens' career aspirations determine the path they follow after high school. As a result, most teens devote a considerable amount of thought to the type of work they would like to do in adulthood. Concerns about career decisions escalate as teens reach the end of their high school years.

One way to describe the career decision-making process is in terms of a series of stages, a model proposed originally by Donald Super (Super, 1971, 1986). First comes the *growth stage* (from birth to 14 years), in which children learn about their abilities and interests. Next is the *exploratory stage* (roughly from age 15 to 24), in which young people begin to look for links between their personal characteristics and those required by various occupations. As Super's theory would predict, research shows that high school seniors are more likely to spend time seriously researching actual careers, as opposed to fantasizing about attractive but improbable career options (e.g., rock star, professional athlete), than high school freshmen are (Fouad, 2007). Nevertheless, only about half of high school students end up pursuing the careers they choose while they are still in school.

Professional career guidance can help teens work through the exploration phase. Career guidance services in high school often include tests that help teens determine their career interests. In addition, many schools make arrangements for students to observe various workplaces. Most schools also have access to online and library resources that are useful to students who are researching career information. (The Career Center in MyDevelopmentLab includes links to numerous resources on careers in child development.)

Career guidance professionals can also administer personality tests that help students determine which occupations best fit their own characteristics. John Holland, whose work has been the most influential in this area, proposes six basic personality types, summarized in Table 14.2 (Holland, 1973, 1992). Holland's basic hypothesis is that each of us tends to choose, and be most successful at, an occupation that matches our personality.

Research in non-Western as well as Western cultures, and with African Americans, Hispanic Americans, and Native Americans as well as Whites in the United States, has generally supported Holland's proposal (e.g., Leong, Austin, Sekaran, & Komarraju, 1998; Tokar, Fischer, & Subich, 1998). Ministers, for example, generally score highest on Holland's social scale, engineers highest on the investigative scale, car salespeople on the enterprising scale, and career army officers on the realistic scale.

Table 14.2 Holland's Personality Types and Work Preferences

Type	Personality Characteristics and Work Preferences
Realistic	Aggressive, masculine, physically strong, often with low verbal or interpersonal skills; prefer mechanical activities and tool use; are often mechanics, electricians, or surveyors
Investigative	Oriented toward thinking (particularly abstract thinking), organizing, and planning; prefer ambiguous, challenging tasks, but are low in social skills; are often scientists or engineers
Artistic	Asocial; prefer unstructured, highly individual activities; are often artists
Social	Extraverted, often need attention; avoid intellectual activity and dislike highly ordered activities, preferring to work with people; often choose service jobs like nurse or educator
Enterprising	Highly verbal and dominating; enjoy organizing and directing others; are persuasive and strong leaders; often choose careers in sales
Conventional	Accurate and precise; like clear guidelines; prefer structured activities and subordinate roles; may choose occupations such as bookkeeper or clerk

Source: Holland, 1973, 1992.

Learning Objective 14.13

What factors influence adolescents' career decisions?

Influences on Career Choices

Most adult career seekers find career counseling to be helpful (Whiston, 2003). However, even when schools offer extensive career guidance services, most high school students do not take advantage of them. It turns out that the most important factors in career choices are family influences, education and intelligence, and gender.

Family Influences In the United States, more than three-fourths of high school students report that their parents are their most important sources of information about careers (Hurley & Thorp, 2002). Moreover, young people tend to choose occupations at the same general social-class level as those of their parents. In part, this effect operates through the medium of education. For example, researchers have found that young adults whose parents are college graduates are less likely to enlist in the military than those whose parents have less education (Bachman, Segal, Freedman-Doan, & O'Malley, 2000). Such findings suggest that parents who have higher-than-average levels of education themselves are more likely to encourage their children to go on to postsecondary education. Such added education, in turn, makes it more likely that the young person will qualify for middle-class jobs, for which a college education is frequently a required credential.

Families also influence job choices through their value systems. In particular, parents who value academic and professional achievement are far more likely to have children who attend college and acquire a professional-level position. This effect is not just social-class difference in disguise. Among working-class families, it is the children of those who place the strongest emphasis on achievement who are most likely to move up into middle-class jobs (Gustafson & Magnusson, 1991). Further, families whose career aspirations for their children are high tend to produce young adults who are more intrinsically motivated as employees (Cotton, Bynum, & Madhere, 1997).

Similarly, parental moral beliefs influence young adults' willingness to enter various occupations (Bregman & Killen, 1999). For example, young adults whose families believe that drinking alcohol is morally wrong are unlikely to choose alcohol-related occupations such as bartending, waiting tables in a restaurant where liquor is served, or working at a liquor store.

Education and Intelligence Education and intelligence also exert interactive influences on teens' career decisions. These interactions strongly influence not just the specific job a young person chooses but also career success over the long haul. The higher a person's intelligence, the more years of education she is likely to complete; the more education she has, the higher the level at which she will enter the job market; the higher the level of entry into the job market, the further she is likely to go over her professional lifetime (Brody, 1992; Kamo, Ries, Farmer, Nickinovich, & Borgatta, 1991).

Intelligence has direct effects on job choice and job success as well. Brighter students are more likely to choose technical or professional careers. And highly intelligent workers are more likely to advance, even if they enter the job market at a lower level than those who are less intelligent (Dreher & Bretz, 1991).

Gender Specific job choice is also strongly affected by gender. Despite the women's movement and despite the vast increase in the proportion of women working, it is still true that sex role definitions designate some jobs as "women's jobs" and some as "men's jobs" (Reskin, 1993; Zhou, Dawson, Herr, & Stukas, 2004). Stereotypically male jobs are more varied, more technical, and higher in both status and income (e.g., business executive, carpenter). Stereotypically female jobs are concentrated in service occupations and are typically lower in status and lower paid (e.g., teacher, nurse, secretary). One-third of all working women hold clerical jobs; another quarter are in health care, teaching, or domestic service.

Children learn these cultural definitions of "appropriate" jobs for men and women in their early years, just as they learn all the other aspects of sex roles. So it is not surprising that most young women and men choose jobs that fit these sex role designations. Nonstereotypical job choices are much more common among young people who see themselves as androgynous or whose parents have unconventional occupations. For instance, young women who choose traditionally masculine careers are more likely to have a mother who has had a long-term career and more likely to define themselves either as androgynous or as masculine (Betz & Fitzgerald, 1987; Fitzpatrick & Silverman, 1989).

Test Prep Center

with PEARSON mydevelopmentlab

PIAGET'S FORMAL OPERATIONAL STAGE

14.1 What are the characteristics of thought in Piaget's formal operational stage? (pp. 420–421)

Piaget proposed a fourth stage of cognitive development in adolescence. The formal operational stage is characterized by the ability to apply basic cognitive operations to ideas and possibilities, in addition to actual objects.

1. Piaget used the pendulum problem to measure adolescents' ability to engage in ______________________.
2. The ability to reason from premises that are not necessarily factually true is called ______________________.

14.2 What are some major research findings regarding Piaget's claims about the formal operational stage? (pp. 421–423)

Researchers have found clear evidence of such advanced forms of thinking in at least some adolescents. But formal operational thinking is not universal, nor is it consistently used by those who are able to do it.

3. Transform this false statement into one that is true: Research has verified all of Piaget's assertions about the formal operational stage.

____

____

14.3 How is formal operational thinking manifested in everyday settings? (pp. 423–425)

David Elkind proposed that hypothetico-deductive thinking is manifested as an exaggerated sense of self-importance, or adolescent egocentrism, which leads teens to base decisions on their personal fables and the judgments of an imaginary audience. Piaget claimed that naïve idealism leads teens to be dissatisfied with the real world. Teens' plans reflect hypothetico-deductive thinking, but they often fail to consider all of the details that are relevant to a decision.

4. Briefly describe each feature of adolescent thought in the table below.

Feature	Description
Adolescent egocentrism	
Imaginary audience	
Personal fable	
Naïve idealism	
Faulty planning	

5. From the Multimedia Library within MyDevelopmentLab, watch the *Adolescent Egocentrism* video and answer the following question.

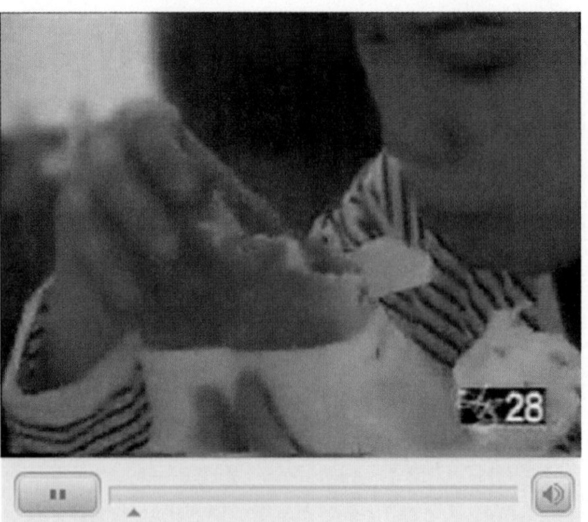

How do these teens use personal fables to justify their unhealthy eating habits?

____

____

6. From the Multimedia Library within MyDevelopmentLab, watch the *Imaginary Audience* video and answer the following question.

How does the girl in the video show that she is influenced by an imaginary audience?

____

____

ADVANCES IN INFORMATION PROCESSING

14.4 In what ways do executive processes improve during adolescence? (pp. 425–426)

Improvements in executive processes lead to improvements in response inhibition, metamemory, and the ability to discriminate between relevant and irrelevant information.

7. From the Multimedia Library within MyDevelopmentLab, go through the *Experiencing the Stroop Effect* activity and answer the following question.

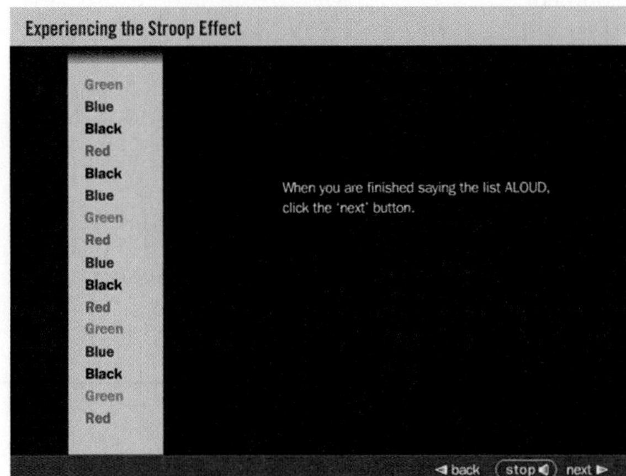

One executive processing skill that is vital to success on the Stroop test is ______________________.

14.5 What do advances in executive processing contribute to academic learning? (pp. 426–427)

Teens' improved executive processes enable them to develop, choose, and transfer learning strategies that are useful in school. In addition, they are better able to understand and remember text as a result of advances in executive processing.

8. What do training studies suggest about the ability of teens to summarize and outline text, compared to that of younger children?

____

____

SCHOOLING

14.6 How do changes in students' goals contribute to the transition to secondary school? (pp. 427–430)

The transition to middle school may be accompanied by changes in children's goal orientation that result in declines in achievement and self-esteem. The high school transition offers many teens more opportunities to pursue special interests and extracurricular activities.

9. Goals that are based on a desire for self-improvement are called ______________________.
10. Goals that are based on a desire to be superior to others are called ______________________.
11. What are ninth-grade academies, and how do at-risk students benefit from attending them?

____

____

14.7 What characteristics distinguish engaged students from those who are disengaged? (pp. 430–433)

Engaged students like school, put forth effort to accomplish academic tasks, and participate in extracurricular activities. They tend to be higher achievers than disengaged students, who don't enjoy school and refrain from participating in both academic and extracurricular activities.

12. Parents of disengaged high school students were more likely than those of engaged students to exhibit a ______________ or ____________ style of parenting.

14.8 What variables predict the likelihood of dropping out of high school? (pp. 433–434)

Those who drop out are more likely to be from low-income families or to be doing poorly in school. Peer influence is also a factor.

13. What are some of the difficulties associated with drop-out estimates?

____

____

14.9 What are the goals of character education? (p. 435)

The purpose of character education is to teach students a common value system and to encourage them to learn to discipline themselves according to the standards of that system.

14. How do advocates of character education overcome the objection that such programs fail to take into account the diversity of views on acceptable behavior in contemporary society?

____

____

15. From the Multimedia Library within MyDevelopmentLab, watch the *Values Education* video and answer the following question.

What do the educators in the video believe about the relationship between teaching values in the home and teaching them at school?

____

____

14.10 What gender and ethnic differences in science and math achievement have been found by researchers? (pp. 435–437)

Female, African American, and Hispanic American high school students score lower on science and math achievement tests and choose to take courses in these disciplines less often than do White and Asian American males. Girls may view success in science and math as unacceptable for women. African American and Hispanic American students may not be getting the preparation they need in middle school for advanced high school math courses.

16. How can educators increase the chances that African American and Hispanic American students will complete college-preparatory classes in high school?

____

____

17. From the Multimedia Library within MyDevelopmentLab, watch the *Gender/Spatial Ability: Nora Newcombe* video and answer the following question.

Does Professor Newcombe believe that gender differences in spatial ability are biological or learned?

____

____

ENTERING THE WORLD OF WORK

14.11 What are the effects of employment on teens' lives? (pp. 437–438)

Teen employment is associated with increased risks of drug use and poor achievement. Jobs that provide teens with meaningful work experience and allow them to learn skills that will transfer to their adult careers may be beneficial to their development.

18. Teens who are employed are (more/less) likely to go to college than teens who do not work are.

19. Only _____ of students report that having a part-time job while in high school helped them choose a career.

14.12 What are the stages in the career decision-making process? (pp. 438–439)

In the growth stage, from birth to 14 years, children learn about their abilities and interests. In the exploratory stage, from 15 to 24 years, teens and young adults look for links between their personal characteristics and those required by occupations that interest them.

20. How can career guidance professionals help teens negotiate Super's career exploration stage?

____

____

21. Match the six personality types defined by Holland to their corresponding work preferences.

_______(1) realistic

_______(2) investigative

_______(3) artistic

_______(4) social

_______(5) enterprising

_______(6) conventional

A. artists

B. service jobs like nurse or educator

C. mechanics, electricians, or surveyors

D. sales

E. bookkeeper or clerk

F. scientists or engineers

14.13 What factors influence adolescents' career decisions? (pp. 440–441)

The career a teen chooses is affected by his or her education, intelligence, family background and resources, family values, and gender. The majority choose jobs that fit the cultural norms for their social class and gender.

22. Briefly describe the ways in which each of the factors listed in the table influences teens' career decisions.

Factor	Influence
Family	
Education	
Intelligence	
Gender	

For answers to the questions in this chapter, turn to page 524. For a list of key terms, turn to page 532.

Succeed with PEARSON **mydevelopmentlab**

Do You Know All of the Terms in This Chapter?
Find out by using the Flashcards. Want more practice? Take additional quizzes, try simulations, and watch video to be sure you are prepared for the test!

Chapter

15

Social and Personality Development in Adolescence

Taking their cue from the pioneering work of psychoanalytic theorist Erik Erikson (1959), some developmentalists believe that the absence of formal *rites of passage*, ceremonies that mark the transition from childhood to adulthood, in industrialized societies makes adolescents more vulnerable to risky behaviors such as alcohol use, unprotected sex, and aggression. Teens who become involved in these activities, say some observers, are attempting to invent their own rites of passage. How adolescents accomplish this goal depends on the peer group with which they identify. For one teenager, the rite may involve preparing for a standardized test such as the PSAT that may win her a college scholarship. For another adolescent, it may involve joining a street gang.

Consideration of rites of passage brings to mind Vygotsky's concept of scaffolding. Adolescents are conscious of the need to transition to adulthood, and they take many steps toward this goal on their own. But they need adults to lead the way and to support them when their steps toward maturity turn out to be missteps, whether that support occurs in the context of formal rites of passage or in more informal ways.

This chapter begins with an examination of the aspects of the transition to adulthood that occur within adolescents themselves. Changes in personal identity and self-concept are fundamental to this transition. Its effects extend beyond the self to include advances in moral judgment and important changes in teens' relationships with their parents, friends, and potential romantic partners.

Learning Objectives

Theories of Social and Personality Development

15.1 What happens during Erikson's identity versus role confusion stage?

15.2 How does Marcia explain identity development?

Self-Concept

15.3 In what way does self-understanding in adolescence differ from that in childhood?

15.4 How does self-esteem change across the teenaged years?

15.5 What are the gender role concepts of adolescents?

15.6 How do minority, biracial, and immigrant teens develop a sense of ethnic identity?

Moral Development

15.7 What are the features of moral reasoning at each of Kohlberg's stages?

15.8 What are some important causes and effects of the development of moral reasoning?

15.9 How has Kohlberg's theory been criticized?

Social Relationships

15.10 What are the features of adolescents' relationships with their parents?

15.11 What are the characteristics of adolescents' friendships?

15.12 How do peer groups change over the teen years?

15.13 How does interest in romantic relationships emerge among heterosexual and homosexual teens?

Theories of Social and Personality Development

Thirteen-year-old Brendon took a deep breath to steady his nerves and punched in Melissa's cell phone number. He continued to breathe deeply as he waited for her to answer. Over the past few minutes, he had attempted to call her three times. However, the fear of rejection overcame him each time, and he punched the END button before she could answer. This time, he was determined to at least say "Hi."

Such dramas are played out every day in the world of young adolescents, and there is no denying the fact that the emergence of romantic interests is a prominent feature of this period of development. For Freud, these interests were the central theme of adolescence. Erikson and other theorists proposed models of adolescent development that were much broader in scope.

Learning Objective 15.1
What happens during Erikson's identity versus role confusion stage?

Psychoanalytic Perspectives

According to Freud, the postpubertal years constitute the last stage of personality development. So both adolescents and adults are in what he called the *genital stage*, the period during which psychosexual maturity is reached. Freud believed that puberty awakens the sexual drive that has lain dormant during the latency stage. Thus, for Freud, the primary developmental task of adolescence is to channel the libido into a healthy sexual relationship.

Erikson, though not denying the importance of achieving sexual maturity, proposed that achievement of a sense of personal identity is a far more important developmental task faced by adolescents. He described *identity* as a sense of self-continuity (Erikson, 1959). More recent theorists, elaborating on his idea, define **identity** as an understanding of one's unique characteristics and how they have been, are, and will be manifested across ages, situations, and social roles. Thus, in Erikson's model, the central crisis of adolescence is **identity versus role confusion.**

identity an understanding of one's unique characteristics and how they have been, are, and will be manifested across ages, situations, and social roles

identity versus role confusion in Erikson's theory, the stage during which adolescents attain a sense of who they are

identity crisis Erikson's term for the psychological state of emotional turmoil that arises when an adolescent's sense of self becomes "unglued" so that a new, more mature sense of self can be achieved

Erikson argued that a child's early sense of identity comes partly "unglued" in early adolescence because of the combination of rapid body growth and the sexual changes of puberty. Erikson claimed that during this period the adolescent's mind is in a kind of moratorium between childhood and adulthood. The old identity will no longer suffice; a new identity must be forged, one that will equip the young person for the myriad roles of adult life—occupational roles, sexual roles, religious roles, and others.

Confusion about all these role choices is inevitable and leads to a pivotal transition Erikson called the *identity crisis*. The **identity crisis** is a period during which an adolescent is troubled by his lack of an identity. Erikson believed that adolescents' tendency to identify with peer groups is a defense against the emotional turmoil engendered by the identity crisis. In a sense, he claimed, teens protect themselves against the unpleasant emotions of the identity crisis by merging their individual identities with that of a group (Erikson, 1980a). The teenaged group thus forms a secure base from which the young person can move toward a unique solution of the identity crisis. Ultimately, however, each teenager must achieve an integrated view of himself, including his own pattern of beliefs, occupational goals, and relationships.

Learning Objective 15.2
How does Marcia explain identity development?

Marcia's Theory of Identity Achievement

Nearly all the current work on the formation of adolescent identity has been based on James Marcia's descriptions of identity statuses, which are rooted in Erikson's general conceptions of the adolescent identity process (Marcia, 1966, 1980). Following one of Erikson's ideas, Marcia argues that adolescent identity formation has two key parts:

a crisis and a commitment. By a crisis, Marcia means a period of decision making when old values and old choices are reexamined. This may occur as a sort of upheaval—the classic notion of a crisis—or it may occur gradually. The outcome of the reevaluation is a commitment to some specific role, value, goal, or ideology.

If you put these two key elements together, as shown in Figure 15.1, you can see that four different identity statuses are possible.

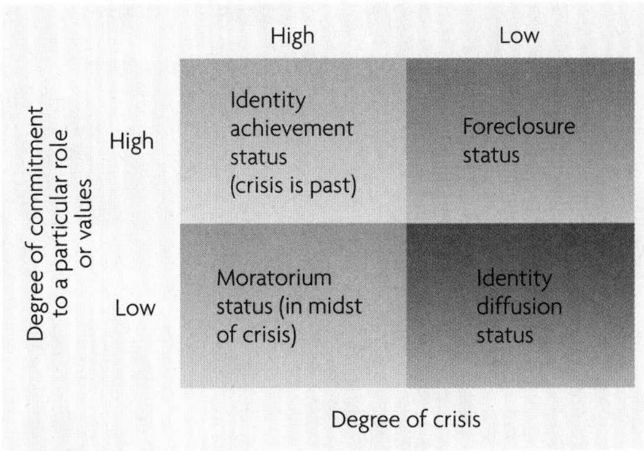

Figure 15.1 The Four Identity Statuses Proposed by Marcia, Based on Erikson's Theory

For a fully achieved identity, the young person must have both examined her values or goals and reached a firm commitment.

(*Source*: Marcia, 1980.)

- **Identity achievement.** The person has been through a crisis and has reached a commitment to ideological, occupational, or other goals.
- **Moratorium.** A crisis is in progress, but no commitment has yet been made.
- **Foreclosure.** The person has made a commitment without having gone through a crisis. No reassessment of old positions has been made. Instead, the young person has simply accepted a parentally or culturally defined commitment.
- **Identity diffusion.** The young person is not in the midst of a crisis (although there may have been one in the past) and has not made a commitment. Diffusion may thus represent either an early stage in the process (before a crisis) or a failure to reach a commitment after a crisis.

THE WHOLE CHILD IN FOCUS

What were Cho's and Michelle's identity statuses at age 18? Find out on page 475.

The whole process of identity formation may occur later than Erikson and Marcia thought, perhaps because cognitive development, or the acquisition of formal operational thinking, is more strongly related to identity formation than either believed. Research suggests that teens who are most advanced in the development of logical thinking and other information-processing skills are also the most likely to have attained Marcia's status of identity achievement (Klaczynski, Fauth, & Swanger, 1998).

There is also evidence that the quest for personal identity continues throughout the lifespan, with alternating periods of instability and stability (Marcia, 2002). For example, a person's sense of being "young" or "old" and her integration of that idea into a sense of belonging to a particular generation appear to change several times over the course of the adolescent and adult years (Sato, Shimonska, Nakazato, & Kawaai, 1997). Consequently, adolescence may be only one period of identity formation among several.

Some research suggests that individuals who have attained Marcia's identity achievement status sometimes regress to other categories (Berzonsky, 2003). This may happen because the achievement status may not be the most adaptive one in every situation. For example, teenagers facing extreme stressors, such as life-threatening illnesses, seem to be optimally adjusted when they adopt the status of foreclosure (Madan-Swain et al., 2000). Accepting others' goals for them, at least temporarily, seems to protect these teens against some of the negative emotional effects of the difficulties they must face. Thus, the idea that progression to identity achievement is the most psychologically healthy response to the identity crisis clearly doesn't apply to some adolescents.

As you might suspect, ideas about adolescent identity development and the kinds of experiences that drive it are firmly rooted in cultural assumptions. For example, in the United States, both parents and teenagers tend to believe that paid employment during adolescence helps adolescents sort out the career-selection aspects of identity development (Greenberger & Steinberg, 1986). Predictably, cross-cultural studies show that teens in the United States spend a great deal more time working than do their peers in other industrialized nations (Larson & Verma, 1999). Such cultural beliefs and the experiences that flow from them are likely to affect the process of identity development.

Clearly, too, the whole concept of an adolescent identity crisis has been strongly influenced by current cultural assumptions in Western societies, in which full adult status is postponed for almost a decade after puberty. In such cultures, young people do not normally or necessarily adopt the same roles or occupations as their parents. Indeed, they are encouraged

identity achievement in Marcia's theory, the identity status achieved by a person who has been through a crisis and reached a commitment to ideological, occupational, or other goals

moratorium in Marcia's theory, the identity status of a person who is in a crisis but who has made no commitment

foreclosure in Marcia's theory, the identity status of a person who has made a commitment without having gone through a crisis; the person has simply accepted a parentally or culturally defined commitment

identity diffusion in Marcia's theory, the identity status of a person who is not in the midst of a crisis and who has made no commitment

In rites of passage programs, African American girls learn about the traditional styles of dress among African women. In the Jewish ceremony called *bar mitzvah* (for boys) or *bat mitzvah* (for girls), 13-year-olds read from the Torah in Hebrew and are admitted to full adult status in the congregation. The Tanzanian boy has had his face painted with white clay as part of an adolescent rite of passage.

to choose for themselves. These adolescents are faced with what may be a bewildering array of options, a pattern that might well foster the sort of identity crisis Erikson described. In less industrialized cultures, there may well be a shift in identity from that of child to that of adult, but without a crisis of any kind. Further, adolescents' search for identity in other cultures may be better supported by cultural initiation rites that clearly, at least in a symbolic sense, separate childhood from adulthood (see *Developmental Science at Home*).

Self-Concept

In Chapter 14, you read that thinking becomes more abstract in adolescence. Thus, you shouldn't be surprised to find that teenagers' self-concepts are a lot more complex than those of younger children.

Learning Objective 15.3

In what way does self-understanding in adolescence differ from that in childhood?

Self-Understanding

You should remember that, through the elementary school years, a child's self-concept becomes more focused on enduring internal characteristics—the *psychological self*. This trend continues in adolescence, with self-definition becoming more abstract. Moreover, cognitive development, particularly the acquisition of formal operational thought, leads teens to theorize about the outcomes they experience. Once theories are formed, adolescents look for evidence to confirm or refute them and adjust their theories accordingly. This back-and-forth process of theorizing, collecting data, and adjusting theoretical propositions enables teens to construct a somewhat stable self-concept by the end of the period.

Advances in self-understanding among adolescents both are facilitated by and contribute to the increasing stability of the Big Five personality traits during this period. As a result, enduring traits such as shyness, or *introversion* in Big Five terminology, show up in adolescents'

DEVELOPMENTAL SCIENCE AT HOME

Rites of Passage Programs

An expression of intense concentration appeared on 13-year-old Roneisha's face as she stood before a mirror, wrapping a brightly colored cloth around her head. She had learned the art of Gele headwrapping just a few hours earlier and wanted to demonstrate it for her mother and younger sister. Headwrapping is just one of many traditional African skills Roneisha learned in a church-based program in which her parents had enrolled her. Roneisha's parents were eager for their children to take part in the program when they learned that its purpose was to provide African American teens and their families with social support during the teen years.

Programs such as the one Roneisha attended have arisen out of concern about the lack of formal rites of passage in Western society. African Americans point out that other minority groups practice rites of passage that connect their young people with a centuries-long cultural heritage—such as the *bar mitzvah* and *bat mitzvah* for Jewish boys and girls and the *quinceañera* for Hispanic girls. By contrast, the institution of slavery separated African Americans from the traditions of their ancestors.

Consequently, many African American churches and other institutions have devised formal initiation rites preceded by a period of instruction in traditional African cultural values and practices, typically called *rites of passage programs*. The goal of such programs is to support African American families' efforts to enhance their adolescent children's sense of racial identity and self-esteem (Harvey & Rauch, 1997; Warfield-Coppock, 1997). Most such programs are implemented over a fairly long period of time, usually a year or more, and include formal instruction for both the teens and their families (Gavazzi & Law, 1997). Many programs target teens in situations that carry especially high risks, such as teens who are incarcerated or in foster care (Gavazzi, Alford, & McKenry, 1996; Harvey & Coleman, 1997).

Research indicates that rites of passage programs can make a difference (Harvey & Hill, 2004). In one program, six underachieving sixth-grade African American boys with histories of school behavior problems participated in a rites of passage program for an entire school year (Bass & Coleman, 1997). In-depth case studies of all the boys revealed that by the end of the year, their classroom behavior had improved considerably, they exhibited less antisocial behavior, and they had acquired a great deal of knowledge about African cultures, symbols, and ideas. A larger group participated in a rites of passage program involving both boys and girls in the fifth and sixth grades, over a 2-year period (Cherry et al., 1998). At the end of this program, participants exhibited higher self-esteem, a stronger sense of racial identity, a lower incidence of school behavior problems, and greater knowledge of African culture.

The experiences of many African American youth in rites of passage programs suggest that there may be some real advantage to providing teens with formal instruction and initiation into adult roles. What many see as a vestige of a bygone era may actually serve a very important function in adolescent identity development.

Questions for Reflection

1. Rites of passage programs include three separate components that may explain their positive effects on teenagers: contact with adults, contact with peers, and information about ethnicity. Which factor do you think is most important and why?
2. When you were a teenager, did you participate in any formal rites of passage, such as a confirmation, bar mitzvah, or quinceañera? If so, what effect did it have on you? If not, in what way do you think such a program might have been helpful to you?

self-descriptions far more often than they do in those of younger children. This change was evident in the replies of a 9-year-old and an 11-year-old to the question "Who am I?" which you may recall from Chapter 12. Internal traits are even more pronounced in this 17-year-old's answer to the same question:

> I am a human being. I am a girl. I am an individual. I don't know who I am. I am a Pisces. I am a moody person. I am an indecisive person. I am an ambitious person. I am a very curious person. I am not an individual. I am a loner. I am an American (God help me). I am a Democrat. I am a liberal person. I am a radical. I am a conservative. I am a pseudoliberal. I am an atheist. I am not a classifiable person (i.e., I don't want to be). (Montemayor & Eisen, 1977, p. 318)

Clearly, this girl's self-concept is even less tied to her physical characteristics or even her abilities than are those of younger children. She is describing abstract traits or ideology. You can see the change very graphically in Figure 15.2, which is based on the answers of all 262 participants in Montemayor and Eisen's study. Each of the answers to the "Who am I?" question was categorized as a reference either to body image or physical properties ("I am tall," "I have blue eyes") or to ideology or belief ("I am a Democrat," "I believe in God"). As you can see, appearance was a highly prominent dimension in the preteen and

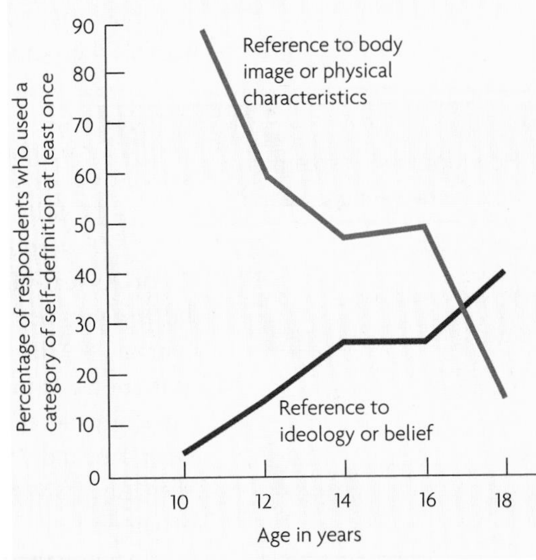

Figure 15.2 Changes in Teens' Self-Descriptions

As they get older, children and adolescents define themselves less and less by what they look like and more and more by what they believe or feel.

(*Source*: Montemayor & Eisen, 1977, from Table 1, p. 316.)

early teen years but became less dominant in late adolescence, a time when ideology and belief became more important. By late adolescence, most teenagers think of themselves in terms of enduring traits, beliefs, personal philosophy, and moral standards (Damon & Hart, 1988).

At the same time, the adolescent's self-concept becomes more differentiated, as she comes to see herself somewhat differently in each of several roles: as a student, as a friend, as a daughter, and as a romantic partner (Harter & Monsour, 1992). Once these self-concepts are formed, they begin to influence adolescents' behavior. For example, teens whose academic self-concepts are strong take more difficult courses in high school than do teens who believe themselves to be less academically able. Further, they tend to select courses in disciplines in which they believe they have the greatest ability and to avoid courses in perceived areas of weakness (Marsh & Yeung, 1997).

Adolescents' academic self-concepts seem to come both from internal comparisons of their performance to a self-generated ideal and from external comparisons to peer performance (Bong, 1998). It also appears that perceived competency in one domain affects how a teenager feels about his ability in other areas. For example, if a high school student fails a math course, it is likely to affect his self-concept in other disciplines as well as in math. This suggests that teens' self-concepts are hierarchical in nature: Perceived competencies in various domains serve as building blocks for creating a global academic self-concept (Cheng, Xiaoyan, & Dajun, 2006; Yeung, Chui, & Lau, 1999).

Social self-concepts also predict behavior. For example, a teenager's family self-concept reflects his beliefs about the likelihood of attaining and/or maintaining satisfactory relationships with family members. Developmentalists have found that adolescents who are estranged from their families, such as runaways, perceive themselves to be less competent in the give-and-take of family relations than do teens who are close to parents and siblings (Swaim & Bracken, 1997). Indeed, the perceived lack of competency in family relations appears to be distinct from other components of self-concept.

Girls and boys also appear to construct the various components of self-concept somewhat differently. For example, a study of teens' evaluations of their own writing abilities found that boys and girls rated themselves as equally capable writers (Pajares & Valiante, 1999). However, the girls scored higher on objective tests of writing ability. The boys appeared to believe that they were better writers than they actually were. These findings raise interesting questions about the degree to which self-concept development is influenced by cultural ideas about sex roles. Perhaps girls display more objectivity about their writing skills because they know that girls are supposed to be better at language skills than boys.

Learning Objective 15.4

How does self-esteem change across the teenage years?

Self-Esteem

Self-esteem shows some interesting shifts during the teenage years. The overall trend is a steady rise in self-esteem through the years of adolescence. The average 19- or 20-year-old has a considerably more positive sense of her global self-worth than she did at age 8 or 11 (Diehl, Vicary, & Deike, 1997; Harter, 1990; Wigfield, Eccles, MacIver, Reuman, & Midgley, 1991). However, the rise to higher self-esteem during adolescence is not continuous. At the beginning of adolescence, self-esteem very often drops rather abruptly. In one study, developmentalists followed a group of nearly 600 Hispanic American, African American, and White youngsters over the 2 years from sixth grade to junior high (Seidman, Allen, Aber, Mitchell, & Feinman, 1994). Researchers found a significant average drop in self-esteem over that period, a decline that occurred in each of the three ethnic groups.

To study the relationship of self-esteem to important developmental outcomes, such as school achievement, researchers often divide teens into four groups based on the stability of their self-esteem ratings across adolescence (Diehl et al., 1997; Zimmerman, Copeland, Shope, & Dielman, 1997). The largest group, about half in most studies, displays consistently high self-esteem throughout adolescence. The self-esteem of those in the second group steadily increases, and the self-esteem ratings of those in the third group are consistently low

DEVELOPMENTAL SCIENCE IN THE CLINIC

A Troublesome Cluster of Traits

Rick was a high school sophomore who could not see that there was anything good about his life or anything that might change in the future. After 2 years in high school, he had failed several classes, and his prospects for graduating on time were growing dim. His generally negative view of the world often led him to experience alternating feelings of rage and despair. He longed to have friends, yet, for reasons that he couldn't understand, he always responded to others with hostility. His hostile feelings led him, in turn, to be unable to participate in small talk and other social rituals that he viewed as pointless. Because such interactions are usually required at the beginning of a friendship, Rick had no friends. His parents thought he might be depressed, so they consulted with a psychologist.

After meeting with Rick a few times, the psychologist agreed that he was depressed. She believed that his depression was the result of the combined effects of a cluster of personality traits, including the introversion and neuroticism dimensions of the Big Five along with low self-esteem (Beautrais, Joyce, & Mulder, 1999). As you'll recall, introversion is the preference for solitary over social activities. Individuals who score high on tests of neuroticism are pessimistic and irritable, and they worry a lot. Most adolescents who show such personality traits resist efforts by parents and friends to help them and are at greater risk than their peers for all kinds of adjustment problems.

The psychologist also ascertained that Rick had an external locus of control. You may recall from the *Developmental Science in the Clinic* discussion in Chapter 14 that teens with an external locus of control attribute the causes of experiences (for example, school failure) to factors outside themselves. Thus, an external locus of control often leads to feelings of powerlessness, like those that Rick experienced, and low self-esteem.

Developmentalists have found that teens across a variety of cultures who are high in introversion and neuroticism, who are low in self-esteem, and who possess an external locus of control have a very negative outlook on life and seem to have little ability or motivation to change their circumstances. For instance, these adolescents are likely to use avoidant coping when they face problems (Gomez, Bounds, Holmberg, Fullarton, & Gomez, 1999; Gomez, Holmberg, Bounds, Fullarton, & Gomez, 1999; Medvedova, 1998). This means that they ignore problems or put off dealing with them. For example, a high school student with these traits who finds out he is failing a class may wait until it is too late to try to do anything about it. However, because he tends to blame others for his problems, he is unlikely to be able to learn from the experience. Such teens get into these situations over and over again and appear to be unable to prevent this or to pull themselves out of trouble in any effective way. The consequence of their negative outlook combined with repeated experiences of disappointment and failure is that these adolescents are prone to depression (del Barrio, Moreno-Rosset, Lopez-Martinez, & Olmedo, 1997; Ge & Conger, 1999). Once depressed, such teens are likely to attempt suicide (Beautrais et al., 1999). Their emotional difficulties are compounded by the fact that most are rejected by peers (Young & Bradley, 1998).

The outlook for teens with this cluster of traits is not bright. Their beliefs about themselves and the social world are resistant to change and persist into adulthood (Gomez, Gomez, & Cooper, 2002; Offer, Kaiz, Howard, & Bennett, 1998). In addition, as adults, they continue to be subject to bouts of depression and a variety of academic, occupational, and relationship difficulties. Consequently, developmentalists are searching for assessment tools and intervention strategies that can be used to identify and help such individuals in middle childhood or early adolescence (Young & Bradley, 1998).

Questions for Reflection

1. What kind of research would be required to test the effectiveness of an intervention program for the type of adolescent described in this discussion?
2. How would theorists on either side of the nature-nurture debate explain the development of this troublesome cluster of traits?

(see *Developmental Science in the Clinic*). Teens in the fourth group enjoy moderate to high self-esteem at the beginning of the period, but it declines steadily as adolescence progresses. One finding of concern is that girls outnumber boys in the third and fourth groups (Zimmerman et al., 1997). In addition, several studies have found that high self-esteem is correlated with positive developmental outcomes. For example, teens with high self-esteem are better able to resist peer pressure, get higher grades in school, and are less likely to be depressed (Repetto, Caldwell, & Zimmerman, 2004).

Gender Roles

Learning Objective 15.5
What are the gender role concepts of adolescents?

Developmentalists use the term **gender role identity** to refer to gender-related aspects of the psychological self. In contrast to younger children, adolescents understand that gender roles are social conventions, so their attitudes toward them are more flexible (Katz & Ksansnak, 1994). Parental attitudes and parental behavior become increasingly important in shaping teens' ideas about gender and sex roles (Castellino, Lerner, Lerner, & von Eye, 1998; Ex & Janssens, 1998; Jackson & Tein, 1998; Raffaelli & Ontai, 2004). In addition, concepts that were largely separate earlier in development, such as beliefs about gender roles and

gender role identity the gender-related aspects of the psychological self

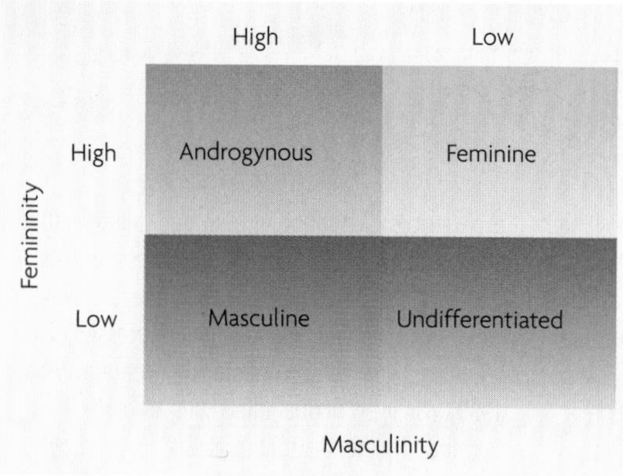

Figure 15.3 **Bem's Gender Role Categories**

This diagram illustrates how the dimensions of masculinity and femininity interact to produce four types of sex role orientation.

sexuality, seem to become integrated into a conceptual framework that teens use to formulate ideas about the significance of gender in personal identity and social relationships (Mallet, Apostolidis, & Paty, 1997).

In the early days of research on gender role identity, psychologists conceived of masculinity and femininity as polar opposites. A person could be masculine or feminine, but couldn't be both. However, theories first advanced in the 1970s by Sandra Bem and others have resulted in a large body of research in support of the notion that masculinity and femininity are separate dimensions and each may be found in varying quantities in the personalities of both men and women (Bem, 1974; Spence & Helmreich, 1978). A male or a female can be high or low on masculinity and femininity. Indeed, if people are categorized as high or low on each of these two dimensions, based on their self-descriptions, four basic gender role types emerge: masculine, feminine, androgynous, and undifferentiated (see Figure 15.3).

Teenaged boys like these may have an easier time achieving high self-esteem than girls of the same age, because both boys and girls seem to place a higher value on certain traditionally "masculine" qualities than on traditionally "feminine" qualities.

The masculine and feminine types are the traditional categories; a person in either of these categories sees himself or herself as high in one and low in the other. A person with a **masculine gender role identity**, according to this view, is one who perceives himself (or herself) as having many traditional masculine qualities and few traditional feminine qualities. A teenager or adult with a **feminine gender role identity** shows the reverse pattern. In contrast, those with an **androgynous gender role identity** see themselves as having both masculine and feminine traits. Individuals with an **undifferentiated gender role identity** describe themselves as lacking both.

Interestingly, research suggests that either an androgynous or a masculine gender role identity is associated with higher self-esteem among both boys and girls (Gurnáková & Kusá, 2004; Woo & Oei, 2006). This finding makes sense in light of the existence of a "masculine bias" in American and other Western societies, which causes both men and women to value traditionally masculine qualities such as independence and competitiveness more than many traditionally female qualities.

THE WHOLE CHILD IN FOCUS

What led Michelle to pursue a career in enginerering? Find out on page 475.

However, cross-cultural research suggests that adoption of an androgynous or masculine orientation by a girl can lead to lower self-esteem. For example, one study of Israeli girls found that preteens who were tomboys and who rated themselves high on masculine personality traits were less popular and had lower self-esteem than their more feminine peers (Lobel, Slone, & Winch, 1997). Consequently, when considering gender roles and gender role identity, it is important to remember that both are very strongly tied to culture. A particular society may value the masculine role more highly but also actively discourage girls from adopting it. Thus, it may not be universally true that teens who adopt the more highly valued gender role identity gain self-esteem.

Learning Objective 15.6

How do minority, biracial, and immigrant teens develop a sense of ethnic identity?

Ethnic Identity

Minority teenagers, especially those of color in a predominantly White culture, face the task of creating two identities in adolescence. Like other teens, they must develop a sense of individual identity that they believe sets them apart from others. In addition, they must develop an **ethnic identity** that includes self-identification as a member of their specific group, commitment to that group and its values and attitudes, and some attitudes (positive or negative) about the group to which they belong. Many minority families support children's ethnic identity development by providing them with specific teaching about how their group differs from the dominant one. Similarly, some families who speak a language different from that of the dominant group support children's ethnic identity development by teaching them the language of their home country. Researchers have found that minority teenagers whose families engage in such practices are likely to develop a strong sense of ethnic identity (Davey, Fish, Askew, & Robila, 2003; Phinney, Romero, Nava, & Huang, 2001).

Psychologist Jean Phinney has proposed that, in adolescence, the development of a complete ethnic identity moves through three stages (Phinney, 1990; Phinney & Rosenthal, 1992). The first stage is an *unexamined ethnic identity*. For some subgroups in U.S. society, such as African Americans and Native Americans, this unexamined identity typically includes the negative images and stereotypes common in the wider culture (see *Developmental Science in the Classroom*). Indeed, it may be especially at adolescence, with the advent of the cognitive ability to reflect and interpret, that the young person becomes keenly aware of how his own group is perceived by the majority.

Phinney's second stage is the *ethnic identity search*. This search is typically triggered by some experience that makes ethnicity relevant—perhaps an example of blatant prejudice or merely the widening experience of high school. At this point, the young person begins to compare his own ethnic group with others, to try to arrive at his own judgments.

This exploration stage is eventually followed by the *ethnic identity achievement* stage, in which adolescents develop strategies for solving conflicts between the competing demands of the dominant culture and those of the ethnic group with which they identify. Most deal with such conflicts by creating two identities, one that they display when they are in the presence of members of the dominant group and another that they exhibit when they are with members of their own group.

masculine gender role identity high self-ratings on masculine traits, low self-ratings on feminine traits

feminine gender role identity low self-ratings on masculine traits, high self-ratings on feminine traits

androgynous gender role identity high self-ratings on both masculine and feminine traits

undifferentiated gender role identity low self-ratings on both masculine and feminine traits

ethnic identity a sense of belonging to an ethnic group

DEVELOPMENTAL SCIENCE IN THE CLASSROOM

Role Models in the Media and in School

Like many adolescents, Carlos idolizes professional athletes. His current hero is baseball player Manny Rodriguez. Carlos identifies with Rodriguez's biography, one that includes the difficulties associated with moving to a new culture and having to learn a new language in mid-adolescence. Like Manny Rodriguez, Carlos's physics teacher also immigrated to the United States when he was a teenager. When his students complain about their lives, Carlos's teacher points out that he had no knowledge of English when he came to the United States at the age of 14, yet he graduated from high school and then worked his way through college. Why does Carlos idolize Manny Rodriguez and other professional athletes rather than his physics teacher? This question has been examined by researchers who are concerned about the ways in which media portrayals of occupational roles influence children's choice of role models.

A good illustration of the complex nature of the influence of models comes from research examining African American children's ideas about which adults they consider to be their role models. Researchers conducted a survey in which 4,500 African American boys aged 10 to 18 were asked to name an important role model outside their own families (Assibey-Mensah, 1997). Investigators thought that these boys would name teachers as important role models because of their frequent interactions with them. However, a large majority of the boys named a professional athlete, and not a single boy named a teacher as an important personal role model (which is astounding when you think of the number of boys who participated in the study). These findings suggest that entertainment media are a more important source of role models for these youths than their real-life experiences with adults. Clearly, neither frequency of interaction with a model nor similarity between the observer and the model explains these findings. However, comparisons of portrayals of teachers to those of athletes in media may help explain why these boys responded as they did.

In entertainment media, teachers are often portrayed as inept, and many popular TV programs geared to young audiences (for example, *South Park* and *The Simpsons*) depict teachers and other school officials as buffoons who are not respected by their students. In contrast, stories about both real and fictional athletes are dominated by themes of fame, wealth, popularity, and achievements such as league championships and record-breaking statistics. Considering the contrast between the two, it isn't surprising that minority boys prefer athletes as role models rather than teachers, even though they know many teachers personally and most likely have no personal interactions with professional athletes.

Questions for Reflection

1. How might frequent interactions make it less likely that someone would be viewed by a child as a role model?
2. In your opinion, to what extent are the concerns highlighted by these researchers equally true for children of other ethnicities?

Young people of color often develop two identities: a psychological sense of self and an ethnic identity. Those who succeed at both tasks often think of themselves as bicultural and have an easier time relating to peers of the same and other ethnicities.

In both cross-sectional and longitudinal studies, Phinney has found that African American teens and young adults do indeed move through these steps or stages toward a clear ethnic identity. The "bicultural" orientation of the last stage has been found to be a consistent characteristic of adolescents and adults who have high self-esteem and enjoy good relations with members of both the dominant culture and their own ethnic group (Yamada & Singelis, 1999).

Biracial Adolescents Biracial adolescents experience a different pathway to ethnic identity, one that highlights the difference between the biological aspects of race and the psychosocial nature of ethnic identity. Studies showing that biracial siblings often develop different ethnic identities highlight this distinction. To explain these surprising findings, psychologist Maria Root (2003), who has studied identity development in biracial teens for two decades, has proposed a theoretical model which includes four sets of factors that interact with a biracial adolescent's personality to shape the development of her ethnic identity.

Hazing and the emotional trauma that it engenders represent one factor. Often, Root says, biracial teens are challenged by the racial group of one parent to prove their "authenticity." Such challenges force them to adopt new music and clothing preferences, change their speech patterns, and reject peers who represent their other parent's group. This kind of hazing, says Root, leads biracial teens to reject the group by whom they are hazed, even if, for the sake of social survival, they outwardly appear to have conformed to it.

Family and neighborhood variables constitute the second and third factors. If a biracial teen is abused or rejected by a parent, she tends to reject the ethnicity of that parent. Moreover, if a biracial adolescent grows up in a neighborhood in which the ethnic group of one of her parents is highly dominant, she is likely to adopt the ethnicity of that dominant group. The fourth factor that influences ethnic identity development in biracial teens is the presence of other salient identities. For example, for teens growing up in military families, the identity of "Army brat" or "Air Force brat" supersedes ethnic identity.

Immigrant Teens Adolescents in immigrant families often feel caught between the culture of their parents and that of their new homes. For example, cultures that emphasize the community rather than the individual view teens' acceptance of family responsibilities as a sign of maturity. A question such as whether a teen should get a job is decided in terms of family needs. If the family needs money, the adolescent might be encouraged to work. However, if the family needs the teenager to care for younger siblings while the parents work, then a part-time job is likely to be forbidden. By contrast, most American parents think that part-time jobs help teens mature and allow their children to work, even if their doing so inconveniences the parents in some way. As a result, an immigrant teen may feel that his parents are preventing him from fitting in with his American peers.

Research involving Asian American teenagers helps to illustrate this point. Psychologists have found that first-generation Asian American teens often feel guilty about responding to the individualistic pressures of North American culture. Their feelings of guilt appear to be based on their parents' cultural norms, which hold that the most mature adolescents are those who take a greater role in the family rather than trying to separate from it (Chen, 1999). Thus, for many Asian American adolescents, achievement of personal and ethnic identity involves balancing the individualistic demands of North American culture against the familial obligations of their parents' cultures. Consequently, many teens in immigrant families develop a bicultural identity (Farver, Bhadha, & Narang, 2002; Phinney, Horenczyk, Liebkind, & Vedder, 2001).

Moral Development

As you read in Chapter 12, Piaget proposed a stage theory of moral reasoning. However, the theorist whose work has had the most powerful impact is psychologist Lawrence Kohlberg (Bergman, 2002; Colby, Kohlberg, Gibbs, & Lieberman, 1983; Kohlberg, 1976, 1981). Moreover, theories of moral reasoning have been important in explanations of adolescent antisocial behavior.

Kohlberg's Theory of Moral Reasoning

Learning Objective 15.7

What are the features of moral reasoning at each of Kohlberg's stages?

You may recall from Chapter 12 that Piaget proposed two stages in the development of moral reasoning. Working from Piaget's basic assumptions, Kohlberg devised a way of measuring moral reasoning based on research participants' responses to moral dilemmas such as the following:

> In Europe, a woman was near death from a special kind of cancer. There was one drug that the doctors thought might save her. It was a form of radium that a druggist in the same town had recently discovered. The drug was expensive to make, but the druggist was charging ten times what the drug cost him to make. He paid $200 for the radium and charged $2000 for a small dose of the drug. The sick woman's husband, Heinz, went to everyone he knew to borrow the money, but he could only get together about $1000. . . . He told the druggist that his wife was dying, and asked him to sell it cheaper or let him pay later. But the druggist said, "No, I discovered the drug and I'm going to make money from it." So Heinz got desperate and broke into the man's store to steal the drug for his wife. (Kohlberg & Elfenbein, 1975, p. 621)

Kohlberg analyzed participants' answers to questions about such dilemmas (for example, "Should Heinz have stolen the drug? Why?") and concluded that there were three levels of moral development, each made up of two substages, as summarized in Table 15.1 on page 458. It is important to understand that what determines the stage or level of a person's moral judgment is not any specific moral choice but the form of reasoning used to justify that choice. For example, either response to Kohlberg's dilemma—that Heinz should steal the drug or that he should not—could be justified with logic at any given stage.

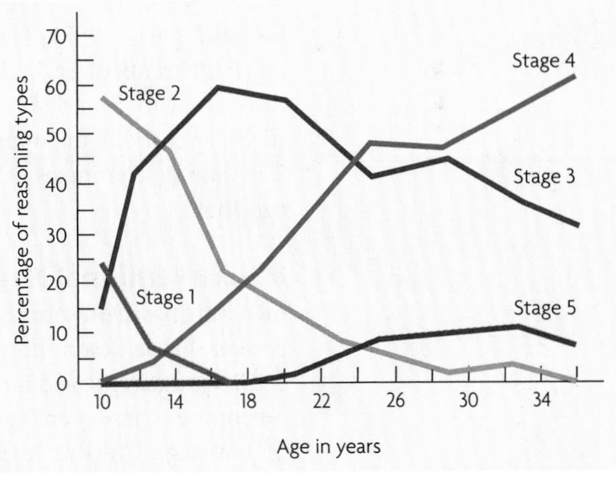

Figure 15.4 Colby and Kohlberg's Longitudinal Study of Moral Reasoning

These findings are from Colby and Kohlberg's long-term longitudinal study of a group of boys who were asked about Kohlberg's moral dilemmas every few years from age 10 through early adulthood. As they got older, the stage or level of their answers changed, with conventional reasoning appearing fairly widely at high school age. Postconventional, or principled, reasoning was not very common at any age.

(*Source*: Figure of "longitudinal study of moral judgement" by A. Colby et al., 1983, Figure 1. p. 46, © The Society for Research in Child Development. Reprinted by permission of Blackwell Publishing.)

Age and Moral Reasoning The stages are correlated somewhat loosely with age. Very few children reason beyond stage 1 or 2, and stages 2 and 3 reasoning are the types most commonly found among adolescents (Walker, de Vries, & Trevethan, 1987). Among adults, stages 3 and 4 are the most common (Gibson, 1990). Two research examples illustrate these overall age trends. The first, shown in Figure 15.4, comes from Kohlberg's own longitudinal study of 58 boys,

Table 15.1 Kohlberg's Stages of Moral Development

Level	Stages	Description
Level I: Preconventional Morality	*Stage 1*: Punishment and Obedience Orientation	The child or teenager decides what is wrong on the basis of what is punished. Obedience is valued for its own sake, but the child obeys because the adults have superior power.
	Stage 2: Individualism, Instrumental Purpose, and Exchange	Children and teens follow rules when it is in their immediate interest. What is good is what brings pleasant results.
Level II: Conventional Morality	*Stage 3*: Mutual Interpersonal Expectations, Relationships, and Interpersonal Conformity	Moral actions are those that live up to the expectations of the family or other significant group. "Being good" becomes important for its own sake.
	Stage 4: Social System and Conscience (Law-and-Order Orientation)	Moral actions are those so defined by larger social groups or the society as a whole. One should fulfill duties one has agreed to and uphold laws, except in extreme cases.
Level III: Postconventional Morality	*Stage 5*: Social Contract Orientation	This stage involves acting so as to achieve the "greatest good for the greatest number." The teenager or adult is aware that most values are relative and laws are changeable, although rules should be upheld in order to preserve the social order. Still, there are some basic absolute values, such as the importance of each person's life and liberty.
	Stage 6: Universal Ethical Principles Orientation	The small number of adults who reason at stage 6 develop and follow self-chosen ethical principles in determining what is right. These ethical principles are part of an articulated, integrated, carefully thought out, and consistently followed system of values and principles.

Sources: Kohlberg, 1976; Lickona, 1978.

first interviewed when they were 10 and then followed for more than 20 years (Colby et al., 1983). Figure 15.5 shows cross-sectional data from a study by Lawrence Walker and his colleagues (1987). They studied 10 boys and 10 girls at each of four ages, interviewing the parents of each child as well. The results of these two studies, although not identical, point to remarkably similar conclusions about the order of emergence of the various stages and about the approximate ages at which they predominate. In both studies, stage 2 reasoning dominates at around age 10, and stage 3 reasoning is most common at about age 16.

Preconventional Reasoning At level I, **preconventional morality**, the child's judgments are based on sources of authority who are close by and physically superior—usually the parents. Just as descriptions of others are largely external at this level, so the standards the child uses to judge rightness or wrongness are external rather than internal. In particular, it is the outcome or consequence of an action that determines the rightness or wrongness of the action.

In stage 1 of this level—*punishment and obedience orientation*—the child relies on the physical consequences of some action to decide whether it is right or wrong. If he is punished, the behavior was wrong; if he is not punished, it was right. He is obedient to adults because they are bigger and stronger.

In stage 2—*individualism, instrumental purpose, and exchange*—the child or adolescent operates on the principle that you should do things that are rewarded and avoid things that are punished. For this reason, the stage is sometimes called *naive hedonism*. If it feels good or brings pleasant results, it is good. Some beginning of concern for other people is apparent during this stage, but only if that concern can be expressed as something that benefits the child or teenager himself as well. So, he can enter into agreements such as "If you help me, I'll help you."

preconventional morality in Kohlberg's theory, the level of moral reasoning in which judgments are based on authorities outside the self

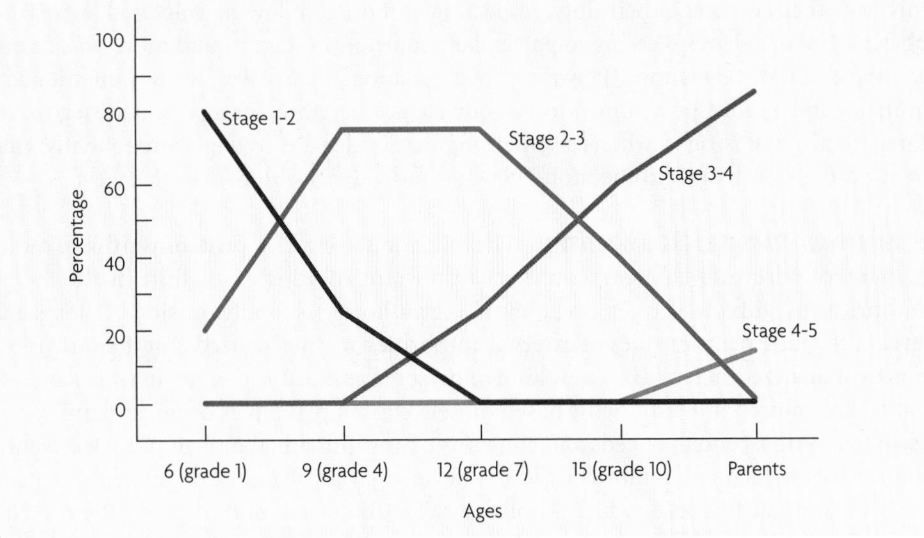

Figure 15.5 **Percentages of Children and Parents Who Show Moral Reasoning at Each of Kohlberg's Stages**

Like the results of Colby and Kohlberg's longitudinal study, cross-sectional data collected by Lawrence Walker and his colleagues suggest that stages 1 and 2 reasoning dominates in the early school years, stages 2 and 3 responses are common from the later elementary through middle school years, and stages 3 and 4 reasoning begins to be predominant in high school and remains so into adulthood.

(*Source*: Walker et al., from Table 1, p. 849. "Moral stages and moral orientations in real-life and hypothetical dilemmas," *Child Development*, 60 (1987), 842–858. © The Society for Research in Child Development. Reprinted by permission of Blackwell Publishing.)

To illustrate, here are some responses to variations of the Heinz dilemma, drawn from studies of children and teenagers in a number of different cultures, all of whom were at stage 2:

> He should steal the [drug] for his wife because if she dies he'll have to pay for the funeral, and that costs a lot. [Taiwan]
>
> [He should steal the drug because] he should protect the life of his wife so he doesn't have to stay alone in life. [Puerto Rico] (Snarey, 1985, p. 221)

Conventional Reasoning At the next major level, the level of **conventional morality**, rules or norms of a group to which the individual belongs become the basis of moral judgments, whether that group is the family, the peer group, a church, or the nation. What the chosen reference group defines as right or good is right or good in the individual's view. Again, very few children exhibit conventional thinking, but many adolescents are capable of this kind of moral reasoning.

Stage 3 (the first stage of level II) is the stage of *mutual interpersonal expectations, relationships, and interpersonal conformity* (sometimes also called the *good boy/nice girl stage*). Regardless of age, individuals who reason at this stage believe that good behavior is what pleases other people. They value trust, loyalty, respect, gratitude, and maintenance of mutual relationships. Andy, a boy Kohlberg interviewed who was at stage 3, said:

> I try to do things for my parents, they've always done things for you. I try to do everything my mother says, I try to please her. Like she wants me to be a doctor and I want to, too, and she's helping me get up there. (Kohlberg, 1964, p. 401)

Another mark of this third stage is that the individual makes judgments based on intentions as well as on outward behavior. If someone "didn't mean to do it," the wrongdoing is seen as less serious than if the person did it "on purpose."

Stage 4, the second stage of the conventional morality level, incorporates the norms of a larger reference group into moral judgments. Kohlberg labeled this the stage of *social system and conscience*. It is also sometimes called the *law-and-order orientation*. People reasoning at

conventional morality in Kohlberg's theory, the level of moral reasoning in which judgments are based on the rules or norms of a group to which the person belongs

THE WHOLE CHILD IN FOCUS

What do Michelle's career plans say about her level of moral development? Find out on page 475.

this stage focus on doing their duty, respecting authority, following rules and laws. The emphasis is less on what is pleasing to particular people (as in stage 3) and more on adhering to a complex set of regulations. However, the regulations themselves are not questioned, and morality and legality are assumed to be equivalent. Therefore, for a person at stage 4, something that is legal is right, whereas something that is illegal is wrong. Consequently, changes in law can effect changes in the moral views of individuals who reason at stage 4.

Postconventional Reasoning The transition to level III, **postconventional morality**, is marked by several changes, the most important of which is a shift in the source of authority. Individuals who reason at level I see authority as totally outside of themselves; at level II, the judgments or rules of external authorities are internalized, but they are not questioned or analyzed; at level III, a new kind of personal authority emerges, in which an individual makes choices and judgments based on self-chosen principles or on principles that are assumed to transcend the needs and concerns of any individual or group. Postconventional thinkers represent only a minority of adults and an even smaller minority of adolescents.

In stage 5 at this level, which Kohlberg called the *social contract orientation*, such self-chosen principles begin to be evident. Rules, laws, and regulations are not seen as irrelevant; they are important ways of ensuring fairness. But people operating at this level also acknowledge that there are times when the rules, laws, and regulations need to be ignored or changed.

The American civil rights movement of the 1950s and 1960s is a good example of stage 5 reasoning in action. *Civil disobedience*—deliberately breaking laws believed to be immoral—arose as a way of protesting racial segregation. For example, in restaurants, African Americans intentionally took seats that were reserved for Whites. It is important to note that the practice of civil disobedience does not usually involve avoiding the penalties that accompany criminal behavior. Indeed, some of the most effective and poignant images from that period of U.S. history are photographs of individuals who surrendered and were jailed for breaking segregation laws. This behavior illustrates the stage 5 view that, as a general principle, upholding the law is important, even though a specific law that is deemed to be immoral can—or even should—be broken when breaking it will serve to promote the common good.

Civil disobedience involves intentionally breaking laws one believes to be immoral. For example, in the early years of the U.S. civil rights movement, African Americans broke laws that excluded them from certain sections of restaurants by "sitting in" at Whites-only lunch counters. Practitioners of civil disobedience do not try to evade the consequences of their actions, because they believe in upholding the law as a general principle even though they view some specific laws as immoral. Thus, the thinking that underlies acts of civil disobedience represents Kohlberg's postconventional level of moral reasoning.

In his original writing about moral development, Kohlberg also included a sixth stage, the *universal ethical principles orientation*. Stage 6 reasoning involves balancing equally valid, but conflicting, moral principles against one another in order to determine which should be given precedence with respect to a specific moral issue. When a person who is arguing against capital punishment says that an individual's right to life is more important than society's right to exact justice from those who are convicted of heinous crimes, this might or might not be an example of stage 6 reasoning. Remember, the key to assessing an individual's stage of moral development is to fully probe the reasoning behind his or her answer to a question about a moral dilemma. Sometimes this kind of probing reveals that arguments that, on first glance, appear to represent stage 6 thinking are actually based on the authority of a religious tradition or a highly respected individual, in which case the reasoning is conventional rather than postconventional. Occasionally, though, the individual making such an argument is able to explain it in terms of a universal ethical principle that must always be adhered to regardless of any other considerations. In the case of opposition

postconventional morality in Kohlberg's theory, the level of moral reasoning in which judgments are based on an integration of individual rights and the needs of society

to the death penalty, the universal ethical principle would be the idea that the maintenance of human life is the highest of all moral principles. Note, however, that a person reasoning at stage 6 would not argue that society has no right to punish criminals. Instead, he or she would say that, in situations where upholding such rights involves termination of a human life, the right to life of the person whose life would be ended takes precedence.

Kohlberg argued that this sequence of reasoning is both universal and hierarchically organized. That is, each stage grows out of the preceding one. Kohlberg did not suggest that all individuals eventually progress through all six stages—or even that each stage is tied to specific ages. But he insisted that the order is invariant and universal. He also believed that the social environment determines how slowly or rapidly individuals move through the stages.

The evidence seems fairly strong that the stages follow one another in the sequence Kohlberg proposed. Long-term longitudinal studies of teenagers and young adults in the United States, Israel, and Turkey show that changes in participants' reasoning nearly always occur in the hypothesized order (Colby et al., 1983; Nisan & Kohlberg, 1982; Snarey, Reimer, & Kohlberg, 1985; Walker, 1989). People do not skip stages, and movement down the sequence rather than up occurs only about 5–7% of the time.

Variations of Kohlberg's dilemmas have been used with children in a wide range of countries, both Western and non-Western, industrialized and nonindustrialized (Snarey, 1985). In every culture, researchers find higher stages of reasoning among older children, but cultures differ in the highest level of reasoning observed. In urban cultures (both Western and non-Western), stage 5 is typically the highest stage observed; in agricultural societies and those in which there is little opportunity for formal education, stage 4 is typically the highest. Collectively, this evidence seems to provide quite strong support for the universality of Kohlberg's stage sequence.

Causes and Consequences of Moral Development

Learning Objective 15.8

What are some important causes and effects of the development of moral reasoning?

The most obvious reason for the general correlations between Kohlberg's stages and chronological age is cognitive development. Specifically, it appears that children must have a firm grasp of concrete operational thinking before they can develop and use conventional moral reasoning. Likewise, formal operational thinking appears to be necessary for advancement to the postconventional level.

To be more specific, Kohlberg and many other theorists suggest that the decline of egocentrism that occurs as an individual moves through Piaget's concrete and formal operational stages is the cognitive-developmental variable that matters most in moral reasoning. The idea is that the greater a child's or adolescent's ability to look at a situation from another person's perspective, the more advanced she is likely to be in moral reasoning. Psychologists use the term **role taking** to refer to this ability (Selman, 1980). Research has provided strong support for the hypothesized link between role taking and moral development (Kuhn, Kohlberg, Languer, & Haan, 1977; Walker, 1980).

Nevertheless, cognitive development isn't enough. Kohlberg thought that the development of moral reasoning also required support from the social environment. Specifically, he claimed that in order to foster mature moral reasoning, a child's or teenager's social environment must provide him with opportunities for meaningful, reciprocal dialogue about moral issues.

Longitudinal research relating parenting styles and family climate to levels of moral reasoning suggests that Kohlberg was right (Pratt, Arnold, & Pratt, 1999). Parents' ability to identify, understand, and respond to children's and adolescents' less mature forms of moral reasoning seems to be particularly important to the development of moral reasoning. This ability on the part of parents is important because people of all ages have difficulty understanding and remembering moral arguments that are more advanced than their own level (Narvaez, 1998). Thus, a parent who can express her own moral views in words

role taking the ability to look at a situation from another person's perspective

that reflect her child's level of understanding is more likely to be able to influence the child's moral development.

As an individual's capacity for moral reasoning grows, so does his ability to think logically about issues in other domains. For example, the complexity of an individual's political reasoning is very similar to the complexity of his moral reasoning (Raaijmakers, Verbogt, & Vollebergh, 1998). Attitudes toward the acceptability of violence also vary with levels of moral reasoning. Individuals at lower levels are more tolerant of violence (Sotelo & Sangrador, 1999).

Perhaps most importantly, teenagers' level of moral reasoning appears to be positively correlated with prosocial behavior and negatively related to antisocial behavior (Schonert-Reichl, 1999). In other words, the highest levels of prosocial behavior are found among teens at the highest levels of moral reasoning (compared to their peers). Alternatively, the highest levels of antisocial behavior are found among adolescents at the lowest levels of moral reasoning.

Learning Objective 15.9

How has Kohlberg's theory been criticized?

Criticisms of Kohlberg's Theory

Criticisms of Kohlberg's theory have come from theorists representing different perspectives.

Culture and Moral Reasoning Cross-cultural research provides strong support for the universality of Kohlberg's stage sequence (Snarey, 1985, 1995). Nevertheless, cross-cultural researchers have argued that his approach is too narrow to be considered truly universal. These critics point out that many aspects of moral reasoning found in non-Western cultures do not fit in well with Kohlberg's approach (Eckensberger & Zimba, 1997). The root of the problem, they say, is that Kohlberg's theory is strongly tied to the idea that justice is an overriding moral principle. To be sure, say critics, justice is an important moral concept throughout the world, and thus it isn't surprising that Kohlberg's stage sequence has been so strongly supported in cross-cultural research. However, these critics argue that the notion that justice supercedes all other moral considerations is what distinguishes Western from non-Western cultures. As these criticisms would predict, research has shown that the responses of individuals in non-Western cultures to Kohlberg's classic dilemmas often include ideas that are not found in his scoring system (Baek, 2002).

For example, in many cultures, respect for one's elders is an important moral principle that often overrides other concerns (Eckensberger & Zimba, 1997). Thus, if researchers alter the Heinz dilemma so that the sick woman is Heinz's mother rather than his wife, Western and non-Western research participants are likely to respond quite differently. Such differences are difficult to explain from the justice-based, stage-oriented perspective of Kohlberg's theory. Advocates for the theory have argued that respect for elders as the basis of moral reasoning represents Kohlberg's conventional level. Critics, by contrast, say that this classification underestimates the true moral reasoning level of individuals from non-Western cultures.

Moral Reasoning and Emotions Researchers studying the link between moral emotions and moral reasoning have also criticized the narrowness of Kohlberg's justice-based approach. Psychologist Nancy Eisenberg, for example, suggests that empathy, the ability to identify with others' emotions, is both a cause and a consequence of moral development (Eisenberg, 2000). Similarly, Eisenberg suggests that a complete explanation of moral development should include age-related and individual variations in the ability to regulate emotions (such as anger) that can motivate antisocial behavior.

Likewise, Carol Gilligan claims that an ethic based on caring for others and on maintaining social relationships may be as important to moral reasoning as ideas about justice are. Gilligan's theory argues that there are at least two distinct "moral orientations": justice and care (Gilligan, 1982; Gilligan & Wiggins, 1987). Each has its own central injunction—not to treat others unfairly (justice) and not to turn away from someone in need (caring). Research suggests that adolescents do exhibit a moral orientation based on care and that care-based reasoning about hypothetical moral dilemmas is related to reasoning about real-life dilemmas (Skoe et al., 1999). In response, Kohlberg acknowledged in his later writings that his theory deals specifically with development of reasoning about justice and does not claim to be a comprehensive account of moral development (Kohlberg, Levine, & Hewer, 1983). Thus, some developmentalists view Gilligan's ideas about moral development as an expansion of Kohlberg's theory rather than a rejection of it (Jorgensen, 2006).

Possible sex differences in moral reasoning are another focus of Gilligan's theory. According to Gilligan, boys and girls learn both justice and care orientations, but girls are more likely to operate from the care orientation whereas boys are more likely to operate from a justice orientation. Because of these differences, girls and boys tend to perceive moral dilemmas quite differently.

Given the emerging evidence on sex differences in styles of interaction and in friendship patterns, Gilligan's hypothesis makes some sense. Perhaps girls, focused more on intimacy in their relationships, judge moral dilemmas by different criteria. But, in fact, research on moral dilemmas has not consistently shown that boys are more likely to use justice reasoning or that girls more often use care reasoning. Several studies of adults have shown such a pattern (e.g., Lyons, 1983; Wark & Krebs, 1996). However, studies of children and teenagers generally have not (Jadack, Hyde, Moore, & Keller, 1995; Smetana, Killen, & Turiel, 1991; Walker et al., 1987). Further, recent evidence suggests that such sex differences, if they exist, may be restricted to North American culture (Skoe et al., 1999).

Moral Reasoning and Behavior Finally, critics have questioned the degree to which moral reasoning predicts moral behavior (Krebs & Denton, 2006). Researchers have found that moral reasoning and moral behavior are correlated, but the relationship is far from perfect. To explain inconsistencies between reasoning and behavior, learning theorists suggest that moral reasoning is situational rather than developmental. They point to a variety of studies to support this assertion.

First, neither adolescents nor adults reason at the same level in response to every hypothetical dilemma (Rique & Camino, 1997). An individual research participant might reason at the conventional level in response to one dilemma and at the postconventional level with respect to another. Second, the types of characters in moral dilemmas strongly influence research participants' responses to them, especially when the participants are adolescents. For example, hypothetical dilemmas involving celebrities as characters elicit much lower levels of moral reasoning from teenagers than those involving fictional characters such as Heinz (Einerson, 1998).

In addition, research participants show disparities in levels of moral reasoning invoked in response to hypothetical dilemmas and real-life moral issues. For example, Israeli Jewish, Israeli Bedouin, and Palestinian youths living in Israel demonstrate different levels of moral reasoning when responding to hypothetical stories such as the Heinz dilemma than they exhibit in discussing the moral dimensions of the long-standing conflicts among their ethnic groups (Elbedour, Baker, & Charlesworth, 1997). Thus, as learning theorists predict, it appears that situational factors may be more important variables for decisions about actual moral behavior than the level of moral reasoning exhibited in response to hypothetical dilemmas.

Adolescents who engage in serious forms of antisocial behavior are less advanced than their peers in moral reasoning because they lack the ability to look at situations from others' points of view.

The consistent finding of low levels of moral reasoning among adolescents who engage in serious forms of antisocial behavior has been of particular interest to developmentalists (Aleixo & Norris, 2000; Ashkar & Kenny, 2007; Cheung, Chan, Lee, Liu, & Leung, 2001; Ma, 2003). As you learned in Chapter 13, *delinquency* is distinguished from other forms of antisocial behavior, such as bullying, on the basis of actual law breaking. Delinquents appear to be behind their peers in moral reasoning because of deficits in role-taking skills. For example, researchers have found that teenagers who can look at actions they are contemplating from their parents' perspective are less likely to engage in delinquent behavior than adolescents who cannot do so (Wyatt & Carlo, 2002). Most delinquent teens seem to be unable to look at their crimes from their victims' perspectives or to assess hypothetical crimes from the victims' perspectives. Thus, programs aimed at helping delinquents develop more mature levels of moral reasoning usually focus on heightening their awareness of the victim's point of view.

Table 15.2 Children's and Adolescents' Comments About How to Solve Disagreements Between Friends

Age	Comments
5-year-olds	"Go away from her and come back later when you're not fighting."
8-year-olds	"Well, if you say something and don't really mean it, then you have to mean it when you take it back."
14-year-olds	"Sometimes you got to get away for a while. Calm down a bit so you won't be so angry. Then get back and try to talk it out."
16-year-olds	"Well, you could talk it out, but it usually fades itself out. It usually takes care of itself. You don't have to explain everything. You do certain things and each of you knows what it means. But if not, then talk it out."

Source: Selman, 1980, pp. 107–113.

Social Relationships

Fifteen-year-old Sheronnah's mother told her long ago that she would not be able to go out on a date until she was 16. Recently, however, a boy at school has begun to pursue Sheronnah, and she has spent untold hours debating the issue with her mother. Her mother has refused to relent, and as a result, Sheronnah is giving her mother the "silent treatment." According to the progression in children's and adolescents' understanding of social conflicts described in Table 15.2, Sheronnah is likely to expect that the division between her mother and herself over the dating issue is a temporary one. Nevertheless, Sheronnah's predicament illustrates the growing importance of peer relationships in adolescence, a trend that is shown in Figure 15.6.

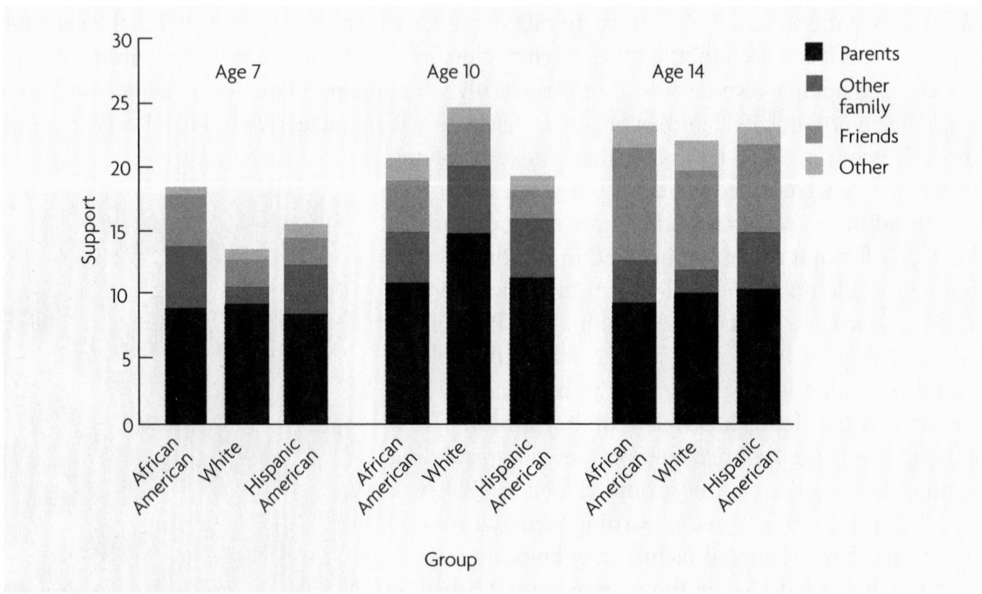

Figure 15.6 Sources of Support for Adolescents

Children and teens from different ethnic groups were asked about the amount and type of support they received from various sources. Note that for teens, friends become more significant sources of support, but parents do not become less important.

(*Source*: Adapted from Figure 2, p. 815, "Convoys of Social Support and Early Adolescence: Structure and Function," by M. Levitt, N. Guacci-Franco, and J. Levitt, from *Developmental Psychology*, 29. Copyright © 1993, by the American Psychological Association.)

Relationships with Parents

Learning Objective 15.10

What are the features of adolescents' relationships with their parents?

Teenagers have two apparently contradictory tasks in their relationships with their parents: to establish autonomy from them and to maintain a sense of relatedness with them. As a result, the frequency of parent-child conflicts increases. This trend has been documented by a number of researchers (e.g., Flannery, Montemayor, & Eberly, 1994; Laursen, 1995). In the great majority of families, these conflicts center around everyday issues such as chores or personal rights—for example, whether the adolescent should be allowed to wear a bizarre hairstyle or whether and when the teen should be required to do chores. Teenagers and their parents also often disagree about the age at which certain privileges—such as dating—ought to be granted and about the amount of parental supervision teenagers need (Cunningham, Swanson, Spencer, & Dupree, 2003; Dekovic, Noom, & Meeus, 1997).

Individual traits of teenagers themselves may contribute to conflicts with parents. The adolescent's temperament, for example, contributes to the amount of conflict. Those who have been difficult from early childhood are the most likely to experience high degrees of conflict with parents in adolescence (Dekovic, 1999). Teens' pubertal status may be a factor as well. Among girls, conflict seems to rise after menarche (Holmbeck & Hill, 1991). Moreover, as noted earlier regarding Asian American teens, cultural factors affect both the degree of parent-teen conflict and perceptions of its meaning.

Despite these conflicts, teenagers' underlying emotional attachment to their parents remains strong on average (refer back to Figure 15.6). A study in the Netherlands suggests that a teenager's bond with her parents may weaken somewhat in the middle of adolescence (ages 15 and 16) and then return to former levels (van Wel, 1994). But virtually all the researchers who have explored this question find that a teenager's sense of well-being or happiness is more strongly correlated with the quality of her attachment to her parents than with the quality of her relationships with peers (e.g., Greenberg, Siegel, & Leitch, 1983; Raja, McGee, & Stanton, 1992). Moreover, research findings regarding the centrality of parent-teen relationships have been consistent across a variety of cultures (Claes, 1998; Okamoto & Uechi, 1999).

Research in several countries has also found that teens who remain closely attached to their parents are the most likely to be academically successful and to enjoy good peer relations (Mayseless & Scharf, 2007; Turnage, 2004; Weimer, Kerns, & Oldenburg, 2004; Zimmermann, 2004). They are also less likely than less securely attached teens to engage in antisocial behavior (Ma, Shek, Cheung, & Oi Bun Lam, 2000). Further, the quality of attachment in early adolescence predicts drug use in later adolescence and early adulthood (Brook, Whiteman, Finch, & Cohen, 2000). Teens who are close to their parents are less likely to use drugs than peers whose bonds with parents are weaker. Thus, even while teenagers are becoming more autonomous, they need their parents to provide a psychological safe base.

Although it is true that the physical changes of puberty are often followed by an increase in the number of conflicts, it is a myth that conflict is the main feature of the parent-adolescent relationship.

Friendships

Learning Objective 15.11

What are the characteristics of adolescents' friendships?

Despite the importance of family relationships to adolescents, it is clear that peer relationships become far more significant in adolescence than they have been at any earlier period. For many, the electronic communication devices that are available today serve as hubs around which their social networks revolve. Many teenagers have one group of friends with whom they communicate by phone, another with whom they exchange online instant messages and email, and yet another with whom they associate through online communities such as myspace.com (Foehr, 2006). As a result, teenagers have a wider range of acquaintances than their parents did in adolescence. However, they do not necessarily have more close friends.

Teens' friendships become increasingly intimate, in the sense that adolescent friends share more and more of their inner feelings and secrets and are more knowledgeable about each other's feelings. Loyalty and faithfulness become more valued characteristics of friendship. However, the ability to display intimacy, loyalty, and faithfulness in the context of a friendship doesn't come automatically with age. In fact, teens vary considerably in these interpersonal skills. The variation may be the result of individual differences in temperament and personality or of teens' experiences with family relationships (Updegraff & Obeidallah, 1999).

Adolescent friendships are also more stable than those of younger children (Bowker, 2004; Degirmencioglu, Urberg, & Tolson, 1998). In one longitudinal study, researchers found that only about 20% of friendships among fourth-graders lasted as long as a year, whereas about 40% of friendships formed by these same youngsters when they were tenth-graders were long-lasting (Cairns & Cairns, 1994). Friendship stability probably increases in adolescence because older teens work harder than younger teens and elementary school children at maintaining positive relationships with friends through negotiation of conflicts (Nagamine, 1999).

THE WHOLE CHILD IN FOCUS

Do Cho and Michelle expect to remain close friends even after they graduate from high school? Find out on page 475.

In addition, teens often choose friends who are committed to the same activities they are. For example, many teens, especially boys, report that peer companionship is their primary motive for playing computer and video games (Chou & Tsai, 2007; Colwell & Kato, 2005). Some studies suggest that shared video game–playing experiences promote the development of a masculine gender role among male teens (Sanford & Madill, 2006). Some developmentalists also argue that playing these games in group settings helps male adolescents learn to channel aggressive and competitive impulses into socially acceptable ways of expressing them (Jansz & Martens, 2005). However, playing violent video games, even in social settings, increases feelings of hostility and decreases sensitivity to violent images (Arriaga, Esteyes, Carneiro, & Monteiro, 2006; Bushman & Huesman, 2006; Carnagey & Anderson, 2005). Thus, the social costs of playing video games may outweigh their benefits.

Finally, adolescents' reasons for ending friendships reflect the influence of individual differences in rate of development of social skills. For example, a change in identity status from a less mature to a more mature level often leads to acquisition of new friends (Akers, Jones, & Coyl, 1998). Likewise, girls seem to prefer friendships with other girls whose romantic status is the same as their own—that is, girls who have boyfriends prefer female friends who also have boyfriends. In fact, a girl who gets a boyfriend is likely to spend less time with female peers and to end long-standing friendships with girls who haven't yet acquired a romantic partner (Zimmer-Gembeck, 1999). For boys, differences in athletic achievements can lead to the end of previously important friendships (Benenson & Benarroch, 1998).

Learning Objective 15.12

How do peer groups change over the teen years?

Peer Groups

Like friendships, peer groups become relatively stable in adolescence (Degirmencioglu, Urberg, & Tolson, 1998). Adolescents typically choose to associate with a group that shares their values, attitudes, behaviors, and identity status (Akers et al., 1998; Mackey & La Greca, 2007; Urberg, Degirmencioglu, & Tolson, 1998). If the discrepancy between their own ideas and those of their friends becomes too great, teens are more likely to switch to a more compatible group of friends than to be persuaded to adopt the first group's values or behaviors (Verkooijen, de Vries, & Nielsen, 2007). Furthermore, teenagers report that when explicit peer pressure is exerted, it is likely to be pressure toward positive activities, such as school involvement, and away from misconduct.

The structure of the peer group also changes over the years of adolescence. The classic, widely quoted early study is that of Dunphy (1963) on the formation, dissolution, and interaction of teenaged groups in a high school in Sydney, Australia, between 1958 and 1960. Dunphy identified two important subvarieties of groups. The first type, which he called a **clique**, is made up of four to six young people who appear to be strongly attached to one another. Cliques have strong cohesiveness and high levels of intimate sharing.

In the early years of adolescence, cliques are almost entirely same-sex groups—a holdover from the preadolescent pattern. Gradually, however, the cliques combine into larger sets that Dunphy called **crowds**, which include both males and females. Finally, the crowd breaks down again into mixed-gender cliques and then into loose associations of couples. In Dunphy's study, the period during which adolescents socialized in crowds was roughly between 13 and 15—the very years when they display the greatest conformity to peer pressure.

More recent researchers on adolescence have changed Dunphy's labels somewhat (Brown, 1990; Brown, Mory, & Kinney, 1994). They use the word *crowd* to refer to the *reputation-based group* with which a young person is identified, either by choice or by peer designation. In U.S. schools, these groups have labels such as "jocks," "brains," "nerds," "dweebs," "punks," "druggies," "toughs," "normals," "populars," "preppies," and "loners." Studies in American junior high and high schools make it clear that teenagers can readily identify each of the major crowds in their school and have quite stereotypical—even caricatured—descriptions of them (e.g., "The partyers goof off a lot more than the jocks do, but they don't come to school stoned like the burnouts do") (Brown et al., 1994, p. 133). Each of these descriptions serves as what Brown calls an *identity prototype*: Labeling others and oneself as belonging to one or more of these groups helps to create or reinforce the adolescent's own identity (Brown et al., 1994). Such labeling also helps the adolescent identify potential friends or foes.

Through the years of junior high and high school, the social system of crowds becomes increasingly differentiated, with more and more distinct groups. For example, in one midwestern U.S. school system, researchers found that junior high students labeled only two major crowds: one small high-status group, called "trendies" in this school, and the great mass of lower-status students, called "dweebs" (Kinney, 1993). A few years later, the same students named five distinct crowds: three with comparatively high social status and two low-status groups ("grits" and "punkers"). By late high school, these students identified seven or eight

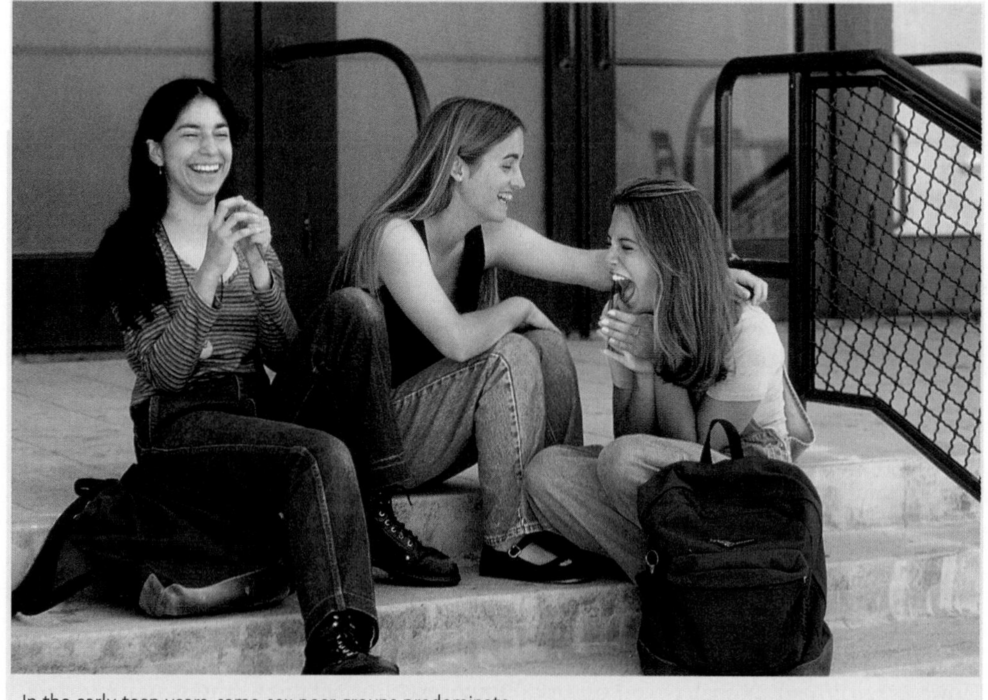
In the early teen years, same-sex peer groups predominate.

clique a group of four to six young people who appear to be strongly attached to one another

crowd a combination of cliques, including both males and females crowds, but the crowds now appeared to be less significant in the social organization of the peer group. These observations support other research that finds that mutual friendships and dating pairs are more central to social interactions in later adolescence than are cliques or crowds (Urberg, Degirmencioglu, Tolson, & Halliday-Scher, 1995).

Learning Objective 15.13

How does interest in romantic relationships emerge among heterosexual and homosexual teens?

Romantic Relationships

Heterosexual and homosexual teens follow somewhat different pathways. For both, the ups and downs associated with early romances are an important theme of development during adolescence.

Heterosexual Teens Most teens display a gradual progression from same-sex friendships to heterosexual relationships. The change happens gradually, but it seems to proceed at a somewhat more rapid pace in girls than in boys. At the beginning of adolescence, teens are still fairly rigid about their preferences for same-sex friends (Bukowski, Sippola, & Hoza, 1999). Over the next year or two, they become more open to opposite-sex friendships (Harton & Latane, 1997; Kuttler, La Greca, & Prinstein, 1999). The skills they gain in relating to opposite-sex peers in such friendships and in mixed-gender groups prepare them for romantic relationships (Feiring, 1999). Thus, although adults often assume that sexual desires are the basis of emergent romantic relationships, it appears that social factors are just as important. In fact, research suggests that social competence in a variety of relationships—with parents, peers, and friends—predicts the ease with which teens move from exclusive same-sex relationships to opposite-sex friendships and romantic relationships (Theriault, 1998).

By 12 or 13, most adolescents have a basic conception of what it means to be "in love," and the sense of being in love is an important factor in adolescent dating patterns (Montgomery & Sorell, 1998). In other words, teenagers prefer to date those with whom they believe they are in love, and they view falling out of love as a reason for ending a dating relationship. In addition, for girls (but not for boys), romantic relationships are seen as a context for self-disclosure. Put another way, girls seem to want more psychological intimacy from these early relationships than their partners do (Feiring, 1999).

Early dating and early sexual activity are more common among the poor of every ethnic group and among those who experience relatively early puberty. Religious teachings and individual attitudes about the appropriate age for dating and sexual behavior also make a difference, as does family structure. Girls with parents who are divorced or remarried, for example, report earlier dating and higher levels of sexual experience than do girls from intact families, and those with a strong religious identity report later dating and lower levels of sexuality (Bingham, Miller, & Adams, 1990; Miller & Moore, 1990). But for every group, these are years of experimentation with romantic relationships.

Homosexual Teens Romantic relationships emerge somewhat differently in the lives of homosexual teens. Researchers have found that today's homosexual teenagers are more comfortable than those in past cohorts about revealing their sexual orientation to their parents and to their peers (Floyd & Bakeman, 2006). Consequently, developmentalists have learned a great deal about the development of a homosexual orientation in the past couple of decades.

One thing that researchers have learned is that homosexual teenagers become aware of same-sex attraction at around age 11 or 12, roughly the same age when their heterosexual peers begin to notice their attraction to the opposite sex (Rosario, Scrimshaw, & Hunter, 2004). In contrast to the trend among heterosexual teens, boys notice and act on same-sex attraction at somewhat earlier ages than girls do (Grov, Bimbi, Nanin, & Parsons, 2006). However, girls who ultimately commit to a homosexual orientation express more certainty about their sexual identity than boys do (Rosario, Scrimshaw, Hunter, & Braun, 2006).

There are many boys and girls, however, who experience some degree of attraction to both sexes prior to self-identifying as gay or lesbian. Thus, many homosexual teens go through a period of sexual discovery that begins with experimentation with heterosexual relationships. Shortly thereafter, these teenagers begin to experiment with same-sex relationships. By age 15 or so, most have classified themselves as primarily heterosexual or committed to a gay, lesbian, or bisexual orientation (Rosario, Scrimshaw, & Hunter, 2004). Many of those who are gay, lesbian, or bisexual participate in clubs and extracurricular activities designed to help sexual minority youth form social connections. In the company of these like-minded peers, gay, lesbian, and bisexual teens meet potential romantic partners and find important sources of social support (Rosario, Scrimshaw, & Hunter, 2004).

Test Prep Center

with PEARSON mydevelopmentlab

THEORIES OF SOCIAL AND PERSONALITY DEVELOPMENT

15.1 What happens during Erikson's identity versus role confusion stage? (p. 448)

A child's early sense of identity becomes partly unglued in early adolescence because of the combination of rapid body growth and puberty. Thus, the teenager must develop a sense of who he is and where he belongs in his culture.

1. According to Erikson, a teen who fails to successfully resolve the identity crisis risks developing a sense of ______________________________.

2. According to Erikson, how does identifying with peer groups help teens resolve the identity crisis?

____

____

15.2 How does Marcia explain identity development? (pp. 448–450)

Building on Erikson's notion of an adolescent identity crisis, Marcia identified four identity statuses: identity achievement, moratorium, foreclosure, and identity diffusion. Identity development is influenced by cognitive development. Thus, the process of identity formation may take place somewhat later than either Erikson or Marcia believed.

3. Classify each of these behaviors as indicative of (A) identity achievement, (B) moratorium, (C) foreclosure, or (D) identity diffusion.

   ______(1) Lucy has decided on a premed major because her mother and grandmother are physicians.

   ______(2) Carl is taking a few college courses in different disciplines to figure out what he wants to major in.

   ______(3) After considering several different options, Rosa has decided to join the Marines after graduation.

   ______(4) Sean dropped out of high school at 16 and has moved from one minimum-wage job to another since then. He gives little thought to his future.

4. From the Multimedia Library within MyDevelopmentLab, watch the *Adolescence: Identity and Role Development* video and answer the following question.

Which of Marcia's identity statuses best describes the girl in the video?

____

SELF-CONCEPT

15.3 In what way does self-understanding in adolescence differ from that in childhood? (pp. 450–452)

Self-definitions become increasingly abstract in adolescence, with more emphasis on enduring internal qualities and ideology.

5. Which of the following characteristics are likely to be included in a teenager's self-description but unlikely to be included in a school-aged child's self-description?

   ______ happy

   ______ honest

   ______ tall

   ______ friendly

   ______ environmentalist

15.4 How does self-esteem change across the teenage years? (pp. 452–453)

Self-esteem drops somewhat at the beginning of adolescence and then rises steadily throughout the teenage years.

6. Transform each false statement into one that is true.

   (A) A child who enters adolescence with high self-esteem will probably maintain this level of self-worth through her teen years.

   ____

   ____

   (B) Boys and girls do not differ with regard to self-esteem.

   ____

   ____

15.5 What are the gender role concepts of adolescents? (pp. 453–454)

Teenagers increasingly define themselves in terms that include both masculine and feminine traits. When high levels of both masculinity and femininity are present, the individual is described as androgynous. Androgyny and a masculine gender role identity are associated with higher self-esteem in both male and female adolescents.

7. Classify each description as indicative of one of the following gender role identities: (A) androgynous, (B) masculine, (C) feminine, or (D) undifferentiated sex role.

   ______(1) Luis views assertiveness as the defining characteristic of his personality.

   ______(2) Sandra's ability to offer compassionate and caring responses to her friends' problems is the trait she feels best defines her personality.

   ______(3) Montel prides himself on responding according to the demands of different situations. If a problem calls for assertiveness, he can tackle it head on. If a problem calls for empathy or patience, he feels that he can handle that as well.

   ______(4) Keisha has a poorly developed sense of self and has trouble describing her identity in terms of personality traits.

15.6 How do minority, biracial, and immigrant teens develop a sense of ethnic identity? (pp. 454–457)

Young people in clearly identifiable minority groups, biracial teens, and teens in immigrant families have the additional task in adolescence of forming an ethnic identity. Phinney proposed a series of ethnic identity stages that are similar to those in Marcia's model of general identity development. Phinney's stages are unexamined ethnic identity, ethnic identity search, and ethnic identity achievement. Biracial teens may be challenged by one parent's group to prove their ethnic authenticity. For immigrant teens, the process of identity development includes reconciling differences in their own and their parents' views of the cultural values of their new and former homes.

8. In the table below, briefly summarize Phinney's stages of ethnic identity development.

Stage	Summary
Unexamined	
Search	
Achievement	

MORAL DEVELOPMENT

15.7 What are the features of moral reasoning at each of Kohlberg's stages? (pp. 457–461)

Kohlberg proposed six stages of moral reasoning, organized into three levels. Preconventional morality relies on external authority: What is punished is bad, and what feels good is good. Conventional morality is based on rules and norms provided by outside groups, such as the family, church, or society. Postconventional morality is based on self-chosen principles. Research evidence suggests that these levels and stages are loosely correlated with age, develop in a specified order, and appear in this same sequence in all cultures studied so far.

9. In the table below, summarize how individuals in each of Kohlberg's stages view society's rules.

Stage	View of Rules
Punishment and Obedience Orientation	
Individualism, Instrumental Purpose, and Exchange	
Mutual Interpersonal Expectations, Relationships, and Interpersonal Conformity	
Social System and Conscience (Law-and-Order Orientation)	
Social Contract Orientation	
Universal Ethical Principles Orientation	

15.8 What are some important causes and effects of the development of moral reasoning? (pp. 461–462)

The acquisition of cognitive role-taking skills is important to moral development, but the social environment is important as well. Specifically, to foster moral reasoning, adults must provide children with opportunities for discussion of moral issues.

10. List the factors that influence progression through Kohlberg's stages.

(A) ______________________________

(B) ______________________________

(C) ______________________________

(D) ______________________________

15.9 How has Kohlberg's theory been criticized? (pp. 462–464)

Kohlberg's theory has been criticized by cross-cultural researchers who argue that his approach is too narrow to be considered universal. Other theorists place more emphasis on learning moral behavior, and still others believe that moral reasoning may be based more on emotional factors than on ideas about justice and fairness. Delinquent teens are usually found to be far behind their peers in both role taking and moral reasoning.

11. Transform each false statement into one that is true.

(A) Kohlberg's stages have been found in all cultures.

____

____

(B) Gilligan's approach to moral development emphasizes justice.

____

____

(C) People who are advanced in moral reasoning are very unlikely to exhibit behavior that society deems to be morally unacceptable.

____

____

12. From the Multimedia Library within MyDevelopmentLab, watch the *Cognition, Emotion, and Motivation Across Cultures: Shinobu Kitayama* video and answer the following question.

How do cultural differences in views of the person and society affect people's reasoning about concepts, such as individual rights, that are emphasized in Kohlberg's approach to moral reasoning?

____

____

SOCIAL RELATIONSHIPS

15.10 What are the features of adolescents' relationships with their parents? (p. 465)

Adolescent-parent interactions typically become somewhat more conflicted in early adolescence, an effect possibly linked to the physical changes of puberty. Strong attachments to parents remain so and are predictive of good peer relations.

13. From the Multimedia Library within MyDevelopmentLab, watch the *Interaction of Cognition and Emotion: Jutta Joormann* video and answer the following question.

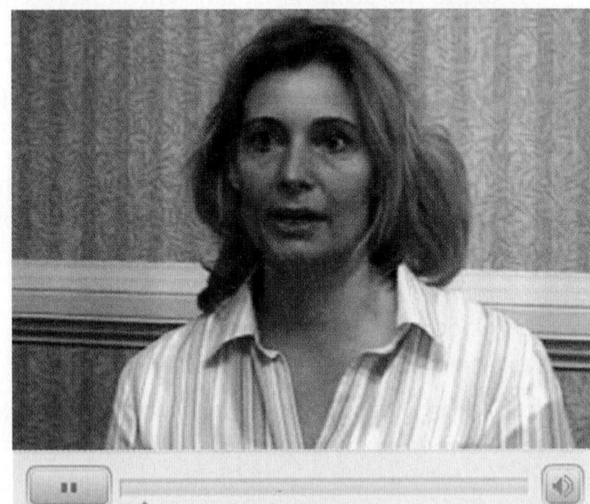

For which teens are conflicts with parents most likely to lead to emotional problems?

____

____

15.11 What are the characteristics of adolescents' friendships? (pp. 465–466)

Teens' friendships become increasingly intimate and stable. Adolescents often choose friends who share their interests.

14. List three characteristics of adolescent friendships.

(A) ______________________________

(B) ______________________________

(C) ______________________________

15.12 How do peer groups change over the teen years? (pp. 466–468)

In the early years of adolescence, cliques are almost entirely same-sex cliques. Between 13 and 15, cliques combine into crowds that include both males and females. This is the time when teens are most susceptible to peer influences. Crowds break down into mixed-gender cliques and then into small groups of couples.

15. Classify each of the following as characteristic of (A) cliques or (B) crowds.

______(1) combinations of smaller groups that includes males and females

______(2) groups of four to six teens who are strongly attached to one another

______(3) reputation-based groups

______(4) usually same-sex groups in early adolescence

______(5) serve as identity prototypes

15.13 How does interest in romantic relationships emerge among heterosexual and homosexual teens? (pp. 468–469)

Heterosexual teens gradually move from same-sex peer groups to heterosexual couples. The feeling of being "in love" is important to the formation of couple relationships. Many homosexual teens experiment with heterosexual and homosexual relationships before committing to a gay, lesbian, or bisexual orientation in mid-adolescence.

16. When do most adolescents have a basic conception of what it means to be "in love"?

____

17. List three factors that are related to ideas about the appropriate age at which to begin dating.

(A) ______________________________

(B) ______________________________

(C) ______________________________

18. When do most homosexual teens become aware of feelings of same-sex attraction?

____

19. From the Multimedia Library within MyDevelopmentLab, watch the *Michael Bailey: Evolution and Sex* video and answer the following question.

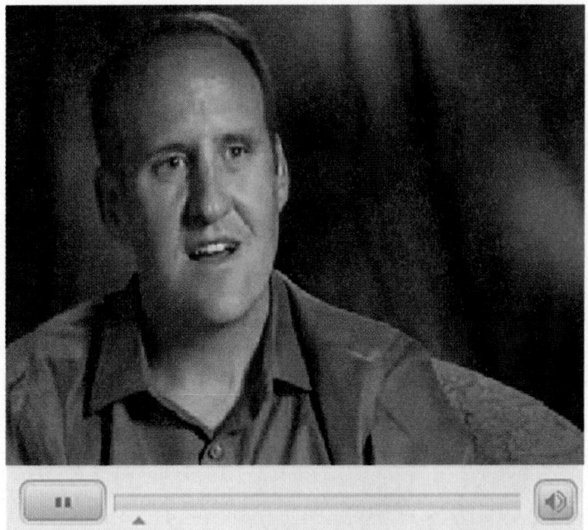

Heterosexual and homosexual males are more interested in ______________, ______________, and ______________ than heterosexual and homosexual females are.

For answers to the questions in this chapter, turn to page 526. For a list of key terms, turn to page 532.

Succeed with PEARSON **mydevelopmentlab**

Do You Know All of the Terms in This Chapter?
Find out by using the Flashcards. Want more practice? Take additional quizzes, try simulations, and watch video to be sure you are prepared for the test!

The Whole Child in Focus

Physical, Cognitive, and Socioemotional Development in Adolescence: An Integrated Review

We met Cho and Michelle at the beginning of this unit (page 382). The girls have remained close friends throughout their teen years and are now ready to graduate from high school. How have they changed, and in what ways have these changes affected their friendship?

The Prefrontal Cortex (p. 387)

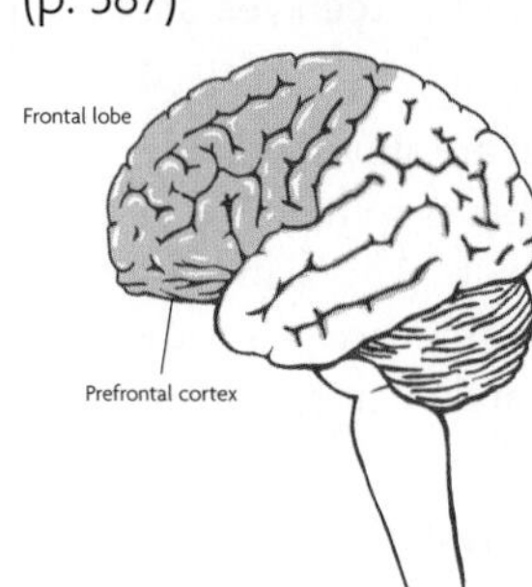

With the maturation of the **prefrontal cortex (PFC)**, the girls' abilities to manage their own thought processes have improved substantially. These advances have supported growth in the girls' capacity for **academic learning**. As a result, both girls seem to be ready to take on the intellectual challenges of college.

Michelle, who had always tended more toward **sensation-seeking** behavior than Cho, had a rough start to high school. In adjusting to her new surroundings, she made a series of decisions that had potentially negative consequences for her well-being. Cho's friendship was instrumental to Michelle's escaping relatively unscathed from her sensation-seeking adventures; following Cho's suggestions to channel her energies into more productive pursuits, Michelle joined the school's extreme sports club and became an avid rock climber.

Thinking about Developmental Pathways

1. It appears from this brief sketch of Cho and Michelle at age eighteen that Cho's progression through the milestones of puberty was slower than that of her peers. How would her peer relationships have been different if she had progressed more rapidly than her peers in this domain? What role might Michelle's support have played in helping her cope under these alternative circumstances?
2. Cho and Michelle are about to graduate from high school and go on to college. Some of their classmates, however, dropped out of school. What kinds of risk and protective factors that are relevant to staying in school were present in these girls' lives? How did these factors interact such that both girls completed high school? How might these same factors have worked to produce different outcomes for them?
3. In what ways might the process of identity development have differed for Cho if she were African American or biracial rather than Asian American?

At thirteen, you'll remember, Cho and Michelle were beginning to display the kind of planning skills that are typical of adolescence. Yet, their plans sometimes failed to take critical details into account. Now that they are eighteen, they are much better able to formulate plans and carry them out. In Piaget's terminology, they have reached the **formal operational stage**, and their capacity for applying **hypothetico-deductive thought** to everyday problems (such as choosing a college) has improved.

Piaget's Cognitive–Developmental Stages (p. 38)

Approximate Ages	Stage
Birth to 24 months	Sensorimotor
24 months to 6 years	Preoperational
6 to 12	Concrete operational
12+	Formal operational

Marcia's Identity Statuses (p. 449)

Degree of commitment to a particular role or values / Degree of crisis

	High	Low
High	Identity achievement status (crisis is past)	Foreclosure status
Low	Moratorium status (in midst of crisis)	Identity diffusion status

Both girls have made decisions about post-secondary education, an important step in their **identity** development. Encouraged by her physics and calculus teachers, Michelle decided to pursue a career in engineering and plans to attend a large university. Cho is less certain about her career and intends to take general education courses at a community college while she explores her options. Marcia would say that Michelle's decision represents **foreclosure**, and Cho's is typical of the **moratorium** status his theory describes.

Bem's Gender Role Categories (p. 454)

Femininity / Masculinity

	High	Low
High	Androgynous	Feminine
Low	Masculine	Undifferentiated

Michelle's decision was also influenced by her sense of **gender role identity**. She knows that women are underrepresented in engineering, and she looks forward to helping to make the profession more diverse.

Cho and Michelle know that, by virtue of having chosen divergent future pathways, their relationship will change after they graduate from high school. Still, **social relationships** are highly valued by both girls. They plan to stay in touch as they transition from adolescence to adulthood, but they are eager to make new friends as well. And the **interpersonal skills** that they have gained from their long-term friendship will, no doubt, serve them well wherever their future endeavors take them.

Kohlberg's Stages of Moral Development (p. 458)

Level	Stages
Level I: Preconventional Morality	**Stage 1:** Punishment and Obedience Orientation **Stage 2:** Individualism, Instrumental Purpose, and Exchange
Level II: Conventional Morality	**Stage 3:** Mutual Interpersonal Expectations, Relationships, and Interpersonal Conformity **Stage 4:** Social System and Conscience (Law and Order)
Level III: Postconventional Morality	**Stage 5:** Social Contract Orientation **Stage 6:** Universal Ethical Principles Orientation

Michelle's interest in balancing individual and social goals also suggests that she is in transition from Kohlberg's **conventional level** of moral reasoning to his **postconventional level** of moral reasoning.

The Whole Child in Action

Apply What You've Learned about Development in Adolescence

Raise Your Virtual Child

Adolescence

1. Summarize the changes that you observed in your virtual child between the ages of 12 and 18 in the physical, cognitive, and socioemotional domains. Which of these changes represent universals and which reflect individual differences?
2. To what extent did your parenting decisions contribute to these changes?
3. Did the virtual child result in decision-related outcomes that you think are valid? Why or why not?
4. Write a brief biographical sketch of your child at age 18, integrating information from all three domains.

This activity requires that you be registered for My Virtual Child *through MyDevelopmentLab.*

Conduct Your Research

Adolescents' Self-Descriptions

You can replicate the classic study of Montemayor and Eisen simply by asking children and teenagers from 10 to 18 years of age to answer the question "Who am I?" (Remember to get parents' permission before involving children in any research project.) In each participant's response, count the number of references to physical characteristics and the number to beliefs or ideology. Plot your results on a graph like the one in Figure 15.2 on page 451. If your results differ from those of Montemayor and Eisen, try to determine what may have influenced your results. It may help to think about how the children you questioned might be different from those in the original study or how children's ideas about the self may have been influenced by historical and cultural changes in the three decades since Montemayor and Eisen's data were collected.

Build Your Portfolio

1. Read one of the novels listed below, and then develop a lesson plan in which high school students who have read the book learn to use Marcia's classification system to think and write about one or more of the characters. Taking into consideration the developmental differences between 14- and 18-year-olds, determine the appropriate grade level for your lesson.
   Atonement (Ian McEwan)
   The Secret Life of Bees (Sue Kidd)
   Little Women (Louisa May Alcott)
   A Tree Grows in Brooklyn (Betty Smith)
   Great Expectations (Charles Dickens)
   The Outsiders (S. E. Hinton)
2. Adolescents are more concerned about how they appear to others than younger children are (look back at the discussion of the imaginary audience). Create a list of ways in which secondary school teachers can recognize outstanding student work without embarrassing their students.

Powered by PEARSON mydevelopmentlab™

www.mydevelopmentlab.com

Explore Possible Careers

Licensed Professional Counselor

A licensed professional counselor (LPC) is a mental health professional who is trained to support individuals' efforts to solve problems associated with normative life events. Examples of normative life events in adolescence include puberty and romantic relationships. Most teens work through problems they have with these events on their own. Sometimes, however, the feelings and thoughts that arise from such events induce feelings of anxiety or even despair. In such cases, LPCs can be of great help to teens and their families. LPCs are also trained to help teens make decisions about postsecondary education and career options. Many work with teens who have eating disorders and other more serious problems. To become an LPC, you must have a master's degree in counseling and be licensed by the state in which you practice. Graduate programs in counseling include courses in theory, counseling methods, statistics, research methods, and psychological testing. Any undergraduate major is acceptable to most graduate programs in counseling, but having majored in psychology is usually an advantage during the application process. A background in psychology also helps prepare you for graduate work in counseling.

Visit the Career Center in MyDevelopmentLab to learn about other careers that rely on child development research.

Volunteer with Children

National Runaway Hotline Volunteer

The National Runaway Switchboard is a nonprofit organization that provides help to teens who have either run away from their homes or been asked to leave home by their parents or guardians (sometimes called "thrown-away kids"). The Switchboard advertises its toll-free telephone hotline, 1-800-RUNAWAY, in urban neighborhoods that attract large numbers of teens who are on their own, on television, in teen magazines, and on the Internet. The ads target teens who are considering running away, as well as those who are already on their own. The volunteers who answer hotline calls direct runaway teens to resources such as temporary shelters where they can find refuge and help those who have not yet left home determine other options that are available to them. To be a hotline volunteer, you must be over the age of 16 and be willing to work 2 to 4 hours a week.

Visit the Career Center in MyDevelopmentLab to learn about other volunteer opportunities that rely on child development research.

HARLEY-DAVIDSON
03

Epilogue

The Process of Development

Any study of child and adolescent development is bound to include thousands of minute details that can be marshaled to answer questions such as *When do the lungs develop? What are the characteristics of babbling? In what order does a child move from pretending with objects to engaging in role play? What are the limits on logical thinking? What are the risk factors for eating disorders?*

All of these details are important, but learning about them can cause students to lose sight of the big picture. Our purpose in providing you with this epilogue is to encourage you take a step back from all the details you have read about in this text and think once again about the overall process of development. We begin by considering the general pattern that is found in every developmental change.

Transitions, Consolidations, and Systems

The process of development can be thought of as a series of alternating periods of rapid growth, or *transition*, that are characterized by disruption and periods of comparative calm, or *consolidation*. Change is obviously going on all the time, but the evidence suggests that there are particular times when changes pile up or when one highly significant change occurs. The change might be a major physiological development such as puberty, a highly significant cognitive change such as the beginning of symbol usage at about 18 months, or some other major shift.

Such a significant change has two related effects. First, in systems theory terms, any change inevitably affects the entire system. Thus, a rapid increase in skill in one area, such as language, demands adaptation in all parts of the developing system. Because a child learns to talk, her social interactions change, her thinking changes, and no doubt even her nervous system changes as new synapses are created and redundant or underused ones are pruned. Similarly, a child's early attachment may affect her cognitive development by altering the way she approaches new situations, and the hormonal changes of puberty often affect parent-child relations.

Eight-month-old Laura has a whole set of new skills and understandings: She can crawl, she has a firm attachment to both parents, she can perhaps understand a few words, and she has a beginning understanding of object permanence. All these more or less simultaneous changes profoundly alter the system that is the child.

Second, in the midst of most major transitions, the child seems to come "unglued" for a while. The old patterns of relationships, of thinking, and of talking don't work very well anymore, and it takes a while to work out new patterns. Erikson frequently used the word *dilemma* to refer to such a period of semiupheaval. Klaus Riegel (1975) once suggested the term *developmental leaps*, which conveys nicely the sense of energy that often accompanies these pivotal periods. Whatever terminology we apply, it is clear that identifying the factors responsible for the ebb and flow of developmental change has been the primary focus of developmental science. Thus, we return to some of the fundamental questions that we raised in Chapters 1 and 2 to see whether we can answer them more clearly for you now that you are familiar with the basic outline of child and adolescent development.

What Are the Major Influences on Development?

Throughout this book, you read about the arguments for and against both nature and nurture as basic explanations of developmental patterns. In every instance, you learned that the real answer lies in the interaction between the two. All of development is a product of various forms of interaction between internal and external influences.

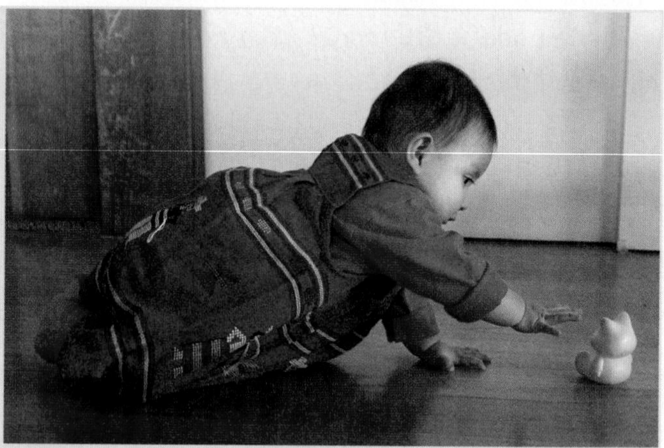

The fact that virtually all babies have some chance to reach for and examine objects does not mean that such experience is unimportant in the child's emerging perceptual or motor skills. Most (if not all) so-called maturational sequences require particular kinds of environmental inputs if they are to occur.

Even in the case of development that appears to be the most clearly biologically determined or influenced, such as physical development or early perceptual development, normal development can occur only if the child is growing in an environment that falls within an adequate or sufficient range. The fact that the vast majority of environments fall within that range in no way reduces the crucial importance of the environment. As John Flavell puts it, "Environmental elements do not become any less essential to a particular form of development just because they are virtually certain to be available for its use" (1985, p. 284). Similarly, even those aspects of development that seem most obviously to be products of the environment, such as the quality of the child's first attachment, rest on a physiological foundation and on instinctive patterns of attachment behaviors. The fact that all normal children possess that foundation and those instincts makes them no less essential for development.

Another point is that the form and extent of the interaction between nature and nurture may well vary as a function of the aspect of development in question. It may help to think of different facets of development along a continuum, with those most fully internally programmed on one end and those most externally influenced on the other.

Physical development defines one end of this continuum, since it is very strongly shaped by internal forces. Given the minimum necessary environment, physical maturational timetables are extremely powerful and consistent, particularly during infancy and adolescence. Next along the continuum is probably language (although some experts might argue with this conclusion, given the possible dependence of language development on prior cognitive developments). Language seems to emerge with only minimal environmental support—though again, the environment must fall within some acceptable range. At the very least, the child must hear language spoken (or see it signed). Still, specific features of the environment seem to matter a bit more in the case of language development than in that of physical development. For example, parents who respond appropriately to their children's vocalizations seem to be able to speed up the process.

Cognitive development falls somewhere in the middle of the continuum. Clearly, powerful internal forces are at work here. As John Flavell expressed it, "There is an impetus to childhood cognitive growth that is not ultimately explainable by this environmental push or that experiential shove" (1985, p. 283). Developmentalists don't yet know whether the impressive regularity of the sequences of cognitive development arises from built-in processes such as assimilation and accommodation, from physiological changes such as synapse formation and pruning, or from some combination of causes. However, developmentalists do know that specific qualities of the environment affect both universals and individual differences in intellectual development. Children who have varied and age-appropriate toys, who receive encouragement for exploration and achievement, and whose parents are responsive to their overtures show faster cognitive development and higher IQ scores.

Socioemotional development lies at the other end of the continuum, where the impact of the environment seems to be the greatest, although even here genetic factors are obviously at work. Some aspects of temperament seem clearly to be built in, or genetic, and attachment behaviors may be programmed into the human genome; both of these inborn factors certainly shape the child's earliest encounters with others. In this developmental area, however, the balance of nature and nurture seems to lean more toward nurture. In particular, the security of the child's attachment and the quality of the child's relationships with others outside of the family seem to be powerfully affected by the specific quality of the interactions within the family.

Does Timing Matter?

It is also important to remember that the impact of any experience can vary, depending on when it occurs during development. This issue has been explored in a variety of ways throughout the book.

Early Experience as Critical

The most pervasive version of the timing question has asked whether the early years of life are a critical or sensitive period for the establishment of many of the trajectories of the child's later development. To borrow Ann Clarke's analogy (Clarke & Clarke, 1976): In the construction of a house, does the shape of the foundation determine the final structure partially or completely, or can later structures be built on the original foundation? Are any flaws or weaknesses in the original foundation permanent, or can they be corrected later, after the house is completed?

There are arguments on both sides. Some psychologists point to the fact that virtually all children successfully complete the sensorimotor period, and even children with mild or moderate degrees of mental retardation achieve some form of Piaget's concrete operations. The term that has been widely used to describe such developmental patterns is *canalization*, a notion borrowed from embryologist C. H. Waddington (1957). Waddington suggested that development can be thought of metaphorically as a marble rolling down a gully on a hillside, as in Figure E.1 (Waddington, 1974). When a gully is narrow and deep, development is said to be

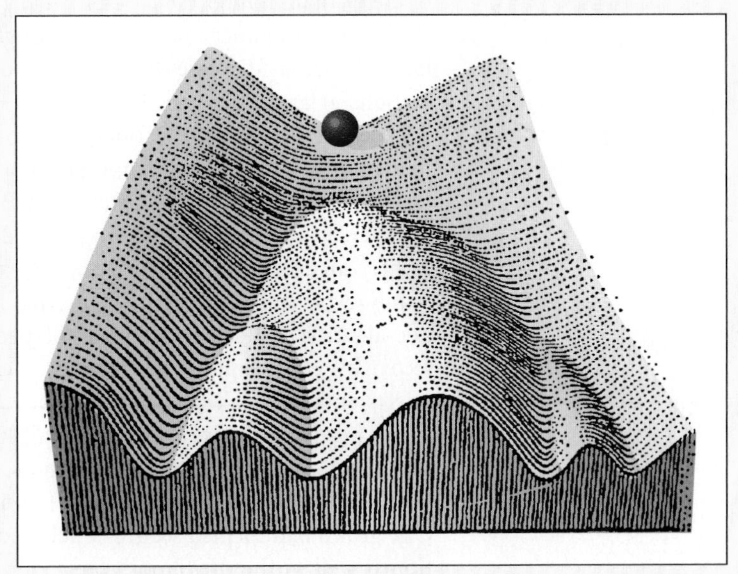

Figure E.1 Waddington's Model of Canalization

A narrow and deep gully depicts strong canalization. If infancy is highly canalized, almost any environment will support or sustain development.

(*Source*: "A catastrophic theory of evolution" by C. H. Waddington in the *Annals of the New York Academy of Science*, 231, pp. 32–42 (1974). Reprinted by permission.)

If infancy is a critical period for some aspects of personality development, then these preschoolers' characters are already well formed. Whether or not this is true remains one of the most crucial theoretical and practical issues in developmental psychology.

highly canalized—the marble will roll down that gully with little deviation. Other aspects of development, in contrast, might be better depicted by much flatter or wider gullies with many side branches, where the marble will be more likely to deviate from a given path. Some developmental scientists argue that in the early years of life, development is highly canalized, with strong "self-righting" tendencies. Even if deflected, the baby's pattern of development rapidly returns to the bottom of the gully and proceeds along the normal track. Such self-righting is illustrated, for example, by the large percentage of low-birth-weight or other initially vulnerable babies who nonetheless catch up to their normal-birth peers in physical and cognitive development by the time they go to school.

On the other side of the argument are a whole group of psychologists—much of whose thinking is rooted in psychoanalytic theory—who see infancy and early childhood as especially formative (e.g., Sroufe, Egeland, Carlson, & Collins, 2005). They note that some prenatal influences are permanent; some effects of early cognitive impoverishment, malnutrition, or abuse may also be long-lasting. There is also a good deal of evidence that early psychological adaptations, such as the quality of the earliest attachment or a child's tendency toward aggressive behavior, tend to persist and shape the child's later experiences in a cumulative way.

It seems likely that both of these perspectives are valid: The early years of life are a sensitive period for some kinds of development and at the same time highly canalized. How can such an apparent paradox be resolved? There are at least two possible ways. First, canalization could be seen not just as a product of powerful built-in programming but as the result of such programming being expressed in a sufficiently supportive environment. When it is viewed this way, a good deal of the apparent paradox disappears (Turkheimer & Gottesman, 1991). It is only when a child's particular environment falls outside the range of sufficiently supportive environments that there is a so-called environmental effect. So, for a child reared in an extremely impoverished orphanage setting or a child who is regularly physically abused, environmental effects can be strongly negative and long-lasting. The earlier such a deviation from a sufficiently supportive environment occurs, the more pervasive the effects seem to be. In this way of looking at critical periods versus canalization, a normally supported infancy may be less pivotal in the pattern of the child's development than minor deviations during toddlerhood or the preschool years. But if the deviations in infancy are extreme enough to deflect the infant from a normal developmental path—as in the case of severe abuse or malnutrition—the effect is larger than for deviations at any other age.

Robert Cairns (1991) offers a second resolution to the paradox when he points out that in any given period, some facets of development may be highly canalized and other facets may be strongly responsive to environmental variation. In infancy, for example, physical, perceptual, and perhaps linguistic development may be strongly canalized, but the development of internal working models of attachment is clearly affected by a child's specific family experiences. Indeed, all internal working models—whether of attachment, of gender identity and self-concept, or of peer relations—are likely to be more powerfully affected by early experiences than by later ones, simply because the model, once formed, affects and filters all later experience.

A particularly nice example of this kind of early effect comes from one of Alan Sroufe's studies of the long-term consequences of attachment security. Sroufe and his colleagues (Sroufe, Egeland, & Kreutzer, 1990) compared two groups of elementary school children. One group had formed secure attachments in infancy but for various reasons had not functioned well in the preschool years. The second group had shown poor adaptation at both ages. When these two groups of children were assessed at elementary school age, Sroufe found that those who had had a good early start "rebounded" better. They had better emotional health and social skills than did those who had had poor adaptation in infancy, even though both groups had functioned poorly as preschoolers. The infancy experience is not totally formative; a child's current circumstances also have a major impact. But, at least with respect to attachment security, early experience leaves a lingering trace.

Psychological Tasks at Different Ages

Another way to think about timing is to identify specific psychological tasks to be dealt with at different ages. Erikson's theory, for example, emphasizes a series of psychological dilemmas. Any experience that affects the way a child resolves a particular task will be formative at that time; at an earlier or later time, the same experience might have much less effect. Alan Sroufe and Michael Rutter (1984) have offered a broader list of age-related issues and tasks, presented in Table E.1. In this way of looking at things, a child is seen as focusing on different aspects of the environment at different times. Thus, during the period from age 1 to 2½, when the child is focused on mastery of the world of objects, the quality and range of inanimate experiences to which the child has access may be of special importance.

Overall, most developmentalists today do not think that any specific age is "critical" for all aspects of development; most do think, though, that for any aspect of development, some ages are more critical than others, and that patterns that affect later experience are set during those times. As Alan Sroufe says, "Development is hierarchical; it is not a blackboard to be erased and written upon again. Even when children change rather markedly, the shadows of the earlier adaptation remain" (1983, p. 73).

The developmental tasks of adolescence are quite different from those that face younger children. Some, such as learning to drive, are associated with the specific cultural context in which a teenager is growing up. Others, such as learning to form and dissolve romantic partnerships, are universal and appear to be strongly linked to milestones in the physical domains (e.g., puberty).

Table E.1 Issues or Tasks in Each of Several Age Periods

Age in Years	Issues or Tasks
0–1	Biological regulation; harmonious interactions with parents and/or caregivers; formation of an effective attachment relationship
1–2½	Exploration, experimentation, and mastery of the world of objects (caregiver as secure base); individuation and autonomy; responding to external control of impulses
3–5	Flexible self-control; self-reliance; initiative; gender identification and gender concept; establishing effective peer contacts (empathy)
6–12	Social understanding (equity, fairness); gender constancy; same-sex friendships; sense of "industry" (competence); school adjustment
13+	Formal operations (flexible perspective taking, "what-if" thinking); loyal friendships (same sex); beginning heterosexual relationships; emancipation; identity

Source: Table 1, p. 22, "The domain of developmental psychopathology" by L. A. Sroufe and M. Rutter, *Child Development, 55* (1984), 17–29. © The Society for Research in Child Development. Reprinted by permission of Blackwell Publishing.

What Is the Nature of Developmental Change?

On balance, it seems likely that developmental change is more qualitative than quantitative. Certainly, over the years of development, the child acquires more vocabulary words, more information-processing strategies. But these tools and skills are used in different ways by older children than they are by younger ones. Further, it seems clear that these qualitative changes occur in sequences. Such sequences are apparent in physical development, in cognitive development, and in social and personality development.

The Issue of Stages

Whether it is meaningful to speak of stages of development is still an open question. Some hierarchically organized stages have certainly been identified, the most obvious example being Kohlberg's stages of moral reasoning. And researchers can certainly find examples of apparently stage-like changes across several developmental areas—for example, at about 18 to 24 months, a child seems to discover the ability to combine symbols, a change that is evident in two-word sentences, in thinking, and in multistep play with other children. There also appears to be a quite stage-like shift between ages 3 and 4, of which the theory of mind is the centerpiece. Nevertheless, each new skill or understanding seems to be acquired in a fairly narrow area first and generalized more fully only later. In fact, one of the things that differentiates a gifted or higher-IQ child from a child with a lower IQ or mental retardation is how quickly and broadly the child generalizes some new concept or strategy to new instances.

Despite this non-stage-like quality of most developmental change, it is nonetheless true that the patterns of relationships, of thinking, and of problem solving of two children of widely different ages (say, a 5-year-old and an 11-year-old) differ in almost every respect. So there is certainly orderliness in the sequences, and there are some links between them, but the stages of cognitive development may not be quite as discrete as Piaget believed them to be.

Continuities in Development

In the midst of all of these sequences, there is also continuity. Each child carries forward some core of individuality. The notion of temperament certainly implies such a core, as does the concept of an internal working model. Thus, the specific behavior exhibited by a child may change—a clinging toddler may not become a clinging 9-year-old—but the underlying attachment model or temperament that led to the clinging will still be at least partially present, manifesting itself in new ways. In particular, it has become increasingly clear that maladaptations often persist over time, as seen in the consistency of high levels of aggression or tantrum behavior and in the persistence of some of the maladaptive social interactions that flow from insecure attachments. The task of developmental scientists is to understand both coherence (consistency) and the underlying patterns of transformation (development).

What Is the Significance of Individual Differences?

The issue of individual continuities emphasizes the fact that development is individual as well as collective. By definition, and as the core of its basic approach, developmental science concerns itself with the typical rather than with deviations from what is expected. Still, you have read about individual differences in virtually every chapter, so you know that both inborn differences and emergent or environmentally produced variations are present for children in every aspect of development. It seems instructive to return to the dimension of individual difference you read about several times—vulnerability versus resilience.

It may be useful to define these concepts somewhat differently than we did in earlier chapters: in terms of the range of environments that will be sufficiently supportive for optimal development. By this definition, a vulnerable infant is one with a narrow range of potentially supportive environments. For such a child, only the most stimulating, most responsive, most adaptive environment will do. When the child's environment falls outside that range, the probability of a poor outcome is greatly increased. A resilient child, in contrast, is one for whom any of a very wide range of environments will support optimal development. A resilient child may thus be more strongly canalized, and a vulnerable child less so.

Some kinds of vulnerabilities are inborn, caused by genetic abnormalities, prenatal trauma or stress, preterm birth, or malnutrition. Any child suffering from these problems will thrive only in a highly supportive environment. You've encountered this pattern again and again throughout the chapters of this book. For example, low-birth-weight infants typically have normal IQs if they are reared in middle-class homes, but they have a high risk of retardation if they are reared in nonstimulating poverty-level homes (Bradley et al., 1994).

As the example of low birth weight suggests, vulnerability does not remain constant throughout life. A more general proposition, which you might think of as a working hypothesis, is that each time a given child's environment falls outside the range of acceptable supportiveness (that is, each time a mismatch occurs between the child's needs and what is available), the child becomes more vulnerable. On the other hand, every time the child's needs are met, the child becomes more resilient. For example, a temperamentally difficult child whose family environment is nonetheless sufficient to foster a secure attachment will become more resilient, more able to handle the next set of tasks; a temperamentally easy child who for some reason develops an insecure attachment will become more vulnerable to later stress or environmental insufficiency.

Furthermore, the qualities of the environment that are critical for a child's optimal development no doubt change as the child passes from one age to another. Responsive and warm interactions with parents seem particularly important in the period from perhaps 6 months to 18 months; richness of cognitive stimulation seems particularly critical between perhaps 1 year and 4 years; opportunities for practicing social skills with peers may be especially crucial at a later age. Thus, as the tasks change with age, the optimal environment changes also. Among other things, this means that the same family may be very good with a child of one age and not so good with a child of another age.

Most generally, the vulnerability/resilience model leads to the conclusion that even the most "vulnerable" child can show improvement if his environment improves markedly. Because some congenitally vulnerable children do not encounter sufficiently supportive environments, their vulnerability continues to increase. For this reason, early problems often persist. At the same time, improvement is possible, even likely. Most children manage to survive and thrive, despite stresses and vulnerabilities.

A Final Point: The Joy of Development

To end both this epilogue and the book on an optimistic note, remember that in the midst of all the "crises" and "transitions" and "vulnerabilities," development has a special joyous quality. When a child masters a new skill, she is not just pleased—she is delighted and will repeat that new skill at length, quite obviously getting vast satisfaction from it. A 5-year-old who learns to draw stars may draw them on everything in sight, including paper, walls, clothes, and napkins, simply because it is so much fun to draw stars. A 10-year-old who learns to do cartwheels will delightedly display this new talent to anyone who will watch and will practice endlessly.

The same joyous quality can be part of the family's development as well. Confronting and moving successfully through any of the periodic and inevitable upheavals in family life can be immensely pleasing. Watching your child progress, liking your child, and enjoying being together are all deeply satisfying parts of rearing children. When parents cry at their son's or daughter's high school graduation or wedding, it is not merely sentiment. It is an expression of that sense of love, pride, and wonderment that they and their children have come so far.

Comprehensive Practice Test

UNIT ONE ■ FOUNDATIONS

Chapter 1
Basic Concepts and Methods

1. The philosophy that proposes that adults can mold children into whatever the adults want them to be is called
   a. morality.
   b. the blank slate.
   c. original sin.
   d. innate goodness.
2. Improvements in children's memory function fall within the _______________ domain of development.
   a. physical
   b. cognitive
   c. social
   d. emotional
3. Which of the following is an example of an inborn bias that is shared by virtually all infants?
   a. crying and snuggling to entice others to care for them
   b. sleeping through the night
   c. not liking solid foods
   d. being easy to soothe when they become distressed
4. When a caterpillar changes into a butterfly, this is an example of a
   a. quantitative change.
   b. continuous change.
   c. cross-species change.
   d. qualitative change.
5. Changes that are common to every individual in a species and are linked to specific ages are called _______________ changes.
   a. normative age-graded
   b. nonnormative
   c. normative history-graded
   d. on-time and off-time
6. Developmental scientists emphasize
   a. the environmental hazards of the place where a person lives.
   b. all of the contexts in which the child is growing.
   c. how much the individual likes his or her environment.
   d. the child's temperament.
7. Sets of statements that propose general principles to explain development are called
   a. theories.
   b. the independent variables.
   c. hypotheses.
   d. the critical periods.
8. Which of the following is the major limitation of the correlational method?
   a. Observer bias is likely.
   b. It studies only single individuals.
   c. It does not tell us about causal relationships.
   d. Research ethics prevent its use in most developmental studies.
9. An experiment is testing the effects of observed violence on children's behavior. One group of children views a violent cartoon. A second group views a humorous nonviolent cartoon. A third group is not exposed to any cartoon. The first group is the
   a. experimental group.
   b. control group.
   c. comparison group.
   d. observational group.
10. Which of the following is an advantage of a longitudinal study?
    a. The research is completed in a short period of time.
    b. The healthiest participants drop out.
    c. The better-educated participants drop out.
    d. It allows the researcher to compare performance by the same people at different ages.
11. A detailed description of a single culture or context based on extensive observation is called
    a. the cohort effect.
    b. ageism.
    c. maturation.
    d. an ethnography.
12. Which of the following ethical standards for research involves the right to information about the potential hazards involved in participating in a study?
    a. knowledge of results
    b. deception
    c. informed consent
    d. confidentiality

Chapter 2
Theories of Development

13. Which term best describes Freud's theory of development?
    a. psychosocial stages
    b. psychoeducational stages
    c. psychosexual stages
    d. psychosomatic stages
14. Which of the following accurately summarizes Erikson's theory?
    a. A poor interpersonal relationship can cause individuals to fixate on problems.
    b. The superego is a more powerful force than the id and drives most behavior.
    c. Without societal pressures to conform to, we would be overly destructive.
    d. Healthy development requires confronting and resolving crises throughout the lifespan.
15. One strength of psychoanalytic theories is that they emphasize
    a. the importance of sexuality in infancy.
    b. links between early childhood and adult development.
    c. rigorous research methods.
    d. the influence of the environment on development.
16. What kind of learning was involved in Watson's Little Albert experiment?
    a. classical conditioning
    b. sensitization
    c. operant conditioning
    d. habituation
17. A consequence that increases behavior is a __________, whereas one that decreases behavior is a __________.
    a. positive reinforcement, negative reinforcement
    b. positive punishment, negative punishment
    c. reinforcement, punishment
    d. reinforcement, extinction
18. Bandura suggests that learning can take place without direct reinforcement. What is this type of learning called?
    a. positive reinforcement
    b. modeling
    c. instrumental conditioning
    d. classical conditioning
19. Some developmentalists argue that learning theories
    a. are based on unethical research studies.
    b. do not provide clinicians with strategies for influencing children's behavior.
    c. do not provide a comprehensive explanation of development.
    d. are less objective and scientific than psychoanalytic theories are.
20. Chris is in elementary school and has learned to solve problems logically. Which of Piaget's stages best describes her level of cognitive development?
    a. concrete operational
    b. sensorimotor
    c. preoperational
    d. formal operational
21. In Vygotsky's theory, what does *scaffolding* mean?
    a. building new schemes
    b. developing a firm sense of self-identity
    c. acquiring new emotional experiences through direct experience
    d. structuring a child's learning experiences to ensure success
22. Information-processing theorists explain Piaget's findings as the result of inefficiencies in children's
    a. schemes.
    b. private speech.
    c. zone of proximal development.
    d. short-term memories.
23. Which of the following is a weakness of Piaget's theory?
    a. He developed innovative methods of studying children's thinking.
    b. He was wrong about the ages at which children develop specific skills.
    c. His theory forced psychologists to think about child development in a new way.
    d. His findings have been replicated in virtually every culture and every cohort of children since the 1920s.
24. __________ study the relative influence of heredity and environment on individual behavior. __________ study inherited traits that aid individual survival. __________ study inherited traits that support the creation and maintenance of survival-oriented social organizations.
    a. Ethologists, Sociobiologists, Behavior geneticists
    b. Behavior geneticists, Ethologists, Sociobiologists
    c. Sociobiologists, Behavior geneticists, Ethologists
    d. Behavior geneticists, Sociobiologists, Ethologists
25. The contexts of Bronfenbrenner's bioecological theory, in order from the largest circle to the smallest, are
    a. macrosystem, exosystem, microsystem, biological context.
    b. microsystem, biological context, macrosystem, exosystem.
    c. biological context, exosystem, microsystem, macrosystem.
    d. macrosystem, biological context, microsystem, exosystem.

26. Which of the following is not one of the criteria of usefulness listed in the text?

a. Does it stimulate thinking and research?
b. Does it explain the basic facts of development?
c. Does it emphasize nature over nurture?
d. Does it generate predictions that can be tested with scientific methods?

27. When developmentalists incorporate multiple theoretical perspectives into explanations of age-related change, they are using an approach known as

a. continuity.
b. eclecticism.
c. rationalism.
d. organismic.

Chapter 3
Prenatal Development and Birth

28. The unique genetic blueprint from the mother and the father that characterizes a specific individual is called a
    a. phenotype.
    b. chromosome.
    c. gamete.
    d. genotype.
29. ___________ is a genetic disorder, whereas ___________ is a chromosomal disorder.
    a. Sickle-cell disease, Huntington's disease
    b. Down syndrome, fragile-X syndrome
    c. Huntington's disease, fragile-X syndrome
    d. Tay-Sachs disease, Huntington's disease
30. The three stages of prenatal development, in order, are
    a. germinal, embryonic, fetal.
    b. viability, organogenesis, germinal.
    c. embryonic, fetal, viability.
    d. embryonic, germinal, fetal.
31. Which statement is not true?
    a. Newborns remember stimuli to which they were exposed prenatally.
    b. Fetuses can distinguish between familiar and novel stimuli as early as the 32nd week.
    c. Female fetuses are more physically active than male fetuses.
    d. Fetuses respond to sounds.
32. Which period of prenatal development is the time of greatest risk for the influence of most teratogens?
    a. the first 8 weeks of gestation
    b. the beginning of the fetal period
    c. the 29th week to the 38th week of development
    d. the time of conception
33. Which of the following is not a typical characteristic of children who have fetal alcohol syndrome?
    a. mild mental retardation
    b. heart defects
    c. learning and behavior difficulties
    d. limb deformities
34. Of the following developing systems of an embryo/fetus, which would be most severely and negatively affected by maternal malnutrition?
    a. musculo-skeletal
    b. reproductive
    c. nervous
    d. cardiovascular
35. Which of the following prenatal diagnostic techniques is usually used during the first trimester of pregnancy and involves extracting cells for laboratory testing?
    a. chorionic villus sampling
    b. amniocentesis
    c. ultrasonography
    d. fetoscopy
36. Which of the following would be true of an infant who had received a score of 10 on the Apgar scale?
    a. The infant is most likely 1 to 2 minutes old.
    b. The infant is most likely 5 minutes old.
    c. The infant is in need of immediate resuscitation to establish a normal breathing pattern.
    d. The infant is in critical condition.
37. Which statement is true about low-birth-weight babies?
    a. Low-birth-weight girls are more likely to show long-term effects than low-birth-weight boys.
    b. Most low-birth-weight babies never catch up to their normal peers.
    c. Low birth weight is not related to the neonate's health.
    d. Low-birth-weight infants show markedly lower levels of responsiveness.

Chapter 4
Physical Development and Health in Infancy and Toddlerhood

1. What is pruning as it relates to development?
   a. a surgical technique for compensating for brain damage
   b. elimination of redundant neural pathways
   c. slowly easing the child off the bottle and onto solid food
   d. a surgery that may alleviate epileptic seizures
2. Baby Jake is 1 week old. He is likely to be ____________ most of the time.
   a. actively awake
   b. quietly awake
   c. asleep
   d. eating
3. What concept explains the fact that the sequences of motor development are virtually the same for all children?
   a. an inborn timetable
   b. growth
   c. accommodation
   d. phenotypical influence
4. Which of the following is not a benefit of breast-feeding?
   a. lower risk of infant mortality
   b. lower risk of intestinal difficulties
   c. better immune system functioning
   d. slower weight gain
5. Macronutrient malnutrition results from a diet that contains
   a. too little iron.
   b. too much vitamin A.
   c. too few calories.
   d. only breast milk.
6. Why do health-care professionals assess infants' motor development during well-baby check-ups?
   a. to determine whether they are healthy enough to receive immunizations
   b. to identify developmental delays as early as possible
   c. to predict the age at which they will display future motor milestones
   d. to make recommendations as to how parents can speed up children's development
7. Which of the following factors or influences is not associated with sudden infant death syndrome?
   a. a history of physical abuse
   b. a history of apnea
   c. sleeping on the stomach on a soft, fluffy item of bedding
   d. smoking by the mother during pregnancy
8. Which of the following has not been proposed as an explanation for group differences in infant mortality?
   a. variations in attentiveness to infant needs
   b. variations in poverty rates
   c. variations in access to prenatal care
   d. variations in the rates of congenital abnormalities
9. Which of the following visual abilities appears to be almost identical in newborns and adults?
   a. tracking
   b. visual acuity
   c. color sensation
   d. scanning of objects
10. At what age do researchers find the ability to hear?
    a. prenatally
    b. first day of life
    c. first week of life
    d. first month of life
11. Which of the following can be used to test an infant's perceptual abilities?
    a. classical conditioning
    b. cross-modal transfer
    c. tracking device
    d. preference technique
12. Nativists' arguments are supported by the fact that
    a. newborns have so many sensory abilities early in life.
    b. animals deprived of light show an increase in perceptual abilities.
    c. animals deprived of auditory stimuli have limited or no auditory perceptual skills.
    d. infants from Iranian orphanages were retarded in the development of perceptual skills.

Chapter 5
Cognitive Development in Infancy and Toddlerhood

13. What is sensorimotor intelligence?
    a. utilizing innate schemes to process incoming information
    b. manipulating symbols to develop more sophisticated schemes
    c. a type of intelligence that is genetically determined
    d. using basic logic to categorize the world
14. Which of the following is a criticism of Piaget's theory?
    a. Piaget overestimated children's abilities.
    b. Piaget did not use all of the advanced techniques that were available to him.
    c. Development occurs in stages, unlike the quantitative changes that Piaget proposed.
    d. Piaget underestimated children's abilities.
15. Which of the following best describes Spelke's views regarding infants' understanding of objects?
    a. Babies are born with certain built-in assumptions that guide their interactions with objects.
    b. Babies construct their understanding of objects through the development and modification of cognitive schemes.
    c. Babies have little understanding of objects until they are at least 1 year old.
    d. Babies learn about objects from watching others manipulate them.
16. Researchers have increased newborns' head turning through the use of reinforcements such as the sound of the mother's voice. This is an example of
    a. classical conditioning.
    b. operant conditioning.
    c. habituation.
    d. schematic learning.
17. Schematic learning assumes that
    a. babies attempt to categorize their experiences.
    b. children cannot learn unless the information is organized for them.
    c. babies will learn only if they are reinforced for exploring.
    d. learning is sequential and orderly.
18. Which of the following is an accurate statement about infant memory?
    a. Infants younger than 6 months do not retain memories.
    b. The expansion of memory is preprogrammed.
    c. Infants develop very general memories for information.
    d. Early infant memory is specific to the context in which it was learned.
19. The theory of language development that proposes that infants learn language because their brains possess innate grammatical structures is called
    a. holophrase acquisition.
    b. nativist explanation.
    c. behaviorist explanation.
    d. language acquisition device.
20. Infant-directed speech is characterized by
    a. complex sentence structure.
    b. a lower pitch.
    c. grammatically incorrect forms.
    d. simplicity.
21. What is the baby's first communicative sound?
    a. ma-ma
    b. cooing
    c. crying
    d. laughing
22. A child who can understand a word that is spoken but cannot yet say the word has
    a. expressive language.
    b. receptive language.
    c. imitation.
    d. innate vocalization.
23. Which of the following is an example of telegraphic speech?
    a. "Daddy" (while pointing to Daddy's shoe)
    b. "Ma-ma"
    c. "Me fall"
    d. "The cookie is good."
24. Most children who are late to talk
    a. also have cognitive delays.
    b. eventually catch up.
    c. are above average in intelligence.
    d. are girls.
25. Which of the following is an accurate statement about infant intelligence tests?
    a. Some studies indicate that babies who habituate quickly when they are 4 or 5 months old are likely to have lower intelligence test scores at later ages.
    b. The Bayley Scales of Infant Development accurately predict a child's intelligence at age 10.
    c. None of the infant intelligence test scores correlate with intelligence test scores at later ages.
    d. Infant intelligence tests measure mostly babies' motor abilities.

Chapter 6
Social and Personality Development in Infancy and Toddlerhood

26. Erikson's first stage of psychosocial development is called
    a. anal.
    b. interdependence.
    c. trust versus mistrust.
    d. oral.
27. Britt feels a strong bond of affection toward her mother. She feels safe with her mother and comforted when she is nearby. Britt is demonstrating what Ainsworth would call
    a. imprinting.
    b. surrogacy.
    c. satiability.
    d. attachment.
28. Which of the following statements about attachment is true?
    a. Infants rarely become attached to fathers.
    b. Babies tend to laugh and wriggle more around their mothers, but their behavior with their fathers is more subtle, such as smiling.
    c. Fathers tend to talk to and smile more at their babies than mothers do.
    d. Synchrony is a critical factor in both mother-infant and father-infant attachment.
29. Callie, age 11 months, went to the circus with her mother. When a clown came bouncing up to Callie's stroller, Callie looked at her mother, alarmed. When Callie's mother began to laugh at the clown, Callie joined in the laughter. Callie's behavior is called
    a. stranger anxiety.
    b. attachment dependence.
    c. social referencing.
    d. affective regulation.
30. Which of the following statements is true?
    a. Securely attached infants have no greater social skills once they reach adolescence than insecurely attached infants.
    b. Attachment relationships are more critical to adult intimate relationships than to other types of relationships.
    c. Securely attached infants often show more dependence on teachers in later years.
    d. Insecure/avoidant infants are less likely as adolescents to act out sexually.
31. Which of the following is *not* one of the dimensions proposed by researchers who study temperament?
    a. inhibition
    b. rhythmicity
    c. persistence
    d. intelligence
32. Which statement best describes research examining the influence of heredity and environment on temperament?
    a. Temperament is determined by heredity.
    b. Temperament is determined by the infant's environment.
    c. Temperament is inborn but is modified by the environment.
    d. Temperament has not been studied sufficiently to allow developmentalists to draw conclusions about the relative influences of heredity and environment on its development.
33. The ________ self is a toddler's understanding that he or she is defined by membership in various categories, such as gender or personality characteristics.
    a. superficial
    b. subjective
    c. existential
    d. objective
34. Which of the following represents one reason why it is difficult to arrive at a definitive conclusion about the effects of nonparental care on infants' development?
    a. Home care and day care have too many differences for the effects to be adequately measured.
    b. Nonparental care is stable in quality.
    c. Nonparental care is more common among low-income children, so effects attributed to it may actually reflect the effects of income.
    d. There is a discrepancy between the levels of stimulation a child would receive at home and in a child-care facility.
35. In children's play areas in day-care centers, ________ of toys is more important than ________ of toys.
    a. quantity; variety
    b. cognitive level; variety
    c. variety; quantity
    d. quality; cleanliness

Chapter 7
Physical Development and Health in Early Childhood

1. The stabilization of growth curves in early childhood enables health-care professionals to
   a. accurately predict children's adult heights.
   b. diagnose health disorders.
   c. identify children who may be abused or neglected.
   d. all of the above
2. Improvement in young children's ability to attend to stimuli is the result of
   a. lateralization of brain functions.
   b. myelination of the reticular formation.
   c. development of the hippocampus.
   d. synaptogenesis and pruning.
3. The fact that handedness is evident in most children ________________ supports the genetic hypothesis.
   a. prenatally
   b. by the end of the first year
   c. by age 4
   d. in the school years
4. Early diagnosis of amblyopia is important because the condition can negatively affect the development of
   a. visual acuity in the good eye.
   b. the reticular formation.
   c. the vestibular sense.
   d. stereopsis.
5. Mild degrees of hearing loss
   a. are unrelated to academic achievement.
   b. can interfere with cognitive development and learning.
   c. are easily and quickly noticed by a child's parents and teachers.
   d. usually do not require correction or amplification.
6. The development of both gross and fine motor skills depends on
   a. instruction by parents and teachers.
   b. advances in underlying fundamental movement skills.
   c. opportunities to practice specific skills, such as running and handwriting.
   d. individual differences in children's interest in physical activities.
7. Which of the following is not something parents can do to prevent bedtime and middle-of-the-night struggles?
   a. Provide children with a transitional object such as a doll or stuffed animal.
   b. Discontinue daytime naps.
   c. Let the child go to bed whenever he or she is very tired.
   d. Provide the child with a predictable daytime schedule.
8. Parents should be concerned with
   a. the quantity of food that children eat, even if this means that they eat high-fat foods.
   b. the quality of food that children eat, since food preferences are often established during the preschool years.
   c. the quantity of food that children eat, because obesity is prevalent during the preschool years.
   d. neither the quality nor the quantity of food that children eat.
9. Which of the following is not a risk factor for child abuse and neglect?
   a. physical disability
   b. poverty
   c. parental depression
   d. being the oldest in a family
10. Children with ______________ display cognitive difficulties, whereas those with ______________ have problems with social relationships.
   a. pervasive developmental disorders, mental retardation
   b. Asperger's disorder, autism
   c. autistic spectrum disorders, pervasive developmental disorders
   d. mental retardation, pervasive developmental disorders

Chapter 8
Cognitive Development in Early Childhood

11. A child is offered a choice between six pieces of candy laid out in a row and four pieces of candy spread farther apart to form a longer row. If the child chooses the longer row with four pieces, we know that the child's thinking is consistent with the characteristics of
   a. preoperational thought.
   b. conservation.
   c. a principle of false belief.
   d. a theory of mind.

12. A set of ideas that describes, explains, and makes predictions about other people's knowledge and behaviors, based on inferences about their mental state, is called a
   a. false belief principle.
   b. theory of mind.
   c. metamemory.
   d. matrix classification.

13. Knowledge about and control of thought processes is called
   a. metacognition.
   b. theory of mind.
   c. cognitive dissonance.
   d. self-concept.

14. According to Vygotsky, ______________ is required for cognitive development.
   a. social interaction
   b. formal education
   c. strong parent-child attachment
   d. metacognition

15. ________________ helps young children acquire new words through the use of categories.
   a. Metacognition
   b. Centration
   c. Fast-mapping
   d. Overregularization

16. What explains a child's use of expressions such as "I sitted down," "goed," or "mouses"?
   a. The child is underextending the verb class.
   b. The child has had insufficient practice with inflections.
   c. The child is recasting language heard in the environment.
   d. The child is overregularizing the rules of language.

17. What is the primary source of children's development of phonological awareness?
   a. word play
   b. exposure to a variety of languages
   c. communication between parent and child
   d. being read to

18. Research indicates that IQ scores
   a. are not related to later school performance.
   b. are predictive of school performance only among White Americans.
   c. are not stable.
   d. are stable if tests are given only a few months or a few years apart.

19. The research on group differences in IQ suggests that there are
   a. no consistent group differences.
   b. consistent group differences that are most likely due to environment.
   c. consistent group differences but they disappear by age 2.
   d. small group differences that are primarily genetic.

20. Tanya attends a preschool where the teachers focus on teaching children the alphabet and letter sounds. Her preschool exemplifies the ____________ approach.
   a. academic
   b. developmental
   c. eclectic
   d. developmentally appropriate practices

21. Which of the following statements about the effects of Head Start and other early childhood programs for disadvantaged children is not true?
   a. Children show gains in IQ scores while enrolled in these programs.
   b. Children who begin an enrichment program in infancy maintain the IQ gains they make in these programs throughout adolescence.
   c. Children in these programs are less likely to repeat a grade and are more likely to graduate from high school.
   d. Children in these programs may have higher rates of criminal behavior and unemployment.

Chapter 9
Social and Personality Development in Early Childhood

22. The text suggests that both Freud and Erikson believed that the key to the social development of 2- to 6-year-olds is
    a. striking a balance between the child's emerging skills and parents' need for control.
    b. the successful development of peer relationships.
    c. whether potty training goes smoothly.
    d. the ability of the parents to give the child freedom to grow.
23. A child who classifies a peer as "nice" or who can describe another's typical behavior patterns, such as by saying "she always eats all her cereal," has developed
    a. social referencing.
    b. person perception.
    c. a gender concept.
    d. prosocial behavior.
24. If you asked preschooler Mariana to describe herself, which of the following answers might you expect?
    a. "I am good at drawing."
    b. "I am a kind person."
    c. "I am a girl."
    d. "I am smart."
25. Which of the following is an example of emotional self-regulation?
    a. Judy is sad, so she turns on the television to watch a favorite cartoon.
    b. Ray gives up on a puzzle that is too difficult for him.
    c. Carol gets angry at her mother and storms out of the room.
    d. When Dorothy pushes her off a swing, Kathy kicks Dorothy.
26. A little boy chooses a toy that he believes is for boys and rejects a shirt based on its color, saying "That's for girls!" He is using ______________ to process information about gender.
    a. gender identity
    b. a gender schema
    c. cross-gender comparison
    d. a gender chromosome
27. Which of the following is the most accurate description of gender identity?
    a. the understanding that you stay the same gender throughout life
    b. a child's ability to label his or her sex correctly and to identify other people as women or men and girls or boys
    c. the recognition that a woman continues to be a woman even if she wears a man's clothes and cuts her hair short
    d. the choice of a pattern of behaviors that is typical or expected for one's sex
28. The interactions of a group of 4-year-old boys playing together most likely would not include
    a. efforts to derail the interactions.
    b. contradicting or interrupting.
    c. boasting and forms of self-display.
    d. behaviors that foster equality and connectedness.
29. Lateefah's father has very high standards and expectations and requires Lateefah to comply with his wishes without discussion. What is the best description of this parental style?
    a. authoritative
    b. permissive
    c. authoritarian
    d. inductive
30. According to research studies, which of the following is an accurate statement about the interrelationships of parenting styles, socioeconomic status, and ethnicity?
    a. Authoritative parenting is preferred by Asian American families.
    b. Families of lower socioeconomic status typically use authoritative parenting strategies.
    c. Single-parent families typically use authoritative parenting strategies.
    d. White teenagers from authoritative families show more self-reliance and less delinquency than do those from nonauthoritative families.
31. Which of the following is not a change in family processes typically experienced by families after divorce?
    a. reduced financial and emotional resources to support the children
    b. disruption and transition of the family system
    c. increased violence
    d. a shift away from authoritative parenting
32. What is the most dominant form of aggression among 4- to 8-year-old children?
    a. verbal
    b. physical
    c. instrumental
    d. hostile
33. During preschool, friendships
    a. shift from day to day.
    b. are based on parallel play experiences.
    c. become more stable.
    d. are common among girls but are rare among boys.

Chapter 10
Physical Development and Health in Middle Childhood

1. The best measure of a child's physical maturity is
   a. height.
   b. weight.
   c. bone age.
   d. body mass index (BMI).
2. During middle childhood, growth in the brain and nervous system results in all of the following *except*
   a. improvements in logic and planning.
   b. increased ability to think hypothetically and reason abstractly.
   c. improvement in ability to control attention.
   d. lateralization of spatial perception.
3. Map reading is an example of which of the following cognitive skills?
   a. spatial perception
   b. relative right-left orientation
   c. metacognition
   d. inductive logic
4. Which of the following is not a significant health risk for most school-aged children in the industrialized world?
   a. motor vehicle accidents
   b. bicycle accidents
   c. infectious diseases
   d. excessive weight gain
5. _______________ is a chronic condition that is responsible for more school absences than any other health problem.
   a. Excessive weight gain
   b. Diabetes
   c. Heart disease
   d. Asthma
6. Which of these children is most likely to be injured?
   a. Allan, a fifth-grader who plays Little League baseball
   b. Shayna, a third-grader who participates in an organized soccer league
   c. Luisa, a second-grader who is on her neighborhood swim team
   d. Charles, a fourth-grader who has been playing on an organized football team since he was 7 years old
7. Which of the following is a strategy that parents of an overweight child should not utilize?
   a. Have the child follow a strict weight-loss diet.
   b. Limit the amount of time the child spends on television, computers, and video games.
   c. Help the child develop good eating habits without overemphasizing cultural norms for thinness.
   d. Encourage the child to be physically active.
8. In type 1 diabetes, blood sugar rises to dangerous levels because
   a. the person's body does not respond to insulin.
   b. the person's pancreas does not produce insulin.
   c. the person is in the habit of eating too many sweets.
   d. the person's blood cells are defective.
9. What does research suggest about the link between access to medical care and socioeconomic group differences in health outcomes among children?
   a. Access to care is the primary cause of such differences.
   b. Access to care is unrelated to such differences.
   c. Access to care is one of several factors that lead to such differences.
   d. Too little is known about the role of access to care to draw conclusions about its connection to group differences in health outcomes.
10. For which of the following have medications proven to be helpful?
    a. oppositional-defiant disorder, attention-deficit/hyperactivity disorder, childhood-onset conduct disorder, and childhood depression
    b. oppositional-defiant disorder, childhood depression, and childhood-onset conduct disorder
    c. attention-deficit/hyperactivity disorder and childhood-onset conduct disorder
    d. attention-deficit/hyperactivity disorder and childhood depression
11. To meet the criteria for a diagnosis of major depressive disorder, a child must experience feelings of sadness that significantly impair her functioning in school or social relationships for at least
    a. 1 week.
    b. 1 month.
    c. 3 months.
    d. 6 months.

Chapter 11
Cognitive Development in Middle Childhood

12. A child who can explain the difference between nouns and verbs is demonstrating
a. concrete operational thinking.
b. metalinguistic skills.
c. metacognitive skills.
d. phonological awareness skills.

13. Four-year-old Surjit thinks that the key to safely crossing any busy street is to run really fast. His 8-year-old brother, Mehta, knows that the speed at which one can safely cross a street is determined by the speed at which traffic is moving, how wide the street is, and several other relevant variables. Mehta's thinking illustrates the principle of
a. reversibility.
b. compensation.
c. identity.
d. decentration.

14. According to Robert Siegler's explanation of children's cognitive development, a child who takes into account only one dimension of a problem is using ________ in the solution sequence.
a. Rule I
b. Rule II
c. Rule III
d. Rule IV

15. School-aged children exhibit better memory function than younger children do. This difference is due largely to the older child's
a. automaticity.
b. executive processes.
c. processing efficiency.
d. all of the above

16. Which of the following statements is most consistent with the balanced approach to reading instruction?
a. Children should be taught to read using systematic and explicit phonics.
b. Whole language methods should be avoided, as they have been found to be ineffective.
c. All instruction should be based on standardized tests.
d. Effective reading instruction includes systematic phonics and the motivational features of whole language methods.

17. Most English-language learners who attend school in the United States receive English instruction in ____________ classes.
a. bilingual education
b. ESL
c. foreign language
d. submersion

18. In which of the following do boys appear to do better than girls?
a. mathematics
b. reading comprehension
c. vocabulary skills
d. speed of information processing

19. A child who approaches a school assignment by focusing on "the big picture" instead of on specific subtasks of the assignment is using a/an ________ learning style.
a. analytical
b. relational
c. inductive
d. deductive

20. What is the most prevalent disability for which U.S. children receive special education services?
a. communication disorder
b. mental retardation
c. serious emotional disturbance
d. learning disability

Chapter 12
Social and Personality Development in Middle Childhood

21. According to Erikson's view of children's psychosocial development in middle childhood, what factor is instrumental in children's development of a sense of industry or inferiority?
    a. their developing relationships with cross-gender friends and peers
    b. their growing independence from their parents
    c. their success or failure at academic tasks
    d. their developing motor skills and athletic accomplishments
22. Trait theorists argue that
    a. emotions are the primary influence on personality development.
    b. temperament evolves into five dimensions of personality by middle childhood.
    c. traits exert less influence on development than other factors do.
    d. emotions play no role in personality development.
23. Bandura's reciprocal determinism model proposes that children's personalities are influenced by
    a. environmental reinforcement.
    b. internal traits.
    c. their own behavior.
    d. interactions of a, b, and c.
24. Which of the following is more likely to be the self-description of a 10-year-old than a 6-year-old?
    a. "I am smart."
    b. "I am better at math than my friend Paul."
    c. "I'm bad."
    d. "My brown hair is curly."
25. What are the key influences on a child's self-esteem in middle childhood?
    a. her skills and abilities in key developmental areas such as academics, sports, and hobbies
    b. the amount of support she receives from important people around her and the discrepancy between what she has achieved and what she desires to achieve
    c. her perceptions about what children of her age should be able to accomplish or achieve
    d. her popularity with other children and her popularity with the adults she knows
26. Which of the following best represents Bandura's concept of self-efficacy?
    a. a child's sense of self-value
    b. a child's understanding of her personality
    c. a child's belief that she can accomplish goals
    d. a child's understanding of others' opinions of her
27. Which of the following best represents the way a school-aged child might describe a friend, rather than the way a preschool-aged child would be likely to describe a friend?
    a. "Miguel is the fastest runner in our class."
    b. "Hoshi is always kind and helpful."
    c. "DeShawna has pigtails in her hair."
    d. "Darryl always sits next to Ms. Jones."
28. According to Piaget, children who are at the beginning of middle childhood are in which stage of moral development?
    a. moral emotional
    b. moral realism
    c. moral judgmental
    d. moral relativism
29. As a result of the development of moral reasoning in middle childhood, children are capable of understanding all of the following *except* that
    a. you can change the rules of a game you are playing as long as all the other players agree to play by the different rules.
    b. accidents are not caused by deliberately "naughty" behavior.
    c. intentions are more important than consequences when the behaviors of others are being judged.
    d. standards of universal fairness dictate that no child should get a treat unless all the children get a treat.
30. Which of the following would be least helpful to parents who want to facilitate their child's development of self-regulation?
    a. Provide discipline through authoritarian parenting.
    b. Provide the child with models of good self-regulation.
    c. Monitor the child's behavior.
    d. Expect the child to demonstrate self-regulatory behavior.
31. Which of the following is not an accurate statement about the peer-group interactions of middle childhood?
    a. During middle childhood, gender is the most important factor in children's selection of friends.
    b. Both girls and boys enjoy rough-and-tumble play in same-sex groups.
    c. Boys' friendships are more focused on competition and dominance than are girls' friendships.
    d. Collaborative and cooperative exchanges are the most common form of communication in girls' and boys' friendships in middle childhood.
32. Which of the following is not a true statement about relational aggression?
    a. Girls are especially likely to use relational aggression against other girls.
    b. Children who use relational aggression are apt to be shunned by their peers.
    c. Children typically are not hurt by relational aggression because it is an indirect form of aggression.
    d. Relational aggression can take the form of expressions of disdain or threats of ostracism.

33. In middle childhood, a popular child most likely
   a. would have a feature or characteristic that made her unusual in comparison to her peers.
   b. would be highly creative.
   c. would be shy.
   d. would be physically attractive and larger than her peers.

34. Which of the following is not a factor that seems to help protect some children from the detrimental effects of poverty?
   a. high IQ
   b. a large network of peers who also are poor
   c. a secure initial attachment to the mother
   d. stable parental employment

35. Which of the following has been associated with playing violent video games?
   a. greater intelligence
   b. greater self-reliance
   c. preference for violent stimuli of all kinds
   d. increase in social skills

Chapter 13
Physical Development and Health in Adolescence

1. The first hormonal milestone of puberty takes place during
   a. infancy.
   b. early childhood.
   c. middle childhood.
   d. adolescence.
2. Changes in the ____________ are responsible for gains in executive processing abilities during the teen years.
   a. brain stem
   b. corpus callosum
   c. hypothalamus
   d. prefrontal cortex
3. Changes in the natural body rhythms of adolescents, called ____________________, may cause adolescents to have difficulty getting up in the morning.
   a. endocrine pulses
   b. circadian rhythms
   c. pubertal cycles
   d. neuronal phases
4. The first observable sign that an adolescent is entering puberty is usually
   a. a sudden growth spurt.
   b. the first menstrual period or ejaculation.
   c. growth of the breasts in girls and facial hair in boys.
   d. changes in facial features.
5. The athletic abilities of teenagers far surpass those of school-aged children because of
   a. joint maturity.
   b. improvements in stamina due to organ growth.
   c. increased muscle mass and strength.
   d. all of the above
6. The average age at which ______________ appear(s) has changed little in the past several decades, but ____________________ appear(s) in younger girls than was common in earlier cohorts.
   a. secondary sex characteristics, menarche
   b. secondary sex characteristics, primary sex characteristics
   c. menarche, secondary sex characteristics
   d. breast buds, ovulation
7. Generally, ____________ puberty is associated with positive outcomes for girls, and ___________ puberty is linked to such outcomes among boys.
   a. late, early
   b. average, early
   c. early, late
   d. average, late
8. Which of the following is not a risk factor for early initiation of sexual activity?
   a. lack of parental monitoring
   b. alcohol and/or substance use
   c. family attitudes toward early sexual activity
   d. participation in sex education classes
9. Which of the following factors helps adolescent mothers overcome the negative effects of teenaged pregnancy?
   a. support from their families
   b. maintaining a romantic relationship with the baby's father
   c. leaving school to make money to support the baby
   d. supportive friends
10. Which of the following has been proposed as a causal factor in the development of a gay, lesbian, or bisexual orientation?
   a. sex education classes
   b. prenatal hormones
   c. cross-gender play in early childhood
   d. peer influences
11. The diets of many teens in the United States are deficient in
   a. carbohydrates.
   b. protein.
   c. fat.
   d. calcium.
12. A vaccine is now available to protect teens and young women against the
   a. human immunodeficiency virus (HIV).
   b. bacteria that cause gonorrhea.
   c. human papilloma virus (HPV).
   d. herpes virus.
13. Some teens may choose to engage in risky behaviors because they possess high levels of a trait called
   a. extraversion.
   b. openness to experience.
   c. sensation seeking.
   d. hyperactivity.
14. Homicide is a more frequent cause of death in ______________ teens than in other groups.
   a. White
   b. Asian American
   c. Hispanic American
   d. African American
15. Which of the following has not been proposed as a causal factor in the development of eating disorders?
   a. emphasis on thinness in the media
   b. brain dysfunction
   c. general tendency toward distorted thinking
   d. drug abuse

Chapter 14
Cognitive Development in Adolescence

16. A teenager who can derive conclusions from hypothetical premises, such as what his mother might say if she finds out that he failed a French test, is engaged in
    a. hypothetico-deductive reasoning.
    b. information processing.
    c. metacognition.
    d. logico-conditional thinking.
17. Research suggests that Piaget
    a. overestimated teens' capacity for formal operational thinking.
    b. underestimated teens' capacity for formal operational thinking.
    c. was on target in claiming that most adolescents exhibit form thinking around age 12 or 13.
    d. failed to identify a form of thinking that distinguishes teens from younger children.
18. A teenager who knows the risks of driving under the influence but still insists on doing it because she would never have an accident is engaging in
    a. an imaginary audience.
    b. a personal fable.
    c. projection.
    d. naïve idealism.
19. Teens are more efficient academic learners than younger children are primarily because of improvements in
    a. metamemory skills.
    b. executive processes.
    c. response inhibition.
    d. all of the above
20. Which of the following is the best example of a child who has task goals for her athletic activities?
    a. Mia hopes to become the best goalie in her high school soccer league.
    b. Tovah wants to improve her personal best time in the 100-meter freestyle swimming event.
    c. Sharinda works hard at free-throw practice because she wants to have the best free-throw percentage on her basketball team.
    d. Robin hopes that her fitness training program will help her become the best tennis player her school has ever had.
21. Which of the following statements about gender and ethnic differences in achievement in science and math is true?
    a. With respect to achievement in math, gender differences are greater than ethnic differences.
    b. With respect to achievement in math, ethnic differences are greater than gender differences.
    c. Girls excel in math but not science.
    d. Intellectually talented girls are encouraged to take courses in sciences such as chemistry and physics rather than zoology or botany.
22. Which of the following factors has not been found to be related to dropping out of high school?
    a. low socioeconomic status
    b. having a peer group that does not value academic achievement
    c. drug use
    d. authoritarian parenting

Chapter 15
Social and Personality Development in Adolescence

23. What is the pivotal transition of adolescence, according to Erikson?
    a. the development of a libido
    b. the development of sexual fixations
    c. an identity crisis
    d. commitment to ideological, occupational, or personal goals

24. Bob has thought about numerous career options. He has had internships in some of the fields he was considering. After all his exploration, he decides to commit himself to a career in sales. James Marcia would describe Bob's status as
    a. identity achievement.
    b. moratorium.
    c. foreclosure.
    d. identity diffusion.

25. Which of the following is an accurate statement about self-esteem during adolescence?
    a. Across the teenaged years, girls consistently have higher self-esteem than boys.
    b. Most teens have high self-esteem at the beginning of adolescence but experience a steady decline in self-esteem during the teenaged years.
    c. Self-esteem typically drops at the beginning of adolescence, but then rises throughout the teenaged years.
    d. Cross-cultural research shows that in all societies, girls who adopt masculine or androgynous characteristics are more popular and have higher self-esteem.

26. When asked "Who are you?" which of the following individuals would be most likely to say "I am a liberal Democrat who opposes the death penalty"?
    a. Chris, age 9
    b. Pat, age 12
    c. Lou, age 15
    d. Hillary, age 18

27. According to Sandra Bem's conceptualization of gender role identity, an individual who gets high scores on both masculinity and femininity scales would be described as having a/an __________ sex role orientation.
    a. androgynous
    b. ambivalent
    c. undifferentiated
    d. transgender

28. Which of the following is not an aspect of the development of an ethnic identity, as identified by Jean Phinney?
    a. an unexamined ethnic identity
    b. an ethnic identity search
    c. an ethnic identity rejection
    d. achievement of an ethnic identity

29. Which of the following is not a level of moral development proposed by Lawrence Kohlberg?
    a. preconventional morality
    b. formal operational morality
    c. conventional morality
    d. postconventional morality

30. Which of the following is least important in the development of moral reasoning?
    a. increased ability to see the perspective of others
    b. a social environment that provides opportunities for meaningful, reciprocal dialogue about moral issues
    c. parents' ability to express moral views in words that reflect a child's level of understanding
    d. successful resolution of Erikson's identity crisis

31. According to Gilligan, the two distinct moral orientations involved in moral reasoning are
    a. justice and empathy.
    b. justice and care.
    c. honesty and sincerity.
    d. right and wrong.

32. Among adolescents, membership in a/an __________ means identification with a reputation-based group of peers, characterized by a label such as "jocks," "brains," or "toughs."
    a. clique
    b. crowd
    c. prototypical identity
    d. achievement identity

33. Jeri is a 12-year-old girl who is sexually attracted to both males and females. Which of the following statements best corresponds to what research would predict about the development of romantic relationships in Jeri's life?
    a. Her romantic relationships will be influenced by the fact that attraction to others of the same sex and self-identification as a homosexual occur simultaneously.
    b. Jeri will probably experiment with both heterosexual and homosexual relationships before committing to a sexual orientation.
    c. She is more likely to hide her attraction to same-sex peers than teenagers in earlier cohorts did.
    d. Jeri will avoid associating with gay and lesbian teens, because they might try to persuade her to commit to a homosexual orientation.

Answers for Test Prep Centers

Chapter 1

AN INTRODUCTION TO HUMAN DEVELOPMENT (pp. 6-9)

1. (1) B (2) A (3) C
2.

Theorist	Methods of Studying Development
Charles Darwin	Baby biographies
G. Stanley Hall	Questionnaires, interviews
Arnold Gesell	Observation laboratories equipped with one-way mirrors, movie cameras

3. Developmental science uses theories and research from many disciplines (e.g., biology, psychology).
4. Adaptive characteristics are acquired through natural selection. Organisms that possess these characteristics outreproduce organisms that do not have them.
5. Since this question asks about students' own experiences, many answers are possible. Here are examples of correct answers for each cell in the table:

	Developmental Event		
Period	Physical	Cognitive	Socioemotional
Infancy (Birth to 2)	Walking	Talking	Attachment
Early childhood (2 to 6)	Riding a tricycle	Making up stories	Cooperative play
Middle childhood (6 to 12)	Writing	Rule-governed games	Long-term friendships
Adolescence (12 to 18)	Puberty	Abstract thinking	Peer groups

KEY ISSUES IN THE STUDY OF HUMAN DEVELOPMENT (pp. 9-13)

6. An inborn bias is an inborn tendency to respond in certain ways. For contemporary developmentalists, inborn biases represent the nature side of the nature-nurture continuum. An internal model of experience is the meaning that a child attaches to a specific experience. This is how most developmentalists think of the nurture side of the nature-nurture continuum.
7. Correlational studies suggested that restricting calories might extend the lifespan. The experiment tested calorie-restricted diets in fruit flies with and without the Sir2 gene and found that calorie restriction extended the lifespan only in the flies that had the gene. Therefore, calorie restriction interacts with genes to extend the lifespan, a finding that fits with the current view that genes and experiential factors interact to affect development.
8. (1) A (2) B (3) B (4) A (5) B

9.

Type of Change	Example
Normative age-graded	Walking, other physical milestones; language acquisition
Normative history-graded	Great Depression
Nonnormative	Genetic disorders; abuse

10. (1) extended family relationships (2) neighborhood (3) school (4) parents' occupations (5) gender

RESEARCH METHODS AND DESIGNS (pp. 13-21)

11. (1) Y (2) N (3) Y (4) Y (5) Y (6) Y
12. Single-parent families are likely to have fewer economic resources to deal with children's problems, so the problems tend to get worse. Parents may experience levels of stress that interfere with effective parenting. Children may have untreated health conditions that cause them to miss school, fall behind in their studies, develop low self-esteem, and, as a result, be more vulnerable to negative peer influences.
13. independent; dependent
14. (1) G (2) E (3) C (4) B (5) A (6) F (7) D (8) H
15.

Method	Advantages	Disadvantages
Cross-sectional	Quick access to data about different age groups	Ignores individual differences; cohort effects
Longitudinal	Tracking of developmental changes over time in individuals	Time-consuming; finding may apply only to group studied
Sequential	Cross-sectional and longitudinal data relevant to same hypotheses	Time-consuming; attrition rates differ across groups

16. Such results would not apply to cultures such as those in the video, in which older adults are more highly valued than they are in European American culture. As noted in the video, children in Native American and Asian American families often have close contact with and receive instruction from their grandparents. Thus, research in societies in which children generally do not experience such interactions with grandparents would not apply to them.
17.

Issue	What Researchers Must Do
Protection from Harm	Avoid research that may cause harm; provide remediation for any possible temporary harmful effects
Informed Consent	Obtain permission from institutions (e.g., schools), parents, and children themselves; allow participants to withdraw
Confidentiality	Keep identities of participants confidential
Knowledge of Results	Provide participants, parents, and institutions with research results
Deception	Provide debriefing if deception is involved

18. No. In some cases, deception is necessary to test a hypothesis. However, ethical guidelines require that participants be informed of the deception as soon as possible after the study ends.

Chapter 2

PSYCHOANALYTIC THEORIES (pp. 27–32)

1. (1) superego (2) id (3) ego
2.

Name of Stage	Age	Focus of Libido	Developmental Task	Characteristics of Fixation in Adulthood
Oral	0–1	Mouth	Weaning	Behaviors that involve the mouth (e.g., swearing)
Anal	1–3	Organs of elimination	Toilet training	Behaviors that involve cleanliness and order
Phallic	3–6	Sex organs	Resolving Oedipus/Electra complex; identifying with same-sex parent	Deviant sexual behavior
Latency	6–12	Libido suppressed	Developing defense mechanisms; identifying with same-sex peers	None
Genital	12+	Sex organs	Mature sexual intimacy	Sincere interest in others; mature sexuality

3.

Name of Stage	Age	Positive Characteristics Gained and Typical Activities	Conflict Associated with Stage
Trust versus mistrust	0–1	Hope; trust in primary caregiver and in one's own ability to make things happen (secure attachment to caregiver is key)	Infants whose care has been erratic or harsh may develop mistrust.
Autonomy versus shame and doubt	1–3	Independence; new physical skills lead to demand for more choices, most often seen as saying "no" to caregivers; child learns self-care skills such as toileting	Toddlers who are not encouraged to develop independence may have self-doubts.
Initiative versus guilt	3–6	Purpose; ability to organize activities around some goal; more assertiveness and aggressiveness	Young children who do not learn to fit in with agemates may develop excessive guilt feelings. (Oedipus/Electra conflict with parent of same sex may lead to guilt.)
Industry versus inferiority	6–12	Competence; cultural skills and norms, including school skills and tool use	Children who fail to learn culturally important skills (e.g., reading) develop a sense of inferiority.
Identity versus role confusion	12–18	Fidelity; adaptation of sense of self to pubertal changes, consideration of future choices, achievement of a more mature sexual identity, and search for new values	Teens who do not develop a sense of identity are confused about their place in the adult world.

Intimacy versus isolation	18–30	Love; person develops intimate relationships beyond adolescent love; many become parents	Young adults who fail to develop intimate relationships feel socially isolated.
Generativity versus stagnation	30–late adult-hood	Care; people rear children, focus on occupational achievement or creativity, and train the next generation; turning outward from the self toward others	Middle-aged adults who do not exhibit generativity become self-absorbed.
Ego integrity versus despair	Late adult-hood	Wisdom; person conducts a life review, integrates earlier stages and comes to terms with basic identity, and develops self-acceptance	Elderly people who do not develop self-acceptance experience despair.

4. The major concepts of psychoanalytic theory (i.e., id, ego, superego) are difficult to test because they are not precisely defined.

LEARNING THEORIES (pp. 32-37)

5. Because of the proximity of the nose to the mouth, a person smells a food just prior to eating it. As a result, the smell of a particular food is a conditioned stimulus that becomes associated with the unconditioned stimulus of the food itself. This association causes the smell to elicit the same response from the digestive system that the food does.
6. UCS: noise; UCR: startle, cry; CS: white rat; CR: startle, cry
7. (1) negative reinforcement (2) positive reinforcement (3) punishment
8. If the father repeatedly does not respond to the child's whining, he is using extinction.
9. Social-cognitive theory emphasizes the cognitive elements of experience; other learning theories do not. One major concept of social-cognitive theory is the idea that people learn from models. To learn from a model, the child has to pay attention to the model, remember what she does, be developmentally capable of performing the observed behavior, and have the motivation to perform the behavior on his/her own.
10. Children who had been exposed to a great deal of aggressive behavior might have viewed Bandura's models as behaving normally and may not have paid sufficient attention to them to learn the behaviors that they modeled.
11. Developmentalists argue that children are not as passive as conditioning theories assume them to be and that social-cognitive theory explains only specific behaviors rather than the overall developmental process.

COGNITIVE THEORIES (pp. 37-41)

12.

Stage	Average Ages	Description
Sensorimotor	0–2	Children use senses and motor activities to learn; object permanence develops.
Preoperational	2–6	Children use symbols.
Concrete operational	6–12	Children learn to think logically about ideas that have concrete referents; conservation.
Formal operational	12+	Teens learn to think about abstract ideas.

13. social interactions
14. The children were capable of completing the puzzles partly on their own but needed the help of an adult to place some of the pieces. (Zone of proximal development = the range of tasks that are too hard for the child to do alone but that he can manage with guidance.)

15. (1) C (2) A (3) B
16. (1) B (2) A (3) C

BIOLOGICAL AND ECOLOGICAL THEORIES (pp. 42-45)

17. Heredity contributes more to intelligence than it does to achievement, because achievement depends to a greater degree on specific experiences.
18. According to ethologists, the forces of evolution have shaped infant crying such that it is irritating to adults. As a result, adults are motivated to care for the infant in order to escape from the irritation they feel when the infant cries.
19. According to sociobiologists, evolution has provided humans with genetic programming that fosters social rules that enhance a group's chances of survival. Prohibition against murder is one such rule. These rules are universal because the hypothesized genetic program that leads societies to create them is also universal in the human species.
20. (1) B (2) C (3) D (4) A

COMPARING THEORIES (pp. 45-47)

21.

Theories	Active/Passive	Nature/Nurture	Continuity/Discontinuity
Psychosexual	Passive	Nature	Discontinuity
Psychosocial	Passive	Both	Discontinuity
Classical Conditioning	Passive	Nurture	Continuity
Operant Conditioning	Passive	Nurture	Continuity
Social-Cognitive	Active	Nurture	Continuity
Cognitive-Developmental	Active	Both	Discontinuity
Sociocultural	Active	Both	Discontinuity
Information-Processing	Active	Both	Both

22. (A) A testable theory is more useful than one that can't be tested scientifically.
    (B) A theory that has heuristic value stimulates discussion and research by those who support and oppose it.
    (C) Useful theories generate solutions to real-world problems.
    (D) The more basic facts about development that a theory can explain, the more useful it is.
23. (1) False (2) True (3) True (4) False (5) True

Chapter 3

CONCEPTION AND GENETICS (pp. 53-59)

1. (1) B (2) F (3) E (4) A (5) C (6) D
2.

Inheritance	Description
Polygenic	Several genes influence a trait.
Genomic imprinting	A gene influences a trait when it is received from one parent but not when it is received from the other.

Mitochondrial	DNA that is in the mitochondria rather than in the nucleus of an ovum influences a trait. DNA is therefore passed only from the mother to the child.
Multi-factorial	Both genetic and environmental factors influence a trait.

GENETIC AND CHROMOSOMAL DISORDERS (pp. 59-61)

3. early in life; recessive; in adulthood; dominant
4. Early interventions for children with Down syndrome include physical, occupational, and speech therapy. Educators also train parents of children with Down syndrome in the use of techniques that will stimulate their children's development.

PREGNANCY AND PRENATAL DEVELOPMENT (pp. 62-70)

5. (1) A (2) C (3) B (4) C (5) C (6) B
6. The fetus is too small.
7. Conception usually occurs in the fallopian tube.
8. Female fetuses advance more rapidly in skeletal development. At birth, female infants are typically 1 to 2 weeks ahead in bone development. Females typically acquire coordination and motor skills earlier than males.
9. (1) N (2) Y (3) Y (4) Y (5) N (6) N (7) Y

PROBLEMS IN PRENATAL DEVELOPMENT (pp. 70-79)

10. embryonic
11. Some pregnant women must take prescription or over-the-counter drugs to treat conditions that threaten their own health and that of their unborn children.
12.

Drug	Effect
Heroin	Miscarriage; premature labor; early death; postnatal addiction and withdrawal symptoms
Cocaine	Difficult to determine because of influence of multiple co-occurring factors such as poor maternal health, poverty, lack of prenatal care, postnatal neglect
Marijuana	Tremors; sleep problem; postnatal lethargy; short stature
Tobacco	Low birth weight; higher risk of learning problems and antisocial behavior
Alcohol	Fetal alcohol syndrome; short stature

13. In the later weeks of the prenatal period, alcohol interferes with the connections between newly formed neurons in the developing brain. As a result, many of the neurons die, and the child is born with brain damage.
14. (1) A, D, F (2) B (3) A, E, F (4) A, C, E (5) E, F, G
15.

Variable	Association with Prenatal Development
Diet	Insufficient folic acid is linked to spina bifida; malnutrition increases risk of low birth weight, learning problems, and obstetrical complications.
Age	Older mothers have more complications, more birth defects in infants, more multiple pregnancies; teen mothers have more problems than mothers in their 20s even when poverty and prenatal care are taken into account.
Chronic illnesses	Depression slows fetal growth and increases risk of premature labor; other health conditions have adverse effects, so mothers should be monitored by specialists in fetal-maternal health.

Environmental hazards	Lead, arsenic, cadmium, anesthetic gases, solvents, and parasites have a variety of negative effects.
Maternal emotions	Some states, such as anxiety, cause hormonal changes that may affect the fetus; the fetuses of highly stressed mothers grow more slowly.

16.

Test	How It Works
Ultrasonography	Image of fetus derived from sound waves; shows physical defects, placement of placenta, etc.; can be done any time during pregnancy
Alpha-fetoprotein	Maternal blood test; helps identify nervous system defects
Chorionic villus sampling	Cells extracted from placenta for testing; used to identify genetic and chromosomal disorders; done during first 8 to 10 weeks
Fetoscopy	Image of fetus from small camera inserted in uterus; used in conjunction with fetal surgery, blood transfusions, bone marrow transplants, fetal blood samples; can be done any time
Fetal blood tests	Blood sample taken from umbilical cord; guided by fetoscopy or ultrasound; used to diagnose infections and other conditions of the fetus
Amniocentesis	Cells extracted from amniotic fluid; used to identify genetic and chromosomal disorders; done between 14 and 16 weeks

BIRTH AND THE NEONATE (pp. 79–86)

17.

Category	Choices Available
Location	Hospital, birthing room in hospital, birth center, home
Pain relief	Analgesics, sedatives, tranquilizers, anesthesia (general or epidural), natural (prepared) childbirth
Birth attendants	Physicians, obstetricians, certified nurse midwives, certified midwives

18. Breastfed babies have a more highly developed sense of taste because they are exposed to the more complex tastes of breast milk.
19. (1) 1 (2) 1 (3) 1 (4) 2 (5) 0 (6) 5
20. A has the best chance (early but appropriate weight for gestational age); B has the poorest chance (full term, small for date).
21. Small sacs inside the lungs of full-term infants expand and allow for the exchange of oxygen and carbon dioxide in the baby's blood. In premature infants, the sacs do not fully expand. The treatment simulates conditions in the womb in which the fetus "breathes" amniotic fluid. Under such conditions, the sacs can fully expand and gases can be exchanged in the lungs.

Chapter 4

PHYSICAL CHANGES (pp. 99–106)

1. (1) A (2) C (3) B

2. Myelination improves the efficiency with which the neurons conduct electrochemical impulses. Myelin serves as an insulator that keeps impulses on track.
3. Some aspects of visual perception, such as the muscles and brain structures needed to control eye movements, are fully mature at birth. Other aspects of perception, such as the ability to predict visual events (e.g., to understand that a ball that rolls behind a screen will appear on the other side), are acquired as the brain matures and the baby interacts with the world.
4. (A) Neonates sleep 80% of the time, evenly divided between day and night; by 8 weeks, amount of sleep per day drops and day/night rhythms appear—babies sleep through two or three 2-hour cycles in sequence without coming to full wakefulness; by 6 months, babies sleep 14 hours, with extended sleep at night and naps during the day.
   (B) Neonates are awake and alert for 2 to 3 hours a day, but total time is unevenly distributed over the 24 hours of each day; over the first 6 months, awake and alert periods become longer and regular periods of sleeping, crying, and eating emerge.
   (C) Crying increases over the first 6 weeks, then tapers off; prompt attention during the first 3 months reduces later crying.
5. The breathing reflex ensures that the newborn's body will get oxygen. The rooting and sucking reflexes help the newborn obtain nutrition through nursing.
6.

Age	Gross Motor Skills	Fine Motor Skills
1 month	Stepping reflex; lifts head slightly	Holds object placed in hand
2–3 months	Lifts head up to 90-degree angle when lying on stomach	Begins to swipe at objects in sight
4–6 months	Rolls over; sits with support; moves on hands and knees ("creeps"); holds head erect while in sitting position	Reaches for and grasps objects
7–9 months	Sits without support; crawls	Transfers objects from one hand to the other
10–12 months	Pulls self up and walks grasping furniture, then walks alone; squats and stoops; plays pat-a-cake	Shows some signs of hand preference; grasps a spoon across palm but has poor aim when moving food to mouth
13–18 months	Walks backward, sideways; runs (14–20 months); rolls ball to adult; claps	Stacks two blocks; puts objects into small container and dumps them out
19–24 months	Walks up and down stairs, two feet per step; jumps with both feet off ground	Uses spoon to feed self; stacks 4 to 10 blocks

7. Motor skills that are universal in adulthood (e.g., sitting, walking) emerge in a fixed sequence among infants across all cultures. Skills that are used little or not at all in adulthood (e.g., crawling) are not universal. In some cultures, infants do not crawl at all, and in others, they crawl after they walk.

HEALTH AND WELLNESS (pp. 106-109)

8. Breast-fed babies have a more highly developed sense of taste because they are exposed to the more complex tastes of breast milk.
9. (1) B (2) D (3) C (4) A
10. Infants need well-baby check-ups to keep track of their growth and development. They also need immunizations.

INFANT MORTALITY (pp. 109-112)

11. (1) N (2) Y (3) N (4) N

12. (1) 1 (2) 3 (3) 6 (4) 2 (5) 5 (6) 4
13. SIDS is two to three times more common among African American and Native American infants, the two groups with the highest rates of infant mortality, than in other groups.

SENSORY SKILLS (pp. 112-115)

14. Vision is the most poorly developed sense at birth. For the first few weeks, babies see clearly at 10 inches. Infants' acuity improves rapidly the first year.
15. Auditory; visual

PERCEPTUAL SKILLS (pp. 115-119)

16. The baby looks at a toy for a while and then looks away. When the toy is presented again, she looks at it briefly. When a new toy is presented, she looks at it much longer.
17. The baby perceives depth but doesn't yet understand that the glass will prevent her from falling. She stops because she perceives the end of the checkered pattern as a "cliff" that she will fall off if she keeps crawling.
18. At 1 week, newborns perceive the location of a sound as well as its volume and pitch. They also prefer high voices. At 2 months, infants startle at sounds and recognize voices. At 4 to 7 months, they turn to follow sounds and deliberately imitate sounds.
19. Intermodal perception speeds the learning of the nature of objects and recognition of new stimuli.
20. (1) A (2) B (3) B (4) A

Chapter 5

COGNITIVE CHANGES (pp. 127-134)

1. (1) A (2) B (3) C (4) A (5) C (6) B
2. Piaget would say that Jarrett is in substage 4 of the sensorimotor stage and is showing the A-not-B error. This error causes babies to look for an object where they last saw it rather than where they saw it go. When Jarrett looks at the spot on the floor where the ball used to be and doesn't see it, he probably remembers that his ball is usually in the toy box.
3. Children adapt their reflexes to explore the world, learn to use their senses and motor skills to manipulate objects, learn to communicate, and explore the world around them, behaving as "little scientists" in Piaget's terms.
4. At 8 months old, the infant would not look for the hidden toys if they were fully hidden from view. If he were able to see part of a toy, however, he would look for it.
5.

Milestone	Findings
Object permanence	Studies that do not depend on infants' motor skills show that babies exhibit "looking" behaviors which suggest that they understand more about objects and how they move than Piaget believed, perhaps as early as 4 months of age.
Imitation	Newborn infants imitate facial expressions. Very young infants may be able to defer imitation for a few minutes. Older infants have greater imitation and deferred imitation abilities than Piaget thought.

6. Spelke's work has shown that babies as young as 2 to 3 months old have expectations about the ways in which objects can move. Baillargeon's studies indicate that infants develop basic hypotheses about the properties of objects and, through experience, modify these hypotheses until they have an accurate understanding of the nature of objects and their movements.

LEARNING, CATEGORIZING, AND REMEMBERING (pp. 134–136)

7. (1) B (2) A (3) C
8. the organization of experiences into expectancies, called schemas, which enable infants to distinguish between familiar and unfamiliar stimuli
9. (1) True (2) False (3) True

THE BEGINNINGS OF LANGUAGE (pp. 136–145)

10. Infants are better able than fluent speakers to recognize concepts that the language they are learning doesn't describe, showing that cognition precedes language and that language shapes cognition.
11. (A) talking to their children often (B) reading to them regularly (C) using a wide range of words in their speech
12. Child-directed speech makes it easier for infants to recognize and imitate the individual sounds that are used in the language they are learning.
13. Constraints on word learning are "hints" built into the human brain that provide infants with language-learning assumptions, such as the idea that some words stand for actions and others stand for objects.
14. naming explosion; Infants learn new words very rapidly and easily generalize them to new situations.
15. (1) Y (2) N (3) Y (4) Y (5) N (6) N
16.

Differences in . . .	Description
Rate	The normal age ranges for all the milestones of language development are very broad. For example, some children use words at 8 months, but others do not do so until 18 months. Some children do not use sentences until age 3.
Style	Toddlers who use an expressive style use mostly words that are linked to social relationships. Those who use a referential style communicate more about objects and the physical environment.

17. (A) The sequence of language development is highly similar across cultures. Cooing always comes before babbling, babbling always comes before words, and words always appear before holophrases. All babies understand language before they can speak it. Babies everywhere utter their first words, on average, at around 12 months of age.
    (B) The specific word order in children's early sentences varies with the language they are learning to speak. Inflections vary in the order in which they are learned as well. Children learning Turkish seem to skip the two-word phase.

MEASURING INTELLIGENCE IN INFANCY (pp. 146–147)

18. (A) Scores on infant intelligence tests are not predictive of scores on later tests because the former depend too much on infants' motor abilities.
    (B) Infant intelligence tests are useful for identifying children who are at risk for serious developmental delays.
    (C) These tests have proven to be useful for infants with conditions, such as cerebral palsy, that cause them to be unable to respond to other infant intelligence tests. Research suggests that they are of limited usefulness with healthy infants, however.

Chapter 6

THEORIES OF SOCIAL AND PERSONALITY DEVELOPMENT (pp. 153–155)

1. (1) A (2) A (3) B (4) A
2. (A) The ethological perspective asserts that infants are born with the tendency to form attachment relationships.

(B) Ethologists claim that the first 2 years are a critical period for the formation of an emotional bond with a caregiver. They claim that this bond shapes those that come after it, including peer relationships. Thus, a peer relationship cannot substitute for attachment to a caregiver.

(C) Ethologists hypothesize that early attachments lead to the development of internal models that guide the development of later socioemotional relationships, even those in adulthood.

ATTACHMENT (pp. 155-163)

3. During the first few weeks, mothers and fathers behave similarly. Afterward, fathers spend more time playing with the baby, and mothers spend more time in caregiving.
4.

Stage	Name of Stage	Age	Attachment Behaviors
1	Nonfocused orienting and signaling	0–3 months	Crying, smiling, making eye contact to draw the attention of anyone with whom infants come in contact
2	Focus on one or more figures	3–6 months	"Come here" signals sent to fewer people, typically those with whom infants spend the most time; less responsiveness to unfamiliar people
3	Secure base behavior	6–24 months	True attachment to primary caregiver; proximity-seeking such as following and clinging to caregivers when anxious, injured, or in need
4	Internal model	24+ months	Anticipating how actions will affect socioemotional bonds with caregivers and others

5. Phase 3: secure base behavior
6. (1) ambivalent (2) secure (3) avoidant (4) disorganized
7. (1) False (2) True (3) True (4) False (5) True
8.

Early and Middle Childhood	Adolescence	Adulthood
More sociable Less "clingy" Less aggressive, disruptive More empathetic	Better social skills More friendships More likely to be leaders Higher self-esteem Less likely to become sexually active at an early age	More sociable Less likely to have sexual dysfunctions More responsive to own children More confident in ability to parent

9. True

PERSONALITY, TEMPERAMENT, AND SELF-CONCEPT (pp. 164-169)

10. (A) Easy children are emotionally positive, have predictable eating and sleeping cycles, are usually happy, and adjust well to change.
    (B) Difficult children display irregular sleeping and eating cycles, emotional negativity, irritability, and resistance to change.
    (C) Slow-to-warm-up children show few intense reactions and are nonresponsive to unfamiliar people.
11. The child makes the transition from her mother to her teacher with no difficulty.
12. Trait theorists see each individual infant's temperament as the result of his profile on several different characteristics. These characteristics interact to produce the child's temperament.

13. frontal lobe asymmetry
14. niche-picking
15.

Component of Self	Behaviors
Subjective/existential	Awareness of existence; effects on objects and people enable baby to separate self from the outside world; object permanence enables her to understand that the self is stable and permanent
Objective/categorical	Awareness of properties of the self and responses to objects and other people in the environment; mirror test suggests objective self-awareness emerges around 21 months, along with a proprietary attitude
Emotional	Awareness of own and others' emotions; babies respond to others' facial expression in first few months, respond to both facial and vocal expressions of emotion by 5 to 7 months, try to elicit positive emotional expressions from others by end of first year; social referencing and ability to deliberately alter his emotional state emerge around baby's first birthday; self-conscious emotions (e.g., embarrassment) appear at same time as self-recognition

EFFECTS OF NONPARENTAL CARE (pp. 169–173)

16. It would be easier, because all children would be enrolled in the same kind of care. In reality, children who are exposed to nonparental care are taken care of by many different kinds of caregivers in a variety of settings. This makes it difficult to study "nonparental care" as a single entity.
17. more enrichment than they would receive at home
18. True
19. Children and senior citizens who need supervision are cared for in the same facility and spend a lot of time together.

Chapter 7

PHYSICAL CHANGES (pp. 185–198)

1. below
2. possible
3. 5th
4. growth hormone
5. (1) B (2) C (3) A
6. Split-brain studies examine neurological functioning in patients in whom the corpus callosum has been severed in order to prevent seizures. These studies make it possible to determine in which hemisphere particular functions, such as those associated with language comprehension and production, are carried out.
7. nature
8. nurture
9. Correlations between left-handedness and developmental problems are due to an underlying factor that, for unknown reasons, contributes to both. Pushing a child to be right-handed will not prevent such problems from developing.
10. (1) A (2) B (3) C (4) D
11. Research suggests that children with mild hearing loss are more likely to have learning problems than children without mild hearing loss.

12.

Age	Gross Motor Skills	Fine Motor Skills
18–24 months	Runs awkwardly; climbs stairs with both feet on each step; pushes and pulls boxes or wheeled toys	Shows clear hand preference; stacks four to six blocks; turns pages one at a time; picks up things without overbalancing; unscrews lid on a jar
2–3 years	Runs easily; climbs on furniture unaided; hauls and shoves big toys around obstacles	Picks up small objects; throws small ball while standing
3–4 years	Walks up stairs one foot per step; skips on two feet; walks on tiptoe; pedals and steers tricycle; walks in any direction pulling large toys	Catches large ball between outstretched arms; cuts paper with scissors; holds pencil between thumb and fingers
4–5 years	Walks up and down stairs one foot per step; stands and runs on tiptoe	Strikes ball with bat; kicks and catches ball; threads beads on a string; grasps pencil properly
5–6 years	Skips on alternate feet; walks on a line; uses slides, swings	Plays ball games well; threads needle and sews large stitches

13. (A) scribble (B) pictorial (C) design (D) shape
14. nightmares
15. night terrors
16. too little

HEALTH AND WELLNESS (pp. 198-207)

17. Dietary fat is needed for brain development in early childhood.
18. Dental care prevents the accumulation of bacteria that cause dental caries.
19. Research shows that mild cases of otitis media often resolve on their own without antibiotics. Overuse of antibiotics is believed to contribute to the development of treatment-resistant strains of bacteria.
20. cosmetics
21. sub-Saharan Africa; HIV/AIDS
22. (A) Most cases of abuse involve children age 4 and younger.
    (B) Risk factors for abuse include sociocultural factors, characteristics of the child, characteristics of the abuser, and family stresses.
    (C) Abuse can be prevented through law enforcement, parent education, and identification of at-risk families by health professionals.

ATYPICAL DEVELOPMENT (pp. 208-212)

23. (A) an intelligence test score in the bottom 2% of the distribution of scores (B) deficits in adaptive functioning
24. The girl's siblings engaged in physical play with her that helped her develop physical skills. In the school setting, the child learned physical and cognitive skills from observing the typically developing children in the class.
25. (A) poor communication skills (B) inability to engage in reciprocal social interactions (C) self-injurious behavior (D) unusual, repetitive behaviors
26. Children with autism show atypical patterns of language and cognitive development in the first 2 years of life. Children with Asperger's syndrome have language and cognitive skills similar to those of typically developing children. Their problems with social relationships

don't show up until they start interacting with peers at age 3 or 4. Even then, they may be characterized as "late bloomers" and go undiagnosed until they reach school age.

Chapter 8

COGNITIVE CHANGES (pp. 220-231)

1. (1) D (2) C (3) E (4) A (5) B
2. centration
3.

Cognitive Ability	Research Findings
Conservation	Most children cannot solve conservation problems until age 5. Younger children can sometimes solve simplified versions of Piaget's conservation tasks.
Egocentrism	Piaget underestimated young children's ability to overcome egocentric thinking. Children as young as 2 and 3 have some ability to understand that another person experiences things differently than they do.
Perspective-taking	At level 1 (age 2 to 3), the child knows that other people experience things differently. At level 2 (age 4 and beyond), the child develops a whole series of complex rules for figuring out precisely what the other person sees or experiences.
Appearance/reality	The young child's movement away from egocentrism seems to be part of a much broader change in her understanding of appearance and reality.

4. false belief
5. (1) D (2) A (3) C (4) B
6. The child has some of the skills needed to complete the puzzle but could not do so on his own without his teacher's guidance. Her hints and demonstrations fill in the gaps in the child's skills so that he can accomplish the goal of putting the puzzle together.

CHANGES IN LANGUAGE (pp. 231-233)

7. Fast-mapping involves the formation of hypotheses about word meanings. When children use words they have acquired through fast-mapping in their own speech, feedback from fluent speakers helps them confirm or correct their hypotheses.
8. Telegraphic speech lacks inflections, prepositions, and articles.
9. (1) N (2) Y (3) N (4) Y

DIFFERENCES IN INTELLIGENCE (pp. 234-239)

10. Guthrie challenges the assumption that it is possible to measure anyone's ability to learn with a paper-and-pencil test.
11. The reaction range is the span within which the environment can affect a trait that is strongly influenced by heredity.
12. Even between twins reared together, the correlation between IQ scores is less than perfect. This shows that the environment has some degree of influence on intelligence.
13. (A) The gap between the average IQ scores of White and African American students has narrowed in recent years.
    (B) Most developmentalists believe that group differences in intelligence test scores are the result of environmental factors.
    (C) The difference falls within the presumed reaction range.
14. Sternberg has found that definitions of intelligence vary across cultures. For example, people in industrialized cultures are more likely to include performance on academic tasks in definitions of intelligence than people in traditional cultures are.

EARLY CHILDHOOD EDUCATION (pp. 240–243)

15. (1) A (2) B (3) A (4) B (5) B (6) A
16. The researcher emphasizes the plasticity of the brain in early childhood. She would probably say that early childhood programs are needed to be sure that disadvantaged children receive the kinds of learning opportunities that are needed for optimal physical and cognitive development.

Chapter 9

THEORIES OF SOCIAL AND PERSONALITY DEVELOPMENT (pp. 249–253)

1. Freud viewed the early childhood period as the time in life when young children, first, gain control of their bodily functions and, second, renegotiate their relationships with their parents to prepare for stepping out into the world of peers.
2. Erikson believed that with too much parental control the child would not have sufficient opportunity to explore and with too little control the child would become unmanageable and fail to learn the skills she would need to get along with peers as well as adults.
3. Children as young as 3 have some understanding of intentions, but they still sometimes judge the "naughtiness" of acts on the basis of the consequences of the action rather than the intentions of the actor.

PERSONALITY AND SELF-CONCEPT (pp. 253–256)

4. Parents who reject a difficult child may cause the child's difficult behavior to become more frequent or intense. Those who respond by helping the child learn to regulate her emotions and behaviors can lessen the potential effects of the child's temperament on her social relationships.
5.

Stage	Description
1: Global empathy	During the first year, if the infant is around someone expressing a strong emotion, he may match that emotion—for example, by beginning to cry when he hears another infant crying.
2: Egocentric empathy	Beginning at about 12 to 18 months of age, when children have developed a fairly clear sense of their separate selves, they respond to another's distress with some distress of their own, but they may attempt to "cure" the other person's problem by offering what they themselves would find most comforting. A child may, for example, show sadness when she sees another child hurt and go get her own mother to help.
3: Empathy for another's feelings	Beginning as young as age 2 or 3 and continuing through elementary school, children note others' feelings, partially match those feelings, and respond to the others' distress in nonegocentric ways. Over these years, children become able to distinguish a wider (and more subtle) range of emotions.
4: Empathy for another's life condition	In late childhood or adolescence, some children develop a more generalized notion of others' feelings and respond not just to the immediate situation but to the others' general situation or plight. Thus, a young person at this level may become more distressed by another person's sadness if she knows that the sadness is chronic or that the person's general situation is particularly tragic than if she sees it as a momentary problem.

GENDER DEVELOPMENT (pp. 256-262)

6. The video showed a lesbian couple whose toddler son consistently chose "boy" toys to play with, even though he had never seen the toys before. The research suggested that imitation of parental role models may be less important in gender development than some people believe.
7. 9–12 months
8. When children understand, later in childhood, that gender rules are social conventions rather than moral rules, they become more flexible. So the rigidity of 5- and 6-year-olds results more from their lack of understanding of social rules in general than from enduring gender stereotypes.
9. Gender differences exist for some highly specific cognitive skills, such as mental rotation, but Sternberg's research suggests that there are no gender differences in general intelligence.

FAMILY RELATIONSHIPS AND STRUCTURE (pp. 262-272)

10.

Age	Change in Attachment Relationship
2–3	Attachment behaviors such as proximity-seeking become less visible.
4	Internal models of attachment influence other relationships.

11. Bowlby would say that children's internal working models of attachment generalize from relationships with their parents to those they have with their peers.
12.

Style	Definition	Effects on Development
Authoritarian	High in control and maturity demands; low in nurturance and communication	Lower achievement, self-esteem, and social skills than with authoritative parenting style
Permissive	High in nurturance; low in maturity demands, control, and communication	Lower achievement; higher aggressiveness
Authoritative	High in nurturance, maturity demands, control, and communication	Most consistently associated with positive outcomes
Uninvolved	Low in nurturance, maturity demands, control, and communication	Poorest outcomes; disturbances in social relationships; poor achievement

13. Among Asian Americans, authoritarian parenting is associated with children's academic achievement. Among Whites and African Americans, authoritarian parenting is associated with lower levels of substance abuse in adolescence.
14. (A) Little is known abut the effects of being raised by grandparents, because most research focuses on the effects of parenting on the grandparents themselves, not on the children.
    (B) Homosexuality is no more frequent among individuals raised in gay or lesbian families than among those raised in other types of families.
15. Father involvement in general is more important than any specific behavior that fathers exhibit.
16. (A) Economic resources decline.
    (B) School performance declines in the first few years after a divorce. Children living in stepparent families have more behavior problems in school and lower grades.
    (C) In the first few years after a divorce, children show more aggressive, defiant, negative, or depressed behavior. Adolescent children of divorced parents are more likely to engage in criminal behavior. Children of divorced parents also have a higher risk of mental health problems in adulthood, may struggle with fears of intimacy in relationships, and are themselves more likely to divorce.

17. Grandparents, aunts, uncles, cousins, and other extended family members often provide financial and emotional support as well as help with child care.

PEER RELATIONSHIPS (pp. 272-277)

18.

Type of Play	Example
Solitary	A child building a block structure alone
Onlooker	A child watching another build a block structure
Parallel	Two children building separate block structures without interacting
Associative	Two children building separate block structures and minimally interacting (e.g., looking at and commenting on the structures)
Cooperative	Two children working together to create a block structure

19. (A) True (B) True (C) False (D) False (E) False
20. a key role
21. Instrumental aggression is more common between 2 and 4. When frustrated, children of this age express themselves by throwing things or hitting other children, actions aimed at gaining some object. Taunting and name calling become more common as children's language skills improve.
22. Prosocial behavior is intentional and voluntary behavior that is intended to help another person. Such behavior becomes more common as children develop more interest in playing with others, around 2 or 3. Turn taking increases with age, but comforting others declines.
23. (A) 4 (B) 18 months (C) 3

Chapter 10

PHYSICAL CHANGES (pp. 289-294)

1. bone age
2.

	Changes
Skeletal system	Bones mature; epiphyses ossify.
Hormones	Adrenal glands produce androgens in higher quantities.
Strength	Increases in muscle mass lead to increases in strength; ratio of strength to body size is greater among boys.
Stamina	Growth of the heart and lungs increases capacity for sustained physical activity.

3. (A) False (B) False (C) True
4. (A) Myelination continues in middle childhood. The myelination of the reticular formation enables older children to be less distractible than those who are younger.
   (B) Lateralization of spatial perception occurs in middle childhood, with complex spatial perception becoming strongly lateralized about age 8.
5. Spatial reasoning scores improved by more than 40%; origami, chess
6. Figure-ground

HEALTH AND WELLNESS (pp. 294-308)

7. 80
8. healthier
9. (1) A (2) B
10. (A) Control the child's environment by avoiding allergens.
    (B) Give the child prescription antihistamine drugs.
    (C) Give the child prescription steroids.
    (D) Treat the child with desensitization therapy.
11. asthma
12. Daily medication for asthma can have negative effects on children's cognitive development.
13. (A) amount of supervision (B) amount of physical activity (C) amount of aggressive or impulsive behavior
14. (A) African American children are more likely to die from homicide than are children in other groups.
    (B) The rate of death due to cancer is higher among Asian American children than any other group.
    (C) The rate of death due to accidents is higher among Native American children than any other group.
15. (1) B (2) C (3) A
16. Busy parents may give their children too much junk food, leading to increases in children's obesity, a risk factor for diabetes.

    A diet that carefully balances carbohydrates and protein can decrease the severity of diabetes or eliminate it altogether. Keeping a child on such a diet may be difficult when parents have little time to prepare meals.
17. (A) parental unemployment (B) parental employment in low-wage occupation (C) low level of parental education (D) lack of access to health care (E) parental tobacco use
18. Multiple answers are possible, including the following: (A) high IQ (B) authoritative parenting (C) an optimistic outlook (D) effective schools (E) secure initial attachment to parent
19. (1) Y (2) N (3) Y (4) N (5) N (6) N (7) Y

ATYPICAL DEVELOPMENT (pp. 308-314)

20. 6 months
21.

Pros	Cons
1. Improved concentration	1. School performance does not always improve.
2. Decreased physical activity	2. Newer drugs may cause changes in thinking that increase the risk of serious mental disorder.
3. Decreased impulsivity	3. Individuals face increased risk of heart attacks and strokes as adults.
4. Improved social behavior	

22. School Psychologist: Improve self-esteem. Teachers: Interact with peers verbally rather than through physical aggression, increase compliance.
23. 8
24. ODD
25. Depression is difficult to diagnose because its symptoms overlap with those of behavioral disorders such as ADHD.

Chapter 11

COGNITIVE CHANGES (pp. 322-329)

1. 60,000
2. (A) Decentration allows children to think about more than one variable when solving problems such as Piaget's conservation tasks.
   (B) Reversibility enables children to mentally reverse processes that result in a change in a substance's appearance but not its quantity.

3. The boy failed to follow the rule because children in the concrete operational stage cannot reason from a premise that is contrary to fact.
4. (1) B (2) A
5. relational complexity
6.

Advances	Benefits
Greater processing efficiency	Makes more efficient use of short-term memory; allows faster processing of information
Automaticity	Frees up space in short-term memory to manage complex problems
Executive processes	Improves ability to devise and carry out alternative ways of processing information
Memory strategies	Improves capacity for remembering information
Expertise	Improves information-processing system efficiency, memory, categorization, creativity

7. (A) organization (B) rehearsal (C) elaboration (D) mnemonic

SCHOOLING (pp. 329–339)

8. The balanced approach to reading instruction includes systematic and explicit instruction in phonics along with other instructional strategies derived from the whole language approach.
9. Teachers should be trained in the principles of literacy acquisition and how to individualize instruction in order to maximize development.
10. (1) D (2) B (3) C (4) A
11. Teachers in diverse classrooms cannot assume that students have the same background knowledge they do or the background knowledge on which the curriculum is based. Language differences may also interfere with teachers' attempts to communicate with students.
12.

Type	Definition
Linguistic	Ability to use language effectively
Logical/mathematical	Facility with numbers and logical problem solving
Musical	Ability to appreciate and produce music
Spatial	Ability to appreciate spatial relationships
Bodily/kinesthetic	Ability to move in a coordinated way, sense of body in space
Naturalist	Ability to make discriminations among things in natural world and patterns/designs of human artifacts
Interpersonal	Sensitivity to behavior, moods, needs of others
Intrapersonal	Ability to understand oneself

13. (1) B (2) C (3) A
14. No, because they don't measure knowledge or performance in real-world settings.
15. (A) awareness of one's own emotions (B) ability to express one's emotions appropriately (C) capacity to channel emotions into the pursuit of goals
16. (1) B (2) G (3) B (4) G
17. (1) A (2) B

18. (A) cultural beliefs (B) teaching methods (C) parental involvement (D) individualized instruction outside of school (E) use of rewards

SCHOOLING FOR CHILDREN WITH SPECIAL NEEDS (pp. 339-347)

19. A brain-imaging test that examines the brain as it is performing different functions may help to identify children with learning disabilities before they fall behind in school.
20. Children with cerebral palsy may require physical assistance with personal care functions and may also require special equipment to be able to write and participate fully in school.
21. (A) articulation (B) voice (C) fluency (D) form (E) content (F) function
22. The teachers said that the speech language pathologist taught him to read in addition to helping him learn to speak.
23. (A) Children with physical disabilities but no learning problems make better academic gains in full-inclusion programs.
    (B) Children with learning disabilities need individualized programs. Special classes or co-teaching arrangements in regular classrooms appear to be particularly helpful to children with learning disabilities.
24. Sternberg argues that the emphasis on "memory" learning in schools causes teachers and administrators to overlook children who are creatively gifted.

Chapter 12

THEORIES OF SOCIAL AND PERSONALITY DEVELOPMENT (pp. 354-356)

1.

Industry	Inferiority
Learning culturally valued skills, such as reading; accomplishing goals	Failing to learn skills; inability to accomplish goals

2. (1) A (2) B (3) D (4) E (5) C
3.

Environmental	Behavioral	Personal
Emotional responses of others; social support	Imitation of models; responses to failure	Beliefs; traits; emotions

SELF-CONCEPT (pp. 356-359)

4. (A) N (B) Y
5. (1) A (2) B
6. (A) mental comparison of ideal/actual selves (B) personal value placed on each component of self-esteem (C) overall support, especially from parents and peers (D) cultural values (E) experiences of success and failure
7. Self-esteem can change in response to others' judgments and changes in a child's experiences of success and failure.

ADVANCES IN SOCIAL COGNITION (pp. 359-361)

8. smart, happy, mean
9. concrete operational thinking

THE SOCIAL WORLD OF THE SCHOOL-AGED CHILD (pp. 361-369)

10.

Factor	Contribution to Self-Regulation
Culture	Groups vary in the ages at which they expect children to be able to regulate their own behavior.
Gender	Parents have higher expectations for girls' self-regulation.
Parenting style	Authoritative parents encourage self-regulation.

11. loneliness, being bullied
12. (1) B (2) G (3) B (4) B (5) G
13. (A) No (B) Yes (C) No
14. ridicule of a peer behind her back, ostracism
15.

Category	Characteristics
Popular	Socially skilled, good communicators, helpful, good leadership skills
Rejected	Avoided by peers, aggressive, withdrawn
Neglected	Ignored by peers, shy, tend to prefer solitary activities

INFLUENCES BEYOND FAMILY AND PEERS (pp. 369-373)

16. (A) poor peer relationships (B) poor school performance (C) poor social skills (D) more behavior problems
17. Professor Gentile was surprised that the children in his study who played violent video games showed increases in aggression over a relatively short period of time (6 months).

Chapter 13

PHYSICAL CHANGES (pp. 386-393)

1.

Gland	Hormone(s)	Influence on Development
Thyroid	Thyroxine	Brain development; growth rate
Adrenal	Adrenal androgen	Secondary sex characteristics in girls
Testes (boys)	Testosterone	Male genitalia (prenatal); primary, secondary sex characteristics in boys
Ovaries (girls)	Estrogen (estradiol)	Menstrual cycle; breast development
Pituitary	Gonadotrophic hormones, growth hormone, thyroid-stimulating hormone	Maturation rate; signals to other glands

2. an acceleration of development at the ends of bones (epiphyses), triggered by hormonal signals.
3. Yes and no. Some signs of puberty are appearing earlier, but the age of menarche has remained stable.
4. (1) B (2) A (3) B (4) A (5) A (6) B
5.

Effects on Boys	Effects on Girls
Occupy leadership roles; more academically and economically successful as adults; increased risk of substance use and depression	May have more negative body image than "on time" girls (may see themselves as fat); increased risk of behavior problems, early sexual activity, and substance use

ADOLESCENT SEXUALITY (pp. 393-400)

6. Sexual activity is poorly defined in that teens who have had sex only once in their lives are classified as "sexually active." Variables such as sexual agency, the ability of teens to make decisions about sexual behavior, reveal more about the role that sexuality plays in adolescents' lives.
7. Her mother had given birth at 17.
8. mental health

ADOLESCENT HEALTH (pp. 400-406)

9. Teens drink less milk and more soda than they did when they were younger.
10. HPV
11. (A) immaturity of the prefrontal cortex (B) the desire to be accepted by peers (C) the need to establish autonomy from parents (D) permissive parenting
12. tobacco
13. impulsivity, risk-taking
14. Boys are five times more likely to be homicide victims than girls are.

ATYPICAL DEVELOPMENT (pp. 406-412)

15. less likely
16. is not
17. underestimate
18. (1) B (2) B (3) C (4) C (5) A (6) A (7) C
19. Anorexia causes the heart to lose its fatty covering and to shrink.
20. Professor Forbes's research shows that teens who are depressed have trouble getting motivated to do positive things and have difficulty recognizing the good things that happen to them.

Chapter 14

PIAGET'S FORMAL OPERATIONAL STAGE (pp. 419-425)

1. systematic problem solving
2. hypothetico-deductive reasoning
3. Research suggests that Piaget's predictions about teens' acquisition of formal operational thinking were overly optimistic. The stage may not be universal and is strongly correlated with education in adulthood.

4.

Feature	Description
Adolescent egocentrism	Belief that one's thoughts, beliefs, and feelings are unique
Imaginary audience	Internalized behavioral standards usually derived from a teen's peer group
Personal fable	Belief that events of one's life are controlled by a mentally constructed autobiography
Naïve idealism	Use of formal operational thinking to mentally construct an ideal world and compare the real world to it
Faulty planning	Failure to anticipate all the contingencies involved in a plan, common in early formal operational thinking

5. None of the teens worry about the dangers of unhealthy eating. One doesn't feel he is in danger since he is skinny now, and the others think they could die from other ailments such as lung cancer from pollution.
6. She worried that everyone at school noticed that her hair was a mess and was talking about her behind her back. In reality, nobody noticed.

ADVANCES IN INFORMATION PROCESSING (pp. 425-427)

7. response inhibition
8. Teens are more likely than younger children to include all the main ideas of a text in their summaries. When they outline a text, they are more likely to include both main ideas and supporting information.

SCHOOLING (pp. 427-437)

9. task goals
10. ability goals
11. Ninth-grade academies are self-contained schools devoted entirely to the ninth grade. They often have schedules that allocate extra time for reading and math classes. Research shows that at-risk students who attend these academies are absent less often, require fewer disciplinary actions, get higher scores on standardized tests, and are more likely than their peers at traditional schools to pass freshman classes.
12. permissive, authoritarian
13. Because of the way they are calculated, drop-out estimates do not take into account how many students eventually go back to school, obtain a GED, or complete high school in the military. Also, it is difficult to gauge the accuracy of the statistics, since government reports define "drop-outs" as all students of secondary school age who are not enrolled in school. Thus, homeschooled students and students who are in alternative programs could be wrongly classified as drop-outs.
14. Surveys show that there are several characteristics, such as basic honesty, that almost all parents agree that children should be encouraged to develop.
15. They believe that values are taught at home and reinforced at school.
16. They can provide students with rigorous transitional classes in eighth and ninth grade.
17. She believes that both biology and learning could contribute to gender differences.

ENTERING THE WORLD OF WORK (pp. 437-441)

18. less
19. 2%

20. Career guidance professionals can arrange for students to observe various workplaces and can direct students to online and library resources that are useful for researching career information. Career guidance professionals can also administer personality tests to help students determine which occupations best fit their own characteristics.
21. (1) C (2) F (3) A (4) B (5) D (6) E
22.

Factor	Influence
Family	Most choose occupations with educational and socioeconomic levels similar to those of parents; family moral standards rule out some choices; family values influence the importance of "moving up," going to college, etc.
Education	Bright teens who do well in school are more likely to choose professional careers that require many years of education.
Intelligence	Intelligence influences career choice through its correlation with school success. Brighter students are also more likely to choose technical or professional careers.
Gender	Many conform to traditional views of "men's jobs" and "women's jobs," but the degree to which a teen's own parents conform to these expectations moderates the effects of the stereotypes.

Chapter 15

THEORIES OF SOCIAL AND PERSONALITY DEVELOPMENT (pp. 448–450)

1. role confusion
2. Teens merge their individual identities with that of a group. The teenaged group thus forms a base of security from which the young person can move toward a unique solution of the identity crisis.
3. (1) C (2) B (3) A (4) D
4. moratorium

SELF-CONCEPT (pp. 450–457)

5. honest, environmentalist
6. (A) Some teens with high levels of self-esteem experience declines in self-esteem during adolescence, while others experience consistently high levels throughout the period.
   (B) Girls are more likely than boys to show either consistently low or declining self-esteem in adolescence.
7. (1) B (2) C (3) A (4) D
8.

Stage	Summary
Unexamined	Integration of society's negative stereotypes into one's sense of identity
Search	Comparisons of one's own group with others; may be triggered by an episode in which attention is drawn to the teen's ethnicity, such as an incidence of blatant racism
Achievement	Development of strategies for solving conflicts between the demands of the dominant culture and those of the teen's own ethnic group

MORAL DEVELOPMENT (pp. 457-464)

9.

Stage	View of Rules
Punishment and Obedience Orientation	Rules should be obeyed because disobedience usually results in punishment.
Individualism, Instrumental Purpose, Exchange	Rules should be obeyed if doing so brings about some kind of material benefit.
Mutual Interpersonal Expectations, Relationships, and Interpersonal Conformity	Rules should be obeyed because obedience is a characteristic of "good" or "nice" people. Conforming to rules and others' expectations is important to the maintenance of harmonious interpersonal relationships.
Social System and Conscience (Law-and-Order Orientation)	Rules should be obeyed in order to maintain the social order and to prevent each person from taking the law into his or her own hands.
Social Contract Orientation	Rules should generally be obeyed to maintain order, but some rules violate individual rights, which are more important than social order. In such cases, disobedience is justified and efforts should be made to change the rules.
Universal Ethical Principles Orientation	There are a few moral principles that transcend all other concerns, whether such concerns are individual or social in nature. Moral issues in which such principles are involved should be dealt with in accordance with these principles.

10. (A) cognitive development (B) role-taking skills (C) social support in the form of reciprocal dialogue about moral issues (D) parents' ability to express their own moral views in ways that make them understandable to children and teenagers
11. (A) All of Kohlberg's preconventional and conventional stages have been found in all cultures, but the postconventional level may be limited to Western cultures that emphasize individual rights over collective concerns.
    (B) Gilligan's approach emphasizes the "ethic of caring" rather than justice.
    (C) Moral development is not strongly related to moral behavior.
12. Some societies emphasize the independence of individuals and view the rights of individuals as more important than social concerns. Such views are similar to those associated with Kohlberg's postconventional level. Thus, people in individualistic societies might be judged to be at the postconventional level when they are actually only expressing the values of their culture. People in interdependent (or collectivist) societies might be unfairly viewed as reasoning at a lower level because of the way their cultures balance individual and social concerns.

SOCIAL RELATIONSHIPS (pp. 464-469)

13. Negative events such as conflicts with parents are most likely to trigger emotional problems such as depression in teens who are high in neuroticism and who tend to ruminate.
14. (A) increased intimacy (B) increased stability (C) shared interests
15. (1) B (2) A (3) B (4) A (5) B
16. by age 12 or 13
17. (A) religious teachings (B) individual attitudes (C) family structure
18. age 11 or 12, which is roughly the same age as for heterosexual attraction
19. casual sex, a partner's looks, pornography

Answers for Practice Tests

UNIT ONE

CHAPTER 1
1. b 2. b 3. a 4. d 5. a 6. b 7. a 8. c 9. a 10. d 11. d 12. c

CHAPTER 2
13. c 14. d 15. b 16. a 17. c 18. b 19. c 20. a 21. d 22. d 23. b 24. b 25. a 26. c 27. b

CHAPTER 3
28. d 29. c 30. a 31. c 32. a 33. d 34. c 35. a 36. b 37. d

UNIT TWO

CHAPTER 4
1. b 2. c 3. a 4. d 5. c 6. b 7. a 8. a 9. c 10. a 11. d 12. a

CHAPTER 5
13. a 14. d 15. a 16. b 17. a 18. d 19. b 20. d 21. c 22. b 23. c 24. b 25. d

CHAPTER 6
26. c 27. d 28. d 29. c 30. b 31. d 32. c 33. d 34. a 35. c

UNIT THREE

CHAPTER 7
1. d 2. b 3. b 4. d 5. b 6. b 7. c 8. b 9. d 10. d

CHAPTER 8
11. a 12. b 13. a 14. a 15. c 16. d 17. a 18. d 19. b 20. a 21. d

CHAPTER 9
22. a 23. b 24. c 25. a 26. b 27. b 28. d 29. c 30. d 31. c 32. a 33. c

UNIT FOUR

CHAPTER 10

1. c 2. b 3. a 4. c 5. d 6. d 7. a 8. b 9. c 10. d 11. d

CHAPTER 11

12. b 13. d 14. a 15. d 16. d 17. b 18. a 19. b 20. d

CHAPTER 12

21. c 22. b 23. d 24. b 25. b 26. c 27. b 28. b 29. d 30. a 31. b 32. c 33. d 34. c

UNIT FIVE

CHAPTER 13

1. c 2. d 3. b 4. a 5. d 6. c 7. a 8. d 9. a 10. b 11. d 12. c 13. c 14. d 15. d

CHAPTER 14

16. a 17. a 18. b 19. d 20. b 21. b 22. d

CHAPTER 15

23. c 24. a 25. c 26. d 27. a 28. c 29. b 30. d 31. b 32. b 33. b

Key Terms by Chapter

Chapter 1

atypical development (p. 11)
case study (p. 15)
cognitive domain (p. 7)
cohort (p. 10)
control group (p. 17)
correlation (p. 16)
critical period (p. 11)
cross-sectional design (p. 18)
dependent variable (p. 17)
developmental science (p. 6)
ecological approach (p. 11)
ethnography (p. 19)
experiment (p. 16)
experimental group (p. 17)
hypothesis (p. 14)
inborn biases (p. 9)
independent variable (p. 17)
laboratory observation (p. 16)
longitudinal design (p. 18)
maturation (p. 7)
naturalistic observation (p. 15)
nature-nurture debate (p. 9)
nonnormative changes (p. 11)
normative age-graded changes (p. 10)
normative history-graded changes (p. 10)
norms (p. 7)
physical domain (p. 7)
qualitative change (p. 10)
quantitative change (p. 10)
research ethics (p. 20)
resilience (p. 12)
sensitive period (p. 11)
sequential design (p. 18)
social clock (p. 10)
socioemotional domain (p. 8)
stages (p. 10)
theories (p. 13)
vulnerability (p. 12)

Chapter 2

accommodation (p. 38)
assimilation (p. 38)
behavior genetics (p. 42)
behaviorism (p. 32)
bioecological theory (p. 44)
classical conditioning (p. 32)
cognitive theories (p. 37)
eclecticism (p. 47)
ego (p. 28)
equilibration (p. 38)
ethology (p. 43)
extinction (p. 35)
id (p. 28)
information-processing theory (p. 40)
learning theories (p. 32)
neo-Piagetian theory (p. 40)
operant conditioning (p. 34)
psychoanalytic theories (p. 28)
psychosexual stages (p. 29)
psychosocial stages (p. 30)
punishment (p. 34)
reinforcement (p. 34)
scheme (p. 37)
social learning (modeling) (p. 35)
sociobiology (p. 43)
sociocultural theory (p. 39)
superego (p. 28)

Chapter 3

amnion (p. 64)
anoxia (p. 83)
axons (p. 67)
cell body (p. 67)
cephalocaudal pattern (p. 64)
cesarean section (c-section) (p. 81)
chromosomes (p. 54)
dendrites (p. 67)
deoxyribonucleic acid (DNA) (p. 54)
dominant-recessive pattern (p. 56)
embryonic stage (p. 64)
fetal stage (p. 66)
gametes (p. 54)
genes (p. 54)
genotype (p. 56)
germinal stage (p. 64)
glial cells (p. 67)
gonads (p. 55)
implantation (p. 64)
low birth weight (LBW) (p. 84)
multi-factorial inheritance (p. 58)
neonate (p. 84)
neurons (p. 64)
organogenesis (p. 66)
phenotype (p. 56)
placenta (p. 64)
polygenic inheritance (p. 58)
proximodistal pattern (p. 64)
synapses (p. 67)
teratogens (p. 70)
umbilical cord (p. 64)
viability (p. 66)
zygote (p. 54)

Chapter 4

adaptive reflexes (p. 102)
auditory acuity (p. 113)
colic (p. 104)
cortex (p. 100)
dishabituation (p. 115)
dynamic systems theory (p. 105)
empiricists (p. 119)
habituation (p. 115)
infant mortality (p. 109)
intermodal perception (p. 118)
myelination (p. 101)
nativists (p. 119)
plasticity (p. 100)
preference technique (p. 115)
primitive reflexes (p. 103)
pruning (p. 100)
reticular formation (p. 102)
sudden infant death syndrome (SIDS) (p. 109)
synapses (p. 100)
synaptogenesis (p. 100)
tracking (p. 113)
visual acuity (p. 112)

Chapter 5

A-not-B error (p. 130)
babbling (p. 140)
Bayley Scales of Infant Development (p. 146)
cooing (p. 140)
deferred imitation (p. 131)
expressive language (p. 141)
expressive style (p. 144)
holophrases (p. 142)
infant-directed speech (IDS) (p. 139)
inflections (p. 142)
intelligence (p. 146)
interactionists (p. 138)
language acquisition device (LAD) (p. 138)
mean length of utterance (MLU) (p. 144)
means-end behavior (p. 129)
naming explosion (p. 142)
object concept (p. 132)
object permanence (p. 129)
primary circular reactions (p. 128)
receptive language (p. 141)
referential style (p. 145)
schematic learning (p. 135)
secondary circular reactions (p. 129)
sensorimotor stage (p. 128)
telegraphic speech (p. 142)
tertiary circular reactions (p. 129)
violation of expectations method (p. 133)

Chapter 6

attachment (p. 155)
attachment theory (p. 154)
emotional self (p. 169)
goodness-of-fit (p. 167)
insecure/ambivalent attachment (p. 158)
insecure/avoidant attachment (p. 158)
insecure/disorganized attachment (p. 158)
niche-picking (p. 166)
objective (categorical) self (p. 168)
personality (p. 164)
secure attachment (p. 158)
separation anxiety (p. 157)
social referencing (p. 157)
stranger anxiety (p. 157)
subjective (existential) self (p. 168)
synchrony (p. 155)
temperament (p. 164)

Chapter 7

Chapter 8

Chapter 9

Chapter 10

Chapter 11

Chapter 12

self-care children (p. 370)
self-efficacy (p. 357)
self-esteem (p. 358)
self-regulation (p. 362)
social status (p. 368)
trait (p. 355)

Chapter 13

adolescence (p. 385)
adolescent growth spurt (p. 388)
adolescent-onset conduct disorder (p. 407)
anorexia nervosa (p. 409)
bulimia nervosa (p. 409)
circadian rhythms (p. 387)
delayed sleep phase syndrome (DSPS) (p. 388)
delinquency (p. 407)
gonadotrophic hormones (p. 386)
menarche (p. 390)
prefrontal cortex (PFC) (p. 387)
primary sex characteristics (p. 390)
puberty (p. 386)
secondary sex characteristics (p. 390)
secular trend (p. 391)
sensation seeking (p. 403)
sexually transmitted disease (STD) (p. 401)
transgendered (p. 400)

Chapter 14

ability goals (p. 428)
academic learning (p. 426)
adolescent egocentrism (p. 423)
character education (p. 435)
disengaged students (p. 430)
engaged students (p. 430)
formal operational stage (p. 419)
hypothetico-deductive reasoning (p. 420)
imaginary audience (p. 424)
naïve idealism (p. 424)
personal fable (p. 423)
systematic problem solving (p. 420)
task goals (p. 428)

Chapter 15

androgynous gender role identity (p. 454)
clique (p. 467)
conventional morality (p. 459)
crowd (p. 467)
ethnic identity (p. 454)
feminine gender role identity (p. 454)
foreclosure (p. 449)
gender role identity (p. 453)
identity (p. 448)
identity achievement (p. 449)
identity crisis (p. 448)
identity diffusion (p. 449)
identity versus role confusion (p. 448)
masculine gender role identity (p. 454)
moratorium (p. 449)
postconventional morality (p. 460)
preconventional morality (p. 458)
role taking (p. 461)
undifferentiated gender role identity (p. 454)

References

ABC News. (2000, August 22). Poll: Americans like public school. Retrieved August 23, 2000 from http://www.abcnews.com.

Abrams, E. J., Matheson, P. B., Thomas, P. A., Thea, D. M., Krasinski, K., Lambert, G., Shaffer, N., Bamji, M., Hutson, D., Grimm, K., Kaul, A., Bateman, D., Rogers, M., & New York City Perinatal HIV Transmission Collaborative Study Group. (1995). Neonatal predictors of infection status and early death among 332 infants at risk of HIV-1 infection monitored prospectively from birth. *Pediatrics, 96*, 451–458.

Accardo, P., Tomazic, T., Fete, T., Heaney, M., Lindsay, R., & Whitman, B. (1997). Maternally reported fetal activity levels and developmental diagnoses. *Clinical Pediatrics, 36*, 279–283.

Adair, R., & Bauchner, H. (1993). Sleep problems in childhood. *Current Problems in Pediatrics, 23*, 147–170.

Adelman, W., & Ellen, J. (2002). Adolescence. In A. Rudolph, R. Kamei, & K. Overby (Eds.), *Rudolph's fundamentals of pediatrics* (3rd ed., pp. 70–109). New York: McGraw-Hill.

Adesman, A. R. (1996). Fragile X syndrome. In A. J. Capute & P. J. Accardo (Eds.), *Developmental disabilities in infancy and childhood, Vol. II: The spectrum of developmental disabilities* (pp. 255–269). Baltimore: Paul H. Brookes.

Administration for Children and Families. (2006). Office of Child Support Enforcement factsheet. Retrieved June 18, 2007 from www.acf.hhs.gov/opa/fact_sheets/cse_factsheet.html.

Agnew, J., Dorn, C., & Eden, G. (2004). Effect of intensive training on auditory processing and reading skills. *Brain & Language, 88*, 21–25.

Ahadi, S. A., & Rothbart, M. K. (1994). Temperament, development, and the big five. In C. F. Halverson, Jr., G. A. Kohnstamm, & R. P. Martin (Eds.), *The developing structure of temperament and personality from infancy to adulthood* (pp. 189–207). Hillsdale, NJ: Erlbaum.

Aiken, L. (1997). *Psychological testing and assessment* (9th ed.). Boston: Allyn & Bacon.

Ainsworth, M. D. S., Blehar, M., Waters, E., & Wall, S. (1978). *Patterns of attachment.* Hillsdale, NJ: Erlbaum.

Ainsworth, M. D. S., & Marvin, R. S. (1995). On the shaping of attachment theory and research: An interview with Mary D. S. Ainsworth (Fall 1994). *Monographs of the Society for Research in Child Development, 60* (244, Nos. 2–3), 3–21.

Akbari, O., Faul, J., Hoyte, E., Berry, G., Wahlstrom, J., Kronenberg, M., DeKruyff, R., & Umetsu, D. (2006). CD4 + invariant T-cell-receptor + natural killer T cells in bronchial asthma. *New England Journal of Medicine, 354*, 1117–1129.

Akers, J., Jones, R., & Coyl, D. (1998). Adolescent friendship pairs: Similarities in identity status development, behaviors, attitudes, and interests. *Journal of Adolescent Research, 13*, 178–201.

Aksu-Koc, A. A., & Slobin, D. I. (1985). The acquisition of Turkish. In D. I. Slobin (Ed.), *The crosslinguistic study of language acquisition: Vol. 1: The data* (pp. 839–878). Hillsdale, NJ: Erlbaum.

Alan Guttmacher Institute. (2004). U.S. teenage pregnancy statistics with comparative statistics for women aged 20–24. Retrieved July 9, 2004 from http://www.guttmacher.org/pubs/teen_stats.html.

Aleixo, P., & Norris, C. (2000). Personality and moral reasoning in young offenders. *Personality & Individual Differences, 28*, 609–623.

Alexander, G., & Hines, M. (1994). Gender labels and play styles: Their relative contribution to children's selection of playmates: *Child Development, 65*, 869–879.

Allen, C., & Kisilevsky, B. (1999). Fetal behavior in diabetic and nondiabetic pregnant women: An exploratory study. *Developmental Psychobiology, 35*, 69–80.

Allen, M. (2004). Reading achievement of students in French Immersion programs. *Educational Quarterly Review, 9*, 25–30.

Al Otaiba, S., Connor, C., Lane, H., Kosanovich, M., Schatschneider, C., Dyrlund, A., Miller, M., & Wright, T. (2008). Reading First kindergarten classroom instruction and students' growth in phonological awareness and letter naming/decoding fluency. *Journal of School Psychology, 46*, 281–314.

Alsaker, F. D., & Olweus, D. (1992). Stability of global self-evaluations in early adolescence: A cohort longitudinal study. *Journal of Research on Adolescence, 2*, 123–145.

Alspaugh, J. (1998). Achievement loss associated with the transition to middle school and high school. *Journal of Educational Research, 92*, 20–25.

Amato, P. R. (1993). Children's adjustment to divorce: Theories, hypotheses, and empirical support. *Journal of Marriage & the Family, 55*, 23–38.

Amato, S. (1998). Human genetics and dysmorphy. In R. Behrman & R. Kliegman (Eds.), *Nelson essentials of pediatrics* (3rd ed., pp. 129–146). Philadelphia: W. B. Saunders.

Ambert, A. (2001). *Families in the new millennium.* Boston: Allyn & Bacon.

Ambuel, B. (1995). Adolescents, unintended pregnancy, and abortion: The struggle for a compassionate social policy. *Current Directions in Psychological Science, 4*, 1–5.

American Academy of Pediatric Dentistry. (2001). Clinical guidelines on management of the developing dentition and occlusion in pediatric dentistry. Retrieved March 29, 2008 from http://www.guideline.gov/summary/summary.aspx?doc_id=7494.

American Academy of Pediatrics (AAP). (1998). Guidance for effective discipline. *Pediatrics, 101*, 723–728.

American Academy of Pediatrics (AAP). (1999). Calcium requirements of infants, children, and adolescents. *Pediatrics, 104*, 1152–1157.

American Academy of Pediatrics (AAP). (2001a). Policy statement: Children, adolescents, and television. *Pediatrics, 107*, 423–426.

American Academy of Pediatrics (AAP). (2001b). Sexuality education for children and adolescents: Committee on psychosocial aspects of child and family health and committee on adolescence. *Pediatrics, 108*, 498–502.

American Academy of Pediatrics (AAP). (2004). Clinical practice guideline: Diagnosis and management of acute otitis media. *Pediatrics, 113*, 1451–1465.

American Academy of Pedatrics (AAP). (2006). *Pediatrics, 118*, 405–420.

American Academy of Pediatrics (AAP). (2008). Poison prevention and treatment. Retrieved March 18, 2008 from http://aap.org/advocacy/releases/poisonpreventiontips.cfm.

American College of Obstetricians and Gynecologists (ACOG). (2001, December 12). ACOG addresses latest controversies in obstetrics. Retrieved April 1, 2004 from http://www.acog.org.

American College of Obstetricians and Gynecologists (ACOG). (2002, November 29). Rubella vaccination recommendation changes for pregnant women. Retrieved April 2, 2004 from http://www.acog.org.

American College of Obstetricians and Gynecologists (ACOG). (2004). *Ethics in obstetrics and gynecology.* Washington, DC: Author.

American Speech-Language-Hearing Association (ASHA). (2008). Noisy toys, dangerous play. Retrieved March 19, 2008 from http://www.asha.org/public/hearing/disorders/noisy_toys.htm.

Anderman, E., Maehr, M., & Midgley, C. (1999). Declining motivation after the transition to middle school: Schools can make a difference. *Journal of Research & Development in Education, 32,* 131–147.

Anderman, E., & Midgley, C. (1997). Changes in achievement goal orientations, perceived academic competence, and grades across the transition to middle-level schools. *Contemporary Educational Psychology, 22,* 269–298.

Anderman, L. (1999). Classroom goal orientation, school belonging and social goals as predictors of students' positive and negative affect following the transition to middle school. *Journal of Research & Development in Education, 32,* 89–103.

Anderman, L., & Anderman, E. (1999). Social predictors of changes in students' achievement goal orientations. *Contemporary Educational Psychology, 24,* 21–37.

Andersen, G. (2001). *Pragmatic markers and sociolinguistic variation.* Philadelphia: John Benjamins Publishing Company.

Anderson, C., & Dill, K. (2000). Video games and aggressive thoughts, feelings, and behavior in the laboratory and in life. *Journal of Personality & Social Psychology, 78,* 772–790.

Anderson, R. (1998). Examining language loss in bilingual children. *Electronic Multicultural Journal of Communication Disorders,* 1.

Anderson, S., Dallal, G., & Must, A. (2003). Relative weight and race influence average age at menarche: Results from two nationally representative surveys of U.S. girls studied 25 years apart. *Pediatrics, 111,* 844–850.

Andersson, H. (1996). The Fagan Test of Infant Intelligence: Predictive validity in a random sample. *Psychological Reports, 78,* 1015–1026.

Andreou, E., & Metallidou, P. (2004). The relationship of academic and social cognition to behaviour in bullying situations among Greek primary school children. *Educational Psychology, 24,* 27–41.

Andrews, G., & Halford, G. (1998). Children's ability to make transitive inferences: The importance of premise integration and structural complexity. *Cognitive Development, 13,* 479–513.

Andrews, G., & Halford, G. (2002). A cognitive complexity metric applied to cognitive development. *Cognitive Psychology, 45,* 153–219.

Anglin, J. M. (1995, March). Word learning and the growth of potentially knowable vocabulary. Paper presented at the biennial meetings of the Society for Research in Child Development, Indianapolis, IN.

Anisfeld, M. (1991). Neonatal imitation. *Developmental Review, 11,* 60–97.

Annett, M. (2003). Do the French and the English differ for hand skill asymmetry? Handedness subgroups in the sample of Doyen and Carlier (2002) and in English schools and universities. *Laterality: Asymmetries of Body, Brain & Cognition, 8,* 233–245.

Annunziato, P. W., & Frenkel, L. M. (1993). The epidemiology of pediatric HIV-1 infection. *Pediatric Annals, 22,* 401–405.

Anshel, M. (1990). *Sport psychology: From theory to practice.* Scottsdale, AZ: Gorsuch Scarisbrick.

Anthony, J., & Lonigan, C. (2004). The nature of phonological awareness: Converging evidence from four studies of preschool and early grade school children. *Journal of Educational Psychology, 96,* 43–55.

Antrop, I., Roeyers, H., Van Oost, P., & Buysse, A. (2000). Stimulation seeking and hyperactivity in children with ADHD. *Journal of Child Psychology, Psychiatry & Allied Disciplines, 41,* 225–231.

Apgar, V. A. (1953). A proposal for a new method of evaluation of the newborn infant. *Current Research in Anesthesia and Analgesia, 32,* 260–267.

Aranha, M. (1997). Creativity in students and its relation to intelligence and peer perception. *Revista Interamericana de Psicologia, 31,* 309–313.

Arditti, J. (1991). Child support noncompliance and divorced fathers: Rethinking the role of paternal involvement. *Journal of Divorce & Remarriage, 14,* 107–120.

Arluk, S., Swain, D., & Dowling, E. (2003). Childhood obesity's relationship to time spent in sedentary behavior. *Military Medicine, 168,* 583–586.

Armbruster, B., Lehr, F., & Osborn, J. (2003). Put reading first: The research building blocks of reading instruction. Retrieved June 20, 2008 from http://www.nifl.gov/partnershipforreading/publications/PFRbooklet.pdf.

Arriaga, P., Esteyes, F., Carneiro, P., & Monteiro, M. (2006). Violent computer games and their effects on state hostility and physiological arousal. *Aggressive Behavior, 32,* 146–158.

Asbjornsen, A., Obrzut, J., Boliek, C., Myking, E., Holmefjord, A., Reisaeter, S., Klausen, O., & Moller, P. (2005). Impaired auditory attention skills following middle-ear infections. *Child Neuropsychology, 11,* 121–133.

Asendorpf, J. B., Warkentin, V., & Baudonnière, P. (1996). Self-awareness and other-awareness. II: Mirror self-recognition, social contingency awareness, and synchronic imitation. *Developmental Psychology, 32,* 313–321.

Ashiabi, G., & O'Neal, K. (2007). Children's health status: Examining the associations among income poverty, material hardship, and parental factors. *PLoS ONE, 2,* e940.

Ashkar, P., & Kenny, D. (2007). Moral reasoning of adolescent male offenders: Comparison of sexual and nonsexual offenders. *Criminal Justice and Behavior, 34,* 108–118.

Aslin, R. (1987). Motor aspects of visual development in infancy. In N. P. Salapatek & L. Cohen (Eds.), *Handbook of infant perception, Vol. 1: From sensation to perception* (pp. 43–113). Orlando, FL: Academic Press.

Aslin, R., Saffran, J., & Newport, E. (1998). Computation of conditional probability statistics by 8-month-old infants. *Psychological Science, 9,* 321–324.

Assibey-Mensah, G. (1997). Role models and youth development: Evidence and lessons from the perceptions of African-American male youth. *Western Journal of Black Studies, 21,* 242–252.

Associated Press. (2007. February 27). Overweight 8-year-old sets off child obesity debate in Britain. Retrieved June 16, 2007 from www.iht.com/articles/ap/2007/02/27/europe/EU-GEN-Britain-Child-Obesity.php.

Astington, J. W., & Jenkins, J. M. (1995, March). Language and theory of mind: A theoretical review and a longitudinal study. Paper presented at the biennial meetings of the Society for Research in Child Development, Indianapolis, IN.

Astington, J. W., & Jenkins, J. M. (1999). A longitudinal study of the relation between language and theory-of-mind development. *Developmental Psychology, 35,* 1311–1320.

Astor, R. (1994). Children's moral reasoning about family and peer violence: The role of provocation and retribution. *Child Development, 65*, 1054–1067.

Auditor General of British Columbia. (2000). Fostering a safe learning environment: How the British Columbia Public School System is doing. Victoria, BC: Author.

Austin, M., Reiss, N., & Burgdorf, L. (2007). ADHD comorbidity. Retrieved September 12, 2008 from http://www.mentalhelp.net/poc/view_doc.php?type=doc&id=13851&cn=3.

Austin, S., Ziyadeh, N., Kahn, J., Camargo, C., Colditz, G., & Field, A. (2004). Sexual orientation, weight concerns, and eating-disordered behaviors in adolescent girls and boys. *Journal of the American Academy of Child & Adolescent Psychiatry, 43*, 1115–1123.

Avis, J., & Harris, P. L. (1991). Belief-desire reasoning among Baka children: Evidence for a universal conception of mind. *Child Development, 62*, 460–467.

Bachman, J. G., Safron, D., Sy, S., & Schulenberg, J. (2003). Wishing to work: New perspectives on how adolescents' part-time work intensity is linked to educational disengagement, substance use, and other problem behaviours. *International Journal of Behavioral Development, 27*, 301–315.

Bachman, J. G., & Schulenberg, J. (1993). How part-time work intensity relates to drug use, problem behavior, time use, and satisfaction among high school seniors: Are these consequences or merely correlates? *Developmental Psychology, 29*, 220–235.

Bachman, J. G., Segal, D., Freedman-Doan, P., & O'Malley, P. (2000). Who chooses military service? Correlates of propensity and enlistment in the U.S. Armed Forces. *Military Psychology, 12*, 1–30.

Baddeley, A. (1998). *Human memory: Theory and practice* (rev. ed.) Boston: Allyn & Bacon.

Baek, H. (2002). A comparative study of moral development of Korean and British children. *Journal of Moral Education, 31*, 373–391.

Bahrick, L., & Lickliter, R. (2000). Intersensory redundancy guides attentional selectivity and perceptual learning in infancy. *Developmental Psychology, 36*, 190–201.

Bailey, J., Brobow, D., Wolfe, M., & Mikach, S. (1995). Sexual orientation of adult sons of gay fathers. *Developmental Psychology, 31*, 124–129.

Bailey, J., Pillard, R., Dawood, K., Miller, M., Farrer, L., Trivedi, S., & Murphy, R. (1999). A family history study of male sexual orientation using three independent samples. *Behavior Genetics, 29*, 7986.

Bailey, S., & Zvonkovic, A. (2003). Parenting after divorce: Nonresidential parents' perceptions of social and institutional support. *Journal of Divorce & Remarriage, 39*, 59–80.

Baillargeon, R. (1987). Object permanence in very young infants. *Developmental Psychology, 23*, 655–664.

Baillargeon, R. (1994). How do infants learn about the physical world? *Current Directions in Psychological Science, 3*, 133–140.

Baillargeon, R., & DeVos, J. (1991). Object permanence in young infants: Further evidence. *Child Development, 62*, 1227–1246.

Baillargeon, R., Spelke, E. S., & Wasserman, S. (1985). Object permanence in five-month-old infants. *Cognition, 20*, 191–208.

Baird, A., Kagan, J., Gaudette, T., Walz, K., Hershlag, N., & Boas, D. (2002). Frontal lobe activation during object permanence: Data from near-infrared spectroscopy. *Neuroimage, 16*, 1120–1125.

Baker, J. M. & Zigmond, N. (1995). The meaning and practice of inclusion for students with learning disabilities: Themes and implications from the five cases. *The Journal of Special Education, 29*, 163–180.

Balaban, M. T. (1995). Affective influences on startle in five-month-old infants: Reactions to facial expressions of emotion. *Child Development, 66*, 28–36.

Baldwin, D. A. (1995, March). Understanding relations between constraints and a socio-pragmatic account of meaning acquisition. Paper presented at the biennial meetings of the Society for Research in Child Development, Indianapolis, IN.

Balfanz, R., & Legters, N. (2004). Locating the dropout crisis. Retrieved June 29, 2008 from http://www.csos.jhu.edu/tdhs/rsch/Locating_Dropouts.pdf.

Ball, E. (1997). Phonological awareness: Implications for whole language and emergent literacy programs. *Topics in Language Disorders, 17*, 14–26.

Bamford, F. N., Bannister, R. P., Benjamin, C. M., Hillier, V. F., Ward, B. S., & Moore, W. M. O. (1990). Sleep in the first year of life. *Developmental Medicine & Child Neurology, 32*, 718–724.

Bandura, A. (1977). *Social learning theory.* Englewood Cliffs, NJ: Prentice-Hall.

Bandura, A. (1982). The psychology of chance encounters and life paths. *American Psychologist, 37*, 747–755.

Bandura, A. (1989). Social cognitive theory. *Annals of Child Development, 6*, 1–60.

Bandura, A. (1997). *Self-efficacy: The exercise of control.* New York: Freeman.

Bandura, A., Ross, D., & Ross, S. A. (1961). Transmission of aggression through imitation of aggressive models. *Journal of Abnormal & Social Psychology, 63*, 575–582.

Bandura, A., Ross, D., & Ross, S. A. (1963). Imitation of film-mediated aggressive models. *Journal of Abnormal & Social Psychology, 66*, 3–11.

Bangerter, A., & Heath, C. (2004). The Mozart effect: Tracking the evolution of a scientific legend. *British Journal of Social Psychology, 43*, 605–623.

Baranchik, A. (2002). Identifying gaps in mathematics preparation that contribute to ethnic, gender, and American/foreign differences in precalculus performance. *Journal of Negro Education, 71*, 253–268.

Barayuga, D. (November 30, 2005). "Ice" addict cleared of killing newborn. Retrieved June 8, 2007 from http://starbulletin.com/2005/11/30/news/story02.html.

Barbarin, O. (1999). Social risks and psychological adjustment: A comparison of African American and South African children. *Child Development, 70*, 1348–1359.

Barber, B., & Olsen, J. (2004). Assessing the transitions to middle and high school. *Journal of Adolescent Research, 19*, 3–30.

Barenboim, C. (1981). The development of person perception in childhood and adolescence: From behavioral comparisons to psychological constructs to psychological comparisons. *Child Development, 52*, 129–144.

Barkin, S., Scheindlin, B., Ip, E., Richardson, I., & Finch, S. (2007). Determinants of parental discipline practices: A national sample from primary care practices. *Clinical Pediatrics, 46*, 64–69.

Barkley, R. (1990). *Attention-deficit hyperactivity disorder.* New York: Guilford Press.

Barlow, J., & Lewandowski, L. (2000, August). Ten-year longitudinal study of preterm infants: Outcomes and predictors. Paper presented at the annual meeting of the American Psychological Association, Washington, DC.

Barnard, K. E., Hammond, M. A., Booth, C. L., Bee, H. L., Mitchell, S. K., & Spieker, S. J. (1989). Measurement and meaning of parent-child interaction. In J. J. Morrison, C. Lord, & D. P. Keating (Eds.), *Applied developmental psychology, Vol. 3* (pp. 40–81). San Diego, CA: Academic Press.

Barness, L., & Curran, J. (1996). Nutrition. In R. E. Behrman, R. M. Kliegman, & A. M. Arvin (Eds.), *Nelson's textbook of pediatrics* (15th ed., pp. 141–184). Philadelphia: Saunders.

Barnett, W. S. (1993). Benefit-cost analysis of preschool education: Findings from a 25-year follow-up. *American Journal of Orthopsychiatry, 63,* 500–508.

Barnett, W. S. (1995). Long-term effects of early childhood programs on cognitive and school outcomes. *The Future of Children, 5* (3), 25–50.

Baron, I. (2003). *Neuropsychological evaluation of the child.* New York: Oxford University Press.

Barr, R., Marrott, H., & Rovee-Collier, C. (2003). The role of sensory preconditioning in memory retrieval by preverbal infants. *Learning & Behavior, 31,* 111–123.

Barrett, G., & Depinet, R. (1991). A reconsideration of testing for competence rather than for intelligence. *American Psychologist, 46,* 1012–1024.

Barron, V., & Menken, K. (2002). What are the characteristics of the bilingual education and ESL teacher shortage? National Clearinghouse for English Language Acquisition & Language Instruction Educational Programs Factsheet. Retrieved June 23, 2004 from http://www.ncela.gwu.edu/expert/faq/14shortage.htm.

Barrow, F., Armstrong, M., Vargo, A., & Boothroyd, R. (2007). Understanding the findings of resilience-related research for fostering the development of African American adolescents. *Child and Adolescent Psychiatric Clinics of North America, 16,* 393–413.

Bartholow, B., Bushman, B., & Sestir, M. (2006). Chronic violent video game exposure and desensitization to violence: Behavioral and event-related brain potential data. *Journal of Experimental Social Psychology, 42,* 532–539.

Bartiss, M. (2007). Convergence insufficiency. Retrieved March 28, 2008 from http://www.emedicine.com/oph/topic553.htm.

Basham, P. (2001). Home schooling: From the extreme to the mainstream. *Public Policy Sources/The Fraser Institute, 51.* Retrieved June 23, 2004 from http://www.fraserinstitute.ca/admin/books/files/homeschool.pdf.

Bass, C., & Coleman, H. (1997). Enhancing the cultural identity of early adolescent male African Americans. *Professional School Counseling, 1,* 48–51.

Bates, E. (1993). Commentary: Comprehension and production in early language development. *Monographs of the Society for Research in Child Development, 58* (3–4, Serial No. 233), 222–242.

Bates, E., Marchman, V., Thal, D., Fenson, L., Dale, P., Reznick, J. S., Reilly, J., & Hartung, J. (1994). Developmental and stylistic variation in the composition of early vocabulary. *Journal of Child Language, 21,* 85–123.

Bates, E., O'Connell, B., & Shore, C. (1987). Language and communication in infancy. In J. D. Osofsky (Ed.), *Handbook of infant development* (2nd ed., pp. 149–203). New York: Wiley.

Bates, J. E. (1989). Applications of temperament concepts. In G. A. Kohnstamm, J. E. Bates, & M. K. Rothbart (Eds.), *Temperament in childhood* (pp. 321–356). Chichester, England: Wiley.

Bauer, P., Schwade, J., Wewerka, S., & Delaney, K. (1999). Planning ahead: Goal-directed problem solving by 2-year-olds. *Developmental Psychology, 35,* 1321–1337.

Baumeister, R., Smart, L., & Boden, J. (1999). Relation of threatened egotism to violence and aggression: The dark side of high self-esteem. In R. Baumeister (Ed.), *The self in social psychology.* Philadelphia: Psychology Press.

Bauminger, N., & Kasari, C. (1999). Brief report: Theory of mind in high-functioning children with autism. *Journal of Autism & Developmental Disorders, 29,* 81–86.

Baumrind, D. (1967). Child care practices anteceding three patterns of preschool behavior. *Genetic Psychology Monographs, 75,* 43–88.

Baumrind, D. (1971). Current patterns of parental authority. *Developmental Psychology Monograph, 4* (1, Part 2).

Baumrind, D. (1972). Socialization and instrumental competence in young children. In W. W. Hartup (Ed.), *The young child: Reviews of research, Vol. 2* (pp. 202–224). Washington, DC: National Association for the Education of Young Children.

Baumrind, D. (1980). New directions in socialization research. *American Psychologist, 35,* 639–652.

Baumrind, D. (1991). Effective parenting during the early adolescent transition. In P. A. Cowan & M. Hetherington (Eds.), *Family transitions* (pp. 111–163). Hillsdale, NJ: Erlbaum.

Bausell, C. (2007). Quality Counts 2007: From cradle to career: Connecting American education from birth to adulthood. *Education Week, 26,* 86–87.

Baydar, N., & Brooks-Gunn, J. (1991). Effects of maternal employment and child-care arrangements on preschoolers' cognitive and behavioral outcomes: Evidence from the children of the National Longitudinal Survey of Youth. *Developmental Psychology, 27,* 932–945.

Baydar, N., Brooks-Gunn, J., & Furstenberg, F. F. (1993). Early warning signs of functional illiteracy: Predictors in childhood and adolescence. *Child Development, 64,* 815–829.

Bayley, N. (1969). *Bayley scales of infant development.* New York: Psychological Corporation.

Bayley, N. (1993). *Bayley scales of infant development: Birth to two years.* San Antonio, TX: Psychological Corporation.

Bayley, N. (2006). *Bayley Scales of Infant and Toddler Development* (3rd ed.). San Antonio, TX: Harcourt Assessment.

Bearce, K., & Rovee-Collier, C. (2006). Repeated priming increases memory accessibility in infants. *Journal of Experimental Child Psychology, 93,* 357–376.

Beaudry, M., Dufour, R., & Marcoux, S. (1995). Relation between infant feeding and infections during the first six months of life. *Journal of Pediatrics, 126,* 191–197.

Beautrais, A., Joyce, P., & Mulder, R. (1999). Personality traits and cognitive styles as risk factors for serious suicide attempts among young people. *Suicide & Life-Threatening Behavior, 29,* 37–47.

Bee, Helen. *The growing child: An applied approach* (2nd ed.). Boston: Allyn & Bacon.

Bee, H. L., Barnard, K. E., Eyres, S. J., Gray, C. A., Hammond, M. A., Spietz, A. L., Snyder, C., & Clark, B. (1982). Prediction of IQ and language skill from perinatal status, child performance, family characteristics, and mother-infant interaction. *Child Development, 53,* 1135–1156.

Behrend, D., Scofield, J., & Kleinknecht, E. (2001) Beyond fast mapping: Young children's extensions of novel words and novel facts. *Developmental Psychology, 37,* 690–705.

Belgrave, F., & Allison, K. (2005). *African American psychology: From Africa to America.* Thousand Oaks, CA: Sage Publications.

Bell, J., & Bromnick, R. (2003). The social reality of the imaginary audience: A ground theory approach. *Adolescence, 38,* 205–219.

Bell, L. G., & Bell, D. C. (1982). Family climate and the role of the female adolescent: Determinants of adolescent functioning. *Family Relations, 31,* 519–527.

Belsky, J. (1985). Prepared statement on the effects of day care. In Select Committee on Children, Youth, and Families, House of Representatives, 98th Congress, Second Session, *Improving child care services: What can be done?* Washington, DC: U.S. Government Printing Office.

Belsky, J. (1992). Consequences of child care for children's development: A deconstructionist view. In A. Booth (Ed.), *Child care in the 1990s: Trends and consequences* (pp. 83–94). Hillsdale, NJ: Erlbaum.

Belsky, J. (2001). Developmental risks (still) associated with early child care. *Journal of Child Psychology & Psychiatry & Allied Disciplines, 42*, 845–859.

Belsky, J. (2002). Quantity counts: Amount of child care and children's socio-emotional development. *Journal of Developmental & Behavioral Pediatrics, 23*, 167–170.

Belsky, J., & Rovine, M. (1988). Nonmaternal care in the first year of life and the security of infant-parent attachment. *Child Development, 59*, 157–167.

Bem, S. L. (1974). The measurement of psychological androgyny. *Journal of Consulting & Clinical Psychology, 42*, 155–162.

Bem, S. L. (1981). Gender schema theory: A cognitive account of sex-typing. *Psychological Review, 88*, 354–364.

Benbow, C. P. (1988). Sex differences in mathematical reasoning ability in intellectually talented preadolescents: Their nature, effects, and possible causes. *Behavioral & Brain Sciences, 11*, 169–232.

Bender, B. G., Harmon, R. J., Linden, M. G., & Robinson, A. (1995). Psychosocial adaptation of 39 adolescents with sex chromosome abonrmalities. *Pediatrics, 96*, 302–308.

Bendersky, M., & Lewis, M. (1994). Environmental risk, biological risk, and developmental outcome. *Developmental Psychology, 30*, 484–494.

Benedetti, W. (April 20, 2007). Were video games to blame for Virginia Tech massacre? Retrieved June 28, 2007 from http://www.msnbc.msn.com/id/18220228/.

Benenson, J. F. (1994). Ages four to six years: Changes in the structures of play networks of girls and boys. *Merrill-Palmer Quarterly, 40*, 478–487.

Benenson, J. F., & Benarroch, D. (1998). Gender differences in responses to friends' hypothetical greater success. *Journal of Early Adolescence, 18*, 192–208.

Benton, J. (2007). Fort Worth charter school in trouble over TAKS cheating. *Dallas Morning News Online.* Retrieved June 25, 2007 from www.dallasnews.com/sharedcontent/dws/dn/latestnews/stories/061507dnmetcheatinglee.3c44589html.

Berg, C., Rapoff, M., Snyder, C., & Belmont, J. (2007). The relationship of children's hope to pediatric asthma treatment adherence. *Journal of Positive Psychology, 2*, 176–184.

Bergeson, T., & Trehub, S. (1999). Mothers' singing to infants and preschool children. *Infant Behavior & Development, 22*, 53–64.

Bergman, R. (2002). Why be moral? A conceptual model from developmental psychology. *Human Development, 45*, 104–124.

Berliner, D., & Biddle, B. (1997). *The manufactured crisis: Myths, fraud, and the attack on America's public schools.* New York: Addison-Wesley.

Bernard, R., & Cohen, L. (2006). Parent anxiety and infant pain during pediatric immunizations. *Journal of Clinical Psychology in Medical Settings, 13*, 285–290.

Bernardo, A., & Calleja, M. (2005). The effects of stating problems in bilingual students' first and second languages on solving mathematical word problems. *Journal of Genetic Psychology, 166* (1), 117–128.

Berndt, T. J., & Keefe, K. (1995). Friends' influence on adolescents' adjustment to school. *Child Development, 66*, 1312–1329.

Berthier, N., DeBlois, S., Poirier, C., Novak, M., & Clifton, R. (2000). Where's the ball? Two- and three-year-olds reason about unseen events. *Developmental Psychology, 36*, 394–401.

Berzonsky, M. (2003). The structure of identity: Commentary on Jane Kroger's view of identity status transition. *Identity, 3*, 231–245.

Betancourt, H., & Lopez, S. R. (1993). The study of culture, ethnicity, and race in American psychology. *American Psychologist, 48*, 629–637.

Betancourt, L., Fischer, R., Gianetta, J., Malmud, E., Brodsky, N. & Hurt, H. (1999). Problem-solving ability of inner-city children with and without in utero cocaine exposure. *Journal of Developmental Disabilities, 20*, 418–424.

Bethus, I., Lemaire, V., Lhomme, M., & Goodall, G. (2005). Does prenatal stress effect latent inhibition? It depends on the gender. *Behavioural Brain Research, 158*, 331–338.

Betz, N. E., & Fitzgerald, L. F. (1987). *The career psychology of women.* Orlando, FL: Academic Press.

Bhatt, R., Wilk, A., Hill, D., & Rovee-Collier, C. (2004). Correlated attributes and categorization in the first half-year of life. *Developmental Psychobiology, 44*, 103–115.

Bialystok, E. (2005). Consequences of bilingualism for cognitive development. In J. Kroll, & A. de Groot (Eds.), *Handbook of bilingualism: Psycholinguistic approaches* (pp. 417–432). New York: Oxford University Press.

Bialystok, E., Shenfield, T., & Codd, J. (2000). Languages, scripts, and the environment: Factors in developing concepts of print. *Developmental Psychology, 36*, 66–76.

Biederman, J., Faraone, S., Jetton, J., Kraus, I., Mick, E., Pert, J., Spencer, T., Weber, W., Wilens, T., Williamson, S., & Zallen, B. (1999). Clinical correlates of ADHD in females: Findings from a large group of girls ascertained from pediatric and psychiatric referral sources. *Journal of the American Academy of Child and Adolescent Psychiatry, 38*, 966–975.

Biederman, J., Monuteaux, M., Doyle, A., Seidman, L., Wilens, T., Ferrero, F., Morgan, C., & Faraone, S. (2004). Impact of executive function deficits and attention-deficit/hyperactivity disorder (ADHD) on academic outcomes in children. *Journal of Consulting and Clinical Psychology, 72*, 757–766.

Biederman, J., Petty, C., Doyle, A., Spencer, T., Henderson, C., Marion, B., Fried, R., & Faraone, S. (2008). Stability of executive function deficits in girls with ADHD: A prospective longitudinal followup study into adolescence. *Developmental Neuropsychology, 33*, 44.

Bigler, R., & Liben, S. (1993). The role of attitudes and interventions in gender-schematic processing. *Child Development, 61*, 1440–1452.

Binet, A., & Simon, T. (1905). Méthodes nouvelles pour le diagnostic du niveau intellectuel des anormaux [New methods for diagnosing the intellectual level of the abnormal]. *L'Anée Psychologique, 11*, 191–244.

Bingham, C. R., Miller, B. C., & Adams, G. R. (1990). Correlates of age at first sexual intercourse in a national sample of young women. *Journal of Adolescent Research, 5*, 18–33.

Birch, D. (1998). The adolescent parent: A fifteen-year longitudinal study of school-age mothers and their children. *International Journal of Adolescent Medicine & Health, 19*, 141–153.

Biringen, Z. (2000). Emotional availability: Conceptualization and research findings. *American Journal of Orthopsychiatry, 70*, 104–114.

Biswas, M. K., & Craigo, S. D. (1994). The course and conduct of normal labor and delivery. In A. H. DeCherney & M. L. Pernoll (Eds.), *Current obstetric and gynecologic diagnosis and treatment* (pp. 202–227). Norwalk, CT: Appleton & Lange.

Bittner, S., & Newberger, E. (1981). Pediatric understanding of child abuse and neglect. *Pediatric Review, 2*, 198.

Black, K. A., & McCartney, K. (1995, March). Associations between adolescent attachment to parents and peer interactions. Paper presented at the biennial meetings of the Society for Research in Child Development, Indianapolis.

Black, M., & Krishnakumar, A. (1999). Predicting height and weight longitudinal growth curves using ecological factors among children with and without early growth deficiency. *Journal of Nutrition, 129*, 539S–543S.

Blackman, J. A. (1990). Update on AIDS, CMV, and herpes in young children: Health, developmental, and educational issues.

In M. Wolraich & D. K. Routh (Eds.), *Advances in developmental and behavioral pediatrics, Vol. 9* (pp. 33–58). London: Jessica Kingsley Publishers.

Blair, C., Greenberg, M., & Crnic, K. (2001). Age-related increases in motivation among children with mental retardation and MA- and CA-matched controls. *American Journal on Mental Retardation, 106*, 511–524.

Blake, I. K. (1994). Language development and socialization in young African-American children. In P. M. Greenfield & R. R. Cocking (Eds.), *Cross-cultural roots of minority child development* (pp. 167–195). Hillsdale, NJ: Erlbaum.

Blake, J., Osborne, P., Cabral, M., & Gluck, P. (2003). The development of communicative gestures in Japanese infants. *First Language, 23*, 3–20.

Blakemore, J., LaRue, A., Olejnik, A. (1979). Sex-appropriate toy preference and the ability to conceptualize toys as sex-role related. *Developmental Psychology, 15*, 339–340.

Blau, G. (1996). Adolescent depression and suicide. In G. Blau & T. Gullotta (Eds.), *Adolescent dysfunctional behavior: Causes, interventions, and prevention* (pp. 187–205). Newbury Park, CA: Sage.

Blickstine, I., Jones, C., & Keith, L. (2003). Zygotic-splitting rates after single-embryo transfers in in vitro fertilization. *New England Journal of Medicine, 348*, 2366–2367.

Block, J. (1971). *Lives through time.* Berkeley, CA: Bancroft.

Block, J., & Robins, R. W. (1993). A longitudinal study of consistency and change in self-esteem from early adolescence to early adulthood. *Child Development, 64*, 909–923.

Bloom, B., & Cohen, R. (2007). Summary health statistics for U.S. children: National Health Interview Survey, 2006. Retrieved March 27, 2008 from http://www.cdc.gov/nchs/data/series/sr_10/sr10_234.pdf.

Bloom, L. (1973). *One word at a time.* The Hague: Mouton.

Bloom, L. (1991). *Language development from two to three.* Cambridge, England: Cambridge University Press.

Bloom, L. (1993). *The transition from infancy to language: Acquiring the power of expression.* Cambridge, England: Cambridge University Press.

Bloom, L. (1997, April). The child's action drives the interaction. Paper presented at the biennial meetings of the Society for Research in Child Development, Washington, DC.

Bloom, L., & Tinker, E. (2001). The intentionality model and language acquisition: Engagement, effort, and the essential tension in development. *Monographs of the Society for Research in Child Development, 66*, 1–89.

Bogenschneider, K., Wu, M., Raffaelli, M., & Tsay, J. (1998). "Other teens drink, but not my kid": Does parental awareness of adolescent alcohol use protect adolescents from risky consequences? *Journal of Marriage & the Family, 60*, 356–373.

Bond, L., Braskamp, D., & Roeber, E. (1996). *The status report of the assessment programs in the United States.* Oakbrook, IL: North Central Regional Educational Laboratory. ERIC No. ED 401 333.

Bong, M. (1998). Tests of the internal/external frames of reference model with subject-specific academic self-efficacy and frame-specific academic self-concepts. *Journal of Educational Psychology, 90*, 102–110.

Borawski, E., Trapl, E., Lovegreen, L., Colabianchi, N., & Block, T. (2005). Effectiveness of abstinence-only intervention in middle school teens. *American Journal of Health Behavior, 29*, 423–434.

Borkowski, M., Hunter, K., & Johnson, C. (2001). White noise and scheduled bedtime routines to reduce infant and childhood sleep disturbances. *Behavior Therapist, 24*, 29–37.

Bornstein, M. H. (1992). Perception across the life span. in M. H. Bornstein & M. E. Lamb (Eds.), *Developmental psychology: An advanced textbook* (3rd ed., pp. 155–210). Hillsdale, NJ: Erlbaum.

Bornstein, M. H., Arterberry, M., & Mash, C. (2005). Perceptual development. In M. H. Bornstein & M. E. Lamb (Eds), *Developmental science: An advanced textbook.* (5th ed., pp. 283–326). Hillsdale, NJ: Erlbaum.

Bornstein, M. H., Tamis-LeMonda, D., Tal, J., Ludemann, P., Toda, S., Rahn, C., Pecheux, M., Azuma, H., & Vardi, D. (1992). Maternal responsiveness to infants in three societies: The United States, France, and Japan. *Child Development, 63*, 808–821.

Boscardin, C., Muthén, B., Francis, D., & Baker, E. (2008). Early identification of reading difficulties using heterogeneous developmental trajectories. *Journal of Educational Psychology, 100*, 192–208.

Bosch, L., & Sebastian-Galles, N. (1997). Native-language recognition abilities in 4-month-old infants from monolingual and bilingual environments. *Cognition, 65*, 33–69.

Bougie, E., Wright, S., & Taylor, D. (2003). Early heritage language education and the abrupt shift to a dominant-language classroom: Impact on the persona and collective esteem of Inuit children in Arctic Québec. *International Journal of Bilingual Education and Bilingualism, 6*, 349–373.

Bowen, J., Gibson, F., & Hand, P. (2002). Educational outcome at 8 years for children who were born extremely prematurely: A controlled study. *Journal of Pediatrics & Child Health, 38*, 438–444.

Bower, B. (2005). Mental meeting of the sexes: Boys' spatial advantage fades in poor families. *Science News, 168*, 21.

Bowerman, M. (1985). Beyond communicative adequacy: From piecemeal knowledge to an integrated system in the child's acquisition of language. In K. E. Nelson (Ed.), *Children's language, Vol. 5* (pp. 369–398). Hillsdale, NJ: Erlbaum.

Bowker, A. (2004). Predicting friendship stability during early adolescence. *Journal of Early Adolescence, 24*, 85–112.

Bowlby, J. (1969). *Attachment and loss, Vol. 1: Attachment.* New York: Basic Books.

Bowlby, J. (1980). *Attachment and loss, Vol. 3: Loss, sadness, and depression.* New York: Basic Books.

Boyan, S., & Termini, A. (2005). *The psychotherapist as parent coordinator in high-conflict divorce: Strategies and techniques.* Binghamton, NY: Haworth Clinical Practice Press.

Bradbury, K., & Katz, J. (2002). Women's labor market involvement and family income mobility when marriages end. *New England Economic Review, Q4*, 41–74.

Bradley, R. H., Caldwell, B. M., Rock, S. L., Barnard, K. E., Gray, C., Hammond, M. A., Mitchell, S., Siegel, L., Ramey, C. D., Gottfried, A. W., & Johnson, D. L. (1989). Home environment and cognitive development in the first 3 years of life: A collaborative study involving six sites and three ethnic groups in North America. *Developmental Psychology, 25*, 217–235.

Bradley, R. H., Whiteside, L., Mundfrom, D., Casey, P., Kelleher, K., & Pope, S. (1994). Early indications of resilience and their relation to experiences in the home environments of low birthweight, premature children living in poverty. *Child Development, 65*, 346–360.

Bradmetz, J. (1999). Precursors of formal thought: A longitudinal study. *British Journal of Developmental Psychology, 17*, 61–81.

Brandon, P. (1999). Determinants of self-care arrangements among school-age children. *Children & Youth Services Review, 21*, 497–520.

Brandon, P., & Hofferth, S. (2003). Determinants of out-of-school childcare arrangements among children in single-mother and two-parent families. *Social Science Research, 32*, 129–147.

Bray, N., Fletcher, K., & Turner, L. (1997). Cognitive competencies and strategy use in individuals with mental retardation. In W. MacLean (Ed.), *Ellis's handbook of mental deficiency* (3rd ed., pp. 197–217). Mahwah, NJ: Erlbaum.

Brazelton, T. B. (1984). *Neonatal Behavioral Assessment Scale.* Philadelphia: Lippincott.

Bregman, G., & Killen, M. (1999). Adolescents' and young adults' reasoning about career choice and the role of parental influence. *Journal of Research on Adolescence, 9*, 253–275.

Bremner, J. (2002). The nature of imitation by infants. *Infant Behavior & Development, 25*, 65–67.

Brennan, F., & Ireson, J. (1997). Training phonological awareness: A study to evaluate the effects of a program of metalinguistic games in kindergarten. *Reading & Writing, 9*, 241–263.

Breslau, N., & Chilcoat, H. (2000). Psychiatric sequelae of low birth weight at 11 years of age. *Biological Psychiatry, 47*, 1005–1011.

Breyer, J., & Winters, K. (2005). *Adolescent brain development: Implications for drug use prevention.* Retrieved April 15, 2008 from http://www.mentorfoundation.org/pdfs/prevention_perspectives/19.pdf.

Bridgeland, J., DiIulio, J., & Morison, K. (2006). The silent epidemic: Perspectives of high school dropouts. Retrieved September 9, 2008 from http://www.gatesfoundation.org/nr/downloads/ed/thesilentepidemic3-06final.pdf.

Britner, S., & Pajares, F. (2006). Sources of science self-efficacy beliefs in middle school students. *Journal of Research in Science Teaching, 43*, 485–499.

Brockington, I. (1996). *Motherhood and mental health.* Oxford, England: Oxford University Press.

Brody, G., Kim, S., Murry, V., & Brown, A. (2003). Longitudinal direct and indirect pathways linking older sibling competence to the development of younger sibling competence. *Developmental Psychology, 39*, 618–628.

Brody, N. (1992). *Intelligence* (2nd ed.). San Diego, CA: Academic Press.

Broman, C., Reckase, M., & Freedman-Doan, C. (2006). The role of parenting in drug use among Black, Latino and White adolescents. *Journal of Ethnicity in Substance Abuse, 5*, 39–50.

Broman, S., Nichols, P., Shaughnessy, P., & Kennedy, W. (1987). *Retardation in young children.* Hillsdale, NJ: Erlbaum.

Bronfenbrenner, U. (1979). *The ecology of human development.* Cambridge, MA: Harvard University Press.

Bronfenbrenner, U. (1993). The ecology of cognitive development: Research models and fugitive findings. In R. H. Wozniak and K. W. Fischer (Eds.), *Development in context: Acting and thinking in specific environments.* Hillsdale, NJ: Erlbaum.

Bronstein, A., Spyker, D., Cantilena, L., Green, J., Rumack, B., & Heard, S. (2007). 2006 annual report of the American Association of Poison Control Centers' National Poison Data System (NPDS). *Clinical Toxicology, 45*, 815–917.

Brook, J., Whiteman, M., Finch, S., & Cohen, P. (2000). Longitudinally foretelling drug use in the late twenties: Adolescent personality and social-environmental antecedents. *Journal of Genetic Psychology, 161*, 37–51.

Brooks-Gunn, J. (1987). Pubertal processes and girls' psychological adaptation. In R. M. Lerner & T. T. Foch (Eds.), *Biological-psychosocial interactions in early adolescence* (pp. 123–154). Hillsdale, NJ: Erlbaum.

Brooks-Gunn, J., Guo, G., & Furstenberg, F. F., Jr. (1993). Who drops out of and who continues beyond high school? A 20-year follow-up of black urban youth. *Journal of Research on Adolescence, 3*, 271–294.

Brooks-Gunn, J., & Warren, M. P. (1985). The effects of delayed menarche in different contexts: Dance and nondance students. *Journal of Youth & Adolescence, 13*, 285–300.

Brown, A., & Day, J. (1983). Macrorules for summarizing text: The development of expertise. *Journal of Verbal Learning & Verbal Behavior, 22*, 1–14.

Brown, B. B. (1990). Peer groups and peer cultures. In S. S. Feldman & G. R. Elliott (Eds.), *At the threshold: The developing adolescent* (pp. 171–196). Cambridge, MA: Harvard University Press.

Brown, B. B., & Huang, B. (1995). Examining parenting practices in different peer contexts: Implications for adolescent trajectories. In L. J. Crockett & A. C. Crouter (Eds.), *Pathways through adolescence* (pp. 151–174). Mahwah, NJ: Erlbaum.

Brown, B. B., Mory, M. S., & Kinney, D. (1994). Casting adolescent crowds in a relational perspective: Caricature, channel, and context. In R. Montemayor, G. R. Adams, & T. P. Gullotta (Eds.), *Personal relationships during adolescence* (pp. 123–167). Thousand Oaks, CA: Sage.

Brown, J., Bakeman, R., Coles, C., Sexson, W., & Demi, A. (1998). Maternal drug use during pregnancy: Are preterm and full-term infants affected differently? *Developmental Psychology, 34*, 540–554.

Brown, R. (1973). *A first language: The early stages.* Cambridge, MA: Harvard University Press.

Brown, R., & Bellugi, U. (1964). Three processes in the acquisition of syntax. *Harvard Educational Review, 334*, 133–151.

Brown, S., Estroff, J., & Barnewolt, C. (2004). Fetal MRI. *Applied Radiology, 33*, 9–25.

Brownell, C. A. (1990). Peer social skills in toddlers: Competencies and constraints illustrated by same age and mixed-age interaction, *Child Development, 61*, 836–848.

Brownwell, H., Griffin, R., Winner, E., Friedman, O., & Happe, F. (2000). Cerebral lateralization and theory of mind. In S. Baron-Cohen, H. Tager-Flusberg, & D. Cohen (Eds.), *Understanding other minds: Perspectives from developmental cognitive neuroscience* (2nd ed.). Oxford, UK: Oxford University Press.

Bruck, M., & Ceci, S. (1997). The suggestibility of young children. *Current Directions in Psychological Science, 6*, 75–79.

Bruck, M., Ceci, S., & Hembrooke, H. (1998). Reliability and credibility of young children's reports: From research to policy and practice. *American Psychologist, 53*, 136–151.

Brückner, H., & Bearman, P. (2005). After the promise: The STD consequences of adolescent virginity pledges. *Journal of Adolescent Health, 36*, 271–278.

Bruer, J. (1999). *The myth of the first three years.* New York: Free Press.

Bryant, P. E., MacLean, M., & Bradley, L. L. (1990). Rhyme, language, and children's reading. *Applied Psycholinguistics, 11*, 237–252.

Bryant, P. E., MacLean, M., Bradley, L. L., & Crossland, J. (1990). Rhyme and alliteration, phoneme detection, and learning to read. *Developmental Psychology, 26*, 429–438.

Buchanan, C. M., Maccoby, E. E., & Dornbusch, S. M. (1991). Caught between parents: Adolescents' experience in divorced homes. *Child Development, 62*, 1008–1029.

Buchanan, P., & Vardaxis, V. (2003). Sex-related and age-related differences in knee strength of basketball players ages 11–17 years. *Journal of Athletic Training, 38*, 231–237.

Bukowski, W., Sippola, L., & Hoza, B. (1999). Same and other: Interdependency between participation in same- and other-sex friendships. *Journal of Youth & Adolescence, 28*, 439–459.

Bullock, M., & Lütkenhaus, P. (1990). Who am I? Self-understanding in toddlers. *Merrill-Palmer Quarterly, 36*, 217–238.

Burgess, S. (2005). The preschool home literacy environment provided by teenage mothers. *Early Child Development & Care, 175*, 249–258.

Burgess, S., Propper, C., & Rigg, J. (2004). The impact of low income on child health: Evidence from a birth cohort study. CASE Paper 85, Center for Analysis of Social Exclusion. Retrieved March 20, 2008 from http://sticerd.lse.ac.uk/dps/case/cp/CASEpaper85.pdf.

Burkham, D., Lee, V., & Smerdon, B. (1997). Gender and science learning early in high school: Subject matter and laboratory experiences. *American Educational Research Journal, 34*, 297–332.

Burn, S., O'Neil, A., & Nederend, S. (1996). Childhood tomboyishness and adult androgeny. *Sex Roles, 34,* 419–428.

Burton, L. (1992). Black grandparents rearing children of drug-addicted parents: Stressors, outcomes, and social service needs. *Gerontologist, 31,* 744–751.

Bus, A., & van IJzendoorn, M. (1999). Phonological awareness and early reading: A meta-analysis of experimental training studies. *Journal of Educational Psychology, 91,* 403–414.

Bushman, B. (2006). Effects of warning and information labels on attraction to television violence in viewers of different ages. *Journal of Applied Social Psychology, 36,* 2073–2078.

Bushman, B., & Huesmann, R. (2006). Short-term and long-term effects of violent media on aggression in children and adults. *Archives of Pediatric Adolescent Medicine, 160,* 348–352.

Buss, A., & Plomin, R. (1984). *Temperament: Early developing personality traits.* Hillsdale, NJ: Erlbaum.

Bussey, K., & Bandura, A. (1992). Self-regulation mechanisms governing gender development. *Child Development, 63,* 1236–1250.

Bussing, R., Menvielle, E., & Zima, B. (1996). Relationship between behavioral problems and unintentional injuries in U.S. children. *Archives of Pediatric and Adolescent Medicine, 150,* 50–56.

Buston, K., & Wood, S. (2000). Non-compliance amongst adolescents with asthma: Listening to what they tell us about self-management. *Family Practice, 17,* 134–138.

Buzi, R., Roberts, R., Ross, M., Addy, R., & Markham, C. (2003). The impact of a history of sexual abuse on high-risk sexual behaviors among females attending alternative schools. *Adolescence, 38,* 595–605.

Cahn, D., Marcotte, A., Stern, R., Arruda, J., Akshoomoff, N., & Leshko, I. (1966). The Boston Qualitative Scoring System for the Rey-Osterrieth Complex Figure: A study of children with attention deficit hyperactivity disorder. *Clinical Neuropsychologist, 10,* 397–406.

Cairns, R. (1991). Multiple metaphors for a singular idea. *Developmental Psychology, 27,* 23–26.

Cairns, R. B., & Cairns, B. D. (1994). *Lifelines and risks: Pathways of youth in our time.* Cambridge, England: Cambridge University Press.

Calhoun, S., & Dickerson Mayes, S. (2005). Processing speed in children with clinical disorders. *Psychology in the Schools, 42,* 333–343.

California Department of Education. (2007, December 6). State schools chief Jack O'Connell releases eighth annual physical fitness test results. Retrieved March 27, 2008 from http://www.cde.ca.gov/ta/tg/pf/documents/pftnewsrelease.doc.

Calkins, S., Dedmon, S., Gill, K., Lomax, L., & Johnson, L. (2002). Frustration in infancy: Implications for emotion regulation, physiological processes, and temperament. *Infancy, 3,* 175–197.

Callaghan, T. (1999). Early understanding and production of graphic symbols. *Child Development, 70,* 1314–1324.

Callaghan, T., & Rankin, M. (2002). Emergence of graphic symbol functioning and the question of domain specificity: A longitudinal training study. *Child Development, 73,* 359–376.

Callahan, K., Rademacher, J., & Hildreth, B. (1998). The effect of parent participation in strategies to improve the homework performance of students who are at risk. *Remedial & Special Education, 19,* 131–141.

Calvert, S., & Kotler, J. (2003). Lessons from children's television: The impact of the Children's Television Act on children's learning. *Applied Developmental Psychology, 24,* 275–335.

Calvert, S., Mahler, B., Zehnder, S., Jenkins, A., & Lee, M. (2003). Gender differences in preadolescent children's online interactions: Symbolic modes of self-presentation and self-expression. *Applied Developmental Psychology, 24,* 627–644.

Camilleri, C., & Malewska-Peyre, H. (1997). Socialization and identity strategies. In J. Berry, P. Dasen, & T. Saraswathi (Eds.), *Handbook of cross-cultural psychology, Vol. 2: Basic processes and human development.* Boston: Allyn & Bacon.

Campbell, A., Shirley, L., & Candy, J. (2004). A longitudinal study of gender-related cognition and behaviour. *Developmental Science, 7,* 1–9.

Campbell, A., Shirley, L., & Caygill, L. (2002). Sex-typed preferences in three domains: Do two-year-olds need cognitive variables? *British Journal of Psychology, 93,* 203–217.

Campbell, F. A., & Ramey, C. T. (1994). Effects of early intervention on intellectual and academic achievement: A follow-up study of children from low-income families. *Child Development, 65,* 684–698.

Campbell, F. A., Ramey, C. T., Pungello, E., Sparling, J., & Miller-Johnson, S. (2002). Early childhood education: Young adult outcomes from the Abecedarian Project. *Applied Developmental Science, 6,* 42–57.

Caplan, G. (1964). *Principles of preventive psychiatry.* New York: Basic Books.

Capron, C., & Duyme, M. (1989). Assessment of effects of socio-economic status on IQ in a full cross-fostering study. *Nature, 340,* 552–554.

Capute, A. J., Palmer, F. B., Shapiro, B. K., Wachtel, R. C., Ross, A., & Accardo, P. J. (1984). Primitive reflex profile: A quantification of primitive reflexes in infancy. *Developmental Medicine & Child Neurology, 26,* 375–383.

Cardon, R., & Fulker, D. (1991). Sources of continuity in infant predictors of later IQ. *Intelligence, 15,* 279–293.

Carey, S., & Bartlett, E. (1978). Acquiring a single new word. *Papers & Reports on Child Language Development, 15,* 17–29.

Carlson, E. A., Sampson, M., & Sroufe, L. A. (2003). Implications of attachment theory and research for developmental-behavioral pediatrics. *Journal of Developmental & Behavioral Pediatrics, 24,* 364–379.

Carlson, E. A., & Sroufe, L. A. (1995). Contribution of attachment theory to developmental psychopathology. In D. Cicchetti & D. J. Conen (Eds.), *Developmental psychopathology, Vol. 1: Theory and methods* (pp. 581–617). New York: Wiley.

Carlson, E. A., Sroufe, L. A., & Egeland, B. (2004). The construction of experience: A longitudinal study of representation and behavior. *Child Development, 75,* 66–83.

Carnagey, N., & Anderson, C. (2005). The effects of reward and punishment in violent video games on aggressive affect, cognition, and behavior. *Psychological Science, 16,* 882–889.

Caron, A. J., & Caron, R. F. (1981). Processing of relational information as an index of infant risk. In S. Friedman & M. Sigman (Eds.), *Preterm birth and psychological development* (pp. 219–240). New York: Academic Press.

Carpenter, S. (2001). Teens' risky behavior is about more than race and family resources. *APA Monitor, 32,* 22–23.

Carrera, M., Kaye, J., Philiber, S., & West, E. (2000). Knowledge about reproduction, contraception, and sexually transmitted infections among young adolescents in American cities. *Social Policy, 30,* 41–50.

Carroll, J., & Snowling, M. (2004). Language and phonological skills in children at high risk of reading difficulties. *Journal of Child Psychology & Psychiatry, 45,* 631–640.

Carson, D., Klee, T. & Perry, C. (1998). Comparisons of children with delayed and normal language at 24 months of age on measures of behavioral difficulties, social and cognitive development. *Infant Mental Health Journal, 19,* 59–75.

Cartwright, C. (2006). You want to know how it affected me? Young adults' perceptions of the impact of parental divorce. *Journal of Divorce & Remarriage, 44,* 125–143.

Carver, P., Egan, S., & Perry, D. (2004). Children who question their heterosexuality. *Developmental Psychology, 40*, 43–53.

Carver, R. P. (1990). Intelligence and reading ability in grades 2–12. *Intelligence, 14*, 449–455.

Casas, J. F., & Mosher, M. (1995, March). *Relational and overt aggression in preschool: "You can't come to my birthday party unless . . . "* Paper presented at the biennial meeting of the Society for Research in Child Development, Indianapolis.

Casasola, M., & Cohen, L. (2000). Infants' association of linguistic labels with causal actions. *Developmental Psychology, 36*, 155–168.

Case, A., Lee, D., & Paxson, C. (2007). The income gradient in children's health: A comment on Currie, Shields and Wheatley Price. NBER Working Paper No. W13495. Retrieved March 19, 2008 from http://ssrn.com/abstract=1021973.

Case, A., Lubotsky, D., & Paxson, C. (2002). Economic status and health in childhood: The origins of the gradient. *American Economic Review, 92*, 1308–1334.

Case, R. (1985). *Intellectual development: Birth to adulthood.* New York: Academic Press.

Case, R. (1991). Stages in the development of the young child's first sense of self. *Developmental Review, 11*, 210–230.

Case, R. (1992). *The mind's staircase: Exploring thought and knowledge.* Hillsdale, NJ: Erlbaum.

Case, R. (1997). The development of conceptual structures. In B. Damon (General Ed.) and D. Kuhn & R. S. Siegler (Series Eds.), *Handbook of child psychology, Vol. 2: Cognitive, language, and perceptual development.* New York: Wiley.

Cashon, C., & Cohen, L. (2000). Eight-month-old infants' perceptions of possible and impossible events. *Infancy, 1*, 429–446.

Caslyn, C., Gonzales, P., & Frase, M. (1999). *Highlights from the Third International Mathematics and Science Study.* Washington, DC: National Center for Education Statistics.

Casper, L., & Smith, K. (2002). Dispelling the myths: Self-care, class, and race. *Journal of Family Issues, 23*, 716–727.

Caspi, A. (2000). The child is father of the man: Personality continuities from childhood to adulthood. *Journal of Personality & Social Psychology, 78*, 158–172.

Caspi, A., & Moffitt, T. (2006). Gene-environment interactions in psychiatry: Joining forces with neuroscience. *Nature Reviews: Neuroscience, 7*, 583–590.

Cassidy, J., & Berlin, L. J. (1994). The insecure/ambivalent pattern of attachment: Theory and research. *Child Development, 65*, 971–991.

Castellino, D., Lerner, J., Lerner, R., & von Eye, A. (1998). Maternal employment and education: Predictors of young adolescent career trajectories. *Applied Developmental Science, 2*, 114–126.

Cato, J., & Canetto, S. (2003). Attitudes and beliefs about suicidal behavior when coming out is the precipitant of the suicidal behavior. *Sex Roles, 49*, 497–505.

Catsambis, S. (1995). Gender, race, ethnicity, and science education in the middle grades. *Journal of Research in Science Teaching, 32*, 243–257.

Caughy, M. O., DiPietro, J. A., & Strobino, D. M. (1994). Day-care participation as a protective factor in the cognitive development of low-income children. *Child Development, 65*, 457–471.

Cavill, S., & Bryden, P. (2003). Development of handedness: Comparison of questionnaire and performance-based measures of preference. *Brain & Cognition, 53*, 149–151.

CBS News. (2004, April 29). Utah C-section mom gets probation. Retrieved March 9, 2008, from http://www.cbsnews.com/stories/2004/03/12/national/printable605537.shtml.

Ceci, S., & Bronfenbrenner, U. (1985). "Don't forget to take the cupcakes out of the oven": Prospective memory, strategic time-monitoring, and context. *Child Development, 56*, 152–164.

Ceci, S. J., & Bruck, M. (1993). Suggestibility of the child witness: A historical review and synthesis. *Psychological Bulletin, 113*, 403–439.

Ceci S., & Bruck, M. (1995). *Jeopardy in the courtroom: A scientific analysis of children's testimony.* Washington, DC: American Psychological Association.

Ceci, S., & Bruck, M. (1998). The ontogeny and durability of true and false memories: A fuzzy trace account. *Journal of Experimental Child Psychology, 71*, 165–169.

Center for Adoption Medicine. (2008). Growth charts. Retrieved June 11, 2008 from http://www.adoptmed.org/topics/growth-charts.html.

Centers for Disease Control (CDC). (1996). Population-based prevalence of perinatal exposure to cocaine—Georgia, 1994. *Morbidity & Mortality Weekly Report, 45*, 887.

Centers for Disease Control (CDC) (2004). Surveillance summaries. *Morbidity & Mortality Weekly Report, 53*, 2–29.

Centers for Disease Control (CDC). (2005). Mental health in the United States: Prevalence of diagnosis and medication treatment for attention-deficit/hyperactivity disorder—United States, 2003. *Morbidity & Mortality Weekly Report, 54*, 842–847.

Centers for Disease Control and Prevention (CDC). (2006a). *HPV vaccine questions and answers.* Retrieved June 29, 2006 from http://www.cdc.gov/std/hpv/STDFact-HPV-vaccine.htm#vaccine.

Centers for Disease Control. (CDC). (2006b). Sudden Infant Death Syndrome (SIDS): Risk factors. Retrieved June 8, 2007 from www.cdc.gov/SIDS/riskfactors.htm.

Centers for Disease Control (CDC). (2006c). Understanding child maltreatment. Retrieved June 14, 2007 from www.cdc.gov/ncipc/pub-res/CMFactsheet.pdf.

Centers for Disease Control (CDC). (2006d). Youth risk behavior surveillance: United States, 2005. *Morbidity & Mortality Weekly Report, 55*, 1–112.

Centers for Disease Control (CDC). (2007a). Defining overweight and obesity. Retrieved June 19, 2008 from http://www.cdc.gov/nccdphp/dnpa/obesity/defining.htm.

Centers for Disease Control (CDC). (2007b). HIV/AIDS surveillance in adolescents and young adults (through 2005). Retrieved April 11, 2008 from http://www.cdc.gov/hiv/topics/surveillance/resources/slides/adolescents/index.htm.

Centers for Disease Control (CDC). (2007c). National estimates of the 10 leading causes of nonfatal injuries treated in hospital emergency rooms in the United States, 2006. Retrieved March 27, 2008 from ftp://ftp.cdc.gov/pub/ncipc/10LC-2004/JPEG/10lc-2004-nonfatal.jpg.

Centers for Disease Control (CDC). (2007d). Sexually transmitted disease surveillance 2006 supplement. Retrieved April 9, 2008 from http://www.cdc.gov/std/Chlamydia2006/CTSurvSupp2006Short.pdf.

Centers for Disease Control (CDC). (2007e). *Suicide: Fact sheet.* Retrieved June 22, 2007 from http://www.cdc.gov/ncipc/factsheets/suifacts.htm.

Centers for Disease Control (CDC). (2008). *Healthy youth 2007.* Retrieved June 25, 2008 from http://www.cdc.gov/HealthyYouth/yrbs/index.htm.

Centers for Disease Control (CDC). (2000). Youth risk behavior surveillance—United States, 1999. *Morbidity & Mortality Weekly Report, 49*, 1–96.

Centers for Disease Control National Immunization Program. (2000, January 21). 2000 childhood immunization schedule. *Morbidity & Mortality Weekly Report, 49*, 35–38.

Ceponiene, R., Kuchnerenko, E., Fellman, V., Renlund, M., Suominen, K., & Naeaetaenen, R. (2002). Event-related potential features indexing central auditory discrimination by newborns. *Cognitive Brain Research, 13*, 101–113.

Cernoch, J. M., & Porter, R. H. (1985). Recognition of maternal axillary odors by infants. *Child Development, 56*, 1593–1598.
Chabris, C. F. (1999). Prelude or requiem for the "Mozart effect"? *Nature, 400*, 826–827.
Chadwick, O., Taylor, E., Taylor, A., Heptinstall, E., et al. (1999). Hyper-activity and reading disability: A longitudinal study of the nature of the association. *Journal of Child Psychology & Psychiatry, 40*, 1039–1050.
Chan, R., Raboy, B., & Patterson, C. (1998). Psychosocial adjustment among children conceived via donor insemination by lesbian and heterosexual mothers. *Child Development, 69*, 443–457.
Chandler, D. (2002). *Semiotics: The basics.* London: Routledge.
Chang, E. (2001). Lifes stress and depressed mood among adolescents: Examining a cognitive-affective mediation model. *Journal of Social & Clinical Psychology, 20*, 416–429.
Chang, L., & Murray, A. (1995, March). *Math performance of 5- and 6-year-olds in Taiwan and the U.S.: Maternal beliefs, expectations, and tutorial assistance.* Paper presented at the biennial meetings of the Society for Research in Child Development, Indianapolis, IN.
Chang, L., Schwartz, D., Dodge, K., & McBride-Chang, C. (2003). Harsh parenting in relation to child emotion regulation and aggression. *Journal of Family Psychology, 17*, 598–606.
Chao, R. (1994). Beyond parental control and authoritarian parenting style: Understanding Chinese parenting through the cultural notion of training. *Child Development, 65*, 1111–1119.
Chapman, J., & Tunmer, W. (1997). A longitudinal study of beginning reading achievement and reading self-concept. *British Journal of Educational Psychology, 67*, 279–291.
Chapman, K., Nicholas, P., & Supramaniam, R. (2006). How much food advertising is there on Australian television? *Health Promotion International, 21*, 172–180.
Charlesworth, W. R. (1992). Darwin and developmental psychology: Past and present. *Developmental Psychology, 28*, 5–16.
Chase-Lansdale, P. L., Cherlin, A. J., & Kiernan, K. E. (1995). The long-term effects of parental divorce on the mental health of young adults: A developmental perspective. *Child Development, 66*, 1614–1634.
Chatlos, J. (1997). Substance use and abuse and the impact on academic difficulties. *Child & Adolescent Clinics of North America, 6*, 545–568.
Cheay, C., & Rubin, K. (2004). European American and mainland Chinese mothers' responses to aggression and social withdrawal in preschoolers. *International Journal of Behavioral Development, 28*, 83–94.
Chen, E. (2004). Why socioeconomic status affects the health of children: A psychosocial perspective. *Current Directions in Psychological Science, 13*, 112–115.
Chen, S. (1997). Child's understanding of secret and friendship development. *Psychological Science (China), 20*, 545.
Chen, X., Rubin, K. H., & Li, Z. (1995). Social functioning and adjustment in Chinese children: A longitudinal study. *Developmental Psychology, 31*, 531–539.
Chen, X., Rubin, K. H., & Sun, Y. (1992). Social reputation and peer relationships in Chinese and Canadian children: A cross-cultural study. *Child Development, 63*, 1336–1343.
Chen, Z. (1999). Ethnic similarities and differences in the association of emotional autonomy and adolescent outcomes: Comparing Euro-American and Asian-American adolescents. *Psychological Reports, 84*, 501–516.
Cheng, G., Xiaoyan, H., & Dajun, Z. (2006). A review of academic self-concept and its relationship with academic achievement. *Psychological Science (China), 29*, 133–136.
Cheour, M., Martynova, O., Naeaetaenen, R., Erkkola, R., Sillanpaeae, M., Kero, P., Raz, A., Kaipio, M., Hiltunen, J., Aaltonen, O., Savela, J., & Haemaelaeinen, H. (2002). Speech sounds learned by sleeping newborns. *Nature, 415*, 599–600.
Cherlin, A. (1992). *Marriage, divorce, remarriage*, Cambridge, MA: Harvard University Press.
Cherlin, A., Chase-Lansdale, P., & McRae, C. (1998). Effects of parental divorce on mental health throughout the life course. *American Sociological Review, 63*, 239–249.
Cherry, V., Belgrave, F., Jones, W., Kennon, D., Gray, F., & Phillips, F. (1998). NTU: An Africentric approach to substance abuse prevention among African American youth. *Journal of Primary Prevention, 18*, 319–339.
Cheung, C., Chan, W., Lee, T., Liu, S., & Leung, K. (2001). Structure of moral consciousness and moral intentions among youth in Hong Kong. *International Journal of Adolescence & Youth, 9*, 83–116.
Chi, M. T. (1978). Knowledge structure and memory development. In R. S. Siegler (Ed.), *Children's thinking: What develops?* (pp. 73–96). Hillsdale, NJ: Erlbaum.
Chiappe, P., Glaeser, B., & Ferko, D. (2007). Speech perception, vocabulary, and the development of reading skills in English among Korean- and English-speaking children. *Journal of Educational Psychology, 99*, 154–166.
Chiappe, P., & Siegel, L. (1999). Phonological awareness and reading acquisition in English- and Punjabi-speaking Canadian children. *Journal of Educational Psychology, 91*, 20–28.
Child Welfare Information Gateway. (2007). Definitions of child abuse and neglect. Retrieved June 15, 2008 from http://www.childwelfare.gov/systemwide/laws_policies/statutes/define.cfm.
Child Welfare Information Gateway. (2008a). Mandatory reporters of child abuse and neglect. Retrieved June 11, 2008 from http://www.childwelfare.gov/systemwide/laws_policies/statutes/manda.cfm.
Child Welfare Information Gateway. (2008b). Recognizing child abuse and neglect: Signs and symptoms. Retrieved June 11, 2008 from http://www.childwelfare.gov/pubs/factsheets/signs.cfm.
Children's Hospital of Philadelphia (2008, March 3). In early childhood, continuous care by one doctor best, study suggests. Retrieved March 18, 2008 from http://www.sciencedaily.com/releases/2008/03/080303072646.htm.
Children spend more time playing video games than watching TV, MSU survey shows. (2004, April 4). Retrieved July 23, 2005 from www.newsroom.msu.edu/site/indexer/1943/content.htm.
Chincotta, D., & Underwood, G. (1997). Estimates, language of schooling and bilingual digit span. *European Journal of Cognitive Psychology, 9*, 325–348.
Choi, S. (2000). Caregiver input in English and Korean: Use of nouns and verbs in book-reading and toy-play contexts. *Journal of Children's Language, 27*, 69–96.
Chomsky, N. (1959). A review of B. F. Skinner's *Verbal Behavior. Language, 35*, 26–129.
Chong, B., Babcook, C., Salamat, M., Nemzek, W., Kroeker, D., & Ellis, W. (1996). A magnetic resonance template for normal neuronal migration in the fetus. *Neurosurgery, 39*, 110–116.
Chou, C., & Tsai, M. (2007). Gender differences in Taiwan high school students' computer game playing. *Computers in Human Behavior, 23*, 812–824.
Christakis, D., Zimmerman, F., DiGiuseppe, D., & McCarty, C. (2004). Early television exposure and subsequent attentional problems in children. *Pediatrics, 113*, 708–713.
Church, M., Eldis, F., Blakley, B., & Bawle, E. (1997) Hearing, language, speech, vestibular, and dento-facial disorders in fetal alcohol syndrome. *Alcoholism: Clinical & Experimental Research, 21*, 227–237.

Ciancio, D., Sadovsky, A., Malabonga, V., Trueblood, L., et al. (1999). Teaching classification and seriation to preschoolers. *Child Study Journal, 29*, 193–205.

Cicchetti, D., Rogosch, F., Maughan, A., Toth, S., & Bruce, J. (2003). False belief understanding in maltreated children. *Development & Psychopathology, 15*, 1067–1091.

Cicchetti, D., & Toth, S. (1998). The development of depression in children and adolescents. *American Psychologist, 53*, 221–241.

Cillessen, A., & Mayeux, L. (2004). From censure to reinforcement: Developmental changes in the association between aggression and social status. *Child Development, 75*, 147–163.

Cillessen, A. H. N., van IJzendoorn, H. W., van Lieshout, C. F. M., & Hartup, W. W. (1992). Heterogeneity among peer-rejected boys: Subtypes and stabilities. *Child Development, 63*, 893–905.

Claes, M. (1998). Adolescents' closeness with parents, siblings, and friends in three countries: Canada, Belgium, and Italy. *Journal of Youth & Adolescence, 27*, 165–184.

Clarke, A. M., & Clarke, A. D. (1976). *Early experience: Myth and evidence.* New York: Free Press.

Clarke-Stewart, A. (1992). Consequences of child care for children's development. In A. Booth (Ed.), *Child care in the 1990s: Trends and consequences* (pp. 63–82). Hillsdale, NJ: Erlbaum.

Cobb, K. (2000, September 3). Breaking in drivers: Texas could join states restricting teens in effort to lower rate of fatal accidents. *Houston Chronicle*, pp. A1, A20.

Cohen-Kettenis, P., & van Goozen, S. (1997). Sex reassignment of adolescent transsexuals: A follow-up study. *American Academy of Child & Adolescent Psychiatry, 36*, 263–271.

Coie, J. D., & Cillessen, A. H. N. (1993). Peer rejection: Origins and effects on children's development. *Current Directions in Psychological Science, 2*, 89–92.

Colby, A., Kohlberg, L., Gibbs, J., & Lieberman, M. (1983). A longitudinal study of moral judgment. *Monographs of the Society for Research in Child Development, 48* (1–2, Serial No. 200).

Cole, M. (1992). Culture in development. In M. H. Bornstein & M. E. Lamb (Eds.), *Developmental psychology: An advanced textbook* (pp. 731–789). Hillsdale, NJ: Erlbaum.

Cole, M. (2005). Culture in development. In M. Bornstein & M. Lamb (Eds.), *Developmental science: An advanced textbook* (5th ed., pp. 45–102). Mahwah, NJ: Erlbaum.

Cole, P., Martin, S., & Dennis, T. (2004). Emotion regulation as a scientific construct: Methodological challenges and directions for child development research. *Child Development, 75*, 317–333.

Coleman, J., Pratt, R., Stoddard, R., Gerstmann, D., & Abel, H. (1997). The effects of the male and female singing and speaking voices on selected physiological and behavioral measures of premature infants in the intensive care unit. *International Journal of Arts Medicine, 5*, 4–11.

Coley, R., & Chase-Lansdale, L. (1998). Adolescent pregnancy and parenthood: Recent evidence and future directions. *American Psychologist, 53*, 152–166.

Collet, J. P., Burtin, P., Gillet, J., Bossard, N., Ducruet, T., & Durr, F. (1994). Risk of infectious diseases in children attending different types of day-care setting. Epicreche Research Group. *Respiration, 61*, 16–19.

Collins, R., Elliott, M., Berry, S., Kanouse, D., Kunkel, D., Hunter, S., & Miu, A. (2004). Watching sex on television predicts adolescent initiation of sexual behavior. *Pediatrics, 114*, 280–289.

Colombo, J. (1993). *Infant cognition: Predicting later intellectual functioning.* Newbury Park, CA: Sage.

Colwell, J., & Kato, M. (2005). Video game play in British and Japanese adolescents. *Simulation & Gaming, 36*, 518–530.

Committee on Infectious Diseases (1996). Recommended childhood immunization schedule. *Pediatrics, 97*, 143–146.

Compas, B. E., Ey, S., & Grant, K. E. (1993). Taxonomy, assessment, and diagnosis of depression during adolescence. *Psychological Bulletin, 114*, 323–344.

Condry, J., & Condry, S. (1976). Sex differences: A study in the eye of the beholder. *Child Development, 47*, 812–819.

Conduct Problems Research Group. (2004). The Fast Track experiment: Translating the developmental model into a prevention design. In J. Kupersmidt & K. Dodge (Eds.), *Children's peer relations: From development to intervention.* (pp. 181–208). Washington, DC: American Psychological Association.

Connolly, K., Dalgleish, M. (1989). The emergence of a tool-using skill in infancy. *Developmental Psychology, 25*, 894–912.

Cooper, R. P., & Aslin, R. N. (1994). Developmental differences in infant attention to the spectral properties of infant-directed speech. *Child Development, 65*, 1663–1677.

Coplan, R., Bowker, A., & Cooper, S. (2003). Parenting daily hassles, child temperament and social adjustment in preschool. *Early Childhood Research Quarterly, 18*, 376–395.

Corbet, A., Long, W., Schumacher, R., Gerdes, J., & Cotton, R. (1995). Double-blind developmental evaluation at 1-year corrected age of 597 premature infants with birth weights from 500 to 1350 grams enrolled in three placebo-controlled trials of prophylactic synthetic surfactant. *Journal of Pediatrics, 126*, S5–S12.

Cornelius, M., Goldschmidt, L., Day, N., & Larkby, C. (2002). Alcohol, tobacco and marijuana use among pregnant teenagers: 6-year follow-up of offspring growth effects. *Neurotoxicology & Teratology, 24*, 703–710.

Cornwell, A., & Feigenbaum, P. (2006). Sleep biological rhythms in normal infants and those at high risk for SIDS. *Chronobiology International, 23*, 935–961.

Corsaro, W., Molinari, L., Hadley, K., & Sugioka, H. (2003). Keeping and making friends: Italian children's transition from preschool to elementary school. *Social Psychology Quarterly, 66*, 272–292.

Costello, E., Sung, M., Worthman, C., & Angold, A. (2007). Pubertal maturation and the development of alcohol use and abuse. *Drug and Alcohol Dependence, 88*, S50–S59.

Cotton, L., Bynum, D., & Madhere, S. (1997). Socialization forces and the stability of work values from late adolescence to early adulthood. *Psychological Reports, 80*, 115–124.

Cottrell, L., Northrup, K., & Wittberg, R. (2007). The extended relationship between child cardiovascular risks and academic performance measures. *Journal of Obesity Research, 15*, 3170–3177.

Coulthard, H., & Harris, G. (2003). Early food refusal: The role of maternal mood. *Journal of Reproductive & Infant Psychology, 21*, 335–345.

Courage, M., & Howe, M. (2002). From infant to child: The dynamics of cognitive change in the second year of life. *Psychological Bulletin, 128*, 250–277.

Coury, D. (2002). Developmental & behavioral pediatrics. In A. Rudolph, R. Kamei, & K. Overby (Eds.), *Rudolph's fundamentals of pediatrics* (3rd ed., pp. 110–124). New York: McGraw-Hill.

Cowan, B. R., & Underwood, M. K. (1995, March). Sugar and spice and everything nice? A developmental investigation of social aggression among girls. Paper presented at the biennial meetings of the Society for Research in Child Development, Indianapolis.

Cramer, P. (2000). Defense mechanisms in psychology today. *American Psychologist, 55*, 637–646.

Cramer-Berness, L. (2006). A comparison of behavioral interventions for infant immunizations. Unpublished dissertation, State University of New York at Binghamton.

Cramond, B. (2004). Can we, should we, need we agree on a definition of giftedness? *Roeper Review, 27*, 15–16.

Crick, N. R., & Dodge, K. (1994). A review and reformulation of social information processing mechanisms in children's social adjustment. *Psychological Bulletin, 115*, 74–101.

Crick, N. R., & Dodge, K. (1996). Social information-processing mechanisms in reactive and proactive aggression. *Child Development, 67*, 993–1002.

Crick, N. R., & Grotpeter, J. K. (1995). Relational aggression, gender, and social-psychological adjustment. *Child Development, 66*, 710–722.

Crittenden, P. M. (1992). Quality of attachment in the preschool years. *Development & Psychopathology, 4*, 209–241.

Crittenden, P. M. (2000). Introduction. In P. Crittenden & A. Claussen (Eds.), *The organisation of attachment relationships: Maturation, culture and context.* Cambridge, UK: Cambridge University Press.

Crittenden, P. M., Partridge, M. F., & Claussen, A. H. (1991). Family patterns of relationship in normative and dysfunctional families. *Development & Psychopathology, 3*, 491–512.

Crncec, R., Wilson, S., & Prior, M. (2006). The cognitive and academic benefits of music to children: Facts and fiction. *Educational Psychology, 26*, 579–594.

Crockenberg, S. (2003). Rescuing the baby from the bathwater: How gender and temperament (may) influence how child care affects child development. *Child Development, 74*, 1034–1038.

Crockenberg, S., Leerkes, E., & Lekka, S. (2007). Pathways from marital aggression to infant emotion regulation: The development of withdrawal in infancy. *Infant Behavior & Development, 30*, 97–113.

Crockenberg, S., & Litman, C. (1990). Autonomy as competence in 2-year-olds: Maternal correlates of child defiance, compliance, and self-assertion. *Developmental Psychology, 26*, 961–971.

Crockett, D. (2003). Critical issues children face in the 2000s. *School Psychology Quarterly, 18*, 446–453.

Crone, E., & van der Molen, M. (2004). Developmental changes in real life decision making: Performance on a gambling task previously shown to depend on the ventromedial prefrontal cortex. *Developmental Neuropsychology, 25*, 251–279.

Crook, C. (1987). Taste and olfaction. In P. Salapatek & L. Cohen (Eds.), *Handbook of infant perception, Vol. 1: From sensation to perception* (pp. 237–264). Orlando, FL: Academic Press.

Crowley, S., Acebo, C., & Carskadon, M. (2006). Sleep, circadian rhythms, and delayed phase in adolescence. *Sleep Medicine, 8*, 602–612.

Cuffe, S., Moore, C., & McKeown, R. (2005). Prevalence and correlates of ADHD symptoms in the National Health Interview Survey. *Journal of Attention Disorders, 9*, 392–401.

Cummings, E. M., & Davies, P. T. (1994). Maternal depression and child development. *Journal of Child Psychology & Psychiatry, 35*, 73–112.

Cummings, E. M., Hollenbeck, B., Iannotti, R., Radke-Yarrow, M., & Zahn-Waxler, C. (1986). Early organization of altruism and aggression: Developmental patterns and individual differences. In C. Zahn-Waxler, E. M. Cummings, & R. Iannotti (Eds.), *Altruism and aggression* (pp. 165–188). Cambridge, England: Cambridge University Press.

Cunningham, M., Swanson, D., Spencer, M., & Dupree, D. (2003). The association of physical maturation with family hassles among African American adolescent males. *Cultural Diversity & Ethnic Minority Psychology, 9*, 276–288.

Currie, A., Shields, M., & Wheatley Price, S. (2004). Is the child health/family income gradient universal? Evidence from England. *Journal of Health Economics, 26*, 213–232.

Currie, J., & Stabile, M. (2003). Socioeconomic status and child health: Why is the relationship stronger for older children? *American Economic Review, 93*, 1813–1823.

Curry, C. (2002). An approach to clinical genetics. In A. Rudolph, R. Kamei, & K. Overby (Eds.), *Rudolph's fundamentals of pediatrics.* (pp. 184–220). New York: McGraw-Hill.

Cushner, K., McClelland, A., & Safford, P. (1992). *Human diversity in education.* New York: McGraw–Hill.

Cuvo, A. (1974). Incentive level influence on overt rehearsal and free recall as a function of age. *Journal of Experimental Child Psychology, 18*, 167–181.

Dahl, G. (2007). Early teen marriage and future poverty. Retrieved June 26, 2008 from http://www.nber.org/papers/w11328.pdf.

D'Alton, M. E., & DeCherney, A. H. (1993). Prenatal diagnosis. *New England Journal of Medicine, 328*, 114–118.

Daly, L. E., Kirke, P. N., Molloy, A., Weir, D. G., & Scott, J. M. (1995). Folate levels and neural tube defects: Implications for prevention. *Journal of the American Medical Association, 274*, 1698–1702.

Daly, M., & Wilson, M. (1996) Violence against stepchildren. *Current Directions in Psychological Science, 5*, 77–81.

Daly, S., & Glenwick, D. (2000). Personal adjustment and perceptions of grandchild behavior in custodial grandmothers. *Journal of Clinical Child Psychology, 29*, 108–118.

Dammeijer, P., Schlundt, B., Chenault, M., Manni, J., & Anteunis, l. (2002). Effects of early auditory deprivation and stimulation on auditory brainstem responses in the rat. *Acta Oto-Laryngologica, 122*, 703–708.

Damon, W. (1977). *The social world of the child.* San Francisco: Jossey-Bass.

Damon, W., & Hart, D. (1988). *Self understanding in childhood and adolescence.* New York: Cambridge University Press.

Danby, S., & Baker, C. (1998). How to be masculine in the block area. *Childhood: A Global Journal of Child Research, 5*, 151–175.

Dark, V. J., & Benbow, C. P. (1993). Cognitive differences among the gifted: A review and new data. In D. Detterman (Ed.), *Current topics in human intelligence: Vol. 3. Individual differences and cognition* (pp. 85–120). Norwood, NJ: Ablex.

Darlington, R. B. (1991). The long-term effects of model preschool programs. In L. Okagaki & R. J. Sternberg (Eds.), *Directors of development* (pp. 203–215). Hillsdale, NJ: Erlbaum.

Davenport, E. (1992). The making of minority scientists and engineers. Invited address presented at the annual meeting of the American Educational Research Association, San Francisco.

Davenport, E., Davison, M., Kuang, H., Ding, S., Kim, S., & Kwak, N. (1998). High school mathematics course-taking by gender and ethnicity. *American Educational Research Journal, 35*, 497–514.

Davey, M., Fish, L., Askew, J., & Robila, M. (2003). Parenting practices and the transmission of ethnic identity. *Journal of Marital & Family Therapy, 29*, 195–208.

Davies, P., & Rose, J. (1999). Assessment of cognitive development in adolescents by means of neuropsychological tasks. *Developmental Neuropsychology, 15*, 227–248.

Dawood, K., Pillard, R., Horvath, C., Revelle, W., & Bailey, J. (2000). Familial aspects of male homosexuality. *Archives of Sexual Behavior, 29*, 155–163.

Dawson, D. A. (1991). Family structure and children's health and well-being: Data from the 1988 National Health Interview Survey on child health. *Journal of Marriage & the Family, 53*, 573–584.

DeBell, M., & Chapman, C. (2006). Computer and Internet use by students in 2003. Retrieved June 20, 2007 from http://nces.ed.gov/pubs2006/2006065.pdf.

DeCasper, A. J., & Fifer, W. (1980). Of human bonding: Newborns prefer their mothers' voices. *Science, 208*, 1174–1176.

DeCasper, A. J., & Lecaneut, J., Busnel, M., Granier-DeFerre, C., & Maugeais, R. (1994). Fetal reactions to recurrent maternal speech. *Infant Behavior & Development, 17,* 159–164.

DeCasper, A. J., & Spence, M. J. (1986). Prenatal maternal speech influences newborns' perception of speech sounds. *Infant Behavior and Development, 9,* 133–150.

Deci, E., Koestner, R., & Ryan, R. (1999). A meta-analytic review of experiments examining the effects of extrinsic rewards on intrinsic motivation. *Psychological Bulletin, 125,* 627–668.

Degirmencioglu, S., Urberg, K., & Tolson, J. (1998). Adolescent friendship networks: Continuity and change over the school year. *Merrill-Palmer Quarterly, 44,* 313–337.

de Haan, M., Luciana, M., Maslone, S. M., Matheny, L. S., & Richards, M. L. M. (1994). Development, plasticity, and risk: Commentary on Huttenlocher, Pollit and Gorman, and Gottesman and Goldsmith. In C. A. Nelson (Ed.), *The Minnesota Symposia on Child Psychology, Vol. 27* (pp. 161–178). Hillsdale, NJ: Erlbaum.

Dekovic, M. (1999). Parent-adolescent conflict: Possible determinants and consequences. *International Journal of Behavioral Development, 23,* 977–1000.

Dekovic, M., Noom, M., & Meeus, W. (1997). Expectations regarding development during adolescence: Parental and adolescent perceptions. *Journal of Youth & Adolescence, 26,* 253–272.

de Lacoste, M., Horvath, D., & Woodward, J. (1991). Possible sex differences in the developing human fetal brain. *Journal of Clinical & Experimental Neuropsychology, 13,* 831.

del Barrio, V., Moreno-Rosset, C., Lopez-Martinez, R., & Olmedo, M. (1997). Anxiety, depression and personality structure. *Personality & Individual Differences, 23,* 327–335.

Dellatolas, G., de Agostini, M., Curt, F., Kremin, H., Letierce, A., Maccario, J., & Lellouch, J. (2003). Manual skill, hand skill asymmetry, and cognitive performances in young children. *Laterality: Asymmetries of Body, Brain & Cognition, 8,* 317–338.

DeLoache, J., & Brown, A. (1987). Differences in the memory-based searching of delayed and normally developing young children. *Intelligence, 11,* 277–289.

DeMars, C. (2000). Test stakes and item format interactions. *Applied Measurement in Education, 13,* 55–77.

Demb, H., & Chang, C. (2004). The use of psychostimulants in children with disruptive behavior disorders and developmental disabilities in a community setting. *Mental Health Aspects of Developmental Disabilities, 7,* 26–36.

DeMulder, E., Denham, S., Schmidt, M., & Mitchell, J. (2000). Q-sort assessment of attachment security during the preschool years: Links from home to school. *Developmental Psychology, 36,* 274–282.

DeNavas-Walt, C., Proctor, B., & Smith, C. (2007). Income, poverty, and health insurance coverage in the United States: 2006. Retrieved June 20, 2008 from http://www.census.gov/prod/2007pubs/p60-233.pdf.

Denham, S. (2006). Social-emotional competence as support for school readiness: What is it and how do we assess it? *Early Education and Development, 17,* 57–89.

Denham, S., Blair, K., DeMulder, E., Levitas, J., Sawyer, K., Auerbach-Major, S., & Queenan, P. (2003). Preschool emotional competence: Pathway to social competence. *Child Development, 74,* 238–256.

Dennis, W. (1960). Causes of retardation among institutional children: Iran. *Journal of Genetic Psychology, 96,* 47–59.

Den Ouden, L., Rijken, M., Brand, R., Verloove-Vanhorick, S. P., & Ruys, J. H. (1991). Is it correct to correct? Developmental milestones in 555 "normal" preterm infants compared with term infants. *Journal of Pediatrics, 118,* 399–404.

DeRegnier, R., Wewerka, S., Georgieff, M., Mattia, F., & Nelson, C. (2002). Influences of postconceptional age and postnatal experience on the development of auditory recognition memory in the newborn infant. *Developmental Psychobiology, 41,* 215–225.

DeSchipper, J., Tevecchio, L., van IJzendoorn, M., & Linting, M. (2003). The relation of flexible child care to quality of center day care and children's socio-emotional functioning: A survey and observational study. *Infant Behavior and Development, 26* (3), 300–325.

Desrochers, S. (2008). From Piaget to specific Genevan developmental models. *Child Development Perspectives, 2,* 7–12.

Deter, H., & Herzog, W. (1994). Anorexia nervosa in a long-term perspective: Results of the Heidelberg-Mannheim study. *Psychosomatic Medicine, 56,* 20–27.

de Villiers, P. A., & de Villiers, J. G. (1992). Language development. In M. H. Bornstein & M. E. Lamb (Eds.), *Developmental psychology: An advanced textbook* (3rd ed., pp. 337–418). Hillsdale, NJ: Erlbaum.

Dezoete, J., MacArthur, B., & Tuck, B. (2003). Prediction of Bayley and Stanford-Binet scores with a group of very low birthweight children. *Child: Care, Health, & Development, 29,* 367–372.

Diagnostic and statistical manual of mental disorders IV: Text revision (DSM-IV TR). (2000). Washington, DC: American Psychiatric Association.

Diagram Group (1977). *Child's body.* New York: Paddington.

Diamond, A. (1991). Neuropsychological insights into the meaning of object concept development. In S. Carey & R. Gelman (Eds.), *The epigenesis of mind: Essays on biology and cognition* (pp. 67–110). Hillsdale, NJ: Erlbaum.

Diehl, L., Vicary, J., & Deike, R. (1997). Longitudinal trajectories of self-esteem from early to middle adolescence and related psychosocial variables among rural adolescents. *Journal of Research on Adolescence, 7,* 393–411.

Diener, M., & Kim, D. (2004). Maternal and child predictors of preschool children's social competence. *Journal of Clinical & Experimental Neuropsychology, 13,* 831.

Dieni, S., & Rees, S. (2003). Dendritic morphology is altered in hippocampal neurons following prenatal compromise. *Journal of Neurobiology, 55,* 41–52.

Diesendruck, G., & Shatz, M. (2001). Two-year-olds' recognition of hierarchies: Evidence from their interpretation of the semantic relation between object labels. *Cognitive Development, 16,* 577–594.

Dietz, W. (2001). Breastfeeding may help prevent childhood overweight. *JAMA: Journal of the American Medical Association, 285,* 2506–2507.

DiMario, F. (2002). The nervous system. In A. Rudolph, R. Kamei, & K. Overby (Eds.), *Rudolph's fundamentals of pediatrics* (3rd ed., pp. 796–846). New York: McGraw-Hill.

D'Imperio, R., Dubow, E., & Ippolito, M. (2000). Resilient and stress-affected adolescents in an urban setting. *Journal of Clinical Child Psychology, 29,* 129–142.

Dinkes, R., Cataldi, E., Lin-Kelly, W., & Snyder, T. (2007). Indicators of school crime and safety 2007. Retrieved June 29, 2008 from http://www.ojp.usdoj.gov/bjs/pub/pdf/iscs07.pdf.

Dion, K., & Berscheid, E. (1974). Physical attractiveness and peer perception among children. *Sociometry, 37,* 1–12.

DiPietro, J., Hodgson, D., Costigan, K., Hilton, S., & Johnson, T. (1996). Fetal neurobehavioral development. *Child Development, 67,* 2553–2567.

DiPietro, J., Hodgson, D., Costigan, K., & Johnson, T. (1996). Fetal antecedents of infant temperament. *Child Development, 67,* 2568–2583.

Dishion, T. J., French, D. C., & Patterson, G. R. (1995). The development and ecology of antisocial behavior. In D. Cicchetti & D. J. Cohen (Eds.), *Developmental psychopathology, Vol. 2: Risk, disorder, and adaptation* (pp. 421–471). New York: Wiley.

Dishion, T. J., Patterson, G. R., Stoolmiller, M., & Skinner, M. L. (1991). Family, school, and behavioral antecedents to early adolescent involvement with antisocial peers. *Developmental Psychology, 27*, 172–180.

Dixon, M., & Kaminska, Z. (2007). Does exposure to orthography affect children's spelling accuracy? *Journal of Research in Reading, 30*, 184–197.

Dixon, S., & Stein, M. (2006). *Encounters with children: Pediatric behavior and development.* Philadelphia: Mosby Elsevier.

Dockett, S., & Smith, I. (1995, March). Children's theories of mind and their involvement in complex shared pretense. Paper presented at the biennial meetings of the Society for Research in Child Development, Indianapolis.

Doctoroff, S. (1997). Sociodramatic script training and peer role prompting: Two tactics to promote sociodramatic play and peer interaction. *Early Child Development & Care, 136*, 27–43.

Dodge, K. (1993). Social-cognitive mechanisms in the development of conduct disorder and depression. *Annual Review of Psychology, 44*, 559–584.

Doh, H., & Falbo, T. (1999). Social competence, maternal attentiveness, and overprotectiveness: Only children in Korea. *International Journal of Behavioral Development, 23*, 149–162.

Dollard, J., Doob, L. W., Miller, N. E., Mowrer, O. H., & Sears, R. R. (1939). *Frustration and aggression.* New Haven, CT: Yale University Press.

Donenberg, G., Emerson, E., Bryant, F., & King, S. (2006). Does substance use moderate the effects of parents and peers on risky sexual behavior? *AIDS Care, 18*, 194–200.

Donnellan, M. B., Trzesniewski, K. H., Robins, R. W., Moffitt, T. E., & Caspi, A. (2005). Low self-esteem is related to aggression, antisocial behavior, and delinquency. *Psychological Science, 16*, 328–335.

Donnerstein, E., Slaby, R. G., & Eron, L. D. (1994). The mass media and youth aggression. In L. D. Eron, J. H. Gentry, & P. Schlegel (Eds.), *Reason to hope: A psychosocial perspective on violence and youth* (pp. 219–250). Washington, DC: American Psychological Association.

Donohew, R., Hoyle, R., Clayton, R., Skinner, W., Colon, S., & Rice, R. (1999). Sensation seeking and drug use by adolescents and their friends: Models for marijuana and alcohol. *Journal of Studies on Alcohol, 60*, 622–631.

Dorn, L., Dahl, R., Williamson, D., Birmaher, B., Axelson, D., Perel, J., Stull, S., & Ryan, N. (2003). Developmental markers in adolescence: Implications for studies of pubertal processes. *Journal of Youth & Adolescence, 32*, 315–324.

Dornbusch, S. M., Ritter, P. L., Liederman, P. H., Roberts, D. F., & Fraleigh, M. J. (1987). The relation of parenting style to adolescent school performance. *Child Development, 58*, 1244–1257.

Douglas, E. (2006). Familial violence socialization in childhood and later life approval of corporal punishment: A cross-cultural perspective. *American Journal of Orthopsychiatry, 76*, 23–30.

Douglas-Hall, A., & Chau, M. (2007). *Basic facts about low-income children, Birth to age 18.* Retrieved March 18, 2008 from http://nccp.org/publications/pub_762.html.

Dowd, J. (2004). Maternal health, health behaviors, and the childhood health gradient. Paper presented at the Office of Population Research, Princeton University, April.

Dowd, J. (2007). Early childhood origins of the income-health gradient: The role of maternal health behaviors. *Social Science and Medicine, 65*, 1202–1213.

Downey, D. (2001). Number of siblings and intellectual development: The resource dilution explanation. *American Psychologist, 56*, 497–504.

Doyle, A. B., & Aboud, F. E. (1995). A longitudinal study of white children's racial prejudice as a social-cognitive development. *Merrill-Palmer Quarterly, 41*, 209–228.

Dreher, G. F., & Bretz, R. D., Jr. (1991). Cognitive ability and career attainment: Moderating effects of early career success. *Journal of Applied Psychology, 76*, 392–397.

Droege, K., & Stipek, D. (1993). Children's use of dispositions to predict classmates' behavior. *Developmental Psychology, 29*, 646–654.

Drum, P. (1985). Retention of text information by grade, ability and study. *Discourse Processes, 8*, 21–52.

Dunphy, D. C. (1963). The social structure of urban adolescent peer groups. *Sociometry, 26*, 230–246.

Duvall, S., Delquadri, J., & Ward, D. (2004). A preliminary investigation of the effectiveness of homeschool instructional environments for students with attention-deficit/hyperactivity disorder. *School Psychology Review, 33*, 140–158.

Dwairy, M. (2008). Parental inconsistency versus parental authoritarianism: Associations with symptoms of psychological disorders. *Journal of Youth and Adolescence, 37*, 616–626.

Dwairy, M., & Menshar, K. (2005). Parenting style, individuation, and mental health of Egyptian adolescents. *Journal of Adolescence, 29*, 103–117.

DYG, Inc. (2004). What grown-ups understand about children: A national benchmark survey. Retrieved June 15, 2007, from www.zerotothree.org/site/DocServer/surveyexecutivesummary.pdf?docID=821&AddInterest=1153.

Dyl, J., Kittler, J., Phillips, K., & Hunt, J. (2006). Body dysmorphic disorder and other clinically significant body image concerns in adolescent psychiatric inpatients: Prevalance and clinical characteristics. *Child Psychiatry and Human Development, 36*, 369–382.

Eagle, R. (1975). Deprivation of early sensorimotor experience and cognition in the severely involved cerebral-palsied child. *Journal of Autism and Developmental Disorders, 15*, 269–283.

Eamon, M., & Mulder, C. (2005). Predicting antisocial behavior among Latino young adolescents: An ecological systems analysis. *American Journal of Orthopsychiatry, 75*, 117–127.

Ecalle, J., Magan, A., & Gibert, F. (2007). Class size effects on literacy skills and literacy interest in first grade: A large-scale investigation. *Journal of School Psychology, 44*, 191–209.

Eccles, J., Jacobs, J., & Harold, R. (1990). Gender role stereotypes, expectancy effects, and parents' socialization of gender differences. *Journal of Social Issues, 46*, 183–201.

Eckensberger, E., & Zimba, R. (1997). The development of moral judgment. In J. Berry, P. Dasen, & T. Saraswathi (Eds.), *Handbook of cross-cultural psychology, Vol. 2* (pp. 299–328). Boston: Allyn & Bacon.

Education Trust. (1996). *Education watch: The 1996 Education Trust state and national data book.* Washington, DC: Author.

Egan, S. K., & Perry, D. G. (1998). Does low self-regard invite victimization? *Developmental Psychology, 34*, 299–309.

Eiden, R., Foote, A., & Schuetze, P. (2007). Maternal cocaine use and caregiving status: Group differences in caregiver and infant risk variables. *Addictive Behaviors, 32*, 465–476.

Einerson, M. (1998). Fame, fortune, and failure: Young girls' moral language surrounding popular culture. *Youth & Society, 30*, 241–257.

Eisenberg, N. (1992). *The caring child.* Cambridge, MA: Harvard University Press.

Eisenberg, N. (2000). Emotion, regulation, and moral development. *Annual Review of Psychology, 51*, 665–697.

Eisenberg, N., Fabes, R. A., Murphy, B., Karbon, M., Smith, M., & Maszk, P. (1996). The relations of children's dispositional empathy-related responding to their emotionality, regulation, and social functioning. *Developmental Psychology, 32*, 195–209.

Eisenberg, N., Fabes, R. A., Murphy, B., Maszk, P., Smith, M., & Karbon, M. (1995). The role of emotionality and regulation in children's social functioning: A longitudinal study. *Child Development, 66*, 1360–1384.

Eisenberg, N., Guthrie, I., Murphy, B., Shepard, S., et al. (1999). Consistency and development of prosocial dispositions: A longitudinal study. *Child Development, 70*, 1360–1372.

Eisenberger, R., Pierce, W., & Cameron, J. (1999). Effects of reward on intrinsic motivation—negative, neutral, and positive: Comment on Deci, Koestner, and Ryan. *Psychological Bulletin, 125*, 677–691.

Elbedour, S., Baker, A., & Charlesworth, W. (1997). The impact of political violence on moral reasoning in children. *Child Abuse & Neglect, 21*, 1053–1066.

Eley, T., Liang, H., Plomin, R., Sham, P., Sterne, A., Williamson, R., & Purcell, S. (2004). Parental familial vulnerability, family environment, and their interactions as predictors of depressive symptoms in adolescents. *Journal of the American Academy of Child Psychiatry, 43*, 298–306.

Ellsworth, C. P., Muir, D. W., & Hains, S. M. J. (1993). Social competence and person-object differentiation: An analysis of the still-face effect. *Developmental Psychology, 29*, 63–73.

Emde, R. N., Plomin, R., Robinson, J., Corley, R., DeFries, J., Fulker, D. W., Reznick, J. S., Campos, J., Kagan, J., & Zahn-Waxler, C. (1992). Temperament, emotion, and cognition at fourteen months: The MacArthur longitudinal twin study. *Child Development, 63*, 1437–1455.

Emery, R., & Laumann-Billings, L. (1998). An overview of the nature, causes, and consequencess of abusive family relationships: Toward differentiating maltreatment and violence. *American Psychologist, 53*, 121–135.

Ensign, J. (1998). Defying the stereotypes of special education: Homeschool students. Paper presented at the annual meeting of the American Education Research Association, San Diego.

Entwisle, D. R., & Alexander, K. L. (1990). Beginning school math competence: Minority and majority comparisons. *Child Development, 61*, 454–471.

Ericsson, K. A., & Crutcher, R. J. (1990). The nature of exceptional performance. In P. B. Baltes, D. L. Featherman, & R. M. Lerner (Eds.), *Life-span development and behavior, Vol. 10* (pp. 188–218). Hillsdale, NJ: Erlbaum.

Erikson, E. H. (1950). *Childhood and society.* New York: Norton.

Erikson, E. H. (1959). *Identity and the life cycle.* New York: Norton (reissued, 1980).

Erikson, E. H. (1963). *Childhood and society* (2nd ed.). New York: Norton.

Erikson, E. H. (1980a). *Identity and the life cycle.* New York: Norton (originally published 1959).

Erikson, E. H. (1980b). Themes of adulthood in the Freud-Jung correspondence. In N. J. Smelser & E. Erikson (Eds.), *Themes of work and love in adulthood* (pp. 43–76). Cambridge, MA: Harvard University Press.

Erikson, E. H. (1982). *The life cycle completed.* New York: Norton.

Erikson, E. H., Erikson, J. M., & Kivnick, H. Q. (1986). *Vital involvement in old age.* New York: Norton.

Eron, L. D., Huesmann, L. R., & Zelli, A. (1991). The role of parental variables in the learning of aggression. In D. J. Pepler & K. H. Rubin (Eds.), *The development and treatment of childhood aggression* (pp. 169–188). Hillsdale, NJ: Erlbaum.

Escorihuela, R. M., Tobena, A., & Fernández-Teruel, A. (1994). Environmental enrichment reverses the detrimental action of early inconsistent stimulation and increases the beneficial effects of postnatal handling on shuttlebox learning in adult rats. *Behavioral Brain Research, 61*, 169–173.

Eskes, T. K. A. B. (1992). Home deliveries in the Netherlands—perinatal mortality and morbidity. *International Journal of Gynecology & Obstetrics, 38*, 161–169.

Eslea, M., Menesini, E., Morita, Y., O'Moore, M., Mora-Merchan, J., Pereira, B., & Smith, P. (2004). Friendship and loneliness among bullies and victims: Data from seven countries. *Aggressive Behavior, 30*, 71–83.

Espy, K., Stalets, M., McDiarmid, M., Senn, T., Cwik, M., & Hamby, A. (2002). Executive functions in preschool children born preterm: Application of cognitive neuroscience paradigms. *Child Neuropsychology, 8*, 83–92.

Etaugh, C., & Liss, M. (1992). Home, school, and playroom: Training grounds for adult gender roles. *Sex Roles, 26*, 129–147.

Evans, G. (2004). The environment of childhood poverty. *American Psychologist, 59*, 77–92.

Evans, R. I. (1969). *Dialogue with Erik Erikson.* New York: Dutton.

Evans, R. I., & Erikson, E. (1967). *Dialogue with Erik Erikson.* New York: Harper & Row.

Ex, C., & Janssens, J. (1998). Maternal influences on daughters' gender role attitudes. *Sex Roles, 38*, 171–186.

Fabes, R. A., Knight, G. P., & Higgins, D. A. (1995, March). Gender differences in aggression: A meta-analytic reexamination of time and age effects. Paper presented at the biennial meetings of the Society for Research in Child Development, Indianapolis.

Fagan, J. F. (2000). A theory of intelligence as processing: Implications for society. *Psychology, Public Policy, & Law, 6*, 168–179.

Fagan, J. F., & Detterman, D. K. (1992). The Fagan Test of Infant Intelligence: A technical summary. *Journal of Applied Developmental Psychology, 13*, 173–193.

Fagan, J. F., & Holland, C. (2002). Equal opportunity and racial differences in IQ. *Intelligence, 30*, 361–387.

Fagan, J. F., & Singer, L. T. (1983). Infant recognition memory as a measure of intelligence. In L. P. Lipsett (Ed.), *Advances in infancy research, Vol. 2* (pp. 31–78). Norwood, NJ: Ablex.

Fagard, J., & Jacquet, A. (1989). Onset of bimanual coordination and symmetry versus asymmetry of movement. *Infant Behavior & Development, 12*, 229–235.

Fagot, B. I., & Hagan, R. (1991). Observations of parent reactions to sex-stereotyped behaviors: Age and sex effects. *Child Development, 62*, 617–628.

Fagot, B. I., & Leinbach, M. D. (1993). Gender-role development in young children: From discrimination to labeling. *Developmental Review, 13*, 205–224.

Fairclough, S., Stratton, G., & Baldwin, B. (2002). The contribution of secondary school physical education to lifetime physical activity. *European Physical Education Review, 8*, 69–84.

Falbo, T. (1992). Social norms and one-child family: Clinical and policy limitations. In F. Boer & J. Dunn (Eds.), *Children's sibling relationships* (pp. 71–82). Hillsdale, NJ: Erlbaum.

Fallis, R., & Opotow, S. (2003). Are students failing school or are schools failing students? Class cutting in high school. *Journal of Social Issues, 59*, 103–119.

Fantuzzo, J., Coolahan, K., & Mendez, J. (1998). Contextually relevant validation of peer play constructs with African American Head Start children: Penn Interactive Peer Play Scale. *Early Childhood Research Quarterly, 13*, 411–431.

Fantuzzo, J., Sekino, Y., & Cohen, H. (2004). An examination of the contributions of interactive peer play to salient classroom competencies for urban Head Start children. *Psychology in the Schools, 41*, 323–336.

Fantz, R. L. (1956). A method for studying early visual development. *Perceptual & Motor Skills, 6*, 13–15.

Farmer, T., Estell, D., Leung, M., Trott, H., Bishop, J., & Cairns, B. (2003). Individual characteristics, early adolescent peer affiliations, and school dropout: An examination of aggressive and popular group types. *Journal of School Psychology, 41*, 217–232.

Farnham-Diggory, S. (1992). *The learning-disabled child.* Cambridge, MA: Harvard University Press.

Farrar, M. J. (1992). Negative evidence and grammatical morpheme acquisition. *Developmental Psychology, 28*, 90–98.

Farver, J. (1996). Aggressive behavior in preschoolers' social networks: Do birds of a feather flock together? *Early Childhood Research Quarterly, 11*, 333–350.

Farver, J., Bhadha, B., & Narang, S. (2002). Acculturation and psychological functioning in Asian Indian adolescents. *Social Development, 11*, 11–29.

Featherman, D. (1980). Schooling and occupational careers: Constancy and change in worldly success. In O. Brim & J. Kagan (Eds.), *Constancy and change in human development* (pp. 675–738). Cambridge, MA: Harvard University Press.

Federal Interagency Forum on Child and Family Statistics (FIFCFS). (2005). America's children in brief: Key national indicators of well-being, 2005. Retrieved May 18, 2007 from www.childstats.gov/pubs.asp.

Federal Interagency Forum on Child and Family Statistics (FIFCFS). (2007). America's children in brief: Key national indicators of well-being, 2007. Retrieved May 12, 2008 from http://childstats.gov/americaschildren/index.asp.

Fein, J., Durbin, D., & Selbst, S. (2002). Injuries & emergencies. In A. Rudolph, R. Kamei, & K. Overby (Eds.), *Rudolph's fundamentals of pediatrics* (3rd ed., pp. 390–436). New York: McGraw-Hill.

Feiring, C. (1999). Other-sex friendship networks and the development of romantic relationships in adolescence. *Journal of Youth & Adolescence, 28*, 495–512.

Feldman, D. (2004). Piaget's stages: The unfinished symphony of cognitive development. *New Ideas in Psychology, 22*, 175–231.

Feldman, R. (2003). Paternal socio-psychological factors and infant attachment: The mediating role of synchrony in father-infant interactions. *Infant Behavior & Development, 25*, 221–236.

Feng, J., Spence, I., & Pratt, J. (2007). Playing an action video game reduces gender differences in spatial cognition. *Psychological Science, 18*, 850–855.

Fenson, L., Dale, P. S., Reznick, J. S., Bates, E., Thal, D. J., & Pethick, S. J. (1994). Variability in early communicative development. *Monographs of the Society for Research in Child Development, 59* (5, Serial No. 242).

Fergusson, D. M., Horwood, L. J., & Lynskey, M. T. (1993). Maternal smoking before and after pregnancy: Effects on behavioral outcomes in middle childhood. *Pediatrics, 92*, 815–822.

Fernald, A., & Kuhl, P. (1987). Acoustic determinants of infant preference for motherese speech. *Infant Behavior & Development, 10*, 279–293.

Field, T. (1995). Psychologically depressed parents. In M. H. Bornstein (Ed.), *Handbook of parenting, Vol. 4: Applied and practical parenting* (pp. 85–99). Mahwah, NJ: Erlbaum.

fightingautism.org. (2008). Number of cases. Retrieved June 10, 2008 from http://www.fightingautism.org/idea/autism.php.

Figueras-Costa, B., & Harris, P. (2001). Theory of mind development in deaf children: A nonverbal test of false belief understanding. *Journal of Deaf Studies and Deaf Education, 6*, 92–102.

Filipek, P., Steinberg-Epstein, R., & Book, T. (2006). Intervention for autism spectrum disorders. *Pediatric Neuropathy, 3*, 207–216.

Findlay, L., Girardi, A., & Coplan, R. (2006). Links between empathy, social behavior, and social understanding. *Early Childhood Research Quarterly, 21*, 347–359.

Findling, R., Feeny, N., Stansbrey, R., Delporto-Bedoya, D., & Demeter, C. (2004). Special articles: Treatment of mood disorders in children and adolescents: Somatic treatment for depressive illnesses in children and adolescents. *Psychiatric Clinics of North America, 27*, 113–137.

Finer, L. (2007). Trends in premarital sex in the United States, 1954–2003. *Public Health Reports, 122*, 73–78.

Fischer, K. W., & Bidell, T. (1991). Constraining nativist inferences about cognitive capacities. In S. Carey & R. Gelman (Eds.), *The epigenesis of mind: Essays on biology and cognition* (pp. 199–236). Hillsdale, NJ: Erlbaum.

Fischer, K. W., & Rose, S. (1994). Dynamic development of coordination of components in brain and behavior: A framework for theory and research. In K. Fischer & G. Dawson (Eds.), *Human behavior and the developing brain* (pp. 3–66). New York: Guilford Press.

Fish, M., Stifter, C. A., & Belsky, J. (1991). Conditions of continuity and discontinuity in infant negative emotionality: Newborn to five months. *Child Development, 62*, 1525–1537.

Fitzgerald, B. (1999). Children of lesbian and gay parents: A review of the literature. *Marriage & Family Review, 29*, 57–75.

Fitzgerald, D., & White, K. (2003). Linking children's social worlds: Perspective-taking in parent-child and peer contexts. *Social Behavior & Personality, 31*, 509–522.

Fitzgerald, M. (2004). The case of Robert Walser. *Irish Journal of Psychological Medicine, 21*, 138–142.

Fitzpatrick, J. L., & Silverman, T. (1989). Women's selection of careers in engineering: Do traditional-nontraditional differences still exist? *Journal of Vocational Behavior, 34*, 266–278.

Flannery, D., Vazsonyi, A., Embry, D., Powell, K., Atha, H., Vesterdal, W., & Shenyang, G. (2000, August). Longitudinal effectiveness of the Peace-Builders' universal school-based violence prevention program. Paper presented at the annual meeting of the American Psychological Association, Washington, DC.

Flannery, D. J., Montemayor, R., & Eberly, M. B. (1994). The influence of parent negative emotional expression on adolescents' perceptions of their relationships with their parents. *Personal Relationships, 1*, 259–274.

Flavell, J. H. (1963). *The developmental psychology of Jean Piaget.* New York: D. Van Nostrand.

Flavell, J. H. (1985). *Cognitive development* (2nd ed.). Englewood Cliffs, NJ: Prentice-Hall.

Flavell, J. H. (1986). The development of children's knowledge about the appearance-reality distinction. *American Psychologist, 41*, 418–425.

Flavell, J. H. (1993). Young children's understanding of thinking and consciousness. *Current Directions in Psychological Science, 2*, 40–43.

Flavell, J. H. (1999). Cognitive development: Children's knowledge about the mind. *Annual Review of Psychology, 50*, 21–45.

Flavell, J. H., Everett, B. A., Croft, K., & Flavell, E. R. (1981). Young children's knowledge about visual perception: Further evidence for the Level 1–Level 2 distinction. *Developmental Psychology, 17*, 99–103.

Flavell, J. H., Green, F. L., & Flavell, E. R. (1990). Developmental changes in young children's knowledge about the mind. *Cognitive Development, 5*, 1–27.

Flavell, J. H., Green, F. L., Wahl, K. E., & Flavell, E. R. (1987). The effects of question clarification and memory aids on young children's performance on appearance-reality tasks. *Cognitive Development, 2*, 127–144.

Floyd, F., & Bakeman, R. (2006). Coming-out across the life course: Implications of age and historical context. *Archives of Sexual Behavior, 35*, 287–297.

Flynn, J. (1999). Searching for justice: The discovery of IQ gains over time. *American Psychologist, 54*, 5–20.

Flynn, J. (2003). Movies about intelligence: The limitations of *g*. *Current Directions in Psychological Science, 12*, 95–99.

Flynn, R. (1999). Myopia. Retrieved March 28, 2008 from http://www2.vhi.ie/topic/myopia.

Foehr, U. (2006). Media multitasking among American youth: Prevalence, predictors and pairings. Menlo Park, CA: Henry J. Kaiser Foundation. Retrieved June 26, 2007 from http://kff.org/entmedia/upload/7592.pdf.

Foley, E. (2002). Drug screening and criminal prosecution of pregnant women. *Journal of Obstetric, Gynecologic, & Neonatal Nursing, 31*, 1331.

Fombonne, E., Zakarian, R., Bennett, A., Meng, L., & McLean-Heywood, D. (2006). Pervasive developmental disorders in Montreal, Quebec, Canada: Prevalence and links with immunizations. *Pediatrics, 118*, e139–e150.

Foorman, B., & Nixon, S. (2006). The influence of public policy on reading research and practice. *Topics in Language Disorders, 26*, 157–171.

Fordham, K., & Stevenson-Hinde, J. (1999). Shyness, friendship quality, and adjustment during middle childhood. *Journal of Child Psychology & Psychiatry & Allied Disciplines, 40*, 757–768.

Fouad, N. (2007). Work and vocational psychology: Theory, research, and counseling. *Annual Review of Psychology, 58*, 543–564.

Foulder-Hughes, L., & Cooke, R. (2003a). Do mainstream schoolchildren who were born preterm have motor problems? *British Journal of Occupational Therapy, 66*, 9–16.

Foulder-Hughes, L., & Cooke, R. (2003b). Motor, cognitive, and behavioural disorders in children born very preterm. *Developmental Medicine & Child Neurology, 45*, 97–103.

Fourn, L., Ducic, S., & Seguin, L. (1999). Smoking and intrauterine growth retardation in the Republic of Benin. *Journal of Epidemiology & Community Health, 53*, 432–433.

Fox, N., Henderson, H., Rubin, K., Calkins, S., & Schmidt, L. (2001). Continuity and discontinuity of behavioral inhibition and exuberance: Psychophysiological and behavioral influences across the first four years of life. *Child Development, 72*, 1–21.

Fox, N. A., Kimmerly, N. L., & Schafer, W. D. (1991). Attachment to mother/attachment to father: A meta-analysis. *Child Development, 62*, 210–225.

Francis, P. L., Self, P. A., & Horowitz, F. D. (1987). The behavioral assessment of the neonate: An overview. In J. D. Osofsky (Ed.), *Handbook of infant development* (2nd ed., pp. 723–779). New York: Wiley-Interscience.

Franco, N., & Levitt, M. (1998). The social ecology of middle childhood: Family support, friendship quality, and self-esteem. *Family Relations: Interdisciplinary Journal of Applied Family Studies, 47*, 315–321.

Frankenburg, W., & Dodds, J. (1990). *Denver Developmental Screening II (Denver II)*. Denver, CO: Denver Developmental Materials.

Fraser, A. M., Brockert, J. E., & Ward, R. H. (1995). Association of young maternal age with adverse reproductive outcomes. *New England Journal of Medicine, 332*, 1113–1117.

Fredriksen, K., Rhodes, J., Reddy, R., & Way, N. (2004). Sleepless in Chicago: Tracking the effects of adolescent sleep loss during the middle school years. *Child Development, 75*, 84–95.

Freeman, C., & Fox, M. (2005). Status and trends in the education of American Indians and Alaska Natives. Retrieved June 27, 2008 from http://nces.ed.gov/pubs2005/2005108.pdf.

Frey, K. S., & Ruble, D. N. (1992). Gender constancy and the "cost" of sex-typed behavior: A test of the conflict hypothesis. *Developmental Psychology, 28*, 714–721.

Friend, M., & Bursuck, W. (2006). *Including students with special needs: A practical guide for classroom teachers*. Boston: Allyn & Bacon.

Frisch, A., Laufer, N., Danziger, Y., Michaelovsky, E., Leor, S., Carel, C., Stein, D., Fenig, S., Mimouni, M., Apter, A., & Weizman, A. (2001). Association of anorexia nervosa with the high activity allele of the COMT gene: A family-based study in Israeli patients. *Molecular Psychiatry, 6*, 243–245.

Fry, R. (2003). Hispanic youth dropping out of U.S. schools: Measuring the challenge. Retrieved June 27, 2008 from http://pewhispanic.org/files/reports/19.pdf.

Fryar, C., Hirsch, R., Porter, K., Kottiri, B., Brody, D., & Louis, T. (2007). Drug use and sexual behaviors reported by adults: 1999–2002. *Vital and Health Statistics, 384*, 1–15.

Fuchs, L., Fuchs, D., & Zumeta, R. (2008). Response to intervention: A strategy for the prevention and identification of learning disabilities. In E. Grigorenko, (Ed.), *Educating individuals with disabilities: IDEIA 2004 and beyond* (pp. 115–135). New York: Spring Publishing Company.

Funk, J., Baldacci, H., Pasold, T., & Baumgardner, J. (2004). Violence exposure in real-life, video games, television, movies, and the Internet: Is there desensitization? *Journal of Adolescence, 27*, 23–39.

Funk, J., Buchman, D., Jenks, J., & Bechtoldt, H. (2003). Playing violent video games, desensitization, and moral evaluation in children. *Journal of Applied Developmental Psychology, 24*, 413–436.

Funk, J., Buchman, D., Myers, B., & Jenks, J. (2000, August). Asking the right questions in research on violent electronic games. Paper presented at the annual meeting of the American Psychological Association, Washington, DC.

Furman, L., Wilson-Costello, D., Friedman, H., Taylor, H., Minich, N., & Hack, M. (2004). The effect of neonatal maternal milk feeding on the neurodevelopmental outcome of very low birth weight infants. *Journal of Developmental & Behavioral Pediatrics, 25*, 247–253.

Furrow, D., & Nelson, K. (1984). Environmental correlates of individual differences in language acquisition. *Journal of Child Language, 11*, 523–534.

Fussell, J., & Burns, K. (2007). Attention deficit/hyperactivity disorder: A case study in differential diagnosis. *Clinical Pediatrics, 46*, 735–737.

Gabbard, C. (2008). *Lifelong motor development*. San Francisco: Benjamin Cummings.

Galambos, N., & Maggs, J. (1991). Out-of-school care of young adolescents and self-reported behavior. *Developmental Psychology, 27*, 644–655.

Galanaki, E. (2004). Teachers and loneliness: The children's perspective. *School Psychology International, 25*, 92–105.

Galassi, J., Gulledge, S., & Cox, N. (1997). Middle school advisories: Retrospect and prospect. *Review of Educational Research, 67*, 301–338.

Gallagher, A., Frith, U., & Snowling, M. (2000). Precursors of literacy delay among children at genetic risk of dyslexia. *Journal of Child Psychology & Psychiatry & Allied Disciplines, 41*, 202–213.

Gamoran, A., Porter, A., Smithson, J., & White, P. (1997). Upgrading high school mathematics instruction: Improving learning opportunities for low-achieving, low-income youth. *Educational Evaluation & Policy Analysis, 19*, 325–338.

Ganchrow, J. R., Steiner, J. E., & Daher, M. (1983). Neonatal facial expressions in response to different qualities and intensities of gustatory stimuli. *Infant Behavior & Development, 6*, 189–200.

Ganong, L., & Coleman, M. (1994). *Remarried family relationships*. Thousand Oaks, CA: Sage Publications.

Garces, E., Thomas, D., & Currie, J. (2002). Longer-term effects of Head Start. *American Economic Review, 92*, 999–1012.

Gardner, A. (2007). ADHD drugs need better warnings on heart, psychiatric risks: FDA. Retrieved June 19, 2007 from www.healthfinder.gov/news/newsstory.asp?docID=602115.

Gardner, H. (1983). *Frames of mind: The theory of multiple intelligence*. New York: Basic Books.

Gardner, H. (2003). Three distinct meaning of intelligence. In R. Sternberg, J. Lautrey, & T. Lubart (Eds.), *Models of intelligence: International perspectives* (pp. 43–54). Washington, DC: American Psychological Association.

Gardner, J., Karmel, B., Freedland, R., Lennon, E., Flory, M., Miroschnichenko, I., Phan, H., Barone, A., & Harm, A. (2006).

Arousal, attention, and neurobehavioral assessment in the neonatal period: Implications for intervention and policy. *Journal of Policy and Practice in Intellectual Disabilities, 3*, 22–32.

Garmezy, N. (1993). Vulnerability and resilience. In D. C. Funder, R. D. Parke, C. Tomlinson-Keasey, & K. Widaman (Eds.), *Studying lives through time: Personality and development* (pp. 377–398). Washington, DC: American Psychological Association.

Garmezy, N., & Rutter, M. (Eds.). (1983). *Stress, coping, and development in children.* New York: McGraw-Hill.

Garnier, H., Stein, J., & Jacobs, J. (1997). The process of dropping out of high school: A 19-year perspective. *American Educational Research Journal, 34*, 395–419.

Gartstein, M., & Rothbart, M. (2003). Studying infant temperament via the revised infant behavior questionnaire. *Infant Behavior & Development, 26*, 64–86.

Gass, K., Jenkins, J., & Dunn, J. (2007). Are sibling relationships protective? A longitudinal study. *Journal of Child Psychology and Psychiatry, 48*, 167–175.

Gathercole, S., Pickering, S., Ambridge, B., & Wearing, H. (2004). The structure of working memory from 4 to 15 years of age. *Developmental Psychology, 40*, 177–190.

Gaultney, J., & Gingras, J. (2005). Fetal rate of behavioral inhibition and preference for novelty during infancy. *Early Human Development, 81*, 379–386.

Gavazzi, S., Alford, K., & McKenry, P. (1996). Culturally specific programs for foster care youth: The sample case of an African American rites of passage program. *Family Relations: Journal of Applied Family & Child Studies, 45*, 166–174.

Gavazzi, S., & Law, J. (1997). Creating definitions of successful adulthood for families with adolescents: A therapeutic intervention from the Growing Up FAST program. *Journal of Family Psychotherapy, 8*, 21–38.

Ge, X., & Conger, R. (1999). Adjustment problems and emerging personality characteristics from early to late adolescence. *American Journal of Community Psychology, 27*, 429–459.

Geary, D., Lin, F., Chen, G., Saults, S., et al. (1999). Contributions of computational fluency to cross-national differences in arithmetical reasoning abilities. *Journal of Educational Psychology, 91*, 716–719.

Gee, C., & Rhodes, J. (1999). Postpartum transitions in adolescent mothers' romantic and maternal relationships. *Merrill-Palmer Quarterly, 45*, 512–532.

Gee, C., & Rhodes, J. (2003). Adolescent mothers' relationship with their children's biological fathers: Social support, social strain and relationship continuity. *Journal of Family Psychology, 17*, 370–383.

Gelman, R. (1972). Logical capacity of very young children: Number invariance rules. *Child Development, 43*, 75–90.

Gentile, D., Lynch, P., Linder, J., & Walsh, D. (2004). The effects of violent video game habits on adolescent hostility, aggressive behaviors, and school performance. *Journal of Adolescence, 27*, 5–22.

George, M. (2001). The challenge of culturally competent health care: Applications for asthma. *Heart & Lung: The Journal of Acute and Critical Care, 30*, 392–400.

Georgieff, M. K. (1994). Nutritional deficiencies as developmental risk factors: Commentary on Pollitt and Gorman. In C. A. Nelson (Ed.), *The Minnesota Symposia on Child Development, Vol. 27* (pp. 145–159). Hillsdale, NJ: Erlbaum.

Gergely, G. (2002). The development of understanding self and agency. In U. Goswami (Ed.). *Blackwell Handbook of Childhood Cognitive Development.* Boston: Blackwell Publishing.

Gerhardstein, P., Liu, J., & Rovee-Collier, C. (1998). Perceptual constraints on infant memory retrieval. *Journal of Experimental Child Psychology, 69*, 109–131.

Gershkoff-Stowe, L., & Hahn, E. (2007). Fast mapping skills in the developing lexicon. *Journal of Speech, Language, and Hearing Research, 50*, 682–696.

Gershoff, E. (2002). Corporal punishment by parents and associated child behaviors and experiences: A meta-analytic and theoretical review. *Psychological Bulletin, 128*, 539–579.

Gesell, A. (1925). *The mental growth of the preschool child.* New York: Macmillan.

Gibbs, R., & Beitel, D. (1995). What proverb understanding reveals about how people think. *Psychological Bulletin, 118*, 133–154.

Gibson, E. J., & Walk, R. D. (1960). The "visual cliff." *Scientific American, 202*, 80–92.

Giedd, J. (2004). Structural magnetic resonance imaging of the adolescent brain. *Annals of the New York Academy of Sciences, 1021*, 77–85.

Giedd, J., Blumenthal, J., & Jeffries, N. (1999). Brain development during childhood and adolescence: A longitudinal MRI study. *Nature Neuroscience, 2*, 861–863.

Gillies, V., & Lucey, H. (2006). "It's a connection you can't get away from": Brothers, sisters and social capital. *Journal of Youth Studies, 9*, 479–493.

Gilligan, C. (1982). *In a different voice: Psychological theory and women's development.* Cambridge, MA: Harvard University Press.

Gilligan, C., & Wiggins, G. (1987). The origins of morality in early childhood relationships. In J. Kagan & S. Lamb (Eds.), *The emergence of morality in young children* (pp. 277–307). Chicago: University of Chicago Press.

Gilman, E. A., Cheng, K. K., Winter, H. R., & Scragg, R. (1995). Trends in rates and seasonal distribution of sudden infant deaths in England and Wales, 1988–1992. *British Medical Journal, 30*, 631–632.

Gilman, S., Abrams, D., & Buka, S. (2003). Socioeconomic status over the life course and stages of cigarette use: Initiation, regular use, and cessation. *Journal of Epidemiology in Community Health, 57*, 802–808.

Glaser, D. (2000). Child abuse and neglect and the brain—a review. *Journal of Child Psychology & Psychiatry & Allied Disciplines, 41*, 97–116.

Glaubke, C., Miller, P., Parker, M., & Espejo, E. (2001). Fair play: Violence, gender, and race in video games. Retrieved June 28, 2007 from http://publications.childrennow.org/assets/pdf/cmp/fairplay/fair-play-video-01.pdf.

Gleitman, L. R., & Gleitman, H. (1992). A picture is worth a thousand words, but that's the problem: The role of syntax in vocabulary acquisition. *Current Directions in Psychological Science, 1*, 31–35.

Gnepp, J., & Chilamkurti, C. (1988). Children's use of personality attributions to predict other people's emotional and behavioral reactions. *Child Development, 50*, 743–754.

Gogtay, N., Giedd, J., Lusk, L., Hayashi, K., Greenstein, D., Vaituzis, A., Nugent, T., Herman, D., Clasen, L., Toga, A., Rapoport, J., & Thompson, P. (2004). Dynamic mapping of human cortical development during childhood through early adulthood. *Proceedings of the National Academy of Sciences, 17*, 17.

Goldberg, W. A. (1990). Marital quality, parental personality, and spousal agreement about perceptions and expectations for children. *Merrill-Palmer Quarterly, 36*, 531–556.

Goldfield, B. A. (1993). Noun bias in maternal speech to one-year-olds. *Journal of Child Language, 20*, 85–99.

Goldfield, B. A., & Reznick, J. S. (1990). Early lexical acquisition: Rate, content, and the vocabulary spurt. *Journal of Child Language, 17*, 171–183.

Golding, J., Emmett, P., & Rogers, I. (1997a). Does breast feeding protect against non-gastric infections? *Early Human Development, 49* (Supp.), S105–S120.

Golding, J., Emmett, P., & Rogers, I. (1997b). Gastroenteritis, diarrhea and breast feeding. *Early Human Development, 49* (Supp.), S83–S103.

Goldstein, R., & Volkow, N. (2002). Drug addiction and its underlying neurobiological basis: Neuroimaging evidence for the involvement of the frontal cortex. *American Journal of Psychiatry, 159*, 1642–1652.

Goleman, D. (1995). *Emotional intelligence.* New York: Bantam.

Golinkoff, R. M., Mervis, C. B., & Hirsh-Pasek, K. (1994). Early object labels: The case for lexical principles. *Journal of Child Language, 21*, 125–155.

Golombok, S., & Fivush, R. (1994). *Gender development.* Cambridge, England: Cambridge University Press.

Golombok, S., & Tasker, F. (1996). Do parents influence the sexual orientation of their children? Findings from a longitudinal study of lesbian families. *Developmental Psychology, 32*, 3–11.

Gomez, R., Bounds, J., Holmberg, K., Fullarton, C., & Gomez, A. (1999). Effects of neuroticism and avoidant coping style on maladjustment during early adolescence. *Personality & Individual Differences, 26*, 305–319.

Gomez, R., Gomez, A., & Cooper, A. (2002). Neuroticism and extraversion as predictors of negative and positive emotional information processing: Comparing Eysenck's, Gray's and Newman's theories. *European Journal of Personality, 16*, 333–350.

Gomez, R., Holmberg, K., Bounds, J., Fullarton, C., & Gomez, A. (1999). Neuroticism and extraversion as predictors of coping styles during early adolescence. *Personality & Individual Differences, 27*, 3–17.

Gonzales, P., Guzman, J., Partelow, L., Pahlke, E., Jocelyin, L., Kastberg, D., & Williams, T. (2004). Highlights from the Trends in International Mathematics and Science Study: TIMSS 2003. Retrieved June 17, 2008 from http://nces.ed.gov/pubsearch/pubsinfo.asp?pubid=2005005.

Goodenough, F. L. (1931). *Anger in young children.* Minneapolis: University of Minnesota Press.

Goodsitt, J. V., Morse, P. A., Ver Hoeve, J. N., & Cowan, N. (1984). Infant speech recognition in multisyllabic contexts. *Child Development, 55*, 903–910.

Goodway, J., & Branta, C. (2003). Influence of a motor skill intervention on fundamental motor skill development of disadvantaged preschool children. *Research Quarterly for Exercise and Sport, 74*, 36–46.

Goodwin, R., & Fitzgibbon, M. (2002). Social anxiety as a barrier to treatment for eating disorders. *International Journal of Eating Disorders, 32*, 103–106.

Gordon, R. (2001). Eating disorders East and West: A culture-bound syndrome unbound. In M. Nasser, M., Katzman, & R. Bordon (Eds.), *Eating disorders and cultures in transition* (pp. 1–23). New York: Taylor & Francis.

Gottesman, I., & Goldsmith, H. (1994). Developmental psychopathology of antisocial behavior: Inserting genes into its ontogenesis and epigenesis. In C. Nelson (Ed.), *Minnesota symposia on child psychology, Vol. 27* (pp. 69–104). Mahwah, NJ: Erlbaum.

Gottman, J. M. (1986). The world of coordinated play: Same- and cross-sex friendship in young children. In J. M. Gottman & J. G. Parker (Eds.), *Conversations of friends: Speculations on affective development* (pp. 139–191). Cambridge, England: Cambridge University Press.

Grabowski, L., Call, K., & Mortimer, J. (2001). Global and economic self-efficacy in the educational attainment process. *Social Psychology Quarterly, 64*, 164–197.

Graham, J., Cohen, R., Zbikowski, S., & Secrist, M. (1998). A longitudinal investigation of race and sex as factors in children's classroom friendship choices. *Child Study Journal, 28*, 245–266.

Graham, S., & Harris, K. (1997). It can be taught, but it does not develop naturally: Myths and realities in writing instruction. *School Psychology Review, 26*, 414–424.

Gralinski, J. H., & Kopp, C. B. (1993). Everyday rules for behavior: Mothers' requests to young children. *Developmental Psychology, 29*, 573–584.

Grall, T. (2007). Custodial mothers and fathers and their child support: 2005. Retrieved March 26, 2008 from http://www.census.gov/prod/2007pubs/p60-234.pdf.

Green, S. (2001). Systemic vs. individualistic approaches to bullying. *Journal of the American Medical Association, 286*, 787.

Green, S., Anderson, E., Doyle, E., & Ridelbach, H. (2006). Divorce. In G. Bear & K. Minke (Eds.), *Children's needs III: Development, prevention, and intervention.* Washington, DC: National Association of School Psychologists.

Green, S., Pring, L., & Swettenham, J. (2004). An investigation of first-order false belief understanding of children with congenital profound visual impairment. *British Journal of Developmental Psychology, 22*, 1–17.

Greenberg, M., & Kusché, C. (2006). Building social and emotional competence: The PATHS curriculum. In S. Jimerson & M. Furlong (Eds.), *Handbook of school violence and school safety: From research to practice* (pp. 395–412). Mahwah, NJ: Erlbaum.

Greenberg, M. T., Siegel, J. M., & Leitch, C. J. (1983). The nature and importance of attachment relationships to parents and peers during adolescence. *Journal of Youth & Adolescence, 12*, 373–386.

Greenberger, E., & Steinberg, L. (1986). *When teenagers work: The psychological and social costs of adolescent employment.* New York: Basic Books.

Greene, K., Krcmar, M., Rubin, D., Walters, L., & Hale, J. (2002). Elaboration in processing adolescent health messages: The impact of egocentrism and sensation seeking on message processing. *Journal of Communication, 52*, 812–831.

Greenfield, P., Brannon, C., & Lohr, D. (1994). Two-dimensional representation of movement through three-dimensional space: The role of video game expertise. *Journal of Applied Developmental Psychology, 15*, 87–104.

Greer, F. (2005). Bone health: It's more than calcium intake. *Pediatrics, 115*, 792–794.

Griffiths, M., & Chandler, D. (1998). Gendered editing and camerawork techniques in advertisements for children's toys on British television. Retrieved July 3, 2006 from http://users.aber.ac.uk/dgc/toyads.html.

Groome, L., Mooney, D., Holland, S., Smith, L., Atterbury, J., & Dykman, R. (1999). Behavioral state affects heart rate response to low-intensity sound in human fetuses. *Early Human Development, 54*, 39–54.

Grossmann, K., Grossmann, K. E., Spangler, G., Suess, G., & Unzner, L. (1985). Maternal sensitivity and newborns' orientation responses as related to quality of attachment in northern Germany. *Monographs of the Society of Research in Child Development, 50* (1–2, Serial No. 209), 233–256.

Grov, C., Bimbi, D., Nanin, J., & Parsons, J. (2006). Race, ethnicity, gender, and generational factors associated with the coming-out process among gay, lesbian, and bisexual individuals. *Journal of Sex Research, 43*, 115–121.

Gruber, J., & Fineran, S. (2008). Comparing the impact of bullying and sexual harassment. *Sex Roles, 58*, in press.

Grusec, J. (1992). Social learning theory and developmental psychology: The legacies of Robert Sears and Albert Bandura. *Developmental Psychology, 28*, 776–786.

Guangyuan, S. (2005). A follow-up study on the effect of attributional training for achievement motivation. *Psychological Science (China), 28*, 52–55.

Guerin, D. W., & Gottfried, A. W. (1994a). Developmental stability and change in parent reports of temperament: A ten-year longitudinal investigation from infancy through preadolescence. *Merrill-Palmer Quarterly, 40*, 334–355.

Guerin, D. W., & Gottfried, A. W. (1994b). Temperamental consequences of infant difficultness. *Infant Behavior & Development, 17*, 413–421.

Guesry, P. (1998). The role of nutrition in brain development. *Preventive Medicine, 27*, 189–194.

Guilford, J. (1967). *The nature of human intelligence.* New York: McGraw-Hill.

Gunnar, M. R. (1994). Psychoendocrine studies of temperament and stress in early childhood: Expanding current models. In J. E. Bates & T. D. Wachs (Eds.), *Temperament: Individual differences at the interface of biology and behavior* (pp. 175–198). Washington, DC: American Psychological Association.

Gunther, M. (1955). Instinct and the learning couple. *Lancet, 1*, 575.

Gunther, M. (1961). Infant behavior at the breast. In B. Foss (Ed.), *Determinants of infant behavior* (pp. 37–44). London: Methuen.

Guralnik, J. M., & Kaplan, G. A. (1989). Predictors of healthy aging: Prospective evidence from the Alameda County Study. *American Journal of Public Health, 79*, 703–708.

Guralnik, J. M., & Paul-Brown, D. (1984). Communicative adjustments during behavior-request episodes among children at different developmental levels. *Child Development, 55*, 911–919.

Gurnáková, J., & Kusá, D. (2004). Gender self-concept in personal theories of reality. *Studia Psychologica, 46*, 49–61.

Gust, D., Strine, T., Maurice, E., Smith, P., Yusuf, H., Wilkinson, M., Battaglia, M., Wright, R., & Schwartz, B. (2004). Underimmunization among children: Effects of vaccine safety concerns on immunization status. *Pediatrics, 114*, 16–22.

Gustafson, S. B., & Magnusson, D. (1991). *Female life careers: A pattern approach.* Hillsdale, NJ: Erlbaum.

Guthrie, R. (2004). *Even the rat was white* (2nd ed.). Boston: Allyn & Bacon.

Gutman, L. (2006). How student and parent goal orientations and classroom goal structures influence the math achievement of African Americans during the high school transition. *Contemporary Educational Psychology, 31*, 44–63.

Guzzetti, B., & Williams, W. (1996). Gender, text, and discussion: Examining intellectual safety in the science classroom. *Journal of Research in Science Teaching, 33*, 5–20.

Gzesh, S. M., & Surber, C. F. (1985). Visual perspective-taking skills in children. *Child Development, 56*, 1204–1213.

Habermas, T., & de Silveira, C. (2008). The development of global coherence in life narratives across adolescence: Temporal, causal, and thematic aspects. *Developmental Psychology, 44*, 707–721.

Hagan, J. (1997). Defiance and despair: Subcultural and structural linkages between delinquency and despair in the life course. *Social Forces, 76*, 119–134.

Haier, R. J., Chueh, D., Touchette, P., Lott, I., Buchsbaum, M. S., MacMillan, D., Sandman, C., LaCasse, L., & Sosa, E. (1995). Brain size and cerebral glucose metabolic rate in nonspecific mental retardation and Down syndrome. *Intelligence, 20*, 191–210.

Hakansson, G., Salameh, E., & Nettelbladt, U. (2003). Measuring language development in bilingual children: Swedish-Arabic children with and without language impairment. *Linguistics, 41*, 255–288.

Hakuta, K., Bialystok, E., & Wiley, E. (2003). Critical-evidence: A test of the critical-period hypothesis for second-language acquisition. *Psychological Science, 14*, 31–38.

Halama, P., & Strízenec, M. (2004). Spiritual, existential or both? Theoretical considerations on the nature of "higher" intelligences. *Studia Psychologica, 46*, 239–253.

Hale, J. (2001). *Learning while black: Creating educational excellence for African American children.* Baltimore, MD: Johns Hopkins University Press.

Halford, G., Bunch, K., & McCredden, J. (2007). Problem decomposability as a factor in complexity of the dimensional change card sort task. *Cognitive Development, 22*, 384–391.

Halford, G. S., Maybery, M. T., O'Hare, A. W., & Grant, P. (1994). The development of memory and processing capacity. *Child Development, 65*, 1338–1356.

Hall, G. (2003, September). Primary elective C-section up 20% from 1999 to 2001. *OB/GYN News.* Retrieved April 1, 2004 from www.imng.com.

Halle, T. (1999). Implicit theories of social interactions: Children's reasoning about the relative importance of gender and friendship in social partner choices. *Merrill-Palmer Quarterly, 45*, 445–467.

Halmi, K. (2003). Classification, diagnosis and comorbidities of eating disorders. In M. Maj, K. Halmi, J. Lopez-Ibor, & N. Sartorius, *Eating disorders* (pp. 1–33). New York: Wiley.

Halpern, C. T., Udry, J. R., Campbell, B., & Suchindran, C. (1993). Testosterone and pubertal development as predictors of sexual activity: A panel analysis of adolescent males. *Psychosomatic Medicine, 55*, 436–447.

Ham, B. (2004, October 29). Hispanic children less likely to get ADHD diagnosis. Retrieved June 20, 2008 from http://www.cfah.org/hbns/news/ADHD10-29-04.cfm.

Hämäläinen, M., & Pulkkinen, L. (1996). Problem behavior as a precursor of male criminality. *Development and Psychopathology, 8*, 443–455.

Hamilton, B., Martin, J., & Ventura, S. (2007). Births: Preliminary data for 2006. *National Vital Statistics Reports, 56*, 1–18.

Hamilton, C. E. (1995, March). Continuity and discontinuity of attachment from infancy through adolescence. Paper presented at the biennial meetings of the Society for Research in Child Development, Indianapolis.

Hammond, M., Landry, S., Swank, P., & Smith, K. (2000). Relation of mothers' affective development history and parenting behavior: Effects on infant medical risk. *American Journal of Orthopsychiatry, 70*, 95–103.

Handelman, L., Rich, M., Bridgemohan, C., & Schneider, L. (2004). Understanding pediatric inner-city asthma: An explanatory model approach. *Journal of Asthma, 41*, 167–177.

Handley-Derry, M., Low, J., Burke, S., Waurick, M., Killen, H., & Derrick, E. (1997). Intrapartum fetal asphyxia and the occurrence of minor deficits in 4- to 8-year-old children. *Developmental Medicine & Child Neurology, 39*, 508–514.

Hanna, E., & Meltzoff, A. N. (1993). Peer imitation by toddlers in laboratory, home, and day-care contexts: Implications for social learning and memory. *Developmental Psychology, 29*, 701–710.

Hannigan, J., O'Leary-Moore, S., & Berman, R. (2007). Postnatal environmental or experiential amelioration of neurobehavioral effects of perinatal alcohol exposure in rats. *Neuroscience & Biobehavioral Reviews, 31*, 202–211.

Hardy, C., & Van Leeuwen, S. (2004). Interviewing young children: Effects of probe structures and focus of rapport-building talk on the qualities of young children's eyewitness statements. *Canadian Journal of Behavioral Science, 36*, 155–165.

Harkness, S. (1998). Time for families. *Anthropology Newsletter, 39*, 1, 4.

Harkness, S., & Super, C. M. (1985). The cultural context of gender segregation in children's peer groups. *Child Development, 56*, 219–224.

Harlow, H., & Zimmerman, R. (1959). Affectional responses in the infant monkey. *Science, 130*, 421–432.

Harris, L. (2003). The status of pregnant women and fetuses in U.S. criminal law. *Journal of the American Medical Association, 289*, 1697–1699.

Harris, P., & Leevers, H. (2005). Pretending, imagery, and self-awareness in autism. In S. Baron-Cohen, H. Tager-Flusberg, & D. Cohen (Eds.), *Understanding other minds: Perspectives from developmental cognitive neuroscience* (2nd ed., pp. 182–202). New York: Oxford University Press.

Harris-Davis, E., & Stallmann-Jorgensen, I. (2006). Addressing overweight in children: A public health perspective. In S. Edelstein (Ed.), *Nutrition in public health* (pp. 139–190). Sudbury, MA: Jones and Bartlett Publishers.

Harrison, A., Wilson, M., Pine, C., Chan, S., & Buriel, R. (1990). Family ecologies of ethnic minority children. *Child Development, 61*, 347–362.

Harrist, A., Zaia, A., Bates, J., Dodge, K., & Pettit, G. (1997). Subtypes of social withdrawal in early childhood: Sociometric status and social-cognitive differences across four years. *Child Development, 68*, 278–294.

Hart, C., Olsen, S., Robinson, C., & Mandleco, B. (1997). The development of social and communicative competence in childhood: Review and a model of personal, familial, and extrafamilial processes. *Communication Yearbook, 20*, 305–373.

Hart, B., & Risley, T. R. (1995). *Meaningful differences in the everyday experience of young American children.* Baltimore: Paul H. Brookes.

Hart, S., Jones, N., Field, T., & Lundy, B. (1999). One-year-old infants of intrusive and withdrawn depressed mothers. *Child Psychiatry & Human Development, 30*, 111–120.

Harter, S. (1987). The determinations and mediational role of global self-worth in children. In N. Eisenberg (Ed.), *Contemporary topics in developmental psychology* (pp. 219–242). New York: Wiley-Interscience.

Harter, S. (1990). Processes underlying adolescent self-concept formation. In R. Montemayor, G. R. Adams, & T. P. Gullotta (Eds.), *From childhood to adolescence: A transitional period?* (pp. 205–239). Newbury Park, CA: Sage.

Harter, S., & Monsour, A. (1992). Developmental analysis of conflict caused by opposing attributes in the adolescent self-portrait. *Developmental Psychology, 28*, 251–260.

Harton, H., & Latane, B. (1997). Social influence and adolescent lifestyle attitudes. *Journal of Research on Adolescence, 7*, 197–220.

Hartup, W. W. (1974). Aggression in childhood: Developmental perspectives. *American Psychologist, 29*, 336–341.

Hartup, W. W. (1996). The company they keep: Friendships and their developmental significance. *Child Development, 67*, 1–13.

Harvey, A., & Coleman, A. (1997). An Afrocentric program for African American males in the juvenile justice system. *Child Welfare, 76*, 197–211.

Harvey, A., & Hill, R. (2004). Afrocentric youth and family rites of passage program: Promoting resilience among at-risk African American youths. *Social Work, 49*, 65–74.

Harvey, A., & Rauch, J. (1997). A comprehensive Afrocentric rites of passage program for black male adolescents. *Health & Social Work, 22*, 30–37.

Harvey, R., Fletcher, J., & French, D. (2001). Social reasoning: A source of influence on aggression. *Clinical Psychology Review, 21*, 447–469.

Hatano, G. (1990). Toward the cultural psychology of mathematical cognition: Commentary. In H. Stevenson & S. Lee (Eds.), *Contexts of achievement. Monographs of the Society for Research in Child Development, 55* (12, Serial No. 221), 108–115.

Hay, D., Payne, A., & Chadwick, A. (2004). Peer relations in childhood. *Journal of Child Psychology & Psychiatry & Allied Disciplines, 45*, 84–108.

Hayne, H., & Rovee-Collier, C. (1995). The organization of reactivated memory in infancy. *Child Development, 66*, 893–906.

Hecht, M., & Eddington, E. (2003). The place and nature of sexuality education in society. In R. Levesque, (Ed.), *Sexuality education: What adolescents' rights require.* New York: Nova Science Publishers.

Heenan, J. (2005). Character education transforms school. Retrieved July 19, 2005 from http://www.cornerstonevalues.org/kew2.htm.

Heinicke, C., Goorsky, M., Moscov, S., Dudley, K., Gordon, J., Schneider, C., & Guthrie, D. (2000). Relationship-based intervention with at-risk mothers: Factors affecting variations in outcome. *Infant Mental Health Journal, 21*, 133–155.

Heinonen, K., Raikkonen, K., & Keltikangas-Jarvinen, L. (2003). Maternal perceptions and adolescent self-esteem: A six-year longitudinal study. *Adolescence, 38*, 669–687.

helpguide.org. (2008). *Anorexia nervosa.* Retrieved April 9, 2008 from http://www.helpguide.org/mental/anorexia_signs_symptoms_causes_treatment.htm#signs.

Helson, R., Mitchell, V., & Moane, G. (1984). Personality and patterns of adherence and nonadherence to the social clock. *Journal of Personality & Social Psychology, 46*, 1079–1096.

Henderson, H., Marshall, P., Fox, N., & Rubin, K. (2004). Psychophysiological and behavioral evidence for varying forms and functions of nonsocial behavior in preschoolers. *Child Development, 75*, 236–250.

Henderson, M., Wight, D., Raab, G., Abraham, C., Parkes, A., Scott, S., & Hart, G. (2007). Impact of a theoretically based sex education programme (SHARE) delivered by teachers on NHS registered conceptions and terminations: Final results of cluster randomised trial. *BMJ: British Medical Journal, 334*, 7585.

Henry, B., Caspi, A., Moffitt, T., Harrington, H., et al. (1999). Staying in school protects boys with poor self-regulation in childhood from later crime: A longitudinal study. *International Journal of Behavioral Development, 23*, 1049–1073.

Henry, B., Caspi, A., Moffitt, T., & Silva, P. (1996). Temperamental and familial predictors of violent and nonviolent criminal convictions: Age 3 to age 18. *Developmental Psychology, 32*, 614–623.

Henry J. Kaiser Family Foundation. (2005). Sex on TV 4. Retrieved June 21, 2007 from http://www.kff.org/entmedia/entmedia110905pkg.cfm.

Hepper, P., Wells, D., & Lynch, C. (2004). Prenatal thumb sucking is related to postnatal handedness. *Neuropsychologia, 43*, 313–315.

Herbert, J., Gross, J., & Hayne, H. (2006). Age-related changes in deferred imitation between 6 and 9 months of age. *Infant Behavior & Development, 29*, 136–139.

Hermes, S., & Keel, P. (2003). The influence of puberty and ethnicity on awareness and internalization of the thin ideal. *International Journal of Eating Disorders, 33*, 465–467.

Hernandez, D. (1997). Child development and the social demography of childhood. *Child Development, 68*, 149–169.

Heron, M. (2007). Deaths: Leading causes for 2004. *National Vital Statistics Reports, 56*, 1–96.

Heron, M., Hoyert, D., Xu, J., Scott, C., & Tejada-Vera, B. (2008). Deaths: Preliminary data for 2006. *National Vital Statistics Reports, 56*, 1–52.

Herrenkohl, E., Herrenkohl, R., Egolf, B., & Russo, M. (1998). The relationship between early maltreatment and teenage parenthood. *Journal of Adolescence, 21*, 291–303.

Hertenstein, M., & Campos, J. (2004). The retention effects of an adult's emotional displays on infant behavior. *Child Development, 75*, 595–613.

Hess, E. H. (1972). "Imprinting" in a natural laboratory. *Scientific American, 227*, 24–31.

Hetherington, E. M. (1991a). Presidential address: Families, lies, and videotapes. *Journal of Research on Adolescence, 1*, 323–348.

Hetherington, E. M. (1991b). The role of individual differences and family relationships in children's coping with divorce and remarriage. In P. A. Cowen & M. Hetherington (Eds.), *Family transitions* (pp. 165–194). Hillsdale, NJ: Erlbaum.

Hetherington, E. M., & Stanley-Hagan, M. M. (1995). Parenting in divorced and remarried families. In M. H. Bornstein (Ed.), *Handbook of parenting, Vol. 3: Status and social conditions of parenting* (pp. 233–254). Mahwah, NJ: Erlbaum.

Higgins, E., & Pittman, T. (2008). Motives of the human animal: Comprehending, managing, and sharing inner states. *Annual Review of Psychology, 59*, 361–386.

Hill, J., Brooks–Gunn, J., & Waldfogel, J. (2003). Sustained effects of high participation in an early intervention for low-birth-weight premature infants. *Developmental Psychology, 39*, 730–744.

Hinde, R. A., Titmus, G., Easton, D., & Tamplin, A. (1985). Incidence of "friendship" and behavior toward strong associates versus nonassociates in preschoolers. *Child Development, 56*, 234–245.

Ho, C., & Bryant, P. (1997). Learning to read Chinese beyond the logographic phase. *Reading Research Quarterly, 32*, 276–289.

Hobbs, J., & Ferth, P. (1993). *The Bounty pregnancy guide.* New York: Bounty Health Care Publishing.

Hodge, K., & Tod, D. (1993). Ethics of childhood sport. *Sports Medicine, 15*, 291–298.

Hodges, E. V. E., Malone, M. J., & Perry, D. G. (1997). Individual risk and social risk as interacting determinants of victimization in the peer group. *Developmental Psychology, 33*, 1032–1039.

Hoeksma, J., Oosterlaan, J., & Schipper, E. (2004). Emotion regulation and the dynamics of feelings: A conceptual and methodological framework. *Child Development, 75*, 354–360.

Hoffman, M. L. (1970). Moral development. In P. Mussen (Ed.), *Carmichael's manual of child psychology, Vol. 2.* New York: Wiley.

Hoffman, M. L. (1982). Development of prosocial motivation: Empathy and guilt. In N. Eisenberg (Ed.), *The development of prosocial behavior* (pp. 281–314). New York: Academic Press.

Hoffman, M. L. (1988). Moral development. In M. Bornstein & M. Lamb (Eds.), *Developmental psychology: An advanced textbook* (2nd ed., pp. 497–548). Hillsdale, NJ: Erlbaum.

Holahan, C. (1988). Relation of life goals at age 70 to activity participation and health and psychological well-being among Terman's gifted men and women. *Psychology and Aging, 3*, 286–291.

Holland, J. L. (1973). *Making vocational choices: A theory of careers.* Englewood Cliffs, NJ: Prentice-Hall.

Holland, J. L. (1992). *Making vocational choices: A theory of vocational personalities and work environments* (2nd ed.). Odessa, FL: Psychological Assessment Resources.

Holmbeck, G. N., & Hill, J. P. (1991). Conflictive engagement, positive affect, and menarche in families with seventh-grade girls. *Child Development, 62*, 1030–1048.

Holmgren, S., Molander, B., & Nilsson, L. (2006). Intelligence and executive functioning in adult age: Effects of sibship size and birth order. *European Journal of Cognitive Psychology, 18*, 138–158.

Holowka, S., Brosseau-Lapré, F., & Petitto, L. (2002). Semantic and conceptual knowledge underlying bilingual babies' first signs and words. *Language Learning, 52*, 205–262.

Hood, M., Conlon, E., & Andrews, G. (2008). Preschool home literacy practices and children's literacy development: A longitudinal analysis. *Journal of Educational Psychology, 100*, 252–271.

Hood, M., & Ellison, R. (2003). Television viewing and change in body fat from preschool to early adolescence: The Framingham Children's Study. *International Journal of Obesity & Related Metabolic Disorders, 27*, 827–833.

Horan, W., Pogge, D., Borgaro, S., & Stokes, J. (1997). Learning and memory in adolescent psychiatric inpatients with major depression: A normative study of the California Verbal Learning Test. *Archives of Clinical Neuropsychology, 12*, 575–584.

Horowitz, F. D. (1990). Developmental models of individual differences. In J. Colombo & J. Fagen (Eds.), *Individual differences in infancy: Reliability, stability, prediction* (pp. 3–18). Hillsdale, NJ: Erlbaum.

Hou, J., Chen, H., & Chen, X. (2005). The relationship of parent-children interaction in the free play session and copy-modeling session with the development of children's behavioral inhibition in Chinese families. *Psychological Science (China), 28*, 820–825.

Houck, G., & Lecuyer-Maus, E. (2004). Maternal limit setting during toddlerhood, delay of gratification and behavior problems at age five. *Infant Mental Health Journal, 25*, 28–46.

House of Commons Work and Pensions Committee. (2006). Child poverty in the UK. Retrieved June 20, 2007 from www.publications.parliament.uk/pa/cm200304/cmselect/cmworpen/85/85.pdf.

Houston, D., & Jusczyk, P. (2003). Infants' long-term memory for the sound patterns of words and voices. *Journal of Experimental Psychology: Human Perception & Performance, 29*, 1143–1154.

Howes, C. (1983). Patterns of friendship. *Child Development, 54*, 1041–1053.

Howes, C. (1987). Social competence with peers in young children: Developmental sequences. *Developmental Review, 7*, 252–272.

Howes, C., & Matheson, C. C. (1992). Sequences in the development of competent play with peers: Social and pretend play. *Developmental Psychology, 28*, 961–974.

Howes, C., Phillips, D. A., & Whitebook, M. (1992). Thresholds of quality: Implications for the social development of children in center-based child care. *Child Development, 63*, 449–460.

Huang, H., & Hanley, J. (1997). A longitudinal study of phonological awareness, visual skills, and Chinese reading acquisition among first-graders in Taiwan. *International Journal of Behavioral Development, 20*, 249–268.

Hubel, D. H., & Weisel, T. N. (1963). Receptive fields of cells in striate cortex of very young, visually inexperienced kittens. *Journal of Neurophysiology, 26*, 994–1002.

Hudziak, J., van Beijsterveldt, C., Bartels, M., Rietveld, M., Rettew, D., Derks, E., & Boomsma, D. (2003). Individual differences in aggression: Genetic analyses by age, gender, and informant in 3-, 7-, and 10-year-old Dutch twins. *Behavior Genetics, 33*, 575–589

Huebner, T., Vioet, T., Marx, I., Konrad, K., Fink, G., Herpetz, S., & Herpetz-Dahlmann, B. (2008). Morphometric brain abnormalities in boys with conduct disorder. *Journal of the American Academy of Child & Adolescent Psychiatry, 47*, 540–547.

Huesmann, L. R., Moise, J., Podolski, C. P., & Eron, L. D. (2003). Longitudinal relations between childhood exposure to media violence and adult aggression and violence 1977–1982. *Developmental Psychology, 39(2)*, 201–221.

Humphrey, N., Curran, A., Morris, E., Farrell, P., & Woods, K. (2007). Emotional intelligence and education: A critical review. *Educational Psychology, 27*, 235–254.

Hunfeld, J., Tempels, A., Passchier, J., Hazebroek, F., et al. (1999). Parental burden and grief one year after the birth of a child with a congenital anomaly. *Journal of Pediatric Psychology, 24*, 515–520.

Hurley, D., & Thorp. J. (2002). Decisions without direction: Career guidance and decision-making among American youth. Retrieved April 13, 2008 from http://www.ferris.edu/careerinstitute/exec.pdf.

Hurry, J., & Sylva, K. (2007). Long-term outcomes of early reading intervention. *Journal of Research in Reading, 30*, 227–248.

Hurwitz, E., Gunn, W. J., Pinsky, P. F., & Schonberger, L. B. (1991). Risk of respiratory illness associated with day-care attendance: A nationwide study. *Pediatrics, 87*, 62–69.

Huth-Bocks, A., Levendosky, A., Bogat, G., & von Eye, A. (2004). The impact of maternal characteristics and contextual variables on infant-mother attachment. *Child Development, 75*, 480–496.

Huttenlocher, J. (1995, April). Children's language in relation to input. Paper presented at the biennial meetings of the Society for Research in Child Development, Indianapolis.

Huttenlocher, P. R. (1994). Synaptogenesis, synapse elimination, and neural plasticity in human cerebral cortex. In C. A. Nelson (Ed.), *The Minnesota Symposia on Child Psychology, Vol. 27* (pp. 35–54). Hillsdale, NJ: Erlbaum.

Huttenlocher, P. R., & Dabholkar, A. (1997). Regional differences in synaptogenesis in human cerebral cortex. *Journal of Comparative Neurology, 387*, 167–178.

Hyde, J. (2005). The gender similarities hypothesis. *American Psychologist, 60*, 581–592.

Hyde, J., Fennema, E., & Lamon, S. (1990), Gender differences in mathematics performance: A meta-analysis. *Psychological Bulletin, 107*, 139–155.

Hyun, O., Lee, W., Yoo, A., Cho, B., Yoo, K., Miller, B., Schvaneveldt, J., & Lau, S. (2002). Social support for two generations of new mothers in selected populations in Korea, Hong Kong, and the United States. *Journal of Comparative Family Studies, 33*, 515–527.

Iaquinta, A. (2006). Guided reading: A research-based response to the challenges of early reading instruction. *Early Childhood Education Journal, 33*, 1573–1707.

Ingoldsby, E., Shaw, D., Owens, E., & Winslow, E. (1999). A longitudinal study of interparental conflict, emotional and behavioral reactivity, and preschoolers' adjustment problems among low-income families. *Journal of Abnormal Child Psychology, 27*, 343–356.

Ingrassia, M. (1993, August 2). Daughters of Murphy Brown. *Newsweek*, 58–59.

Inhelder, B., & Piaget, J. (1958). *The growth of logical thinking from childhood to adolescence.* New York: Basic Books.

Isabella, R. A. (1995). The origins of infant-mother attachment: Maternal behavior and infant development. *Annals of Child Development, 10*, 57–81.

Itier, R., & Taylor, M. (2004). Face inversion and contrast-reversal effects across development: In contrast to the expertise theory. *Developmental Science, 7*, 246–260.

Izard, C. E., Fantauzzo, C. A., Castle, J. M., Haynes, O. M., Rayias, M. F., & Putnam, P. H. (1995). The ontogeny and significance of infants' facial expressions in the first 9 months of life. *Developmental Psychology, 31*, 997–1013.

Izard, C. E., & Harris, P. (1995). Emotional development and developmental psychopathology. In D. Cicchetti & D. J. Cohen (Eds.), *Developmental psychopathology, Vol. 1: Theory and methods* (pp. 467–503). New York: Wiley.

Jackson, D., & Tein, J. (1998). Adolescents' conceptualization of adult roles: Relationships with age, gender, work goal, and maternal employment. *Sex Roles, 38*, 987–1008.

Jacobs, J., Finken, L., Griffin, N., & Wright, J. (1998). The career plans of science-talented rural adolescent girls. *American Educational Research Journal, 35*, 681–704.

Jacobsen, T., & Hofmann, V. (1997). Children's attachment representations: Longitudinal relations to school behavior, and academic competency in middle childhood and adolescence. *Developmental Psychology, 33*, 703–710.

Jacobsen, T., Husa, M., Fendrich, M., Kruesi, M., & Ziegenhain, U. (1997). Children's ability to delay gratification: Longitudinal relations to mother-child attachment. *Journal of Genetic Psychology, 158*, 411–426.

Jadack, R. A., Hyde, J. S., Moore, C. F., & Keller, M. L. (1995). Moral reasoning about sexually transmitted diseases. *Child Development, 66*, 167–177.

Jambunathan, S., & Burts, D. (2003). Comparison of perception of self-competence among five ethnic groups of preschoolers in the U.S. *Early Childhood Education, 173*, 651–660.

Janosz, M., Le Blanc, M., Boulerice, B., & Tremblay, R. (2000). Predicting different types of school dropouts: A typological approach with two longitudinal samples. *Journal of Educational Psychology, 92*, 171–190.

Jansz, J., & Martens, L. (2005). Gaming at a LAN event: The social context of playing video games. *New Media & Society, 7*, 333–355.

Javo, C., Ronning, J., Heyerdahl, S., & Rudmin, F. (2004). Parenting correlates of child behavior problems in a multiethnic community sample of preschool children in northern Norway. *European Child & Adolescent Psychiatry, 13*, 8–18.

Jendrek, M. (1993). Grandparents who parent their grandchildren: Effects on lifestyle. *Journal of Marriage & the Family, 55*, 609–621.

Jenkins, J., & Buccioni, J. (2000). Children's understanding of marital conflict and the marital relationship. *Journal of Child Psychology & Psychiatry & Allied Disciplines, 41*, 161–168.

Jenkins, J. M., & Astington, J. W. (1996). Cognitive factors and family structure associated with theory of mind development in young children. *Developmental Psychology, 32*, 70–78.

Jenks, K., van Lieshout, E., & de Moor, J. (2008). Arithmetic achievement in children with cerebral palsy or spina bifida meningomyelocele. *Remedial and Special Education*, in press.

Jensen, A., & Whang, P. (1994). Speed of accessing arithmetic facts in long-term memory: A comparison of Chinese-American and Anglo-American children. *Contemporary Educational Psychology, 19*, 1–12.

Jeynes, W. (2007). The impact of parental remarriage on children: A meta-analysis. *Marriage & Family Review, 40*, 75–102.

Jimerson, S. (1999). On the failure of failure: Examining the association between early grade retention and educational and employment outcomes during late adolescence. *Journal of School Psychology, 37*, 243–272.

Jimerson, S., Egeland, B., Sroufe, A., & Carlson, B. (2001). A prospective longitudinal study of high school dropouts examining multiple predictors across development. *Journal of School Psychology, 38*, 525–549.

Jin, Y., Jing, J., Morinaga, R., Miki, K., Su, X., & Chen, X. (2002). A comparative study of theory of mind in Chinese and Japanese children. *Chinese Mental Health Journal, 16*, 446–448.

Jirtle, R., & Weidman, J. (2007). Imprinted and more equal. *American Scientist, 95*, 143–149.

John, O. P., Caspi, A., Robins, R. W., Moffitt, T. E., & Stouthamer-Loeber, M. (1994). The "little five": Exploring the nomological network of the five-factor model of personality in adolescent boys. *Child Development, 65*, 160–178.

Johnson, E., & Breslau, N. (2000). Increased risk of learning disabilities in low birth weight boys at age 11 years. *Biological Psychiatry, 47*, 490–500.

Johnson, H., Nusbaum, B., Bejarano, A., & Rosen, T. (1999). An ecological approach to development in children with prenatal drug exposure. *American Journal of Orthopsychiatry, 69*, 448–456.

Johnson, M. (2003). Development of human brain functions. *Biological Psychiatry, 54*, 1312–1316.

Johnston, D., Shah, M., & Shields, M. (2007, April). Handedness, time use and early childhood development. IZA Discussion Paper No. 2752.

Johnston, L., O'Malley, P., Bachman, J., & Schulenberg, J. (2007). Monitoring the Future: National results on adolescent drug use: Overview of key findings. NIH Publication No. 07-6202. Retrieved June 22, 2007 from http://monitoringthefuture.org/pubs/monographs/overview2006.pdf.

Jones, M. C. (1924). A laboratory study of fear: The case of Peter. *Pedagogical Seminary, 31*, 308–315.

Jones, S., & Zigler, E. (2002). The Mozart effect: Not learning from history. *Journal of Applied Developmental Psychology, 23*, 355–372.

Jonsson, P. (2003). The new face of homeschooling. *Christian Science Monitor Online.* Retrieved June 23, 2004, from http://www.csmonitor.com/2003/0429/p01s01-ussc.html.

Jorgensen, G. (2006). Kohlberg and Gilligan: Duet or duel? *Journal of Moral Education, 35*, 179–196.

Jorgenson, S. (1993). Adolescent pregnancy and parenting. In T. Gullotta, G. Adams, & R. Montemayor (Eds.), *Adolescent sexuality* (pp. 103–140). Thousand Oaks, CA: Sage Publications.

Joseph, K., Young, D., Dodds, L., O'Connell, C., Allen, V., Chandra, S., & Allen, A. (2003). Changes in maternal characteristics and obstetric practice and recent increases in primary cesarean delivery. *Obstetrics and Gynecology, 102*, 791–800.

Joseph, R. (2000). Fetal brain behavior and cognitive development. *Developmental Review, 20*, 81–98.

Josse, D., Thibault, H., Bourdais, C., Mirailles, P., Pireyre, E., Surgal, L., Gerboin-Reyrolles, P., & Chauliac, M. (1999). Iron deficiency and psychomotor development in young children in a child health centre: Assessment with revised version of the Brunet-Lezine scale. *Approche Neuropsychologique des Apprentissages chez l'Enfant, 11*, 21–27.

Judson, T., & Nishimori, T. (2005). Concepts and skills in high school calculus: An examination of a special case in Japan and the United States. *Journal for Research in Mathematics, 36*, 24–43.

Jusczyk, P., & Hohne, E. (1997). Infants' memory for spoken words. *Science, 277.*

Jusczyk, P., Houston, D., & Newsome, M. (1999). The beginnings of word segmentation in English-learning infants. *Cognitive Psychology, 39*, 159–207.

Jussim, L., & Eccles, J. (1992). Teacher expectations II: Construction and reflection of student achievement. *Journal of Personality & Social Psychology, 63*, 947–961.

Kagan, J., & Herschkowitz, N. (2005). *A young mind in a growing brain.* Hillsdale, NJ: Erlbaum.

Kagan, J., Snidman, N., & Arcus, D. (1993). On the temperamental categories of inhibited and uninhibited children. In K. H. Rubin & J. B. Asendorpf (Eds.), *Social withdrawal, inhibition, and shyness in childhood* (pp. 19–28). Hillsdale, NJ: Erlbaum.

Kahana-Kalman, R., & Walker-Andrews, A. (2001). The role of person familiarity in young infants' perception of emotional expressions. *Child Development, 72*, 352–369.

Kail, R. (1990). *The development of memory in children* (3rd ed.). New York: Freeman.

Kail, R. (1991). Processing time declines exponentially during childhood and adolescence. *Developmental Psychology, 27*, 259–266.

Kail, R. (1997). Processing time, imagery, and spatial memory. *Journal of Experimental Child Psychology, 64*, 67–78.

Kail, R., & Ferrer, E. (2007). Processing speed in childhood and adolescence: Longitudinal models for examining developmental change. *Child Development, 78*, 1760–1770.

Kail, R., & Hall, L. K. (1994). Processing speed, naming speed, and reading. *Developmental Psychology, 30*, 949–954.

Kail, R., & Hall, L. K. (1999). Sources of developmental change in children's word-problem performance. *Journal of Educational Psychology, 91*, 660–668.

Kaiser Family Foundation. (2004). Children, the digital divide, and federal policy. Retrieved September 9, 2008 from http://www.kff.org/entmedia/loader.cfm?url=/commonspot/security/getfile.cfm&PageID=46360.

Kaltiala-Heino, R., Kosunen, E., & Rimpela, M. (2003). Pubertal timing, sexual behaviour and self-reported depression in middle adolescence. *Journal of Adolescence, 26*, 531–545.

Kamo, Y., Ries, L. M., Farmer, Y. M., Nickinovich, D. G., & Borgatta, E. F. (1991). Status attainment revisited. The National Survey of Families and Households. *Research on Aging, 13*, 124–143.

Kanemura, H., Aihara, M., Aoki, S., Araki, T., & Nakazawa, S. (2004). Development of the prefrontal lobe in infants and children: A three-dimensional magnetic resonance volumetric study. *Brain and Development, 25*, 195–199.

Kaplan, P., Bachorowski, J., Smoski, M., & Zinser, M. (2001). Role of clinical diagnosis and medication use in effects of maternal depression on infant-directed speech. *Infancy, 2*, 537–548.

Kaplowitz, P., & Oberfield, S. (1999). Reexamination of the age limit for defining when puberty is precocious in girls in the United States: Implications for evaluation and treatment. *Pediatrics, 104*, 936–941.

Karmiloff-Smith, A. (1991). Beyond modularity: Innate constraints and developmental change. In S. Carey & R. Gelman (Eds.), *The epigenesis of mind: Essays on biology and cognition* (pp. 171–197). Hillsdale, NJ: Erlbaum.

Katz, P. A., & Ksansnak, K. R. (1994). Developmental aspects of gender role flexibility and traditionality in middle childhood and adolescence. *Developmental Psychology, 30*, 272–282.

Kauffman, J. (2005). *Characteristics of emotional and behavioral disorders of children and youth.* Upper Saddle River, NJ: Pearson Prentice-Hall.

Kaufman, A., & Kaufman, N. (1983). *Kaufman assessment battery for children (KABC).* Circle Pines, MN: American Guidance Service.

Kaufman, A., & Kaufman, N. (2004). *Kaufman assessment battery for children (KABC) II.* Bloomington, MN: Pearson AGS.

Kaufman, J., Kaufman, A., Kaufman-Singer, J., & Kaufman, N. (2005). The Kaufman Assessment Battery for Children–Second Edition and the Kaufman Adolescent and Adult Intelligence Test. In D. Flanagan & P. Harrison (Eds.), *Contemporary intellectual assessment: Theories, tests, and issues* (pp. 344–370). New York: Guilford Press.

Kaufman, M. (1997). The teratogenic effects of alcohol following exposure during pregnancy, and its influence on the chromosome constitution of the pre-ovulatory egg. *Alcohol & Alcoholism, 32*, 113–128.

Keech, R. (2002). Ophthalmology. In A. Rudolph, R. Kamei, & K. Overby (Eds.), *Rudolph's fundamentals of pediatrics* (3rd ed., pp. 847–862). New York: McGraw-Hill.

Keen, R. (2003). Representation of objects and events: Why do infants look so smart and toddlers look so dumb? *Current Directions in Psychological Science, 12*, 79–83.

Kellogg, R. (1970). *Analyzing children's art.* Palo Alto, CA: National Press Books.

Kemper, K. (1996). *The holistic pediatrician.* New York: HarperCollins.

Kendall-Tackett, K., Williams, L., & Finkelhor, D. (1993). Impact of sexual abuse on children: A review and synthesis of recent empirical studies. *Psychological Bulletin, 113*, 164–180.

Kendler, K., Thornton, L., Gilman, S., & Kessler, R. (2000). Sexual orientation in a U.S. national sample of twin and nontwin sibling pairs. *American Journal of Psychiatry, 157*, 1843–1846.

Kennedy, D. M. (1995). Glimpses of a highly gifted child in a heterogeneous classroom. *Roeper Review, 17*, 164–168.

Kent, L., Doerry, U., Hardy, E., Parmar, R., Gingell, K., Hawai, Z., Kirley, A., Lowe, N., Fitzgerald, M., Gill, M., & Craddock, N. (2002). Evidence that variation at the serotonin transporter gene influences susceptibility to attention deficit hyperactivity disorder (ADHD): Analysis and pooled analysis. *Molecular Psychiatry, 7*, 908–912.

Kercsmar, C. (1998). The respiratory system. In R. Behrman & R. Kliegman (Eds.), *Nelson essentials of pediatrics* (3rd ed). Philadelphia: W. B. Saunders.

Kerns, K., Don, A., Mateer, C., & Streissguth, A. (1997). Cognitive deficits in nonretarded adults with fetal alcohol syndrome. *Journal of Learning Disabilities, 30*, 685–693.

Kerr, C., McDowell, B., & McDonough, S. (2007). The relationship between gross motor function and participation restriction in children with cerebral palsy: An exploratory analysis. *Child: Care, Health and Development, 33*, 22–27.

Khan, M. (2007). Emotional and behavioral effects, including addictive potential, of video games: Report of the AMA Council on Science and Public Health. Retrieved June 28, 2007 from http://www.ama-assn.org/ama1/pub/upload/mm/467/csaph12a07.doc.

Khanna, G., & Kapoor, S. (2004). Secular trend in stature and age at menarche among Punjabi Aroras residing in New Delhi, India. *Collegium Antropologicum, 28*, 571–575.

Kickbusch, I. (2001). Health literacy: Addressing the health and education divide. *Health Promotion International, 16*, 289–297.

Kilbride, H., Castor, C., Hoffman, E., & Fuger, K. (2000). Thirty-six month outcome of prenatal cocaine exposure for term or near-term infants: Impact of early case management. *Journal of Developmental Pediatrics, 21*, 19–26.

Kilpatrick, S. J., & Laros, R. K. (1989). Characteristics of normal labor. *Obstetrics & Gynecology, 74*, 85–87.

Kim, K., Relkin, N., Lee, K., & Hirsch, J. (1997). Distinct cortical areas associated with native and second languages. *Nature, 388*, 171–174.

Kim, S. (1997). Relationships between young children's day care experience and their attachment relationships with parents and socioemotional behavior problems. *Korean Journal of Child Studies, 18*, 5–18.

Kinney, D. A. (1993). From "nerds" to "normals": Adolescent identity recovery within a changing social system. *Sociology of Education, 66*, 21–40.

Kinzl, J., Mangweth, B., Traweger, C., & Biebl, W. (1996). Sexual dysfunction in males: Significance of adverse childhood experiences. *Child Abuse & Neglect, 20*, 759–766.

Kirk, S., Gallagher, J., & Anastasiow, N. (1993). *Educating exceptional children* (7th ed.). Boston: Houghton Mifflin.

Kirkcaldy, B., Siefen, G., Surall, D., & Bischoff, R. (2004). Predictors of drug and alcohol abuse among children and adolescents. *Personality & Individual Differences, 36*, 247–265.

Klaczynski, P., Fauth, J., & Swanger, A. (1998). Adolescent identity: Rational vs. experiential processing, formal operations, and critical thinking beliefs. *Journal of Youth & Adolescence, 27*, 185–207.

Klahr, D. (1992). Information-processing approaches to cognitive development. In M. H. Bernstein & M. E. Lamb (Eds.), *Developmental psychology: An advanced textbook* (3rd ed., pp. 273–335). Hillsdale, NJ: Erlbaum.

Klar, A. (2003). Human handedness and scalp hair-whorl direction develop from a common genetic mechanism. *Genetics, 165*, 269–276.

Klass, P., & Costello, E. (2003). *Quirky kids: Understanding and helping your child who doesn't fit in: When to worry and when not to worry.* New York: Ballantine Books.

Klauda, S., & Guthrie, J. (2008). Relationships of three components of reading fluency to reading comprehension. *Journal of Educational Psychology, 100*, 310–321.

Kliegman, R. (1998). Fetal and neonatal medicine. In R. Behrman & R. Klieg-man (Eds.), *Nelson essentials of pediatrics* (3rd ed., pp. 167–225). Philadelphia: W. B. Saunders.

Klomsten, A., Skaalvik, E., & Espnes, G. (2004). Physical self-concept and sports: Do gender differences still exist? *Sex Roles: A Journal of Research, 50*, 119–127.

Knecht, S. (2004). Does language lateralization depend on the hippocampus? *Brain, 127*, 1229–1236.

Kobayashi, M., Glover, G., & Temple, E. (2008). Switching language switches mind: Linguistic effects on developmental neural bases of "theory of mind." *Social Cognitive and Affective Neuroscience, 3*, 62–70.

Kobayashi, M., Haynes, C., Macaruso, P., Hook, P., & Kato, J. (2005). Effects of mora deletion, nonword repetition, rapid naming, and visual search performance on beginning reading in Japanese. *Annals of Dyslexia, 55*, 105–128.

Kochanek, K., & Martin, J. (2004). Supplemental analyses of recent trends in infant mortality. Retrieved April 13, 2004 from http://www.cdc.gov.

Kochanek, K., & Smith, B. (2004). Deaths: Preliminary data for 2002. *National Vital Statistics Report: Volume 52.* Hyattsville, Maryland: National Center for Health Statistics. Retrieved April 13, 2004 from http://www.cdc.gov.

Kochanska, G. (1997a). Multiple pathways to conscience for children with different temperaments: From toddlerhood to age 5. *Developmental Psychology, 33*, 228–240.

Kochanska, G. (1997b). Mutually responsive orientation between mothers and their young: Implications for early socialization. *Child Development, 68*, 94–112.

Kochanska, G., Murray, K., & Coy, K. (1997). Inhibitory control as a contributor to conscience in childhood: From toddler to early school age. *Child Development, 68*, 263–277.

Kochanska, G., Murray, K., Jacques, T., Koenig, & A., Vandegeest, K. (1996). Inhibitory control in young children and its role in emerging internalization. *Child Development, 67*, 490–507.

Koenen, K., Moffitt, T., Poulton, R., Martin, J., & Caspi, A. (2007). Early childhood factors associated with the development of post-traumatic stress disorder: Results from a longitudinal birth cohort. *Psychological Medicine, 37*, 181–192.

Koenig, A., Cicchetti, D., & Rogosch, F. (2004). Moral development: The association between maltreatment and young children's prosocial behaviors and moral transgressions. *Social Development, 13*, 97–106.

Koeppe, R. (1996). Language differentiation in bilingual children: The development of grammatical and pragmatic competence. *Linguistics, 34*, 927–954.

Kohlberg, L. (1964). Development of moral character and moral ideology. In M. L. Hoffman & L. W. Hoffman (Eds.), *Review of child development research, Vol. 1* (pp. 283–332). New York: Russell Sage Foundation.

Kohlberg, L. (1966). A cognitive-developmental analysis of children's sex-role concepts and attitudes. In E. E. Maccoby (Ed.), *The development of sex differences* (pp. 82–172). Stanford, CA: Stanford University Press.

Kohlberg, L. (1976). Moral stages and moralization: The cognitive developmental approach. In T. Lickona (Ed.), *Moral development and behavior: Theory, research, and social issues* (pp. 31–53). New York: Holt.

Kohlberg, L. (1981). *Essays on moral development, Vol. 1: The philosophy of moral development.* New York: Harper & Row.

Kohlberg, L., & Elfenbein, D. (1975). The development of moral judgments concerning capital punishment. *American Journal of Orthopsychiatry, 54*, 614–640.

Kohlberg, L., Levine, C., & Hewer, A. (1983). *Moral stages: A current formulation and a response to critics.* Basel, Switzerland: S. Karger.

Kohlberg, L., & Ullian, D. Z. (1974). Stages in the development of psychosexual concepts and attitudes. In R. C. Friedman, R. M. Richart, & R. L. Vande Wiele (Eds.), *Sex differences in behavior* (pp. 209–222). New York: Wiley.

Kohler, P., Manhart, L., & Lafferty, W. (2008). Abstinence-only and comprehensive sex education and the initiation of sexual activity and teen pregnancy. *Journal of Adolescent Health, 42,* 344–351.

Koppehaver, D., Hendrix, M., & Williams, A. (2007). Toward evidence-based literacy interventions for children with severe and multiple disabilities. *Seminars in Speech & Language, 28,* 79–90.

Koskinen, P., Blum, I., Bisson, S., Phillips, S., et al. (2000). Book access, shared reading, and audio models: The effects of supporting the literacy learning of linguistically diverse students in school and at home. *Journal of Educational Psychology, 92,* 23–36.

Kost, K. (1997). The effects of support on the economic well-being of young fathers. *Families in Society, 78,* 370–382.

Kostanski, M., Fisher, A., & Gullone, E. (2004). Current conceptualisation of body image dissatisfaction: Have we got it wrong? *Journal of Child Psychology and Psychiatry, 45,* 1317–1325.

Krakovsky, M. (2005, February 2). Dubious Mozart effect remains music to many Americans' ears. *Stanford Report.* Retrieved May 3, 2005 from http://newservice.stanford.edu/news/2005/february2/mozart-0202.

Krebs, D., & Denton, K. (2006). Explanatory limitations of cognitive-developmental approaches to morality. *Psychological Review, 113,* 672–675.

Kristensen, P., & Bjerkedal, T. (2007). Explaining the relation between birth order and intelligence. *Science, 316,* 1717.

Ku, S., Kang, J., Kim, H., Kim, Y., Jee, B., Suh, C., Choi, Y., Kim, J., Moon, S., & Kim, S. (2006). Age at menarche and its influencing factors in North Korean female refugees. *Human Reproduction, 21,* 833–836.

Kuhn, D. (1992). Cognitive development. In M. H. Bornstein & M. E. Lamb (Eds.), *Developmental psychology: An advanced textbook* (3rd ed., pp. 211–272). Hillsdale, NJ: Erlbaum.

Kuhn, D. (2008). Formal operations from a twenty-first century perspective. *Human Development, 51,* 48–55.

Kuhn, D., Kohlberg, L., Languer, J., & Haan, N. (1977). The development of formal operations in logical and moral judgment. *Genetic Psychology Monographs, 95,* 97–188.

Kurdek, L. A., & Fine, M. A. (1994). Family acceptance and family control as predictors of adjustment in young adolescents: Linear, curvilinear, or interactive effects? *Child Development, 65,* 1137–1146.

Kuttler, A., La Greca, A., & Prinstein, M. (1999). Friendship qualities and social-emotional functioning of adolescents with close, cross-sex friendships. *Journal of Research on Adolescence, 9,* 339–366.

La Freniere, P., Strayer, F. F., & Gauthier, R. (1984). The emergence of same-sex affiliative preferences among preschool peers. A developmental/ethological perspective. *Child Development, 55,* 1958–1965.

Laird, R., Pettit, G., Dodge, K., & Bates, J. (1999). Best friendships, group relationships, and antisocial behavior in early adolescence. *Journal of Early Adolescence, 19,* 413–437.

Lakatos, K., Nemoda, Z., Birkas, E., Ronai, Z., Kovacs, E., Ney, K., Toth, I., Sasvari-Szekely, M., & Gervai, J. (2003). Association of D4 dopamine receptor gene and serotonin transporter romoter polymorphisms with infants' response to novelty. *Molecular Psychiatry, 8,* 90–97.

Lam, C., Lam, M., Shek, D., & Tang, V. (2004). Coping with economic disadvantage. A qualitative study of Chinese adolescents from low-income families. *International Journal of Adolescent Medicine and Health, 16,* 343–357.

Lamb, M. E. (1981). The development of father-infant relationships. In M. E. Lamb (Ed.), *The role of the father in child development* (2nd ed., pp. 459–488). New York: Wiley.

Lamb, M. E., Bornstein, M. H., & Teti, D. (2002). *Development in infancy: An introduction.* Mahwah, NJ: Erlbaum.

Lamb, M. E., & Lewis, C. (2005). The role of parent-child relationships in child development. In M. H. Bornstein & M. E. Lamb (Eds.), *Developmental science: An advanced textbook* (5th ed., pp. 429–468). Hillsdale, NJ: Erlbaum.

Lamb, M. E., Sternberg, K. J., & Prodromidis, M. (1992). Nonmaternal care and the security of infant-mother attachment: A reanalysis of the data. *Infant Behavior & Development, 15,* 71–83.

Lamborn, S. D., Mounts, N. S., Steinberg, L., & Dornbusch, S. M. (1991). Patterns of competence and adjustment among adolescents from authoritative, authoritarian, indulgent, and neglectful families. *Child Development, 62,* 1049–1065.

Landry, S. H., Garner, P. W., Swank, P. R., & Baldwin, C. D. (1996). Effects of maternal scaffolding during joint toy play with preterm and full-term infants. *Merrill-Palmer Quarterly, 42,* 177–199.

Langer, G., Arnedt, C., & Sussman, D. (2004). Primetime Live poll: American sex survey analysis. Retrieved June 22, 2007 from http://abcnews.go.com/Primetime/PollVault/story?id=156921&page=1.

Langlois, J. H., Roggman, L. A., & Rieser-Danner, L. A. (1990). Infants' differential social responses to attractive and unattractive faces. *Developmental Psychology, 26,* 153–159.

Larson, R. (2000). Toward a psychology of positive youth development. *American Psychologist, 55,* 170–183.

Larson, R., & Verma, S. (1999). How children and adolescents spend time across the world: Work, play, and developmental opportunities. *Psychological Bulletin, 125,* 701–736.

Lau, A., Uba, A., & Lehman, D. (2002). Infectious diseases. In A. Rudolph, R. Kamei, & K. Overby (Eds.), *Rudolph's fundamentals of pediatrics* (3rd ed., pp. 289–399). New York: McGraw-Hill.

Lauritsen, M., Pedersen, C., & Mortensen, P. (2004). The incidence and prevalence of pervasive developmental disorders: A Danish population-based study. *Psychological Medicine, 34,* 1339–1346.

Laursen, B. (1995). Conflict and social interaction in adolescent relationships. *Journal of Research on Adolescence, 5,* 55–70.

Lawrence, V., Houghton, S., Douglas, G., Durkin, K., Whiting, K., & Tannock, R. (2004). Children with ADHD: Neuropsychological testing and real-world activities. *Journal of Attention Disorders, 7,* 137–149.

Layton, L., Deeny, K., Tall, G., & Upton, G. (1996). Researching and promoting phonological awareness in the nursery class. *Journal of Research in Reading, 19,* 1–13.

Leaper, C. (1991). Influence and involvement in children's discourse: Age, gender, and partner effects. *Child Development, 62,* 797–811.

Lederer, J. (2000). Reciprocal teaching of social studies in inclusive elementary classrooms. *Journal of Learning Disabilities, 33,* 91–106.

Lederman, R., & Mian, T. (2003). The Parent-Adolescent Relationship Education (PARE) program: A curriculum for prevention of STDs and pregnancy in middle school youth. *Behavioral Medicine, 29,* 33–41.

Legendre, G. (2006). Early child grammars: Qualitative and quantitative analysis of morphosyntactic production. *Cognitive Science, 30,* 803–835.

Legerstee, M., Pomerleau, A., Malcuit, G., & Feider, H. (1987). The development of infants' responses to people and a doll: Implications for research in communication. *Infant Behavior & Development, 10,* 81–95.

Leichtman M., & Ceci S. (1995). The effects of stereotypes and suggestions on preschoolers' reports. *Developmental Psychology, 31,* 568–578.

Lenhart, A., Arafeh, S., Smith, A., & Macgill, A. (2008). Writing, technology, and teens. Retrieved June 29, 2008 from http://www.pewinternet.org/pdfs/PIP_Writing_Report_FINAL3.pdf.

Leong, F., Austin, J., Sekaran, U., & Komarraju, M. (1998). An evaluation of the cross-cultural validity of Holland's theory: Career choices by workers in India. *Journal of Vocational Behavior, 52,* 441–455.

Leve, L. D., & Fagot, B. I. (1995, April). The influence of attachment style and parenting behavior on children's prosocial behavior with peers. Paper presented at the biennial meetings of the Society for Research in Child Development, Indianapolis.

Levine, J., Pollack, H., & Comfort, M. (2001). Academic and behavioral outcomes among the children of young mothers. *Journal of Marriage & Family, 63,* 355–369.

LeVine, R. (1974). Parental goals: A cross-cultural view. *Teachers College Record, 76,* 226–239.

Levitt, M. J., Guacci-Franco, N., & Levitt, J. L. (1993). Convoys of social support in childhood and early adolescence: Structure and function. *Developmental Psychology, 29,* 811–818.

Levy, G. D., & Fivush, R. (1993). Scripts and gender: A new approach for examining gender-role development. *Developmental Review, 13,* 126–146.

Lewis, C., & Lamb, M. E. (2003). Fathers' influences on children's development: The evidence from two-parent families. *European Journal of Psychology of Education, 18,* 211–228.

Lewis, C. C. (1981). How adolescents approach decisions: Changes over grades seven to twelve and policy implications. *Child Development, 52,* 538–544.

Lewis, M. (1990). Social knowledge and social development. *Merrill-Palmer Quarterly, 36,* 93–116.

Lewis, M. (1991). Ways of knowing: Objective self-awareness of consciousness. *Developmental Review, 11,* 231–243.

Lewis, M., Allesandri, S. M., & Sullivan, M. W. (1992). Differences in shame and pride as a function of children's gender and task difficulty. *Child Development, 63,* 630–638.

Lewis, M., & Brooks, J. (1978). Self-knowledge and emotional development. In M. Lewis & L. A. Rosenblum (Eds.), *The development of affect* (pp. 205–226). New York: Plenum.

Lewis, M., Sullivan, M. W., Stanger, C., & Weiss, M. (1989). Self development and self-conscious emotions. *Child Development, 60,* 146–156.

Lewis, M. D. (1993). Early socioemotional predictors of cognitive competence at 4 years. *Developmental Psychology, 29,* 1036–1045.

Lewis, V. (2002). *Development and disability* (2nd ed.). Malden, MA: Blackwell Publishing.

Li, S., Lindenberger, B., Aschersleben, G., Prinz, W., & Baltes, P. (2004). Transformations in the couplings among intellectual abilities and constituent cognitive processes across the life span. *Psychological Science, 15,* 155–163.

Lickona, T. (1978). Moral development and moral education. In J. M. Gallagher & J. J. A. Easley (Eds.), *Knowledge and development, Vol. 2* (pp. 21–74). New York: Plenum.

Lickona, T. (1983). *Raising good children.* New York: Bantam Books.

Lickona, T. (2004). *Character matters: How to help our children develop good judgment, integrity, and other essential virtues.* New York: Simon & Schuster.

Lieberman, M., Doyle, A., & Markiewicz, D. (1999). Developmental patterns in security of attachment to mother and father in late childhood and early adolescence: Associations with peer relations. *Child Development, 70,* 202–213.

Li-Grining, C. (2007). Effortful control among low-income preschoolers in three cities: Stability, change, and individual differences. *Developmental Psychology, 43,* 208–221.

Lillard, A. (2006a). Guided participation: How mothers structure and children understand pretend play. In A. Göncü & S. Gaskins (Eds.), *Play and development: Evolutionary, sociocultural, and functional perspectives* (pp. 131–153). The Jean Piaget symposium series. Mahwah, NJ: Erlbaum.

Lillard, A. (2006b). The socialization of theory of mind: Cultural and social class differences in behavior explanation. In A. Alessandro, O. Sempio-Liverta, & A. Marchetti (Eds.), *Theory of mind and language in developmental contexts* (pp. 65–76). New York: Spring Science and Business Media.

Lillard, A. S., & Flavell, J. H. (1992). Young children's understanding of different mental states. *Developmental Psychology, 28,* 626–634.

Lindsay, D. S., & Read, J. D. (1994). Psychotherapy and memory of childhood sexual abuse: A cognitive perspective. *Applied Cognitive Psychology, 8,* 281–338.

Linnet, K., Dalsgaard, S., Obel, C., Wisborg, K., Henriksen, T., Rodriquez, A., Kotimaa, A., Moilanen, I., Thomsen, P., Olsen, J., & Jarvelin, M. (2003). Maternal lifestyle factors in pregnancy risk of attention deficit hyperactivity disorder and associated behaviors: Review of the current evidence. *American Journal of Psychiatry, 160,* 1028–1040.

Lippa, R. (2005). *Gender, nature, and nurture.* Hillsdale, NJ: Erlbaum.

Lippé, R., Perchet, C., & Lassonde, M. (2007). Electrophysical markers of visocortical development. *Cerebral Cortex, 17,* 100–107.

Liu, D., & Wellman, H. (2004). Scaling of theory-of-mind tasks. *Child Development, 75,* 523–541.

Liu, D., Wellman, H., Tardif, T., & Sabbagh, M. (2008). Theory of mind development in Chinese children: A meta-analysis of false-belief understanding across cultures and languages. *Developmental Psychology, 44,* 523–531.

Livesley, W. J., & Bromley, D. B. (1973). *Person perception in childhood and adolescence.* London: Wiley.

Livingstone, S., & Helsper, E. (2006). Does advertising literacy mediate the effects of advertising on children? A critical examination of two linked research literatures in relation to obesity and food choice. *Journal of Communication, 56,* 560–584.

Lobel, T., Slone, M., & Winch, G. (1997). Masculinity, popularity, and self-esteem among Israeli preadolescent girls. *Sex Roles, 36,* 395–408.

Loeb, S., Fuller, B., Kagan, S., & Carrol, B. (2004). Child care in poor communities: Early learning effects of type, quality, and stability. *Child Development, 75,* 47–65.

Loehlin, J. C., Horn, J. M., & Willerman, L. (1994). Differential inheritance of mental abilities in the Texas Adoption Project. *Intelligence, 19,* 325–336.

Lopez-Alarcon, M., Villapando, S., & Fajardo, A. (1997). Breast-feeding lowers the frequency and duration of acute respiratory infection and diarrhea in infants under six months of age. *Journal of Nutrition, 127,* 436–443.

Lorenz, K. (1935). The companion in the bird's world. The fellow-member of the species as releasing factor of social behavior. *Journal for Ornithology, 83,* 137–213.

Love, J., Harrison, L., Sagi-Schwartz, A., van IJzendoorn, M., Ross, C., Ungerer, J., Raikes, H., Brady-Smith, C., Boller, K., Brooks-Gunn, J., Constantine, J., Kisker, E., Paulsell, D., & Chazan-Cohen, R. (2003). Child care quality matters: How conclusions may vary with context. *Child Development, 74,* 1021–1033.

Lubart, T. (2003). In search of creative intelligence. In R. Sternberg, J. Lautrey, & T. Lubart (Eds.), *Models of intelligence for the next millenium* (pp. 279–292). Washington, DC: American Psychological Association.

Lubinski, D., & Benbow, C. P. (1992). Gender differences in abilities and preferences among the gifted: Implications for the math-science pipeline. *Current Directions in Psychological Science, 1,* 61–66.

Ludwig, J., & Miller, D. (2007). Does Head Start improve children's life chances? Evidence from a regression discontinuity design. *Quarterly Journal of Economics, 122*, 159–208.

Luna, B., Garver, K., Urban, T., Lazar, N., & Sweeney, J. (2004). Maturation of cognitive processes from late childhood to adulthood. *Child Development, 75*, 1357–1372.

Luster, T., & McAdoo, H. P. (1995). Factors related to self-esteem among African American youths: A secondary analysis of the High/Scope Perry Preschool data. *Journal of Research on Adolescence, 5*, 451–467.

Luthar, S. S., & Zigler, E. (1992). Intelligence and social competence among high-risk adolescents. *Development & Psychopathology, 4*, 287–299.

Lynam, D., Moffitt, T., & Stouthamer-Loeber, M. (1993). Explaining the relation between IQ and delinquency: Class, race, test motivation, school failure, or self-control? *Journal of Abnormal Psychology, 102*, 187–196.

Lynch, R. (2004). Surfactant and RDS in premature infants. *Journal of the Federation of American Societies for Experimental Biology, 18*, 1624.

Lyons, N. P. (1983). Two perspectives: On self, relationships, and morality. *Harvard Educational Review, 53*, 125–145.

Lyons-Ruth, K. (1996). Attachment relationships among children with aggressive behavior problems: The role of early disorganized attachment patterns. *Journal of Consulting and Clinical Psychology, 64*, 64–73.

Lytton, H., & Romney, D. M. (1991). Parents' differential socialization of boys and girls: A meta-analysis. *Psychological Bulletin, 109*, 267–296.

Ma, H. (2003). The relation of moral orientation and moral judgment to prosocial and antisocial behaviour of Chinese adolescents. *International Journal of Psychology, 38*, 101–111.

Ma, H., Shek, D., Cheung, P., & Oi Bun Lam, C. (2000). Parental, peer and teacher influences on the social behavior of Hong Kong Chinese adolescents. *Journal of Genetic Psychology, 161*, 65–78.

Maccoby, E. E. (1980). *Social development: Psychological growth and the parent-child relationship.* New York: Harcourt Brace Jovanovich.

Maccoby, E. E. (1988). Gender as a social category. *Developmental Psychology, 24*, 755–765.

Maccoby, E. E. (1990). Gender and relationships: A developmental account. *American Psychologist, 45*, 513–520.

Maccoby, E. E. (1995). The two sexes and their social systems. In P. Moen, G. H. Elder, Jr., & K. Lüscher (Eds.), *Examining lives in context: Perspectives on the ecology of human development* (pp. 347–364). Washington, DC: American Psychological Association.

Maccoby, E. E., & Jacklin, C. N. (1987). Gender segregation in childhood. In H. W. Reese (Ed.), *Advances in child development and behavior, Vol. 20* (pp. 239–288). Orlando, FL: Academic Press.

Maccoby, E. E., & Lewis, C. (2003). Less day care or different day care? *Child Development, 74*, 1069–1075.

Maccoby, E. E., & Martin, J. A. (1983). Socialization in the context of the family: Parent-child interaction. In E. M. Hetherington (Ed.), *Handbook of child psychology: Socialization, personality, & social development, Vol. 4* (pp. 1–102). New York: Wiley.

MacDorman, M., & Atkinson, J. (1999, July 30). Infant mortality statistics from the 1997 period. Linked birth/infant death data set. *National Vital Statistics Reports, 47*(23), 1–24.

MacIver, D. J., Reuman, D. A., & Main, S. R. (1995). Social structuring of the school: Studying what is, illuminating what could be. *Annual Review of Psychology, 46*, 375–400.

Mackey, E., & La Greca, A. (2007). Adolescents' eating, exercise, and weight control behaviors: Does peer crowd affiliation play a role? *Journal of Pediatric Psychology, 32*, 13–23.

Mackintosh, N. (2007). Review of race differences in intelligence: An evolutionary hypothesis. *Intelligence, 35*, 94–96.

MacMaster, F., & Kusumakar, V. (2004). MRI study of the pituitary gland in adolescent depression. *Journal of Psychiatric Research, 38*, 231–236.

MacMillan, D., & Reschly, D. (1997). Issues of definition and classification. In W. MacLean (Ed.), *Ellis's handbook of mental deficiency* (3rd ed., pp. 686–724). Mahwah, NJ: Erlbaum.

Macrae, C., & Bodenhausen, G. (2000). Social cognition: Thinking categorically about others. *Annual Review of Psychology, 51*, 93–120.

Madan-Swain, A., Brown, R., Foster, M., Verga, R., et al. (2000). Identity in adolescent survivors of childhood cancer. *Journal of Pediatric Psychology, 25*, 105–115.

Madison, C., Johnson, J., Seikel, J., Arnold, M., & Schultheis, L. (1998). Comparative study of the phonology of preschool children prenatally exposed to cocaine and multiple drugs and non-exposed children. *Journal of Communication Disorders, 31*, 231–244.

Madsen, K., Hviid, A., Vestergaard, M., Schendel, D., Wohlfahrt, J., Thorsen, P., Olsen, J., & Melbye, M. (2003). A population-based study of measles, mumps, rubella vaccination and autism. *New England Journal of Medicine, 347*, 1477–1482.

Madsen, K., Lauritsen, M., Pederson, C., Thorsen, P., Plesner, A., Andersen, P., & Mortensen, P. (2003). Thimerosal and the occurrence of autism: Negative ecological evidence from Danish population-based data. *Pediatrics, 112*, 604–606.

Magarey, A., Daniels, L., Boulton, T., & Cockington, R. (2003). Predicting obesity in early adulthood from childhood and parental obesity. *International Journal of Obesity & Related Metabolic Disorders, 27*, 505–513.

Magiera, K., & Zigmond, N. (2005). Co-teaching in middle school classrooms under routine conditions: Does the instructional experience differ for students with learning disabilities in co-taught and solo-taught classes? *Learning Disabilities Research & Practice, 20*, 79–85.

Maguire, M., & Dunn, J. (1997). Friendships in early childhood and social understanding. *International Journal of Behavioral Development, 21*, 669–686.

Mah, L., Arnold, M., & Grafman, J. (2004). Impairment of social perception associated with lesions of the prefrontal cortex. *American Journal of Psychiatry, 161*, 1247–1255.

Main, M., & Hesse, E. (1990). Parents' unresolved traumatic experiences are related to infant disorganized attachment status: Is frightened and/or frightening parental behavior the linking mechanism? In M. T. Greenberg, D. Cicchetti, & E. M. Cummings (Eds.), *Attachment in the preschool years: Theory, research, and intervention* (pp. 161–182). Chicago: University of Chicago Press.

Main, M., & Solomon, J. (1990). Procedures for identifying infants as disorganized/disoriented during the Ainsworth Strange Situation. In M. T. Greenberg, D. Cicchetti, & E. M. Cummings (Eds.), *Attachment in the preschool years: Theory, research, and intervention* (pp. 121–160). Chicago: University of Chicago Press.

Maitel, S., Dromi, E., Sagi, A., & Bornstein, M. (2000). The Hebrew Communicative Development Inventory: Language-specific properties and cross-linguistic generalizations. *Journal of Child Language, 27*, 43–67.

Maki, P., Veijola, J., Rantakallio, P., Jokelainen, J., Jones, P., & Isohanni, M. (2004). Schizophrenia in the offspring of antenatally depressed mothers: A 31-year follow-up of the Northern Finland 1966 Birth Cohort. *Schizophrenia Research, 66*, 79–81.

Malabonga, V., & Pasnak, R. (2002). Hierarchical categorization by bilingual Latino children: Does a basic-level bias exist? *Genetic, Social, & General Psychology Monographs, 128*, 409–441.

Malina, R. M. (1990). Physical growth and performance during the transition years. In R. Montemayor, G. R. Adams, & T. P. Gullotta (Eds.), *From childhood to adolescence: A transitional period?* (pp. 41–62). Newbury Park, CA: Sage.

Malinosky-Rummel, R., & Hansen, D. (1993). Long-term consequences of childhood physical abuse. *Psychological Bulletin, 114,* 68–79.

Mallet, P., Apostolidis, T., & Paty, B. (1997). The development of gender schemata about heterosexual and homosexual others during adolescence. *Journal of General Psychology, 124,* 91–104.

Maratsos, M. (1998). The acquisition of grammar. In W. Damon (Ed.), *Handbook of child psychology, Vol. 2: Cognition, perception, and language* (5th ed., pp. 421–466). New York: Wiley.

Maratsos, M. (2000). More overregularizations after all: New data and discussion of Marcus, Pinker, Ullman, Hollander, Rosen, & Xu. *Journal of Child Language, 27,* 183–212.

March of Dimes. (2004). Environmental risks and pregnancy. Retrieved September, 21, 2004 from http://www.marchofdimes.com/professionals/681_9146.asp.

Marcia, J. E. (1966). Development and validation of ego identity status. *Journal of Personality & Social Psychology, 3,* 551–558.

Marcia, J. E. (1980). Identity in adolescence. In J. Adelson (Ed.), *Handbook of adolescent psychology* (pp. 159–187). New York: Wiley.

Marcia, J. E. (2002). Identity and psychosocial development in adulthood. *Identity, 2,* 7–28.

Marcus, D. E., & Overton, W. F. (1978). The development of cognitive gender constancy and sex role preferences. *Child Development, 49,* 434–444.

Marcus, R. F. (1986). Naturalistic observation of cooperation, helping, and sharing and their association with empathy and affect. In C. Zahn-Waxler, E. M. Cummings, & R. Iannotti (Eds.), *Altruism and aggression: Biological and social origins* (pp. 256–279). Cambridge, England: Cambridge University Press.

Marean, G. C., Werner, L. A., & Kuhl, P. K. (1992). Vowel categorization by very young infants. *Developmental Psychology, 28,* 396–405.

Margolin, G., & Gordis, E. (2000). The effects of family and community violence on children. *Annual Review of Psychology, 51,* 445–479.

Markey, C., Markey, P., & Tinsley, B. (2003). Personality, puberty, and preadolescent girls' risky behaviors: Examining the predictive value of the Five-Factor Model of personality. *Journal of Research in Personality, 37,* 405–419.

Markman, E. M. (1992). Constraints on word learning: Speculations about their nature, origins, and domain specificity. In M. R. Gunnar & M. Maratsos (Eds.), *Minnesota Symposia on Child Psychology, Vol. 25* (pp. 59–101). Hillsdale, NJ: Erlbaum.

Marsh, H., Craven, R., & Debus, R. (1999). Separation of competency and affect components of multiple dimensions of academic self-concept: A developmental perspective. *Merrill-Palmer Quarterly, 45,* 567–601.

Marsh, H., & Yeung, A. (1997). Coursework selection: Relations to academic self-concept and achievement. *American Educational Research Journal, 34,* 691–720.

Marshall, N., Coll, C., Marx, F., McCartney, K., Keefe, N., & Ruh, J. (1997). After-school time and children's behavioral adjustment. *Merrill-Palmer Quarterly, 43,* 497–514.

Martin, C. L. (1991). The role of cognition in understanding gender effects. In H. W. Reese (Ed.), *Advances in child development and behavior, Vol. 23* (pp. 113–150). San Diego, CA: Academic Press.

Martin, C. L. (1993). New directions for investigating children's gender knowledge. *Developmental Review, 13,* 184–204.

Martin, C. L., & Halverson, C. F., Jr. (1981). A schematic processing model of sex typing and stereotyping in children. *Child Development, 52,* 1119–1134.

Martin, C. L., & Little, J. K. (1990). The relation of gender understanding to children's sex-typed preferences and gender stereotypes. *Child Development, 61,* 1427–1439.

Martin, C., L. & Ruble, D. (2002). Cognitive theories of early gender development. *Psychological Bulletin, 128,* 903–933.

Martin, C. L., Wood, C. H., & Little, J. K. (1990). The development of gender stereotype components. *Child Development, 61,* 1891–1904.

Martin, J. (1995). Birth characteristics for Asian or Pacific Islander subgroups, 1992. *Monthly Vital Statistics Report, 43* (10, Supplement).

Martin, J., & D'Augelli, A. (2003). How lonely are gay and lesbian youth? *Psychological Reports, 93,* 486.

Martin, J., Hamilton, B., Sutton, P., Ventura, S., Menacker, F., & Kirmeyer, S. (2006). Births: Final data for 2004. *National Vital Statistics Reports, 55,* 1–102.

Martin, J., Hamilton, B., Sutton, P., Ventura, S., Menacker, F., & Munson, M. (2005). Births: Final data for 2003. *National Vital Statistics Reports, 54,* 1–116.

Martin, R. P., Noyes, J., Wisenbaker, J. & Huttunen, M. (1999). Prediction of early childhood negative emotionality and inhibition from maternal distress during pregnancy. *Merrill-Palmer Quarterly, 45,* 370–391.

Martin, R. P., Wisenbaker, J., & Huttunen, M. (1994). Review of factor analytic studies of temperament measures based on the Thomas-Chess structural model: Implications for the Big Five. In C. F. Halverson, Jr., G. A. Kohnstamm, & R. P. Martin (Eds.), *The developing structure of temperament and personality from infancy to adulthood* (pp. 157–172). Hillsdale, NJ: Erlbaum.

Martino, S., Elliott, M., Collins, R., Kanouse, D., & Berry, S. (2008). Virginity pledges among the willing: Delays in first intercourse and consistency of condom use. *Journal of Adolescent Health, 43,* in press.

Martorano, S. C. (1977). A developmental analysis of performance on Piaget's formal operations tasks. *Developmental Psychology, 13,* 666–672.

Mascolo, M. F., & Fischer, K. W. (1995). Developmental transformations in appraisals for pride, shame, and guilt. In J. P. Tangney & K. W. Fischer (Eds.), *Self-conscious emotions: The psychology of shame, guilt, embarrassment, and pride* (pp. 64–113). New York: Guilford Press.

Mason, M., & Chuang, S. (2001). Culturally-based after-school arts programming for low-income urban children: Adaptive and preventive effects. *Journal of Primary Prevention, 22,* 45–54.

Masten, A. S., Best, K. M., & Garmezy, N. (1990). Resilience and development: Contributions from the study of children who overcome adversity. *Development & Psychopathology, 2,* 425–444.

Masten, A. S. & Coatsworth, D. (1998). The development of competence in favorable and unfavorable environments: Lessons from research on successful children. *American Psychologist, 53,* 205–220.

Maszk, P., Eisenberg, N., & Guthrie, I. (1999). Relations of children's social status to their emotionality and regulation: A short-term longitudinal study. *Merrill-Palmer Quarterly, 454,* 468–492.

Mathew, A., & Cook, M. (1990). The control of reaching movements by young infants. *Child Development, 61,* 1238–1257.

Matson, J. (2008). A review of behavioral treatment for self-injurious behavior of persons with autism spectrum disorders. *Behavior Modification, 32,* 61–76.

Matthews, T. (2005). Racial/ethnic disparities in infant mortality: United States, 1995–2002. *Morbidity & Mortality Weekly Report, 54,* 553–556.

Mattson, S., & Riley, E. (1999). Implicit and explicit memory functioning in children with heavy prenatal alcohol exposure. *Journal of the International Neuropsychological Society, 5,* 462–471.

Mattson, S., Riley, E., Gramling, L., Delis, D., & Jones, K. (1998). Neuropsychological comparison of alcohol-exposed children with or without physical features of fetal alcohol syndrome. *Neuropsychology, 12*, 146–153.

Maughan, B., Pickles, A., & Quinton, D. (1995). Parental hostility, childhood behavior, and adult social functioning. In J. McCord (Ed.), *Coercion and punishment in long-term perspectives* (pp. 34–58). Cambridge, England: Cambridge University Press.

Maurer, D., & Maurer, C. (1988). *The world of the newborn.* New York: Basic Books.

Mayes, L., Cicchetti, D., Acharyya, S., & Zhang, H. (2003). Developmental trajectories of cocaine-and-other-drug-exposed and non-cocaine-exposed children. *Journal of Developmental & Behavioral Pediatrics, 24*, 323–335.

Mayeux, L., & Cillissen, A. (2003). Development of social problem solving in early childhood: Stability, change, and associations with social competence. *Journal of Genetic Psychology, 164*, 153–173.

Mayseless, O., & Scharf, M. (2007). Adolescents' attachment representations and their capacity for intimacy in close relationships. *Journal of Research on Adolescence, 17*, 23–50.

McAlister, A., & Peterson, C. (2006). Mental playmates: Siblings, executive functioning and theory of mind. *British Journal of Developmental Psychology, 24*, 733–751.

McAllister, D., Kaplan, B., Edworthy, S., Martin, L., et al. (1997). The influence of systemic lupus erythematosus on fetal development: Cognitive, behavioral, and health trends. *Journal of the International Neurological Society, 3*, 370–376.

McBride-Chang, C., & Ho, C. (2000). Developmental issues in Chinese children's character acquisition. *Journal of Educational Psychology, 92*, 50–55.

McBride-Chang, C., Shu, H., Zhou, C., & Wagner, R. (2004). Morphological awareness uniquely predicts young children's Chinese character recognition. *Journal of Educational Psychology, 96*, 743–751.

McCabe, K., Hough, R., Wood, P., & Yeh, M. (2001). Childhood and adolescent onset conduct disorder: A test of the developmental taxonomy. *Journal of Abnormal Child Psychology, 29*, 305–316.

McCall, R. B. (1993). Developmental functions for general mental performance. In D. K. Detterman (Ed.), *Current topics in human intelligence, Vol. 3: Individual differences and cognition* (pp. 3–30). Norwood, NJ: Ablex.

McClintock, M. K., and Herdt, G. (1996). Rethinking puberty: The development of sexual attraction. *Current Directions in Psychological Science, 5*, 181.

McCrae, R., Costa, P., Ostendorf, F., & Angleitner, A. (2000). Nature over nurture: Temperament, personality, and life span development. *Journal of Personality & Social Psychology, 78*, 173–186.

McCune, L. (1995). A normative study of representational play at the transition to language. *Developmental Psychology, 31*, 198–206.

McDonald, J. (1997). Language acquisition: The acquisition of linguistic structure in normal and special populations. *Annual Review of Psychology, 48*, 215–241.

McFayden-Ketchumm, S., Bates, J., Dodge, K., & Pettit, G. (1996). Patterns of change in early childhood aggressive-disruptive behavior: Gender differences in predictions from early coercive and affectionate mother-child interactions. *Child Development, 67*, 2417–2433.

McGrath, M., & Sullivan, M. (2002). Birth weight, neonatal morbidities, and school age outcomes in full-term and preterm infants. *Issues in Comprehensive Pediatric Nursing, 25*, 231–254.

McGregor, K., Sheng., L., & Smith, B. (2005). The precocious two-year-old: Status of the lexicon and links to the grammar. *Journal of Child Language, 32*, 563–585.

McHale, S., Crouter, A., & Tucker, C. (1999). Family context and gender role socialization in middle childhood: Comparing girls to boys and sisters to brothers. *Child Development, 70*, 990–1004.

McKay, S., Gravel, J., & Tharpe, A. (2008). Amplification considerations for children with minimal or mild bilateral hearing loss and unilateral hearing loss. *Trends in Amplification, 12*, 43–54.

McKelvie, P., & Low, J. (2002). Listening to Mozart does not improve children's spatial ability: Final curtains for the Mozart effect. *British Journal of Developmental Psychology, 20*, 241–258.

McKown, C., & Weinstein, R. (2003). The development and consequences of stereotype consciousness in middle childhood. *Child Development, 74*, 498–515.

McLanahan, S., & Sandefur, G. (1994). *Growing up with a single parent: What hurts, what helps.* Cambridge, MA: Harvard University Press.

Measles Initiative. (2007). Measles deaths in Africa plunge by 91 percent. Retrieved June 11, 2008 from http://www.measlesinitiative.org/index3.asp.

Mediascope Press. (1999). *Substance use in popular movies and music*/Issue Brief Series. Studio City, CA: Mediascope Inc.

Mediascope Press. (2000). *Teens, sex and the media*/Issue Brief Series. Studio City, CA: Mediascope Inc.

Medvedova, L. (1998). Personality dimensions—"little five "—and their relationships with coping strategies in early adolescence. *Studia Psychologica, 40*, 261–265.

Mehta, M., Goodyer, I., & Sahakian, B. (2004). Methylphenidate improves working memory and set-shifting in AD/HD: Relationships to baseline memory capacity. *Journal of Child Psychology & Psychiatry & Allied Disciplines, 45*, 293–305.

Mei, Z., Grummer-Strawn, L., Thompson, D., & Dietz, W. (2004). Shifts in percentiles of growth during early childhood: Analysis of longitudinal data from California Child Health and Development Study. *Pediatrics, 113*, 617–627.

Melby, J. N., & Conger, R. D. (1996). Parental behaviors and adolescent academic performance: A longitudinal analysis. *Journal of Research on Adolescence, 6*, 113–137.

Melot, A., & Houde, O. (1998). Categorization and theories of mind: the case of the appearance/reality distinction. *Cahiers de Psychologie Cognitive/Current Psychology of Cognition, 17*, 71–93.

Meltzoff, A. N. (1988). Infant imitation and memory: Nine-month-olds in immediate and deferred tasks. *Child Development, 59*, 217–225.

Meltzoff, A. N. (1995). Understanding the intentions of others: Re-enactment of intended acts by 18-month-old children. *Developmental Psychology, 31*, 838–850.

Merikangas, K. R., & Angst, J. (1995). The challenge of depressive disorders in adolescence. In M. Rutter (Ed.), *Psychosocial disturbances in young people: Challenges for prevention* (pp. 131–165). Cambridge, England: Cambridge University Press.

Merrick, J., & Morad, M. (2002). Adolescent pregnancy in Israel. *International Journal of Adolescent Medicine, 14*, 161–164.

Merson, M. (2006). The HIV/AIDS pandemic at 25: The global response. *New England Journal of Medicine, 354*, 2414–2417.

Meschyan, G., & Hernandez, A. (2002). Is native-language decoding skill related to second-language learning? *Journal of Educational Psychology, 94*, 14–22.

Meyer, M. (1998). Perceptual differences in fetal alcohol syndrome affect boys performing a modeling task. *Perceptual & Motor Skills, 87*, 784–786.

Meyer-Bahlburg, H. F. L., Ehrhardt, A. A., Rosen, L. R., Gruen, R. S., Veridiano, N. P., Vann, F. H., & Neuwalder, H. F. (1995). Prenatal estrogens and the development of homosexual orientation. *Developmental Psychology, 31*, 12–21.

Miller, B. C., Benson, B., & Galbraith, K. (2001). Family relationships and adolescent pregnancy risk: A research synthesis. *Developmental Review, 21*, 1–38.

Miller, B. C., & Moore, K. A. (1990). Adolescent sexual behavior, pregnancy, and parenting: Research through the 1980s. *Journal of Marriage & the Family, 52*, 1025–1044.

Miller, B. C., Norton, M., Curtis, T., Hill, E., Schvaneveldt, P., & Young, M. (1998). The timing of sexual intercourse among adolescents: Family, peer, and other antecedents: Erratum. *Youth & Society, 29*, 390.

Miller, P., Eisenberg, N., Fabes, R., & Shell, R. (1996). Relations of moral reasoning and vicarious emotion to young children's prosocial behavior toward peers and adults. *Developmental Psychology, 29*, 3–18.

Miller, P., Wang, S., Sandel, T., & Cho, G. (2002). Self-esteem as folk theory: A comparison of European American and Taiwanese mothers' beliefs. *Science & Practice, 2*, 209–239.

Miller-Johnson, S., Coie, J., Maumary-Gremaud, A., & Bierman, K. (2002). Peer rejection and aggression and early starter models of conduct disorder. *Journal of Abnormal Child Psychology, 30*, 217.

Mills, D., Coffey-Corina, S., & Neville, H. (1994). Variability in cerebral organization during primary language acquisition. In G. Dawson & K. Fischer (Eds.), *Human behavior and the developing brain.* New York: Guilford Press.

Mischel, W. (1966). A social learning view of sex differences in behavior. In E. E. Maccoby (Ed.), *The development of sex differences* (pp. 56–81). Stanford, CA: Stanford University Press.

Mischel, W. (1970). Sex typing and socialization. In P. H. Mussen (Ed.), *Carmichael's manual of child psychology, Vol. 2* (pp. 3–72). New York: Wiley.

Mishra, R. (1997). Cognition and cognitive development. In J. Berry, P. Dasen, & T. Saraswathi (Eds.), *Handbook of cross-cultural psychology* (2nd ed., pp. 143–176). Boston: Allyn & Bacon.

Mishra, R. (2001). Cognition across cultures. In D. Matsumoto (Ed.), *The handbook of culture and psychology* (pp. 119–135). New York: Oxford University Press.

Mitchell, P. R., & Kent, R. D. (1990). Phonetic variation in multisyllable babbling. *Journal of Child Language, 17*, 247–265.

Mizuta, I., Zahn-Waxler, C., Cole, P., & Hiruma, N. (1996). A cross-cultural study of preschoolers' attachment: Security and sensitivity in Japanese and U.S. dyads. *International Journal of Behavioral Development, 19*, 141–159.

Moen, P., & Erickson, M. A. (1995). Linked lives: A transgenerational approach to resilience. In P. Moen, G. H. Elder, Jr., & K. Lüscher (Eds.), *Examining lives in context: Perspectives on the ecology of human development* (pp. 169–210). Washington, DC: American Psychological Association.

Mohanty, A. & Perregaux, C. (1997). Language acquisition and bilingualism. In J. Berry, P. Dasen, & T. Saraswath (Eds.), *Handbook of cross-cultural psychology, Vol. 2.* Boston: Allyn & Bacon.

Mohsin, M., Wong, F., Bauman, A., & Bai, J. (2003). Maternal and neonatal factors influencing premature birth and low birth weight in Australia. *Journal of Biosocial Science, 35*, 161–174.

Mokdad, A., Ford, E., Bowman, B., Dietz, W., Vinicor, F., Bales, V., & Marks, J. (2003). Prevalence of obesity, diabetes, and obesity-related health risk factors, 2001. *Journal of the American Medical Association, 289*, 76–79.

Monk, C., Webb, S., & Nelson, C. (2001). Prenatal neurobiological development: Molecular mechanisms and anatomical change. *Developmental Neuropsychology, 19*, 211–236.

Montemayor, R., & Eisen, M. (1977). The development of self-conceptions from childhood to adolescence. *Developmental Psychology, 13*, 314–319.

Montero, I., & De Dios, M. (2006). Vygotsky was right: An experimental approach to the relationship between private speech and task performance. *Estudios de Psicologíia, 27*, 175–189.

Montgomery, M., & Sorel, G. (1998). Love and dating experience in early and middle adolescence: Grade and gender comparisons. *Journal of Adolescence, 21*, 677–689.

Moon, C., & Fifer, W. P. (1990). Syllables as signals for 2-day-old infants. *Infant Behavior & Development, 13*, 377–390.

Mooney, L., Knox, D., & Schacht, C. (2000). *Understanding social problems* (2nd ed.). Thousand Oaks, CA: Wadsworth.

Moore, C., Barresi, J., & Thompson, C. (1998). The cognitive basis of future-oriented prosocial behavior. *Social Development, 7*, 198–218.

Moore, D. (2001). Reassessing emotion recognition performance in people with mental retardation: A review. *American Journal on Mental Retardation, 106*, 481–502.

Moore, K. L. (1998). *The developing human: Clinically oriented embryology* (6th ed.). Philadelphia: Saunders.

Moore, K. L., & Persaud, T. V. N. (1993). *The developing human: Clinically oriented embryology* (5th ed.). Philadelphia: Saunders.

Morgan, B., Finan, A., Yarnold, R., Petersen, S., Horsfield, M., Rickett, A., & Wailoo, M. (2002). Assessment of infant physiology and neuronal development using magnetic resonance imaging. *Child: Care, Health, & Development, 28*, 7–10.

Morgan, J. L. (1994). Converging measures of speech segmentation in preverbal infants. *Infant Behavior & Development, 17*, 389–403.

Morrison, W., & Legters, N. (2001). Creating a ninth grade success academy: Guidebook for the talent development high school. Baltimore, MD: Johns Hopkins University Center for Research on the Education of Students Placed at Risk.

Morrissette, P. (1999). Post-traumatic stress disorder in child sexual abuse: Diagnostic and treatment considerations. *Child & Youth Care Forum, 28*, 205–219.

Morrongiello, B. A. (1988). Infants' localization of sounds along the horizontal axis: Estimates of minimum audible angle. *Developmental Psychology, 24*, 8–13.

Morrongiello, B. A., Fenwick, K. D., & Chance, G. (1990). Sound localization acuity in very young infants: An observer-based testing procedure. *Developmental Psychology, 24*, 75–84.

Morse, P. A., & Cowan, N. (1982). Infant auditory and speech perception. In T. M. Field, A. Houston, H. C. Quay, L. Troll, & G. E. Finley (Eds.), *Review of human development* (pp. 32–61). New York: Wiley.

Mortimer, J. T., & Finch, M. D. (1996). Work, family, and adolescent development. In J. T. Mortimer & M. D. Finch (Eds.), *Adolescents, work, and family: An intergenerational developmental analysis* (pp. 1–24). Thousand Oaks, CA: Sage.

Mortimer, J. T., Finch, M. D., Dennehy, K., Lee, C., & Beebe, T. (1995, March). *Work experience in adolescence.* Paper presented at the biennial meetings of the Society for Research in Child Development, Indianapolis, IN.

Mortimer, J. T., & Harley, C. (2002). The quality of work and youth mental health. *Work & Occupations, 29*, 166–197.

Mortimer, J. T., Zimmer-Gembeck, M., Holmes, M., & Shanahan, M. (2002). The process of occupational decision making: Patterns during the transition to adulthood. *Journal of Vocational Behavior, 61*, 439–465.

Mott, J., Crowe, P., Richardson, J., & Flay, B. (1999). After-school supervision and adolescent cigarette smoking: Contributions of the setting and intensity of after-school self-care. *Journal of Behavioral Medicine, 22*, 35–58.

Mounts, N. S., & Steinberg, L. (1995). An ecological analysis of peer influence on adolescent grade point average and drug use. *Developmental Psychology, 31*, 915–922.

Mueller, U., Overton, W., & Reene, K. (2001). Development of conditional reasoning: A longitudinal study. *Journal of Cognition & Development, 2,* 27–49.

Muir-Broaddus, I. (1997). The effects of social influences and psychological reactance on children's responses to repeated questions. Paper presented at the biennial meetings of the Society for Research on Child Development, Indianapolis.

Munroe, R. H., Shimmin, H. S., & Munroe, R. L. (1984). Gender understanding and sex role preference in four cultures. *Developmental Psychology, 20,* 673–682.

Murnen, S., Smolak, L., Mills, J., & Good, L. (2003). Thin, sexy women and strong, muscular men: Grade-school children's responses to objectified images of women and men. *Sex Roles, 49,* 427–437.

Murray, B. (1998, June). Dipping math scores heat up debate over math teaching. *APA Monitor, 29,* 34–35.

Murray, J., Liotti, M., Ingmundson, P., Mayberg, H., Pu U., Zamarripa, F., Liu, Y., Woldorff, M., Gao, J., & Fox, P. (2006). Children's brain activations while viewing televised violence revealed by MRO. *Media Psychology, 8,* 25–37.

Murray, J., & Youniss, J. (1968). Achievement of inferential transitivity and its relation to serial ordering. *Child Development, 39,* 1259–1268.

Murray, L., Sinclair, D., Cooper, P., Ducournau, P., et al. (1999). The socio-emotional development of 5-year-old children of postnatally depressed mothers. *Journal of Child Psychology & Psychiatry & Allied Disciplines, 40,* 1259–1271.

Mutch, L., Leyland, A., & McGee, A. (1993). Patterns of neuropsychological function in a low-birth-weight population. *Developmental Medicine & Child Neurology, 35,* 943–956.

Muter, V., Hulme, C., Snowling, M., & Stevenson, J. (2004). Phonemes, rimes, vocabulary, and grammatical skills as foundations of early reading development: Evidence from a longitudinal study. *Developmental Psychology, 40,* 665–681.

Mwamwenda, T. (1999). Undergraduate and graduate students' combinatorial reasoning and formal operations. *Journal of Genetic Psychology, 160,* 503–506.

Nagamine, S. (1999). Interpersonal conflict situations: Adolescents' negotiation processes using an interpersonal negotiation strategy model: Adolescents' relations with their parents and friends. *Japanese Journal of Educational Psychology, 47,* 218–228.

Nagy, W., Berninger, V., Abbott, R., Vaughan, K., & Vermeulen, K. (2004). Relationship of morphology and other language skills to literacy skills in at-risk second-grade readers and at-risk fourth-grade writers. *Journal of Educational Psychology, 96,* 730–742.

Namka, L. (2002). What the research literature says about corporal punishment. Retrieved June 15, 2007 from http://www.angriesout.com/parents10.htm.

Narvaez, D. (1998). The influence of moral schemas on the reconstruction of moral narratives in eighth graders and college students. *Journal of Educational Psychology, 90,* 13–24.

Nation, K., & Snowling, M. (2004). Beyond phonological skills: Broader language skills contribute to the development of reading. *Journal of Research in Reading, 27,* 342–356.

National Abortion and Reproductive Rights Action League. (1997). *Limitations on the rights of pregnant women.* Retrieved March 5, 2001 from http://www.naral.org/publications/facts.

National Academies of Science Food and Nutrition Board. (2005). *Dietary reference intakes for energy, carbohydrate, fiber, fat, fatty acids, cholesterol, protein, and amino acids (macronutrients).* Washington, DC: National Academies Press. Retrieved March 25, 2008 from http://books.nap.edu/openbook.php?record_id=10490&page=R1.

National Association for the Education of Young Children (NAEYC). (2006). Developmentally appropriate practice in early childhood programs serving children from birth through age 8. Retrieved March 21, 2008 from http://www.naeyc.org/about/positions/dap1.asp.

National Cancer Institute. (2006). Breast cancer and the environment research centers chart new territory. Retrieved June 21, 2007 from http://www.nci.nih.gov/ncicancerbulletin/NCI_Cancer_Bulletin_081506/page9.

National Cancer Institute. (2007). Incidence and mortality rate trends. Retrieved June 19, 2008 from http://planning.cancer.gov/disease/Pediatric-Snapshot.pdf.

National Center for Chronic Disease Prevention and Health Promotion. (2000). Obesity epidemic increases dramatically in the United States. Retrieved August 23, 2000 from http://www.cdc.gov.

National Center for Education Statistics (NCES). (1997). *Condition of education/1997.* Washington, DC: U.S. Department of Education.

National Center for Education Statistics (NCES). (2003a). *The nation's report card: Mathematics highlights 2003.* Washington, DC: U.S. Department of Education, NCES 2004–451.

National Center for Education Statistics (NCES). (2006a). Digest of education statistics 2005. NCES 2006-030. Retrieved June 22, 2007 from http://nces.ed.gov/programs/digest/d05/

National Center for Education Statistics (NCES). (2006b). How many students with disabilities receive services? Retrieved June 19, 2007 from http://nces.ed.gov/fastfacts/display.asp?id=64

National Center for Education Statistics (NCES). (2006c). 2005 Math Results. Retrieved May 18, 2007 from http://nces.ed.gov/nationsreportcard/nrc/reading_math_2005/s0017.asp?printver=

National Center for Education Statistics (NCES). (2006d). 2005 Reading Results. Retrieved May 18, 2007 from http://nces.ed.gov/nationsreportcard/nrc/reading_math_2005/s0002.asp?printver=

National Center for Educational Statistics (NCES). (2008). *The condition of education 2008.* Retrieved June 27, 2008 from http://nces.ed.gov/programs/coe/.

National Center for Health Statistics (NCES). (2003). Births: Final data for 2002. Retrieved June 18, 2004 from http://www.cdc.gov/nchs/pressroom/3facts/teenbirth.htm.

National Center for Health Statistics (NCHS). (2005). Health, United States, 2005. Retrieved July 5, 2007 from www.cdc.gov/nchs/data/hus/hus05.pdf#053.

National Center for Health Statistics (NCHS). (2006). *Health, United States, 2006.* Hyattsville, MD: Author.

National Center for Health Statistics. (NCHS). (2007a). Deaths by place of death, age, race, and sex: United States, 1999–2004. Retrieved August 3, 2007 from www.cdc.gov/nchs/datawh/statab/unpubd/mortabs/gmwk309_10.htm.

National Center for Health Statistics (NCHS). (2007b). Health, United States 2007. Retrieved July 6, 2008 from www.cdc.gov/nchs/hus.htm.

National Center for Health Statistics (NCHS). (2007c). Prevalence of over-weight among children and adolescents: United States 2003–2004. Retrieved June 19, 2007 from www.cdc.gov/nchs/products/pubs/pubd/hestats/overweight/overwght_child_03.htm

National Center for Injury Prevention and Control (NCIPC). (2000). *Fact book for the year 2000.* Washington, DC: Author.

National Highway Traffic Safety Administration (NHTSA). (2006). Traffic safety facts 2005 data: Young drivers. Retrieved April 9, 2008 from http://www-nrd.nhtsa.dot.gov/pdf/nrd-30/NCSA/TSF2005/810630.pdf.

National Institute for Health Care Management Foundation. (2004). Obesity in young children: Impact and intervention. Retrieved March 27, 2008 from http://www.nihcm.org/~nihcmor/pdf/OYCbrief.pdf.

National Institute of Child Health and Human Development (NICHD) Early Child Care Research Network. (1998). The effects of infant child care on mother-infant attachment security: Results of the NICHD study of early child care. *Child Development, 68*, 860–879.

National Institute of Child Health and Human Development (NICHD) Early Child Care Research Network. (1999). Chronicity of maternal depressive symptoms, maternal sensitivity, and child functioning at 36 months. *Developmental Psychology, 35*, 1297–1310.

National Institute of Child Health and Human Development (NICHD) Early Child Care Research Network. (2003). Does amount of time spent in child care predict socioemotional adjustment during the transition to kindergarten? *Child Development, 74*, 976–1005.

National Institute of Child Health and Human Development (NICHD) Early Child Care Research Network. (2004). Are child developmental outcomes related to before- and after-school care arrangements? Results from the NICHD Study of Early Child Care. *Child Development, 75*, 280–295.

National Institute of Child Health and Human Development (NICHD) Early Child Care Research Network. (2006). Child-care effect sizes for the NICHD Study of Early Child Care and Youth Development. *American Psychologist, 61*, 99–116.

National Institute of Mental Health (NIMH). (2001). *The numbers count: Mental disorders in America.* NIMH Report No. 01-4584. Washington DC: Author.

National Library of Medicine. (2008). Color vision deficiency. Genetics Home Reference. Retrieved August 14, 2008 from http//ghr.nlm.nih.gov/condition/colorvisiondeficiency.

National Middle School Association (NMSA). (2004). Small schools and small learning communities. Retrieved June 22, 2007 from http://www.nmsa.org/AboutNMSA/PositionStatements/SmallSchools/tabid/293/Default.aspx.

National Safe Kids Campaign. (2000). *Get into the game: A national survey of parent's knowledge, attitudes and self-reported behaviors concerning sports safety.* Washington (DC): Author.

Naude, H., & Pretorius, E. (2003). Investigating the effects of asthma medication on the cognitive and psychosocial functioning of primary school children with asthma. *Early Child Development & Care, 173*, 699–709.

Needlman, R. (1996). Growth and development. In W. Nelson, R. Behrman, R. Kliegman, & A. Marvin (Eds.), *Nelson textbook of pediatrics*. Philadelphia: W. B. Saunders.

Neild, R., & Balfanz, R. (2006). An extreme degree of difficulty: The educational demographics of urban neighborhood high schools. *Journal of Education for Students Placed at Risk, 11*, 123–141.

Neill, M. (1998). High stakes tests do not improve student learning. Retrieved October 21, 1998 from http://www.fairtest.org.

Neill, M. (2000). Too much harmful testing? *Educational Measurement: Issues & Practice, 16*, 57–58.

Neisser, U., Boodoo, G., Bouchard, T. J., Jr., Boykin, A. W., Brody, N., Ceci, S. J., Halpern, D. F., Loehlin, J. C., Perloff, R., Sternberg, R. J., & Urbina, S. (1996). Intelligence: Knowns and unknowns. *American Psychologist, 51*, 77–101.

Neitzel, C., & Stright, A. (2003). Mothers' scaffolding of children's problem solving: Establishing a foundation of academic self-regulatory competence. *Journal of Family Psychology, 17*, 147–159.

Nelson, C., Haan, M., & Thomas, K. (2006). *Neuroscience of cognitive development: The role of experience and the developing brain.* New York: Wiley.

Nelson, K. (1973). Structure and strategy in learning to talk. *Monographs of the Society for Research in Child Development, 38* (Serial No. 149).

Nelson, K. (1977). Facilitating children's syntax acquisition. *Developmental Psychology, 13*, 101–107.

Nelson, S. (1980). Factors influencing young children's use of motives and outcomes as moral criteria. *Child Development, 51*, 823–829.

Nemours Foundation. (2007). Common sleep problems. Retrieved June 25, 2008 from http://kidshealth.org/teen/your_body/take_care/sleep.html.

Neshat-Doost, H., Taghavi, M., Moradi, A., Yule, W., & Dalgleish, T. (1998). Memory for emotional trait adjectives in clinically depressed youth. *Journal of Abnormal Psychology, 107*, 642–650.

Neugebauer, R., Hoek, H., & Susser, E. (1999). Prenatal exposure to wartime famine and development of antisocial personality disorder in early adulthood. *Journal of the American Medical Association, 282*, 455–462.

Neumark-Sztainer, D., Wall, M., Eisenberg, M., Story, M., & Hannan, P. (2006). Overweight status and weight control behaviors in adolescents: Longitudinal and secular trends from 1999 to 2004. *Preventive Medicine, 43*, 52–59.

Newcomb, A. F., & Bagwell, C. L. (1995). Children's friendship relations: A meta-analytic review. *Psychological Bulletin, 117*, 306–347.

Newcomb, A. F., Bukowski, W. M., & Pattee, L. (1993). Children's peer relations: A meta-analytic review of popular, rejected, neglected, controversial, and average sociometric status. *Psychological Bulletin, 113*, 99–128.

Newman, D., Caspi, A., Moffitt, T., & Silva, P. (1997). Antecendents of adult interpersonal functioning: Effects of individual differences in age 3 temperament. *Developmental Psychology, 33*, 206–217

Newschaffer, C., Falb, M., & Gurney, J. (2005). National autism prevalence trends from United States special education data. *Pediatrics, 115*, e277–e282.

New York City Children's Services. (2008). Children's services immigrant community group initiative fights child abuse and neglect. Retrieved June 11, 2008 from http://www.nyc.gov/html/acs/html/pr_archives/pr08_04_14.shtml.

Ng, B., & Wiemer-Hastings, P. (2005). Addiction to the internet and online gaming. *Cyberpsychological Behavior, 8*, 110–113.

Ni, Y. (1998). Cognitive structure, content knowledge, and classificatory reasoning. *Journal of Genetic Psychology, 159*, 280–296.

Nicholson, J. (1998). Inborn errors of metabolism. In R. Behrman & R. Kliegman (Eds.), *Nelson essentials of pediatrics* (3rd ed., pp. 147–166). Philadelphia: W. B. Saunders.

Nicklaus, S., Boggio, V., & Issanchou, S. (2005). Gustatory perceptions in children. *Archives of Pediatrics, 12*, 579–584.

Nightingale, E. O., & Goodman, M. (1990). *Before birth. Prenatal testing for genetic disease.* Cambridge, MA: Harvard University Press.

Nijhuis, J. (2003). Fetal behavior. *Neurobiology of Aging, 24*, S41–S46.

Nilsson, E., Gillberg, C., Gillberg, I., & Rastam, M. (1999). Ten-year follow-up of adolescent-onset anorexia nervosa: Personality disorders. *Journal of the American Academy of Child & Adolescent Psychiatry, 38*, 1389–1395.

Nisan, M., & Kohlberg, L. (1982). Universality and variation in moral judgment: A longitudinal and cross-sectional study in Turkey. *Child Development, 53*, 865–876.

Norman, R., Bradshaw, D., Schneider, M., Pieterse, D., & Groenewald, P. (2000). Revised burden of disease estimates for the comparative risk factor assessment, South Africa 2000. Retrieved June 11, 2008 from fightingautism.org. (2008). Number of cases. Retrieved June 10, 2008 from http://www.mrc.ac.za/bod/bodestimate.pdf.

Nucci, L., & Smetana, J. (1996). Mothers' concepts of young children's areas of personal freedom. *Child Development, 67,* 1870–1886.

Nussbaum, A., & Steele, C. (2007). Situational disengagement and persistence in the face of adversity. *Journal of Experimental Social Psychology, 43,* 127–134.

Oates, J. (1998). Risk factors for infant attrition and low engagement in experiments and free-play. *Infant Behavior & Development, 21,* 569.

O'Beirne, H., & Moore, C. (1995, March). Attachment and sexual behavior in adolescence. Paper presented at the biennial meetings of the Society for Research in Child Development, Indianapolis, IN.

O'Brien, M. (1992). Gender identity and sex roles. In V. B. Van Hasselt & M. Hersen (Eds.), *Handbook of social development: A lifespan perspective* (pp. 325–345). New York: Plenum.

Offer, D., Kaiz, M., Howard, K., & Bennett, E. (1998). Emotional variables in adolescence and their stability and contribution to the mental health of adult men: Implications for early intervention strategies. *Journal of Youth & Adolescence, 27,* 675–690.

Office of Educational Research and Improvement (OERI). (1998). *The educational system in Japan: Case study findings.* Washington, DC: U.S. Department of Education.

Office of Juvenile Justice and Delinquency Prevention. (2006). Juvenile offenders and victims: 2006 report. Retrieved April 12, 2008 from http://ojjdp.ncjrs.gov/ojstatbb/nr2006/index.html.

Offord, D. R., Boyle, M. H., & Racine, Y. A. (1991). The epidemiology of antisocial behavior in childhood and adolescence. In D. J. Pepler & K. H. Rubin (Eds.), *The development and treatment of childhood aggression* (pp. 31–54). Hillsdale, NJ: Erlbaum.

Ogbu, J. (1990). Cultural models, identity and literacy. In J. W. Stigler, R. A. Shweder, & G. Hendt (Eds.), *Cultural psychology: Essays on comparative human development* (pp. 520–541). Hillsdale, NJ: Erlbaum.

Okamoto, K., & Uechi, Y. (1999). Adolescents' relations with parents and friends in the second individuation process. *Japanese Journal of Educational Psychology, 47,* 248–258.

O'Leary, S., Slep, A. S., & Reid, M. (1999). A longitudinal study of mothers' overreactive discipline and toddlers' externalizing behavior. *Journal of Abnormal Child Psychology, 27,* 331–341.

Olivan, G. (2003). Catch-up growth assessment in long-term physically neglected and emotionally abused preschool age male children. *Child Abuse & Neglect, 27,* 103–108.

Oller, D. K. (1981). Infant vocalizations: Exploration and reflectivity. In R. E. Stark (Ed.), *Language behavior in infancy and early childhood* (pp. 85–104). New York: Elsevier North-Holland.

Oller, D. K., Eilers, R., Urbano, R., & Cobo-Lewis, A. (1997). Development of precursors to speech in infants exposed to two languages. *Journal of Child Language, 24,* 407–425.

Olson, H., Feldman, J., Streissguth, A., Sampson, P., & Bookstein, F. (1998). Neuropsychological deficits in adolescents with fetal alcohol syndrome: Clinical findings. *Alcoholism: Clinical & Experimental Research, 22,* 1998–2012.

Olson, S. L., Bates, J. E., & Kaskie, B. (1992). Caregiver-infant interaction antecedents of children's school-age cognitive ability. *Merrill-Palmer Quarterly, 38,* 309–330.

Olweus, D. (1995). Bullying or peer abuse at school: Facts and intervention. *Current Directions in Psychological Science, 4,* 196–200.

Omiya, A., & Uchida, N. (2002). The development of children's thinking strategies: The retrieval of alternatives based on the categorization with conditional reasoning tasks. *Japanese Journal of Psychology, 73,* 10–17.

Ompad, D., Strathdee, S., Celentano, D., Latkin, C., Poduska, J., Kellam, S., & Ialongo, N. (2006). Predictors of early initiation of vaginal and oral sex among urban young adults in Baltimore, Maryland. *Archives of Sexual Behavior, 35,* 53–65.

O'Neill, D. K., Astington, J. W., & Flavell, J. H. (1992). Young children's understanding of the role that sensory experiences play in knowledge acquisition. *Child Development, 63,* 474–490.

Oosterlaan, J., Geurts, H. M., Knol, D. J., & Sergeant, J. A. (2005). Low basal salivary cortisol is associated with teacher reported conduct disorder symptoms. *Psychiatry Research, 134,* 1–10.

Orchard, T., Costacou, T., Kretowski, A., & Nesto, R. (2006). Type 1 diabetes and coronary artery disease. *Diabetes Care, 29,* 2528–2538.

Organization of Teratology Information Specialists. (2005). Acetaminophen and pregnancy. Retrieved June 7, 2007 from www.otispregnancy.org/pdf/acetaminophen.pdf.

Ornoy, A. (2002). The effects of alcohol and illicit drugs on the human embryo and fetus. *Israel Journal of Psychiatry & Related Sciences, 39,* 120–132.

Osher, D., Dwyer, K., & Jackson, S. (2004). *Safe, supportive and successful schools.* Boston: Sopris West Educational Services.

Osorio-O'Dea, P. (2001). CRS report for Congress: Bilingual education. Retrieved June 23, 2008 from http://www.policyalmanac.org/education/archive/bilingual.pdf.

Ostoja, E., McCrone, E., Lehn, L., Reed, T., & Sroufe, L. A. (1995, March). Representations of close relationships in adolescence: Longitudinal antecedents from infancy through childhood. Paper presented at the biennial meetings of the Society for Research in Child Development, Indianapolis.

Overby, K. (2002). Pediatric health supervision. In A. Rudolph, R. Kamei, & K. Overby (Eds.), *Rudolph's fundamentals of pediatrics* (3rd ed., pp. 1–69). New York: McGraw-Hill.

Overmeyer, S., & Taylor, E. (1999). Principles of treatment for hyperkinetic disorder: Practice approaches for the U.K. *Journal of Child Psychology & Psychiatry & Allied Disciplines, 40,* 1147–1157.

Ozmon, H. A., & Craver, S. M. (1986). *Philosophical foundations of education.* Columbus, OH: Merrill.

Paarlberg, K., Vingerhoets, A. J., Passchier, J., Dekker, G., & van Geign, H. (1995). Psychosocial factors and pregnancy outcome: A review with emphasis on methodological issues. *Journal of Psychosomatic Research, 39,* 563–595.

Paasche-Orlow, M., Riekert, K., Bilderback, A., Chanmugam, A., Hill, P., Rand, C., Brancati, F., & Krishnan, J. (2005). Tailored education may reduce health literacy disparities in asthma self-management. *American Journal of Respiratory and Critical Care Medicine, 172,* 980–986.

Pagani, L., Boulerice, B., Tremblay, R., & Vitaro, F. (1997). Behavioural development in children of divorce and remarriage. *Journal of Child Psychology & Psychiatry & Allied Disciplines, 38,* 769–781.

Painter, M., & Bergman, I. (1998). Neurology. In R. Behrman & R. Kliegman (Eds.), *Nelson essentials of pediatrics* (3rd ed., pp. 694–745). Philadelphia: W. B. Saunders.

Pajares, F., & Graham, L. (1999). Self-efficacy, motivation constructs, and mathematics performance of entering middle school students. *Contemporary Educational Psychology, 24,* 124–139.

Pajares, F., & Valiante, G. (1999). Grade level and gender differences in the writing self-beliefs of middle school students. *Contemporary Educational Psychology, 24,* 390–405.

Paley, V. (1986). *Mollie is three: Growing up in school.* Chicago: University of Chicago Press.

Parault, S., & Schwanenflugel, P. (2000). The development of conceptual categories of attention during the elementary school years. *Journal of Experimental Child Psychology, 75,* 245–262.

Parent, S., Tillman, G., Jule, A., Skakkebaek, N., Toppari, J., & Bourguignon, J. (2003). The timing of normal puberty and the age limits of sexual precocity: Variations around the world, secular trends, and changes after migration. *Endocrine Review, 24,* 668–693.

Parke, R. D. (2004). The Society for Research in Child Development at 70: Progress and promise. *Child Development, 75,* 1–24.

Parke, R. D., & Tinsley, B. R. (1981). The father's role in infancy: Determinants of involvement in caregiving and play. In M. E. Lamb (Ed.), *The role of the father in child development* (2nd ed., pp. 429–458). New York: Wiley.

Parrila, R., Kirby, J., & McQuarrie, L. (2004). Articulation rate, naming speed, verbal short-term memory, and phonological awareness: Longitudinal predictors of early reading development? *Scientific Studies of Reading, 8,* 3–26.

Parten, M. (1932). Social participation among preschool children. *Journal of Abnormal and Social Psychology, 27,* 243–269.

Pascalis, O., de Schonen, S., Morton, J., Derulle, C., & Fabre-Grenet, M. (1995). Mother's face recognition by neonates: A replication and extension. *Infant Behavior and Development, 18,* 79–85.

Pasquini, E., Corriveau, K., Koenig, M., & Harris, P. (2007). Preschoolers monitor the relative accuracy of informants. *Developmental Psychology, 43,* 1216–1226.

Patterson, C. (2006). Children of lesbian and gay parents. *Current Directions in Psychological Science, 15,* 241–244.

Patterson, G. R. (1980). Mothers: The unacknowledged victims. *Monographs of the Society for Research in Child Development, 45* (Serial No. 186).

Patterson, G. R., Capaldi, D., & Bank, L. (1991). An early starter model for predicting delinquency. In D. J. Pepler & K. H. Rubin (Eds.), *The development and treatment of childhood aggression* (pp. 139–168). Hillsdale, NJ: Erlbaum.

Patterson, G. R., DeBaryshe, B. D., & Ramsey, E. (1989). A developmental perspective on antisocial behavior. *American Psychologist, 44,* 329–335.

Patterson, J. (1998). Expressive vocabulary of bilingual toddlers: Preliminary findings. *Multicultural Electronic Journal of Communication Disorders, 1.* Retrieved April 11, 2001 from www.asha.ucf.edu/patterson.html.

Pauen, S. (2000). Early differentiation within the animate domain: Are humans something special? *Journal of Experimental Child Psychology, 75,* 134–151.

Pauen, S. (2002). The global-to-basic level shift in infants' categorical thinking: First evidence from a longitudinal study. *International Journal of Behavioral Development, 26,* 492–499.

Peasant, E. (2007). Crossing the bridge from eighth to tenth grade: Can ninth grade schools make it better? Unpublished dissertation.

Pederson, D. R., & Moran, G. (1995). A categorical description of infant-mother relationships in the home and its relation to Q-sort measures of infant-mother interaction. *Monographs of the Society for Research in Child Development, 60* (244, Nos. 2–3), 111–132.

Pederson, D. R., Moran, G., Sitko, C., Campbell, K., Ghesquire, K., & Acton, H. (1990). Maternal sensitivity and the security of infant-mother attachment: A Q-sort study. *Child Development, 61,* 1974–1983.

Pediatric Nutrition Surveillance. (2005). National summary of health indicators. Retrieved June 14, 2007 from www.cdc.gov/pednss/pednss_tables/pdf/national_table2.pdf.

Pedlow, R., Sanson, A., Prior, M., & Oberklaid, F. (1993). Stability of maternally reported temperament from infancy to 8 years. *Developmental Psychology, 29,* 998–1007.

Pegg, J. E., Werker, J. F., & McLeod, P. J. (1992). Preference for infant-directed over adult-directed speech: Evidence from 7-week-old infants. *Infant Behavior & Development, 15,* 325–345.

Peisner-Feinberg, E. S. (1995, March). Developmental outcomes and the relationship to quality of child care experiences. Paper presented at the biennial meetings of the Society for Research in Child Development, Indianapolis.

Pelletier, L., Dion, S., & Levesque, C. (2004). Can self-determination help protect women against sociocultural influences about body image and reduce their risk of experiencing bulimic symptoms? *Journal of Social & Clinical Psychology, 23,* 61–88.

Pelligrini, A., & Smith, P. (1998). Physical activity play: The nature and function of a neglected aspect of play. *Child Development, 69,* 577–598.

Pennington, B., Moon, J., Edgin, J., Stedron, J., & Nadel, L. (2003). The neuropsychology of Down syndrome: Evidence for hippocampal dysfunctions. *Child Development, 74,* 75–93.

Peoples, C. E., Fagan, J. F., III, & Drotar, D. (1995). The influence of race on 3-year-old children's performance on the Stanford-Binet: Fourth edition. *Intelligence, 21,* 69–82.

Pereverzeva, M., Hui-Lin Chien, S., Palmer, J., & Teller, D. (2002). Infant photometry: Are mean adult isoluminance values a sufficient approximation to individual infant values? *Vision Research, 42,* 1639–1649.

Persson, A., & Musher-Eizenman, D. (2003). The impact of a prejudice-prevention television program on young children's ideas about race. *Early Childhood Research Quarterly, 18,* 530–546.

Pesonen, A., Raikkonen, K., Strandberg, T., Kelitikangas-Jarvinen, L., & Jarvenpaa, A. (2004). Insecure adult attachment style and depressive symptoms: Implications for parental perceptions of infant temperament. *Infant Mental Health Journal, 25,* 99–116.

Petersen, A. C., Compas, B. E., Brooks-Gunn, J., Stemmler, M., Ey, S., & Grant, K. E. (1993). Depression in adolescence. *American Psychologist, 48,* 155–168.

Petersen, A. C., & Taylor, B. (1980). The biological approach to adolescence. In J. Adelson (Ed.), *Handbook of adolescent psychology* (pp. 117–158). New York: Wiley.

Peterson, C., & Bell, M. (1996). Children's memory for traumatic injury. *Child Development, 67,* 3045–3070.

Peterson, C., & Siegal, M. (1999). Representing inner worlds: Theory of mind in autistic, deaf, and normal hearing children. *Psychological Science, 10,* 126–129.

Peterson, C., Wellman, H., & Liu, D. (2005). Steps in theory of mind development for children with deafness or autism. *Child Development, 76,* 502–517.

Peterson, L., Ewigman, B., & Kivlahan, C. (1993). Judgments regarding appropriate child supervision to prevent injury: The role of environmental risk and child age. *Child Development, 64,* 934–950.

Pettit, G. S., Clawson, M. A., Dodge, K. A., & Bates, J. E. (1996). Stability and change in peer-rejected status: The role of child behavior, parenting, and family ecology. *Merrill-Palmer Quarterly, 42,* 295–318.

Pettit, G. S., Laird, R., Bates, J. E., & Dodge, K. A. (1997). Patterns of after-school care in middle childhood: Risk factors and developmental outcomes. *Merrill-Palmer Quarterly, 43,* 515–538.

Pezdek, K., Blandon-Gitlin, I., & Moore, C. (2003). Children's face recognition memory: More evidence for the cross-race effect. *Journal of Applied Psychology, 88,* 760–763.

Phelps, L., Wallace, N., & Bontrager, A. (1997). Risk factors in early child development: Is prenatal cocaine/polydrug exposure a key variable? *Psychology in the Schools, 34,* 245–252.

Philadelphia Education Fund. (2003). Year three of the Talent Development High School Initiative in Philadelphia: Results from five schools. Retrieved June 29, 2008 from http://www.philaedfund.org/pdfs/K-8%20Report.pdf.

Phillips, A., Wellman, H., & Spelke, E. (2002). Infants' ability to connect gaze and emotional expression to intentional action. *Cognition, 85,* 53–78.

Phillips, D., Schwean, V., & Saklofske, D. (1997). Treatment effect of a school-based cognitive-behavioral program for aggressive children. *Canadian Journal of School Psychology, 13*, 60–67.

Phillipsen, L. (1999). Associations between age, gender, and group acceptance and three components of friendship quality. *Journal of Early Adolescence, 19*, 438–464.

Phinney, J. S. (1990). Ethnic identity in adolescents and adults: Review of research. *Psychological Bulletin, 108*, 499–514.

Phinney, J. S., Horenczyk, G., Liebkind, K., & Vedder, P. (2001). Ethnic identity, immigration, and well-being: An interactional perspective. *Journal of Social Issues, 57*, 493–510.

Phinney, J. S., Romero, I., Nava, M., & Huang, D. (2001). The role of language, parents, and peers in ethnic identity among adolescents in immigrant families. *Journal of Youth & Adolescence, 30*, 135–153.

Phinney, J. S., & Rosenthal, D. A. (1992). Ethnic identity in adolescence: Process, context, and outcome. In G. R. Adams, T. P. Gullotta, & R. Montemayor (Eds.), *Adolescent identity formation* (pp. 145–172). Newbury Park, CA: Sage.

Piaget, J. (1932). *The moral judgment of the child.* New York: Macmillan.

Piaget, J. (1952). *The origins of intelligence in children.* New York: International Universities Press.

Piaget, J. (1954). *The construction of reality in the child.* New York: Basic Books. (Originally published 1937.)

Piaget, J. (1965). *The moral judgment of the child.* New York: Free Press.

Piaget, J. (1970). Piaget's theory. In P. H. Mussen (Ed.), *Carmichael's manual of child psychology, Vol. 1* (3rd ed., pp. 703–732). New York: Wiley.

Piaget, J. (1977). *The development of thought: Equilibration of cognitive structures.* New York: Viking.

Piaget, J., & Inhelder, B. (1969). *The psychology of the child.* New York: Basic Books.

Pianta, R. C., & Egeland, B. (1994). Predictors of instability in children's mental test performance at 24, 48, and 96 months. *Intelligence, 18*, 145–163.

Pickens, J. (1994). Perception of auditory-visual distance relations by 5-month-old infants. *Developmental Psychology, 30*, 537–544.

Pickering, L., Granoff, D., Erickson, J., Masor, M., Cordle, C., Schaller, J., Winship, T., Paule, C., & Hilty, M. (1998). Modulation of the immune system by human milk and infant formula containing nucleotides. *Pediatrics, 101*, 242–249.

Pierce, M., & Leon, D. (2005). Age at menarche and adult BMI in the Aberdeen children of the 1950s cohort study. *American Journal of Clinical Nutrition, 82*, 733–739.

Pike, J., & Jennings, N. (2005). The effects of commercials on children's perceptions of gender appropriate toy use. *Sex Roles, 52*, 83–91.

Pilgrim, C., Luo, Q., Urberg, K., & Fang, X. (1999). Influence of peers, parents, and individual characteristics on adolescent drug use in two cultures. *Merrill-Palmer Quarterly, 45*, 85–107.

Pillow, B. (1999). Children's understanding of inferential knowledge. *Journal of Genetic Psychology, 160*, 419–428.

Pine, J. M., Lieven, E. V. M., & Rowland, C. F. (1997). Stylistic variation at the "single-word" stage: Relations between maternal speech characteristics and children's vocabulary composition and usage. *Child Development, 68*, 807–819.

Pinker, S. (1994). *The language instinct: How the mind creates language.* New York: HarperCollins.

Pinker, S. (2002). *The blank slate.* New York: Viking.

Plomin, R. (1990). *Nature and nurture: An introduction to behavior genetics.* Pacific Grove, CA: Brooks/Cole.

Plomin, R., Emde, R. N., Braungart, J. M., Campos, J., Corley, R., Fulker, D. W., Kagan, J., Reznick, J. S., Robinson, J., Zahn-Waxler, C., & DeFries, J. C. (1993). Genetic change and continuity from fourteen to twenty months: The MacArthur longitudinal twin study. *Child Development, 64*, 1354–1376.

Plomin, R., Reiss, D., Hetherington, E. M., & Howe, G. W. (1994). Nature and nurture: Genetic contributions to measures of the family environment. *Developmental Psychology, 30*, 32–43.

Plomin, R., & Rende, R. (1991). Human behavioral genetics. *Annual Review of Psychology, 42*, 161–190.

Plucker, J. (1999). Is the proof in the pudding? Reanalyses of Torrance's (1958 to present) longitudinal data. *Creativity Research Journal, 12*, 103–115.

Polka, L., & Werker, J. F. (1994). Developmental changes in perception of nonnative vowel contrasts. *Journal of Experimental Psychology: Human Perception & Performance, 20*, 421–435.

Pollack, L., Stewart, S., & Thompson, T. (2007). Trends in childhood cancer mortality: United States, 1990–2004. *Morbidity and Mortality Weekly Report, 56*, 1257–1261.

Pollitt, E., & Gorman, K. S. (1994). Nutritional deficiencies as developmental risk factors. In C. A. Nelson (Ed.), *The Minnesota Symposia on Child Development, Vol. 27* (pp. 121–144). Hillsdale, NJ: Erlbaum.

Pomerantz, E., & Ruble, D. (1998). The role of maternal control in the development of sex differences in child self-evaluative factors. *Child Development, 69*, 458–478.

Pomerleau, A., Malcuit, G., Turgeon, L., & Cossette, L. (1997). Effects of labelled gender on vocal communication of young women with 4-month-old infants. *International Journal of Psychology, 32*, 65–72.

Pomerleau, A., Scuccimarri, C., & Malcuit, G. (2003). Mother-infant behavioral interactions in teenage and adult mothers during the first six months postpartum: Relations with infant development. *Infant Mental Health Journal, 24*, 495–509.

Population Resource Center. (2004). Latina teen pregnancy: Problems and prevention. Retrieved October 27, 2004 from http://www.prcds.org/summaries/latinapreg04/latinapreg04.html.

Porac, C., & Friesen, I. (2000). Hand preference side and its relation to hand preference switch history among old and oldest-old adults. *Developmental Neuropsychology, 17*, 222–239.

Posner, J., & Vandell, D. (1994). Low-income children's after-school care: Are there beneficial effects of after-school programs? *Child Development, 65*, 440–456.

Posthuma, D., de Geus, E., & Boomsma, D. (2003). Genetic contributions to anatomical, behavioral, and neurophysiological indices of cognition. In R. Plomin, J. DeFries, I. Craig, & P. McGuffin (Eds.), *Behavioral genetics in the postgenomic era* (pp. 141–161). Washington, DC: American Psychological Association.

Poulin, F., & Boivin, M. (1999). Proactive and reactive aggression and boys' friendship quality in mainstream classrooms. *Journal of Emotional & Behavioral Disorders, 7*, 168–177.

Poulin, F., & Boivin, M. (2000). The role of proactive and reactive aggression in the formation and development of boys' friendships. *Developmental Psychology, 36*, 233–240.

Poulson, C. L., Nunes, L. R. D., & Warren, S. F. (1989). Imitation in infancy: A critical review. In H. W. Reese (Ed.), *Advances in child development and behavior, Vol. 22* (pp. 272–298). San Diego, CA: Academic Press.

Poureslami, I., Rootman, I., Balka, E., Devarakonda, R., Hatch, J., & FitzGerald, M. (2007). A systematic review of asthma and health literacy: A cultural-ethnic perspective in Canada. *Medscape General Medicine, 9*, 40.

Powlishta, K. K. (1995). Intergroup processes in childhood: Social categorization and sex role development. *Developmental Psychology, 31*, 781–788.

Pozzi, M. (2003). The use of observation in the psychoanalytic treatment of a 12-year-old boy with Asperger's syndrome. *The International Journal of Psychoanalysis, 84*, 1333–1349.

Prat-Sala, M., Shillcock, R., & Sorace, A. (2000). Animacy effects on the production of object-dislocated descriptions by Catalan-speaking children. *Journal of Child Language, 27,* 97–117.

Pratt, M., Arnold, M., & Pratt, A. (1999). Predicting adolescent moral reasoning from family climate: A longitudinal study. *Journal of Early Adolescence, 19,* 148–175.

Premack, D. (1959). Toward empirical behavior laws: I. Positive reinforcement. *Psychological Review, 66,* 219–233.

Prentice, A. (1994). Extended breast-feeding and growth in rural China. *Nutrition Reviews, 52,* 144–146.

Pressley, M., & Dennis-Rounds, J. (1980). Transfer of a mnemonic keyword strategy at two age levels. *Journal of Educational Psychology, 72,* 575–582.

Pressman, E., DiPietro, J., Costigan, K., Shupe, A., & Johnson, T. (1998). Fetal neurobehavioral development: Associations with socioeconomic class and fetal sex. *Developmental Psychobiology, 33,* 79–91.

Price, C., & Kunz, J. (2003). Rethinking the paradigm of juvenile delinquency as related to divorce. *Journal of Divorce & Remarriage, 39,* 109–133.

Prince, A. (1998). Infectious diseases. In R. Behrman & R. Kliegman (Eds.), *Nelson essentials of pediatrics* (3rd ed., pp. 315–418). Philadelphia: W. B. Saunders.

Prinstein, M., & La Greca, A. (1999). Links between mothers' and children's social competence and associations with maternal adjustment. *Journal of Clinical Child Psychology, 28,* 197–210.

Provasi, J., Dubon, C., & Bloch, H. (2001). Do 9- and 12-month-olds learn means-ends relation by observing? *Infant Behavior & Development, 24,* 195–213.

Pulkkinen, L. (1982). Self-control and continuity from childhood to late adolescence. In P. Baltes & O. G. Brim, Jr. (Eds.), *Life span development and behavior, Vol. 4* (pp. 64–107). New York: Academic Press.

Puma, M., Bell, S., Cook, R., Heid, C., Lopez, M., & Zill, N. (2005). *Head Start impact study: First year findings.* Washington, DC: U.S. Department of Health and Human Services.

Puzzanchera, C., Adams, B., Snyder, H., & Kang, W. (2007). Easy access to FBI arrest statistics 1994–2005. Retrieved September 19, 2008 from http://ojjdp.ncjrs.gov/ojstatbb/ezaucr/.

Pynoos, H., Steinberg, A., & Wraith, R. (1995). A developmental model of childhood traumatic stress. In D. Cicchetti & D. Cohen (Eds.), *Developmental psychopathology, Vol 2: Risk, disorder, and adaptation.* New York: Wiley.

Quick Stats: Prevalence of HPV infection among sexually active females aged 14 to 59 years. (2007). *Morbidity and Mortality Weekly Report, 56,* 852.

Raaijmakers, Q., Verbogt, T., & Vollebergh, W. (1998). Moral reasoning and political beliefs of Dutch adolescents and young adults. *Journal of Social Issues, 54,* 531–546.

Rabasca, L. (1999, October). Ultra-thin magazine models found to have little negative effect on adolescent girls. *APA Monitor Online 30.* Retrieved January 16, 2001 from http://www.apa.org/monitor/oct99.

Raffaelli, M., & Ontai, L. (2004). Gender socialization in Latino/a families: Results from two retrospective studies. *Sex Roles, 50,* 287–299.

Ragnarsdottir, H., Simonsen, H., & Plunkett, K. (1999). The acquisition of past tense morphology in Icelandic and Norwegian children: An experimental study. *Journal of Child Language, 26,* 577–618.

Rahman, A., Lovel, H., Bunn, J., Igbal, A., & Harrington, R. (2004). Mothers' mental health and infant growth: A case-control study from Rawalpindi, Pakistan. *Child: Care, Health, & Development, 30,* 21–27.

Rahman, Q., & Wilson, G. (2003). Born gay? The psychobiology of human sexual orientation. *Personality and Individual Differences, 34,* 1337–1382.

Raja, S. N., McGee, R., & Stanton, W. R. (1992). Perceived attachments to parents and peers and psychological well-being in adolescence. *Journal of Youth & Adolescence, 21,* 471–485.

Ramey, C. T. (1992). High-risk children and IQ: Altering intergenerational patterns. *Intelligence, 16,* 239–256.

Ramey, C. T. (1993). A rejoinder to Spitz's critique of the Abecedarian experiment. *Intelligence, 17,* 25–30.

Ramey, C. T., & Campbell, F. A. (1987). The Carolina Abecedarian Project: An educational experiment concerning human malleability. In J. J. Gallagher & C. T. Ramey (Eds.), *The malleability of children* (pp. 127–140). Baltimore: Paul H. Brookes.

Ramey, C. T., & Ramey, S. (1998). Early intervention and early experience. *American Psychologist, 53,* 109–120.

Rask-Nisillä, L., Jokinen, E., Pirjo, T., Tammi, A., Lapinleimu, H., Rönnemaa, T., Viikari, J., Seppänen, R., Korhonen, T., Tuominen, J., Välimäki, I., & Simell, O. (2000). Neurological development of 5-year-old children receiving a low-saturated fat, low-cholesterol diet since infancy: A randomized controlled trial. *Journal of the American Medical Association, 284,* 993–1000.

Rauscher, F. H., Shaw, G. L., & Ky, K. N. (1993). Music and spatial task performance. *Nature, 365,* 611.

Ray, B. (1999). *Home schooling on the threshold: A survey of research at the dawn of the new millennium.* Washington, DC: Home Education Research Institute.

Rego, A. (2006). The alphabetic principle, phonics, and spelling: Teaching students the code. In J. Schumm (Ed.), *Reading assessment and instruction for all learners* (pp. 118–162). New York: Guilford Press.

Reid, P., & Roberts, S. (2006). Gaining options: A mathematics program for potentially talented at risk adolescent girls. *Merrill-Palmer Quarterly, 52,* 288–304.

Reiner, W., & Gearhart, J. (2004). Discordant sexual identity in some genetic males with cloacal extrophy assigned to female sex at birth. *The New England Journal of Medicine, 350,* 333–341.

Reisman, J. E. (1987). Touch, motion, and proprioception. In P. Salapatek & L. Cohen (Eds.), *Handbook of infant perception, Vol. 1: From sensation to perception* (pp. 265–304). Orlando, FL: Academic Press.

Reiss, D. (1998). Mechanisms linking genetic and social influences in adolescent development: Beginning a collaborative search. *Current Directions in Psychological Science, 6,* 100–105.

Remafedi, G., Resnick, M., Blum, R., & Harris, L. (1998). Demography of sexual orientation in adolescents. *Pediatrics, 89,* 714–721.

Remsberg, K., Demerath, E., Schubert, C., Chumlea, W., Sun, S., & Siervoge, R. (2004). Early menarche and the development of cardiovascular disease risk factors in adolescent girls: The Fels Longitudinal Study. *Journal of Clinical Endocrinology & Metabolism, 90,* 2718–2724.

Repetto, P., Caldwell, C., & Zimmerman, M. (2004). Trajectories of depressive symptoms among high risk African-American adolescents. *Journal of Adolescent Health, 35,* 468–477.

Reskin, B. (1993). Sex segregation in the workplace. *Annual Review of Sociology, 19,* 241–270.

Reynolds, M., Schieve, L., Martin, J., Jeng, G., & Macaluso, M. (2003). Trends in multiple births conceived using assisted reproductive technology, United States, 1997–2000. *Pediatrics, 111,* 1159–1162.

Rholes, W. S., & Ruble, D. N. (1984). Children's understanding of dispositional characteristics of others. *Child Development, 55,* 550–560.

Ricci, C., Beal, C., & Dekle, D. (1995). The effect of parent versus unfamiliar interviewers on young witnesses' memory and identification accuracy. Paper presented at the biennial meetings of the Society for Research in Child Development, Indianapolis.

Richardson, G., Conroy, M., & Day, N. (1996). Prenatal cocaine exposure: Effects on the development of school-aged children. *Neurotoxicology & Teratology, 18*, 627–634.

Riegel, K. (1975). Adult life crises: A dialectic interpretation of development. In N. Datan & L. Ginsberg (Eds.), *Lifespan developmental psychology: Normative life crises* (pp. 99–128). New York: Academic Press.

Riegle-Crumb, C., Farkas, G., & Muller, C. (2006). The role of gender and friendship in advanced course taking. *Sociology of Education, 79*, 206–228.

Rique, J., & Camino, C. (1997). Consistency and inconsistency in adolescents' moral reasoning. *International Journal of Behavioral Development, 21*, 813–836.

Roberts, R., & Mather, N. (1995). The return of students with learning disabilities to regular classrooms: A sellout? *Learning Disabilities Research & Practice, 10*, 46–58.

Robinson, H. (1981). The uncommonly bright child. In M. Lewis & L. Rosenblum (Eds.), *The uncommon child* (pp. 57–82). New York: Plenum Press.

Robinson, N., Lanzi, R., Weinberg, R., Ramey, S., & Ramey, C. (2002). Family factors associated with high academic competence in former Head Start children at third grade. *Gifted Child Quarterly, 46*, 278–290.

Roche, A. F. (1979). Secular trends in human growth, maturation, and development. *Monographs of the Society for Research in Child Development, 44* (3–4, Serial No. 179).

Rock, A., Trainor, L., & Addison, T. (1999). Distinctive messages in infant-directed lullabies and play songs. *Developmental Psychology, 35*, 527–534.

Roderick, M., & Camburn, E. (1999). Risk and recovery from course failure in the early years of high school. *American Educational Research Journal, 36*, 303–343.

Rodkin, P., Farmer, T., Pearl, R., & Van Acker, R. (2000). Heterogeneity of popular boys: Antisocial and prosocial configurations. *Developmental Psychology, 36*, 14–24.

Rodrigo, M., Janssens, J., & Ceballos, E. (1999). Do children's perceptions and attributions mediate the effects of mothers' child rearing actions? *Journal of Family Psychology, 13*, 508–522.

Rodriguez, B., Fujimoto, W., Mayer-Davis, E., Imperatore, G., Williams, D., Bell, R., Wadwa, P., Palla, S., Liu, L., Kershnar, A., Daniels, S., & Linder, B. (2006). Prevalence of cardiovascular disease risk factors in U.S. children and adolescents with diabetes: The SEARCH for Diabetes in Youth study, *Diabetes Care, 29*, 1891–1896.

Roediger, H. (2008). Relativity of remembering: Why the laws of memory vanished. *Annual Review of Psychology, 59*, 225–254.

Roer-Strier, D., & Rivlis, M. (1998). Timetable of psychological and behavioural autonomy expectations among parents from Israel and the former Soviet Union. *International Journal of Psychology, 33*, 123–135.

Roeser, R., & Eccles J. (1998). Adolescents' perceptions of middle school: Relation to longitudinal changes in academic and psychological adjustment. *Journal of Research on Adolescence, 8*, 123–158.

Rogers, J. L., Rowe, D. C., & May, K. (1994). DF analysis of NLSY IQ/Achievement data: Nonshared environmental influences. *Intelligence, 19*, 157–177.

Rogoff, B. (1991). *Apprenticeship in thinking: Cognitive development in social context.* New York: Oxford University Press.

Rogosch, F., Cicchetti, D., & Aber, J. (1995). The role of child maltreatment in early deviations in cognitive and affective processing abilities and later peer relationship problems. *Development & Psychopathology, 7*, 591–609.

Rolls, E. (2000). Memory systems in the brain. *Annual Review of Psychology, 51*, 599–630.

Root, M. (2003). Racial identity development and persons of mixed race heritage. In M. Root & M. Kelly (Eds.), *The multiracial child resource book: Living complex identities* (pp. 34–41). Seattle, WA: Mavin Foundation.

Rosander, K., & von Hofsten, C. (2004). Infants' emerging ability to represent occluded object motion. *Cognition, 91*, 1–22.

Rosario, M., Schrimshaw, E., & Hunter, J. (2004). Ethnic/racial differences in the coming-out process of lesbian, gay, and bisexual youths: A comparison of sexual identity development over time. *Cultural Diversity and Ethnic Minority Psychology, 10*, 215–228.

Rosario, M., Schrimshaw, E., Hunter, J., & Braun, L. (2006). Sexual identity development among lesbian, gay, and bisexual youths: Consistency and change over time. *Journal of Sex Research, 43*, 46–58.

Rose, A., & Asher, S. (2004). Children's strategies and goals in response to help-giving and help-seeking tasks within a friendship. *Child Development, 75*, 749–763.

Rose, R. J. (1995). Genes and human behavior. *Annual Review of Psychology, 56*, 625–654.

Rose, S. A., & Feldman, J. F. (1995). Prediction of IQ and specific cognitive abilities at 11 years from infancy measures. *Developmental Psychology, 31*, 685–696.

Rose, S. A., Feldman, J. F., & Jankowski, J. (2004). Infant visual recognition memory. *Developmental Review, 24*, 74–100.

Rose, S. A., & Ruff, H. A. (1987). Cross-modal abilities in human infants. In J. D. Osofsky (Ed.), *Handbook of infant development* (2nd ed., pp. 318–362). New York: Wiley-Interscience.

Rosenbaum, J. E. (1984). *Career mobility in a corporate hierarchy.* New York: Academic Press.

Rosenberg, M. (1986). Self-concept from middle childhood through adolescence. In J. Suls & A. G. Greenwald (Eds.), *Psychological perspectives on the self, Vol. 3* (pp. 107–136). Hillsdale, NJ: Erlbaum.

Rosenberg, M. (2003). Recognizing gay, lesbian, and transgender teens in a child and adolescent psychiatry practice. *Journal of the American Academy of Child and Adolescent Psychiatry, 42*, 1517–1521.

Rosenblith, J. F. (1992). *In the beginning* (2nd ed.). Thousand Oaks, CA: Sage.

Rosenkrantz, S., Aronson, S., & Huston, A. (2004). Mother-infant relationship in single, cohabiting, and married families: A case for marriage? *Journal of Family Psychology, 18*, 5–18.

Rosenthal, J., Rodewald, L., McCauley, M., Berman, S., Irigoyen, M., Sawyer, M., Yusuf, H., Davis, R., & Kalton, G. (2004). Immunization coverage levels among 19- to 35-month-old children in 4 diverse, medically under-served areas of the United States. *Pediatrics, 113*, e296–e302.

Rosenthal, S., & Gitelman, S. (2002). Endocrinology. In A. Rudolph, R. Kamei, & K. Overby (Eds.), *Rudolph's fundamentals of pediatrics* (3rd ed., pp. 747–795). New York: McGraw-Hill.

Rosenthal, S., Lewis, L., Succop, P., & Burklow, K. (1997). Adolescent girls' perceived prevalence of sexually transmitted diseases and condom use. *Journal of Developmental & Behavioral Pediatrics, 18*, 158–161.

Rosenvinge, J., Matinussen, M., & Ostensen, E. (2000). The comorbidity of eating disorders and personality disorders: A meta-analytic review of studies published between 1983 and 1998. *Eating and Weight Disorders: Studies on Anorexia, Bulimia, and Obesity, 5*, 52–61.

Rosser, J. (1994). *Cognitive development: Psychological and biological perspectives.* Boston: Allyn & Bacon.

Rostosky, S., Owens, G., Zimmerman, R., & Riggle, E. D. (2003). Associations among sexual attraction status, school belonging, and alcohol and marijuana use in rural high school students. *Journal of Adolescence, 26*, 741–751.

Rothbart, M. K., Ahadi, S., & Evans, D. (2000). Temperament and personality: Origins and outcomes. *Journal of Personality & Social Psychology, 78*, 122–135.

Rothbart, M. K., Derryberry, D., & Posner, M. I. (1994). A psychobiological approach to the development of temperament. In J. E. Bates & T. D. Wachs (Eds.), *Temperament: Individual differences at the interface of biology and behavior* (pp. 83–116). Washington, DC: American Psychological Association.

Rothbart, M. K., & Putnam, S. (2002). Temperament and socialization. In L. Pulkkinen & A. Caspi (Eds.), *Paths to successful development: Personality in the life course* (pp. 19–45). New York: Cambridge University Press.

Rotter, J. (1990). Internal versus external control of reinforcement: A case history of a variable. *American Psychologist, 45*, 489–493.

Rovee-Collier, C. (1993). The capacity for long-term memory in infancy. *Current Directions in Psychological Science, 2*, 130–135.

Rowe, D. (2002). IQ, birth weight, and number of sexual partners in White, African American, and mixed race adolescents. *Population & Environment: A Journal of Interdisciplinary Studies, 23*, 513–524.

Roy, E., Bryden, P., & Cavill, S. (2003). Hand differences in pegboard performance through development. *Brain & Cognition, 53*, 315–317.

Rubin, K., Burgess, K., Dwyer, K., & Hastings, P. (2003). Predicting preschoolers' externalizing behaviors from toddler temperament, conflict, and maternal negativity. *Developmental Psychology, 39*, 164–176.

Rubin, K., Burgess, K., & Hastings, P. (2002). Stability and social-behavioral consequences of toddlers' inhibited temperament and parenting behaviors. *Child Development, 73*, 483–495.

Rubin, K. H., Fein, G. G., & Vandenberg, B. (1983). Play. In E. M. Hetherington (Ed.), *Handbook of child psychology: Socialization, personality, and social development, Vol. 4* (pp. 693–774). New York: Wiley.

Rubin, K. H., Hymel, S., Mills, R. S. L., & Rose-Krasnor, L. (1991). Conceptualizing different developmental pathways to and from social isolation in childhood. In D. Cicchetti & S. L. Toth (Eds.), *Internalizing and externalizing expressions of dysfunction: Rochester Symposium on Developmental Psychopathology, Vol. 2* (pp. 91–122). Hillsdale, NJ: Erlbaum.

Ruble, D. N. (1987). The acquisition of self-knowledge: A self-socialization perspective. In N. Eisenberg (Ed.), *Contemporary topics in developmental psychology* (pp. 243–270). New York: Wiley-Interscience.

Ruble, D. N., & Dweck, C. S. (1995). Self-conceptions, person conceptions, and their development. In N. Eisenberg (Ed.), *Social development.* Thousand Oaks, CA: Sage.

Rule, A., & Stewart, R. (2002). Effects of practical life materials on kindergartners' fine motor skills. *Early Childhood Education Journal, 30*, 9–13.

Rushton, J., & Jensen, A. (2006). The totality of available evidence shows the race IQ gap still remains. *Psychological Science, 17*, 921–922.

Rushton, J., & Rushton, E. (2003). Brain size, IQ, and racial-group differences: Evidence from musculoskeletal traits. *Intelligence, 31*, 139–155.

Rushton, J., Skuy, M., & Fridjhon, P. (2003). Performance on Raven's Advanced Progressive Matrices by African, East Indian, and White engineering students in South Africa. *Intelligence, 31*, 123–137.

Rutter, M. (1987). Continuities and discontinuities from infancy. In J. D. Osofsky (Ed.), *Handbook of infant development* (2nd ed., pp. 1256–1296). New York: Wiley-Interscience.

Rutter, M. (2005). Incidence of autism spectrum disorders: Changes over time and their meaning. *Acta Paediatrica, 94*, 2–15.

Rutter, M., Dunn, J., Plomin, R., Simonoff, E., Pickles, A., Maughan, B., Ormel, J., Meyer, J., & Eaves, L. (1997). Integrating nature and nurture: Implications of person-environment correlations and interactions for developmental psychopathology. *Development & Psychopathology, 9*, 335–364.

Ryder, J., Tunmer, W., & Greaney, K. (2008). Explicit instruction in phonemic awareness and phonemically based decoding skills as an intervention strategy for struggling readers in whole language classrooms. *Reading and Writing, 21*, 349–369.

Rys, G., & Bear, G. (1997). Relational aggression and peer relations: Gender and developmental issues. *Merrill-Palmer Quarterly, 43*, 87–106.

Sagi, A. (1990). Attachment theory and research from a cross-cultural perspective. *Human Development, 33*, 10–22.

Sagi, A., van IJzendoorn, M. H., & Koren-Karie, N. (1991). Primary appraisal of the Strange Situation: A cross-cultural analysis of preseparation episodes. *Developmental Psychology, 27*, 587–596.

Sak, U., & Maker, C. (2006). Developmental variation in children's creative mathematical thinking as a function of schooling, age, and knowledge. *Creativity Research, 18*, 279–291.

Saltz, R. (1979). Children's interpretation of proverbs. *Language Arts, 56*, 508–514.

Saluja, G., Iachan, R., Scheidt, P., Overpeck, M., Sun, W., & Giedd, J. (2004). Prevalence of and risk factors for depressive symptoms among young adolescents. *Archives of Pediatric & Adolescent Medicine, 158*, 760–765.

Sanchez, B. (2008). Communication disorders. Retrieved June 22, 2008 from http://psychologytoday.com/conditions/commdisorder.html.

Sanchez, R., Crismon, M., Barner, J., Bettinger, T., & Wilson, J. (2005). Assessment of adherence measures with different stimulants among children and adolescents. *Pharmacotherapy, 25*, 909–917.

Sandman, C., Wadhwa, P., Chicz-DeMet, A., Porto, M., & Garite, T. (1999). Maternal corticotropin-releasing hormone and habituation in the human fetus. *Developmental Psychobiology, 34*, 163–173.

Sandman, C., Wadhwa, P., Hetrick, W., Porto, M., & Peeke, H. (1997). Human fetal heart rate dishabituation between thirty and thirty-two weeks. *Child Development, 68*, 1031–1040.

Sandnabba, N., & Ahlberg, C. (1999). Parents' attitudes and expectations about children's cross-gender behavior. *Sex Roles, 40*, 249–263.

Sandson, T., Bachna, K., & Morin, M. (2000). Right hemisphere dysfunction in ADHD: Visual hemispatial inattention and clinical subtype. *Journal of Learning Disabilities, 33*, 83–90.

Sandvig, C. (2006). The internet at play: Child users of public internet connections. *Journal of Computer-Mediated Communication, 11*, 932–956.

Sanford, K., & Madill, L. (2006). Resistance through video game play: It's a boy thing. *Canadian Journal of Education, 29*, 287–306.

Santelli, J., Ott, M., Lyon, M., Rogers, J., & Summers, D. (2006). Abstinence-only education policies and programs: A position paper of the Society for Adolescent Medicine. *Journal of Adolescent Health, 38*, 83–87.

Sato, S., Shimonska, Y., Nakazato, K., & Kawaai, C. (1997). A life-span developmental study of age identity: Cohort and gender differences. *Japanese Journal of Developmental Psychology, 8,* 88–97.

Sattler, J. (2008). *Assessment of children: Cognitive foundations* (5th ed.). San Diego, CA: Jerome M. Sattler, Publisher, Inc.

Saudino, K. J., & Plomin, R. (1997). Cognitive and temperamental mediators of genetic contributions to the home environment during infancy. *Merrill-Palmer Quarterly, 43,* 1–23.

Savage, M., & Holcomb, D. (1999). Adolescent female athletes' sexual risk-taking behaviors. *Journal of Youth & Adolescence, 28,* 583–594.

Savage, S., & Gauvain, M. (1998). Parental beliefs and children's everyday planning in European-American and Latino families. *Journal of Applied Developmental Psychology, 19,* 319–340.

Savin-Williams, R., & Ream, G. (2003). Suicide attempts among sexual-minority male youth. *Journal of Clinical Child & Adolescent Psychology, 32,* 509–522.

Scarr, S. (1997). Why child care has little impact on most children's development. *Current Directions in Psychological Science, 6,* 143–147.

Scarr, S., & Eisenberg, M. (1993). Child care research: Issues, perspectives, and results. *Annual Review of Psychology, 44,* 613–644.

Scarr, S., & McCartney, K. (1983). How people make their own environments: A theory of genotype/environment effects. *Child Development, 54,* 424–435.

Scarr, S., & Weinberg, R. A. (1983). The Minnesota adoption studies: Genetic differences and malleability. *Child Development, 54,* 260–267.

Scarr, S., Weinberg, R. A., & Waldman, I. D. (1993). IQ correlations in trans-racial adoptive families. *Intelligence, 17,* 541–555.

Schaffer, H., & Emerson, P. (1964). The development of social attachments in infancy. *Monographs of the Society for Research in Child Development, 29* (3, Serial No. 94).

Schatschneider, C., Fletcher, J., Francis, D., Carlson, C., & Foorman, B. (2004). Kindergarten prediction of reading skills: A longitudinal comparative analysis. *Journal of Educational Psychology, 96,* 265–282.

Schechter, R., & Grether, J. (2008). Continuing increases in autism reported to California's developmental services system: Mercury in retrograde. *Archives of General Psychiatry, 65,* 19.

Scheiman, M., Mitchell, L., Cotter, S., Cooper, J., Kulp, M., Rouse, M., Borsting, E., London, R., & Wensveen, J. (2005). A randomized clinical trial of treatments for convergence insufficiency in children. *Archives of Opthalmology, 123,* 14–24.

Schmidt, M., DeMulder, E., & Denham, S. (2002). Kindergarten social-emotional competence: Developmental predictors and psychosocial implications. *Early Child Development & Care, 172,* 451–461.

Schmidt, P. (2000, January 21). Colleges prepare for the fallout from state testing policies. *Chronicle of Higher Education, 46,* A26–A28.

Schmitz, S., Fulker, D., Plomin, R., Zahn-Waxler, C., Emde, R., & DeFries, J. (1999). Temperament and problem behavior during early childhood. *International Journal of Behavioral Development, 23,* 333–355.

Schneider, B., Hieshima, J. A., Lee, S., & Plank, S. (1994). East-Asian academic success in the United States: Family, school, and community explanations. In P. M. Greenfield & R. R. Cocking (Eds.), *Cross-cultural roots of minority child development* (pp. 323–350). Hillsdale, NJ: Erlbaum.

Schonert-Reichl, K. (1999). Relations of peer acceptance, friendship adjustment, and social behavior to moral reasoning during early adolescence. *Journal of Early Adolescence, 19,* 249–279.

Schothorst, P., & van Engeland, H. (1996). Long-term behavioral sequelae of prematurity. *Journal of the American Academy of Child & Adolescent Psychiatry, 35,* 175–183.

Schraf, M., & Hertz-Lazarowitz, R. (2003). Social networks in the school context: Effects of culture and gender. *Journal of Social & Personal Relationships, 20,* 843–858.

Schredl, M., Barthold, C., & Zimmer, J. (2006). Dream recall and nightmare frequency: A family study. *Perceptual and Motor Skills, 102,* 878–880.

Schuler, M., & Nair, P. (1999). Frequency of maternal cocaine use during pregnancy and infant neurobehavioral outcome. *Journal of Pediatric Psychology, 24,* 511–514.

Schuler, M., Nair, P., & Black, M. (2002). Ongoing maternal drug use, parenting attitudes, and a home intervention: Effects on mother-child interaction at 18 months. *Journal of Developmental & Behavioral Pediatrics, 23,* 87–94.

Schull, W., & Otake, M. (1997). Cognitive function and prenatal exposure to ionizing radiation. *Teratology, 59,* 222–226.

Schulz, K., & Sisk, C. (2006). Pubertal hormones, the adolescent brain, and the maturation of social behaviors: Lessons from the Syrian hamster. *Molecular and Cellular Endocrinology, 254/255,* 120–126.

Schwartz, R. M., Anastasia, M. L., Scanlon, J. W., & Kellogg, R. J. (1994). Effect of surfactant on morbidity, mortality, and resource use in newborn infants weighing 500 to 1500 g. *New England Journal of Medicine, 330,* 1476–1480.

Schwebel, D., Rosen, C., & Singer, J. (1999). Preschoolers' pretend play and theory of mind: The role of jointly constructed pretence. *British Journal of Developmental Psychology, 17,* 333–348.

Schweinle, A., & Wilcox, T. (2003). Intermodal perception and physical reasoning in young infants. *Infant Behavior & Development, 27,* 246–265.

Scott, J. (1998). Hematology. In R. Behrman & R. Kliegman (Eds.), *Nelson essentials of pediatrics* (3rd ed., pp. 545–582). Philadelphia: W. B. Saunders.

Sebanc, A. (2003). The friendship features of preschool children: Links with prosocial behavior and aggression. *Social Development, 12,* 249–268.

Seidman, E., Allen, L., Aber, J. L., Mitchell, C., & Feinman, J. (1994). The impact of school transitions in early adolescence on the self-system and perceived social context of poor urban youth. *Child Development, 65,* 507–522.

Seifer, R., Schiller, M., Sameroff, A. J., Resnick, S., & Riordan, K. (1996). Attachment, maternal sensitivity, and infant temperament during the first year of life. *Developmental Psychology, 32,* 12–25.

Seiler, N. (2002). Is teen marriage a solution? Retrieved June 26, 2008 from http://www.clasp.org/publications/teenmariage02-20.pdf.

Sellers, A., Burns, W., & Guyrke, J. (2002). Differences in young children's IQs on the Wechsler Preschool and Primary Scale of Intelligence-Revised as a function of stratification variables. *Neuropsychology, 9,* 65–73.

Selman, R. L. (1980). *The growth of interpersonal understanding.* New York: Academic Press.

Semrud-Clikeman, M., Nielsen, K., Clinton, A., Sylvester, L., et al. (1999). An intervention approach for children with teacher- and parent-identified attentional difficulties. *Journal of Learning Disabilities, 32,* 581–590.

Seo, S. (2006). A study of infant developmental outcome with a sample of Korean working mothers of infants in poverty: Implications for early intervention programs. *Early Childhood Education Journal, 33,* 253–260.

Serbin, L. A., Poulin-Dubois, D., Colbourne, K., Sen, M., & Eichstedt, J. (2001). Gender stereotyping in infancy: Visual preferences for and knowledge of gender-stereotyped toys in the second year. *International Journal of Behavioral Development, 25,* 7–15.

Serbin, L. A., Powlishta, K. K., & Gulko, J. (1993). The development of sex typing in middle childhood. *Monographs of the Society for Research in Child Development, 58* (2, Serial No. 232).

Serdula, M. K., Ivery, D., Coates, R. J., Freedman, D. S., Williamson, D. F., & Byers, T. (1993). Do obese children become obese adults? A review of the literature. *Preventive Medicine, 22*, 167–177.

Serpell, R., & Hatano, G. (1997). Education, schooling, and literacy. In J. Berry, P. Dasen, & T. Saraswathi (Eds.), *Handbook of cross-cultural psychology, Vol. 2: Basic processes and human development.* Needham Heights, MA: Allyn & Bacon.

Shakib, S. (2003). Female basketball participation. *American Behavioral Scientist, 46*, 1405–1422.

Shames, R. (2002). Allergy: Mechanisms & disease processes. In A. Rudolph, R. Kamei, & K. Overby (Eds.), *Rudolph's fundamentals of pediatrics* (3rd ed., pp. 728–746). New York: McGraw Hill.

Share, D., & Leiken, M. (2004). Language impairment at school entry and later reading disability: Connections at lexical versus supralexical levels of reading. *Scientific Studies of Reading, 8*, 87–110.

Sharma, A., Dorman, M., & Kral, A. (2005). The influence of a sensitive period on central auditory development of children with unilateral and bilateral cochlear implantation. *Hearing Research, 203*, 134–143.

Sharma, A., Dorman, M., & Spahr, T. (2002). A sensitive period for the development of the central auditory system in children with cochlear implants. *Ear and Hearing, 23*, 532–539.

Sharma, V., & Sharma, A. (1997). Adolescent boys in Gujrat, India: Their sexual behavior and their knowledge of acquired immunodeficiency syndrome and other sexually transmitted diseases. *Journal of Developmental & Behavioral Pediatrics, 18*, 399–404.

Shaw, D. S., Kennan, K., & Vondra, J. I. (1994). Developmental precursors of externalizing behavior: Ages 1 to 3. *Developmental Psychology, 30*, 355–364.

Shochat, L. (2003). *Our Neighborhood*: Using entertaining children's television to promote interethnic understanding in Macedonia. *Conflict Resolution Quarterly, 21*, 79–93.

Shore, C. (1986). Combinatorial play, conceptual development, and early multiword speech. *Developmental Psychology, 22*, 184–190.

Shu, H., Anderson, R., & Wu, N. (2000). Phonetic awareness: Knowledge of orthography-phonology relationships in the character acquisition of Chinese children. *Journal of Educational Psychology, 92*, 56–62.

Shum, D., Neulinger, K., O'Callaghan, M., & Mohay, H. (2008). Attentional problems in children born very preterm or with extremely low birth weight at 7–9 years. *Archives of Clinical Neuropsychology, 23*, 103–112.

Siegal, M. (1987). Are sons and daughters treated more differently by fathers than by mothers? *Developmental Review, 7*, 183–209.

Siegel, B. (1996). Is the emperor wearing clothes? Social policy and the empirical support for full inclusion of children with disabilities in the preschool and early elementary grades. *Social Policy Report, Society for Research in Child Development, 10(2–3)*, 2–17.

Siegler, R. S. (1994). Cognitive variability: A key to understanding cognitive development. *Current Directions in Psychological Science, 3*, 1–5.

Siegler, R. S., & Chen, Z. (2002). Development of rules and strategies: Balancing the old and the new. *Journal of Experimental Child Psychology, 81*, 446–457.

Sigman, M., & McGovern, C. (2005). Improvement in cognitive and language skills from preschool to adolescence in autism. *Journal of Autism and Developmental Disorders, 35*, 15–23.

Sigman, M., Neumann, C., Carter, E., Cattle, D. J., D'Souza, S., & Bwibo, N. (1988). Home interactions and the development of Embu toddlers in Kenya. *Child Development, 59*, 1251–1261.

Sijuwade, P. (2003). A comparative study of family characteristics of Anglo American and Asian American high achievers. *Journal of Applied Social Psychology, 33*, 445–454.

Silver, J. (2003). Movie day at the Supreme Court or "I know it when I see it": A history of the definition of obscenity. Retrieved June 28, 2007 from http://library.findlaw.com/2003/May/15/132747.html.

Simard, V. (2008). Longitudinal study of preschool sleep disturbance. *Archives of Pediatrics & Adolescent Medicine, 162*, 360–367.

Simons, R. L., Robertson, J. F., & Downs, W. R. (1989). The nature of the association between parental rejection and delinquent behavior. *Journal of Youth & Adolescence, 18*, 297–309.

Simpkins, S., Davis-Kean, P., & Eccles, J. (2006). Math and science motivation: A longitudinal examination of the links between choices and beliefs. *Developmental Psychology, 42*, 70–83.

Sims, M., Hutchins, T., & Taylor, M. (1997). Conflict as social interaction: Building relationship skills in child care settings. *Child & Youth Care Forum, 26*, 247–260.

Singh, A., Mulder, J., Twisk, W., van Mechelen, M., & Chinapaw, M. (2008). Tracking of childhood overweight into adulthood: A systematic review of the literature. *Obesity Reviews, 9*, in press.

Singh, S., & Darroch, J. (2000). Adolescent pregnancy and childbearing: Levels and trends in industrialized countries. *Family Planning Perspectives, 32*, 14–23.

Singh, S., Wulf, D., Samara, R., & Cuca, Y. (2000). Gender differences in the timing of first intercourse: Data from 14 countries. *International Family Planning Perspectives, 26*, 21–28, 43.

Skaalvik, E., & Valas, H. (1999). Relations among achievement, self-concept and motivation in mathematics and language arts: A longitudinal study. *Journal of Experimental Education, 67*, 135–149.

Skinner, B. F. (1953). *Science and human behavior.* New York: Macmillan.

Skinner, B. F. (1957). *Verbal behavior.* New York: Prentice Hall.

Skinner, B. F. (1980). The experimental analysis of operant behavior: A history. In R. W. Riebes & K. Salzinger (Eds.), *Psychology: Theoretical-historical perspectives.* New York: Academic Press.

Skoe, E., Hansen, K., Morch, W., Bakke, I., Hoffman, T., Larsen, B., & Aasheim, M. (1999). Care-based moral reasoning in Norwegian and Canadian early adolescents: A cross-national comparison. *Journal of Early Adolescence, 19*, 280–291.

Skwarchuk, S., & Anglin, J. (2002). Children's acquisition of the English cardinal number words: A special case of vocabulary development. *Journal of Educational Psychology, 97*, 107–125.

Slaby, R. G., & Frey, K. S. (1975). Development of gender constancy and selective attention to same-sex models. *Child Development, 46*, 849–856.

Slater, A. (1995). Individual differences in infancy and later IQ. *Journal of Child Psychology & Psychiatry, 36*, 69–112.

Slobin, D. I. (1985a). Introduction: Why study acquisition crosslinguistically? In D. I. Slobin (Ed.), *The crosslinguistic study of language acquisition, Vol. 1: The data* (pp. 3–24). Hillsdale, NJ: Erlbaum.

Slobin, D. I. (1985b). Crosslinguistic evidence for the language-making capacity. In D. I. Slobin (Ed.), *The crosslinguistic study of language acquisition, Vol. 2: Theoretical issues* (pp. 1157–1256). Hillsdale, NJ: Erlbaum.

Smetana, J. G., Killen, M., & Turiel, E. (1991). Children's reasoning about interpersonal and moral conflicts. *Child Development, 62*, 629–644.

Smetana, J. G., Schlagman, N., & Adams, P. (1993). Preschool children's judgments about hypothetical and actual transgressions. *Child Development, 64*, 202–214.

Smith, C., & Farrington, D. (2004). Continuities in antisocial behavior and parenting across three generations. *Journal of Child Psychology and Psychiatry, 45,* 230–247.

Smith, D. (2007). *Introduction to special education* (6th ed.). Boston: Pearson Allyn & Bacon.

Smith, D., & Mosby, G. (2003). Jamaican child-rearing practices: The role of corporal punishment. *Adolescence, 38,* 369–381.

Smith, J., & Joyce, C. (2004). Mozart versus new age music: Relaxation states, stress, and ABC relaxation theory. *Journal of Music Therapy, 41,* 215–224.

Smith, L., Fagan, J., & Ulvund, S. (2002). The relation of recognition memory in infancy and parental socioeconomic status to later intellectual competence. *Intelligence, 30,* 247–259.

Smith, P., Smees, R., & Pelligrini, A. (2004). Play fighting and real fighting: Using video playback methodology with young children. *Aggressive Behavior, 30,* 164–173.

Smock, P. J. (1993). The economic costs of marital disruption for young women over the past two decades. *Demography, 30,* 353–371.

Smokowski, P., Mann, E., Reynolds, A., & Fraser, M. (2004). Childhood risk and protective factors and late adolescent adjustment in inner city minority youth. *Children and Youth Services Review, 26,* 63–91.

Smoll, F. L., & Schutz, R. W. (1990). Quantifying gender differences in physical performance: A developmental perspective. *Developmental Psychology, 26,* 360–369.

Snarey, J. R. (1985). Cross-cultural universality of social-moral development: A critical review of Kohlbergian research. *Psychological Bulletin, 97,* 202–232.

Snarey, J. R. (1995). In communitarian voice: The sociological expansion of Kohlbergian theory, research, and practice. In W. M. Kurtines & J. L. Gerwitz (Eds.), *Moral development: An introduction* (pp. 109–134). Boston: Allyn & Bacon.

Snarey, J. R., Reimer, J., & Kohlberg, L. (1985). Development of social-moral reasoning among kibbutz adolescents: A longitudinal cross-sectional study. *Developmental Psychology, 21,* 3–17.

Snow, C. E. (1997, April). Cross-domain connections and social class differences: Two challenges to nonenvironmentalist views of language development. Paper presented at the biennial meetings of the Society for Research in Child Development, Washington, DC.

Society for Assisted Reproductive Technology (SART). (2004). Guidelines on number of embryos transferred: Committee report. Retrieved August 18, 2004, from http://www.sart.org.

Society for Assisted Reproductive Technology (SART). (2008a). All SART member clinics: Clinic summary report. Retrieved March 5, 2008 from https://www.sartcorsonline.com/rptCSR_PublicMultYear.aspx?ClinicPKID=0.

Society for Assisted Reproductive Technology (SART). (2008b). Success rates. Retrieved March 5, 2008 from http://www.sart.org/Guide_SuccessRates.html.

Sodian, B., Taylor, C., Harris, P., & Perner, J. (1991). Early deception and the child's theory of mind: False trails and genuine markers. *Child Development, 62,* 468–483.

Sodoro, J., Allinder, R., & Rankin-Erickson, J. (2002). Assessment of phonological awareness: Review of methods and tools. *Educational Psychology Review, 14,* 223–260.

Soken, N., & Pick, A. (1999). Infants' perception of dynamic affective expressions: Do infants distinguish specific expressions? *Child Development, 70,* 1275–1282.

Sola, A., Rogido, M., & Partridge, J. (2002). The perinatal period. In A. Rudolph, R. Kamei, & K. Overby (Eds.) *Rudolph's fundamentals of pediatrics* (3rd ed., pp. 125–183). New York: McGraw-Hill.

Soori, H., & Bhopal, R. (2002). Parental permission for children's independent outdoor activities: Implications for injury prevention. *European Journal of Public Health, 12,* 104–109.

Sophian, C. (1995). Representation and reasoning in early numerical development: Counting, conservation, and comparisons between sets. *Child Development, 66,* 557–559.

Sotelo, M., & Sangrador, J. (1999). Correlations of self-ratings of attitude towards violent groups with measures of personality, self-esteem, and moral reasoning. *Psychological Reports, 84,* 558–560.

Sowell, E., Peterson, B., Thompson, P., Welcome, S., Henkenius, A., & Toga, A. (2003). Mapping cortical change across the human life span. *Nature Neuroscience, 6,* 309–315.

Spelke, E. S. (1979). Exploring audible and visible events in infancy. In A. D. Pick (Ed.), *Perception and its development: A tribute to Eleanor J. Gibson* (pp. 221–236). Hillsdale, NJ: Erlbaum.

Spelke, E. S. (1982). Perceptual knowledge of objects in infancy. In J. Mehler, E. C. T. Walker, & M. Garrett (Eds.), *Perspectives on mental representation* (pp. 409–430). Hillsdale, NJ: Erlbaum.

Spelke, E. S. (1991). Physical knowledge in infancy: Reflections on Piaget's theory. In S. Carey & R. Gelman (Eds.), *The epigenesis of mind: Essays on biology and cognition* (pp. 133–169). Hillsdale, NJ: Erlbaum.

Spelke, E. S., von Hofsten, C., & Kestenbaum, R. (1989). Object perception in infancy: Interaction of spatial and kinetic information for object boundaries. *Developmental Psychology, 25,* 185–196.

Spence, J. T., & Helmreich, R. L. (1978). *Masculinity and femininity.* Austin: University of Texas Press.

Spiers, P. S., & Guntheroth, W. G. (1994). Recommendations to avoid the prone sleeping position and recent statistics for Sudden Infant Death Syndrome in the United States. *Archives of Pediatric & Adolescent Medicine, 148,* 141–146.

Spiker, D. (1990). Early intervention from a developmental perspective. In D. Cicchetti & M. Beeghly (Eds.), *Children with Down syndrome: A developmental perspective* (pp. 424–448). New York: Cambridge University Press.

Spreen, O., Risser, A., & Edgell, D. (1995). *Developmental neuropsychology.* New York: Oxford University Press.

Sroufe, L. A. (1983). Infant-caregiver attachment and patterns of adaptation in preschool: The roots of maladaptation and competence. In M. Perlmutter (Ed.), *The Minnesota symposia on child psychology, Vol. 16* (pp. 41–84). Hillsdale, NJ: Erlbaum.

Sroufe, L. A., Carlson, E., & Schulman, S. (1993). Individuals in relationships: Development from infancy through adolescence. In D. C. Funder, R. D. Parke, C. Tomlinson-Keasey, & K. Widaman (Eds.), *Studying lives through time: Personality and development* (pp. 315–342). Washington, DC: American Psychological Association.

Sroufe, L. A., Egeland, B., Carlson, E., & Collins, W. (2005). *The development of the person: The Minnesota study of risk and adaptation from birth to adulthood.* New York: Guilford Publications.

Sroufe, L. A., Egeland, B., & Kreutzer, T. (1990). The fate of early experience following developmental change: Longitudinal approaches to individual adaptation in childhood. *Child Development, 61,* 1363–1373.

Sroufe, L. A., & Rutter, M. (1984). The domain of developmental psychopathology. *Child Development, 55,* 17–29.

Staff, J., & Kreager, D. (2007). Too cool for school? Peer status and high school dropout. Paper presented at the annual meeting of the American Sociological Association, New York, August.

Stainback, S., & Stainback, W. (1985). The merger of special and regular education: Can it be done? A response to Lieberman and Mesinger. *Exceptional Children, 51,* 517–521.

Standley, J. (2002). A meta-analysis of the efficacy of music therapy for premature infants. *Journal of Pediatric Nursing, 17,* 107–113.

Stattin, H., & Klackenberg-Larsson, I. (1993). Early language and intelligence development and their relationship to future criminal behavior. *Journal of Abnormal Psychology, 102,* 369–378.

Steele, C., & Aronson, J. (1995). Stereotype threat and the intellectual test performance of African Americans. *Journal of Personality & Social Psychology, 69,* 797–811.

Steele, J., & Mayes, S. (1995). Handedness and directional asymmetry in the long bones of the human upper limb. *International Journal of Osteoarchaeology, 5,* 39–49.

Steele, K. M., Bass, K. E., & Crook, M. D. (1999). The mystery of the Mozart effect: Failure to replicate. *Psychological Science, 10,* 366–369.

Steele, M., Hodges, J., Kaniuk, J., Hillman, S., & Henderson, K. (2003). Attachment representations and adoption: Associations between maternal states of mind and emotion narratives in previously maltreated children. *Journal of Child Psychotherapy, 29,* 187–205.

Stein, K., Roeser, R., & Markus, H. (1998). Self-schemas and possible selves as predictors and outcomes of risky behaviors in adolescents. *Nursing Research, 47,* 96–106.

Steinberg, L. (1986). Latchkey children and susceptibility to peer pressure: An ecological analysis. *Developmental Psychology, 22,* 433–439.

Steinberg, L. (1996). *Beyond the classroom: Why school reform has failed and what parents need to do.* New York: Simon & Schuster.

Steinberg, L., Blatt-Eisengart, I., & Cauffman, E. (2006). Patterns of competence and adjustment among adolescents from authoritative, authoritarian, indulgent, and neglectful homes: A replication in a sample of serious juvenile offenders. *Journal of Research on Adolescence, 16,* 47–58.

Steinberg, L., Elmen, J. D., & Mounts, N. S. (1989). Authoritative parenting, psychosocial maturity, and academic success among adolescents. *Child Development, 60,* 1424–1436.

Steinberg, L., Fletcher, A., & Darling, N. (1994). Parental monitoring and peer influences on adolescent substance use. *Pediatrics, 93,* 1060–1064.

Steinberg, L., Lamborn, S. D., Dornbusch, S. M., & Darling, N. (1992). Impact of parenting practices on adolescent achievement: Authoritative parenting, school involvement, and encouragement to succeed. *Child Development, 63,* 1266–1281.

Steinberg, L., Mounts, N. S., Lamborn, S. D., & Dornbusch, S. D. (1991). Authoritative parenting and adolescent adjustment across varied ecological niches. *Journal of Research on Adolescence, 1,* 19–36.

Steiner, J. E. (1979). Human facial expressions in response to taste and smell stimulation. In H. W. Reese & L. P. Lipsitt (Eds.), *Advances in child development and behavior, Vol. 13* (pp. 257–296). New York: Academic Press.

Sternberg, R. J. (1988). *The triarchic mind: A new theory of intelligence.* New York: Viking Press.

Sternberg, R. J. (2002). A broad view of intelligence: The theory of successful intelligence. *Consulting Psychology Journal: Practice and Research, 55,* 139–154.

Sternberg, R. J., & Davidson, J. E. (1985). Cognitive development in the gifted and talented. In F. Horowitz & M. O'Brien (Eds.), *The gifted and talented: Developmental perspectives* (pp. 37–74). Washington, DC: American Psychological Association.

Sternberg, R. J., & Grigorenko, E. (2006). Cultural intelligence and successful intelligence. *Group & Organization Management, 31,* 37–39.

Sternberg, R. J., Wagner, R., Williams, W., & Horvath, J. (1995). Testing common sense. *American Psychologist, 50,* 912–927.

Stevenson, H. (1994). Moving away from stereotypes and preconceptions: Students and their education in East Asia and the United States. In P. M. Greenfield & R. R. Cocking (Eds.), *Cross-cultural roots of minority child development* (pp. 315–322). Hillsdale, NJ: Erlbaum.

Stevenson, H. W., & Lee, S. (1990). Contexts of achievement: A study of American, Chinese, and Japanese children. *Monographs of the Society for Research in Child Development, 55* (1–2, Serial No. 221).

Stevenson, M., Rimajova, M., Edgecombe, D., & Vickery, K. (2003). Childhood drowning: Barriers surrounding private swimming pools. *Pediatrics, 111,* e119.

Stigler, J. W., Lee, S., & Stevenson, H. W. (1987). Mathematics classrooms in Japan, Taiwan, and the United States. *Child Development, 58,* 1272–1285.

Stigler, J. W., & Stevenson, H. W. (1991). How Asian teachers polish each lesson to perfection. *American Educator* (Spring), 12–20, 43–47.

Stipek, D., Gralinski, J., & Kopp, C. (1990). Self-concept development in the toddler years. *Developmental Psychology, 26,* 972–977.

St. James-Roberts, I., Bowyer, J., Varghese, S., & Sawdon, J. (1994). Infant crying patterns in Manila and London. *Child: Care, Health & Development, 20,* 323–337.

Stormshak, E., Bierman, K., McMahon, R., Lengua, L., et al. (2000). Parenting practices and child disruptive behavior problems in early elementary school. *Journal of Clinical Child Psychology, 29,* 17–29.

Strauss, S., & Altwerger, B. (2007). The logographic nature of English alphabetics and the fallacy of direct intensive phonics instruction. *Journal of Early Childhood Literacy, 7,* 299–319.

Strayer, F. F. (1980). Social ecology of the preschool peer group. In A. Collins (Ed.), *Minnesota symposia on child psychology, Vol. 13* (pp. 165–196). Hillsdale, NJ: Erlbaum.

Strayer, J., & Roberts, W. (2004). Empathy and observed anger and aggression in five-year-olds. *Social Development, 13,* 1–13.

Streissguth, A. P., Aase, J. M., Clarren, S. K., Randels, S. P., LaDue, R. A., & Smith, D. F. (1991). Fetal alcohol syndrome in adolescents and adults. *Journal of the American Medical Association, 265,* 1961–1967.

Striano, T., & Rochat, P. (1999). Developmental link between dyadic and triadic social competence in infancy. *British Journal of Developmental Psychology, 17,* 551–562.

Stroganova, T., Posikera, I., Pushina, N., & Orekhova, E. (2003). Lateralization of motor functions in early human ontogeny. *Human Physiology, 29,* 48–58.

Stunkard, A. J., Harris, J. R., Pedersen, N. L., & McClearn, G. E. (1990). The body-mass index of twins who have been reared apart. *New England Journal of Medicine, 322,* 1483–1487.

Sturm, J., & Seery, C. (2007). Speech and articulatory rate of school-aged children in conversation and narrative contexts. *Language, Speech, and Hearing Services in Schools, 38,* 47–59.

Styne, D., & Glaser, N. (2002). Endocrinology. In R. Behrman & R. Klingman (Eds.), *Nelson essentials of pediatrics* (4th ed., pp. 711–766). Philadelphia: W. B. Saunders.

Suizzo, M., & Stapleton, L. (2007). Home-based parental involvement in young children's education: Examining the effects of maternal education across U.S. ethnic groups. *Educational Psychology, 27,* 1–24.

Sulkes, S. (1998). Developmental and behavioral pediatrics. In R. Behrman & R. Kliegman (Eds.), *Nelson essentials of pediatrics* (3rd ed., pp. 1–55). Philadelphia: W. B. Saunders.

Sullivan, K., Zaitchik, D., & Tager-Flusberg, H. (1994). Preschoolers can attribute second-order beliefs. *Developmental Psychology, 30,* 395–402.

Super, D. E. (1971). A theory of vocational development. In H. J. Peters & J. C. Hansen (Eds.), *Vocational guidance and career development* (pp. 111–122). New York: Macmillan.

Super, D. E. (1986). Life career roles: Self-realization in work and leisure. In D. T. H. & Associates (Eds.), *Career development in organizations* (pp. 95–119). San Francisco: Jossey-Bass.

Susman, E. J., Inoff-Germain, G., Nottelmann, E. D., Loriaux, D. L., Cutler, G. B., Jr., & Chrousos, G. P. (1987). Hormones, emotional dispositions, and aggressive attributes in young adolescents. *Child Development, 58,* 1114–1134.

Susser, E., & Lin, S. (1992). Schizophrenia after prenatal exposure to the Dutch hunger winter of 1944–45. *Archives of General Psychiatry, 49,* 983–988.

Suzuki, L., & Aronson, J. (2005). The cultural malleability of intelligence and its impact on the racial/ethnic hierarchy. *Psychology, Public Policy, & Law, 11,* 320–327.

Sveum, K. (2008). Delayed sleep phase syndrome and the menstrual cycle. Paper presented at the annual meeting of the Associated Sleep Professionals Society, Baltimore, MD, June.

Svrakic, N., Svrakic, D., & Cloninger, C. (1996). A general quantitative theory of personality development: Fundamentals of a self-organizing psychobiological complex. *Development & Psychopathology, 8,* 247–272.

Swaim, K., & Bracken, B. (1997). Global and domain-specific self-concepts of a matched sample of adolescent runaways and nonrunaways. *Journal of Clinical Child Psychology, 26,* 397–403.

Swanson, L., & Kim, K. (2007). Working memory, short-term memory, and naming speed as predictors of children's mathematical performance. *Intelligence, 35,* 151–168.

Sweeting, H., & West, P. (2002). Gender differences in weight related concerns in early to late adolescence. *Journal of Family Issues, 23,* 728–747.

Syska, E., Schmidt, R., & Schubert, J. (2004). The time of palatal fusion in mice: A factor of strain susceptibility to teratogens. *Journal of Cranio-mascillofacial Surgery, 32,* 2–4.

Szeinberg, A., Borodkin, K., & Dagan, Y. (2006). Melatonin treatment in adolescents with delayed sleep phase syndrome. *Clinical Pediatrics, 45,* 809–818.

Taga, K., Markey, C., & Friedman, H. (2006). A longitudinal investigation of associations between boys' pubertal timing and adult behavioral health and well-being. *Journal of Youth and Adolescence, 35,* 401–411.

Tagliamonte, S., & Denis, D. (2008). Linguistic ruin? LOL! Instant messaging and teen language. *American Speech, 83,* 3–34.

Talmor, R., Reiter, S., & Feigin, N. (2005). Factors relating to regular education teacher burnout in inclusive education. *European Journal of Special Needs Education, 20,* 215–229.

Tanner, J. M. (1990). *Fetus into man: Physical growth from conception to maturity.* Cambridge, MA: Harvard University Press.

Tan-Niam, C., Wood, D., & O'Malley, C. (1998). A cross-cultural perspective on children's theories of mind and social interaction. *Early Child Development & Care, 144,* 55–67.

Tardif, T., So, C., & Kaciroti, N. (2007). Language and false belief: Evidence for general, not specific, effects in Cantonese-speaking preschoolers. *Developmental Psychology, 43,* 318–340.

Tardif, T., & Wellman, H. (2000). Acquisition of mental state language in Mandarin- and Cantonese-speaking children. *Developmental Psychology, 36,* 25–43.

Tasbihsazan, R., Nettelbeck, T., & Kirby, N. (2003). Predictive validity of the Fagan Test of Infant Intelligence. *British Journal of Developmental Psychology, 21,* 585–597.

Task Force on Sudden Infant Death Syndrome. (2005). The changing concept of Sudden Infant Death Syndrome: Diagnostic coding shifts, controversies regarding the sleeping environment, and new variables to consider in reducing risk. *Pediatrics, 116,* 1245–1255.

Taveras, E., Li, R., Grummer-Strawn, L., Richardson, M., Marshall, R., Rêgo, V., Miroshnik, I., & Lieu, T. (2004). Opinions and practices of clinicians associated with continuation of exclusive breastfeeding, *Pediatrics, 113,* e283–e290.

Temko, N. (2005). Anti-bullying protests force policy u-turn. Retrieved June 20, 2007 from www.guardian.co.uk/child/story/0,7369,1557999,00.html

Terlecki, M., & Newcombe, N. (2005). How important is the digital divide? The relation of computer and video game usage to gender differences in mental rotation ability. *Sex Roles, 53,* 433–441.

Terman, L. (1916). *The measurement of intelligence.* Boston: Houghton Mifflin.

Terman, L. (1925). *Genetic studies of genius: Vol. 1. Mental and physical traits of a thousand gifted children.* Stanford, CA: Stanford University Press.

Terman, L., & Merrill, M. A. (1937). *Measuring intelligence: A guide to the administration of the new revised Stanford-Binet tests.* Boston: Houghton Mifflin.

Terman, L., & Oden, M. (1959). *Genetic studies of genius: Vol. 5. The gifted group at mid-life.* Stanford, CA: Stanford University Press.

Terrisse, B. (2000). The resilient child: Theoretical perspectives and a review of the literature. Paper presented to the Council of Ministers of Education, Canada, Ottawa, Ontario, April.

Tershakovec, A. & Stallings, V. (1998). Pediatric nutrition and nutritional disorders. In R. Behrman & R. Kliegman (Eds.), *Nelson essentials of pediatrics* (3rd ed.). Philadelphia: W. B. Saunders.

Teti, D., & Candelaria, M. (2002). Parenting competence. In M. Bornstein (Ed.), *Handbook of parenting* (Vol. 4, pp. 149–180). Mahwah, NJ: Erlbaum.

Teti, D. M., Gelfand, D. M., Messinger, D. S., & Isabella, R. (1995). Maternal depression and the quality of early attachment: An examination of infants, preschoolers, and their mothers. *Developmental Psychology, 31,* 364–376.

Thal, D., & Bates, E. (1990). Continuity and variation in early language development. In J. Colombo & J. Fagen (Eds.), *Individual differences in infancy: Reliability, stability, prediction* (pp. 359–385). Hillsdale, NJ: Erlbaum.

Thal, D., Tobias, S., & Morrison, D. (1991). Language and gesture in late talkers: A 1-year follow-up. *Journal of Speech & Hearing Research, 34,* 604–612.

Thapar, A., Fowler, T., Rice, F., Scourfield, J., van den Bree, M., Thomas, H., Harold, G., & Hay, D. (2003). Maternal smoking during pregnancy and attention deficit hyperactivity disorder symptoms in offspring. *American Journal of Psychiatry, 160,* 1985–1989.

Tharp, R. G., & Gallimore, R. (1988). *Rousing minds to life.* New York: Cambridge University Press.

Tharpe, A. (2006). The impact of minimal and mild hearing loss on children. Retrieved March 19, 2008 from http://www.medicalhomeinfo.org/screening/EHDI/June_26_2006_FINAL_MildHearingLoss.pdf.

Tharpe, A. (2007). Assessment and management of minimal, mild, and unilateral hearing loss in children. Retrieved June 10, 2008 from http://www.audiologyonline.com/articles/article_detail.asp?article_id=1889.

Thelen, E. (1995). Motor development: A new synthesis. *American Psychologist, 50,* 79–95.

Thelen, E., & Adolph, K. E. (1992). Arnold L. Gesell: The paradox of nature and nurture. *Developmental Psychology, 28,* 368–380.

Theriault, J. (1998). Assessing intimacy with the best friend and the sexual partner during adolescence: The PAIR-M inventory. *Journal of Psychology, 132*, 493–506.

Thierer, A. (2003). Regulating video games: Parents or Uncle Sam? Retrieved June 28, 2007 from www.cato.org/pub_display.php?pub_id=3167.

Thomas, A., & Chess, S. (1977). *Temperament and development.* New York: Brunner/Mazel.

Thomas, D., Townsend, T., & Belgrave, F. (2003). The influence of cultural and racial identification on the psychosocial adjustment of inner-city African American children in school. *American Journal of Community Psychology, 32*, 217–228.

Thomas, J., Yan, J., & Stelmach, G. (2000). Movement substructures change as a function of practice in children and adults. *Journal of Experimental Child Psychology, 75*, 228–244.

Thomas, M. (2000). *Comparing theories of development* (5th ed.). Pacific Grove, CA: Brooks/Cole.

Thomas, R. M. (Ed.). (1990). *The encyclopedia of human development and education: Theory, research, and studies.* Oxford, England: Pergamon Press.

Thompson, G., & Joshua-Shearer, M. (2002). In retrospect: What college undergraduates say about their high school education. *High School Journal, 85*, 1–15.

Thompson, L., Fagan, J., & Fulker, D. (1991). Longitudinal prediction of specific cognitive abilities from infant novelty preference. *Child Development, 62*, 530–538.

Thompson, R., & Goodvin, R. (2005). The individual child: Temperament, emotion, self, and personality. In M. Bornstein & M. Lamb (Eds.), *Developmental science: An advanced textbook* (5th ed.). Hillsdale, NJ: Erlbaum.

Thorn, A., & Gathercole, S. (1999). Language-specific knowledge and short-term memory in bilingual and non-bilingual children. *Quarterly Journal of Experimental Psychology: Human Experimental Psychology, 52A*, 303–324.

Thorne, B. (1986). Girls and boys together . . . but mostly apart: Gender arrangements in elementary schools. In W. W. Hartup & Z. Rubin (Eds.), *Relationships and development* (pp. 167–184). Hillsdale, NJ: Erlbaum.

Tiedemann, J. (2000). Parents' gender stereotypes and teachers' beliefs as predictors of children's concept of their mathematical ability in elementary school. *Journal of Educational Psychology, 92*, 144–151.

Timimi, S., & Leo, J. (2009). *Rethinking ADHD.* London: Palgrave Macmillan.

Todd, R. D., Swarzenski, B., Rossi, P. G., & Visconti, P. (1995). Structural and functional development of the human brain. In D. Cicchetti & D. J. Cohen (Eds.), *Developmental psychopathology: Vol. 1. Theory and methods* (pp. 161–194). New York: Wiley.

Tokar, D., Fischer, A., & Subich, L. (1998). Personality and vocational behavior: A selective review of the literature, 1993–1997. *Journal of Vocational Behavior, 53*, 115–153.

Tomasello, M. (1999). *The cultural origins of human cognition.* Cambridge, MA: Harvard University Press.

Tomasi, P., Siracusano, S., Monni, A., Mela, G., & Delitala, G. (2001). Decreased nocturnal urinary antidiuretic hormone excretion in enuresis is increased with imipramine. *British Journal of Urology International, 88*, 932–937.

Tomblin, J., Smith, E., & Zhang, X. (1997). Epidemiology of specific language impairment: Prenatal and perinatal risk factors. *Journal of Communication Disorders, 30*, 325–344.

Tomlinson-Keasey, C., Eisert, D. C., Kahle, L. R., Hardy-Brown, K., & Keasey, B. (1979). The structure of concrete operational thought. *Child Development, 50*, 1153–1163.

Toomela, A. (1999). Drawing development: Stages in the representation of a cube and a cylinder. *Child Development, 70*, 1141–1150.

Torgesen, J., Wagner, R., Rashotte, C., Rose, E., et al. (1999). Preventing reading failure in young children with phonological processing disabilities: Group and individual responses to instruction. *Journal of Educational Psychology, 91*, 594–603.

Torrance, P. (1998). *Torrance Tests of Creative Thinking.* Bensenville, IL: Scholastic Testing Service.

Tortora, G., & Grabowski, S. (1993). *Principles of anatomy and physiology.* New York: HarperCollins.

Trautner, H., Gervai, J., & Nemeth, R. (2003). Appearance-reality distinction and development of gender constancy understanding in children. *International Journal of Behavioral Development, 27*, 275–283.

Traverso, A., Ravera, G., Lagattolla, V., Testa, S., & Adami, G. (2000). Weight loss after dieting with behavioral modification for obesity: The predicting efficiency of some psychometric data. *Eating and Weight Disorders: Studies on Anorexia, Bulimia, and Obesity, 5*, 102–107.

Trehub, S. E., & Rabinovitch, M. S. (1972). Auditory-linguistic sensitivity in early infancy. *Developmental Psychology, 6*, 74–77.

Tremblay, R. E., Masse, L. C., Vitaro, F., & Dobkin, P. L. (1995). The impact of friends' deviant behavior on early onset of delinquency: Longitudinal data from 6 to 13 years of age. *Development and Psychopathology, 7*, 649–667.

Tronick, E. Z., Morelli, G. A., & Ivey, P. K. (1992). The Efe forager infant and toddler's pattern of social relationships: Multiple and simultaneous. *Developmental Psychology, 28*, 568–577.

Turic, D., Robinson, L., Duke, M., Morris, D. W., Webb, V., Hamshere, M., Milham, C., Hopkin, E., Pound, K., Fernando, S., Grierson, A., Easton, M., Williams, N., Van Den Bree, M., Chowdhury, R., Gruen, J., Krawczak, M., Owen, M. J., O'Donovan, M. C., & Williams, J. (2004). Linkage disequilibrium mapping provides further evidence of a gene for reading disability on chromosome 6p21.3–22. *Molecular Psychiatry, 8*, 176–185.

Turkheimer, E., & Gottesman, I. (1991). Individual differences and the canalization of human behavior. *Developmental Psychology, 27*, 18–22.

Turnage, B. (2004). African American mother-daughter relationships mediating daughter's self-esteem. *Child & Adolescent Social Work Journal, 21*, 155–173.

Tynan, D. (2008). Oppositional defiant disorder. Retrieved March 30, 2008 from http://www.emedicine.com/ped/TOPIC2791.HTM.

Udry, J. R., & Campbell, B. C. (1994). Getting started on sexual behavior. In A. S. Rossi (Ed.), *Sexuality across the life course* (pp. 187–208). Chicago: University of Chicago Press.

Uecker, A., & Nadel, L. (1996). Spatial locations gone awry: Object and spatial memory deficits in children with fetal alcohol syndrome. *Neuropsychologia, 34*, 209–223.

Umetsu, D. (1998). Immunology and allergy. In R. Behrman & R. Kleigman (Eds.), *Nelson essentials of pediatrics* (3rd ed.). Philadelphia: W. B. Saunders.

Underwood, M. K. (1997). Peer social status and children's understanding of the expression and control of positive and negative emotions. *Merrill-Palmer Quarterly, 43*, 610–634.

Underwood, M. K., Coie, J. D., & Herbsman, C. R. (1992). Display rules for anger and aggression in school-age children. *Child Development, 63*, 366–380.

Ungerer, J. A., & Sigman, M. (1984). The relation of play and sensorimotor behavior to language in the second year. *Child Development, 55*, 1448–1455.

UNICEF. (2008). The state of the world's children: 2008. Retrieved June 11, 2008 from http://www.unicef.org/sowc08/.

United States Consumer Product Safety Commission. (2005). *2004 Product summary report.* Washington, DC: Author.

Uno, D., Florsheim, P., & Uchino, B. (1998). Psychosocial mechanisms underlying quality of parenting among Mexican-American and White adolescent mothers. *Journal of Youth & Adolescence, 27,* 585–605.

Updegraff, K., & Obeidallah, D. (1999). Young adolescents' patterns of involvement with siblings and friends. *Social Development, 8,* 52–69.

Urban, J., Carlson, E., Egeland, B., & Sroufe, L. A. (1991). Patterns of individual adaptation across childhood. *Development and Psychopathology, 3,* 445–460.

Urberg, K. A., Degirmencioglu, S. M., & Pilgrim, C. (1997). Close friend and group influence on adolescent cigarette smoking and alcohol use. *Developmental Psychology, 33,* 834–844.

Urberg, K. A., Degirmencioglu, S. M., & Tolson, J. M. (1998). Adolescent friendship selection and termination: The role of similarity. *Journal of Social & Personal Relationships, 15,* 703–710.

Urberg, K. A., Degirmencioglu, S. M., Tolson, J. M., & Halliday-Scher, K. (1995). The structure of adolescent peer networks. *Developmental Psychology, 31,* 540–547.

U.S. Bureau of Labor Statistics. (2007). Current population survey. Retrieved June 27, 2008 from http://www.bls.gov/cps/home.htm.

U.S. Census Bureau. (1998). *Statistical abstract of the United States: 1998.* Washington, DC: U.S. Government Printing Office.

U.S. Census Bureau. (2003a). Married-couple and unmarried-partner households: 2000. Retrieved August 18, 2004 from http://www.census.gov.

U.S. Census Bureau. (2003b). *Statistical abstract of the United States: 2003.* Washington, DC: U.S. Government Printing Office.

U.S. Department of Education. (2002). *24th annual report to Congress on the implementation of the Individuals with Disabilities Education Act.* Washington, DC: Author.

U.S. Department of Education. (2004). No Child Left Behind: Introduction. Retrieved September 21, 2004 from http://www.ed.gov/print/nclb/overview/intro/index.html.

U.S. Department of Health and Human Services. (1999). *Mental health: A report of the Surgeon General.* Retrieved April 11, 2008 from http://www.surgeongeneral.gov/library/mentalhealth/home.html.

U.S. Department of Health and Human Services. (2008). Annual update of the HHS poverty guidelines. Retrieved March 12, 2008 from http://aspe.hhs.gov/poverty/08fedreg.htm.

U.S. Department of the Treasury. (2008). Income mobility in the U.S. from 1996 to 2005. Retrieved March 13, 2008 from http://www.treas.gov/offices/tax-policy/library/incomemobilitystudy03-08revise.pdf.

U.S. Food and Drug Administration (FDA). (2004, October 15). Suicidality in children and adolescents being treated with antidepressant medication. Retrieved May 12, 2005 from http://www.fda.gov/cder/drug/antidepressants/SSRIPHA200410.htm.

Usher, E., & Pajares, F. (2006). Sources of academic and self-regulatory efficacy beliefs of entering middle school students. *Contemporary Educational Psychology, 31,* 125–141.

Uylings, H. (2006). Development of the human cortex and the concept of "critical" or "sensitive" periods. *Language Learning, 56,* 59–90.

Vaeisaenen, L. (1998). Family grief and recovery process when a baby dies. *Psychiatria Fennica, 29,* 163–174.

Valanides, N., & Markoulis, D. (2000). The acquisition of formal operational schemata during adolescence: A cross-national comparison. *International Journal of Group Tensions, 29,* 135–162.

Valdez-Menchaca, M. C., & Whitehurst, G. J. (1992). Accelerating language development through picture book reading: A systematic extension to Mexican day care. *Developmental Psychology, 28,* 1106–1114.

Valenza, E., Leo, I., Gava, L., & Simion, F. (2006). Perceptual completion in newborn human infants. *Child Development, 77,* 1810–1821.

Valleroy, L., MacKellar, D., Karon, J., Rosen, D., McFarland, W., Shehan, D., Stoyanoff, S., LaLota, M., Celentano, D., Koblin, B., Thieded, H., Katz, M., Torian, L., & Janssen, R. (2000). HIV prevalence and associated risks in young men who have sex with men. *Journal of the American Medical Association, 284,* 198–204.

van Beijsterveldt, C., Bartels, M., Hudziak, J., & Boomsma, D. (2003). Causes of stability of aggression from early childhood to adolescence: A longitudinal genetic analysis in Dutch twins. *Behavior Genetics, 33,* 591–605.

van Beijsterveldt, C., Hudziak, J., & Boomsma, D. (2005). Short- and long-term effects of child care on problem behaviors in a Dutch sample of twins. *Twin Research and Human Genetics, 8,* 250–258.

van den Boom, D. C. (1994). The influence of temperament and mothering on attachment and exploration: An experimental manipulation of sensitive responsiveness among lower-class mothers with irritable infants. *Child Development, 65,* 1457–1477.

van den Boom, D. C. (1995). Do first-year intervention effects endure? Follow-up during toddlerhood of a sample of Dutch irritable infants. *Child Development, 66,* 1798–1816.

Van den Broek, P., Lynch, J., Naslund, J., Ievers-Landis, C., & Verduin, K. (2004). The development of comprehension of main ideas in narratives: Evidence from the selection of titles. *Journal of Educational Psychology, 96,* 707–718.

van der Meer, V., Rikkers-Mutsaerts, E., Sterk, P., Thiadens, H., Assendelft, W., & Sont, J. (2006). Compliance and reliability of electronic PEF monitoring in adolescents with asthma. *Thorax, 61,* 457–458.

van der Molen, M., & Molenaar, P. (1994). Cognitive psychophysiology: A window to cognitive development and brain maturation. In G. Dawson & K. Fischer (Eds.), *Human behavior and the developing brain* (pp. 456–492). New York: Guilford Press.

Vandewater, E., Shim, M., & Caplovitz, A. (2004). Linking obesity and activity level with children's television and video game use. *Journal of Adolescence, 27,* 71–85.

van IJzendoorn, M. H. (1995). Adult attachment representations, parental responsiveness, and infant attachment: A meta-analysis on the predictive validity of the Adult Attachment Interview. *Psychological Bulletin, 117,* 387–403.

van IJzendoorn, M. H. (2005). Attachment in social networks: Toward an evolutionary social network model. *Human Development, 48,* 85–88.

van IJzendoorn, M. H., & Kroonenberg, P. M. (1988). Cross-cultural patterns of attachment: A meta-analysis of the Strange Situation. *Child Development, 59,* 147–156.

Van Lange, P., DeBruin, E., Otten, W., & Joireman, J. (1997). Development of prosocial, individualistic, and competitive orientations: Theory and preliminary evidence. *Journal of Personality & Social Psychology, 73,* 733–746.

Van Mierlo, J., & Van den Bulck, J. (2004). Benchmarking the cultivation approach to video game effects: A comparison of the correlates of TV viewing and game play. *Journal of Adolescence, 27,* 97–111.

van Wel, F. (1994). "I count my parents among my best friends": Youths' bonds with parents and friends in the Netherlands. *Journal of Marriage & the Family, 56,* 835–843.

van Wormer, K., & McKinney, R. (2003). What schools can do to help gay/lesbian/bisexual youth: A harm reduction approach. *Adolescence, 38,* 409–420.

Vartanian, L. (2000). Revisiting the imaginary audience and personal fable constructs of adolescent egocentrism: A conceptual review. *Adolescence, 35,* 639–661.

Vartanian, L. (2001). Adolescents' reactions to hypothetical peer group conversations: Evidence for an imaginary audience? *Adolescence, 36*, 347–380.

Verkooijen, K., de Vries, N., & Nielsen, G. (2007). Youth crowds and substance use: The impact of perceived group norm and multiple group identification. *Psychology of Addictive Behaviors, 21*, 55–61.

Vermeer, H., & van IJzendoorn, M. (2006). Children's elevated cortisol levels at daycare. *Early Childhood Research Quarterly, 21*, 390–401.

Viadero, D. (2007). Teachers say NCLB has changed classroom practice. *Education Week, 26*, 6.

Vida, J. (2005). Treating the "wise baby." *American Journal of Psychoanalysis, 65*, 3–12.

Vikat, A., Rimpela, A., Kosunen, E., & Rimpela, M. (2002). Sociodemographic differences in the occurrence of teenage pregnancies in Finland in 1987–1998: A follow up study. *Journal of Epidemiology & Community Health, 56*, 659–670.

Viner, R. (2002). Is puberty getting earlier in girls? *Archives of Disease in Childhood, 86*, 8–10.

Visscher, W., Feder, M., Burns, A., Brady, T., & Bray, R. (2003). The impact of smoking and other substance use by urban women on the birthweight of their infants. *Substance Use & Misuse, 38*, 1063–1093.

Visser, S., & Lesesne, C. (2005). Mental health in the United States: Prevalence of diagnosis and medication treatment for attention-deficit/hyperactivity disorder: United States, 2003. *Morbidity and Mortality Weekly Report, 54*, 842–847.

Vitaro, F., Tremblay, R., Kerr, M., Pagani, L., & Bukowski, W. (1997). Disruptiveness, friends' characteristics, and delinquency in early adolescence: A test of two competing models of development. *Child Development, 68*, 676–689.

Vogin, J. (2005). Taking medication while pregnant. Retrieved June 7, 2007 from http://www.medicinenet.com/script/main/art.asp?articlekey=51639.

Vuchinich, S., Bank, L., & Patterson, G. R. (1992). Parenting, peers, and the stability of antisocial behavior in preadolescent boys. *Developmental Psychology, 28*, 510–521.

Vyrostek, S., Annest, J., & Ryan, G. (2004). Surveillance for fatal and nonfatal injuries: United States, 2001. *Morbidity & Mortality Weekly Report, 53*, 1–57.

Wachs, T. (1975). Relation of infants' performance on Piaget scales between twelve and twenty-four months and their Stanford-Binet performance at thirty-one months. *Child Development, 46*, 929–935.

Waddington, C. (1957). *The strategy of the genes.* London: Allen.

Waddington, C. (1974). A catastrophe theory of evolution. *Annals of the New York Academy of Science, 231*, 32–41.

Walden, T. A. (1991). Infant social referencing. In J. Garber & K. A. Dodge (Eds.), *The development of emotion regulation and dysregulation* (pp. 69–88). Cambridge, England: Cambridge University Press.

Walker, H., Messinger, D., Fogel, A., & Karns, J. (1992). Social and communicative development in infancy. In V. B. V. Hasselt & M. Hersen (Eds.), *Handbook of social development: A lifespan perspective* (pp. 157–181). New York: Plenum.

Walker, L. J. (1980). Cognitive and perspective-taking prerequisites for moral development. *Child Development, 51*, 131–139.

Walker, L. J. (1989). A longitudinal study of moral reasoning. *Child Development, 60*, 157–160.

Walker, L. J., de Vries, B., & Trevethan, S. D. (1987). Moral stages and moral orientations in real-life and hypothetical dilemmas. *Child Development, 58*, 842–858.

Walker, M., & Stickgold, R. (2006). Sleep, memory, and plasticity. *Annual Review of Psychology, 57*, 139–166.

Walker-Andrews, A. S. (1997). Infants' perception of expressive behaviors: Differentiation of multimodal information. *Psychological Bulletin, 121*, 437–456.

Walker-Andrews, A. S., & Kahana-Kalman, R. (1999). The understanding of pretence across the second year of life. *British Journal of Developmental Psychology, 17*, 523–536.

Walker-Andrews, A. S., & Lennon, E. (1991). Infants' discrimination of vocal expressions: Contributions of auditory and visual information. *Infant Behavior & Development, 14*, 131–142.

Wallerstein, J., & Lewis, J. (1998). The long-term impact of divorce on children: A first report from a 25-year study. *Family & Conciliation Courts Review, 36*, 368–383.

Walton, G. E., Bower, N. J. A., & Bower, T. G. R. (1992). Recognition of familiar faces by newborns. *Infant Behavior & Development, 15*, 265–269.

Walusinski, O., Kurjak, A., Andonotopo, W., & Azumendi, G. (2005). Fetal yawning: A behavior's birth with 4D US revealed. *The Ultrasound Review of Obstetrics & Gynecology, 5*, 210–217.

Wang, C., & Chou, P. (1999). Risk factors for adolescent primigravida in Kaohsium county, Taiwan. *American Journal of Preventive Medicine, 17*, 43–47.

Wang, C., & Phinney, J. (1998). Differences in child rearing attitudes between immigrant Chinese mothers and Anglo-American mothers. *Early Development & Parenting, 7*, 181–189.

Wang, D., Kato, N., Inaba, Y., Tango, T., et al. (2000). Physical and personality traits of preschool children in Fuzhou, China: Only child vs. sibling. *Child: Care, Health & Development, 26*, 49–60.

Wang, X., Dow-Edwards, D., Anderson, V., Minkoff, H., & Hurd, Y. (2004). In utero marijuana exposure associated with abnormal amygdala dopamine D-sub-2 gene expression in the human fetus. *Biological Psychiatry, 56*, 909–915.

Wang, Y. (2002). Is obesity associated with early sexual maturation? A comparison of the association in American boys versus girls. *Pediatrics, 110*, 903–910.

Wang, Y., Bleich, S., & Gortmaker, S. (2008). Increasing caloric contribution from sugar-sweetened beverages and 100% fruit juices among US children and adolescents. *Pediatrics, 121*, e1604–e1614.

Wang, Y., & Lobstein, T. (2006). Worldwide trends in childhood overweight and obesity. *International Journal of Pediatric Obesity, 1*, 11–25.

Wang, Y., & Ollendick, T. (2001). A cross-cultural and developmental analysis of self-esteem in Chinese and Western children. *Clinical Child & Family Psychology Review, 4*, 253–271.

Ward, S. L., & Overton, W. F. (1990). Semantic familiarity, relevance, and the development of deductive reasoning. *Developmental Psychology, 26*, 488–493.

Wardle, J., Carnell, S., Haworth, C., & Plomin, R. (2008). Evidence for a strong genetic influence on childhood adiposity despite the force of the obesogenic environment. *American Journal of Clinical Nutrition, 87*, 398–404.

Wardle, J., & Cooke, L. (2008). Genetic and environmental determinants of children's food preferences. *British Journal of Nutrition, 99* (S1), S15–S21.

Warfield-Coppock, N. (1997). The balance and connection of manhood and womanhood training. *Journal of Prevention & Intervention in the Community, 16*, 121–145.

Wark, G. R., & Krebs, D. L. (1996). Gender and dilemma differences in real-life moral judgment. *Developmental Psychology, 32*, 220–230.

Warren, S., Gunnar, M., Kagan, J., Anders, T., Simmens, S., Rones, M., Wease, S., Aron, E., Dahl, R., & Sroufe, A. (2003). Maternal panic disorder: Infant temperament, neurophysiology, and parenting behaviors. *Journal of the American Academy of Child & Adolescent Psychiatry, 42*, 814–825.

Wartner, U. B., Grossman, K., Fremmer-Bombik, E., & Suess, G. (1994). Attachment patterns at age six in south Germany: Predictability from infancy and implications for preschool behavior. *Child Development, 65*, 1014–1027.

Waseem, M. (2007). Otitis media. Retrieved March 18, 2008 from http://www.emedicine.com/ped/TOPIC1689.HTM.

Watamura, S., Donzella, B., Alwin, J., & Gunnar, M. (2003). Morning-to-afternoon increases in cortisol concentrations for infants and toddlers at child care: Age differences and behavioral correlates. *Child Development, 74*, 1006–1020.

Waters, E., Merrick, S., Treboux, D., Crowell, J., & Albersheim, L. (2003). Attachment security in infancy and early adulthood: A twenty-year longitudinal study. In M. Hertzig & E. Farber (Eds.), *Annual progress in child psychiatry and child development: 2000–2001* (pp. 63–72). New York: Brunner-Routledge.

Waters, E., Treboux, D., Crowell, J., Merrick, S., & Albersheim, L. (1995, March). From the Strange Situation to the Adult Attachment Interview: A 20-year longitudinal study of attachment security in infancy and early adulthood. Paper presented at the biennial meetings of the Society for Research in Child Development, Indianapolis.

Watson, A., Nixon, C., Wilson, A., & Capage, L. (1999). Social interaction skills and theory of mind in young children. *Developmental Psychology, 35*, 386–391.

Watson, J. B. (1930). *Behaviorism.* New York: Norton.

Waxman, S. R., & Kosowski, T. D. (1990). Nouns mark category relations: Toddlers' and preschoolers' word-learning biases. *Child Development, 61*, 1461–1473.

Webster, B., & Bishaw, A. (2007). Income, earnings, and poverty data from the 2006 American Community Survey. Retrieved June 27, 2008 from http://www.census.gov/prod/2007pubs/acs-08.pdf.

Webster-Stratton, C., & Reid, M. (2003). Treating conduct problems and strengthening social and emotional competence in young children: The Dina Dinosaur treatment program. *Journal of Emotional & Behavioral Disorders, 11*, 130–143.

Wechsler, D. (2002). *The Wechsler preschool and primary scale of intelligence* (3rd ed.). San Antonio, TX: The Psychological Corporation.

Weimer, B., Kerns, K., & Oldenburg, C. (2004). Adolescents' interactions with a best friend: Associations with attachment style. *Journal of Experimental Psychology, 88*, 102–120.

Weinberg, R. A. (1989). Intelligence and IQ: Landmark issues and great debates. *American Psychologist, 44*, 98–104.

Weinberg, R. A., Scarr, S., & Waldman, I. D. (1992). The Minnesota transracial adoption study: A follow-up of IQ test performance. *Intelligence, 16*, 117–135.

Weindrich, D., Jennen-Steinmetz, C., Laucht, M., & Schmidt, M. (2003). Late sequelae of low birthweight: Mediators of poor school performance at 11 years. *Developmental Medicine & Child Neurology, 45*, 463–469.

Weinfield, N., & Egeland, B. (2004). Continuity, discontinuity, and coherence in attachment from infancy to late adolescence: Sequelae of organization and disorganization. *Attachment & Human Development, 6*, 73–97.

Weinstock, L. (1999). Gender differences in the presentation and management of social anxiety disorder. *Journal of Clinical Psychiatry, 60*, 9–13.

Weisner, T., & Wilson-Mitchell, J. (1990). Nonconventional family lifestyles and sex typing in six-year-olds. *Child Development, 62*, 1915–1933.

Welch-Ross, M. (1997). Mother-child participation in conversation about the past: Relationships to preschoolers' theory of mind. *Developmental Psychology, 33*, 618–629.

Wellman, H. M. (1982). The foundations of knowledge: Concept development in the young child. In S. G. Moore & C. C. Cooper (Eds.), *The young child: Reviews of research, Vol. 3* (pp. 115–134). Washington, DC: National Association for the Education of Young Children.

Wellman, H. M., Cross, D., & Watson, J. (2001). Meta-analysis of theory-of-mind development: The truth about false belief. *Child Development, 72*, 655–684.

Wentzel, K. R., & Asher, S. R. (1995). The academic lives of neglected, rejected, popular, and controversial children. *Child Development, 66*, 754–763.

Werker, J. F., Pegg, J. E., & McLeod, P. J. (1994). A cross-language investigation of infant preference for infant-directed communication. *Infant Behavior & Development, 17*, 323–333.

Werner, E. E. (1995). Resilience in development. *Current Directions in Psychological Science, 4*, 81–85.

Werner, E. E., & Smith, R. S. (1992). *Overcoming the odds: High risk children from birth to adulthood.* Ithaca, NY: Cornell University Press.

Werner, L. A., & Gillenwater, J. M. (1990). Pure-tone sensitivity of 2- to 5-week-old infants. *Infant Behavior & Development, 13*, 355–375.

West, P., Sweeting, H., & Ecob, R. (1999). Family and friends' influences on the uptake of regular smoking from mid-adolescence to early adulthood. *Addiction, 97*, 1397–1411.

Wetzel, N., Widmann, A., Berti, S., & Schröger, E. (2006). The development of involuntary and voluntary attention from childhood to adulthood: A combined behavioral and event-related potential study. *Clinical Neurophysiology, 117*, 2191–2203.

Whiston, S. (2003). Career counseling: 90 years old yet still healthy and vital. *Career Development Quarterly, 52*, 35–42.

White, W. H. (1992). G. Stanley Hall: From philosophy to developmental psychology. *Developmental Psychology, 28*, 25–34.

Whitehurst, G. J., Arnold, D. S., Epstein, J. N., Angell, A. L., Smith, M., & Fischel, J. E. (1994). A picture book reading intervention in day care and home for children from low-income families. *Developmental Psychology, 30*, 679–689.

Whitehurst, G. J., Falco, F. L., Lonigan, C. J., Fischel, J. E., DeBaryshe, B. D., Valdez-Menchaca, M. C., & Caulfield, M. (1988). Accelerating language development through picture book reading. *Developmental Psychology, 24*, 552–559.

Whitehurst, G. J., Fischel, J. E., Crone, D. A., & Nania, O. (1995, March). First year outcomes of a clinical trial of an emergent literacy intervention in Head Start homes and classrooms. Paper presented at the biennial meetings of the Society for Research in Child Development, Indianapolis.

Wiehe, V. (2003). Empathy and narcissism in a sample of child abuse perpetrators and a comparison sample of foster parents. *Child Abuse & Neglect, 27*, 541–555.

Wiesner, M., Kim, H., & Capaldi, D. (2005). Developmental trajectories of offending: Validation and prediction to young adult alcohol use, drug use, and depressive symptoms. *Development and Psychopathology, 17*, 251–270.

Wigfield, A., Eccles, J. S., MacIver, D., Reuman, D. A., & Midgley, C. (1991). Transitions during early adolescence: Changes in children's domain-specific self-perceptions and general self-esteem across the transition to junior high school. *Developmental Psychology, 27*, 552–565.

Williams, J. E., & Best, D. L. (1990). *Measuring sex stereotypes: A multination study* (rev. ed.). Newbury Park, CA: Sage.

Williams-Mbengue, N. (2003). Safe havens for abandoned infants. Retrieved June 18, 2007 from www.ncsl.org/programs/cyf/slr268.htm.

Wilson, G., & Sysko, R. (2006). Cognitive-behavioral therapy for adolescents with bulimia nervosa. *European Eating Disorders Review, 14*, 8–16.

Wilson, H., & Donenberg, G. (2004). Quality of parent communication about sex and its relationship to risky sexual behavior among youth in psychiatric care: A pilot study. *Journal of Child Psychology & Psychiatry & Allied Disciplines, 45*, 387–395.

Wilson, W. J. (1995). Jobless ghettos and the social outcome of youngsters. In P. Moen, G. H. Elder, Jr., & K. Lüscher (Eds.), *Examining lives in context: Perspectives on the ecology of human development* (pp. 527–543). Washington, DC: American Psychological Association.

Wiltenburg, M. (2003). Safe haven. Retrieved June 18, 2007 from www.csmonitor.com/2003/0724/p14s02-lifp.html.

Wimmer, H., Mayringer, H., & Landerl, K. (1998). Poor reading: A deficit in skill-automatization or a phonological deficit? *Scientific Studies of Reading, 2*, 321–340.

Winner, E. (1997). Exceptionally high intelligence and schooling. *American Psychologist, 52*, 1070–1081.

Wolpe, J. (1958). *Psychotherapy by reciprocal inhibition.* Palo Alto, CA: Stanford University Press.

Wong, C., & Tang, C. (2004). Coming out experiences and psychological distress of Chinese homosexual men in Hong Kong. *Archives of Sexual Behavior, 33*, 149–157.

Wong, D. (1993). *Whaley & Wong's essentials of pediatric nursing.* St. Louis, MO: Mosby-Yearbook, Inc.

Woo, M., & Oei, T. (2006). The MMPI-2 gender-masculine and gender-feminine scales: Gender roles as predictors of psychological health in clinical patients. *International Journal of Psychology, 41*, 413–422.

Woolley, M., & Grogan-Kaylor, A. (2006). Protective family factors in the context of neighborhood: Promoting positive school outcomes. *Family Relations, 55*, 93–104.

World Health Organization (WHO). (2005). World health 2005. Retrieved March 19, 2008 from http://www.who.int/whr/2005/en/.

Worrell, F. (1997). Predicting successful or non-successful at-risk status using demographic risk factors. *High School Journal, 81*, 46–53.

Wright, C., & Birks, E. (2000). Risk factors for failure to thrive: A population-based survey. *Child: Care, Health & Development, 26*, 5–16.

Wu, T., Mendola, P., & Buck, G. (2002). Ethnic differences in the presence of secondary sex characteristics and menarche among U.S. girls: The Third National Health and Nutrition Examination Survey, 1988–1994.

Wyatt, J., & Carlo, G. (2002). What will my parents think? Relations among adolescents' expected parental reactions, prosocial moral reasoning and prosocial and antisocial behaviors. *Journal of Adolescent Research, 17*, 646–666.

Xie, H., Cairns, R., & Cairns, B. (1999). Social networks and configurations in inner-city schools: Aggression, popularity, and implications for students with EBD. *Journal of Emotional & Behavioral Disorders, 7*, 147–155.

Yairi, E., & Ambrose, N. (2004). Stuttering: Recent developmental and future directions. *ASHS Leader, 10*, 4–5, 14–15.

Yamada, A., & Singelis, T. (1999). Biculturalism and self-construal. *International Journal of Intercultural Relations, 23*, 697–709.

Yazzie-Mintz, E. (2007). *Voices of students on engagement.* Retrieved June 27, 2008 from http://ceep.indiana.edu/hssse/pdf/HSSSE_2006_Report.pdf.

Yen, K. (2006). Amblyopia. Retrieved March 14, 2008 from http://www.emedicine.com/oph/TOPIC316.HTM.

Yeung, A., Chui, H., & Lau, I. (1999). Hierarchical and multidimensional academic self-concept of commercial students. *Contemporary Educational Psychology, 24*, 376–389.

Yirmiya, N., Eriel, O., Shaked, M., & Solomonica-Levi, D. (1998). Meta-analyses comparing theory of mind abilities of individuals with autism, individuals with mental retardation, and normally developing individuals. *Psychological Bulletin, 124*, 283–307.

Yirmiya, N., & Shulman, C. (1996). Seriation, conservation, and theory of mind abilities in individuals with autism, individuals with mental retardation, and normally developing children. *Child Development, 67*, 2045–2059.

Yirmiya, N., Solomonica-Levi, D., Shulman, C., & Pilowsky, T. (1996). Theory of mind abilities in individuals with autism, Down syndrome, and mental retardation of unknown etiology: The role of age and intelligence. *Journal of Child Psychology & Psychiatry & Allied Disciplines, 37*, 1003–1014.

Yonas, A., Elieff, C., & Arterberry, M. (2002). Emergence of sensitivity to pictorial depth cues: Charting development in individual infants. *Infant Behavior & Development, 25*, 495–514.

Yonas, A., & Owsley, C. (1987). Development of visual space perception. In P. Salpatek & L. Cohen (Eds.), *Handbook of infant perception, Vol. 2: From perception to cognition* (pp. 80–122). Orlando, FL: Academic Press.

Young, A. (1997). I think, therefore I'm motivated: The relations among cognitive strategy use, motivational orientation and classroom perceptions over time. *Learning & Individual Differences, 9*, 249–283.

Young, C. (2002). New look at "deadbeat dads." Retrieved June 16, 2007 from www.reason.com/news/printer/31886.html.

Young, M., & Bradley, M. (1998). Social withdrawal: Self-efficacy, happiness, and popularity in introverted and extroverted adolescents. *Canadian Journal of School Psychology, 14*, 21–35.

Young, S., Fox, N., & Zahn-Waxler, C. (1999). The relations between temperament and empathy in 2-year-olds. *Developmental Psychology, 35*, 1189–1197.

Yuill, N. (1997). English children as personality theorists: Accounts of the modifiability, development, and origin of traits. *Genetic, Social & General Psychology Monographs, 123*, 5–26.

Zahn-Waxler, C., & Radke-Yarrow, M. (1982). The development of altruism: Alternative research strategies. In N. Eisenberg (Ed.), *The development of prosocial behavior* (pp. 109–138). New York: Academic Press.

Zahn-Waxler, C., Radke-Yarrow, M., Wagner, E., & Chapman, M. (1992). Development of concern for others. *Developmental Psychology, 28*, 126–136.

Zakriski, A., & Coie, J. (1996). A comparison of aggressive-rejected and nonaggressive-rejected children's interpretation of self-directed and other-directed rejection. *Child Development, 67*, 1048–1070.

Zamboni, B. (2006). Therapeutic considerations in working with the family, friends, and partners of transgendered individuals. *The Family Journal, 14*, 174–179.

Zelazo, N. A., Zelazo, P. R., Cohen, K. M., & Zelazo, P. D. (1993). Specificity of practice effects on elementary neuromotor patterns. *Developmental Psychology, 29*, 686–691.

Zelazo, P., Helwig, C., & Lau, A. (1996). Intention, act, and outcome in behavioral prediction and moral judgment. *Child Development, 67*, 2478–2492.

Zhang, R., & Yu, Y. (2002). A study of children's coordinational ability for outcome and intention information. *Psychological Science* (China), *25*, 527–530.

Zhou, L., Dawson, M., Herr, C., & Stukas, S. (2004). American and Chinese college students' predictions of people's occupations, housework responsibilities, and hobbies as a function of cultural and gender influences. *Sex Roles, 50*, 463.

Zhou, Z., & Boehm, A. (2004). American and Chinese children's understanding of basic relational concepts in directions. *Psychology in the Schools, 41*, 261–272.

Zigler, E., & Finn-Stevenson, M. (1993). *Children in a changing world: Developmental and social issues.* Pacific Grove, CA: Brooks/Cole.

Zigler, E., & Hodapp, R. M. (1991). Behavioral functioning in individuals with mental retardation. *Annual Review of Psychology, 42*, 29–50.

Zimmer-Gembeck, M. (1999). Stability, change and individual differences in involvement with friends and romantic partners among adolescent females. *Journal of Youth & Adolescence, 28*, 419–438.

Zimmerman, C. (2000). The development of scientific reasoning skills. *Developmental Review, 20*, 99–149.

Zimmerman, M., Copeland, L., Shope, J., & Dielman, T. (1997). A longitudinal study of self-esteem: Implications for adolescent development. *Journal of Youth & Adolescence, 26*, 117–141.

Zimmermann, P. (2004). Attachment representations and characteristics of friendship relations during adolescence. *Journal of Experimental Child Psychology, 88*, 83–101.

Zoghbi, H. (2003). Postnatal neurodevelopmental disorders: Meeting at the synapse? *Science, 302*, 826–830.

Zola, S., & Squire, L. (2003). Genetics of childhood disorders: Learning and memory: Multiple memory systems. *Journal of the American Academy of Child and Adolescent Psychiatry, 42*, 504–506.

Glossary

A-not-B error (p. 130) substage 4 infants' tendency to look for an object in the place where it was last seen (position A) rather than in the place to which they have seen a researcher move it (position B)

ability goals (p. 428) goals based on a desire to be superior to others

academic approach (p. 240) an approach to early childhood education that provides children with instruction in skills needed for success in school

academic learning (p. 426) the type of learning that is required in school, where information is often presented without a real-world context

accommodation (p. 38) changing a scheme as a result of some new information

achievement test (p. 333) a test designed to assess specific information learned in school

adaptive reflexes (p. 102) reflexes, such as sucking, that help newborns survive

adolescence (p. 385) the transitional period between childhood and adulthood

adolescent egocentrism (p. 423) an adolescent's belief that her or his thoughts, beliefs, and feelings are unique

adolescent growth spurt (p. 388) a period during which a teenager grows rapidly to near-adult stature, usually the first observable sign of puberty

adolescent-onset conduct disorder (p. 407) a pattern of behavior that begins at age 11 or later and includes high levels of aggression, argumentativeness, bullying, disobedience, irritability, and threatening and loud behavior

aggression (p. 274) behavior intended to harm another person or damage an object

allergies (p. 296) immune reactions to substances called allergens

altruism (p. 276) acts motivated by the desire to help another person without expectation of reward

amblyopia (p. 191) a disorder in which the brain suppresses information from one of the eyes ("lazy eye")

amnion (p. 64) fluid-filled sac in which the fetus floats until just before it is born

analytical style (p. 336) a style of learning that involves defining learning goals and following orderly steps to reach them

androgynous gender role identity (p. 454) high self-ratings on both masculine and feminine traits

animism (p. 222) the attribution of the characteristics of living organisms to nonliving objects

anorexia nervosa (p. 409) an eating disorder characterized by self-starvation

anoxia (p. 83) oxygen deprivation experienced by a fetus during labor and/or delivery

Asperger's syndrome (p. 210) a disorder in which children have age-appropriate language and cognitive skills but are incapable of engaging in normal social relationships

assimilation (p. 38) the process of using a scheme to make sense of an event or experience

association areas (p. 292) parts of the brain where sensory, motor, and intellectual functions are linked

associative play (p. 273) a type of play in which children both play alone and engage in brief periods of interactive play with peers

asthma (p. 296) a chronic lung disease, characterized by sudden, potentially fatal attacks of breathing difficulty

at-risk-for-overweight (p. 301) a term that characterizes a child whose BMI is between the 85th and 95th percentiles

attachment (p. 155) the emotional bond between parents and infants, from which infants derive security

attachment theory (p. 154) the view that infants are biologically predisposed to form emotional bonds with caregivers and that the characteristics of those bonds shape later social and personality development

attention-deficit hyperactivity disorder (ADHD) (p. 308) a behavior disorder that causes children to have difficulty attending to and completing tasks, as well as controlling impulses

atypical development (pp.11, 208) development that deviates from the typical developmental pathway in a direction that is harmful to the individual; developmental pathways, persisting for 6 months or longer, that are different from those of most children and/or are at the extreme end of the continuum for that behavior

auditory acuity (p. 113) how well one can hear

authoritarian parenting style (p. 264) a style of parenting that is high in control and maturity demands but low in nurturance and communication

authoritative parenting style (p. 264) a style of parenting that is high in nurturance, maturity demands, control, and communication

autistic disorders (p. 210) a group of disorders that are characterized by limited or nonexistent language skills, an inability to engage in reciprocal social relationships, and a severely limited range of interests

automaticity (p. 327) the ability to recall information from long-term memory without using short-term memory capacity

axons (p. 67) tail-like extensions of neurons

babbling (p. 140) the repetitive vocalizing of consonant-vowel combinations by an infant

balanced approach (p. 330) an approach to reading instruction that combines systematic and explicit phonics instruction with other strategies, derived from the whole language approach, for helping children acquire literacy

Bayley Scales of Infant Development (p. 146) the best-known and most widely used test of infant "intelligence"

behavior genetics (p. 42) the study of the role of heredity in individual differences

behaviorism (p. 32) the view that defines development in terms of behavior changes caused by environmental influences

bilingual education (p. 331) an approach to second-language education in which children receive instruction in two different languages

bioecological theory (p. 44) Bronfenbrenner's theory that explains development in terms of relationships between individuals and their environments, or interconnected contexts

BMI-for-age (p. 301) a measure that compares an individual child's BMI against established norms for his or her age group and sex

bone age (p. 209) a measure of a child's physical maturation that is based on x-rays of the hand and wrist

bulimia nervosa (p. 409) an eating disorder characterized by binge eating and purging

case study (p. 15) an in-depth examination of a single individual

cell body (p. 67) the part of a neuron that contains the nucleus and is the site of vital cell functions

centration (p. 222) a young child's tendency to think of the world in terms of one variable at a time

cephalocaudal pattern (p. 64) growth that proceeds from the head downward

cesarean section (c-section) (p. 81) delivery of an infant through incisions in the abdominal and uterine walls

character education (p. 435) a curriculum that teaches students culturally acceptable ways of behaving

child abuse (p. 203) physical or psychological injury that results from an adult's intentional exposure of a child to potentially harmful physical stimuli, sexual acts, or neglect

childhood-onset conduct disorder (p. 312) a behavior disorder involving high levels of aggression, argumentativeness, bullying, disobedience, irritability, and threatening and loud behavior that begin before age 10

chromosomes (p. 54) strings of genetic material in the nuclei of cells

circadian rhythms (p. 387) the regular fluctuation of bodily functions within each 24-hour period

class inclusion (p. 324) the understanding that subordinate classes are included in larger, superordinate classes

classical conditioning (p. 32) learning that results from the association of stimuli

clique (p. 467) a group of four to six young people who appear to be strongly attached to one another

cognitive domain (p. 7) changes in thinking, memory, problem-solving, and other intellectual skills

cognitive theories (p. 37) theories that emphasize mental processes in development, such as logic and memory

cohort (p. 10) a group of individuals who share the same historical experiences at the same times in their lives

colic (p. 104) an infant behavior pattern involving intense daily bouts of crying totaling 3 or more hours a day

communication disorders (p. 343) problems with speech or language that interfere with a child's education

concrete operational stage (p. 323) Piaget's third stage of cognitive development, during which children construct schemes that enable them to think logically about objects and events in the real world

conservation (p. 222) the understanding that matter can change in appearance without changing in quantity

control group (p. 17) the group in an experiment that receives either no special treatment or a neutral treatment

conventional morality (p. 459) in Kohlberg's theory, the level of moral reasoning in which judgments are based on the rules or norms of a group to which the person belongs

convergence insufficiency (p. 295) the inability to move both eyes inward to the degree required for focusing on near objects

cooing (p. 140) making repetitive vowel sounds, particularly the *uuu* sound

cooperative play (p. 273) a type of play in which several children work together to accomplish a goal

corpus callosum (p. 188) the brain structure through which the left and right sides of the cerebral cortex communicate

correlation (p. 16) a relationship between two variables that can be expressed as a number ranging from −1.00 to +1.00

cortex (p. 100) the convoluted gray matter that wraps around the midbrain and is involved in perception, body movement, thinking, and language

creativity (p. 335) the ability to produce original, appropriate, and valuable ideas and/or solutions to problems

critical period (p. 11) a specific period in development when an organism is especially sensitive to the presence (or absence) of some particular kind of experience

cross-gender behavior (p. 261) behavior that is atypical for one's own sex but typical for the opposite sex

cross-sectional design (p. 18) a research design in which groups of people of different ages are compared

crowd (p. 467) a combination of cliques, including both males and females

cumulative risk (p. 305) the overall risk resulting from interactions over time among risk factors that influence children's health

decentration (p. 323) thinking that takes multiple variables into account

deductive logic (p. 324) a type of reasoning, based on hypothetical premises, that requires predicting a specific outcome from a general principle

deferred imitation (p. 131) imitation that occurs in the absence of the model who first demonstrated it

delayed sleep phase syndrome (DSPS) (p. 388) a disturbance of circadian rhythms that is manifested as a pattern of staying up until 3:00 or 4:00 a.m. and being sleepy in the daytime, regardless of how many hours the person sleeps

delinquency (p. 407) a narrow category of behavior problems that includes intentional law breaking

dendrites (p. 67) branch-like protrusions from the cell bodies of neurons

dental caries (p. 200) tooth decay (cavities) caused by bacteria

deoxyribonucleic acid (DNA) (p. 54) chemical material that makes up chromosomes and genes

dependent variable (p. 17) the characteristic or behavior that is expected to be affected by the independent variable

depression (p. 314) feelings of sadness or despair that persist for more than 6 months

design stage (p. 196) Kellogg's third stage, in which children mix several basic shapes to create more complex designs

developmental approach (p. 240) an approach to early childhood education that supports children's achievement of naturally occurring milestones

developmental disabilities (p. 342) conditions that impair children's functioning in school and will prevent them from living independently as adults

developmental science (p. 6) the application of scientific methods to the study of age-related changes in behavior, thinking, emotion, and personality

developmentally appropriate practices (p. 241) early childhood education practices based on an understanding of developmental universals, individual differences, and contextual variables

diabetes (p. 302) a disorder of carbohydrate metabolism

disengaged students (p. 430) secondary school students who do not enjoy school and do not participate in school activities

dishabituation (p. 115) responding to a somewhat familiar stimulus as if it were new

divergent thinking (p. 335) the ability to produce multiple solutions to problems that have no clear answer

dominant-recessive pattern (p. 56) pattern of inheritance in which a single dominant gene influences a person's phenotype but two recessive genes are necessary to produce an associated trait

dynamic systems theory (p. 105) the view that several factors interact to influence development

dyslexia (p. 341) problems in reading or the inability to read

early childhood education (p. 240) educational programs for children between birth and 8 years

eclecticism (p. 47) the use of multiple theoretical perspectives to explain and study human development

ecological approach (p. 11) the view that children's development must be studied and understood within the contexts in which it occurs

ego (p. 28) according to Freud, the thinking element of personality

egocentrism (p. 222) a young child's belief that everyone sees and experiences the world the way she or he does

embryonic stage (p. 64) the second stage of prenatal development, from week 2 through week 8, during which the embryo's organ systems form

emotional intelligence (p. 335) a type of intelligence that includes awareness of one's own emotions, the ability to express emotions appropriately, and the ability to channel emotions to accomplish goals

emotional regulation (p. 254) the ability to control emotional states and emotion-related behavior

emotional self (p. 169) a toddler's identification of emotions expressed in others' faces and ability to regulate emotion

empathy (p. 255) the ability to identify with another person's emotional state

empiricists (p. 119) theorists who argue that perceptual abilities are learned

endocrine system (p. 188) glands (including the adrenals, thyroid, pituitary, testes, and ovaries) that secrete hormones governing overall physical growth and sexual maturation

engaged students (p. 430) secondary school students who enjoy school and are involved in all aspects of it

English-as-a-second-language (ESL) program (p. 332) an approach to second-language education in which children attend classes to learn English for part of the day and then academic classes conducted entirely in English for the other part of the day

English-language learners (ELLs) (p. 331) school children who do not speak English well enough to function in English-only classes

equilibration (p. 38) the process of balancing assimilation and accommodation to create schemes that fit the environment

ethnic identity (p. 454) a sense of belonging to an ethnic group

ethnography (p. 19) a detailed description of a single culture or context

ethology (p. 43) a perspective on development that emphasizes genetically determined survival behaviors presumed to have evolved through natural selection

excessive weight gain (p. 300) a pattern in which children gain more weight in a year than is appropriate for their height, age, and sex

executive processes (p. 327) information-processing skills that involve devising and carrying out strategies for remembering and solving problems

experiment (p. 16) a study that tests a causal hypothesis

experimental group (p. 17) the group in an experiment that receives the treatment the experimenter thinks will produce a particular effect

expertise (p. 328) the amount of knowledge one possesses about a particular topic

expressive language (p. 141) the ability to use sounds, signs, or symbols to communicate meaning

expressive style (p. 144) a style of word learning characterized by low rates of noun-like terms and high use of personal-social words and phrases

extended family (p. 272) a social network of parents, grandparents, aunts, uncles, cousins, and so on

extinction (p. 35) the gradual elimination of a behavior through repeated nonreinforcement

false belief principle (p. 225) an understanding that enables a child to look at a situation from another person's point of view and determine what kind of information will cause that person to have a false belief

fast-mapping (p. 231) the ability to categorically link new words to real-world referents

feminine gender role identity (p. 454) low self-ratings on masculine traits, high self-ratings on feminine traits

fetal stage (p. 66) the third stage of prenatal development, from week 9 to birth, during which growth and organ refinement take place

field of vision (p. 191) the amount of the environment that can be seen without moving the eyes

figurative schemes (p. 221) mental representations of the basic properties of objects in the child's world

figure-ground perception (p. 294) the ability to discriminate between a moving object and its background

finger differentiation (p. 194) the ability to touch each finger on a hand with the thumb of that hand

Flynn effect (p. 239) the phenomenon of average IQ scores increasing in every racial group throughout the industrialized world during the 19th and 20th centuries

foreclosure (p. 449) in Marcia's theory, the identity status of a person who has made a commitment without having gone through a crisis; the person has simply accepted a parentally or culturally defined commitment

formal operational stage (p. 419) the fourth of Piaget's stages, during which adolescents learn to reason logically about abstract concepts

fundamental movement skills (p. 193) basic patterns of movement that underlie gross motor skills such as running

gametes (p. 54) cells that unite at conception (ova in females; sperm in males)

gender (p. 256) the psychological and social associates and implications of biological sex

gender constancy (p. 257) the understanding that gender is a component of the self that is not altered by external appearance

gender identity (p. 258) the ability to correctly label oneself and others as male or female

gender role identity (p. 453) the gender-related aspects of the psychological self

gender schema theory (p. 257) an information-processing approach to gender concept development that asserts that people use a schema for each gender to process information about themselves and others

gender stability (p. 258) the understanding that gender is a stable, lifelong characteristic

genes (p. 54) pieces of genetic material that control or influence traits

genotype (p. 56) the unique genetic blueprint of each individual

germinal stage (p. 64) the first stage of prenatal development, beginning at conception and ending at implantation (approximately 2 weeks)

giftedness (p. 346) exceptional ability, such as very high intelligence and/or musical, artistic, mathematical, or spatial talents

glial cells (p. 67) the "glue" that holds neurons together to give form to the structures of the nervous system

gonadotrophic hormones (p. 386) hormones that stimulate the growth of ovaries in girls and testes in boys

gonads (p. 55) sex glands (ovaries in females; testes in males)

goodness-of-fit (p. 167) the degree to which an infant's temperament is adaptable to his or her environment, and vice versa

grammar explosion (p. 232) a period during which children rapidly acquire grammatical speech

growth curve (p. 187) the pattern and rate of growth exhibited by a child over time

growth hormone (GH) (p. 188) the pituitary hormone that controls the growth process

guided participation (p. 230) an intervention strategy in which children become teachers' apprentices rather than passive recipients of instruction

habituation (p. 115) a decline in attention that occurs because a stimulus has become familiar

handedness (p. 189) the tendency to rely primarily on the right or left hand

Head Start (p. 242) community-based early childhood education programs for economically disadvantaged children that are funded by the federal government

hippocampus (p. 189) the brain structure that is involved in the transfer of information to long-term memory

holophrases (p. 142) combinations of gestures and single words used to convey more meaning than can be conveyed by just the word alone

hormones (p. 188) substances that are secreted by glands and that govern physical growth and sexual maturation

hostile aggression (p. 275) aggression used to hurt another person or gain an advantage

hypothesis (p. 14) a testable prediction based on a theory

hypothetico-deductive reasoning (p. 420) the ability to derive conclusions from hypothetical premises

id (p. 28) in Freud's theory, the part of the personality that comprises a person's basic sexual and aggressive impulses; it contains the libido and motivates a person to seek pleasure and avoid pain

identity (p. 448) an understanding of one's unique characteristics and how they have been, are, and will be manifested across ages, situations, and social roles

identity achievement (p. 449) in Marcia's theory, the identity status achieved by a person who has been through a crisis and reached a commitment to ideological, occupational, or other goals

identity crisis (p. 448) Erikson's term for the psychological state of emotional turmoil that arises when an adolescent's sense of self becomes "unglued" so that a new, more mature sense of self can be achieved

identity diffusion (p. 449) in Marcia's theory, the identity status of a person who is not in the midst of a crisis and who has made no commitment

identity versus role confusion (p. 448) in Erikson's theory, the stage during which adolescents attain a sense of who they are

imaginary audience (p. 424) an internalized set of behavioral standards usually derived from a teenager's peer group

implantation (p. 64) attachment of the blastocyst to the uterine wall

inborn biases (p. 9) the notion that children are born with tendencies to respond in certain ways

inclusive education (p. 345) a general term for education programs in which children with disabilities are taught in regular classrooms

independent variable (p. 17) the presumed causal element in an experiment

individualized educational plan (IEP) (p. 340) an instructional program that has been designed to meet a child's unique needs

inductive discipline (p. 265) a discipline strategy in which parents explain to children why a punished behavior is wrong

inductive logic (p. 323) a type of reasoning in which general principles are inferred from specific experiences

infant-directed speech (IDS) (p. 139) the simplified, high-pitched speech used by adults with infants and young children

infant mortality (p. 109) death within the first year of life

inflections (p. 142) additions to words that change their meaning (e.g., the *s* in toys, the *ed* in waited)

information-processing theory (p. 40) a theoretical perspective that explains how the mind manages information

ingrowth stage (p. 230) Vygotsky's fourth stage, in which children 6 and older have fully internalized private speech

insecure/ambivalent attachment (p. 158) a pattern of attachment in which the infant shows little exploratory behavior, is greatly upset when separated from the mother, and is not reassured by her return or efforts to comfort him or her

insecure/avoidant attachment (p. 158) a pattern of attachment in which an infant avoids contact with the parent and shows no preference for the parent over other people

insecure/disorganized attachment (p. 158) a pattern of attachment in which an infant seems confused or apprehensive and shows contradictory behavior, such as moving toward the mother while looking away from her

instrumental aggression (p. 275) aggression used to gain an object

intelligence (p. 146) the ability to take in information and use it to adapt to the environment

intelligence quotient (IQ) (p. 234) the ratio of mental age to chronological age; also, a general term for any kind of score derived from an intelligence test

interactionists (p. 138) theorists who argue that language development is a subprocess of general cognitive development and is influenced by both internal and external factors

intermodal perception (p. 118) formation of a single perception of a stimulus based on information from two or more senses

invented spelling (p. 233) a strategy used by young children with good phonological awareness skills when they write

laboratory observation (p. 16) observation of behavior under controlled conditions

language acquisition device (LAD) (p. 138) an innate language processor, theorized by Chomsky, that contains the basic grammatical structure of all human language

lateralization (p. 188) the functional specialization of the left and right hemispheres of the cerebral cortex

learning disability (p. 341) a disorder in which a child has difficulty mastering a specific academic skill, even though she or he possesses normal intelligence and no physical or sensory handicaps

learning theories (p. 32) theories that assert that development results from an accumulation of experiences

lifetime physical activities (p. 307) sports or activities that are relatively easy to pursue into adulthood because they can be done alone or with only one or two others

longitudinal design (p. 18) a research design in which people in a single group are studied at different times in their lives

low birth weight (LBW) (p. 84) newborn weight below 5.5 pounds

major depressive disorder (MDD) (p. 314) feelings of deep sadness that last 6 months or longer and are accompanied by disturbances of sleeping and eating and difficulty concentrating

masculine gender role identity (p. 454) high self-ratings on masculine traits, low self-ratings on feminine traits

maturation (p. 7) the gradual unfolding of a genetically programmed sequential pattern of change

mean length of utterance (MLU) (p. 144) the average number of meaningful units in a sentence

means-end behavior (p. 129) purposeful behavior carried out in pursuit of a specific goal

memory strategies (p. 328) learned methods for remembering information

menarche (p. 390) the beginning of the menstrual cycle

mental retardation (p. 208) low levels of intellectual functioning (usually defined as an IQ score below 70) combined with significant problems in adaptive behavior

metacognition (p. 229) knowledge about how the mind thinks and the ability to control and reflect on one's own thought processes

metalinguistic skills (p. 322) the capacity to think and talk about language

metamemory (p. 229) knowledge about how memory works and the ability to control and reflect on one's own memory function

moral realism stage (p. 360) the first of Piaget's stages of moral development, in which children believe that rules are inflexible

moral relativism stage (p. 361) the second of Piaget's stages of moral development, in which children understand that many rules can be changed through social agreement

moratorium (p. 449) in Marcia's theory, the identity status of a person who is in a crisis but who has made no commitment

multi-factorial inheritance (p. 58) inheritance affected by both genes and the environment

myelination (p. 101) a process in neuronal development in which sheaths made of a substance called myelin gradually cover individual axons and electrically insulate them from one another to improve the conductivity of the nerve

myopia (p. 294) a condition that results in blurred distant vision

naïve idealism (p. 424) the use of hypothetico-deductive thinking to conceive of an ideal world and compare the real world to it

naive psychology stage (p. 230) Vygotsky's second stage, in which 2- to 3-year-olds use language but do not understand its symbolic nature

naming explosion (p. 142) the period when toddlers experience rapid vocabulary growth, typically beginning between 16 and 24 months

nativists (p. 119) theorists who claim that perceptual abilities are inborn

naturalistic observation (p. 15) the process of studying people in their normal environments

nature-nurture debate (p. 9) the debate about the relative contributions of biological processes and experiential factors to development

neglect (p. 203) the failure of caregivers to provide emotional and physical support for a child

neglected children (p. 368) children who are neither preferred nor avoided by most other children in a group

neonate (p. 84) term for babies between birth and 1 month of age

neo-Piagetian theory (p. 40) an approach that uses information-processing principles to explain the developmental stages identified by Piaget

neurons (p. 64) specialized cells of the nervous system

niche-picking (p. 166) the process of selecting experiences on the basis of temperament

night terrors (p. 197) frightening dreams that usually happen within a couple of hours of a child's going to sleep and do not fully awaken the child

nightmares (p. 197) frightening dreams that usually happen early in the morning and awaken the child

nonnormative changes (p. 11) changes that result from unique, unshared events

normative age-graded changes (p. 10) changes that are common to every member of a species

normative history-graded changes (p. 10) changes that occur in most members of a cohort as a result of factors at work during a specific, well-defined historical period

norms (p. 7) average ages at which developmental milestones are reached

object concept (p. 132) an infant's understanding of the nature of objects and how they behave

object permanence (p. 129) the understanding that objects continue to exist when they can't be seen

objective (categorical) self (p. 168) a toddler's understanding that he or she is defined by various categories such as gender or qualities such as shyness

onlooker play (p. 273) a type of play in which children watch another child playing

operant conditioning (p. 34) learning to repeat or stop behaviors because of their consequences

operational efficiency (p. 228) a neo-Piagetian term that refers to the maximum number of schemes that can be processed in working memory at one time

operative schemes (p. 221) mental representations that enable children to understand the logical connections among objects in their world and to reason about the effects of any changes on them

oppositional defiant disorder (ODD) (p. 312) a behavior disorder involving a pattern of negative, defiant, disobedient, and hostile behavior toward parents and other authority figures that is established prior to age 8

organogenesis (p. 66) process of organ development

otitis media (OM) (p. 201) an inflammation of the middle ear that is caused by a bacterial infection

overregularization (p. 232) attachment of regular inflections to irregular words, such as the substitution of *goed* for *went*

overweight (p. 301) a term that characterizes a child whose BMI is at the 95th percentile

parallel play (p. 273) a type of play in which children play side by side but do not interact

parenting styles (p. 263) the characteristic strategies that parents use to manage children's behavior

percentile rank (p. 186) the percentage of individuals whose scores on a measure are equal to or less than those of the individual child who is being described

permissive parenting style (p. 264) a style of parenting that is high in nurturance but low in maturity demands, control, and communication

person perception (p. 251) the ability to classify others according to categories such as traits, age, gender, and race

personal fable (p. 423) the belief that the events of one's life are controlled by a mentally constructed autobiography

personality (p. 164) a pattern of responding to people and objects in the environment

pervasive developmental disorders (PDDs) (p. 209) a group of disorders that are characterized by the inability to form social relationships

phenotype (p. 56) an individual's particular set of observable characteristics

phonological awareness (p. 233) children's understanding of the sound patterns of the language they are acquiring and knowledge of that language's system for representing sounds with letters

physical domain (p. 7) changes in the size, shape, and characteristics of the body

pictorial stage (p. 196) Kellogg's fourth stage, in which children begin to draw pictures of objects or events from real life

pituitary gland (p. 188) gland that governs the endocrine system and provides hormonal triggers for release of hormones from other glands

placenta (p. 64) specialized organ that allows substances to be transferred from mother to embryo and from embryo to mother, without their blood mixing

plasticity (p. 100) the ability of the brain to change in response to experience

polygenic inheritance (p. 58) pattern of inheritance in which many genes influence a trait

popular children (p. 368) children who are preferred as playmates by most other children in a group

postconventional morality (p. 460) in Kohlberg's theory, the level of moral reasoning in which judgments are based on an integration of individual rights and the needs of society

preconventional morality (p. 458) in Kohlberg's theory, the level of moral reasoning in which judgments are based on authorities outside the self

preference technique (p. 115) a research method in which a researcher keeps track of how long a baby looks at each of two objects shown

prefrontal cortex (PFC) (p. 387) the part of the frontal lobe that is just behind the forehead and is responsible for executive processing

preoperational stage (p. 220) Piaget's second stage of cognitive development, during which children become proficient in the use of symbols in thinking and communicating but still have difficulty thinking logically

primary circular reactions (p. 128) Piaget's phrase to describe a baby's simple repetitive actions in substage 2 of the sensorimotor stage, organized around the baby's own body

primary sex characteristics (p. 390) the sex organs: ovaries, uterus, and vagina in the female; testes and penis in the male

primitive reflexes (p. 103) reflexes, controlled by "primitive" parts of the brain, that disappear during the first year of life

primitive stage (p. 230) Vygotsky's first stage, in which children between birth and age 2 think nonverbally and learn through conditioning

private speech stage (p. 230) Vygotsky's third stage, in which 3- to 6-year-olds use utterances based on internalized speech routines for self-instruction and self-monitoring

processing efficiency (p. 327) the ability to make efficient use of short-term memory capacity

prosocial behavior (p. 276) behavior intended to help another person

proximodistal pattern (p. 64) growth that proceeds from the middle of the body outward

pruning (p. 100) the process of eliminating unused synapses

psychoanalytic theories (p. 28) theories proposing that developmental change happens because of the influence of internal drives and emotions on behavior

psychological self (p. 356) an understanding of one's stable internal traits

psychosexual stages (p. 29) Freud's five stages of personality development through which children move in a fixed sequence determined by maturation; the libido is centered in a different body part in each stage

psychosocial stages (p. 30) Erikson's eight stages, or crises, of personality development in which inner instincts interact with outer cultural and social demands to shape personality

puberty (p. 386) a collective term for the physical changes that culminate in sexual maturity

punishment (p. 34) anything that follows a behavior and causes it to stop

qualitative change (p. 10) a change in kind or type

quantitative change (p. 10) a change in amount

reaction range (p. 238) a range, established by one's genes, between upper and lower boundaries for traits such as intelligence; one's environment determines where, within those limits, one will fall

receptive language (p. 141) comprehension of spoken language

reciprocal determinism (p. 355) Bandura's model in which personal, behavioral, and environmental factors interact to influence personality development

referential style (p. 145) a style of word learning characterized by emphasis on things and people and their naming and description

reinforcement (p. 34) anything that follows a behavior and causes it to be repeated

rejected children (p. 368) children who are avoided by most other children in a group

relational aggression (p. 367) aggression aimed at damaging another person's self-esteem or peer relationships

relational complexity (p. 326) the number of elements in a problem and the complexity of the relationships among the elements

relational style (p. 336) a style of learning that involves focusing on the "big picture" instead of on the details of a task

relative right-left orientation (p. 293) the ability to identify right and left from multiple perspectives

research ethics (p. 20) guidelines researchers follow to protect the rights of animals used in research and humans who participate in studies

resilience (p. 12) factors within the individual or the environment that moderate or prevent the negative effects of vulnerabilities

response to intervention (RTI) (p. 342) a three-tier plan for helping children who fall behind in school

retaliatory aggression (p. 367) aggression to get back at someone who has hurt you

reticular formation (p. 102) the part of the brain that regulates attention

reversibility (p. 323) the understanding that both physical actions and mental operations can be reversed

role taking (p. 461) the ability to look at a situation from another person's perspective

scaffolding (p. 230) provision, by an adult or an older child, of the guidance and assistance needed by a preschooler to accomplish tasks within the zone of proximal development

schematic learning (p. 135) organization of experiences into expectancies, called schemas, which enable infants to distinguish between familiar and unfamiliar stimuli

scheme (p. 37) in Piaget's theory, an internal cognitive structure that provides an individual with a procedure to use in a specific circumstance

scribble stage (p. 196) the first of Kellogg's stages of drawing, in which children draw dots, horizontal and vertical lines, curved or circular lines, and zigzags

scripts (p. 229) cognitive structures that guide the performance of routine behaviors that involve a fixed sequence of events

secondary circular reactions (p. 129) repetitive actions in substage 3 of the sensorimotor period, oriented around external objects

secondary sex characteristics (p. 390) body parts such as breasts in females and pubic hair in both sexes

secular trend (p. 391) a change, such as the decline in average age of menarche or increase in average height, that occurs in developing nations when nutrition and health improve

secure attachment (p. 158) a pattern of attachment in which an infant readily separates from the parent, seeks proximity when stressed, and uses the parent as a safe base for exploration

selective attention (p. 292) the ability to focus cognitive activity on the important elements of a problem or situation

self-care children (p. 370) children who are at home by themselves after school for an hour or more each day

self-efficacy (p. 357) the belief in one's capacity to cause an intended event to occur or to perform a task

self-esteem (p. 358) a global evaluation of one's own worth

self-regulation (p. 362) the ability to conform to parental standards of behavior without direct supervision

semiotic (symbolic) function (p. 220) the understanding that one object or behavior can represent another

sensation seeking (p. 403) a desire to experience increased levels of arousal such as those that accompany fast driving or the "highs" associated with drugs

sensitive period (p. 11) a span of months or years during which a child may be particularly responsive to specific forms of experience or particularly influenced by their absence

sensorimotor stage (p. 128) Piaget's first stage of development, in which infants use information from their senses and motor actions to learn about the world

separation anxiety (p. 157) expressions of discomfort, such as crying, when separated from an attachment figure

sequential design (p. 18) a research design that combines cross-sectional and longitudinal comparisons of development

seriation task (p. 326) a problem that requires the ability to use a rule to put an array of objects in order

sex-typed behavior (p. 260) different patterns of behavior exhibited by boys and girls

sexually transmitted disease (STD) (p. 401) a disease that is spread by sexual contact

shape stage (p. 196) Kellogg's second stage, in which children intentionally draw shapes such as circles, squares, or X shapes

short-term storage space (STSS) (p. 228) neo-Piagetian theorist Robbie Case's term for the child's working memory

social clock (p. 10) a set of age norms that defines a sequence of normal life experiences

social-cognitive theory (p. 250) the theoretical perspective that social and emotional development in early childhood is related to improvements in the cognitive domain

social learning (modeling) (p. 35) learning that results from seeing a model reinforced or punished for a behavior

social referencing (p. 157) an infant's use of others' facial expressions as a guide to his or her own emotions

social skills (p. 274) a set of behaviors that usually lead to being accepted as a play partner or friend by others

social status (p. 368) an individual child's classification as popular, rejected, or neglected

sociobiology (p. 43) the study of society using the methods and concepts of biology; when used by developmentalists, an approach that emphasizes genes that aid group survival

sociocultural theory (p. 39) Vygotsky's view that complex forms of thinking have their origins in social interactions rather than in an individual's private explorations

socioeconomic status (SES) (p. 305) a collective term that includes the economic, occupational, and educational factors that influence a family's relative position in society

socioemotional domain (p. 8) change in variables that are associated with the relationship of an individual to the self and others

solitary play (p. 273) a type of play in which children play by themselves

spatial cognition (p. 293) the ability to infer rules from and make predictions about the movement of objects in space

spatial perception (p. 293) the ability to identify and act on relationships between objects in space

speech-language pathologist (SLP) (p. 344) professional trained to diagnose communication disorders and to help children overcome them

stages (p. 10) qualitatively distinct periods of development

stamina (p. 290) the capacity for extended physical activity

standardized test (p. 333) a test on which each individual's performance is evaluated by comparing his or her score to the average score attained by a large sample of similar individuals

stereopsis (p. 191) the capacity to perceive depth by integrating separate images sent to the brain by the eyes into a single, three-dimensional image

strabismus (p. 191) a disorder of alignment of the two eyes in which one or both eyes are turned in or out

stranger anxiety (p. 157) expressions of discomfort, such as clinging to the mother, in the presence of strangers

structured immersion (p. 331) an approach to second-language instruction in which basic instruction is solely in English and a bilingual teacher translates only when absolutely necessary

stuttering (p. 345) a disorder of fluency in which children's speech features repeated sounds

subjective (existential) self (p. 168) an infant's awareness that she or he is a separate person who endures through time and space and can act on the environment

submersion (p. 332) the integration of non–English-speaking children into English-only classes

sudden infant death syndrome (SIDS) (p. 109) a phenomenon in which an apparently healthy infant dies suddenly and unexpectedly

superego (p. 28) Freud's term for the part of personality that is the moral judge

synapses (pp. 67, 100) tiny spaces across which neural impulses flow from one neuron to the next

synaptogenesis (p. 100) the process of synapse development

synchrony (p. 155) a mutual, interlocking pattern of attachment behaviors shared by a parent and child

systematic and explicit phonics (p. 329) planned, specific instruction in sound-letter correspondences

systematic problem solving (p. 420) the process of finding a solution to a problem by testing single factors

task goals (p. 428) goals based on a desire for self-improvement

telegraphic speech (p. 142) simple two-word sentences that usually include a noun and a verb

temperament (p. 164) predispositions, such as activity level, that are present at birth and form the foundations of personality

teratogens (p. 70) substances, such as viruses and drugs, that can cause birth defects

tertiary circular reactions (p. 129) the deliberate experimentation with variations of previous actions that occurs in substage 5 of the sensorimotor period

theories (p. 13) sets of statements that propose general principles of development

theory of mind (p. 225) a set of ideas constructed by a child or adult to describe, explain, and make predictions about other people's knowledge and behavior, based on inferences about their mental states

theory of multiple intelligences (p. 334) Howard Gardner's theory that there are eight types of intelligence

Title I preschool programs (p. 242) early childhood education programs for economically disadvantaged children that are based in public schools

tracking (p. 113) the smooth movements of the eye used to follow the track of a moving object

trait (p. 355) a stable pattern of responding to situations

transductive logic (p. 222) causal inference based only on the temporal relationship between two events (if event B happened shortly after event A, then A caused B)

transgendered (p. 400) descriptive of a person whose psychological gender is the opposite of his or her biological sex

transitivity (p. 326) the ability to make inferences about logical relationships in an ordered set of stimuli

triarchic theory of intelligence (p. 334) Robert Sternberg's theory that intelligence includes three components: contextual, experiential, and componential

type 1 diabetes (p. 303) a type of diabetes in which the pancreas fails to produce insulin

type 2 diabetes (p. 303) a type of diabetes in which the pancreas produces insulin, but the body does not respond to it

umbilical cord (p. 64) organ that connects the embryo to the placenta

undifferentiated gender role identity (p. 454) low self-ratings on both masculine and feminine traits

uninvolved parenting style (p. 264) a style of parenting that is low in nurturance, maturity demands, control, and communication

vestibular sense (p. 192) the body's sense of its position in space

viability (p. 66) ability of the fetus to survive outside the womb

violation of expectations method (p. 133) a research strategy in which researchers move an object in one way after having taught an infant to expect it to move in another

visual acuity (p. 112) how well one can see details at a distance

vulnerability (p. 12) factors within the individual or the environment that increase the risk of poor developmental outcomes

whole language approach (p. 330) an approach to reading instruction that places more emphasis on the meaning of written language than on its structure

zone of proximal development (p. 230) the range of tasks that are too difficult for children to do alone but that they can manage with guidance

zygote (p. 54) single cell created when sperm and ovum unite

Name Index

C

D

E

F

I

J

T

X

Y

Z

Subject Index

C

H

I

Q

R

S

T

U

V

W

X

Y

Z

Photo Credits

Milestones (insert)

Physical (L to R): © Elizabeth Crews/The Image Works; © iStockphoto.com/Michael Blackburn, © Laura Dwight/Mira.com, © Elizabeth Crews/The Image Works, © Myrleen Ferguson Cate/PhotoEdit, © Niamh Baldock/Alamy, © Tony Freeman/PhotoEdit, (top) © Ellen B. Senisi/The Image Works, (bottom) © iStockphoto/Brian McEntire, © Ed Quinn/Corbis; *Cognitive* (L to R): Courtesy of Carolyn Rovee-Collier, © Tim Brown/Stone/Getty Images, © T. Lindfors/Lindfors Photography, © James Shaffer/PhotoEdit; *Socioemotional* (L to R): © Joseph Pobereskin/Getty Images, © Myrleen Ferguson Cate/PhotoEdit, (top) © Eastcott/Momatiuk/The Image Works, (bottom) © Rolf Bruderer/Corbis, © Myrleen Ferguson Cate/PhotoEdit, © Adams Picture Library t/a apl/Alamy.

Timeline (insert)

Plato, Descartes, H. Mann, Horace Mann School, W. James, M. Mead, and E. Erikson: Library of Congress; *Aristotle, G. S. Hall, and D. Wechsler*: National Library of Medicine; *M. Montessori*: © Bettman/CORBIS; *J. Watson, R. Raynor, and Little Albert*: Benjamin Harris, Ph.D.; *J. Piaget*: © Bill Anderson/Photo Researchers; *B.F. Skinner*: © Bettman/CORBIS; *L. Kohlberg*: Harvard University News Office; *A. Bandura, M. Ainsworth, and Supreme Court*: Pearson Education/PH College; *Harlow monkeys*: USDA/Animal and Plant Health Inspection Service; *R. Guthrie*: Archives of the History of American Psychology—The Robert V. Guthrie Papers; *Even the Rat Was White*: Pearson Education/Allyn & Bacon; *A Nation at Risk*: U.S. Department of Education.

Pages vi-vii, 3R, 92B: © Mark Hall/Taxi/Getty Images; viii-ix, 97R, 178: © photos.com/Jupiter Images; x-xi, 183R, 282: © rubberball/Getty Images; xii-xiii, 287R, 378L: © David Deas/DK Stock/Getty Images; xiv-xv, 383R, 474: © Michael Stuckey/Comstock/Corbis; 2L: © iStockphoto.com/Rhienna Cutler; 2R: © iStockphoto.com/Yvonne Chamberlain; 3L: © George Doyle/Stockbyte/Getty Images; 4: © Bob Daemmrich/The Image Works; 7: © AMNH Special Collections, 11L: © Michael Krasowitz/Taxi/Getty Images; 11R: © Mel Yates/Taxi/Getty Images; 13: © Nathan Benn/Corbis; 15: © Laura Dwight/PhotoEdit; 19: © Michael Doolittle/The Image Works; 26: © Felicia Martinez/PhotoEdit; 31: © Peter M. Fisher/Corbis; 35T: © Ken Heyman/Woodfin Camp & Associates, Inc.; 35BL: © Kathy Sloane/Photo Researchers, Inc.; 35BR: © LWA-Dann Tardif/Corbis; 37: © Bill Anderson/Photo Researchers, Inc.; 38: © Tim Brown/Stone/Getty Images; 39T: © T. Lindfors/Lindfors Photography; 39B: © David Young-Wolff/PhotoEdit; 43: © Nina Leen/Getty Images/Time Life Pictures; 45: © Jose Luis Pelaez, Inc./Corbis; 52: © iStockphoto.com/Sean O'Riordan Photographer; 54: © Michael Clancy; 55T: © Biophoto Associates/Photo Researchers, Inc.; 55(BL and BR): © Addenbrookes Hospital/Photo Researchers, Inc.; 61: © Mark Richards/PhotoEdit; 63T, 92T: © UHB Trust/Stone/Getty Images; 63B: © stockbyte/Getty Images; 65 (sperm/egg): © Profs. P.M. Motta & J. Van Blerkom/Photo Researchers, Inc.; 65 (zygote): © Lennart Nilsson/Albert Bonniers Forlag AB; 65 (embryo and 12-week fetus): © Claude Edelmann/Photo Researchers, Inc.; 65 (14-week fetus): © James Stevenson/Photo Researchers, Inc.; 65 (well-developed fetus): © Petit Format/Photo Researchers, Inc.; 67 (L and R): Courtesy of Dr. Olivier Walusinski, www.yawning.info; 68: Reprinted with permission of Anderson Publishing Ltd from Brown, S.D., Estroff, J.A. & Barnewolt, C.E.,

Fetal MRI. Applied Radiology, 2004, 33(2), pp 9-25, Fig. 2. © Anderson Publishing Ltd.; 74: © 2000 George Steinmetz/Courtesy of the San Francisco AIDS Foundation; 76: © REALITATEA TV/AFP/Getty Images; 78: © Keith Brofsky/Getty Images; 79T: © Sean Sprague/Stock Boston; 79B: © Margaret Miller/Photo Researchers, Inc.; 80: © Purestock/Getty Images; 84: © Jonathan Nourok/PhotoEdit; 94: © Bill Aron/PhotoEdit; 95T: © Andersen Ross/Brand X/Corbis; 95B: © Stockbyte/Getty Images; 96L: © iStockphoto.com/Michael Blackburn; 96C: © Jose Luis Pelaez, Inc./Blend Images/Getty Images; 96R: © IMAGEMORE Co., Ltd./Getty Images; 97L: © iStockphoto.com/Karen Struthers; 98: © iStockphoto.com/arsenic; 102: © Richard Meats/Getty Images; 106T: © Elizabeth Crews Photography; 106C: © Laura Dwight/PhotoEdit; 106B: © Myrleen Ferguson Cate/PhotoEdit; 108: © Photo Network/Alamy; 113: ©Jonathan Nourok/PhotoEdit; 114: Source: Steiner, J.E., "Human Facial Expressions in Response to Taste and Smell Stimulation," in *Advances in Child Development and Behavior*, Vol. 13, H.W. Reese and L.P. Lipsitt, eds. © 1979 by Academic Press. By permission.; 116: © Mark Richards/PhotoEdit; 118: © Elizabeth Crews/The Image Works; 119: © Laura Dwight/Mira.com; 126: © G. Baden/zefa/Corbis; 129: © Laura Dwight/PhotoEdit; 130: © thislife pictures/Alamy; 132: From Meltzoff & Moore, SCIENCE 198:75 (1977). Reprinted with permission from AAAS.; 136: Courtesy of Carolyn Rovee-Collier; 140: © Picture Partners/Alamy; 141: © Michael Newman/PhotoEdit; 146: © Laura Dwight Photography; 152: © Tetra Images/Getty Images; 154: © Martin Rogers/Woodfin Camp & Associates, Inc.; 155: © Lynne J. Weinstein/Woodfin Camp & Associates, Inc.; 156: © Laura Dwight/PhotoEdit; 157, 179: © Laura Dwight/PhotoEdit; 166: © Gabe Palmer/Corbis; 168: © Joseph Pobereskin/Getty Images; 169: © Laurance Monneret/Stone/Getty Images; 171: © Syracuse Newspapers/Dick Blume/The Image Works; 180: © Ellen B. Senisi; 181T: © ALI JAREKJI/Reuters /Landov; 181B: © Melanie Stetson Freeman/The Christian Science Monitor via Getty Images; 182L: © Stockbyte/Getty Images; 182C: © David Young-Wolff/PhotoEdit; 182R: © Bob Thomas/Stone/Getty Images; 183L: © Jack Hollingsworth/Photodisc/Getty Images; 184: © Niamh Baldock/Alamy; 186: © Tony Freeman/PhotoEdit; 192: © iStockphoto/Brian McEntire; 194: © iStockphoto/ND1939; 195TL: © Sharon Dominick/Getty Images; 195TR: © Ellen B. Senisi/The Image Works; 195 (B): © Bill Bachmann/Alamy; 200: © Rebecca Emery/Getty Images; 209: © Ellen B. Senisi/The Image Works; 218: © David Young-Wolff/PhotoEdit; 224: © Spencer Grant/PhotoEdit; 227: © Edward Parker/Alamy; 232: © Will Faller; 242: © Paul Conklin/PhotoEdit; 248: © Bill Bachmann/The Image Works; 250: © Larry Williams/Corbis; 254: © Chris Knapton/Alamy; 258: Courtesy of Jerry and Denise Boyd; 259T, 283: © Index Stock/Alamy; 259C: © Mary Kate Denny/PhotoEdit; 259B: © Sunstar/Photo Researchers, Inc.; 261T: © AGB Photo/Alamy; 261B: © Sue Ann Miller/Stone/Getty Images; 262: © Ben Blankenburg/Corbis; 268: © Rayes/Digital Vision/Getty Images; 270: © Tom & Dee Ann McCarthy/Corbis; 271L: © Cindy Charles/PhotoEdit; 271R: © Rachel Epstein/PhotoEdit; 275: © Myrleen Ferguson Cate/PhotoEdit; 277: © Danita Delimont/Alamy; 284: © Annie Engel/zefa/Corbis; 285T: © JUPITERIMAGES/Comstock Images/Alamy; 285B: © Jeff Greenberg/Alamy; 286L: © iStockphoto.com/Rich Legg; 286R: © iStockphoto.com/Wendy Shiao Photos; 287L: Copyright © Michael Newman/PhotoEdit; 287C: © iStockphoto.com/Morgan Lane Photography; 288: © Bob Daemmrich/PhotoEdit; 293, 379T: © Tetra Images/Alamy; 294, 379B: © Jeff Kaufman/Taxi/Getty Images; 302: © Michael Newman/PhotoEdit; 307: © Image Source/Getty Images; 308: © Keith Wood/Stone/Getty Images; 314: © iStockphoto/Mikael Damkier; 320: © Michael Newman/PhotoEdit; 328: © Alistair Berg/Digital Vision/Getty Images; 329L: © A. Ramey/Woodfin Camp & Associates, Inc.; 329C: © Joseph Sohm/Visions of America/Corbis; 329R: © Shehzad Noorani/Woodfin Camp & Associates, Inc.; 336, 378R: © Fancy/Veer/Corbis; 337: © Andy Sacks/Stone/Getty Images; 341: © Michael Newman/PhotoEdit; 352: © JUPITERIMAGES; 358: © David Young-Wolff/PhotoEdit; 361 and 362: © Michael Newman/PhotoEdit; 365T: © Rolf Bruderer/Corbis; 365B: © Mary Kate Denny/PhotoEdit; 366: © Eastcott/Momatiuk/The Image Works; 369: © Bill Aron/PhotoEdit; 370: © Stewart Cohen/Taxi/Getty Images; 371: © Corbis RF/Alamy; 380: compilation of 4 images from

© iStockphoto/Petko Danov; 381T: © Realistic Reflections/Getty Images; 381B: © AP Photo/Denis Poroy; 382L: © Bob Daemmrich Photography; 382R: © Diamond Images/Getty Images; 383L: © David Young-Wolff/PhotoEdit; 383C: © Tom Stewart/Corbis; 384: © Bubbles Photolibrary/Alamy; 389: © David Young-Wolff/PhotoEdit; 391: © FogStock LLC/Index Open; 394: © Maria Taglienti-Molinari/Brand X/Corbis; 399: © Ed Quinn/Corbis; 403: Photo by Joel Warren/© Disney Channel/Courtesy Everett Collection; 410: © Tony Freeman/PhotoEdit; 418: © Bob Daemmrich/PhotoEdit; 420: © James Shaffer/PhotoEdit; 427: © Scott Cunningham/PH Merrill Publishing; 428: © AP Photo/Daniel R. Patmore; 430: © Will & Deni McIntyre/Photo Researchers, Inc.; 438: © Peter Hvizdak/The Image Works; 446: © Lee Snider/The Image Works; 450L: © Adams Picture Library t/a apl/Alamy; 450C: © Bill Aron/PhotoEdit; 450R: © Carl & Ann Purcell/Corbis; 454: © Myrleen Ferguson Cate/PhotoEdit; 456T: © Kris Timken/Blend Images/Getty Images; 456B: © Will & Deni McIntyre/Corbis; 460: © Bettmann/Corbis; 463: © John Neubauer/PhotoEdit; 465: © Penny Tweedie/Stone/Getty Images; 467: © David Young-Wolff/Stone/Getty Images; 476: © Stockbyte/Getty Images; 477T: © Mary Kate Denny/PhotoEdit; 477B: © Tim Boyle/Getty Images; 478: © Fabio Cardoso/Maxx Images; 479: © Laura Dwight Photography; 480: © Elizabeth Crews/The Image Works; 482: © David Young-Wolff/PhotoEdit; 483T: © John Eastcott/StockBoston; 483B: © Spencer Grant/PhotoEdit.